The Rand McNally Encyclopedia of Military Aircraft
1914 to the Present

The Rand McNally Encyclopedia of
Military Aircraft

1914 to the Present

Enzo Angelucci

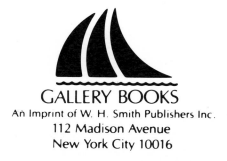

GALLERY BOOKS
An Imprint of W. H. Smith Publishers Inc.
112 Madison Avenue
New York City 10016

conceived and edited by
ENZO ANGELUCCI

written by
PAOLO MATRICARDI

created by
ADRIANO ZANNINO

Editor-in-chief
SERENELLA GENOESE ZERBI

Editors
Armando Castro, Daniela Luciano

under the technical supervision of
Giorgio Apostolo
Bruno Benvenuti

Head of production
Bruno Bazzoni

color illustrations by
Nicole Arolse, Vincenzo Cosentino,
Valeria Matricardi, Studio Kromos

black and white illustrations by
Daniela Dazzi, Paolo Riccioni,
Benedetto Tavi, Claudio Tatangelo

cutaway drawings on pages 38, 62, 168, 254, 308, 400, 448
by kind permission of Pilot Press

The Publisher would like to extend his sincere thanks to the
Museums of Aviation and to the Press Offices of aeronautical
industries throughout the world for their help in supplying data,
information and photographic material which have contributed to
the making of this book.

Translated from the Italian by S.M. Harris
Additional material translated by Valerie Palmer

This updated 1990 edition is published by The Military Press,
distributed by Outlet Book Company, Inc., a Random House Company,
225 Park Avenue South, New York, New York 10003

Library of Congress Cataloging in Publication Data
Atlante enciclopedico degli aerei militari del mondo
    dal 1914 a oggi. English. The Rand McNally encyclopedia
    of military aircraft 1914–1980

Translation of: Atlante Enciclopedico degli aerei militari
    del mondo dal 1914 a oggi.
    Reprint. Originally published: Chicago: Rand McNally, 1981.
    Bibliography: p.
    Includes indexes.
    I. Airplanes, Military-History. I. Angelucci, Enzo.
    II. Matricardi, Paolo. III. Title.

LCG1240. A8413 1983 358.4'183'09 83—752
ISBN 0 517 05655—0   8 7 6 5 4 3 2 1

Printed and bound in Italy by Arnoldo Mondadori Editore Officine Grafiche, Verona

This book, together with its companion volume on civil aviation, is the result of six years' concentrated study by a team of sixteen contributors who have given us the benefit of their flair and expertise on the subject.

We had set ourselves a somewhat ambitious goal: that of compiling a reference book which would be a concise and comprehensive source of information on all aircraft worthy of mention, giving a very wide range of facts together with as much detail as possible – such as technical data, national markings, three-views, photographs and historical background. In thirty years of enthusiastic interest in the field of aviation we had never succeeded in finding an "atlas" or an encyclopaedia which could furnish, in however compressed a form, ready answers to questions on the aircraft, both past and present, of each nation. This book, therefore, attempts to fill this gap and to be of help to those who share our enthusiasm, providing them with a basic guideline and point of departure from which to pursue more advanced and specialised research.

This volume deals with over eight hundred types of military aircraft: all those belonging to the past which we consider deserve a place in history and all the important aircraft of the present day. The absence of certain famous military aircraft may appear surprising but is explained by the fact that it was thought more appropriate to include them in the volume dealing with civil aircraft in such cases where the importance of the aircraft is more in its association with the development of civil aviation than the weapons of war.

There will be those, no doubt, who will accuse us of "unforgivable" omissions. Our choice was made from the many thousands of military aircraft constructed, even if they had only reached prototype stage. This process of selection entailed many awkward problems but we believe that for each era and each nation we have "rendered unto Caesar that which is Caesar's".

The assembly of this work has been a hard task for all the team of contributors, and for the publishers too. It is hoped that its effect will be to spread knowledge and insight into that exciting phenomenon, aviation; in the meanwhile the story continues to unfold as new and ever more sophisticated aircraft take shape on the designers' drawing boards. After less than eighty years of evolution, our most advanced aircraft are capable of travelling three times as fast as sound itself – and some are even spacecraft too.

The authors of this book and all those who have contributed towards it dedicate their work to all who man or manage the aircraft, be they pilots or test pilots, designers or engineers. It is also dedicated to the governments of this world, in order to remind them that the warplane can only be considered to have served its purpose in the deepest sense if it reaches the stage of being taken out of service without having been to war. The past has fallen short of this ideal; but there is still hope for the future.

Enzo Angelucci

CONTENTS

The numbers in **bold** to the right of the main contents column indicate page numbers of the illustrations; the numbers in normal type refer to pages where the corresponding texts will be found.

In the series of scale views of aircraft, two different scales have been used. For aircraft from 1914 to 1937 the scale is 3 m = 2.16 cm (Plates 1, 9, 48 and 61); for aircraft after 1935 the scale is 4 m = 2.16 cm (Plates 78, 115, 141, 157, 165, 184, 209, 222, 236 and 237).

In the "Entry into Service" plates, a common scale applies to all the drawings within one plate, and to all the plates within one chapter. Thus in chapter 2 plates 49 and 62 are on the same scale, in chapter 3 plates 75, 116, 158 and 166, and in chapter 4 plates 185, 210, 223 and 238.

Country abbreviations are as follows:
A - Austria; **AUS** - Australia; **B** - Belgium; **BR** - Brazil; **CDN** - Canada; **CH** - Switzerland; **CS** - Czechoslovakia; **F** - France; **G** - Federal Republic of Germany; **GB** - Britain; **I** - Italy; **IL** - Israel; **IND** - India; **J** - Japan; **NL** - Netherlands; **PL** - Poland; **R** - Romania; **RA** - Argentina; **S** - Sweden; **SF** - Finland; **SP** - Spain; **USSR** - Soviet Union; **USA** - United States of America; **YU** - Yugoslavia.

INTRODUCTION

Thursday, 17th December 1903. No description can equal a photograph taken that day on a beach, near Kill Devil dune, four miles south of Kitty Hawk, in Dare County, North Carolina. The background is blurred, the horizon obscured by a wintry mist; in the foreground and to the right on the vast expanse of sand can be seen two boxes, a shovel, a can; from the left to the centre a long wooden rail; at the end of the rail – a metre off the ground, barely in the air, is an ungainly aeroplane with large, pale wings, propellers turning and a man lying face downwards in the pilot's position; on the extreme right is a second figure wearing a jacket and cap, stretching forward towards the machine, as though to support it. The two men are Orville and Wilbur Wright; the aeroplane is their *Flyer I*, the occasion the first powered flight in history.

The photograph was taken at 10.35 by John T. Daniels, a Kill Devil coast-guard station employee, one of the five witnesses called by Orville and Wilbur to be present at the birth of modern aviation. It was Orville who, before getting into the pilot's position of *Flyer I*, had asked Daniels to take the photograph – "but only if the machine gets off the ground". The first flight lasted exactly 12 seconds. In the ensuing hour and a half the two brothers took turns in three further attempts, during the last of which *Flyer I* managed to travel 852 feet (260 metres) in the air, piloted by Wilbur, remaining aloft for 59 seconds. This was more than sufficient to make the claim and to uphold it, in the face of any challenge, that a machine driven by a man had managed to take to the air for the first time, in controlled flight and to land in a place no lower than its take-off point.

This date, the circumstances and participants, together with the photograph, all represent the starting point of the history of aviation. This was the moment that began the history of the modern aeroplane and ended long centuries of myth and fantasy, and the guesswork of early experiments in flight. There is no doubt however that those centuries of myth and guesswork made their contribution to the Wright brothers' success, and that the new trail they were about to blaze could never have been possible without the long and tortuous path followed by their predecessors.

Man's first dreams of flight are lost in the remote annals of history. In the earliest evidence, flight is the exclusive attribute of the gods, as in the winged figures found in prehistoric wall-paintings. Similar images are handed down to us through Egyptian mythology, or the flying bulls and horses of ancient Assyria and the Greek myths. For many, the story of human flight begins with the legend of Daedalus and Icarus, whose wings were made of birds' feathers held together with wax, and the tragic fate which spared only the older and wiser of the two.

But it is not only the Mediterranean civilisations which thus sought to defy the laws of nature. In 2200 BC the Chinese emperor Shin launched himself from the top of a tower and was more fortunate than Icarus, since he managed to reach the ground unharmed, by using two large straw hats. Towards 1500 BC the Persian king Kai Kawus is said to have made a legendary voyage through the air in a chariot pulled by eagles. Tradition has it that Alexander the Great carried out a very similar exploit, when he wished to visit the celestial regions, which he did aboard a wicker basket drawn by mythical griffons. The Celtic legend of King Bladud of Brittany also takes up the theme of human flight, telling how one day man wished to test his own magic powers and tried to fly, attaching two wings to his shoulders.

Beyond the confines of myth and legend, there is no lack of historical records of similar but ill-fated experiments. The first dates from AD 852 and concerns the Muslim divine, Armen Firman of Cordoba; whilst in 1020 the Anglo-Saxon Benedictine monk Eilmer jumped from the roof of Malmesbury Abbey. In 1496 it was the turn of the elderly Nuremberg chorister Senecio; and then in 1503 that of the mathematician Giovanni Battista Danti of Perugia; later, in 1628 Paolo Guidotti of Lucca launched himself into the air with a pair of wings made of whalebone and birds' feathers. The list is long.

This age-old fascination remained in the realm of fantasy for a long time – even though, besides wings and flying chariots, there were in fact plenty of practical examples that could have suggested a rational approach to the problem: windmills, in use since ancient Chinese times, are no more than remote precursors of the propeller, as was Archimedes' screw; kites, which had originated in China and had then been revived in medieval Europe, were long unrecognised as the forerunners of the glider. In western civilisation at a time when intellectual enquiry was the exclusive province of philosophy and religion, Leonardo da Vinci (1452–1519) was the first to apply scientific reasoning to the problem of flight.

Leonardo however was still influenced – paradoxically – by the same fascination which had obsessed his predecessors. His mistake was to maintain that only by imitating birds could man fly: preoccupied with this principle he devoted all his research to one particular mechanism, the ornithopter, with which he tried to attain lift by using moving or flapping wings. It was only towards the end of his life that Leonardo understood the impracticability of these attempts, and guessed that the real solution lay in adopting a fixed wing. By then it was too late for him to develop the idea.

Leonardo's underestimation of the energy needed to power such a machine meant that almost twenty years of study and observation which he had carried out from 1486 were misdirected. He considered that a man's muscular strength alone would be sufficient to lift the ornithopter from the ground together with its occupant, by means of the complicated mechanism of the wings. Leonardo thought of just one solution to this problem – in some of his ornithopter and helicopter sketches, a spring is shown which was to augment the pilot's own muscle-power, but there was not enough time left to him to explore this.

Notwithstanding these limitations, da Vinci did contribute a vast wealth of ideas. Many of his recorded theories, which cover 5,000 pages and include 150 drawings, were centuries ahead of his time: principles and methods which were subsequently to be revived and used to turn the ancient dream of flight into reality. These include some of the details of aircraft structure; the parachute; various control systems; and the concept of the propeller itself.

Leonardo was to remain an isolated phenomenon of genius. His records were in fact lost for nearly three centuries (it was only in 1797 that some of them came to light for the first time). During this long intervening period of time, myth and fantasy regained the upper hand, as though nothing had happened. Flying men and winged ships once more filled the expositions and treatises of the learned. In 1670 the Jesuit Francesco de Lana de Terzi (1631–87) of Brescia described with a wealth of detail a flying-machine in which lift would be assured by four empty wooden spheres, and its flight by a sail, to which suitable controls were attached.

The Brazilian Jesuit Lourenço de Gusmão (1686–1724) designed a large glider in the shape of a bird, which he named *Passarola* and with which, we are told, he carried out experiments in 1709. Flying-machines with fixed wings and rotating wings were designed in 1764 by the German Merchior Bauer, and in 1781 by the Frenchman, Blanchard. In 1781 another German, Karl-Friedrich Meerwein, experimented with a form of glider-ornithopter.

And then, while scientists, enthusiasts and scholars were busy searching for the scientific principles which would lead to the great achievement, the conquest of the sky took place without their help altogether. It was not wings or propellers, not the complicated structure of a flying-machine that did the trick. It was a relatively simple device, based on nothing more than a good idea – the balloon.

The historic date was 21st November 1783. On that date at 1.54 pm in Paris, two men left the ground for the first time, aboard a hot-air balloon. It was oval in shape, almost 50 feet (15 metres) wide and about 72 feet (22 metres) high; and the men were Jean-François Pilâtre de Rozier, a professor of chemistry, and the Marquis François d'Arlandes, a major in the army. This achievement was the brilliant and inspired work of two French brothers, Joseph-Michel Montgolfier (1740–1810) and Jacques-Etienne Montgolfier (1745–99), who owned a paper-mill at Annonay, near Lyons. They had observed how smoke rose, and had noted how paper containers, when placed near a furnace, tended to float upwards. From this it was but a short step to construct a sufficiently large and very light container, capable of holding a considerable volume of hot air.

After a series of experiments carried out in September 1782, a large balloon 33 feet (10 metres) in diameter was successfully tested on 4th June 1783. On 9th September of the same year, at Versailles, a second balloon was launched with a sheep, a goose and a chicken on board. In front of an enthusiastic crowd, this balloon covered nearly 2 miles (about 3 km) and brought its occupants safely back to earth. Two months later, with a third balloon, the Montgolfier brothers staged Pilâtre de Rozier's and the Marquis d'Arlandes' historic ascent.

The *Montgolfier* hot-air balloon (as it was immediately

named in honour of its inventors), was soon joined by another type of balloon, in which hydrogen was used – "the inflammable air" discovered seventeen years previously by the Englishman, Henry Cavendish. Jacques-Alexandre César Charles (1746–1823), the French academician, was the first to experiment with this, and the hydrogen balloon (named the *Charlière*, after him) flew from the Tuileries gardens on 1st December 1783 and covered 27 miles (43 km) without mishap.

After this early success, the "lighter-than-air" mania spread everywhere, like an epidemic. In Italy, the first ascent was made on 25th February 1784 at Milan by Paolo Andreani and the Gerli brothers in a *Montgolfier*. And then in Scotland, on 27th August, James Tytler of Edinburgh made the first free-flight balloon ascent in Britain. Less than five months later, on 5th January 1785, the Frenchman Jean-Pierre Blanchard and the American John Jeffries managed to cross the English Channel in a balloon of 27 feet (8.3 metres) diameter. It was Blanchard who made the first balloon ascent in the United States at Philadelphia on 9th January 1793. A year later, the balloon officially became military equipment: it was the French who used it for aerial observation of artillery fire.

What effect did the unexpected and dazzling success of lighter-than-air flight have on the painstaking research into the heavier-than-air machines? Scientifically its contribution was negligible. From the point of view of public interest, the enthusiasm and the attention of all Europe were monopolised by the balloon. Scholars and scientists redoubled their efforts to carry their experiments further. The end of the eighteenth and the first half of the nineteenth centuries were marked by many notable advances.

Sir George Cayley (1773–1857), an Englishman with many interests, had a considerable influence on this field. His contribution was considered by many to be comparable to that of Leonardo da Vinci. Cayley's research concerned the mechanical principles of flight – the relationships, that is, between weight, power, drag and thrust. Moving away for the first time from da Vinci's bird-imitative concepts of flight, we enter the world of modern aviation.

Cayley commenced his experiments in 1796 with a little model helicopter. Eight years later, this scholar applied his theories to the construction of the first true aeroplane of history: a very small glider about 5 feet (1.5 metres) long, with a fixed wing set at an angle of 6 degrees; it had a cruciform tail-plane fixed to the fuselage by flexible joints, and movable ballast was used to control the centre of gravity.

In 1809 Cayley built a slightly larger glider, which was made to fly successfully. After having produced a number of models, Cayley scaled up his experiments to full-size gliders. The erudite Englishman came very close to success; he made experiments with his first full scale glider in 1849, putting the ten-year-old son of a servant aboard. He launched the second in 1853 from a hill-top, and this time the occupant was John Appleby, his coachman, who glided for some 32 feet (10 metres) before landing with a crash.

These experiments apart, Cayley's role was important for his dissemination of theory, resulting from his studies and research, in the scientific reviews of the period. His most important publication appeared in 1809–10 under the title *On Aerial Navigation*; in this the principles of aerodynamics were discussed, as well as their application and function. Cayley also faced the problem of propulsion, and having established that muscular force would never be enough for mechanical flight, he came to the conclusion that the only element now lacking was an internal combustion engine: only with this would it finally be possible to turn the ancient dream into reality.

Cayley's reasoning was undoubtedly far ahead of his time, but his influence had no immediate practical impact. Indeed, for most of the nineteenth century, ideas of winged men persisted; and projects and experiments with bizarre flying-ships were pursued. Slowly, however, significant advances were being made. In 1842 the Englishman William Samuel Henson (1812–88) designed and patented a flying-machine which had an enormous influence on aeronautical opinion, even though the "Aerial steam carriage" was never constructed. The aircraft, based on Cayley's theories, was to be powered by a 25–30 hp steam engine and represented the first design in history of a fixed-wing, propeller-driven aircraft.

Together with his friend John Stringfellow (1799–1883), Henson made a scale model which was tested in the years 1845–47, but the trials were disappointing. Henson abandoned everything and soon afterwards emigrated to the United States. Stringfellow, however, was not discouraged: he persisted with the experiments and, in 1868, he built the original triplane, equipped with a small steam-engine which he had constructed himself. Although this machine did not fly, the engine received due recognition.

Research into an efficient propulsion unit was a dominant theme of the second half of the century. In many cases, as in the experiments of the Frenchmen, Alphonse Pénaud (1850–80) and Victor Tatin (1843–1913), this research came to be associated with the development of important theories in aerodynamics. There was no lack of volunteers for the adventure of flight in a mechanically-powered machine, as for example the French naval officer, Félix du Temple (1823–90) who in 1874 tested his monoplane, powered by a steam-engine with a traction propeller. Du Temple, taking off from a downward-sloping ramp, managed to leave the ground and achieved 32 feet (10 metres) of uncontrolled flight. A similar exploit took place in Russia in 1881, when a captain in the Imperial Navy, Alexandr F. Mozhaiski, took off in a steam-powered monoplane of his own design. Research and countless attempted flights did, however, make two things clear: that the steam engine was not a suitable power-source for mechanical flight; and that the best means of propulsion was the propeller.

These conclusions had been confirmed by significant developments in lighter-than-air craft which, by using a propeller, had become dirigible in horizontal flight in 1852. The first recorded dirigible was tested on 24th September

1852 by the Frenchman, Henri Giffard (1825–82); the airship was driven by a propeller linked to a small steam-engine. In the years which followed, the problem of devising a suitable power unit was tackled with little success.

The piston engine provided the answer, and it was only in 1898 that the modern dirigible could be flown, the *No. 1* of the Brazilian, Alberto Santos-Dumont (1873–1932) who both built it and tried it out in Paris. Santos-Dumont's experiments were widely copied, especially in Germany, and it was at this time that Ferdinand von Zeppelin (1838–1917), the German engineer, became active.

But to return to the heavier-than-air craft: before the piston engine was to make the aeroplane possible, there was still one last problem to solve, that of the wing, and consequently, that of controlled flight. The experiments and studies of the German, Otto Lilienthal (1848–96); the Australian, Lawrence Hargrave (1850–1915); the Scotsman, Percy Sinclair Pilcher (1867–99) and Octave Chanute (1832–1910), a Frenchman who had US citizenship, all had an influence in this direction. Although Lilienthal was the first man in the world to take to the air in a glider, it was the other three men who developed volplaning theory to the point where a completely controllable machine could be built, and it was Chanute in particular who directly influenced and encouraged the Wright brothers in their work.

The final success of Orville and Wilbur Wright on the morning of 17th December 1903 had been preceded by two other attempted flights, the last belonging to what was by then a bygone era: these were experiments of the Frenchman Clément Ader (1841–1925) and of the American Samuel Pierpont Langley (1834–1906). The former built and tried out two flying machines, the *Eole* and the *Avion III*; only the *Eole* managed to get about 4 inches (10 cm) off the ground and cover about 164 feet (50 metres) on 9th October 1890; this had a propeller powered by a steam engine. On 7th October and 8th December 1903, Langley tried to make his *Aerodrome* fly, from a pontoon on the Potomac River; it was a tandem monoplane powered by a petrol engine driving two propellers: it crashed on both occasions.

Once the myths had been shattered, and the dreams had become reality, the Wrights' actual achievement aroused less enthusiasm than had been expected. The exploit at Kitty Hawk met with great scepticism in America, which drove the two pioneers to devote themselves to building improved versions of their *Flyer*. A second aircraft made its appearance in May 1904; and a third, definitive, model in the following year.

Until 1908, Orville and Wilbur Wright were not seen in public on an airfield again. This respite allowed aviators in Europe to make up for lost time, and for the aeroplane to be further developed. Following the news from America, enthusiasm almost reached the point of frenzy. In 1904 the Frenchman Ferdinand Ferber perfected a glider with efficient controls. Similar experiments were conducted by such well-known people as Louis Blériot, Gabriel Voisin, Robert Esnault-Pelterie and Ernest Archdeacon. On 23rd October 1906 Alberto Santos-Dumont in his *14 bis* won the prize of 3,000 francs awarded for the first aircraft in Europe to fly for more than 82 feet (25 metres). Santos-Dumont went on to fly 650 feet (200 metres) on 12th November of that year. On 9th November 1907 Henri Farman flew for more than a minute.

In Germany, the era of heavier-than-air flight began with the *Ellehammer IV* in June 1908. 23rd July 1909 was the historic date for Britain: the aeroplane was Alliott Verdon Roe's *Triplane I*.

It was an era of many "firsts": the first major air show, at Rheims in 1909; the first heavier-than-air crossing of the English Channel by Louis Blériot on 25th July 1909: the first records, made at the Rheims air show, by Glenn Curtiss for speed, Henri Farman for distance and Hubert Latham for altitude; and the first fatal accident, which befell Lt T. E. Selfridge of the US Army on 17th September 1908 in a *Wright A*.

At the end of the first decade of the new century, interest in aviation had spread round the world. Gradually the aeroplane was considered to be no longer a fairground attraction or a plaything of madmen, but a useful and dependable vehicle which had come of age. It was now that thought was given to putting it to military use. The Italians were the first to transform the aeroplane into a weapon, transforming military tactics and strategy, and even changing the very role of ground forces. This was expressed by Maj Giulio Douhet in 1909, who wrote: "At present we are fully conscious of the importance of the sea. In the near future, it will be no less vital to achieve supremacy in the air." The first practical application took place barely two years later in the Italian conquest of Libya (the first reconnaissance flight was carried out on 23rd October 1911 by Capt Carlo Piazza, and the first bombing raid on 1st November by 2nd Lt Giulio Giudotti).

What could be more useful in a Europe which had already heard the rumblings of approaching world war? The pioneering days, filled with enthusiasm, had flashed by, borne along under the impetus of their own excitement. They abruptly gave way to the sombre years of the war. The aeroplane, however, was not to lose its leading role, but was to occupy the forefront of the stage.

1. THE FIRST WORLD WAR:

FROM A DUBIOUS EXPERIMENT TO A DECISIVE FACTOR IN VICTORY

Douhet's perceptions on the future of the aeroplane as a weapon, and Italy's experience in Libya, where the aeroplane had been put to combat use for the first time, aroused little immediate interest. Apart from those already mentioned, there were numerous demonstrations of the military use of the aeroplane (suffice it to recall the experiments of Glenn Curtiss in 1910 and 1911 in the United States, when the famous pioneer carried out tests involving both bombing and warship-based use). The general staffs of most armies were still so committed to traditional strategy that they regarded the aeroplane with great scepticism. Thus it came about that at the outbreak of the First World War in August 1914 aviation was still in an embryonic stage of development.

The few available aeroplanes were in no sense combat aircraft; they had been conceived in the pioneering days, and any changes they had undergone since then had not equipped them for offensive or defensive use. The first aircraft to be used in the war were frail, slow and of limited range, and their operational use was confined to occasional reconnaissance, out of range of ground forces and never far from their own lines.

This state of affairs, however, lasted for only a few months; it was soon changed by the harsh necessities of war. Earlier scepticism gave way to an almost obsessive interest in the aeroplane. Aircraft designers and manufacturers – who only shortly before had been regarded as fanatics in a world of their own – were now encouraged in every way; the aircraft industry expanded rapidly. Both quality and quantity came to be in great demand. This was the beginning of an era of unchecked progress, which lasted for five long years at the end of which the aeroplane had really come of age.

For all practical purposes the warplane came into being at the end of 1914, with the adoption of the machine gun. In the early stages of the war reconnaissance planes, used for observation of enemy troop movements and of artillery fire, used to come into close confrontation with each other. Although these aircraft were unarmed, battle was joined, using whatever weapons were to hand, such as pistols and rifles, many of which had been specially adapted for use by air crews; some also carried steel darts to throw at the enemy's fabric-covered planes, and even hooks suspended on cables, a device invented by Captain Alexandr Alexandrovich Kazakov, Russia's leading air ace of the war.

The advent of the machine gun put an end to this heroic period of warfare, and with it the armed reconnaissance plane came into being. In the beginning these aircraft had the gun located in the observer's cockpit, but operational use soon showed that this siting made it impossible to counter frontal attacks, because the plane's own structure limited the field of fire. On the other hand, a forward-firing machine gun would be obstructed by the propeller disc.

In the absence of any form of synchronisation of the rate of fire of the gun and the turning of the propeller (this was only achieved in 1915), various expedients were introduced. One solution, quite widely used, was to mount the gun on top of the upper wing, thus avoiding the propeller; another was to design the aircraft with a rear-mounted pusher-propeller, so that the machine gun could be positioned in the nose. In both cases, however, there were drawbacks; in the former it was difficult to sight and control the gun (especially when it was necessary to reload or unjam it); in the latter, performance was generally inferior to puller-propeller aircraft.

The next development was the arming of the reconnaissance plane with a small bomb-load, usually anti-personnel. The emergence of new aircraft which could carry heavier loads, and which were more stable in flight, made this feasible. These could not be described accurately as real bombers (it was only in the following years that the heavy bombers went into action in any numbers), but the aeroplane proved beyond question that it could fulfil this new role successfully.

The reconnaissance plane and the bomber were soon joined by another type of combat aircraft: the fighter, designed for one task only – to engage the enemy in aerial combat. It was consequently fast, manoeuvrable, well-armed and a single-seater. The development of effective aircraft of this type was, however, dependent upon solving the problem of firing forward through the propeller disc, since in this way the plane's armament could be used to the greatest effect, enabling the pilot to aim the machine gun directly forward. Thus man, plane and weapon were all aligned together to make the most effective combination.

The Frenchman Roland Garros was the first person to attempt this solution, installing in 1915 a fixed machine gun in a Morane-Saulnier L, together with rudimentary deflector-plates fixed to the propeller-blades in the line of fire; their function was to deflect any bullets which would not have cleared the rotating propeller. This was known as the deflector plate system, and its success made Morane & Saulnier's monoplane a very effective fighter, the first real fighter in aeronautical history.

This was, however, still a period of temporary expedients. The Germans, inspired by Garros' work, pressed forward to the final stage by devising an effective synchronising device and fitting it to their aircraft industry's most manoeuvrable monoplane, the Fokker E. This made it the definitive fighter of its day, which when it reached the front (in the summer of 1915) immediately changed the balance of power in the air, to the disadvantage of the Allies.

It was at this time that the immense military potential of the aeroplane was first fully recognised. The fighter was seen as one of the decisive weapons of the war. It was a means of countering any menace from the air, be it bombers, reconnaissance planes or sudden air-ground attacks. If one had at one's disposal more powerful and faster fighters than those of the enemy, one possessed the means of achieving air supremacy. From 1915 onwards, this objective was one of the top priorities for all the countries involved in the conflict.

The introduction of the Fokker monoplane signalled the start of an out-and-out race between the two opposing sides.

Air supremacy was lost and regained time and again in a desperate see-saw which continued until the end of the war. The period known to the British as the "Fokker Scourge" first began on 1st August 1915, the date of a brilliantly successful mission by two future air aces, Oswald Boelcke and Max Immelmann, and reached its apogee in February when the latest model, the E.IV, arrived at the front and joined its predecessors in operational use. At this stage, German fighters were scoring success after success against the slow and poorly-armed Allied aircraft. The British B.E.2cs in particular proved easy victims, since they lacked manoeuvrability and were very vulnerable when attacked from the rear.

Early in 1916 the balance slowly swung back in favour of the Allies. Two British fighters (the F.E.2b and the D.H.2, which both outclassed the Fokkers in speed, rate of climb and handling) and two French fighters (the Nieuport 11 and 17) were the first to bring about this reversal of fortunes. Air superiority was regained and consolidated by the first Allied planes with forward-flying synchronised machine guns, among them the Spad S.VII, the best example of aeronautical engineering of the time.

The Germans, however, reacted quickly and very effectively. They produced fighters which were, technically speaking, exceptional – such as the Albatros D.I, D.II and D.III and the Halberstadt D.II and D.III. Renewed vigour and greater flexibility were introduced in the structure of the air force, which was regrouped into independent squadrons (called *Jagdstaffeln* or *Jasta*), manned by very experienced pilots able to take full advantage of the potential of these new aircraft. The results of this drive soon made themselves felt and, for the second time, the onset of winter saw the Germans in control of the air. The Allies had to wait until the spring and summer of 1917 before they caught up, when such fighters as Britain's Sopwith Camel, Sopwith Triplane, R.A.F. S.E.5 and Bristol Fighter, and France's Spad S. XIII came into service.

From this point onwards until the end of the war, air supremacy remained once and for all with the Allies. By now, it was not merely a question of quality, but even more of quantity. Even though the Germans made supreme efforts in aircraft production, putting superb planes into service (such as the Fokker D.VII and D.VIII, the Roland D.VI and the Pfalz D.XII), they only succeeded in gaining a temporary advantage. In the spring of 1918 the Allies had 10,000 combat planes against 2,390; a ratio of 4:1 in their favour.

The fighter plane did play a decisive role in determining the outcome of the war; and after its years of non-stop development in all aspects of its engineering and technology, the aviation world had been changed profoundly. Engine and airframe construction had advanced almost beyond recognition, stimulated by ever-increasing demands for speed and power.

Engine design had been following two different paths in the French and German aircraft industries at the outbreak of war. The French had concentrated mainly on developing the rotary engine, which had first been produced in satisfactory form in France by the Seguin brothers in the pioneering days. Germany had concentrated on the stationary liquid-cooled inline engine. Both types had advantages and drawbacks in military use. The rotary engine, whose cylinders and entire engine casing rotated on a central camshaft, thus driving the propeller, was very compact and had fewer vulnerable parts, and being light had an excellent power-to-weight ratio; it was extremely suitable for light and manoeuvrable aircraft. On the other hand, it was not always reliable, was heavy on fuel (and even more so on oil) and produced less power.

The typical six cylinder inline engines of Mercedes, Benz and Austro-Daimler were robust, reliable and powerful, but had the disadvantage, at least in the first years of war, of being too heavy and thereby reducing manoeuvrability. These limitations became evident from the earliest days of air combat, where agility was of prime importance.

The rotary engine, which produced high torque and, because of the rotation of the engine's mass, had a strong gyroscopic effect, lent the aeroplane great manoeuvrability, which expert pilots could put to good advantage in combat, but was potentially lethal for a novice pilot. The Germans fully understood the implications of this and, copying the French, developed their own range of rotary engines, the most famous of these being the Oberursel which was based on the Le Rhône. It was put into some of their most outstanding fighters, in particular the Fokker E.

With the passing of the years, both types of engine underwent constant upgrading, but the two stories ended differently. The rotary engine achieved a maximum output of 200 hp, and then disappeared from the scene. On the other hand the Germans continued to improve their inline engines throughout the war, and for a long time these were valid alternatives to the new generation of radial and liquid-cooled V engines.

Britain became pre-eminent in the manufacture of the latter type in 1915 with the Rolls-Royce V-12 series of engines. Previously, the British aeronautical industry had lacked an entirely domestically produced power unit, and had had to rely on French engines, either imported or manufactured under licence. The V-8 Hispano-Suiza, which had improved upon all previously recorded power-to-weight ratios, was also highly satisfactory. The V-12 Liberty, designed in the US in 1917 by the Packard Motor Corporation, was with 400 hp the most powerful of the whole war.

Naturally, the demand for more and more power directly influenced design, aircraft construction techniques and materials. Wood and fabric gradually gave way to part-plywood, then to wooden monocoque fuselages, which were followed by steel-tube frames, fabric-covered at first, and later covered with aluminium. Excellent monoplanes were produced, including the all-metal Junkers J.1 of 1915, which indicates the ease and confidence which designers were beginning to acquire. The typical fighter of 1918 was a biplane, with tractor propeller, a 220 hp engine, with combat speeds of 125–130 mph (200–210 km/h) at an altitude of nearly 20,000 feet (6,000 metres), armed with two synchronised machine guns. Such an aircraft was the result of four years of remarkable progress, and there was little about it which resembled the slow and fragile planes which had begun the war in the air in 1914.

The second half of the war saw the emergence of the bomber, the development of which was parallel to that of the fighter. The first operational use in 1915 of the large three-engine Italian Caproni and the four-engine Russian Sikorsky Ilya Mouromets had clearly shown that the bomber need not be confined to tactical use; these were the forerunners of all the strategic bombers of the war. Britain and Germany immediately took up the challenge: the former with the first models of the Handley Page, the latter with the A.E.G., Gotha, Friedrichshafen and Zeppelin Staaken. It was the Germans who began a form of warfare which was to become so deadly in the future: the prolonged bombing of a single objective, starting with raids at night on London and southern England in 1917. Aeroplanes combined forces with the large Zeppelin airships on these missions. This particular combination, of the lighter and heavier-than-air craft, was to be the worst source of terror from the air for the civil population.

In what way did the various nations in the war adapt their systems to the needs of long years of conflict? What was the effect on the development of their aircraft industries, and of their air forces?

There is no doubt that France, the pioneer of European aviation, led the way for the Allies. In 1914 the French aviation industry was the most advanced in the world, and her contribution was crucial to the establishment and maintenance of air power with which to confront that of the Central Powers. In the early years of the war, France supplied aircraft and engines to her allies, and in the later years of the war put formidable aircraft into the struggle. Furthermore, France enjoyed the prestige of having recognised the military potential of the aircraft very early on. Apart from the pioneers and researchers in the armed forces who had given so much encouragement to the development of the aeroplane, the ministry of war itself had recognised its combat potential, and as early as 12th July 1909 had bought a Wright biplane. Fifteen months later in October 1910 the armed forces had already acquired thirty aircraft of various types, and another sixty-one were on order from the manufacturers.

In 1911 the tradition of military air shows was started, and not only was this idea taken up by other nations, but it also proved a great stimulus for the aviation industry, where production levels quickly rose, the numbers involved being very high for the period: 1,350 aircraft in 1911, 1,425 in 1912 and 1,294 in 1913. The organisation of the French air force was changed and divided into three commands on 28th August 1912, with bases at Versailles, Rheims and Lyons. Two years later, when war was declared, the air force comprised 25 squadrons (aeroplanes and balloons had been placed under separate commands in February 1914; whilst in March 1913 the naval air service had been created,

equipped with eight seaplanes and a few airships and balloons). Twenty-one of these squadrons were made up of six two-seaters, making a total of 138 combat aircraft of various types in service. As the war went on, aircraft were grouped according to their operational roles: single- and two-seat fighters, day and night bombers, and long-range planes. On Armistice Day the *Aviation militaire* had 6,000 aircraft, 6,417 pilots and 1,682 observers out of a total strength of 80,000 personnel. The naval air service had 1,264 aircraft of which 870 were warplanes, 58 airships, 198 balloons, and 11,000 men. Total aircraft production reached 51,000 in all.

The experience of another major air power, Britain, was similar to that of the French. On 9th August 1914, five days after the declaration of war, the Royal Flying Corps was able to deploy 63 assorted aircraft, 105 pilots and 755 other airmen. From this small group originated one of the world's most redoubtable air forces. The concept of the aeroplane in a military role had been accepted since the early pioneering days, actively canvassed by three artillery officers (Lt L. D. L. Gibbs, Capt J. D. B. Fulton and Capt B. Dickson), who, in 1910, succeeded in arranging the first courses for training pilots. On 28th February 1911 the Royal Engineers formed the Air Battalion consisting of two companies, one equipped with balloons, the other with five aircraft – the first air unit of the Army. The Royal Flying Corps was founded on 13th April 1912, under the control of the Army; it comprised naval and military wings and the Central Flying School. On 23rd June 1914 the Royal Navy took a similar step in forming the Royal Naval Air Service. The structure evolved further on 1st April 1918 with the constitution of Royal Air Force (which absorbed the RFC and the RNAS) as an independent service. In October 1918 the RAF had a strength of 291,748, and had 22,171 aircraft, of which 3,300 were in front-line service. To achieve this remarkable total, the British aviation industry turned out 55,000 aircraft of all types during the war years, with maximum production levels running at 3,500 aircraft a month when the most intense efforts were being made.

Of the enemy nations, Germany was the direct adversary of these two great powers. When one considers Germany's achievement in setting up, running efficiently and greatly expanding the complex structure needed for aerial warfare, it was certainly impressive. At the beginning of the war, their aircraft were slow and unarmed, intended only to be used for aerial observation and reconnaissance of ground forces. In line with the general view, the Germans too had treated the idea of incorporating aircraft into the traditional armed forces with a measure of scepticism. Aviation was at the outset under the control of the army, responsible to the High Command, and divided into units (*Feldflieger-abteilungen* – each normally of six aeroplanes).

It soon developed into an independent service, and its structure and organisation were subject to constant change as proved necessary in the light of operational experience. The naval air service developed in a similar fashion, being under the command of the Imperial Navy. Towards the end of the war, Germany had attained considerable power in the air, and the effective strength of the air force was continually reinforced by an industrial machine which was working flat out. To the very last, Germany continued to field exceptional aircraft in large numbers. The growth in numbers produced is the most significant indicator of this achievement: from 24 aircraft built in 1911, rising to 136 in 1912, to 446 in 1913, to 1,348 in 1914, 4,532 in 1915 and 8,182 in 1916. The last two years of the war witnessed their supreme effort – 19,746 aircraft in 1917 and 14,123 in 1918. The total number of all types of aircraft produced during the war years was 48,537.

Italy and Austria were also in direct confrontation. When Italy entered the war after a year's delay, she found herself with an air force which, although well-trained and combat-ready, could not be considered to be on a par with those of the other powers, who were already battle-seasoned after considerable fighting experience. The first dozen squadrons at the front were issued with a varied collection of French planes: out of a total of 86, there were 37 Blériots, 27 Nieuports and 22 Farmans. Although there had been a growing interest in heavier-than-air craft since 1911, resulting in the formation of the *Servizio Aeronautico* on 27th June 1912 as part of the Army, and the creation that October of the seaplane unit of the navy – *Sezione Idroplani della Marina* – domestic industry had not yet managed to manufacture military aircraft which could compete with the French. In fact, a feature of the evolution of Italian aviation (which saw the formation of the *Corpo Aeronautico Militare* on 7th January 1915) was the massive number of French aircraft used for much of the war, especially fighters. The only exceptions were naval aircraft and bombers, where Macchi's and Caproni's best designs placed Italy in a pre-eminent position. It was only in 1918 that the first Italian-produced fighters started to go into service, yet their influence on the course of the war was quite considerable. Anyhow, from 1916 onwards things improved: industry managed to produce 1,255 aircraft and operational units totalled 49 squadrons of which 13 were bomber squadrons, 22 reconnaissance, 9 fighter and five were for the defence of areas of particular strategic importance. In 1917, production reached a total of 3,861 aircraft; and the service was reorganised and simplified: each Italian army had an air force unit attached, while a separate force came under the direct control of the High Command. At the time of the Armistice, 1,683 aircraft were in front-line service, and total production had reached a figure of 11,986.

When the war began the position in Austria was very similar to that in Italy; the air force consisted of 36 aircraft, 1 airship and 10 balloons. The exigencies of war spurred the army to frantic efforts, to reorganise and strengthen its air force, and Austria was soon able to put good aircraft of Austrian manufacture into service, together with others of German design built under licence. In 1917 the air force was reorganised into three types of unit: *Aufklärungskompagnien* of observation and reconnaissance planes (each of 8–10 Type C two-seaters and 3 or 4 escort fighters); *Jagdkompagnien* of fighters (16–20 aircraft); and *Geschwadern* or *Fliegerkompagnien* of 10 bombers and 4 escort fighters. Unlike the army air force, the naval air force suffered from a persistent lack of material.

Separate mention must be made of Russia and the United States, two nations which played a relatively minor part in the war in the air. The former suffered not only from the inferior products of her aircraft industry, but also from the internal turmoil that led up to the revolution of 1917, which hampered any significant development. The only exceptions were Igor Sikorsky's advanced multi-engined bombers, which were used in a strategic role. Apart from this, the Imperial Air Service, which at the outbreak of war had 24 aircraft, 12 airships and 46 balloons, also received several hundred planes of French design which had been made under licence, as well as those imported direct from France, Britain and the United States. Thus the Russians had to fight from a position of inferiority.

The United States felt the consequences of the delay in implementing organisation and development plans in military aviation. Up to 1911 the only aircraft was the Flyer A which Orville Wright had managed to sell to the Army in August 1909. On 18th July 1914 military aviation had received recognition with the formation of the Aviation Section of the Signal Corps; and only in the ensuing two years was approval given for a vast reorganisation programme which involved increased personnel, production, and the founding of flying schools. When the United States declared war on 9th April 1917, its air force was less than 250 aircraft strong (these being quite unsuitable for combat) with 1,087 airmen. Only in 1918 did the American Expeditionary Force's air arm get itself rationally organised on the front under the command of Gen William Mitchell, and it used only French equipment. At the end of the war, this force totalled 45 squadrons, with a strength of 740 aircraft, about 800 pilots and 500 observers.

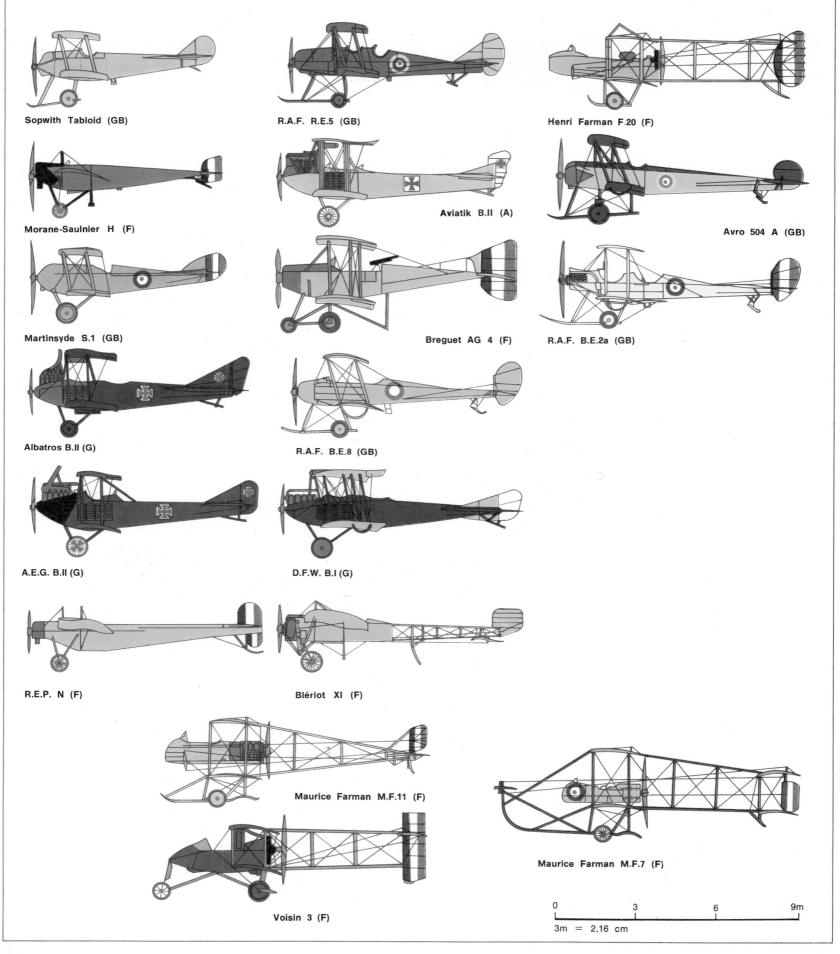

Sopwith Tabloid (GB)

R.A.F. R.E.5 (GB)

Henri Farman F.20 (F)

Morane-Saulnier H (F)

Aviatik B.II (A)

Avro 504 A (GB)

Martinsyde S.1 (GB)

Breguet AG 4 (F)

R.A.F. B.E.2a (GB)

Albatros B.II (G)

R.A.F. B.E.8 (GB)

A.E.G. B.II (G)

D.F.W. B.I (G)

R.E.P. N (F)

Blériot XI (F)

Maurice Farman M.F.11 (F)

Maurice Farman M.F.7 (F)

Voisin 3 (F)

0   3   6   9m

3m = 2,16 cm

Plate 2

French aircraft at the outbreak of war: 1914

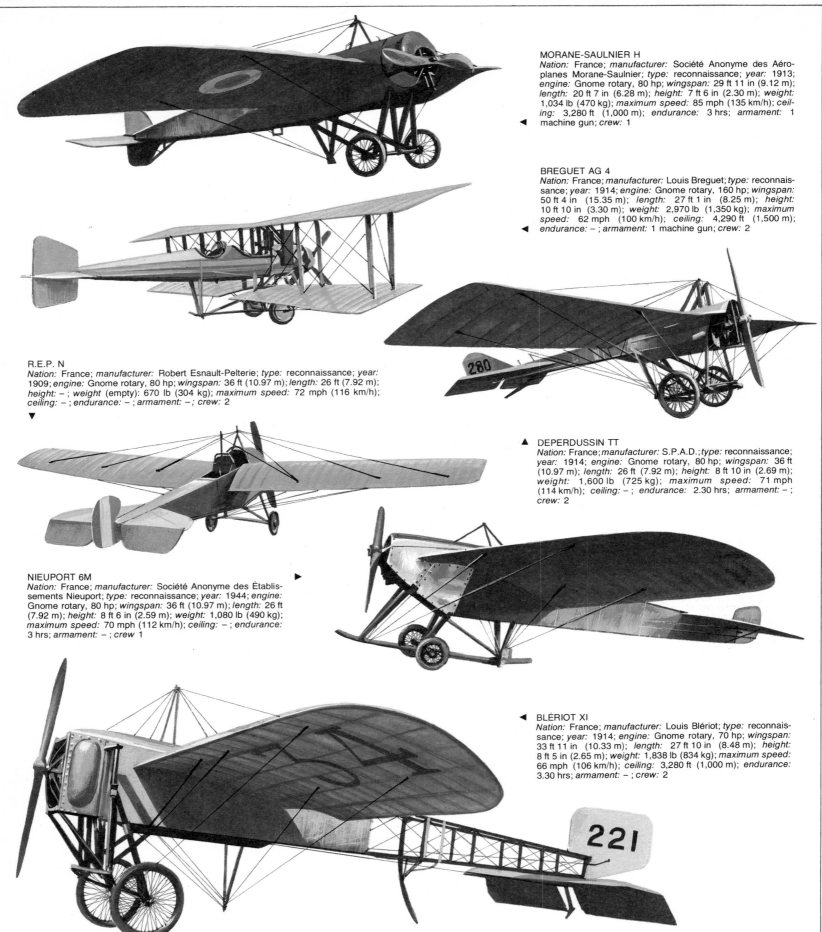

MORANE-SAULNIER H
Nation: France; *manufacturer:* Société Anonyme des Aéroplanes Morane-Saulnier; *type:* reconnaissance; *year:* 1913; *engine:* Gnome rotary, 80 hp; *wingspan:* 29 ft 11 in (9.12 m); *length:* 20 ft 7 in (6.28 m); *height:* 7 ft 6 in (2.30 m); *weight:* 1,034 lb (470 kg); *maximum speed:* 85 mph (135 km/h); *ceiling:* 3,280 ft (1,000 m); *endurance:* 3 hrs; *armament:* 1 machine gun; *crew:* 1

BREGUET AG 4
Nation: France; *manufacturer:* Louis Breguet; *type:* reconnaissance; *year:* 1914; *engine:* Gnome rotary, 160 hp; *wingspan:* 50 ft 4 in (15.35 m); *length:* 27 ft 1 in (8.25 m); *height:* 10 ft 10 in (3.30 m); *weight:* 2,970 lb (1,350 kg); *maximum speed:* 62 mph (100 km/h); *ceiling:* 4,290 ft (1,500 m); *endurance:* – ; *armament:* 1 machine gun; *crew:* 2

R.E.P. N
Nation: France; *manufacturer:* Robert Esnault-Pelterie; *type:* reconnaissance; *year:* 1909; *engine:* Gnome rotary, 80 hp; *wingspan:* 36 ft (10.97 m); *length:* 26 ft (7.92 m); *height:* – ; *weight* (empty): 670 lb (304 kg); *maximum speed:* 72 mph (116 km/h); *ceiling:* – ; *endurance:* – ; *armament:* – ; *crew:* 2

DEPERDUSSIN TT
Nation: France; *manufacturer:* S.P.A.D.; *type:* reconnaissance; *year:* 1914; *engine:* Gnome rotary, 80 hp; *wingspan:* 36 ft (10.97 m); *length:* 26 ft (7.92 m); *height:* 8 ft 10 in (2.69 m); *weight:* 1,600 lb (725 kg); *maximum speed:* 71 mph (114 km/h); *ceiling:* – ; *endurance:* 2.30 hrs; *armament:* – ; *crew:* 2

NIEUPORT 6M
Nation: France; *manufacturer:* Société Anonyme des Établissements Nieuport; *type:* reconnaissance; *year:* 1944; *engine:* Gnome rotary, 80 hp; *wingspan:* 36 ft (10.97 m); *length:* 26 ft (7.92 m); *height:* 8 ft 6 in (2.59 m); *weight:* 1,080 lb (490 kg); *maximum speed:* 70 mph (112 km/h); *ceiling:* – ; *endurance:* 3 hrs; *armament:* – ; *crew* 1

BLÉRIOT XI
Nation: France; *manufacturer:* Louis Blériot; *type:* reconnaissance; *year:* 1914; *engine:* Gnome rotary, 70 hp; *wingspan:* 33 ft 11 in (10.33 m); *length:* 27 ft 10 in (8.48 m); *height:* 8 ft 5 in (2.65 m); *weight:* 1,838 lb (834 kg); *maximum speed:* 66 mph (106 km/h); *ceiling:* 3,280 ft (1,000 m); *endurance:* 3.30 hrs; *armament:* – ; *crew:* 2

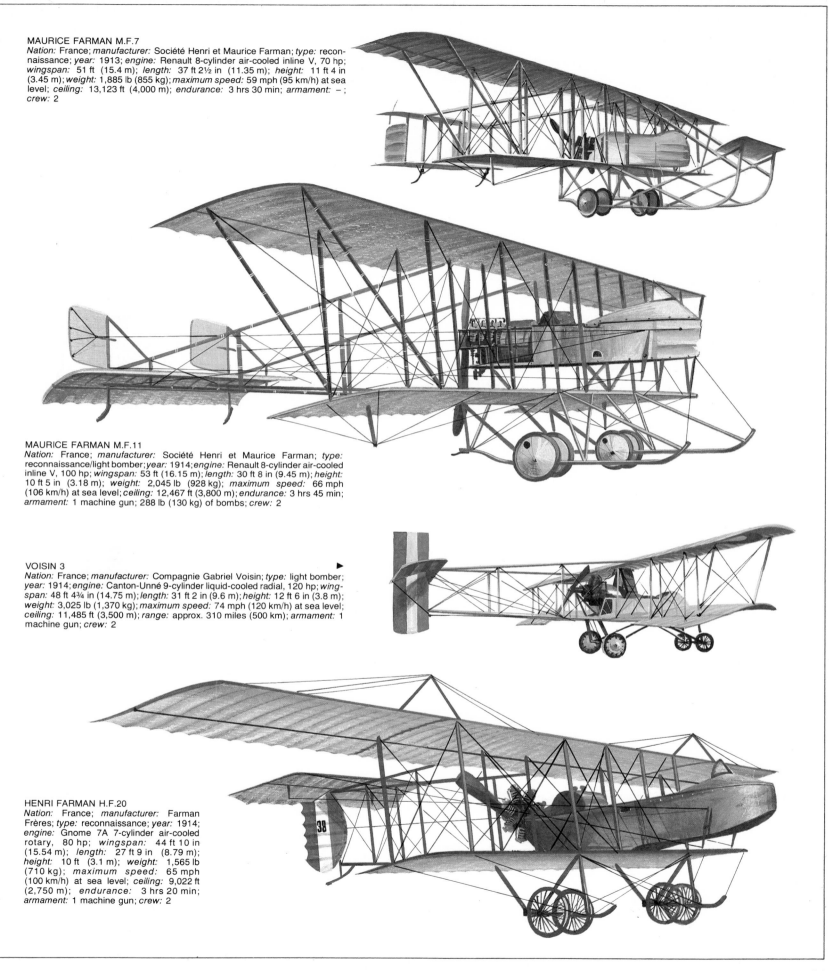

MAURICE FARMAN M.F.7
Nation: France; *manufacturer:* Société Henri et Maurice Farman; *type:* reconnaissance; *year:* 1913; *engine:* Renault 8-cylinder air-cooled inline V, 70 hp; *wingspan:* 51 ft (15.4 m); *length:* 37 ft 2½ in (11.35 m); *height:* 11 ft 4 in (3.45 m); *weight:* 1,885 lb (855 kg); *maximum speed:* 59 mph (95 km/h) at sea level; *ceiling:* 13,123 ft (4,000 m); *endurance:* 3 hrs 30 min; *armament:* – ; *crew:* 2

MAURICE FARMAN M.F.11
Nation: France; *manufacturer:* Société Henri et Maurice Farman; *type:* reconnaissance/light bomber; *year:* 1914; *engine:* Renault 8-cylinder air-cooled inline V, 100 hp; *wingspan:* 53 ft (16.15 m); *length:* 30 ft 8 in (9.45 m); *height:* 10 ft 5 in (3.18 m); *weight:* 2,045 lb (928 kg); *maximum speed:* 66 mph (106 km/h) at sea level; *ceiling:* 12,467 ft (3,800 m); *endurance:* 3 hrs 45 min; *armament:* 1 machine gun; 288 lb (130 kg) of bombs; *crew:* 2

VOISIN 3 ▶
Nation: France; *manufacturer:* Compagnie Gabriel Voisin; *type:* light bomber; *year:* 1914; *engine:* Canton-Unné 9-cylinder liquid-cooled radial, 120 hp; *wingspan:* 48 ft 4¾ in (14.75 m); *length:* 31 ft 2 in (9.6 m); *height:* 12 ft 6 in (3.8 m); *weight:* 3,025 lb (1,370 kg); *maximum speed:* 74 mph (120 km/h) at sea level; *ceiling:* 11,485 ft (3,500 m); *range:* approx. 310 miles (500 km); *armament:* 1 machine gun; *crew:* 2

HENRI FARMAN H.F.20
Nation: France; *manufacturer:* Farman Frères; *type:* reconnaissance; *year:* 1914; *engine:* Gnome 7A 7-cylinder air-cooled rotary, 80 hp; *wingspan:* 44 ft 10 in (15.54 m); *length:* 27 ft 9 in (8.79 m); *height:* 10 ft (3.1 m); *weight:* 1,565 lb (710 kg); *maximum speed:* 65 mph (100 km/h) at sea level; *ceiling:* 9,022 ft (2,750 m); *endurance:* 3 hrs 20 min; *armament:* 1 machine gun; *crew:* 2

Plate 4

British aircraft at the outbreak of war: 1914

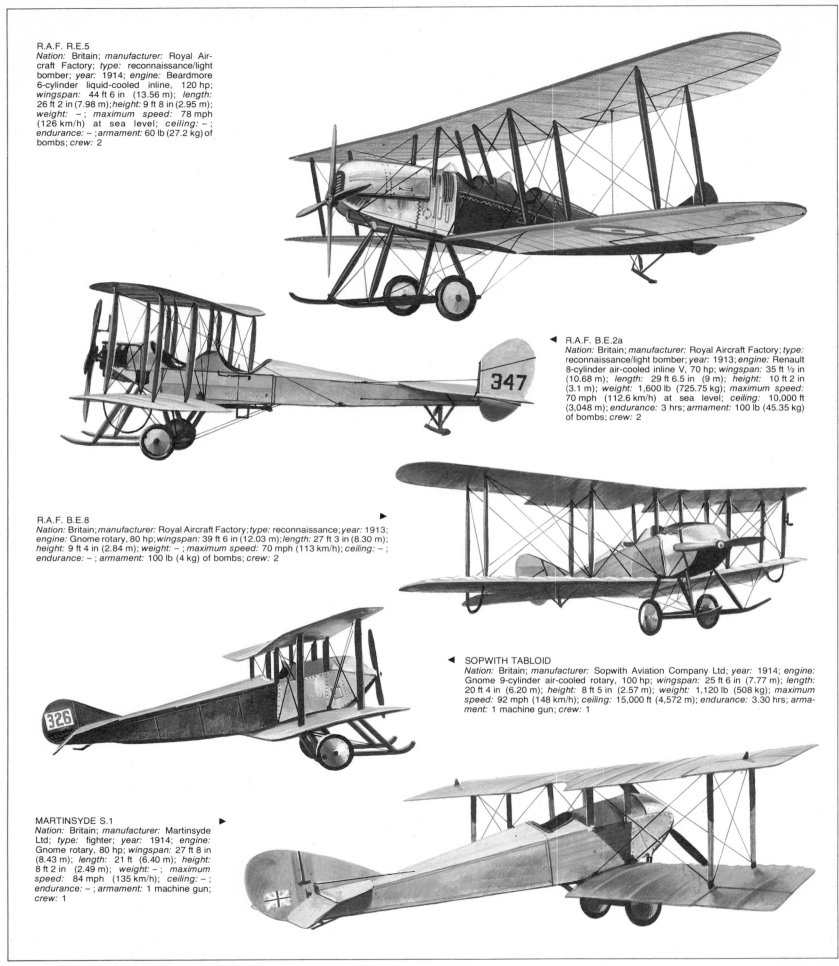

R.A.F. R.E.5
Nation: Britain; *manufacturer:* Royal Aircraft Factory; *type:* reconnaissance/light bomber; *year:* 1914; *engine:* Beardmore 6-cylinder liquid-cooled inline, 120 hp; *wingspan:* 44 ft 6 in (13.56 m); *length:* 26 ft 2 in (7.98 m); *height:* 9 ft 8 in (2.95 m); *weight:* – ; *maximum speed:* 78 mph (126 km/h) at sea level; *ceiling:* – ; *endurance:* – ; *armament:* 60 lb (27.2 kg) of bombs; *crew:* 2

◄ **R.A.F. B.E.2a**
Nation: Britain; *manufacturer:* Royal Aircraft Factory; *type:* reconnaissance/light bomber; *year:* 1913; *engine:* Renault 8-cylinder air-cooled inline V, 70 hp; *wingspan:* 35 ft ½ in (10.68 m); *length:* 29 ft 6.5 in (9 m); *height:* 10 ft 2 in (3.1 m); *weight:* 1,600 lb (725.75 kg); *maximum speed:* 70 mph (112.6 km/h) at sea level; *ceiling:* 10,000 ft (3,048 m); *endurance:* 3 hrs; *armament:* 100 lb (45.35 kg) of bombs; *crew:* 2

R.A.F. B.E.8 ►
Nation: Britain; *manufacturer:* Royal Aircraft Factory; *type:* reconnaissance; *year:* 1913; *engine:* Gnome rotary, 80 hp; *wingspan:* 39 ft 6 in (12.03 m); *length:* 27 ft 3 in (8.30 m); *height:* 9 ft 4 in (2.84 m); *weight:* – ; *maximum speed:* 70 mph (113 km/h); *ceiling:* – ; *endurance:* – ; *armament:* 100 lb (4 kg) of bombs; *crew:* 2

◄ **SOPWITH TABLOID**
Nation: Britain; *manufacturer:* Sopwith Aviation Company Ltd; *year:* 1914; *engine:* Gnome 9-cylinder air-cooled rotary, 100 hp; *wingspan:* 25 ft 6 in (7.77 m); *length:* 20 ft 4 in (6.20 m); *height:* 8 ft 5 in (2.57 m); *weight:* 1,120 lb (508 kg); *maximum speed:* 92 mph (148 km/h); *ceiling:* 15,000 ft (4,572 m); *endurance:* 3.30 hrs; *armament:* 1 machine gun; *crew:* 1

MARTINSYDE S.1 ►
Nation: Britain; *manufacturer:* Martinsyde Ltd; *type:* fighter; *year:* 1914; *engine:* Gnome rotary, 80 hp; *wingspan:* 27 ft 8 in (8.43 m); *length:* 21 ft (6.40 m); *height:* 8 ft 2 in (2.49 m); *weight:* – ; *maximum speed:* 84 mph (135 km/h); *ceiling:* – ; *endurance:* – ; *armament:* 1 machine gun; *crew:* 1

AVRO 504A
Nation: Britain; *manufacturer:* A. V. Roe &
Co Ltd; *type:* reconnaissance/light bomber;
year: 1914; *engine:* Gnome 7-cylinder air-
cooled rotary, 80 hp; *wingspan:* 36 ft
(10.97 m); *length:* 29 ft 5 in (8.97 m);
height: 10 ft 5 in (3.18 m); *weight:* 1,574 lb
(714 kg); *maximum speed:* 82 mph
(132 km/h) at sea level; *ceiling:* 12,000 ft
(3,658 m); *endurance:* 4 hrs 30 mins;
armament: 1 machine gun; 80 lb (36.3 kg)
of bombs; *crew:* 2

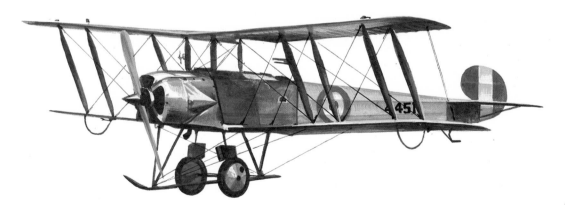

AVRO 504B
Nation: Britain; *manufacturer:* A. V. Roe &
Co Ltd; *type:* reconnaissance/light bomber;
year: 1914; *engine:* Gnome rotary, 80 hp;
wingspan: 36 ft (10.97 m); *length:* 29 ft 5 in
(8.97 m); *height:* 10 ft 5 in (3.18 m); *weight:*
1,574 lb (714 kg); *maximum speed:*
62 mph (100 km/h); *ceiling:* 13,000 ft
(3,950 m); *endurance:* 4.30 hrs; *armament:*
1 machine gun, 80 lb (36 kg) of bombs;
crew: 2

AVRO 504J
Nation: Britain; *manufacturer:* A. V. Roe &
Co Ltd; *type:* trainer; *year:* 1916; *engine:*
Gnome rotary, 100 hp; *wingspan:* 36 ft
(10.97 m); *length:* 29 ft 5 in (8.97 m);
height: 10 ft 5 in (3.18 m); *weight:* 1,825 lb
(828 kg); *maximum speed:* 95 mph
(153 km/h); *ceiling:* 13,000 ft (3,950 m);
endurance: 3 hrs; *armament:* – ; *crew:* 2

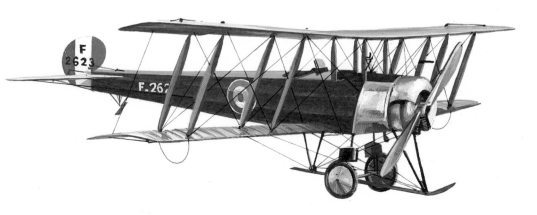

AVRO 504K
Nation: Britain; *manufacturer:* A. V. Roe &
Co Ltd; *type:* night fighter; *year:* 1918;
engine: Le Rhône 9-cylinder air-cooled rotary, 110 hp; *wingspan:* 36 ft (10.97 m);
length: 29 ft 5 in (8.97 m); *height:* 10 ft 5 in
(3.18 m); *weight:* 1,829 lb (830 kg); *maximum speed:* 95 mph (153 km/h) at sea
level; *ceiling:* 16,000 ft (4,877 m); *endurance:* 3 hrs; *armament:* 1 machine gun;
crew: 1

Plate 6　　　　　　　　　　　　　　　　　　　　**German and Austrian aircraft at the outbreak of war: 1914**

D.F.W. BI
Nation: Germany; *manufacturer:* Deutsche Flugzeug-Werke GmbH; *type:* reconnaissance; *year:* 1914; *engine:* Mercedes 6-cylinder, 100 hp; *wingspan:* 45 ft 11¼ in (14 m); *length:* 27 ft 6¾ in (8.4 m); *height:* 9 ft 10 in (3 m); *weight:* 2,233 lb (1,015 kg); *maximum speed:* 75 mph (120 km/h); *ceiling:* 9,840 ft (3,000 m); *endurance:* 4 hrs; *armament:* none; *crew:* 2 ▶

AVIATIK BI
Nation: Germany; *manufacturer:* Automobil und Aviatikwerke AG; *type:* reconnaissance; *year:* 1914; *engine:* Mercedes 6-cylinder inline liquid-cooled 100 hp; *wingspan:* 45 ft 10 in (13.97 m); *length:* 26 ft 2 in (7.97 m); *height:* 10 ft 10 in (3.30 m); *weight:* 2,400 lb (1,088 kg); *maximum speed:* 62 mph (100 km/h); *ceiling:* – ; *endurance:* 4 hrs; *armament:* – ; *crew:* 2 ▲

AVIATIK BII
Nation: Austria; *manufacturer:* Österreichische-Ungarische Flugzeugfabrik Aviatik; *type:* reconnaissance; *year:* 1915; *engine:* Austro-Daimler 6-cylinder inline liquid-cooled, 120 hp; *wingspan:* 46 ft (14.02 m); *length:* 26 ft (8 m); *height:* 10 ft 6 in (3.20 m); *weight:* 1,917 lb (870 kg); *maximum speed:* 68 mph (109 km/h); *ceiling:* 8,140 ft (2,500 m); *endurance:* 4 hrs; *armament:* 44 lb (20 kg) of bombs; *crew:* 2 ▼

ALBATROS BII
Nation: Germany; *manufacturer:* Albatros Werke GmbH; *type:* reconnaissance; *year:* 1914; *engine:* Mercedes 6-cylinder liquid-cooled inline, 100 hp; *wingspan:* 42 ft (12.8 m); *length:* 25 ft ½ in (7.63 m); *height:* 10 ft 4 in (3.15 m); *weight:* 2,356 lb (1,071 kg); *maximum speed:* 66 mph (105 km/h) at sea level; *ceiling:* 9,840 ft (3,000 m); *endurance:* 4 hrs; *armament:* — ; *crew:* 2 ▼

A.E.G. BII
Nation: Germany; *manufacturer:* Allgemeine Elektrizitäts Gesellschaft; *type:* reconnaissance; *year:* 1914; *engine:* Mercedes BII 6-cylinder liquid-cooled inline, 120 hp; *wingspan:* 42 ft 7 in (13 m); *length:* 25 ft 7 in (7.8 m); *height:* 10 ft 2 in (3.1 m); *weight:* – ; *maximum speed:* – ; *ceiling:* – : *armament:* none; *crew:* 2 ▲

◀ **GOTHA-TAUBE LE-3**
Nation: Germany; *manufacturer:* Gothaer Waggonfabrik AG; *type:* reconnaissance; *year:* 1914; *engine:* Mercedes D1, 6-cylinder inline liquid-cooled, 100 hp; *wingspan:* 47 ft 7 in (14.50 m); *length:* 32 ft 10 in (10 m); *height:* — ; *weight:* 2,257 lb (1,086 kg); *maximum speed:* 60 mph (96 km/h); *ceiling:* – ; *endurance:* 4 hrs; *armament:* – ; *crew:* 2

Plate 2
French aircraft at the outbreak of war: 1914

The 138 aeroplanes which, at the outbreak of hostilities, constituted the French air force, were something of a mixed bag. Many of them had not been built specifically for military use and in appearance and performance were no different from the frail monoplanes and biplanes which up to a few months previously were to be seen in large numbers at airfields and aviation rallies.

The Morane-Saulnier H, for example, was derived directly from the family of monoplanes which Léon Morane and Raimond Saulnier had created from 1911 onwards and was to to become famous in the following year with the long-distance flights of Roland Garros (which included a flight from Tunis to Rome on 18th December 1912). The model H was produced in 1913, together with a twin-seater version of slightly larger dimensions, model G; and according to some sources 26 were built for the *Aviation militaire*, who used some of them during the first months of the war.

Considerably greater quantities of the two-seat version were made: 94 aircraft were supplied to the air force, and a number were also built in seaplane configuration. The combat use of both models was rather limited, although it is interesting that ten of them went into service with the Royal Flying Corps. The Morane-Saulnier nevertheless has its niche in the history of military aviation: from it a famous fighter was indirectly developed: the German Fokker E.1 of 1915.

Antony Fokker copied a Morane-Saulnier H, bought second-hand in 1913, when building his M.5 monoplane, which with synchronisation of the machine gun and propeller became a revolutionary combat aircraft. Léon Morane and Raimond Saulnier, meanwhile, carried on with the development of their series of monoplanes and their model L which appeared at the beginning of the war was the first aircraft to prove superior to its German contemporaries.

The first months of the war also saw in action the last examples of the biplanes built by Louis Breguet from 1912 onwards. Two of these in particular, designated Breguet AG 4, can be considered as the first real warplanes of the French pioneer-constructor. These aeroplanes incorporated armour plating for the protection of the pilot whilst a manually-aimed machine gun could be installed for the second member of the crew. The aircraft, however, had a very short operational life as did the few examples of the Deperdussin TT monoplane, which at the outbreak of hostilities equipped two squadrons of the French *Aviation militaire*. They were clearly inadequate for war use, being frail and unarmed. An attempt to equip the pilot with a machine gun had been made in February 1914, with the installation of a mounting for the weapon in the nose, high enough to permit firing above the propeller; but the experiment was not followed up.

A more successful aeroplane was the R.E.P. N, derived from an earlier model which had met with similar success to that of Deperdussin's aeroplanes. This was the military version of the civil aeroplane originally built by Robert Esnault-Pelterie in 1909, which went on to break numerous records. In August 1914 the R.E.P. N equipped a squadron of the *Aviation militaire* and a second unit was formed in the first months of the war. These aircraft remained in service until the early part of 1915 and, although unarmed, gave good service. The observer of course could carry personal weapons; and in fact on 2nd March 1915 an R.E.P. N succeeded in bringing down an Aviatik near Lanevin with a rifle.

The French, Russian and Italian air forces also used a monoplane which in its military role was as successful as it had been in civilian use, the Nieuport 6M. This aircraft had taken the speed record on 21st June 1911, at 133 km/h (83 mph); while this showed the advantage of its clean aerodynamic lines, it was also very sturdy. For conversion to military use the Nieuport 6M was not changed much and at the beginning of the war equipped a squadron of the *Aviation militaire*. In

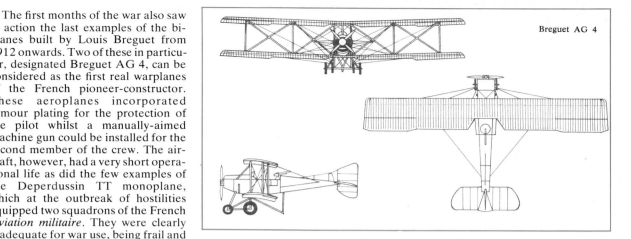

Breguet AG 4

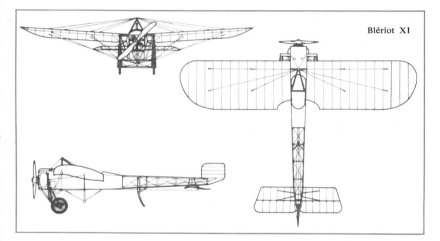

Blériot XI

Italy and in Russia these aeroplanes were kept in service longer: four Italian squadrons were equipped with Nieuports at the time of Italy's entry into the war against the Austro-Hungarian Empire, and the monoplanes were only replaced after some months. In the Russian air force the use of the Nieuport 6M continued for almost the whole of 1915.

The Blériot XI was built in five versions and 132 were manufactured: this monoplane was made famous by Louis Blériot's feat, when on 25th July 1909 he managed to fly it across the Channel from France to England. The aircraft was only fragile in appearance, and showed that it had considerable potential, and with various structural modifications and more powerful engines proved to be suitable for military use, to which it was first put in 1910 in France and in Italy, and in 1912 in Britain. At the outbreak of the World War the *Aviation militaire* used the Blériot XI in at least eight squadrons; seven squadrons of the Royal Flying Corps were equipped with it when they arrived in France, and six squadrons of the Italian air force flew Blériots at the time of Italy's entry into the war.

The five basic variants differed in their carrying capacity and in the power of their engines: the XI Militaire and the XI Artillerie were single-seaters with 50 hp Gnome rotary engines, the XI-2 Artillerie and the XI-2 Génie were twin-seaters with 70 hp Gnome rotary engines; the CI-3 was a three-seater with a 140 hp Gnome engine. Italy's Blériot monoplanes were manufactured under licence by the Società Italiana Transaerea (SIT).

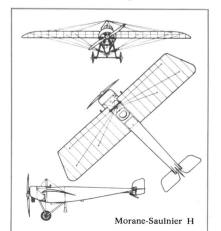

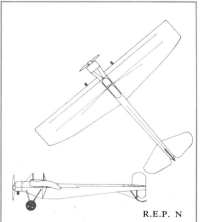

Morane-Saulnier H

R.E.P. N

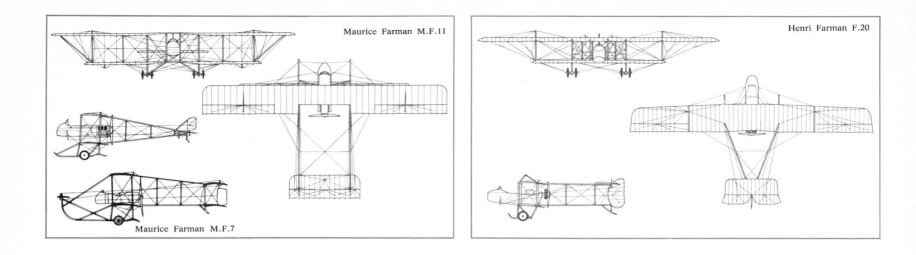

Maurice Farman M.F.11

Henri Farman F.20

Maurice Farman M.F.7

Plate 3
French aircraft at the outbreak of war: 1914

Apart from the various types derived from the pioneering models, France also had aeroplanes specifically built for military use. With continual updating and improvement these were built in large quantities and used to equip the other Allied air forces as well.

The designs of the Farman brothers were particularly successful. Henri Farman, the great French aeronautical pioneer, had gone into business in 1912 with his brother Maurice, also a brilliant aeronautical designer. Together they formed a company at Billancourt, on the basis that each of the two was to follow up his own ideas and develop his own designs. This division of labour in a lively, go-ahead company was the main factor in their success. The two brothers made their preparations in anticipation of the war and when it came their factory stood ready for mass production. The Farman works was the only one able to accept orders on a large scale in August 1914 without radical reorganisation. Production centred on two models, the Maurice Farman M.F.7 and the Henri Farman F.20, both developed from 1913 onwards.

The first of these marked the beginning of a successful series which remained in front-line service with the air forces of the Allies throughout most of 1915. The M.F.7 still resembled the biplanes of the prewar years but despite its ageing appearance it could do an effective job. In service from 1913 with the French and British air forces, it lasted for the first year of the war mainly as an observation aircraft. In May 1915 the M.F.7s were replaced by the improved and more powerful Maurice Farman M.F.11, designed in 1914. Apart from aerodynamic and structural improvements, this aircraft carried an observer's machine gun and a small bomb load. It was an M.F.11 of the Royal Naval Air Service which carried out the first night bombing mission of the war on 21st December 1914 over Ostend. In Italy the M.F.11 was built under licence by SIA and equipped 24 squadrons.

Less successful, though as widely used, were the aircraft of Henri Farman. The Series 20 planes were underpowered and could only be used in observation flights. The weight of the machine gun was simply too much for the engine, and so all but the simplest, safest operations were out of the question. However, simply because it was one of the few aeroplanes available in large numbers, the Series 20

Farman were in operational service from the first day of the war until the summer of 1915 when they were relegated to use as trainers.

The four most widely-used variants, differing in wingspan and length of fuselage, were the F.20, F.21, F.22 and F.23 which were produced almost simultaneously. Apart from the French, British, Russian and Romanian air forces, these aircraft also served with the Belgian, Dutch and Italian air forces where they were built under licence. In Italy the F.22 was built by Savoia in seaplane versions as well. The Italian-built models were mainly powered by Fiat A.10 or Colombo engines, both of 100 hp. Another important biplane, powered with a pusher propeller, was the Voisin 3. This machine, which ran to several variants and was built in hundreds, was the standard bomber of the first years of the war. Also designated Model LA, the Voisin 3 began service as a daytime bomber and later took on a night bomber role. The French air force received 800 of them, the Belgian air force about 30, and the Russians a small number. The Royal Flying Corps used about 100 Voisin 3s, of which 50 were built under licence. In Italy 112 were constructed by Società Italiana Transaerea and went into service with five squadrons of the Italian air force in 1915 and 1916.

Apart from its intrinsic merits, notably its great structural rigidity, Gabriel Voisin's biplane was famed for one special achievement: the first aircraft of the French air force to shoot down an enemy aircraft was a Voisin 3. It brought down a German Aviatik, on the 5th October 1914, near Rheims.

Voisin 3

Plate 4
British aircraft at the outbreak of war: 1914

Britain, like other countries, was fielding transitional aircraft for the first few months of the war, with pioneer designs from the days before aerial war had become a matter of real experience. Among the aircraft already in production at the outbreak of war were biplanes of the B.E. series, built by the Royal Aircraft Factory (R.A.F.).

Slow, very lightly armed, and not very manoeuvrable, these aircraft, which dated from 1912, were often at a disadvantage against more modern adversaries. The series had started with the B.E.1 designed by Geoffrey de Havilland and F. M. Green, which had flown for the first time on 1st January 1912. In the following month the B.E.2 had appeared, proving superior to other aircraft which were being tested by the Army at the time. It had managed to break the British altitude record at 3,218.7 metres (10,560 feet).

The beginning of war found a new model in service in three squadrons of the Royal Flying Corps, with an improved skin and with a better fuel system; this was the B.E.2a. These aircraft were widely used for reconnaissance and as bombers, in the latter role carrying a 45 kg (100 lb) bomb or three smaller bombs. The B.E., however, was not armed with a machine gun and during its operational service in France showed itself to be easy prey for the more powerful and manoeuvrable German fighters. Later on came the B.E.8, developed in 1913 with a slightly more powerful rotary engine. Their operational value was limited by the fact that these planes could only carry 45 kg (100 lb) of bombs with the pilot as the only crew. The bombload was even smaller if a two-man crew was carried. Defence was entrusted to the observer, who used a pistol or rifle.

The R.A.F. (Royal Aircraft Factory) R.E.5 biplane was similarly a basic reconnaissance plane. It appeared in 1914 with two squadrons of the Royal Flying Corps. While not famed for its manoeuvrability, this plane too was unarmed: the observer carried personal weapons, and there was provision for a maximum load of 27 kg (60 lb) of small bombs.

The R.E.5, soon hopelessly out of its depth with improving enemy aircraft, had to be withdrawn and used at home for experimental flights. One R.E.5, converted to a single-seater and given greater wingspan, reached an altitude of 5,182 metres (17,000 feet) in July 1914. Another was used to test a new 152.4 kg (335 lb) bomb.

Manoeuvrability and speed, which had been amply demonstrated in competitions, were the main characteristics of the Sopwith Tabloid, four of

which had been sent to France shortly after the outbreak of war. Production of the military version of the aircraft which had won the 1914 Schneider trophy had started in the spring, and the total produced reached 40. The aircraft turned out to be of little use as a warplane, still lacking adequate armament. One pilot of a Tabloid succeeded in bringing down a German aeroplane by circling round it and throwing steel darts at it, but there are no records of significant performance in aerial combat. It was later used as a light bomber, although the most it could carry was a small load of 9 kg (20 lb) bombs.

Very similar to the Tabloid, although generally inferior, was another contemporary aeroplane, the Martinsyde S.1, which served on the Western front as a fast reconnaissance plane. Delivered in small numbers to each squadron, it remained in service until the summer of 1915. Only 60 of this aircraft were built.

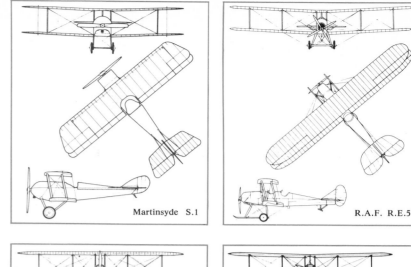

Martinsyde S.1

R.A.F. R.E.5

R.A.F. B.E.2a

R.A.F. B.E.8

Plate 5
The Avro 504 — in service from the first to the last day of the war: 1914–18

The Avro 504 was one of the best British aircraft of the period. In its long career this biplane, designed in 1913, was used in a multitude of roles – trainer, fighter, reconnaissance, bomber and night fighter, and in each of these it distinguished itself. Over 10,000 Avro 504s were built in all, and several versions continued in service after the war. These were used in civil aviation and as trainers right through to the 1930s, some still flying when the Second World War broke out. A 504 is preserved in flying condition at the Shuttleworth collection. In its first version the Avro 504 flew at 130.2 km/h (80 mph) and established an altitude record of 4,395 metres (14,420 feet). The widespread competition use to which the prototype was submitted for publicity purposes led to an order for 12 aircraft from the War Office in the summer of 1913, followed a year later by an order for another seven for the Royal Naval Air Service. The outbreak of war saw these aircraft in service in the role of reconnaissance aircraft and light bombers. One of these planes was unfortunate enough to be the first British aircraft to be shot down in combat, on 22nd August 1914.

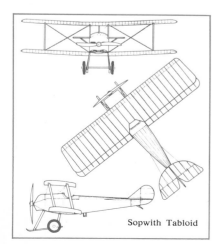

Sopwith Tabloid

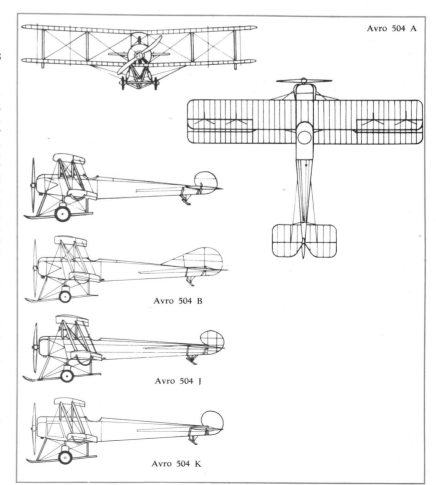

Avro 504 A

Avro 504 B

Avro 504 J

Avro 504 K

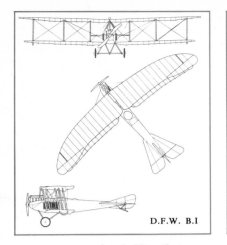

D.F.W. B.I

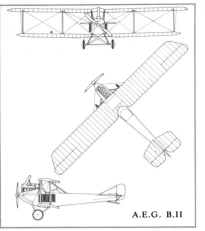

A.E.G. B.II

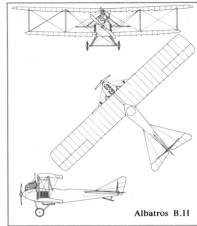

Albatros B.II

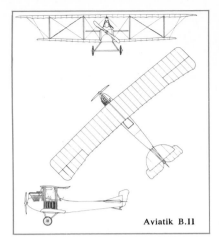

Aviatik B.II

The basic model was soon followed by successive variants, improving the aircraft in the light of wartime experience. The Avro 504 A, with strengthened and modified ailerons, was built for the RFC and was accompanied by a parallel version, the Avro 504 B for the Royal Naval Air Service. The latter had its wing structure strengthened later and was distinguishable by the installation of a broad fin forward of the tailplane. While these aircraft were widely used for training, many went out after a special quarry, the airship. It was the menace of the German Zeppelin which gave rise to two new models, the 504 C and the 504 D, in which an attempt was made to convert the aeroplane into a fighter, covering over the rear cockpit and making it a single-seater. The space thus freed was used for a fuel tank enabling the aircraft to remain in the air for eight hours, more than twice as long as the previous version. Eighty examples of the 504 C were made for the RNAS, as against the six 504 D ordered by the RFC.

The next variant was the 504 E of 1916, of which only 10 were built, with increased power and generally improved performance.

These continual updatings did not prevent the Avro 504 from becoming obsolete as a combat aircraft, unable to face newer enemy aircraft which had appeared in the meantime. In 1916 the 504 J was built, designed expressly as a trainer, which was supplied to the first flying school of the RFC on Salisbury Plain.

The 504 J soon became very widely used, while in order to adapt the airframe to newly-developed engines it was necessary to put another variant into production, the 504 K, with universal engine-bearer struts capable of housing any rotary engine in produc-

tion at the time. Once again the 504 was able to take on a combat role, in the last year of the war to defend the British mainland against night raids by Zeppelins. The conversion was not very different from the other combat conversion, the 504 C: the rear cockpit was covered over and the aircraft was armed with a Lewis gun, fitted over the upper centre section. Thus, from a two-seat trainer, the Avro 504 K was again a single-seat night fighter. Performance was considerably improved thanks to the adoption of a 110 hp Le Rhône rotary engine. Thus equipped, the aircraft was put into service with six home defence squadrons in the North London sector during 1918.

At the end of the war 226 504s were still in service with five units. To these must be added 2,267 Avro 504s of various models in service with flying schools. The total with the Royal Air Force on 31st October 1918 was 2,999, a number which was exceptional and higher than that of any other type of aircraft built during the course of the war.

Plate 6
German and Austrian aircraft at the outbreak of war: 1914

At the beginning of the war German aviation had a similar status to that of the Allies; German authorities had also been sceptical about the military value of the aeroplane, and those machines which were in service were regarded as a minor weapon and kept under the control of the army commanders, with little if any autonomy. They too were slow and unarmed aircraft, serving as observation and

reconnaissance for the ground forces. The biplane was clearly the prevailing type, apart from the Igor Etrich-designed Taube (= dove). Its name was derived from the distinctive shape of its wing, and the aeroplane had been designed long before the war, in 1910. In the years leading up to the war it was made in very large quantities in several factories, including Albatros, Gotha, Rumpler and D.F.W.

The D.F.W. (Deutsch Flugzeug-Werke) B.1 was a biplane whose general configuration echoed that of the Taube, and it too was ready to go into service at the outbreak of war. It could easily be seen that D.F.W. designers had been influenced by the dove wing shape of the Taube, and by all accounts the curvature of the wings did increase stability and the aircraft flew very well. The D.F.W. B.1 stayed in service until 1915 and was then relegated to training.

The career of the Aviatik B.I and B.II was longer, lasting until the beginning of 1916. There were two Aviatik companies, one in Austria and one in Leipzig.

The Austrian works produced the B.II, and one result of Austria's late entry into the war was that the full scale, large quantity production of these aircraft was to start much later than the German plane. The Aviatik B.I on the other hand went into service with reconnaissance units at the very outbreak of war. The two types differed mainly in the structure of the rudder and the elevator and also in engine power.

The operational activity of the A.E.G. B.II on the other hand was limited to the early months of the war, after which it was quickly superseded by more modern aircraft, even though it was developed in 1914. However, in 1915 another version, the type C, was

developed which was produced in considerable numbers in 1915 and 1916 and widely used until the end of the war.

The great name of Albatros came to be known at the start of the war in the form of the Albatros B.II, forerunner of a whole family of combat planes which have left their mark on the history of military aviation. The Albatros B.II was designed by Ernst Heinkel and showed its excellence by setting an altitude record of 4,500 metres (14,765 feet) at the very outset of its career. It was produced and used on a vast scale and was probably the most widely deployed German reconnaissance plane of the first year of the war. From 1915 onwards it was switched to training, in which it continued for the duration.

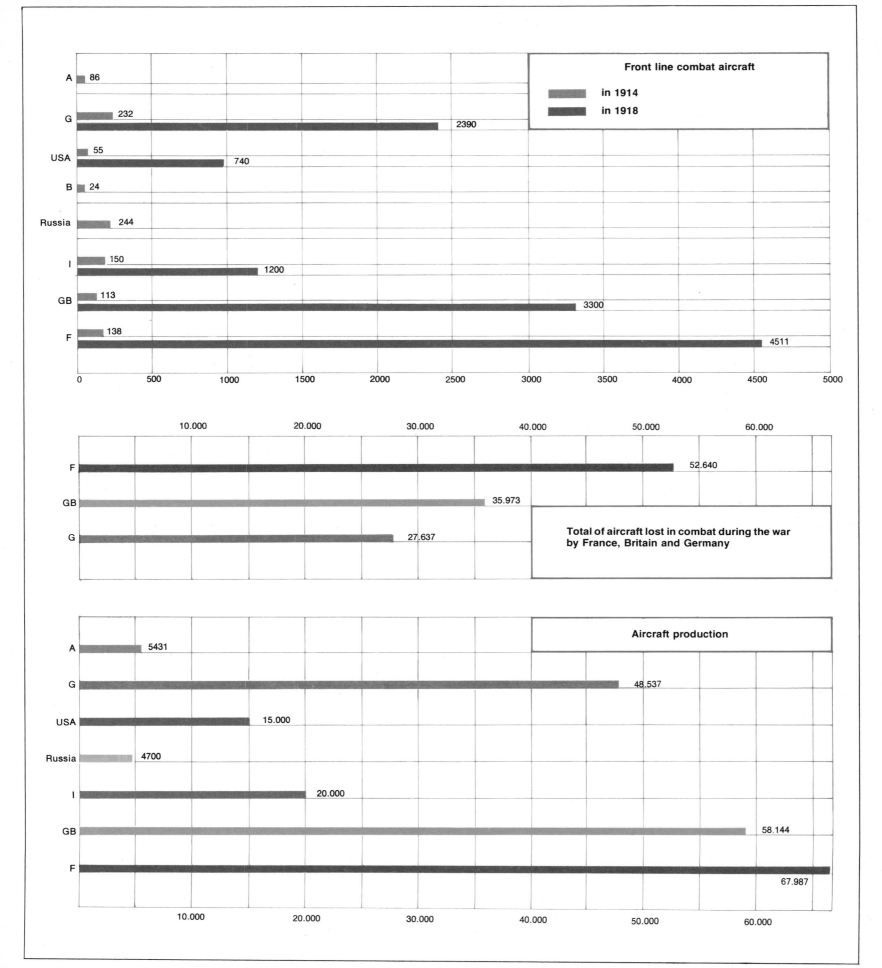

Front line combat aircraft
- in 1914
- in 1918

A	86
G	232 / 2390
USA	55 / 740
B	24
Russia	244
I	150 / 1200
GB	113 / 3300
F	138 / 4511

Total of aircraft lost in combat during the war by France, Britain and Germany

F	52.640
GB	35.973
G	27.637

Aircraft production

A	5431
G	48.537
USA	15.000
Russia	4700
I	20.000
GB	58.144
F	67.987

Plate 8

National markings in the First World War

Austro-Hungarian Empire – 1914

Austro-Hungarian Empire – 1915

Germany – 1915

Germany – 1916

Britain – Royal Naval Air Service – 1914

Britain – Royal Flying Corps – 1915

United States – 1917

United States – 1918

Imperial Russia – 1914

Imperial Russia – 1914 (navy)

Italy – 1915

Italy – 1915

Switzerland (neutral)

Sweden (neutral)

Austro-Hungarian Empire – 1914

Bulgaria – 1915

Germany – 1918

Germany – 1918

Britain – Royal Flying Corps – 1915

Britain – Royal Flying Corps – 1918 (night)

France

Belgium

Imperial Russia – 1916

Portugal

Japan

Turkey

China

The Netherlands – 1916

35

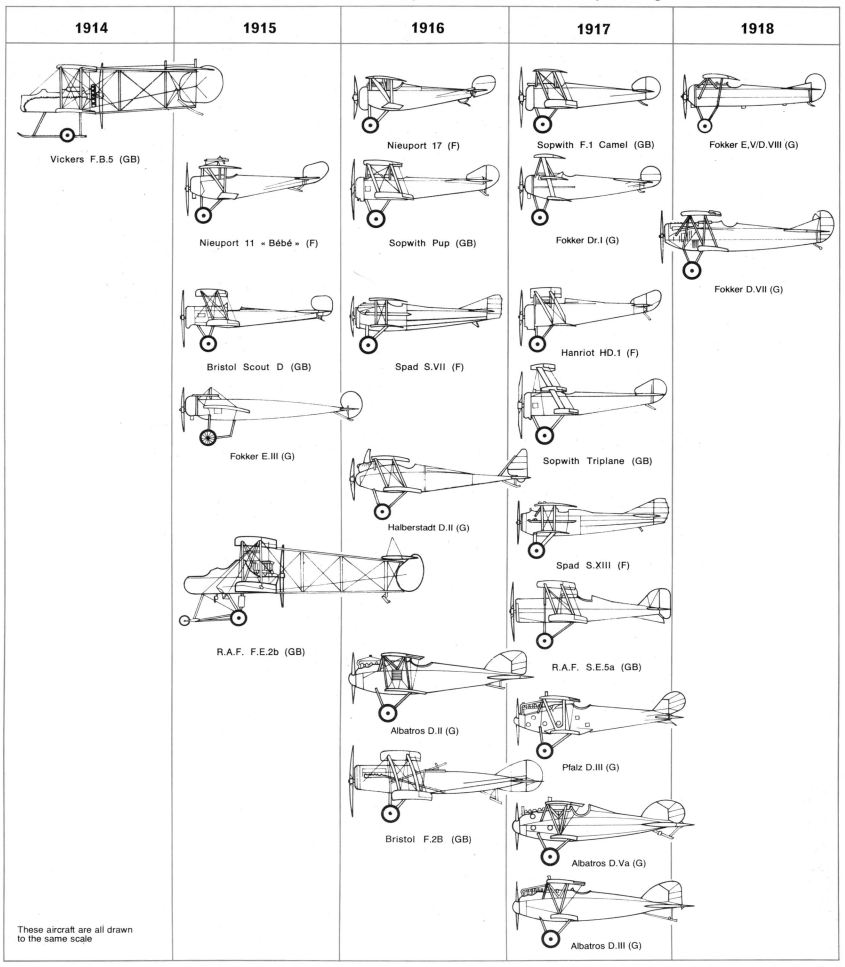

1914	1915	1916	1917	1918

Vickers F.B.5 (GB)

Nieuport 11 « Bébé » (F)

Bristol Scout D (GB)

Fokker E.III (G)

R.A.F. F.E.2b (GB)

Nieuport 17 (F)

Sopwith Pup (GB)

Spad S.VII (F)

Halberstadt D.II (G)

Albatros D.II (G)

Bristol F.2B (GB)

Sopwith F.1 Camel (GB)

Fokker Dr.I (G)

Hanriot HD.1 (F)

Sopwith Triplane (GB)

Spad S.XIII (F)

R.A.F. S.E.5a (GB)

Pfalz D.III (G)

Albatros D.Va (G)

Albatros D.III (G)

Fokker E,V/D.VIII (G)

Fokker D.VII (G)

These aircraft are all drawn
to the same scale

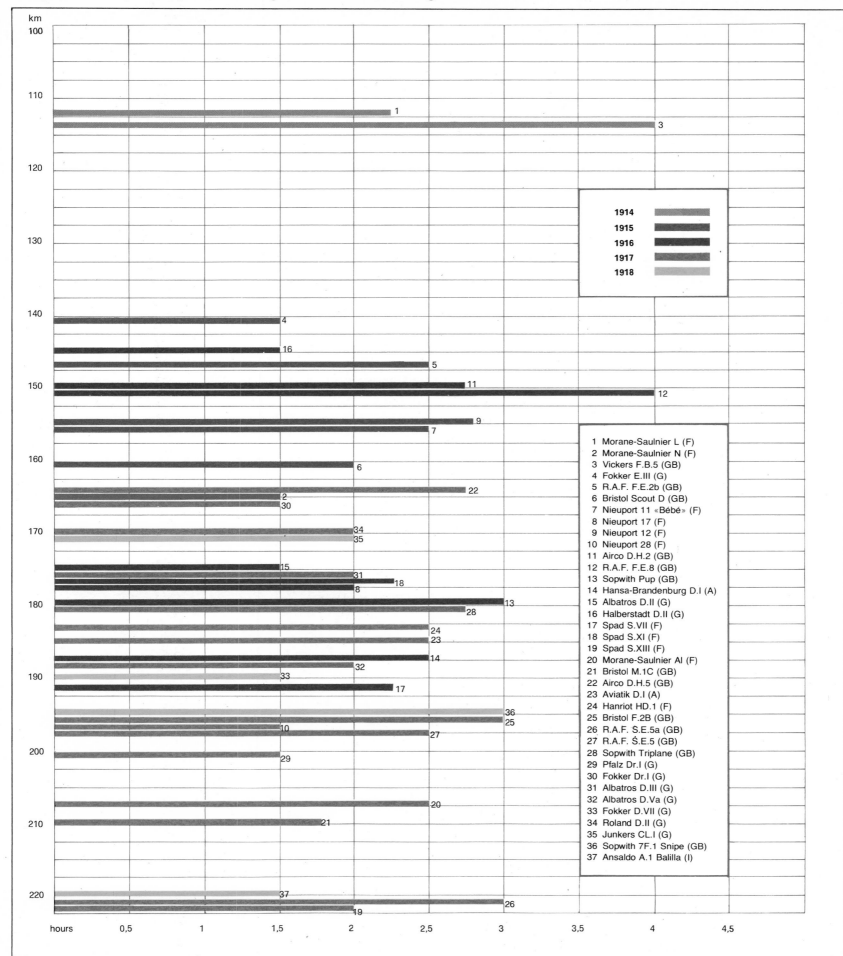

km

100

110

120

130

140

150

160

170

180

190

200

210

220

1914
1915
1916
1917
1918

1 Morane-Saulnier L (F)
2 Morane-Saulnier N (F)
3 Vickers F.B.5 (GB)
4 Fokker E.III (G)
5 R.A.F. F.E.2b (GB)
6 Bristol Scout D (GB)
7 Nieuport 11 «Bébé» (F)
8 Nieuport 17 (F)
9 Nieuport 12 (F)
10 Nieuport 28 (F)
11 Airco D.H.2 (GB)
12 R.A.F. F.E.8 (GB)
13 Sopwith Pup (GB)
14 Hansa-Brandenburg D.I (A)
15 Albatros D.II (G)
16 Halberstadt D.II (G)
17 Spad S.VII (F)
18 Spad S.XI (F)
19 Spad S.XIII (F)
20 Morane-Saulnier AI (F)
21 Bristol M.1C (GB)
22 Airco D.H.5 (GB)
23 Aviatik D.I (A)
24 Hanriot HD.1 (F)
25 Bristol F.2B (GB)
26 R.A.F. S.E.5a (GB)
27 R.A.F. S.E.5 (GB)
28 Sopwith Triplane (GB)
29 Pfalz Dr.I (G)
30 Fokker Dr.I (G)
31 Albatros D.III (G)
32 Albatros D.Va (G)
33 Fokker D.VII (G)
34 Roland D.II (G)
35 Junkers CL.I (G)
36 Sopwith 7F.1 Snipe (GB)
37 Ansaldo A.1 Balilla (I)

hours   0,5   1   1,5   2   2,5   3   3,5   4   4,5

Plate 12   **Anatomy of a First World War fighter: the Fokker Dr.I**

Fokker Dr.I

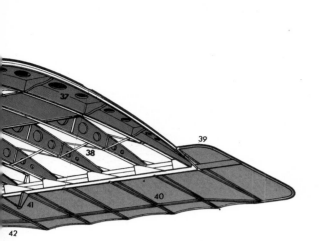

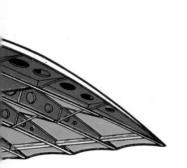

Fokker Dr.1

1 Starboard upper wing tip
2 Wing panel fabric covering
3 Starboard upper interplane strut
4 Aileron cable run
5 Two-bladed wooden propeller
6 Starboard centre wing
7 Lower interplane strut
8 Propeller hub fixing bolts
9 Ventilated engine cowling
10 Oberursel Ur II (Le Rhône) nine-cylinder rotary engine
11 Engine compartment fireproof bulkhead
12 Engine bearer struts
13 Reduction gearbox
14 Plywood side fairing panel
15 Carburettor
16 Rudder pedal bar
17 Pilot's footboards
18 Compass mounting
19 Control column
20 Control column-mounted secondary throttle control
21 Gun firing cables
22 Ammunition boxes
23 Fuel tank (20-Imp gal/91 litre capacity)
24 Wing spar box construction
25 Centre wing/fuselage attachments
26 Fuel filler cap
27 Twin 7.92 mm LMG 08/15 machine guns
28 Ring-and-bead gunsights
29 Diagonal wire bracing
30 Centre section V-struts
31 Aileron cables
32 V-strut attachment
33 Plywood covered leading edge
34 Upper wing spar box
35 Wing ribs
36 Port upper interplane strut
37 Wing tip construction
38 Rib bracing tapes
39 Aileron horn balance
40 Welded steel tube aileron construction
41 Aileron control horn
42 Wire trailing edge
43 Port centre wing construction
44 Interplane strut attachment
45 Wing-root cut-out forward and downward visibility

46 Machine gun breaches
47 Padded cockpit coaming
48 Engine instruments
49 Engine throttle and fuel cock controls
50 Pilot's seat
51 Sliding seat adjustment
52 Welded steel-tube fuselage construction
53 Aft end of plywood side fairing panel
54 Plywood top decking
55 Port lower interplane strut
56 Fuselage top longeron
57 Horizontal spacers
58 Port lower wing tip
59 Wing tip skid
60 Tailplane centre section mounting
61 Welded steel tube tailplane construction
62 Rudder horn balance
63 Steel tube leading edge
64 Elevator horn balance
65 Steel tube elevator construction
66 Rudder fabric covering
67 Sternpost
68 Rudder control horn
69 Elevator control horn
70 Tailskid hinge mounting
71 Steel-shod tailskid
72 Elastic cord shock absorbers
73 Fuselage vertical spacers
74 Lifting handles
75 Fuselage fabric covering
76 Diagonal wire bracing (double wires)
77 Tailplane control cables
78 Fuselage bottom longeron
79 Control cable guides
80 Mounting step
81 Seat support frame
82 Dust proof fabric bulkhead
83 Pilot's floor
84 Control column mounting shaft
85 Lower wing centre section spar box
86 Undercarriage strut attachments
87 Main undercarriage V-struts
88 Port mainwheel
89 Wheel disc fabric covering
90 Wheel spokes
91 Pivoted half-axle
92 Axle fairing construction
93 Axle spar box
94 Elastic cord shock absorbers
95 Starboard mainwheel
96 Tyre valve access
97 Starboard lower wing tip skid

Plate 13   **The fighter appears at the end of 1914 . . .**

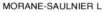

MORANE-SAULNIER L
Nation: France; *manufacturer:* Morane-Saulnier; *type:*
fighter reconnaissance; *year:* 1913; *engine:* Gnome
rotary, 80 hp; *wingspan:* 36 ft 9 in (11.2 m); *length:*
22 ft 6¾ in (6.88 m); *height:* 12 ft 10½ in (3.93 m);
weight: 1,441 lb (655 kg); *maximum speed:* 71.5 mph
(115 km/h) at 6,560 ft (2,000 m); *ceiling:* 13,123 ft
(4,000 m); *endurance:* 2 hrs 30 mins; *armament:* 1
machine gun; few bombs; *crew:* 1–2

MORANE-SAULNIER N
Nation: France; *manufacturer:* Aéroplanes Morane-
Saulnier; *type:* fighter; *year:* 1914; *engine:* Le Rhône 9C
9-cylinder air-cooled rotary, 80 hp; *wingspan:*
26 ft 8½ in (8.15 m); *length:* 19 ft 1½ in (5.83 m);
height: 7 ft 4½ in (2.25 m); *weight:* 976 lb (444 kg);
maximum speed: 90 mph (144 km/h); *ceiling:* 13,123 ft
(4,000 m); *endurance:* 1 hr 30 mins; *armament:* 1
machine gun; *crew:* 1

VICKERS FB.5
Nation: Britain; *manufacturer:* Vickers Ltd; *type:* fighter;
year: 1914; *engine:* Gnome Monosoupape 9-cylinder
air-cooled rotary, 100 hp; *wingspan:* 36 ft 6 in
(11.13 m); *length:* 27 ft 2 in (8.28 m); *height:* 11 ft 6 in
(3.51 m); *weight:* 2,050 lb (930 kg); *maximum speed:*
70 mph (113 km/h) at 5,000 ft (1,524 m); *ceiling:*
9,000 ft (2,743 m); *endurance:* 4 hrs 30 mins; *armament:* 1–2 machine guns; *crew:* 2

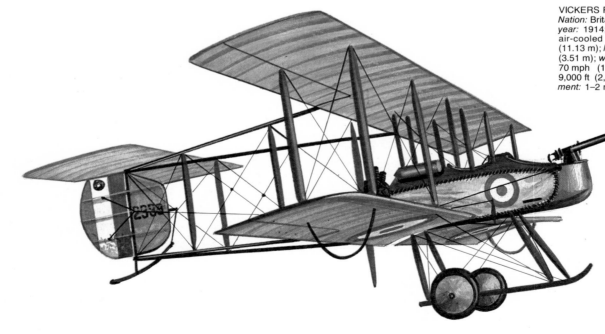

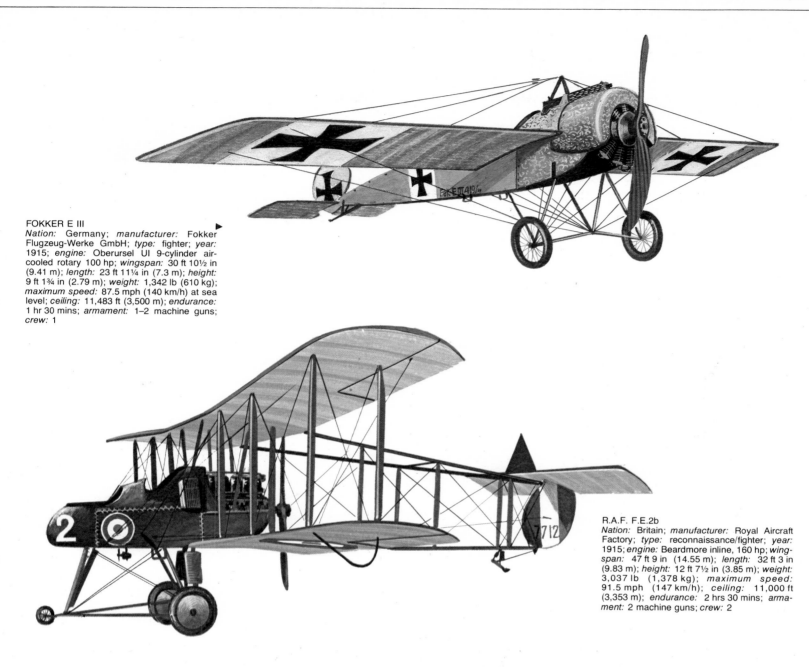

FOKKER E III ▶
Nation: Germany; *manufacturer:* Fokker
Flugzeug-Werke GmbH; *type:* fighter; *year:*
1915; *engine:* Oberursel UI 9-cylinder air-
cooled rotary 100 hp; *wingspan:* 30 ft 10½ in
(9.41 m); *length:* 23 ft 11¼ in (7.3 m); *height:*
9 ft 1¾ in (2.79 m); *weight:* 1,342 lb (610 kg);
maximum speed: 87.5 mph (140 km/h) at sea
level; *ceiling:* 11,483 ft (3,500 m); *endurance:*
1 hr 30 mins; *armament:* 1–2 machine guns;
crew: 1

R.A.F. F.E.2b
Nation: Britain; *manufacturer:* Royal Aircraft
Factory; *type:* reconnaissance/fighter; *year:*
1915; *engine:* Beardmore inline, 160 hp; *wingspan:* 47 ft 9 in (14.55 m); *length:* 32 ft 3 in
(9.83 m); *height:* 12 ft 7½ in (3.85 m); *weight:*
3,037 lb (1,378 kg); *maximum speed:*
91.5 mph (147 km/h); *ceiling:* 11,000 ft
(3,353 m); *endurance:* 2 hrs 30 mins; *armament:* 2 machine guns; *crew:* 2

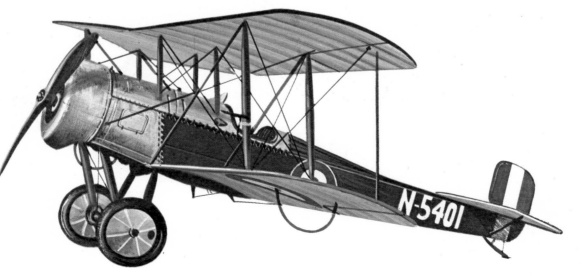

BRISTOL SCOUT D
Nation: Britain; *manufacturer:* British & Colonial
Aeroplane Co Ltd; *type:* fighter; *year:* 1915;
engine: Le Rhône 9-cylinder air-cooled rotary,
80 hp; *wingspan:* 24 ft 7 in (7.49 m); *length:*
20 ft 8 in (6.3 m); *height:* 8 ft 6 in (2.6 m);
weight: (empty): 760 lb (345 kg); *Weight*
(loaded): 1,250 lb (567 kg); *maximum speed:*
100 mph (161 km/h) at sea level; *ceiling:*
16,000 ft (4,877 m); *endurance:* 2 hrs; *armament:* 1 machine gun; *crew:* 1

Plate 15　　　　　　　　　　　　　　　　**Nieuport's great fighters — in service from 1915 to 1918**

NIEUPORT 12
Nation: France; *manufacturer:* Société Anonyme des Etablissements Nieuport; *type:* fighter/reconnaissance; *year:* 1915; *engine:* Clerget 9B 9-cylinder air-cooled rotary, 130 hp; *wingspan:* 29 ft 7½ in (9.03 m); *length:* 23 ft 6 in (7.3 m); *height:* 8 ft 11 in (2.67 m); *weight:* 2,028 lb (920 kg); *maximum speed:* 98 mph (155 km/h) at sea level; *ceiling:* 15,420 ft (4,700 m); *endurance:* 2 hrs 45 mins; *armament:* 1–2 machine guns; *crew:* 1-2

NIEUPORT 11 "BÉBÉ" ▶
Nation: France; *manufacturer:* Société Anonyme des Etablissements Nieuport; *type:* fighter; *year:* 1915; *engine:* Le Rhône 9 C 9-cylinder air-cooled rotary, 80 hp; *wingspan:* 24 ft 9 in (7.55 m); *length:* 19 ft ⅓ in (5.8 m); *height:* 8 ft ½ in (2.45 m); *weight:* 1,060 lb (480 kg); *maximum speed:* 97 mph (156 km/h) at sea level; *ceiling:* 15,090 ft (4,600 m); *endurance:* 2 hrs 30 mins; *armament:* 1 machine gun; *crew:* 1

◀ **NIEUPORT 17**
Nation: France; *manufacturer:* Société Anonyme des Etablissements Nieuport; *type:* fighter; *year:* 1916; *engine:* Le Rhône 9J 9-cylinder air-cooled rotary, 110 hp; *wingspan:* 26 ft 10 in (8.17 m); *length:* 18 ft 11 in (5.77 m); *height:* 8 ft (2.44 m); *weight:* 1,246 lb (565 kg); *maximum speed:* 110 mph (177 km/h) at 6,560 ft (2,000 m); *ceiling:* 17,390 ft (5,300 m); *endurance:* 2 hrs; *armament:* 1 machine gun; *crew:* 1

NIEUPORT 28
Nation: France; *manufacturer:* Société Anonyme des Etablissements Nieuport; *type:* fighter; *year:* 1917; *engine:* Gnome Monosoupape 9N 9-cylinder air-cooled rotary, 160 hp; *wingspan:* 26 ft 9 in (8.15 m); *length:* 21 ft (6.40 m); *height:* 8 ft 1¾ in (2.5 m); *weight:* 1,627 lb (737 kg); *maximum speed:* 122 mph (196 km/h); *ceiling:* 16,995 ft (5,180 m); *endurance:* 1 hr 30 mins; *armament:* 2 machine guns; *crew:* 1　▶

NIEUPORT 27
Nation: France; *manufacturer:* Société Anonyme des Etablissements Nieuport; *type:* fighter; *year:* 1917; *engine:* Le Rhône 9Jb 9-cylinder air-cooled rotary, 120 hp; *wingspan:* 26 ft 11 in (8.18 m); *length:* 19 ft 2¼ in (5.85 m); *height:* 8 ft (2.43 m); *weight:* 1,289 lb (585 kg); *maximum speed:* 116 mph (187 km/h); *ceiling:* 18,210 ft (5,550 m); *endurance:* 1 hr 30 mins; *armament:* 2 machine guns; *crew:* 1

NIEUPORT-DELAGE 29
Nation: France; *manufacturer:* Société Anonyme des Etablissements Nieuport; *type:* fighter; *year:* 1918; *engine:* Hispano-Suiza 8Fb 8-cylinder liquid-cooled inline V, 300 hp; *wingspan:* 32 ft 1¼ in (9.79 m); *length:* 21 ft 5 in (6.5 m); *height:* 9 ft 1½ in (2.77 m); *weight:* 2,420 lb (1,096 kg); *maximum speed:* 147.5 mph (237 km/h); *ceiling:* 26,900 ft (8,200 m); *range:* 360 miles (480 km); *armament:* 2 machine guns; *crew:* 1

AIRCO D.H.2
Nation: Britain; *manufacturer:* Aircraft Manufacturing Co
Ltd; *type:* fighter; *year:* 1916; *engine:* Gnome Monosoupape 9-cylinder air-cooled rotary, 100 hp; *wingspan:*
28 ft 3 in (8.61 m); *length:* 25 ft 2½ in (7.68 m); *height:* 9 ft
6½ in (2.91 m) *weight:* 1,441 lb (653.6 kg); *maximum
speed:* 93 mph (150 km/h); *ceiling:* 14,000 ft (4,267 m);
endurance: 2 hrs 45 mins; *armament:* 1 machine gun;
crew: 1

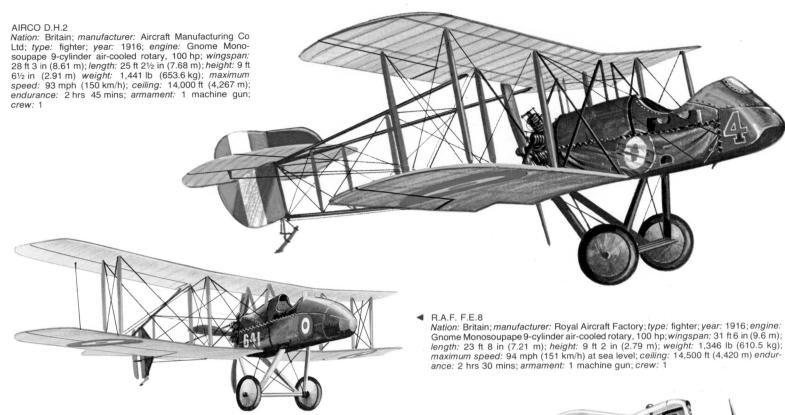

◄ R.A.F. F.E.8
Nation: Britain; *manufacturer:* Royal Aircraft Factory; *type:* fighter; *year:* 1916; *engine:*
Gnome Monosoupape 9-cylinder air-cooled rotary, 100 hp; *wingspan:* 31 ft 6 in (9.6 m);
length: 23 ft 8 in (7.21 m); *height:* 9 ft 2 in (2.79 m); *weight:* 1,346 lb (610.5 kg);
maximum speed: 94 mph (151 km/h) at sea level; *ceiling:* 14,500 ft (4,420 m) *endurance:* 2 hrs 30 mins; *armament:* 1 machine gun; *crew:* 1

SOPWITH PUP
Nation: Britain; *manufacturer:* Sopwith Aviation Co Ltd; *type:* fighter; *year:* 1916;
engine: Le Rhône 9C 9-cylinder air-cooled rotary, 80 hp; *wingspan:* 26 ft 6 in (8.08 m);
length: 19 ft 3¾ in (5.89 m); *height:* 9 ft 5 in (2.87 m); *weight:* 1,225 lb (555.7 kg);
maximum speed: 111.5 mph (179 km/h); *ceiling:* 17,500 ft (5,334 m); *endurance:*
3 hrs; *armament:* 1 machine gun; *crew:* 1
▼

HANSA-BRANDENBURG D I ▲
Nation: Austria; *manufacturer:* Phönix Flugzeug-Werke AG & Ungarische Flugzeugfabrik AG; *type:* fighter; *year:* 1916; *engine:* Austro-Daimler 6-cylinder liquid-cooled inline,
160 hp; *wingspan:* 27 ft 10¾ in (8.51 m); *length:* 20 ft 10 in (6.35 m); *height:* 9 ft 2¼ in
(2.79 m); *weight:* 2,024 lb (917 kg); *maximum speed:* 116 mph (187 km/h); *ceiling:*
16,405 ft (5,000 m); *endurance:* 2 hrs 30 mins; *armament:* 1 machine gun; *crew:* 1

ALBATROS D II
Nation: Germany; *manufacturer:* Albatros Werke GmbH; *type:* fighter; *year:* 1916;
engine: Mercedes D III 6-cylinder liquid-cooled inline, 160 hp; *wingspan:* 27 ft 10¾ in
(8.5 m); *length:* 24 ft 3 in (7.4 m); *height:* 8 ft 6½ in (2.95 m); *weight:* 1,954 lb (888 kg);
maximum speed: 109 mph (175 km/h); *ceiling:* 17,060 ft (5,200 m); *endurance:* .1 hr
30 mins; *armament:* 2 machine guns; *crew:* 1
▼

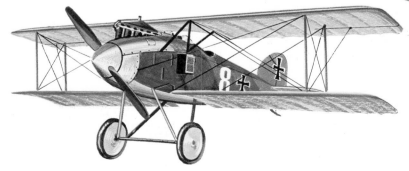

HALBERSTADT D II ▲
Nation: Germany; *manufacturer:* Halberstädter Flugzeug-Werke GmbH; *type:* fighter;
year: 1916; *engine:* Mercedes D II 6-cylinder liquid-cooled inline, 120 hp; *wingspan:*
28 ft 10½ in (8.8 m); *length:* 23 ft 11½ in (7.3 m); *height:* 8 ft 9 in (2.66 m); *weight:*
1,696 lb (771 kg); *maximum speed:* 90 mph (145 km/h); *ceiling:* 13,123 ft (4,000 m);
endurance: 1 hr 30 mins; *armament:* 1 machine gun; *crew:* 1

Plate 17

In 1916 the best fighters go into service: the Spads

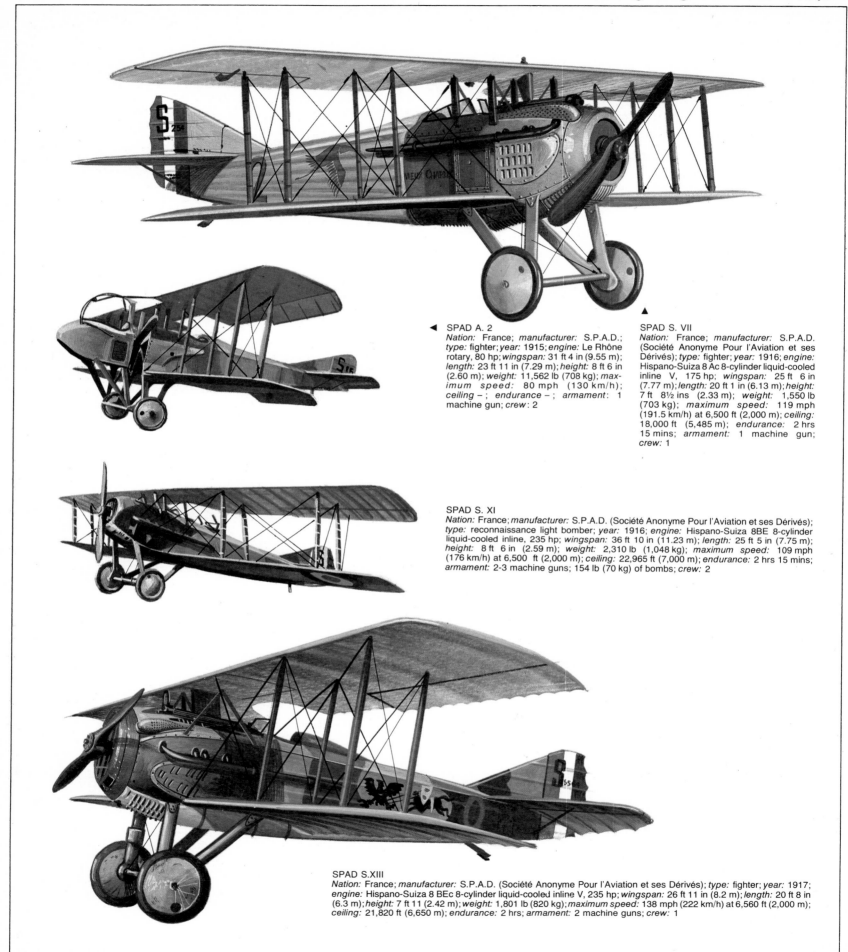

SPAD A. 2
Nation: France; *manufacturer:* S.P.A.D.; *type:* fighter; *year:* 1915; *engine:* Le Rhône rotary, 80 hp; *wingspan:* 31 ft 4 in (9.55 m); *length:* 23 ft 11 in (7.29 m); *height:* 8 ft 6 in (2.60 m); *weight:* 11,562 lb (708 kg); *maximum speed:* 80 mph (130 km/h); *ceiling –; endurance –; armament:* 1 machine gun; *crew:* 2

SPAD S. VII
Nation: France; *manufacturer:* S.P.A.D. (Société Anonyme Pour l'Aviation et ses Dérivés); *type:* fighter; *year:* 1916; *engine:* Hispano-Suiza 8 Ac 8-cylinder liquid-cooled inline V, 175 hp; *wingspan:* 25 ft 6 in (7.77 m); *length:* 20 ft 1 in (6.13 m); *height:* 7 ft 8½ ins (2.33 m); *weight:* 1,550 lb (703 kg); *maximum speed:* 119 mph (191.5 km/h) at 6,500 ft (2,000 m); *ceiling:* 18,000 ft (5,485 m); *endurance:* 2 hrs 15 mins; *armament:* 1 machine gun; *crew:* 1

SPAD S. XI
Nation: France; *manufacturer:* S.P.A.D. (Société Anonyme Pour l'Aviation et ses Dérivés); *type:* reconnaissance light bomber; *year:* 1916; *engine:* Hispano-Suiza 8BE 8-cylinder liquid-cooled inline, 235 hp; *wingspan:* 36 ft 10 in (11.23 m); *length:* 25 ft 5 in (7.75 m); *height:* 8 ft 6 in (2.59 m); *weight:* 2,310 lb (1,048 kg); *maximum speed:* 109 mph (176 km/h) at 6,500 ft (2,000 m); *ceiling:* 22,965 ft (7,000 m); *endurance:* 2 hrs 15 mins; *armament:* 2-3 machine guns; 154 lb (70 kg) of bombs; *crew:* 2

SPAD S.XIII
Nation: France; *manufacturer:* S.P.A.D. (Société Anonyme Pour l'Aviation et ses Dérivés); *type:* fighter; *year:* 1917; *engine:* Hispano-Suiza 8 BEc 8-cylinder liquid-cooled inline V, 235 hp; *wingspan:* 26 ft 11 in (8.2 m); *length:* 20 ft 8 in (6.3 m); *height:* 7 ft 11 (2.42 m); *weight:* 1,801 lb (820 kg); *maximum speed:* 138 mph (222 km/h) at 6,560 ft (2,000 m); *ceiling:* 21,820 ft (6,650 m); *endurance:* 2 hrs; *armament:* 2 machine guns; *crew:* 1

MORANE-SAULNIER A1
Nation: France; *manufacturer:* Morane-Saulnier; *type:* fighter; *year:* 1917; *engine:* Gnome Monosoupape 9N 9-cylinder air-cooled rotary, 150 hp; *wingspan:* 27 ft 11 in (8.51 m); *length:* 18 ft 6½ in (5.65 m); *height:* 7 ft 10¼ in (2.4 m); *weight:* 1,483 lb (673.9 kg); *maximum speed:* 138 mph (220.6 km/h); *ceiling:* 22,965 ft (7,000 m); *endurance:* 2 hrs 30 mins; *armament:* 2 machine guns; *crew:* 1

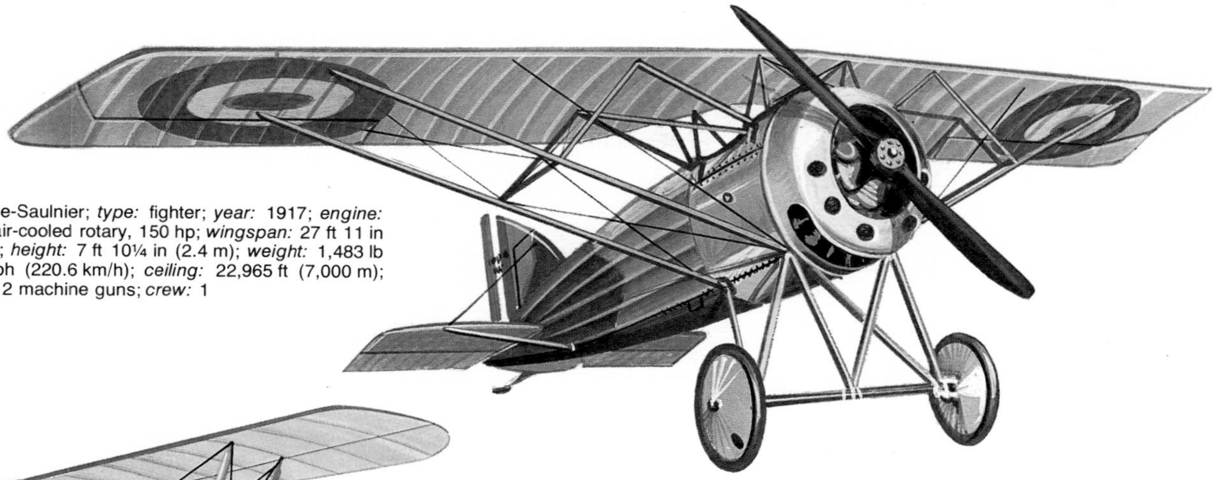

BRISTOL M. 1C
Nation: Britain; *manufacturer:* British & Colonial Aeroplane Co Ltd; *type:* fighter; *year:* 1917; *engine:* Le Rhône 9J 9-cylinder air-cooled rotary, 110 hp; *wingspan:* 30 ft 9 in (9.37 m); *length:* 20 ft 5½ in (6.24 m); *height:* 7 ft 9½ in (2.37 m); *weight:* 1,348 lb (611.5 kg); *maximum speed:* 130 mph (209 km/h) at sea level; *ceiling:* 20,000 ft (6,096 m); *endurance:* 1 hr 45 mins; *armament:* 1 machine gun; *crew:* 1

▼

AIRCO D.H.5
Nation: Britain; *manufacturer:* Aircraft Manufacturing Co Ltd; *type:* fighter; *year:* 1917; *engine:* Le Rhône 9J rotary, 110 hp; *wingspan:* 25 ft 8 in (7.82 m); *length:* 22 ft (6.71 m); *height:* 9ft 1½ in (2.78 m); *weight:* 1,492 lb (677 kg); *maximum sped:* 102 mph (164 km/h); *ceiling:* 16,000 ft (4,877 m); *endurance:* 2 hrs 45 mins; *armament:* 1 machine gun; *crew:* 1

▲

◄ **AVIATIK D I**
Nation: Austria; *manufacturer:* Österreichische-Ungarische Flugzeugfabrik Aviatik; *type:* fighter; *year:* 1917; *engine:* Austro-Daimler 6-cylinder liquid-cooled inline, 200 hp; *wingspan:* 26 ft 3 in (8 m); *length:* 22 ft 9½ in (9.65 m); *height:* 8 ft 2 in (2.48 m); *weight:* 1,878 lb (852 kg); *maximum speed:* 115 mph (185 km/h); *ceiling:* 20,177 ft (6,150 m); *endurance:* 2 hrs 30 mins; *armament:* 2 machine guns; *crew:* 1

HANRIOT HD.1
Nation: France; *manufacturer:* Société Anonyme des Appareils d'Aviation Hanriot; *type:* fighter; *year:* 1917; *engine:* Le Rhône 9JB 9-cylinder air-cooled rotary, 120 hp; *wingspan:* 28 ft 6½ in (8.7 m); *length:* 19 ft 2¼ in (5.85 m); *height:* 9 ft 7¾ in (2.94 m); *weight:* 1,334 lb (605 kg); *maximum speed:* 115 mph (184 km/h) at sea level; *ceiling:* 20,670 ft (6,000 m); *endurance:* 2 hrs 30 mins; *armament:* 1 machine gun; *crew:* 1

Plate 19

Classic British fighters of 1917

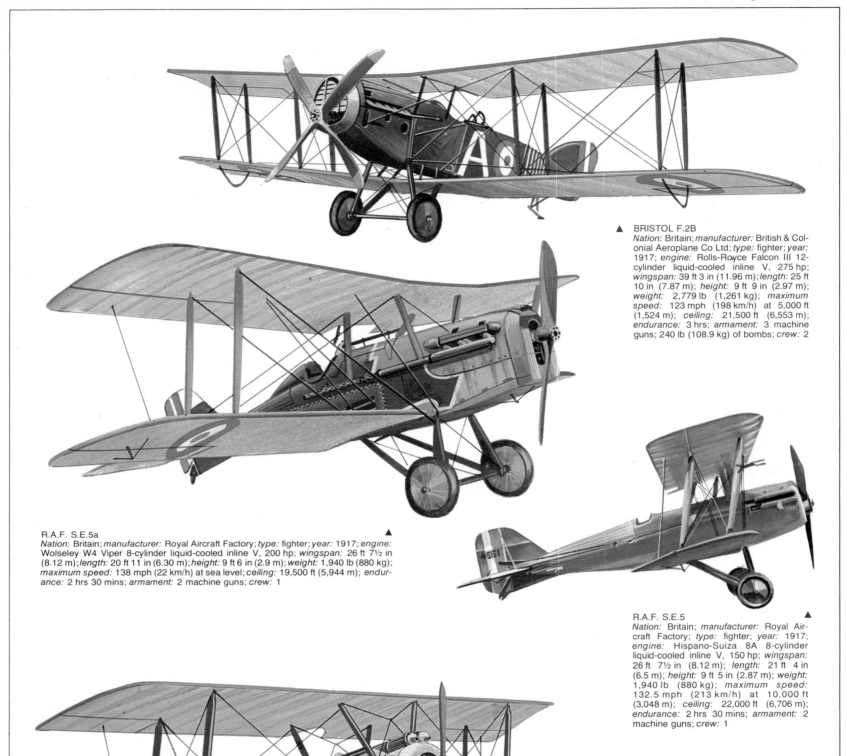

▲ BRISTOL F.2B
Nation: Britain; *manufacturer:* British & Colonial Aeroplane Co Ltd; *type:* fighter; *year:* 1917; *engine:* Rolls-Royce Falcon III 12-cylinder liquid-cooled inline V, 275 hp; *wingspan:* 39 ft 3 in (11.96 m); *length:* 25 ft 10 in (7.87 m); *height:* 9 ft 9 in (2.97 m); *weight:* 2,779 lb (1,261 kg); *maximum speed:* 123 mph (198 km/h) at 5,000 ft (1,524 m); *ceiling:* 21,500 ft (6,553 m); *endurance:* 3 hrs; *armament:* 3 machine guns; 240 lb (108.9 kg) of bombs; *crew:* 2

R.A.F. S.E.5a ▲
Nation: Britain; *manufacturer:* Royal Aircraft Factory; *type:* fighter; *year:* 1917; *engine:* Wolseley W4 Viper 8-cylinder liquid-cooled inline V, 200 hp; *wingspan:* 26 ft 7½ in (8.12 m); *length:* 20 ft 11 in (6.30 m); *height:* 9 ft 6 in (2.9 m); *weight:* 1,940 lb (880 kg); *maximum speed:* 138 mph (22 km/h) at sea level; *ceiling:* 19,500 ft (5,944 m); *endurance:* 2 hrs 30 mins; *armament:* 2 machine guns; *crew:* 1

R.A.F. S.E.5 ▲
Nation: Britain; *manufacturer:* Royal Aircraft Factory; *type:* fighter; *year:* 1917; *engine:* Hispano-Suiza 8A 8-cylinder liquid-cooled inline V, 150 hp; *wingspan:* 26 ft 7½ in (8.12 m); *length:* 21 ft 4 in (6.5 m); *height:* 9 ft 5 in (2.87 m); *weight:* 1,940 lb (880 kg); *maximum speed:* 132.5 mph (213 km/h) at 10,000 ft (3,048 m); *ceiling:* 22,000 ft (6,706 m); *endurance:* 2 hrs 30 mins; *armament:* 2 machine guns; *crew:* 1

◄ SOPWITH F.1 CAMEL
Nation: Britain; *manufacturer:* Sopwith Aviation Company Limited; *type:* fighter; *year:* 1917; *engine:* Clerget 9B 9-cylinder air-cooled rotary, 130 hp; *wingspan:* 28 ft (8.53 m); *length:* 18 ft 9 in (5.72 m); *height:* 8 ft 6 in (2.59 m); *weight:* 1,453 lb (659 kg); *maximum speed:* 115 mph (185 km/h) at 6,500 ft (1,981 m); *ceiling:* 19,000 ft (5,774 m); *endurance:* 2 hrs 30 mins; *armament:* 2 machine guns; *crew:* 1

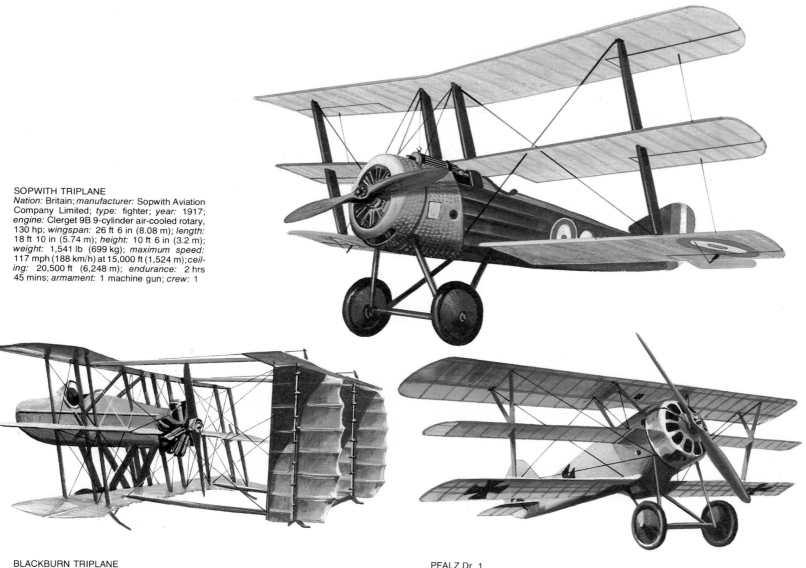

SOPWITH TRIPLANE
Nation: Britain; *manufacturer:* Sopwith Aviation
Company Limited; *type:* fighter; *year:* 1917;
engine: Clerget 9B 9-cylinder air-cooled rotary,
130 hp; *wingspan:* 26 ft 6 in (8.08 m); *length:*
18 ft 10 in (5.74 m); *height:* 10 ft 6 in (3.2 m);
weight: 1,541 lb (699 kg); *maximum speed:*
117 mph (188 km/h) at 15,000 ft (1,524 m); *ceiling:* 20,500 ft (6,248 m); *endurance:* 2 hrs
45 mins; *armament:* 1 machine gun; *crew:* 1

BLACKBURN TRIPLANE
Nation: Britain; *manufacturer:* Blackburn Aeroplane & Motor Co Ltd; *type:* fighter; *year:*
1917; *engine:* Clerget 9Z rotary, 110 hp; *wingspan:* 24 ft (7.32 m); *length:* 21 ft 5 in
(6.53 m); *height:* – ; *weight:* 1,500 lb (680 kg); *maximum speed:* – ; *ceiling:* – ; *endurance:* 3 hrs; *armament:* 1 machine gun; *crew:* 1

PFALZ Dr. 1
Nation: Germany; *manufacturer:* Pfalz Flugzeug-Werke GmbH; *type:* fighter; *year:*
1917; *engine:* Siemens-Halske rotary, 160 hp; *wingspan:* 28 ft (8.53 m); *length:* 18 ft
(5.48 m); *height:* 8 ft 10 in (2.69 m); *weight:* 1,551 lb (703 kg); *maximum speed:*
125 mph (201 km/h); *ceiling:* 19,680 ft (6,000 m); *endurance:* 1 hr 30 mins; *armament:*
2 machine guns; *crew:* 2

FOKKER Dr. 1
Nation: Germany; *manufacturer:* Fokker
Flugzeug-Werke GmbH; *type:* fighter; *year:*
1917; *engine:* Thulin-built Le Rhône 9J
9-cylinder air-cooled rotary, 110 hp; *wingspan:*
23 ft 7½ in (7.19 m); *length:* 18 ft 11 in
(5.77 m); *height:* 9 ft 8 in (2.95 m); *weight:*
1,289 lb (586 kg); *maximum speed:* 103 mph
(165 km/h) at 13,123 ft (4,000 m); *ceiling:*
19,685 ft (6,000 m); *endurance:* 1 hr 30 mins;
armament: 2 machine guns; *crew:* 1

Plate 21

German fighters of 1917

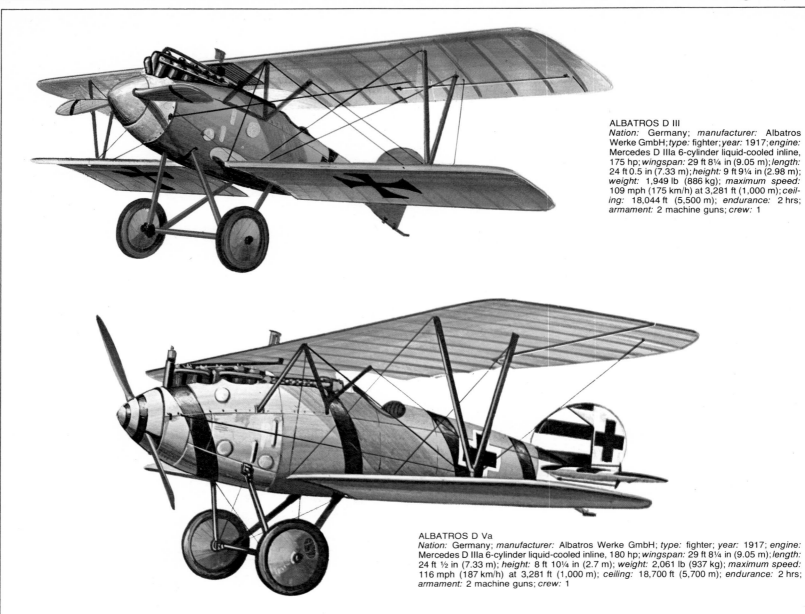

ALBATROS D III
Nation: Germany; *manufacturer:* Albatros Werke GmbH; *type:* fighter; *year:* 1917; *engine:* Mercedes D IIIa 6-cylinder liquid-cooled inline, 175 hp; *wingspan:* 29 ft 8¼ in (9.05 m); *length:* 24 ft 0.5 in (7.33 m); *height:* 9 ft 9¼ in (2.98 m); *weight:* 1,949 lb (886 kg); *maximum speed:* 109 mph (175 km/h) at 3,281 ft (1,000 m); *ceiling:* 18,044 ft (5,500 m); *endurance:* 2 hrs; *armament:* 2 machine guns; *crew:* 1

ALBATROS D Va
Nation: Germany; *manufacturer:* Albatros Werke GmbH; *type:* fighter; *year:* 1917; *engine:* Mercedes D IIIa 6-cylinder liquid-cooled inline, 180 hp; *wingspan:* 29 ft 8¼ in (9.05 m); *length:* 24 ft ½ in (7.33 m); *height:* 8 ft 10¼ in (2.7 m); *weight:* 2,061 lb (937 kg); *maximum speed:* 116 mph (187 km/h) at 3,281 ft (1,000 m); *ceiling:* 18,700 ft (5,700 m); *endurance:* 2 hrs; *armament:* 2 machine guns; *crew:* 1

HALBERSTADT CL II
Nation: Germany; *manufacturer:* Halberstädter Flugzeug Werke GmbH; *type:* ground attack; *year:* 1917; *engine:* Mercedes D III, 160 hp; *wingspan:* 35 ft 4 in (10.77 m); *length:* 23 ft 11½ in (7.3 m); *height:* 9 ft ¼ in (2.75 m); *weight:* 2,493 lb (1,133 kg); *maximum speed:* 103 mph (165 km/h) at 16,405 ft (5,000 m); *ceiling:* 16,700 ft (5,090 m); *endurance:* 3 hrs; *armament:* 2–3 machine guns; 110 lb (50 kg) of bombs; *crew:* 2

▼

PFALZ D III
Nation: Germany; *manufacturer:* Pfalz Flugzeug-Werke GmbH; *type:* fighter; *year:* 1917; *engine:* Mercedes D III 6-cylinder liquid-cooled inline, 160 hp; *wingspan:* 30 ft 10 in (9.4 m); *length:* 22 ft 9¾ m (6.95 m); *height:* 8 ft 9 in (2.67 m); *weight:* 2,056 lb (933 kg); *maximum speed:* 102.5 mph (165 km/h) at 9,842 ft (3,000 m); *ceiling:* 16,995 ft (5,180 m); *endurance:* 2 hrs 30 mins; *armament:* 2 machine guns; *crew:* 1

▲

FOKKER D VII
Nation: Germany; *manufacturer:* Fokker
Fleugzeug-Werke GmbH; *type:* fighter; *year:*
1918; *engine:* Mercedes D III 6-cylinder liquid-
cooled inline, 160 hp; *wingspan:* 29 ft 3½ in
(8.9 m); *length:* 22 ft 11½ in (7 m); *height:* 9 ft
2¼ in (2.75 m); *weight:* 1,870 lb (850 kg);
maximum speed: 124 mph (200 km/h) at sea
level; *ceiling:* 19,685 ft (6,000 m); *endurance:*
1 hr 30 mins; *armament:* 2 machine guns;
crew: 1

FOKKER E V/D VIII
Nation: Germany; *manufacturer:* Fokker
Flugzeug-Werke GmbH; *type:* fighter; *year:*
1918; *engine:* Oberursel UR II 9-cylinder air-
cooled rotary, 110 hp; *wingspan:* 27 ft 6¾ in
(8.4 m); *length:* 19 ft 4 in (5.865 m); *height:* 9 ft
3 in (2.82 m); *weight:* 1,238 lb (562 kg); *maximum speed:* 115 mph (185 km/h) at sea level;
ceiling: 20,670 ft (6,300 m); *endurance:* 1 hr
30 mins); *armament:* 2 machine guns; *crew:* 1

SIEMENS-SCHUCKERT D III
Nation: Germany; *manufacturer:* Siemens-
Schuckert Werke; *type:* fighter; *year:* 1918;
engine: Siemens-Halske Sh III 11-cylinder air-
cooled rotary, 160 hp; *wingspan:* 27 ft 8 in
(8.43 m); *length:* 18 ft 8¼ in (5.7 m); *height:* 9 ft
2¼ in (2.8 m); *weight:* 1,595 lb (725 kg); *maximum speed:* 112 mph (180 km/h); *ceiling:*
26,246 ft (8,000 m); *endurance:* 2 hrs; *armament:* 2 machine guns; *crew:* 1

Plate 23   **The last German and Austrian fighters of the war: 1918**

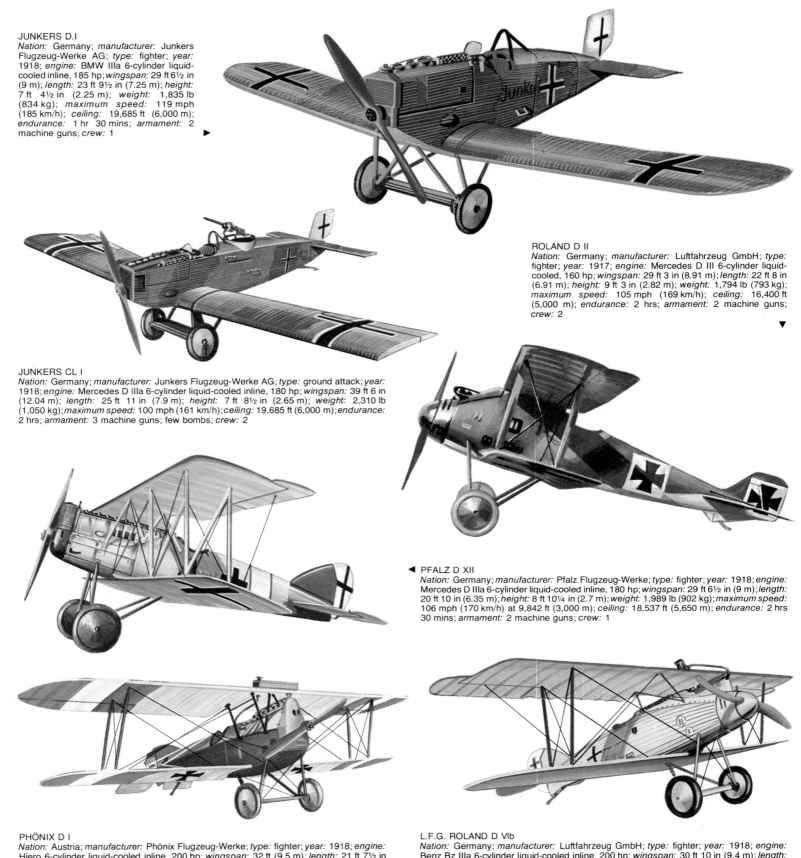

JUNKERS D.I
Nation: Germany; *manufacturer:* Junkers Flugzeug-Werke AG; *type:* fighter; *year:* 1918; *engine:* BMW IIIa 6-cylinder liquid-cooled inline, 185 hp; *wingspan:* 29 ft 6½ in (9 m); *length:* 23 ft 9½ in (7.25 m); *height:* 7 ft 4½ in (2.25 m); *weight:* 1,835 lb (834 kg); *maximum speed:* 119 mph (185 km/h); *ceiling:* 19,685 ft (6,000 m); *endurance:* 1 hr 30 mins; *armament:* 2 machine guns; *crew:* 1

ROLAND D II
Nation: Germany; *manufacturer:* Luftfahrzeug GmbH; *type:* fighter; *year:* 1917; *engine:* Mercedes D III 6-cylinder liquid-cooled, 160 hp; *wingspan:* 29 ft 3 in (8.91 m); *length:* 22 ft 8 in (6.91 m); *height:* 9 ft 3 in (2.82 m); *weight:* 1,794 lb (793 kg); *maximum speed:* 105 mph (169 km/h); *ceiling:* 16,400 ft (5,000 m); *endurance:* 2 hrs; *armament:* 2 machine guns; *crew:* 2

JUNKERS CL I
Nation: Germany; *manufacturer:* Junkers Flugzeug-Werke AG; *type:* ground attack; *year:* 1918; *engine:* Mercedes D IIIa 6-cylinder liquid-cooled inline, 180 hp; *wingspan:* 39 ft 6 in (12.04 m); *length:* 25 ft 11 in (7.9 m); *height:* 7 ft 8½ in (2.65 m); *weight:* 2,310 lb (1,050 kg); *maximum speed:* 100 mph (161 km/h); *ceiling:* 19,685 ft (6,000 m); *endurance:* 2 hrs; *armament:* 3 machine guns; few bombs; *crew:* 2

PFALZ D XII
Nation: Germany; *manufacturer:* Pfalz Flugzeug-Werke; *type:* fighter; *year:* 1918; *engine:* Mercedes D IIIa 6-cylinder liquid-cooled inline, 180 hp; *wingspan:* 29 ft 6½ in (9 m); *length:* 20 ft 10 in (6.35 m); *height:* 8 ft 10¼ in (2.7 m); *weight:* 1,989 lb (902 kg); *maximum speed:* 106 mph (170 km/h) at 9,842 ft (3,000 m); *ceiling:* 18,537 ft (5,650 m); *endurance:* 2 hrs 30 mins; *armament:* 2 machine guns; *crew:* 1

PHÖNIX D I
Nation: Austria; *manufacturer:* Phönix Flugzeug-Werke; *type:* fighter; *year:* 1918; *engine:* Hiero 6-cylinder liquid-cooled inline, 200 hp; *wingspan:* 32 ft (9.5 m); *length:* 21 ft 7½ in (6.62 m); *height:* 9 ft 2 in (2.79 m); *weight:* 1,775 lb (805 kg); *maximum speed:* 112.5 mph (180 km/h); *ceiling:* 19,685 ft (6,000 m); *endurance:* 2 hrs; *armament:* 2 machine guns; *crew:* 1

L.F.G. ROLAND D VIb
Nation: Germany; *manufacturer:* Luftfahrzeug GmbH; *type:* fighter; *year:* 1918; *engine:* Benz Bz IIIa 6-cylinder liquid-cooled inline, 200 hp; *wingspan:* 30 ft 10 in (9.4 m); *length:* 20 ft 8¾ in (6.322 m); *height:* 9 ft 2¼ in (2.8 m); *weight:* 1,892 lb (860 kg); *maximum speed:* 114 mph (182 km/h); *ceiling:* 19,685 ft (6,000 m); *endurance:* 2 hrs; *armament:* 2 machine guns; *crew:* 1

SOPWITH 7F.1 SNIPE
Nation: Britain; *manufacturer:* Sopwith Aviation Co Ltd; *type:* fighter; *year:* 1918; *engine:* Bentley BR2 9-cylinder air-cooled rotary, 230 hp; *wingspan:* 30 ft (9.14 m); *length:* 19 ft 10 in (6.05 m); *height:* 9 ft 6 in (2.9 m); *weight:* 2,020 lb (916 kg); *maximum speed:* 121 mph (195 km/h); *ceiling:* 19,500 ft (5,944 m); *endurance:* 3 hrs; *armament:* 2 machine guns; *crew:* 1

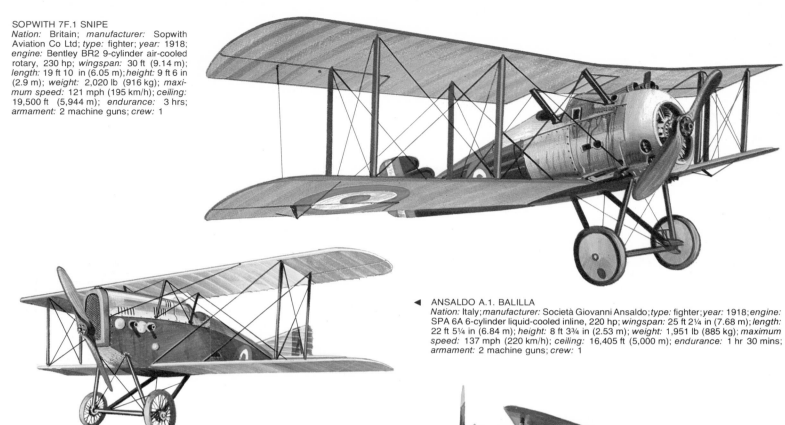

◄ ANSALDO A.1. BALILLA
Nation: Italy; *manufacturer:* Società Giovanni Ansaldo; *type:* fighter; *year:* 1918; *engine:* SPA 6A 6-cylinder liquid-cooled inline, 220 hp; *wingspan:* 25 ft 2¼ in (7.68 m); *length:* 22 ft 5¼ in (6.84 m); *height:* 8 ft 3¾ in (2.53 m); *weight:* 1,951 lb (885 kg); *maximum speed:* 137 mph (220 km/h); *ceiling:* 16,405 ft (5,000 m); *endurance:* 1 hr 30 mins; *armament:* 2 machine guns; *crew:* 1

▲

MARTINSYDE F.4. BUZZARD
Nation: Britain; *manufacturer:* Martinsyde Ltd; *type:* fighter; *year:* 1918; *engine:* Hispano-Suiza 8 F, 8-cylinder V liquid-cooled, 300 hp; *wingspan:* 32 ft 9 in (9.99 m); *length:* 25 ft 6 in (7.76 m); *height:* 8 ft 10 in (2.69 m); *weight:* 2,398 lb (1,087 kg); *maximum speed:* 140 mph (213 km/h); *ceiling:* – ; *endurance:* – ; *armament:* 2 machine guns; *crew:* 2

AUSTIN-BALL A.F.B.1
Nation: Britain; *manufacturer:* Austin Motor Co Ltd; *type:* fighter; *year:* 1918; *engine:* Hispano-Suiza 8-cylinder, liquid-cooled, 200 hp; *wingspan:* 30 ft (9.14 m); *length:* 21 ft 6 in (6.55 m); *height:* 9 ft 3 in (2.84 m); *weight:* 2,077 lb (942 kg); *maximum speed:* 138 mph (222 km/h); *ceiling:* 22,000 ft (6,700 m); *endurance:* 2¼ hrs; *armament:* 2 machine guns; *crew:* 1

▼

PACKARD LE PÈRE-LUSAC 11
Nation: USA; *manufacturer:* Packard Motor Car Co; *type:* fighter; *year:* 1918; *engine:* Liberty 12A 12-cylinder liquid-cooled inline V, 400 hp; *wingspan:* 41 ft 7 in (12.67 m); *length:* 25 ft 6 in (7.77 m); *height:* 9 ft 6 in (2.9 m); *weight:* 3,746 lb (1,699 kg); *maximum speed:* 132 mph (212 km/h) at 2,000 ft (610 m); *ceiling:* 20,000 ft (6,096 m); *range:* 320 miles (515 km); *armament:* 4 machine guns; *crew:* 2

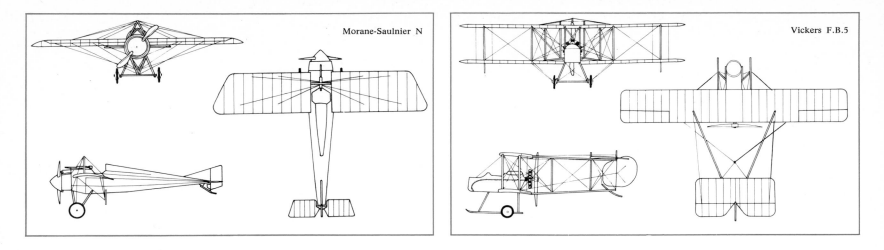

Morane-Saulnier N

Vickers F.B.5

Plates 13 and 14
The fighter is born at the end of
1914 . . . and in 1915 it makes its mark

Under the pressure of war the aeroplane was soon transformed into a much more deadly weapon. The machine gun was responsible for this transformation and the first armed reconnaissance aircraft – their armament being primarily defensive – were soon joined by an aircraft which had been expressly designed for air attack: the fighter. It was on a Morane-Saulnier L at the beginning of 1915 that a fixed machine gun was fired from an aircraft in flight for the first time. This weapon – a Hotchkiss 8 mm – was installed just behind the engine cowling and fired through the propeller disc by means of a simple device, two steel deflector plates being fixed on the propeller blades in line with the trajectory of the bullets. Though rudimentary, this system did turn the Morane-Saulnier L into the war's first effective fighter.

The originator of this device, the well-known French pilot Roland Garros, demonstrated how useful it was by shooting down five aircraft in the first three weeks of April 1915. The Morane-Saulnier was the first of a long line of monoplane fighters based on the Morane-Saulnier G and H, two

aircraft of 1913. Its design was completed during 1913 (without the forward firing weapon) and at the outbreak of war the *Aviation militaire* ordered large numbers of the L for service as reconnaissance planes. Its excellent flight characteristics, which were superior to those of the Aviatik and the Albatros, led to the first experiments, not counting the early rifle and pistol duels, in aerial combat. Then came Garros' experiments with a machine gun. Among the many pilots who had their baptism of fire in the Morane-Saulnier L was George Marie Guynemer, a corporal at that time, who was to become one of the aces of the war. On 19th July 1915 Guynemer shot down a German two-seater using the machine gun.

The Type L, of which 600 were built, was followed in 1914 by the LA and P, which were the larger, more powerful and better armed. The Morane-Saulnier P was the more widely used of the two and, as well as serving as a reconnaissance plane in the French air force, it saw service with the British forces up to 1916–17; total production was 565 aircraft.

The Type N had not been quite so good. Its design was more advanced than its predecessors, having very clean lines and being very fast and manoeuvrable, but it was its very speed (particularly on landing) that was to make the Type N unpopular with its pilots. This, and the extreme

sensitivity of the controls, made it strictly an expert pilot's model.

Only 49 examples were built before the N was replaced in 1916 by the improved Type AC, which was slightly larger and had a more powerful engine.

British engineers were also meanwhile trying to solve the problem of getting a machine gun to fire forwards on an aircraft, and their first solution was entirely different from the French one – they built an aircraft with the machine gun at the front and the propeller at the back – the "pusher propeller". The first RFC squadron to be formed specifically as a fighter unit was equipped with aircraft of this type, the Vickers F.B.5, nicknamed the "Gunbus", with the gunner's position in the nose of the aircraft. This arrangement, which gave a very wide field of fire, was developed by Vickers from 1913 onward with the Type 18 biplane. This machine was gradually perfected through two experimental variants until the F.B.5 was produced in 1914. The first examples reached the squadrons towards the end of the year and the aircraft was used on the Western front during the summer of 1915.

Germany shook the Allied air forces out of any complacency they may have acquired with the forward-firing aircraft – the Germans soon had their own, and much better. This was the Fokker F monoplane, and when it arrived it was to have a profound effect

on the whole balance of air power. It carried a devastating new weapons system, for in this aircraft the world's first efficient synchronising device enabled a fixed machine gun to fire through the propeller disc. Allied aircraft had nothing to offer in resistance to this, and indeed besides the advantage of a better armament the Fokker was a very agile monoplane, and had little difficulty in its encounters with the slow and unmanoeuvrable biplanes of its enemies.

In the early days of 1916, in the face of the continual destruction of their reconnaissance aircraft, the Royal Flying Corps ordered that every aircraft on a mission behind German lines should be escorted by three other machines. The synchronisation mechanism, perhaps in part a response to the deflector plates of the Morane-Saulnier L, was perfected by Antony Fokker in the spring of 1915 and installed in an M.5.K monoplane. The modified aircraft went into service immediately.

Three models were developed which differed in engine power and wingspan. Of these, the Fokker E.III (this being the military designation of the machine) was the best: it appeared in August 1915, and helped to prolong German air supremacy during the first months of 1916, until the arrival of the new French and British fighters at the front gradually started to tilt the balance back again.

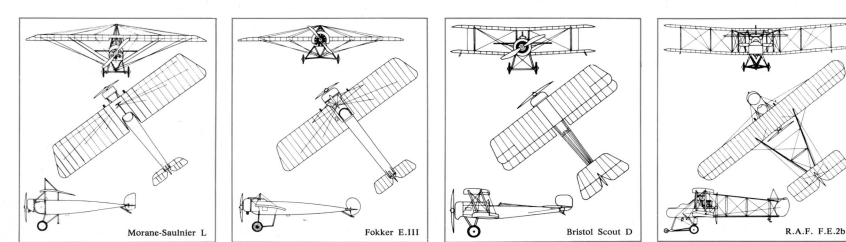

Morane-Saulnier L

Fokker E.III

Bristol Scout D

R.A.F. F.E.2b

One of the Fokker monoplane's principal opponents was the British R.A.F. F.E.2b fighter. This was a very different aircraft both in appearance and in armament but on the whole was able to deal with the "Fokker scourge". The F.E.2b was a twin-seater biplane with a pusher propeller thus similar to the Vickers F.B.5. Its main advantage was that it carried twin machine guns, as opposed to the single machine gun of the Fokker E.III. It was an F.E.2B which on 18th June 1916, near Annay, shot down the Fokker of the great German ace Max Immelmann, who had by then notched up fifteen victories. The F.E.2bs went into service in the summer of 1915 and were withdrawn about a year later and relegated to night bombing, when the new German Albatros biplanes arrived.

Britain's first aircraft in service with a synchronised machine gun was the Bristol Scout, which also had to be withdrawn in the summer of 1916. After three previous variants the Bristol Scout model D, which had modified structure and larger tailplanes, was first deployed in November 1915. The Scout was designed by Frank Barnwell towards the end of 1913 and the prototype immediately became famous for its speed: on 23rd February 1914, piloted by Harry Busteed, it reached 153 km/h (95 mph). This however was not enough to make the small biplane an efficient warplane. Although it did have the honour of being the first British aircraft to receive a synchronised machine gun, in March 1916, other more modern aircraft were ready to go into service and the Bristol Scout D was already near the end of its time.

Plate 15
Nieuport's great fighters — in service from 1915 to 1918

Among the Allied aircraft which succeeded in challenging German air supremacy was a small and agile French biplane, the first member of a long and effective fighter series which was to become famous in the course of the war, the Nieuport 11. Nicknamed Bébé (Baby) because of its small size, hundreds of these aircraft were built (in Italy alone Macchi built 646 under licence) which served on all fronts under the colours of the main Allied powers. The basic design was developed by Gustave Delage in 1914 in time to take part in the Gordon Bennett Cup in the speed class. The outbreak of war meant that the competititon was cancelled but the excellent qualities of the aeroplane ensured that it was immediately ordered in fighter configuration, both by the British and by the French. Put into service in the summer of 1915, the Bébé showed it was fast and manoeuvrable and able to stand up to the Fokker monoplane. During the course of the Battle of Verdun in February 1916, with the best French pilots such as Guynemer, De Rose and Nungesser, the Nieuport 11 inflicted heavy losses on the enemy, forcing a radical change in German tactics. Although the Bébé remained in service in Italy until the summer of 1917, on the Western front it was replaced in 1916 by the more powerful Nieuport 16, an aeroplane which was reminiscent of the two preceding transitional models (Nieuport 10 and Nieuport 12) which had originally been designed as twin-seat biplanes.

From March of that year onwards Delage's most famous design made its appearance, the Nieuport 17. A logical evolution of the Bébé, this aircraft was larger, much sturdier, better armed and considerably faster. These characteristics led to its widespread operational use and the Nieuport 17 emerged as one of the outstanding combat aircraft of its time, and without doubt one of the most useful Allied fighters before the arrival of the Spad S.VII. It was soon put into service with the French, British, Dutch, Belgian, Russian and Italian air forces (150 were built under licence by Macchi) and the Nieuport 17 became the favourite aircraft of the great aces of the period, such as Britain's Ball and Bishop and the French aces Nungesser and Guynemer, Fonck and Navarre. The fighter showed its mettle in the terrible battles of the Somme and the Isonzo, fighting hard against Fokker E monoplanes, Halberstadt D.IIs and even against Albatros D.Is.

Nieuport 11 « Bébé »   Nieuport 12

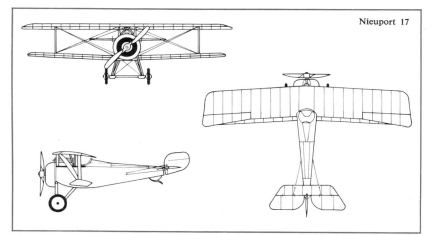
Nieuport 17

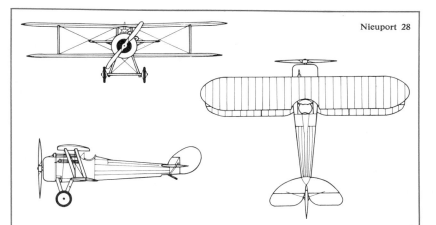
Nieuport 28

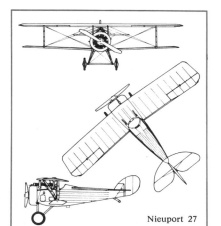
Nieuport 27

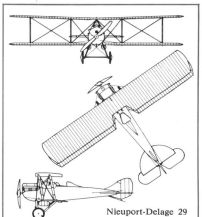
Nieuport-Delage 29

Airco D.H.2

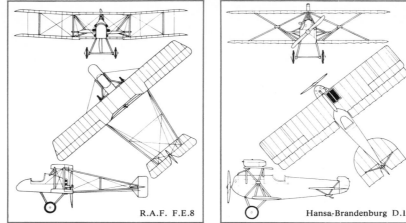

R.A.F. F.E.8

Hansa-Brandenburg D.1

Delage attempted to improve his design still further and went on to produce the Nieuport 24 and the Nieuport 27, but these were not really competitive, largely because the Allies were by then taking delivery of the first outstanding Spads. The Americans purchased these later Nieuports (about 400 drawn from the two types) for use as trainers. The Nieuport 28 ended up in the same way, as it was a generally uninspiring machine, Delage having completely broken away from his previous design formula. The Americans bought 297 and put them into service in the last two months of the war.

The Nieuport-Delage 29 was designed in the 1920s and did not see combat service. Gustave Delage dropped his earlier construction techniques once and for all, this time successfully, and a powerful inline engine and better streamlining helped to make this aeroplane a success. It was used in France, Belgium, Italy, Switzerland and Japan.

Plate 16
Fighters of 1916

Meanwhile in Britain many designers still insisted on sticking to the biplane formula with pusher propeller for fighters. The R.A.F. F.E.2b and the Airco D.H.2 were certainly successful against the Fokker monoplanes. The D.H.2 was the second design of Geoffrey de Havilland for the Aircraft Manufacturing Company and the prototype had flown in July 1915. In the absence of a method of synchronising the machine gun, De Havilland had followed the Vickers formula of 1913, producing a plane which was very agile and fast – the fact that it was a single-seater helped to improve performance. In February 1916 the D.H.2 was delivered to 24 Squadron RFC which had been the first in France to be issued with single-seat Scouts. The pilots of this unit soon learned to handle the new biplane and on 2nd April scored their first victory. On 25th of the same month they shot down their first Fokker and this exploit helped to raise morale. The D.H.2,

however, revealed its limitations when the new German fighters arrived and it fought from then onwards at a disadvantage until the summer of 1917. 450 of them were constructed.

Altogether less satisfactory was a similar aeroplane, the R.A.F. F.E.8, designed by J. Kenworth of the Royal Aircraft Factory. The prototype flew in October 1915 and production commenced at the beginning of the following year, but the F.E.8 did not reach units until August 1916 because of serious flight stability and engine development problems which delayed its entry into service. At that time the new German Albatros D.I and D.II fighters had already been developed and it was clear that the pusher propeller biplane formula was already outdated. The R.A.F. F.E.8 remained in the front line until half way through 1917, and 295 were built.

Germany fielded a transitional aircraft in 1916, the Hansa-Brandenburg D.I, designed in Germany by Ernst Heinkel but manufactured in Austria by the Phönix and Ufag companies which each produced approximately 100 of these aircraft in separate series, differing in the type and power of their engines. The aircraft had poor flight stability and limited visibility for the pilot, and its entry into service in the autumn of 1916 was plagued by a series of accidents which earned it the pilots' nickname "the Coffin".

Nevertheless the Hansa-Brandenburg D.I. was widely used by the Austrian air force until half way through 1917.

The German Halberstadt D.II can also be considered a transitional machine. It went into service in the summer of 1916 and was much used on the Western front until the arrival of the new Albatros fighters. The Halberstadt was first assigned to escort duties and two later variants were developed, the D.III and the D.IV. The first two models were the most widely used, mainly at the end of 1916 and in the early months of 1917. They were then relegated to use as trainers.

The aircraft which won back air supremacy for the Germans – lost by the Fokker monoplane in spring 1916 – was a handsome biplane which appeared at the front in the autumn: the D series Albatros. The first version of this aircraft, the D.I, was developed in the month of August by Robert Thelen of Albatros Flugzeug-Werke. This was the first German fighter which, as well as carrying two fixed synchronised forward-firing machine guns, was consistently reliable. After the D.I the German air forces received the first models of a second variant, the Albatros D.II which was better and more powerful, and then came the D.III which really decided the issue.

The Albatros D.I and D.II had an opponent to be reckoned with in a small British biplane, the Sopwith Pup, developed from the personal aircraft of the Sopwith Aviation Company's test pilot, Harry Hawker. This swift and nimble machine appeared in February 1916 and was initially ordered for the Royal Naval Air Service. The Pup began to reach the Western front towards the end of the year and in a short time a number of the Royal Flying Corps units were equipped with it. Its excellent qualities made it superior to many German fighter types in front line service at the time (in some ways even to the Albatros D.III) and it had many successes in battle. The Pup served throughout 1917 and then started to be withdrawn from combat units. During its career the aircraft was also used in a naval version.

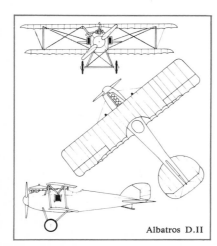

Albatros D.II

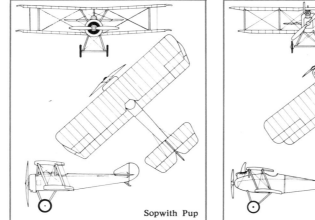

Sopwith Pup

Halberstadt D.II

Plate 17
In 1916 the best fighters go into service: the Spads

The Nieuport 11 and 17 which had done so much to counter German air superiority were joined in the autumn of 1916 by a new, high performance combat aircraft, the Spad S.VII, a plane which represented the pinnacle of air technology in the first half of the war. It was designed by Louis Béchereau, who in 1912 had designed the Deperdussin. He had stayed on as chief designer after Deperdussin was taken over by Louis Blériot, and in 1915 he created the first Spad fighter, the A.2. This was not a brilliantly successful aircraft but it had individuality, being a biplane with a turret, forward of the engine, in which the observer sat armed with a machine gun. This was Béchereau's first unusual and impractical solution to the implicit problems of mounting a forward-firing weapon. Notwithstanding the limitations of the aircraft, 100 were built which saw limited service with the French air force and were used for a longer period by the Russinas.

Béchereau's first great aircraft was the S.VII, taking full advantage of synchronised firing and designed around a new engine, a V-8 designed by the Swiss engineer Marc Birkigt for Hispano-Suiza, which was the forerunner of a long line of engines, gradually supplanting the rotary engine which had already achieved its best.

The engine was contained in a metal cowling which ended in a circular section front radiator and gave a very streamlined fuselage. The prototype of the S.VII flew for the first time in April 1916 and immediately made an impression with its good performance – 196 km/h (122 mph) at sea level, taking only 15 minutes to reach 3,000 m (9,840 ft) although the engine was not supercharged. The French authorities ordered 268 of them immediately and many other orders and applications to produce under licence came from abroad. Delivery to squadrons started on 2nd September.

Production of the S.VII soon ran into thousands (5,600 built in France alone) and as they came off the assembly line they were distributed amongst the Allied air forces. The Spad arrived in Italy in March 1917 and the first units there to be equipped with it were Italy's 77 and 91 squadrons, the latter commanded by Francesco Baracca. This great air ace achieved his first victory in a S.VII on 13th May and a few days later on 21st May he shot down his twelfth enemy plane. The Spad S.VII was certainly Baracca's favourite aircraft and he continued to use it even after its more powerful successor, the Spad S.XIII, had appeared. Béchereau had designed this version towards the end of 1916 when more powerful versions of the Hispano-Suiza engine went into production.

The S.XIII echoed the general lines of its predecessor but was larger, more robust and better armed with its two forward-firing synchronised Vickers machine guns instead of the single machine gun of the S.VII. The prototype flew on 4th April 1917 and the aircraft was immediately accepted as the replacement for the earlier Spads and the later types of Nieuport in the French air forces.

Deliveries to units started towards the end of May and before long more than 80 squadrons had the S.XIII. In the hands of the great aces of the time (Fonck, Nungesser and Guynemer) it reversed the balance of air power once again and gave superiority to the Allies. The United States, Belgium, Britain and Italy also adopted the new French aircraft, eleven squadrons of these nations receiving them. However, it was not always greeted with such great enthusiasm as its forerunner: indeed Italian pilots preferred the more handy Hanriot HD.1 to the heavy S.XIII which, although an excellent gun-platform and exceptionally tough and powerful, was less manoeuvrable and less dependable at low speeds. However the enormously wide use of the last Spad model is illustrated by the volume of its production: in all nine French aircraft manufacturers constructed 8,472 of this aircraft.

There was also a twin-seat Spad, which did not meet with such success, the Spad S.XI, which Béchereau first built in September 1916 as a light reconnaissance bomber. The aircraft was always plagued by the unreliability of its engine (a new version which still had development troubles) and was not a stable flyer, being rather over-sensitive to the distribution of armament loads. It went into service in 1917 but earned a reputation for being difficult to handle and was withdrawn from front-line service in June of the following year.

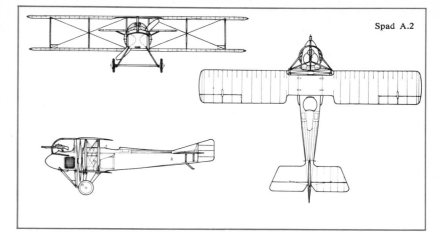

Spad A.2

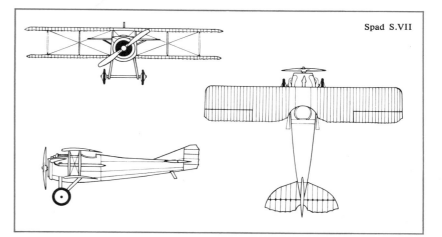

Spad S.VII

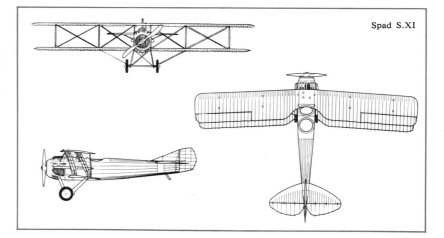

Spad S.XI

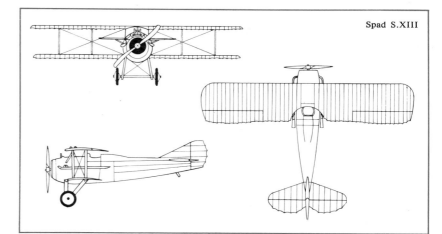

Spad S.XIII

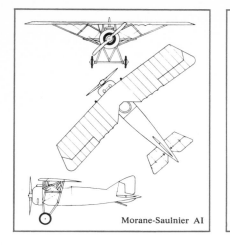

Morane-Saulnier AI

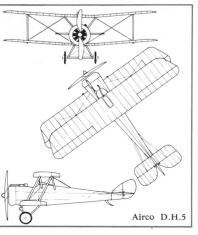

Airco D.H.5

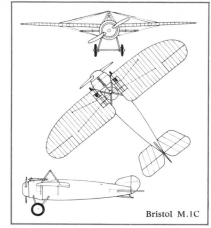

Bristol M.1C

Plate 18
Five fighters of 1917: beautiful but unlucky

The greatness of the various Nieuports and Spads rather overshadowed the good qualities of several contemporary fighters. In France for example the Hanriot HD.1 was a small, agile combat plane which, having been turned down by the *Aviation militaire*, found its way to other Allied units: Italy and Belgium appreciated its merits if others didn't. It was constructed in 1916 by Pierre Dupont and the aeroplane immediately demonstrated its excellent flight characteristics and great manoeuvrability. After its rejection by the French military authorities, towards the end of 1916, Italy showed interest in building the Hanriot fighter under licence and a first consignment of 100 was ordered from Macchi. The first HD.1s were delivered in the new year and the aircraft started to reach units in the early summer. The Hanriot HD.1 proved very sturdy and manoeuvrable although it was slightly less fast than the Brandenburg D.1 and the various Albatros aircraft. The overall superiority of the HD.1 was shown in numerous instances during the war, amongst which was the air battle on 26th December 1917 at Istrana, when the Hanriots of Italy's 6 group shot down eleven German reconnaissance aircraft without loss. The aircraft was adopted as the standard Italian fighter and Macchi, who received an order for a further 1,700 of them, built 831 before the war ended. At the time of its most concentrated use the HD.1 equipped sixteen of the eighteen operational fighter squadrons.

In Belgium the Hanriot HD.1 went into service in August 1917 and was used up to 1926. The Belgian airmen even preferred it to the Sopwith Camel, which was offered to them at the beginning of 1918 but rejected. The HD.1 was the aircraft in which the

great Belgian ace, Willy Coppens de Houthulst, achieved most of his 37 victories.

Another of France's fighters, less successful although good enough for 1,210 examples to be built, was the Morane-Saulnier A1, designed towards the middle of 1917 by Robert and Léon Morane and Raimond Saulnier.

It was a high-wing monoplane with a very streamlined fuselage and modern lines, of which three versions were developed which differed in their armament and engine. The first deliveries were made in the month of September, but barely two months after the beginning of its operational use the aircraft was withdrawn from front line service and relegated to training. The authorities justified this decision on the grounds of inadequate power and suspicions of structural weakness.

The Bristol M.1C, a British monoplane of 1917, also fell victim to similar criticism of its structural safety. This fighter was designed by F. S. Barnwell and was very advanced for its time and very fast at 212km/h (132 mph), achieved by the prototype powered by a rotary engine of only 110 hp; it was also extremely manoeuvrable. However, the Bristol monoplane was never used on the Western front

because of its high landing speed which, the authorities feared, made it dangerous.

Another British aircraft of the period was an unusual biplane designed by Geoffrey de Havilland, the Airco H.D.5. Its most unusual feature was the upper wing, which was back-staggered in order to give the pilot better visibility. It went into service in May 1917 but was switched to training the following January because of its poor performance at high altitude owing to the engine's insufficient power.

Problems in engine overheating plagued the career of the first entirely Austrian-built fighter of the war, the Aviatik D.1. Designed by Julius von Berg, it appeared in prototype form at the beginning of 1917; 700 examples were constructed to replace the unsatisfactory Hansa Brandenburg D.1.

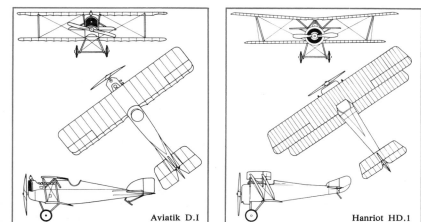

Aviatik D.I

Hanriot HD.1

Plate 19
British classics of 1917

It was in the last two years of the war that the British aircraft industry managed to bridge the quality gap between British and French fighters matching at last the various Nieuports and Spads which bravely faced the enemy. The Bristol F.2B had been conceived as a reconnaissance plane and was handicapped by being a two-seater, but surprisingly enough it managed to become well known for its superior capabilities and made its mark as one of the most useful fighters of the war. It had been developed in March 1916 by Frank S. Barnwell and the prototype of the first version, the F.2A, had flown on 9th September. The F.2A's first encounter with the enemy was nothing less than sheer tragedy. On 5th April 1917 near Douai in France, six Bristol F.2As were attacked by an equal number of Albatros D.IIIs and were all shot down. This crushing defeat was at first attributed to shortcomings of the aircraft, but afterwards eye witnesses described how the pilots had been flying this fighter as if it were an ordinary two-seater with a manually-aimed rear machine gun, so twelve terribly unlucky airmen died because they had not even been instructed in the advantages and tactics of the forward-firing weapon.

The subsequent version, the F.2B, was the one most widely approved. It was structurally improved and had longer range and a more powerful engine; it went into service in the summer of 1917, and 3,101 were built during the course of the war. After the war this number rose to a total of 5,500 and the aircraft flew with the RAF until 1932.

Two variants of a fighter which can be considered one of the very best of the war were built in a total of 5,025, all produced between the end of 1916

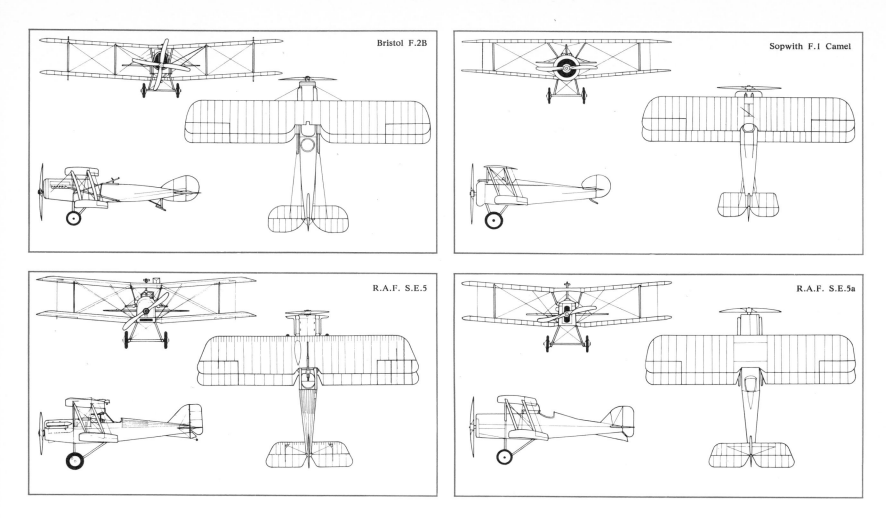

Bristol F.2B

Sopwith F.1 Camel

R.A.F. S.E.5

R.A.F. S.E.5a

and 1918. The R.A.F. S.E.5 and S.E.5a, during the course of their busy operational career, showed that they were better than the more heavily armed German aircraft, from the Albatros D.III and D.V to the Pfalz D.III and the Fokker Dr.I. It was in this plane that heroes such as Mannock, Bishop and McCudden scored most of their victories. The second of these was the main version. Only 58 of the S.E.5 were in fact built, being replaced quickly by the more powerful S.E.5a. The S.E.5 design had been created in the summer of 1916 by the design team of H. P. Folland, J. Kenworthy and F. W. Goodden. A tragic accident happened on 25th January, 1917 in which Frank W. Goodden lost his life; the S.E.5 which he was flying shed its wings and crashed. Suspicions of structural defects led to an enquiry, which discovered that there had been a failure in the main wing aileron and production was therefore halted. The defect was cured and the result was the S.E.5a.

A well remembered companion of the S.E.5a was the Sopwith F.1 Camel. This small and very lively biplane, whose nickname derived from the humped shape of a fairing which covered the twin machine guns, which of course were synchronised and fired forwards, displayed exceptional qualities as a combat aircraft: it accounted for 1,294 enemy aircraft in its one year of operational use. It was developed in

the last months of 1916 by Herbert Smith, the prototype flying on 22nd December. Deliveries to squadrons started in 1917 and the Camels were out in strength at the time of the intense fighting in the summer.

First reactions of the pilots to the new fighter were not, however, entirely favourable, as it was extremely difficult for the novice to handle the fierce torque produced by the powerful rotary engine. This fighter called for experienced pilots but once its habits were mastered its behaviour proved to be of great advantage in aerial combat. In all, 5,490 Camels were built, by Sopwith and eight other firms.

Plate 20
The triplanes join battle: 1917

From February to July 1917 one of the most unusual British fighters, the Sopwith Triplane, served on the Western front. It had a short but brilliant career, ending when the triplane gave up its place to the more useful and conventional Camel, which came from the same designer, Herbert Smith. The six short months of the Sopwith Triplane's activity had managed to cause some alarm to the enemy and drove the Germany industry to desperate efforts to catch up: the new British fighter's superiority in speed and manoeuvrability was clear.

The design work had started in 1916, more or less at the same time as that of the Blackburn Triplane which, when the time came for its proving trials in March 1917, turned out to be a complete failure; the prototype of the triplane had flown on 29th March. Test flights carried out in France awakened such enthusiasm that an order for 400 was placed, but later part of the order had to be cancelled as in the event only the RNAS accepted the triplane. The navy's units soon achieved their first successes and in particular the Canadian ace, Raymond Collishaw, made his name with the Sopwith Triplane: between May and

June 1917 he shot down seven enemy planes and damaged another 17. However, as the Camel gradually reached units of the RNAS the career of the Triplane drew to a close. In October only one squadron was still equipped with it. Production totalled 144.

Meanwhile Germany's efforts bore fruit. Fourteen aircraft manufacturers had been directed to build an effective triplane and among the prototypes, which included the Pfalz Dr.1 of which 10 were constructed, the most successful design was that of Reinhold Platz for the Fokker Flugzeug-Werke. The Fokker Dr.1, when it had completed its test flights, was immediately put into production with an order for 318 examples. In the meantime two of the four pre-series aircraft had been given to *Jagdgeschwader 1* of Manfred von Richthofen, the most dreaded German fighter unit of the war, known as the "Flying Circus" because of the lurid colourings of its aircraft. Flown by Werner Voss, the Fokker Triplane quickly achieved success with a first victory on 30th August 1917 and another twenty in less than three weeks of operational use. The entry into service of the Dr.1 production series models, however, was held up until November because of a structural defect in the upper wing, which caused some machines which had already been delivered to be recalled to the works for modification. The largest

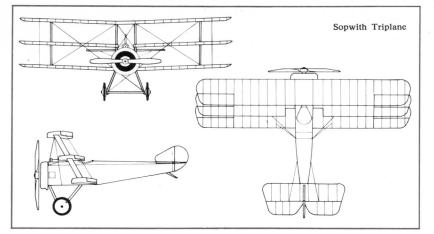

Sopwith Triplane

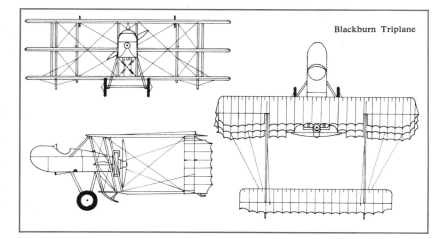

Blackburn Triplane

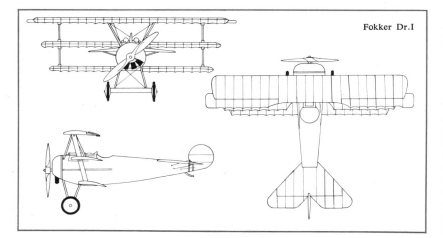

Fokker Dr.I

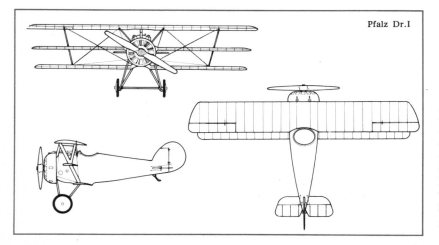

Pfalz Dr.I

number of these aircraft to be in action was in May 1917 when 171 aircraft were in service; then the assembly lines were switched to production of the new Fokker D.VII biplanes.

Although the Dr. 1 was allocated to many front line units who used it with success, it is most strongly associated with Manfred von Richthofen, the "Red Baron", and *Jagdgeschwader 1*. It was in a Fokker Dr.1 (number 425/17) that von Richthofen was killed at 10.35 on the morning of 21st April 1918. The aircraft crashed into no man's land on the outskirts of Sailly-le-Sec in the Somme valley in France.

Plate 21
German fighters of 1917

The second phase of German air supremacy reached its culmination thanks to a new fighter which joined the already excellent Albatros D.II and shared its success. Without doubt the D.III represented the best combat aircraft to be produced by Albatros, and from the moment of its entry into service in January 1917 it began to reach all the re-structured fighter squadrons of the German air force, gradually replacing the D.I and the D.II versions until its high point was reached with 446 operational machines at the front in November 1917. The Albatros D.III was the aircraft which enabled pilots such as Manfred von Richthofen, Werner Voss, Ernst Udet, Eduard von Schleich and Bruno Lörzer to achieve many of the victories which made them the greatest German air aces of the war. The need to replace the D.II with an aircraft with better performance was emphasised by the great impression made by the French Nieuport 17 fighter. The designer of this new model, R. Thelen, chose to install a more powerful engine in the D.II fuselage, and constructed a 1½ V-strut wing similar to that of the

French aircraft. The power unit chosen was the supercharged version of the Mercedes D.III, which could give good power at high altitude. The aircraft which resulted from this combination was a biplane with even more elegant and neat lines than its predecessor, giving excellent performance at high altitude and which had a rate of climb definitely superior to the D.II.

Mass production began immediately and among the first units to receive the new fighter was *Jasta 1* commanded by von Richthofen. In the spring of 1917 all thirty-seven *Jagdstaffeln* at the front were equipped to a greater or lesser degree with Albatros D.IIIs and the aircraft eventually became the standard equipment of the fighter squadrons even after the appearance of its successor, the D.V. German air supremacy reached its height in April 1917, a month which the Albatros's activity was to give the name of "Bloody April".

The German aircraft maintained its combat superiority for the whole of the second half of the year and only gradually lost it with the arrival of the Spad S.XIII, Sopwith Triplane and Camel and the S.E.5s. Production of the D.III ended at the beginning of 1918 after about 800 of them had been constructed.

In the summer of 1917 the D.III was joined by another improved version, the D.V. The great success of the former had encouraged Albatros to develop a more powerful variant of this fighter so that it could stand up to the newer French and British aircraft. The D.V reached units in July, three months before another version which received some structural strengthening but otherwise was not very different, the D.Va. Although they were given a more powerful Mercedes engine and some aerodynamic refinement, the D.V and the D.Va did not perform very differently from their predecessor. These two variants were, however, constructed in large numbers; the maximum number of the Albatros D.Vs at the front was approximately 500 in the month of November 1917, while the D.Va reached its greatest numbers in May

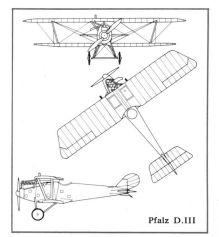

Pfalz D.III

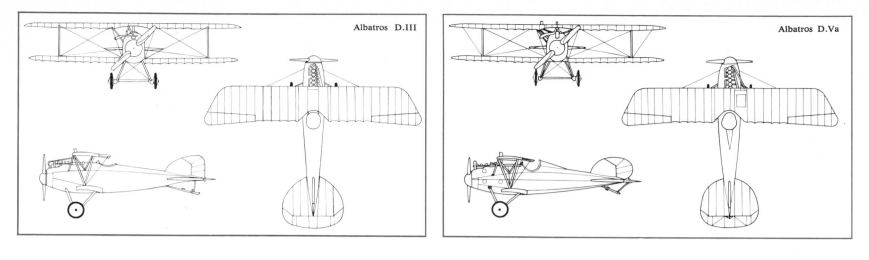

Albatros D.III

Albatros D.Va

1918, when there were 1,000 of them at the front.

The great qualities of the Albatros D.III and D.V somewhat obscured another excellent contemporary fighter, the Pfalz D.III, which reached units in August 1917. Drawing on the experience gained during the construction under licence of the Roland fighter, Pfalz Flugzeug-Werke had decided to design its own original aircraft. The work had been entrusted to Rudolf Gehringer and the prototype appeared in the spring of 1917. Although it smacked of the configuration of the Roland aircraft, Pfalz's D.III was much sturdier and better thought-out, and it had neater lines. When in service, however, the Pfalz D.III suffered mainly from comparison with the contemporary Albatros D.Va and the Fokker D.VII, whose performance it could not equal. Later, in its improved D.IIIa version, the Pfalz fighter was really able to help in re-establishing Germany's air supremacy. About 1,000 aircraft of the two variants were constructed.

Still in the summer of 1917, a new aircraft arrived at the front which was not exclusively designed as a fighter, but was mainly for ground attack: the Halberstadt CL.II. The aircraft had been designed immediately after the introduction of the CL class of twin-seaters, which were mainly meant to be used as army support and co-operation planes. It was in this role

rather than that of a fighter that the Halberstadt CL.II excelled. With its two or three machine guns and its ability to drop 10 kg (22 lb) anti-personnel bombs, it was well able to carry out co-operation and close support tasks. In the first months of 1918 all the *Schlachtstaffeln* (German assault squadrons) were equipped with the Halberstadt and the use of the aircraft severely undermined the morale of Allied infantry. In 1918 an improved version appeared as well, the CL.IV, which was more manoeuvrable.

Plate 22
Great German fighters, joining a war which was already lost: 1918

The last year of the war saw the German aircraft industry working at full stretch. It was this frantic phase that gave birth to what are considered to be the best German fighters to take part in the war.

The Fokker D.VII was the best of them all. In service from April 1918, it showed itself to be generally superior to the Spads, S.E.5as and Sopwith Camels and its great value as a combat aircraft was indirectly implied by the terms of the Armistice: one of the clauses of the treaty specifically mentioned the Fokker D.VII among the war material which the defeated country had to hand over to the victors.

The design of the D.VII was also initiated by Reinhold Platz who had produced the Dr.1 triplane. Work started towards the end of 1917 in response to a specification which called for a D type fighter powered by a Mercedes 160 hp engine. The Fokker V.11 prototype (this was the constructor's designation of the aircraft) was submitted for the competition which the German war ministry held at Adlershof in the months of January and February 1918. The machine

easily outclassed all the other participants (about 30) and won the pilots' enthusiasm, and in particular that of Manfred von Richthofen. The Red Baron in fact personally suggested certain modifications. Orders were immediately placed for 400 from Fokker and a substantial number from Albatros and OAW. Soon orders totalled 2,000 out of which, however, only 1,000 were built before the end of the war.

The first consignments went to *Jagdgeschwader 1* of Manfred von Richthofen since it was the normal practice to deliver new aircraft to the best units at the front and, within each unit, to the most experienced pilots. Gradually the various Albatros and Pfalz aeroplanes were replaced by the Fokker D.VII and many weeks had to pass before the lesser units managed to obtain the new fighter. One month before the Armistice 800 D.VIIs were in the front line, flying with almost all combat units. Amongst the qualities of the aircraft which appealed to the pilots, quite apart from its speed, sturdiness and manoeuvrability, were its exceptional rate of climb and outstanding performance at high altitude. These qualities were still further improved in the F version which appeared in August and was powered by a BMW IIIa 185 hp engine. Although its maximum speed was not much higher than that of the basic model, the D.VIIF could maintain its

engine power up to 6,000 m (19,670 ft). The rate of climb was also improved: the D.VIIF took 14 minutes to reach 5,000 m (16,400 ft) as against 38 minutes and 5 seconds of the Mercedes-engined D.VII.

The D.VII was not Fokker's last contribution to the war effort. In the summer of 1918 at the next competition for fighters at Adlershof, three prototypes of a new creation of Reinhold Platz were submitted: the Fokker E.V/D.VIII. The three machines (constructor's designations V.26/28) were quite differently conceived from their predecessors: they were high-wing monoplanes, two of them powered by rotary engines, and all remarkable for their great structural simplicity. they proved to be the best of the entries in the competition and a large quantity of them was immediately ordered with a first order for 400.

At first the E.V aircraft was to be powered by an Oberursel 145 hp rotary engine or by a 200 hp Goebel Goe engine, but because of delays in developing both these engines, it was powered by a Thulin Le Rhône 110 hp engine or alternatively by the Oberursel Ur.11 of the same horsepower. The first aircraft were delivered at the end of July and went into operational service with *Jagdstaffel 6* a week later. As fate would have it, their entry into service was bedevilled by problems reminiscent of those

Halberstadt CL.II

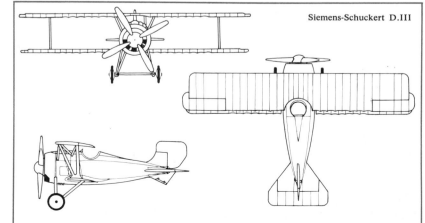

Siemens-Schuckert D.III

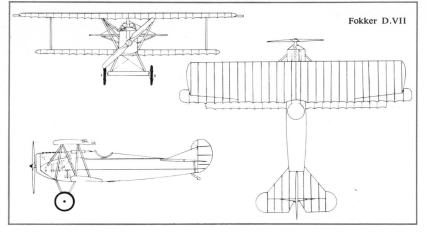

Fokker D.VII

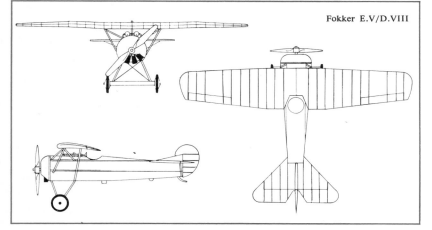

Fokker E.V/D.VIII

Plate 23
The last German and Austrian fighters of the war: 1918

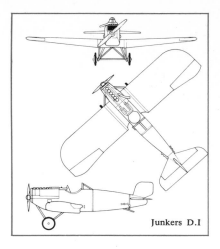

Junkers D.I

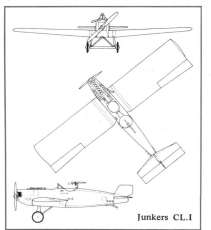

Junkers CL.I

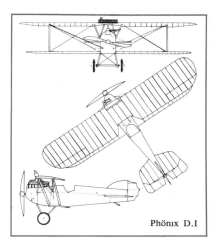

Phönix D.I

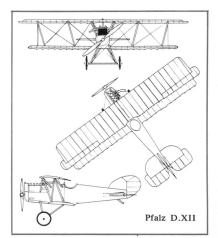

Pfalz D.XII

In the last year of the war the Central Powers produced machines which, whilst they did not achieve the fame of the Albatros and Fokker aeroplanes, provided a useful yardstick for measuring the quality of the German industry's output. To the numerous fighters of the D series was added, in March 1918, an aircraft which from many points of view was revolutionary, the Junkers D.1. Apart from its monoplane formula, this machine also introduced another unusual (for the time) construction technique: it was all-metal, both airframe and covering; the latter was in corrugated duralumin, a material which was to be adopted by Junkers in the years to come as well. It was derived from the J.1 model of 1915 (the first aircraft in the world to be entirely constructed of metal) and some later developments. The Junkers D.1 was powerful, fast and manoeuvrable. Its operational use, however, was limited by the difficulties of construction inevitable in an industry which was used to working with wood and fabric and which affected the numbers produced: only 41.

From the D.1, a twin-seat version, the CL.1, was developed, which was larger and better armed and which brought out more clearly the potential of the basic model. Although it was not meant for air combat, the Junkers Cl.1 ended up by proving to be the best assault aircraft produced in Germany during the war. Designed like its predecessor by Hugo Junkers, it flew in prototype form on 4th March 1918 and was immediately put into production. The same practical difficulties which had slowed up the construction of the D.1 also limited the numbers of CL.1s, of which only 47 came off the assembly lines. As a result, its operational use was very brief. But not so brief, however, that the outstanding merits of the machine were unappreciated; in particular its armament since, apart from its three machine guns, the aircraft had bomb bays along its fuselage carrying anti-personnel grenades to be used on ground attack missions.

In the summer another fighter, the Pfalz D.XII, had a very short period of service but did not match up to its contemporary, the Fokker D.VII. The Roland D.VIb had a similar career: it was built in limited numbers as a special measure to make up any shortage that might be caused by delays in delivery of the Fokker fighters, while the enquiry into the D.VII went on. The Roland D.VIIb was visibly derived from the earlier designs of the company, amongst which were the Roland D.II and D.IIa of 1917 of which 300 had been constructed but

affecting the triplane Dr.1 in October 1917, only this time with dire consequences. Three aircraft literally fell out of the sky within two weeks; their wings failed. The Fokker E.Vs were grounded and on 24th August a commission of enquiry was begun. Meanwhile production was halted. Its verdict was not that the structure itself was to blame, but that unsuitable materials and faults in workmanship were responsible.

When production was resumed, there was a new designation for the aircraft (perhaps for psychological reasons) which became the D.VIII. The new series, delayed as it was, reached the front in the last ten days of October and the aircraft became operational only on the 24th of that month. In barely three weeks' use in the war and in spite of the insufficient power of the Le Rhône and Oberursel engines (which it had proved impossible to replace by more powerful types) the D.VIII gave a very good account of itself in combat. Although it was not as manoeuvrable as the triplane Dr.1, the aircraft was much more manoeuvrable than its predecessor the D.VII. The pilots appreciated its good flight qualities.

The Siemens-Schuckert was another excellent fighter of 1918, of which two versions went into service, both with rotary engines. The first of these was designated D.III and it was ordered in December 1917. Its

development had begun in the spring of that year under Harold Wolff, who based it on the new Siemens-Halske Sh.III rotary engine of 160 hp. These prototypes had been tested by June and in proving flights they had shown themselves to be very manoeuvrable and capable of high rates of climb. Eighty of the D.III type were built, and these were supplied to eight fighter squadrons and some home defence squadrons as well as two flying schools. In August 1918 the final version, the D.IV, appeared, which was better and more powerful than its predecessor. 123 of them were constructed.

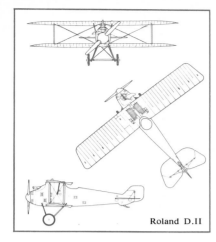

Roland D.II

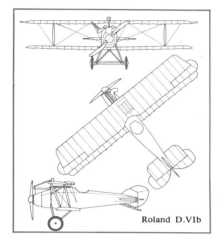

Roland D.VIb

which in practice were not equal to the Albatros fighters.

In Austria as well, this crucial stage of the war caused the industry to build a new fighter, the Phönix D.1 which appeared in February 1918. Three models were constructed in a total of 50 aircraft, and it revealed itself as an adversary to be reckoned with by the Italian Hanriots and Spads.

Plate 24
The last Allied fighters, arriving too late: 1918

Among the Allies as well, the last days of the war saw many worthwhile new warplanes put into the field. The great majority of these were not able to demonstrate their good points but only because – fortunately – the war came to an end.

In Britain the Sopwith 7F.1 Snipe merits special mention; it was designed to replace the Camel and came to be considered the best Allied fighter in service at the time of the Armistice. The Snipe was "custom-built" by Herbert Smith especially for the new rotary engine, the 230 hp Bentley BR2 engine. The Camel's general lines were echoed in this design: the characteristic rounded fuselage was even more accentuated in this model, and it kept the same tail-plane. It had two-bay wings of extended span and had more complex struts with wide cut-outs in the upper centre section in order to improve visibility. The Snipe was ordered into production at the beginning of 1918 and the first aircraft went to France in March, in time to equip three squadrons of the RAF. In operational use the fighter showed itself to be extremely manoeuvrable and tough and had an excellent rate of climb, even though its maximum speed was not exceptional. About 1,500 of them were constructed and it became the standard fighter of the Royal Air Force in the days immediately following the war.

The Martinsyde F.4 Buzzard was another British fighter which, however, did not manage to survive the conflict, although it undoubtedly deserved better. Only 50 of them were completed, in spite of a series of orders among which one was for 1,500 to be constructed in the United States. After the war the choice of the Sopwith Snipe put paid to any hopes of continuing production. The unlucky career of the F.4 recalled that of its predecessor, the Martinsyde F.3 of 1917 which, in spite of its excellent qualities, was not built in quantity because of the scarcity of Rolls-Royce Falcon engines, on which the Bristol fighter had a prior claim.

Also in 1917, the existence of more effective warplanes of which production was already well under way blocked development of another very good combat aircraft, the Austin-Ball A.F.B.1, which was completed in August 1917. The design had been drawn up with the collaboration of Capt Albert Ball, the British air ace, who had contributed his own experience as a pilot. In test flights, the fighter proved outstanding, clearly even superior to the S.E.5a. But it was precisely because of commitments to the S.E.5a – and the Sopwith Camel – that the authorities could not consider the investment needed for a new production line for the A.F.B.1.

In the United States the development of a combat aircraft for the Western front came to fruition in 1918. The Packard Le Père-Lusac, the first escort fighter designed in the USA during the war period, was designed by Capt G. Le Père of the French air force mission to the United States. The prototype started proving trials in September 1918 and was so good that it won an order for mass production (approximately 4,500 commissioned from the Packard Motor Company of Detroit). Only 27 aeroplanes, however, were completed before the Armistice and of these only two reached the front for operational trials. The Lusac II (its acronym stood for Le Père US Army Combat) was sturdy, well-armed, fast and manoeuvrable, and had an excellent rate of climb.

The first Italian-designed fighter of the war, the Ansaldo A.1 Balilla, also only reached the front in very small numbers. It was created in 1917 by Brezzi, one of Ansaldo's engineers, and the fighter was tested at length by the well-known pilots of the time, amongst them Baracca, and showed that its most outstanding merit was speed. Production totalled 108, many of which were exported after the war.

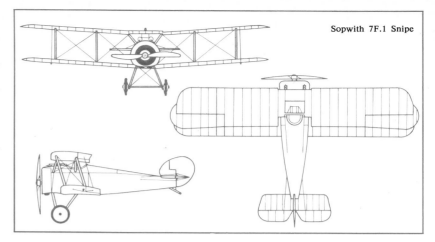

Sopwith 7F.1 Snipe

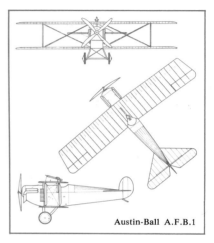

Austin-Ball A.F.B.1

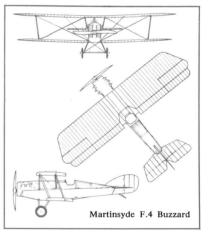

Martinsyde F.4 Buzzard

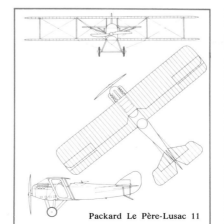

Packard Le Père-Lusac 11

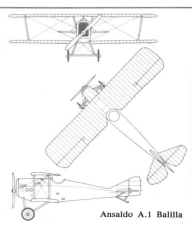

Ansaldo A.1 Balilla

Plate 25

Anatomy of a First World War bomber

Handley Page 0/400

1 Twin 0.303 in (7.62 mm)
  Lewis guns
2 Rotatable Scarff ring
3 Gunner's cockpit (plywood
  construction)
4 Folding seat
5 Slat flooring
6 Entry hatch to gunner's
  cockpit
7 ASI pitot tube
8 Negative lens
9 Rudder pedals
10 Control wheel
11 Clear Pyralin windshield
12 Padded cockpit coaming
13 Pilot's seat
14 Observer's seat
15 Slat flooring

16 Light-bomb rack (manual)
17 Batteries
18 Trap-type forward entry door
19 Fabric lacing
20 Transparent panel
21 Plywood turtle-deck
22 Aluminium fairing
23 Steel propeller hub
24 Brass tip sheathing
25 Four-blade walnut propeller
26 Radiator filler cap
27 Radiator
28 360 hp Rolls-Royce Eagle VIII
  engine
29 Exhaust manifold
30 Nacelle bracing strut/control
  spar

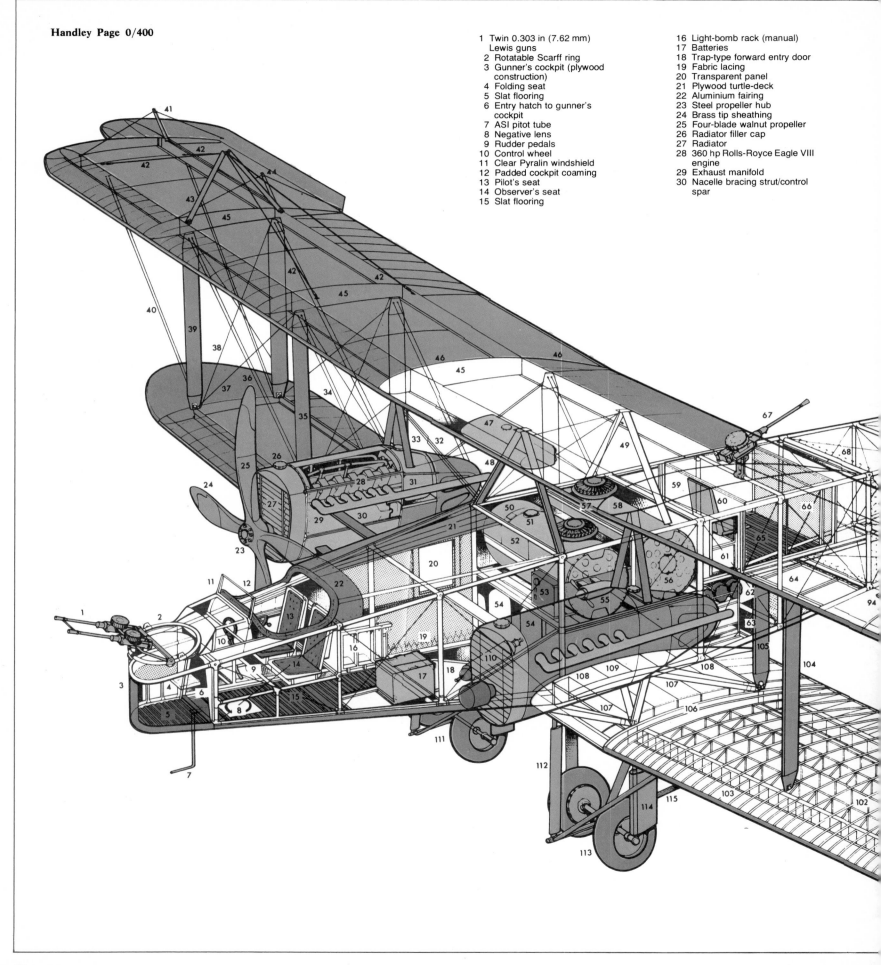

31 Oil tank. 15 Imp gal (68 litre) in
   each nacelle
32 Rigging lines
33 Streamlined steel struts
34 Double flying cable braces
35 Spruce/plywood inner strut
36 Double flying cable braces
37 Single landing cable brace
38 Single stagger cables
39 Spruce/plywood outer strut
40 Double flying braces
41 Outer aileron control horn
42 Cabane braces (four point)
43 Steel cabane
44 Inner aileron control horn
45 Solid end ribs
46 Wing dihedral break-line

47 Gravity-feed fuel tanks in
   leading edge, two of 12-Imp
   gal (54.5 litre) capacity
48 Centre-section streamlined
   forward cabane strut
49 Centre-section streamlined aft
   cabane strut
50 Forward cylindrical fuel tank
   (held by web straps), capacity
   130 Imp gal (581 litre)
51 Filler cap
52 Cross member
53 Engine control pulley cluster
54 Centre-section main
   bomb-bay
55 Six volt wind-driven generator
   (port and starboard)
56 Perforated baffle plate

57 Air-driven fuel pumps
58 Aft fuel tank, capacity 130 Imp
   gal (59 litre)
59 Solid rib at dihedral break-line
60 Dorsal gunner's seat
61 Glazed panel
62 Lewis drum racks
63 Ventral gun position
64 Glazed panel
65 Gun compartment floor
66 Plywood bulkheads
67 Lewis gun
68 Fabric lacing
69 Cable pulley
70 Fuselage frame
71 Multi-strand cable bracing
72 Elevator control cable
73 Tail strut

74 Starboard rudder
75 Upper tail surface
76 Elevator control lever
77 Fixed surface centre-section
78 Upper elevator
79 Port rudder structure
80 Lower elevator
81 Lower tail surface
82 Rudder longeron
83 Tail ballast
84 Rear navigation light
85 Strut
86 Vertical stabiliser
87 Steel attachment point
88 Faired struts
89 Tail skid
90 Tail access panel
91 Lifting points (stations 10 & 12)
92 Port steel cabane
93 Main rear longeron
94 Main forward longeron
95 Plywood covering
96 Steel fitting
97 Solid drag strut
98 Wing structure
99 Port aileron structure
100 Port outer interplane struts
    (plywood-covered spruce)
101 Lower mainplane end rib
102 Wing structure
103 Leading-edge rib construction
104 Port inner interplane struts
    (plywood-covered spruce)
105 Hinge strut
106 Lower mainplane dihedral
    break-line
107 Steel tube engine nacelle
    support struts
108 Wing/fuselage attachment
    points
109 Wing root walkway
110 Fire extinguisher
111 Starboard undercarriage
112 Undercarriage forward strut
113 Port twin mainwheels
114 Faired rubber chord shock
    strut
115 Aft strut

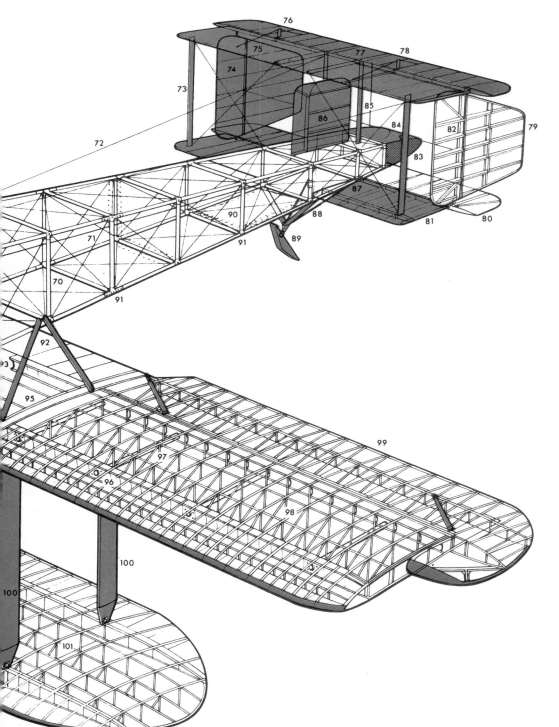

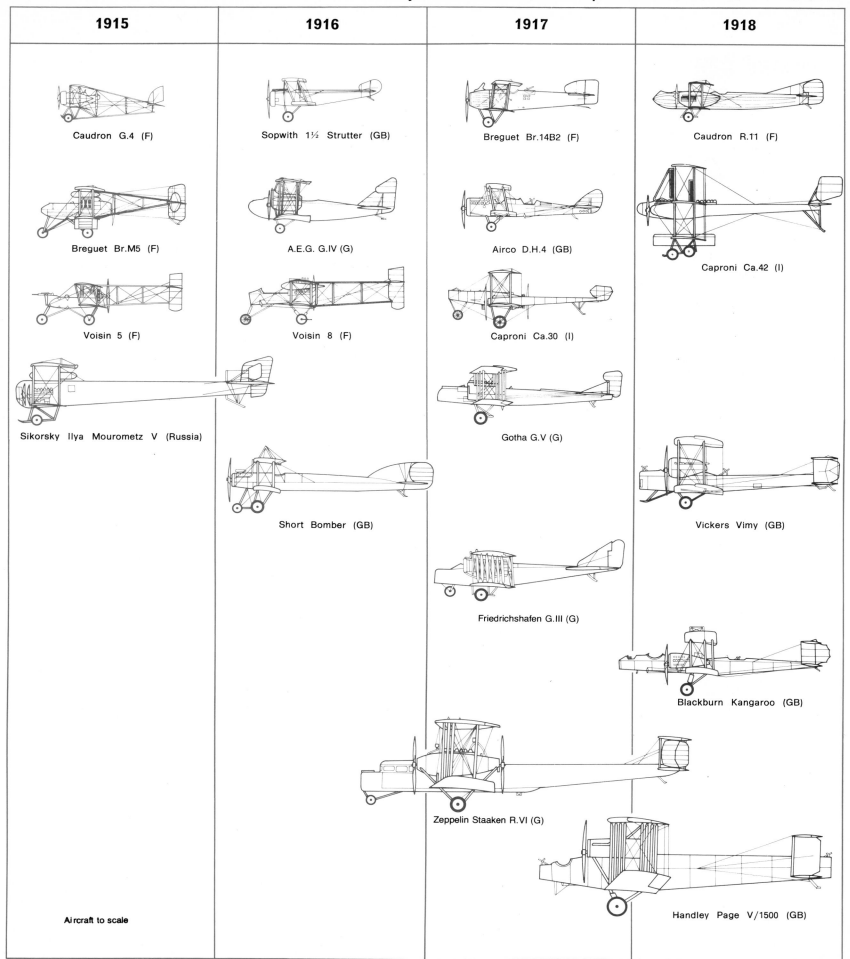

1915	1916	1917	1918

Caudron G.4 (F)

Sopwith 1½ Strutter (GB)

Breguet Br.14B2 (F)

Caudron R.11 (F)

Breguet Br.M5 (F)

A.E.G. G.IV (G)

Airco D.H.4 (GB)

Caproni Ca.42 (I)

Voisin 5 (F)

Voisin 8 (F)

Caproni Ca.30 (I)

Sikorsky Ilya Mourometz V (Russia)

Gotha G.V (G)

Short Bomber (GB)

Vickers Vimy (GB)

Friedrichshafen G.III (G)

Blackburn Kangaroo (GB)

Zeppelin Staaken R.VI (G)

Aircraft to scale

Handley Page V/1500 (GB)

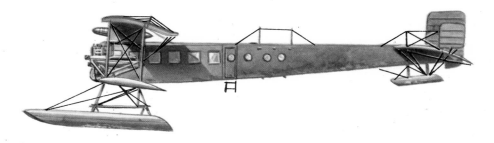

BOLSHOI BAL'TISKY B
Nation: Russia; *manufacturer:* R.B.V.Z.; *type:* trainer; *year:*
1913; *engine:* 4 Argus 6-cylinder liquid-cooled inline, 100 hp
each; *wingspan:* 90 ft 3 in (27.50 m); *length:* 66 ft 3 in
(20.20 m); *height:* – ; *weight:* 7,826 lb (3,550 kg); *maximum
speed:* 53 mph (85 km/h); *ceiling:* – ; *endurance:* – ; *armament:* – ; *crew:* 3

SIKORSKY ILYA MOUROMETZ A
Nation: Russia; *manufacturer:* R.B.V.Z.; *type:* trainer; *year:*
1914; *engine:* 2 Argus 6-cylinder liquid-cooled inline 100 hp, 2
radial Salmson, 140 hp each; *wingspan:* 113 ft 2 in (34.50 m);
length: 67 ft 3 in (20.50 m); *height:* – ; *weight:* 10,580 lb
(4,800 kg); *maximum speed:* 65 mph (105 km/h); *ceiling:*
5,900 ft (1,800 m); *endurance:* 5 hrs; *armament:* – ; *crew:* 4

SIKORSKY ILYA MOUROMETZ E
Nation: Russia; *manufacturer:* R.B.V.Z.; *type:* heavy bomber;
year: 1917; *engine:* four Renault 12-cylinder liquid-cooled inline
Vs, 270 hp each; *wingspan:* 124 ft 8 in (38 m); *length:* 57 ft 5 in
(17.5 m); *height:* – ; *weight:* 15,432 lb (7,000 kg); *maximum
speed:* 85 mph (137 km/h); *ceiling:* 13,120 ft (4,000 m); *endurance:* 5 hrs; *armament:* 7 machine guns, 1,760 lb (800 kg) of
bombs; *crew:* 7

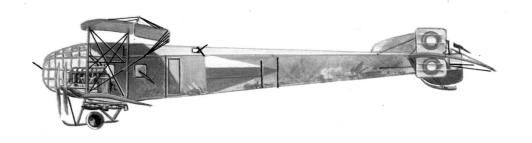

SIKORSKY ILYA MOUROMETZ V
Nation: Russia; *manufacturer:* R.B.V.Z.; *type:* heavy bomber;
year: 1915; *engine:* four Sunbeam 8-cylinder liquid-cooled
inline Vs, 150 hp each; *wingspan:* 97 ft 9 in (29.8 m); *length:*
56 ft 1½ in (17.1 m); *height:* 15 ft 6 in (4.72 m); *weight:*
10,117 lb (4,589 kg); *maximum speed:* 75 mph (121 km/h);
ceiling: 9,840 ft (3,000 m); *endurance:* 5 hrs; *armament:* 3-7
machine guns; 1,150 lb (522 kg) of bombs; *crew:* 4-7

Plate 28

The need for bombers arises in 1915

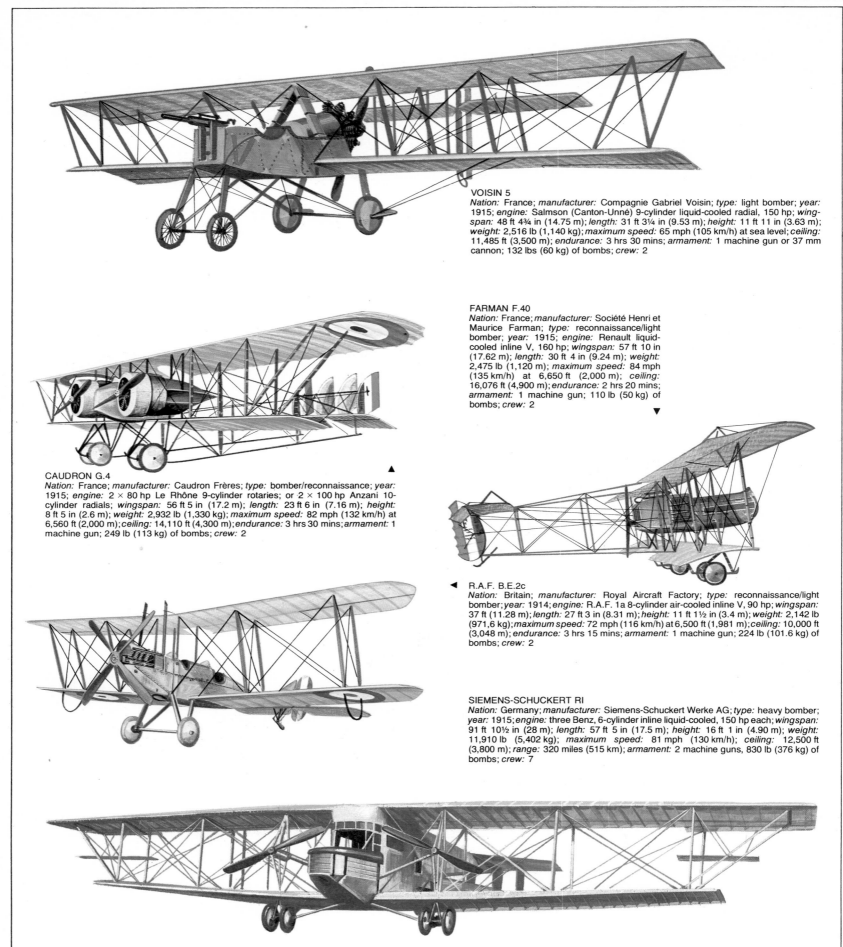

VOISIN 5
Nation: France; *manufacturer:* Compagnie Gabriel Voisin; *type:* light bomber; *year:* 1915; *engine:* Salmson (Canton-Unné) 9-cylinder liquid-cooled radial, 150 hp; *wingspan:* 48 ft 4¾ in (14.75 m); *length:* 31 ft 3¼ in (9.53 m); *height:* 11 ft 11 in (3.63 m); *weight:* 2,516 lb (1,140 kg); *maximum speed:* 65 mph (105 km/h) at sea level; *ceiling:* 11,485 ft (3,500 m); *endurance:* 3 hrs 30 mins; *armament:* 1 machine gun or 37 mm cannon; 132 lbs (60 kg) of bombs; *crew:* 2

FARMAN F.40
Nation: France; *manufacturer:* Société Henri et Maurice Farman; *type:* reconnaissance/light bomber; *year:* 1915; *engine:* Renault liquid-cooled inline V, 160 hp; *wingspan:* 57 ft 10 in (17.62 m); *length:* 30 ft 4 in (9.24 m); *weight:* 2,475 lb (1,120 kg); *maximum speed:* 84 mph (135 km/h) at 6,650 ft (2,000 m); *ceiling:* 16,076 ft (4,900 m); *endurance:* 2 hrs 20 mins; *armament:* 1 machine gun; 110 lb (50 kg) of bombs; *crew:* 2

CAUDRON G.4
Nation: France; *manufacturer:* Caudron Frères; *type:* bomber/reconnaissance; *year:* 1915; *engine:* 2 × 80 hp Le Rhône 9-cylinder rotaries; or 2 × 100 hp Anzani 10-cylinder radials; *wingspan:* 56 ft 5 in (17.2 m); *length:* 23 ft 6 in (7.16 m); *height:* 8 ft 5 in (2.6 m); *weight:* 2,932 lb (1,330 kg); *maximum speed:* 82 mph (132 km/h) at 6,560 ft (2,000 m); *ceiling:* 14,110 ft (4,300 m); *endurance:* 3 hrs 30 mins; *armament:* 1 machine gun; 249 lb (113 kg) of bombs; *crew:* 2

R.A.F. B.E.2c
Nation: Britain; *manufacturer:* Royal Aircraft Factory; *type:* reconnaissance/light bomber; *year:* 1914; *engine:* R.A.F. 1a 8-cylinder air-cooled inline V, 90 hp; *wingspan:* 37 ft (11.28 m); *length:* 27 ft 3 in (8.31 m); *height:* 11 ft 1½ (3.4 m); *weight:* 2,142 lb (971,6 kg); *maximum speed:* 72 mph (116 km/h) at 6,500 ft (1,981 m); *ceiling:* 10,000 ft (3,048 m); *endurance:* 3 hrs 15 mins; *armament:* 1 machine gun; 224 lb (101.6 kg) of bombs; *crew:* 2

SIEMENS-SCHUCKERT RI
Nation: Germany; *manufacturer:* Siemens-Schuckert Werke AG; *type:* heavy bomber; *year:* 1915; *engine:* three Benz, 6-cylinder inline liquid-cooled, 150 hp each; *wingspan:* 91 ft 10½ in (28 m); *length:* 57 ft 5 in (17.5 m); *height:* 16 ft 1 in (4.90 m); *weight:* 11,910 lb (5,402 kg); *maximum speed:* 81 mph (130 km/h); *ceiling:* 12,500 ft (3,800 m); *range:* 320 miles (515 km); *armament:* 2 machine guns, 830 lb (376 kg) of bombs; *crew:* 7

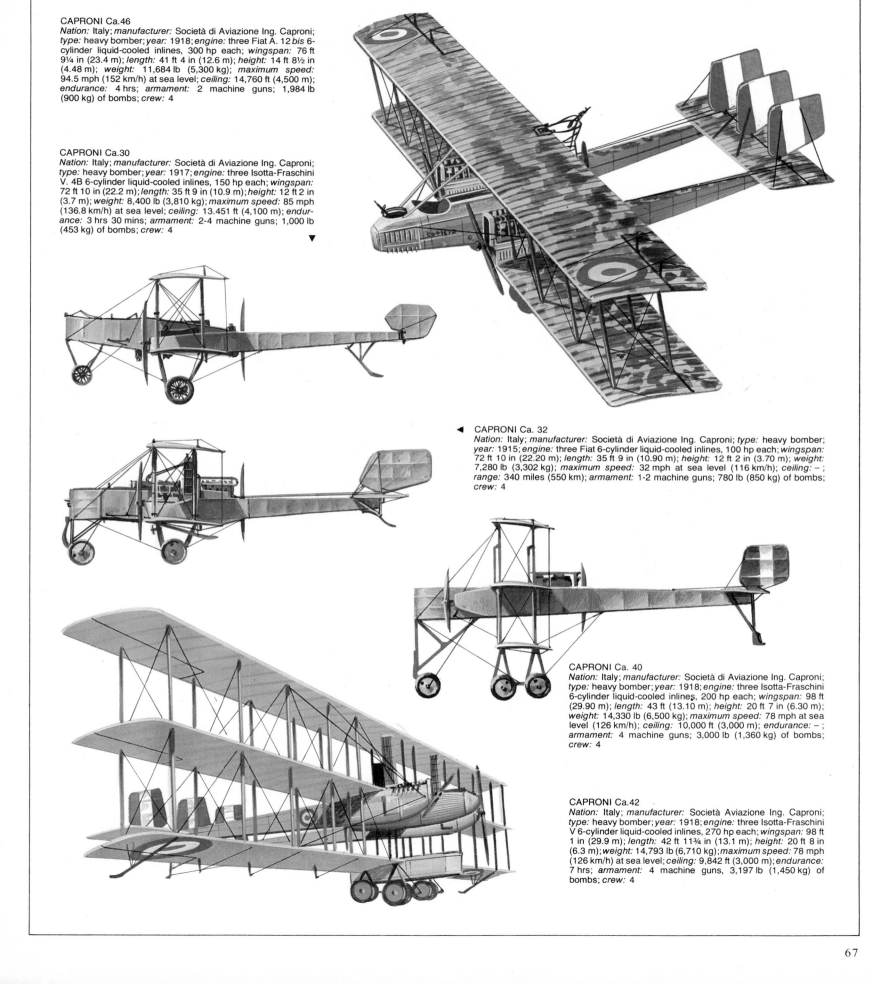

CAPRONI Ca.46
Nation: Italy; *manufacturer:* Società di Aviazione Ing. Caproni; *type:* heavy bomber; *year:* 1918; *engine:* three Fiat A. 12 *bis* 6-cylinder liquid-cooled inlines, 300 hp each; *wingspan:* 76 ft 9¼ in (23.4 m); *length:* 41 ft 4 in (12.6 m); *height:* 14 ft 8½ in (4.48 m); *weight:* 11,684 lb (5,300 kg); *maximum speed:* 94.5 mph (152 km/h) at sea level; *ceiling:* 14,760 ft (4,500 m); *endurance:* 4 hrs; *armament:* 2 machine guns; 1,984 lb (900 kg) of bombs; *crew:* 4

CAPRONI Ca.30
Nation: Italy; *manufacturer:* Società di Aviazione Ing. Caproni; *type:* heavy bomber; *year:* 1917; *engine:* three Isotta-Fraschini V. 4B 6-cylinder liquid-cooled inlines, 150 hp each; *wingspan:* 72 ft 10 in (22.2 m); *length:* 35 ft 9 in (10.9 m); *height:* 12 ft 2 in (3.7 m); *weight:* 8,400 lb (3,810 kg); *maximum speed:* 85 mph (136.8 km/h) at sea level; *ceiling:* 13.451 ft (4,100 m); *endurance:* 3 hrs 30 mins; *armament:* 2-4 machine guns; 1,000 lb (453 kg) of bombs; *crew:* 4 ▼

◄ **CAPRONI Ca. 32**
Nation: Italy; *manufacturer:* Società di Aviazione Ing. Caproni; *type:* heavy bomber; *year:* 1915; *engine:* three Fiat 6-cylinder liquid-cooled inlines, 100 hp each; *wingspan:* 72 ft 10 in (22.20 m); *length:* 35 ft 9 in (10.90 m); *height:* 12 ft 2 in (3.70 m); *weight:* 7,280 lb (3,302 kg); *maximum speed:* 32 mph at sea level (116 km/h); *ceiling:* – ; *range:* 340 miles (550 km); *armament:* 1-2 machine guns; 780 lb (850 kg) of bombs; *crew:* 4

CAPRONI Ca. 40
Nation: Italy; *manufacturer:* Società di Aviazione Ing. Caproni; *type:* heavy bomber; *year:* 1918; *engine:* three Isotta-Fraschini 6-cylinder liquid-cooled inlines, 200 hp each; *wingspan:* 98 ft (29.90 m); *length:* 43 ft (13.10 m); *height:* 20 ft 7 in (6.30 m); *weight:* 14,330 lb (6,500 kg); *maximum speed:* 78 mph at sea level (126 km/h); *ceiling:* 10,000 ft (3,000 m); *endurance:* – ; *armament:* 4 machine guns; 3,000 lb (1,360 kg) of bombs; *crew:* 4

CAPRONI Ca.42
Nation: Italy; *manufacturer:* Società Aviazione Ing. Caproni; *type:* heavy bomber; *year:* 1918; *engine:* three Isotta-Fraschini V 6-cylinder liquid-cooled inlines, 270 hp each; *wingspan:* 98 ft 1 in (29.9 m); *length:* 42 ft 11¾ in (13.1 m); *height:* 20 ft 8 in (6.3 m); *weight:* 14,793 lb (6,710 kg); *maximum speed:* 78 mph (126 km/h) at sea level; *ceiling:* 9,842 ft (3,000 m); *endurance:* 7 hrs; *armament:* 4 machine guns, 3,197 lb (1,450 kg) of bombs; *crew:* 4

Plate 30

Bombers of 1916

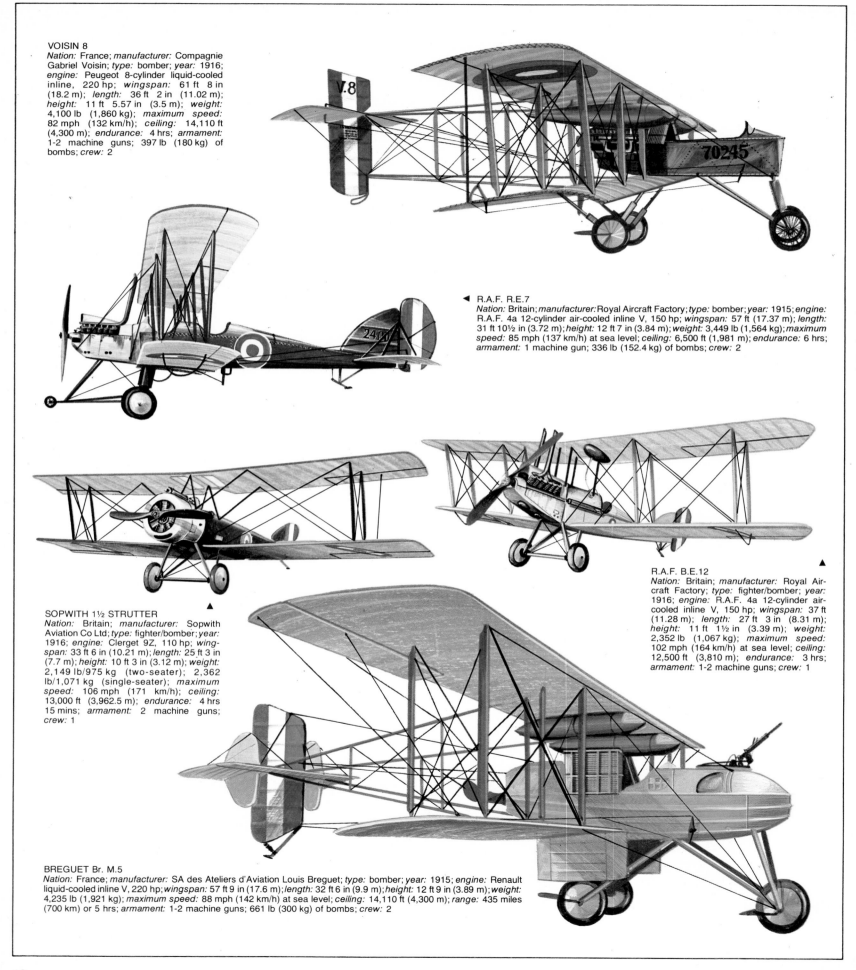

VOISIN 8
Nation: France; *manufacturer:* Compagnie Gabriel Voisin; *type:* bomber; *year:* 1916; *engine:* Peugeot 8-cylinder liquid-cooled inline, 220 hp; *wingspan:* 61 ft 8 in (18.2 m); *length:* 36 ft 2 in (11.02 m); *height:* 11 ft 5.57 in (3.5 m); *weight:* 4,100 lb (1,860 kg); *maximum speed:* 82 mph (132 km/h); *ceiling:* 14,110 ft (4,300 m); *endurance:* 4 hrs; *armament:* 1-2 machine guns; 397 lb (180 kg) of bombs; *crew:* 2

◄ **R.A.F. R.E.7**
Nation: Britain; *manufacturer:* Royal Aircraft Factory; *type:* bomber; *year:* 1915; *engine:* R.A.F. 4a 12-cylinder air-cooled inline V, 150 hp; *wingspan:* 57 ft (17.37 m); *length:* 31 ft 10½ in (3.72 m); *height:* 12 ft 7 in (3.84 m); *weight:* 3,449 lb (1,564 kg); *maximum speed:* 85 mph (137 km/h) at sea level; *ceiling:* 6,500 ft (1,981 m); *endurance:* 6 hrs; *armament:* 1 machine gun; 336 lb (152.4 kg) of bombs; *crew:* 2

R.A.F. B.E.12 ▲
Nation: Britain; *manufacturer:* Royal Aircraft Factory; *type:* fighter/bomber; *year:* 1916; *engine:* R.A.F. 4a 12-cylinder air-cooled inline V, 150 hp; *wingspan:* 37 ft (11.28 m); *length:* 27 ft 3 in (8.31 m); *height:* 11 ft 1½ in (3.39 m); *weight:* 2,352 lb (1,067 kg); *maximum speed:* 102 mph (164 km/h) at sea level; *ceiling:* 12,500 ft (3,810 m); *endurance:* 3 hrs; *armament:* 1-2 machine guns; *crew:* 1

SOPWITH 1½ STRUTTER
Nation: Britain; *manufacturer:* Sopwith Aviation Co Ltd; *type:* fighter/bomber; *year:* 1916; *engine:* Clerget 9Z, 110 hp; *wingspan:* 33 ft 6 in (10.21 m); *length:* 25 ft 3 in (7.7 m); *height:* 10 ft 3 in (3.12 m); *weight:* 2,149 lb/975 kg (two-seater); 2,362 lb/1,071 kg (single-seater); *maximum speed:* 106 mph (171 km/h); *ceiling:* 13,000 ft (3,962.5 m); *endurance:* 4 hrs 15 mins; *armament:* 2 machine guns; *crew:* 1

BREGUET Br. M.5
Nation: France; *manufacturer:* SA des Ateliers d'Aviation Louis Breguet; *type:* bomber; *year:* 1915; *engine:* Renault liquid-cooled inline V, 220 hp; *wingspan:* 57 ft 9 in (17.6 m); *length:* 32 ft 6 in (9.9 m); *height:* 12 ft 9 in (3.89 m); *weight:* 4,235 lb (1,921 kg); *maximum speed:* 88 mph (142 km/h) at sea level; *ceiling:* 14,110 ft (4,300 m); *range:* 435 miles (700 km) or 5 hrs; *armament:* 1-2 machine guns; 661 lb (300 kg) of bombs; *crew:* 2

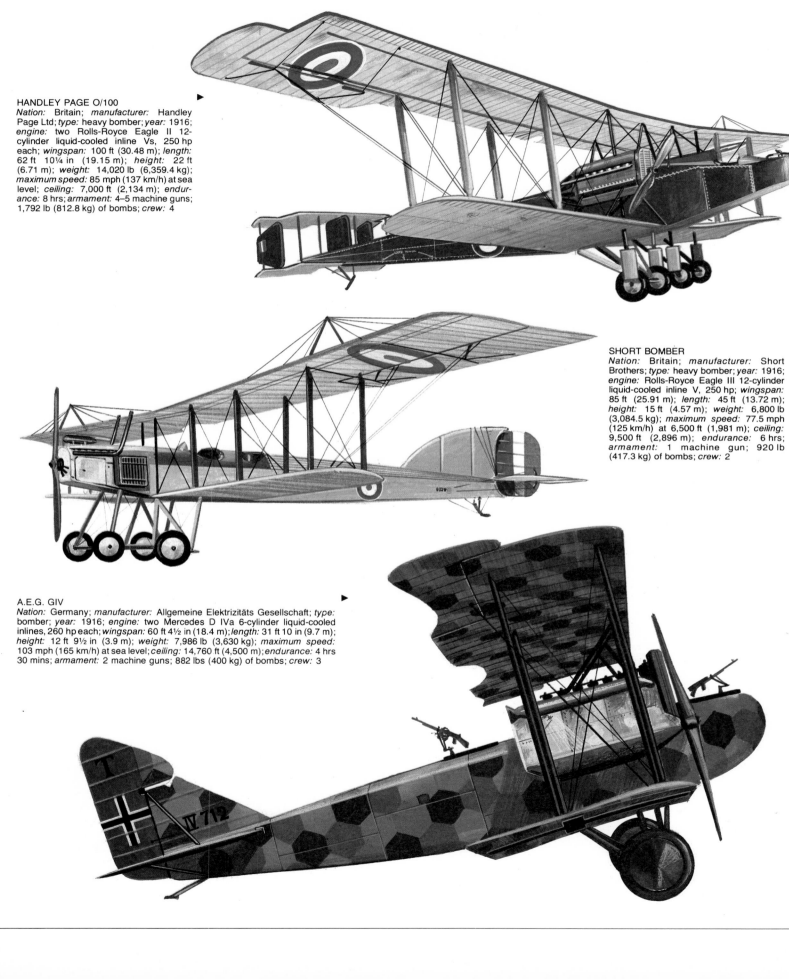

HANDLEY PAGE O/100
Nation: Britain; *manufacturer:* Handley Page Ltd; *type:* heavy bomber; *year:* 1916; *engine:* two Rolls-Royce Eagle II 12-cylinder liquid-cooled inline Vs, 250 hp each; *wingspan:* 100 ft (30.48 m); *length:* 62 ft 10¼ in (19.15 m); *height:* 22 ft (6.71 m); *weight:* 14,020 lb (6,359.4 kg); *maximum speed:* 85 mph (137 km/h) at sea level; *ceiling:* 7,000 ft (2,134 m); *endurance:* 8 hrs; *armament:* 4–5 machine guns; 1,792 lb (812.8 kg) of bombs; *crew:* 4

SHORT BOMBER
Nation: Britain; *manufacturer:* Short Brothers; *type:* heavy bomber; *year:* 1916; *engine:* Rolls-Royce Eagle III 12-cylinder liquid-cooled inline V, 250 hp; *wingspan:* 85 ft (25.91 m); *length:* 45 ft (13.72 m); *height:* 15 ft (4.57 m); *weight:* 6,800 lb (3,084.5 kg); *maximum speed:* 77.5 mph (125 km/h) at 6,500 ft (1,981 m); *ceiling:* 9,500 ft (2,896 m); *endurance:* 6 hrs; *armament:* 1 machine gun; 920 lb (417.3 kg) of bombs; *crew:* 2

A.E.G. GIV
Nation: Germany; *manufacturer:* Allgemeine Elektrizitäts Gesellschaft; *type:* bomber; *year:* 1916; *engine:* two Mercedes D IVa 6-cylinder liquid-cooled inlines, 260 hp each; *wingspan:* 60 ft 4½ in (18.4 m); *length:* 31 ft 10 in (9.7 m); *height:* 12 ft 9½ in (3.9 m); *weight:* 7,986 lb (3,630 kg); *maximum speed:* 103 mph (165 km/h) at sea level; *ceiling:* 14,760 ft (4,500 m); *endurance:* 4 hrs 30 mins; *armament:* 2 machine guns; 882 lbs (400 kg) of bombs; *crew:* 3

Plate 32

German heavy bombers of 1917

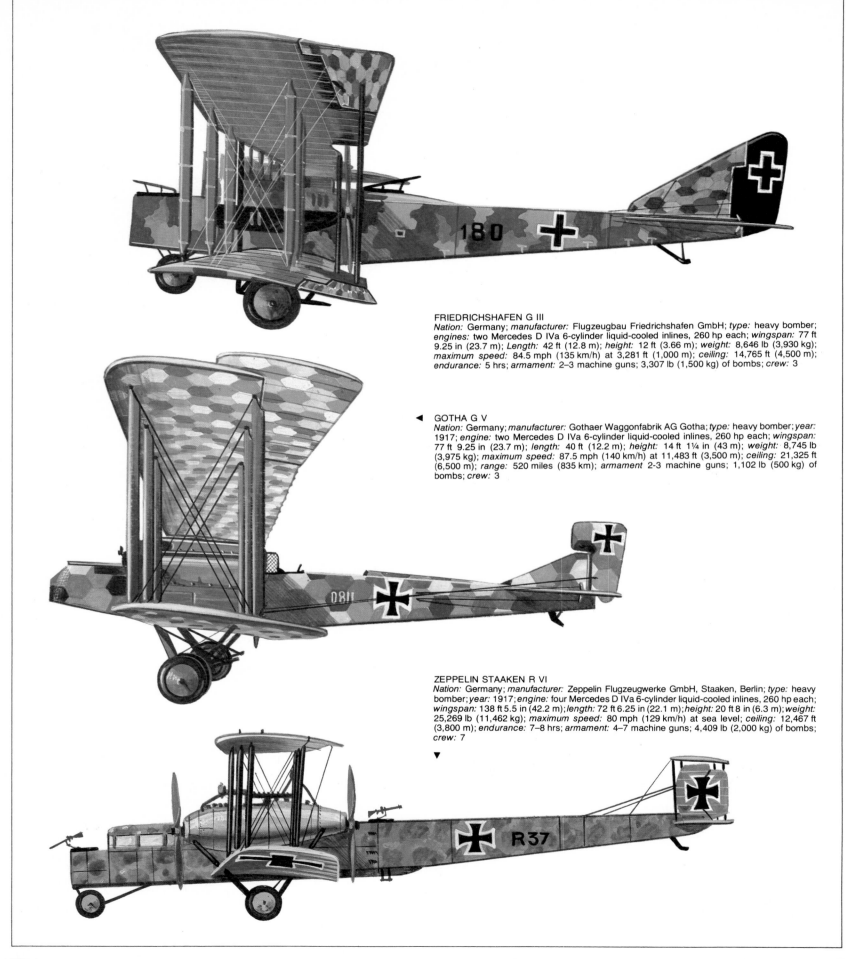

FRIEDRICHSHAFEN G III
Nation: Germany; *manufacturer:* Flugzeugbau Friedrichshafen GmbH; *type:* heavy bomber; *engines:* two Mercedes D IVa 6-cylinder liquid-cooled inlines, 260 hp each; *wingspan:* 77 ft 9.25 in (23.7 m); *Length:* 42 ft (12.8 m); *height:* 12 ft (3.66 m); *weight:* 8,646 lb (3,930 kg); *maximum speed:* 84.5 mph (135 km/h) at 3,281 ft (1,000 m); *ceiling:* 14,765 ft (4,500 m); *endurance:* 5 hrs; *armament:* 2–3 machine guns; 3,307 lb (1,500 kg) of bombs; *crew:* 3

◄ **GOTHA G V**
Nation: Germany; *manufacturer:* Gothaer Waggonfabrik AG Gotha; *type:* heavy bomber; *year:* 1917; *engine:* two Mercedes D IVa 6-cylinder liquid-cooled inlines, 260 hp each; *wingspan:* 77 ft 9.25 in (23.7 m); *length:* 40 ft (12.2 m); *height:* 14 ft 1¼ in (43 m); *weight:* 8,745 lb (3,975 kg); *maximum speed:* 87.5 mph (140 km/h) at 11,483 ft (3,500 m); *ceiling:* 21,325 ft (6,500 m); *range:* 520 miles (835 km); *armament* 2-3 machine guns; 1,102 lb (500 kg) of bombs; *crew:* 3

ZEPPELIN STAAKEN R VI
Nation: Germany; *manufacturer:* Zeppelin Flugzeugwerke GmbH, Staaken, Berlin; *type:* heavy bomber; *year:* 1917; *engine:* four Mercedes D IVa 6-cylinder liquid-cooled inlines, 260 hp each; *wingspan:* 138 ft 5.5 in (42.2 m); *length:* 72 ft 6.25 in (22.1 m); *height:* 20 ft 8 in (6.3 m); *weight:* 25,269 lb (11,462 kg); *maximum speed:* 80 mph (129 km/h) at sea level; *ceiling:* 12,467 ft (3,800 m); *endurance:* 7–8 hrs; *armament:* 4–7 machine guns; 4,409 lb (2,000 kg) of bombs; *crew:* 7

▼

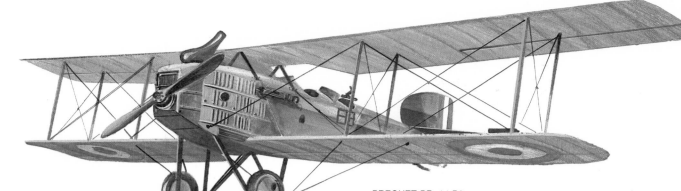

BREGUET BR. 14 B2
Nation: France; *manufacturer:* SA des Ateliers d'Aviation Louis Breguet; *type:* bomber; *year:* 1917; *engine:* Renault 12 Fox 12-cylinder liquid-cooled inline V, 300 hp; *wingspan:* 47 ft 1¼ in (14.36 m); *length:* 29 ft (8.87 m); *height:* 10 ft 10 in (3.3 m); *weight:* 3,892 lb (1,765 kg); *maximum speed:* 110 mph (177 km/h) at 6,560 ft (2,000 m); *ceiling:* 19,030 ft (5,800 m); *endurance:* 2 hrs 45 mins; *armament:* 2–3 machine guns; 661 lb (300 kg) of bombs; *crew:* 2

SOPWITH T.1 CUCKOO
Nation: Britain; *manufacturer:* Sopwith Aviation Co; *type:* torpedo-bomber; *year:* 1917; *engine:* Hispano-Suiza 8-cylinder V liquid-cooled, 200 hp; *wingspan:* 46 ft 9 in (14.25 m); *length:* 28 ft 6 in (8.69 m); *height:* 10 ft 11 in (3.35 m); *weight:* 3,572 lb (1,620 kg); *maximum speed:* 104 mph (166 km/h) at 6,450 ft (1,981 m); *ceiling:* 15,600 ft (4,755 m); *endurance:* 4 hrs; *armament:* 1 torpedo; *crew:* 1

▼

AIRCO D.H.6
Nation: Britain; *manufacturer:* Aircraft Manufacturing Co Ltd; *type:* light bomber; *year:* 1917; *engine:* R.A.F.1a 8-cylinder V air-cooled, 90 hp; *wingspan:* 35 ft 11 in (10.95 m); *length:* 27 ft 3 in (8.32 m); *height:* 10 ft 9 in (3.27 m); *weight:* 2,027 lb (920 kg); *maximum speed:* 66 mph at 6,500 ft (106 km/h at 2,000 m); *ceiling:* – ; *endurance:* – ; *armament:* 100 lb (45 kg) of bombs; *crew:* 1

▲

PAUL SCHMITT 7
Nation: France; *manufacturer:* Paul Schmitt; *type:* light bomber; *year:* 1917; *engine:* Renault 8-cylinder V liquid-cooled, 200 hp; *wingspan:* 57 ft 11 in (17.65 m); *length:* 31 ft 6 in (9.60 m); *height:* 11 ft 9 in (3.58 m); *weight:* 4,615 lb (2,093 kg); *maximum speed:* 84 mph (135 km/h); *ceiling:* 14,000 ft (4,300 m); *endurance:* 5 hrs; *armament:* 2–3 machine guns, 330 lb (150 kg) of bombs; *crew:* 2

▶

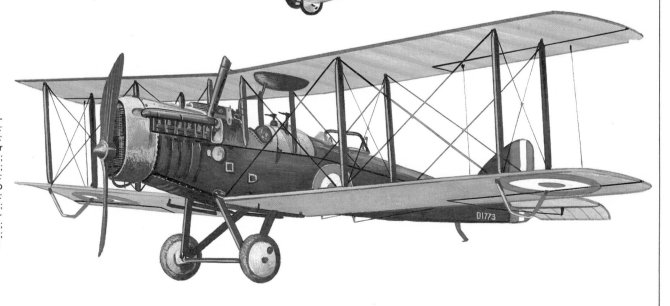

AIRCO D.H.4
Nation: Britain; *manufacturer:* Aircraft Manufacturing Co Ltd; *type:* bomber; *year:* 1917; *engine:* Rolls-Royce Eagle VII 12-cylinder liquid-cooled inline V, 375 hp; *wingspan:* 42 ft 4.5 in (12.92 m); *length:* 30 ft 8 in (9.35 m); *height:* 11 ft (3.35 m); *weight:* 3,472 lb (1,575 kg); *maximum speed:* 143 mph (230 km/h) at sea level; *ceiling:* 23,500 ft (7,163 m); *endurance:* 6 hrs 45 mins (maximum); *armament:* 2–4 machine guns; 460 lb (208.7 kg) of bombs; *crew:* 2

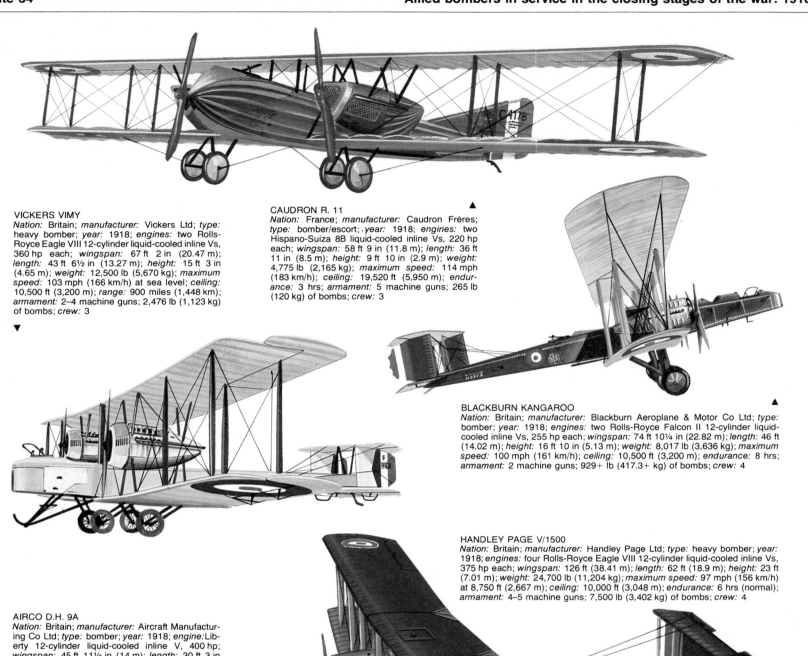

VICKERS VIMY
Nation: Britain; *manufacturer:* Vickers Ltd; *type:*
heavy bomber; *year:* 1918; *engines:* two Rolls-
Royce Eagle VIII 12-cylinder liquid-cooled inline Vs,
360 hp each; *wingspan:* 67 ft 2 in (20.47 m);
length: 43 ft 6½ in (13.27 m); *height:* 15 ft 3 in
(4.65 m); *weight:* 12,500 lb (5,670 kg); *maximum
speed:* 103 mph (166 km/h) at sea level; *ceiling:*
10,500 ft (3,200 m); *range:* 900 miles (1,448 km);
armament: 2–4 machine guns; 2,476 lb (1,123 kg)
of bombs; *crew:* 3

CAUDRON R. 11
Nation: France; *manufacturer:* Caudron Frères;
type: bomber/escort; *year:* 1918; *engines:* two
Hispano-Suiza 8B liquid-cooled inline Vs, 220 hp
each; *wingspan:* 58 ft 9 in (11.8 m); *length:* 36 ft
11 in (8.5 m); *height:* 9 ft 10 in (2.9 m); *weight:*
4,775 lb (2,165 kg); *maximum speed:* 114 mph
(183 km/h); *ceiling:* 19,520 ft (5,950 m); *endurance:* 3 hrs; *armament:* 5 machine guns; 265 lb
(120 kg) of bombs; *crew:* 3

BLACKBURN KANGAROO
Nation: Britain; *manufacturer:* Blackburn Aeroplane & Motor Co Ltd; *type:*
bomber; *year:* 1918; *engines:* two Rolls-Royce Falcon II 12-cylinder liquid-
cooled inline Vs, 255 hp each; *wingspan:* 74 ft 10¼ in (22.82 m); *length:* 46 ft
(14.02 m); *height:* 16 ft 10 in (5.13 m); *weight:* 8,017 lb (3,636 kg); *maximum
speed:* 100 mph (161 km/h); *ceiling:* 10,500 ft (3,200 m); *endurance:* 8 hrs;
armament: 2 machine guns; 929+ lb (417.3+ kg) of bombs; *crew:* 4

HANDLEY PAGE V/1500
Nation: Britain; *manufacturer:* Handley Page Ltd; *type:* heavy bomber; *year:*
1918; *engines:* four Rolls-Royce Eagle VIII 12-cylinder liquid-cooled inline Vs,
375 hp each; *wingspan:* 126 ft (38.41 m); *length:* 62 ft (18.9 m); *height:* 23 ft
(7.01 m); *weight:* 24,700 lb (11,204 kg); *maximum speed:* 97 mph (156 km/h)
at 8,750 ft (2,667 m); *ceiling:* 10,000 ft (3,048 m); *endurance:* 6 hrs (normal);
armament: 4–5 machine guns; 7,500 lb (3,402 kg) of bombs; *crew:* 4

AIRCO D.H. 9A
Nation: Britain; *manufacturer:* Aircraft Manufacturing Co Ltd; *type:* bomber; *year:* 1918; *engine:* Liberty 12-cylinder liquid-cooled inline V, 400 hp;
wingspan: 45 ft 11½ in (14 m); *length:* 30 ft 3 in
(9.22 m); *height:* 11 ft 4 in (3.45 m); *weight:*
4,645 lb (2,107 kg); *maximum speed:* 123 mph
(198 km/h) at sea level; *ceiling:* 18,000 ft (5,486 m);
endurance: 5 hrs 15 mins; *armament:* 2–3 machine
guns; 460–660 lb (208.7–299.4 kg) of bombs; *crew:*
2

Plate 27
Russia introduces the four-engine heavy bomber: 1914

Plate 28
The need for bombers arises in 1915

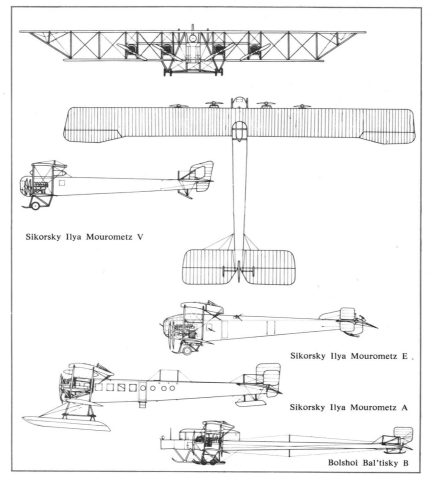

Sikorsky Ilya Mourometz V

Sikorsky Ilya Mourometz E

Sikorsky Ilya Mourometz A

Bolshoi Bal'tisky B

The first giants of the air came into existence in the country which was perhaps the least advanced in aeronautics among the war's main combatants: Czarist Russia. The credit for this went to a young and brilliant designer, Ignor Ivanovich Sikorsky, whose name was to continue to be heard in the West in the years to come. It was in 1912 that Sikorsky – at that time chief designer of the RBVZ, the Russo-Baltic Railway Factories, one of Russia's largest industries – started an ambitious programme for the production of a large multi-engined transport aeroplane. The first of these aircraft, which had only two engines, flew without great success at the beginning of May 1913, but once it was modified with the installation of another two power units in tandem it was flown for 10 minutes on the evening of 13th May. If was unofficially named Bolshoi Bal'tisky Type B (Great Baltic). Yet more modifications were carried out in the installation of the giant biplane's engines: the four 100 hp Argus units, each driving a puller propeller, were installed in separate gondolas. In this configuration the aircraft was renamed Russkyi Vitiaz (Russian Knight) and resumed its proving flights on 23rd July 1913 with very good results.

Stimulated by this initial success, Sikorsky drew on this machine for a four-engine plane of larger dimensions which had a completely redesigned fuselage. On 12th February 1914 the new giant managed to set up an awesome record for its time: it climbed to 2,000 m (6,560 ft) above Moscow and flew for five hours at over 100 km/h (62 mph) average speed, carrying sixteen passengers and a dog. The war potential of the aircraft was clear to all and it was named Ilya Mourometz after a legendary Russian hero. Ten of the four-engine planes were immediately ordered in an adaptation for military use. The outbreak of war meant that this number was increased to 80 and the production models were built in the factories of RBVZ.

The name Ilya Mourometz was used for all five principal versions of the aircraft. The first series model (called Ilya Mourometz A) was purchased by the Imperial Navy, who equipped it with floats and used it widely. This aircraft was followed by a second which was almost identical except for the fact that it had landing-gear and more powerful engines; production then went on to a variant which was specially conceived as a bomber, the Ilya Mourometz V of 1915, of which 32 were built. At the end of the year the assembly lines started to built the first thirty series G aircraft, which had improved armament and in which modifications were made to the fuselage and wings. A few aircraft of the E version followed, which had their engines once more installed in tandem and a smaller wingspan, and in 1917 a dozen aircraft of the final variant, which was the largest and most powerful, were manufactured: the Ilya Mourometz E. In this version a marked improvement in performance was brought about by the adoption of Renault 220 hp engines (constructed under licence in Russia); and with a full bomb-load and a total weight of 7 tonnes, the four engines of the E series could reach a maximum speed of 137 km/h (85 mph).

The wide variety and the difficulties that follow from a lack of standardisation of engines used in the Ilya Mourometz aircraft were typical of Russia's aviation industry at that time. Russia depended almost totally on foreign industry for aero engines and lack of supplies forced the constructors to adapt the aircraft to whatever engines were available at the time. Thus machines were powered by Salmson, Sunbeam, Argus, Renault and RBVZ engines and some aircraft even had two pairs of different engines installed on the inner and outer wing sections.

The first stages of the operational career of the Ilya Mourometz were not greatly distinguished, as this was the time of the relatively inferior first two models. After a few slight technical hitches slowing production for a while, a special bomber unit was formed in December 1914, the *Eskadra Vozdushnykh Korablei* (Squadron of Flying Ships), which became operational in February of the following year from a base in Poland. The first bombing raid took place on 15th February with a raid on East Prussia and from that day up to the Revolution of 1917 the Ilya Mourometz played a formidable wartime role, making over four hundred raids on Germany and Lithuania. During the course of this very intensive use only two aircraft were lost, which is by any standards a remarkable safety record. In 1916 Britain and France both applied for permission to build this renowned aircraft under licence, but without result.

The Russian experiment with heavy bombers remained a somewhat isolated phenomenon of the war, with only one similar development which could be compared happening in Italy at about the same time.

In France, in the early phase of the war, the role of the bomber was entrusted to lighter aircraft which, with only a small load capacity, were most suitable for tactical bombing. The most widely used bomber was the Voisin biplane, whose origins went back to the pre-war period. The type 3, of which 100 were constructed, equipped nearly all the Allied air forces and in 1915 another two versions followed, the Voisin 4 and the Voisin 5. They differed from the basic model mainly in certain small structural modifications, in the adoption of more powerful engines, and in the possibility of installing a Hotchkiss 37 mm or 47 mm cannon in the nose instead of a machine gun. This armament, useless in aerial combat, was found very effective against ground targets.

The Voisin 4 and 5, like their predecessor, were not produced in large numbers: 200 of the type 4 were completed in all, and 350 of type 5. From this latter variant was derived the final version of the aircraft, the Voisin 6, which was almost identical to its predecessor except in its engine, which was more powerful.

The development of Gabriel Voisin's biplane was accompanied in the first stages of the war by new aircraft from Henri and Maurice Farman. After a whole series of separate designs, the brothers had decided to join forces and had produced a new biplane which incorporated the best features of their earlier models: this was the Farman F.40. It appeared in 1915 but proved to be rather ineffectual in combat, mainly due to its inadequate armament: a single forward-firing Lewis gun and only a limited bomb-load. However, the Farman F.40 stayed in the front line for a year and was then relegated to the less demanding role of night bomber and finally to that of trainer. The basic F.40 model was developed in another five principal versions, designated F.41, F.46, F.56, F.60 and F.61 – differing from each other in their engines and in their wingspans.

These variants served not only with the French air force, but were also used by the Belgians.

A more successful aircraft than the Farman series, appearing at the front in November 1915, was the Caudron G.4 bomber. This was designed by two brothers, Gaston and René Caudron,

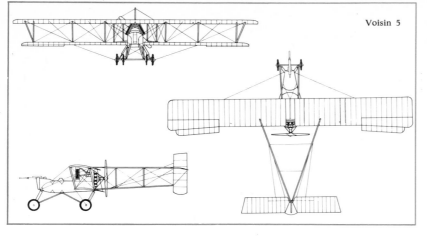

Voisin 5

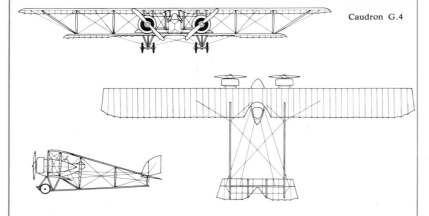

Caudron G.4

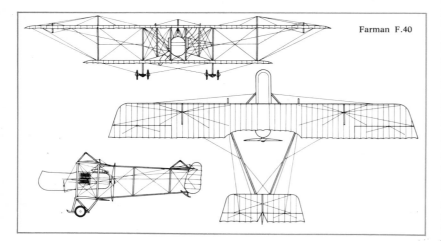

Farman F.40

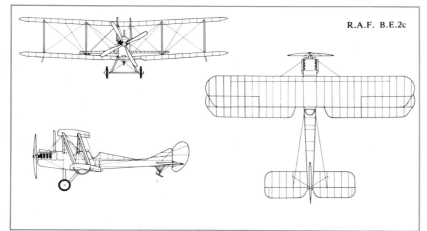

R.A.F. B.E.2c

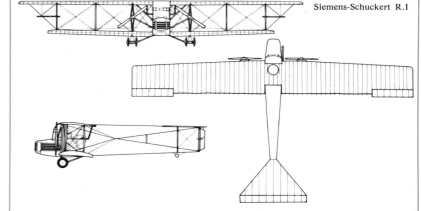

Siemens-Schuckert R.I

and was a large twin-engined biplane derived more or less directly from a preceding model, the single-engined G.3 reconnaissance plane of 1914, of which 100 had been built and which had been used by Britain, Belgium, Italy and Russia, as well as France. The Caudron G.4 flew in prototype form in March 1915, and after a rather slow development phase, it became operational with the *Aviation militaire*.

Although it had little defensive armament, the Caudron bomber soon gained a reputation as an aircraft of good performance (especially rate of climb) and for being totally reliable. Like the G.3 this aircraft aroused the interest of the Allies and was used by Britain and Italy; between 1917 and 1918 the Italians had 51 of them built by the AER factory. The Caudrons of the Royal Flying Corps were put to concentrated use in 1916 and early 1917 in day and night bombing attacks over Belgium against the enemy seaplane and Zeppelin bases. The G.4 was followed in 1916 by the G.6 which represented a transitional model before the advent of the new Caudron bombers of the R series, of completely new design.

In Britain as well, in the early part of the war, no efforts were spared to construct a serviceable bomber. Among the first attempts were the Royal Aircraft Factory's biplanes of the B.E. series. The B.E.2s of 1913 were succeeded in the following year by the first models of a new version, the B.E.2c, which corrected certain serious shortcomings of the B.E.2a, which was badly underpowered and underarmed, and in general its performance was inadequate, especially when confronted with the more mobile and powerful German fighters. In designing the new aircraft all the weak points which had emerged from the operational use of the B.E.2a were borne in mind and the result was a more manoeuvrable, better-armed aircraft with increased bomb carrying capacity, although only a little faster. The engine was changed to one developed by the Royal Aircraft Factory, which was more powerful than the Renault which had been used until

then. The wings were completely redesigned and had more efficient ailerons. The first B.E.2cs arrived at the front towards the end of 1914 and in the following year, as production proceeded, these aircraft equipped a wing of the Royal Naval Air Services and twelve squadrons of the Royal Flying Corps. Even the B.E.2cs, however, found themselves outclassed by enemy aircraft. Strangely they were kept in service up till 1917, before being relegated to training and home defence.

If France and Britain were slow to produce an effective bomber, Germany was quicker off the mark. They already fielded a larger bomber, the Siemens-Schuckert, in 1915. This aircraft was a forerunner of the Gothas, Friedrichshafens and Zeppelins that came later. Seven examples of this early bomber were built, featuring three engines enclosed within the fuselage and driving two propellers which were placed between the wings. This aircraft remained in service up to 1917.

Plate 29
The great Caproni bombers: in service from 1915 to 1918

Thirty-two Caproni Ca.42s were built, six of which were supplied to the Royal Naval Air Service, who returned them to Italy at the end of the war. When in service, the triplane was mainly used for night bombing missions but in the last months of the war it also took part in daytime raids, such as those which were carried out during the battle of Vittorio Veneto. Among the versions derived from it (very few of which were built), the Ca.43 was for the navy, a twin-float seaplane which could carry two torpedoes. The Ca.51 and the Ca.52 were also important, both having biplane tails with a rear machine gun position.

The name of Caproni, like that of Sikorsky, is synonymous with the first heavy bombers. Italy and Russia together were the first nations to develop this kind of warfare and the first Caproni, forerunner of an entire family of multi-engined aircraft, appeared in 1913, at a time when such things were unheard of outside Russia. The Ca.30, the first three-engined Caproni, was notable for the adoption of three Gnome-Rhône 80 hp engines placed inside the fuselage: one connected direct to a pusher propeller, the others powering two tractor propellers through driveshafts. In practice this arrangement of the engines turned out to be too complicated and so Caproni built a more conventional aircraft, the Ca.31, which flew in 1914.

The first operational machines, however, were the Caproni Ca.32s (military designation Ca.2) which were similar to the Ca.31 except for their engines, which were 100 hp inline engines. The Ca.32s carried out the first Italian bombing raid of the war on 25th August 1915. These machines, of which 164 were built, were followed in 1917 by the first of the 269 Caproni Ca.33s (military designation Ca.3) which had more powerful engines, improved performance and greater bomb-load.

Apart from numerous squadrons of the *Corpo Aeronautico Militare*, and the first torpedo bomber squadrons of the navy, two units of the French air force were equipped with Ca.33s constructed under licence by Esnault-Pelterie. Although the Ca.33s remained in service up to the end of the war, at the beginning of 1918 they began to be joined at the front by three new versions grouped together under the military designation of Ca.5. These were the Ca.44, the Ca.45 and the Ca.46. These last two variants were produced in large numbers and their improvement over the bombers of the Ca.3 series lay mainly in their engines and consequently in their performance. Overall, before the end of the war, 225 Capronis of Series 5 were constructed. Production licences were granted to France, Britain and the United States.

Among the biplanes of the Series 3 and those of the Series 5 there appeared several triplane models which were given the military designation of Ca.4. The change in design was intended to increase the combat potential of the aircraft. The result was a machine which was even larger and which did not possess exceptional performance but could accurately drop considerable quantities of bombs on

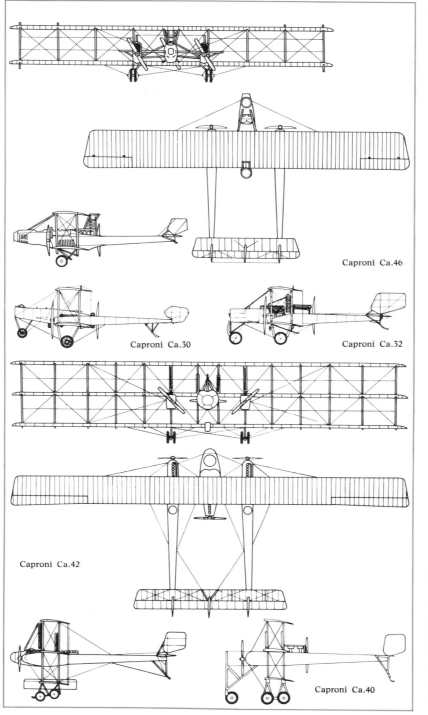

Caproni Ca.46

Caproni Ca.30

Caproni Ca.32

Caproni Ca.42

Caproni Ca.40

distant targets. The first triplane of the Ca.4 series was designated Ca.40 by its manufacturer. Apart from the three large wings, the aircraft was still reminiscent of the earlier biplanes in the configuration of its fuselage and tailplane. The armament had been improved, especially the defensive guns. The Ca.40 encountered development problems and in particular suffered from a noticeable lack of power. Only three were built before production went on to a new version, the Ca.41, which had a modified fuselage and more powerful engines. The

final variant, however, was the Ca.42, which had changes made to its fuselage and a different engine. Several engines were used, from the Isotta Fraschini 270 hp to the Fiat and American Liberty engines, each of 400 hp. This increase in power made possible an increase in armament, and in some aircraft the number of machine guns was doubled, adopting twin installations instead of single ones in the tail turrets. The bombs, which were carried in specially shaped racks between the wheels of the massive undercarriage, weighed up to 1,450 kg (3,197 lb).

Plate 30
Bombers of 1916

Meanwhile France and Britain pressed on with their search for an efficient bomber. The Voisins, Caudrons and Farmans were joined by new aircraft, but not very different in design and effectiveness. The Breguet Br.M5, for instance, which although adapted from a previous Louis Breguet model, the BU-3, was chosen in October 1915 in a French government competititon aiming to find a bomber capable of striking at the town of Essen which was the home of some of Germany's strategic industries. Two versions of the Br.M5 were built, their military designations being 4B.2 and 5Ca.2 respectively, differing mainly in their armament.

The Breguet 4B.2 was a pure bomber, armed with a Hotchkiss or Lewis machine gun in the forward part of the fuselage and carrying Michelin bomb-racks on the lower wing which held up to forty 7 kg (15 lb) bombs. The Breguet 5Ca.2, on the other hand, was not built as a bomber but for the role of bomber escort: it had a 37 mm Hotchkiss gun in the nose and a fixed rear-firing gun on the upper wing. The rear-firing gun was found to be completely useless in aerial combat and was soon replaced with another machine gun.

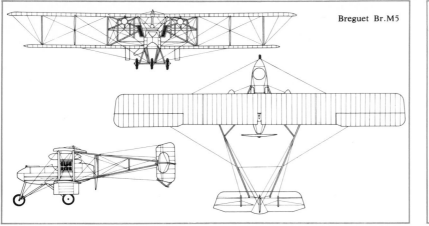

Breguet Br.M5

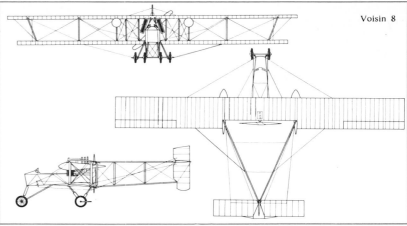

Voisin 8

At the outset the Breguet 4B.2 was used as a daytime bomber but the shortcomings resulting from its old-fashioned design led to its being relegated after a time to night bombing. Although it could carry a reasonable bomb-load the aircraft was slow, vulnerable and clumsy in take-off and landing. Its final relegation to this less dangerous activity was effected in October 1916 after a disastrous raid on Oberndorf. Even as a night bomber, the Breguet biplane proved unreliable, mainly because of bad visibility for the pilot.

Towards the end of 1916 another light but mediocre French bomber appeared, the Voisin 8, which was intended by Gabriel Voisin to repeat the success of his designs of 1914 and 1915. Although it was better armed and had better overall performance than its two forerunners the Voisin 8 was always plagued by problems with its Peugeot engine, and these shortcomings, which were never completely eliminated, curtailed the operational use of the aircraft. In the end the engine was replaced by a 300 hp

Renault engine and this led on to the next model, the Type 10, which apart from structural improvements had better performance and could carry almost double the bomb-load. About 1,100 of the Voisin 8 were built, as well as a version which was armed with a forward-firing cannon as had been done with the Voisin 4 and 5 and with the Breguet bombers.

Among other light bombers, an aircraft which was specially constructed in Britain to drop a new bomb weighing 152.4 kg (335 lb), the R.A.F. R.E.7 turned out not to be a great success. It was delivered from the middle of 1915 onwards. This aircraft was derived from the R.E.5 reconnaissance planes of 1914, some of which had been used for testing the new bomb and its release mechanism. The first squadrons equipped with this bomber went to the lines at the beginning of 1916 in France but bombing missions only started after six months, the aircraft meanwhile simply being used as a reconnaissance plane, probably because of its unsatisfactory performance in an offensive role.

In the late summer the R.E.7 was replaced by the B.E.12 and withdrawn from the line: but not, perhaps surprisingly, before 250 of them had been built. During the course of production an unsuccessful attempt had been made to improve its performance by installing more powerful engines. The R.A.F. B.E.12 was also disappointing. The biplane had been designed as a fighter with the intention of confronting the fearsome Fokker monoplane, but after only a few weeks in service it was quickly relegated to light bombing in September 1916.

The Sopwith 1½-Strutter on the other hand was a good multirole plane, and it pointed the way forward to the outstanding Pup fighter. Designed in 1915, the aircraft went into service in the first months of the following year and served on all fronts in large numbers (1,520 constructed in Britain and 4,200 in France) up to the beginning of 1918. Its versatility was shown by the fact that apart from its use as a fighter it was also used as a light bomber: in this latter role it was changed to a single-seater.

Plate 31
Heavy bombers of 1916

Britain's tardiness compared with Russia and Italy in constructing heavy bombers was finally remedied in 1916 when the first effective aircraft of this type went into service, the large twin-engined Handley-Page.

The Handley-Page was preceded by a transitional aircraft, the Short Bomber, derived from a seaplane which was widely used by the Royal Navy from 1915 onwards. This aircraft in its original form (Short 184) had been conceived as a torpedo-bomber and it was in this role that on 12th August 1915 it had achieved a notable success in sinking an enemy ship in the Dardanelles with a torpedo, which was the first time in history that such a feat had been performed. Production for naval use was very large (900 were constructed in all) and, stimulated by this success, Short decided to develop a landplane from the basic model, and thus to provide a bomber.

The first aircraft resembled the seaplane very closely but later ones had considerable modifications made to the fuselage: it was in this final configuration that the Short Bombers went into squadron service in the spring of 1916. Eighty-three of them were constructed, which remained in front line service until April of the following year.

In November 1916 the first of the "real" heavy British bombers arrived – the Handley-Page O/100: this aircraft had been ordered, designed and constructed with the precise aim of reaching and bombing Germany, and was the result of a very demanding specification from the Air Board. It appeared so impressive, even on the drawing board, that 40 were ordered before any prototype had ever flown. The model O/100 was followed into production by an improved variant, designated O/400, of which 550 were

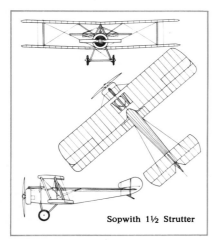

Sopwith 1½ Strutter

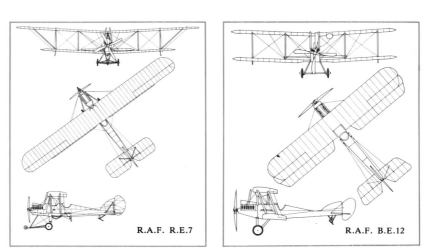

R.A.F. R.E.7

R.A.F. B.E.12

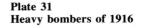

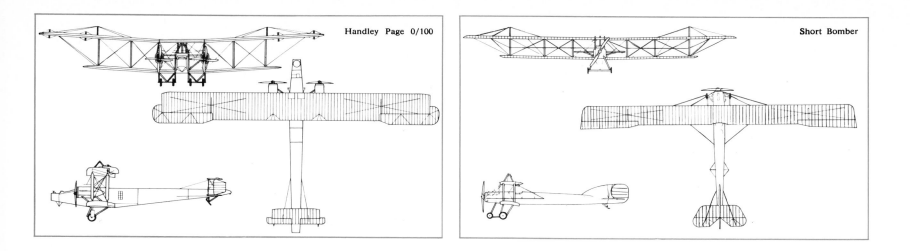

Handley Page 0/100

Short Bomber

built during the course of the war and which went into service on the Western front in the spring of 1917. Together, the two models were widely used for the duration of the war for systematic bombing of military targets in zones occupied by the Germans. In particular the Handley-Page O/400 was also used in 1918 to bomb targets in Germany's Saar and Ruhr industrial centres. In operational use the O/100 bombers were employed for a few months for daytime patrol missions but with the advent of the O/400 they flew in a series of massive night-time raids while the more powerful model replaced them for more dangerous daytime operations. At the end of the war the RAF had an operational force of 259·Handley-Page O/400s.

Differences between the two models of the bomber were not great: the most noticeable lay in the type and power of the engines (about 100 hp more in the O/400) and also in the positioning of the fuel tanks, which in the later model were transferred from the engine gondolas to the fuselage for obvious safety reasons. The structure of the aircraft was very complex and a most unusual feature was in the design of the wings which could be folded backwards in the region of the engines,

so that the aircraft could be parked in normal hangars.

The career of the Handley-Page O/400 did not come to an end with the war. The Royal Air Force, which by then had of course more modern and efficient bombers at its disposal, kept them in service until 1920, after a simple conversion – for carrying VIP passengers. Four more Handley-Page O/400s went into commercial use, pioneering the first intercontinental routes which were subsequently operated by Imperial Airways.

A later variant of the Handley-Page, the O/700 transport, made use of all this experience in larger aircraft but was not built in large numbers; the aircraft were all sold to China and South Africa.

Germany did not get a really worthwhile heavy bomber until 1917 when the Gotha, the Friedrichshafen and the Zeppelin appeared, but in 1916 she already had many medium bombers which were very effective. Among these were the twin-engined G series planes constructed by the Allgemeine Elektrizitätsgesellschaft between 1915 and 1918. The most widely used member of this family was the A.E.G. G.IV which went into service towards the end of 1916. This air-

craft included the best features of its predecessors the G.I, G.II and G.III, and was equipped with more powerful and reliable engines. The G.IV also had a mixed wood and steel tubing structure, the steel tubing forming the wing-frames, which were of a new design with a dihedral on the lower wing and wingflaps on the upper wing.

Because of its limited range and relatively low operational ceiling, the G.IV was mainly used for tactical bombing. Having served on the Eastern front, for example in Romania and Macedonia, and on the Western front, the units which had the A.E.G. bomber carried out a long series of night missions towards the end of 1917 aimed at Italian cities, the main targets being Venice, Padua, Verona and Treviso. In March 1918 the A.E.G. G.IV went back to the Western front and remained there until the end of the war. In August 1918 50 bombers of this type were still flying night raids behind enemy lines. Experimental version were also developed – the G.IVb with wider wingspan; the G.IVk with a biplane tail, armoured engine and a 20 mm cannon; and finally the G.V, too late to take part in combat.

Plate 32
German heavy bombers of 1917

In 1917 Germany brought a new generation of heavy bombers into the field. The Friedrichshafen, Gotha and Zeppelin Staaken were notorious for their depredations on Allied troops, while the Gotha and Zeppelin Staaken came to be well enough known to the citizens of London, who for a whole year were subjected to night-time visits from these deadly German giants.

The Friedrichshafen G.III went into service in February 1917. It was preceded by two variants, the G.I. and the G.II of 1914 and 1916 respectively, which represented the first steps towards this definitive version. The G.III was a larger plane than its two predecessors and driven by more powerful engines, and its sturdy form was able to carry a very large quantity of bombs. It went into service with three bomber groups of the German air force, joining its contemporary the Gotha G.V. in night bombing raids. In the summer of 1917 the Friedrichshafens of *Kagohl I* (*Kampfgeschwader der Obersten Heeresleitung* – High Command Bomber Group) started a series of night-time raids on the British forces at Dunkirk, causing very heavy damage. A number of bombing missions were flown to Paris in the following months.

At the beginning of 1918 the G.III was joined by a modified verson, the G.IIIa, which was equipped with a biplane tail and had other structural modifications. The manufacture of these two types, under licence by Hansa and Daimler, eventually totalled 338.

The Friedrichshafen's best known companion at arms was the Gotha G.V. This twin-engined bomber had been preceded, in the first months of 1917, by the G.IV of which about 230 had been built and which from May onwards had made daytime raids on

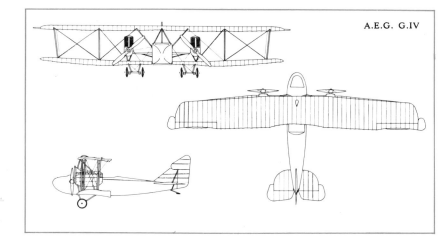

A.E.G. G.IV

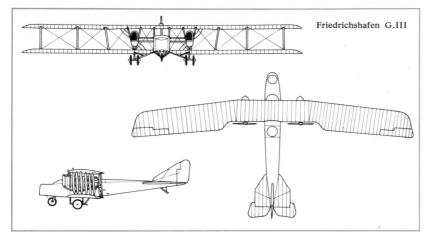

Friedrichshafen G.III

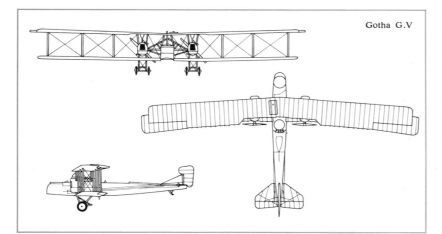

Gotha G.V

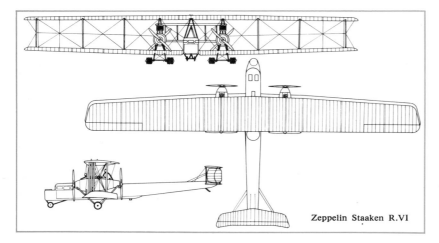

Zeppelin Staaken R.VI

lion damage (in 1917 prices). The psychological effect on the civilian population, however, was considerable, by now unnerved and harassed by continual raids by night and by day. In one of these, on 16th February 1918, a Zeppelin dropped the first 1,000 kg (2,200 lb) bomb, hitting the Royal Hospital in Chelsea and causing dozens of dead and wounded.

Germany's big bombers had their origins in a major effort of new development on the part of Zeppelin, resulting in the first *Riesenflugzeug* (giant aeroplane), the V.G.O. I, in late 1914. From this three-engined plane developed the similar V.G.O. II, the V.G.O. III which had six engines, the R.1V, the R.V. and the R.VII, which all remained at prototype stage. Series production was finally commenced on the R.VI, the definitive model. Eighteen aircraft of this type were built, two of them also equipped with an additional engine which powered the compressors of the aircraft's superchargers. This modification was intended to increase the aircraft's operational ceiling and was successful: the system made it possible to reach 6,000 m (19,686 ft) fully loaded.

Plate 33
Allied bombers of 1917

In the last stages of the war the Allies put excellent light bombers into the field, alongside the large multi-engine aircraft. In France, the Breguet Br.14 was particularly successful, and had gone into production at the beginning of 1917, nearly 5,500 being built before the war came to an end. This figure reached a record total of 8,000 in 1926, when assembly lines were shut down. The exceptionally long life

of this aeroplane was due not only to the merits of its design but also to the many innovations in construction technique such as the use of duralumin in the airframe which was introduced by Louis Breguet. The contribution which the aircraft of Series 4 made to the Allied war effort in the last years of the conflict was considerable, mainly due to the aircraft's great versatility. From the two basic versons – the Br.14A2 reconnaissance and the Br.14B2 bomber – numerous variants were developed: night bomber, air ambulance and even a seaplane version.

The prototype of the Breguet 14 flew on 21 November 1916 and the first production version was the reconnaissance model of which 508 were ordered in the first months of 1917. The bomber model followed which was also ordered in great numbers. Both went into squadron service in the summer of 1917 and were also used by the Belgian air force and the American Expeditionary Force. The latter bought 376 of these aircraft in 1918.

A contemporary of the Breguet 14 (although its design went back to 1915) was an ill-fated single-engine bomber, the Paul Schmitt 7, whose lack of success was mainly due to its very lengthy development phase (nearly a year and a half) which delayed the start of production. Once at the front, these aircraft proved difficult to handle and were very vulnerable to fighter attack; moreover, their long wings made them difficult to fly in close formation and provide one another with effective mutual support. After a few months the units which had been equipped with the Paul Schmitt 7s were issued with more modern bombers.

In Britain an excellent single-engined biplane bomber, the Airco D.H.4, had a similar success, both in terms of quality and numbers produced, to the French Breguet 14. The Airco was considered the best of its class, and its claim to fame was that it was the only British aircraft to be constructed in the United States which saw active service in the war. Out of the 6,295 built over two-thirds, 4,846,

targets in Britain. The G.V differed from its predecessors in having more powerful engines and better performance. It was a very easy machine to handle, especially considering its size; it was well-armed and was very difficult to shoot down. Its one shortcoming was structural weakness, especially in its undercarriage, so that to land the aircraft not only extreme care but specially-prepared landing fields were required. More Gothas were lost in accidents than in combat: while 24 were shot down during the course of the raids on London, 36 aircraft were destroyed in unsuccessful landing. In order to rectify the weakness in the landing-gear to some extent, one of

the two minor versions of the G.V, the G.Va, was equipped with two additional wheels under the nose. The other variant, the G.Vb, had a biplane tail which improved the rear gunner's field of fire.

From 17th December 1917 raids on London involved a new, more terrifying weapon: the Zeppelin Staaken R.VI, a real giant of a four-engine aeroplane, which in the course of 52 raids succeeded in delivering 2,772 bombs totalling 196 tonnes. Material damage was not particularly devastating, especially when compared with similar strategic bombing raids in the Second World War and in Indochina: 857 killed, 2,058 wounded, £1.5 mil-

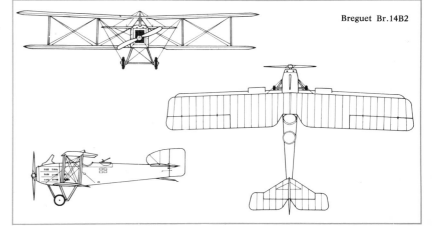

Breguet Br.14B2

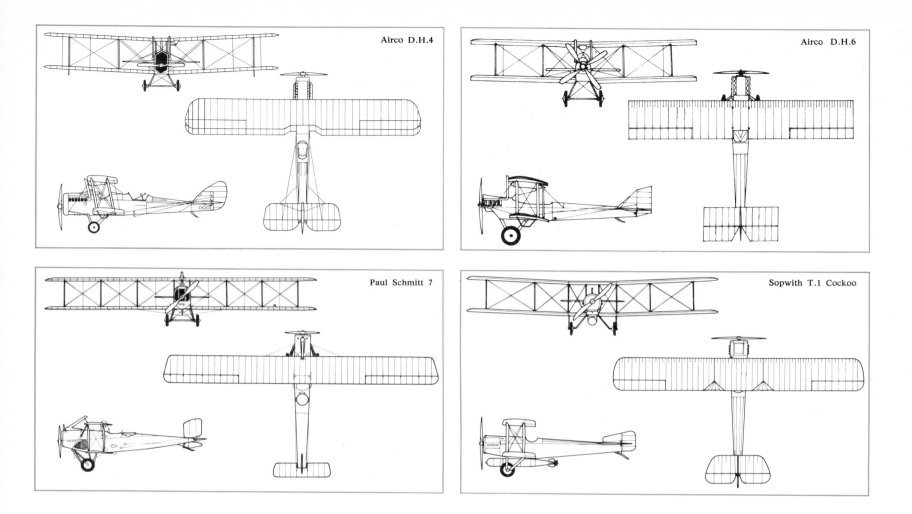

Airco D.H.4

Airco D.H.6

Paul Schmitt 7

Sopwith T.1 Cockoo

were manufactured in the USA and this proportion would have been far higher had not the Armistice ended a massive production run which would have added another 7,502 aeroplanes to those which were completed. The Americans called it the "Liberty plane" after the Liberty 400 hp engine which powered it; the aircraft arrived in time to see service with 13 squadrons of the AEF in the last months of the war.

The D.H.4 was designed in 1916 by Geoffrey de Havilland and after a long search for an effective power unit, the first production model finally appeared early in 1917. The aircraft went into operational use in France in March, and in a short time ten British bomber squadrons had them. Up to the end of the war the D.H.4 served on all fronts in many roles, and remained in service in the United States up to 1932.

In 1917 Britain also carried out the first fruitful experiments with naval bombers. One example was the Airco D.H.6, which had been designed as a trainer but was used for coastal defence from the end of 1917 onwards, after being adapted as a bomber. The Sopwith T.I Cuckoo was a real torpedo bomber but it arrived on the scene too late: on 31st October 1918 the RAF had taken delivery of

only 61 out of the 150 which were to be built. Furthermore, none of these units could be considered operational at that date.

Plate 34
Allied bombers in service in the closing stages of the war: 1918

The great success of the Airco D.H.4 as a light bomber led the Air Board to search for a successor with a longer range. The principal aim was to have an effective bomber which could reach and hit German territory in retaliation for the increasingly frequent German raids on Britain. De Havilland therefore designed the Airco D.H.9, a biplane which, although it kept the general lines of its predecessor, had a

different engine. It was the power unit, paradoxically, which limited the operational capacities of the new aircraft, so much so that it was in fact inferior to the plane which it was meant to replace. The D.H.9 became operational in December 1917, but was not up to the job and was replaced at the end of August 1918 by the first models of a much-improved version, the D.H.9A in which all the first model's problems had been eradicated by the adoption of an American Liberty 400 hp engine. The new aircraft, however, arrived almost too late to have

much effect on the war. Of the D.H.9, 400 were built, and 2,500 of the D.H.9A.

The last heavy bombers to be constructed in Britain were the Blackburn Kangaroo, the Handley-Page V/1500 and the Vickers Vimy which were all enormous aircraft for their day. These were built in response to the needs of the final stages of the war, but as events turned out they had to forgo the crucial strategic roles for which they were designed. The one partial exception was the Blackburn Kangaroo, a large twin-engined aeroplane which

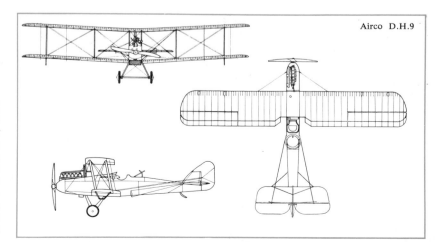

Airco D.H.9

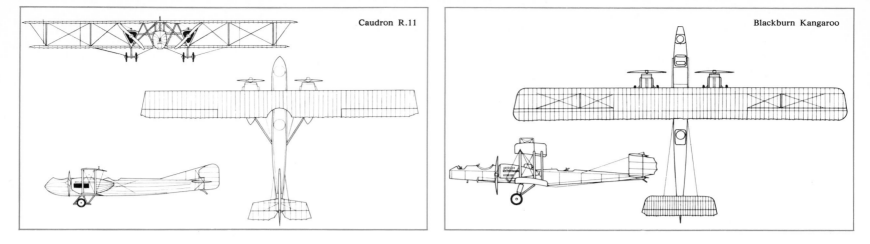

Caudron R.11

Blackburn Kangaroo

began as a naval reconnaissance and bomber seaplane, and was later converted to a landplane. Sixteen Kangaroos did go into action from April 1918 onwards, sinking one German submarine and damaging another four in the North Sea. After 1918 these aircraft were used for many years for passenger flights, for training and as transports.

The Vickers Vimy also became more well-known after the war than during it. It had been designed to have sufficient range to attack Berlin. Only three aircraft reached the Independent Force before the Armistice cut short the wartime career of this large twin-engine aircraft. The project had begun in the late spring of 1917 and three prototypes had been ordered in August. The first of these was flown on 30th November and was put through a long series of test flights. In March 1918 the first order was placed for 150 and others followed, increasing this total, on paper, to 1,000.

In the drastic post-war retrenchment, manufacture was limited to 221, all of which were used in the post-war years. The chief distinction of the

Vimy was in breaking the record for long-distance flight, on more than one occasion. It performed the first non-stop crossing of the Atlantic, in June 1919. John Alcock and Arthur Whitten-Brown flew the 3,032 km (1,884 miles) in a specially modified aircraft from St John's, Newfoundland to Clifden in Northern Ireland. Another remarkable long-distance flight took place in November 1919 from Britain to Australia, covering a distance of 17,912 km (11,130 miles) in just under 136 flying hours by the Australian brothers Ross and Keith Smith.

One of the grandest of the British aircraft of the war was the first British four-engine plane, the Handley-Page V/1500, but it reached only three units before the Armistice. This aircraft design was based on the same specification as the Vimy, which required it to be able to reach Berlin from airfields in eastern England. The first flight of the prototype took place in May 1918 and the second aeroplane was ready in June. The aircraft was impressive because of its great size and its heavy armament. It had six machine

guns and for the first time in a British plane there were guns in the tail. The bomb-load was as much as thirty 113 kg (250 lb) bombs and it could carry two giant bombs weighing 1,497 kg (3,300 lb) each.

The war potential of this aircraft was, without doubt, exceptional and orders soon reached a total of 225. The end of the war, however, abruptly changed these plans: only 35 of the four-engine planes left the assembly lines and, unlike the Vickers Vimy, these aircraft remained in service for only a relatively short time. The only war mission carried out by the V/1500 was in India in May 1919, to put down an insurrection on the North West Frontier.

France did not build bombers of such a size and performance as her Allies across the Channel during the war. One of her last bombers to apear at the front was the Caudron R.11, which did not become a major success. The aircraft, the final model of the R series bombers designed by René Caudron from 1915 onwards, was built to replace the R.4 type which, although robust, resilient and modern,

had shown serious inadequacies in performance and bomb-load. The R.11 was smaller and lighter and had more powerful engines, and went into service in April 1918, being first intended for night bombing. After a certain time, however, the aircraft was found inadequate for that stage of the war and was transferred to the role of bomber escort.

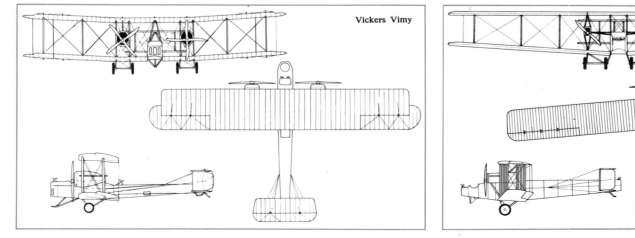

Vickers Vimy

Handley Page V/1500

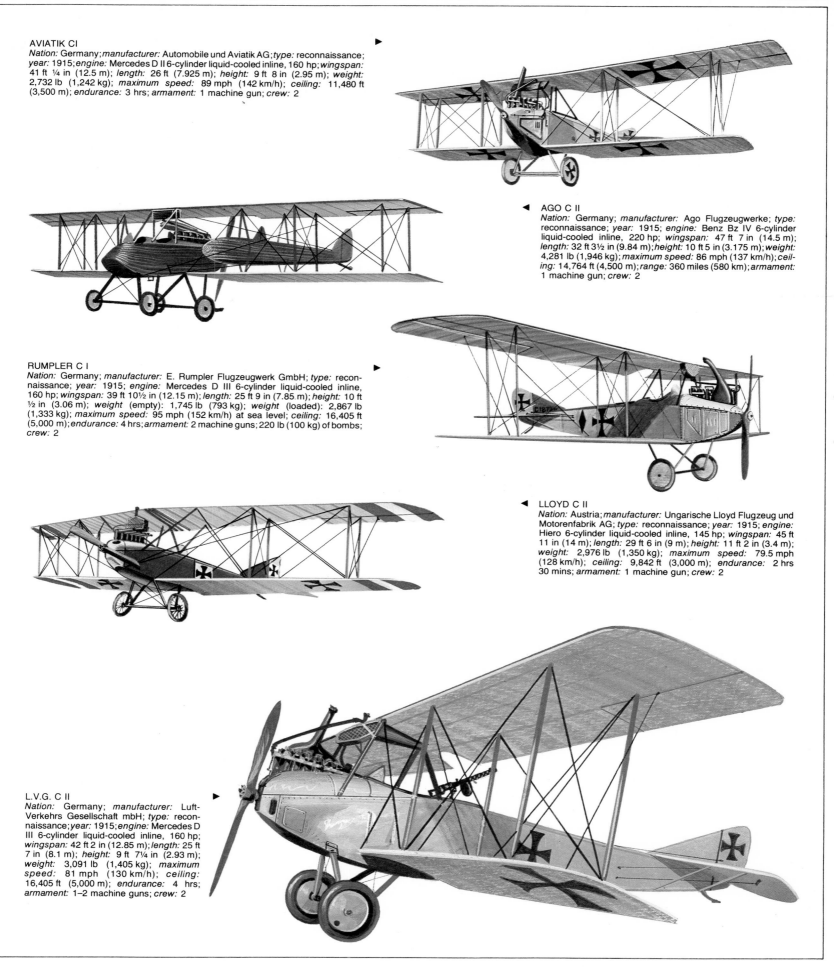

AVIATIK C I
Nation: Germany;*manufacturer:* Automobile und Aviatik AG;*type:* reconnaissance;
year: 1915;*engine:* Mercedes D II 6-cylinder liquid-cooled inline, 160 hp;*wingspan:*
41 ft ¼ in (12.5 m); *length:* 26 ft (7.925 m); *height:* 9 ft 8 in (2.95 m); *weight:*
2,732 lb (1,242 kg); *maximum speed:* 89 mph (142 km/h); *ceiling:* 11,480 ft
(3,500 m); *endurance:* 3 hrs; *armament:* 1 machine gun; *crew:* 2

AGO C II
Nation: Germany; *manufacturer:* Ago Flugzeugwerke; *type:*
reconnaissance; *year:* 1915; *engine:* Benz Bz IV 6-cylinder
liquid-cooled inline, 220 hp; *wingspan:* 47 ft 7 in (14.5 m);
length: 32 ft 3½ in (9.84 m);*height:* 10 ft 5 in (3.175 m);*weight:*
4,281 lb (1,946 kg); *maximum speed:* 86 mph (137 km/h);*ceiling:* 14,764 ft (4,500 m);*range:* 360 miles (580 km);*armament:*
1 machine gun; *crew:* 2

RUMPLER C I
Nation: Germany; *manufacturer:* E. Rumpler Flugzeugwerk GmbH; *type:* reconnaissance; *year:* 1915; *engine:* Mercedes D III 6-cylinder liquid-cooled inline,
160 hp; *wingspan:* 39 ft 10½ in (12.15 m); *length:* 25 ft 9 in (7.85 m); *height:* 10 ft
½ in (3.06 m); *weight* (empty): 1,745 lb (793 kg); *weight* (loaded): 2,867 lb
(1,333 kg); *maximum speed:* 95 mph (152 km/h) at sea level; *ceiling:* 16,405 ft
(5,000 m);*endurance:* 4 hrs;*armament:* 2 machine guns; 220 lb (100 kg) of bombs;
crew: 2

LLOYD C II
Nation: Austria;*manufacturer:* Ungarische Lloyd Flugzeug und
Motorenfabrik AG; *type:* reconnaissance; *year:* 1915; *engine:*
Hiero 6-cylinder liquid-cooled inline, 145 hp; *wingspan:* 45 ft
11 in (14 m); *length:* 29 ft 6 in (9 m); *height:* 11 ft 2 in (3.4 m);
weight: 2,976 lb (1,350 kg); *maximum speed:* 79.5 mph
(128 km/h); *ceiling:* 9,842 ft (3,000 m); *endurance:* 2 hrs
30 mins; *armament:* 1 machine gun; *crew:* 2

L.V.G. C II
Nation: Germany; *manufacturer:* Luft-
Verkehrs Gesellschaft mbH; *type:* reconnaissance;*year:* 1915;*engine:* Mercedes D
III 6-cylinder liquid-cooled inline, 160 hp;
wingspan: 42 ft 2 in (12.85 m);*length:* 25 ft
7 in (8.1 m); *height:* 9 ft 7¼ in (2.93 m);
weight: 3,091 lb (1,405 kg); *maximum
speed:* 81 mph (130 km/h); *ceiling:*
16,405 ft (5,000 m); *endurance:* 4 hrs;
armament: 1–2 machine guns; *crew:* 2

Plate 36

Reconnaissance aircraft of 1916

LEBED 12
Nation: Russia; *manufacturer:* VA Lebedev; *type:* reconnaissance; *year:* 1916; *engine:* Salmson, 150 hp; *wingspan:* 43 ft 1¾ in (13.15 m); *length:* 26 ft 1 in (7.95 m); *height:* – ; *weight:* 2,674 lb (1,213 kg); *maximum speed:* 83 mph (134 km/h); *ceiling:* 11,482 ft (3,500 m); *endurance:* 3 hrs; *armament:* 1 machine gun; 220 lb (90.7 kg) of bombs; *crew:* 2

A.E.G. C IV
Nation: Germany; *manufacturer:* Allgemeine Elektrizitäts Gesellschaft; *type:* reconnaissance; *year:* 1916; *engine:* Mercedes D III 6-cylinder liquid-cooled inline, 160 hp; *wingspan:* 44 ft 2 in (13.46 m); *length:* 23 ft 5½ in (7.15 m); *height:* 11 ft (3.35 m); *weight:* 2,464 lb (1,120 kg); *maximum speed:* 99 mph (158 km/h); *ceiling:* 16,405 ft (5,000 m); *endurance:* 4 hrs; *armament:* 2 machine guns; 220 lb (100 kg) of bombs; *crew:* 2

▼

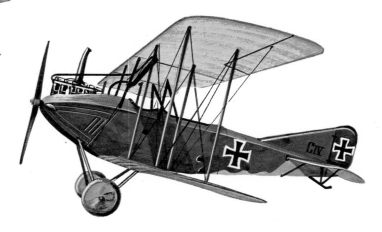

HANSA-BRANDENBURG C I
Nation: Austria; *manufacturer:* Phönix Flugzeug-Werke AG & Ungarische Flugzeugfabrik AG; *type:* reconnaissance; *year:* 1916; *engine:* Austro-Daimler 6-cylinder liquid-cooled inline, 160 hp; *wingspan:* 40 ft 2¼ in (12.25 m); *length:* 27 ft 8¾ in (8.45 m); *height:* 10 ft 11 in (3.32 m); *weight:* 2,888 lb (1,310 kg); *maximum speed:* 87 mph (140 km/h); *ceiling:* 19,028 ft (5,800 m); *endurance:* 3 hrs; *armament:* 2 machine guns; 132 lb (60 kg) of bombs; *crew:* 2

▲

LOHNER C I
Nation: Austria; *manufacturer:* Jakob Lohner AG; *type:* reconnaissance; *year:* 1916; *engine:* Austro-Daimler 6-cylinder liquid-cooled inline, 160 hp; *wingspan:* 44 ft 1½ in (13.46 m); *length:* 30 ft 3 in (9.22 m); *height:* 10 ft 8 in (3.25 m); *weight:* 2,998 lb (1,360 kg); *maximum speed:* 85 mph (137 km/h) at sea level; *ceiling:* 11,482 ft (3,500 m); *endurance:* 3 hrs; *armament:* 1 machine gun; *crew:* 2

▼

▲

D.F.W. C V
Nation: Germany; *manufacturer:* Deutsche Flugzeug-Werke; *type:* reconnaissance; *year:* 1916; *engine:* Benz Bz IV 6-cylinder liquid-cooled inline, 200 hp; *wingspan:* 43 ft 6½ in (13.27 m); *length:* 25 ft 10 in (7.875 m); *height:* 10 ft 8 in (3.25 m); *weight:* 3,146 lb (1,430 kg); *maximum speed:* 97 mph (155 km/h) at 3,281 ft (1,000 m); *ceiling:* 16,405 ft (5,000 m); *endurance:* 3 hrs 30 mins; *armament:* 2 machine guns; 220 lb (100 kg) of bombs; *crew:* 2

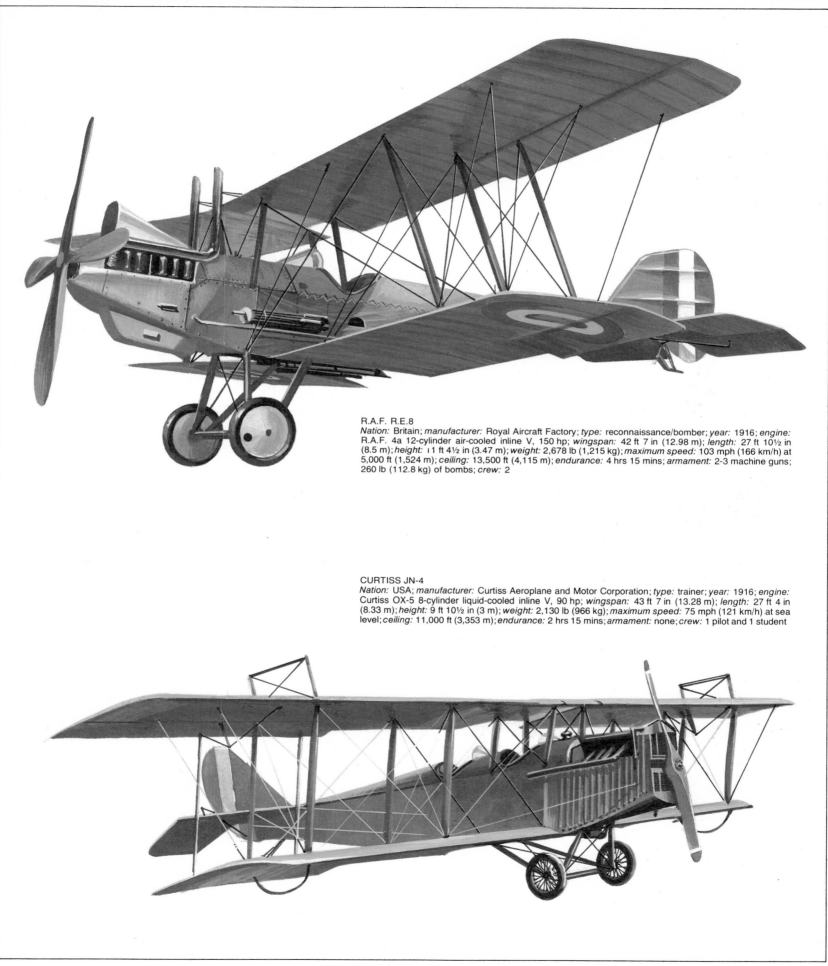

R.A.F. R.E.8
Nation: Britain; *manufacturer:* Royal Aircraft Factory; *type:* reconnaissance/bomber; *year:* 1916; *engine:* R.A.F. 4a 12-cylinder air-cooled inline V, 150 hp; *wingspan:* 42 ft 7 in (12.98 m); *length:* 27 ft 10½ in (8.5 m); *height:* 11 ft 4½ in (3.47 m); *weight:* 2,678 lb (1,215 kg); *maximum speed:* 103 mph (166 km/h) at 5,000 ft (1,524 m); *ceiling:* 13,500 ft (4,115 m); *endurance:* 4 hrs 15 mins; *armament:* 2-3 machine guns; 260 lb (112.8 kg) of bombs; *crew:* 2

CURTISS JN-4
Nation: USA; *manufacturer:* Curtiss Aeroplane and Motor Corporation; *type:* trainer; *year:* 1916; *engine:* Curtiss OX-5 8-cylinder liquid-cooled inline V, 90 hp; *wingspan:* 43 ft 7 in (13.28 m); *length:* 27 ft 4 in (8.33 m); *height:* 9 ft 10½ in (3 m); *weight:* 2,130 lb (966 kg); *maximum speed:* 75 mph (121 km/h) at sea level; *ceiling:* 11,000 ft (3,353 m); *endurance:* 2 hrs 15 mins; *armament:* none; *crew:* 1 pilot and 1 student

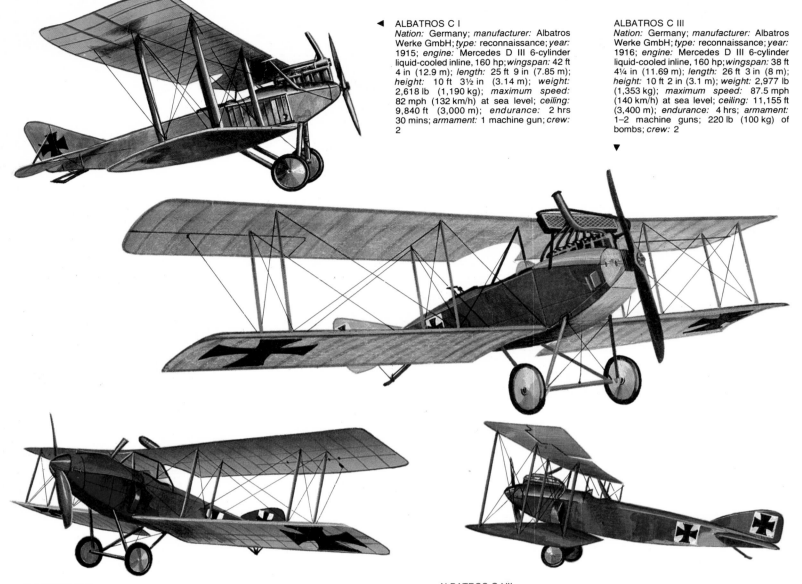

◄ ALBATROS C I
Nation: Germany; *manufacturer:* Albatros Werke GmbH; *type:* reconnaissance; *year:* 1915; *engine:* Mercedes D III 6-cylinder liquid-cooled inline, 160 hp; *wingspan:* 42 ft 4 in (12.9 m); *length:* 25 ft 9 in (7.85 m); *height:* 10 ft 3½ in (3.14 m); *weight:* 2,618 lb (1,190 kg); *maximum speed:* 82 mph (132 km/h) at sea level; *ceiling:* 9,840 ft (3,000 m); *endurance:* 2 hrs 30 mins; *armament:* 1 machine gun; *crew:* 2

ALBATROS C III
Nation: Germany; *manufacturer:* Albatros Werke GmbH; *type:* reconnaissance; *year:* 1916; *engine:* Mercedes D III 6-cylinder liquid-cooled inline, 160 hp; *wingspan:* 38 ft 4¼ in (11.69 m); *length:* 26 ft 3 in (8 m); *height:* 10 ft 2 in (3.1 m); *weight:* 2,977 lb (1,353 kg); *maximum speed:* 87.5 mph (140 km/h) at sea level; *ceiling:* 11,155 ft (3,400 m); *endurance:* 4 hrs; *armament:* 1–2 machine guns; 220 lb (100 kg) of bombs; *crew:* 2

▼

ALBATROS C V
Nation: Germany; *manufacturer:* Albatros Werke GmbH; *type:* reconnaissance; *year:* 1916; *engine:* Mercedes D IV 8-cylinder liquid-cooled inline, 220 hp; *wingspan:* 41 ft 11¼ in (12.78 m); *length:* 29 ft 4½ in (8.95 m); *height:* 11 ft 8 in (3.56 m); *weight:* 2,387 lb (1,585 kg); *maximum speed:* 106 mph (170 km/h); *ceiling:* 16,405 ft (5,000 m); *endurance:* 3 hrs 15 mins; *armament:* 2 machine guns; 220 lb (100 kg) of bombs; *crew:* 2

ALBATROS C VII
Nation: Germany; *manufacturer:* Albatros Werke GmbH; *type:* reconnaissance; *year:* 1916; *engine:* Benz Bz IV 6-cylinder liquid-cooled inline, 200 hp; *wingspan:* 41 ft 11¼ in (12.78 m); *length:* 28 ft 6½ in (8.7 m); *height:* 11 ft 11¾ in (3.6 m); *weight:* 3,410 lb (1,550 kg); *maximum speed:* 106 mph (170 km/h) at sea level; *ceiling:* 16,405 ft (5,000 m); *endurance:* 3 hrs 20 mins; *armament:* 2 machine guns; small bomb-load; *crew:* 2

ALBATROS C X
Nation: Germany; *manufacturer:* Albatros Werke GmbH; *type:* reconnaissance; *year:* 1917; *engine:* Mercedes D IVa 6-cylinder liquid-cooled inline, 260 hp; *wingspan:* 47 ft 1½ in (14.36 m); *length:* 30 ft ¼ in (9.15 m); *height:* 11 ft 2 in (3.4 m); *weight:* 3,669 lb (1,668 kg); *maximum speed:* 109.5 mph (175 km/h) at sea level; *ceiling:* 16,405 ft (5,000 m); *endurance:* 3 hrs 25 mins; *armament:* 2 machine guns; light bomb-load; *crew:* 2

ALBATROS C XII
Nation: Germany; *manufacturer:* Albatros Flugzeug Werke GmbH; *type:* reconnaissance; *year:* 1918; *engine:* Mercedes D IVa 6-cylinder liquid-cooled inline, 260 hp; *wingspan:* 47 ft 2 in (14.37 m); *length:* 29 ft ½ in (8.85 m); *height:* 10 ft 8 in (3.25 m); *weight:* 3,606 lb (1,639 kg); *maximum speed:* 109 mph (175 km/h) at sea level; *ceiling:* 16,405 ft (5,000 m); *endurance:* 3 hrs 15 mins; *armament:* 2 machine guns; *crew:* 2

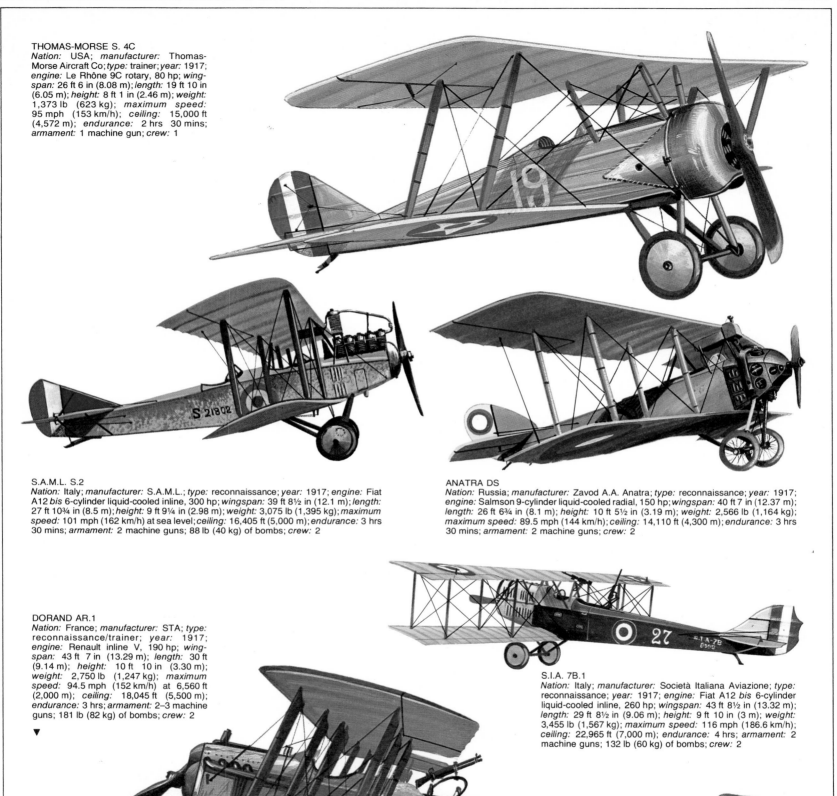

THOMAS-MORSE S. 4C
Nation: USA; *manufacturer:* Thomas-Morse Aircraft Co; *type:* trainer; *year:* 1917; *engine:* Le Rhône 9C rotary, 80 hp; *wingspan:* 26 ft 6 in (8.08 m); *length:* 19 ft 10 in (6.05 m); *height:* 8 ft 1 in (2.46 m); *weight:* 1,373 lb (623 kg); *maximum speed:* 95 mph (153 km/h); *ceiling:* 15,000 ft (4,572 m); *endurance:* 2 hrs 30 mins; *armament:* 1 machine gun; *crew:* 1

S.A.M.L. S.2
Nation: Italy; *manufacturer:* S.A.M.L.; *type:* reconnaissance; *year:* 1917; *engine:* Fiat A12 *bis* 6-cylinder liquid-cooled inline, 300 hp; *wingspan:* 39 ft 8½ in (12.1 m); *length:* 27 ft 10¾ in (8.5 m); *height:* 9 ft 9¼ in (2.98 m); *weight:* 3,075 lb (1,395 kg); *maximum speed:* 101 mph (162 km/h) at sea level; *ceiling:* 16,405 ft (5,000 m); *endurance:* 3 hrs 30 mins; *armament:* 2 machine guns; 88 lb (40 kg) of bombs; *crew:* 2

ANATRA DS
Nation: Russia; *manufacturer:* Zavod A.A. Anatra; *type:* reconnaissance; *year:* 1917; *engine:* Salmson 9-cylinder liquid-cooled radial, 150 hp; *wingspan:* 40 ft 7 in (12.37 m); *length:* 26 ft 6¾ in (8.1 m); *height:* 10 ft 5½ in (3.19 m); *weight:* 2,566 lb (1,164 kg); *maximum speed:* 89.5 mph (144 km/h); *ceiling:* 14,110 ft (4,300 m); *endurance:* 3 hrs 30 mins; *armament:* 2 machine guns; *crew:* 2

DORAND AR.1
Nation: France; *manufacturer:* STA; *type:* reconnaissance/trainer; *year:* 1917; *engine:* Renault inline V, 190 hp; *wingspan:* 43 ft 7 in (13.29 m); *length:* 30 ft (9.14 m); *height:* 10 ft 10 in (3.30 m); *weight:* 2,750 lb (1,247 kg); *maximum speed:* 94.5 mph (152 km/h) at 6,560 ft (2,000 m); *ceiling:* 18,045 ft (5,500 m); *endurance:* 3 hrs; *armament:* 2–3 machine guns; 181 lb (82 kg) of bombs; *crew:* 2

S.I.A. 7B.1
Nation: Italy; *manufacturer:* Società Italiana Aviazione; *type:* reconnaissance; *year:* 1917; *engine:* Fiat A12 *bis* 6-cylinder liquid-cooled inline, 260 hp; *wingspan:* 43 ft 8½ in (13.32 m); *length:* 29 ft 8½ in (9.06 m); *height:* 9 ft 10 in (3 m); *weight:* 3,455 lb (1,567 kg); *maximum speed:* 116 mph (186.6 km/h); *ceiling:* 22,965 ft (7,000 m); *endurance:* 4 hrs; *armament:* 2 machine guns; 132 lb (60 kg) of bombs; *crew:* 2

Plate 40

Italian reconnaissance aircraft and trainers of 1918

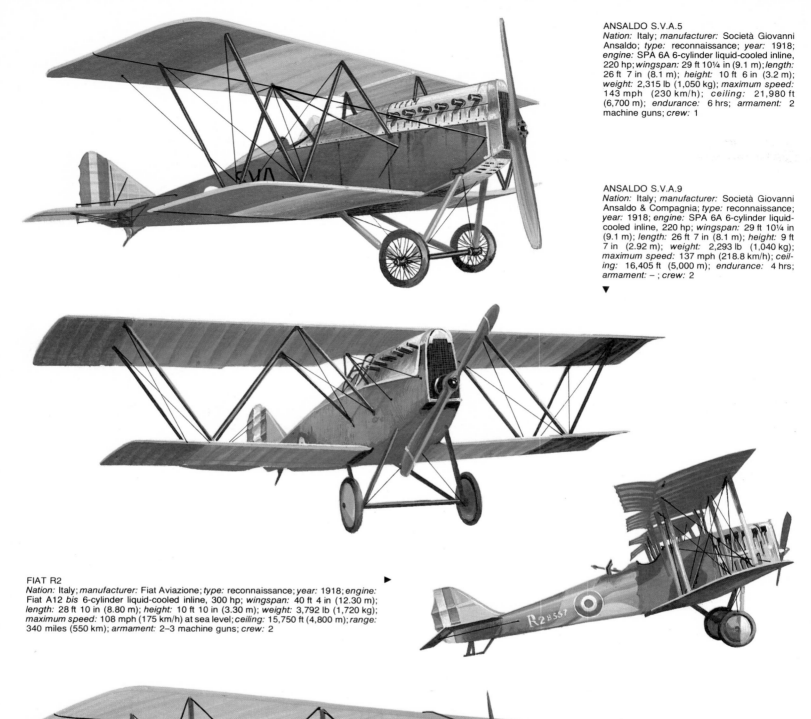

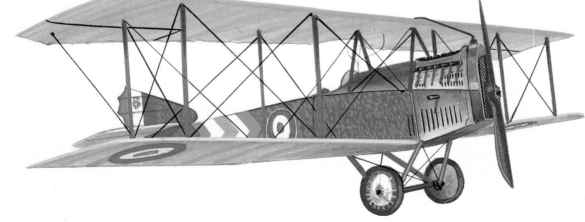

ANSALDO S.V.A.5
Nation: Italy; *manufacturer:* Società Giovanni Ansaldo; *type:* reconnaissance; *year:* 1918; *engine:* SPA 6A 6-cylinder liquid-cooled inline, 220 hp; *wingspan:* 29 ft 10¼ in (9.1 m); *length:* 26 ft 7 in (8.1 m); *height:* 10 ft 6 in (3.2 m); *weight:* 2,315 lb (1,050 kg); *maximum speed:* 143 mph (230 km/h); *ceiling:* 21,980 ft (6,700 m); *endurance:* 6 hrs; *armament:* 2 machine guns; *crew:* 1

ANSALDO S.V.A.9
Nation: Italy; *manufacturer:* Società Giovanni Ansaldo & Compagnia; *type:* reconnaissance; *year:* 1918; *engine:* SPA 6A 6-cylinder liquid-cooled inline, 220 hp; *wingspan:* 29 ft 10¼ in (9.1 m); *length:* 26 ft 7 in (8.1 m); *height:* 9 ft 7 in (2.92 m); *weight:* 2,293 lb (1,040 kg); *maximum speed:* 137 mph (218.8 km/h); *ceiling:* 16,405 ft (5,000 m); *endurance:* 4 hrs; *armament:* – ; *crew:* 2
▼

FIAT R2
Nation: Italy; *manufacturer:* Fiat Aviazione; *type:* reconnaissance; *year:* 1918; *engine:* Fiat A12 *bis* 6-cylinder liquid-cooled inline, 300 hp; *wingspan:* 40 ft 4 in (12.30 m); *length:* 28 ft 10 in (8.80 m); *height:* 10 ft 10 in (3.30 m); *weight:* 3,792 lb (1,720 kg); *maximum speed:* 108 mph (175 km/h) at sea level; *ceiling:* 15,750 ft (4,800 m); *range:* 340 miles (550 km); *armament:* 2–3 machine guns; *crew:* 2
▶

POMILIO PE
Nation: Italy; *manufacturer:* Fabbrica Aeroplani Ing. O. Pomilio & Compagnia; *type:* reconnaissance; *year:* 1918; *engine:* Fiat A12, 260 hp; *wingspan:* 38 ft 8½ in (11.78 m); *length:* 29 ft 4 in (8.94 m); *height:* 11 ft (3.35 m); *weight:* 3,391 lb (1,538 kg); *maximum speed:* 120 mph (194 km/h); *ceiling:* 16,405 ft (5,000 m); *endurance:* 3 hrs 30 mins; *armament:* 2 machine guns; *crew:* 2

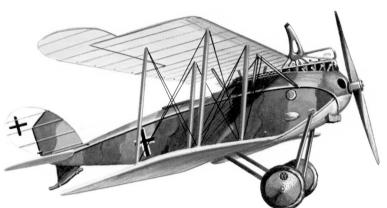

UFAG C I
Nation: Austria; *manufacturer:* Ungarische Flugzeugfabrik; *type:* reconnaissance; *year:* 1918; *engine:* Hiero 6-cylinder liquid-cooled inline, 230 hp; *wingspan:* 35 ft 2 in (10.69 m); *length:* 23 ft 7½ in (7.2 m); *height:* 9 ft 7 in (2.92 m); *weight:* 2,315 lb (1,050 kg); *maximum speed:* 118 mph (190 km/h); *ceiling:* 16,075 ft (4,900 m); *endurance:* 3 hrs; *armament:* 2–3 machine guns; *crew:* 2

HALBERSTADT C V
Nation: Germany; *manufacturer:* Halberstädter Flugzeug-Werke GmbH; *type:* photographic reconnaissance; *year:* 1918; *engine:* Benz Bz IV 6-cylinder liquid-cooled inline 220 hp; *wingspan:* 44 ft 8¾ in (13.62 m); *length:* 22 ft 8½ in (6.92 m); *height:* 11 ft ¼ in (3.36 m); *weight:* 2,730 lb (1,365 kg); *maximum speed:* 106 mph (170 km/h); *ceiling:* 16,405 ft (5,000 m); *endurance:* 3 hrs 30 mins; *armament:* 2 machine guns; *crew:* 2

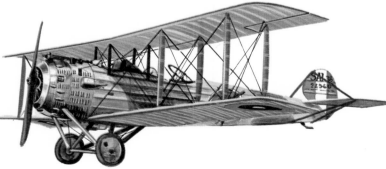

PHÖNIX C I
Nation: Austria; *manufacturer:* Phönix Flugzeug-Werke; *type:* reconnaissence; *year:* 1918; *engine:* Hiero 6-cylinder liquid-cooled inline, 230 hp; *wingspan:* 36 ft 1 in (10.99 m); *length:* 24 ft 8 in (7.52 m); *height:* 9 ft 8 in (2.95 m); *weight:* 2,436 lb (1,105 kg); *maximum speed:* 110 mph (177 km/h) at sea level; *ceiling:* 17,715 ft (5,400 m); *endurance:* 3 hrs 30 mins; *armament:* 2 machine guns; 110 lb (50 kg) of bombs; *crew:* 2

HANNOVER CL. IIIa
Nation: Germany; *manufacturer:* Hannoversche Waggonfabrik AG; *type:* reconnaissance; *year:* 1918; *engine:* Argus AS III 6-cylinder inline liquid-cooled, 180 hp; *wingspan:* 38 ft 5 in (11.70 m); *length:* 24 ft 10 in (7.58 m); *height:* 9 ft 2 in (2.80 m); *weight:* 2,378 lb (1,081 kg); *maximum speed:* 103 mph (165 km/h) at 16,400 ft (5,000 m); *ceiling:* 24,600 ft (7,500 m); *endurance:* 3 hrs; *armament:* 3 machine guns; *crew:* 2

◄ SALMSON 2
Nation: France; *manufacturer:* Société Salmson; *type:* reconnaissance; *year:* 1918; *engine:* Salmson (Canton-Unné) 9-cylinder liquid-cooled radial, 260 hp; *wingspan:* 38 ft 8½ in (11.8 m); *length:* 27 ft 10¾ in (8.5 m); *height:* 9 ft 6¼ in (2.9 m); *weight:* 2,954 lb (1,340 kg); *maximum speed:* 115 mph (185 km/h); *ceiling:* 20,505 ft (6,250 m); *endurance:* 3 hrs; *armament:* 2–3 machine guns; *crew:* 2

STANDARD E-1
Nation: USA; *manufacturer:* Standard Aircraft Corp; *type:* trainer; *year:* 1918; *engine:* Le Rhône 9-cylinder air-cooled rotary, 80 hp; *wingspan:* 24 ft (7.32 m); *length:* 18 ft 10 in (5.74 m); *height:* 7 ft 10 in (2.39 m); *weight:* 1,144 lb (519 kg); *maximum speed:* 100 mph (161 km/h); *ceiling:* 14,800 ft (4,511 m); *endurance:* 2 hrs 30 mins; *armament:* none; *crew:* 1

Plate 42

Flying boats and seaplanes of 1915–16

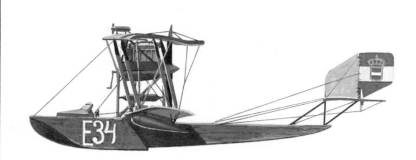

LOHNER E
Nation: Austria; *manufacturer:* Jacob Lohner Werke & Co; *type:* reconnaissance; *year:* 1914; *engine:* Hiero 6-cylinder inline liquid-cooled, 85 hp; *wingspan:* 53 ft 2 in (16.20 m); *length:* 33 ft 8 in (10.25 m); *height:* 12 ft 8 in (3.85 m); *weight:* 3,747 lb (1,700 kg); *maximum speed:* 65 mph (105 km/h); *ceiling:* 13,120 ft (4,000 m); *endurance:* 4 hrs; *armament:* – ; *crew:* 2

MACCHI L. 1
Nation: Italy; *manufacturer:* SA Nieuport-Macchi; *type:* reconnaissance; *year:* 1915; *engine:* Isotta-Fraschini V4a 6-cylinder inline liquid-cooled, 150 hp; *wingspan:* 53 ft 10 in (16.40 m); *length:* 33 ft 8 in (10.25 m); *height:* 12 ft 8 in (3.85 m); *weight:* 3,747 lb (1,700 kg); *maximum speed:* 68 mph (110 km/h); *ceiling:* 14,760 ft (500 m); *endurance:* 4 hrs; *armament:* 1 machine gun; *crew:* 2

RUMPLER 6B 1
Nation: Germany; *manufacturer:* E. Rumpler Flugzeug-Werke GmbH; *type:* fighter; *year:* 1916; *engine:* Mercedes D III 6-cylinder liquid-cooled inline, 160 hp; *wingspan:* 40 ft ½ in (12.2 m); *length:* 29 ft 8½ in (9.05 m); *height:* 11 ft 6 in (3.5 m); *weight:* 2,508 lb (1,140 kg); *maximum speed:* 95 mph (153 km/h) at sea level; *ceiling:* 16,405 ft (5,000 m); *endurance:* 4 hrs; *armament:* 1 machine gun; *crew:* 1

▼

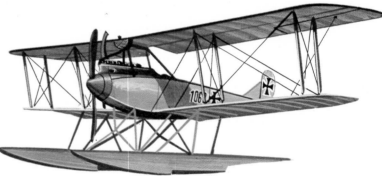

F.B.A. Type C
Nation: France; *manufacturer:* Franco-British Aviation; *type:* reconnaissance; *year:* 1915; *engine:* Clerget 9-cylinder air-cooled rotary, 130 hp; *wingspan:* 44 ft 11 in (13.70 m); *length:* 28 ft 10 in (8.79 m); *height:* 11 ft 2 in (3.4 m); *weight:* 2,072 lb (940 kg); *maximum speed:* 68 mph (110 km/h) at sea level; *ceiling:* 11,480 ft (3,500 m); *range:* 186 m (300 km); *armament:* 1 machine gun; *crew:* 2

HANSA-BRANDENBURG K.D.W.
Nation: Germany; *manufacturer:* Hansa und Brandenburgische Flugzeug-Werke GmbH; *type:* fighter; *year:* 1916; *engine:* Benz Bz III 6-cylinder liquid-cooled inline, 150 hp; *wingspan:* 30 ft 4¼ in (9.25 m); *length:* 26 ft 3 in (8 m); *height:* 11 ft (3.35 m); *weight:* 2,662 lb (1,210 kg); *maximum speed:* 106 mph (170 km/h) at sea level; *ceiling:* 13,123 ft (4,000 m); *endurance:* 3 hrs; *armament:* 1–2 machine guns; *crew:* 1

▼

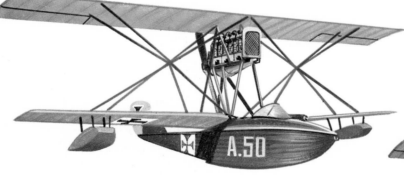

HANSA-BRANDENBURG CC
Nation: Austria; *manufacturer:* Phönix Flugzeug-Werke AG; *type:* fighter; *year:* 1916; *engine:* Benz Bz III 6-cylinder liquid-cooled inline, 150 hp; *wingspan:* 30 ft 6 in (9.3 m); *length:* 25 ft 1 in (7.65 m); *height:* 10 ft 6 in (3.2 m); *weight:* 2,989 lb (1,356 kg); *maximum speed:* 108.75 mph (175 km/h); *ceiling:* – ; *endurance:* 3 hrs 30 mins; *armament:* 1 machine gun; *crew:* 1

▲

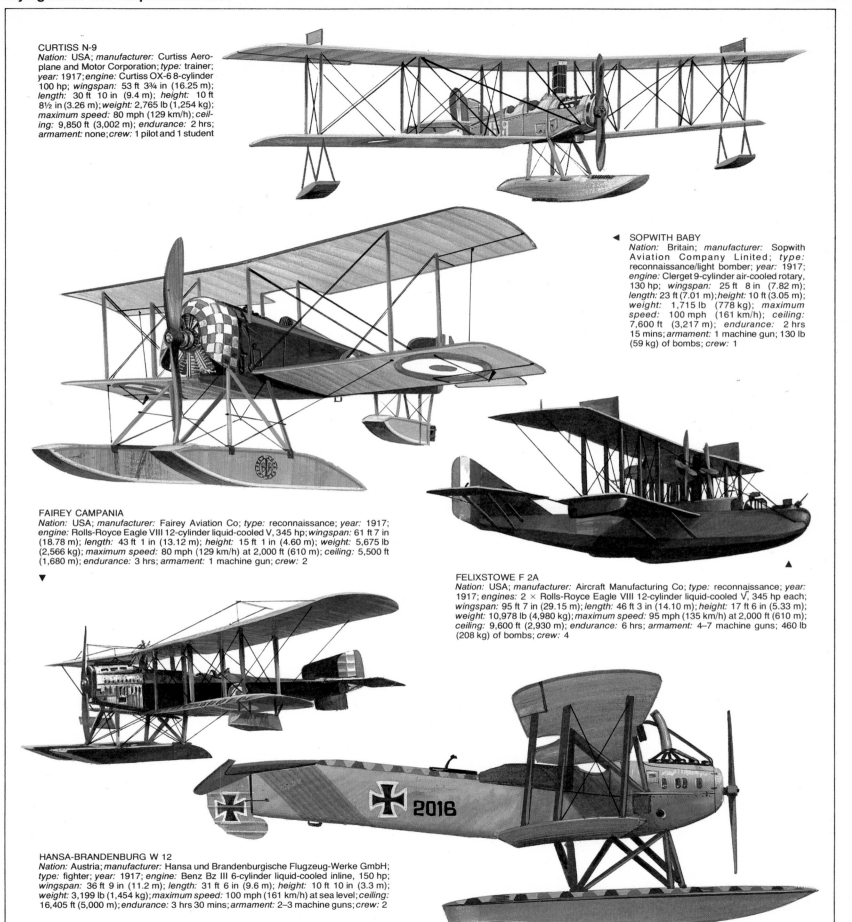

CURTISS N-9
Nation: USA; *manufacturer:* Curtiss Aeroplane and Motor Corporation; *type:* trainer; *year:* 1917; *engine:* Curtiss OX-6 8-cylinder 100 hp; *wingspan:* 53 ft 3¾ in (16.25 m); *length:* 30 ft 10 in (9.4 m); *height:* 10 ft 8½ in (3.26 m); *weight:* 2,765 lb (1,254 kg); *maximum speed:* 80 mph (129 km/h); *ceiling:* 9,850 ft (3,002 m); *endurance:* 2 hrs; *armament:* none; *crew:* 1 pilot and 1 student

◄ SOPWITH BABY
Nation: Britain; *manufacturer:* Sopwith Aviation Company Limited; *type:* reconnaissance/light bomber; *year:* 1917; *engine:* Clerget 9-cylinder air-cooled rotary, 130 hp; *wingspan:* 25 ft 8 in (7.82 m); *length:* 23 ft (7.01 m); *height:* 10 ft (3.05 m); *weight:* 1,715 lb (778 kg); *maximum speed:* 100 mph (161 km/h); *ceiling:* 7,600 ft (3,217 m); *endurance:* 2 hrs 15 mins; *armament:* 1 machine gun; 130 lb (59 kg) of bombs; *crew:* 1

FAIREY CAMPANIA
Nation: USA; *manufacturer:* Fairey Aviation Co; *type:* reconnaissance; *year:* 1917; *engine:* Rolls-Royce Eagle VIII 12-cylinder liquid-cooled V, 345 hp; *wingspan:* 61 ft 7 in (18.78 m); *length:* 43 ft 1 in (13.12 m); *height:* 15 ft 1 in (4.60 m); *weight:* 5,675 lb (2,566 kg); *maximum speed:* 80 mph (129 km/h) at 2,000 ft (610 m); *ceiling:* 5,500 ft (1,680 m); *endurance:* 3 hrs; *armament:* 1 machine gun; *crew:* 2

▼

FELIXSTOWE F 2A
Nation: USA; *manufacturer:* Aircraft Manufacturing Co; *type:* reconnaissance; *year:* 1917; *engines:* 2 × Rolls-Royce Eagle VIII 12-cylinder liquid-cooled V, 345 hp each; *wingspan:* 95 ft 7 in (29.15 m); *length:* 46 ft 3 in (14.10 m); *height:* 17 ft 6 in (5.33 m); *weight:* 10,978 lb (4,980 kg); *maximum speed:* 95 mph (135 km/h) at 2,000 ft (610 m); *ceiling:* 9,600 ft (2,930 m); *endurance:* 6 hrs; *armament:* 4–7 machine guns; 460 lb (208 kg) of bombs; *crew:* 4

▲

HANSA-BRANDENBURG W 12
Nation: Austria; *manufacturer:* Hansa und Brandenburgische Flugzeug-Werke GmbH; *type:* fighter; *year:* 1917; *engine:* Benz Bz III 6-cylinder liquid-cooled inline, 150 hp; *wingspan:* 36 ft 9 in (11.2 m); *length:* 31 ft 6 in (9.6 m); *height:* 10 ft 10 in (3.3 m); *weight:* 3,199 lb (1,454 kg); *maximum speed:* 100 mph (161 km/h) at sea level; *ceiling:* 16,405 ft (5,000 m); *endurance:* 3 hrs 30 mins; *armament:* 2–3 machine guns; *crew:* 2

Plate 44

Flying boats and seaplanes of 1918

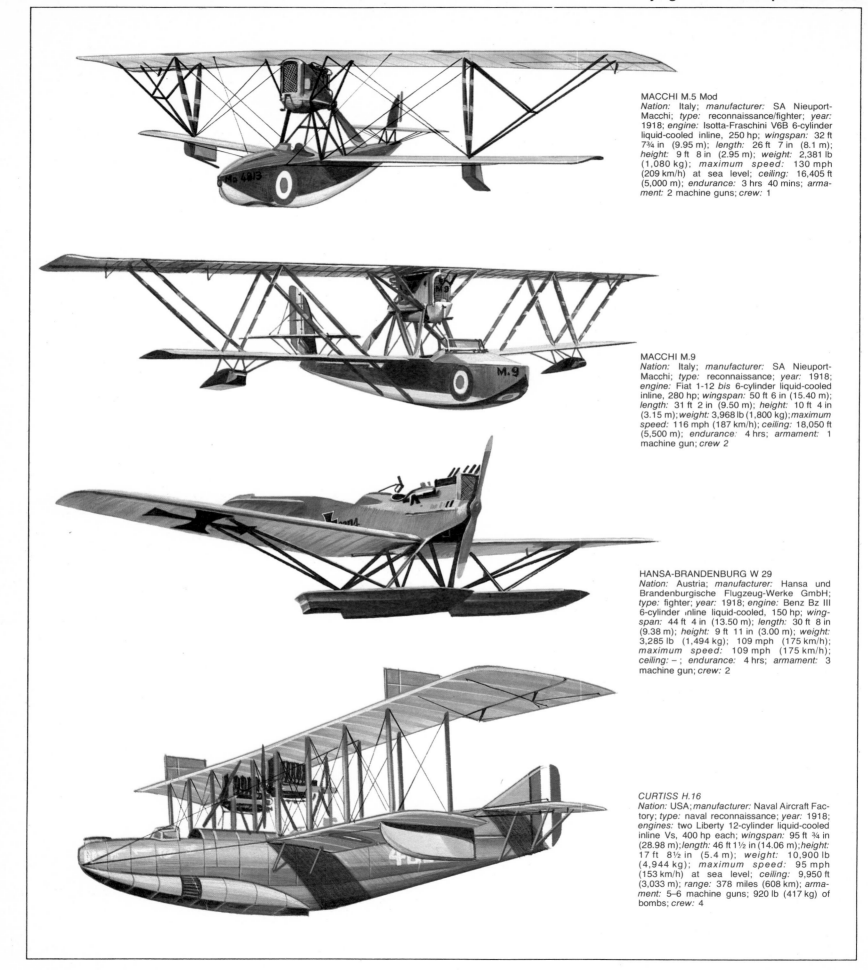

MACCHI M.5 Mod
Nation: Italy; *manufacturer:* SA Nieuport-Macchi; *type:* reconnaissance/fighter; *year:* 1918; *engine:* Isotta-Fraschini V6B 6-cylinder liquid-cooled inline, 250 hp; *wingspan:* 32 ft 7¾ in (9.95 m); *length:* 26 ft 7 in (8.1 m); *height:* 9 ft 8 in (2.95 m); *weight:* 2,381 lb (1,080 kg); *maximum speed:* 130 mph (209 km/h) at sea level; *ceiling:* 16,405 ft (5,000 m); *endurance:* 3 hrs 40 mins; *armament:* 2 machine guns; *crew:* 1

MACCHI M.9
Nation: Italy; *manufacturer:* SA Nieuport-Macchi; *type:* reconnaissance; *year:* 1918; *engine:* Fiat 1-12 *bis* 6-cylinder liquid-cooled inline, 280 hp; *wingspan:* 50 ft 6 in (15.40 m); *length:* 31 ft 2 in (9.50 m); *height:* 10 ft 4 in (3.15 m); *weight:* 3,968 lb (1,800 kg); *maximum speed:* 116 mph (187 km/h); *ceiling:* 18,050 ft (5,500 m); *endurance:* 4 hrs; *armament:* 1 machine gun; *crew* 2

HANSA-BRANDENBURG W 29
Nation: Austria; *manufacturer:* Hansa und Brandenburgische Flugzeug-Werke GmbH; *type:* fighter; *year:* 1918; *engine:* Benz Bz III 6-cylinder inline liquid-cooled, 150 hp; *wingspan:* 44 ft 4 in (13.50 m); *length:* 30 ft 8 in (9.38 m); *height:* 9 ft 11 in (3.00 m); *weight:* 3,285 lb (1,494 kg); 109 mph (175 km/h); *maximum speed:* 109 mph (175 km/h); *ceiling:* –; *endurance:* 4 hrs; *armament:* 3 machine gun; *crew:* 2

CURTISS H.16
Nation: USA; *manufacturer:* Naval Aircraft Factory; *type:* naval reconnaissance; *year:* 1918; *engines:* two Liberty 12-cylinder liquid-cooled inline Vs, 400 hp each; *wingspan:* 95 ft ¾ in (28.98 m); *length:* 46 ft 1½ in (14.06 m); *height:* 17 ft 8½ in (5.4 m); *weight:* 10,900 lb (4,944 kg); *maximum speed:* 95 mph (153 km/h) at sea level; *ceiling:* 9,950 ft (3,033 m); *range:* 378 miles (608 km); *armament:* 5–6 machine guns; 920 lb (417 kg) of bombs; *crew:* 4

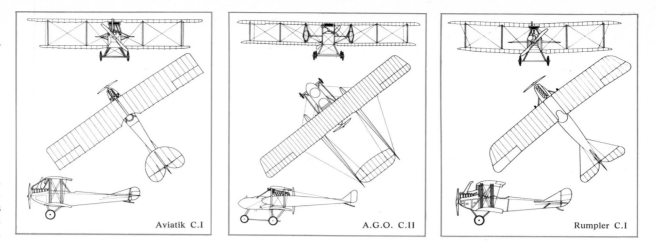

Aviatik C.I

A.G.O. C.II

Rumpler C.I

The first unarmed reconnaissance aircraft to be put into service by the Germans at the outbreak of hostilities soon gave way to more powerful machines which, more importantly, were fitted with a machine gun as standard weapon.

Aircraft of this type were then grouped together under a precise category (armed reconnaissance biplanes) and designated Type C. The first types were generally more or less directly derived from their immediate predecessors of the B category, but as further models were developed by various aircraft industries, these aircraft became very effective and efficient warplanes.

After the B.I and the B.II which were built in 1914 and widely used in the first months of war on the Western and Eastern fronts, Aviatik developed its C.I in 1915. It was an almost direct descendant: the biplane retained the general lines and structural characteristics of its forerunners, even keeping the back-to-front arrangement of the cockpits (the pilot behind and the observer in front) which had originally been conceived specially to make the observer's task easier. This arrangement had to be abandoned once manually-armed machine guns were used in the sub-series C.Ia. The following series, which differed in type and power of engine, were designated C.II and C.III and were constructed in the largest numbers. The Type C Aviatik was mainly used during 1916.

The development of another contemporary reconnaissance plane was similar, and unusual amongst German aircraft in its biplane configuration with pusher propeller and two tailplanes: this was the A.G.O. This formula, though considered old-fashioned, worked well, since it led to a fast, manoeuvrable aircraft with long range. Of the three versions which were developed between 1915 and 1916, the best was the C.II, which during its year in service won the unstinting praise of the pilots.

An even greater success attended the careers of a family of C type reconnaissance planes manufactured by L.V.G. from 1915 onwards in six different versions. The first variant was the C.I, derived from the preceding B type, and appearing at the front towards the middle of 1915. At the end of the year the improved version, the C.II, appeared and the two models served with many units, staying in front line service up to 1916. Apart from reconnaissance these aircraft also carried out light bombing missions: it was in this capacity on 28th November 1916 that a C.II managed to reach London in daylight and dropped its six 10 kg (22 lb) bombs on Victoria Station, causing chaos but little damage.

The C.III and C.IV variants, of which limited numbers were produced, were followed in the last two years of the war by the C.V and C.VI which met with success similar to that of the first two models. These aircraft differed substantially from their predecessors since they were created by a different designer, but they proved equally worthwhile; they served over the lines in such large numbers that in August 1918 no less than 500 were flying.

Another very efficient aircraft was the Rumpler. Their C.I, which appeared at the beginning of 1915, even stayed in service until February 1918 and was used in great numbers on all fronts and in every sort of climate. Tough, fast, well-armed and very difficult to shoot down, the Rumpler C.I made a great contribution to the German war effort. It was the first to fly photographic reconnaissance missions.

Another Rumpler which was built and constructed on a vast scale was the C.IV of 1917. Benefiting from a particularly appropriate engine, this variant showed, in an even more accentuated form, the excellent qualities of its predecessor, especially in speed, range and general resilience. The C.IVs were mainly used as long-range reconnaissance and intruder planes; it was specially suitable for the intruder role because of the large bomb-load which the aircraft could carry without its performance suffering very much.

On the Italian and Romanian fronts the Lloyd type Cs built in Austria were used, five versions of which were in service during the first two and a half years of the war. The Lloyd C.II (100 manufactured) appeared in 1915. This was followed by the C.III and the C.IV in which an attempt was made to improve general performance by the adoption of more powerful engines. In spite of these efforts, however, the Lloyd type Cs never managed to make much impression; they were always considered mediocre machines and of limited use.

Plate 36
Reconnaissance aircraft of 1916

Another type C reconnaissance plane built in Austria by Lohner, a manufacturer which was very well known for its seaplanes, was just as unsatisfactory. The Lohner C.I reached reconnaissance units at the beginning of 1916 and remained in service for the whole of the year. It was never particularly noted for its performance although it was the final version of a succession of aircraft designed from 1913 onwards.

The Hansa-Brandenburg C.1 was much more impressive and although it was designed in Germany by Ernst Heinkel it was built in Austria by Phönix and Ufag. Eighteen production series were turned out which, apart from minor structural details, used different and increasingly powerful engines. The biplane went into service in the spring of 1916 and was widely used for reconnaissance, observation, artillery spotting and light bombing missions up to the end of the war. Its good overall handling

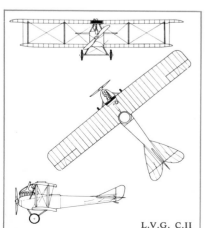

L.V.G. C.II

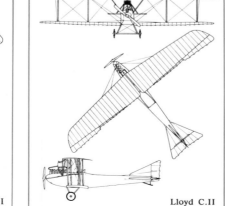

Lloyd C.II

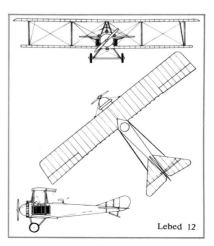

Lebed 12

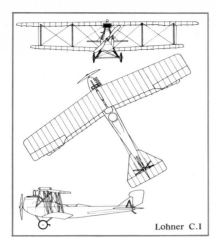

Lohner C.I

Hansa-Brandenburg C.I

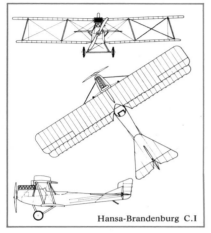

A.E.G. C.IV

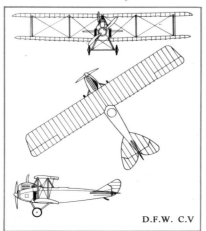

D.F.W. C.V

qualities made it a favourite with the crews, whilst its performance was continually being improved as the various production series were equipped with more and more powerful engines.

Meanwhile in Germany, 1916 was the year in which industry put some of the best type C reconnaissance planes into the field. Amongst these was the A.E.G. C.IV, which soon became well known. Although it had been developed from its predecessor, the C.II, of which it echoed the structure and general lines, this aircraft had a wider wingspan and a very much more efficient engine. The A.E.G. C.IV went into service in the spring of 1916 and served up to the middle of 1918, distinguishing itself by its performance. It was used on all fronts and was held to be so useful that it was also ordered in a specially adapted night bomber version. This was designated the C.IVN and developed towards the end of 1916: it could carry six 50 kg (110 lb) bombs.

A similar success was enjoyed by the D.F.W. C.V, produced in 1916 and put into service in the summer of that year. Over 1,000 of them were constructed (a record figure for German aircraft during the war) and it remained in front-line service up to the first months of 1918. Its performance was so impressive that in the hands of expert pilots it could evade the most modern enemy fighters. The D.F.W. C.V was directly derived from the preceding C.IV model. It was identical in size but it was powered by a 200 hp Benz (against the 150 hp engine of the C.IV) which noticeably improved its speed. The two aircraft were the main models amongst all type Cs manufactured by D.F.W. during the war years and with their very good flight qualities they became extremely popular with the crews.

In 1916 the first reconnaissance plane to be designed and constructed in Russia came on the scene: the Lebed 12. The real prototype of this aircraft was the type 11, built the year before and copied from a captured German Albatros B.II, by Vladimir A. Lebedey, a pioneer of Russian aviation who, having learned to fly in France in 1910, set up an aircraft construction company in his own country. The Lebed 11 was not very satisfactory and so it was followed by the type 12, which made its maiden flight on 28th December 1915. 225 of this aircraft were ordered but its development turned out to be so beset by difficulties that its entry into service was delayed until the autumn of 1916. Even after its arrival at the front the aircraft still had handling problems.

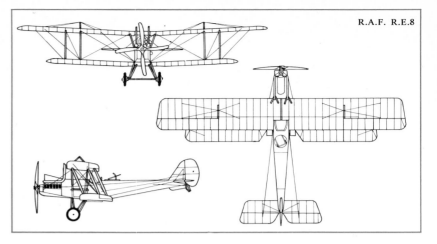

R.A.F. R.E.8

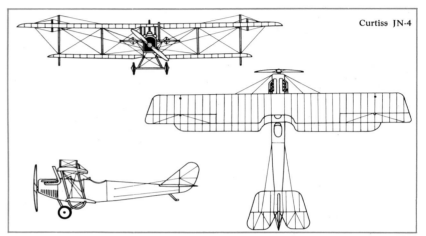

Curtiss JN-4

Plate 37
Two classic training and reconnaissance aircraft of 1916

On the Allied side, the autumn of 1916 saw the entry into service of the aircraft which was the most widely-used British twin-seater on the Western front: the R.A.F. R.E.8. This rapidly acquired the rhyming nickname Harry Tate. 4,099 of them were built, a remarkable number for those days, and this biplane whilst not exceptional (mainly because of unsatisfactory manoeuvrability which made it vulnerable to enemy fighters) was generally good enough to remain in service in all operational theatres until the Armistice. After its original role of reconnaissance plane, the R.E.8 was soon used as a day and night bomber, and for army co-operation and ground attack.

The project, which was started off towards the end of 1915, was dictated by the necessity of replacing the B.E.2c which was insufficiently armed and not very manoeuvrable. The first prototype flew on 17th June 1916 and production commenced in August. The aircraft did show some improvement where armament was concerned,

but its manoeuvrability was really quite poor and similar to that of the machine which it was supposed to replace. In spite of this the R.E.8 went into service and once it had gone through an initial phase of structural alterations which led to considerable changes in the tailplane, it soon went to sixteen reconnaissance squadrons. Of the 4,099 manufactured, 22 were supplied to the Belgian air force, who used them after replacing the engines. Apart from serving on the Western front, the R.A.F. R.E.8 was used by two British squadrons in Italy, two in Mesopotamia, two in Palestine, and three Home Defence squadrons.

A small biplane built in the USA never saw action, but gave good service in training thousands of pilots and became very well known later, in the 1920s: the Curtiss JN-4, the principal production model of an aircraft of which thousands were built. The specification from the United States Army called for a trainer biplane with a puller propeller and was issued in 1914: the Curtiss model was chosen and a small number of them were ordered the following year. In 1916 the principal production variant appeared, designated JN-4, of which enormous numbers were built: 701 by Curtiss; 1,260 by Canadian Aeroplanes of Toronto: 781 of the JN-4A

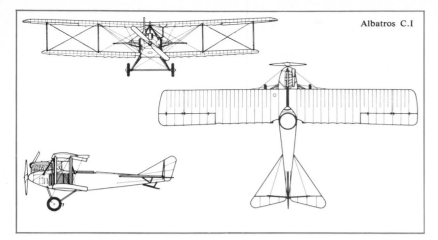

Albatros C.I

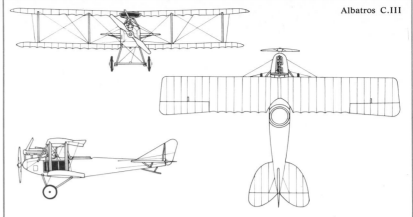

Albatros C.III

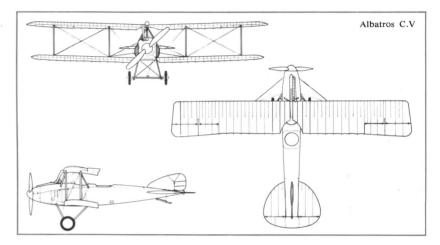

Albatros C.V

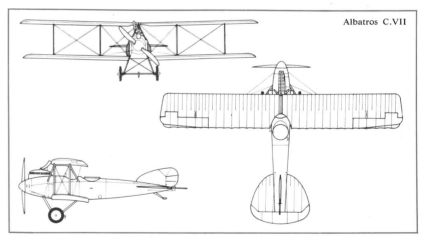

Albatros C.VII

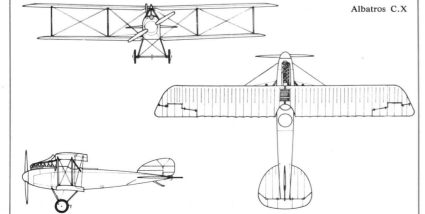

Albatros C.X

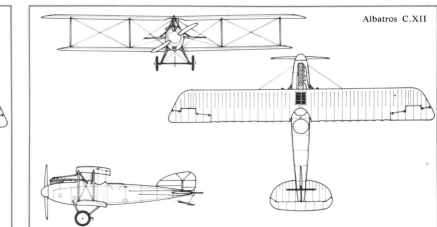

Albatros C.XII

model; 2,765 of the JN-4D, and 929 of the JN-4H. These aircraft were all, in the various production series, subjected to structural modifications in order to improve their performance. In the JN-4H an engine of nearly twice the power of the original engine was installed, enabling it to train pilots for flying increasingly higher performance aircraft. Total procurement of the last version, the JN-6H, was 1,035.

Plate 38
Albatros reconnaissance aircraft —
still in service on the last day of the war:
1915–18

Up to the day of the Armistice the Albatros C series reconnaissance aircraft were used on all fronts by the German air force, winning fame for themselves as the most widely deployed aircraft of all. They were the direct descendants of the unarmed B type two-seat biplanes and the first

C.Is were developed at the beginning of 1915. Their design was mainly derived from Ernst Heinkel's B.II of 1914. They kept the original structure and the excellent flight characteristics of their predecessors. The considerable power of the engine (greater than that of the most widely used Allied engines of the time) and the forward firing machine gun made this a fearsome adversary and it was employed with great success. At that time Germany's future fighter aces, including Oswald Boelcke and Manfred von Richthofen, both flew their first missions in Albatros C.Is.

Towards the end of the year an improved version, the C.III, appeared, and this was also derived from a B series model (the B.III of 1914), echoing the general lines and the structure of the tailplane of that aircraft. The result was an even faster machine, which was also sturdier and more manoeuvrable than the C.1 and was subsequently constructed in greater numbers than any other C type Albatros. The aeroplane went into service at the beginning of 1916 and remained in use until the following year, being widely employed for observation, photo-reconnaissance and as a light bomber, carrying 90 kg (200 lb) of bombs.

The C.IV variant was merely a transitional aircraft of which few were built. It appeared at the beginning of 1916 before a completely redesigned version, the C.V. This aircraft was slightly larger than the C.III and had a new, more powerful engine and its fuselage had more refined aerodynamic lines. It was this new engine, however, which ruined the operational career of the C.V. It was of an unusual design (an 8-cylinder inline instead of the traditional 6 cylinders) and suffered from continual development troubles which exacerbated piloting problems and were never ironed out. In spite of this 400 C.Vs were built before being replaced by the following C.VII variant. This too was a compromise design which was, nevertheless, constructed in large numbers, staying in service until the first months of 1917.

Best results were at last achieved with the C.X version, which appeared towards the middle of 1917 and which represented the pinnacle of the basic airframe's development. The success of this aircraft was mainly due to the adoption of the new Mercedes D.4a 260 hp engine (in which a return had been made to the conventional 6 cylinders) which made for excellent performance and very good load-carrying capacity. The Albatros C.X remained in service with reconnaissance and observation units until the middle of 1918 in all operational theatres.

The experience gained with the C.X made possible the achievement of the final model, the C.XII, which was the best of all the type C planes. While its engine was the same as that of the C.X, the aircraft profited greatly from its studied aerodynamic lines. It was operational until the last day of the war in a brilliant combat career.

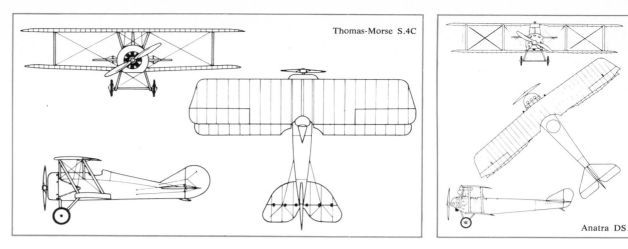
Thomas-Morse S.4C

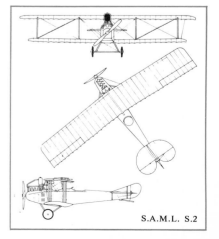
Anatra DS

Plate 39
Reconnaissance aircraft and trainers of 1917

In the penultimate year of the war many reconnaissance aircraft were developed. In France, for instance, the Dorand AR.1 was widely used and ultimately equipped as many as eighteen observation squadrons on the French and Italian fronts. In 1916 the French government had issued a specification to the aviation industry for a biplane with puller propeller which could replace the Farman reconnaissance plane. None of the manufacturers were very enthusiastic apart from Colonel Dorand, who submitted an up dated version of one of his 1914 biplanes, the Type DO.1. The new aircraft retained the general lines of its predecessor, with back-staggered wings, but it was driven by a much more powerful engine. The Dorand AR.1 completed trials in September 1916 and was sent to observation units in April 1917. An improved version of this aircraft was also constructed, the AR.2 A2, powered by a Renault 200 h.p. engine, which was notable for its wing-mounted radiators.

In Italy, two new designs were to lead to the S.I.A. 7B.1 and the S.A.M.L. S.2. The 7B.1 was produced in 1917 by the Società Italiana Aviazione, a subsidiary of Fiat. The designers were Savoia and Verduzio, who had designed the famous S.V.A. built by Ansaldo. It was immediately put into production and the reconnaissance plane went into service towards the end of the year and proved very fast and manoeuvrable. In operational use, however, the 7B.1 developed disturbing weaknesses in its wing structure and was withdrawn from the front in July 1918.

The second reconnaissance machine was designed between 1916 and 1917 by the Società Aeronautica Meccanica Lombarda, which until that time had been the main Italian constructor of the German Aviatik B.1 biplane. The basic model, which was developed around the Fiat A-12 260 hp engine, was called the S.1, and was followed by another version, the S.2, which had smaller wings, simplified structure and more powerful armament and engine. Both these aircraft were used a great deal on the lines and served with sixteen reconnaissance squadrons in Italy, Albania and Macedonia. Total production, including aeroplanes built under licence by other Italian com-

panies, reached 600. Some S.2s, instead of carrying a small bomb-load, carried a camera, whilst others were equipped with dual controls and used for training.

In 1917 Russia created another original reconnaissance plane, following the Lebed 12 of the preceding year. This was the Anatra DS produced by the company of the same name in Odessa, founded by the Italian banker, A. Anatra. It appeared at the front towards the middle of the year but the DS remained in production for only a few months and about 70 of them were built. The aircraft was derived from the preceding D type of 1916 which had proved a failure because of structural weaknesses, and because of its unsatisfactory engine. In the following model the engine problems were resolved by adopting a Salmson 150 hp radial.

In the United States, meanwhile, in June of 1917 a new trainer appeared, to join the already famous Curtiss JN-4: the Thomas Morse S4. Although fewer were constructed (597), the S4 scored a distinct success and was adopted by the army as an advanced trainer. The aircraft had more outstanding qualities than the JN-4 and this promoted its civil use when the war was over.

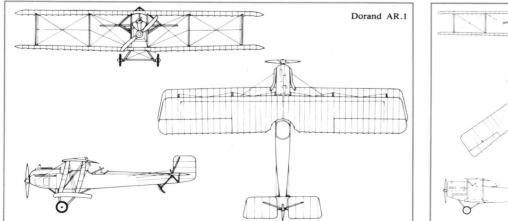
Dorand AR.1

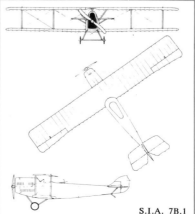
S.I.A. 7B.1

S.A.M.L. S.2

Plate 40
Italian reconnaissance aircraft and trainers of 1918

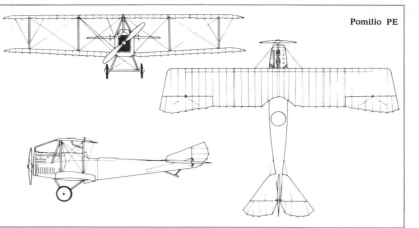
Pomilio PE

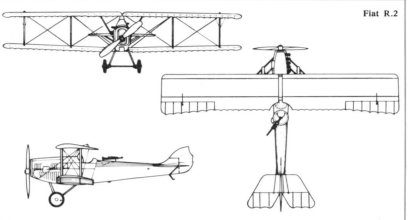
Fiat R.2

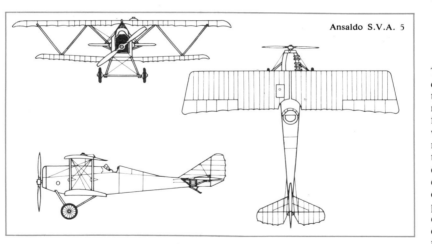
Ansaldo S.V.A. 5

Among the reconnaissance planes of the war undoubtedly the best of the last years was Italian. The S.V.A. 5 which, while it owed a lot of its fame to the historic raid on Vienna, was indeed an exceptional aircraft for its time – fast, sturdy and with long range. It was developed in 1917 by Umberto Savoia and Rodolfo Verduzio, with the collaboration of Celestino Rosatelli, the future creator of so many famous aircraft, and the prototype made its first flight on 19th March of that year. At the end of proving flights only one drawback had been revealed: the aircraft was not manoeuvrable enough to be used as a fighter and in consequence was developed as a reconnaissance plane.

The first production version was the S.V.A. 4 which was followed immediately afterwards by the S.V.A. 5. The differences between the two aircraft lay mainly in the capacity of their fuel tanks, and consequently in their endurance: four hours for the former and six for the latter; and there were differences in armament. In service from February 1918 onwards, the S.V.A. single-seaters equipped six reconnaissance squadrons and carried out a number of important missions; among these was the reconnaissance of Friedrichshafen, completed by Locatelli and Ferrarin on 21st May 1918, a flight of about 700 km (435 miles).

At the same time as the single-seaters, two two-seat variants were developed, designated S.V.A. 9 and S.V.A. 10. The first was for use as a trainer, with no armament, dual controls and shorter range than the type 5. The second was constructed for armed

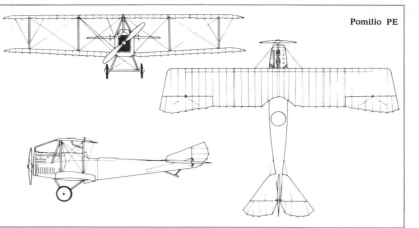
Ansaldo S.V.A. 9

reconnaissance and light bombing and went into service in the last months of the war.

The operational career of the S.V.A.s, of which 2,000 were constructed, went on long after the war and continued until the 1930s.

Apart from Ferrarin and Masiero's historic Rome–Tokyo race which covered 18,105 km (11,250 miles) in 109 flying hours and was undertaken from February to May 1920, the wartime exploit which gave the S.V.A. international fame was a mission to Vienna on 9th August 1918. Eight aircraft of 87 Squadron, which had set off just before 6 am from their base at San Pelagio, reached Vienna at 9.20 am

and for half an hour circled above the Austrian capital at 800 m (2,625 ft) dropping leaflets and taking photographs. The aeroplanes, all S.V.A. 5s, returned at 12.40 pm, after flying more than 1,000 kms (620 miles) out of which over 800 km (498 miles) were over enemy territory.

Another Italian reconnaissance plane, not as distinguished as the S.V.A. but effective all the same, was the Pomilio PE, which was produced in large numbers, 1,616 being made during the war. This aircraft represented the culmination of a series of two-seat reconnaissance biplanes constructed by the Fabbrica Aeroplani Ingegner O. Pomilio of Turin during

1917 and 1918. From its Type PC PD predecessors, the PE kept the mixed wood and metal airframe but it had different, larger tailplanes. It proved to be a very fast aircraft, with high rate of climb, and was widely used for reconnaissance and artillery spotting: it was supplied to thirty squadrons in various versions. The Pomilio PE was also produced in the United States by the Italian company's local subsidiary, and powered by Liberty 400 hp engines.

Only for a brief period, however, did the Fiat R2 see service on the lines; this was put into production in 1918 and 500 were ordered. It was designed by Celestino Rosatelli and the R.2 was the first aircraft to carry the Fiat name. Its design was meant to overcome the structural weaknesses of another aircraft, the S.I.A. 7B2, construction of which had been handed over to Fiat after it had taken over the Società Italiana Aviazione. Only 129 R.2s were built but the aircraft stayed in service until 1925.

Plate 41
The last reconnaissance aircraft and trainers of the war: 1918

The final year of the war saw the last combat aircraft make their entry on the scene. Among the German reconnaissance planes which reached the front in 1918, the Halberstadt C.V. was widely used for photo-reconnaissance. It was derived from the C.III of 1917 and had the same designer, Karl Theiss. The C.V. was equipped with a supercharged version of the Benz Bz.IV engine, which could provide 220 hp at altitude. The cameras were installed on the observer's cockpit floor. The prototype appeared at the beginning of 1918 and stayed in service up to the end of the war. During the course of production, which was entrusted to Aviatik, B.F.W. and D.F.W. as well as the original manufacturer, various models were developed, the most interesting of which was the C.VIII which had an operational ceiling of 9,000 m (29,530 ft).

The Hannover CL.IIIa was used not only for reconnaissance but also as an escort and close support plane. It appeared at the front at the beginning of 1918. The aircraft was the most widely used version, with 537 built, of this successful family of aircraft, developed by Hannoversche Waggonfabrik from 1917 onwards. One of its noteworthy features was the biplane

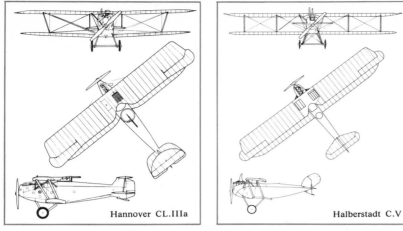

Hannover CL.IIIa

Halberstadt C.V

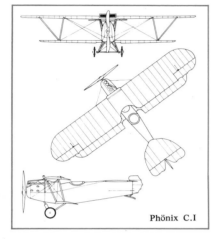

Phönix C.I

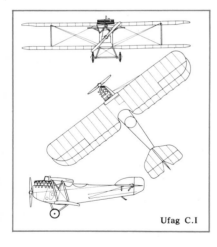

Ufag C.I

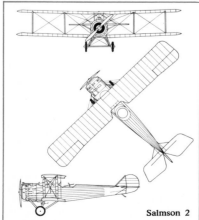

Salmson 2

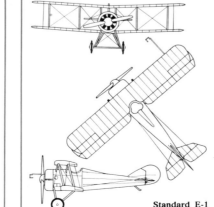

Standard E-1

tail, designed to eliminate blind angles for the observer's aim. The CL.IIIa was very manoeuvrable and easy to fly, and was most used in the summer and autumn of the last year of the war.

In Austria two aircraft which were derived from the same basic design had busy operational careers up to the end of the war: the Phönix C.1 and the Ufag C.1, both developed from the Hansa-Brandenburg C.II designed in Germany in 1916 by Ernst Heinkel. Constructed independently by Phönix Flugzeug-Werke and by Ungarische Flugzeugfabrik AG, the two machines were very different, which became evident during the course of comparative tests in 1917.

For instance, the Ufag C.1 was inferior in take off to the Phönix, in rate of climb and performance at altitude but, on the other hand, it was much faster than its rival and much more manoeuvrable. As a result, both designs were chosen for production and the two types put to different operational uses: the Phönix for high-altitude reconnaissance, the Ufag for observation at lower altitude and army co-operation. The aircraft arrived at the front in the spring of 1918 and 100 and 150 respectively of them were built. Of the two, the Phönix was the more long-lived: after the end of the war it was constructed in Sweden under licence and the thirty planes built stayed in service up to 1920.

In France, one of the most widely used reconnaissance planes of the last year of the war was the Salmson 2, an aircraft designed in 1917 by the Société des Moteurs Salmson around a new radial Canton-Unné engine of which Salmson had the production rights. The Salmson 2 went through its proving flights together with the Breguet 14 and the Spad S.XI and went into service at the beginning of 1918. The French air force used it with twenty-four squadrons and the United States forces with eleven. A total of 3,200 were built, of which 705 went to the Americans. The aircraft proved an excellent reconnaissance plane and its versatility meant that it also carried out successful day bombing and ground-attack missions.

America's urgent need was for an effective combat aircraft, and all efforts went to make up this deficiency. Even so, the last American aircraft to appear before the end of the war, the Standard E-1, did not make a good fighter. Two prototypes were delivered in 1918 but they were slow and clearly under-powered, and these shortcomings were never put right. The 168 built were used as trainers. The design had been drawn up at the beginning of 1917 by the Standard Aircraft Corporation of Elizabeth, New Jersey, a company which built European aircraft under licence.

Plate 42
Flying boats and seaplanes of 1915–16

During the course of the war maritime reconnaissance and patrol functions were demonstrated to be just as important as those of the fighter and the land bomber. They were needed in the operational theatres to the north and south of the European mainland, such as the North Sea and the Adriatic. The Austrians and the Italians in particular, who were both Adriatic powers, each developed a whole series of seaplanes from the very beginning of the war which confronted each other throughout hostilities.

Among the most well known old-established Austrian constructors of marine aircraft was Jacob Lohner of Vienna who in 1914 built a biplane flying boat which was to become the forerunner of a prolific family of flying boats manufactured throughout the

war. The first to be put into series production was the Lohner E, of which about 40 were built and from which were derived the more powerful and widely used flying boats of the L series, 108 of which left the assembly lines up to 1916.

The importance of these aircraft did not arise only from their widespread operational use, but also from the influence which they had on the development of Italy's flying boats, all built by Macchi. The first Macchi flying boat, the L.I of 1915, was a copy of the Lohner L based on a captured example. Macchi built 140 of these.

Rivals of the Macchi flying boats were the British and French machines. France's F.B.A. C, for instance, was built in large numbers, not only for the French navy but also for the Russian and Italian navies. The following Type H proved even better and 982 were manufactured under licence in Italy.

Although the Allies used flying boats mainly for reconnaissance duties, marine patrol and anti-submarine warfare, enemy flying boats which were especially designed for use as fighters appeared more or less at the same time. The best of this type went into service in 1916. Similar to the Hansa-Brandenburg KDW, they were constructed especially to defend the flying-boat bases of the Adriatic and the North Sea. The Hansa-Brandenburg biplane was designed by Ernst Heinkel and derived from an earlier landplane. About 60 of them were built in five production batches which had increasingly powerful engines.

The Rumpler 6B.1 was also developed from a landplane and appeared in the summer of 1916. 38 of these biplanes were completed at a very slow rate of production, the last of which was delivered at the end of May 1917. 50 aircraft of the 6B.2 variant followed, which had a greater wing-span and other structural changes, and were delivered up to January 1918. The Rumpler seaplane was not regarded as the equal of the KDW and it was mainly used from North Sea and Black Sea bases. Another Hansa-Brandenburg flying boat, the CC, saw wide use in the Adriatic. It had been

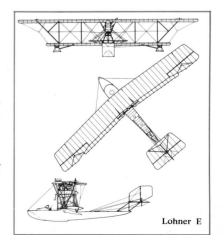

Lohner E

Hansa-Brandenburg CC

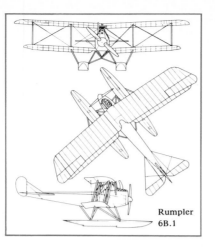

Rumpler 6B.1

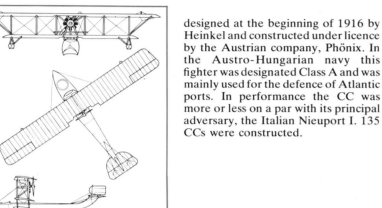

F.B.A. C

Hansa-Brandenburg KDW

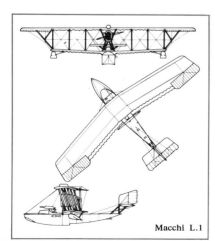

Macchi L.1

designed at the beginning of 1916 by Heinkel and constructed under licence by the Austrian company, Phönix. In the Austro-Hungarian navy this fighter was designated Class A and was mainly used for the defence of Atlantic ports. In performance the CC was more or less on a par with its principal adversary, the Italian Nieuport I. 135 CCs were constructed.

Plate 43
Flying boats and seaplanes of 1917

In 1917 another excellent German flying-boat fighter made its appearance, the Hansa-Brandenburg W.12. Again designed by Ernst Heinkel, in the last months of the previous year, this aircraft was conceived in response to the navy's request for a naval fighter which could defend itself against attacks from the rear. In consequence Heinkel chose the formula of a two-seat biplane with the observer in a rear cockpit armed with a machine gun with a wide field of fire. Production of the W.12 reached a total of 145, delivered from April 1917 to March of the following year. This fighter was held in high esteem by its enemies and it was joined, from the end of 1917 onwards, by an improved version, the W.19, with which it shared its operational tasks up to the end of the war.

In Allied quarters a small British seaplane, the Sopwith Baby, was widely used. It was derived from the Tabloid which had won the Schneider Trophy in 1914 and of which the Royal Naval Air Service had ordered 136 for observation and maritime patrol. 457 were built and served until the end of the war from the Royal Navy's coastal bases and from aircraft car-

riers, and were therefore sent to all operational theatres as one of the reconnaissance and anti-submarine planes. It was much used over the Channel and the North Sea, and in the Mediterranean, Egypt, Palestine and Italy. The small seaplane carried out its tasks for a long time, making a considerable contribution to the fight against enemy submarines. In Italy the Baby was constructed under licence by Ansaldo.

At this time the British were improving their techniques in the use of aircraft carriers and carrier-based machines, which led to a reduced emphasis on the smaller seaplane; while for long-range reconnaissance larger, multi-engined aircraft were planned.

In 1917 the first aircraft designed for carrier-based use, the Fairey Campania, appeared, a biplane whose name derived from the transatlantic liner, HMS *Campania*, which had been converted into the carrier on which it served. After the first two prototypes production totalled 62, which stayed in service until 1919.

An important large flying boat was the Felixstowe F.2A: a large biplane derived from the American Curtiss H-12 Large America, which indeed set the basic formula for all British maritime aircraft up to the 1930s. From November 1917 to March 1918 as many as 170 of this twin-engine plane were ordered and delivered. In service the Felixstowe F.2As were widely used with great success for patrol duties in the North Sea. They were particularly effective against submarines and against the German Zeppelins.

The use of seaplanes was by now so widespread that it was necessary to produce seaplane trainers; amongst the Allied trainers, the American Curtiss N-9 was widely employed, 450 being built which remained in service with the US Army and Navy flying schools up to 1927. The aircraft was developed towards the end of 1916 by Curtiss, and it was based on another trainer, the JN-4B which was already in production, modifying its structure and equipping it with a more powerful engine. The N-9s went into service at the beginning of 1917.

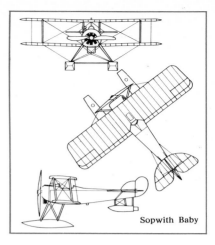

Sopwith Baby

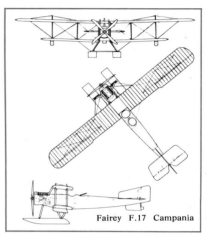

Fairey F.17 Campania

Hansa-Brandenburg W.12

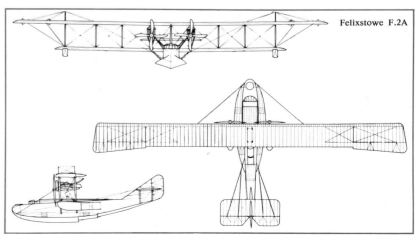

Felixstowe F.2A

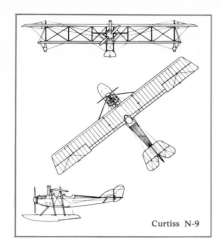

Curtiss N-9

Meanwhile among the small float-planes, the models developed by Macchi following the Type L.1 had made their mark due to their excellent qualities. In 1918 two of the best seaplanes of this family appeared, the Macchi M.5 and the Macchi M.9 which were a fighter and armed reconnaissance plane. The former in particular, with 270 built, proved so useful and such a good warplane that it managed to compete successfully with land fighters of the time. In the course of their career, which lasted up to the end of the war, the M.5s were joined by a more powerful model, M.5 Mod equipped with an Isotta-Fraschini 250 hp engine. The Macchi M.9, how-ever, which was developed from the M.8 two-seater of 1917, only flew in a few missions before the war came to an end. The 30 constructed stayed in service until 1923.

Among the last German seaplane fighters was the Hansa-Brandenburg W.29, considered to be the best of the naval warplane designs of Ernst Heinkel. It was a totally new aircraft, a monoplane, offering all the improved performance that came by eliminating the extra drag which was inevitable with biplanes. The performance of the W.29 really was impressive. The 78 constructed mainly served from North Sea bases and were held in healthy respect by their enemies.

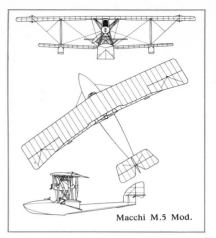

Macchi M.5 Mod.

Plate 44
Flying boats and seaplanes of 1918

In the field of landplanes, the contribution of American industry to the war was practically nil. This was amply compensated for by the remarkable effect which the great flying boats of Glenn Curtiss had in the maritime sector, which were widely used by the British, especially in the North Sea to counter German submarines. The design had been drawn up by Curtiss in 1914 with the intention of producing an aircraft which could cross the Atlantic. The American pioneer was working with an ex-Royal Navy pilot, John C. Porte, who had ambitions of performing this feat. The war, how-ever, put an end to this ambitious plan, and Porte went back home and managed to get the Admiralty to purchase two America flying boats which were prepared for the crossing. The aircraft, which were designated H-4, were delivered at the end of the year and met with such success that orders were placed for ten of them to begin with and then for a further fifty. Their operational use was so satisfactory that Britain also ordered the succeeding variants of the H-4, more powerful, larger, and better-armed.

One useful successor was the H-12, of which 50 were ordered and which was called the Large America to distinguish it from the H-4, which was then called the Small America. The H-12s built for the Royal Navy were equipped with Rolls-Royce Eagle 1 250 hp engines instead of the original Liberty 300 hp engines which were installed in models constructed for the American navy. Towards the end of 1917 a new variant, even larger and better-armed, made its appearance, the H-16 of which 76 were ordered by Britain. Before the end of the war the RNAS obtained fifteen H-16s which joined the aircraft of earlier versions. They remained in service until 1921.

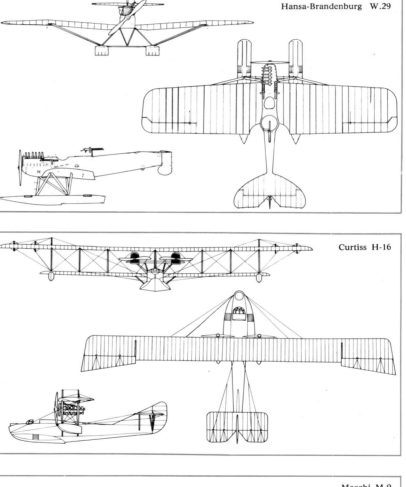

Hansa-Brandenburg W.29

Curtiss H-16

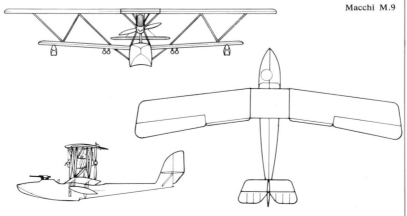

Macchi M.9

Lighter-than-air craft were put to very wide use during the First World War. Their most traditional role was an obvious one, dating back to the last years of the preceding century when they were first used for observation. A hydrogen-filled balloon was floated above the battlefield anchored to the ground by cables or attached to balloon-beds. From inside the airship's car, at a considerable height above the ground, one or two observers would keep track of the movements of the enemy's forces and would then direct their own artillery accordingly. This system worked well but it did have one major drawback: when a wind was blowing it was impossible to control the balloon and the car rocked and rotated so violently that the observer could stay in it for only short periods of time.

Towards the end of the century two German officers, August von Parseval and H. Bartsch von Sigsfield, managed to solve this problem. They designed a cylindrical shaped captive balloon which was flown in much the same way as a kite and inclined at 30–40 degrees into the wind; this enabled the air pressure itself to stabilise the balloon, which was also controlled by the attachment of two small sails plus a large air-containing sac located at its rear end to act as a rudder and keep it heading into the wind.

Parseval and Sigsfield had started their experiments in 1893 and these continued for five years. Once the best configuration had been decided upon, the *Drachenballon*, or "kite balloon" as this new observation balloon was called, was put into regular production. It proved so effective that it could be used at heights varying between 1,000 m (3,280 ft) and 2000 m (6,560 ft) in a 65 km/h (40 knot) wind. By the time the First World War broke out, the German army had a considerable number of these captive balloons and normally used them for the direction of artillery fire.

France was the next nation to adopt this innovation, using experience gained on the Western front. In 1914, using German designs as a starting point, Capt Albert Caquot developed a more streamlined captive balloon with three tails, one vertical and two lateral, attached at intervals of 120°, thus improving stabilisation. The Caquot balloon soon became standard equipment for the French army and navy and four basic models were built, with volumes of 750, 820, 930 and 1,000 cubic metres. Depending on the number of crew in the car (up to three) operational altitude varied between 500 m (1,640 ft) and 1,000 m (3,280 ft). The observers were issued

with parachutes and could jump to safety in the event of the balloon coming under attack.

A considerable number of these balloons were used by the Allies who set up an efficient network of observation posts along the entire front. In Britain a new method of passive defence was developed, using captive balloons, which was implemented in 1917. The system involved putting up a series of balloons which were joined together by steel cables; from these linking cables others trailed down to the ground, thus constituting a serious obstacle to any enemy aircraft attempting to fly into that particular air space. The best combination was to have three balloons joined together by a horizontal cable 900 m (2,950 ft) long, from which a series of steel wires measuring approximately 300 m (985 ft) hung downwards. Uninterrupted barrages of this type were put up to form protective barriers around large cities: London, for instance, had a barrage stretching for about 82 km (50 miles) by the middle of 1918.

Among the numerous balloons that were available for barrage purposes, the Italian Avorio-Prassone balloon, developed in 1915, was considered by the British to be the best of its kind. Before they had these British experiments were copied by France, Germany and Italy. The most ambitious plan was undoubtedly that of the French, who aimed to put up a system of 150 barrages, each comprising ten balloons. The war ended, however, before production had got very far.

While balloons had proved their military value in this passive defensive role, their mobile equivalents, the airships, made their mark as strategic weapons alongside the bomber aeroplanes. Most of the nations in the First World War adopted these machines, which continually increased in size and power, but the Germans led the way in developing them and in exploiting their potential to the fullest extent. The first Zeppelin first saw active service during the night of 19th January 1915, in a raid up the Humber estuary. This was the L3, which was a giant airship measuring 158 m (520 ft) in length, powered by three 200 hp engines and which, on this particular mission, carried eight 50 kg (110 lb) bombs and ten 28 kg (62 lb) incendiary bombs. This airship's career ended a month later on 17th February, when bad weather forced it to land in Denmark during a reconnaissance mission and it was destroyed by the crew.

In Italy, one of the most effective types of airship to be used in a bomber role was the series M, whose prototype M-1 flew in 1912. A total of nineteen airships of this class were produced which were built until 1918 and mainly used for night bombing missions. The series M airships were of semi-rigid construction and were manufactured by the Stabilimento Costruzionia Aeronautiche di Roma.

In Britain, airships were mainly used for maritime reconnaissance and anti-submarine warfare. There were several series of class SS (Submarine Scout) airships and the SS-3 of 1915 was built on much the same lines as the first series. This was a non-rigid type, of relatively modest dimensions; about 150 were constructed during the war, many of which were used by France and Italy. There were several production series which had different engines and increased capacity. The last, and best, was the SSZ of 1917, of which 93 were built.

Apart from the SS class Britain also developed two other non-rigid types of dirigibles: the Coastal class and the North Sea class. Of the former, which began in 1915, ten were later modified, enlarged, and thus turned into a fourth class, the C Star class. These were constructed in 1918, following the completion of 26 Coastal class airships; by then longer-range airships with higher speeds were needed to protect convoys from attack by German submarines. The C Star airships could carry a 20 per cent greater load while they could also climb faster. Speed increased from 75 km/h (46 mph) to 90 km/h (56 mph).

An even better performance was achieved with the sixteen North Sea class airships built in 1917 and 1918; these were the best airships Britain made during the war and they were used not only for convoy escort duties but also for liaison with the navy. They also had much longer operational ranges, which varied from 24 hours to almost 50 hours. The endurance record for this class of airship was set by the North Sea NS-11 early in 1919: 101 hours 50 minutes.

Unlike Germany, Britain only adopted rigid construction airships towards the end of the war and even then only in very limited numbers. A first attempt had been made in 1914 to construct effective airships of this type when the N.9 dirigible was built, but hesitation by the authorities had led to the programme falling a long way behind schedule and the airship only flew on 16th November 1916. Some months, earlier, however, a new programme had been initiated which allowed for the construction of ten larger airships. The first of these was designated N.23 and this became the designation of a new class of airship. Work commended on the project in June 1916 and the airship had its maiden flight in August 1917. The operational career of this dirigible, and that of the only two others like it which were completed, was very limited and was mainly confined to patrol flights over the North Sea and in the event it was more extensively used for training.

In Germany the development of the Zeppelin airships continued almost uninterruptedly throughout the war, the aim of producing ever larger and more powerful machines with increased war potential and better per-

formance. The various models which were developed during the war years (which reached a total of 115 in all) increased in carrying capacity and in engine power. Streamlining was constantly refined and improved by such modifications as those introduced in the L.48 of 1917, the first Zeppelin to have a control car designed to reduce drag. This process of perfecting the airship culminated in the construction of three airships of the X Class (the L.70, the L.71 and the L.72) of 1918.

Tests indicated that an airship of this type could carry out bombing missions on Britain with a 3,630 kg (8,000 lb) bomb-load. Such a mission was, however, never accomplished. On the night of 5th August 1918, during the L.70's first bombing raid on Britain, it was attacked by a de Havilland D.H.4 and shot down in flames. The L.71 met with a different fate, as did the L.72: the former was seized by Britain as reparation and survived until 30th June 1920; the latter was handed over to France after the Armistice and continued to fly until 21st December 1923, when it went down over the sea during a storm and was wrecked.

Plate 45

Balloons and airships: 1912–15

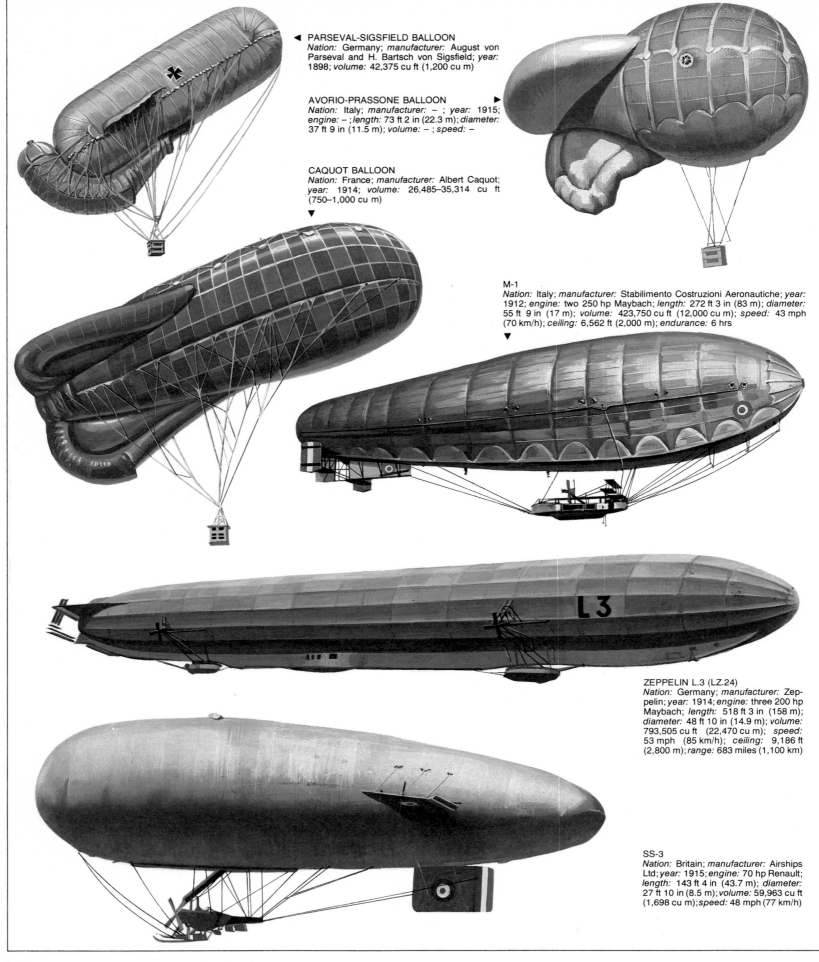

PARSEVAL-SIGSFIELD BALLOON
Nation: Germany; *manufacturer:* August von Parseval and H. Bartsch von Sigsfield; *year:* 1898; *volume:* 42,375 cu ft (1,200 cu m)

AVORIO-PRASSONE BALLOON
Nation: Italy; *manufacturer:* – ; *year:* 1915; *engine:* – ;*length:* 73 ft 2 in (22.3 m); *diameter:* 37 ft 9 in (11.5 m); *volume:* – ; *speed:* –

CAQUOT BALLOON
Nation: France; *manufacturer:* Albert Caquot; *year:* 1914; *volume:* 26,485–35,314 cu ft (750–1,000 cu m)

M-1
Nation: Italy; *manufacturer:* Stabilimento Costruzioni Aeronautiche; *year:* 1912; *engine:* two 250 hp Maybach; *length:* 272 ft 3 in (83 m); *diameter:* 55 ft 9 in (17 m); *volume:* 423,750 cu ft (12,000 cu m); *speed:* 43 mph (70 km/h); *ceiling:* 6,562 ft (2,000 m); *endurance:* 6 hrs

ZEPPELIN L.3 (LZ.24)
Nation: Germany; *manufacturer:* Zeppelin; *year:* 1914; *engine:* three 200 hp Maybach; *length:* 518 ft 3 in (158 m); *diameter:* 48 ft 10 in (14.9 m); *volume:* 793,505 cu ft (22,470 cu m); *speed:* 53 mph (85 km/h); *ceiling:* 9,186 ft (2,800 m); *range:* 683 miles (1,100 km)

SS-3
Nation: Britain; *manufacturer:* Airships Ltd; *year:* 1915; *engine:* 70 hp Renault; *length:* 143 ft 4 in (43.7 m); *diameter:* 27 ft 10 in (8.5 m); *volume:* 59,963 cu ft (1,698 cu m); *speed:* 48 mph (77 km/h)

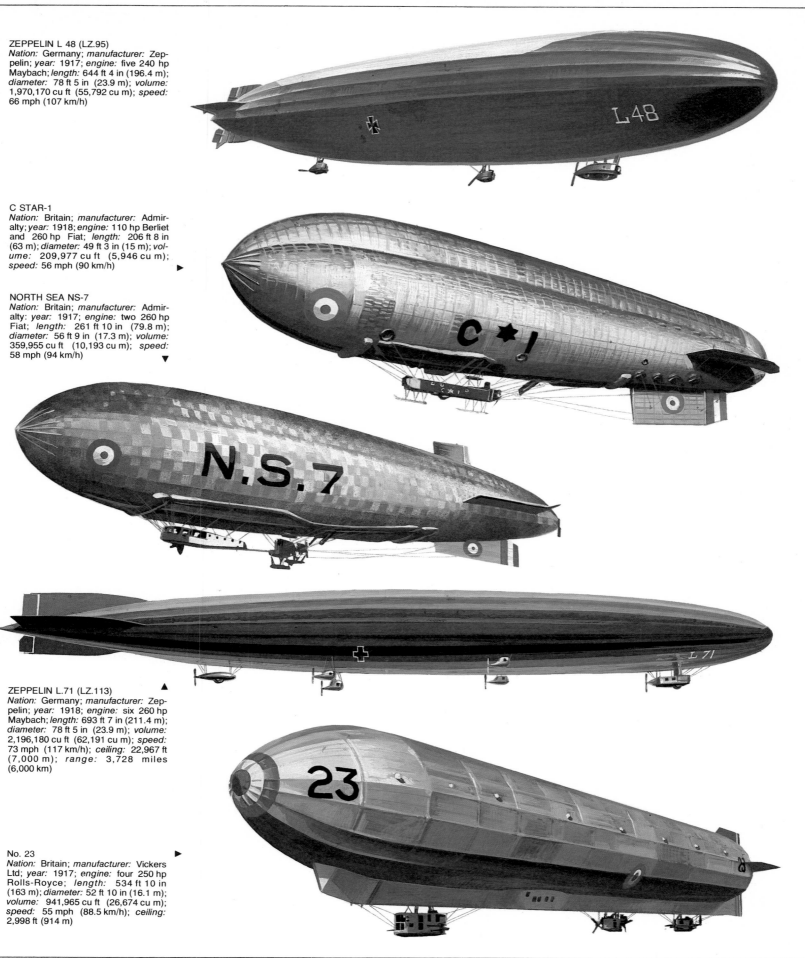

ZEPPELIN L 48 (LZ.95)
Nation: Germany; *manufacturer:* Zeppelin; *year:* 1917; *engine:* five 240 hp Maybach; *length:* 644 ft 4 in (196.4 m); *diameter:* 78 ft 5 in (23.9 m); *volume:* 1,970,170 cu ft (55,792 cu m); *speed:* 66 mph (107 km/h)

C STAR-1
Nation: Britain; *manufacturer:* Admiralty; *year:* 1918; *engine:* 110 hp Berliet and 260 hp Fiat; *length:* 206 ft 8 in (63 m); *diameter:* 49 ft 3 in (15 m); *volume:* 209,977 cu ft (5,946 cu m); *speed:* 56 mph (90 km/h)

NORTH SEA NS-7
Nation: Britain; *manufacturer:* Admiralty: *year:* 1917; *engine:* two 260 hp Fiat; *length:* 261 ft 10 in (79.8 m); *diameter:* 56 ft 9 in (17.3 m); *volume:* 359,955 cu ft (10,193 cu m); *speed:* 58 mph (94 km/h)

ZEPPELIN L.71 (LZ.113)
Nation: Germany; *manufacturer:* Zeppelin; *year:* 1918; *engine:* six 260 hp Maybach; *length:* 693 ft 7 in (211.4 m); *diameter:* 78 ft 5 in (23.9 m); *volume:* 2,196,180 cu ft (62,191 cu m); *speed:* 73 mph (117 km/h); *ceiling:* 22,967 ft (7,000 m); *range:* 3,728 miles (6,000 km)

No. 23
Nation: Britain; *manufacturer:* Vickers Ltd; *year:* 1917; *engine:* four 250 hp Rolls-Royce; *length:* 534 ft 10 in (163 m); *diameter:* 52 ft 10 in (16.1 m); *volume:* 941,965 cu ft (26,674 cu m); *speed:* 55 mph (88.5 km/h); *ceiling:* 2,998 ft (914 m)

Plate 47

Engines of the First World War

◄ GNOME MONOSOUPAPE 100 hp 1914 (France)
This engine was very widely used as an alternative to the Le Rhône engine which was similar in design. The 80 hp and 100 hp Gnome Monosoupape rotaries powered a whole generation of Allied warplanes and were built under licence in Britain, the United States and Italy. The two models differed mainly in the number of cylinders – seven in the 80 hp type A and nine in the 100 hp type B. Both had the same internal dimensions, with bore of 100 mm and stroke of 150 mm. Maximum engine speed was 1,200 rpm

HISPANO-SUIZA A 1915 (Spain) ►
At the time of its appearance it was hailed as "the greatest engine in the world" and the Hispano-Suiza was certainly revolutionary; for the first time the German aero-engine industry's supremacy, gained through the success of its rotary engines, was successfully challenged. The basic model A developed 150 hp but later versions almost doubled this. The Hispano-Suiza was a liquid-cooled V-8 engine with bore and stroke of 120 mm and 130 mm, and maximum power was at 1,700 rpm. Its dry weight was 206 kg (454 lb). This engine was built under licence in France, Britain and the United States

▲
CLERGET 9B 1915 (France)
The series of rotary engines developed by Clerget were manufactured in considerable numbers and France was not the only country to make wide use of them. After the first 80 hp 7-cylinder engines the 110–140 hp 9-cylinder models were soon developed and these saw very widespread use throughout the war. The model 9B developed 130 hp in normal use – 135 hp emergency maximum. Bore and stroke were 120 mm and 160 mm, maximum power was at 1,250 rpm, and the maximum all-up weight was 173 kg (380 lb)

MERCEDES 180 hp 1917 (Germany)
The Mercedes engine was made famous by some of the most well-known German fighters of the latter part of the war and was a liquid-cooled vertical 6-cylinder inline engine, a layout which was adopted by the manufacturer from the very beginning of the war onwards. Bore was 140 mm, stroke 160 mm and engine capacity 14.776 litres; maximum power was developed at 1,400 rpm. Dry weight was 300 kg (660 lb)

AUSTRO-DAIMLER 200 hp 1917 (Austria)
Together with the Hiero the engines manufactured by the Austrian Daimler company were among the most outstanding of the war. This was a liquid-cooled 6-cylinder inline engine which was continually improved leading to increasingly powerful versions. The 200 hp model was the last to be put into general use before the end of the war. Bore and stroke were 135 mm and 175 mm respectively; maximum power was developed at 1,400 rpm. Dry weight was 330 kg (727 lb), height was 115 cm and the engine was 172 cm long
▼

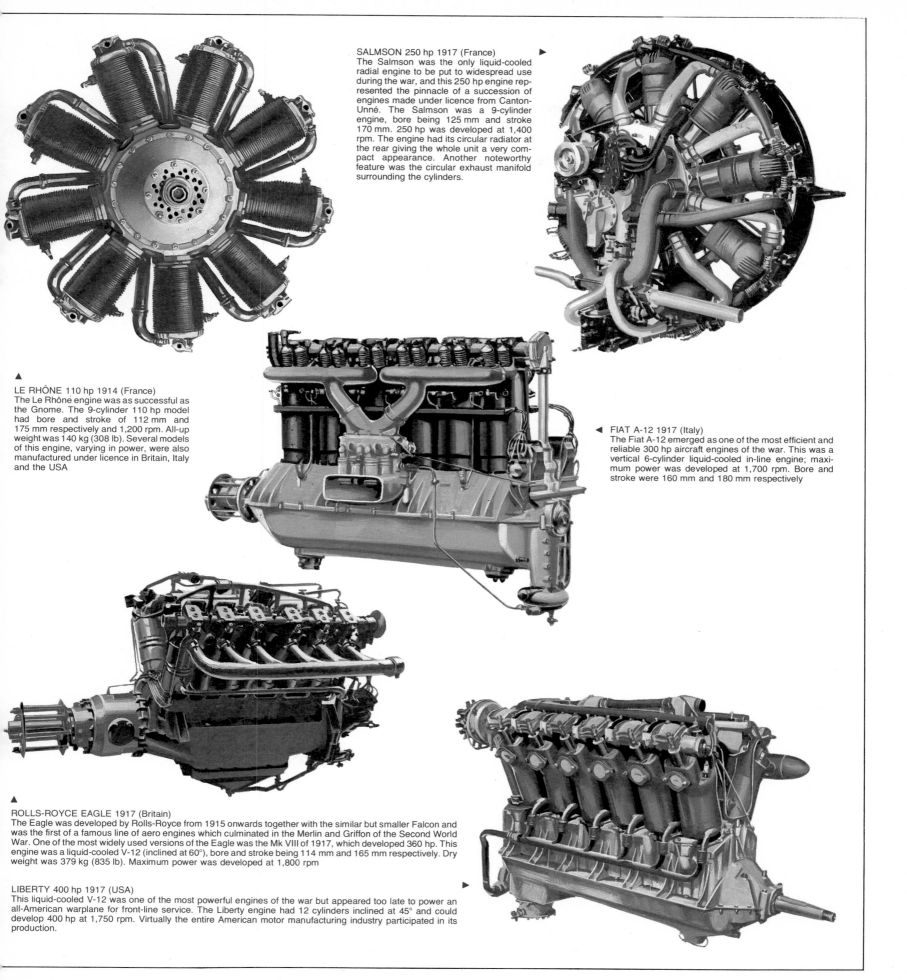

SALMSON 250 hp 1917 (France)
The Salmson was the only liquid-cooled radial engine to be put to widespread use during the war, and this 250 hp engine represented the pinnacle of a succession of engines made under licence from Canton-Unné. The Salmson was a 9-cylinder engine, bore being 125 mm and stroke 170 mm. 250 hp was developed at 1,400 rpm. The engine had its circular radiator at the rear giving the whole unit a very compact appearance. Another noteworthy feature was the circular exhaust manifold surrounding the cylinders.

LE RHÔNE 110 hp 1914 (France)
The Le Rhône engine was as successful as the Gnome. The 9-cylinder 110 hp model had bore and stroke of 112 mm and 175 mm respectively and 1,200 rpm. All-up weight was 140 kg (308 lb). Several models of this engine, varying in power, were also manufactured under licence in Britain, Italy and the USA

FIAT A-12 1917 (Italy)
The Fiat A-12 emerged as one of the most efficient and reliable 300 hp aircraft engines of the war. This was a vertical 6-cylinder liquid-cooled in-line engine; maximum power was developed at 1,700 rpm. Bore and stroke were 160 mm and 180 mm respectively

ROLLS-ROYCE EAGLE 1917 (Britain)
The Eagle was developed by Rolls-Royce from 1915 onwards together with the similar but smaller Falcon and was the first of a famous line of aero engines which culminated in the Merlin and Griffon of the Second World War. One of the most widely used versions of the Eagle was the Mk VIII of 1917, which developed 360 hp. This engine was a liquid-cooled V-12 (inclined at 60°), bore and stroke being 114 mm and 165 mm respectively. Dry weight was 379 kg (835 lb). Maximum power was developed at 1,800 rpm

LIBERTY 400 hp 1917 (USA)
This liquid-cooled V-12 was one of the most powerful engines of the war but appeared too late to power an all-American warplane for front-line service. The Liberty engine had 12 cylinders inclined at 45° and could develop 400 hp at 1,750 rpm. Virtually the entire American motor manufacturing industry participated in its production.

Photographic appendix

R.A.F. B.E.2c-1914, GB (plate 28)

R.A.F. F.E.2b-1915, GB (plate 19)

R.A.F. R.E.8-1916, GB (plate 37)

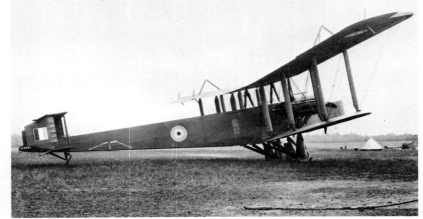

Handley-Page O/100-1916, GB (plate 31)

Bristol F.2B-1917, GB (plate 19)

R.A.F. S.E.5a-1917, GB (plate 19)

Sopwith F.1 Camel-1917, GB (plate 19)

Sopwith 7F.1 Snipe-1918, GB (plate 24)

Curtiss JN-4-1916. GB (plate 37)

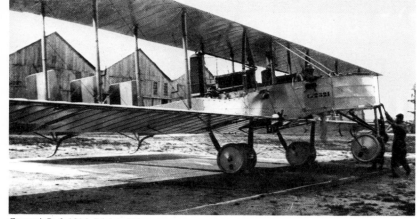

Caproni Ca.3-1916, I (plate 29)

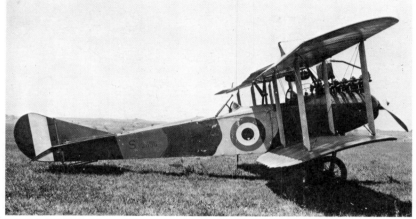

S.A.M.L. S.2-1917, I (plate 39)

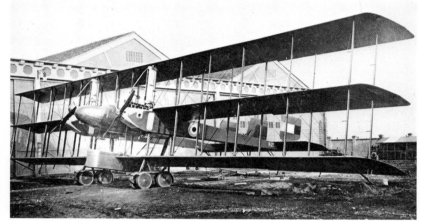

Caproni Ca.4-1917, I (plate 29)

Ansaldo S.V.A. 5, I (plate 40)

Pomilio PE-1918, I (plate 40)

Macchi M.5-1918, I (plate 44)

A.E.G. C.II-1915, G (plate 92)

105

Photographic appendix

Fokker E.III-1915, G (plate 14)

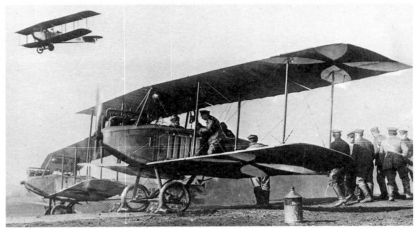

Aviatik B.I-1915, G (plate 6)

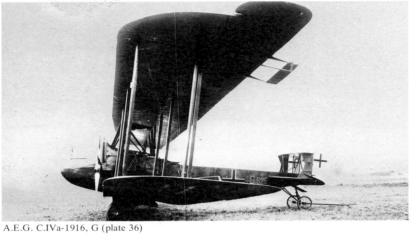

A.E.G. C.IVa-1916, G (plate 36)

Pfalz D.IIIa-1916, G (plate 21)

Siemens-Schuckert D.III-1917, G (plate 22)

Junkers CL.I-1917, G (plate 23)

Fokker D.VII-1918, G (plate 22)

Pfalz D.XII-1918, G (plate 23)

106

Blériot XI-1914, F (plate 2)

Caudron G.4-1915, F (plate 28)

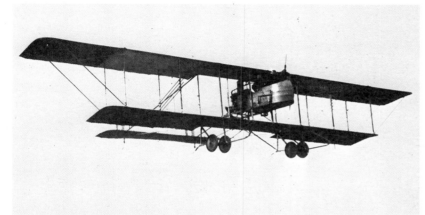

Maurice Farman M.F.11-1915, F (plate 3)

Nieuport 11 «Bébé»-1915, F (plate 15)

Voisin 10-1916, F (plate 76)

Hanriot HD.1-1917, F (plate 18)

Breguet Br.14-1917, F (plate 33)

Spad S.XIII-1917, F (plate 17)

2.

MILITARY AVIATION BETWEEN THE TWO WORLD WARS

With peace a new phase began in the story of aviation. The overwhelming pressures of war had given production a momentum which seemed unstoppable. Yet the brake was suddenly applied. In the space of a few months, armies demobilised, weapons were consigned to depots and stores, airfields became immense and silent parking-lots, and the aviation industry abruptly cut down its output and almost came to a halt. The time had come, after over four years of war, to repair shattered economies and to devote every effort to reconstruction. The aeroplane was not immune to the process – quite the reverse. It too was affected by events and adapted itself accordingly. The war, which was now a closed chapter, had brought about advances in aeronautical techniques which as late as 1914 had seemed to be pure fantasy. The aeroplane had grown up, it was now seen in a different light, and it was put to peaceful uses.

The twenty years that followed were marked by two basic tendencies: a general sluggishness in the development of military aviation until the beginning of the 1930s, and during that period the growth in importance of civil and commercial aviation, then in its infancy. In a major shift of emphasis, it was civil aviation which became the determining factor in the development of the aeroplane. The discovery that aviation could be put to wider uses and the harsh realities of commercial competition both stimulated the peacetime industry, in much the same way as war had stimulated military aircraft production. At the same time, emulating the feats of the pioneering years, competition flying bettered those achievement and reawakened the spirit of adventure; it also stimulated research into improvements in airframes, materials and engines.

It is impossible to trace the evolution of the military aircraft without considering, if only briefly, the enormous contribution made by twenty years of competitive events in Europe and the USA. The air races (the Schneider Trophy in Europe, the National Air Races in North America), long-distance competitions, and attempts to beat records, apart from their immediate consequences, led on each occasion to the solution of technical problems, and this slowly but ceaselessly aided the development of aircraft and engines.

The engine showed the most obvious results of this progress. The rotary engine completely disappeared, and the unremitting search for higher and higher speeds led to the adoption of the static V-engine, which during the First World War was first produced by Britain and France, with promising results. None of the aeronautically advanced nations failed to take this direction. France used the final versions of the Hispano-Suiza engine for competitions; Britain refined and perfected the long series of Rolls-Royce engines; Italy eventually produced the Fiat AS6 engine which took the world speed record for seaplanes. The United States, too, after the introduction of the V-12 Liberty engine, developed the very sophisticated and powerful Curtiss engines. Beginning in the middle twenties, America's aircraft industry saw the widespread adoption of the radial engine, and its commercial success.

In the case of airframes and components too, the stimulus furnished by competitions led to similar progress. One has only to recall the transformation undergone by propellers, where metal replaced wood and the variable-pitch mechanism was invented. In addition, the undercarriage became retractable in response to the need for clean aerodynamic lines. Then, perhaps most important of all, the biplane was generally displaced by the monoplane; this only came about because of research into more advanced construction techniques required by competitive events, the Schneider Trophy in particular.

All this was, however, only very gradually applied to military aviation, at any rate in the first ten years of peace. One has only to recall that in spite of all these innovations, the fighter remained virtually unchanged up to the 1930s, inherited in the same form as it had emerged from the First World War: a biplane or high-wing monoplane with open cockpit, fixed undercarriage and two synchronised machine guns firing through the propeller hub. Certainly its general performance was much improved, but in essence it remained the same. The picture altered as soon as the world became aware of tensions which foreshadowed another war. The aeroplane was once more the focal point of attention for strategists and politicians. Then the progress of the postwar years of enthusiasm was absorbed into military aircraft production. With a new incentive at hand, each country responded to the very utmost of its ability.

In Britain the end of the First World War saw a drastic cut in defence spending, and consequently, an abrupt reduction in the RAF's establishment, both in men and aircraft. This position persisted for a long time, due mainly to the government's stringent budgeting. A few months after the Armistice, the RAF's 188 war-time front-line squadrons were reduced to 33 and these were nearly all stationed in the colonies. Up to the autumn of 1922 only one squadron of already obsolete Sopwith Snipes formed Britain's home air defence. In December 1933, the total of front-line aircraft was 833.

A similar situation was found in naval aviation. At the end of 1919 the Royal Naval Air Service had only 3 units: one of fighters, one of reconnaissance planes, and one of torpedo-bombers. In January 1924 (three months before the RNAS became the Fleet Air Arm) there were 78 aircraft in service. This rose to 144 by September 1930 and to 156 in 1932.

Only in the second half of the 1930s was there an improvement in quantity and quality. In 1937 the RAF (divided for operational purposes into Fighter, Bomber and Coastal Command) already had its first modern monoplane in service, the Hurricane, and was on the point of acquiring the Spitfire. Amongst their bombers, the most representative were the twin-engined Blenheim, Hampden, Wellington and Whitley, some already in squadron service, others on the point of becoming operational. The modernisation of the Fleet Air Arm, however, was much slower, and it was only in 1939 that it became an independent service. The military theory behind the rearmament of the RAF was based on the premise that the bomber's role was specifically strategic, and that of the fighter, defensive. Industry coped very well with the sudden expansion thrust upon it, and in 1938 it succeeded in producing a total of 4,000 aircraft, and was preparing for the even more ambitious targets which it would have to meet in the coming years.

In France, the *Aviation militaire* had been reduced to about 180 squadrons immediately after the Treaty of Versailles in 1919, most of which were to serve in the colonial possessions. This was a reliable air force which was kept up to strength for a longer period than those of the other Allied powers, largely because the French were convinced that such a force was necessary to ensure that the terms of the peace treaty were respected. For a certain length of time, therefore, a good supply of new types was forthcoming, for example the Nieuport-Delage 29 and the Wibault 7 monoplane fighters, facilitated by the healthy state of the aircraft industry. Later, under the delusion that the League of Nations could successfully enforce international disarmament, all strengthening of military aviation was shelved.

This was the first of a series of political miscalculations, being followed by another, after the failure of the Disarmament Conference which began on 2nd February 1932: in the new rearmament against the threat from Germany, priority was placed on the army at the expense of the air force. Thus it was that on the eve of another world war France certainly had an impressive line of fortifications on the ground, but was quite unprepared in the air. This is illustrated by the fact that it was only in 1936 that the air force was reconstituted as a separate service with the formation of the *Armée de l'Air*. It was in the same year that the aircraft industry underwent a much needed reorganisation, with nationalisation aimed at co-ordination of production. On 15th July 1939, as a very belated afterthought, a French ministerial order allocated 69 per cent of the military budget to aviation. This investment was never to yield the hoped-for return; for then the objective was too distant and the war too close.

Germany, the traditional enemy, had developed her air power along quite different lines. The Armistice of 1918 and the Treaty of Versailles in 1919 stipulated the complete disbandment of the German air force. The terms of the Treaty provided for the confiscation of all military equipment, which included 20,000 aircraft and 27,000 engines and which was all placed under the control of a specially formed commission; a complete ban on any aircraft for Germany's armed forces: and a ban on the design, financing and construction of any military aircraft. Only private industry was permitted to built aircraft, which had to be civil aircraft and must be of limited size and performance.

These were harsh restrictions for a nation which had formerly been one of the strongest air powers. However, after a few years under these conditions they in fact began to make their mark in the new sphere of commercial aviation. In 1922 they were able to take advantage of the lapsing of some of the limitations imposed by the Treaty of Versailles and reorganised their industry. Famous aircraft manufacturers such as Junkers, Dornier and Heinkel were already operating through subsidiaries abroad, and they were joined in 1924 by Focke-Wulf, in 1925 by Arado and in 1926 by Messerschmitt. This was the year when all restrictions imposed at Versailles came to an end, and a great period of growth began, still ostensibly in the name of commercial aviation. Work was started on aircraft of very advanced design. Deutsche Lufthansa, recently formed by the merger of Junkers and Aero Lloyd, operated the new aircraft. The expansion of civil aviation made it possible to get manufacturing under way, to rebuild administrative and operating structures; while pilots, aircrew and specialists could openly be trained in large numbers. Prior to this it is known that training took place discreetly with gliders; and the Germans also ran a secret pilot training scheme in the Soviet Union.

Thus arose Germany's new air force: the *Luftwaffe*. Its existence was officially revealed on 1st March 1935, but it had been built up in secret in the preceding year, following Hitler's rise to power in 1933. During its secret phase the *Luftwaffe* had quite boldly hidden under the cover of civil aviation. Masquerading as commercial aircraft, some of the *Luftwaffe*'s most famous and widely used bombers appeared – the Junkers Ju.86, the Dornier Do.17 and the Heinkel He.111. Then there was the Junkers Ju.52, the ubiquitous military transport which, before flying with military markings, was both famous and successful as a civil airliner.

No such reticence was shown, however, with other combat planes. Among the fighters, the Messerschmitt Bf.109, one of the best aircraft of its time, was even entered for air races and thus publicly revealed its merits. At the end of 1935 the *Luftwaffe* had approximately 1,000 aircraft in service, and 20,000 personnel, and production was running at the rate of 300 a month. It was undoubtedly a flying start for what was to become within a few years the most powerful air force in the world. The first test in battle followed shortly afterwards in the Spanish Civil War.

In Italy, as elsewhere, the surge in production during the last stages of the First World War had ceased with the coming of peace. Military aviation went into a stagnant phase which only ended in 1923, when a separate service, the *Regia Aeronautica*, was formed on 28th March. Interest in the aeroplane began to reawaken, encouraged by the work of theorists such as Giulio Douhet. In 1921 he published a book entitled *Il Dominio dell' Aria* which aroused worldwide interest. The aircraft industry, after virtually ceasing production for four years, was now asked to prepare itself to meet the military requirements of a new regime – 1922 being the year in which Mussolini was brought to power – while at the same time orders for civilian aircraft were on the increase. A revival began to take place. Italian aircraft began to be entered for international competitions and gained some records, for ocean and other long distance flights.

This growth in Italy's aviation was not confined to peacetime activities: there was some military action too. In the mid 1920s an insurrection had to be put down in Libya, one of Italy's possessions; and in 1935 Italy invaded Abyssinia. Then in the following year, 1936, the Spanish Civil War broke out, and Italy intervened on the fascist side.

It was looked on as a test for assessing the performance of the Italian air force's hardware, and with hindsight it is clear that Italy sadly misinterpreted the results of that test. This miscalculation led the Italian air force to be seriously unprepared for the Second World War. Experts concluded that the aircraft which had been so successful in Spain, including the Savoia-Marchetti S.M.79 and S.M.81 bombers, and the Fiat B.20 bomber and C.R.32 and G.50 fighters, would be capable of holding their own in another world conflict. As a result, production of some models was continued for too long, and thinking on manufacturing and operational techniques, which ought to have been discredited by a correct analysis of the Spanish experience, remained entrenched.

The Americans had fallen behind during the First World War, and now it was up to them to make up for lost time. Obvious unpreparedness had been revealed, when fighting alongside their allies, upon whose material and equipment they had been totally dependent. Industry responded fairly quickly, although there was some resistance to the reorganisation that had to be put into effect. After the end of the war, the Air Service, which had enjoyed a brief period of autonomy (from 20th May 1918) came back under direct command of the Army on 4th June 1920. In that year Congress cut funds and reduced the USAAS to 27 squadrons, instead of the 87 which had been planned. The strenuous protests of Gen William "Billy" Mitchell (who had commanded the air units of the AEF in the war) were in vain. He tried to convince the general staff that they should review their strategic thinking so as to give the air force a dominant role. The persistence of this high-ranking officer only led to his being courtmartialled and dismissed from the service.

The US Army Air Corps was formed on 2nd July 1926, and with it began a programme of re-equipment and an increase in personnel of 1,650 officers and 15,000 other ranks. This took place rather slowly, although the Army Air Corps did well in those years in competitive flying and air displays, participating alongside the navy.

The army and naval air services found themselves in a state of rivalry, which may have been based on feelings of resentment about the unequal status given to the two forces. The Naval Flying Corps, created on 1st July 1915, had managed to remain a more viable organisation than the USAAS, even after it had lost much of its strength in severe demobilisation cuts. Its ability to continue at a higher level of activity than the USAAS was due mainly to the formation of the Bureau of Aeronautics under the Department of the Navy. The bureau had charge of all naval aviation and had powers to co-ordinate its development with that of the fleet.

In contrast, the USAAC had to wait until 1st March 1935 for the creation of a parallel structure within the US Army. The effect of this, and of certain other obstacles in the political world, was that during the thirties, whilst there were very significant developments in civil aviation, military aviation received little encouragement and received equipment which was clearly unsuitable for the war which was by then drawing near. Production of military aircraft was markedly below capacity in this whole decade, with only 1,800 aircraft made in 1938 and 2,195 in the following year.

Two other nations achieved positions of importance as air powers between the two wars, Japan and the USSR. The former managed to do this unnoticed by the western world, and during the decade immediately preceding the war succeeded in establishing a really impressive military machine.

Development was gradual, and during its early phase Japan acquired a great deal of technical help from France, Britain and Germany. The results of this could be seen by the beginning of the 1930s, when her aircraft industry was firmly established and quite independent. Japanese aircraft emerged which were actually superior in many cases to those of contemporary western design; and the chief customers were the army and navy. This activity was greatly speeded up during the three years preceding Japan's entry into the war. Besides encouraging further production, the military orders enabled a streamlining to take place throughout the industry, making it very efficient, flexible and competitive, ready to work flat out to meet future needs. Production rose from the 445 planes built in 1930 to 952 in 1935, 1,181 in 1936, 1,511 in 1937, 3,201 in 1938 and 4,467 in 1939.

In the Soviet Union the aviation industry, like all the other industries, went through a great crisis from the year 1917, but reconstruction got under way and from 1924 a reorganised and effective aircraft industry grew up.

The strength of Soviet air forces in 1931 is estimated to have been about 1,000 aircraft. In 1935 this rose to 4,000, and included aircraft which were definitely as advanced as any produced elsewhere, such as the Polikarpov I-16 fighter and the Tupolev SB-2 bomber. In fact these aircraft were the best the USSR was able to build before the outbreak of war, and further advances were only to be made in the 1940s.

Plate 48

Scale view of selected interwar fighters

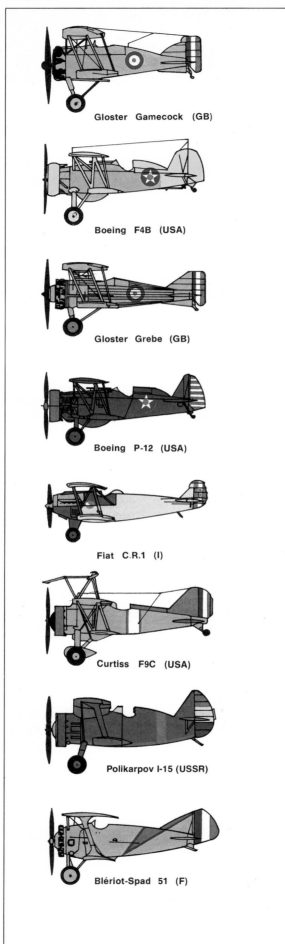

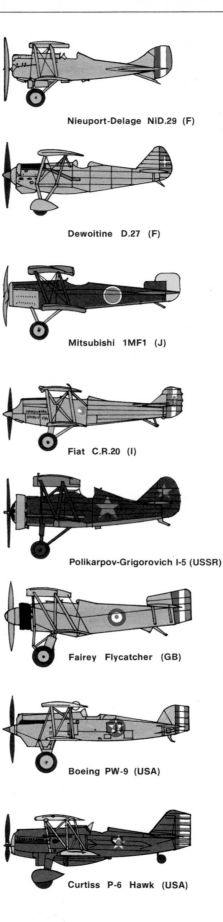

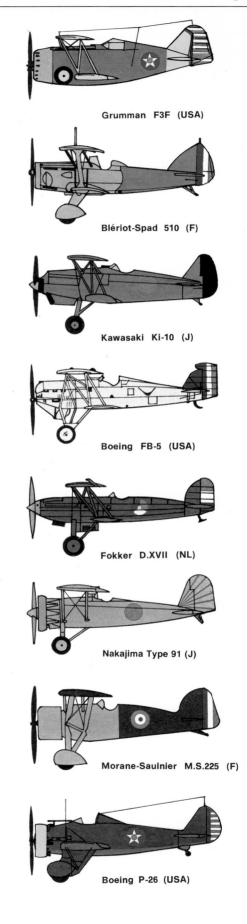

Gloster Gamecock (GB)

Nieuport-Delage NiD.29 (F)

Grumman F3F (USA)

Boeing F4B (USA)

Dewoitine D.27 (F)

Blériot-Spad 510 (F)

Gloster Grebe (GB)

Mitsubishi 1MF1 (J)

Kawasaki Ki-10 (J)

Boeing P-12 (USA)

Fiat C.R.20 (I)

Boeing FB-5 (USA)

Fiat C.R.1 (I)

Polikarpov-Grigorovich I-5 (USSR)

Fokker D.XVII (NL)

Curtiss F9C (USA)

Fairey Flycatcher (GB)

Nakajima Type 91 (J)

Polikarpov I-15 (USSR)

Boeing PW-9 (USA)

Morane-Saulnier M.S.225 (F)

Blériot-Spad 51 (F)

Curtiss P-6 Hawk (USA)

Boeing P-26 (USA)

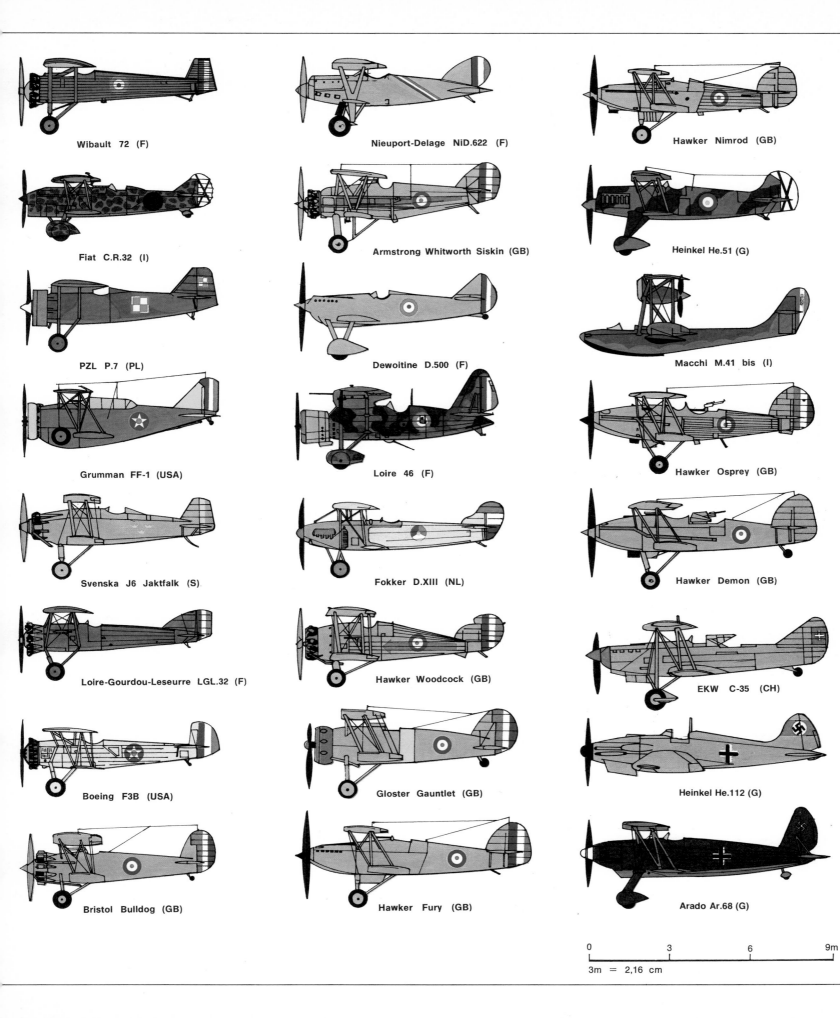

Wibault 72 (F)

Nieuport-Delage NiD.622 (F)

Hawker Nimrod (GB)

Fiat C.R.32 (I)

Armstrong Whitworth Siskin (GB)

Heinkel He.51 (G)

PZL P.7 (PL)

Dewoitine D.500 (F)

Macchi M.41 bis (I)

Grumman FF-1 (USA)

Loire 46 (F)

Hawker Osprey (GB)

Svenska J6 Jaktfalk (S)

Fokker D.XIII (NL)

Hawker Demon (GB)

Loire-Gourdou-Leseurre LGL.32 (F)

Hawker Woodcock (GB)

EKW C-35 (CH)

Boeing F3B (USA)

Gloster Gauntlet (GB)

Heinkel He.112 (G)

Bristol Bulldog (GB)

Hawker Fury (GB)

Arado Ar.68 (G)

0   3   6   9m

3m = 2,16 cm

Plate 49

Entry into service of the most important interwar fighters

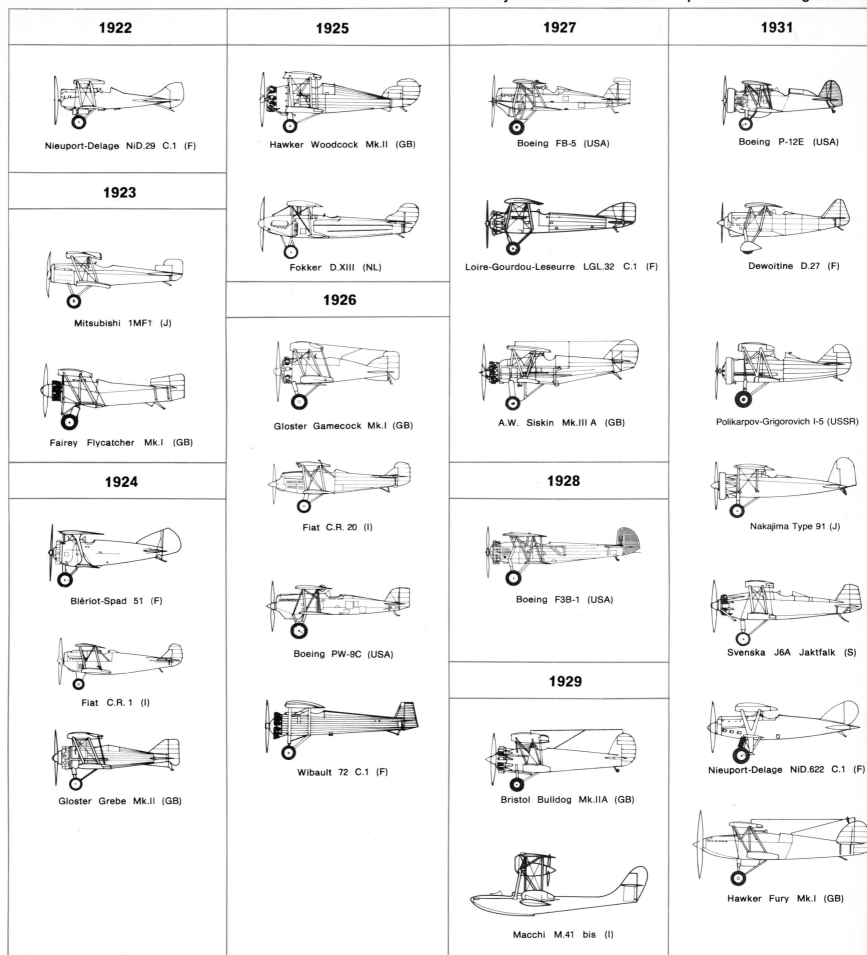

1922	1925	1927	1931

Nieuport-Delage NiD.29 C.1 (F)

Hawker Woodcock Mk.II (GB)

Boeing FB-5 (USA)

Boeing P-12E (USA)

1923

Mitsubishi 1MF1 (J)

Fokker D.XIII (NL)

Loire-Gourdou-Leseurre LGL.32 C.1 (F)

Dewoitine D.27 (F)

1926

Fairey Flycatcher Mk.I (GB)

Gloster Gamecock Mk.I (GB)

A.W. Siskin Mk.III A (GB)

Polikarpov-Grigorovich I-5 (USSR)

1924

Blériot-Spad 51 (F)

Fiat C.R. 20 (I)

1928

Nakajima Type 91 (J)

Fiat C.R. 1 (I)

Boeing PW-9C (USA)

Boeing F3B-1 (USA)

Svenska J6A Jaktfalk (S)

1929

Gloster Grebe Mk.II (GB)

Wibault 72 C.1 (F)

Bristol Bulldog Mk.IIA (GB)

Nieuport-Delage NiD.622 C.1 (F)

Macchi M.41 bis (I)

Hawker Fury Mk.I (GB)

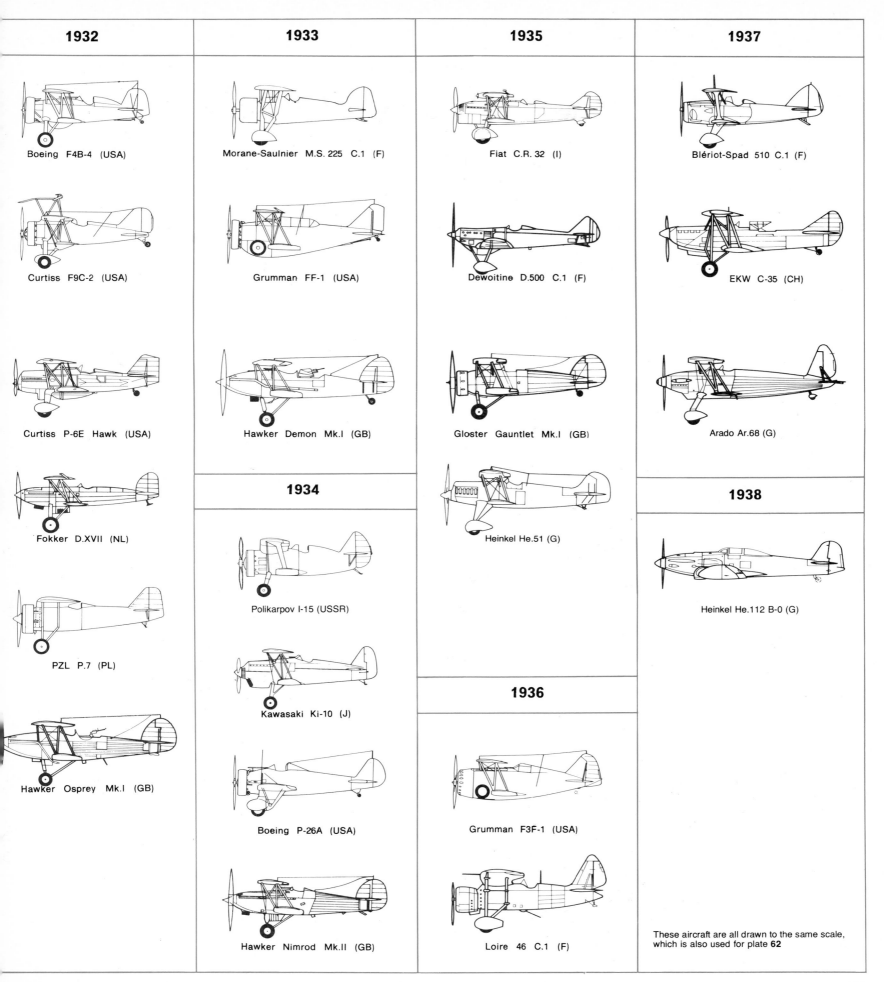

1932

Boeing F4B-4 (USA)

Curtiss F9C-2 (USA)

Curtiss P-6E Hawk (USA)

Fokker D.XVII (NL)

PZL P.7 (PL)

Hawker Osprey Mk.I (GB)

1933

Morane-Saulnier M.S. 225 C.1 (F)

Grumman FF-1 (USA)

Hawker Demon Mk.I (GB)

1934

Polikarpov I-15 (USSR)

Kawasaki Ki-10 (J)

Boeing P-26A (USA)

Hawker Nimrod Mk.II (GB)

1935

Fiat C.R. 32 (I)

Dewoitine D.500 C.1 (F)

Gloster Gauntlet Mk.I (GB)

Heinkel He.51 (G)

1936

Grumman F3F-1 (USA)

Loire 46 C.1 (F)

1937

Blériot-Spad 510 C.1 (F)

EKW C-35 (CH)

Arado Ar.68 (G)

1938

Heinkel He.112 B-0 (G)

These aircraft are all drawn to the same scale, which is also used for plate **62**

115

BLÉRIOT-SPAD 51
Nation: France; *manufacturer:* Blériot Aéronautique; *type:* fighter;
year: 1924; *engine:* Gnome-Rhône Jupiter 9-cylinder air-cooled
radial, 380 hp; *wingspan:* 31 ft 1 in (9.47 m); *length:* 21 ft 2 in
(6.45 m); *height:* 10 ft 2 in (3.10 m); *weight:* 3,595 lb (1,631 kg);
maximum speed: 143 mph (231 km/h) at 16,400 ft (5,000 m); *ceiling:* 29,530 ft (9,000 m); *endurance:* – ; *armament:* 2 machine
guns; *crew:* 1

NIEUPORT-DELAGE NiD 29 C1
Nation: France; *manufacturer:* Société Anonyme des Etablissements Nieuport; *type:* fighter; *year:* 1922; *engine:* Hispano-Suiza
8FB 8-cylinder liquid-cooled V, 300 hp; *wingspan:* 31 ft 10 in
(9.70 m); *length:* 21 ft 4 in (6.50 m); *height:* 8 ft 2 in (2.50 m);
weight: 2,628 lb (1,192 kg); *maximum speed:* 132 mph (213 km/h)
at 13,120 ft (4,000 m); *ceiling:* 25,260 ft (7,700 m); *range:* 360
miles (580 km); *armament:* 2 machine guns; *crew:* 1

LOIRE-GOURDOU-LESEURRE LGL 32 C 1
Nation: France; *manufacturer:* Loire-Gourdou-Leseurre; *type:* fighter; *year:* 1927;
engine: Gnome-Rhône Jupiter 9Ac 9 cylinder air-cooled radial, 420 hp; *wingspan:* 40 ft
(12.20 m); *length:* 24 ft 9 in (7.55 m); *height:* 9 ft 1 in (2.95 m); *weight:* 3,033 lb
(1,376 kg); *maximum speed:* 147 mph (237 km/h) at 16,400 ft (5,000 m); *ceiling:*
28,700 ft (8,750 m); *range:* 310 miles (500 km); *armament:* 4 machine guns; *crew:* 1

WIBAULT 72 C 1
Nation: France; *manufacturer:* Chantiers Aéronautiques Wibault;
type: fighter; *year:* 1926; *engine:* Gnome-Rhône Jupiter 9Ac
9-cylinder air-cooled radial, 420 hp; *wingspan:* 35 ft 11 in
(10.95 m); *length:* 24 ft 5 in (7.45 m); *height:* 9 ft 8 in (2.96 m);
weight: 3,183 lb (1,444 kg); *maximum speed:* 141 mph (227 km/h)
at 16,400 ft (5,000 m); *ceiling:* 26,575 ft (8,100 m); *range:* 373
miles (600 km); *armament:* 2 machine guns; *crew:* 1

POTEZ 25 A 2
Nation: France; *manufacturer:* Société des Aéroplanes H. Potez; *type:* reconnaissance;
year: 1925; *engine:* Lorraine-Dietrich 12-cylinder at V liquid-cooled, 450 hp; *wingspan:*
46 ft 7 in (14.19 m); *length:* 30 ft 2 in (9.19 m); *height:* 11 ft 11 in (3.65 m); *weight:*
4,316 lb (1,958 kg); *maximum speed:* 137 mph (220 km/h); *ceiling:* 23,620 ft
(7,200 m); *range:* 410 miles (660 km); *armament:* 2 machine guns; 600 lb (272 kg) of
bombs; *crew:* 2

NIEUPORT-DELAGE NiD 622 C 1
Nation: France; *manufacturer:* Société Anonyme des Etablissements Nieuport; *type:* fighter; *year:* 1931; *engine:* Hispano-Suiza
12Md 12-cylinder at V liquid-cooled, 500 hp; *wingspan:* 39 ft 5 in
(12.00 m); *length:* 25 ft (7.63 m); *height:* 9 ft 10 in (3.00 m); *weight:*
4,052 lb (1,838 kg); *maximum speed:* 154 mph (248 km/h) at
16,400 ft (5,000 m); *ceiling:* 25,260 ft (7,700 m); *range:* 404 miles
(650 km); *armament:* 2 machine guns; *crew:* 1

◀ DEWOITINE D 27
Nation: France; *manufacturer:* EKW; *type:* fighter; *year:* 1931; *engine:* Hispano-Suiza 12Mc 12-cylinder at V liquid-cooled, 500 hp; *wingspan:* 32 ft 2 in (9.80 m); *length:* 21 ft 4 in (6.50 m); *height:* 9 ft 2 in (2.79 m); *weight:* 3,046 lb (1,382 kg); *maximum speed:* 194 mph (312 km/h); *ceiling:* 30,185 ft (9,200 m); *range:* 373 miles (600 km); *armament:* 2 machine guns; *crew:* 1

MORANE-SAULNIER MS 225 C 1
Nation: France; *manufacturer:* Morane-Saulnier; *type:* fighter; *year:* 1933; *engine:* Gnome-Rhône 9Kbrs 9-cylinder air-cooled radial, 440 hp; *wingspan:* 34 ft 5 in (10.56 m); *length:* 23 ft 6 in (7.24 m); *height:* 10 ft 8 in (3.30 m); *weight:* 3,484 lb (1,581 kg); *maximum speed:* 207 mph (333 km/h) at 13,120 ft (4,000 m); *ceiling:* 32,810 ft (10,000 m); *range:* 435 miles (700 km); *armament:* 2 machine guns; *crew:* 1 ▶

◀ DEWOITINE D 500 C 1
Nation: France; *manufacturer:* Société Aéronautique Française; *type:* fighter; *year:* 1935; *engine:* Hispano-Suiza 12Kbrs 12-cylinder at V liquid-cooled, 690 hp; *wingspan:* 39 ft 8 in (12.00 m); *length:* 25 ft 5 in (7.74 m); *height:* 11 ft 11 in (3.63 m); *weight:* 3,770 lb (1,710 kg); *maximum speed:* 223 mph (359 km/h) at 13,120 ft (4,000 m); *ceiling:* 36,090 ft (11,000 m); *range:* 535 miles (860 km); *armament:* 4 machine guns; *crew:* 1

BLÉRIOT-SPAD 510 C 1 ▶
Nation: France; *manufacturer:* Blériot Aéronautique; *type:* fighter; *year:* 1937; *engine:* Hispano-Suiza 12Xbrs 12-cylinder at V liquid-cooled, 690 hp; *wingspan:* 29 ft (8.84 m); *length:* 23 ft 4 in (7.10 m); *height:* 11 ft 2 in (3.41 m); *weight:* 3,957 lb (1,795 kg); *maximum speed:* 231 mph (372 km/h) at 9,840 ft (3,000 m); *ceiling:* 32,645 ft (9,950 m); *range:* 435 miles (700 km); *armament:* 4 machine guns; *crew:* 1

◀ LOIRE 46 C1
Nation: France; *manufacturer:* SNCAO; *type:* fighter; *year:* 1936; *engine:* Gnome-Rhône 14KFS 14-cylinder air-cooled radial, 930 hp; *wingspan:* 38 ft 9 in (11.80 m); *length:* 25 ft 6 in (7.76 m); *height:* 13 ft 9 in (4.18 m); *weight:* 4,376 lb (1,985 kg); *maximum speed:* 255 mph (410 km/h) at 13,120 ft (4,000 m); *ceiling:* 34,450 ft (10,500 m); *range:* 465 miles (750 km); *armament:* 4 machine guns; *crew:* 1

Plate 52

British fighters of the twenties: 1924–29

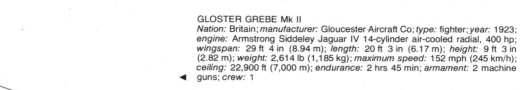

GLOSTER GREBE Mk II
Nation: Britain; *manufacturer:* Gloucester Aircraft Co; *type:* fighter; *year:* 1923; *engine:* Armstrong Siddeley Jaguar IV 14-cylinder air-cooled radial, 400 hp; *wingspan:* 29 ft 4 in (8.94 m); *length:* 20 ft 3 in (6.17 m); *height:* 9 ft 3 in (2.82 m); *weight:* 2,614 lb (1,185 kg); *maximum speed:* 152 mph (245 km/h); *ceiling:* 22,900 ft (7,000 m); *endurance:* 2 hrs 45 min; *armament:* 2 machine guns; *crew:* 1

HAWKER WOODCOCK Mk II
Nation: Britain; *manufacturer:* H. G. Hawker Engineering Co; *type:* fighter; *year:* 1925; *engine:* Bristol Jupiter IV 9-cylinder air-cooled radial, 420 hp; *wingspan:* 32 ft 6 in (9.91 m); *length:* 26 ft 2 in (7.98 m); *height:* 9 ft 11 in (3.02 m); *weight:* 2,979 lb (1,351 kg); *maximum speed:* 138 mph (220 km/h); *ceiling:* 20,000 ft (6,100 m); *range:* 270 miles (435 km); *armament:* 2 machine guns; *crew:* 1

ARMSTRONG WHITWORTH SISKIN Mk III A
Nation: Britain; *manufacturer:* Armstrong Whitworth Aircraft Ltd; *type:* fighter; *year:* 1927; *engine:* Armstrong Siddeley Jaguar IV 14-cylinder air-cooled radial, 425 hp; *wingspan:* 33 ft 2 in (10.11 m); *length:* 25 ft 4 in (7.72 m); *height:* 10 ft 2 in (3.10 m); *weight:* 3,012 lb (1,366 kg); *maximum speed:* 156 mph (251 km/h); *ceiling:* 27,000 ft (8,230 m); *range:* 280 miles (450 km); *armament:* 2 machine guns; *crew:* 1

GLOSTER GAMECOCK Mk I
Nation: Britain; *manufacturer:* Gloucestershire Aircraft Co; *type:* fighter; *year:* 1925; *engine:* Bristol Jupiter VI 9-cylinder air-cooled radial, 425 hp; *wingspan:* 29 ft 9 in (9.08 m); *length:* 19 ft 8 in (5.99 m); *height:* 9 ft 8 in (2.94 m); *weight:* 2,863 lb (1,299 kg); *maximum speed:* 155 mph (250 km/h) at 5,000 ft (1,500 m); *ceiling:* 22,000 ft (6,700 m); *range:* 365 miles (587 km); *armament:* 2 machine guns; *crew:* 1

BRISTOL BULLDOG Mk IIA
Nation: Britain; *manufacturer:* Bristol Aeroplane Co; *type:* fighter; *year:* 1929; *engine:* Bristol Jupiter VII F 9-cylinder air-cooled radial, 490 hp; *wingspan:* 33 ft 11 in (10.33 m); *length:* 25 ft 2 in (7.67 m); *height:* 9 ft 10 in (2.99 m); *weight:* 3,503 lb (1,589 kg); *maximum speed:* 174 mph (280 km/h) at 10,000 ft (3,000 m); *ceiling:* 27,000 ft (8,200 m); *endurance:* – ; *armament:* 2 machine guns; 80 lb (35 kg) of bombs; *crew:* 1

HAWKER FURY I
Nation: Britain; *manufacturer:* Hawker Aircraft Ltd;
type: fighter; *year:* 1931; *engine:* Rolls-Royce Kestrel IIS 12-cylinder liquid-cooled V, 525 hp; *wingspan:* 30 ft (9.14 m); *length:* 26 ft 8 in (8.12 m);
height: 10 ft 2 in (3.09 m); *weight:* 3,490 lb
(1,580 kg); *maximum speed:* 207 mph (333 km/h)
at 14,000 ft (4,200 m); *ceiling:* 28,000 ft (8,500 m);
range: 305 miles (490 km); *armament:* 2 machine
guns; *crew:* 1

HAWKER DEMON
Nation: Britain; *manufacturer:* Hawker Aircraft Ltd;
type: fighter; *year:* 1931; *engine:* Rolls-Royce Kestrel V 12-cylinder liquid-cooled V, 584 hp; *wingspan:* 37 ft 3 in (11.35 m); *length:* 29 ft 7 in
(9.01 m); *height:* 10 ft 5 in (3.17 m); *weight:*
4,464 lb (2,025 kg); *maximum speed:* 182 mph
(293 km/h) at 16,400 ft (5,000 m); *ceiling:* 27,500 ft
(8,300 m); *endurance:* 2 hrs 30 min; *armament:* 3
machine guns; *crew:* 2

GLOSTER GAUNTLET Mk 1
Nation: Britain; *manufacturer:* Gloster Aircraft Co;
type: fighter; *year:* 1935; *engine:* Bristol Mercury VI
S2 9-cylinder air-cooled radial, 645 hp; *wingspan:*
32 ft 9 in (9.99 m); *length:* 26 ft 2 in (8.05 m);
height: 10 ft 4 in (3.12 m); *weight:* 3,970 lb
(1,801 kg); *maximum speed:* 230 mph (370 km/h)
at 15,800 ft (4,825 m); *ceiling:* 33,500 ft
(10,210 m); *range:* 460 miles (740 km); *armament:*
2 machine guns; *crew:* 1

Plate 54   **Fighters of the United States Army Air Corps: 1926–34**

BOEING PW-9C
Nation: USA; *manufacturer:* Boeing Airplane Co; *type:* fighter; *year:* 1926; *engine:* Curtiss D-12D 12-cylinder at V liquid-cooled, 435 hp; *wingspan:* 32 ft (9.75 m); *length:* 23 ft 1 in (7.04 m); *height:* 8 ft 8 in (2.64 m); *weight:* 3,170 lb (1,438 kg); *maximum speed:* 165 mph (265 km/h); *ceiling:* 20,175 ft (6,150 m); *endurance:* 2 hrs 35 min; *armament:* 2 machine guns; *crew:* 1

CURTISS P-6E Hawk
Nation: USA; *manufacturer:* Curtiss Aeroplane and Motor Co; *type:* fighter; *year:* 1932; *engine:* Curtiss V-1750-23, 12-cylinder at V liquid-cooled, 700 hp; *wingspan:* 31 ft 6 in (9.60 m); *length:* 23 ft 2 in (7.06 m); *height:* 8 ft 10 in (2.72 m); *weight:* 3,392 lb (1,538 kg); *maximum speed:* 198 mph (319 km/h); *ceiling:* 24,700 ft (7,530 m); *range:* 285 miles (460 km); *armament:* 2 machine guns; *crew:* 1

BOEING P-12E
Nation: USA; *manufacturer:* Boeing Airplane Co; *type:* fighter; *year:* 1931; *engine:* Pratt & Whitney Wasp 9-cylinder radial air-cooled, 500 hp; *wingspan:* 30 ft (9.14 m); *length:* 20 ft 3 in (6.17 m); *height:* 9 ft (2.74 m); *weight:* 2,690 lb (1,220 kg); *maximum speed:* 189 mph (304 km/h) at 7,000 ft (2,135 m); *ceiling:* 26,300 ft (8,020 m); *range:* 585 miles (941 km); *armament:* 2 machine guns; *crew:* 1

BOEING P-26A
Nation: USA; *manufacturer:* Boeing Airplane Co; *type:* fighter; *year:* 1934; *engine:* Pratt and Whitney Wasp 9-cylinder radial air-cooled, 600 hp; *wingspan:* 27 ft 11 in (8.52 m); *length:* 23 ft 7 in (7.18 m); *height:* 10 ft (3.05 m); *weight:* 2,955 lb (1,340 kg); *maximum speed:* 234 mph (377 km/h) at 7,500 ft (2,300 m); *ceiling:* 27,400 ft (8,300 m); *range:* 620 miles (1,000 km); *armament:* 2 machine guns; 110 lb (50 kg) of bombs; *crew:* 1

BOEING F3B-1
Nation: USA; *manufacturer:* Boeing Airplane Co;
type: fighter; *year:* 1928; *engine:* Pratt & Whitney
Wasp 9-cylinder radial air-cooled, 415 hp; *wing-span:* 33 ft (10.06 m); *length:* 24 ft 10 in (7.57 m);
height: 9 ft 2 in (2.79 m); *weight:* 2,945 lb
(1,336 kg); *maximum speed:* 157 mph (253 km/h);
ceiling: 21,500 ft (6,550 m); *range:* 340 miles
(547 km); *armament:* 2 machine guns; *crew:* 1

CURTISS F9C-2
Nation: USA; *manufacturer:* Curtiss Aeroplane and
Motor Co; *type:* fighter; *year:* 1932; *engine:* Wright
Whirlwind 9-cylinder radial air-cooled, 420 hp;
wingspan: 25 ft 6 in (7.77 m); *length:* 20 ft 1 in
(2.16 m); *height:* 7 ft 1 in (2.16 m); *weight:* 2,752 lb
(1,248 kg); *maximum speed:* 177 mph (284 km/h)
at 4,000 ft (1,220 m); *ceiling:* 19,200 ft (5,800 m);
range: 360 miles (590 km); *armament:* 2 machine
guns; *crew:* 1

BOEING F4B-4
Nation: USA; *manufacturer:* Boeing Airplane Co;
type: fighter; *year:* 1932; *engine:* Pratt & Whitney
9-cylinder radial air-cooled, 550 hp; *wingspan:*
30 ft (9.14 m); *length:* 20 ft 1 in (6.12 m); *height:* 9 ft
4 in (2.84 m); *weight:* 3,611 lb (1,637 kg); *maxi-mum speed:* 188 mph (302 km/h) at 6,000 ft
(1,800 m); *ceiling:* 26,900 ft (8,200 m); *range:* 585
miles (940 km); *armament:* 2 machine guns;
crew: 1

BOEING FB-5
Nation: USA; *manufacturer:* Boeing
Airplane Co; *type:* fighter; *year:* 1927;
engine: Packard 2A-1500 12-cylinder
at V liquid-cooled, 520 hp; *wingspan:*
32 ft (9.75 m); *length:* 23 ft 5 in
(7.14 m); *height:* 8 ft 2 in (2.49 m);
weight: 2,835 lb (1,286 kg); *maximum
speed:* 159 mph (256 km/h); *ceiling:*
18,925 ft (5,770 m); *range:* 390 miles
(628 km); *armament:* 2 machine guns;
crew: 1

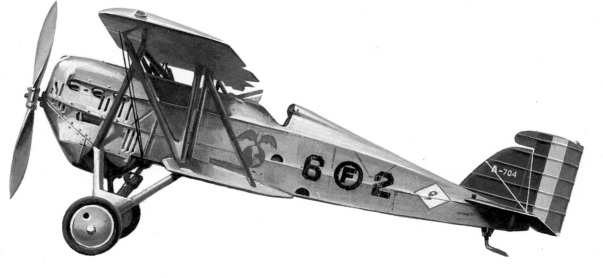

Plate 56

Fighters of the US Navy and the Royal Navy: 1923–36

FAIREY FLYCATCHER Mk 1
Nation: Britain; *manufacturer:* Fairey Aviation Ltd; *type:* fighter (landplane); *year:* 1923; *engine:* Armstrong Siddeley Jaguar III, 14-cylinder radial, air-cooled, 400 hp; *wingspan:* 29 ft (8.84 m); *length:* 23 ft (7.01 m); *height:* 12 ft (3.65 m); *weight:* 3,028 lb (1,373 kg); *maximum speed:* 134 mph (215 km/h) at 5,000 ft (1,500 m); *ceiling:* 20,600 ft (6,200 m); *range:* 260 miles (420 km); *armament:* 2 machine guns; 80 lb (36 kg) of bombs; *crew:* 1

HAWKER OSPREY Mk 1
Nation: Britain; *manufacturer:* Hawker Aircraft Ltd; *type:* fighter; *year:* 1932; *engine:* Rolls-Royce Kestrel II MS 12-cylinder at V liquid-cooled, 630 hp; *wingspan:* 37 ft (11.28 m); *length:* 29 ft 4 in (8.94 m); *height:* 10 ft 5 in (3.17 m); *weight:* 4,950 lb (2,245 kg); *maximum speed:* 168 mph (270 km/h) at 5,000 ft (1,525 m); *ceiling:* 23,500 ft (7,160 m); *endurance:* – ; *armament:* 2 machine guns; *crew:* 2

HAWKER NIMROD Mk II
Nation: Britain; *manufacturer:* Hawker Aircraft Ltd; *type:* fighter; *year:* 1935; *engine:* Rolls-Royce Kestrel IIS 12-cylinder at V liquid-cooled, 590 hp; *wingspan:* 33 ft 6 in (10.21 m); *length:* 27 ft (8.23 m); *height:* 9 ft 9 in (2.97 m); *weight:* 4,258 lb (1,944 kg); *maximum speed:* 195 mph (314 km/h) at 14,000 ft (4,265 m); *ceiling:* 26,000 ft (7,925 m); *endurance:* 2 hrs 5 min; *armament:* 2 machine guns; 80 lb (36 kg) of bombs; *crew:* 1

GRUMMAN FF-1
Nation: USA; *manufacturer:* Grumman Engineering Co; *type:* fighter; *year:* 1933; *engine:* Wright Cyclone 9-cylinder radial air-cooled, 700 hp; *wingspan:* 34 ft 6 in (10.51 m); *length:* 24 ft 6 in (7.46 m); *height:* 11 ft 1 in (3.63 m); *weight:* 4,830 lb (2,190 kg); *maximum speed:* 207 mph (333 km/h) at 4,000 ft (1,220 m); *ceiling:* 21,000 ft (6,400 m); *range:* 920 miles (1,480 km); *armament:* 3 machine guns; *crew:* 2

GRUMMAN F3F-1
Nation: USA; *manufacturer:* Grumman Aircraft Engineering Co; *type:* fighter; *year:* 1935; *engine:* Pratt & Whitney Twin Wasp Jr 14-cylinder radial air-cooled, 700 hp; *wingspan:* 32 ft (9.75 m); *length:* 23 ft 3 in (7.08 m); *height:* 9 ft 4 in (2.84 m); *weight:* 4,121 lb (1,869 kg); *maximum speed:* 231 mph (372 km/h); *ceiling:* 28,500 ft (8,600 m); *range:* 530 miles (850 km); *armament:* 2 machine guns; 110 lb (50 kg) of bombs; *crew:* 1

◀ MITSUBISHI 1MF1
Nation: Japan; *manufacturer:* Mitsubishi Jukogyo KK; *type:* fighter; *year:* 1923; *engine:* Hispano-Mitsubishi 8-cylinder V liquid-cooled, 300 hp; *wingspan:* 30 ft 6 in (9.30 m); *length:* 22 ft (6.71 m); *height:* 9 ft 8 in (2.95 m); *weight:* 2,510 lb (1,140 kg); *maximum speed:* 147 mph (237 km/h) at 6,500 ft (2,000 m); *ceiling:* 23,000 ft (7,000 m); *endurance:* 2 hrs 30 min; *armament:* 2 machine guns; *crew:* 1

NAKAJIMA ARMY TYPE 91
Nation: Japan; *manufacturer:* Nakajima Hikoki KK; *type:* fighter; *year:* 1931; *engine:* Bristol Jupiter-Nakajima 9-cylinder radial air-cooled, 500 hp; *wingspan:* 36 ft 1 in (10.99 m); *length:* 23 ft 10 in (7.26 m); *height:* 9 ft 2 in (2.79 m); *weight:* 3,370 lb (1,530 kg); *maximum speed:* 186 mph (299 km/h) at 6,500 ft (2,000 m); *ceiling:* 29,500 ft (9,000 m); *range:* 370 miles (600 km); *armament:* 2 machine guns; *crew:* 1 ▶

KAWASAKI Ki-10
Nation: Japan; *manufacturer:* Kawasaki KK; *type:* fighter; *year:* 1935; *engine:* Kawasaki Ha9 IIa 12-cylinder V liquid-cooled, 850 hp; *wingspan:* 31 ft 4 in (9.55 m); *length:* 23 ft 7 in (7.20 m); *height:* 9 ft 10 in (3.00 m); *weight:* 3,640 lb (1,650 kg); *maximum speed:* 250 mph (400 km/h) at 9,800 ft (3,000 m); *ceiling:* 32,800 ft (10,000 m); *range:* 680 miles (1,100 m); ◀ *armament:* 2 machine guns; *crew:* 1

POLIKARPOV-GRIGOROVICH I-5
Nation: USSR; *manufacturer:* State Industries; *type:* fighter; *year:* 1931; *engine:* M22 9-cylinder radial air-cooled, 480 hp; *wingspan:* 33 ft 7 in (10.24 m); *length:* 22 ft 3 in (6.78 m); *height:* 9 ft 9 in (2.98 m); *weight:* 2,767 lb (1,355 kg); *maximum speed:* 173 mph (278 km/h); *ceiling:* 23,950 ft (7,300 m); *range:* 410 miles (660 km); *armament:* 2 machine guns; *crew:* 1 ▶

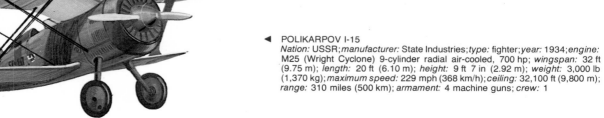

◀ POLIKARPOV I-15
Nation: USSR; *manufacturer:* State Industries; *type:* fighter; *year:* 1934; *engine:* M25 (Wright Cyclone) 9-cylinder radial air-cooled, 700 hp; *wingspan:* 32 ft (9.75 m); *length:* 20 ft (6.10 m); *height:* 9 ft 7 in (2.92 m); *weight:* 3,000 lb (1,370 kg); *maximum speed:* 229 mph (368 km/h); *ceiling:* 32,100 ft (9,800 m); *range:* 310 miles (500 km); *armament:* 4 machine guns; *crew:* 1

Plate 58

Italian fighters: 1924–35

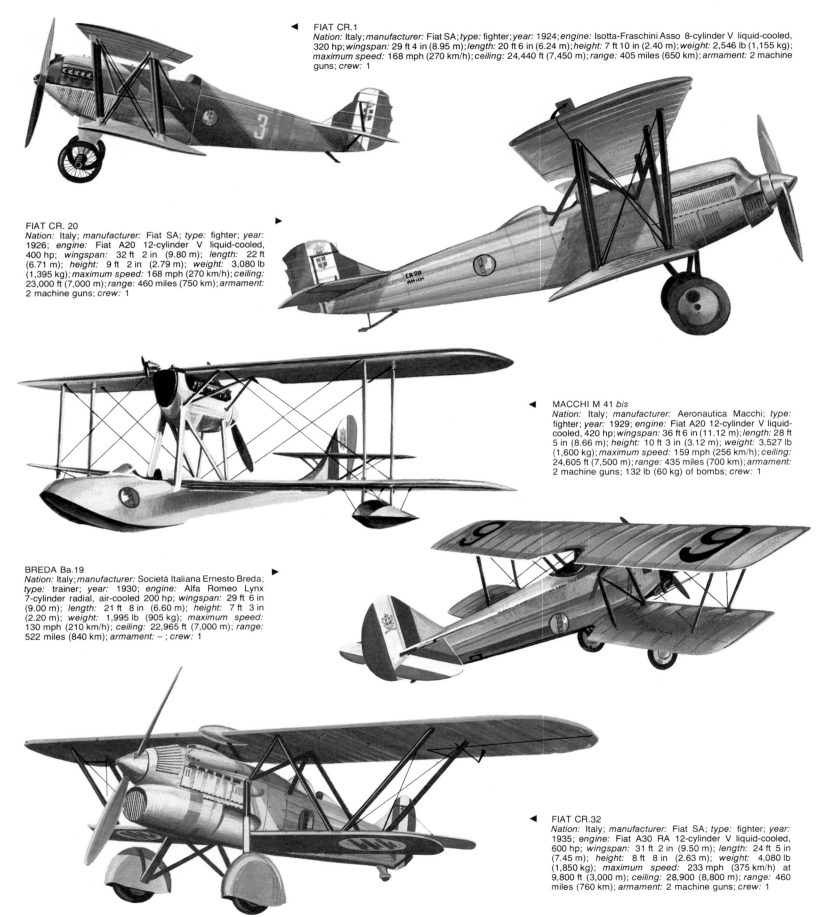

◄ FIAT CR.1
Nation: Italy; *manufacturer:* Fiat SA; *type:* fighter; *year:* 1924; *engine:* Isotta-Fraschini Asso 8-cylinder V liquid-cooled, 320 hp; *wingspan:* 29 ft 4 in (8.95 m); *length:* 20 ft 6 in (6.24 m); *height:* 7 ft 10 in (2.40 m); *weight:* 2,546 lb (1,155 kg); *maximum speed:* 168 mph (270 km/h); *ceiling:* 24,440 ft (7,450 m); *range:* 405 miles (650 km); *armament:* 2 machine guns; *crew:* 1

FIAT CR. 20 ▶
Nation: Italy; *manufacturer:* Fiat SA; *type:* fighter; *year:* 1926; *engine:* Fiat A20 12-cylinder V liquid-cooled, 400 hp; *wingspan:* 32 ft 2 in (9.80 m); *length:* 22 ft (6.71 m); *height:* 9 ft 2 in (2.79 m); *weight:* 3,080 lb (1,395 kg); *maximum speed:* 168 mph (270 km/h); *ceiling:* 23,000 ft (7,000 m); *range:* 460 miles (750 km); *armament:* 2 machine guns; *crew:* 1

◄ MACCHI M 41 *bis*
Nation: Italy; *manufacturer:* Aeronautica Macchi; *type:* fighter; *year:* 1929; *engine:* Fiat A20 12-cylinder V liquid-cooled, 420 hp; *wingspan:* 36 ft 6 in (11.12 m); *length:* 28 ft 5 in (8.66 m); *height:* 10 ft 3 in (3.12 m); *weight:* 3,527 lb (1,600 kg); *maximum speed:* 159 mph (256 km/h); *ceiling:* 24,605 ft (7,500 m); *range:* 435 miles (700 km); *armament:* 2 machine guns; 132 lb (60 kg) of bombs; *crew:* 1

BREDA Ba.19 ▶
Nation: Italy; *manufacturer:* Società Italiana Ernesto Breda; *type:* trainer; *year:* 1930; *engine:* Alfa Romeo Lynx 7-cylinder radial, air-cooled 200 hp; *wingspan:* 29 ft 6 in (9.00 m); *length:* 21 ft 8 in (6.60 m); *height:* 7 ft 3 in (2.20 m); *weight:* 1,995 lb (905 kg); *maximum speed:* 130 mph (210 km/h); *ceiling:* 22,965 ft (7,000 m); *range:* 522 miles (840 km); *armament:* – ; *crew:* 1

◄ FIAT CR.32
Nation: Italy; *manufacturer:* Fiat SA; *type:* fighter; *year:* 1935; *engine:* Fiat A30 RA 12-cylinder V liquid-cooled, 600 hp; *wingspan:* 31 ft 2 in (9.50 m); *length:* 24 ft 5 in (7.45 m); *height:* 8 ft 8 in (2.63 m); *weight:* 4,080 lb (1,850 kg); *maximum speed:* 233 mph (375 km/h) at 9,800 ft (3,000 m); *ceiling:* 28,900 (8,800 m); *range:* 460 miles (760 km); *armament:* 2 machine guns; *crew:* 1

◄ HEINKEL He.51
Nation: Germany; *manufacturer:* Ernst Heinkel AG; *type:* fighter; *year:* 1934; *engine:* BMW VI, 12-cylinder V, liquid-cooled 750 hp; *wingspan:* 36 ft 1 in (10.99 m); *length:* 27 ft 6 in (8.38 m); *height:* 10 ft 6 in (3.20 m); *weight:* 4,200 lb (1,900 kg); *maximum speed:* 205 mph (330 km/h); *ceiling:* 25,200 ft (7,700 m); *range:* 350 miles (570 km); *armament:* 2 machine guns; *crew:* 1

ARADO Ar 68 E-1 ►
Nation: Germany; *manufacturer:* Arado Flugzeugwerke GmbH; *type:* fighter; *year:* 1937; *engine:* Junkers Jumo 219 Ea 12-cylinder V liquid-cooled, 680 hp; *wingspan:* 36 ft 1 in (11.00 m); *length:* 31 ft 2 in (9.50 m); *height:* 10 ft 10 in (3.30 m); *weight:* 4,453 lb (2,020 kg); *maximum speed:* 208 mph (335 km/h) at 8,695 ft (2,650 m); *ceiling:* 26,575 ft (8,100 m); *range:* 310 miles (500 km); *armament:* 2 machine guns; *crew:* 1

◄ FOCKE WULF Fw.56 A-1
Nation: Germany; *manufacturer:* Focke Wulf Flugzeugbau GmbH; *type:* trainer; *year:* 1936; *engine:* Argus As10G 8-cylinder V air-cooled, 240 hp; *wingspan:* 34 ft 7 in (10.54 m); *length:* 25 ft 1 in (7.65 m); *height:* 8 ft 4 in (2.54 m); *weight:* 2,172 lb (985 kg); *maximum speed:* 166 mph (267 km/h); *ceiling:* 20,340 ft (6,200 m); *range:* 230 miles (370 km); *armament:* 2 machine guns; 66 lb (30 kg) of bombs; *crew:* 1

HEINKEL He.112 B-0 ►
Nation: Germany; *manufacturer:* Ernst Heinkel AG; *type:* fighter; *year:* 1938; *engine:* Junkers Jumo 210 Ea 12-cylinder V liquid-cooled, 680 hp; *wingspan:* 29 ft 10 in (9.10 m); *length:* 30 ft 6 in (9.30 m); *height:* 12 ft 7 in (3.84 m); *weight:* 4,960 lb (2,250 kg); *maximum speed:* 317 mph (510 km/h) at 15,420 ft (4,700 m); *ceiling:* 27,890 ft (8,500 m); *range:* 683 miles (1,100 km); *armament:* 4 machine guns; 132 lb (60 kg) of bombs; *crew:* 1

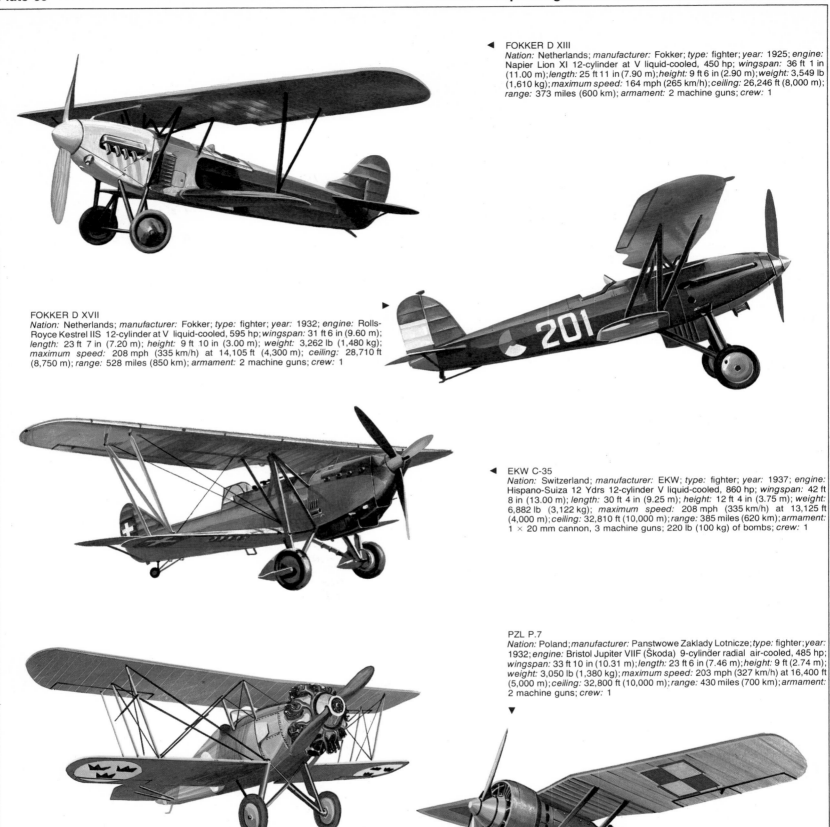

◀ **FOKKER D XIII**
Nation: Netherlands; *manufacturer:* Fokker; *type:* fighter; *year:* 1925; *engine:*
Napier Lion XI 12-cylinder at V liquid-cooled, 450 hp; *wingspan:* 36 ft 1 in
(11.00 m); *length:* 25 ft 11 in (7.90 m); *height:* 9 ft 6 in (2.90 m); *weight:* 3,549 lb
(1,610 kg); *maximum speed:* 164 mph (265 km/h); *ceiling:* 26,246 ft (8,000 m);
range: 373 miles (600 km); *armament:* 2 machine guns; *crew:* 1

FOKKER D XVII
Nation: Netherlands; *manufacturer:* Fokker; *type:* fighter; *year:* 1932; *engine:* Rolls-
Royce Kestrel IIS 12-cylinder at V liquid-cooled, 595 hp; *wingspan:* 31 ft 6 in (9.60 m);
length: 23 ft 7 in (7.20 m); *height:* 9 ft 10 in (3.00 m); *weight:* 3,262 lb (1,480 kg);
maximum speed: 208 mph (335 km/h) at 14,105 ft (4,300 m); *ceiling:* 28,710 ft
(8,750 m); *range:* 528 miles (850 km); *armament:* 2 machine guns; *crew:* 1

◀ **EKW C-35**
Nation: Switzerland; *manufacturer:* EKW; *type:* fighter; *year:* 1937; *engine:*
Hispano-Suiza 12 Ydrs 12-cylinder V liquid-cooled, 860 hp; *wingspan:* 42 ft
8 in (13.00 m); *length:* 30 ft 4 in (9.25 m); *height:* 12 ft 4 in (3.75 m); *weight:*
6,882 lb (3,122 kg); *maximum speed:* 208 mph (335 km/h) at 13,125 ft
(4,000 m); *ceiling:* 32,810 ft (10,000 m); *range:* 385 miles (620 km); *armament:*
1 × 20 mm cannon, 3 machine guns; 220 lb (100 kg) of bombs; *crew:* 1

PZL P.7
Nation: Poland; *manufacturer:* Panstwowe Zaklady Lotnicze; *type:* fighter; *year:*
1932; *engine:* Bristol Jupiter VIIF (Škoda) 9-cylinder radial air-cooled, 485 hp;
wingspan: 33 ft 10 in (10.31 m); *length:* 23 ft 6 in (7.46 m); *height:* 9 ft (2.74 m);
weight: 3,050 lb (1,380 kg); *maximum speed:* 203 mph (327 km/h) at 16,400 ft
(5,000 m); *ceiling:* 32,800 ft (10,000 m); *range:* 430 miles (700 km); *armament:*
2 machine guns; *crew:* 1
▼

SVENSKA J 6A JAKTFALK
Nation: Sweden; *manufacturer:* Svenska Aero AB; *type:* fighter; *year:* 1931; *engine:*
Bristol Jupiter VIIF 9-cylinder radial air-cooled, 500 hp; *wingspan:* 28 ft 10 in (8.80 m);
length: 24 ft 7 in (7.50 m); *height:* 11 ft 4 in (3.46 m); *weight:* 3,240 lb (1,470 kg);
maximum speed: 193 mph (310 km/h) at 14,700 ft (4,500 m); *ceiling:* 26,200 ft
(8,000 m); *range:* 340 miles (550 km); *armament:* 2 machine guns; *crew:* 1

Plate 50
France takes the lead in postwar development of the fighter: 1922–31

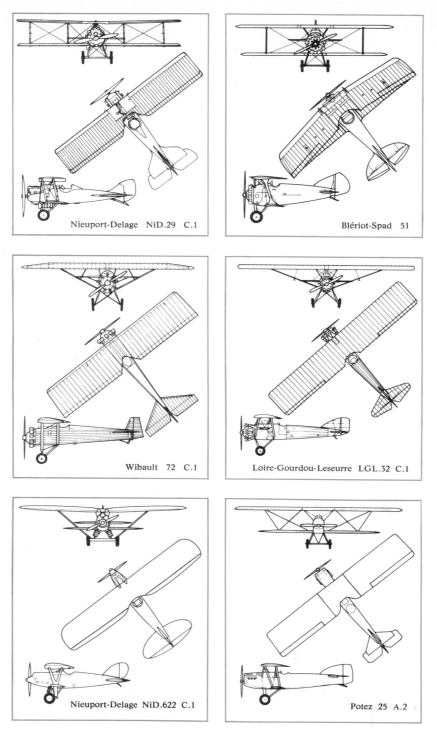

Nieuport-Delage NiD.29 C.1

Blériot-Spad 51

Wibault 72 C.1

Loire-Gourdou-Leseurre LGL.32 C.1

Nieuport-Delage NiD.622 C.1

Potez 25 A.2

Whilst restructuring her industry and armed forces in line with peacetime needs, France put an excellent fighter into service from 1922 onwards which had been designed too late to see service in the war: the Nieuport-Delage NiD.29 C.1. This machine was directly descended from Gustave Delage's outstanding aircraft of 1918. In 1921 changes had been made to the wings and to the ailerons, and once it had successfully carried out its proving trials it was accepted as the standard fighter of the air force. The NiD.29 C.1 stayed in service until 1928 and was also very successfully exported; Spain took 30 of them, of which ten were built under licence; Belgium 108, out of which 87 were built under licence; Italy 181, of which she built 175 under licence; Japan 609, and Sweden 9. A total of 250 were built to meet France's own needs.

The Blériot-Spad 51 however was only sold abroad. This was a fast and neat biplane which had been produced within the rearmament programme of 1923. It was designed by André Herbemont and was not used by the French air force. The 50 aircraft of the first production series (the first prototype flew on 16th June 1924) all went to meet an order from Poland, who received them in 1925–26. In the autumn of 1928, after the fourth prototype had appeared with a more powerful engine on 30th August 1928, another ten aircraft were constructed but only two of these were exported, one to Turkey and the other to the Soviet Union.

The comprehensive programmes of modernisation which were undertaken by the military authorities bore their first fruits in the official 1925 competition, in which a fast all-metal monoplane came to the fore, the Wibault 7, the prototype of which had flown the year before. Six pre-series models were ordered for proving trials and at the end of tests the fighter was accepted as a high-altitude interceptor. The standard production version was designated Wibault 72 C.1 and the first of 60 built went into service during 1926. The operational career of these aircraft continued until just before the outbreak of the Second World War. Series 7 Wibaults were also exported to Bolivia and Brazil; Britain and Poland bought construction licences. Procurement for France's own forces was 36, comprising models 74 and 75 which were fighters and fighter-reconnaissance planes for carrier-borne use.

Another contemporary monoplane in the same category as the Wibault which was also chosen by the military authorities after the competition of 1925 was the Loire-Gourdou-Leseurre LGL.32 C.1. The aircraft was the first to be produced by the merged Gourdou-Leseurre and Ateliers Chantiers de la Loire companies, who had merged in 1925, and the prototype had been completed very rapidly. After the construction of 16 pre-series models which were used for proving trials, the fighter was ordered in large numbers (orders totalled 350) and went into service towards the end of 1927, staying in front line use as an interceptor until the middle of the 1930s. The LGL.32 C.1 also had great export success: it was bought by Romania (50 in 1928); by Turkey (12 in 1930); and by Spain (8 in 1936).

Another series of excellent front line aircraft from Nieuport-Delage was the biplane Series 62, which had emerged from the aeronautical competitions of the early 1920s. The most important of these was the NiD.62 C.1 of 1928, of which 345 were built for the air force. The next variant to be produced in large numbers was the NiD.622 C.1, which had a more powerful engine, a metal propeller and modified ailerons; it went into service in 1931 and 330 were delivered. Fifty more powerful NiD.629 C.1s also saw service with the French air force. The Series 62 Nieuport-Delage were exported to Peru and Belgium.

Another contemporary biplane, the Potez 25, was not a fighter but was very widely used and produced in large numbers; it was also well-known for its numerous sporting achievements and its commercial career. It appeared in 1925 and this versatile aircraft was produced in very large numbers, over 4,000 being constructed in two basic versions: the A.2 reconnaissance plane and the B.2 bomber. It was in service with the air force until the mid-1930s (the reconnaissance variant was the most widely used) and the Potez 25 was used by 21 other nations, many of them building it under licence.

Plate 51
French fighters of the thirties: 1931–37

The French continued to modernise their warplanes uninterruptedly throughout the thirties. The well-known constructor Emile Dewoitine played a very important part in this process and in 1935 he supplied the renamed *Armée de l'Air* with its first modern monoplane fighter, the D.500. Before arriving at this point, Dewoitine had been through some hard times. In 1927, due to lack of orders, he had been forced to close down his business and move to Switzerland. There he had continued to design aircraft and about a year later had produced an interesting fighter monoplane, the D.27, on the basis of knowledge acquired from earlier models. The aircraft was accepted by the Swiss army and production was entrusted to the government factories. Sixty-six D.27s equipped the small Swiss air force from 1931 onwards.

In that year Dewoitine went back to France and formed a new company, the Société Aéronautique Française, and recommended limited production for the French air force of a derivative model, the D.37. In 1932 the designer

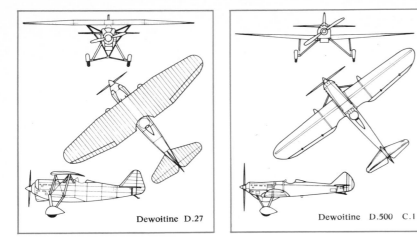

Dewoitine D.27

Dewoitine D.500 C.1

Plate 52
**British fighters of the twenties:
1924–29**

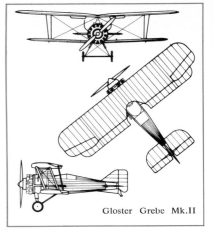

Gloster Grebe Mk.II

Morane-Saulnier M.S.225 C.1

started on the development of the D.500 C.1 along the lines of specifications issued two years earlier by the air ministry. The first prototype of this elegant low-wing, all metal monoplane flew on 18th June and at the end of proving trials was ordered into production. The D.500s went into service in 1935 flanked by the more powerful D.501 version. In all 308 were built including the prototypes. This fighter was joined in service from 1934 onwards by 120 D.510s which were more powerful and structurally stronger, and which remained in service until the Second World War.

The Dewoitine fighters flew side by side with the *Armée de l'Air*'s other contemporary machines. In 1933 the first of 55 Morane-Saulnier M.S.225 C.1s were delivered. This small and sturdy high-wing monoplane (the prototype of which had appeared in 1932) was mainly chosen because of its excellent manoeuvrability, but it never played a very important role. The Loire 46 C.1 had much the same sort of career: this was a high-wing monoplane with the distinctive "gull-wing" which had appeared in prototype form on 1st September 1934, and went into service two years later. The 70 aircraft built were in fact always plagued by engine faults and by problems of structural weakness in the landing gear. The Loire 46 C.1 was withdrawn from front-line service from December 1938 and relegated to training.

The operational career of the last biplane to be put into service by the French air force was even shorter and ironically restricted by the same shortcomings: this was the Blériot-Spad 510. The 510 entered service in July 1937 and was withdrawn from front-line duties in August, being relegated to second-line squadrons. The prototype flew on 6th January 1933 and production (which totalled 60) commenced at the end of 1933.

In Britain, after a pause immediately after the war for the necessary restructuring of the armed forces, major efforts were made to re-equip the air force.

In the RAF one of the first new generation fighters was the Gloster Grebe, a small and very handy biplane, designed by H. P. Folland, which replaced the by now obsolete Sopwith Snipes. The Grebe Mk I prototype made its first appearance in June 1923 at the RAF annual Hendon Air Display and its manoeuvrability made a strong impression. It was chosen to re-equip several fighter squadrons and was put into production under the designation of Grebe Mk II. 112 of these aircraft were constructed which remained in service from 1924 onwards, staying in front line service for four years. During the course of its career the Gloster Grebe gave ample proof of its great aerobatic talents, especially with 25 Squadron which gave a spectacular display at Hendon in 1925.

In that same year, another fighter biplane went into service, the Hawker Woodcock, the first aircraft of this type to be produced by a new company, Hawker Engineering, which was to become world-famous in years to come. The first prototype appeared in 1924 and was immediately followed by a second, which was exhibited at the Hendon Air Display of that year. This aircraft impressed the Air Ministry which ordered the production of a large number for the RAF. The series models were designated Woodcock Mk II and went into service in May 1925, and up to April 1927 62 had been constructed. The Woodcock remained in front-line service for three years.

In the meantime, H. P. Folland had designed a new fighter model basically derived from the Grebe; this was the Gamecock. It differed from its predecessor in having a redesigned fuselage and tailplane, a more powerful engine and improved armament. The first prototype was flown in February 1925 and had been followed by two other experimental machines. The RAF ordered a large production batch of 82 (designated Gamecock Mk I) which went into operational use in May 1926 and stayed in front line service until June 1931. These were equipped with a Bristol Jupiter VI 425 hp engine which was more reliable than the Armstrong Siddeley Jaguar which had been used in the Gloster Grebe.

As was the case with the Grebe, the

Hawker Woodcock Mk.II

Gloster Gamecock Mk.I

Gamecock became well-known for outstanding aerobatics and this made it very popular with the pilots of the time. The aircraft was also the last wooden biplane fighter to serve with the RAF. The construction licence for an improved version of the Gamecock was sold to Finland in 1927.

Another important contemporary combat aircraft was the Armstrong Whitworth Siskin, a biplane which, together with the Grebe, also went to re-equip units of the RAF immediately after the war. The development of the Siskin began in the very early 1920s and its development was pro-

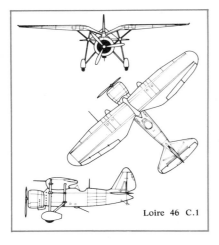

Loire 46 C.1

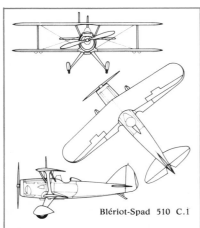

Blériot-Spad 510 C.1

Armstrong Whitworth Siskin Mk.IIIA

commenced immediately afterwards and 302 fighters and 58 trainers were completed. The first were designated Mk II (48 built) and Mk IIA (254) and these had a stronger undercarriage and airframe, and a more powerful engine. 58 of the second Bulldog TM were built.

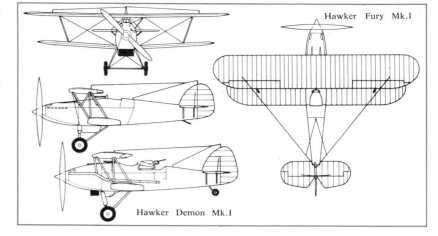

Hawker Fury Mk.I

Hawker Demon Mk.I

tracted; after the first prototype, trainer and fighter variants were produced. A series of important structural modifications to the wing and to the fuselage led to the final version, the Siskin Mk III, which appeared in prototype form on 24th March 1924 and was immediately put into production for the RAF; 70 left the assembly lines and they first reached units in the month of May.

The operational career of this new fighter was given considerable impetus three years later with the arrival of a new variant which was to become the most widely used, the Mk III A. The prototype had flown for the first time on 20th October 1925, and showed itself to be generally much better than the preceding model. This was mainly due to its more powerful engine (over 100 hp more) and to the reduced dihedral of the upper wings. Production of the Siskin Mk III was started in 1926 and Bristol and Gloster also participated; procurement totalled over 350. This fighter remained in service until October 1932.

The Siskin was joined from May 1929 by a new, more powerful machine: the Bristol Bulldog, a biplane which was to represent the spearhead of the RAF's forces until 1936. The first prototype had flown on 17th May 1927 and had been followed on 21st January 1928 by a second pre-series model. Production was

Plate 53
British fighters of the thirties: 1931–35

Whilst the Bristol Bulldog, fast, powerful and extremely manoeuvrable as it was, was one of the very best radial-engined fighter biplanes, the Hawker Fury, which came shortly afterwards, represented the most successful application at that time of inline engine technology used in this type of aircraft. The Fury was more or less directly derived from another excellent combat biplane, the Hart of 1928, which revolutionised the concept of the bomber. The designer was Sydney Camm, who had found no difficulty in repeating in the Fury the meticulous aerodynamic formula and type of engine which lay behind the Hart's success. Indeed, since this was a straight fighter, the results were even better.

The Fury prototype flew for the first time on 25th March 1931, and its performance was impressive especially in speed, rate of climb and manoeuvrability. The prototype also retained its predecessor's fabric-covered metal structure with all-metal forward fuselage and the neatly housed Rolls-Royce Kestrel engine. Production was immediately started for the RAF and the first unit to receive the new fighter was 43 Squadron in May 1931. A total of 117 Fury Mk Is were built up to 1935 and their front line service came to an end in 1939, when they were replaced by the Hawker Hurricane.

The career of the Fury was given a second lease of life in 1936, when the Hawker assembly lines completed the first of a new version, the Mk II, developed in order to make the most of the exceptional speed of the fighter, which in its first variant already exceeded by over 50 km/h (31 mph) the top speed of any other interceptor of the RAF. The most noteworthy features of the Fury Mk II were its

engine, a Rolls-Royce Kestrel 640 hp version, and its general streamlining. When the first production model had its inaugural flight on 3rd December 1936 it showed an increase of 8 per cent in speed and 34 per cent in rate of climb over its predecessor. Hawker completed a first batch of 23 aircraft and subsequently General Aircraft built another 75. The Fury Mk II stayed in front line service until January 1939.

Meanwhile, Sydney Camm had developed another fighter which echoed the design of the Hart bomber: the Hawker Demon. The aircraft had been requested at the beginning of the thirties by the Air Ministry in view of the Hart's excellent performance: in effect they wanted an interceptor which could equal its performance. The designer adopted the simplest solution; he converted the bomber into a two-seat fighter, thus reverting to an old tradition which had not been followed in the RAF since the Bristol fighter of 1917. He armed it more powerfully and put in a Rolls-Royce Kestrel 584 hp engine, almost 60 hp more than the Hart's engine. The aircraft was test-flown in March 1931 and production was started in the following year. The first operational unit to have the Demon Mk I was 23 Squadron which took delivery of the fighters in April 1933. Gradually, as production progressed (234 built in total as at

December 1937) use was more extensive and this aircraft remained in front-line service for a further six years. They were withdrawn during 1939. Among the most interesting modifications to which the Demon was subjected in the course of its career was one made in 1936: in order to increase its firepower, a hydraulically driven turret was installed in the rear cockpit. This version was called the Turret-Demon.

The line of radial engine powered fighters included one other notable plane: the Gloster Gauntlet, the last open-cockpit fighter to serve with the RAF. The Gauntlet had a long gestation period, attaining its final form only after the appearance of numerous preliminary models which proved unsatisfactory. The prototype appeared in the spring of 1933 and was ordered into production as the Gauntlet Mk I (24 built) from September onwards and went into service in May 1935. Only a month later the assembly lines had started up production of a second version, the Mk II, which differed considerably from its predecessor in methods of construction as a result of the merger of Gloster with Hawker-Siddeley; 204 were completed in two lots. These aircraft went into front line service in May 1936 and remained there until the beginning of the Second World War. The Gauntlet Mk I was withdrawn in 1938.

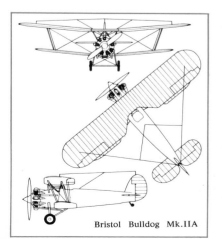

Bristol Bulldog Mk.IIA

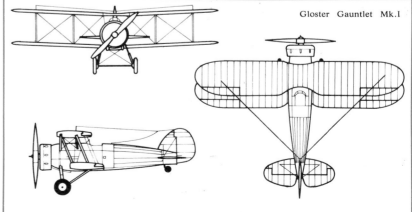

Gloster Gauntlet Mk.I

Plate 54
Fighters of the United States Army Air
Corps: 1926–34

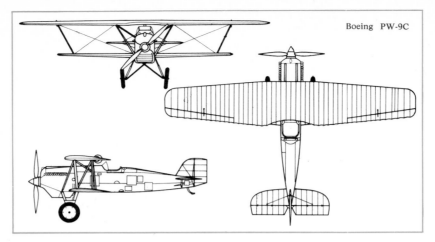

Boeing PW-9C

The end of the First World War found the United States very busy building up its own air forces, after slow progress during the war years. The army and the navy spared no efforts – stimulated by the rivalry between these two services – to improve industrial production which grew increasingly efficient in satisfying their requirements.

In the fighter class one of the first machines to go into service with units of the USAAC was the Boeing PW-9, a small and handy biplane driven by a powerful V-12 Curtiss engine. The first prototype developed privately by Boeing flew on 29th April 1923, and after a series of proving trials, of which some were carried out by military pilots, it was accepted by the USAAC together with another two experimental models. Production was started in September 1924 and the first of thirty series aircraft, designated PW-9, reached units a year later. Towards the end of 1925 the second version was developed, the PW-9A, in which detail changes were made, and of which 25 were built and immediately afterwards the assembly lines started to build a further 40 aircraft of the third variant, the PW-9C. This fighter went into service during 1926 and was joined after some time by 16 of the last series to be ordered by the army, the PW-9D, which had modified undercarriage and rudder.

In October 1928 a new aircraft was ordered following the success of two prototypes in the National Air Races of the preceding year. This was a category P(Pursuit) plane, the Curtiss P-6 Hawk. The fighter had been developed from a long line of machines of this type built by Curtiss from 1924 onwards, both for the army and for the navy (designated respectively P-1 and F6C). In 1927 the new model had been especially built for competitive flying and in essence it differed from its predecessor in being powered by a Curtiss Conqueror 600 hp engine.

The interest of the military authorities took concrete form with an order for nine pre-series aircraft (designated YP-6) and for nine of the initial production series (P-6A). After entering into service these aircraft were modified in 1932, receiving a new type of engine and being redesignated P-6D. Also in 1932 came yet another variant, the P-6E, which had an even more powerful engine together

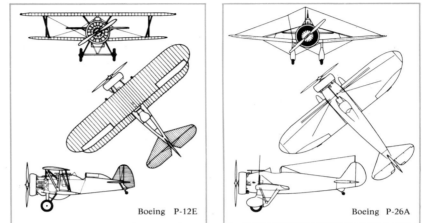

Boeing P-12E

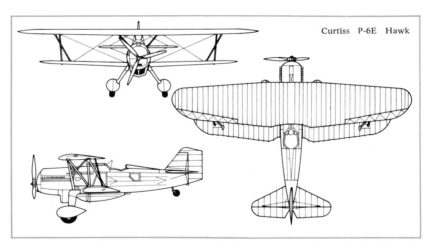

Boeing P-26A

Curtiss P-6E Hawk

with structural and aerodynamic improvements.

Its rivalry with the navy did not stop the US Army from adopting, towards the end of the 1930s, a new single-seat fighter which had been especially built at the request of the US Navy: the Boeing P-12 (designated F4B by the Navy). The two prototypes of this small and handy biplane had been developed privately by Boeing and the first of these had flown on 25th June 1928. Once accepted by the US Navy these aircraft had been put into production with an initial order for 27, which went into service in the following year, equipping squadrons based on the aircraft carriers USS *Lexington* and *Langley*.

It was at this stage that the USAAC, who had at first rejected the Boeing fighter, went back on their decison and ordered nine aircraft, designating them P-12, and a prototype (XP-12A) which had modified undercarriage and wings. This slight quantity of machines led to large orders for later variants, which joined those in production for

the US Navy. The Army received 90 P-12Bs; 96 P-12Cs, which again had new modifications to the undercarriage, and a Townend Ring engine cowling; 110 P-112Es, which entered service in 1931 with more powerful engines and a metal fuselage; and 25 P-12Fs, which were given a new engine.

The change from the biplane to the monoplane was marked in 1934 by the entry into service of the Boeing P-26 Peashooter, so-called because of its bulbous lines and its stubby radial engine. The P-26, which was also the USAAC's first all-metal monoplane, had arisen from close collaboration between Boeing and the army. The prototype flew on 20th March 1932 and had been subjected to a long series of tests and operational proving flights. 111 of the first production version, designated P-26A, were built and were followed by 25 aircraft of the second version, the P-26B, which had a more powerful engine. The P-26s went into service at the beginning of 1934 and for almost five years they represented the front-line equipment of fighter units both in the continental United States as well as the Panama Canal zone and Hawaii.

Plate 55
Fighters of the US Navy: 1927–32

The navy did not lag behind the army in its interest in the PW-9 Boeing fighter, and placed its own order immediately after production was started for the USAAC. This was in early 1925, and the order was for 16 of the new fighters, which were delivered later that year and early in 1926.

These aircraft were not adapted for carrier use and were therefore used by land-based Marine Corps squadrons. The gap was filled by the succeeding variants, the FB-2, FB-3 and the FB-4, of which small numbers were built and which led to the perfecting of the final production model, the FB-5 which appeared in prototype form in October 1926. Two Boeing FB-2s were built which had a stronger airframe and landing gear in order better to meet the demands of shipborne use; three FB-3s were constructed in which the landing gear was interchangeable with twin floats; only one prototype was built of the FB-4, which was powered by a Wright radial engine. 27 of the final FB-5 model, however, were constructed, and were all delivered in January 1927; they went to two squadrons on board the aircraft carrier USS *Langley* and to two squadrons on board the carrier USS *Lexington*.

Collaboration between the US Navy and Boeing remained just as close after the production of the FB series, whch had been Boeing's first carrier-borne fighter. Working from the basis of the single FB-4 prototype, which was subsequently further modified by the installation of Pratt & Whitney's new Wasp radial engine and designated FB-6, Boeing prepared a new prototype powered by this promising engine and submitted it to the navy towards the end of 1926. The aircraft, Model 69 (first flight on 3rd November) was accepted under the designation XF2B-1 and after proving trials was put into production with an order for 32. These machines were delivered from January 1928 onwards and went into service on board the aircraft carrier USS *Saratoga*.

A month later the prototype of a new fighter appeared which had been developed jointly in the course of the preceding year: the Boeing F3B-1, a much more powerful aircraft. The F3B-1, 74 of which were built, flew from USS *Langley*, *Saratoga* and *Lexington* from 1928 onwards, and represented the final confirmation of the radial engine's effectiveness.

The US Navy's choice continued to influence the USAAC. Another first class fighter biplane had appeared in 1928 built by Boeing, the F4B, which was perhaps the most renowned of this family of aeroplanes. The first order came from the US Navy, for 27 F4B-1s to serve with the USS *Lexington* and *Langley*. Such was the enthusiasm displayed by the navy that the army soon placed an order for the F4B "sight unseen", and the fighter went into army service under the designation P-12.

In June 1930 the US Navy ordered 41 F4B-2s, which were similar to the army's P-12C and went into service at the beginning of the following year on board the USS *Lexington* and *Saratoga*. In April 1931 21 F4B-3s, which had metal fuselages, were ordered, and in January of the following year 92 F4B-4s with modified tail-

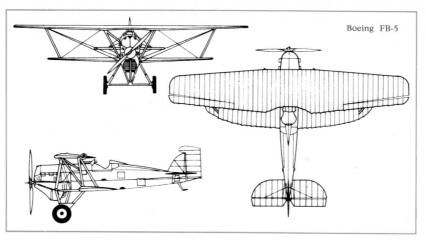

Boeing FB-5

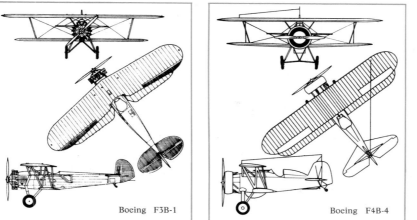

Boeing F3B-1   Boeing F4B-4

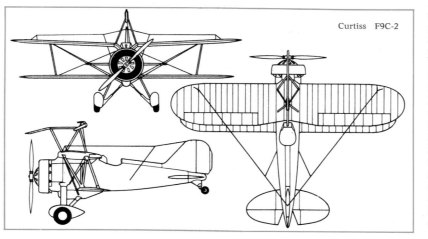

Curtiss F9C-2

planes were ordered. This final version of the small Boeing fighter remained in front-line service up till the end of 1937 at which time it started to be replaced by the more modern Grumman biplanes.

The US Navy carried out a number of experiments during the twenties and thirties to explore the possibility of using aircraft in combination with an airship. A small parasite fighter made by Curtiss, the F9C Sparrowhawk, originally meant for carrier-

based use, was modified to be launched and retrieved in flight from an airship. The fighter was accommodated in a special hangar in the stern of the airship. The first experiment was carried out on 27th October 1931 with the prototype XF9C-1, with good results, so another experimental aircraft was ordered as well as six series aircraft, the F9C-2. These were delivered in 1931 and tested with the airships *Akron* and *Macon*, again with encouraging results. These experi-

ments came to an end, however, after the destruction of the two airships in flying accidents, in 1933 and 1935.

Plate 56
Fighters of the US Navy and the Royal Navy: 1923–36

The early thirties saw a new American manufacturer who began making naval aircraft: Grumman, a name which soon became synonymous with carrier-borne fighters. Grumman's many years of collaboration with the US Navy began on 2nd April 1931, with the signing of a contract for the FF-1, the first military aircraft to be equipped with retractable undercarriage. This small and fast twin-seat biplane did not go into large-scale production in spite of this innovation. It was considered to be a transitional model, and as such built in relatively small numbers. The prototype, XFF-1, which had flown towards the end of 1931, had been followed by a second model, adapted for reconnaissance and designated XSF-1. Production totalled 27 fighters and 33 reconnaissance planes, all for the USS *Lexington*. The two types went into service in June 1933 and March 1934 respectively, and were withdrawn from front-line service towards the end of 1936.

The success of the FF-1 opened up the way for further, larger orders. On 2nd November 1932 the US Navy placed an order for a prototype of a new carrier-borne fighter, similar in general structure to the preceding model but more compact and which was a single-seater. This was the XF2F-1 and it made its first flight on 18th October 1933, which satisfied the navy well enough for an order to be placed for 54 series models. The first Grumman F2F-1s reached units at the beginning of 1935 and remained with them for another five years. The fighter squadron VF-2B on board the USS *Lexington* kept its F2F-1s until 1940, despite various new versions of the little Grumman fighter which had appeared in the meantime.

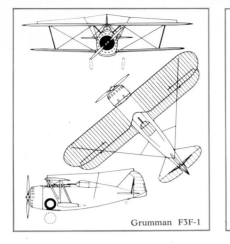

Grumman F3F-1

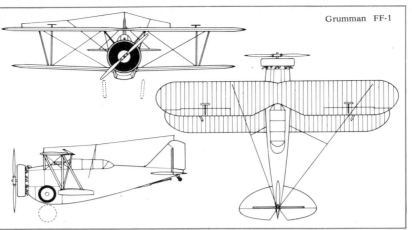

Grumman FF-1

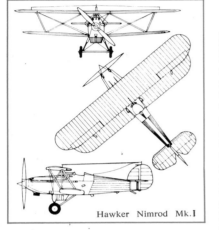

Hawker Nimrod Mk. I

Hawker Osprey Mk. I

Fairey Flycatcher

In the early months of 1935 the next prototype, XF3F-1, started its proving flights. This was really an F2F-1 with larger fuselage and wings. Although the two examples of the original prototype were destroyed in an accident, a third prototype carried out the tests with great success and the aircraft was put into production with an order for 54. The first F3F-1s reached units at the beginning of 1936 and flew with them until 1940. In January 1937 a new version was built, equipped with a more powerful engine, and was to be the model produced in the largest numbers, the F3F-2, of which 81 were built, going into service in 1938. The final variant was the F3F-3 which had an even more powerful engine. Twenty-seven were built, deliveries of which started at the end of 1938. This aircraft had the briefest operational career of all the aircraft of this family, lasting little more than a year, and it was the last biplane fighter of both the US Navy and of Grumman. The following model was to be the F4F Wildcat.

But the US Navy was not the only one to develop a worthwhile line of carrier-borne combat aircraft. A similar effort, with similarly good results, was made by the Fleet Air Arm during the twenties and thirties. The first new generation postwar fighter was the Fairey Flycatcher, a small, sturdy and swift biplane which remained in front line service from 1923 to 1934, and until 1932 was the only carrier-borne fighter in use. The prototype appeared in 1922, in response to a request from the Air Ministry which called for a single-seater multirole fighter in seaplane and amphibious configuration and a carrier version with arrestergear. Production started in 1923 and continued until 1930, building a total of 193, which served in the aircraft carriers HMS *Argus*, *Courageous*, *Eagle*, *Furious* and *Hermes*.

The Flycatcher's successor was the Hawker Nimrod, which was really another member of the family of Harts and Furies developed by Sydney Camm at the end of the 1930s: the Nimrod was the naval version of the Fury, although much modified. The

prototype flew on 2nd September 1931, and production was started with an order for 56 Nimrod Mk Is. These aircraft were followed by 30 of the Mk II series, which were structurally modified and which appeared in 1934.

The Nimrods remained in service from 1932 to 1939. They were joined in operations by another derivant of the Hart: the Hawker Osprey which was a carrier-borne version of the RAF's bomber. With the introduction of this fast biplane in November 1932, the Fleet Air Arm began a new category of aircraft: the two-seat fighter-reconnaissance plane. The Osprey was tested during 1931 and 129 were constructed up to 1935: 37 Mk Is, 14 Mk IIs, 52 Mk IIIs which had metal propellers, 26 Mk IVs which received more powerful engines. The Ospreys were in service until 1939.

Plate 57
The most important interwar Soviet and Japanese fighters: 1923–35

It was not only the great industrial powers who strove to develop modern air forces; there was great aeronautical activity in some other countries, considered then to be in the rearguard of aviation. During the twenties and thirties Japan and the Soviet Union built up the industrial structures which were

to enable them to catch up with aviation in the more advanced nations.

Japan had no aeronautical technology and spared no expense to acquire it from other countries. Numerous types of aircraft constructed in Europe were bought and analysed; foreign experts were invited to train engineers and workers. This was a gradual process, which started to show results at the beginning of the 1930s. One of the typical products of this phase of "apprenticeship" was the Mitsubishi 1MF, the first carrier-borne fighter of the Imperial Navy, the work of none other than the English designer Herbert Smith, the creator of some of the greatest combat aircraft built by Sopwith during the First World War.

Smith went to Japan in 1921 to assess the needs of the navy for a fighter to be used with the first Japanese aircraft carrier, the *Hosho*. His aircraft appeared towards the end of the year and, after proving flights, was put into production under the designation of Type 10. The first take-offs and landings on carriers took place in February 1923 and some months later the fighter went into squadron service. Production, which went through seven variants, reached a total of 128 up till 1928. The Mitsubishi 1MF stayed in front line service until the following year.

In 1931 the first entirely Japanese-produced fighter went to the army, the Nakajima 91. The specification had been issued in 1927 and after the prototype had been initially refused the military authorities had reversed their decision and had accepted the aircraft with some changes. It was in service from December 1931, and the Type 91 replaced the French Nieuport-Delage NiD.29 C.1 fighter produced under licence by Nakajima, which was front-line equipment at the time. 320 of the Type 91 were constructed.

The age of the biplane came to a close in Japan in 1935 when units received the Kawasaki Ki-10. This small and very handy fighter had been flown for the first time in March, and during proving flights it had shown that it was very much better than a more modern contender, another monoplane built by Nakajima and entered in the same competition. 300 Ki-10a were built up till 1937 and stayed in front-line service until the eve of the Second World War, taking part in the war against China.

In the Soviet Union a significant contribution to the development of effective fighter models was made by Nikolai Polikarpov, one of the youngest designers of the new Russian school. In 1923 Polikarpov had produced the first Russian-built fighter, the I-1, and through successive models which included the I-3 of 1928, he had ended up with a machine which was really exceptional for its time, the model I-5, developed in collaboration with D. P. Grigorovitch. The new aircraft, which was fast, tough, manoeuvrable and powerfully armed, flew

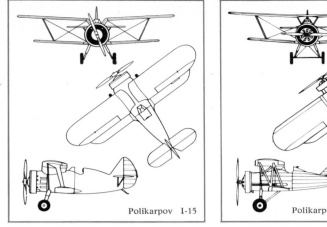

Polikarpov I-15

Polikarpov-Grigorovich I-5

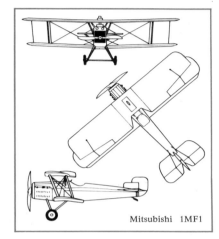

Mitsubishi 1MF1

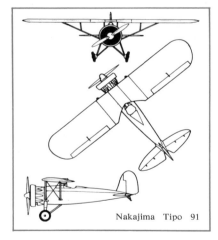

Nakajima Tipo 91

Kawasaki Ki-10

for the first time on 22nd May 1930, and after a series of small modifications it was put into mass production; about 800 Polikarpov-Grigorovitch I-5s left the assembly lines and stayed in service from 1931 until the outbreak of the war.

But the most impressive of Polikarpov's designs was the I-15, designed and flown for the first time in 1933 and which made its mark as one of the best fighters of its class at that time. It was in service from the end of 1934 and was tested in action two years later in Spain, flying with the Republicans. Production reached over 500 aircraft and mainly comprised two versions, apart from the basic model: the I-15*bis*, which was better armed and had increased fuel capacity and modified upper wings, and the I-15*ter*, which appeared in 1938 and was notable mainly for its retractable undercarriage and its 1,000 hp engine.

Plate 58
Italian fighters: 1924–35

The first fighter aircraft which was completely designed and constructed in Italy and which went into service after the end of the First World War was also the first to be designed by Celestino Rosatelli, whose initials C.R. (actually they stood for Caccia Rosatelli) appeared on a whole generation of combat aircraft.

The Fiat C.R.1 was developed in 1923 and the prototype was built around one of the best engines of the time, the 300 hp Hispano-Suiza 42. Once trials had been completed, an Italian-built engine was chosen for series production, the Isotta-Fraschini Asso which was slightly more powerful at 320 hp. The rest of the aircraft was not changed in any significant way. The most unusual feature of the machine was also retained: the span of the lower wing was considerably greater than that of the upper wing. This departure from the usual conventional wing arrangement did not stop the C.R.1 from being a spectacularly good aerobatic plane. About 100 Fiat C.R.1s were built which started to go into service with fighter units of the *Regia Aeronautica* from 1924.

Rosatelli's next aeroplane was also extremely manoeuvrable and went into service with the *Regia Aeronautica* – the Fiat C.R.20 of 1926. This fighter was developed from a prototype, C.R.10, which had been built two years earlier and which represented a major step forward. The C.R.20 came to be a classic of the twenties and thirties, having both excellent general performance and extremely advanced design: among other things, it had an all-metal structure, the first time Rosatelli had tried this out. The prototype's test flights were immediately followed by series production which continued for five years and reached about 400 in total. The C.R.20 remained in service from 1926 until the eve of the Second World War.

The C.R.20 saw action up to 1927 in the last stages of Italy's reconquest of Libya, and was still in front-line service in the Italian campaign in Ethiopia of 1936, even though by then more modern fighter aircraft had appeared. Among the versions derived from it were the C.R.20 B trainer of 1927; the C.R.20 I floatplane; the C.R.20*bis* which had better undercarriage and equipment; and the high altitude C.R.20 AQ with a 420 hp engine. The final variant was the C.R.20 Asso which had a 450 hp engine.

Rosatelli's greatest aircraft of the 1930s was the C.R.32 biplane fighter, which was extremely modern. Its development began in 1931 and proceeded from the basis of a series which had just been built, the C.R.30. The new fighter was smaller than its predecessor, with smaller wings and many minor improvements, although it had the same power unit: the Fiat A.30 RA 600 hp V-12 water-cooled

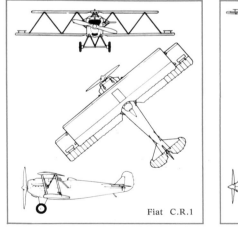

Fiat C.R.1

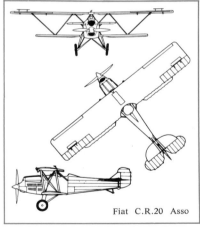

Fiat C.R.20 Asso

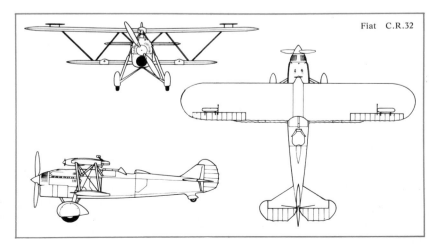

Fiat C.R.32

engine. The prototype flew for the first time on 28th April 1933, demonstrating many excellent qualities.

The following year series production was started and in the spring of 1935 the first models began reaching units. After 383 aircraft of the first series had been built, the assembly lines went on to build 328 of the C.R. 32*bis* series, from 1937 onwards. At the same time 100 of the C.R. 32*ter* series were built, and 401 of the C.R. 32 *quater* series. These variants differed in their armament, in structure, and in streamlining. Production continued until the spring of 1939 when the C.R.32 was replaced by the C.R.42.

The C.R.32 first saw action in Spain from 1936 onwards where a force of 380 of these aircraft was sent to back up the Nationalist *Aviación del Tercio*. At the outbreak of the Second World War C.R.32s were used in Greece, in the Mediterranean and in East Africa. The 177 combat-ready aircraft at the beginning of the war remained with units until April 1941.

Italy's flying boat fighters included the Macchi M.41*bis*, a biplane which had been introduced in 1927. Eight of this very reputable series of aircraft were still in service on the eve of the Second World War.

Another Italian aircraft, very much in the style of the early thirties, was the aerobatic trainer plane, the Breda Ba.19, a machine which was favoured by aerobatic units of the *Regia Aeronautica* from 1930, until the entry into service of the C.R.32. Its prototype, which appeared in 1928, could reach 228 km/h (137 mph) and had a 220 hp engine.

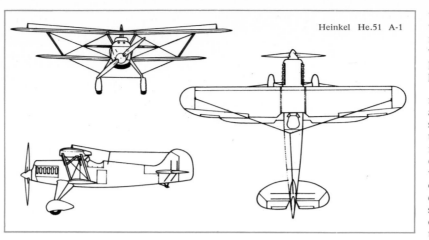

Heinkel He.51 A-1

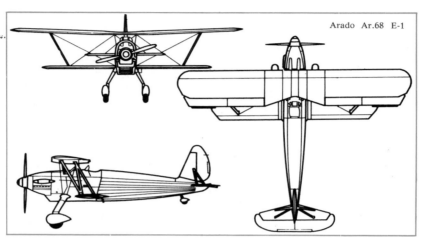

Arado Ar.68 E-1

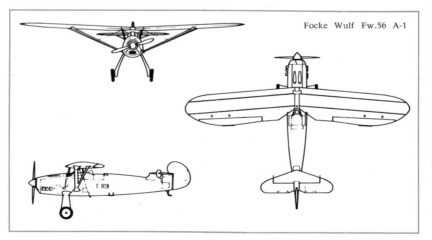

Focke Wulf Fw.56 A-1

were withdrawn from front-line service in 1938. The Heinkel was quite manoeuvrable and fast and was armed with two machine guns, but in combat proved inferior to the Soviet Polikarpov I-15 fighters.

The Heinkel biplane was then replaced by the Arado Ar.68, which appeared in prototype form in the summer of 1934. The development of this machine was delayed by difficulty in choosing an engine: two of the four experimental models were equipped with 750 hp BMW VI engines, the others by 610 hp Junkers Jumo 210 A engines. The second of these was chosen for the first series, the Ar.68 E, but delays in delivery led to the introduction of the BMW and the examples with this engine were designated Ar.68 F. Thus the first aircraft to go into service, in the summer of 1936, were the Ar.68 F series, and a few months later the assembly lines switched to production of the version with a Jumo engine.

The first Ar.68 E-1s reached units in the spring of 1937 but by this time the new and revolutionary Messerschmitt Bf.109 monoplane fighter was already well into its proving trials, and against the Messerschmitt the biplanes of an older generation stood little chance. So it was that the Arado Ar.68 had only a very brief career: and it was the very last biplane of the *Luftwaffe*.

Before the Bf.109 made its appearance the monoplane formula had been tried out with other aircraft. Among these the Focke Wulf Fw.56 gives a good illustration of the progression from one formula to another. This was one of the first of Kurt Tank's designs, the creator of some of the most outstanding German fighters of the Second World War. The first prototype of this elegant single-seat high-wing monoplane appeared in November 1933, and after a series of tests which led to various structural changes (especially in the landing gear) it was ready to undergo the official proving trials in February of the following year. These ended in the summer of 1935 and the Focke Wulf Fw.56 was ordered into production in the A-1 version.

The principal function of this air-

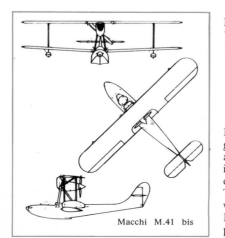

Macchi M.41 bis

Plate 59
The *Luftwaffe* is formed and prepares for war: 1935–37

In Germany military aviation made great strides in the early thirties, when an unprecedented growth of the whole industrial base made possible the clandestine creation of the *Luftwaffe*. The potential of this new armed force was fully demonstrated by the Heinkel He.51, the penultimate biplane to be produced for German military avia-

tion, which was seen in action in Spain from July 1936: first six aircraft, then more travelled to the war in batches until a total of 135 were in service, with both the Nationalist air force and the German Condor Legion.

The He.51 prototype had flown in the summer of 1933 and at the end of test flights had been chosen as the front-line fighter of the *Luftwaffe*. The first production version, the He.51 A-1, had started to leave the assembly lines in April 1935 and in that same month deliveries to operational units began. Production continued through various series which were continually improved and totalled about 700 by the end of production. The He.51s

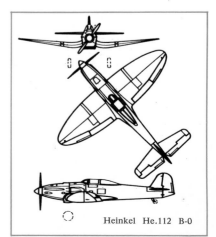

Heinkel He.112 B-0

craft was to be that of an advanced trainer, since there were more powerful aircraft available to be used in operational roles; and in this role the Fw.56 was very widely and successfully used. The exact production total is not known but it is supposed that 900–1,000 of them were constructed up to 1940. These served not only with the *Luftwaffe* but also with the air forces of Austria, Bulgaria and Hungary. In German flying schools the Focke Wulf Fw.56 survived for a great part of the Second World War.

An unsuccessful competitor of the Bf.109 was the Heinkel He.112, developed in the first half of the thirties for the competitive events organised by the *Luftwaffe* in order to find an advanced fighter. The first prototype flew in the summer of 1935 and was followed by another six experimental aircraft. Production was agreed for a batch of thirty (He.112 B-O) which were handed over to the *Luftwaffe* in 1938 for operational tests. Seventeen of these saw combat in the Spanish Civil War under the Nationalist colours, but in spite of its good overall performance the fighter was not chosen for the *Luftwaffe*, being eclipsed by the Bf.109. Only another 24 aircraft were built (of which 11 were the B-1 variant with a different engine) which were sold to Romania towards the end of 1939. They were used during the invasion of the Soviet Union and for the defence of Bucharest. The last of these aircraft were taken out of front-line service in 1942.

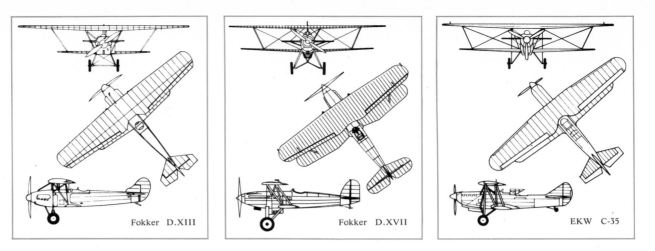

Fokker D.XIII

Fokker D.XVII

EKW C-35

Plate 60
Minor European fighters of the twenties and thirties: 1925–32

Among the great European designers Anton Fokker was one of the most prolific. At the end of the First World War he returned to his native Holland, taking refuge from defeated Germany where he had built the best German combat aircraft of the war. Fokker recommenced his work in Holland and from the new company which he founded, excellent designs soon started to emerge, in progression from the last outstanding fighter of the war, the D.VII.

Surprisingly perhaps, this activity was not hindered in any way by the Dutch government, and Fokker resumed military production, at first supported only by export orders but, as we shall see, with Netherlands orders soon enough. The first successful Dutch made Fokker, the D.XI of 1923, was bought by the USSR, who took 126 examples which were all to be used for the secret training of German military pilots. Other purchases were by Spain, Argentina, Romania, Switzerland and the USA. A total of 178 D.XIs were built. The following D.XIII had a similar career; this was a fighter developed from a prototype D.XII of 1924 which had been intended to attract orders from the USA. It was fast and had excellent overall performance and 50 Fokker D.XIIIs were built, which were bought by the USSR for Germany.

The first orders for the Dutch air force were placed with Fokker in 1929 and were for a new type of fighter, the D.XVI. Fifteen examples of this fast, manoeuvrable biplane were bought by the *Luchtvaartafdeling* (LVA) while another six were exported. In 1932 the military authorities accepted another Fokker design, the D.XVII, of which eleven were constructed. This aircraft remained in service, although only with flying schools, until 1940.

Even neutral Switzerland felt she had to equip herself with a new combat aircraft and in 1934 ordered the Federal EKW factories to develop the design of a twin-seater which could be used not only as a fighter but also for reconnaissance and tactical support. Two blueprints were prepared; the first, the C-36, was for a metal monoplane of fairly advanced design; the other, C-35, for a conventional biplane. The biplane was chosen for production: two prototypes appeared in 1936 and at the end of proving trials 80 C-35s were ordered. They went into service at the end of 1937 and survived until the late 1940s.

Another good combat aircraft made in a neutral country was Sweden's Svenska J6A Jaktfalk. This was tested with a British Bristol Bulldog fighter during its 1929 proving trials and showed that it was considerably better than its rival, which was at that time one of the best combat planes available. The Jaktfalk prototype flew in October 1929 and was bought by the Swedish Government in January of the following year. Two other prototypes equipped with Bristol Jupiter engines instead of the Armstrong Siddeley Jaguars of the first prototype were ordered in the summer of 1930,

and from these the production aircraft were derived, a total of 15, which went into service in 1931, and were in use until 1940.

In a development that will be of interest to the motoring historian, the company that received the order, Svenska Aero AB, otherwise known as Saab, went into the hands of a receiver in the middle of the production run, only completing eight aircraft. The remainder were constructed by ASJ, who bought Saab, and redesignated their seven examples J6B.

One of the well-known fighters of the 1930s was the Polish PZL P.7 designed by Zigmund Pulaski. Derived from the P.1 of 1929, the P.7's main difference lay in its engine, which in the P.1 was a Hispano-Suiza V-12. 150 P.7s were built which went to equip front-line fighter squadrons of the Polish air force in 1932. It was fast, manoeuvrable and well-armed, and the P.7 was powered by a 485 hp Bristol Jupiter VIIF radial engine, built under licence by Škoda.

The PZL P.7 was a single-seater gull-wing monoplane which stayed in service until the Second World War. The first unit to receive them was the Kosciuszko Squadron.

Svenska J6A Jaktfalk

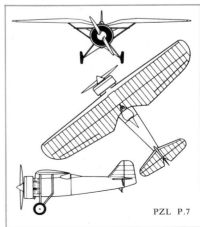

PZL P.7

Plate 61

Scale view of selected bombers, reconnaissance aircraft and trainers of the interwar years

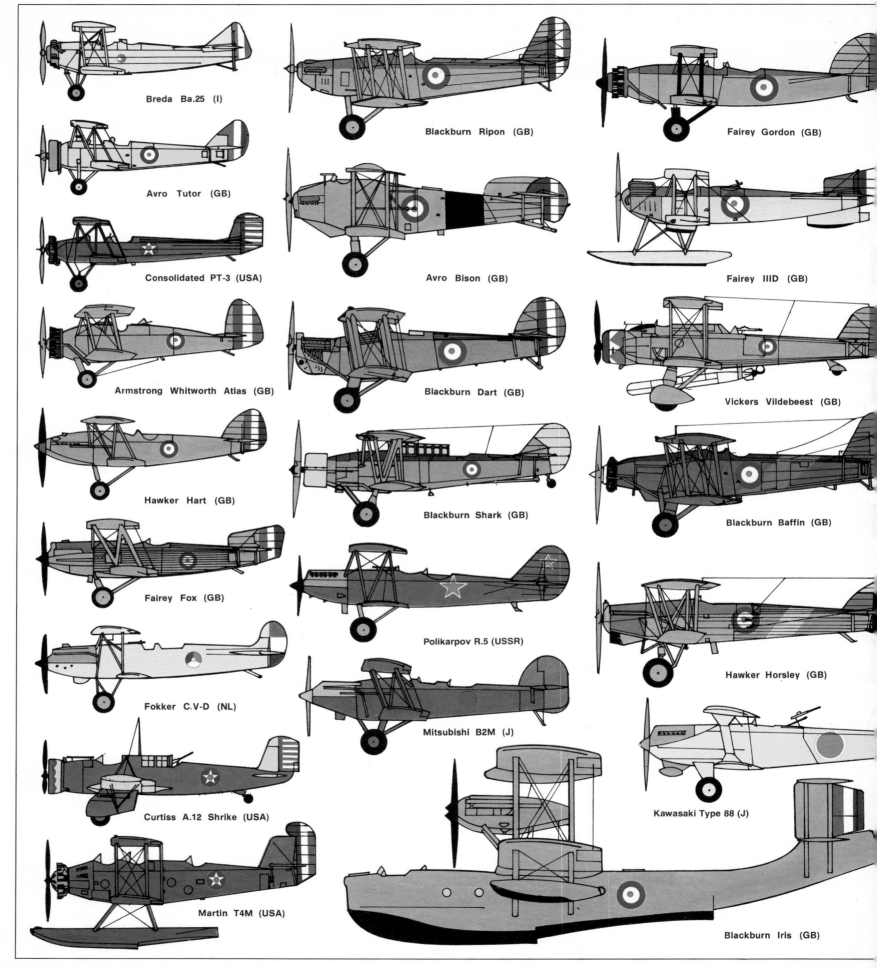

Breda Ba.25 (I)

Avro Tutor (GB)

Consolidated PT-3 (USA)

Armstrong Whitworth Atlas (GB)

Hawker Hart (GB)

Fairey Fox (GB)

Fokker C.V-D (NL)

Curtiss A.12 Shrike (USA)

Martin T4M (USA)

Blackburn Ripon (GB)

Avro Bison (GB)

Blackburn Dart (GB)

Blackburn Shark (GB)

Polikarpov R.5 (USSR)

Mitsubishi B2M (J)

Fairey Gordon (GB)

Fairey IIID (GB)

Vickers Vildebeest (GB)

Blackburn Baffin (GB)

Hawker Horsley (GB)

Kawasaki Type 88 (J)

Blackburn Iris (GB)

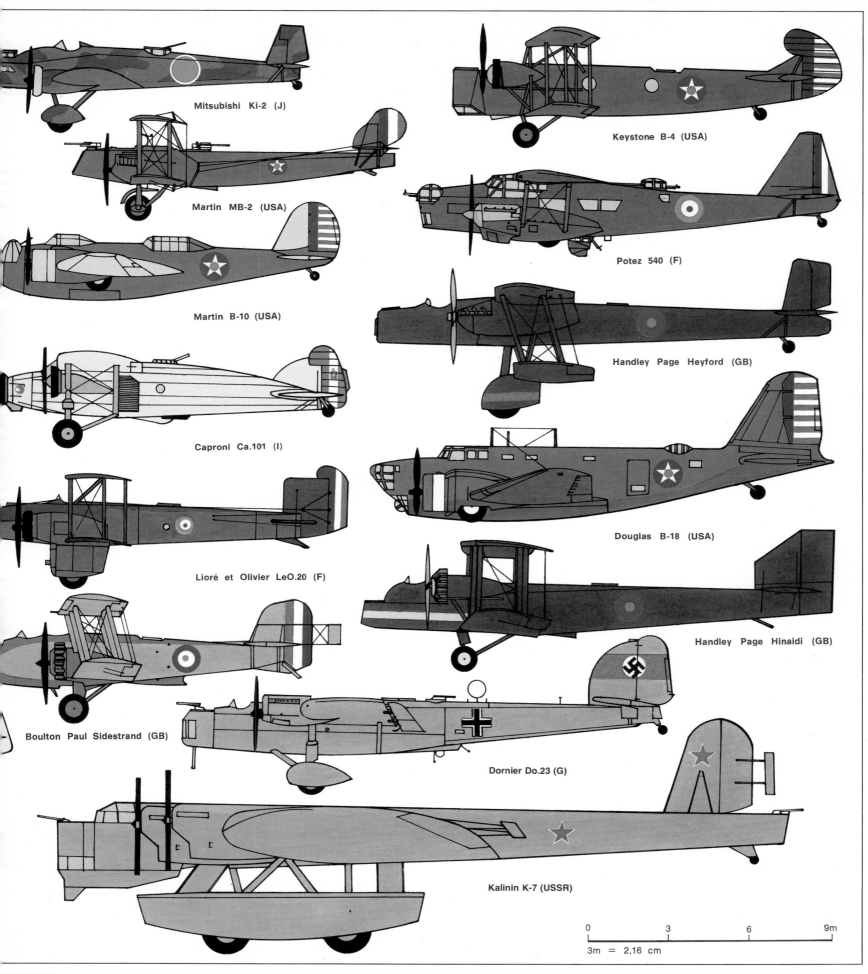

Mitsubishi Ki-2 (J)

Martin MB-2 (USA)

Martin B-10 (USA)

Caproni Ca.101 (I)

Lioré et Olivier LeO.20 (F)

Boulton Paul Sidestrand (GB)

Keystone B-4 (USA)

Potez 540 (F)

Handley Page Heyford (GB)

Douglas B-18 (USA)

Handley Page Hinaidi (GB)

Dornier Do.23 (G)

Kalinin K-7 (USSR)

0   3   6   9m

3m = 2,16 cm

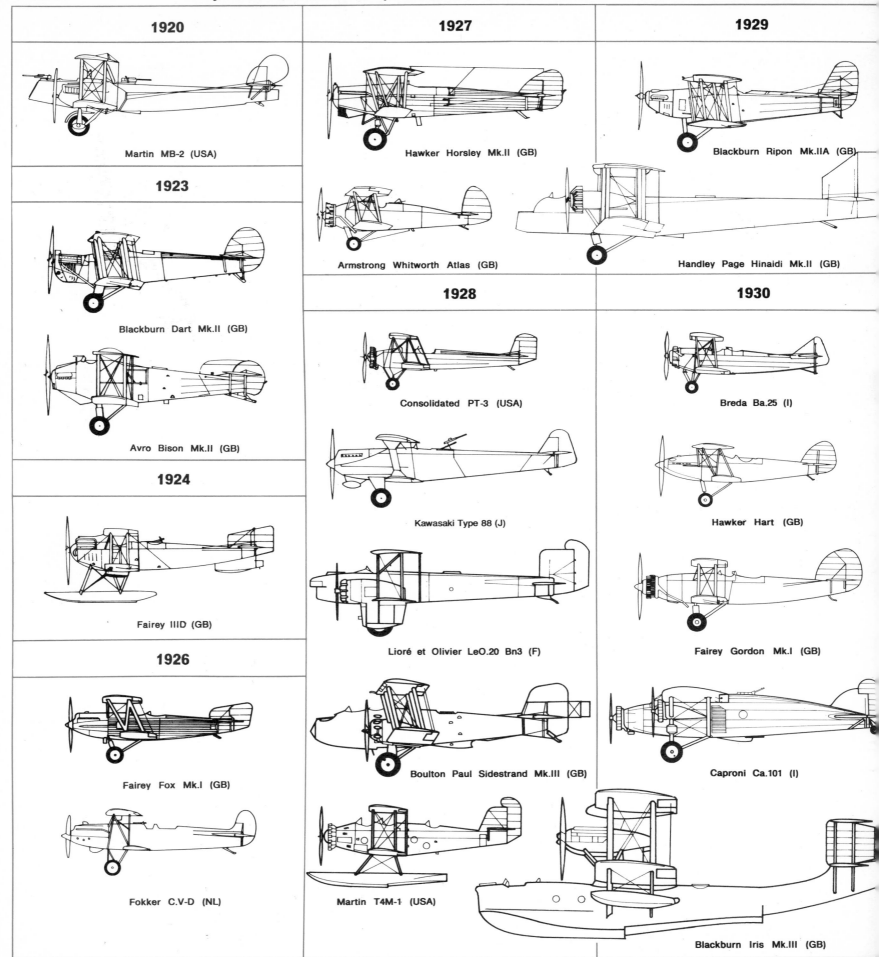

1920

Martin MB-2 (USA)

1923

Blackburn Dart Mk.II (GB)

Avro Bison Mk.II (GB)

1924

Fairey IIID (GB)

1926

Fairey Fox Mk.I (GB)

Fokker C.V-D (NL)

1927

Hawker Horsley Mk.II (GB)

Armstrong Whitworth Atlas (GB)

1928

Consolidated PT-3 (USA)

Kawasaki Type 88 (J)

Lioré et Olivier LeO.20 Bn3 (F)

Boulton Paul Sidestrand Mk.III (GB)

Martin T4M-1 (USA)

1929

Blackburn Ripon Mk.IIA (GB)

Handley Page Hinaidi Mk.II (GB)

1930

Breda Ba.25 (I)

Hawker Hart (GB)

Fairey Gordon Mk.I (GB)

Caproni Ca.101 (I)

Blackburn Iris Mk.III (GB)

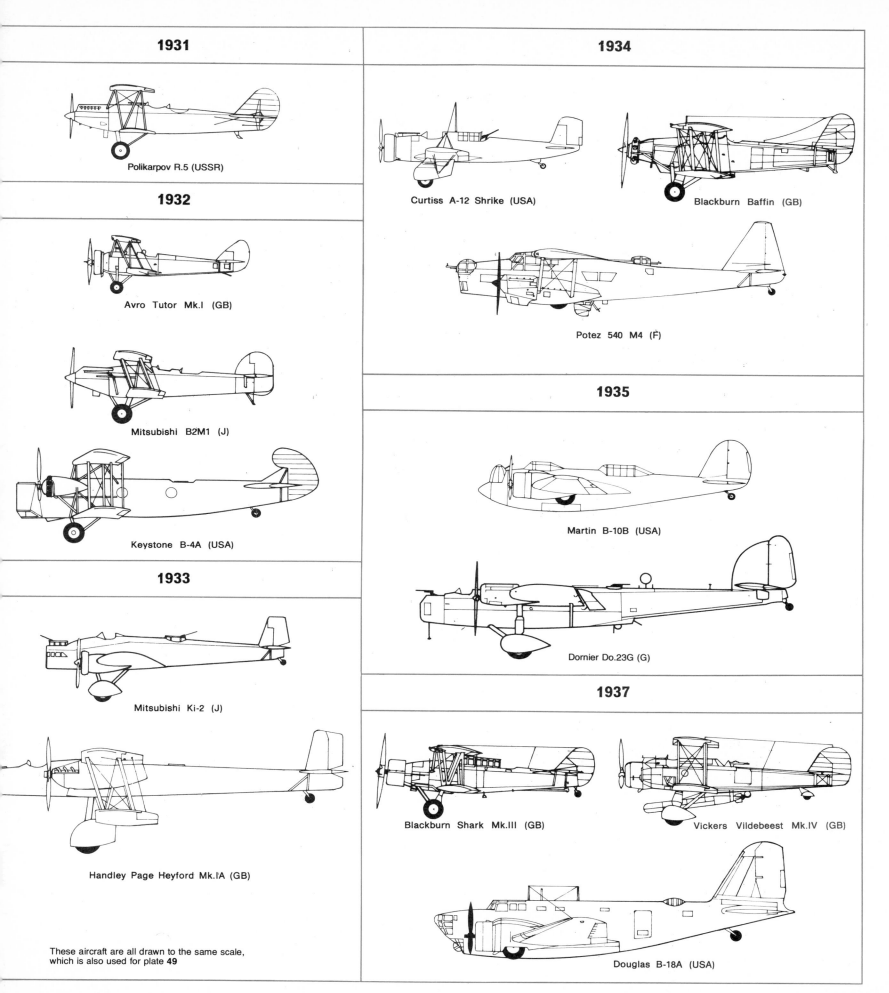

1931

Polikarpov R.5 (USSR)

1932

Avro Tutor Mk.I (GB)

Mitsubishi B2M1 (J)

Keystone B-4A (USA)

1933

Mitsubishi Ki-2 (J)

Handley Page Heyford Mk.IA (GB)

These aircraft are all drawn to the same scale, which is also used for plate **49**

1934

Curtiss A-12 Shrike (USA)

Blackburn Baffin (GB)

Potez 540 M4 (F)

1935

Martin B-10B (USA)

Dornier Do.23G (G)

1937

Blackburn Shark Mk.III (GB)

Vickers Vildebeest Mk.IV (GB)

Douglas B-18A (USA)

Plate 63

British bombers of the twenties: 1924–29

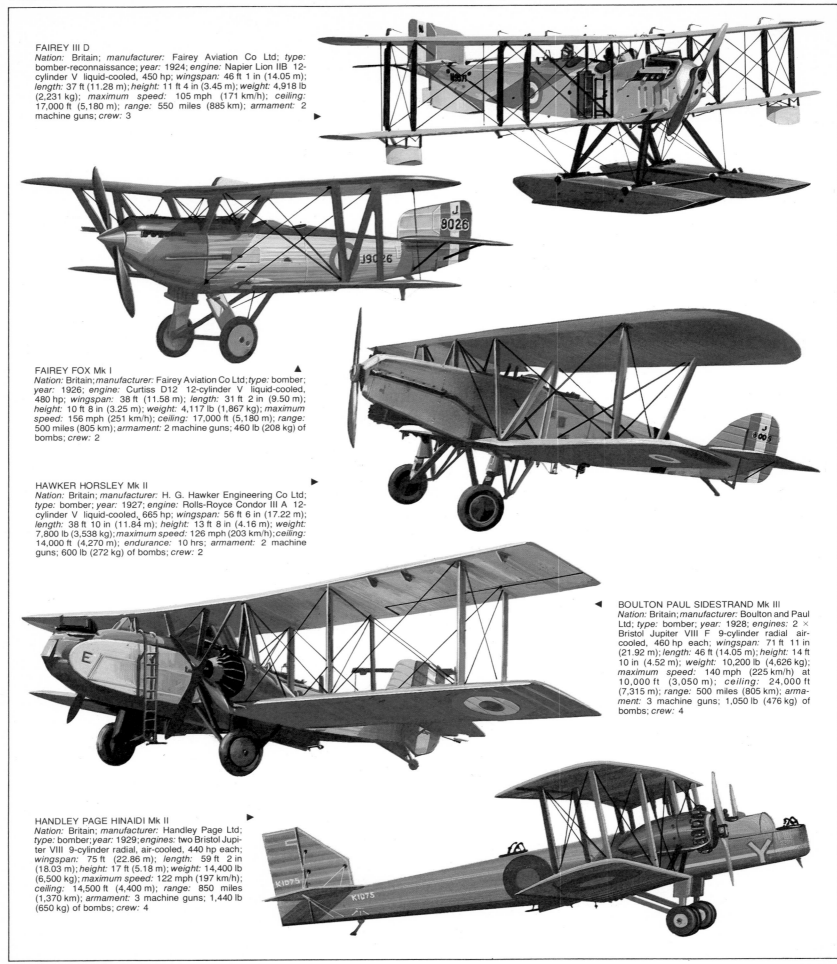

FAIREY III D
Nation: Britain; *manufacturer:* Fairey Aviation Co Ltd; *type:* bomber-reconnaissance; *year:* 1924; *engine:* Napier Lion IIB 12-cylinder V liquid-cooled, 450 hp; *wingspan:* 46 ft 1 in (14.05 m); *length:* 37 ft (11.28 m); *height:* 11 ft 4 in (3.45 m); *weight:* 4,918 lb (2,231 kg); *maximum speed:* 105 mph (171 km/h); *ceiling:* 17,000 ft (5,180 m); *range:* 550 miles (885 km); *armament:* 2 machine guns; *crew:* 3

FAIREY FOX Mk I
Nation: Britain; *manufacturer:* Fairey Aviation Co Ltd; *type:* bomber; *year:* 1926; *engine:* Curtiss D12 12-cylinder V liquid-cooled, 480 hp; *wingspan:* 38 ft (11.58 m); *length:* 31 ft 2 in (9.50 m); *height:* 10 ft 8 in (3.25 m); *weight:* 4,117 lb (1,867 kg); *maximum speed:* 156 mph (251 km/h); *ceiling:* 17,000 ft (5,180 m); *range:* 500 miles (805 km); *armament:* 2 machine guns; 460 lb (208 kg) of bombs; *crew:* 2

HAWKER HORSLEY Mk II
Nation: Britain; *manufacturer:* H. G. Hawker Engineering Co Ltd; *type:* bomber; *year:* 1927; *engine:* Rolls-Royce Condor III A 12-cylinder V liquid-cooled, 665 hp; *wingspan:* 56 ft 6 in (17.22 m); *length:* 38 ft 10 in (11.84 m); *height:* 13 ft 8 in (4.16 m); *weight:* 7,800 lb (3,538 kg); *maximum speed:* 126 mph (203 km/h); *ceiling:* 14,000 ft (4,270 m); *endurance:* 10 hrs; *armament:* 2 machine guns; 600 lb (272 kg) of bombs; *crew:* 2

BOULTON PAUL SIDESTRAND Mk III
Nation: Britain; *manufacturer:* Boulton and Paul Ltd; *type:* bomber; *year:* 1928; *engines:* 2 × Bristol Jupiter VIII F 9-cylinder radial air-cooled, 460 hp each; *wingspan:* 71 ft 11 in (21.92 m); *length:* 46 ft (14.05 m); *height:* 14 ft 10 in (4.52 m); *weight:* 10,200 lb (4,626 kg); *maximum speed:* 140 mph (225 km/h) at 10,000 ft (3,050 m); *ceiling:* 24,000 ft (7,315 m); *range:* 500 miles (805 km); *armament:* 3 machine guns; 1,050 lb (476 kg) of bombs; *crew:* 4

HANDLEY PAGE HINAIDI Mk II
Nation: Britain; *manufacturer:* Handley Page Ltd; *type:* bomber; *year:* 1929; *engines:* two Bristol Jupiter VIII 9-cylinder radial, air-cooled, 440 hp each; *wingspan:* 75 ft (22.86 m); *length:* 59 ft 2 in (18.03 m); *height:* 17 ft (5.18 m); *weight:* 14,400 lb (6,500 kg); *maximum speed:* 122 mph (197 km/h); *ceiling:* 14,500 ft (4,400 m); *range:* 850 miles (1,370 km); *armament:* 3 machine guns; 1,440 lb (650 kg) of bombs; *crew:* 4

HAWKER HART
Nation: Britain; *manufacturer:* H. G. Hawker Engineering Co Ltd; *type:* bomber; *year:* 1930; *engine:* Rolls-Royce Kestrel IB 12-cylinder V liquid-cooled, 525 hp; *wingspan:* 37 ft 3 in (11.35 m); *length:* 29 ft 4 in (8.94 m); *height:* 10 ft 5 in (3.17 m); *weight:* 4,554 lb (2,065 kg); *maximum speed:* 184 mph (296 km/h); *ceiling:* 21,300 ft (6,500 m); *range:* 470 miles (760 km); *armament:* 2 machine guns; 500 lb (226 kg) of bombs; *crew:* 2

VICKERS VILDEBEEST Mk IV
Nation: Britain; *manufacturer:* Vickers Ltd; *type:* torpedo-bomber; *year:* 1937; *engine:* Bristol Perseus VIII 9-cylinder radial air-cooled, 825 hp; *wingspan:* 49 ft (14.93 m); *length:* 37 ft 8 in (11.48 m); *height:* 14 ft 8 in (4.47 m); *weight:* 8,500 lb (3,855 kg); *maximum speed:* 156 mph (251 km/h); *ceiling:* 17,000 ft (5,180 m); *range:* 630 miles (1,015 km); *armament:* 2 machine guns, 1 torpedo, or 2,200 lb (1,000 kg) of bombs; *crew:* 2

HANDLEY PAGE HEYFORD Mk IA
Nation: Britain; *manufacturer:* Handley Page Ltd; *type:* bomber; *year:* 1933; *engine:* two Rolls-Royce Kestrel IIIS, 12-cylinder V, liquid-cooled, 575 hp each; *wingspan:* 75 ft (22.86 m); *length:* 58 ft (17.67 m); *height:* 17 ft 6 in (5.33 m); *weight:* 16,900 lb (7,700 kg); *maximum speed:* 142 mph (228 km/h) at 13,000 ft (3,900 m); *ceiling:* 21,000 ft (6,400 m); *range:* 900 miles (1,500 km); *armament:* 3 machine guns, 2,800 lb (1,300 kg) of bombs; *crew:* 4

FAIREY GORDON Mk I
Nation: Britain; *manufacturer:* Fairey Aviation Co Ltd; *type:* bomber; *year:* 1930; *engine:* Armstrong Siddeley Panther IIA 14-cylinder radial air-cooled, 525 hp; *wingspan:* 45 ft 9 in (13.94 m); *length:* 36 ft 8 in (11.17 m); *height:* 14 ft 2 in (4.31 m); *weight:* 5,900 lb (2,675 kg); *maximum speed:* 143 mph (233 km/h) at 3,000 ft (914 m); *ceiling:* 22,000 ft (6,700 m); *range:* 600 miles (965 km); *armament:* 2 machine guns; 460 lb (208 kg) of bombs; *crew:* 2

HAWKER HIND Mk I
Nation: Britain; *manufacturer:* Hawker Aircraft Ltd; *type:* bomber; *year:* 1935; *engine:* Rolls-Royce Kestrel V 12-cylinder V liquid-cooled, 640 hp; *wingspan:* 37 ft 3 in (11.35 m); *length:* 29 ft 7 in (9.02 m); *height:* 10 ft 7 in (3.23 m); *weight:* 5,298 lb (2,403 kg); *maximum speed:* 186 mph (299 km/h) at 16,400 ft (5,000 m); *ceiling:* 26,400 ft (8,050 m); *range:* 430 miles (690 km); *armament:* 2 machine guns; 500 lb (227 kg) of bombs; *crew:* 2

Plate 65

Torpedo-bombers of the Fleet Air Arm: 1923–37

BLACKBURN DART Mk II
Nation: Britain; *manufacturer:* Blackburn Aeroplane and Motor Co Ltd; *type:* torpedo-bomber; *year:* 1923; *engine:* Napier Lion IIB 12-cylinder V liquid-cooled, 450 hp; *wingspan:* 45 ft 6 in (13.86 m); *length:* 35 ft 4 in (10.77 m); *height:* 12 ft 11 in (3.94 m); *weight:* 6,370 lb (2,895 kg); *maximum speed:* 107 mph (172 km/h) at 3,000 ft (915 m); *ceiling:* 12,700 ft (3,870 m); *range:* 285 miles (460 km); *armament:* 1 torpedo at 1,653 lb (750 kg); *crew:* 1

AVRO BISON Mk II
Nation: Britain; *manufacturer:* A. V. Roe & Co Ltd; *type:* reconnaissance; *year:* 1923; *engine:* Napier Lion 12-cylinder at V liquid-cooled, 480 hp; *wingspan:* 46 ft (14.02 m); *length:* 36 ft (10.97 m); *height:* 14 ft 2 in (4.32 m); *weight:* 6,132 lb (2,781 kg); *maximum speed:* 110 mph (177 km/h); *ceiling:* 12,000 ft (3,660 m); *range:* 360 miles (580 km); *armament:* 2 machine guns; *crew:* 3-4

BLACKBURN RIPON Mk IIA
Nation: Britain; *manufacturer:* Blackburn Aeroplane and Motor Co Ltd; *type:* torpedo bomber; *year:* 1929; *engine:* Napier Lion XI A 12-cylinder at V liquid-cooled, 570 hp; *wingspan:* 44 ft 10 in (13.66 m); *length:* 36 ft 9 in (10.97 m); *height:* 13 ft 4 in (4.06 m); *weight:* 7,405 lb (3,359 kg); *maximum speed:* 126 mph (203 km/h); *ceiling:* 10,000 ft (3,050 m); *range:* 815 miles (1,310 km); *armament:* 2 machine guns, 1 torpedo at 1,635 lb (750 kg); *crew:* 2

BLACKBURN BAFFIN
Nation: Britain; *manufacturer:* Blackburn Aeroplane and Motor Co Ltd; *type:* torpedo-bomber; *year:* 1934; *engine:* Bristol Pegasus IM 3 9-cylinder radial air-cooled, 565 hp; *wingspan:* 45 ft 6 in (13.86 m); *length:* 38 ft 3 in (11.66 m); *height:* 13 ft 5 in (4.09 m); *weight:* 7,610 lb (3,452 kg); *maximum speed:* 136 mph (219 km/h) at 6,500 ft (1,980 m); *ceiling:* 15,000 ft (4,570 m); *range:* 450 miles (725 km); *armament:* 2 machine guns, 1 torpedo at 1,576 lb (715 kg) or 2,000 lb (907 kg) of bombs; *crew:* 2

BLACKBURN SHARK Mk III
Nation: Britain; *manufacturer:* Blackburn Aeroplane and Motor Co Ltd; *type:* torpedo-bomber; *year:* 1937; *engine:* Armstrong Siddeley Tiger VI 14-cylinder radial air-cooled, 760 hp; *wingspan:* 46 ft (14.02 m); *length:* 35 ft 2 in (10.72 m); *height:* 12 ft 1 in (3.68 m); *weight:* 8,050 lb (3,651 kg); *maximum speed:* 152 mph (245 km/h) at 6,500 ft (1,980 m); *ceiling:* 16,400 ft (5,000 m); *range:* 625 miles (1,005 km); *armament:* 2 machine guns, 1 torpedo at 1,576 lb (715 kg); *crew:* 2-3

MARTIN MB-2

Nation: USA; *manufacturer:* Glenn L. Martin Co;
type: bomber; *year:* 1920; *engine:* two Liberty
12 12-cylinder V, liquid-cooled, 420 hp each;
wingspan: 74 ft 2 in (22.60 m); *length:* 42 ft 8 in
(13.00 m); *height:* 14 ft 8 in (4.47 m);
weight: 12,064 lb (5,472 kg); *maximum speed:*
100 mph (160 km/h); *ceiling:* 8,500 ft
(2,600 m); *range:* 560 miles (900 km); *armament:* 5 machine guns; 3,000 lb (1,360 kg) of
bombs; *crew:* 4

KEYSTONE B-4A

Nation: USA; *manufacturer:* Keystone Aircraft
Co; *type:* bomber; *year:* 1932; *engine:* two Pratt
& Whitney Hornet 9-cylinder radial air-cooled,
575 hp each; *wingspan:* 74 ft 9 in (22.78 m);
length: 48 ft 10 in (14.88 m) *height:* 15 ft 9 in
(4.80 m); *weight:* 13,200 lb (6,000 kg); *maximum speed:* 121 mph (195 km/h); *ceiling:*
14,000 ft (4,300 m); *range:* 855 miles
(1,376 km); *armament:* 3 machine guns;
2,500 lb (1,130 kg) of bombs; *crew:* 5

MARTIN B-10B

Nation: USA; *manufacturer:* Glenn L. Martin Co;
type: bomber; *year:* 1935; *engine:* two Wright
Cyclone 9-cylinder radial air-cooled, 775 hp
each; *wingspan:* 70 ft 6 in (21.49 m); *length:*
44 ft 9 in (13.63 m); *height:* 11 ft 5 in (3.48 m);
weight: 16,400 lb (7,430 kg); *maximum speed:*
213 mph (343 km/h); *ceiling:* 24,200 ft
(7,300 m); *range:* 600 miles (960 km); *armament:* 3 machine guns; 2,260 lb (1,025 kg) of
bombs; *crew:* 4

DOUGLAS B-18 A

Nation: USA; *manufacturer:* Douglas Aircraft Co; *type:* bomber; *year:* 1937; *engine:* 2
Wright R-1820-53 Cyclone 9-cylinder radial air-cooled, 1,000 hp each; *wingspan:* 89 ft
6 in (27.28 m); *length:* 57 ft 10 in (17.63 m); *height:* 15 ft 2 in (4.62 m); *weight:* 27,672 lb
(12,552 kg); *maximum speed:* 226 mph (364 km/h) at 10,000 ft (3,050 m); *ceiling:* 27,150 ft
(8,275 m); *range:* 1,200 miles (1,931 km); *armament:* 3 machine guns; 6,500 lb (2,948 kg)
of bombs; *crew:* 6

CURTISS A-12 SHRIKE
Nation: USA; *manufacturer:* Curtiss Aeroplane and Motor Co; *type:* attack; *year:* 1934; *engine:* Wright Cyclone 9-cylinder radial air-cooled, 690 hp; *wingspan:* 44 ft (13.41 m); *length:* 32 ft 3 in (9.83 m); *height:* 9 ft 4 in (2.84 m); *weight:* 5,900 lb (2,670 kg); *maximum speed:* 175 mph (282 km/h); *ceiling:* 15,150 ft (4,620 m); *endurance:* 3½ hrs; *armament:* 4 machine guns; 400 lb (180 kg) of bombs; *crew:* 2

MARTIN T4M-1
Nation: USA; *manufacturer:* Glenn L. Martin Co; *type:* torpedo-bomber; *year:* 1928; *engine:* Pratt & Whitney R-1690-24 Hornet 9-cylinder radial air-cooled, 525 hp; *wingspan:* 53 ft (16.15 m); *length:* 35 ft 7 in (10.85 m); *height:* 14 ft 9 in (4.50 m); *weight:* 8,071 lb (3,661 kg); *maximum speed:* 114 mph (183 km/h); *ceiling:* 10,150 ft (3,095 m); *range:* 363 miles (585 km); *armament:* 2 machine guns, 1 torpedo at 1,618 lb (734 kg); *crew:* 3

CURTISS BF2C-1 GOSHAWK
Nation: USA; *manufacturer:* Curtiss-Wright Corp; *type:* attack; *year:* 1934; *engine:* Wright R-1820-04 Cyclone 9-cylinder radial air-cooled, 700 hp; *wingspan:* 31 ft 6 in (9.60 m); *length:* 23 ft (7.01 m); *height:* 10 ft 10 in (3.30 m); *weight:* 5,086 lb (2,307 kg); *maximum speed:* 285 mph (459 km/h) at 8,000 ft (2,440 m); *ceiling:* 27,000 ft (8,230 m); *range:* 797 miles (1,280 km); *armament:* 2 machine guns; 474 lb (215 kg) of bombs; *crew:* 1

CURTISS SBC-4 HELLDIVER
Nation: USA; *manufacturer:* Curtiss-Wright Corp; *type:* bomber; *year:* 1939; *engine:* Wright R-1820-34 Cyclone 9-cylinder radial air-cooled, 950 hp; *wingspan:* 34 ft (10.36 m); *length:* 28 ft 4 in (8.63 m); *height:* 12 ft 7 in (3.83 m); *weight:* 7,632 lb (3,462 kg); *maximum speed:* 273 mph (381 km/h) at 15,200 ft (4,635 m); *ceiling:* 27,300 ft (8,320 m); *range:* 590 miles (950 km); *armament:* 2 machine guns; 1,000 lb (454 kg) of bombs; *crew:* 2

LIORÉ ET OLIVIER Le. O 20 Bn3
Nation: France; *manufacturer:* Etablissements Lioré et Olivier; *type:* bomber; *year:* 1928; *engine:* 2 Gnome-Rhône 9 Ady 9-cylinder radial air-cooled, 420 hp; *wingspan:* 73 ft (22.25 m); *length:* 45 ft 4 in (13.87 m); *height:* 16 ft 7 in (5.05 m); *weight:* 11,684 lb (5,300 kg); *maximum speed:* 124 mph (200 km/h); *ceiling:* 18,865 ft (5,750 m); *range:* 621 miles (1,000 km); *armament:* 4 machine guns; 2,300 lb (1,040 kg) of bombs; *crew:* 4-5

BLOCH 200 BN 4
Nation: France; *manufacturer:* Avions Marcel Bloch; *type:* bomber; *year:* 1934; *engine:* 2 Gnome-Rhône 14 Kirs 14-cylinder radial air-cooled, 870 hp each; *wingspan:* 73 ft 8 in (22.45 m); *length:* 52 ft 6 in (16.00 m); *height:* 12 ft 10 in (3.92 m); *weight:* 16,050 lb (9,280 kg); *maximum speed:* 143 mph (230 km/h) at 14,100 ft (4,300 m); *ceiling:* 22,640 ft (6,000 m); *range:* 621 miles (1,000 km); *armament:* 3 machine guns; 3,300 lb (1,500 kg) of bombs; *crew:* 4-5

POTEZ 540 M 4
Nation: France; *manufacturer:* Société des Aéroplanes Henry Potez; *type:* bomber; *year:* 1934; *engine:* 2 Hispano-Suiza 12 Kirs 12-cylinder V, liquid-cooled, 690 hp each; *wingspan:* 72 ft 6 in (22.10 m); *length:* 53 ft 2 in (16.20 m); *height:* 12 ft 9 in (3.88 m); *weight:* 13,115 lb (5,950 kg); *maximum speed:* 193 mph (310 km/h) at 13,125 ft (4,000 m); *ceiling:* 32,810 ft (10,000 m); *range:* 745 miles (1,200 m); *armament:* 5 machine guns; 220 lb (100 kg) of bombs; *crew:* 4

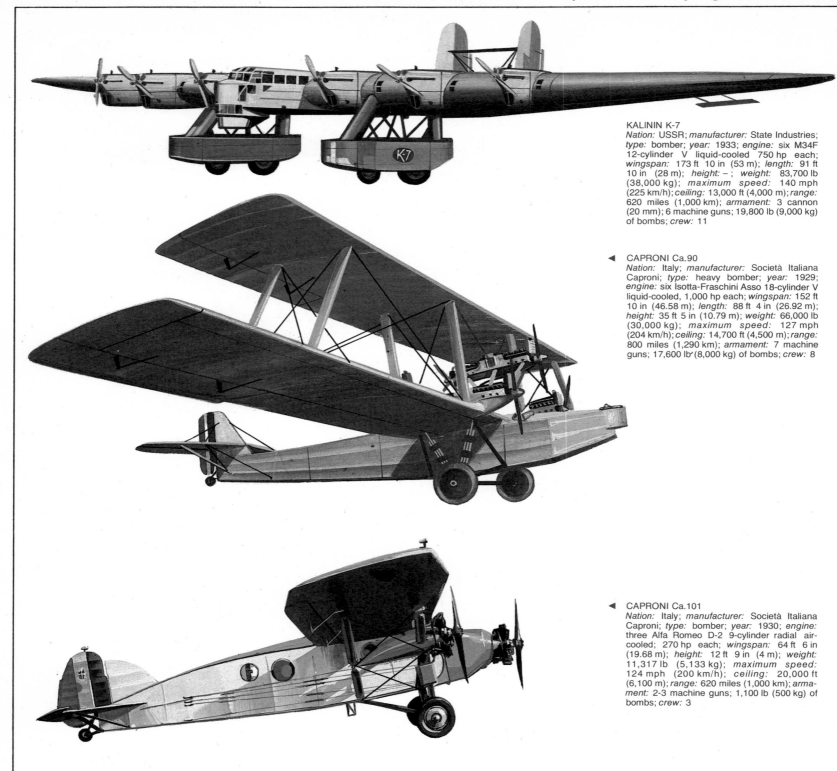

KALININ K-7
Nation: USSR; *manufacturer:* State Industries; *type:* bomber; *year:* 1933; *engine:* six M34F 12-cylinder V liquid-cooled 750 hp each; *wingspan:* 173 ft 10 in (53 m); *length:* 91 ft 10 in (28 m); *height:* – ; *weight:* 83,700 lb (38,000 kg); *maximum speed:* 140 mph (225 km/h); *ceiling:* 13,000 ft (4,000 m); *range:* 620 miles (1,000 km); *armament:* 3 cannon (20 mm); 6 machine guns; 19,800 lb (9,000 kg) of bombs; *crew:* 11

◄ **CAPRONI Ca.90**
Nation: Italy; *manufacturer:* Società Italiana Caproni; *type:* heavy bomber; *year:* 1929; *engine:* six Isotta-Fraschini Asso 18-cylinder V liquid-cooled, 1,000 hp each; *wingspan:* 152 ft 10 in (46.58 m); *length:* 88 ft 4 in (26.92 m); *height:* 35 ft 5 in (10.79 m); *weight:* 66,000 lb (30,000 kg); *maximum speed:* 127 mph (204 km/h); *ceiling:* 14,700 ft (4,500 m); *range:* 800 miles (1,290 km); *armament:* 7 machine guns; 17,600 lb (8,000 kg) of bombs; *crew:* 8

◄ CAPRONI Ca.101
Nation: Italy; *manufacturer:* Società Italiana Caproni; *type:* bomber; *year:* 1930; *engine:* three Alfa Romeo D-2 9-cylinder radial air-cooled; 270 hp each; *wingspan:* 64 ft 6 in (19.68 m); *height:* 12 ft 9 in (4 m); *weight:* 11,317 lb (5,133 kg); *maximum speed:* 124 mph (200 km/h); *ceiling:* 20,000 ft (6,100 m); *range:* 620 miles (1,000 km); *armament:* 2-3 machine guns; 1,100 lb (500 kg) of bombs; *crew:* 3

CAPRONI Ca.310
Nation: Italy; *manufacturer:* Società Italiana Caproni; *type:* reconnaissance; *year:* 1937; *engine:* 2 Piaggio P VIII C 35 7-cylinder radial air-cooled, 470 hp each; *wingspan:* 53 ft 2 in (16.20 m); *length:* 40 ft 1 in (12.20 m); *height:* 11 ft 7 in (3.52 m); *weight:* 10,251 lb (4,650 kg); *maximum speed:* 227 mph (365 km/h); *ceiling:* 22,965 ft (7,000 m); *range:* 1,025 miles (1,650 km); *armament:* 3 machine guns; 882 lb (400 kg) of bombs; *crew:* 3

LETOV SM 1
Nation: Czechoslovakia; *manufacturer:* Letov;
type: bomber; *year:* 1921; *engine:* Hiero L
6-cylinder inline, 230 hp; *wingspan:* 43 ft 4 in
(13.20 m); *length:* 27 ft 3 in (8.30 m); *height:*
10 ft 2 in (3.10 m); *weight:* 3,031 lb (1,355 kg);
maximum speed: 120 mph (194 km/h) at
6,560 ft (2,000 m); *ceiling:* 19,685 ft (6,000 m);
range: 445 miles (715 km); *armament:* 2
machine guns; 265 lb (120 kg) of bombs;
crew: 2

MITSUBISHI B2M1
Nation: Japan; *manufacturer:* Mitsubishi
Jukogyo KK; *type:* torpedo-bomber; *year:* 1932;
engine: Hispano-Mitsubishi 12-cylinder V
liquid-cooled, 600 hp; *wingspan:* 49 ft 11 in
(15.22 m); *length:* 33 ft 8 in (10.27 m); *height:*
12 ft 2 in (3.71 m); *weight:* 7,900 lb (3,600 kg);
maximum speed: 132 mph (213 km/h); *ceiling:*
14,700 ft (4,500 m); *range:* 600 miles (960 km);
armament: 2 machine guns; 1,700 lb (800 kg)
of bombs; *crew:* 2

MITSUBISHI Ki-2
Nation: Japan; *manufacturer:* Mitsubishi
Jukogyo KK; *type:* bomber; *year:* 1933; *engine:*
two Nakajima Kotobuki 9-cylinder radial air-
cooled, 570 hp each; *wingspan:* 65 ft 6 in
(19.96 m); *length:* 41 ft 4 in (12.60 m); *height:*
15 ft 2 in (4.64 m); *weight:* 10,040 lb (4,550 kg);
maximum speed: 158 mph (255 km/h) at
9,800 ft (3,000 m); *ceiling:* 23,000 ft (7,000 m);
range: 560 miles (900 km); *armament:* 2
machine guns; 660 lb (300 kg) of bombs;
crew: 3

DORNIER Do.23G
Nation: Germany; *manufacturer:* Dornier
Werke GmbH; *type:* bomber; *year:* 1935;
engine: 2 BMW VI U 12-cylinder V liquid-
cooled, 750 hp; *wingspan:* 84 ft (25.60 m);
length: 61 ft 8 in (18.78 m); *height:* 17 ft 8 in
(5.40 m); *weight:* 19,290 lb (8,750 kg); *maximum speed:* 162 mph (260 km/h) at 9,840 ft
(3,000 m); *ceiling:* 13,780 ft (5,800 m); *range:*
745 miles (1,200 km); *armament:* 3 machine
guns; 2,200 lb (1,000 kg) of bombs; *crew:* 4

CURTISS SOC-1 SEAGULL
Nation: USA; *manufacturer:* Curtiss-Wright Co; *type:* reconnaissance; *year:* 1935; *engine:* Pratt & Whitney R-1340-18 Wasp 9-cylinder radial air-cooled 600 hp; *wingspan:* 36 ft (10.97 m); *length:* 31 ft 5 in (9.63 m); *height:* 14 ft 9 in (4.49 m); *weight:* 5,437 lb (2,466 kg); *maximum speed:* 165 mph (266 km/h) at 5,000 ft (1,525 m); *ceiling:* 14,000 ft (4,542 m); *range:* 679 miles (1,087 km); *armament:* 2 machine guns; 650 lb (295 kg) of bombs; *crew:* 2

VOUGHT O2U-1 CORSAIR
Nation: USA; *manufacturer:* Chance Vought Co; *type:* reconnaissance; *year:* 1927; *engine:* Pratt & Whitney Wasp 9-cylinder radial air-cooled, 450 hp; *wingspan:* 34 ft 6 in (10.51 m); *length:* 24 ft 5 in (7.45 m); *height:* 10 ft (3.08 m); *weight:* 3,635 lb (1,649 kg); *maximum speed:* 150 mph (241 km/h); *ceiling:* 18,700 ft (5,700 m); *range:* 610 miles (980 km); *armament:* 2–3 machine guns; *crew:* 2

LOENING OL-9
Nation: USA; *manufacturer:* Keystone-Loening; *type:* reconnaissance; *year:* 1927; *engine:* Pratt & Whitney R-1030-4 Wasp 9-cylinder radial air-cooled, 450 hp; *wingspan:* 45 ft (13.72 m); *length:* 34 ft 9 in (10.59 m); *height:* 12 ft 9 in (3.89 m); *weight:* 5,404 lb (2,451 kg); *maximum speed:* 122 mph (196 km/h); *ceiling:* 14,300 ft (4,350 m); *range:* 625 miles (1,000 km); *armament:* – ; *crew:* 2

BLACKBURN IRIS Mk III
Nation: Britain; *manufacturer:* Blackburn Aeroplane and Motor Co; *type:* reconnaissance; *year:* 1930; *engine:* 3 Rolls-Royce Condor IIIB 12-cylinder V liquid-cooled 675 hp each; *wingspan:* 97 ft (29.57 m); *length:* 67 ft 5 in (20.54 m); *height:* 25 ft 6 in (7.77 m); *weight:* 29,000 lb (13,154 kg); *maximum speed:* 118 mph (190 km/h); *ceiling:* 10,000 ft (3,050 m); *range:* 470 miles (756 km); *armament:* 3 machine guns; 2,000 lb (907 kg) of bombs; *crew:* 5

ARMSTRONG WHITWORTH ATLAS
Nation: Britain; *manufacturer:* Armstrong Whitworth Aircraft Ltd; *type:* army co-operation; *year:* 1927; *engine:* Armstrong Siddeley Jaguar IV C 14-cylinder radial air-cooled, 450 hp; *wingspan:* 39 ft 6 in (12.04 m); *length:* 28 ft 6 in (8.68 m); *height:* 10 ft 6 in (3.20 m); *weight:* 4,018 lb (1,823 kg); *maximum speed:* 142 mph (228 km/h); *ceiling:* 16,800 ft (5,120 m); *range:* 480 miles (770 km); *armament:* 2 machine guns; 448 lb (203 kg) of bombs; *crew:* 2

POLIKARPOV R-5
Nation: USSR; *manufacturer:* State Industries; *type:* reconnaissance; *year:* 1931;
engine: M17 12-cylinder V liquid-cooled,
680 hp; *wingspan:* 50 ft 10 in (15.50 m);
length: 34 ft 8 in (10.55 m); *height:* 10 ft 8 in
(3.25 m); *weight:* 6,515 lb (2,955 kg);
maximum speed: 142 mph (228 km/h) at
9,800 ft (3,000 m); *ceiling:* 21,000 ft
(6,400 m); *range:* 500 miles (800 km);
armament: 2 machine guns; 530 lb (240 kg)
of bombs; *crew:* 2

FOKKER C VD
Nation: Netherlands; *manufacturer:* Fokker; *type:* reconnaissance; *year:* 1926; *engine:*
Bristol Jupiter 9-cylinder V air-cooled, 450 hp; *wingspan:* 41 ft (12.50 m); *length:* 31 ft
4 in (9.55 m); *height:* 11 ft 6 in (3.50 m); *weight:* 4,222 lb (1,915 kg); *maximum speed:*
200 mph (320 km/h); *ceiling:* 19,600 ft (6,000 m); *range:* 740 miles (1,200 km); *armament:* 2 machine guns; *crew:* 2

▼

MUREAUX M.117 R.2B2　　　　▲
Nation: France; *manufacturer:* Mureaux; *type:* reconnaissance; *year:* 1935; *engine:*
Hispano-Suiza 12-cylinder V liquid-cooled, 860 hp; *wingspan:* 50 ft 6 in (15.40 m);
length: 33 ft 4 in (10.18 m); *height:* 11 ft 2 in (3.44 m); *weight:* 7,605 lb (3,450 kg)
(loaded); *maximum speed:* 197 mph (317 km/h) at 11,483 ft (3,500 m); *ceiling:*
26,246 ft (8,000 m); *range:* 4,921 miles (1,500 km); *armament:* 5 machine guns, 882 lb
(400 kg) of bombs; *crew:* 2

AERO A-11
Nation: Czechoslovakia; *manufacturer:* Aero Tovarna Letadel; *type:* reconnaissance;
year: 1923; *engine:* Walter W IV 8-cylinder V liquid-cooled, 240 hp; *wingspan:* 41 ft
11 in (12.77 m); *length:* 26 ft 11 in (8.20 m); *height:* 10 ft 2 in (3.10 m); *weight:* 3,260 lb
(1,480 kg); *maximum speed:* 133 mph (214 km/h) at 8,200 ft (2,500 m); *ceiling:*
23,600 ft (7,200 m); *range:* 460 miles (750 km); *armament:* 1 machine gun; *crew:* 2

▼

NIN HAI　　　　▲
Nation: China; *manufacturer:* Naval Air Establishment; *type:* reconnaissance; *year:*
1933; *engine:* Jimpu 7-cylinder radial air-cooled, 130 hp; *wingspan:* 30 ft 2 in
(9.20 m); *length:* 22 ft 11 in (7.00 m); *height:* 9 ft 8 in (2.96 m); *weight:* 1,803 lb
(817 kg); *maximum speed:* 177 mph (110 km/h); *ceiling:* 12,200 ft (3,700 m); *range:*
418 miles (673 km); *crew:* 1

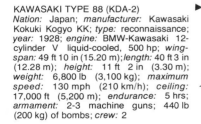

KAWASAKI TYPE 88 (KDA-2)　　▶
Nation: Japan; *manufacturer:* Kawasaki
Kokuki Kogyo KK; *type:* reconnaissance;
year: 1928; *engine:* BMW-Kawasaki 12-
cylinder V liquid-cooled, 500 hp; *wingspan:* 49 ft 10 in (15.20 m); *length:* 40 ft 3 in
(12.28 m); *height:* 11 ft 2 in (3.30 m);
weight: 6,800 lb (3,100 kg); *maximum
speed:* 130 mph (210 km/h); *ceiling:*
17,000 ft (5,200 m); *endurance:* 5 hrs;
armament: 2-3 machine guns; 440 lb
(200 kg) of bombs; *crew:* 2

Plate 73

Trainers and general purpose aircraft: 1928–32

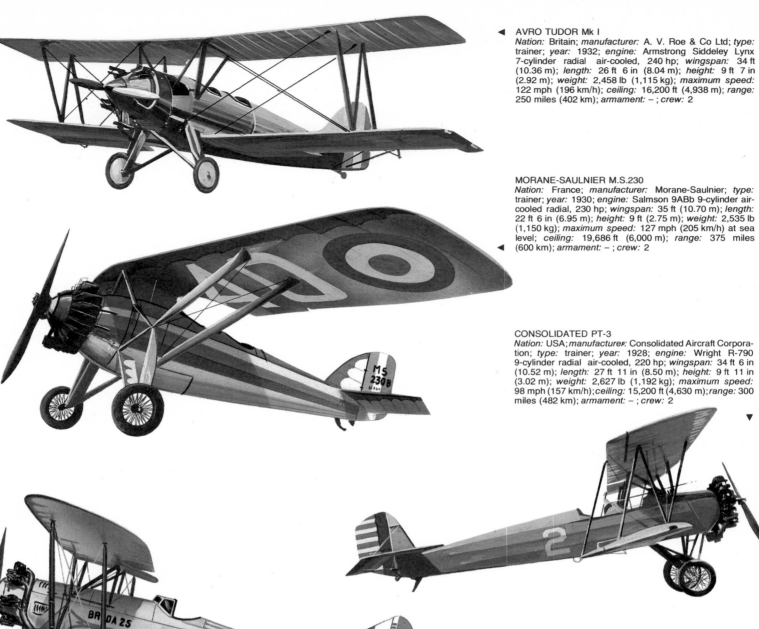

◄ AVRO TUDOR Mk I
Nation: Britain; *manufacturer:* A. V. Roe & Co Ltd; *type:* trainer; *year:* 1932; *engine:* Armstrong Siddeley Lynx 7-cylinder radial air-cooled, 240 hp; *wingspan:* 34 ft (10.36 m); *length:* 26 ft 6 in (8.04 m); *height:* 9 ft 7 in (2.92 m); *weight:* 2,458 lb (1,115 kg); *maximum speed:* 122 mph (196 km/h); *ceiling:* 16,200 ft (4,938 m); *range:* 250 miles (402 km); *armament:* – ; *crew:* 2

MORANE-SAULNIER M.S.230
Nation: France; *manufacturer:* Morane-Saulnier; *type:* trainer; *year:* 1930; *engine:* Salmson 9ABb 9-cylinder air-cooled radial, 230 hp; *wingspan:* 35 ft (10.70 m); *length:* 22 ft 6 in (6.95 m); *height:* 9 ft (2.75 m); *weight:* 2,535 lb (1,150 kg); *maximum speed:* 127 mph (205 km/h) at sea level; *ceiling:* 19,686 ft (6,000 m); *range:* 375 miles (600 km); *armament:* – ; *crew:* 2 ◄

CONSOLIDATED PT-3
Nation: USA; *manufacturer:* Consolidated Aircraft Corporation; *type:* trainer; *year:* 1928; *engine:* Wright R-790 9-cylinder radial air-cooled, 220 hp; *wingspan:* 34 ft 6 in (10.52 m); *length:* 27 ft 11 in (8.50 m); *height:* 9 ft 11 in (3.02 m); *weight:* 2,627 lb (1,192 kg); *maximum speed:* 98 mph (157 km/h); *ceiling:* 15,200 ft (4,630 m); *range:* 300 miles (482 km); *armament:* – ; *crew:* 2 ▼

BREDA Ba.25
Nation: Italy; *manufacturer:* Società Italiana Ernesto Breda; *type:* trainer; *year:* 1930; *engine:* Alfa Romeo Lynx 7-cylinder radial air-cooled, 220 hp; *wingspan:* 32 ft 10 in (10 m); *length:* 26 ft 3 in (8 m); *height:* 9 ft 6 in (2.90 m); *weight:* 2,204 lb (1,000 kg); *maximum speed:* 127 mph (205 km/h); *ceiling:* 16,075 ft (4,900 m); *range:* 248 miles (400 km); *armament:* – ; *crew:* 2

WESTLAND WAPITI Mk IIA
Nation: Britain; *manufacturer:* Westland Aircraft Ltd; *type:* liaison; *year:* 1931; *engine:* Bristol Jupiter VIII 9-cylinder radial air-cooled, 550 hp; *wingspan:* 46 ft 5 in (14.14 m); *length:* 32 ft 6 in (9.90 m); *height:* 11 ft 10 in (3.60 m); *weight:* 5,400 lb (2,450 kg); *maximum speed:* 135 mph (217 km/h) at 5,000 ft (1,525 m); *ceiling:* 20,600 ft (6,280 m); *range:* 360 miles (579 km); *armament:* 2 machine guns; 500 lb (227 kg) of bombs; *crew:* 2 ▶

Plate 63
British bombers of the twenties:
1924–29

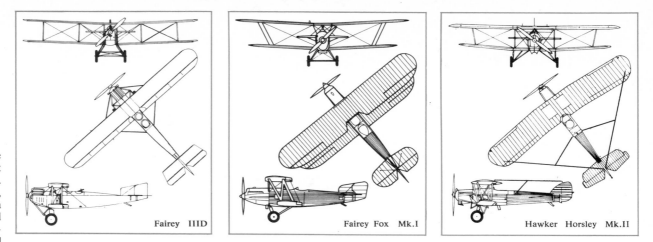

Fairey IIID

Fairey Fox Mk.I

Hawker Horsley Mk.II

The British made some notable improvements in the field of light bombers during the 1920s and 1930s. One of the most versatile aircraft, which could be used equally well as a reconnaissance plane or bomber and had both landplane and seaplane versions, was the Fairey IIID, a tough and efficient biplane used both by the RAF and the Royal Naval Air Service. The Fairey IIID was directly developed from the model IIIC of 1918, which in turn had been derived from the Fairey III seaplane of 1917.

The prototype flew for the first time in August 1920 and was driven by a 375 hp Rolls-Royce Eagle VIII engine, but most of the production aircraft were powered by 450 hp Napier Lion engines. The first of 207 Fairey IIIDs to be built reached units during 1924. The majority of these aircraft were used by the Royal Naval Air Service, as a landplane on board aircraft carriers and in a seaplane version for catapult launching, which kept them in service until 1930; but the RAF also used a certain number.

From 1st March to 21st June four Fairey IIIDs of the Royal Air Force successfully carried out a spectacular long distance formation flight from Northolt to Capetown returning to Lee-on-Solent across Greece, Italy and France. No serious problems were encountered at all on the 22,366 km (13,900 mile) marathon. Another Fairey aircraft, the Fox, was based on the idea of building a light bomber with generally better performance than contemporary fighters. This was a private project and the fast biplane showed the merits of its design and its advanced streamlining very clearly during proving trials in October 1925 which were carried out for the RAF; the Fox prototype showed it was faster by at least 80 km/h (50 mph) than other light bombers in service, and it could also outfly contemporary fighters. This excellent performance was mainly due to its American Curtiss D.12 engine with its small streamlined engine housing. The prototype, which flew for the first time on 3rd January 1925, was followed however by only 28 production aircraft, Fox Mk Is, which went into service in 1926.

A contemporary of the Fairey Fox was the Hawker Horsley, another biplane designed to be used either as a day bomber or a torpedo bomber. The prototype appeared in 1925 and at the end of proving trials it was chosen for production. This started in July 1926 and continued until November 1931, turning out 128 aircraft sub-divided

into two main series: the Mk I, of entirely wooden construction, and the Mk II of mixed construction. There was also a final series which was all-metal.

The first Hawker Horsleys went into service with bomber units of the RAF during 1927, and then the torpedo-bomber version reached units in June of the following year. These aircraft were mainly used in the Far East (India and Singapore) and stayed in the front line until 1935. The Horsleys were taken out of home-based bomber service in 1934.

Among twin-engine medium bomb-

ers, a class of which the most recent example had been the de Havilland of 1919, the first postwar aircraft was the Boulton Paul Sidestrand, a large but very manoeuvrable biplane which appeared in prototype in 1926. Production was limited to equipping one squadron, only 18 Sidestrands being built which went into service in April 1928 with 101 Squadron, flying until the end of 1934. The principal series were the Mk II and the Mk III which had different engines.

Between 1926 and 1933 the RAF's heavy night bombers included two types produced by Handley Page, the

Hyderabad and the Hinaidi, the last examples of a generation which belonged to the First World War. The Hinaidi was an improved and more powerful version of the Hyderabad, which had appeared in prototype form in October 1923. The Hinaidi prototype flew on 26th March 1927 and was put into production as the Mk II after significant structural changes had been carried out. The RAF received 33 of them which went into service in 1929, serving until November 1933. A transport version was also developed which could carry 23 troops and was used in India.

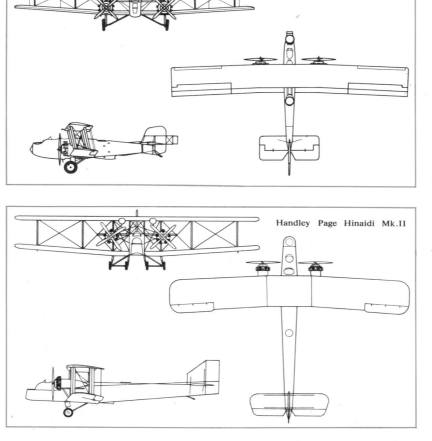

Boulton Paul Sidestrand Mk.III

Handley Page Hinaidi Mk.II

Plate 64
British bombers of the thirties:
1930–37

The Hinaidi's successor was the Handley Page Heyford, the last biplane heavy bomber to serve with the RAF. Designed in 1927 this aircraft's orginality lay in the high-set fuselage which was attached flush to the underside of the upper wings, and the prototype appeared in June 1930, being ordered into production two years later. The assembly lines kept up production until September 1936, building 122 aircraft in four principal series. The Mk I was followed by the Mk IA (minor improvements, 38 built) and by the Mk II powered by 640 hp

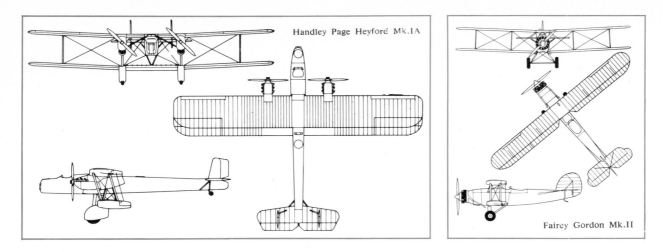

Handley Page Heyford Mk.IA

Fairey Gordon Mk.II

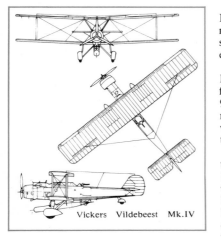

Vickers Vildebeest Mk.IV

Hawker Hart

Hawker Hind

Rolls-Royce Kestrel engines, with new engine nacelles, of smaller cross section and better form, and more efficient fuel consumption.

The last production series was the Mk III, of which 70 were built. The first Heyfords went into service with 99 squadron in July 1933; they remained in service up to 1937 in which year they were relegated to training.

It was in 1937 that the last variant, the Mk IV, of one of the most famous British torpedo-bombers of the 1930s went into service, the Vickers Vildebeest, an aircraft which, although dating back to 1933, ended up by becoming one of the few aircraft of its generation to fight in the Second World War. In Singapore the Vildebeest faced the Japanese invaders in 1941 and the last survivors were destroyed in Sumatra in March of the following year. The prototype of this large and heavy biplane, which was ordered as a replacement for the Hawker Horsley, had flown in 1932. Production had started the following year and had totalled 152 aircraft in three main series. In December 1936 a further contract was placed for 57 Vildebeest Mk IVs which had a different engine and propeller. These aircraft remained in production until December 1937.

But the RAF's most prominent bomber of the thirties was the little Hawker Hart; a biplane which completely revolutionised the concept of bombing with its exceptional performance and from which sprang an entire generation of combat aircraft. The Hart prototype flew in June 1928, and after a series of tests and comparisons with other aircraft, it was chosen by the RAF: its success was mainly due to a particularly happy choice of engine and to the sophisticated streamlining achieved by its designer, Sydney Camm.

Deliveries of the first series aircraft started in January 1930, and production was soon increased by contracts with other firms, Armstrong Whitworth building 149, Vickers 112 and Gloster 40, in addition to the 151 aircraft built by Hawker. A further 500 aircraft were built in trainer versions. Among other variants were the Hart

C, a general purpose aircraft, the Hart India and the Hart Special, both the latter being tropicalised versions. Eight more Harts were exported to Estonia in 1933 and another four to Sweden the year after; and between 1935 and 1936 the Swedish state factories built another 24 Harts powered by Bristol Pegasus radial engines.

At the end of 1935 another Hawker aeroplane, the Hind, started to replace the Hart as a front-line fighter with the RAF. This appeared in prototype on 12th September 1934, and was in essence an improved Hart with a more powerful engine and better aerodynamics. This was the last biplane light bomber of the RAF; 528 of them were built, which remained operational until 1938.

Another contemporary light bomber was withdrawn in the same year, the Fairey Gordon, the final member of the family which had started with the Fairey III of 1917. The Gordon had appeared and entered production in 1930. 160 were constructed in two principal series. The second of these, the Mk II of 1933, was characterised by modifications to the fuselage, tailplane and ailerons. It was powered by an Armstrong Siddeley radial engine which meant that its general performance was better than that of its predecessor, the Fairey IIIF.

Plate 65
Torpedo-bombers of the Fleet Air Arm: 1923–37

Like the RAF, the Royal Naval Air Service (up to April 1934, thereafter the Fleet Air Arm) began from the postwar years to develop its own specialised aircraft types. The first types of aircraft were for carrier based use, mainly reconnaissance and general purpose planes. Amongst them was the ugly Avro Bison, which was in service from April 1923 until 1929; 53 were built in two production series. A much more aggressive type of aircraft soon started to be built: the torpedo-bomber. Among the aircraft manufacturers, Blackburn was the one which made the largest contribution to the growth of this particular type.

The Blackburn Dart of 1923 was the first model of a long family of assault biplanes which ended with the Shark ten years later. The Dart appeared in prototype form in 1921 and stayed in production until 1927 with a total of 117 being built. This was not an exceptional aircraft and it had distinctly mediocre performance, but it was easy to fly and safe when taking off and landing, and this made it the ideal platform for experiments in torpedo techniques, and for training. Clear proof of

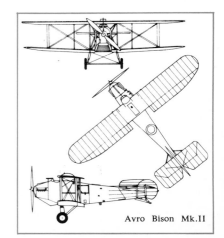

Avro Bison Mk.II

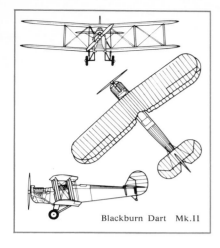

Blackburn Dart Mk.II

Blackburn Ripon

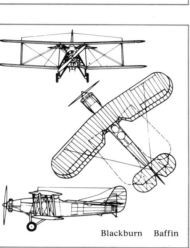

Blackburn Shark Mk.III

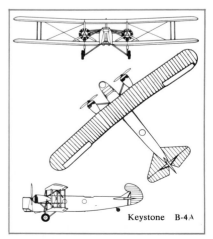

Blackburn Baffin

126. The final version (Shark Mk III) appeared in 1937, by which time the first Fairey Swordfish Mk Is had already gone into service. The last Shark was distinguished from the first two by the adoption of a glazed canopy. Production totalled 95.

The Sharks had a short life in squadron service and towards the middle of 1938 they were withdrawn and relegated to training, a role which they filled for a good part of the Second World War. A seaplane version was made, which served aboard HMS *Repulse* and *Warspite*.

built another 50, 35 and 25 aircraft respectively. The MB-2 stayed in service up to 1927.

The following most widely used aircraft were those built by Keystone from the middle of the 1920s onwards. The first production aircraft – designated LB-5 following the classification system – set the basic configuration for the entire series, which included numerous other variants, all of which had small structural modifications, used different engines, and in some cases had twin tailplanes in order to improve the rear gunner's field of fire. Just under 250 of the Keystone bombers were built, the last production models being the B-4A and the B-6A, both of 1932, of which 25 and 39 were built. They had single tailplanes and were powered either by Pratt & Whitney Hornet or by Wright Cyclone 575 hp radial engines.

In 1932 the prototype of one of the last bombers of the interwar generation, the Martin B-10, appeared, an aircraft which incorporated the best technology of the time. The operational career of this aircraft, however, was relatively brief due to the development and appearance of more modern bombers, amongst which was the Boeing B-17, which immediately made it appear obsolete. The Martin B-10 was directly derived from the B-9 (which had been the first all-metal American monoplane bomber) and was a private venture of Martin's. In

this usefulness is the fact that the Dart stayed in service for ten years, from 1923 onwards, before being relegated entirely to training.

In 1929 the Dart biplane began to be replaced by a new Blackburn model, the Ripon. The prototype of this more powerful biplane appeared on 17th April 1926, and at the end of proving trials the aircraft was immediately put into production. This fell into two principal sub-series, the Mk II and the Mk IIA which differed in detail, and continued until the end of 1933 when the 96th aircraft was completed. The Blackburn Ripon was a very versatile aircraft. Apart from its use as an assault aircraft it could be used for long-range reconnaissance; in this role the machine guns were removed and supplementary fuel tanks fitted so that the aircraft had endurance of fourteen hours. These planes remained in service up to January 1934, in which month replacement by the Blackburn Baffin began.

The real difference in these machines lay in their engines: for the first time Blackburn abandoned use of the liquid-cooled inline engine in favour of a radial. In the Baffin, the Napier Lion of the Ripon was replaced by a 565 hp Bristol Pegasus radial engine which, although of the same power as its predecessor, was much more reliable, simpler and easier to

maintain. The two Blackburn Baffin prototypes appeared in 1932 and 1933 and in the September of 1933 series production was started, which only totalled 29 aircraft. These machines were soon joined by another 68 Ripons with the new radial engine. The aircraft stayed in front-line service until December 1936, when they were phased out in favour of the Fairey Swordfish. Compared with the Ripon, the Baffin gave a very marginal improvement in performance. they were finally taken out of service in September 1937.

The appearance of the Swordfish torpedo-bombers, whose operational life continued well into the Second World War, also rendered obsolete the Baffin's successor, the Shark, the last biplane to be constructed by Blackburn for the Fleet Air Arm. This was a private venture and the prototype had made its maiden flight on 24th August 1933; once proving trials and operational tests had been carried out, the aircraft was accepted and ordered into production with a contract for 16 being signed in August of the following year.

The first Shark Mk I went into service in May 1935. A month later a new contract had been signed for three aircraft of the second series (Mk II) and another two orders in September 1935 and January 1936 brought the total to

Plate 66
USAAC bombers: 1920–37

The history of the United States air arm between the two wars was to highlight the evolution of multi-engine bombers, an area of technology in which the American aircraft industry had no previous experience. It was to further the achievement of an all-American aircraft that in 1917, whilst the First World War was still being fought, the American government asked Martin to develop a twin-engined bomber with better performance than the Handley Page O/400 which at that time was being built in the United States under licence.

The basic model was designated MB-1 and the prototype flew in August the following year. In 1919 an improved version of this plane was developed, especially designed as a night bomber; this was the MB-2 which had more powerful engines and structural improvements. A year later the army issued its first purchase order for 20, which were given the designation of MB-S-1, and implemented a production programme within a short time in which Curtiss, LWF Engineering and Aeromarine were also involved. These three manufacturers

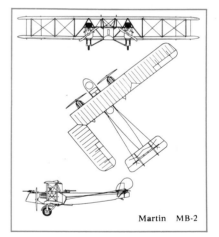

Martin MB-2

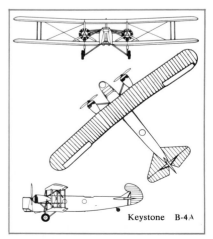

Keystone B-4A

153

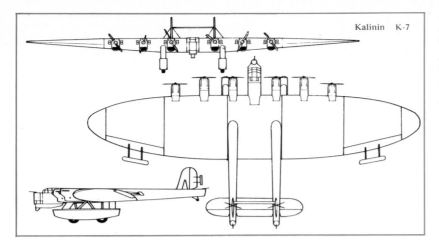

Kalinin K-7

Revolution, the Russian aeronautical industry had been restructured and reorganised, and the previous Russian interest in multi-engined aircraft was reawakened. The chief models of this time were the Tupolev ANT 9 of 1929 and the Tupolev ANT 14 of 1931, two transports of notable dimensions whose construction served at least to develop the necessary technology and to provide experience, both in construction and in service. The industry continued to evolve into the 1930s with alternating successes and failures.

Among the designs which were not successful was the Kalinin K-7 of 1933, a gigantic six-engine aircraft with wingspan of 53 m (174 ft) and take-off weight of 38 tonnes. This experimental military aircraft was the work of the designer K. Alexevitch Kalinin. Its proposed armament was also unusual – three 20 mm cannon and six machine guns as defensive armament, and 9 tonnes of bombs. The fate of the Kalinin K-7, however, was decided at prototype stage when one of the twin booms succumbed to vibration and the prototype crashed in November 1933, three months after its first flight on 11th August.

An Italian aircraft of the same category also failed to pass the prototype stage, although it was very much more promising: the Caproni Ca.90 of 1929, a six-engine biplane which, at the time of its construction, was the largest landplane in the world. The Ca.90 was built at a time when the *Aeronautica Militare* showed a very strong interest in developing heavy multi-engined bombers. As such this machine answered the purpose very well, having all-up power of 6,000 hp, 7 machine guns, 8 tonnes of bombs and a range of almost 1,300 km (800 miles). The flight characteristics of the Ca.90 were demonstrated in 1930 on a record-breaking flight carrying 10,000 kg (22,050 lb) of payload; the bomber reached 3,256 m (10,683 ft) altitude and stayed aloft for 3 hours and 31 minutes. In the event the early interest of the military authorities was not followed up and the Ca.90 remained as a prototype.

Caproni's enthusiasm for giant aircraft ended during the 1930s and the company returned to more orthodox designs. A series of aircraft which met with great success and which, in spite of their outdated appearance, were to stay in service until the Second World War, was the Ca.101 and Ca.133. While the Ca.133s were used only as transports, both for civil and military use, the Ca.101 served as a bomber in Africa. Designed in 1930, the aircraft was developed in various versions which had different engines: Alfa Romeo 200 hp, Piaggio Stella 370 hp and Walter Castor 240 hp. They were in single, twin-engine and three-engine variants. Some models were used as airliners on the East African routes.

A three-engine military version, powered by Alfa-Romeo 270 hp radial engines, equipped some night bomber squadrons of the *Regia Aeronautica* and were first used in action in the invasion of Ethiopia, subsequently remaining in service up to the Second World War.

In 1936 Caproni started construction of the Ca.309–Ca.314 family, one of the most prolific and serviceable series of light aircraft ever to be manufactured by the Italian aircraft industry. A variant which marked the transition towards the final and definitive model of the 1940s was the Ca.310 of 1937. It was given the name Libeccio after Italy's south-west wind, and embodied major changes from the preceding version, the Ca.309 which was also named the Ghibli or desert wind. Twin 470 hp Piaggio radial engines were installed in the Libeccio which had a retractable undercarriage and generally modernised airframe. Apart from its very busy operational use with reconnaissance units of the *Regia Aeronautica*, the Ca.310 was also used in Yugoslavia, Hungary, Norway, and by some Latin American nations.

Plate 70
Japanese, German and Czechoslovak bombers: 1921–35

During the period between the two wars those countries whose aeronautical industries had been of secondary importance in the previous decade made efforts to develop their aviation. In Czechoslovakia Letov was the company which in November 1918 took over the factories of what had been known under Austro-Hungarian rule as the Aircraft Establishment. The first bomber of the independent Czechoslovakia was the Sm.1, developed from 1919, and in its general configuration it was very reminiscent of the First World War aircraft.

The Sm.1 was a two-seat bomber/reconnaissance biplane armed with two machine guns, one manually aimed, of mixed construction using wood and fabric. The engine had also originated during the war, a 230 hp 6-cylinder inline Austrian Hiero engine, one of the classic aero engines of its time. After the prototype's first flight in April 1920, production was commenced and 90 aircraft were completed in two different variants. The second of these, the S-2, was constructed by Aero, featuring a German Maybach Mb.IV 260 hp engine; there were also some smaller changes.

Japan was at this time pursuing its policy of collaboration with foreign aeronautical manufacturers, mainly European, putting a biplane torpedo-bomber into service in 1932 which had been designed by the British firm of Blackburn. The pre-production phase of this project had been put out to tender in 1928 and two other British companies, Sopwith and Handley Page, had competed for the job. Blackburn built a prototype in 1929 and delivered it to the Japanese authorities in February of the following year. In Japan, after the construction of another three prototypes, series production was started by Mitsubishi and the aircraft was delivered to units under the designation of B2M. Up to 1935, 104 had been constructed in two main series, the B2M1 and the B2M2, which differed from each other in improvements and modifications of various types which were aimed at facilitating maintenance.

The Ki-2, an aircraft of Japanese design which was largely an imitation of the German Junkers K.37, was a twin-engine bomber developed by the army air force in 1932, and this was also entrusted to Mitsubishi. The prototype was completed in the spring of 1933 and immediately underwent proving trials. No major modifications were necessary, but a small alteration was required in the forward fuselage; towards the end of 1933 the aircraft was officially accepted. Production of the Ki-2 fell into two variants, the

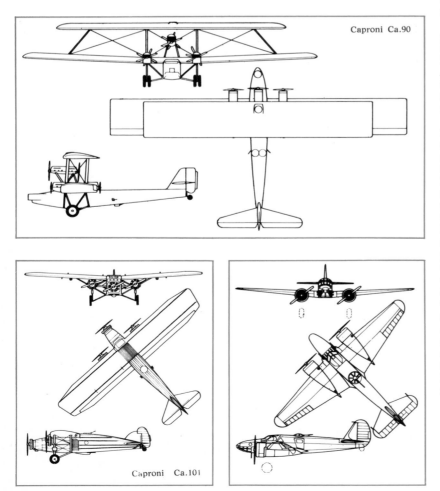

Caproni Ca.90

Caproni Ca.101

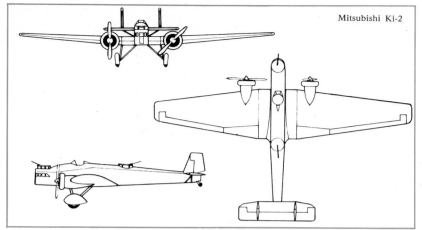

Mitsubishi Ki-2

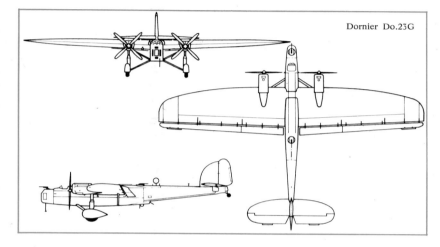

Dornier Do.23G

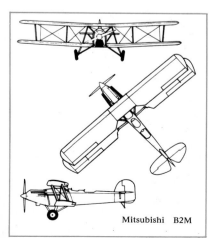

Mitsubishi B2M

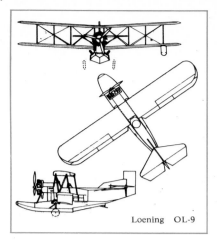

Loening OL-9

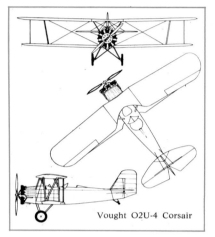

Vought O2U-4 Corsair

Ki-2-1, of which 113 were built up to 1936, and the Ki-2-2, of which 61 were built up to 1938. The last version was a considerable improvement on the original as it had a retractable undercarriage, closed cockpit and other detail changes. The Ki-2 was deployed in the war against China, and

many models were still in service, although only as trainers, at the outbreak of the Second World War.

In Germany, in the rapid but veiled creation of the future *Luftwaffe*, the first of the disguised bombers appeared in 1934; ostensibly a civilian freighter, the Dornier Do.23 was clearly designed as a military aircraft from the beginning. The origins of this ugly and angular twin-engine plane with fixed undercarriage went back to 1931, in which year the design of the model F (subsequently designated Do.11) was officially announced as a freight carrier.

Subsequent versions were built to eliminate many shortcomings in the aircraft, resulting in the Do.13 of 1933, and in the following year, the prototype Do.23 which was much sturdier, more robust and of simpler design than its predecessors. The production variant was designated Do.23G and started to reach units in October 1935. However, even in this aircraft the inherent shortcomings of the design were never rectified, and were responsible for its unsatisfactory performance. At the end of 1935 the Do.23G was taken out of production after 200 had been completed. The aircraft was replaced some time afterwards by the more modern Do.17, the Ju.86 and the He.111. The twin-engine Dornier was relegated to secondary tasks, surviving until the Second World War.

In the years between the two wars the main emphasis of technical advance was on the pure combat planes, the fighter and the bomber. But the development of reconnaissance aircraft was not neglected. This had been the role of the first ever military aircraft at the beginning of the century, and it had not ceased to be a crucial one.

In the United States, one of the most widely used families of reconnaissance planes in the 1920s was that built by Loening for the army and navy. The biplanes all had similar fuselages with the central float fitting flush under the fuselage giving aerodynamic advantages. Production was first started for the USAAC after the flight of the prototype XCOA-1 in July 1924. The army received a total of nine of the first variant, fifteen of the second variant, designated OA-1A with modified structure of tailplanes, nine of the third, OA-1B, ten of the OA-1C which had further modification of the tailplanes, and eight of the OA-2, the last variant, which was driven by a more powerful engine.

The US Navy designated its aircraft with the letters OL; two OL-1s were put into service; five OL-2s; four OL-3s and six OL-4s; twenty-eight OL-6s; forty OL-8 and OL-8As, and twenty-six OL-9s. These aircraft different from each other in structural details and in their engines. From the variant OL-8A onwards, Loening reconnaissance planes were fitted with a 450 hp Pratt and Whitney radial engine instead of the liquid-cooled engines which had been used in earlier versions.

Another series of reconnaissance planes which became standard equipment for the navy were the Vought O2U Corsairs, the first aircraft in the history of the US Navy to be manufactured by this company and the first to be powered by an engine which was to become famous: the Pratt & Whitney Wasp. The prototype was flown in 1926 and ordered into production immediately afterwards under the designation of O2U-1. It was followed by 130 series aircraft which started to go into squadron service the following year. In 1928 the second variant O2U-2 appeared, slightly modified in structural details, of which 37 were built. Eighty O2U-3s and forty O2U-4s followed, mainly notable for the increase in upper wing dihedral. The Corsair, which stayed in service until the early 1930s, was mainly valued for its versatility for it could be used as a landplane or floatplane.

The same versatility was shown by another widely-used reconnaissance aircraft of the US Navy, the Curtiss

SOC Seagull, the prototype of which was ordered in the summer of 1933. It was modern, with enclosed cockpit, and had good general performance, and this tough biplane was also the last aircraft of its type to be supplied by Curtiss to the Navy. The prototype flew for the first time in April 1934, and was put into production under the designation of SOC-1.

The first of the 135 aircraft constructed were delivered to units in November 1935, and subsequently the assembly lines built forty SOC-2s in landplane configuration and eighty-three SOC-3s which were powered by a different engine. Another 64 aircraft were built by the Naval Aircraft Factory and numbered SON-1. Finally, Curtiss built three more SOC-4s which resembled their predecessors closely but were for the US Coast Guard. During the course of their long career, which lasted until 1944, although interrupted for a year, the Seagulls served as reconnaissance planes with the American fleets.

Britain did not lag behind the United States in the development of reconnaissance planes. One of the most useful and versatile aircraft of this type in the second half of the 1920s was the Armstrong Whitworth Atlas, a sturdy biplane which was also the first aircraft specifically designed for army co-operation to go into service with the RAF. The prototype was flown on 10th May 1925, and the first

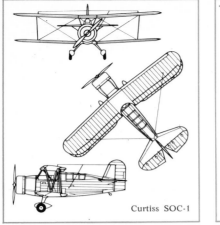

Curtiss SOC-1

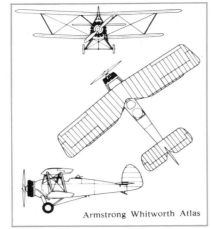

Armstrong Whitworth Atlas

Aero A.11

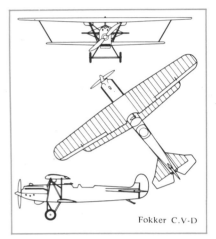

Fokker C.V-D

units began to operate the new aircraft in October 1927. A total of 449 were built up till 1933, 146 of which were trainers, and the aircraft stayed in service for another two years.

From 1930 to 1934 the RAF kept its largest aircraft of the time in service for marine reconnaissance, the Blackburn Iris, a three-engined flying boat which had made its name in 1927 and 1928 with spectacular long distance flights. The RAF's version was the Mk III which appeared in prototype on 21st November 1929 and of which only four were built, equipping only one unit. In its military role the Blackburn Iris again won fame for exceptionally long flights, both in distance and endurance.

Plate 72
Reconnaissance aircraft of the twenties and thirties: 1923–33

In Czechoslovakia the Letov Sm.1 and S-2 were replaced from 1920 onwards by a new biplane, the Aero A.11. This versatile aircraft was one of the first produced by Aero Továrna Létadel, the company which, together with Létov, made a great contribution to the rebirth of the Czechoslovak aviation industry immediately after the end of the First World War. Until October 1918 Aero had constructed the Austrian Phönix fighters under licence and at the time of reorganisation it started to develop its own designs. The A.11 was the first of these to be successfully manufactured and used with the Czechoslovak air force. It proved so useful that 440 were built in more than twenty different models. Apart from the day and night reconnaissance versions, bomber versions were developed (Ab.11 and Ab.11N, night and day bombers); trainers (A.25, A.24 and A.21) and a target tug, the A.29. The latter was equipped with floats and was the first seaplane to be built in Czechoslovakia. Aero biplanes stayed in service for the whole of the 1920s.

The Dutch Fokker C.V had a much longer life: this was an excellent and versatile biplane which served under the colours of a dozen nations and stayed in service in the Netherlands up till the German invasion in 1940. The prototype of this aircraft was flown for the first time in May 1924, and immediately showed its excellent performance. The success of the Fokker C.V and its wide use were mainly linked to the fact that it was extremely easy to maintain and was very versatile. In order to enhance the adaptability of the machine for the most widely differing uses, Fokker provided in the design for interchangeable wings and engines.

The first versions (constructed in limited numbers) were the C.V-A, the C.V-B and the C.V-C which had liquid-cooled inline engines. In 1926 two other variants appeared, the C.V-D and the C.V-E, which had a modified wing structure and wingspan and could be fitted with radial engines. Apart from serving with the Dutch air force the C.V was sold and constructed under licence in various other countries: in Denmark (C.V-A and C.V-B); in Hungary (C.V-D); in Italy (C.V-E manufactured by Imam under the designation of Ro.1); Norway (C.V-D and C.V-E); Sweden (C.V-D and C.V-E) and Switzerland (C.V-D and C.V-E).

The success of the Fokker C.V was eclipsed on the world scale by a similar type of plane built in the Soviet Union, the Polikarpov R.5, which stayed in service from 1931 until the Second World War and was constructed in enormous numbers – about 6,000 aircraft in various civil and military variants. The R.5 prototype was built in 1928 by a design bureau headed by Nicolai N. Polikarpov and put into production in 1930 as a light reconnaissance bomber. Among the other military versions worthy of note was that of 1931 for ground attack (armed with as many as seven machine guns) and the R.5T of 1935, a single-seat torpedo bomber. Among the numerous variants for civil use were those for passenger transport built for Aeroflot and for training.

In France the Mureaux family of reconnaissance planes were developed from 1928 onwards under the designation R.2, and these made their mark throughout the 1930s as standard equipment of the air force; they were still in service at the outbreak of the Second World War. Its forerunner was the type 110 whose maiden flight was in April 1931 but the versions produced in the largest numbers were the type 115 and the type 117 (1935), of which 122 and 117 were constructed up till 1936 and 1939 respectively.

In Japan one of the most useful and longest-serving reconnaissance planes of the 1920s was the Kawasaki Type 88, a fast and agile biplane designed by the German engineer Richard Vogt. In 1923 he had been invited to be the chief designer of Kawasaki so that he could provide the company with the technology it lacked at the time. The

Type 88 was one of this German designer's first contributions. The prototype appeared at the beginning of 1927 and six months later went into production. The army air force put no fewer than 300 of them into service and kept them operational for about ten years.

Still in Asia, one of the few original designs achieved in China was the small carrier-borne seaplane, the Nin Hai, named after the cruiser on which it was to serve. The prototype was built under the supervision of a member of the Naval Aircraft Establishment, T. T. Mar, whose full name is not known, and the aircraft appeared in 1933. Its most noteworthy feature was its folding wings, which meant that it could be stowed easily on board a warship. Apart from this the Nin Hai was a plane of very modest performance.

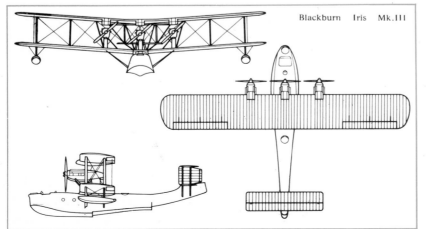

Blackburn Iris Mk.III

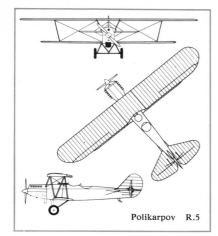

Polikarpov R.5

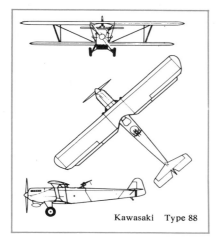

Kawasaki Type 88

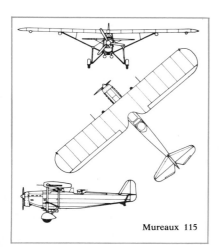

Mureaux 115

Plate 73
Trainers and general purpose aircraft: 1928–32

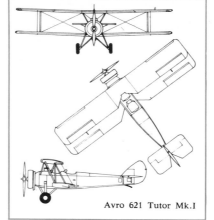

Avro 621 Tutor Mk.I

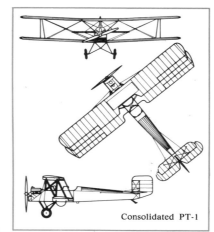

Consolidated PT-1

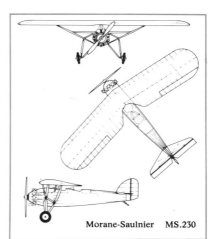

Morane-Saulnier MS.230

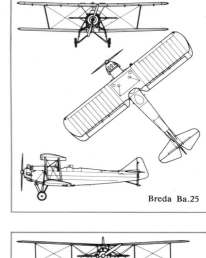

Breda Ba.25

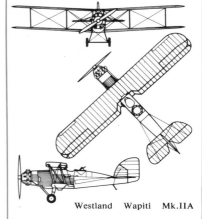

Westland Wapiti Mk.IIA

The activity of the flying schools, both civil and military, underwent enormous expansion in the interwar period, first as a continuation of the intense aeronautical activity of the last ten years of the war, and later within the context of the reorganisation and modernisation of the air forces.

In the RAF the problem of finding a substitute for the obsolescent though still effective and useful Avro 504 was solved in 1932 when, after three years of comparative tests on various models, another Avro biplane, the type 621 Tutor, was chosen. Production of this new trainer was started in 1931 and went on uninterruptedly up to May 1936. Apart from about 50 aircraft for the civil mark and about 40 constructed for export, almost all the Tutors went to the RAF which bought over 400 of them. Amongst these, 14 were in seaplane configuration. The first flying school to receive the Tutors was the Central Flying School in 1932.

In the United States a similar problem faced the Army's air force at the beginning of the 1920s with the need to replace the outdated Curtiss Jenny. One of the most widely used series of trainers of the period was the one built by Consolidated and designated PT by the Army and NY by the Navy. The prototype appeared in 1923; this was not an original design but a re-think of the Dayton-Wright TW-3 biplane, construction of which had been taken over by Consolidated after the failure of the former company. The main modification was to the seating of the crew of two who now sat one behind the other and not side by side as had been the case in the TW-3.

Production started in 1925 with the PT-1, of which 221 were constructed. Other main variants were the PT-3 of 1928 which had a Wright radial engine and modified tailplane, of which 130 were built, and the PT-4 of 1929 which was much the same as its predecessor and of which 100 were delivered. The corresponding naval variants were the NY-1 (76 aircraft built with Wright R-790 hp radial engines), the NY-2 (186 with wider wingspan and more powerful engine, and a further 25 trainers with armament), and the NY-3 (23 were built with more powerful engines). The Consolidated trainer remained in service until 1939.

In France one of the most widely used trainers of the 1930s was the Morane-Saulnier M.S. 230, designed during 1929, which flew the following year. This tough high-wing monoplane was used in great numbers in military flying schools and also had considerable export success: about 1,100 in various versions were built which flew in many countries and production under licence was also undertaken in Belgium and Portugal.

In Italy the most widely used basic trainer of the 1930s was the Breda Ba.25, a robust and agile biplane which appeared at the beginning of 1930. It was constructed in numerous versions (differing mainly in their engines) and the Ba.25 equipped the flying schools of the *Regia Aeronautica* and was also exported to China, Ethiopia and Paraguay. The Ba.25 was joined in service by a more powerful derivation, the single-seat Ba.28, which was similar but was powered by a Piaggio 390 hp radial engine and was used for advanced training and acrobatics.

A noteworthy general purpose aircraft was the Westland Wapiti, which the RAF found invaluable during the ten years until the eve of the Second World War. In appeared in prototype at the beginning of 1927 and this tough and versatile biplane remained in production until August 1932, 517 being built in various models. The model which was most used in the colonies and which saw the most widespread operational use was the Mk IIA of 1931 which had an all-metal structure and was powered by a Bristol Jupiter 550 hp radial engine. Among the tasks which the Wapiti carried out with particular efficiency was army co-operation and reconnaissance. Some were also used on bombing missions.

1940, was the first great air battle of the Second World War. It was also the British aircraft industry's greatest trial of strength. All of Britain's resources, productive capacity and ability faced a life-and-death test before an audience on the ground whose whole future depended on the outcome, and whose gratitude went out to the defending airmen. For the enemy, it was the very first setback that fascism had encountered.

With the threat of invasion staved off, the British were able to organise a large increase in aircraft production. It was at this time the most famous aircraft of the RAF took to the air, amongst them the best versions of the Spitfire and the Mosquito; the heavy strategic bombers such as the Halifax and the Lancaster which were to be so effective in the destruction of the Third Reich's war machine. The first steps were taken in pursuit of a new ambitious objective: the creation of a jet-engine combat aircraft. Even though the Meteor only went into service in the last months of the war and although it was preceded by the German Me.262, Britain had the distinction of being the only Allied nation to achieve this during the war.

The aircraft industry notched up impressive annual production totals: 15,000 aircraft in 1940, 20,100 in 1941, 23,671 in 1942, 26,263 in 1943, 29,220 in 1944. At the end of the war the total number of aircraft of all types to be built had reached 125,254.

Whilst the RAF had the lion's share of this expansion, the strengthening of the Fleet Air Arm came about more slowly. In September 1939 (the Fleet Air Arm had become a separate service in May of that year) only 340 aircraft were in the service, 225 of which were carrier-based and generally inferior to those of the RAF. The Fleet Air Arm had to wait until 1942 for its modernisation to get under way with the first models of the Sea Hurricane and the Seafire. Subsequently, with the arrival of the most effective American aircraft, numbers were also greatly increased. In August 1945 the Fleet Air Arm had 1,300 planes in the front line out of an overall total of 11,500 aircraft.

The last great power to join the allied fight against the Third Reich was the Soviet Union. The pact with Germany, signed on 23rd August 1939, had last for only two years when, on 22nd June 1941, Hitler launched Operation Barbarossa. Initial German successes outstripped all predictions and, once again, this was due to air power: in the first nine hours of the invasion the *Luftwaffe* virtually wiped out the Soviet air forces, destroying 1,200 aircraft, 800 of them on the ground. Apart from the surprise factor (Hitler had issued no ultimatum before the onslaught) this staggering aggressive success was mainly due to the inferiority of Soviet aircraft; many front line aircraft had been made as far back as the mid 1930s.

Only at the beginning of 1942 did the USSR recover from this crushing blow when, having rebuilt her aircraft industry, she started to manufacture more up-to-date aircraft and to step up the tempo of production. A major contribution was also made by United States and British industry supplying the Soviet Union's armed forces. In all, from 1942 to 1944 no fewer than 14,833 aircraft of every type reached the Soviet Union. Among these were high-quality aeroplanes such as the British Hurricane and Spitfire fighters and the American P-47 Thunderbolt fighter and B-25 and A-20 medium bombers. Soviet designers before long managed to make up for lost time and produced excellent combat aircraft which in many ways were superior to those of the opposing forces: the Petlyakov Pe-2 bomber, the Ilyushin Il-2 and Il-10 close support and attack planes, the Yakovlev Yak-3 and Yak-9 and the Lavochkin La-5 and La-7 fighters. Production for the army air force and for the navy's air force rose from 8,000 aircraft in 1942 to 18,000 and 30,000 in 1943 and 1944, reaching 25,000 in the remaining months of the war in 1945.

France's role as an air power only survived the brief space of ten months, from 3rd September 1939 when, together with Britain, she declared war on Germany, until 22nd June 1940 when the Armistice was signed. At the outbreak of war the *Armée de l'Air* had a total of 1,400 combat-ready aircraft but of these almost two-thirds were obsolete. This was the price France had to pay for the lack of priority given to air defence, and consequent delays in reorganising the aircraft industry to prepare it for its necessary task. As the war began to take its course the supply of aircraft improved somewhat but not significantly. Although recourse was had to foreign aircraft to gain time and in spite of some really effective fighters coming into service (such as the Morane-Saulnier M.S.406 and, in very small numbers, the Dewoitine D.520) only 1,501 modern aircraft were in service on 10th May 1940, of which 784 were fighters. The *Armée de l'Air* fought valiantly but there was little it could do; on 14th June German troops entered Paris and eight days later the Armistice was signed.

And then there was the mighty neighbour, Germany, armed to the teeth from the start. When Hitler lit the fuse of war on 1st September 1939, he had the most powerful air force in the world and it was hardened from combat experience in Spain, where the civil war had ended only six months previously. The *Luftwaffe* had 4,840 front-line aircraft including 1,750 bombers and 1,200 fighters. This force was kept up to strength by an aircraft industry which was already producing 1,000 planes a month and which in 1939 was to produce no less than 8,300 aircraft of all types. Success followed on success: after Poland came Denmark and Norway, then the Netherlands, Belgium, Luxembourg and finally France. Only at the shores of the English Channel did the *Blitzkrieg* halt.

The Battle of Britain revealed a weakness in the theoretical basis of German military planning. The essence of German air planning at that time, unquestioned after its successful application in Spain, consisted of the use of medium day-time bombers as the main strategic weapon, and ground attack aircraft as the main tactical weapon.

Three-and-a-half months of air warfare against Britain showed that what had applied in the Spanish Civil War was quite inappropriate against a technically well equipped enemy, in quite a different kind of war. Facing a determined stand by the RAF, the He.III and Do.17 bombers lacked adequate defensive armament and what they had was of limited range. This made it necessary for the escorting Bf.109 fighters to stay in close formation with the bombers, who needed their constant protection; the fighters were thus unable to carry out any wider manoeuvres and so they could not serve with their full effectiveness. In addition, the Ju.87 Stuka, which had spread so much terror in Poland, Belgium and France, was completely at the mercy of the Spitfires and Hurricanes. The *Luftwaffe* lacked a heavy bomber, too, but in spite of the lessons of war Germany never equipped itself with an effective plane in this category.

Whatever their weaknesses, the Germans did continue to manufacture enormous quantities of aircraft, and adapted their designs all the time. Serving as it was on fronts half way round the world, the *Luftwaffe* could only achieve what it did with the backing of a vast industry which kept up very high levels of production throughout the Allied bombardments and in the face of shortages of strategic materials and fuel in the last years of the war. In 1940 10,800 aircraft of all types were constructed; 11,800 in the following year; 15,600 in 1942; 25,500 in 1943 and 39,800 in 1944; 8,000 aircraft were constructed in the first five months of 1945. Under the noses of its enemies Germany managed to become the first nation in the world to build and put into service a jet fighter aircraft. The Messerschmitt Me.262 made its appearance in the second half of 1944, followed shortly afterwards by the Arado Ar.234 and in the last months of the fighting by the Heinkel He.162.

Japan's experience was similar but compressed into three years and eight months of war. On the outbreak of war in the Pacific the Japanese air forces were of a very high standard and, above all, their potential was almost unknown to the Western powers. On 7th December 1941, the date of Pearl Harbor, the Imperial Army Air Force comprised approximately 1,500 combat-ready aircraft, whilst the navy's air force had about 1,400 aircraft. The naval air force was entrusted with the task of neutralising the US fleet, which it was to achieve with its carried-based units, while its land-based aircraft were used in a supporting role in the invasion of the Pacific islands. Most Japanese aircraft were of modern design; and they were flown by pilots and crews of fanatical enthusiasm and determination. After their initial ferocious success momentum was sustained until the second half of 1942, with their enemies in disarray. Air supremacy was lost, first by the navy's air force in the great air-sea battles of 1942, then by the army's air force as the sheer numbers of Japan's enemies, in the lengthening war, began to have their effect.

After this turning point the Japanese had to sustain a defensive war in which they were gradually driven back inside their sphere of expansion until they were reduced to fighting for the survival of their own homeland. Right up to the very end, however, the effort they put up was massive. After a total production of 4,768 aircraft in 1940, 5,088

were built in 1941 (of which 1,080 were fighters and 1,461 bombers); this rose to 8,861 in 1942 (2,935 fighters and 2,433 bombers); 16,693 in 1943 (7,147 fighters and 4,189 bombers); 28,180 in 1944 (13,811 fighters and 4,189 bombers); in the eight months left of the war in 1945 the assembly lines turned out 11,066 combat planes of which 5,474 were fighters and 1,934 were bombers. The greatest losses of aircraft were sustained in the desperate attempt to defend Japan from American raids and in the suicide missions of the last months of the war.

Italy was the third Axis power, without doubt the weakest and least prepared to contend with the strain of the war. On 10th June 1940, when Italy entered the war, joining Germany against France and Britain, the *Regia Aeronautica* had 3,296 aircraft distributed over Italy, the Aegean and Libya. Only just over half of these, however, could be considered combat-ready and numbered 1,796 comprising 783 bombers, 594 fighters, 268 spotter planes and 151 reconnaissance planes. It was still a force to be reckoned with in numbers but in quality it left much to be desired. This was not considered to be of great consequence by the highest generals, one of whom declared that "Italy would need several thousand dead before she sat down at the negotiating table".

Never was prophecy proved to be more false. From its unsuccessful operations in France onwards, the full extent of the *Regia Aeronautica*'s inadequacies was clearly revealed. Then the failed Italian missions in the Battle of Britain undertaken by the *Corpo Aereo Italiano* were even more conclusive. Handicapped by an inefficient industry, Italy was foundering in the midst of a war with enemies attacking on all sides. Mussolini and his ministers were under severe pressure, but help came from the Germans, who supplied the engines vitally needed by the Italian aircraft industry to build modern and powerful aircraft. The recovery benefited the fighter most of all, leading to the appearance of some Italian aircraft which could really contend with the opposition.

On the production front, however, success still eluded Italian aircraft manufacturers and this proved to be the weakness of the whole policy of war. Aggressive plans were no more than a waste of breath, and the war itself was a waste of lives. In 1940 a total of 3,257 aircraft were built; 3,503 in 1941; 2,818 in 1942 and 1,930 in the first eight months of 1943. On 8th September 1943 only 887 Italian aircraft were left.

After that date the toll was even heavier; Italy was divided and Italian airmen fought for opposing sides. In the south the airmen of the Balkan Air Force managed to reach the Allies and join them, and then continued to give their lives until the last day of the war. In the north, those who had chosen to cling to the German cause perished with the air force of the *Repúbblica Sociale Italiana*, trying to stem the irresistible tide of the American and British bombers.

Plate 75

Entry into service of the most important fighters of the Second World War

1937	1938	1939	1940	1941
Gloster Gladiator (GB)	Supermarine Spitfire (GB)	Messerschmitt Bf.109 (G)	Bristol Beaufighter (GB)	Focke Wulf Fw.190 (G)
Hawker Hurricane (GB)		Fiat C.R.42 (I)	Dewoitine D.520 (F)	Macchi M.C.202 (I)
Polikarpov I-16 (USSR)		Messerschmitt Bf.110 (G)	Grumman F4F Wildcat (USA)	Bell P-39 Airacobra (USA)
		Macchi M.C.200 (I)	Nakajima Ki-43 Hayabusa (J)	Curtiss P-40 Warhawk (USA)
		Nakajima Ki-27 (J)	Mitsubishi A6M Reisen (J)	Mikoyan-Gurevich MiG-3 (USSR)
				Lavochkin LaGG-3 (USSR)

These aircraft are all drawn to the same scale which is also used for plates **116**, **143**, **158** and **166**

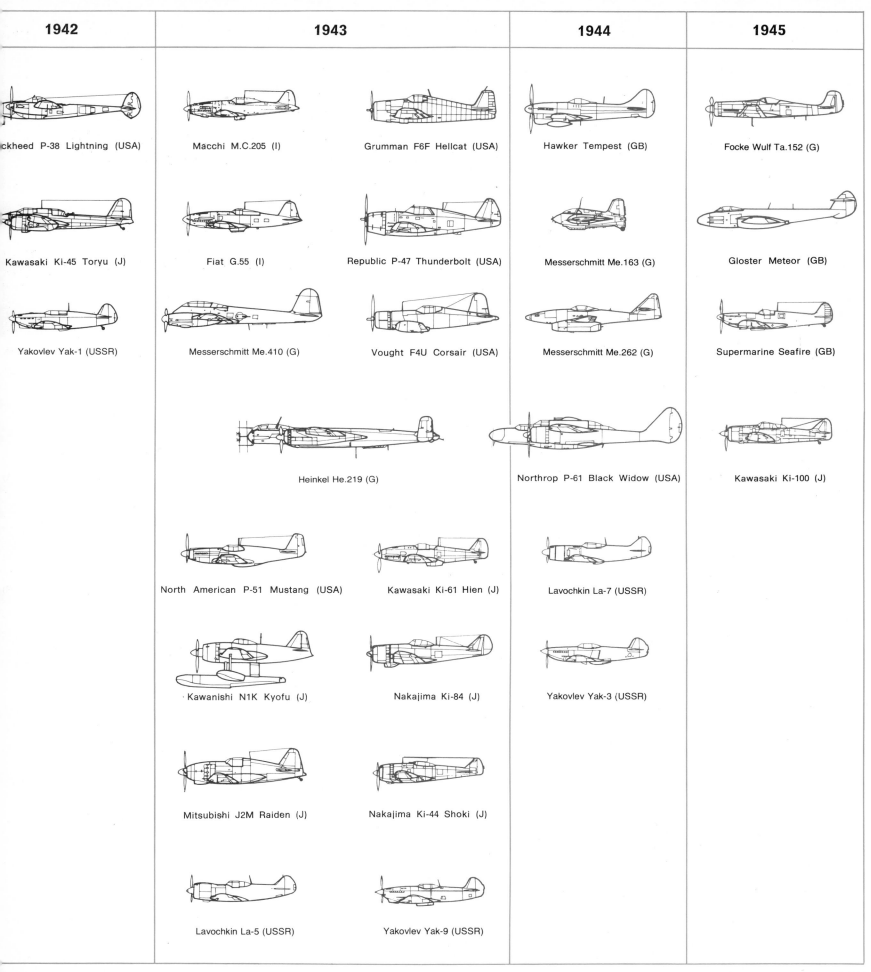

1942	1943	1944	1945

Lockheed P-38 Lightning (USA)

Macchi M.C.205 (I)

Grumman F6F Hellcat (USA)

Hawker Tempest (GB)

Focke Wulf Ta.152 (G)

Kawasaki Ki-45 Toryu (J)

Fiat G.55 (I)

Republic P-47 Thunderbolt (USA)

Messerschmitt Me.163 (G)

Gloster Meteor (GB)

Yakovlev Yak-1 (USSR)

Messerschmitt Me.410 (G)

Vought F4U Corsair (USA)

Messerschmitt Me.262 (G)

Supermarine Seafire (GB)

Heinkel He.219 (G)

Northrop P-61 Black Widow (USA)

Kawasaki Ki-100 (J)

North American P-51 Mustang (USA)

Kawasaki Ki-61 Hien (J)

Lavochkin La-7 (USSR)

Kawanishi N1K Kyofu (J)

Nakajima Ki-84 (J)

Yakovlev Yak-3 (USSR)

Mitsubishi J2M Raiden (J)

Nakajima Ki-44 Shoki (J)

Lavochkin La-5 (USSR)

Yakovlev Yak-9 (USSR)

Plate 76

National markings: 1936–45

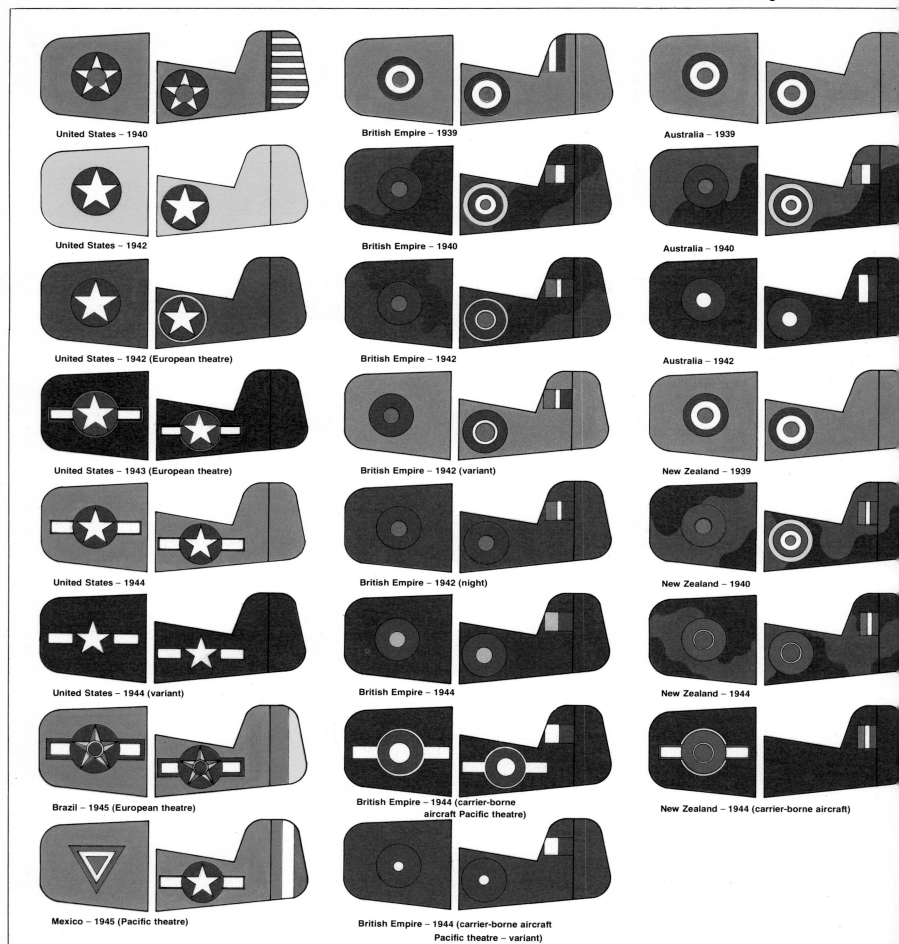

United States – 1940

United States – 1942

United States – 1942 (European theatre)

United States – 1943 (European theatre)

United States – 1944

United States – 1944 (variant)

Brazil – 1945 (European theatre)

Mexico – 1945 (Pacific theatre)

British Empire – 1939

British Empire – 1940

British Empire – 1942

British Empire – 1942 (variant)

British Empire – 1942 (night)

British Empire – 1944

British Empire – 1944 (carrier-borne
aircraft Pacific theatre)

British Empire – 1944 (carrier-borne aircraft
Pacific theatre – variant)

Australia – 1939

Australia – 1940

Australia – 1942

New Zealand – 1939

New Zealand – 1940

New Zealand – 1944

New Zealand – 1944 (carrier-borne aircraft)

France – 1939

France – 1941 (Free French
air force)

France – 1941 (Vichy air force)

The Netherlands – 1939

The Netherlands – 1940

The Netherlands – 1942 (Far East theatre)

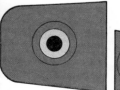

Belgium – 1940

USSR

USSR (variant)

USSR (variant)

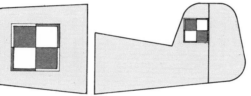

Poland – 1939

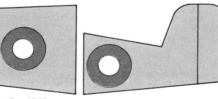

Denmark – 1940

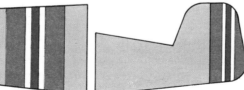

Norway – 1940

Greece – 1940

Czechoslovakia – 1938

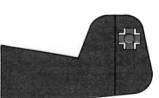

Slovakia – 1940

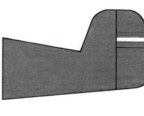

Slovakia – 1943

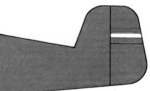

Yugoslavia – 1941

Croatia – 1942

Croatia – 1944

Yugoslavia – 1944

Yugoslavia – 1945

Plate 76 (continued)

National markings: 1936–45

Germany – 1938

Germany – 1939

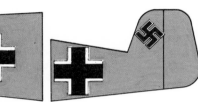

Germany – 1940

Germany – 1944

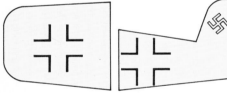

Germany – 1944 (alternative schemes)

Finland – 1939

Finland – 1944

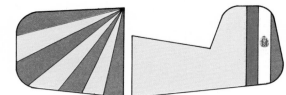

Italy – 1936

Italy – 1939

Italy – 1940

Italy – 1944 (Co-belligerent Air Force)

Italy – 1944 (RSI)

Italy – 1945 (RSI)

Iraq

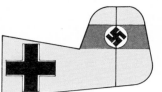

Bulgaria – 1939

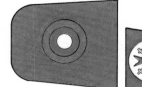

Bulgaria – 1940

Bulgaria – 1944

Romania – 1941

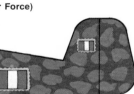

Romania – 1944

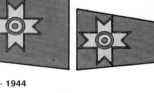

Hungary – 1941

Hungary – 1944

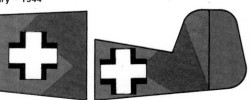

Hungary – 1944 (variant)

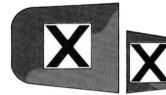

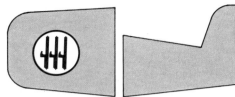

 Japan

 Austria – 1938

 Spain – 1937 (Republican)

 Japan (variant)

 Egypt

 Spain – 1937 (Nationalist)

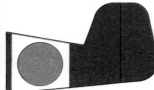 Japan – 1944 (variant)

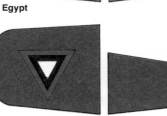 Estonia – 1937

 Spain – 1939

 China

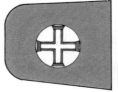 Latvia – 1937

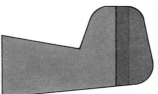 Portugal

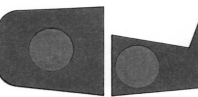 China – Nanking Government

 Lithuania – 1937

 Sweden

 Cochin-China

 Philippines – 1941

 Switzerland

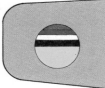 Manchuria

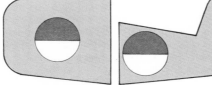 Indonesia – 1945 (Provisional Government)

 Turkey

Plate 79

MORANE-SAULNIER 406
Nation: France; *manufacturer:* SNCAO; *type:* fighter; *year:* 1938; *engine:* Hispano-Suiza 12 Y 12-cylinder V liquid-cooled, 860 hp; *wingspan:* 34 ft 10 in (10.65 m); *length:* 26 ft 9 in (8.15 m); *height:* 9 ft 3 in (2.82 m); *weight:* 6,000 lb (2,720 kg) (loaded); *maximum speed:* 302 mph (486 km/h) at 16,400 ft (5,000 m); *ceiling:* 30,840 ft (9,400 m); *range:* 497 miles (800 km); *armament:* 1 × 20 mm gun; 2 machine guns; *crew:* 1

POTEZ 630
Nation: France; *manufacturer:* SNCAN; *type:* fighter; *year:* 1938; *engine:* two Hispano-Suiza 14 Hbs 14-cylinder radial air-cooled, 640 hp each; *wingspan:* 52 ft 6 in (16.00 m); *length:* 36 ft 4 in (11.07 m); *height:* 11 ft 10½ in (3.61 m); *weight:* 8,488 lb (3,845 kg) (loaded); *maximum speed:* 280 mph (450 km/h) at 13,120 ft (4,000 m); *ceiling:* 32,800 ft (10,000 m); *range:* 760 miles (1,225 km); *armament:* 2 × 20 mm cannon; 1 machine gun; *crew:* 3

BLOCH 152
Nation: France; *manufacturer:* SNCASO; *type:* fighter; *year:* 1939; *engine:* Gnome-Rhône 14N 14-cylinder radial air-cooled, 1,060 hp; *wingspan:* 34 ft 7 in (10.54 m); *length:* 29 ft 10 in (9.10 m); *height:* 12 ft 11 in (3.95 m); *weight:* 5,908 lb (2,676 kg) (loaded); *maximum speed:* 320 mph (515 km/h) at 13,120 ft (4,000 m); *ceiling:* 32,800 ft (10,000 m); *range:* 373 miles (600 km); *armament:* 4 machine guns; *crew:* 1

CAUDRON C. 714
Nation: France; *manufacturer:* Caudron; *type:* fighter; *year:* 1939; *engine:* Renault 12 RO-3 12-cylinder V air-cooled, 450 hp; *wingspan:* 29 ft 5 in (8.96 m); *length:* 27 ft 11 in (8.50 m); *height:* 9 ft 5 in (2.87 m); *weight:* 3,858 lb (1,748 kg) (loaded); *maximum speed:* 303 mph (487 km/h) at 13,120 ft (4,000 m); *ceiling:* 30,000 ft (9,100 m); *range:* 559 miles (900 km); *armament:* 4 machine guns; *crew:* 1

HANRIOT NC 600
Nation: France; *manufacturer:* SNCAC; *type:* fighter; *year:* 1939; *engine:* two Gnome-Rhône MO/01 14 cylinder radial air-cooled, 700 hp each; *wingspan:* 41 ft 11 in (12.77 m); *length:* 28 ft 10½ in (8.78 m); *height:* 10 ft 3 in (3.12 m); *weight:* 8,818 lb (3,995 kg) (loaded); *maximum speed:* 337 mph (542 km/h) at 16,400 ft (5,000 m); *ceiling:* 26,250 ft (8,000 m); *range:* 534 miles (860 km); *armament:* 3 × 20 mm guns; 2 machine guns; *crew:* 2

FOKKER D XXI
Nation: Netherlands; *manufacturer:* Fokker; *type:* fighter; *year:* 1938; *engine:* Bristol Mercury VIII 9-cylinder radial air-cooled 760 hp; *wingspan:* 36 ft 1 in (11.00 m); *length:* 26 ft 11 in (8.20 m); *height:* 9 ft 8 in (2.95 m); *weight:* 4,519 lb (2,050 kg) (loaded); *maximum speed:* 286 mph (460 km/h); *ceiling:* 36,100 ft (11,000 m); *range:* 590 miles (950 km); *armament:* 4 machine guns; *crew:* 1

FOKKER G.1A
Nation: Netherlands; *manufacturer:* Fokker; *type:* fighter; *year:* 1938; *engine:* two Bristol Mercury VIII 9-cylinder radial air-cooled, 830 hp each; *wingspan:* 56 ft 3 in (17.15 m); *length:* 37 ft 9 in (11.50 m); *height:* 11 ft 2 in (3.40 m); *weight:* 10,582 lb (4,970 kg) (loaded); *maximum speed:* 295 mph (475 km/h); *ceiling:* 30,500 ft (9,300 m); *range:* 876 miles (1,409 km); *armament:* 9 machine guns; 660 lb (299 kg) of bombs; *crew:* 3

FOKKER D XXIII
Nation: Netherlands; *manufacturer:* Fokker; *type:* fighter; *year:* 1939; *engine:* two Walter Sagitta I-SR 12-cylinder inline air-cooled, 540 hp each; *wingspan:* 37 ft 9 in (11.50 m); *length:* 35 ft 1 in (11.70 m); *height:* 10 ft 11 in (3.34 m); *weight:* 6,600 lb (2,990 kg) (loaded); *maximum speed:* 326 mph (524 km/h); *ceiling:* 29,520 ft (9,000 m); *range:* 560 miles (900 km); *armament:* 4 machine guns; *crew:* 1

AVIA B-534
Nation: Czechoslovakia; *manufacturer:* Avia; *type:* fighter; *year:* 1935; *engine:* Avia-Hispano-Suiza 12 Ydrs 12-cylinder V liquid-cooled, 850 hp; *wingspan:* 30 ft 10 in (9.40 m); *length:* 26 ft 11 in (8.20 m); *height:* 9 ft 2 in (2.79 m); *weight:* 4,365 lb (1,980 kg) (loaded); *maximum speed:* 245 mph (394 km/h) at 14,435 ft (4,400 m); *ceiling:* 34,875 ft (10,600 m); *range:* 373 miles (600 km); *armament:* 4 machine guns; *crew:* 1

IKARUS IK-2
Nation: Yugoslavia; *manufacturer:* Ikarus AD; *type:* fighter; *year:* 1937; *engine:* Hispano-Suiza 12 Ycrs 12-cylinder V liquid-cooled, 860 hp; *wingspan:* 37 ft 5 in (11.40 m); *length:* 25 ft 10 in (7.88 m); *height:* 12 ft 7 in (3.84 m); *weight:* 4,255 lb (1,930 kg) (loaded); *maximum speed:* 266 mph (428 km/h) at 16,400 ft (5,000 m); *ceiling:* 34,450 ft (10,500 m); *range:* 248 miles (400 km); *armament:* 1 × 20 mm cannon; 2 machine guns; *crew:* 1

PZL P.24
Nation: Poland; *manufacturer:* Pantswowe Zaklady Lotnicze; *type:* fighter; *year:* 1935; *engine:* Gnome-Rhône 14 N7 14-cylinder radial air-cooled, 930 hp; *wingspan:* 35 ft 2½ in (10.75 m); *length:* 24 ft 7½ in (7.52 m); *height:* 8 ft 10 in (2.70 m); *weight:* 4,167 lb (1,890 kg) (loaded); *maximum speed:* 254 mph (408 km/h) at 14,763 ft (4,490 m); *ceiling:* 29,527 ft (9,000 m); *range:* 497 miles (800 km); *armament:* 2 × 20 mm cannon; 2 machine guns; 220 lb (100 kg) of bombs; *crew:* 1

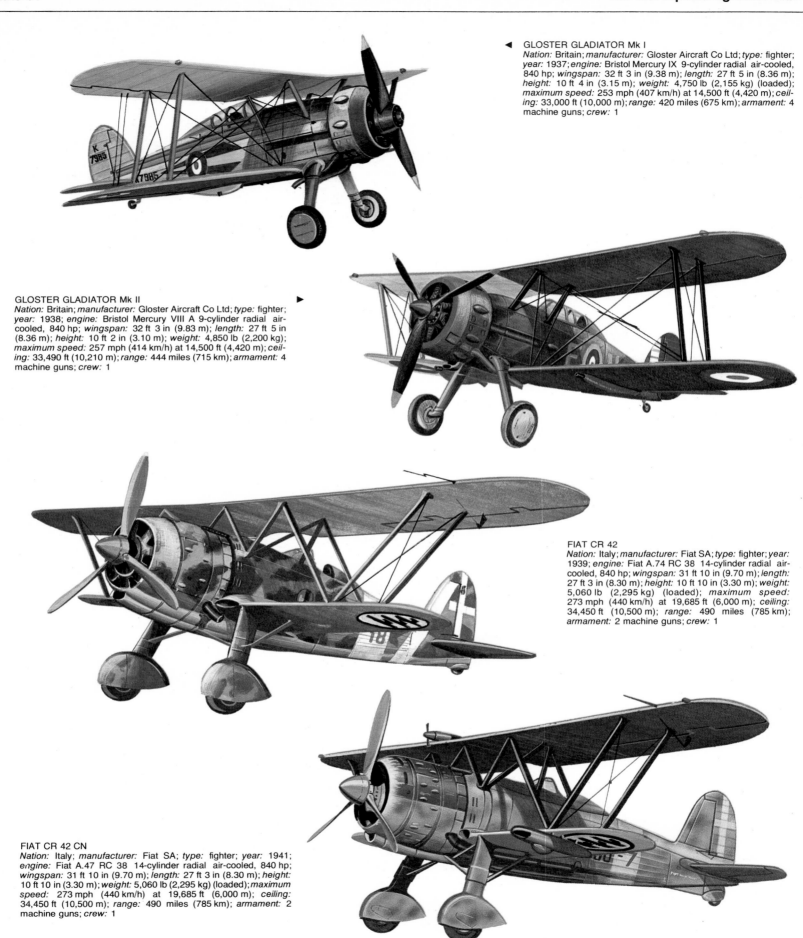

◄ **GLOSTER GLADIATOR Mk I**
Nation: Britain; *manufacturer:* Gloster Aircraft Co Ltd; *type:* fighter;
year: 1937; *engine:* Bristol Mercury IX 9-cylinder radial air-cooled,
840 hp; *wingspan:* 32 ft 3 in (9.38 m); *length:* 27 ft 5 in (8.36 m);
height: 10 ft 4 in (3.15 m); *weight:* 4,750 lb (2,155 kg) (loaded);
maximum speed: 253 mph (407 km/h) at 14,500 ft (4,420 m); *ceiling:* 33,000 ft (10,000 m); *range:* 420 miles (675 km); *armament:* 4
machine guns; *crew:* 1

GLOSTER GLADIATOR Mk II   ▶
Nation: Britain; *manufacturer:* Gloster Aircraft Co Ltd; *type:* fighter;
year: 1938; *engine:* Bristol Mercury VIII A 9-cylinder radial air-
cooled, 840 hp; *wingspan:* 32 ft 3 in (9.83 m); *length:* 27 ft 5 in
(8.36 m); *height:* 10 ft 2 in (3.10 m); *weight:* 4,850 lb (2,200 kg);
maximum speed: 257 mph (414 km/h) at 14,500 ft (4,420 m); *ceiling:* 33,490 ft (10,210 m); *range:* 444 miles (715 km); *armament:* 4
machine guns; *crew:* 1

FIAT CR 42
Nation: Italy; *manufacturer:* Fiat SA; *type:* fighter; *year:*
1939; *engine:* Fiat A.74 RC 38 14-cylinder radial air-
cooled, 840 hp; *wingspan:* 31 ft 10 in (9.70 m); *length:*
27 ft 3 in (8.30 m); *height:* 10 ft 10 in (3.30 m); *weight:*
5,060 lb (2,295 kg) (loaded); *maximum speed:*
273 mph (440 km/h) at 19,685 ft (6,000 m); *ceiling:*
34,450 ft (10,500 m); *range:* 490 miles (785 km);
armament: 2 machine guns; *crew:* 1

FIAT CR 42 CN
Nation: Italy; *manufacturer:* Fiat SA; *type:* fighter; *year:* 1941;
engine: Fiat A.47 RC 38 14-cylinder radial air-cooled, 840 hp;
wingspan: 31 ft 10 in (9.70 m); *length:* 27 ft 3 in (8.30 m); *height:*
10 ft 10 in (3.30 m); *weight:* 5,060 lb (2,295 kg) (loaded); *maximum
speed:* 273 mph (440 km/h) at 19,685 ft (6,000 m); *ceiling:*
34,450 ft (10,500 m); *range:* 490 miles (785 km); *armament:* 2
machine guns; *crew:* 1

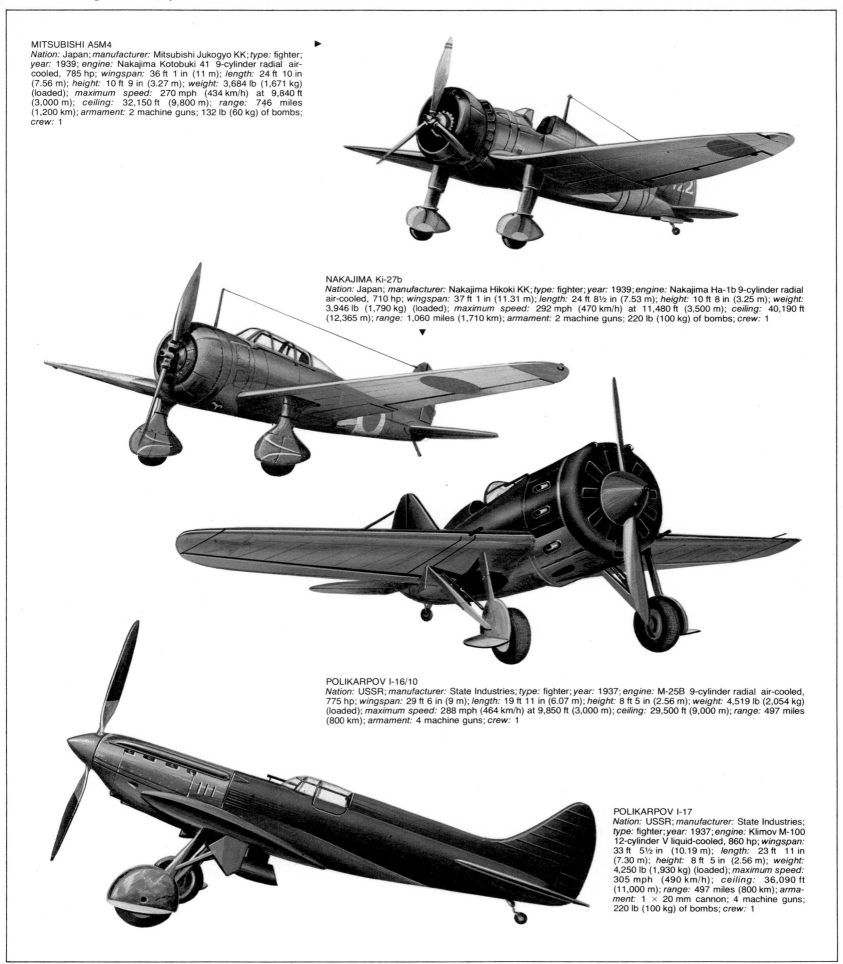

MITSUBISHI A5M4
Nation: Japan; *manufacturer:* Mitsubishi Jukogyo KK; *type:* fighter; *year:* 1939; *engine:* Nakajima Kotobuki 41 9-cylinder radial air-cooled, 785 hp; *wingspan:* 36 ft 1 in (11 m); *length:* 24 ft 10 in (7.56 m); *height:* 10 ft 9 in (3.27 m); *weight:* 3,684 lb (1,671 kg) (loaded); *maximum speed:* 270 mph (434 km/h) at 9,840 ft (3,000 m); *ceiling:* 32,150 ft (9,800 m); *range:* 746 miles (1,200 km); *armament:* 2 machine guns; 132 lb (60 kg) of bombs; *crew:* 1

NAKAJIMA Ki-27b
Nation: Japan; *manufacturer:* Nakajima Hikoki KK; *type:* fighter; *year:* 1939; *engine:* Nakajima Ha-1b 9-cylinder radial air-cooled, 710 hp; *wingspan:* 37 ft 1 in (11.31 m); *length:* 24 ft 8½ in (7.53 m); *height:* 10 ft 8 in (3.25 m); *weight:* 3,946 lb (1,790 kg) (loaded); *maximum speed:* 292 mph (470 km/h) at 11,480 ft (3,500 m); *ceiling:* 40,190 ft (12,365 m); *range:* 1,060 miles (1,710 km); *armament:* 2 machine guns; 220 lb (100 kg) of bombs; *crew:* 1

POLIKARPOV I-16/10
Nation: USSR; *manufacturer:* State Industries; *type:* fighter; *year:* 1937; *engine:* M-25B 9-cylinder radial air-cooled, 775 hp; *wingspan:* 29 ft 6 in (9 m); *length:* 19 ft 11 in (6.07 m); *height:* 8 ft 5 in (2.56 m); *weight:* 4,519 lb (2,054 kg) (loaded); *maximum speed:* 288 mph (464 km/h) at 9,850 ft (3,000 m); *ceiling:* 29,500 ft (9,000 m); *range:* 497 miles (800 km); *armament:* 4 machine guns; *crew:* 1

POLIKARPOV I-17
Nation: USSR; *manufacturer:* State Industries; *type:* fighter; *year:* 1937; *engine:* Klimov M-100 12-cylinder V liquid-cooled, 860 hp; *wingspan:* 33 ft 5½ in (10.19 m); *length:* 23 ft 11 in (7.30 m); *height:* 8 ft 5 in (2.56 m); *weight:* 4,250 lb (1,930 kg) (loaded); *maximum speed:* 305 mph (490 km/h); *ceiling:* 36,090 ft (11,000 m); *range:* 497 miles (800 km); *armament:* 1 × 20 mm cannon; 4 machine guns; 220 lb (100 kg) of bombs; *crew:* 1

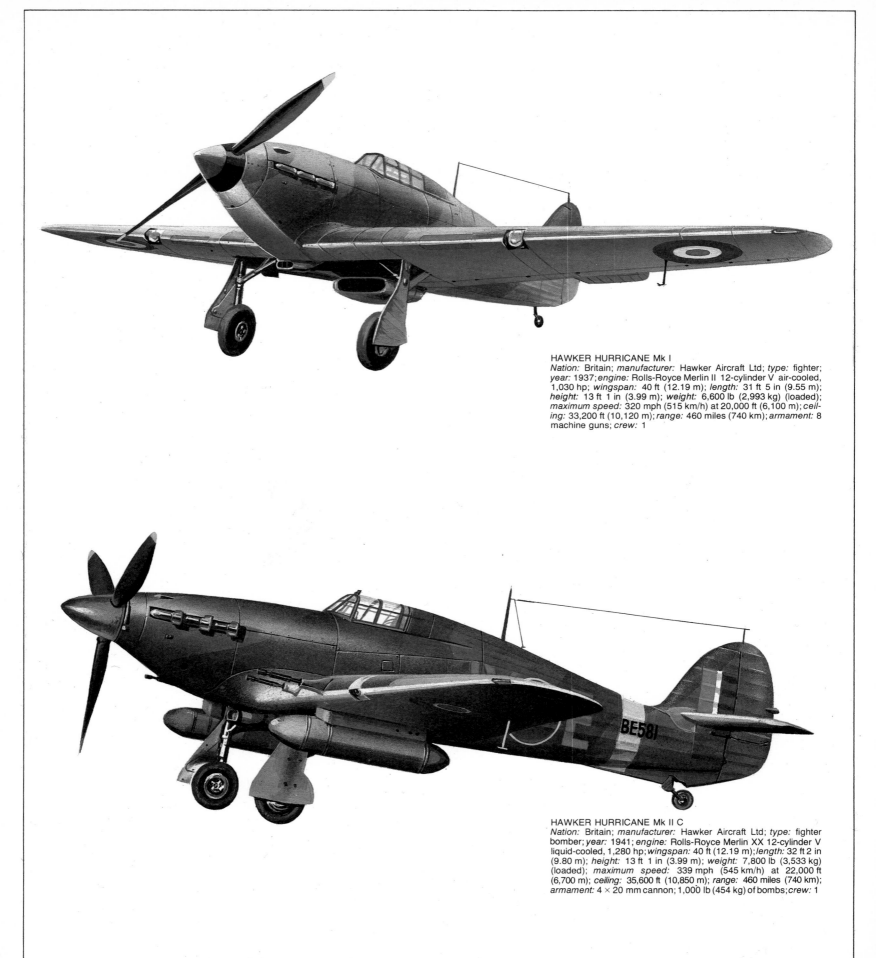

HAWKER HURRICANE Mk I
Nation: Britain; *manufacturer:* Hawker Aircraft Ltd; *type:* fighter;
year: 1937; *engine:* Rolls-Royce Merlin II 12-cylinder V air-cooled,
1,030 hp; *wingspan:* 40 ft (12.19 m); *length:* 31 ft 5 in (9.55 m);
height: 13 ft 1 in (3.99 m); *weight:* 6,600 lb (2,993 kg) (loaded);
maximum speed: 320 mph (515 km/h) at 20,000 ft (6,100 m); *ceiling:* 33,200 ft (10,120 m); *range:* 460 miles (740 km); *armament:* 8
machine guns; *crew:* 1

HAWKER HURRICANE Mk II C
Nation: Britain; *manufacturer:* Hawker Aircraft Ltd; *type:* fighter
bomber; *year:* 1941; *engine:* Rolls-Royce Merlin XX 12-cylinder V
liquid-cooled, 1,280 hp; *wingspan:* 40 ft (12.19 m); *length:* 32 ft 2 in
(9.80 m); *height:* 13 ft 1 in (3.99 m); *weight:* 7,800 lb (3,533 kg)
(loaded); *maximum speed:* 339 mph (545 km/h) at 22,000 ft
(6,700 m); *ceiling:* 35,600 ft (10,850 m); *range:* 460 miles (740 km);
armament: 4 × 20 mm cannon; 1,000 lb (454 kg) of bombs; *crew:* 1

SUPERMARINE SPITFIRE Mk I
Nation: Britain; *manufacturer:* Supermarine Division of Vickers-Armstrong Ltd; *type:* fighter; *year:* 1938; *engine:* Rolls-Royce Merlin II 12-cylinder V liquid-cooled, 1,030 hp; *wingspan:* 36 ft 10 in (11.22 m); *length:* 29 ft 11 in (9.12 m); *height:* 11 ft 5 in (3.48 m); *weight:* 5,332 lb (2,415 kg) (loaded); *maximum speed:* 355 mph (571 km/h) at 19,000 ft (5,800 m); *ceiling:* 34,000 ft (10,360 m); *range:* 500 miles (805 km); *armament:* 8 machine guns; *crew:* 1

SUPERMARINE SPITFIRE Mk VB
Nation: Britain; *manufacturer:* Supermarine Division of Vickers-Armstrong Ltd; *type:* fighter; *year:* 1941; *engine:* Rolls-Royce Merlin 45 12-cylinder V liquid-cooled, 1,440 hp; *wingspan:* 36 ft 10 in (11.22 m); *length:* 29 ft 11 in (9.12 m); *height:* 11 ft 5 in (3.43 m); *weight:* 6,417 lb (2,911 kg) (loaded); *maximum speed:* 374 mph (602 km/h) at 13,000 ft (4,000 m); *ceiling:* 37,000 ft (11,280 m); *range:* 470 miles (750 km); *armament:* 2 × 20 mm cannon; 4 machine guns; *crew:* 1

SUPERMARINE SPITFIRE Mk IX
Nation: Britain; *manufacturer:* Supermarine Division of Vickers-Armstrong Ltd; *type:* fighter; *year:* 1942; *engine:* Rolls-Royce Merlin 61 12-cylinder V liquid-cooled, 1,515 hp; *wingspan:* 36 ft 10 in (11.22 m); *length:* 30 ft 6 in (9.30 m); *height:* 11 ft 5 in (3.48 m); *weight:* 7,500 lb (3,400 kg) (loaded); *maximum speed:* 408 mph (656 km/h) at 25,000 ft (7,620 m); *ceiling:* 44,000 ft (13,400 m); *range:* 434 miles (700 km); *armament:* 2 × 20 mm cannon; 4 machine guns; *crew:* 1

SUPERMARINE SPITFIRE Mk XIV
Nation: Britain; *manufacturer:* Supermarine Division of Vickers-Armstrong Ltd; *type:* fighter; *year:* 1944; *engine:* Rolls-Royce Griffon 65 12-cylinder V liquid-cooled, 2,050 hp; *wingspan:* 36 ft 10 in (11.22 m); *length:* 32 ft 8 in (9.95 m); *height:* 12 ft 8 in (3.86 m); *weight:* 8,500 lb (3,850 kg) (loaded); *maximum speed:* 448 mph (721 km/h) at 26,000 ft (7,900 m); *ceiling:* 44,500 ft (13,560 m); *range:* 460 miles (740 km); *armament:* 2 × 20 mm cannon; 4 machine guns; 1,000 lb (454 kg) of bombs; *crew:* 1

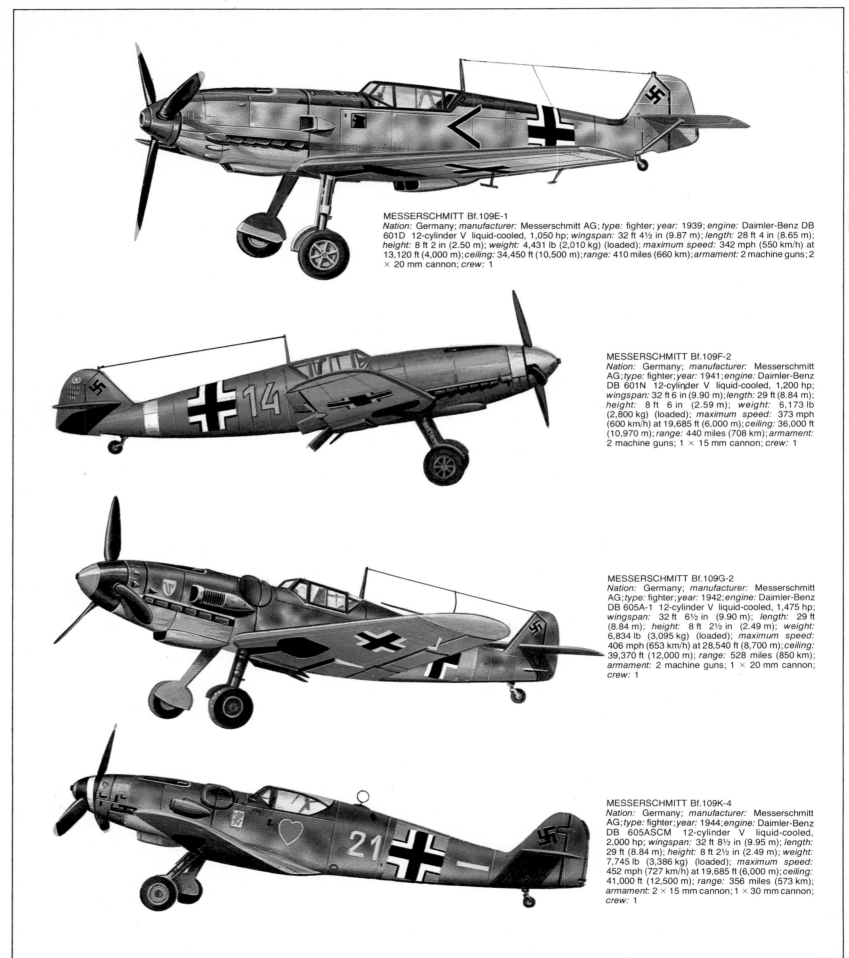

MESSERSCHMITT Bf.109E-1
Nation: Germany; *manufacturer:* Messerschmitt AG; *type:* fighter; *year:* 1939; *engine:* Daimler-Benz DB 601D 12-cylinder V liquid-cooled, 1,050 hp; *wingspan:* 32 ft 4½ in (9.87 m); *length:* 28 ft 4 in (8.65 m); *height:* 8 ft 2 in (2.50 m); *weight:* 4,431 lb (2,010 kg) (loaded); *maximum speed:* 342 mph (550 km/h) at 13,120 ft (4,000 m); *ceiling:* 34,450 ft (10,500 m); *range:* 410 miles (660 km); *armament:* 2 machine guns; 2 × 20 mm cannon; *crew:* 1

MESSERSCHMITT Bf.109F-2
Nation: Germany; *manufacturer:* Messerschmitt AG; *type:* fighter; *year:* 1941; *engine:* Daimler-Benz DB 601N 12-cylinder V liquid-cooled, 1,200 hp; *wingspan:* 32 ft 6 in (9.90 m); *length:* 29 ft (8.84 m); *height:* 8 ft 6 in (2.59 m); *weight:* 6,173 lb (2,800 kg) (loaded); *maximum speed:* 373 mph (600 km/h) at 19,685 ft (6,000 m); *ceiling:* 36,000 ft (10,970 m); *range:* 440 miles (708 km); *armament:* 2 machine guns; 1 × 15 mm cannon; *crew:* 1

MESSERSCHMITT Bf.109G-2
Nation: Germany; *manufacturer:* Messerschmitt AG; *type:* fighter; *year:* 1942; *engine:* Daimler-Benz DB 605A-1 12-cylinder V liquid-cooled, 1,475 hp; *wingspan:* 32 ft 6½ in (9.90 m); *length:* 29 ft (8.84 m); *height:* 8 ft 2½ in (2.49 m); *weight:* 6,834 lb (3,095 kg) (loaded); *maximum speed:* 406 mph (653 km/h) at 28,540 ft (8,700 m); *ceiling:* 39,370 ft (12,000 m); *range:* 528 miles (850 km); *armament:* 2 machine guns; 1 × 20 mm cannon; *crew:* 1

MESSERSCHMITT Bf.109K-4
Nation: Germany; *manufacturer:* Messerschmitt AG; *type:* fighter; *year:* 1944; *engine:* Daimler-Benz DB 605ASCM 12-cylinder V liquid-cooled, 2,000 hp; *wingspan:* 32 ft 8½ in (9.95 m); *length:* 29 ft (8.84 m); *height:* 8 ft 2½ in (2.49 m); *weight:* 7,745 lb (3,386 kg) (loaded); *maximum speed:* 452 mph (727 km/h) at 19,685 ft (6,000 m); *ceiling:* 41,000 ft (12,500 m); *range:* 356 miles (573 km); *armament:* 2 × 15 mm cannon; 1 × 30 mm cannon; *crew:* 1

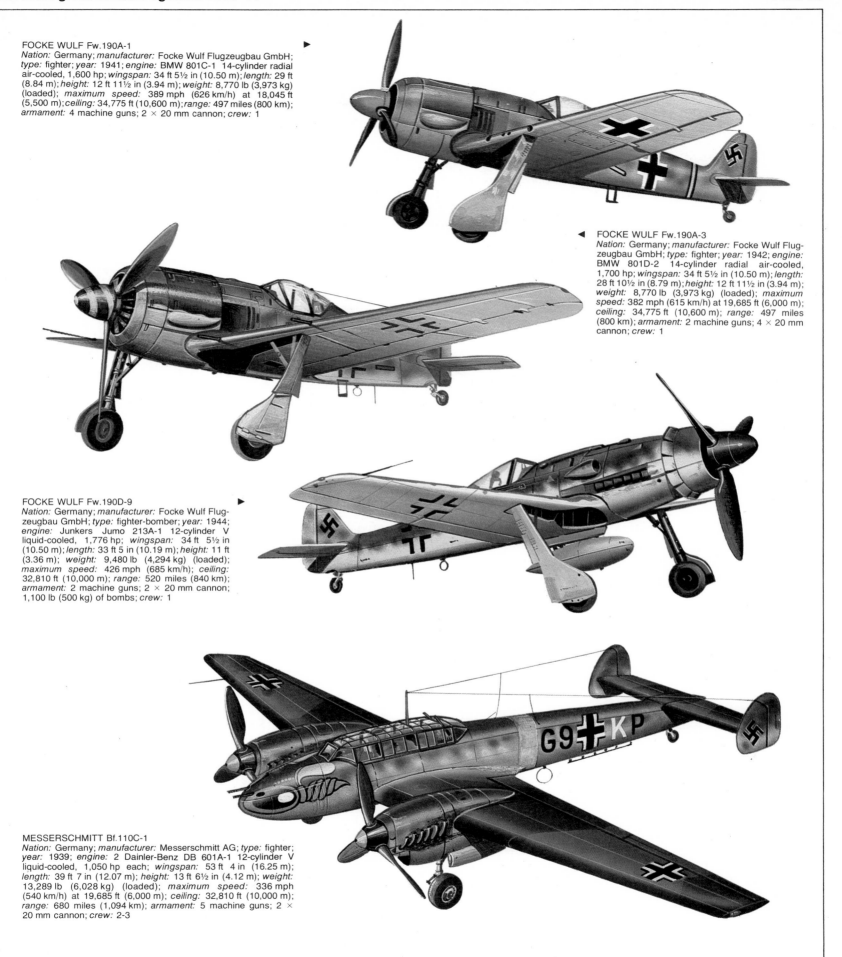

FOCKE WULF Fw.190A-1
Nation: Germany; *manufacturer:* Focke Wulf Flugzeugbau GmbH;
type: fighter; *year:* 1941; *engine:* BMW 801C-1 14-cylinder radial
air-cooled, 1,600 hp; *wingspan:* 34 ft 5½ in (10.50 m); *length:* 29 ft
(8.84 m); *height:* 12 ft 11½ in (3.94 m); *weight:* 8,770 lb (3,973 kg)
(loaded); *maximum speed:* 389 mph (626 km/h) at 18,045 ft
(5,500 m); *ceiling:* 34,775 ft (10,600 m); *range:* 497 miles (800 km);
armament: 4 machine guns; 2 × 20 mm cannon; *crew:* 1

FOCKE WULF Fw.190A-3
Nation: Germany; *manufacturer:* Focke Wulf Flugzeugbau GmbH; *type:* fighter; *year:* 1942; *engine:*
BMW 801D-2 14-cylinder radial air-cooled,
1,700 hp; *wingspan:* 34 ft 5½ in (10.50 m); *length:*
28 ft 10½ in (8.79 m); *height:* 12 ft 11½ in (3.94 m);
weight: 8,770 lb (3,973 kg) (loaded); *maximum
speed:* 382 mph (615 km/h) at 19,685 ft (6,000 m);
ceiling: 34,775 ft (10,600 m); *range:* 497 miles
(800 km); *armament:* 2 machine guns; 4 × 20 mm
cannon; *crew:* 1

FOCKE WULF Fw.190D-9
Nation: Germany; *manufacturer:* Focke Wulf Flugzeugbau GmbH; *type:* fighter-bomber; *year:* 1944;
engine: Junkers Jumo 213A-1 12-cylinder V
liquid-cooled, 1,776 hp; *wingspan:* 34 ft 5½ in
(10.50 m); *length:* 33 ft 5 in (10.19 m); *height:* 11 ft
(3.36 m); *weight:* 9,480 lb (4,294 kg) (loaded);
maximum speed: 426 mph (685 km/h); *ceiling:*
32,810 ft (10,000 m); *range:* 520 miles (840 km);
armament: 2 machine guns; 2 × 20 mm cannon;
1,100 lb (500 kg) of bombs; *crew:* 1

MESSERSCHMITT Bf.110C-1
Nation: Germany; *manufacturer:* Messerschmitt AG; *type:* fighter;
year: 1939; *engine:* 2 Dainler-Benz DB 601A-1 12-cylinder V
liquid-cooled, 1,050 hp each; *wingspan:* 53 ft 4 in (16.25 m);
length: 39 ft 7 in (12.07 m); *height:* 13 ft 6½ in (4.12 m); *weight:*
13,289 lb (6,028 kg) (loaded); *maximum speed:* 336 mph
(540 km/h) at 19,685 ft (6,000 m); *ceiling:* 32,810 ft (10,000 m);
range: 680 miles (1,094 km); *armament:* 5 machine guns; 2 ×
20 mm cannon; *crew:* 2-3

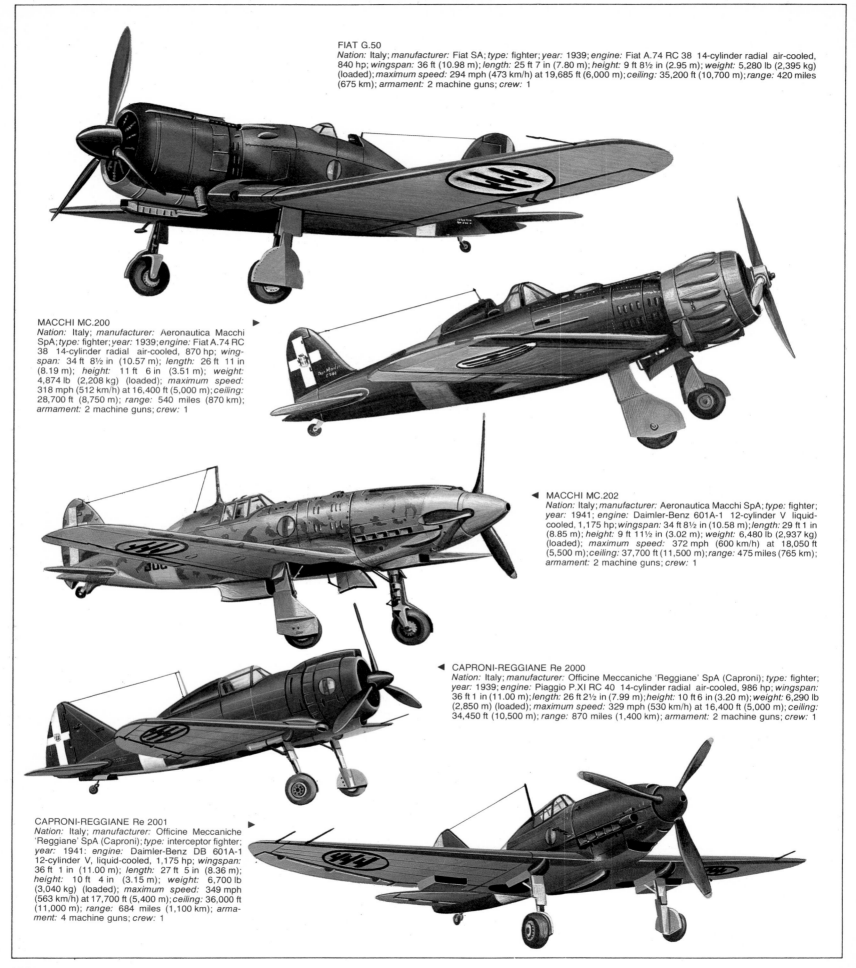

FIAT G.50
Nation: Italy; *manufacturer:* Fiat SA; *type:* fighter; *year:* 1939; *engine:* Fiat A.74 RC 38 14-cylinder radial air-cooled, 840 hp; *wingspan:* 36 ft 7 in (10.98 m); *length:* 25 ft 7 in (7.80 m); *height:* 9 ft 8½ in (2.95 m); *weight:* 5,280 lb (2,395 kg) (loaded); *maximum speed:* 294 mph (473 km/h) at 19,685 ft (6,000 m); *ceiling:* 35,200 ft (10,700 m); *range:* 420 miles (675 km); *armament:* 2 machine guns; *crew:* 1

MACCHI MC.200
Nation: Italy; *manufacturer:* Aeronautica Macchi SpA; *type:* fighter; *year:* 1939; *engine:* Fiat A.74 RC 38 14-cylinder radial air-cooled, 870 hp; *wingspan:* 34 ft 8½ in (10.57 m); *length:* 26 ft 11 in (8.19 m); *height:* 11 ft 6 in (3.51 m); *weight:* 4,874 lb (2,208 kg) (loaded); *maximum speed:* 318 mph (512 km/h) at 16,400 ft (5,000 m); *ceiling:* 28,700 ft (8,750 m); *range:* 540 miles (870 km); *armament:* 2 machine guns; *crew:* 1

MACCHI MC.202
Nation: Italy; *manufacturer:* Aeronautica Macchi SpA; *type:* fighter; *year:* 1941; *engine:* Daimler-Benz 601A-1 12-cylinder V liquid-cooled, 1,175 hp; *wingspan:* 34 ft 8½ in (10.58 m); *length:* 29 ft 1 in (8.85 m); *height:* 9 ft 11½ in (3.02 m); *weight:* 6,480 lb (2,937 kg) (loaded); *maximum speed:* 372 mph (600 km/h) at 18,050 ft (5,500 m); *ceiling:* 37,700 ft (11,500 m); *range:* 475 miles (765 km); *armament:* 2 machine guns; *crew:* 1

CAPRONI-REGGIANE Re 2000
Nation: Italy; *manufacturer:* Officine Meccaniche 'Reggiane' SpA (Caproni); *type:* fighter; *year:* 1939; *engine:* Piaggio P.XI RC 40 14-cylinder radial air-cooled, 986 hp; *wingspan:* 36 ft 1 in (11.00 m); *length:* 26 ft 2½ in (7.99 m); *height:* 10 ft 6 in (3.20 m); *weight:* 6,290 lb (2,850 m) (loaded); *maximum speed:* 329 mph (530 km/h) at 16,400 ft (5,000 m); *ceiling:* 34,450 ft (10,500 m); *range:* 870 miles (1,400 km); *armament:* 2 machine guns; *crew:* 1

CAPRONI-REGGIANE Re 2001
Nation: Italy; *manufacturer:* Officine Meccaniche 'Reggiane' SpA (Caproni); *type:* interceptor fighter; *year:* 1941; *engine:* Daimler-Benz DB 601A-1 12-cylinder V, liquid-cooled, 1,175 hp; *wingspan:* 36 ft 1 in (11.00 m); *length:* 27 ft 5 in (8.36 m); *height:* 10 ft 4 in (3.15 m); *weight:* 6,700 lb (3,040 kg) (loaded); *maximum speed:* 349 mph (563 km/h) at 17,700 ft (5,400 m); *ceiling:* 36,000 ft (11,000 m); *range:* 684 miles (1,100 km); *armament:* 4 machine guns; *crew:* 1

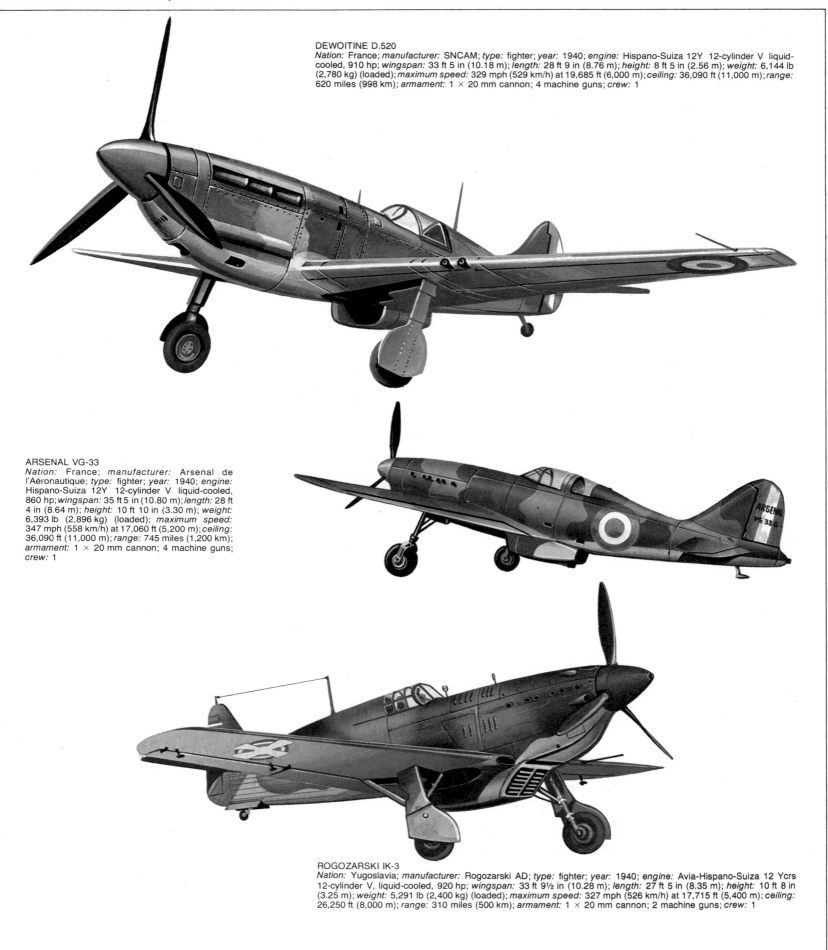

DEWOITINE D.520
Nation: France; *manufacturer:* SNCAM; *type:* fighter; *year:* 1940; *engine:* Hispano-Suiza 12Y 12-cylinder V liquid-cooled, 910 hp; *wingspan:* 33 ft 5 in (10.18 m); *length:* 28 ft 9 in (8.76 m); *height:* 8 ft 5 in (2.56 m); *weight:* 6,144 lb (2,780 kg) (loaded); *maximum speed:* 329 mph (529 km/h) at 19,685 ft (6,000 m); *ceiling:* 36,090 ft (11,000 m); *range:* 620 miles (998 km); *armament:* 1 × 20 mm cannon; 4 machine guns; *crew:* 1

ARSENAL VG-33
Nation: France; *manufacturer:* Arsenal de l'Aéronautique; *type:* fighter; *year:* 1940; *engine:* Hispano-Suiza 12Y 12-cylinder V liquid-cooled, 860 hp; *wingspan:* 35 ft 5 in (10.80 m); *length:* 28 ft 4 in (8.64 m); *height:* 10 ft 10 in (3.30 m); *weight:* 6,393 lb (2,896 kg) (loaded); *maximum speed:* 347 mph (558 km/h) at 17,060 ft (5,200 m); *ceiling:* 36,090 ft (11,000 m); *range:* 745 miles (1,200 km); *armament:* 1 × 20 mm cannon; 4 machine guns; *crew:* 1

ROGOZARSKI IK-3
Nation: Yugoslavia; *manufacturer:* Rogozarski AD; *type:* fighter; *year:* 1940; *engine:* Avia-Hispano-Suiza 12 Ycrs 12-cylinder V, liquid-cooled, 920 hp; *wingspan:* 33 ft 9½ in (10.28 m); *length:* 27 ft 5 in (8.35 m); *height:* 10 ft 8 in (3.25 m); *weight:* 5,291 lb (2,400 kg) (loaded); *maximum speed:* 327 mph (526 km/h) at 17,715 ft (5,400 m); *ceiling:* 26,250 ft (8,000 m); *range:* 310 miles (500 km); *armament:* 1 × 20 mm cannon; 2 machine guns; *crew:* 1

Plate 89

British fighters of 1940

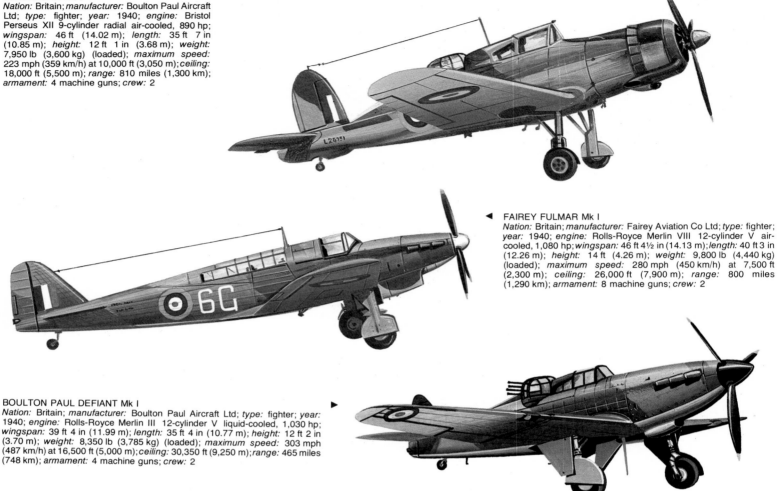

BLACKBURN ROC
Nation: Britain; *manufacturer:* Boulton Paul Aircraft Ltd; *type:* fighter; *year:* 1940; *engine:* Bristol Perseus XII 9-cylinder radial air-cooled, 890 hp; *wingspan:* 46 ft (14.02 m); *length:* 35 ft 7 in (10.85 m); *height:* 12 ft 1 in (3.68 m); *weight:* 7,950 lb (3,600 kg) (loaded); *maximum speed:* 223 mph (359 km/h) at 10,000 ft (3,050 m); *ceiling:* 18,000 ft (5,500 m); *range:* 810 miles (1,300 km); *armament:* 4 machine guns; *crew:* 2

FAIREY FULMAR Mk I
Nation: Britain; *manufacturer:* Fairey Aviation Co Ltd; *type:* fighter; *year:* 1940; *engine:* Rolls-Royce Merlin VIII 12-cylinder V air-cooled, 1,080 hp; *wingspan:* 46 ft 4½ in (14.13 m); *length:* 40 ft 3 in (12.26 m); *height:* 14 ft (4.26 m); *weight:* 9,800 lb (4,440 kg) (loaded); *maximum speed:* 280 mph (450 km/h) at 7,500 ft (2,300 m); *ceiling:* 26,000 ft (7,900 m); *range:* 800 miles (1,290 km); *armament:* 8 machine guns; *crew:* 2

BOULTON PAUL DEFIANT Mk I
Nation: Britain; *manufacturer:* Boulton Paul Aircraft Ltd; *type:* fighter; *year:* 1940; *engine:* Rolls-Royce Merlin III 12-cylinder V liquid-cooled, 1,030 hp; *wingspan:* 39 ft 4 in (11.99 m); *length:* 35 ft 4 in (10.77 m); *height:* 12 ft 2 in (3.70 m); *weight:* 8,350 lb (3,785 kg) (loaded); *maximum speed:* 303 mph (487 km/h) at 16,500 ft (5,000 m); *ceiling:* 30,350 ft (9,250 m); *range:* 465 miles (748 km); *armament:* 4 machine guns; *crew:* 2

BRISTOL BEAUFIGHTER Mk IF
Nation: Britain; *manufacturer:* Bristol Aeroplane Co Ltd; *type:* fighter; *year:* 1940; *engine:* two Bristol Hercules XI 14-cylinder radial air-cooled, 1,400 hp each; *wingspan:* 57 ft 10 in (17.63 m); *length:* 41 ft 4 in (12.50 m); *height:* 15 ft 10 in (4.83 m); *weight:* 21,000 lb (9,500 kg) (loaded); *maximum speed:* 321 mph (516 km/h) at 15,800 ft (4,800 m); *ceiling:* 26,500 ft (8,000 m); *range:* 1,170 miles (1,890 km); *armament:* 4 × 20 mm cannon; 6 machine guns; *crew:* 2

BRISTOL BEAUFIGHTER Mk X
Nation: Britain; *manufacturer:* Bristol Aeroplane Co Ltd; *type:* fighter-bomber; *year:* 1943; *engine:* two Bristol Hercules XVII 14-cylinder radial air-cooled, 1,770 hp each; *wingspan:* 57 ft 10 in (17.63 m); *length:* 42 ft 6 in (12.95 m); *height:* 15 ft 10 in (4.83 m); *weight:* 25,200 lb (11,430 kg) (loaded); *maximum speed:* 330 mph (531 km/h) at 1,300 ft (400 m); *ceiling:* 29,000 ft (8,800 m); *range:* 1,470 miles (2,365 km); *armament:* 4 × 20 mm cannon; 1 × 2,127 lb (964 kg) torpedo; 500 lb (226 kg) of bombs; *crew:* 2

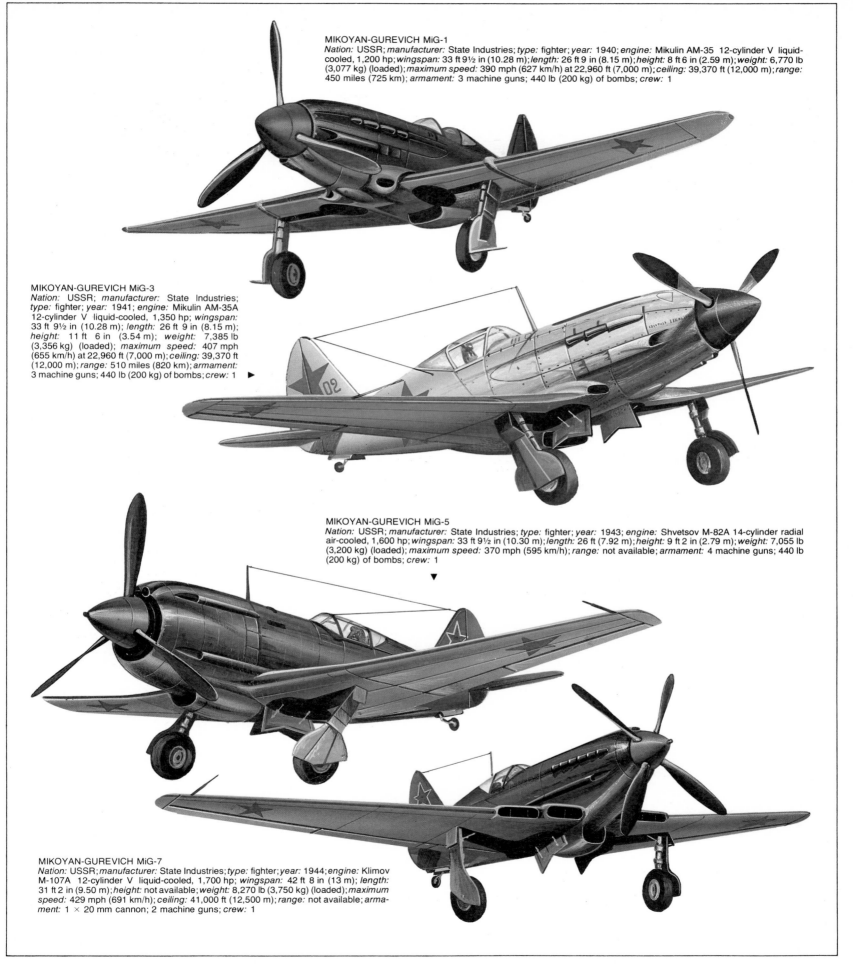

MIKOYAN-GUREVICH MiG-1
Nation: USSR; *manufacturer:* State Industries; *type:* fighter; *year:* 1940; *engine:* Mikulin AM-35 12-cylinder V liquid-cooled, 1,200 hp; *wingspan:* 33 ft 9½ in (10.28 m); *length:* 26 ft 9 in (8.15 m); *height:* 8 ft 6 in (2.59 m); *weight:* 6,770 lb (3,077 kg) (loaded); *maximum speed:* 390 mph (627 km/h) at 22,960 ft (7,000 m); *ceiling:* 39,370 ft (12,000 m); *range:* 450 miles (725 km); *armament:* 3 machine guns; 440 lb (200 kg) of bombs; *crew:* 1

MIKOYAN-GUREVICH MiG-3
Nation: USSR; *manufacturer:* State Industries; *type:* fighter; *year:* 1941; *engine:* Mikulin AM-35A 12-cylinder V liquid-cooled, 1,350 hp; *wingspan:* 33 ft 9½ in (10.28 m); *length:* 26 ft 9 in (8.15 m); *height:* 11 ft 6 in (3.54 m); *weight:* 7,385 lb (3,356 kg) (loaded); *maximum speed:* 407 mph (655 km/h) at 22,960 ft (7,000 m); *ceiling:* 39,370 ft (12,000 m); *range:* 510 miles (820 km); *armament:* 3 machine guns; 440 lb (200 kg) of bombs; *crew:* 1 ▶

MIKOYAN-GUREVICH MiG-5
Nation: USSR; *manufacturer:* State Industries; *type:* fighter; *year:* 1943; *engine:* Shvetsov M-82A 14-cylinder radial air-cooled, 1,600 hp; *wingspan:* 33 ft 9½ in (10.30 m); *length:* 26 ft (7.92 m); *height:* 9 ft 2 in (2.79 m); *weight:* 7,055 lb (3,200 kg) (loaded); *maximum speed:* 370 mph (595 km/h); *range:* not available; *armament:* 4 machine guns; 440 lb (200 kg) of bombs; *crew:* 1
▼

MIKOYAN-GUREVICH MiG-7
Nation: USSR; *manufacturer:* State Industries; *type:* fighter; *year:* 1944; *engine:* Klimov M-107A 12-cylinder V liquid-cooled, 1,700 hp; *wingspan:* 42 ft 8 in (13 m); *length:* 31 ft 2 in (9.50 m); *height:* not available; *weight:* 8,270 lb (3,750 kg) (loaded); *maximum speed:* 429 mph (691 km/h); *ceiling:* 41,000 ft (12,500 m); *range:* not available; *armament:* 1 × 20 mm cannon; 2 machine guns; *crew:* 1

Plate 91   **The Zero – the best Japanese fighter of the war: 1940–45**

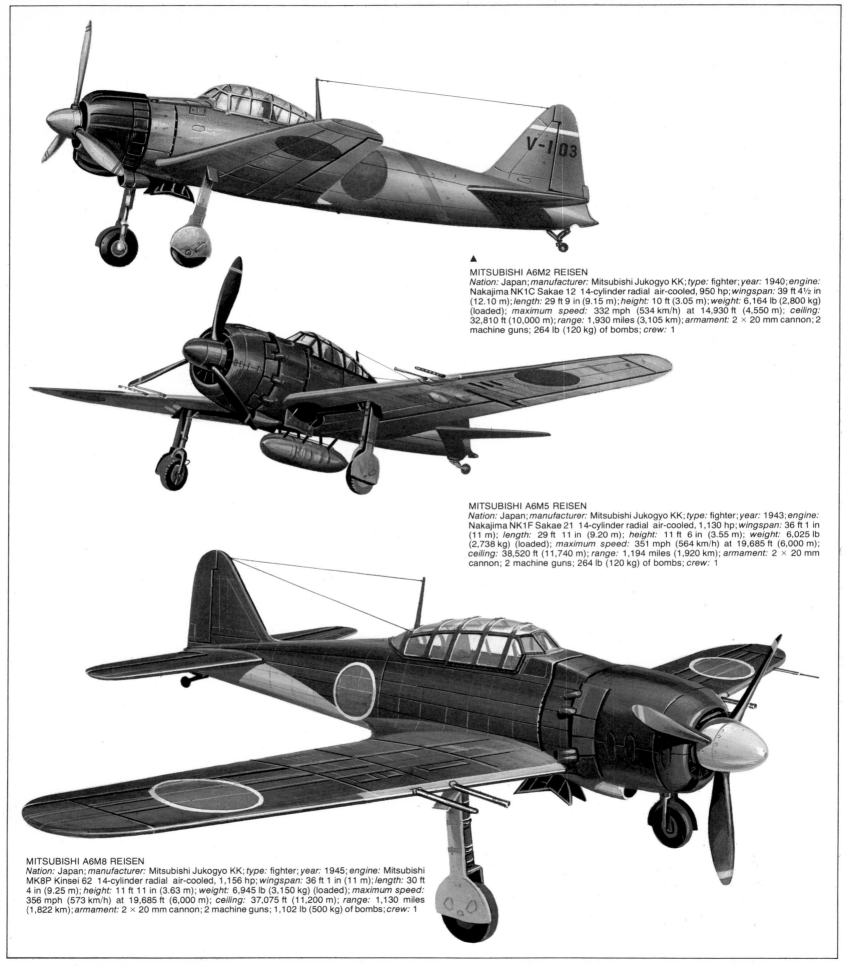

▲
MITSUBISHI A6M2 REISEN
Nation: Japan;*manufacturer:* Mitsubishi Jukogyo KK;*type:* fighter;*year:* 1940;*engine:*
Nakajima NK1C Sakae 12 14-cylinder radial air-cooled, 950 hp;*wingspan:* 39 ft 4½ in
(12.10 m);*length:* 29 ft 9 in (9.15 m);*height:* 10 ft (3.05 m);*weight:* 6,164 lb (2,800 kg)
(loaded); *maximum speed:* 332 mph (534 km/h) at 14,930 ft (4,550 m); *ceiling:*
32,810 ft (10,000 m);*range:* 1,930 miles (3,105 km);*armament:* 2 × 20 mm cannon; 2
machine guns; 264 lb (120 kg) of bombs; *crew:* 1

MITSUBISHI A6M5 REISEN
Nation: Japan;*manufacturer:* Mitsubishi Jukogyo KK;*type:* fighter;*year:* 1943;*engine:*
Nakajima NK1F Sakae 21 14-cylinder radial air-cooled, 1,130 hp;*wingspan:* 36 ft 1 in
(11 m); *length:* 29 ft 11 in (9.20 m); *height:* 11 ft 6 in (3.55 m); *weight:* 6,025 lb
(2,738 kg) (loaded); *maximum speed:* 351 mph (564 km/h) at 19,685 ft (6,000 m);
ceiling: 38,520 ft (11,740 m); *range:* 1,194 miles (1,920 km); *armament:* 2 × 20 mm
cannon; 2 machine guns; 264 lb (120 kg) of bombs; *crew:* 1

MITSUBISHI A6M8 REISEN
Nation: Japan;*manufacturer:* Mitsubishi Jukogyo KK;*type:* fighter;*year:* 1945;*engine:* Mitsubishi
MK8P Kinsei 62 14-cylinder radial air-cooled, 1,156 hp;*wingspan:* 36 ft 1 in (11 m);*length:* 30 ft
4 in (9.25 m); *height:* 11 ft 11 in (3.63 m); *weight:* 6,945 lb (3,150 kg) (loaded); *maximum speed:*
356 mph (573 km/h) at 19,685 ft (6,000 m); *ceiling:* 37,075 ft (11,200 m); *range:* 1,130 miles
(1,822 km);*armament:* 2 × 20 mm cannon; 2 machine guns; 1,102 lb (500 kg) of bombs;*crew:* 1

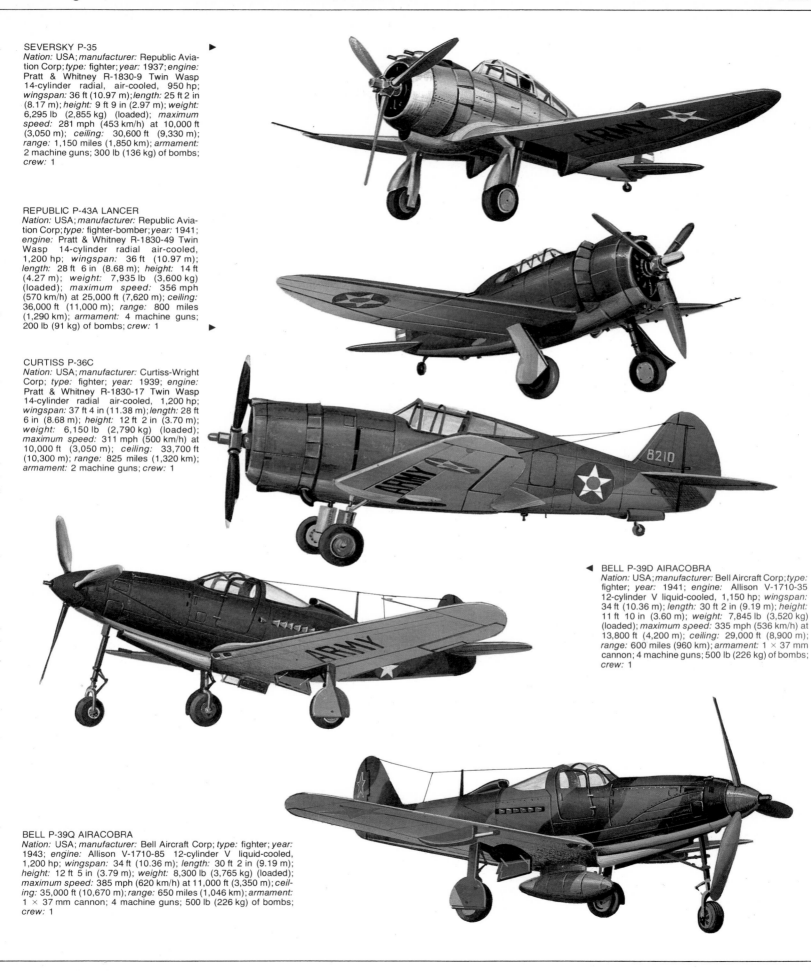

SEVERSKY P-35
Nation: USA; *manufacturer:* Republic Aviation Corp; *type:* fighter; *year:* 1937; *engine:* Pratt & Whitney R-1830-9 Twin Wasp 14-cylinder radial, air-cooled, 950 hp; *wingspan:* 36 ft (10.97 m); *length:* 25 ft 2 in (8.17 m); *height:* 9 ft 9 in (2.97 m); *weight:* 6,295 lb (2,855 kg) (loaded); *maximum speed:* 281 mph (453 km/h) at 10,000 ft (3,050 m); *ceiling:* 30,600 ft (9,330 m); *range:* 1,150 miles (1,850 km); *armament:* 2 machine guns; 300 lb (136 kg) of bombs; *crew:* 1

REPUBLIC P-43A LANCER
Nation: USA; *manufacturer:* Republic Aviation Corp; *type:* fighter-bomber; *year:* 1941; *engine:* Pratt & Whitney R-1830-49 Twin Wasp 14-cylinder radial air-cooled, 1,200 hp; *wingspan:* 36 ft (10.97 m); *length:* 28 ft 6 in (8.68 m); *height:* 14 ft (4.27 m); *weight:* 7,935 lb (3,600 kg) (loaded); *maximum speed:* 356 mph (570 km/h) at 25,000 ft (7,620 m); *ceiling:* 36,000 ft (11,000 m); *range:* 800 miles (1,290 km); *armament:* 4 machine guns; 200 lb (91 kg) of bombs; *crew:* 1

CURTISS P-36C
Nation: USA; *manufacturer:* Curtiss-Wright Corp; *type:* fighter; *year:* 1939; *engine:* Pratt & Whitney R-1830-17 Twin Wasp 14-cylinder radial air-cooled, 1,200 hp; *wingspan:* 37 ft 4 in (11.38 m); *length:* 28 ft 6 in (8.68 m); *height:* 12 ft 2 in (3.70 m); *weight:* 6,150 lb (2,790 kg) (loaded); *maximum speed:* 311 mph (500 km/h) at 10,000 ft (3,050 m); *ceiling:* 33,700 ft (10,300 m); *range:* 825 miles (1,320 km); *armament:* 2 machine guns; *crew:* 1

BELL P-39D AIRACOBRA
Nation: USA; *manufacturer:* Bell Aircraft Corp; *type:* fighter; *year:* 1941; *engine:* Allison V-1710-35 12-cylinder V liquid-cooled, 1,150 hp; *wingspan:* 34 ft (10.36 m); *length:* 30 ft 2 in (9.19 m); *height:* 11 ft 10 in (3.60 m); *weight:* 7,845 lb (3,520 kg) (loaded); *maximum speed:* 335 mph (536 km/h) at 13,800 ft (4,200 m); *ceiling:* 29,000 ft (8,900 m); *range:* 600 miles (960 km); *armament:* 1 × 37 mm cannon; 4 machine guns; 500 lb (226 kg) of bombs; *crew:* 1

BELL P-39Q AIRACOBRA
Nation: USA; *manufacturer:* Bell Aircraft Corp; *type:* fighter; *year:* 1943; *engine:* Allison V-1710-85 12-cylinder V liquid-cooled, 1,200 hp; *wingspan:* 34 ft (10.36 m); *length:* 30 ft 2 in (9.19 m); *height:* 12 ft 5 in (3.79 m); *weight:* 8,300 lb (3,765 kg) (loaded); *maximum speed:* 385 mph (620 km/h) at 11,000 ft (3,350 m); *ceiling:* 35,000 ft (10,670 m); *range:* 650 miles (1,046 km); *armament:* 1 × 37 mm cannon; 4 machine guns; 500 lb (226 kg) of bombs; *crew:* 1

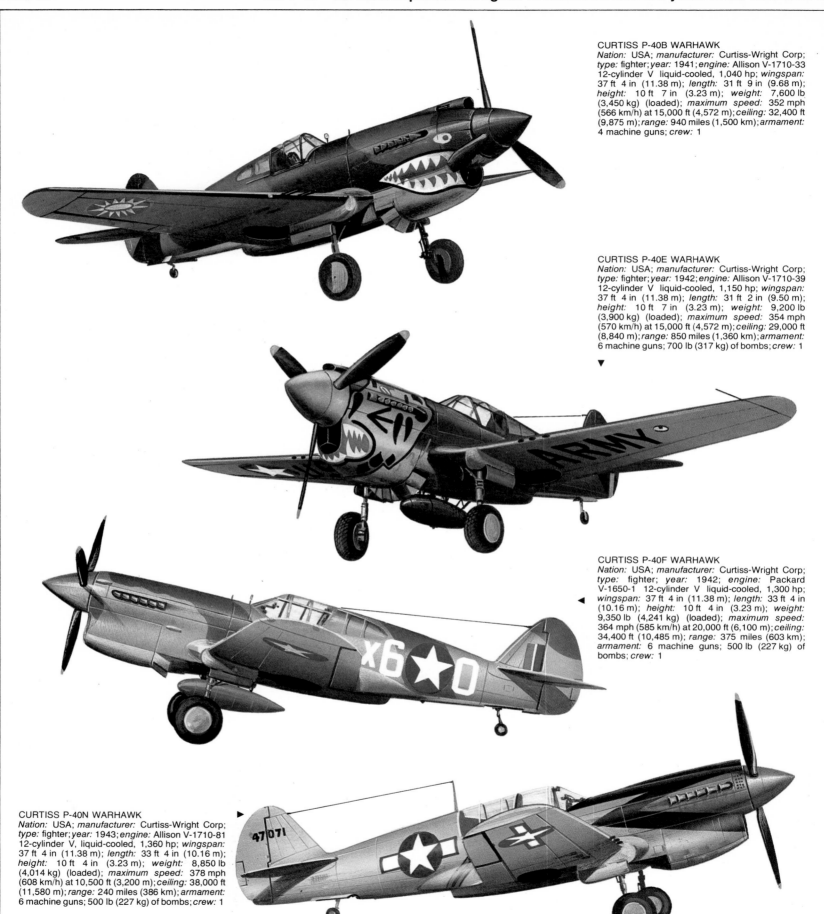

CURTISS P-40B WARHAWK
Nation: USA; *manufacturer:* Curtiss-Wright Corp; *type:* fighter; *year:* 1941; *engine:* Allison V-1710-33 12-cylinder V liquid-cooled, 1,040 hp; *wingspan:* 37 ft 4 in (11.38 m); *length:* 31 ft 9 in (9.68 m); *height:* 10 ft 7 in (3.23 m); *weight:* 7,600 lb (3,450 kg) (loaded); *maximum speed:* 352 mph (566 km/h) at 15,000 ft (4,572 m); *ceiling:* 32,400 ft (9,875 m); *range:* 940 miles (1,500 km); *armament:* 4 machine guns; *crew:* 1

CURTISS P-40E WARHAWK
Nation: USA; *manufacturer:* Curtiss-Wright Corp; *type:* fighter; *year:* 1942; *engine:* Allison V-1710-39 12-cylinder V liquid-cooled, 1,150 hp; *wingspan:* 37 ft 4 in (11.38 m); *length:* 31 ft 2 in (9.50 m); *height:* 10 ft 7 in (3.23 m); *weight:* 9,200 lb (3,900 kg) (loaded); *maximum speed:* 354 mph (570 km/h) at 15,000 ft (4,572 m); *ceiling:* 29,000 ft (8,840 m); *range:* 850 miles (1,360 km); *armament:* 6 machine guns; 700 lb (317 kg) of bombs; *crew:* 1
▼

CURTISS P-40F WARHAWK
Nation: USA; *manufacturer:* Curtiss-Wright Corp; *type:* fighter; *year:* 1942; *engine:* Packard V-1650-1 12-cylinder V liquid-cooled, 1,300 hp; *wingspan:* 37 ft 4 in (11.38 m); *length:* 33 ft 4 in (10.16 m); *height:* 10 ft 4 in (3.23 m); *weight:* 9,350 lb (4,241 kg) (loaded); *maximum speed:* 364 mph (585 km/h) at 20,000 ft (6,100 m); *ceiling:* 34,400 ft (10,485 m); *range:* 375 miles (603 km); *armament:* 6 machine guns; 500 lb (227 kg) of bombs; *crew:* 1

CURTISS P-40N WARHAWK
Nation: USA; *manufacturer:* Curtiss-Wright Corp; *type:* fighter; *year:* 1943; *engine:* Allison V-1710-81 12-cylinder V, liquid-cooled, 1,360 hp; *wingspan:* 37 ft 4 in (11.38 m); *length:* 33 ft 4 in (10.16 m); *height:* 10 ft 4 in (3.23 m); *weight:* 8,850 lb (4,014 kg) (loaded); *maximum speed:* 378 mph (608 km/h) at 10,500 ft (3,200 m); *ceiling:* 38,000 ft (11,580 m); *range:* 240 miles (386 km); *armament:* 6 machine guns; 500 lb (227 kg) of bombs; *crew:* 1

SUPERMARINE SEAFIRE Mk IIC
Nation: Britain; *manufacturer:* Supermarine Division of Vickers-Armstrong Ltd; *type:* fighter; *year:* 1942; *engine:* Rolls-Royce Merlin 45 12-cylinder V liquid-cooled, 1,340 hp; *wingspan:* 36 ft 8 in (11.17 m); *length:* 30 ft (9.14 m); *height:* 11 ft 2 in (3.41 m); *weight:* 7,000 lb (3,170 kg) (loaded); *maximum speed:* 333 mph (536 km/h) at 5,000 ft (1,500 m); *ceiling:* 32,000 ft (9,750 m); *range:* 755 miles (1,215 km); *armament:* 2 × 20 mm cannon; 4 machine guns; *crew:* 1

SUPERMARINE SEAFIRE Mk XV
Nation: Britain; *manufacturer:* Supermarine Division of Vickers-Armstrong Ltd; *type:* fighter; *year:* 1945; *engine:* Rolls-Royce Griffon VI 12-cylinder V liquid-cooled, 1,850 hp; *wingspan:* 36 ft 10 in (11.22 m); *length:* 32 ft 3 in (9.83 m); *height:* 10 ft 8 in (3.25 m); *weight:* 8,000 lb (3,628 kg) (loaded); *maximum speed:* 383 mph (616 km/h) at 13,500 ft (4,110 m); *ceiling:* 35,500 ft (10,810 m); *range:* 640 miles (1,029 km); *armament:* 2 × 20 mm cannon; 4 machine guns; *crew:* 1

FAIREY FIREFLY Mk I
Nation: Britain; *manufacturer:* Fairey Aviation Co Ltd; *type:* fighter; *year:* 1943; *engine:* Rolls-Royce Griffon IIB 12-cylinder V liquid-cooled, 1,730 hp; *wingspan:* 44 ft 6 in (13.56 m); *length:* 37 ft 7 in (11.46 m); *height:* 13 ft 7 in (4.14 m); *weight:* 14,020 lb (6,350 kg) (loaded); *maximum speed:* 316 mph (508 km/h) at 14,000 ft (4,250 m); *ceiling:* 28,000 ft (8,500 m); *range:* 1,300 miles (2,100 km); *armament:* 4 × 20 mm cannon; *crew:* 2

Plate 95

Russian efforts to compete on equal terms: 1941–43

LAVOCHKIN LaGG-3
Nation: USSR; *manufacturer:* State Industries; *type:* fighter; *year:* 1941; *engine:* Klimov M-105PF 12-cylinder V liquid-cooled, 1,210 hp; *wingspan:* 32 ft 2 in (9.80 m); *length:* 29 ft 1 in (8.86 m); *height:* 8 ft 10 in (2.69 m); *weight:* 7,032 lb (3,190 kg) (loaded); *maximum speed:* 348 mph (560 km/h) at 16,400 ft (5,000 m); *ceiling:* 31,500 ft (9,690 m); *range:* 404 miles (650 km); *armament:* 1 × 20 mm cannon; 3 machine guns; 440 lb (200 kg) of bombs; *crew:* 1

LAVOCHKIN La-7
Nation: USSR; *manufacturer:* State Industries; *type:* fighter; *year:* 1944; *engine:* Shvetsov M-82FN 14-cylinder radial air-cooled, 1,850 hp; *wingspan:* 32 ft 2 in (9.80 m); *length:* 28 ft 2½ in (8.58 m); *height:* 9 ft 2 in (2.79 m); *weight:* 7,496 lb (3,400 kg) (loaded); *maximum speed:* 423 mph (680 km/h) at 21,000 ft (6,400 m); *ceiling:* 34,450 ft (10,500 m); *range:* 395 miles (635 km); *armament:* 3 × 20 mm cannon; 441 lb (200 kg) of bombs; *crew:* 1

LAVOCHKIN La-5FN
Nation: USSR; *manufacturer:* State Industries; *type:* fighter; *year:* 1943; *engine:* Shvetsov M-82FN 14-cylinder radial air-cooled, 1,640 hp; *wingspan:* 32 ft 2 in (9.80 m); *length:* 28 ft 5 in (8.65 m); *height:* 8 ft 4 in (2.56 m); *weight:* 7,406 lb (3,360 kg) (loaded); maximum *speed:* 402 mph (647 km/h) at 16,400 ft (5,000 m); *ceiling:* 32,800 ft (10,000 m); *range:* 475 miles (766 km); *armament:* 2 × 20 mm cannon; 662 lb (300 kg) of bombs; *crew:* 1

YAKOVLEV Yak-1
Nation: USSR; *manufacturer:* State Industries; *type:* fighter; *year:* 1942; *engine:* Klimov M-105PA 12-cylinder liquid-cooled, 1,100 hp; *wingspan:* 32 ft 10 in (10 m); *length:* 27 ft 9½ in (8.48 m); *height:* 8 ft 8 in (2.64 m); *weight:* 6,217 lb (2,820 kg) (loaded); *maximum speed:* 360 mph (580 km/h) at 16,400 ft (5,000 m); *ceiling:* 32,810 ft (10,000 m); *range:* 528 miles (850 km); *armament:* 1 × 20 mm cannon; 2 machine guns; *crew:* 1 ▶

YAKOVLEV Yak-9D
Nation: USSR; *manufacturer:* State Industries; *type:* fighter; *year:* 1943; *engine:* Klimov M-105PF 12-cylinder V liquid-cooled, 1,360 hp; *wingspan:* 32 ft 11½ in (10.03 m); *length:* 28 ft 1 in (8.55 m); *height:* 9 ft 10 in (3.05 m); *weight:* 6,867 lb (3,115 kg) (loaded); *maximum speed:* 374 mph (600 km/h) at 6,560 ft (2,000 m); *ceiling:* 32,800 ft (10,000 m); *range:* 808 miles (1,300 km); *armament:* 1 × 20 mm cannon; 1 machine gun; *crew:* 1 ◀

GRUMMAN F4F-3 WILDCAT
Nation: USA; *manufacturer:* Grumman Aircraft Engineering Corp; *type:* fighter; *year:* 1940; *engine:*
Pratt & Whitney R-1830-76 Twin Wasp 14-cylinder radial air-cooled, 1,200 hp; *wingspan:* 38 ft
(11.58 m); *length:* 28 ft 9 in (8.76 m); *height:* 11 ft 10 in (3.60 m); *weight:* 7,000 lb (3,176 kg)
(loaded); *maximum speed:* 331 mph (531 km/h) at 21,300 ft (6,500 m); *ceiling:* 37,500 ft
(11,430 m); *range:* 845 miles (1,360 km); *armament:* 6 machine guns; 200 lb (91 kg) of bombs;
crew: 1

GRUMMAN F4F-4 WILDCAT
Nation: USA; *manufacturer:* Grumman Aircraft Engineering Corp;
type: fighter; *year:* 1941; *engine:* Pratt & Whitney R-1830-86 Twin
Wasp 14-cylinder radial air-cooled, 1,200 hp; *wingspan:* 38 ft
(11.58 m); *length:* 28 ft 9 in (8.76 m); *height:* 11 ft 10 in (3.60 m);
weight: 7,952 lb (3,560 kg) (loaded); *maximum speed:* 318 mph
(512 km/h) at 19,400 ft (5,900 m); *ceiling:* 34,900 ft; (10,640 m);
range: 770 miles (1,240 km); *armament:* 6 machine guns; 200 lb
(91 kg) of bombs; *crew:* 1

BREWSTER F2A-3 BUFFALO
Nation: USA; *manufacturer:* Brewster Aeronautical Corp; *type:*
fighter-bomber; *year:* 1941; *engine:* Wright R-1820-40 Cyclone
9-cylinder radial air-cooled, 1,200 hp; *wingspan:* 35 ft (10.67 m);
length: 26 ft 4 in (8.02 m); *height:* 12 ft 1 in (3.66 m); *weight:*
7,159 lb (3,247 kg) (loaded); *maximum speed:* 321 mph (517 km/h)
at 16,500 ft (5,030 m); *ceiling:* 33,200 ft (10,120 m); *range:* 965
miles (1,553 km); *armament:* 4 machine guns; 220 lb (91 kg) of
bombs; *crew:* 1

LOCKHEED P-38F LIGHTNING
Nation: USA; *manufacturer:* Lockheed Aircraft Corp; *type:* fighter;
year: 1942; *engine:* two Allison V-1710-49 12-cylinder V liquid-
cooled, 1,250 hp each; *wingspan:* 52 ft (15.85 m); *length:* 37 ft
10 in (11.53 m); *height:* 9 ft 10 in (2.99 m); *weight:* 20,000 lb
(9,065 kg) (loaded); *maximum speed:* 395 mph (636 km/h) at
25,000 ft (7,620 m); *ceiling:* 39,000 ft (11,880 m); *range:* 1,425
miles (2,000 km); *armament:* 1 × 20 mm cannon; 4 machine guns;
2,000 lb (900 kg) of bombs; *crew:* 1

LOCKHEED P-38J LIGHTNING
Nation: USA; *manufacturer:* Lockheed Aircraft Corp; *type:* fighter; *year:* 1943; *engine:*
two Allison V-1710-91 12-cylinder V
liquid-cooled, 1,425 hp; *wingspan:* 52 ft
(15.85 m); *length:* 37 ft 10 in (11.53 m);
height: 9 ft 10 in (2.99 m); *weight:* 21,600 lb
(9,798 kg) (loaded); *maximum speed:*
414 mph (666 km/h) at 25,000 ft (7,620 m);
ceiling: 44,000 ft (13,400 m); *range:* 2,260
miles (3,600 km); *armament:* 1 × 20 mm
cannon; 4 machine guns; 3,200 lb
(1,450 kg) of bombs; *crew:* 1

Plate 97

Japanese fighters for a war of aggression: 1940–42

NAKAJIMA Ki-43-Ia HAYABUSA
Nation: Japan; *manufacturer:* Nakajima Hikoki KK; *type:* fighter; *year:* 1940; *engine:* Nakajima Ha-25 14-cylinder radial air-cooled, 980 hp; *wingspan:* 37 ft 6 in (11.43 m); *length:* 29 ft (8.85 m); *height:* 10 ft 9 in (3.29 m); *weight:* 5,695 lb (2,598 kg) (loaded); *maximum speed:* 308 mph (495 km/h) at 13,120 ft (4,000 m); *ceiling:* 38,500 ft (11,750 m); *range:* 745 miles (1,200 km); *armament:* 2 machine guns; 66 lb (30 kg) of bombs; *crew:* 1

NAKAJIMA Ki-43-IIb HAYABUSA
Nation: Japan; *manufacturer:* Nakajima Hikoki KK; *type:* fighter; *year:* 1942; *engine:* Nakajima Ha-115 14-cylinder radial air-cooled, 1,150 hp; *wingspan:* 35 ft 7 in (10.50 m); *length:* 29 ft 3 in (8.92 m); *height:* 10 ft.9 in (3.29 m); *weight:* 6,450 lb (2,932 kg) (loaded); *maximum speed:* 329 mph (530 km/h) at 13,125 ft (4,000 m); *ceiling:* 36,750 ft (11,200 m) *range:* 1,095 miles (1,760 km); *armament:* 2 machine guns; 1,102 lb (500 kg) of bombs; *crew:* 1

KAWASAKI Ki-45 KAIa TORYU
Nation: Japan; *manufacturer:* Kawasaki Kokuki Kogyo KK; *type:* fighter; *year:* 1942; *engine:* two Nakajima Ha-25 14-cylinder radial air-cooled, 1,050 hp each; *wingspan:* 49 ft 3 in (15.02 m); *length:* 34 ft 9 in (10.60 m); *height:* 12 ft 2 in (3.70 m); *weight:* 12,081 lb (5,491 kg) (loaded); *maximum speed:* 340 mph (547 km/h) at 22,965 ft (7,000 m); *ceiling:* 35,200 ft (10,730 m); *range:* 1,404 miles (2,260 km); *armament:* 1 × 20 mm cannon; 3 machine guns; 1,100 lb (500 kg) of bombs; *crew:* 2

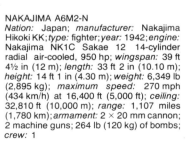

NAKAJIMA A6M2-N
Nation: Japan; *manufacturer:* Nakajima Hikoki KK; *type:* fighter; *year:* 1942; *engine:* Nakajima NK1C Sakae 12 14-cylinder radial air-cooled, 950 hp; *wingspan:* 39 ft 4½ in (12 m); *length:* 33 ft 2 in (10.10 m); *height:* 14 ft 1 in (4.30 m); *weight:* 6,349 lb (2,895 kg); *maximum speed:* 270 mph (434 km/h) at 16,400 ft (5,000 m); *ceiling:* 32,810 ft (10,000 m); *range:* 1,107 miles (1,780 km); *armament:* 2 × 20 mm cannon; 2 machine guns; 264 lb (120 kg) of bombs; *crew:* 1

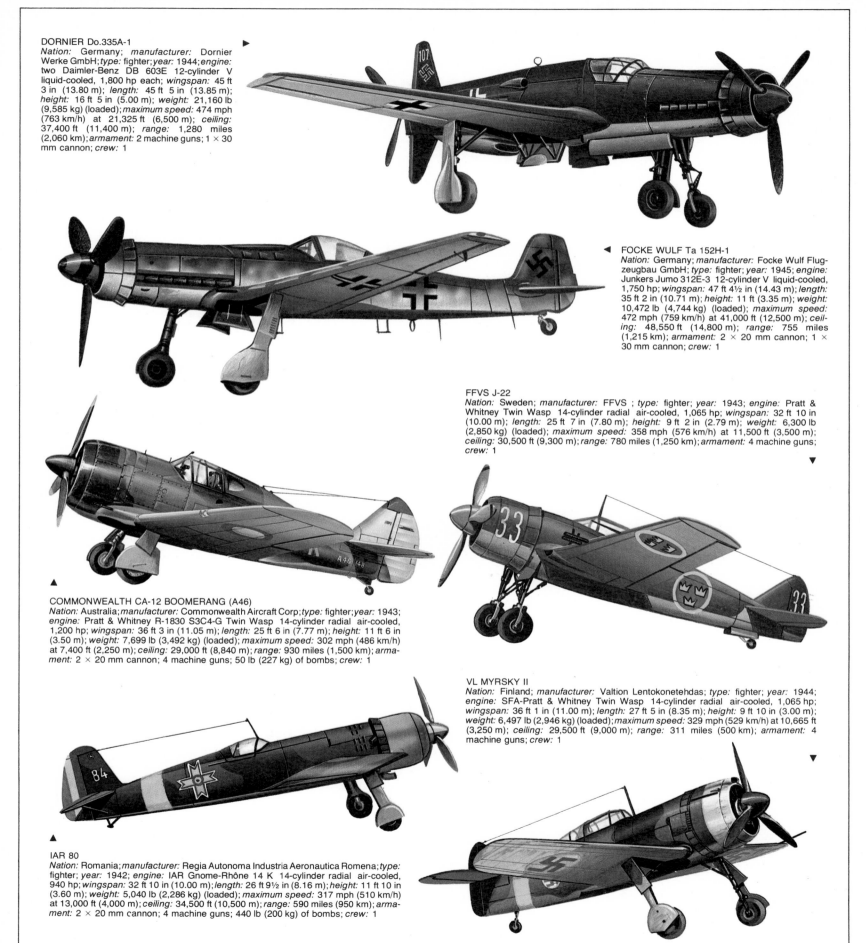

DORNIER Do.335A-1
Nation: Germany; *manufacturer:* Dornier Werke GmbH; *type:* fighter; *year:* 1944; *engine:* two Daimler-Benz DB 603E 12-cylinder V liquid-cooled, 1,800 hp each; *wingspan:* 45 ft 3 in (13.80 m); *length:* 45 ft 5 in (13.85 m); *height:* 16 ft 5 in (5.00 m); *weight:* 21,160 lb (9,585 kg) (loaded); *maximum speed:* 474 mph (763 km/h) at 21,325 ft (6,500 m); *ceiling:* 37,400 ft (11,400 m); *range:* 1,280 miles (2,060 km); *armament:* 2 machine guns; 1 × 30 mm cannon; *crew:* 1

FOCKE WULF Ta 152H-1
Nation: Germany; *manufacturer:* Focke Wulf Flug-zeugbau GmbH; *type:* fighter; *year:* 1945; *engine:* Junkers Jumo 312E-3 12-cylinder V liquid-cooled, 1,750 hp; *wingspan:* 47 ft 4½ in (14.43 m); *length:* 35 ft 2 in (10.71 m); *height:* 11 ft (3.35 m); *weight:* 10,472 lb (4,744 kg) (loaded); *maximum speed:* 472 mph (759 km/h) at 41,000 ft (12,500 m); *ceiling:* 48,550 ft (14,800 m); *range:* 755 miles (1,215 km); *armament:* 2 × 20 mm cannon; 1 × 30 mm cannon; *crew:* 1

FFVS J-22
Nation: Sweden; *manufacturer:* FFVS ; *type:* fighter; *year:* 1943; *engine:* Pratt & Whitney Twin Wasp 14-cylinder radial air-cooled, 1,065 hp; *wingspan:* 32 ft 10 in (10.00 m); *length:* 25 ft 7 in (7.80 m); *height:* 9 ft 2 in (2.79 m); *weight:* 6,300 lb (2,850 kg) (loaded); *maximum speed:* 358 mph (576 km/h) at 11,500 ft (3,500 m); *ceiling:* 30,500 ft (9,300 m); *range:* 780 miles (1,250 km); *armament:* 4 machine guns; *crew:* 1

COMMONWEALTH CA-12 BOOMERANG (A46)
Nation: Australia; *manufacturer:* Commonwealth Aircraft Corp; *type:* fighter; *year:* 1943; *engine:* Pratt & Whitney R-1830 S3C4-G Twin Wasp 14-cylinder radial air-cooled, 1,200 hp; *wingspan:* 36 ft 3 in (11.05 m); *length:* 25 ft 6 in (7.77 m); *weight:* 7,699 lb (3,492 kg) (loaded); *maximum speed:* 302 mph (486 km/h) at 7,400 ft (2,250 m); *ceiling:* 29,000 ft (8,840 m); *range:* 930 miles (1,500 km); *armament:* 2 × 20 mm cannon; 4 machine guns; 50 lb (227 kg) of bombs; *crew:* 1

VL MYRSKY II
Nation: Finland; *manufacturer:* Valtion Lentokonetehdas; *type:* fighter; *year:* 1944; *engine:* SFA-Pratt & Whitney Twin Wasp 14-cylinder radial air-cooled, 1,065 hp; *wingspan:* 36 ft 1 in (11.00 m); *length:* 27 ft 5 in (8.35 m); *height:* 9 ft 10 in (3.00 m); *weight:* 6,497 lb (2,946 kg) (loaded); *maximum speed:* 329 mph (529 km/h) at 10,665 ft (3,250 m); *ceiling:* 29,500 ft (9,000 m); *range:* 311 miles (500 km); *armament:* 4 machine guns; *crew:* 1

IAR 80
Nation: Romania; *manufacturer:* Regia Autonoma Industria Aeronautica Romena; *type:* fighter; *year:* 1942; *engine:* IAR Gnome-Rhône 14 K 14-cylinder radial air-cooled, 940 hp; *wingspan:* 32 ft 10 in (10.00 m); *length:* 26 ft 9½ in (8.16 m); *height:* 11 ft 10 in (3.60 m); *weight:* 5,040 lb (2,286 kg) (loaded); *maximum speed:* 317 mph (510 km/h) at 13,000 ft (4,000 m); *ceiling:* 34,500 ft (10,500 m); *range:* 590 miles (950 km); *armament:* 2 × 20 mm cannon; 4 machine guns; 440 lb (200 kg) of bombs; *crew:* 1

Plate 99

Great Italian fighters which arrived too late: 1943

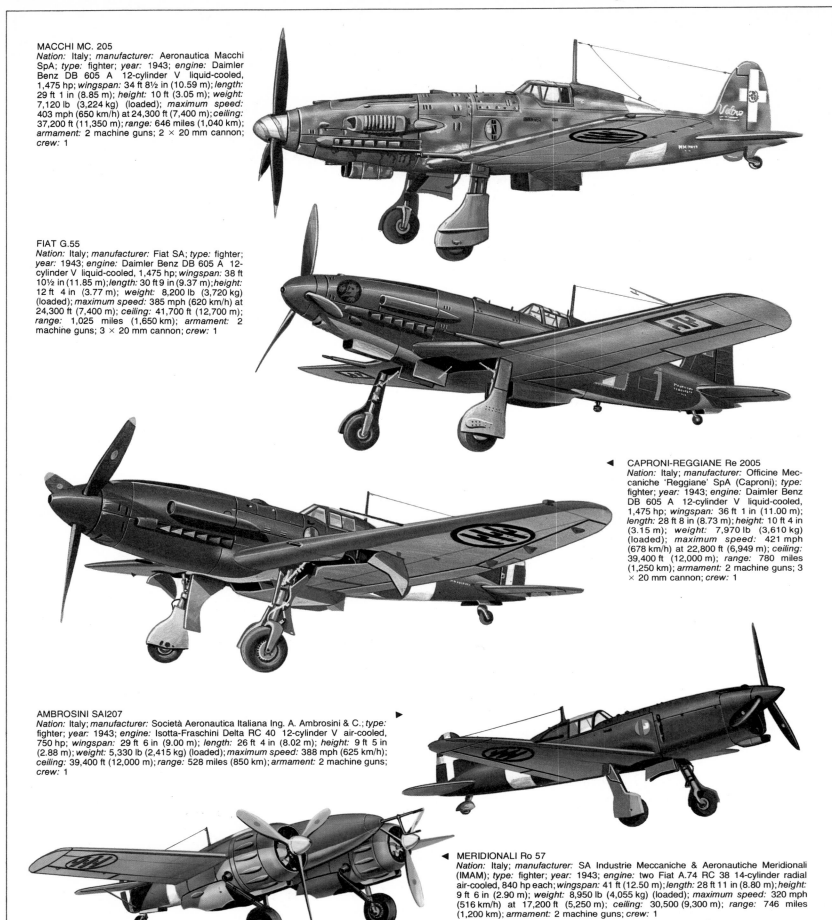

MACCHI MC. 205
Nation: Italy; *manufacturer:* Aeronautica Macchi SpA; *type:* fighter; *year:* 1943; *engine:* Daimler Benz DB 605 A 12-cylinder V liquid-cooled, 1,475 hp; *wingspan:* 34 ft 8½ in (10.59 m); *length:* 29 ft 1 in (8.85 m); *height:* 10 ft (3.05 m); *weight:* 7,120 lb (3,224 kg) (loaded); *maximum speed:* 403 mph (650 km/h) at 24,300 ft (7,400 m); *ceiling:* 37,200 ft (11,350 m); *range:* 646 miles (1,040 km); *armament:* 2 machine guns; 2 × 20 mm cannon; *crew:* 1

FIAT G.55
Nation: Italy; *manufacturer:* Fiat SA; *type:* fighter; *year:* 1943; *engine:* Daimler Benz DB 605 A 12-cylinder V liquid-cooled, 1,475 hp; *wingspan:* 38 ft 10½ in (11.85 m); *length:* 30 ft 9 in (9.37 m); *height:* 12 ft 4 in (3.77 m); *weight:* 8,200 lb (3,720 kg) (loaded); *maximum speed:* 385 mph (620 km/h) at 24,300 ft (7,400 m); *ceiling:* 41,700 ft (12,700 m); *range:* 1,025 miles (1,650 km); *armament:* 2 machine guns; 3 × 20 mm cannon; *crew:* 1

◄ **CAPRONI-REGGIANE Re 2005**
Nation: Italy; *manufacturer:* Officine Meccaniche 'Reggiane' SpA (Caproni); *type:* fighter; *year:* 1943; *engine:* Daimler Benz DB 605 A 12-cylinder V liquid-cooled, 1,475 hp; *wingspan:* 36 ft 1 in (11.00 m); *length:* 28 ft 8 in (8.73 m); *height:* 10 ft 4 in (3.15 m); *weight:* 7,970 lb (3,610 kg) (loaded); *maximum speed:* 421 mph (678 km/h) at 22,800 ft (6,949 m); *ceiling:* 39,400 ft (12,000 m); *range:* 780 miles (1,250 km); *armament:* 2 machine guns; 3 × 20 mm cannon; *crew:* 1

AMBROSINI SAI207
Nation: Italy; *manufacturer:* Società Aeronautica Italiana Ing. A. Ambrosini & C.; *type:* fighter; *year:* 1943; *engine:* Isotta-Fraschini Delta RC 40 12-cylinder V air-cooled, 750 hp; *wingspan:* 29 ft 6 in (9.00 m); *length:* 26 ft 4 in (8.02 m); *height:* 9 ft 5 in (2.88 m); *weight:* 5,330 lb (2,415 kg) (loaded); *maximum speed:* 388 mph (625 km/h); *ceiling:* 39,400 ft (12,000 m); *range:* 528 miles (850 km); *armament:* 2 machine guns; *crew:* 1

◄ **MERIDIONALI Ro 57**
Nation: Italy; *manufacturer:* SA Industrie Meccaniche & Aeronautiche Meridionali (IMAM); *type:* fighter; *year:* 1943; *engine:* two Fiat A.74 RC 38 14-cylinder radial air-cooled, 840 hp each; *wingspan:* 41 ft (12.50 m); *length:* 28 ft 11 in (8.80 m); *height:* 9 ft 6 in (2.90 m); *weight:* 8,950 lb (4,055 kg) (loaded); *maximum speed:* 320 mph (516 km/h) at 17,200 ft (5,250 m); *ceiling:* 30,500 (9,300 m); *range:* 746 miles (1,200 km); *armament:* 2 machine guns; *crew:* 1

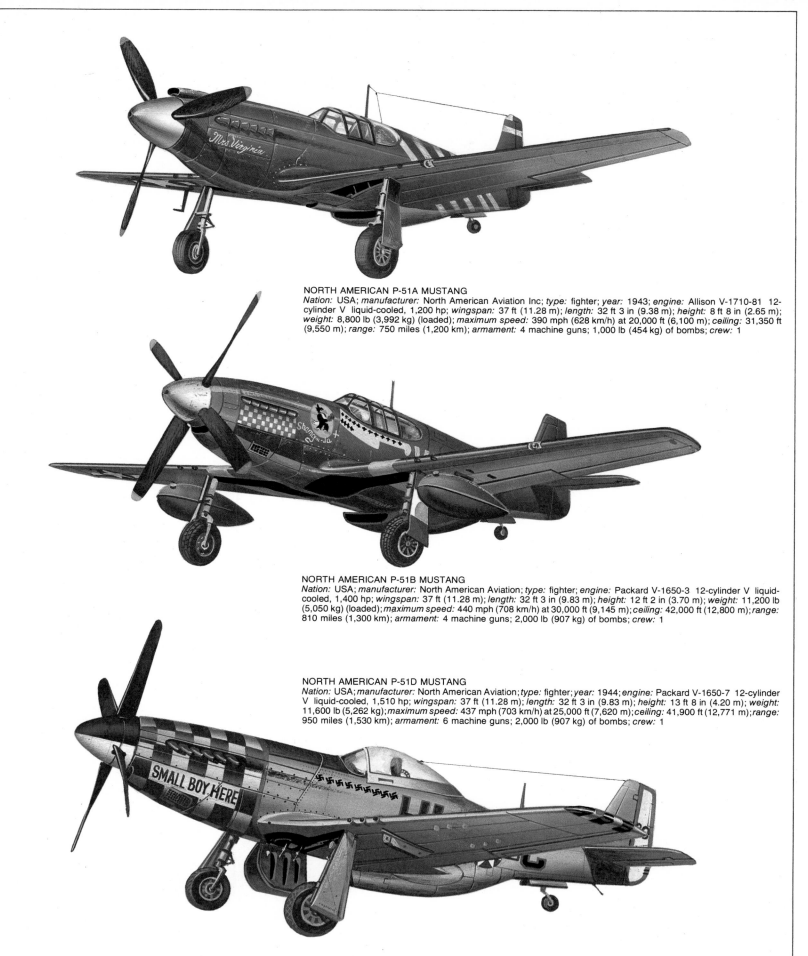

NORTH AMERICAN P-51A MUSTANG
Nation: USA; *manufacturer:* North American Aviation Inc; *type:* fighter; *year:* 1943; *engine:* Allison V-1710-81 12-cylinder V liquid-cooled, 1,200 hp; *wingspan:* 37 ft (11.28 m); *length:* 32 ft 3 in (9.38 m); *height:* 8 ft 8 in (2.65 m); *weight:* 8,800 lb (3,992 kg) (loaded); *maximum speed:* 390 mph (628 km/h) at 20,000 ft (6,100 m); *ceiling:* 31,350 ft (9,550 m); *range:* 750 miles (1,200 km); *armament:* 4 machine guns; 1,000 lb (454 kg) of bombs; *crew:* 1

NORTH AMERICAN P-51B MUSTANG
Nation: USA; *manufacturer:* North American Aviation; *type:* fighter; *engine:* Packard V-1650-3 12-cylinder V liquid-cooled, 1,400 hp; *wingspan:* 37 ft (11.28 m); *length:* 32 ft 3 in (9.83 m); *height:* 12 ft 2 in (3.70 m); *weight:* 11,200 lb (5,050 kg) (loaded); *maximum speed:* 440 mph (708 km/h) at 30,000 ft (9,145 m); *ceiling:* 42,000 ft (12,800 m); *range:* 810 miles (1,300 km); *armament:* 4 machine guns; 2,000 lb (907 kg) of bombs; *crew:* 1

NORTH AMERICAN P-51D MUSTANG
Nation: USA; *manufacturer:* North American Aviation; *type:* fighter; *year:* 1944; *engine:* Packard V-1650-7 12-cylinder V liquid-cooled, 1,510 hp; *wingspan:* 37 ft (11.28 m); *length:* 32 ft 3 in (9.83 m); *height:* 13 ft 8 in (4.20 m); *weight:* 11,600 lb (5,262 kg); *maximum speed:* 437 mph (703 km/h) at 25,000 ft (7,620 m); *ceiling:* 41,900 ft (12,771 m); *range:* 950 miles (1,530 km); *armament:* 6 machine guns; 2,000 lb (907 kg) of bombs; *crew:* 1

Plate 101

Fighters for the Mikado's army: 1943–44

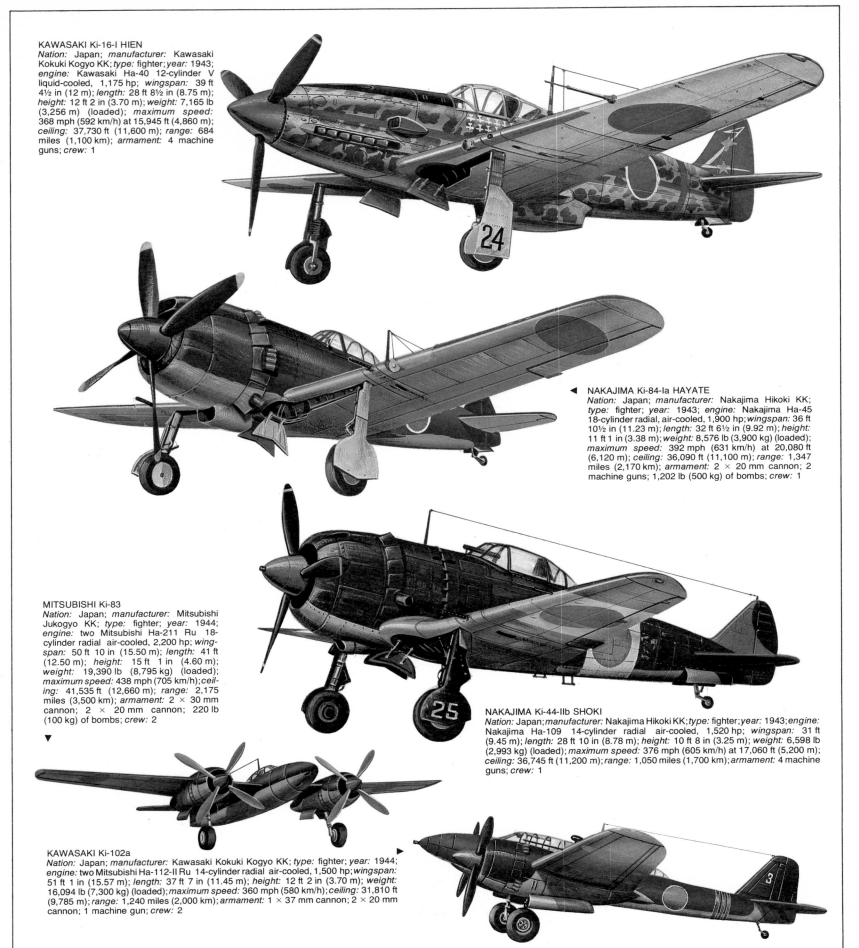

KAWASAKI Ki-16-I HIEN
Nation: Japan; *manufacturer:* Kawasaki Kokuki Kogyo KK; *type:* fighter; *year:* 1943; *engine:* Kawasaki Ha-40 12-cylinder V liquid-cooled, 1,175 hp; *wingspan:* 39 ft 4½ in (12 m); *length:* 28 ft 8½ in (8.75 m); *height:* 12 ft 2 in (3.70 m); *weight:* 7,165 lb (3,256 m) (loaded); *maximum speed:* 368 mph (592 km/h) at 15,945 ft (4,860 m); *ceiling:* 37,730 ft (11,600 m); *range:* 684 miles (1,100 km); *armament:* 4 machine guns; *crew:* 1

NAKAJIMA Ki-84-Ia HAYATE
Nation: Japan; *manufacturer:* Nakajima Hikoki KK; *type:* fighter; *year:* 1943; *engine:* Nakajima Ha-45 18-cylinder radial, air-cooled, 1,900 hp; *wingspan:* 36 ft 10½ in (11.23 m); *length:* 32 ft 6½ in (9.92 m); *height:* 11 ft 1 in (3.38 m); *weight:* 8,576 lb (3,900 kg) (loaded); *maximum speed:* 392 mph (631 km/h) at 20,080 ft (6,120 m); *ceiling:* 36,090 ft (11,100 m); *range:* 1,347 miles (2,170 km); *armament:* 2 × 20 mm cannon; 2 machine guns; 1,202 lb (500 kg) of bombs; *crew:* 1

MITSUBISHI Ki-83
Nation: Japan; *manufacturer:* Mitsubishi Jukogyo KK; *type:* fighter; *year:* 1944; *engine:* two Mitsubishi Ha-211 Ru 18-cylinder radial air-cooled, 2,200 hp; *wingspan:* 50 ft 10 in (15.50 m); *length:* 41 ft (12.50 m); *height:* 15 ft 1 in (4.60 m); *weight:* 19,390 lb (8,795 kg) (loaded); *maximum speed:* 438 mph (705 km/h); *ceiling:* 41,535 ft (12,660 m); *range:* 2,175 miles (3,500 km); *armament:* 2 × 30 mm cannon; 2 × 20 mm cannon; 220 lb (100 kg) of bombs; *crew:* 2

NAKAJIMA Ki-44-IIb SHOKI
Nation: Japan; *manufacturer:* Nakajima Hikoki KK; *type:* fighter; *year:* 1943; *engine:* Nakajima Ha-109 14-cylinder radial air-cooled, 1,520 hp; *wingspan:* 31 ft (9.45 m); *length:* 28 ft 10 in (8.78 m); *height:* 10 ft 8 in (3.25 m); *weight:* 6,598 lb (2,993 kg) (loaded); *maximum speed:* 376 mph (605 km/h) at 17,060 ft (5,200 m); *ceiling:* 36,745 ft (11,200 m); *range:* 1,050 miles (1,700 m); *armament:* 4 machine guns; *crew:* 1

KAWASAKI Ki-102a
Nation: Japan; *manufacturer:* Kawasaki Kokuki Kogyo KK; *type:* fighter; *year:* 1944; *engine:* two Mitsubishi Ha-112-II Ru 14-cylinder radial air-cooled, 1,500 hp; *wingspan:* 51 ft 1 in (15.57 m); *length:* 37 ft 7 in (11.45 m); *height:* 12 ft 2 in (3.70 m); *weight:* 16,094 lb (7,300 kg) (loaded); *maximum speed:* 360 mph (580 km/h); *ceiling:* 31,810 ft (9,785 m); *range:* 1,240 miles (2,000 km); *armament:* 1 × 37 mm cannon; 2 × 20 mm cannon; 1 machine gun; *crew:* 2

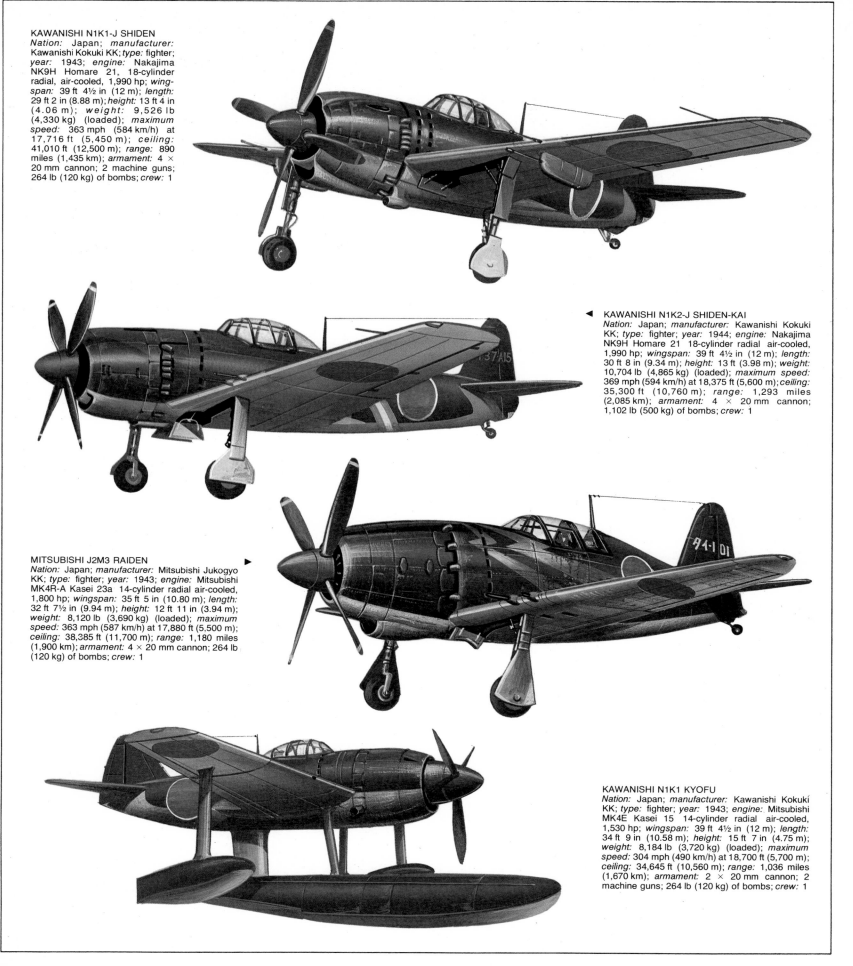

KAWANISHI N1K1-J SHIDEN
Nation: Japan; *manufacturer:* Kawanishi Kokuki KK; *type:* fighter; *year:* 1943; *engine:* Nakajima NK9H Homare 21, 18-cylinder radial, air-cooled, 1,990 hp; *wingspan:* 39 ft 4½ in (12 m); *length:* 29 ft 2 in (8.88 m); *height:* 13 ft 4 in (4.06 m); *weight:* 9,526 lb (4,330 kg) (loaded); *maximum speed:* 363 mph (584 km/h) at 17,716 ft (5,450 m); *ceiling:* 41,010 ft (12,500 m); *range:* 890 miles (1,435 km); *armament:* 4 × 20 mm cannon; 2 machine guns; 264 lb (120 kg) of bombs; *crew:* 1

◄ **KAWANISHI N1K2-J SHIDEN-KAI**
Nation: Japan; *manufacturer:* Kawanishi Kokuki KK; *type:* fighter; *year:* 1944; *engine:* Nakajima NK9H Homare 21 18-cylinder radial air-cooled, 1,990 hp; *wingspan:* 39 ft 4½ in (12 m); *length:* 30 ft 8 in (9.34 m); *height:* 13 ft (3.98 m); *weight:* 10,704 lb (4,865 kg) (loaded); *maximum speed:* 369 mph (594 km/h) at 18,375 ft (5,600 m); *ceiling:* 35,300 ft (10,760 m); *range:* 1,293 miles (2,085 km); *armament:* 4 × 20 mm cannon; 1,102 lb (500 kg) of bombs; *crew:* 1

MITSUBISHI J2M3 RAIDEN ►
Nation: Japan; *manufacturer:* Mitsubishi Jukogyo KK; *type:* fighter; *year:* 1943; *engine:* Mitsubishi MK4R-A Kasei 23a 14-cylinder radial air-cooled, 1,800 hp; *wingspan:* 35 ft 5 in (10.80 m); *length:* 32 ft 7½ in (9.94 m); *height:* 12 ft 11 in (3.94 m); *weight:* 8,120 lb (3,690 kg) (loaded); *maximum speed:* 363 mph (587 km/h) at 17,880 ft (5,500 m); *ceiling:* 38,385 ft (11,700 m); *range:* 1,180 miles (1,900 km); *armament:* 4 × 20 mm cannon; 264 lb (120 kg) of bombs; *crew:* 1

KAWANISHI N1K1 KYOFU
Nation: Japan; *manufacturer:* Kawanishi Kokukí KK; *type:* fighter; *year:* 1943; *engine:* Mitsubishi MK4E Kasei 15 14-cylinder radial air-cooled, 1,530 hp; *wingspan:* 39 ft 4½ in (12 m); *length:* 34 ft 9 in (10.58 m); *height:* 15 ft 7 in (4.75 m); *weight:* 8,184 lb (3,720 kg) (loaded); *maximum speed:* 304 mph (490 km/h) at 18,700 ft (5,700 m); *ceiling:* 34,645 ft (10,560 m); *range:* 1,036 miles (1,670 km); *armament:* 2 × 20 mm cannon; 2 machine guns; 264 lb (120 kg) of bombs; *crew:* 1

Plate 103

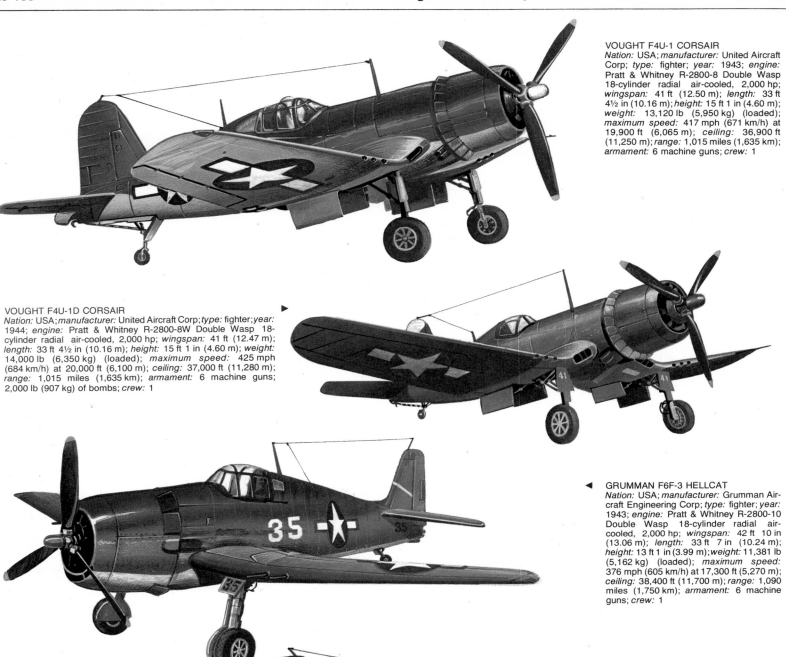

VOUGHT F4U-1 CORSAIR
Nation: USA; *manufacturer:* United Aircraft Corp; *type:* fighter; *year:* 1943; *engine:* Pratt & Whitney R-2800-8 Double Wasp 18-cylinder radial air-cooled, 2,000 hp; *wingspan:* 41 ft (12.50 m); *length:* 33 ft 4½ in (10.16 m); *height:* 15 ft 1 in (4.60 m); *weight:* 13,120 lb (5,950 kg) (loaded); *maximum speed:* 417 mph (671 km/h) at 19,900 ft (6,065 m); *ceiling:* 36,900 ft (11,250 m); *range:* 1,015 miles (1,635 km); *armament:* 6 machine guns; *crew:* 1

VOUGHT F4U-1D CORSAIR
Nation: USA; *manufacturer:* United Aircraft Corp; *type:* fighter; *year:* 1944; *engine:* Pratt & Whitney R-2800-8W Double Wasp 18-cylinder radial air-cooled, 2,000 hp; *wingspan:* 41 ft (12.47 m); *length:* 33 ft 4½ in (10.16 m); *height:* 15 ft 1 in (4.60 m); *weight:* 14,000 lb (6,350 kg) (loaded); *maximum speed:* 425 mph (684 km/h) at 20,000 ft (6,100 m); *ceiling:* 37,000 ft (11,280 m); *range:* 1,015 miles (1,635 km); *armament:* 6 machine guns; 2,000 lb (907 kg) of bombs; *crew:* 1

GRUMMAN F6F-3 HELLCAT
Nation: USA; *manufacturer:* Grumman Aircraft Engineering Corp; *type:* fighter; *year:* 1943; *engine:* Pratt & Whitney R-2800-10 Double Wasp 18-cylinder radial air-cooled, 2,000 hp; *wingspan:* 42 ft 10 in (13.06 m); *length:* 33 ft 7 in (10.24 m); *height:* 13 ft 1 in (3.99 m); *weight:* 11,381 lb (5,162 kg) (loaded); *maximum speed:* 376 mph (605 km/h) at 17,300 ft (5,270 m); *ceiling:* 38,400 ft (11,700 m); *range:* 1,090 miles (1,750 km); *armament:* 6 machine guns; *crew:* 1

GRUMMAN F6F-5 HELLCAT
Nation: USA; *manufacturer:* Grumman Aircraft Engineering Corp; *type:* fighter; *year:* 1944; *engine:* Pratt & Whitney R-2800-10W Double Wasp 18-cylinder radial air-cooled, 2,000 hp; *wingspan:* 42 ft 10 in (13.06 m); *length:* 33 ft 7 in (10.24 m); *height:* 13 ft 1 in (3.99 m); *weight:* 15,400 lb (6,970 kg) (loaded); *maximum speed:* 380 mph (610 km/h) at 23,400 ft (7,120 m); *ceiling:* 37,300 ft (11,370 m); *range:* 1,040 miles (1,670 km); *armament:* 6 machine guns; 2,000 lb (907 kg) of bombs; *crew:* 1

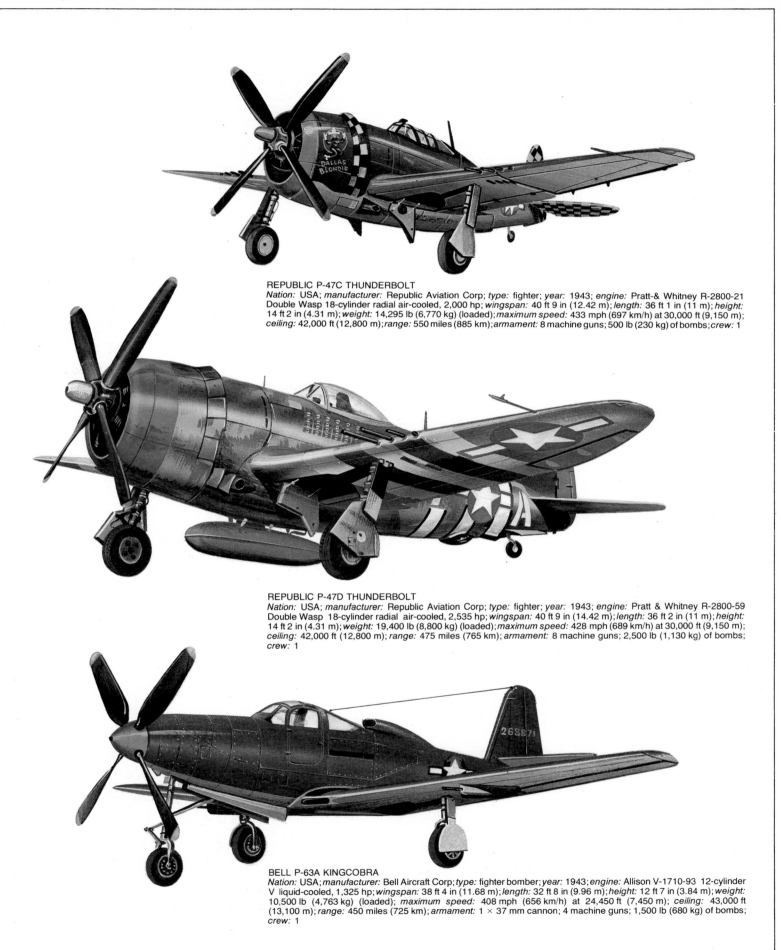

REPUBLIC P-47C THUNDERBOLT
Nation: USA; *manufacturer:* Republic Aviation Corp; *type:* fighter; *year:* 1943; *engine:* Pratt-& Whitney R-2800-21 Double Wasp 18-cylinder radial air-cooled, 2,000 hp; *wingspan:* 40 ft 9 in (12.42 m); *length:* 36 ft 1 in (11 m); *height:* 14 ft 2 in (4.31 m); *weight:* 14,295 lb (6,770 kg) (loaded); *maximum speed:* 433 mph (697 km/h) at 30,000 ft (9,150 m); *ceiling:* 42,000 ft (12,800 m); *range:* 550 miles (885 km); *armament:* 8 machine guns; 500 lb (230 kg) of bombs; *crew:* 1

REPUBLIC P-47D THUNDERBOLT
Nation: USA; *manufacturer:* Republic Aviation Corp; *type:* fighter; *year:* 1943; *engine:* Pratt & Whitney R-2800-59 Double Wasp 18-cylinder radial air-cooled, 2,535 hp; *wingspan:* 40 ft 9 in (14.42 m); *length:* 36 ft 2 in (11 m); *height:* 14 ft 2 in (4.31 m); *weight:* 19,400 lb (8,800 kg) (loaded); *maximum speed:* 428 mph (689 km/h) at 30,000 ft (9,150 m); *ceiling:* 42,000 ft (12,800 m); *range:* 475 miles (765 km); *armament:* 8 machine guns; 2,500 lb (1,130 kg) of bombs; *crew:* 1

BELL P-63A KINGCOBRA
Nation: USA; *manufacturer:* Bell Aircraft Corp; *type:* fighter bomber; *year:* 1943; *engine:* Allison V-1710-93 12-cylinder V liquid-cooled, 1,325 hp; *wingspan:* 38 ft 4 in (11.68 m); *length:* 32 ft 8 in (9.96 m); *height:* 12 ft 7 in (3.84 m); *weight:* 10,500 lb (4,763 kg) (loaded); *maximum speed:* 408 mph (656 km/h) at 24,450 ft (7,450 m); *ceiling:* 43,000 ft (13,100 m); *range:* 450 miles (725 km); *armament:* 1 × 37 mm cannon; 4 machine guns; 1,500 lb (680 kg) of bombs; *crew:* 1

MESSERSCHMITT Me.262A-1a
Nation: Germany; *manufacturer:* Messerschmitt
AG; *type:* fighter; *year:* 1944; *engine:* two Junkers
Jumo 004B-1, 1,980 lb (898 kg) thrust; *wingspan:*
40 ft 11½ in (12.48 m); *length:* 34 ft 9½ in
(10.60 m); *height:* 12 ft 7 in (3.84 m); *weight:*
14,101 lb (6,396 kg) (loaded); *maximum speed:*
540 mph (869 km/h) at 19,685 ft (6,000 m); *ceiling:*
37,565 ft (11,450 m); *range:* 652 miles (1,050 km);
armament: 4 × 30 mm cannon; *crew:* 1

MESSERSCHMITT Me.163B-1a
Nation: Germany; *manufacturer:* Messerschmitt
AG; *type:* interceptor fighter; *year:* 1944; *engine:*
Walter HWK 509A-2, 3,750 lb (1,700 kg) thrust;
wingspan: 30 ft 7 in (9.32 m); *length:* 18 ft 8 in
(5.70 m); *height:* 9 ft (2.74 m); *weight:* 8,707 lb
(3,950 kg); *maximum speed:* 596 mph (959 km/h);
ceiling: 39,500 ft (12,039 m); *endurance:* 7½
minutes; *armament:* 2 × 20 mm cannon; *crew:* 1

HEINKEL He.162A-2
Nation: Germany; *manufacturer:* Ernst Heinkel AG;
type: fighter; *year:* 1945; *engine:* BMW 003E-1
axial-flow turbojet, 1,764 lb (800 kg) thrust; *wingspan:* 23 ft 7½ in (7.20 m); *length:* 29 ft 8 in
(9.04 m); *height:* 8 ft 6 in (2.59 m); *weight:* 5,740 lb
(2,600 kg) (loaded); *maximum speed:* 521 mph
(838 km/h) at 19,690 ft (6,000 m); *ceiling:* 39,400 ft
(12,000 m); *range:* 606 miles (975 km); *armament:*
2 × 20 mm cannon; *crew:* 1

BACHEM Ba.349B-1
Nation: Germany; *manufacturer:* Bachem-Werke
GmbH; *type:* interceptor fighter; *year:* 1945; *engine:*
Walter HWK 509C-1 bi-fuel rocket, 4,400 lb
(1,995 kg) thrust; *wingspan:* 13 ft 1½ in (3.39 m);
length: 19 ft 9 in (6.02 m); *height:* 7 ft 4½ in
(2.24 m); *weight:* 4,920 lb (2,230 kg) (loaded);
maximum speed 620 mph (997 km/h) at 16,400 ft
(5,000 m); *ceiling:* 45,920 ft (13,996 m); *range:*
36¼ miles (58 km); *armament:* 24 × 73 mm
rockets; *crew:* 1

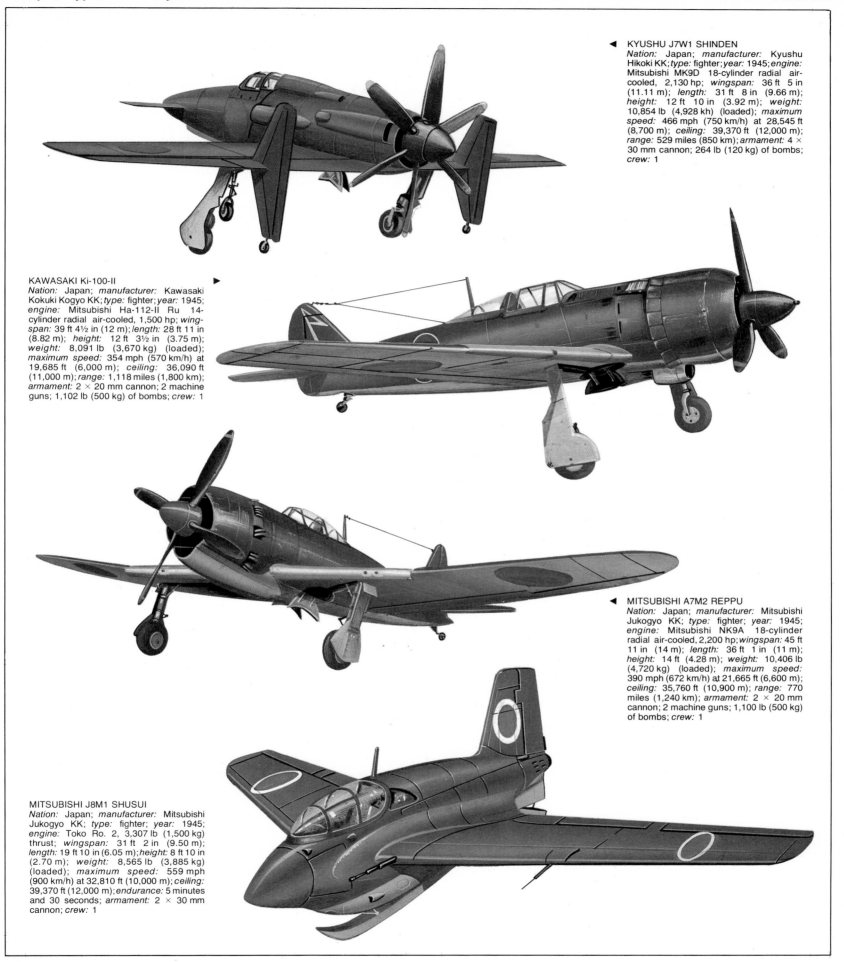

◀ **KYUSHU J7W1 SHINDEN**
Nation: Japan; *manufacturer:* Kyushu Hikoki KK; *type:* fighter; *year:* 1945; *engine:* Mitsubishi MK9D 18-cylinder radial air-cooled, 2,130 hp; *wingspan:* 36 ft 5 in (11.11 m); *length:* 31 ft 8 in (9.66 m); *height:* 12 ft 10 in (3.92 m); *weight:* 10,854 lb (4,928 kh) (loaded); *maximum speed:* 466 mph (750 km/h) at 28,545 ft (8,700 m); *ceiling:* 39,370 ft (12,000 m); *range:* 529 miles (850 km); *armament:* 4 × 30 mm cannon; 264 lb (120 kg) of bombs; *crew:* 1

KAWASAKI Ki-100-II ▶
Nation: Japan; *manufacturer:* Kawasaki Kokuki Kogyo KK; *type:* fighter; *year:* 1945; *engine:* Mitsubishi Ha-112-II Ru 14-cylinder radial air-cooled, 1,500 hp; *wingspan:* 39 ft 4½ in (12 m); *length:* 28 ft 11 in (8.82 m); *height:* 12 ft 3½ in (3.75 m); *weight:* 8,091 lb (3,670 kg) (loaded); *maximum speed:* 354 mph (570 km/h) at 19,685 ft (6,000 m); *ceiling:* 36,090 ft (11,000 m); *range:* 1,118 miles (1,800 km); *armament:* 2 × 20 mm cannon; 2 machine guns; 1,102 lb (500 kg) of bombs; *crew:* 1

◀ **MITSUBISHI A7M2 REPPU**
Nation: Japan; *manufacturer:* Mitsubishi Jukogyo KK; *type:* fighter; *year:* 1945; *engine:* Mitsubishi NK9A 18-cylinder radial air-cooled, 2,200 hp; *wingspan:* 45 ft 11 in (14 m); *length:* 36 ft 1 in (11 m); *height:* 14 ft (4.28 m); *weight:* 10,406 lb (4,720 kg) (loaded); *maximum speed:* 390 mph (672 km/h) at 21,665 ft (6,600 m); *ceiling:* 35,760 ft (10,900 m); *range:* 770 miles (1,240 km); *armament:* 2 × 20 mm cannon; 2 machine guns; 1,100 lb (500 kg) of bombs; *crew:* 1

MITSUBISHI J8M1 SHUSUI
Nation: Japan; *manufacturer:* Mitsubishi Jukogyo KK; *type:* fighter; *year:* 1945; *engine:* Toko Ro. 2, 3,307 lb (1,500 kg) thrust; *wingspan:* 31 ft 2 in (9.50 m); *length:* 19 ft 10 in (6.05 m); *height:* 8 ft 10 in (2.70 m); *weight:* 8,565 lb (3,885 kg) (loaded); *maximum speed:* 559 mph (900 km/h) at 32,810 ft (10,000 m); *ceiling:* 39,370 ft (12,000 m); *endurance:* 5 minutes and 30 seconds; *armament:* 2 × 30 mm cannon; *crew:* 1

Plate 107

The first British and American jet fighters: 1944–45

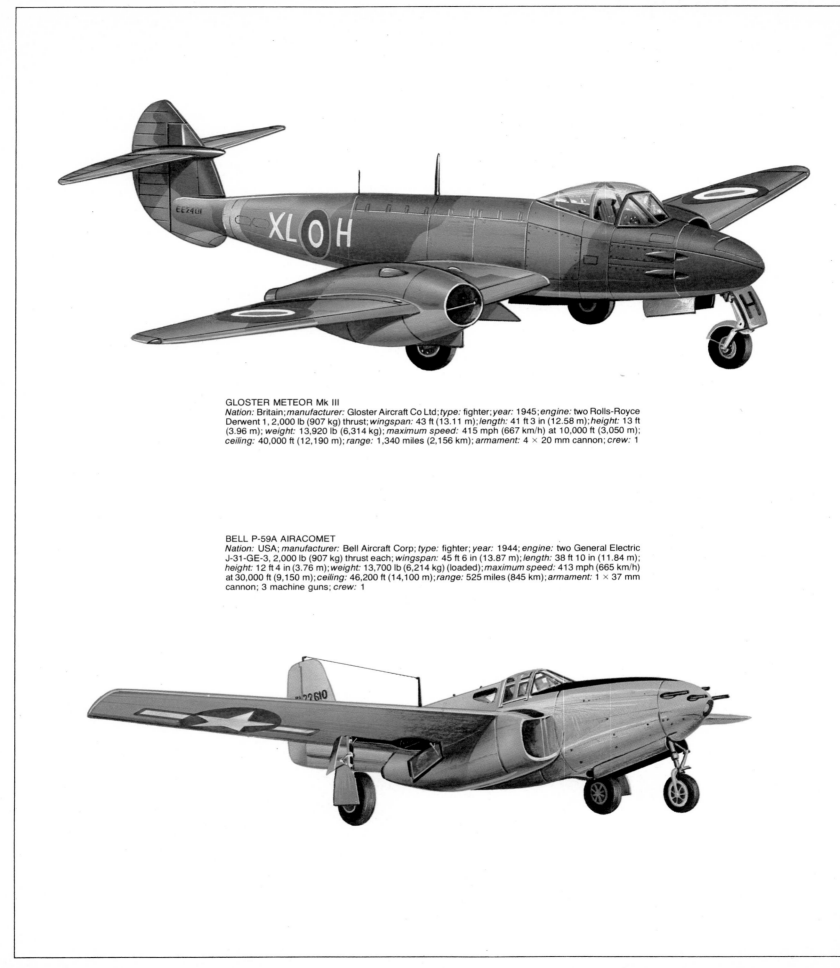

GLOSTER METEOR Mk III
Nation: Britain; *manufacturer:* Gloster Aircraft Co Ltd; *type:* fighter; *year:* 1945; *engine:* two Rolls-Royce Derwent 1, 2,000 lb (907 kg) thrust; *wingspan:* 43 ft (13.11 m); *length:* 41 ft 3 in (12.58 m); *height:* 13 ft (3.96 m); *weight:* 13,920 lb (6,314 kg); *maximum speed:* 415 mph (667 km/h) at 10,000 ft (3,050 m); *ceiling:* 40,000 ft (12,190 m); *range:* 1,340 miles (2,156 km); *armament:* 4 × 20 mm cannon; *crew:* 1

BELL P-59A AIRACOMET
Nation: USA; *manufacturer:* Bell Aircraft Corp; *type:* fighter; *year:* 1944; *engine:* two General Electric J-31-GE-3, 2,000 lb (907 kg) thrust each; *wingspan:* 45 ft 6 in (13.87 m); *length:* 38 ft 10 in (11.84 m); *height:* 12 ft 4 in (3.76 m); *weight:* 13,700 lb (6,214 kg) (loaded); *maximum speed:* 413 mph (665 km/h) at 30,000 ft (9,150 m); *ceiling:* 46,200 ft (14,100 m); *range:* 525 miles (845 km); *armament:* 1 × 37 mm cannon; 3 machine guns; *crew:* 1

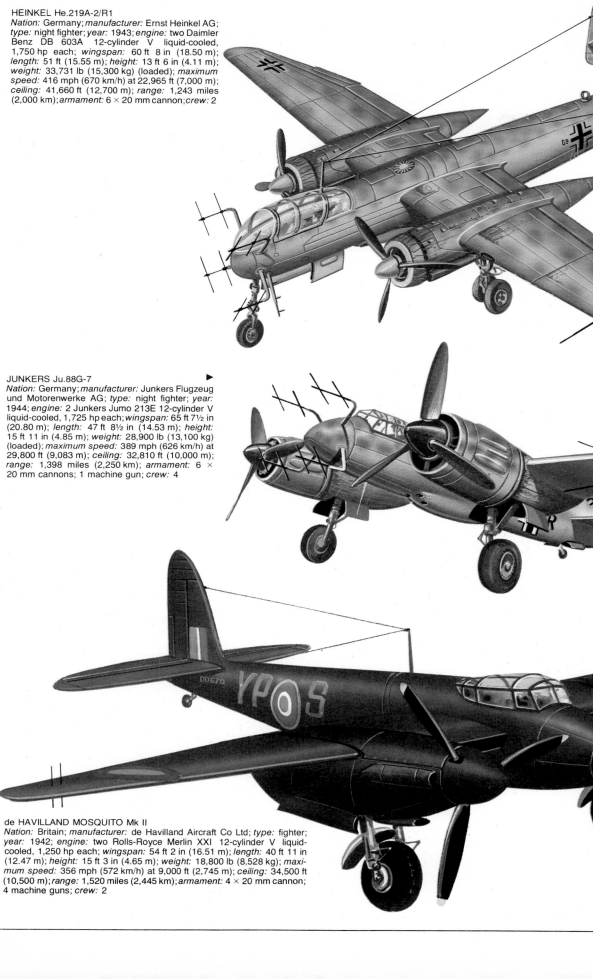

HEINKEL He.219A-2/R1
Nation: Germany; *manufacturer:* Ernst Heinkel AG;
type: night fighter; *year:* 1943; *engine:* two Daimler
Benz DB 603A 12-cylinder V liquid-cooled,
1,750 hp each; *wingspan:* 60 ft 8 in (18.50 m);
length: 51 ft (15.55 m); *height:* 13 ft 6 in (4.11 m);
weight: 33,731 lb (15,300 kg) (loaded); *maximum
speed:* 416 mph (670 km/h) at 22,965 ft (7,000 m);
ceiling: 41,660 ft (12,700 m); *range:* 1,243 miles
(2,000 km); *armament:* 6 × 20 mm cannon; *crew:* 2

JUNKERS Ju.88G-7   ►
Nation: Germany; *manufacturer:* Junkers Flugzeug
und Motorenwerke AG; *type:* night fighter; *year:*
1944; *engine:* 2 Junkers Jumo 213E 12-cylinder V
liquid-cooled, 1,725 hp each; *wingspan:* 65 ft 7½ in
(20.80 m); *length:* 47 ft 8½ in (14.53 m); *height:*
15 ft 11 in (4.85 m); *weight:* 28,900 lb (13,100 kg)
(loaded); *maximum speed:* 389 mph (626 km/h) at
29,800 ft (9,083 m); *ceiling:* 32,810 ft (10,000 m);
range: 1,398 miles (2,250 km); *armament:* 6 ×
20 mm cannons; 1 machine gun; *crew:* 4

de HAVILLAND MOSQUITO Mk II
Nation: Britain; *manufacturer:* de Havilland Aircraft Co Ltd; *type:* fighter;
year: 1942; *engine:* two Rolls-Royce Merlin XXI 12-cylinder V liquid-
cooled, 1,250 hp each; *wingspan:* 54 ft 2 in (16.51 m); *length:* 40 ft 11 in
(12.47 m); *height:* 15 ft 3 in (4.65 m); *weight:* 18,800 lb (8,528 kg); *maximum speed:* 356 mph (572 km/h) at 9,000 ft (2,745 m); *ceiling:* 34,500 ft
(10,500 m); *range:* 1,520 miles (2,445 km); *armament:* 4 × 20 mm cannon;
4 machine guns; *crew:* 2

Plate 109

Second generation night fighters: 1943–45

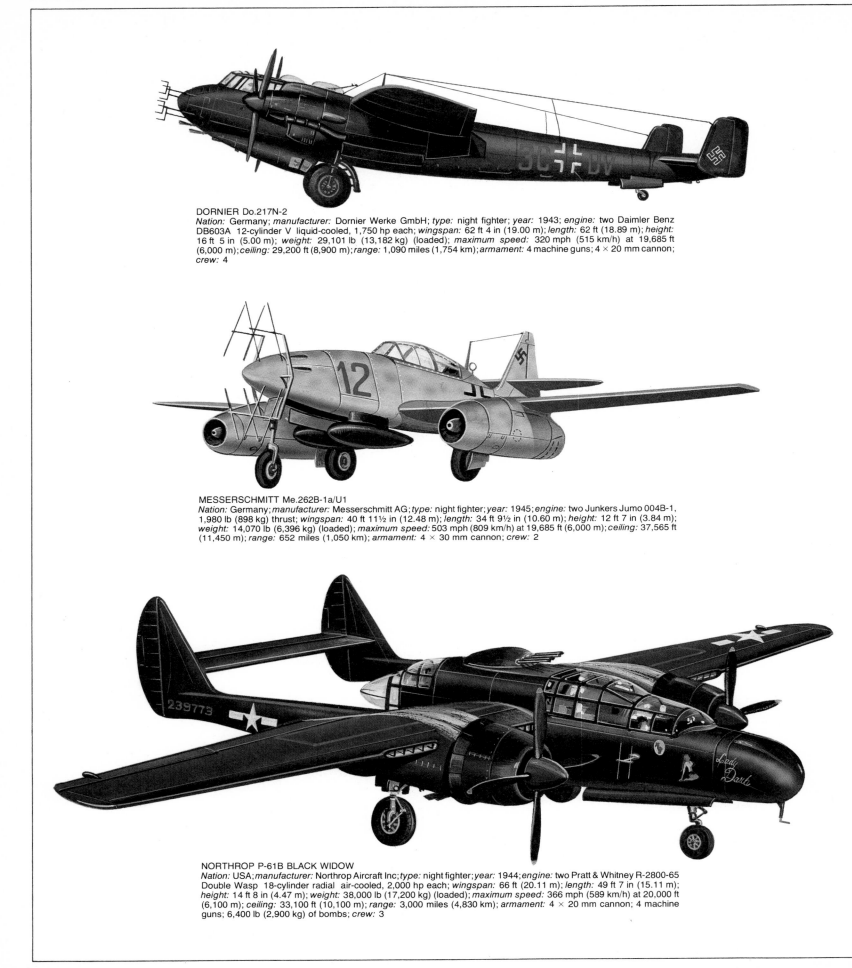

DORNIER Do.217N-2
Nation: Germany; *manufacturer:* Dornier Werke GmbH; *type:* night fighter; *year:* 1943; *engine:* two Daimler Benz DB603A 12-cylinder V liquid-cooled, 1,750 hp each; *wingspan:* 62 ft 4 in (19.00 m); *length:* 62 ft (18.89 m); *height:* 16 ft 5 in (5.00 m); *weight:* 29,101 lb (13,182 kg) (loaded); *maximum speed:* 320 mph (515 km/h) at 19,685 ft (6,000 m); *ceiling:* 29,200 ft (8,900 m); *range:* 1,090 miles (1,754 km); *armament:* 4 machine guns; 4 × 20 mm cannon; *crew:* 4

MESSERSCHMITT Me.262B-1a/U1
Nation: Germany; *manufacturer:* Messerschmitt AG; *type:* night fighter; *year:* 1945; *engine:* two Junkers Jumo 004B-1, 1,980 lb (898 kg) thrust; *wingspan:* 40 ft 11½ in (12.48 m); *length:* 34 ft 9½ in (10.60 m); *height:* 12 ft 7 in (3.84 m); *weight:* 14,070 lb (6,396 kg) (loaded); *maximum speed:* 503 mph (809 km/h) at 19,685 ft (6,000 m); *ceiling:* 37,565 ft (11,450 m); *range:* 652 miles (1,050 km); *armament:* 4 × 30 mm cannon; *crew:* 2

NORTHROP P-61B BLACK WIDOW
Nation: USA; *manufacturer:* Northrop Aircraft Inc; *type:* night fighter; *year:* 1944; *engine:* two Pratt & Whitney R-2800-65 Double Wasp 18-cylinder radial air-cooled, 2,000 hp each; *wingspan:* 66 ft (20.11 m); *length:* 49 ft 7 in (15.11 m); *height:* 14 ft 8 in (4.47 m); *weight:* 38,000 lb (17,200 kg) (loaded); *maximum speed:* 366 mph (589 km/h) at 20,000 ft (6,100 m); *ceiling:* 33,100 ft (10,100 m); *range:* 3,000 miles (4,830 km); *armament:* 4 × 20 mm cannon; 4 machine guns; 6,400 lb (2,900 kg) of bombs; *crew:* 3

HENSCHEL Hs 123A-1
Nation: Germany; *manufacturer:* Henschel Flugzeugw. AG; *type:* ground-attack fighter; *year:* 1936; *engine:* BMW 132 Dc 9-cylinder radial air-cooled, 880 hp; *wingspan:* 34 ft 5 in (10.50 m); *length:* 27 ft 4 in (8.33 m); *height:* 10 ft 6 in (3.21 m); *weight:* 4,888 lb (2,200 kg) (loaded); *maximum speed:* 212 mph (317 km/h) at 3,940 ft (1,200 m); *ceiling:* 29,525 ft (9,000 m); *range:* 534 miles (860 km); *armament:* 2 machine guns; 440 lb (200 kg) of bombs; *crew:* 1 ▶

HENSCHEL Hs 129B-1
Nation: Germany; *manufacturer:* Henschel Flugzeugw. AG; *type:* ground attack; *year:* 1942; *engine:* two Gnome-Rhône 14M 14-cylinder radial air-cooled, 700 hp each; *wingspan:* 46 ft 7 in (14.20 m); *length:* 32 ft (9.73 m); *height:* 10 ft 8 in (3.25 m); *weight:* 11,574 lb (5,243 kg) (loaded); *maximum speed:* 253 mph (407 km/h) at 12,570 ft (3,800 m); *ceiling:* 29,530 ft (9,000 m); *range:* 428 miles (690 km); *armament:* 6 machine guns; 2 × 20 mm cannon; 1 × 30 mm cannon; *crew:* 1 ▼

ILYUSHIN Il-10
Nation: USSR; *manufacturer:* State Industries; *type:* attack; *year:* 1944; *engine:* Mikulin AM-42 12-cylinder V liquid-cooled, 2,000 hp; *wingspan:* 43 ft 11½ in (13.54 m); *length:* 36 ft 9 in (11.30 m); *height:* 11 ft 6 in (3.50 m); *weight:* 14,409 lb (6,550 kg) (loaded); *maximum speed:* 311 mph (550 km/h); *ceiling:* 24,606 ft (7,570 m); *range:* 621 miles (1,000 km); *armament:* 3 × 20 mm cannon; 2 machine guns; *crew:* 2
▼

YAKOVLEV Yak-3
Nation: USSR; *manufacturer:* State Industries; *type:* attack fighter; *year:* 1944; *engine:* Klimov M-105PF-2 12-cylinder V liquid-cooled, 1,300 hp; *wingspan:* 30 ft 2 in (9.20 m); *length:* 27 ft 11 in (8.50 m); *height:* 7 ft 11 in (2.40 m); *weight:* 5,864 lb (2,660 kg) (loaded); *maximum speed:* 403 mph (648 km/h) at 16,400 ft (5,000 m); *ceiling:* 35,430 ft (10,900 m); *range:* 560 miles (900 km); *armament:* 1 × 20 mm cannon; 2 machine guns; *crew:* 1

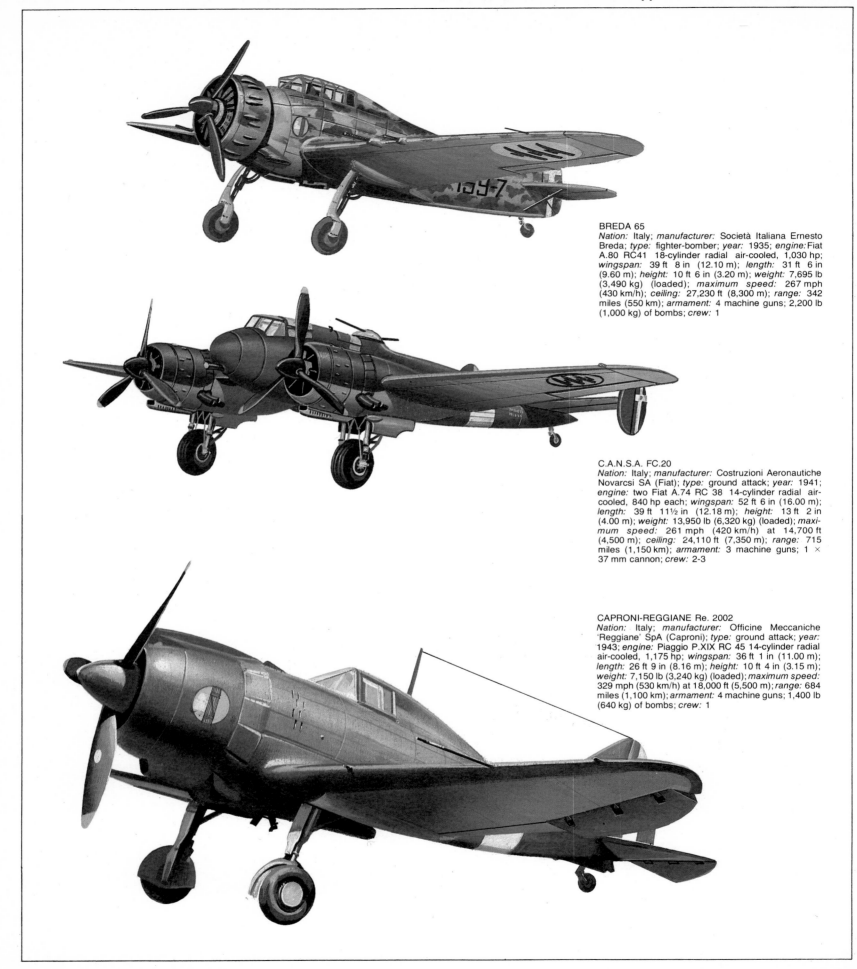

BREDA 65
Nation: Italy; *manufacturer:* Società Italiana Ernesto Breda; *type:* fighter-bomber; *year:* 1935; *engine:* Fiat A.80 RC41 18-cylinder radial air-cooled, 1,030 hp; *wingspan:* 39 ft 8 in (12.10 m); *length:* 31 ft 6 in (9.60 m); *height:* 10 ft 6 in (3.20 m); *weight:* 7,695 lb (3,490 kg) (loaded); *maximum speed:* 267 mph (430 km/h); *ceiling:* 27,230 ft (8,300 m); *range:* 342 miles (550 km); *armament:* 4 machine guns; 2,200 lb (1,000 kg) of bombs; *crew:* 1

C.A.N.S.A. FC.20
Nation: Italy; *manufacturer:* Costruzioni Aeronautiche Novarcsi SA (Fiat); *type:* ground attack; *year:* 1941; *engine:* two Fiat A.74 RC 38 14-cylinder radial air-cooled, 840 hp each; *wingspan:* 52 ft 6 in (16.00 m); *length:* 39 ft 11½ in (12.18 m); *height:* 13 ft 2 in (4.00 m); *weight:* 13,950 lb (6,320 kg) (loaded); *maximum speed:* 261 mph (420 km/h) at 14,700 ft (4,500 m); *ceiling:* 24,110 ft (7,350 m); *range:* 715 miles (1,150 km); *armament:* 3 machine guns; 1 × 37 mm cannon; *crew:* 2-3

CAPRONI-REGGIANE Re. 2002
Nation: Italy; *manufacturer:* Officine Meccaniche 'Reggiane' SpA (Caproni); *type:* ground attack; *year:* 1943; *engine:* Piaggio P.XIX RC 45 14-cylinder radial air-cooled, 1,175 hp; *wingspan:* 36 ft 1 in (11.00 m); *length:* 26 ft 9 in (8.16 m); *height:* 10 ft 4 in (3.15 m); *weight:* 7,150 lb (3,240 kg) (loaded); *maximum speed:* 329 mph (530 km/h) at 18,000 ft (5,500 m); *range:* 684 miles (1,100 km); *armament:* 4 machine guns; 1,400 lb (640 kg) of bombs; *crew:* 1

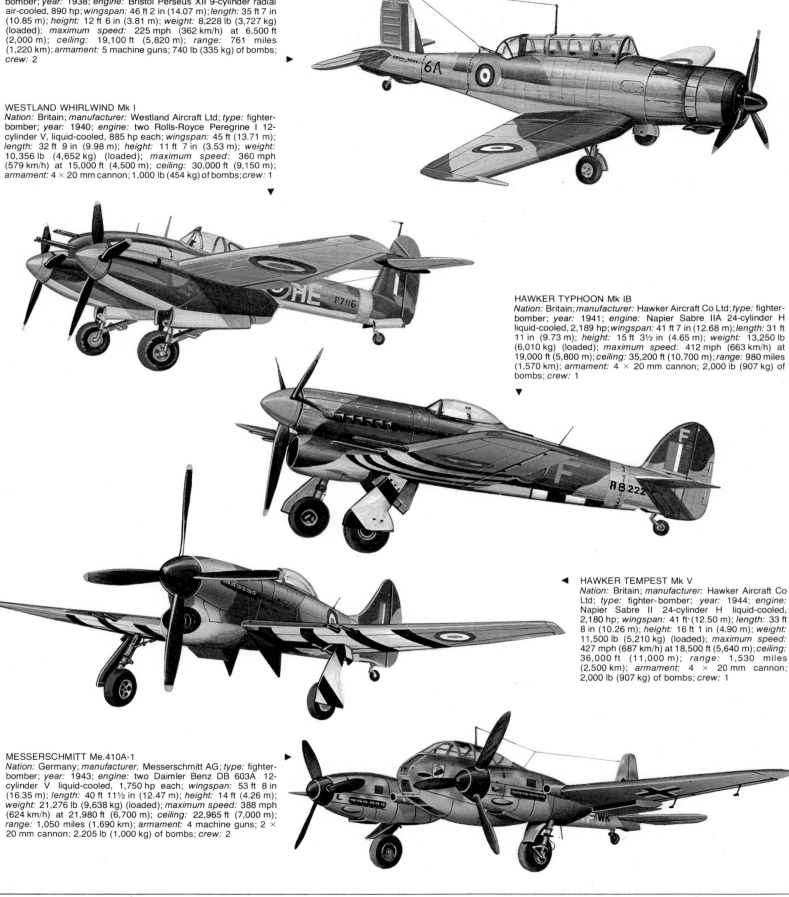

BLACKBURN SKUA Mk II
Nation: Britain; *manufacturer:* Blackburn Aircraft Ltd; *type:* fighter-bomber; *year:* 1938; *engine:* Bristol Perseus XII 9-cylinder radial air-cooled, 890 hp; *wingspan:* 46 ft 2 in (14.07 m); *length:* 35 ft 7 in (10.85 m); *height:* 12 ft 6 in (3.81 m); *weight:* 8,228 lb (3,727 kg) (loaded); *maximum speed:* 225 mph (362 km/h) at 6,500 ft (2,000 m); *ceiling:* 19,100 ft (5,820 m); *range:* 761 miles (1,220 km); *armament:* 5 machine guns; 740 lb (335 kg) of bombs; *crew:* 2

WESTLAND WHIRLWIND Mk I
Nation: Britain; *manufacturer:* Westland Aircraft Ltd; *type:* fighter-bomber; *year:* 1940; *engine:* two Rolls-Royce Peregrine I 12-cylinder V, liquid-cooled, 885 hp each; *wingspan:* 45 ft (13.71 m); *length:* 32 ft 9 in (9.98 m); *height:* 11 ft 7 in (3.53 m); *weight:* 10,356 lb (4,652 kg) (loaded); *maximum speed:* 360 mph (579 km/h) at 15,000 ft (4,500 m); *ceiling:* 30,000 ft (9,150 m); *armament:* 4 × 20 mm cannon; 1,000 lb (454 kg) of bombs; *crew:* 1

HAWKER TYPHOON Mk IB
Nation: Britain; *manufacturer:* Hawker Aircraft Co Ltd; *type:* fighter-bomber; *year:* 1941; *engine:* Napier Sabre IIA 24-cylinder H liquid-cooled, 2,189 hp; *wingspan:* 41 ft 7 in (12.68 m); *length:* 31 ft 11 in (9.73 m); *height:* 15 ft 3½ in (4.65 m); *weight:* 13,250 lb (6,010 kg) (loaded); *maximum speed:* 412 mph (663 km/h) at 19,000 ft (5,800 m); *ceiling:* 35,200 ft (10,700 m); *range:* 980 miles (1,570 km); *armament:* 4 × 20 mm cannon; 2,000 lb (907 kg) of bombs; *crew:* 1

HAWKER TEMPEST Mk V
Nation: Britain; *manufacturer:* Hawker Aircraft Co Ltd; *type:* fighter-bomber; *year:* 1944; *engine:* Napier Sabre II 24-cylinder H liquid-cooled, 2,180 hp; *wingspan:* 41 ft (12.50 m); *length:* 33 ft 8 in (10.26 m); *height:* 16 ft 1 in (4.90 m); *weight:* 11,500 lb (5,210 kg) (loaded); *maximum speed:* 427 mph (687 km/h) at 18,500 ft (5,640 m); *ceiling:* 36,000 ft (11,000 m); *range:* 1,530 miles (2,500 km); *armament:* 4 × 20 mm cannon; 2,000 lb (907 kg) of bombs; *crew:* 1

MESSERSCHMITT Me.410A-1
Nation: Germany; *manufacturer:* Messerschmitt AG; *type:* fighter-bomber; *year:* 1943; *engine:* two Daimler Benz DB 603A 12-cylinder V liquid-cooled, 1,750 hp each; *wingspan:* 53 ft 8 in (16.35 m); *length:* 40 ft 11½ in (12.47 m); *height:* 14 ft (4.26 m); *weight:* 21,276 lb (9,638 kg) (loaded); *maximum speed:* 388 mph (624 km/h) at 21,980 ft (6,700 m); *ceiling:* 22,965 ft (7,000 m); *range:* 1,050 miles (1,690 km); *armament:* 4 machine guns; 2 × 20 mm cannon; 2,205 lb (1,000 kg) of bombs; *crew:* 2

Plate 79
French fighters: 1938–39

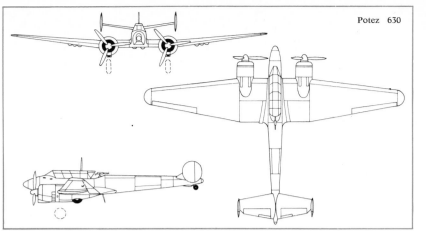

Potez 630

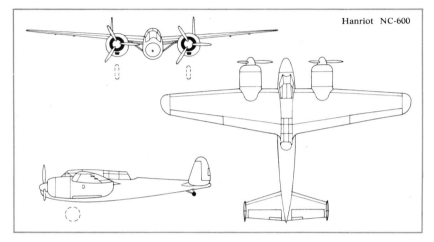

Hanriot NC-600

The first modern fighter of the French air force, the Morane-Saulnier M.S.406, was also the most widely known French combat plane of the Second World War. Its renown was not so much due to its performance, which although good was noticeably inferior to that of the contemporary German Messerschmitt, but rather to its intense and wide-ranging operational activity, including its appearance in large numbers in the Battle of France. The M.S.406 was given priority and had a long production run of 1,081 units. The quick pace of production is demonstrated by the fact that in September 1939, fifteen months after the first flight of the final prototype, 600 planes had already left the assembly lines.

The forerunner of all the Morane-Saulnier M.S.406 aircraft had appeared as far back as 1935. In August of that year the M.S.405 had been tested in great secrecy, an aeroplane which had revealed excellent characteristics and performance in every respect from the very first flights, especially in maximum speed, which ranged between 489 km per hour (303 mph) at 4,000 m (13,120 ft) and 402 km/h (249 mph) at sea level. At the Brussels Air Show in June 1937 it was claimed that the new fighter was the "best in the world". After the construction of a second prototype and an order for 15 pre-production models, the fourth M.S.405 became the definitive prototype. With a modified engine and propeller, the first M.S.406 flew on 20th May 1938 and began to reach the squadrons in December. After the Armistice many models remained with the Vichy air force; others were given to Finland by the Germans.

The Potez 63 family was just as numerous; production reached the highest number of aircraft achieved by the French industry during the war, more than 1,100 aircraft of different variants being constructed by June

1940. This clean-lined and modern twin-engine machine served as a fighter, a bomber and a reconnaissance plane. Its development began in 1935 and the first prototype flew in April the following year; the Potez 630 started to come off the production lines in February 1938. This variant was a heavy fighter, whilst the 631 was to be a night fighter. The principal models which became operative in the units of the French Air Force were the 633, as a light bomber and for ground attack, and the 63.11, for reconnaissance. At the end of 1942 dozens of examples of the Potez twin-engine were requisitioned by the Germans and given to the Axis allies. The Italian Air Force, in particular, used several

Potez 63.11s for training.

Returning to the pure fighters, one of the most intensively used aeroplanes in the last weeks of fighting before the Armistice was the Bloch MC-152. Derived from the mediocre Bloch MV-1151, of which fewer than one hundred models had been constructed up to the outbreak of war, this little single-seater was not an exceptional aircraft; its main limitations lay in its lack of manoeuvrability at high altitude, its short range and in a marked inferiority compared with its most direct rival the Messerschmitt Bf.109. The prototype of the Bloch MC-152 had flown at the beginning of 1938 and production in wartime totalled 614 aircraft. Many of these

remained in service in the fighter units of the Vichy government.

Two other combat aircraft were produced between 1938 and 1939: the Caudron C.714 and the Hanriot NC-600. These two very dissimilar fighters were not without merit and potential, but each suffered the same fate of cancellation at an early stage.

The Caudron C.714 was derived from the competition aircraft produced by Marcel Riffard in the first half of the thirties, and as such it was a light and fast machine, very convenient due to its simplicity of construction, the use of non-strategic materials and the short time needed to build it. After the flight of the prototype in September 1938, two orders were placed, each for one hundred aircraft; but the contract was cancelled in the following year because the French air force discovered some characteristics which were thought unsatisfactory. The few dozen aircraft completed equipped a unit formed by Polish pilots who had fled to France.

The Hanriot NC-600 was produced in only two prototypes before the whole programme was abandoned. This lively twin-engined aircraft, which was fairly fast and powerfully armed, revealed its excellent features from its very first flight in 1939, reaching 542 km/h (336 mph) at an altitude of 5,000 m (16,400 ft). The aircraft was equipped with two Gnome-Rhône engines of 700 hp each, which were enclosed in extremely aerodynamic cowlings. But the French military authorities stopped the project even though they may perhaps not have taken into consideration the potential of this aircraft.

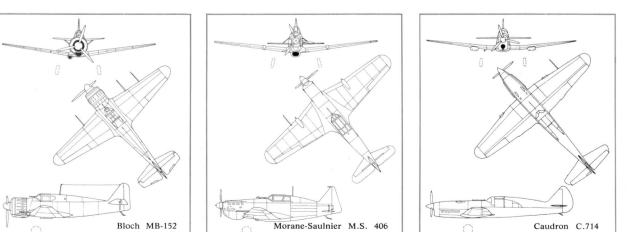

Bloch MB-152

Morane-Saulnier M.S. 406

Caudron C.714

Plate 80
Fighters facing the *Luftwaffe*, obsolete and outnumbers: 1935–39

Germany's *Blitzkrieg*, based on a massive superiority of forces in the field, proved to be particularly destructive of the air forces of the minor powers, which were equipped at that time with outdated aircraft, and in any case possessed only limited numbers of them. This was true of the Netherlands, whose excellent aircraft only managed to slow down the German invasion by a few days. The Fokker D.XXIs fought right up to the end. These fighters were modern and manoeuvrable monoplanes which were both fast and powerfully armed, but the Dutch aircraft industry had only managed to complete 39 models by the outbreak of war. The project had been set in motion in 1936: this was the only aircraft to keep a fixed undercarriage, but apart from this it was totally competitive with its more battle-seasoned adversaries. D.XXIs of Dutch manufacture had the Bristol Mercury radial engine, which varied between 645 and 760 hp, but in those which were constructed under licence in Finland the engine was an American Pratt & Whitney Twin Wasp of 1,050 hp. The Finnish air force put approximately 100 Fokker D.XXIs into service, seven of which had been bought directly in Holland, the others produced under licence. These aircraft remained in the front line for a long time making a notable contribution.

Another excellent combat aircraft which fought against the German invasion saw even less of the war: the Fokker G.1A. Only 36 models of this heavy fighter were constructed and just over twenty were operational on 10th May 1940. Many of these were destroyed on the ground; the others managed to take to the air, but they were all shot down except for one. This sole survivor enabled two Fokker pilots to escape to England a year later. The G.1A had flown for the first time on 16th March 1937, and on its appearance had been particularly impressive because of the fire power concentrated in the nose which consisted of eight machine guns. Another machine gun, manually aimed, was sited in the tail cone. This heavy armament did not detract in any way from the flight characteristics and performance of the aircraft.

The D.XXIII, another brilliant Fokker of the immediate prewar period, remained a prototype. It was one of the most interesting Fokkers of the last prewar years but never went into production because the only model constructed was destroyed by German bombing. Designed in 1938, the D.XXIII was a twin-engine single-seat fighter of revolutionary

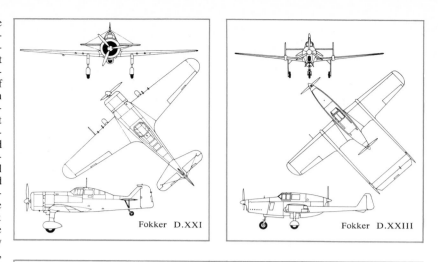

Fokker D.XXI

Fokker D.XXIII

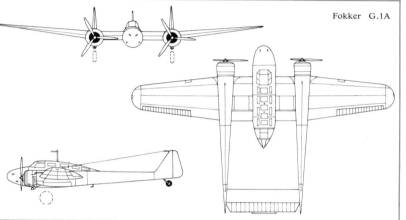

Fokker G.1A

appearance: a twin-boom monoplane with tricycle undercarriage. The pilot was positioned between the two engines, one of which drove a puller propeller and the other a pusher.

The prototype was presented to the public at the Paris Air Show of November 1938 and the first flight took place in May of the following year. This aircraft, however, was never perfected; engineers were slowed down by difficult problems in the cooling system of the rear engine, and by a malfunction of the variable pitch mechanism of the propellers. This lost them several months and the outbreak of war put an end to any further development.

Not modern, but still able to fight

the monoplanes of the *Luftwaffe*, was the Avia B.534, a small and manoeuvrable biplane of which 445 were constructed and which for four years, from 1935 until 1938, remained the standard fighter of the Czechoslovak Air Force. The project was started in 1932 by František Novotny and the prototype appeared in August of the following year. The Avia B.534 was a single-seat biplane with an all-metal structure and mixed covering, and was armed with four machine guns. Its excellent flight characteristics were fully demonstrated at the International Aeronautical Rally at Zürich in 1937; in all the main competitions the B.534 came second, beaten only by the Messerschmitt Bf.109.

The success of the Avia biplane was matched by another contemporary aircraft constructed in Poland, the PZL P.24, a machine that was exported to Turkey, Romania, Bulgaria and Greece. The P.24 represented the latest development in the series of high wing monoplane fighters with a characteristic seagull wing, which had originated with the PZL P.1 of 1929. The prototype flew in March 1933 and, compared with its direct predecessor (the PZL P.11 of 1931), was characterised by a more powerful engine and armament and by a completely enclosed cockpit. Similar to the PZL in general lines, with exception of the engine, was a combat aircraft produced in Yugoslavia between 1933 and 1937: the Ikarus IK-2. Twelve aircraft were completed and eight of these were used in 1941 to oppose the German invasion.

Plate 81
The last biplane fighters: 1937–39

Theoretically, the era of the biplane fighter came to an end in the middle of the thirties. In practice, the momentum of the conflict meant that obsolescent aircraft remained in the front line well into the 1940s, in anachronistic co-existence with much more modern powerful and faster fighters. The last operational biplane fighters were the British Gloster Gladiator and the Italian Fiat C.R.42: the former was only replaced in 1941, the latter was still being used at the time of the Italian surrender in 1943.

In 1934 the Gladiator was introduced to replace the ageing Bristol Bulldog and Gloster Gauntlet, based on a detailed Air Ministry specification which was issued in 1930, which called for a new fighter capable of flying at 400 km/h (248 mph) and armed with four machine guns. The construction of the prototype, entrusted to a working party headed by H. P. Folland, was commenced in the spring of that year and the aircraft, which was designated SS 37, flew for the first time in September 1934, and from the very first tests it performed brilliantly. On 3rd April 1935 the Royal Air Force took over the aircraft

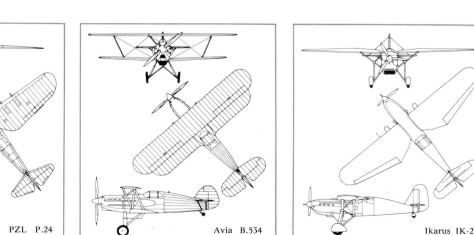

PZL P.24

Avia B.534

Ikarus IK-2

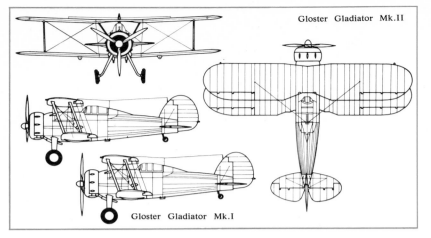

Gloster Gladiator Mk.II

Gloster Gladiator Mk.I

for operational proving flights, and three months later the first order was placed for 23 machines, followed by an order for a further 186 in September of that year. Production was soon under way, and by the spring of 1940, 527 Gladiators, in three models, had left the assembly lines. Of these, as many as 216 were exported to the various European countries (Belgium, Sweden, Norway, Latvia, and Lithuania) and to Iraq and even to China.

The first model, which was called the Gladiator Mk I, was given the go-ahead in July 1936 and went into service at the beginning of January 1937. Soon the second production series made its appearance, the Mk II, in which the wooden two-blade propeller was replaced by a metal fixed-pitch triple-bladed propeller. From this model a carrier-based machine was also derived – called the Sea Gladiator – different only in the adoption of an arrester gear, structural reinforcements for the application of the catapult, and the installation of a dinghy in the ventral undercarriage fairing.

On the outbreak of war, together with the Spitfires which were sparingly deployed on home ground for defence against a possible invasion, the Gladiators faced the *Luftwaffe* in France and in Norway, suffering from their overall inferiority compared with the modern German fighters. Subse-

quently sent to less demanding fronts, they fought in the Mediterranean and in Africa until 1941. The Sea Gladiators played a particularly distinguished role in the defence of Malta in June 1940.

If the Gladiator was the last biplane fighter of the RAF, the last one of all was the Fiat C.R.42. Unlike the Gloster biplane which soon went out of production and was only kept in service for the direst emergencies, Celestino Rosatelli's Falco was produced uninterruptedly throughout the whole period between February 1939 until the Italian Armistice in June 1943. As many as 1,781 machines came off the assembly lines and production took precedence over that of other more modern and more effective fighters, such as the Fiat G.50, the Macchi M.C.200 and M.C.202, although in reality the Italian air force undoubtedly had greater need of these more up-to-date aircraft. This choice had been made as a result of experience dating back to the Civil War in Spain, from which aeronautical engineers and strategists had mistakenly inferred that, for air combat, lightness and manoeuvrability were to be preferred to speed, robustness and firepower.

The prototype of the C.R.42 flew on 23rd May 1938 and the test flights were successful. The first Italian air force purchase order for 200 machines was followed by orders from Hungary

(50), Belgium (34) and Sweden (72). A year later the Falco became operational with the 53rd group, and at the time of Italy's entry into the war there were approximately 300 aircraft in front-line service. Intensive uninterrupted use was made of them on all fronts: from France to Greece, the Mediterranean and North Africa.

The last recorded combats between biplanes took place in North Africa before the arrival of the Hurricanes and Spitfires, the adversaries of the C.R.42s being none other than the British Gloster Gladiators themselves. With the appearance of the new fighters the Falco was destined for other less demanding roles, although not necessarily less important: as bomber escorts and reconnaissance planes, and for observation, ground attack and as night fighters. For the night fighter role the C.R.42s were modified by the installation of a radio: the aircraft could also be fitted with flame-dampers on the engine exhausts, though this device was not always adopted.

The operational use of Falco nightfighters was fairly limited, although units were stationed in many Italian cities.

Plate 82
Transitional fighters in Japan and the USSR: 1937–39

The earliest forewarnings of the coming of the Second World War gave a sudden impetus to the aircraft industries of the great powers. In the second half of the thirties Japan completed a large part of the mighty arsenal which was to last her until August 1945. The requirements of the Imperial Navy and the Imperial Army stimulated industry immensely, and increased volume and profitability enabled the Japanese manufacturers to break free from their former dependence on western technology. Two fighters marked this phase. They were the Mitsubishi A5M and the Nakajima Ki-27; aircraft which were substantially similar, each of which gave way to successors which were to achieve great prominence in battle: the Mitsubishi A6M Reisen (the awe-inspiring Zero) and the Nakajima Ki-43 Hayabusa.

Code-named CLAUDE by the Allies, the Mitsubishi A5M was developed at the beginning of 1934, to a Navy specification calling for an interceptor fighter of small proportions able to fly at 350 km/h (217 mph), with the ability to reach 5,000 m (16,400 ft) in 6½ minutes, and armed with two machine guns. The prototype, designed by Jiro Horikoshi, flew for the first time on 4th February 1935 and, after a long series of proving flights, went into production in the following year. The A5M4 variant went into production in 1939. 1,094 aircraft were produced in several variants.

More than three times that number, 3,399 aircraft, were built in parallel production for the Army of the Nakajima Ki-27, which was the Army's equivalent of the Mitsubishi. This fighter was largely similar to the Mitsubishi, being a low-wing, all-metal monoplane configuration design with fixed undercarriage, and it was of very similar dimensions and performance. Like the A5M, the Ki-27 brilliantly filled its transitional role, during the period when the biplane fighter type was being superseded by the first monoplane fighters of the Imperial Armed Forces.

The Ki-27 project was conceived in 1935, following an army specification, in competition with Kawasaki and Mitsubishi. In October and December of that year the first two prototypes

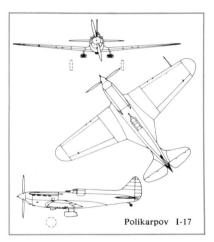

Polikarpov I-17

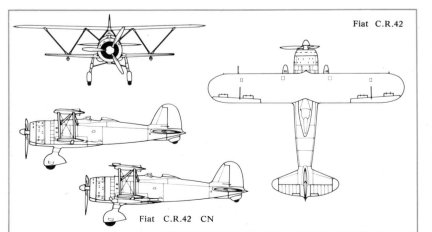

Fiat C.R.42

Fiat C.R.42 CN

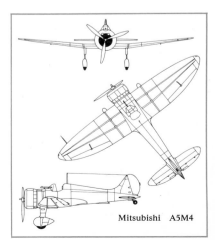

Mitsubishi A5M4

made their appearance and faced their rivals, the Mitsubishi Ki-33 and the Kawasaki Ki-28, in a long series of comparative tests. The Nakajima emerged the victor, mainly due to its exceptional manoeuvrability. Production was started towards the end of 1937 and carried on through various models, the Ki-27b going into production in 1939.

The Ki-27 had its operational debut in China in March 1938, and in the following year was used against the Russians in Manchuria. In these combats the little fighter showed itself to be superior to the Polikarpov I-15 Soviet biplane but was at a noticeable disadvantage when confronted by the Polikarpov I-16 monoplane. At the time of Japan's entry into the war, in December 1941, the Ki-27 was still used by many front-line units. In the Allied code it went under the name of NATE in the Eastern Pacific theatre of operations, and as ABDUL in the India–China–Burma theatre.

One of the first adversaries with which the Nakajima Ki-27 joined battle was the revolutionary (for the period) Soviet Polikarpov I-16. The USSR had also undergone the difficult transition from the biplane to the monoplane in the middle of the thirties, but here progress was particularly rapid, and in the case of the I-16 did indeed represent a major breakthrough which brought great credit to Nikolai Polikarpov.

When it appeared in prototype form, on 31st December 1933, this small and stubby fighter did not fail to astonish the aviation world. At a time when the most industrially advanced nations were starting to reflect upon the limitations of the biplane, Soviet engineers – who certainly until then had enjoyed none of the advantages of a hyper-efficient industrial base – had turned out the world's first cantilever monoplane fighter, complete with retractable landing gear. About 20,000 machines of various models were constructed during the course of a little less than ten years, and after their operational debut in 1937 in Spain, where the I-16/10 appeared, the Polikarpov fighter came through the first phase of the Second World War and remained in front-line use until the summer of 1943. The I-16 came to be known as "Rat" by the Spanish nationalists. Some 200 aircraft were supplied to Nationalist China who used them against the Japanese.

Polikarpov reassessed and improved the concept in his next project, the I-17, the prototype of which was presented on 1st September 1934. Again this was a very modern fighter, with its inline engine, retractable landing gear and good overall aerodynamics. The Polikarpov I-17 started to reach units in 1937, but only a very limited number were used in the war, and then only until 1942.

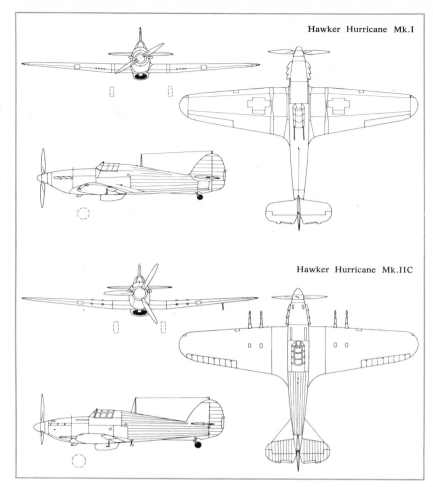

Hawker Hurricane Mk.I

Hawker Hurricane Mk.IIC

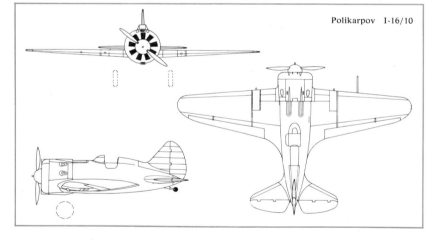

Polikarpov I-16/10

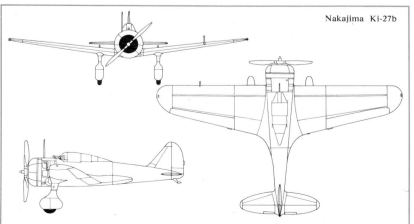

Nakajima Ki-27b

Plate 83
The Hurricane — Britain's first classic of the Second World War: 1937

The first monoplane fighter of the Royal Air Force. The first to be armed with eight machine guns. The first to exceed 300 mph (480 km/h). But it is not for these undisputed records that the Hawker Hurricane is remembered. Sydney Camm's fighter will always be associated with the Battle of Britain in which it shared the main action against the *Luftwaffe* with the Spitfire. Not intended as the main aircraft to take the role of a dogfighter in straight combat, the Hurricane's value lay in its great versatility: during its long career on all fronts it was used as a night fighter, fighter-bomber and even as a ground attack aircraft, armed with rockets and anti-tank guns. The production figures are in themselves proof of its great qualities; the assembly lines turned out no fewer than 14,233 aircraft in the various models, from 1936 to 1944.

Sydney Camm, the creator of other classic fighters of the second half of the twenties, had started the Hurricane project in January 1934. Camm had at first begun work on the design of a monoplane that would use the Rolls-Royce Goshawk engine, but then he

learnt that Rolls-Royce had developed a V-12 engine which had excellent prospects, and he changed his plans in order to accommodate the new engine. This engine was the Merlin which was to become famous with the Hurricane and the Spitfire.

The prototype of the Hurricane flew for the first time on 6th November 1935. In spite of certain shortcomings in the engine, which was still undergoing its own finishing touches, the results of the first flight tests were remarkable: the top registered speed was 506 km/h (314 mph) at 5,000 m (16,400 ft) whilst the climb from take-off to 4,500 m (14,760 ft) showed a time of 5 minutes 7 seconds. Although they had as yet no official order, Hawker made ready for mass production on their own initiative.

The order was not long in coming; on 3rd June 1936 a first consignment of 600 machines was ordered; other orders followed this one, each more substantial. The first Hurricane Mk 1s left the assembly lines in October 1937 and were delivered to the first squadron of Fighter Command two months later. At the outbreak of war, 497 Hurricanes were in service with 18 squadrons. On the eve of the Battle of Britain the number of squadrons had gone up to 26, and in the first days of August it was up to 32, whilst 19 squadrons were equipped with Spitfires. The difference in size and performance of the two aircraft was reflected in their different tactical roles. The Spitfire took on the German fighters, whilst the Hurricane's task was to confront the bombers.

Hawker then perfected a new model of the fighter, the Mk II, due to come into service in August 1940. Three versions were produced in this series. The Mark IIA still carried eight machine guns in the wings while the Mark IIC 1941 was equipped with four 20 mm cannon. Other modifications included the option of drop tanks under the wings, and for the Hurricane's activity as a fighter-bomber it could be fitted with couplings for two 500 lb (227 kg) bombs, or else for its ground attack role it could take rockets, being incidentally the first monoplane to be equipped with this type of armament. Then came the Mk IID, with two 40 mm guns.

The last production model was the Mk IV which appeared in March 1943, designed especially for ground attack: it had a universal wing which could take every projected type of armament. The Hurricane was also very widely used at sea, and all the main models were navalised. The Sea Hurricanes also flew from merchant ships as fighter-bombers to protect convoys from the four-engined German Condors.

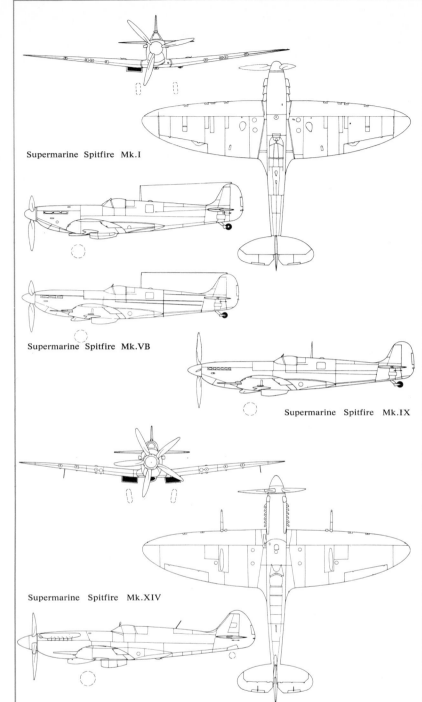

Supermarine Spitfire Mk.I

Supermarine Spitfire Mk.VB

Supermarine Spitfire Mk.IX

Supermarine Spitfire Mk.XIV

Plate 84
The Spitfire — in service from start to finish: 1938

Perhaps no aeroplane achieved such fame as that of the Supermarine Spitfire. This unequalled British fighter was one of the best all-round aircraft to emerge during the Second World War. By virtue of constant improvements which lasted for the whole duration of production, the Spitfire always kept a margin of superiority over its adversaries and, in its final form, remained in front-line

service with the Royal Air Force well into the fifties. All in all 20,351 Spitfires were constructed in about 40 different models, a number exceeding that of the production of any other British plane.

The Spitfire had its origins in the series of seaplanes which were created by Reginald J. Mitchell in the second half of the twenties and culminated in the Supermarine S6B, winner of the last Schneider Trophy race on 13th September 1931. The Spitfire embodied many of the technical elements of the earlier aircraft resulting

from the application of aerodynamics to aircraft design.

Mitchell's prowess in designing the Supermarine seaplanes of the late twenties brought him into association with Henry Royce and the two engineers achieved esteem and recognition in their parallel careers. The Spitfire when it came was the fruit of their association, being Mitchell's application of Royce's Merlin engine, derived from the Type R engine of the seaplane which could produce 2,350 hp. The project got under way in 1934, and after a series of modi-

fications a prototype took shape. This flew for the first time on 5th March 1936. From the very first test flights its performance outstripped all expectations and in the month of June, at the end of the official test flights, an order came through for 310 aircraft. This was followed by massive orders which by October 1939 had reached a total of 4,000 aircraft, which made it absolutely imperative to divide up the vast production programme among all the principal aircraft manufacturers in Britain.

The first production series, Mk I, went into production in 1937 and the new fighters became operative with Fighter Command in June 1938. At the outbreak of war only 9 squadrons had Spitfires, but this became 19 in the period immediately preceding the Battle of Britain during which the Spitfire played a leading role alongside the Hurricane.

Towards the end of 1940 a new series came into service, the Mk II, powered by a more powerful Merlin engine, and constructed in two principal models: the Mk IIA with 8 machine guns and the Mk IIB with four machine guns and two 20 mm cannon. The first photographic reconnaissance models appeared at this time, designated Mk IV. In March 1941 the construction of a more powerful variant was started, Mk V, which was divided into two sub-types according to armament, with the addition of a third (the Mk VC) which was equipped with a universal wing on which could be accommodated all foreseeable kinds of weapons. The Spitfire Mk VC was the first to be used as a fighter-bomber and the first to be widely used overseas. The Mk V aircraft were equipped with a more powerful Rolls-Royce Merlin engine (1,440 hp) which increased the speed of the aircraft to 602 km/h (374 mph) at an altitude of 4,000 m (13,120 ft).

In July 1942 the Mark IX series made its appearance, purpose-built to challenge the superiority of the German Focke Wulf Fw.190 fighter, and was produced in different models for high, medium and low altitudes. Other models were developed concurrently: amongst them the Mk VI and the Mk VII high altitude interceptors, and the Mk VIII and Mk XVI which resembled the Mk IX but which were powered by a Merlin engine built under licence by Packard in the USA.

In 1943 a new Rolls-Royce engine (the Griffon) gave a new zest to the Spitfire. The first to carry this exceptional engine were the aircraft of the Mk XII series, produced to counter the latest Focke Wulf Fw.190 models at low altitudes. The Mk XIV on the other hand was conceived as an interceptor, with a great 5-bladed propeller able to withstand the strain of an output of 2,050 hp, and one of the fastest Spitfires of the war: not only could it offer a serious challenge to the latest types of German jet fighters, it was also able to attack the V-1.

The Spitfire continued to evolve until its later series were too late to serve in the war. Among these was the Mk XVIII, which was noteworthy because of its preformed cowling, and the Mk XIX which was a photographic reconnaissance plane. In the period immediately after the war the final redesignated models made their appearance: these were the F.21, F.22 and F.24. The last operational mission was carried out on 1st April 1954 by a PR19 Spitfire of 81 Squadron: 18 years and one month after the first prototype flight.

Plate 85
The Bf.109 — 35,000 of them are not enough to win the war: 1939

For five years, after its appearance in 1935, the Messerschmitt Bf.109 was the best fighter in the world. Designed at a time when many designers were still thinking in terms of biplanes, it suddenly swept Germany to the forefront of the field of military aircraft and became the forerunner of all the most modern fighter planes of the Second World War. It was indeed one of the great fighters of the war.

Its appearance acted as the signal for a race for mastery of the air, in a similar fashion to what had happened during the First World War. Its main adversary was the British Supermarine Spitfire, and in a way, the course of evolution of each of these two aircraft was determined by the evolution of the other. Just as in the case of the Spitfire, constant efforts were lavished on the Messerschmitt Bf.109 to improve it and make it more powerful. All that the final model K had in common with the prototype was its general configuration of construction: apart from this it was an utterly different and superior aircraft. Production, which went on uninterruptedly from 1936 to 1945, comprised many basic models and innumerable sub-types; ultimately a total of 35,000 aircraft were constructed; the highest overall number of fighter planes produced in the Second World War.

The Bf.109 project was started in the summer of 1934, in response to a request from the German air ministry

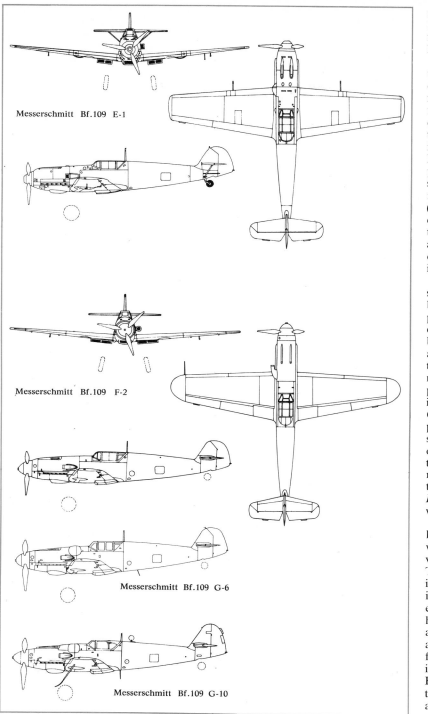

Messerschmitt Bf.109 E-1

Messerschmitt Bf.109 F-2

Messerschmitt Bf.109 G-6

Messerschmitt Bf.109 G-10

for a monoplane interceptor to replace the Heinkel He.51 and the Arado Ar.68 which were in service with the fighter squadrons of the *Luftwaffe*. The designers Willy Messerschmitt and Walter Rethel produced a prototype in which they had made it their aim to combine the smallest structure compatible with the most powerful engine available. The result was an elegant low-wing monoplane, with enclosed cockpit and retractable undercarriage, powered by a Rolls-Royce Kestrel V engine with 695 hp at

take-off, driving a single-blade wooden propeller.

Comparative test flights with the other three aircraft which had been constructed in response to the same specification – the Arado Ar.80, the Heinkel He.112 and the Focke Wulf Fw.159 – took place in October 1935 and saw the Messerschmitt prototype emerge as the winner, and this was subsequently ordered in a pre-series of 10 aircraft. In these aircraft many modifications were carried out to the armament, and the engine was

replaced with a German one, the Junkers Jumo 610 hp 210 A engine. The first production models (the Bf.109B) left the assembly lines in February 1937 and four months later were sent to Spain. Their baptism of fire confirmed the Bf.109 as the best fighter of the time. This success was further enhanced by a number of successes at the International Aeronautics Rally in 1937 at Zürich and again in November of the same year when a Bf.109 equipped with a specially prepared engine, giving 1,650 hp for short bursts, beat the world speed record, bringing it to 610.43 km/h (380 mph). Naturally this aircraft could not really be compared to operational aircraft, but German propaganda made good use of the event to enhance the already remarkable ability of the new fighter.

The B series was followed by the C series (with improved armament) and by the D series, the latter also being powered by a Daimler Benz DB 600 engine. These last series only came to be constructed in very small numbers, a transitional stage in the progression towards the first variant that was mass-produced, the Bf.109E. This production series was typified by the installation of the Daimler Benz DB 601 engine which, as well as being powerful and reliable, was very well suited to the airframe. The first aircraft of the E-1 variant were completed at the beginning of 1939 and production reached 1,540 units before the end of the year. At the outbreak of war the *Luftwaffe* fighter units were equipped with this aircraft.

Experience in the Battle of Britain led to a new series, the F series, equipped with a more powerful engine and very much improved aerodynamics. The Bf.109Fs, which came into service in January 1941, showed themselves in certain situations to be superior even to the Spitfire Mk V, especially at high altitudes. In 1942 the Bf.109G appeared, higher powered and better armed. The limits to which the airframe could be stretched were reached in 1943 with the appearance of the Bf.109K: power had been increased to 2,000 hp and in operational use this aircraft showed itself quite able to face a new generation of Allied fighters, much more modern and sophisticated though they were.

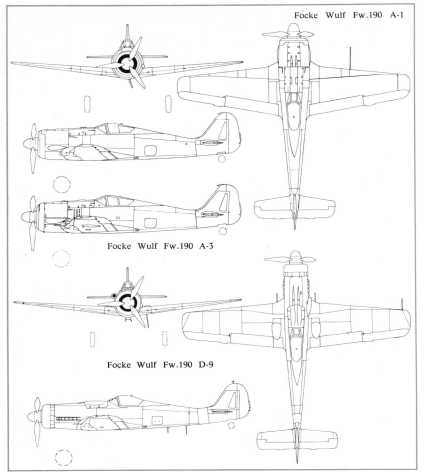

Focke Wulf Fw.190 A-1

Focke Wulf Fw.190 A-3

Focke Wulf Fw.190 D-9

Plate 86
Two more great German fighters: 1939–44

The Focke Wulf came into being to complement the Messerschmitt Bf.109. The Fw.190 was another success story for the German aircraft industry. These two aircraft marked the high point in Germany's development of weapons throughout all the *Luftwaffe*'s theatres of operations round the world, up to the end of the war; and they were Germany's most significant contribution in the struggle for air supremacy. 13,367 Fw.109s

were built in some 10 versions as interceptors, and 6,634 as fighter-bombers, and they distinguished themselves on all fronts, right up to the last days of the Third Reich.

It was in the autumn of 1937 that the German air ministry suggested to Focke Wulfe that they should develop a design for an interceptor fighter to be produced concurrently with the Messerschmitt Bf.109. At the head of the design team was Kurt Tank, technical director of the company, and he put together two alternative ways to meet the specification: one approach used the Daimler Benz DB 601 inline engine, the other was based on BMW's type 139 18-cylinder radial engine, which at that time was still being per-

fected. The second of these was favoured, and three prototypes were made ready, the first of which flew on 1st June 1939. Apart from overheating problems in the engine the flight tests went very well, and development was speeded up with the construction of other prototypes. The fifth 190 finally achieved the necessary performance, thanks to the adoption of a new BMW 14-cylinder radial engine which had replaced the type 139. 40 pre-series machines were immediately ordered and were used in the lengthy test flights and evaluations which were to transform the prototype into a fully operational aircraft.

The aircraft of the first production series, the Fw.190 A-1, went into service in July 1941, showing a marked superiority to their opposite number, the Spitfire Mk V, especially in speed and manoeuvrability. The A-2 and A-3 models followed, differing in engine power and armament. In 1942 the A-4 appeared, and in the following year the A-5, A-6 and A-7. The last model of the A series was the A-8, the main modifications being made to the engine. All these models were constructed in numerous sub-series, different in armament and in use. The F series, in which the fighter was transformed into a fighter-bomber, appeared towards the end of 1942, followed by the G series.

The final model was the Fw.190 D, which appeared at the beginning of 1944 and with this variant the Focke Wulf aircraft underwent considerable change; the BMW radial engine was discontinued, and a Junkers Jumo inline engine was adopted, which could give 2,240 hp for an emergency boost. At the same time, the general appearance of the aircraft remained largely unchanged. The rounded line of the nose was preserved by installing an annular radiator which could fit into the cowling which had enclosed the radial engine. In this form the fighter reached what was perhaps its maximum development and showed that it could compete with the American P-51D Mustang which was without doubt the best fighter plane to emerge from the war. Of the D model alone, 700 Fw.109s were constructed up to 1945.

Another ambitious Messerschmitt project mooted at the same time as the Bf.109 was found, when built, to be ineffective in its intended role. The Bf.110 Zerstörer (destroyer) was designed in 1934 to meet a request from the *Luftwaffe* for a strategic long-range fighter. The Bf.110 was too heavy and not manoeuvrable enough to compete with the fast and agile Hurricanes and Spitfires, showing itself to be ineffectual in close combat. Once it had been accepted for what it really was, a tough and versatile aeroplane, the Bf.110 was used with success as a fighter-bomber, reconnaissance plane, and above all as a night fighter. The prototype flew on 12th May 1936 after lengthy proving flights had

been carried out with pre-series aircraft, and the first mass-production aircraft, the C and D models, appeared in 1939. The reverses of the Battle of Britain had an influence on the conception of the E and F models which were the first in which the aircraft was adapted to roles other than that of a pure interceptor: those of ground attack and fighter-bomber. Night fighter marks were re-introduced, having previously been introduced with the D model, and reached their ultimate expression in 1942, with the Bf.110 G-4, which was equipped with radar. Total procurement of the Bf.110 reached about 6,050.

Plate 87
First and second generation Italian fighters of the Second World War: 1939–41

The progression from the biplane to the monoplane formula was marked in Italy by another Fiat fighter, a contemporary project to that of the C.R. 42 – the G.50 Freccia. A typical product of a transitional phase, this aircraft never possessed any exciting characteristics. Although robust and quite manoeuvrable, it was not particularly fast, and above all it suffered from inadequate armament, which had become typical of Italian fighters by the beginning of the war.

The blueprint was drawn up in 1935 by Giuseppe Gabrielli and in 1936 was entered in a competition held to select designs for a ministerial specification for an interceptor. The prototype flew on 26th February 1937 and a year later the G.50 started comparative test flights with its competitor, the Macchi M.C. 200. Although Gabrielli's fighter was shown to be generally inferior, when modified it was thought good enough for production. It was then sent for operational evaluation in Spain from January 1939 onwards, and then the G.50 was delivered to the forces. At the outbreak of war two groups of 118 aircraft were supplied with the Freccia and the aircraft took part in the war in France. Following this, it was introduced to all theatres of operation. Production reached a total of 783 machines.

The Macchi M.C. 200 Saetta was greatly superior and, up to 1941, it held its own as front-line fighter of the *Regia Aeronautica*. Mario Castoldi had been a designer in 1937, the "father" of the most successful Italian seaplanes. He had drawn on experience

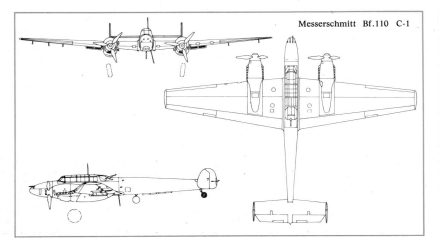

Messerschmitt Bf.110 C-1

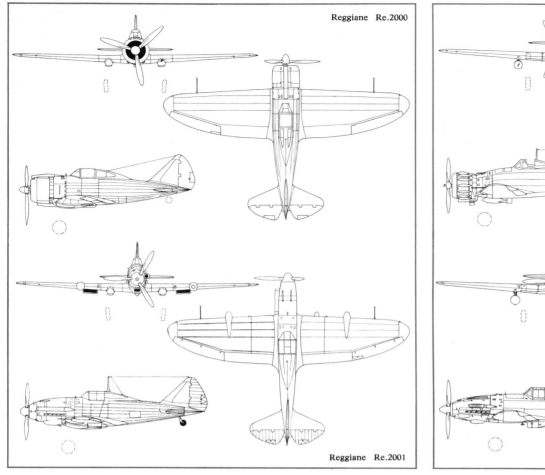

Reggiane Re.2000

Reggiane Re.2001

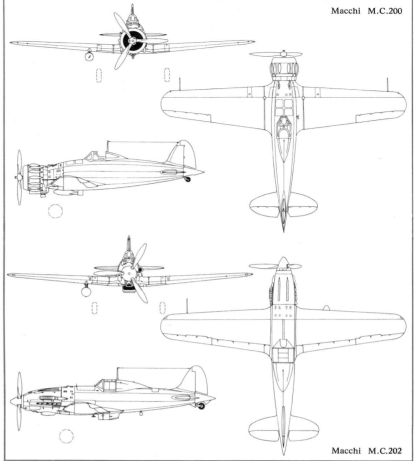

Macchi M.C.200

Macchi M.C.202

gained in producing the M.39 (winner of the 1926 Schneider Trophy) and the M.C. 72 (holder of the world speed record in its class) in what was to be his first fighter plane. The M.C.200 prototype flew on 24th December 1937, and after winning the ministerial competition in 1938 it was ordered in large numbers. The first aircraft started to leave the assembly lines in the summer of 1939 and at the outbreak of war 144 machines were in use with fighter squadrons. With the appearance of its more modern successor, the M.C. 101, towards the end of 1941, the Saetta was gradually withdrawn from the front line. From June 1939 until July 1942, production totalled 1,151 aircraft.

The last fighter of that generation had a humbler history – at least in Italy. This was the Reggiane Re.2000, the prototype of which had appeared on 24th May 1939. Although it represented very interesting technical solutions which made it a more modern and useful aircraft than the G.50 and the M.C. 200, it did not meet the requirements of the ministerial specification and was turned down. Production for export was, however, authorised and paradoxically it was with two foreign nations, Hungary, who had 262 machines, and Sweden with 60, that the Re.2000 gave brilliant service. In Italy the Re.2000 was used as a carrier-based aeroplane in the larger vessels of the navy, but in

this role it saw little combat service.

Then a great qualitative jump forward, finally enabling the Italian aircraft industry to overcome the disparity between it and those of the other great powers in the war, was represented by a new design of Mario Castoldi, the M.C. 202 Folgore. Overall this fighter was shown to be the best Italian fighter of the war, not only for its excellent qualities but because of the extensive use that was made of it and the number manufactured, exceeding 1,100 machines. The prototype flew on 10th August 1940, and from the first test flights it was obvious that the M.C. 202 was a real thoroughbred.

Its principal merit without doubt lay in the use of an entirely new engine which represented a complete break with the tradition of using engines of Italian manufacture: the Daimler Benz DB 601 liquid-cooled V-12 engine giving 1,174 hp on take-off. The M.C. 202 Folgore was the first Italian fighter to use an inline instead of a radial engine.

Operational use of the Macchi M.C. 202 started in Libya in November 1941 and its employment was soon extended all along the North African front, the Balkan front, in the Mediterranean theatre, and on the Russian front, continuing without interruption through the war.

The success of the Folgore eclipsed another good contemporary aircraft,

the Reggiane Re.2001, which was developed after the failure of the Re.2000. The German DB 601 engine was also used in this fighter but priority for allocation of funds was given to the Macchi and this severely limited production at the Reggiane factories. The Re.2001 prototype flew in July 1940 and operational use of the aircraft commenced in December 1941. The 237 completed machines were used mainly as night fighters and fighter-bombers.

Plate 88
Too few and too late to stop the Bf.109s: 1940

Few historians doubt the fact that, if France had not been forced to surrender in June 1940, her aviation industry would have been well able to measure up to the massive strength of the *Luftwaffe*. One of the aircraft which had

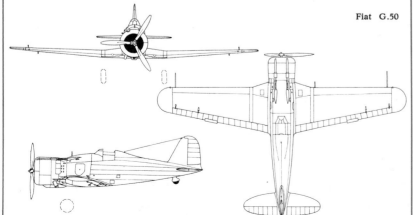

Fiat G.50

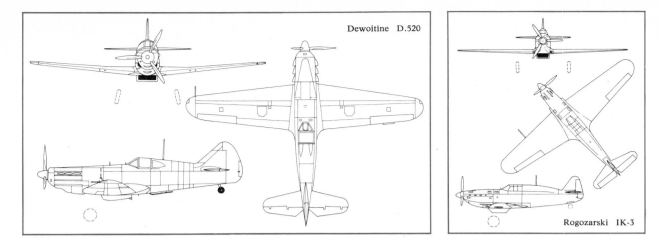

Dewoitine D.520

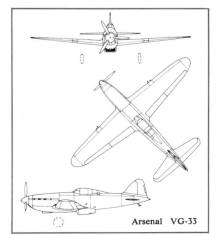

Arsenal VG-33

Rogozarski IK-3

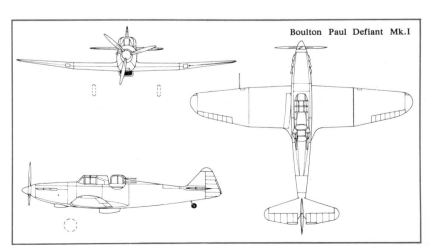

Boulton Paul Defiant Mk.I

the potential to achieve this was the Dewoitine D.520, a fighter of great promise, unanimously considered as the best aircraft of its kind produced by the French aviation industry during the Second World War and which, had it not fallen victim to events, could have had as illustrious a career as its British and German counterparts.

A demonstration of the usefulness of the D.520 was given on 21st April 1940, during a direct comparative test flight with a Messerschmitt Bf.109 E-3 which had been forced down undamaged on French soil: the Dewoitine fighter showed itself to be inferior to its counterpart in terms of pure speed but markedly superior in manoeuvrability. And yet only 36 out of 775 D.520 aircraft which were produced during the war were at the front on 10th May 1940, not enough to have any noticeable effect.

The D.520 originated in 1936, privately manufactured by Emile Dewoitine. The project was not officially accepted by the military authorities until 3rd April 1938, due to the fact that production orders had already been placed for the Morane-Saulnier fighter, and the construction of another, similar machine could not, apparently, be justified. The first D.520 prototype flew on 2nd October 1938, but did not make a favourable impression. Indeed, because of the form of the radiators, serious overheating problems occurred and, furth-

ermore, excessive drag prevented the aircraft from reaching the projected speeds, stipulated in the production order at 520 km/h (323 mph) in horizontal flight.

The prototype was modified, with the adoption of a single ventral radiator, and further modifications were carried out in the second aircraft. In this form, and armed, the D.520 surpassed all expectations, reaching top speeds of 550 km/h (393 mph) at an altitude of 5,200 m (17,060 ft) and taking 12 minutes 53 seconds to climb to 8,000 m (26,250 ft).

The first order for 200 aircraft was placed in April 1939, and in June a second order for a further 510 followed. In April 1940 orders totalled 2,320 aircraft, to be delivered at a rate of 350 a month. Production, however, was slow and on 25th June – the date of the Armistice – 437 machines had been completed. The assembly lines remained in production until December 1942, under German management, and the fighter also pursued its career in service with the *Luftwaffe*, with the Italian Air Force, and the Bulgarian and Romanian air forces, as well as with Free French units.

Another excellent fighter was the Arsenal VG-33, developed from 1937 onwards, but production of which was to be stopped by the war. Developed by the Arsenal de l'Aéronautique, the VG-33 was a light fighter built of non-strategic materials (wood), and powerfully armed: a 20 mm cannon and four machine guns. The prototype, which flew for the first time in the spring of 1939, showed excellent performance, reaching a top speed of 558 km/h (346 mph) during official test flights in August 1939. The Arsenal was put into production and 160 examples were completed, but in June 1940 hardly a dozen of these were ready for operational service.

The German invasion also put an end to aircraft manufacturing in Yugoslavia, where work was in progress on the production of a good fighter which would have been capable of opposing the *Luftwaffe*: the Rogozarski IK-3. Designed by the same Ljubomir Ilic and Kosta Sivcev

who had created the Ikarus IK-2, the aircraft flew in great secrecy in prototype form in the spring of 1938. Twelve machines were handed over for operational evaluation and work on the second batch of 25 machines had hardly started when the course of the war put a stop to all activity. The IK-3, a single-seater monoplane with the same general lines as the British Hurricane, was much more manoeuvrable than the Messerschmitt Bf.109 and had similar armament.

Plate 89
British fighters of 1940

Used operationally side by side with the Hurricane and the Spitfire, the most famous fighters of RAF Fighter Command, were other aircraft which the Fleet Air Arm used to fill similar roles. But, especially in the first years

of the war, these were always very inferior and outclassed. The Boulton Paul Defiant, for example, was a fighter which was designed and developed to a tactical concept which broke with tradition, i.e. the use of a two-seat fighter with its armament entirely concentrated in a dorsal turret, comprising four manually worked machine guns instead of the previous fixed machine gun.

In service from May 1940, the Defiant had some initial successes against bombers, but it soon became clear that it was quite unsuitable for straight combat, both for its poor performance and for its inability to attack or to defend itself adequately against more agile and powerful enemy fighters. In practice, it was difficult for the gunner to synchronise his own movements with those of the pilot. After some months on operations the Defant was relegated to the less demanding role of night fighter and subsequently to that of target tug. 1,064 of these aircraft were constructed.

The Fleet Air Arm's equivalent of the Boulton Paul Defiant was the Blackburn Roc, a fighter which was derived from a previous design of Blackburn that became the Skua, the Royal Navy's first monoplane. The Roc met with the same lack of success as the Defiant and for the same reasons. After only a few months in service – and not on aircraft carriers but from naval land bases – it was relegated to secondary roles as a trainer and target tug. Work had begun on the project in 1936 and the prototype had flown on 23rd December 1938. Production, which was stopped in August 1940, totalled 136 aircraft.

A notable step forward was made by the Fleet Air Arm in June 1940, when the first models of a new fighter, the Fairey Fulmar, went into service. In this aircraft a return had been made to the traditional positioning of armament. Indeed, although it was not a machine of particularly brilliant performance, the Fairey Fulmar's armament was its strong point: 8 wing-mounted machine guns with a fire power equalling that of the Hurricanes and Spitfires of the RAF. The prototype had flown on 4th January 1940 and production had got under way immediately: by 1943 602 aircraft in two production series had left the assembly lines. The first mark used a Rolls-Royce Merlin VIII 1,080 hp engine, the second a 1,300 hp Merlin XX engine. Although they did not on the whole show themselves to be very fast and manoeuvrable, the Fairey Fulmars did however give ample proof of their operational value.

In September 1940 a completely different aircraft made its appearance, destined to fill a role of primary importance right up till the end of the war: the Bristol Beaufighter, one of the most powerful and versatile fighter aircraft ever turned out by the British aircraft industry in the Second World War. It started off as a long range heavy fighter, for both day and night use: the Beaufighter (also referred to as "The Beau") ultimately became a fighter-bomber, torpedo bomber, and ground attack and anti-shipping aircraft. In all these roles it showed itself to be extremely effective and deadly, to the point that it came to be called "whispering death" by the Japanese. As many as 5,562 of these fighters, in numerous models, were completed up to September 1945 and many of them remained in service with the RAF until 1950.

The project evolved towards the end of 1938 and the prototype had flown for the first time on 17th July of the following year. The first production series was the Mk IF, which started to reach Fighter Command units in September 1940, as a night fighter. A special model was produced as a day fighter – the Mk IC, destined for Coastal Command. The second production series was again intended for use as a night fighter (the Mk IIF, of which 450 planes were produced) a feature of which was the adoption of two Rolls-Royce Merlin XX engines instead of the Hercules radials. A return was made to these engines in the most important subsequent series, the Mk VI. Of this series, of which 1,832 planes were produced, two models were built: the Mk VIF for Fighter Command and Mk VIC for Coastal Command. These latter planes profited from the great versatility of the design: rockets and torpedoes became part of the armament and the fast twin-engine aircraft were tried out with success in an anti-shipping and anti-submarine role.

The last production series, the Mk X of 1943 of which 2,205 were constructed, was devoted almost exclusively to these duties, and was reserved for Coastal Command, since night fighting duties had been entrusted to the de Havilland Mosquito.

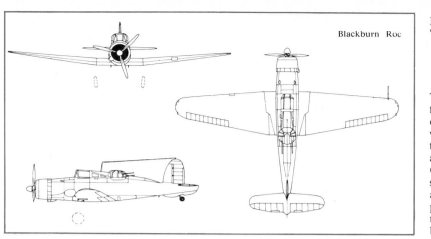
Blackburn Roc

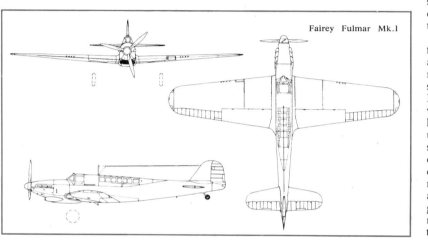
Fairey Fulmar Mk.I

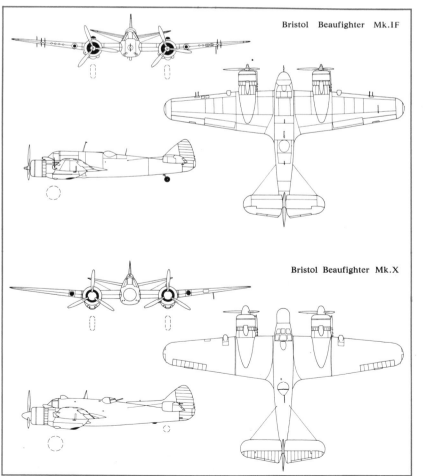
Bristol Beaufighter Mk.IF

Bristol Beaufighter Mk.X

Plate 90.
The MiG, a Russian fighter for all seasons: 1940–44

The first wartime generation Soviet fighter was also the first to result from collaboration between two designers who were to become world famous for their long-running series of fighter aircraft: Artem Mikoyan and Mikhail Gurevich. The MiG-1 and its successors of the war years were not in absolute terms the best fighters to be produced by the Soviet Union during the course of the Second World War, but, although constructed in fairly small numbers overall, they made a considerable impact on the course of the war.

The MiG-1 prototype flew for the first time in March 1940, and immediately gave proof of excellent performance, particularly in speed greatly superior to that of the various types of Polikarpov fighters which were in service at the time. The aircraft was a low-wing monoplane, with retractable undercarriage, mixed wood/metal structure and canvas skin. It was powered by a Mikulin AM 35 1,200 hp engine, which drove a three-blade metal variable pitch propeller. It was armed with two 7.62 mm machine guns, one 12.7 mm gun and had a maximum bomb-capacity equivalent to 200 kg (440 lb).

Production was started immediately and 2,100 aircraft were completed before the MiG-1 was replaced by its more modern successor, the MiG-3. This aircraft went into service towards the end of 1941 and its design earned Mikoyan and Gurevich the Stalin Prize for that year, in consideration of the outstanding contribution they had made to the Soviet aeronautical industry. Athough it was not an outstanding fighter plane in the strictest sense of the term, the MiG-3 did have certain features which enabled it to be used in the role of a high altitude interceptor, in order to oppose the German fighters of the time.

The MiG-3 differed mainly from its direct predecessor as regards its engine and in range. Indeed, while keeping the same structure and general design of a single-engine single seater, with low wings, retractable undercarriage and liquid-cooled engine, the MiG-3 used a more powerful V-12 Mikulin AM 35A engine and was equipped with a supplementary fuel tank which improved its operational capabilities. Other minor modifications, which tended to improve the flight performance and manoeuvrability of the aircraft, were made to the cockpit (which was now equipped with a rear window to enlarge the pilot's field of vision and was completely enclosed), the wing (the rear of which had increased dihedral), the propeller (replaced with one of a more efficient type) and the ventral radiator.

The structure of the MiG-3 was still

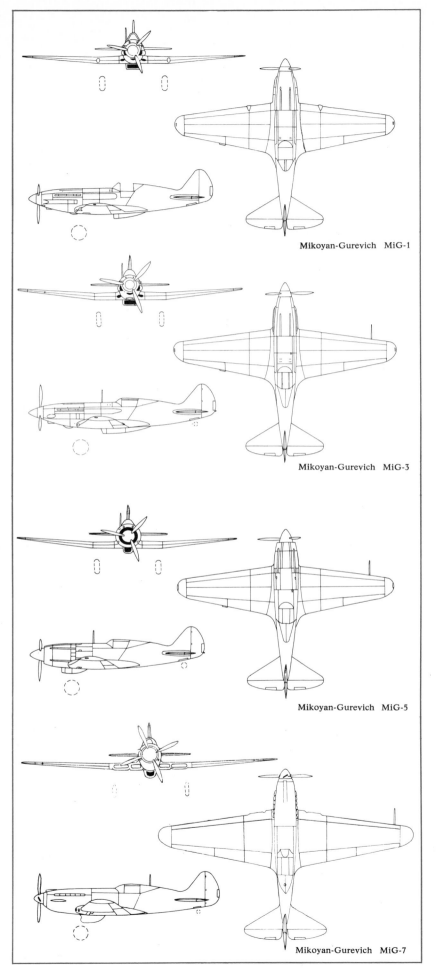

Mikoyan-Gurevich MiG-1

Mikoyan-Gurevich MiG-3

Mikoyan-Gurevich MiG-5

Mikoyan-Gurevich MiG-7

mixed and the skin was in wood and aluminium, like the MiG-1. The armament, too, was identical: two 7.62 mm ShKas machine guns, a Beresin 12.7 mm gun and a maximum bomb-load of 200 kg (440 lb). Speed and range, however, were noticeably better: from 627 km/h (390 mph) at 7,000 m (22,970 ft) altitude to 655 km/h (407 mph) at the same altitude, while the range was almost half as great again as that of the MiG-1.

From the time the MiG-3 started operations it immediately showed its real potential. Above 5,000 m (16,400 ft) altitude the aircraft gave its best performance and it was fit to face all comers: at lower altitudes, however, it showed a noticeable reduction in speed and manoeuvrability which meant that it was at a disadvantage compared with the fighters of the *Luftwaffe*. Another shortcoming when it was used in battle was the inadequacy of its armament: the two small-calibre machine guns were clearly insufficient: an effort was therefore made to remedy this by installing two 12.7 mm Beresin Bs under the wings.

Production of the MiG-3 was not long-lived: towards the end of 1941 the assembly lines were closed down, in part because construction of the AM 35A engine was being superseded by the more powerful AM 38 which was intended for the Ilyushin Il-1. The fighter stayed in service until the last months of 1943. At that time it had already been replaced by the more up-to-date Yakovlev and Lavochkin, but it remained useful for tactical high altitude reconnaissance.

It was the entry of this new and efficient aircraft which meant that Mikoyan and Gurevich's next aircraft, the MiG-5, was only a limited success. Being in direct competition with the Lavochkin La-5, the MiG-5 suffered from being outclassed by its contemporary and only a small number were produced, remaining in service for a brief period in 1943. The MiG-5 prototype flew in 1942: it preserved the structure of its predecessor, with the exception of variations made necessary by the adoption of the Shvetsov M 82A radial engine in place of the V-12 AM 35A.

The two designers returned to the inline engine in the next model, the MiG-7, the prototype of which appeared towards the end of 1944. The fighter had been commissioned with the specific aim of producing a high-altitude interceptor, able to shoot down German reconnaissance planes. The MiG-7 fulfilled these requirements, but very few were made because by that time the danger from enemy reconnaissance aircraft had diminished. The development of the MiG-7 did play an important part in the next technical advance for high-level aircraft: among Soviet aircraft it was the first with a completely pressurised cockpit.

Plate 91
The Zero: the best Japanese fighter of the war: 1940–45

Spitfire, Messerschmitt Bf.109 and P-51 Mustang. If Western technology of the forties managed to find its fullest expression in these three great fighters, Japan, the latecomer in the history of aviation, did not lag behind. For the entire duration of the war, the Japanese kept a distinguished aircraft in production, without doubt the most famous of those which fought in the Pacific: the Mitsubishi A6M, renamed Zero unofficially by the Allies and ZEKE in the official identification code. These aircraft were present in large numbers in every zone and theatre of operations, influencing the course of the war in the early years when, with their definite superiority over the enemy fighters, they became the very symbol of Japanese power and the main instrument used in implementing Japan's expansionist strategy. Even when, from half way through 1942, the balance of power in the air started to pass gradually into Allied hands, the Zero continued to carry out unceasing missions. The assembly lines completed 10,499 machines in many models between March 1939 and August 1945, a total reached by no other Japanese plane during the war.

The Imperial Navy's specification which led to the creation of the Mitsubishi A6M was submitted to Mitsubishi and to Nakajima in May 1937. At first both factories responded positively, but after a few months only Mitsubishi remained in the running. This was due to the fact that in October the military authorities changed the original requirement to a large extent, following combat experience gained in China, and the new specification was regarded as unattainable by Nakajima's engineers, who abandoned the programme.

The fighter was to have: a maximum speed of 500 km/h (311 mph) at an altitude of 4,000 metres (13,120 ft); climbing speed of 9½ minutes to reach 3,000 metres (9,840 ft); a maximum range of 8 hours at economic cruising speed and with auxiliary fuel tanks, and a combat endurance of 2 hours; to be able to take off in a very restricted space; to be no less manoeuvrable than the fighter that it was to replace (the Mitsubishi A5M which at the time was just coming into service); an armament of two machine guns of 7.7 mm and two guns of 20 mm plus a capacity for 60 kg (132 lb) of bombs.

The chief designer of Mitsubishi, Jiro Horikoshi, did not let himself be discouraged by these requirements, which made necessary an outstanding effort of research and experimentation, and he achieved his objective. A little under a year after the original specification had been issued, on 1st April 1939, Horikoshi's first prototype took to the air: with Katsuzo Shima at the controls, the A6M1 did not merely fulfil requirements, it exceeded them.

Encouraged by his success, Horikoshi installed a more powerful engine in the third prototype, A6M2, and by means of this in tests on 28th December 1939 he made an extremely good impression on the navy. The Zero was put into mass production directly after evaluation tests. The first A6M2s became operational in July 1940, and two months later were given their baptism of fire in China.

On Japan's entry into the war, the Zeros comprised the spearhead of the seaborne carrier based force and from Pearl Harbor onwards, up to the Battle of Midway in June 1942, they maintained undisputed air superiority. The turning point, which came after this historic battle, was occasioned not only by the grave losses suffered and the difficulty of replacing machines and pilots which had been shot down, but also by the gradual recovery of their enemies and the appearance of a new and more powerful Allied aircraft.

It was just at the time of the Battle of Midway that the second main model of the Zero, the A6M3, which a more powerful engine and armament, went into service. Under the pressure of the war, the designers made an even more determined effort to improve the aircraft and, in the autumn of 1943, the A6M5 model reached the forces. Perhaps the most effective model of the series, this had been developed to challenge the American Hellcat and Corsair, which were superior in power and armament. But by this time the balance had swung too far in favour of the Allies: not even the A6M5 fought on equal terms. A last attempt was made in 1945 with the production of the final model, the A6M8, equipped with a Mitsubishi Kinsei 1,560 hp engine, which was 60 per cent more powerful than the Mitsubishi A6M2. The prototype appeared in April but the vicissitudes of war and the chaotic state of Japanese industry hindered the ambitious production planning, in which provision was made for the construction of 6,300 machines.

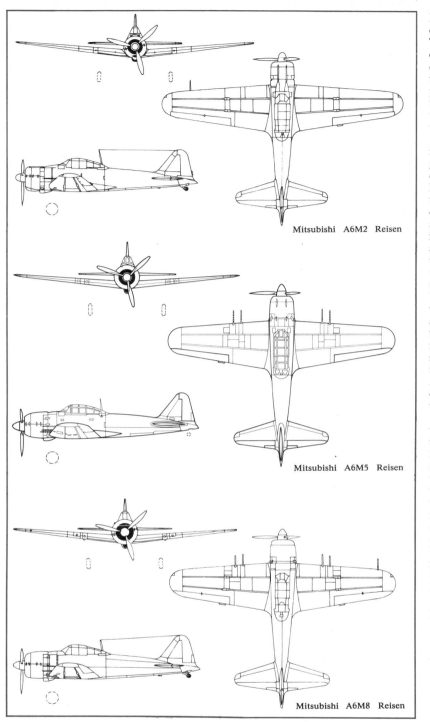

Mitsubishi A6M2 Reisen

Mitsubishi A6M5 Reisen

Mitsubishi A6M8 Reisen

Plate 92
American fighters in service at the time of Pearl Harbor: 1937–41

Pearl Harbor, and the consequent entry of the United States into the war, found the American aviation industry at something of a disadvantage. Even its latest fighters, such as the Bell P-39 and the Curtiss P-40, were scarcely competitive with enemy equivalents.

The Bell P-39 Airacobra had been through its disappointing moments, especially following the enthusiasm which had accompanied its appearance in 1937. The prototype of this fighter aircraft was ordered in the October of that year, on the basis of an ambitious design remarkable for the originality of its armament: a 37 mm cannon installed in the extreme nose and firing through the hub of the propeller. This solution had dictated the entire structure of the aircraft, leading the design engineers (headed by Robert Wood) towards other just as original and revolutionary solutions. The engine was installed in the centre of the fuselage behind the pilot and drove a long propeller shaft: and the tricycle landing gear, which was completely retractable, was positioned under the nose, the first time such an undercarriage position had ever been used in a fighter.

The prototype flew for the first time in April 1939 and showed that it had great qualities, both in horizontal and climbing flight. However, there followed a series of modifications which transformed the thoroughbred into a carthorse; the most significant change, and the one which was mainly responsible for the aircraft's lack of success as an interceptor, was the replacement of the supercharged engine with an unsupercharged one; this resulted in a serious lack of power at high altitude. What made matters worse, the aircraft was now heavier with its armament and armour plating installed, although these were exactly as specified originally. Thus modified the prototype suffered a noticeable decline in its performance. However, on the 10th August 1939 the Bell fighter was ordered in mass and the first P-39Cs were delivered in January 1941.

The following model, P-39D, of which 675 were produced, was offered to the RAF, who rejected it. Several hundred of these aircraft went to the Soviet Union and about 250 went to the USAAC in December 1941. From the time of the USA's entry into the war until the appearance of its more modern successors (the P-38, P-47 and P-51) the Airacobra fought alongside the Curtiss P-40 in the front line, both in Europe and in the Pacific. Various models were subsequently produced and the last ones, the P-39N and P-39Q, were all supplied to the Soviet Union. Out of the 9,558 Airacobras produced, the USSR received as many as 4,773, which were used for tactical support.

The first P-39s were sent into the war side by side with other fighters of earlier design which were clearly outdated. The Seversky P-35 was one example, produced in 1936 by Alexander Kartveli, the future maker of the classic P-47 Thunderbolt. Of the 177 P-35s he constructed, 40 were exported to Sweden and 60 were used in the Philippines at the end of 1941.

Also exported in large numbers was the Curtiss P-36, the A and C models of which first reached American squadrons in 1938 and 1939: this aircraft had been designed in 1934, and shared the honour with the P-35 of being the first monoplane fighter of the American Army Air Corps. Its operational career was not outstanding, the P-36 already being clearly outclassed as far back as the outbreak of the war. Nor were any great hopes fulfilled by a new design that Kartveli completed in 1940 on the basis of the P-35: the P-43 Lancer. Inadequate as a fighter, this aircraft was converted to photographic

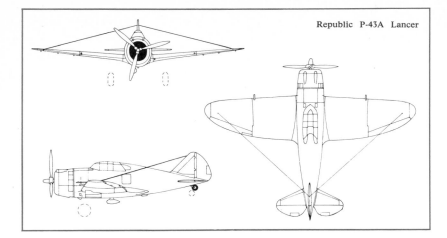

Republic P-43A Lancer

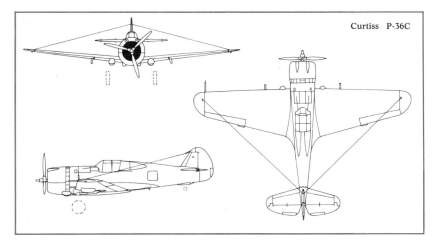

Curtiss P-36C

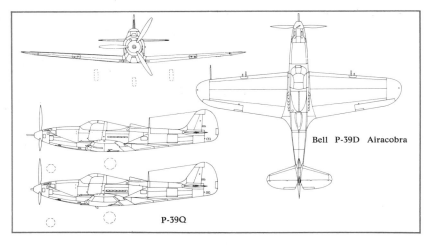

Bell P-39D Airacobra

P-39Q

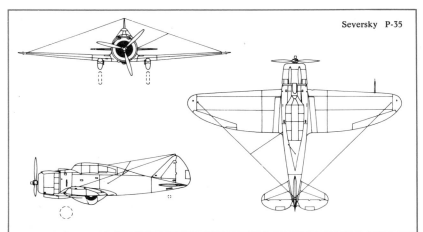

Seversky P-35

reconnaissance in 1942. Out of the 272 aircraft constructed in two main models, the only ones which saw action were the 103 sent to China.

Plate 93
P-40, the most important US fighter of America's first two years in the war: 1941–43

The most important American fighter of the USA's first 2 years in the war was without doubt the Curtiss P-40 Warhawk. Its importance lay mainly in its sheer numbers, for it was not without shortcomings and these remained throughout the long operational life of the aircraft.

When war broke out with Japan the P-40 was the only aircraft of its type capable of being produced in large enough quantities and at short enough notice for the national emergency that was to hand: and as such the P-40 was constructed in enormous numbers which held the fort until the arrival of more effective fighters. Even then, after the appearance of the P-38, P-47 and P-51, P-40s continued to pour out of the factories, ever in demand by the Allies: from 1939 to 1944 13,753 aircraft in ten models were constructed and they were kept in service all through the war on all fronts, in Europe, Africa, the Pacific and Russia.

The XP-40 design took shape in March 1937, with the objective of utilising the 1,200 hp Allison V-1710, which was a liquid-cooled V-12, in the airframe of the P-36A, which at the time had just come into production. The prototype flew in October 1938 and the War Department were well enough pleased with its performance to order the construction of an initial consignment of 524 aircraft on 27th April 1939. The Government's choice, although justified by the fact that Curtiss was the most ready to go into mass production, caused a storm of controversy in American aviation. Other constructors claimed that their prototypes were more suitable, and felt that they had been deprived of this important contract by some kind of fraud: the $12.9 million contract was the largest aviation order since 1918.

In spite of the controversy, produc-

tion got under way: the first P-40s of the first production series appeared in the spring of 1940 and about 20 of them were sent to the American air force before the end of September. At the same time another 140 aircraft of the export model, originally ordered by France, were taken over by Britain, who called them the Tomahawk Mk I and used them for training. They were slightly better than the Hurricane but not as good as the Spitfire, nor the Bf.109E, which was more important – that was the one they would have had to fight if they had been used on the lines.

The second model was the P-40B of 1941, known to the RAF as the Tomahawk Mk II, which was better armed, and carried armour plating for the pilot and self-sealing fuel tanks. These aircraft first saw action in British hands in North Africa, and in American hands at Pearl Harbor and in China. In China, between December 1941 and July 1942, the "Flying Tigers" of Gen Clair Chennault's American Volunteer Group gave the Curtiss fighter its moment of glory. Decorated with a motif of shark's teeth painted on the nose, the P-40Bs brought down 286 Japanese aircraft in six months of operations, with a loss of 23 of their own number.

After the 131 P-40Bs and a few P-40Cs which were of inferior performance, the D series arrived which had a different engine. The 582 that were constructed almost all went to the RAF, where they were called the Kittyhawk I. The P-40E followed, one of the models that were produced in large numbers. It was a more powerful plane and had a heavier armament, and 23,000 aircraft were constructed. These aircraft were the first to serve with the USAAF in Europe, in the Mediterranean theatre.

Still in 1941, the P-40F followed, 1,311 examples being constructed. In this version at last the problem of mediocre engine performance had been solved, by installing a Rolls-Royce Merlin engine manufactured under licence by Packard in the USA. The performance at high altitude improved noticeably, but the new engine was not available in large quantities since priority had been given for its use in the P-51 Mustang.

Subsequent attempts were made to improve the characteristics of the aircraft and led to the production of the K, L and M models, in which an effort was made to lighten the airframe in various ways. The final model, and the one constructed in the greatest numbers at 5,219 aircraft, was the P-40N of 1943 which benefited from all the experience of the previous lightweight versions while also taking advantage of more powerful Allison engines, so that it was a faster aircraft. These were the last P-40s to be used by the USAAF. The Americans exported more than they used, sending large numbers to Britain, the USSR, South Africa, Australia and China.

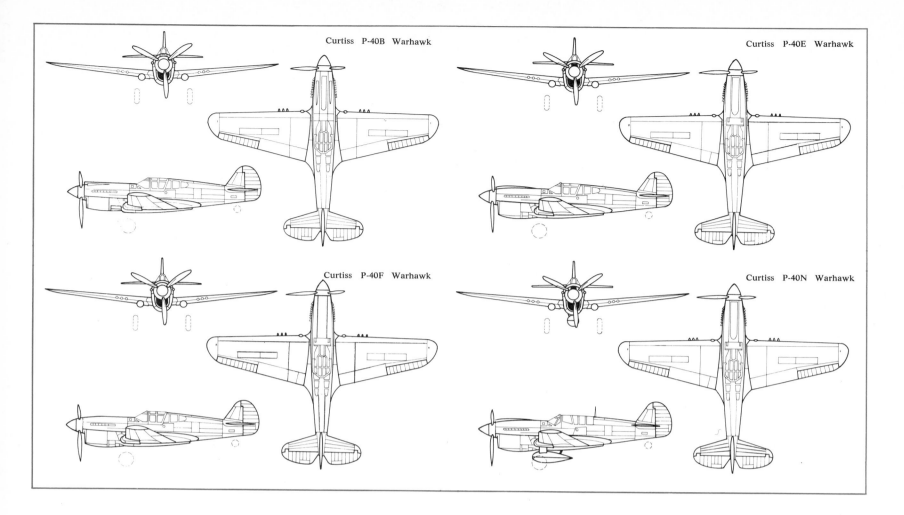

Curtiss P-40B Warhawk

Curtiss P-40E Warhawk

Curtiss P-40F Warhawk

Curtiss P-40N Warhawk

Plate 94
New Fighters for the Fleet Air Arm:
1942–43

Britain's carrier-based fighters evolved at a pace which was markedly slower than that of their land-based equivalents. In 1938 the RAF possessed two of the best fighters in the world, the Hurricane and the Spitfire, while the Fleet Air Arm was still in the age of the biplane. The Fairey Fulmar and the Blackburn Roc, which went into service in 1940, were still far from reaching the standard of their land-based contemporaries. A remedy to this situation was found towards the end of 1941 when it was decided to produce a navalised model of the most famous aircraft of the Royal Air Force – the Spitfire.

A new family of carrier-based fighters was born, the Seafires, which developed side by side with the aircraft that formed the spearhead of the RAF.

The first Seafires, of which about 150 were constructed and which were derived from the Spitfire Mk VB and designated Mk IB, were constructed quite quickly and so were ready in time to take part in operations in North Africa in November 1942, on board the aircraft carrier HMS *Furious*. Meanwhile the first 400 Seafire Mk IICs were delivered, and they went into service in the ensuing months. This model was characterised by the adoption of a universal wing, type C, the same as that of the Spitfire Mk V, which could accommodate all foreseeable types of armament. The Seafire Mk IICs had also had their landing gear strengthened and were fitted with rockets for assisted take-off.

The largest production series was the Mk III of 1943. In this series, which saw over 1,100 aircraft completed from April 1943 to July 1945, a serious defect was at last removed – it was the first version with folding wings, which are indispensable for easy stowage and movement on board the carrier. Special variants of the Seafire Mk III were adapted for photographic reconnaissance and for low altitude operations, as had been the case with the Mk IIC, but the Mk III's innovation was a fighter-bomber variant, which carried bomb racks under the fuselage and wings,

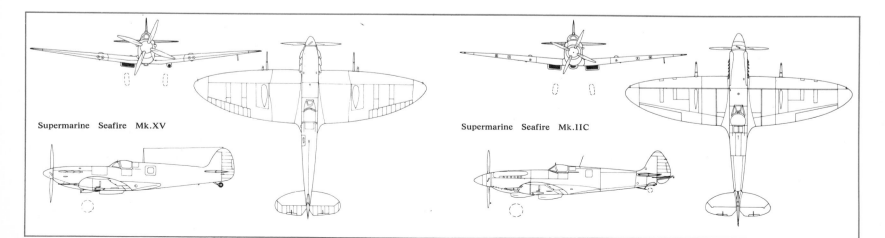

Supermarine Seafire Mk.XV

Supermarine Seafire Mk.IIC

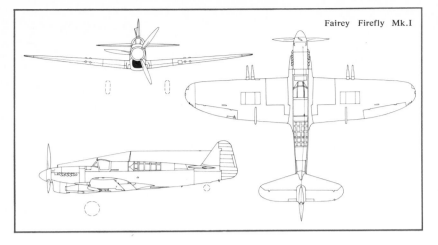

Fairey Firefly Mk.I

capable of carrying one 226 kg (500 lb) bomb or two 113 kg (250 lb) bombs. The Mk IIIs served with the fleet up to the end of the war.

The end of the war meant that the second generation of Seafires missed an active part in the fighting. Like the Spitfire, the new Griffon engine in place of the Merlin revitalised the Seafire, but the first Griffon-powered Seafire, the Mk XV, saw only a brief period of operational service in the last days of the war. It was not in carrier based service.

The prototype flew for the first time in 1944, and besides the installation of the Rolls-Royce Griffon engine it differed from preceding models in the arrangement and capacity of its fuel tanks and in the replacement of the arrester gear under the fuselage by another mechanism which was installed in the extreme end of the tail. The first Mk XVs went into service in May 1945, and a total of 390 aircraft were produced. Four months later they were joined by an improved model, the Mk XVII, of which 232 were made. Principal differences lay in the modification of the rear of the fuselage by the adoption of a bubble hood and the reinforcement of the undercarriage struts.

The last Seafire models imitated the evolution of the Spitfire in the postwar period. The navy's redesignated models F.45 (50 aircraft), F.46 (24 aircraft) and F.47 (90 aircraft) corresponded to the F.21, F.22 and F.24 of the Spitfire. The F.45 and F.46 were transitional, having the wing of the corresponding Spitfire without any modification, and not a folding wing. The fully navalised model which did have folding wings was the F.47, and this was the last to be used in combat service: this was in June 1950 on board the aircraft carrier HMS *Triumph*, in a very intense operational tour off the Korean coast. These Seafires remained in front-line service for another year; they were kept with the reserve forces and finally taken out of service in 1952.

A more direct descendant of the Fulmar was used side by side with the Seafire, the Fairey Firefly, designed according to traditional Fleet Air Arm criteria, which saw the twin-seat reconnaissance plane as indispensable on board aircraft carriers, even if its performance was clearly limited in comparison with a single-seater. The prototype flew on 22nd December 1941 and was followed by three more experimental aircraft. Production of the Mk I series got under way towards the end of the following year and it became operational in October 1943 on board the aircraft carrier HMS *Indefatigable*.

Used mainly in the Pacific, the Firefly showed itself to be very versatile and generally a good aircraft. They could serve as day and night fighters, as reconnaissance planes or as fighter-bombers, and 950 of them were constructed before they were replaced by the more modern Mk IV, which went into service after the war. The most notable wartime actions in which the Firefly served were the sinking of the *Tirpitz* in Norwegian waters in the summer of 1944, and the destruction of the Japanese-held oil refineries in Sumatra in January 1945. In both of these actions the aircraft flew from the aircraft carrier HMS *Indefatigable*.

Plate 95
Russian efforts to compete on equal terms: 1941–43

Gradually the Soviet aircraft industry made up their initial disadvantage and, as the war followed its course, managed to produce excellent fighter aircraft. After Mikoyan and Gurevich, another designer was to become prominent at this time: Semyon Alexsevich Lavochkin. The first fighter which bore his name, even if its designation code also included the initials of his two assistants Gorbunov and Gudkov, was the LaGG-3, which made its appearance as a prototype on 30th March 1939. If it could not be considered exceptional, this aircraft played its part in the development of Soviet military aviation. For almost a year following Germany's attack, the Russians gained experience of mass production with the LaGG-3 which was produced and used in great numbers; and its airframe was still the basis of the La-5 and the La-7, aircraft which contributed significantly to re-establishing air supremacy on the eastern front.

When the LaGG-3 went into the first battles of Russia's war in 1941, Semyon Lavochkin was already preparing an improved design. The factor which radically changed the unremarkable characteristics of the LaGG-3 was a new engine, the Shvetsov M 82 double-banked 15-cylinder radial engine which could give 1,600 hp on take-off in its initial version. It was not difficult to replace the Klimov liquid-cooled engine in the aircraft with the new air-cooled one and, from the very first test flights, it was obvious that the new version represented a marked improvement.

The increased power and the saving in weight which resulted from the absence of a cooling system made up for the increase in drag caused by the enlarged frontal section, and yielded higher performance. In speed alone, an increase of about 50 km/h (31 mph) was registered.

Shvetsov-powered aircraft immediately replaced the LaGG-3 on the assembly lines and the first of these, which were really hybrids and were designated LaGG-5, simply consisted of LaGG-3 airframes in which the radial engine was installed. These aircraft reached the forces very quickly, whilst all awaited the completion of the definitive La-5 model, which saw action in the spring of 1942. Production quickly reached its maximum and, at the time of the Battle of Stalingrad, Lavochkin's new fighter was all along the front.

Meanwhile the designer was working to complete an improved model, which reached the forces in 1943. This was the La-5FN, in which the principal

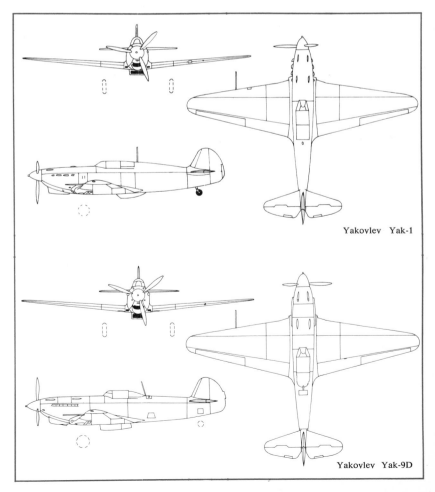

Yakovlev Yak-1

Yakovlev Yak-9D

differences lay in the adoption of a fuel injection engine, of greater power; in the progression from a completely wooden airframe to a mixed wood and metal airframe and in the improvement of some controls.

The La-5FN was followed a year after by a later model, called the La-7, in which aerodynamic improvements had been made, and which had a more powerful engine and increased armament. In an attempt, later on, to improve performance, a certain number of La-7s were given an auxiliary rocket engine in the rear section of the fuselage: the resultant increase in speed was 10–15 per cent. As had happened with the La-5, a two-seater model of the La-7 was constructed, La-7 UTI, used for training, liaison and observation.

The transition to an entirely metal airframe took place in the La-9, which was constructed by Lavochkin in 1944 and sent to the forces in the last days of the war. The aircraft was totally different even if the exterior looked like its predecessors; it had a completely redesigned wing, a 1,870 hp engine, and 4 cannon were added to its armament. Its performance was on a level with the best contemporary Allied fighters. After the war the La-9 was in turn developed into the final La-11, remembered as the last piston-engine fighters of the VVS.

In its whole history the Lavochkin fighter was produced in a total of 15,000 aircraft of all versions.

Another great Russian designer put his name on an equally significant family of fighters to that designed by Lavochkin: Aleksandr Sergeivic Yakovlev. His first aircraft, the Yak-1, which went into service in the first months of 1942, earned him the Order of Lenin, a prize of 100,000 roubles, and a car. The Yak-1 was the forerunner of a series of aircraft of which 30,000 were to be manufactured in total and which were to be the spearhead of the Soviet fighter force for the whole of the war.

After the Yak-7B of 1942, Yakovlev's most successful interceptor was the Yak-9, which was built in the largest numbers of all the Yakovlevs and led to a sub-series which was to continue into the 1950s. The Yak-9 went into service in August 1942 and its variants included the 9B and 9T which could be used both as a fighter-bomber and assault aircraft, and the most well-known variant was the 9D with increased fuel tank capacity and therefore a very long range. These aircraft were intended mainly as escorts for American bomber formations which flew from British bases to raid the oil installations in Romania. Yak-9s were supplied in various versions to foreign units fighting the Germans. Among these were the Polish 1st Warsaw Fighter Regiment and the French Groupe de Chasse Normandy-Niemen.

The last model to be developed during the war was the Yak-9U, although it was not in time to see action. It was a completely new aircraft opening the way for production of the final postwar model, the Yak-9P, which saw action in Korea.

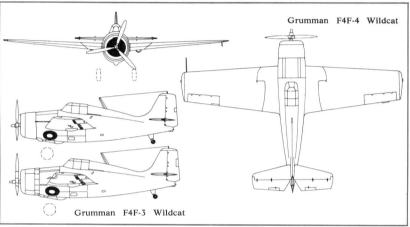

Brewster F2A-3 Buffalo

Grumman F4F-4 Wildcat

Grumman F4F-3 Wildcat

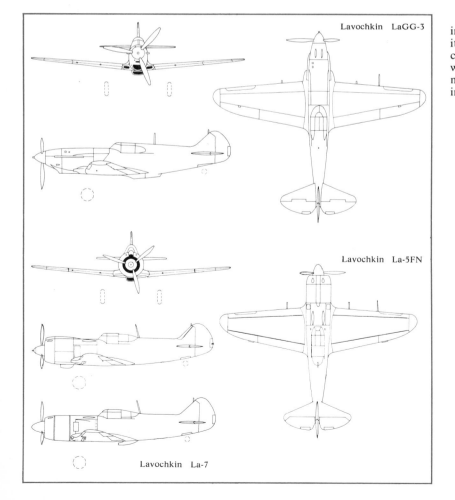

Lavochkin LaGG-3

Lavochkin La-5FN

Lavochkin La-7

Plate 96
The first effective fighters of the US Navy and the US Air Force: 1940–43

In US naval aviation the definitive step from the biplane to the monoplane was marked in 1940 by the Grumman F4F Wildcat, the first of the prolific family of "Cats" which came from Grumman through several decades. The F4F was the founder of a series of excellent carrier-based fighters which saw service during the war in the Pacific. Although it was inferior to its adversary, the Mitsubishi A6M Reisen, the Wildcat had to fulfil a central role in the conflict up to 1943. About 8,000 of these aircraft were made and the F4F was also used by the Fleet Air Arm, under the name of the Martlet.

Oddly enough, the F4F had begun as a biplane. In the early days of 1936 when the previous Grumman carrier-based fighter, the F3F, was in its proving flights, a feasibility study was started for a successor. The US Navy had encouraged competition for the design, ordering prototypes from both Brewster and Grumman. The Brewster design, the F2A Buffalo, was a monoplane, and as such the very first to be ordered by the navy. Although it was not appreciated widely, in fact the differences between these two prototypes were only superficial. At the same time the navy were still not convinced by the revolutionary formula, the monoplane, and their wish was to play safe and stay with the biplane; they still feared that the monoplane structure might fail. But then events proved their point: the measured performance of the F3F, now new in service, was compared with the estimated performance of the biplane version of the F4F, only to show that there was very little difference between the two. If any improvement was to come, it must be through the monoplane formula: and so, while the contract was still for tender, in July 1936 the navy asked Grumman to make the transformation, alter their design and build a monoplane.

The first prototype flew on 2nd September 1937. In proving fights the XF4F-2 appeared to be inferior to the Brewster XF2A-1. In June 1938 the Buffalo was declared the winner and went into production but three months later Grumman was authorised to develop a second prototype. The XF4F-3 appeared on 2nd February of the following year and was immediately seen to be far superior, due mostly to having a new engine. After evaluation flights the Wildcat was at last accepted and an initial consignment of 54 aircraft was ordered.

Even before the US Navy was to receive its first F4F-3s in December 1940, the British Navy was first to put the new fighter into service, with a consignment of 81 aircraft, in the summer of 1940. These aircraft came from an order which had been placed by France before the outbreak of the war in Europe: they saw action in December, over Scapa Flow.

A year later the Wildcat began its active service in American colours, at Pearl Harbor; by then a total of 183 F4F-3s and 65 F4F-3As were in service with both the US Navy and the US Marine Corps.

In 1941 the second model, which was to become the principal production model, made its appearance: the

F4F-4. The prototype had flown on 14th April and the first planes of this series were delivered at the end of the year. From 1942 onwards they began to replace their predecessors and remained the only carrier-based front-line fighters of the USA. They remained in production up to August 1945, and the two last models, the FM-1 and FM-2, were made by General Motors. Some of these also went to Britain's Fleet Air Arm.

Whilst the career of the Wildcat was particularly outstanding, the aircraft which had beaten the Grumman fighter in the competition of 1938 turned out to be sadly lacking when used in operational service. The Brewster F2A Buffalo, in fact, disappeared from the US Navy and the US Marine Corps in the short space of a few months and the 507 completed aircraft went, in large part, to Britain, Finland, and to the Netherlands, who used them in combat with disastrous results. The production models were the F2A-1 (54 made), the F2A-2 (325) and the F2A-3 (128). This last model, especially, suffered from the further burden imposed on an already poor performance by increased armament.

A contemporary of the Grumman Wildcat was another important fighter which was adopted by the USAAF, the Lockheed P-38 Lightning. A very original and controversial aircraft, this fast and powerful twin-engine plane remained a crucially important element in the American aerial arsenal for the entire war. In production from 1940 to 1945, manufacture of this aircraft totalled overall 9,923 in various models, which saw action on all fronts and in very different roles from that first intended, illustrating the great value of the design: photographic reconnaissance plane, fighter-bomber, night fighter. War records attribute to the P-38 the credit for shooting down more Japanese aircraft than any other American aircraft, and among these aircraft in April 1943 was the one which was carrying Admiral

Yamamoto, the originator of the plan to attack Pearl Harbor.

The specification which led to the creation of the Lightning was issued in 1937. The requirements were: a high altitude interceptor capable of doing 580 mph (360 mph) at 6,100 m (20,000 ft) and 467 km/h (290 mph) at sea level and able to reach optimum altitude in 6 minutes. Many of the companies chosen held that these specifications could not be achieved, but the chief designers of Lockheed, H. L. Hubbard and Clarence "Kelly" Johnson, were not discouraged and among the many possible solutions they ended up by choosing the least orthodox, that of twin engines with twin booms.

The first XP-38 flew on 27th January 1939 and, in order to further impress the military authorities, the prototype made a spectacular coast to coast crossing of the American continent on 11th February, achieving this in the record time of 7 hours and 2 minutes. This exploit had its desired result and two months later the aircraft was ordered to be put into production. The first 30 P-38s conformed to the structure of the prototype, but with the P-38D which followed the optimum configuration was achieved. In November 1941 the P-38E appeared, with more powerful armament and, at the beginning of the next year, the P-38F, which was the first to be used on a large scale; it was deployed in large numbers in Europe towards the middle of 1942 and in North Africa in November.

The G and H models followed (1,082 G models and 601 H models were made), and then came the P-38J, the second biggest production total (2,970) and one of the most widely used and very effective with its more powerful engines and greater armament. In these aircraft the positioning of the radiators was modified and consequently the appearance of the engine nacelles was changed too. The largest production numbers were achieved with the P-38L (3,923)

which were equipped with even more powerful engines. Both the J and the L were also used as bombers, with the adoption of a glazed nose for the bomb-aimer.

The last Lightning was the P-38M, designed as a night fighter and equipped with radar. The radar operator was installed in an extra cockpit fitted behind and slightly above the pilot's cockpit.

Plate 97
Japanese fighters for a war of aggression: 1940–42

The Nakajima Ki-43 Hayabusa, also known as OSCAR in the Allied code, was in the front line from the first to the last day of the war and was the first modern fighter of the Japanese army air force. It was an unpalatable surprise to the Allies on the outbreak of war in the Pacific. Fast, very agile and present in large numbers (5,919 aircraft of various models left the assembly lines) the Hayabusa ended its career in the desperate suicide missions of the last year of the war and, although little suited to the task, in the interception of American bombers during their massive raids on the Japanese homeland.

The specifications which led to the creation of the Ki-43 were issued by the army in 1937, and for the first time it was not thrown open to competition between the various manufacturers; an order went straight to Nakajima because the new fighter was to replace the Ki-27, which was already in production there.

The design was entrusted to a working party headed by Hideo Itokawa and, in exactly one year, the first prototype was ready to fly. This took place in the first days of January 1939 and was followed by a long series of tests and proving flights, in which two other prototypes and ten pre-series aircraft also took part; these flights and tests lasted for the whole of 1940.

The early models, of which 716 were built, were designated Ki-43-I and Ki-43-IB and differed only in their armament. They were followed in 1942 by a very much improved model, Ki-43-II, which eventually accounted for the larger part of the

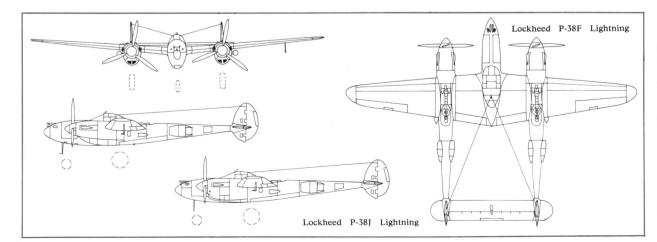

Lockheed P-38F Lightning

Lockheed P-38J Lightning

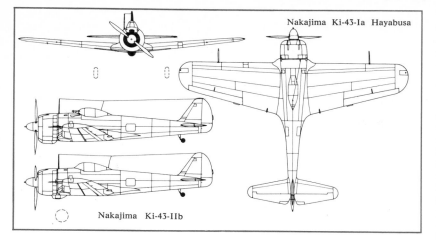

Nakajima Ki-43-Ia Hayabusa

Nakajima Ki-43-IIb

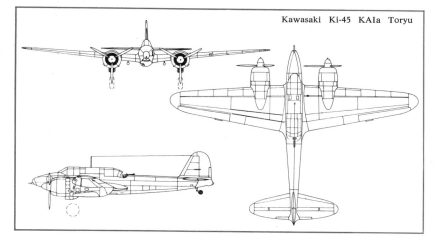

Kawasaki Ki-45 KAIa Toryu

Imperial Army as an interceptor, it was the only one that was able to counter the massive American bombing raids with any success. In all, between August 1941 and July 1945, 1,701 of these aircraft left the assembly lines.

The first prototype appeared in January 1939 but it immediately showed two serious problems: its engine was inefficient and its aerodynamics were poor, so that test flights had to be suspended. The aircraft was substantially redesigned and it was not until May 1941, when the first of three new prototypes appeared, that its final form began to emerge. Designated the Ki-45 KAI (that is, modified) it was for some time used for ground attack (Ki-45 KAIa and Ki-45 KAIb, which differed in armament), and only afterwards with the Ki-45 KAIc model was it used as a night fighter. In common with its German counterparts, this model had two additional oblique, upward-firing machine guns. In the Allied code the Ki-45s were identified by the name of NICK.

In 1942 another single-seat fighter appeared which had been expressly made to answer the needs of the military bases scattered in the little islands of the Pacific, where it was impossible to construct airstrips: this was the Nakajima A6M2-N. Known to the Allies by the code name RUFE, this aircraft was none other than a seaplane model of the carrier-based Mit-

subishi A6M Reisen fighter, the renowned Zero. Between 1941 and 1943, 327 aircraft of this model were produced which were in use up to the end of the war, carrying out their task effectively. In spite of its large floats, its performance compared with that of the Zero was, in fact, only slightly inferior.

Plate 98
German, Romanian, Finnish, Swedish and Australian fighters: 1942–45

A very worthy adversary of Japan's fighters was to be found in a small and warlike Australian aircraft, the Commonwealth CA-12 Boomerang, which

production of this aircraft. The main difference, compared with earlier models, lay in the use of a more powerful engine driving a three-blade, variable pitch metal propeller in place of the single-blade propeller of the Ki-43-I. Aerodynamic improvements were also made and for the first time some armour plating for the pilot and rudimentary self-sealing fuel tanks were introduced. Three models were constructed of the Ki-43-II, the IIa, and the IIb and the KAI; this last incorporated all the various modifications adopted in the course of development.

The final model, manufactured in 1944, was the Ki-43-III, which remained in production until the end of the war. Powered by a 1,250 hp engine, it was undoubtedly the best of the whole series but was produced in the smallest numbers.

Numerically, the Ki-43 was the most significant fighter aircraft of the Imperial Army's air force and it served on all fronts where the Japanese fought. Even though its superiority over Allied fighters did not last for long, the Hayabusa had moments of glory in Malaya, Java and Sumatra, where it seemed almost invincible against the few and outdated Allied aircraft. Its best characteristic was always its manoeuvrability which was simply superb compared with the American fighters of the day.

A contemporary design to the Ki-43 was a substantially different aircraft, the heavy twin-engine fighter, the Kawasaki Ki-45 Toryu (Dragon Slayer). Designed in 1937 to meet a government requirement which was modelled on similar Western achievements, the Toryu suffered from a very long period of development, which only ended in the spring of 1941. Once in service, it was used for much of its career for tasks quite at variance with those for which it had been designed. Only in the last year of the war did it have its moment of success in a role which suited it. A night fighter which had been supplied to the

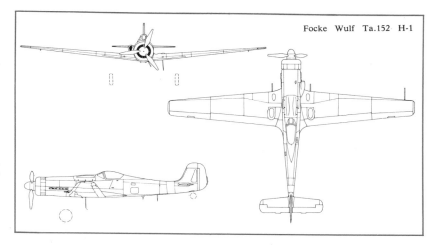

Focke Wulf Ta.152 H-1

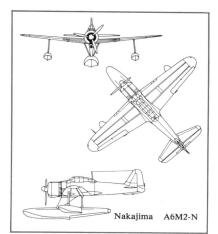

Nakajima A6M2-N

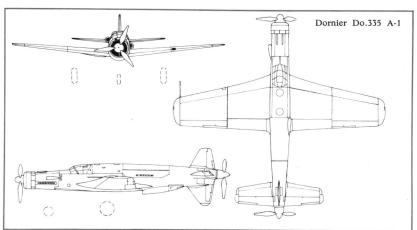

Dornier Do.335 A-1

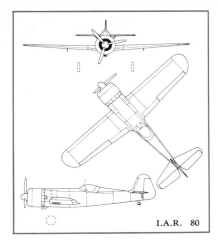

I.A.R. 80

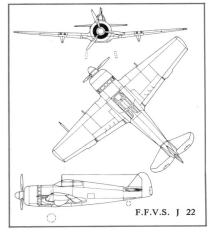

F.F.V.S. J 22

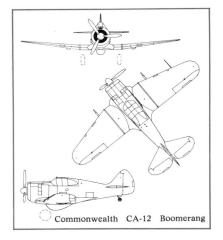

Commonwealth CA-12 Boomerang

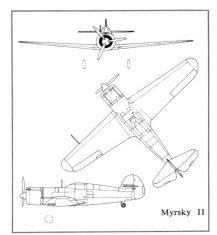

Myrsky II

was also given the designation A46 in the RAAF. Although it was not able to compete well in every respect with the more powerful Japanese aircraft, the Boomerangs showed themselves to be unequalled in tactical use from the middle of 1943, especially in New Guinea, until the arrival of more effective fighter craft from the United States and Britain.

The CA-12 was the only entirely Australian aeroplane to be used in operations during the war and it was designed and constructed within a very brief space of time, from 21st December 1941 to 29th May 1942. Such was Australia's response to the threat of the Japanese invasion. 250 aircraft were produced, which remained in the front line until the last day of the war.

To return to the west, here a desperate struggle for air supremacy was unfolding. The Germans were, in the last years of the war, producing more and more powerful well-armed aircraft as a counter to the ever-increasing Allied strategic bombing. The Dornier Do.335 for instance was designed for interception, an original twin-engine which never became operational. It was endowed with exceptional qualities, especially speed, and the prototype of this aircraft flew in September 1943, but the task of perfecting it proved long and laborious and was also delayed by the scepticism which the originality of the design awakened in the minds of the military authorities. The first production version A-1 appeared towards the end of 1944 and the course of the war put a stop to any subsequent development.

The operational activity of another exceptional interceptor, the Ta.152, was also hampered; this was the final development of the project which had led to the conception of the Focke Wulf Fw.190. It, too, was produced by Kurt Tank, in response to a specific request from the German air ministry. The fighter was essentially conceived for combat and very high altitudes in which domain the Allied bombers held almost complete sway in the last year of the war.

Tank prepared two designs (designated Ta. 152B and H) which differed mainly in wingspan. Of the two the Ta.152H was undoubtedly the more interesting. Its speed at high altitudes was greater than that of any enemy fighter: 748 km/h (465 mph) at 9,150 m (30,000 ft) and 959 km/h (595 mph) at 12,500 m (41,000 ft); its service ceiling was almost 15,000 m (49,200 ft) and, at this height as well, its performance was still exceptional.

The prototype had its maiden flight towards the end of 1944 and the production series of the Ta.152H-I aircraft, which started in January 1945, reach a total of approximately 150. No fighter unit, however, was completely equipped with this aeroplane and its operational activity was reduced on the whole to that of protecting landing strips for the Me.262, in order to ward off the Allied fighters trying to take advantage of the vulnerable moment of take-off to shoot down the jet aeroplanes which otherwise they could not match.

Side by side with the great powers those nations which traditionally played a lesser part in the field of aeronautics did not spare any effort to produce fighter aircraft which they could throw into the maelstrom of the conflict. Romania, for example, put the only fighter of its own original production during the Second World War, the IAR 80, into service in 1942. The prototype flew for the first time towards the end of 1938 and was designed using the experience gained during manufacture under licence of the PZL P.24, of which the rear portion of the fuselage had been adopted, and also the tailplanes and the engines with the corresponding mounting and cowling. The forward and central parts of the fuselage and the wing were, however, completely new. The armament was very powerful and consisted of four 7.7 mm machine guns and two 20 mm cannon. About 120 of the IAR 80 were constructed and remained in service until 1944.

Neutral Sweden also produced a fighter of original design, spurred by the necessity of having at its disposal an efficient air force with which to defend its neutrality. This aircraft was the F.F.V.S. J 22, the prototype of which flew in September 1942. This was a neat single-seater which resembled the German Fw.190 very closely and was of mixed construction in wood and metal and powered by a Pratt & Whitney Twin Wasp 1,065 hp radial engine built under licence. The first production model of the J 22 flew in September 1943 and deliveries to units started two months later. Production amounted to 198 aircraft.

One of the few fighters designed and constructed in Finland during the war years, the Myrsky II, was also powered by a Pratt & Whitney engine constructed under licence in Sweden. This was designed in 1941 and only went into active service in 1944. The four machine guns with which it was armed were mounted in the fuselage and were synchronised to fire through the propeller disc. 50 examples were produced in all.

Plate 99
Great Italian fighters which arrived too late: 1943

The last generation of Italian fighters of the war, the so-called Series V, appeared too late to have any effect on the outcome of the war, which by this time was already predictable. The Macchi M.C. 205, the Fiat G.55 and the Reggiane Re.2005 appeared to be extremely useful aircraft and equalled if they did not surpass the best products of the American, British and German aircraft industries. The three designs, although dissimilar from each other, were linked by a single factor: the German Daimler Benz DB 605 A engine, giving 1,478 hp on take-off, an exceptional power unit which made it possible to produce fighter aircraft of a high standard. Of the three aircraft, the Macchi M.C. 205 Veltro was the first to benefit from the new engine and the only one to have a consistent and effective operational use in the *Regia Aeronautica* before the Armistice.

The prototype of the Veltro (Greyhound) which was designed by Mario Castoldi, flew for the first time on 19th April 1942. The fact that it was derived from the Macchi M.C. 202 was obvious. The new

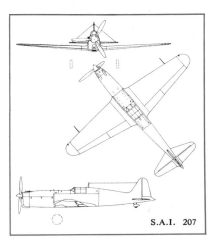

S.A.I. 207

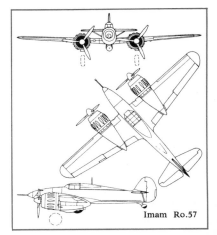

Imam Ro.57

fighter could be distinguished externally from its predecessor by the different configuration of the engine cowling and by the fitting of a circular section oil-cooler. Apart from this it was identical to the Folgore although the Veltro's increased power made it clearly superior in performance: 651 km/h (405 mph) in horizontal flight which was reached by the prototype; 4 minutes 52 seconds to reach 6,000 m (19,690 ft); in its fire power – for the first time 20 mm wing-mounted cannon were used in an Italian fighter; in its manoeuvrability – the increase in power improved on the already noteworthy handling of the 202, especially at medium to low altitudes.

The Veltro was immediately ordered in quantity but production progressed only slowly because of the ever-increasing disruption in the supply of strategic materials and engines. Between October 1942 and September 1943 about 200 models of this aircraft left the assembly lines and reached the *Regia Aeronautica* units, in addition to the 112 that up to March 1944 went to the air force of the RSI (the Italian Social Republic, which followed the fall of fascism in Italy).

The Macchi M.C. 205 went into operational service in April 1943 and was mainly used in the Mediterranean and in Sicily at the time of the Allied landings. After 8th September 1943, 37 aircraft were re-mustered with the Co-Belligerent Air Force and were in active service up to the end of the war, particularly on the Yugoslav front. In the north, the 112 aircraft constructed up to May 1944 joined the 29 aircraft which had escaped and these formed the nucleus of the fighter units of the RSI.

The Fiat G 55 Centauro fought mainly in the air force of the RSI, the *Aviazione Nazionale Repubblicana*. This was the second Series V to be produced. The prototype of this aeroplane, which was generally considered to be the very best and among the more effective of the entire war period, flew on 30th April 1942, but the first production models (about 30) only went into operational service with the *Regia Aeronautica* in June of 1943.

The situation immediately after the Armistice was, however, very different in the north. Twenty of the G 55 Centauro aircraft joined the first *Gruppo Caccia Terrestre* (1st Fighter Wing) of the RSI and subsequently the aircraft (about 130) were all used in the fighter units with which they were kept in active service up to the end of the war. The aircraft, designed by Giuseppe Gabrielli, was powerful, fast and robust and it showed itself to be an unequalled interceptor at high altitudes, and in the air battles which were fought out in the north in the last year of the war they came into confrontation with the best British and American fighters – Spitfires, Mustangs, Thunderbolts and Lightnings. On each occasion the Fiat G.55

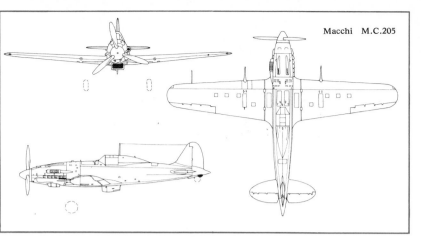

Macchi M.C.205

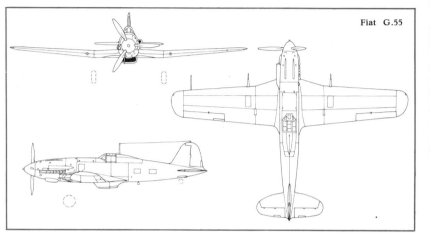

Fiat G.55

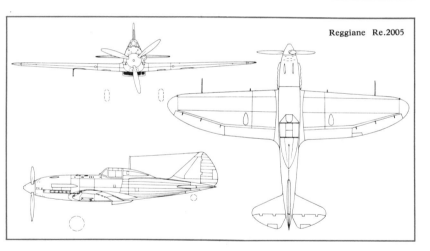

Reggiane Re.2005

proved that it was a fearsome antagonist and not to be understimated. Compared with the Macchi M.C. 205 the Fiat fighter was considerably faster above 7,000 m (22,970 ft), more modern and more powerfully armed. It had two 12.7 mm synchronised machine guns firing through the propeller disc; two 20 mm cannon in the wings and a third cannon which fired through the propeller hub.

The third Series V fighter, the Reggiane Re.2005 Sagittario, had a very brief operational career (from May 1943) since it suffered from a structural defect in the rear fuselage which led to the suspension of flights on 26th August 1943, whilst awaiting

technical modifications which were never carried out. This drawback, which would have been easy to remedy in normal times, was the only unfavourable feature of the Sagittario when compared with its two contemporaries. Apart from this, the Re.2005 was in some ways, such as manoeuvrability, definitely better than its most direct competitor, the Fiat G 55.

The prototype, which made its official flight on 9th May 1942, struck observers as the best fighter to come out of the Reggiane factory and did indeed represent the culmination of a long series which had evolved from the Re.2000 of 1939. Mass production (in the official programme 750 Reggiane

2000, 600 Fiat G 55 and 250 Macchi M.C. 205 were envisaged, a choice which led to a great waste of time and energy) was not, however, immediately authorised. The air ministry first ordered 16 zero series models, then another 18 pre-series aircraft, and only in February 1943 gave the green light for the main order.

The only Sagittarios which left the assembly lines were the first 29. Their operational use took place mainly in Campania and in Sicily and, at the time of the Armistice, the few Reggiane 2005s which survived were destroyed by the crews of the *Regia Aeronautica*. Six were used for training in the RSI air units, others (probably 13) were seized by the Germans and taken to Germany.

The industrial effort of Italy's last year in the war also gave life to other interesting designs. Among these was the one that led to the SAI 207, a light interceptor of completely wooden construction whch was capable of excellent performance in consideration of its engine power, which was of barely 750 hp. This aircraft answered the need for a low-cost fighter which would not use strategic materials and yet which was effective as a fighter. In practice, however, production was limited to a dozen models.

The Imam Ro.57, however, was a complete failure. This was a heavy twin-engine fighter which had been designed as far back as 1939 but left in cold storage up to 1942. When the programme was resumed because of wartime demands, the aircraft was already obsolete. However, a small number were produced in two models: an interceptor and another for ground attack.

Plate 100
The Mustang — perhaps the best fighter of all: 1943–45

It was in the second half of the war that the aircraft which has been unanimously described as the best fighter of the Second World War appeared, the North American P-51 Mustang. This superb aircraft, in its last variants, was one of the most advanced and successful aircraft powered by the piston engine, and was the product of two technologies which were ahead of their time: the United States aeronautics industry which succeeded in achieving the construction of an airframe which was very advanced in structure and aerodynamics in the brief period of 117 days, and also the technology of the British motor industry which with its famous Rolls-Royce Merlin engine supplied the ideal complement. Indeed the Mustang would have been doomed to obscurity had it not been fitted with the British engine.

The project which was to bring the P-51 into being was conducted from the very beginning in the spirit of collaboration between Britain and the United States. In April 1940 the British Purchasing Commission which had been sent to the United States, in its feverish search for good fighter planes, made a proposal to North American that they should construct the Curtiss P-40 fighter under licence for the RAF. This idea was not to the liking of the President of the company, J. H. "Dutch" Kindelberger, who rejoined that his company was capable of constructing a fighter plane equipped with the same engine as the P-40 (Allison V-1710 liquid-cooled V-12) but superior to the P-40.

This counter-proposal was accepted by the British who stipulated only one condition: that the prototype should be completed without fail within 120 days, given the gravity of the situation in Europe. This deadline was fulfilled with time to spare: the designers Raymond Rice and Edgar Schmued managed to complete the NA-73X (as the prototype was designated) three days before the deadline. The first flight took place on 26th October 1940 and the aeroplane, which was distinguished by great purity of line, revealed something more than good general features, demonstrating that it was superior in speed to the Curtiss P-40 by about 40 km/h (25 mph).

Meanwhile the contract for 320 aircraft for the RAF had been approved by the American government on the understanding that two aircraft would be delivered to the USAAC for proving flights. The first production series fighter flew on 1st May 1941 and was taken over by North American for proving flights. The second arrived in Britain in November, where it was given the official designation of Mustang Mk I. These aircraft, which were considered far superior to any other American fighter, were put into service in April 1942 and used for tactical reconnaissance.

More or less at the same time the British ordered 300 examples of the aircraft, differing only in certain details of equipment and in the armament carried. In the United States, after an initial period of lack of interest (a mere 50 Mustangs had been adapted to photographic reconnaissance), the military authorities placed a large order for 500 of a version which had been specially adapted as a dive-bomber and which had been designated A-36A. These aircraft were delivered between September 1942 and March 1943. They were followed

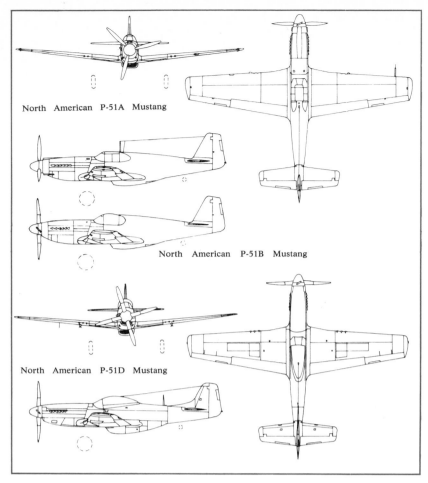

North American P-51A Mustang

North American P-51B Mustang

North American P-51D Mustang

by another order for 310 P-51As, deliveries of which started in the spring of 1943.

The Mustang, however, was still far from having reached its ideal configuration. The idea which brought this aircraft to its final form came almost simultaneously to the British engineers and to their trans-atlantic colleagues: in Britain four Mustang aircraft were handed over to Rolls-Royce so that they could undergo a series of tests with the Merlin 61 engine: in the United States two aircraft were entrusted to North American in order that they should carry out the same exercise with the version of the Merlin engine which was constructed under licence by Packard and designated V-6150-3.

In September 1942 the first prototype to be equipped with this engine appeared, designated the P-51B. Among its performance figures can be quoted: 708 km/h (440 mph) at 9,145 m (30,000 ft) and 5 minutes and 54 seconds to climb to 6,100 m (20,000 ft) altitude. This was a considerable leap forward when compared with the 628 km/h (390 mph) at 6,100 m and the time in excess of 9 minutes which the P-51A had needed to climb to the same altitude. The aircraft was immediately put into mass production in the summer of 1943 and constructed at Inglewood as the P-51B (1,988 built) and in the new Dallas factory as the P-51C (1,750).

The British, who received 1,000 P-51s, called these aircraft the Mustang Mk III. The first P-51B went into service with the US 8th Air Force stationed in England on 1st December 1943.

In the spring of 1944 the largest production model of the war made its appearance, the P-51D. On the basis of the RAF's experiments with its Mustang Mk IIIs in which, in order to improve the pilot's visibility, a streamlined frameless teardrop canopy was installed (called the Malcolm Sliding Canopy after its inventor), North American had decided to tackle the problem of visibility once and for all. In the P-51D the rear part of the fairing of the pilot's cockpit was eliminated and a sponson was added to compensate for the reduction in lateral surface and the pilot's cabin was covered with a completely transparent bubble hood. 7,956 Mustang P-51Ds were built and with 1,700 hp reached a speed of 703 km/h (437 mph) at an altitude of 7,620 m (25,000 ft).

The last variant, the P-51H, completed in time to take part in the last operations against Japan and of which 555 were built was, however, the fastest: 784 km/h (487 mph) at an altitude of 7,600 m (24,935 ft).

The operational career of the Mustang went far beyond its constant use on all fronts during the Second World War. It was in service with the air forces of about 20 countries and it was

in use in Korean War and was only replaced by the first jet fighters. Overall, in its various versions, production reached 15,686 models.

Plate 101
Fighters for the Mikado's army: 1943–44

In the Pacific theatre of operations the Japanese effort to add to and renew their first-line fighters was intense and it continued for the whole duration of the war. In the army air force, the Nakajima Ki-43 Hayabusa was a useful aircraft and kept in production in versions that were continually brought up to date and given greater power, but in spite of this it belonged to a generation of fighter aircraft which had been conceived before the war and, as such, was incapable of maintaining its initial superiority when faced with the new Allied fighters, in particular the American fighters. The first models of a completely new aircraft reached units in February of 1943: an aircraft which completely broke away from the traditional design philosophy of the Japanese industry.

The Kawasaki Ki-61 Hien (TONY in Allied code) was the only fighter put into action by the Japanese during the course of the war which was equipped with a liquid-cooled engine. So unusual did the Hien appear to its enemies that it was at first mistaken for an aircraft of German or Italian origin. In fact, apart from the engine (which was none other than a licence-manufactured Daimler Benz DB 601 A), the design was completely original. Work had been started in April 1940 at the same time as the acquisition by Kawasaki of the construction rights of the German engine.

The designers, Takeo Doi and Shin Owada, had completed the prototype before the end of the following year and the first flight had taken place in December 1941. It was precisely the engine, however, which was the Achilles heel of the new fighter, which from all other points of view was excellent. This engine was difficult to perfect and subject to continual damage and breakdown and was also characterised by inherent defects which were never eliminated.

Between August 1942 and August 1945 3,078 examples of the Hien were constructed in four principal versions. Among these, after the initial variant, the Ki-61-I, the most important were the Ki-61-KAIc which appeared in January 1943 and the Ki-61-II KAI in September of the same year. The latter had a 1,500 hp engine which enabled the aircraft to achieve its best overall performance.

Between 1942 and 1943 two other new fighter aircraft appeared in the front line, more orthodox than the Ki-61, but nonetheless useful. Indeed the Nakajima Ki-84 Hayate (FRANK in the Allied code) and the Nakajima Ki-44 Shoki (TOJO) proved themselves to be among the best combat aircraft produced in Japan in the course of the entire war.

In particular the Ki-44 showed that it was an outstanding interceptor, due to its excellent maximum speed and climbing rate. The first prototype took to the air in August 1940. It was a very small aircraft, as small an airframe as could be constructed around the large radial 1,250 hp Nakajima Ha-41 engine. After a long period of development in order to improve the aerodynamics of the aircraft, the Ki-44 was accepted by the army in September 1942.

Barely 40 examples were constructed of the initial variant Ki-44-I: immediately afterwards production was switched to the Ki-44-II version which had a more powerful engine, more powerful armament and still further improved performance. The aircraft of the second series, Ki-44-IIb, showed itself to be the best of all: maximum speed of 605 km/h (376 mph) at 5,200 m (17,060 ft) with a climbing time to 5,000 m (16,400 ft) of 4 minutes and 17 seconds.

These aircraft were used mainly in the defence of Japan and were armed with 20 mm, 37 mm and 40 mm cannon in the Ki-44-IIc series. They succeeded in scoring notable successes against the American bombers.

The last variant which appeared in prototype form in June 1943 was the Ki-44-III, which had a Nakajima Ha-145 engine giving 2,000 hp on take-off. Although two sub-types were produced which differed in armament, this aeroplane was constructed in only small numbers. In fact production was suspended at the end of 1944 in favour of the Ki-84 Hayate. In all, 1,225 examples of the Shoki were constructed.

The reasons behind the decision to give priority to the production of the Ki-84 in the last year of the war were based on the general performance of this Nakajima design. Above all, the Hayate was not so difficult to handle as the Shoki, the poor control of which was caused by the high wing loading of the aircraft. The Ki-84 had been designed during 1942 and 1943, and in the summer of 1943 the first models of a pre-series production of 83 reached the test pilots for proving flights.

In October an experimental unit was equipped with the new aircraft and, given the promising results obtained under operational conditions, it was decided to start immediately with mass-production through a vast programme which involved various aircraft manufacturers. Desperate efforts were made in this direction: despite the chaos and the destruction caused by the American bombing, as many as 3,514 of the Ki-84 were completed in a year and a half. After the basic version Ki-84-I, the Ki-84-II was added in 1944, partially constructed in non-strategic materials. Other variants were considered in the last months of the war, but remained at the drawing-board stage.

The development of another very promising combat fighter, the Mitsubishi Ki-83, was similarly blocked in the course of the war. This elegant twin-engine aircraft appeared in prototype form on 18th November 1944 and was intended to carry out the role of long-range escort fighter. Its performance was impressive in every respect: 705 km/h (438 mph) at 9,000 m (29,530 ft), armed with 4 cannon, and with a manoeuvrability which equalled that of the best of its single-engine contemporaries.

A similar heavy fighter, on the other hand, appeared in 1944 of which 238 were constructed. The Kawasaki Ki-102 (Allied code-name RANDY) had been designed towards the end of 1943 in order to replace the Ki-45 Toryu in all its functions. Three versions had been envisaged: the Ki-102a (26 constructed) as a fighter; the Ki-102b (238) for ground attack; the Ki-102c (which remained at prototype stage) as a night fighter. The disastrous turn of events in the war put a stop to any subsequent development.

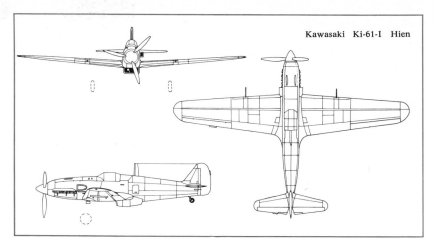

Kawasaki Ki-61-I Hien

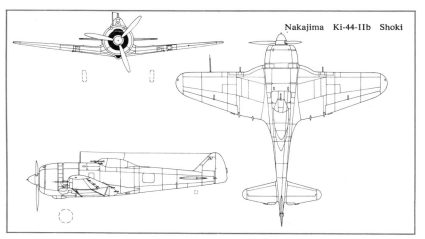

Nakajima Ki-44-IIb Shoki

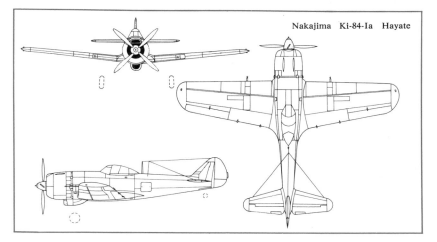

Nakajima Ki-84-Ia Hayate

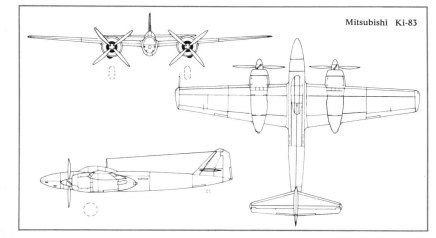

Mitsubishi Ki-83

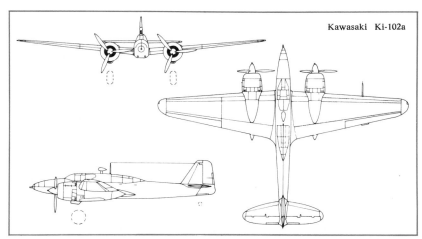

Kawasaki Ki-102a

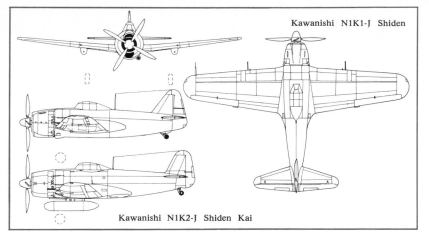
Kawanishi N1K1-J Shiden

Kawanishi N1K2-J Shiden Kai

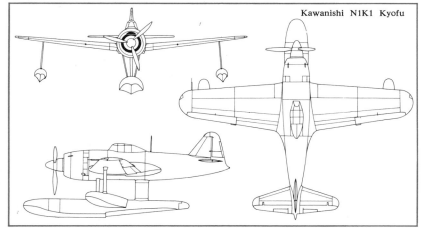
Kawanishi N1K1 Kyofu

**Plate 102
Fighters for the Japanese Navy: 1943–44**

The Japanese Navy, in spite of having at its disposal various versions of the famous Zero fighter, also continually improved and added to the power of its front-line fighters. The aircraft turned out by Kawanishi in the last years of the war were particularly interesting, and made their mark among the best produced by Japanese industry in the course of the war. The N1K1-J and the N1K2-J Shiden and Shiden KAI types (in practice two versions of the same aircraft) were among the few Japanese fighter aircraft which were capable of competing on equal terms with the more effective aircraft of their adversaries such as the American Hellcat and Corsair. Although production totalled 1,435 examples in the last two years of the war, the use of these machines was always sporadic and above all made difficult by the critical condition in which Japan found itself at the time, besieged and confronted with the military might of the Allies.

Perhaps unique in the history of fighter aircraft, these excellent land-based fighters were derived from a seaplane. The idea which gave rise to the production of the N1K1-J came to the engineers of Kawanishi at the end of 1941, when the first prototype of

the seaplane fighter Kawanishi N1K Kyofu was at an advanced stage of design. The project for a seaplane fighter had been ordered by the Imperial Navy in 1940 and the first prototype had flown on 6th May 1942, showing that it had excellent general performance. Moreover, the Kyofu (REX in Allied code) in spite of a very long development period and successive delays in production which led to only 89 series N1K1s being completed, fully justified expectations during the course of its brief operational service between 1943 and 1944. From this N1K design, therefore, the Kawanishi engineers adapted and modified the prototypes of land-based fighters, the first example of which took

to the air on 27th December 1941.

This initiative had been taken without official authorisation and when Kawanishi offered one of the 5 experimental models to the Navy, having completed these models for testing and proving flights, they found it was received with a great deal of scepticism. It took until 1943 for the aeroplane to be officially accepted and put into production after a series of modifications to the engine and to the undercarriage. Its entry into service, however, was subsequently delayed by difficulties which were encountered in the training of pilots and by logistical problems. But in the end, once it was operational, the GEORGE (this was the Allied code-name for the N1K1-Z Shiden) justified the foresight of its designers, and showed itself to be a superb aircraft and regarded with a good deal of respect by Allied pilots.

There were still, however, numerous defects which had to be eliminated and, most important among them, that of the main landing gear, which had a very complicated mechanism, and poor forward visibility particularly for landing and taking off. On 31st December 1943 a new version of the fighter, the N1K2-J Shiden KAI flew for the first time. In fact this was a very different aircraft from its predessor, of which the wing, the engine and the armament were all that was retained. The most noteworthy modification lay in the lowering of the wing to the level of the lower fuselage in order to shorten and simplify the landing gear and thus improve forward visibility. This had made it necessary to redesign the fuselage and the tailplane. The new fighter, however, accomplished its proving flights superbly well and was accepted by the fleet without reservations. Production was started in June 1944, but in spite of a vast programme, the high production levels which had been envisaged were not attained: only 415 aircraft left the assembly lines before the end of the year.

The successor to the Shiden obscured that of another promising contemporary fighter, the Mitsubishi J2M Raiden, production of which was slowed down on purpose to the very minimum in June 1944 in favour of the

N1K2-J. From the time of its appearance as a prototype, in February 1942, the Raiden had been dogged by a series of problems connected mainly with the engine and the undercarriage. Attempts to find solutions to these shortcomings had first slowed down the development stage and then even led to the suspension of the production of the first series. Towards the end of 1943 the principal variant, the J2M3, appeared which, although improved, was not competitive with the Kawanishi fighter. It was this which led to the decision to slow down its production. Overall, 476 Raidens (JACK in Allied code) left the assembly lines. The greater part of these were used defending Japan against American bombing in the last desperate months of the conflict.

**Plate 103
Fighters which helped the US Navy to achieve victory: 1943–44**

On the Pacific front, air supremacy was finally achieved by the United States in 1943 when the two best carrier-based fighters of the war appeared in the front line, the Vought 4FU Corsair and the Grumman F6F Hellcat. In particular the Corsair went down in history as the very best of its type and in certain aspects was even better than the P-51 Mustang. The principal data of the operational career of this powerful fighter plane are a witness to its success: it remained in production for over 10 years and in service up to 1965; 12,681 aircraft were produced in numerous versions; in the course of the war in the Pacific theatre of operations alone, the Corsairs shot down 2,140 enemy aircraft in a total of 64,051 missions against only 189 losses.

The project got under way at the beginning of 1938 following a request from the US Navy which on 30th June ordered the construction of a prototype. The head designer of Vought, Tex B. Beisel, designed the aircraft starting with the basic idea of marrying the most powerful engine available (the new Pratt & Whitney XR-2800 Double Wasp, an 18-cylinder radial

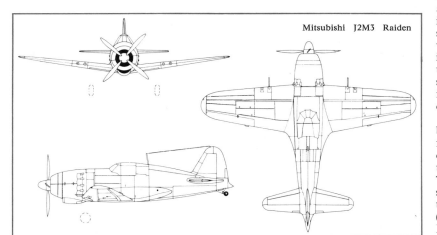
Mitsubishi J2M3 Raiden

engine of 2,000 hp which was being perfected at that time) with the smallest compatible airframe.

The result of this approach made its maiden flight on 29th May 1940, immediately revealing great potential: on 1st October the XF4U-1 reached 650 km/h (404 mph) thus becoming the first fighter produced in the USA to exceed 400 mph. The production programme, however, encountered a series of difficulties whilst perfecting the aircraft: in order to increase its fire-power it was vital to relocate the fuel tanks and this meant that the cockpit was repositioned some 90 cms (35.4 inches) further aft at the expense of forward visibility. It was precisely this last feature which subsequently led to a delay of over a year in the carrier-based use of the Corsair.

On 30th June 1941 an initial contract for 584 F4U-1s was signed and the first production model appeared a year later. Before the end of 1942 the US Navy received 178 aircraft but waited until April 1944 before declaring the fighter to be acceptable for carrier operations. The Corsair, therefore, first saw combat with land-based Marine Corps squadrons; it saw operations on 13th February 1943 at Guadalcanal.

In the meantime production was going ahead. With the sub-series F4U-1A, a different type of canopy was introduced in order to improve the pilot's vision, while with the F4U-1D of 1944 a more powerful engine and armament were introduced. These last Corsairs were to be built in the greatest numbers, 4,102 by Vought; 3,808 by Goodyear (who called them the FG-1); 735 by Brewster (who called them the F3A-1).

Britain received 2,012 of them and New Zealand 370. The final version of the war period was the F4U with a 2,450 hp engine, only a few of which saw operational service before the end of hostilities with Japan. However, a total of 2,356 aircraft were constructed up to 1st August 1947 and this was followed by 509 F4U-5s (more powerful engine and armament apart from structural modifications), by 110 AU-1s (tactical support version) and by 94 F4U-7s which were produced for the French who intended to use them in Indochina.

The production of the Grumman F6F Hellcat on the other hand was limited to the war period. The assembly lines for this aircraft were closed in November 1945 after completing 12,272 aircraft. This was an equal number to that of the Corsairs, but concentrated into only 3 years of production. This shows the much more massive use that the US Navy and the US Marine Corps made of the Hellcat during the course of the war. And in this case as well the figures tell an impressive story: of the 6,477 enemy aircraft destroyed in combat by this aircraft, as many as 4,947 fell victim to the carrier-based F6Fs.

The contract for production of two

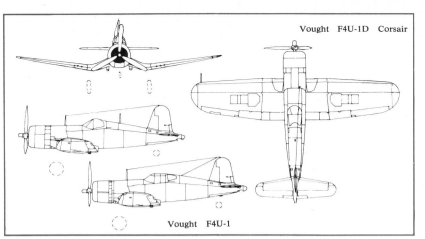

Vought F4U-1D Corsair

Vought F4U-1

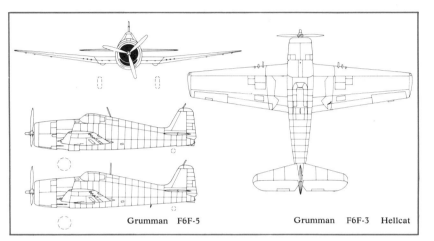

Grumman F6F-5

Grumman F6F-3 Hellcat

prototypes of a new carrier-based fighter which was to replace the F4F Wildcat was signed by Grumman on 30th June 1941. The programme went ahead very quickly and the first prototype flew on 26th June 1942. Production was started within the year and on 16th January 1943 the first delivery reached the aircraft carrier, the USS *Essex*. Little more than seven months later the F6F-3s went into action for the first time over Marcus Island.

In the meantime, production continued at a steady rate. In the course of 1943 2,545 F6F-3s were delivered and units of the British Fleet Air Arm were also re-equipped with these, receiving 252 of them which they called the Hellcat Mk I, putting them into service in July 1943. Before production was switched to the F6F-5 model in April 1944, 4,405 F6F-3s were completed. Of these, 223 were equipped as night-fighters: they were designated F6F-3E and F6F-3N, and were equipped with radar on a wing pod.

The first Hellcat of the largest production variant, the F6F-5, flew on 4th April 1944. These aircraft differed from their predecessors in their engine, in having extra armour, in their armament, and in structural details. The F6F-5s (7,868 of these aircraft were built) were also adapted as night-fighters in the same way as the F6F-3. 1,434 of the F6F-5N series

were built, the modifications being carried out on the assembly line. The British Royal Navy received a total of 932 F6F-5s, of which 70 were equipped with radar, and they called them the Hellcat Mk II. A last sub-type of which only a few were built was the photographic reconnaissance plane, the F6F-5P.

From the attack on 31st August 1943 against the Japanese installations on Marcus Island onwards, the operational career of the Hellcat continued unchecked. It participated in all the air-sea and amphibious operations and these F6Fs earned themselves a lasting reputation, particularly after they had fully demonstrated their superiority over the Japanese fighters and over the Zero in particular.

Plate 104
The USAF's last fighters of the Second World War: 1943

Another combat aircraft which contributed in a noteworthy manner towards consolidating Allied supremacy in the last two years of the war was the Republic P-47 Thunderbolt. This is considered to be the greatest of the heavy single-engine, single-seat fighters constructed during the course of the war. The Thunderbolt showed itself to be an exceptional bomber escort and ground-attack bomber. A total of 15,683 of these aircraft were constructed and saw widespread operational use from the first months of 1943 onwards. After fighting on all fronts the Thunderbolt survived the war and was used in the air forces of some 15 countries.

The P-47 represented the culmination of a line of aircraft which had started way back in 1936 with the Seversky P-35 and which had evolved by the way of the unfortunate P-43 Lancer. Shortly after beginning the latter project in 1939, Alexander Kartveli, the head designer of Republic, also started work on two other aircraft derived from it. They were designated respectively the AP-4 and the AP-10 and they differed from each other substantially.

The former was driven by a very powerful radial engine while the latter was redesigned around the V-12 liquid-cooled Allison engine and was conceived as a light fighter of small dimensions. It was from the second of these, paradoxically, that the Thunderbolt originated: massive and weighing almost 9 tonnes on take-off.

When Kartveli submitted the AP-10 project to the technical branch of the USAAC on 1st August 1939 they turned it down with the request that he should develop a larger and more powerful version. In November the company drew up a contract for two prototypes (to be designated XP-47 and XP-47A), also powered by the liquid-cooled Allison. The idea, however, was mistaken from the outset in that the first experiences of the war in Europe had already started to impose new requirements in armament, performance, and armour for a fighter aircraft, demands which the Allison engine, with its inferior power and its mediocre performance at high altitude, was not capable of satisfying. Becoming aware of all this, Kartveli drew up an alternative design incorporating the most powerful engine available, the new Pratt & Whitney Double Wasp 2,000 hp radial. The proposal was submitted to the army in June 1940 and accepted without reservation. The XP-47B prototype was bought off the drawing-board with an initial order for 772 aircraft.

The aircraft flew for the first time on

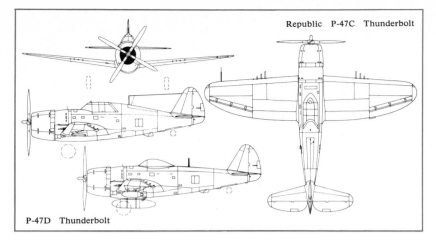

Republic P-47C Thunderbolt

P-47D Thunderbolt

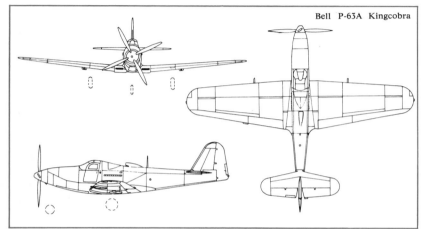

Bell P-63A Kingcobra

Plate 105
The Germans are the first to put jet fighters into service: 1944–45

The final effort of the Third Reich was mainly concentrated on the airborne interceptor. It could scarcely be otherwise since the main threat was formed by the continuous, devastating incursions of the Allied bombers into German air space. On 28th July 1944, over Merseburg, formations of American B-17s found themselves confronted by a new and revolutionary adversary: a small and very fast fighter powered in a completely unconventional way which made lightning attacks. This was the Messerschmitt Me.163 Komet, a rocket-powered interceptor whose entry into combat service started a new phase of the war in the air, giving the Germans the edge over the Allies in technical terms, and which, had it been introduced a year earlier, could well have had a great effect on the course of the war. And yet the Me.163 arrived too late and its brief career was drastically curtailed in Germany's death agony, the scarcity of fuel, production difficulties and the lack of time left in which to perfect the aircraft and train the pilots properly.

In all, little more than 300 of these aircraft left the assembly lines before production was interrupted: the

majority of these were of the B-1a model (237 aircraft in 1944 and 42 in January 1945), the only model to be operational. This project was started towards the end of 1938 by Alexander Lippisch and Helmuth Walter: the former was responsible for the design of the airframe, drawing on his long experience gained from 1926 onwards in the study of glider wings; the latter had perfected the revolutionary jet engine which bore his name.

The first prototype flew on 13th August 1941, the first of the Me.163b series on 21st February two years later and the first operational flight took place on 13th May 1944 from the Bad Zwischenahn base. The Me.163 took off by means of a jettisonable take-off trolley and landed on a skid like a glider, without any power.

But the Germans unveiled other surprises for the Allied strategists who were already alarmed by the appearance of the Komet. In the autumn of 1944 American bomber formations began to be attacked by another revolutionary fighter: the Messerschmitt Me.262, a jet fighter, the first to be operational in the history of aviation, an aircraft which brought to an end the age of the piston engine and propeller and which opened that of the modern fighter plane. The Me.262 could certainly have had a much bigger effect on the course of the war if it had been used in the role to which it was best suited, that of a pure interceptor.

6th May the following year and in March 1942 the first aircraft of the production series started to leave the assembly line. 170 P-47Bs and 602 P-47Cs were produced and also an experimental aircraft equipped with a pressurised cockpit – the P-47E.

The Thunderbolt went into service in January 1943 with the 56th Fighter Group of the US 8th Air Force based in Britain and immediately shows its great qualities in combat; the fighters had very high speed and rate of climb, heavy firepower, and were exceptionally sturdy.

Production of the P-47 really reached its zenith with the appearance of the P-47D variant which was constructed in the largest numbers. It was equipped with engines that were more powerful at high altitude and in emergency and with a notable increase in weaponry.

Thunderbolts were built in numerous production runs. From the P-47D-25 onwards an important modification was adopted similar to that introduced in the P-51 Mustang: the installation of a completely transparent bubble hood which ensured visibility of 360 degrees for the pilot. The P-47Ds were the first to see service in the Pacific with the USAAF units and also the first to be delivered in quantity to Allied air forces: foremost amongst them were the Soviet Union which received 195 of these aircraft, Britain, Brazil, Mexico, and Free French units.

The final variant, which was not in time to be used *en masse* in the conflict, was the P-47N. Designed especially to meet the demands of the war in the Pacific theatre, only 1,800 were built. It had more powerful armament, a more powerful engine and increased range. The last deliveries took place in December 1945.

The Bell P-63 Kingcobra, the final derivative of the P-39 Airacobra family, went in large numbers to the Soviet Union, over two-thirds (2,400) of the production which had totalled 3,303 up to 1945. In fact the USAAF never considered this aircraft to be of much use and only employed it as a target tug. The aircraft had flown for the first time in December 1942 and was derived from the P-39 in structure and in general configuration; the difference lay in the wing, in the tailplanes and in the engine. 1,725 of the P-63A model were built.

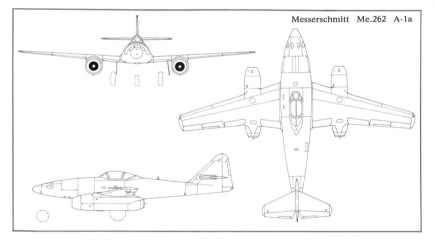

Messerschmitt Me.262 A-1a

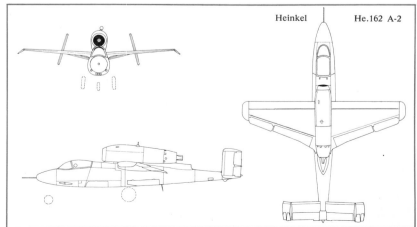

Heinkel He.162 A-2

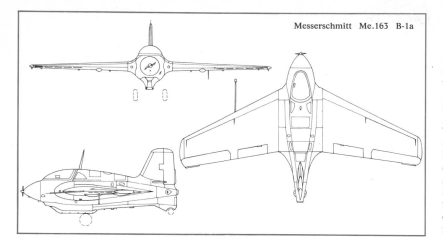

Messerschmitt Me.163 B-1a

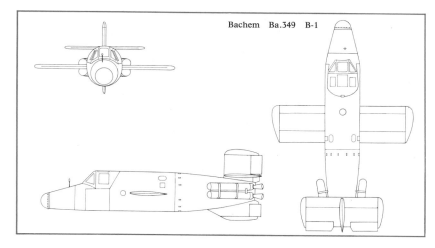

Bachem Ba.349 B-1

Apart from this there was yet another prototype, one more desperate weapon which was thrown into the fray by the Germans in the last months of the war: the Bachem Ba.349. This was, properly speaking, a piloted rocket armed with a battery of 73 mm rockets in the fuselage and powered by a Walter 509 2,000 kg thrust engine. The method of operation was simple and radical: take-off from a vertical launching ramp and attainment of operational altitude by means of an automatic pilot, seeking out the target and attacking it under the control of the pilot, who then abandoned the aircraft by means of a parachute after the rocket engine had burned itself out.

The unmanned flight was carried out by a prototype in December 1944 and the operational test flight only took place on 28th February 1945. This however came to an unfortunate end with the destruction of the aircraft and the death of the test pilot.

Plate 106
Last prototypes of the Japanese war machine: 1945

Similar in every way to the German industrial effort in the last months of the war was the desperate Japanese search for a fighter aircraft capable of halting – or at least of mitigating – the growing and continuous menace of the Allied bombardment. The last fighter which the Imperial Army put into the field was the Kawasaki Ki-100, a machine which, although it was a lash-up conversion of the last model of the Ki-61, proved itself to be one of the best high-altitude interceptors during its few months of operation. The 396 aircraft which were completed between February and August 1945 all saw concentrated operational service, particularly against the American bomber formations.

The spur which led to the building of the Ki-100 was, on a technical level, the continuing unreliability of the series of liquid-cooled engines which Japanese industry made under licence from Germany. Production of these power units had been so inadequate that in the second half of 1944 the availability of Ki-61 airframes had greatly outstripped that of the engines which should have been installed in them. Consequently, in November,

Instead production was spread over a series of variants in which attempts were made to adapt the aircraft in various ways, first as a bomber then as a night fighter. The result of this policy, which originated with Hitler himself, was that out of the 1,430 aircraft produced in the last months of the war only a small proportion (less than a quarter) saw operational use and therefore made a very insignificant impact on the progress of the war.

The project had been started off towards the end of 1938: the aircraft was to be powered by a pair of new jet engines which were in course of development at BMW and Junkers. Delays in perfecting these revolutionary power units affected the progress of the project to a great extent and it was 18th July 1942 before the first test flight could be successfully accomplished. The fighter was demonstrated to Hermann Göring on 23rd July 1943 and on 26th November to Hitler himself: he insisted that the aircraft should be used as a bomber and this decision further held up production.

The first pre-series models were ready in the spring of 1944. The initial variant, designated A-1a, was equipped with four 30 mm cannon. It was followed by the A-1a/U1, U/2 and U/3 sub-types, the first having six cannon, the second and the third being designed for all-weather fighting and photographic reconnaissance. Subsequently the bomber versions were

produced, the Me.262 A-2a with a 2,200 lb (1,000 kg) bomb-load, and the Me.262 A-3a in a ground attack role. In October 1944 the final transformation of the aircraft into a night fighter was begun, as a two-seater equipped with radar.

In spite of this excessive diversification of production, the Me.262 showed itself to be an exceptional aircraft: faster than any other existing aircraft, manoeuvrable and heavily armed. These aircraft in fact represented the *Luftwaffe*'s swansong.

The Germans did not succeed in putting their other jet interceptor into action. This was the Heinkel He.162 Salamander, which was simpler and less costly than the Me.262 but no less effective. Progress from drawing board to flight took barely three months, between September and December 1944. The first prototype flew on 6th December followed by two more and by 31 pre-series models which were all tested in January 1945.

The production models were designated He.162A-2, but in practice they saw little if any action. Production schedules envisaged 4,000 planes a month but only about 100 were completed. The Heinkel He.162's structure was somewhat unusual. The engine (an 800 kg thrust BMW) was mounted on top of the fuselage. It had slanted twin tailplanes and the pilot's cockpit was equipped with an ejector seat.

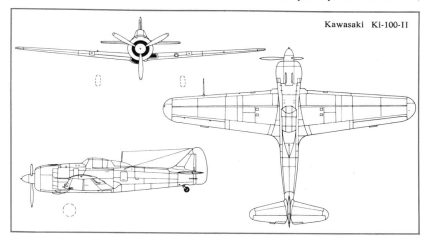

Kawasaki Ki-100-II

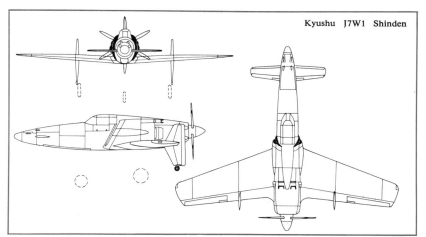

Kyushu J7W1 Shinden

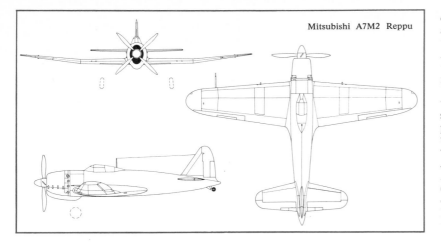

Mitsubishi A7M2 Reppu

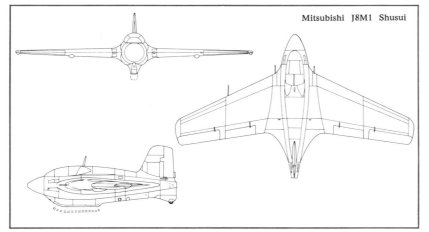

Mitsubishi J8M1 Shusui

whilst awaiting the engines, it was decided to use the numerous Ki-61-II KAIs and to install a different power unit in them. This was the Mitsubishi Ha-112-II, a 1,500 hp radial engine of sufficiently small diameter to fit the slim fuselage of the Ki-61.

The first flight of the "new" fighter took place on 1st February 1945, and production was immediately started with the use of 275 airframes which had already been prepared for the Ki-61-II KAI. In the event performance of the Ki-100 did not turn out to be very different from that of its predecessor but, if nothing else, the aircraft was at least free of any serious problems. The first production version was made in two principal series, the Ia and the Ib, and this latter was constructed from the start as a Ki-100 (106 produced). In an attempt to improve performance at high altitude still further, Kawasaki started to develop a second variant in the month of March, the Ki-100-II, aerodynamically improved and with an up-rated engine. The first prototype flew in May 1945, and was joined by two further aircraft before the end of the war.

The Mitsubishi A-7M Reppu, however, was never used operationally. According to the Imperial Navy's plans, it was meant to replace the Mitsubishi A6M as a carrier-based fighter. The specification for its production was actually issued in 1940 but only 9 prototypes and 1 production model

were completed before the end of the war. This almost unbelievable delay was caused first by continual postponements of the project due to the priority given to other models, and then by disputes between the designer, Jiro Horikoshi (the "father" of the Zero) and the technical branch of the Navy, on the choice of the most suitable engine; and finally as a direct result of wartime events. The A7M2 prototype flew on 13th October 1944. The one and only production model was called SAM in Allied code.

The desperate need for an interceptor fighter of high performance pushed Japanese industry to the most unusual expedients. One of these was an aircraft which was undoubtedly unique: the Kyushu J7W Shinden which, with its undoubtedly original configuration, became the only aircraft in the world of the "canard" type (that is, with the elevators positioned at the front extremity of the fuselage instead of at the rear), and was ordered into mass production during the later years of the Second World War. The vicissitudes of the last months of the war, however, prevented the achievement of such a project which was based on a monthly production rate of 150 aircraft. Only two Shinden prototypes were completed and the first of these (J7W1) flew (for a total of 45 minutes) on 3rd August 1945, 12 days before the Japanese surrender.

The Mitsubishi J8M Shusui was a

direct copy of a German design, being a Messerschmitt Me.163b constructed under licence in Japan. The Mitsubishi J8M even copied the jettisoned trolley system take-off and sprung skid landing system from the German model. Unlike its Luftwaffe twin, however, this rocket-powered aircraft did not see operational service. Out of the 7 prototypes which Mitsubishi managed to complete in the last months of the war, only one was flown (J8M1 on 7th July 1945) and with disastrous results. An unexpected failure of the engine (this too built under licence) while climbing immediately after take-off, led to the crash of the aeroplane and the death of the test pilot. The engineers finally managed to discover the cause of the accident (defective installation of the fuel system) and modified the other 6 prototypes. By then, however, the war was over.

Plate 107
The first British and American jet fighters: 1944–45

The Germans were not alone in research and development of a jet engine which could be installed in a fighter aircraft: the British and the Americans followed with tenacity and speed along this new path of technology that led the way into a new era.

In Britain the project that led to the creation of the Gloster Meteor, the only Allied jet fighter which went into service before the end of the war, was

started in August 1940, in the midst of the Battle of Britain. The designer, George Carter, chose the twin-engine formula, because the first types of turbojet of that period, then at the experimental stage, were not powerful enough to supply sufficient thrust to ensure the necessary high performance of an interceptor. Eight prototypes were constructed which were used for a long time for experiments with the new engine. The first to fly was the fifth model on 5th March 1943, powered by Halford H1 engines.

For the record, the first flight of a jet aircraft in Britain took place on 15th May 1941, when an experimental model of a Gloster, the E.28/39, powered by a single Whittle W1 engine rated at 390 kg thrust was successfully tested; in Germany, the Heinkel He.178 first flew in 1939, the world's first jet flight.

The engine of the Meteor Mark I, the W2B/23, was one of the turbojets derived from the Whittle W1, and was developed and constructed by Rolls-Royce under the name of Welland. It gave a thrust of 1,700 lb (770 kg). The first 20 Meteors ordered by the RAF were delivered by the end of June 1944, and went into service in the following month. They flew combat missions almost immediately: on 27th July the first sortie was made against the V-1 flying bombs and on 4th August one of these was destroyed. The pursuit of the V-1s continued throughout the summer and mainly served to train pilots and ground crews in the use of the new fighters and in the study of operational tactics.

Meanwhile a new variant, the Mk III, had been perfected (200 built) with more powerful engines (two Rolls-Royce 1,995 lbs (905 kg) thrust engines capable of the longer range of 2,156 km (1,340 miles) and able to reach 793 km/h (493 mph) at an altitude of 9,150 m (30,000 ft). In January 1945 these aircraft were sent to Belgium and thus became the first Allied jet fighters in service on the Continent. Their operational activity was initially limited to territory in Allied hands but in the last months of

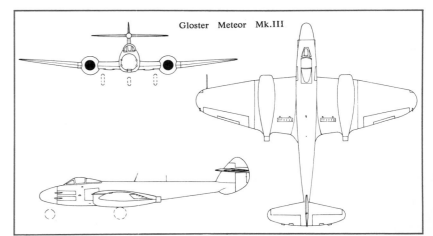

Gloster Meteor Mk.III

the war the Meteors also took part in missions over Germany. The British fighter, however, because of its noticeably inferior performance compared with the Messerschmitt Me.262, never succeeded in directly challenging its principal adversary.

The Bell P-59 Airacomet, on the other hand, the first jet warplane to be perfected in the USA, never saw active service. The project was started in 1941 at the request of the technical service of the USAAF, who had been told of the programmes of development and construction being carried out in Britain on turbojets. On 5th September the Bell Aircraft Corporation was requested to design a fighter aircraft to be powered by the revolutionary new engine. The programme was carried out in secret and in order to disguise this enterprise the aircraft was given the designation XP-59A, which had previously been assigned to a piston-engine fighter design on which Bell was already working. The construction of the first of the three prototypes started in the spring of 1942. 13 pre-series aircraft followed which were designated YP-59A. The test flights started on 1st October, carried out by Bell's chief test pilot, Robert M. Stanley.

No particular problems hindered the development of the airframe and soon the pre-series models were in use testing the engines in flight. Engines of ever-increasing power were installed in the production models: General Electric's 1-16 (subsequently designated J-31) having a thrust of 1,600 lb (725 kg) in the XP-59A were replaced by 2,000 lb (907 kg) thrust engines in the 20 aircraft of the first P-59A series and by engines of still higher power in the 30 P-59B series, the second and last version to be constructed.

The technical expertise which the USAAF and the aircraft industry gained through the Airacomets served mainly to prepare the ground for the achievement of the first true jet fighter of the United States air force, the Lockheed P-80 Shooting Star. Indeed, the development of this aircraft, which was much more impressive than the P-59, led to the cancellation of the

planned construction of a further 300 Airacomets. The operational career of the Airacomet was then limited to training, and it was assigned to a special unit set up for training crews in combat tactics and flying techniques.

Plate 108
The first radar-equipped night fighters: 1942–44

The night fighter assumed an increasingly important role in the course of the war, a role which was closely linked to the stepping-up of strategic bombing, both in aircraft numbers and weight of bombs dropped. The massive bomber formations were less vulnerable by night, opposed only by the anti-aircraft batteries who tried to locate them with searchlights. On the other hand the conventional day fighters were also hindered from attaining their full potential, mainly by the difficulty of locating targets. The equipment which resolved these difficulties once and for all was radar, which was perfected almost simultaneously by the British and the Germans for airborne use.

In Britain, the first aircraft to use radar for night interception with great success was the de Havilland Mosquito, an exceptional aircraft designed in 1938 and destined to become almost synonymous with the RAF in the course of the war, along with the Spitfire and the Hurricane. The fighter version (which was developed after the original bomber version and before the reconnaissance version) was designated Mosquito Mk II and

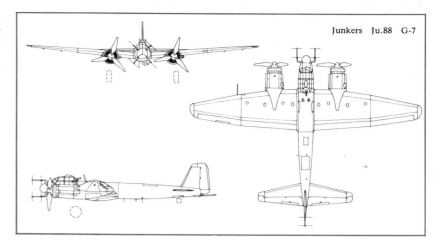

Junkers Ju.88 G-7

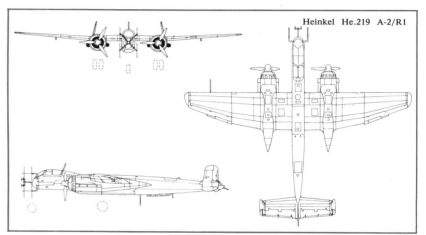

Heinkel He.219 A-2/R1

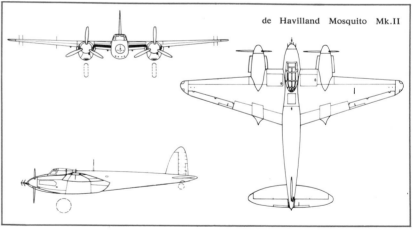

de Havilland Mosquito Mk.II

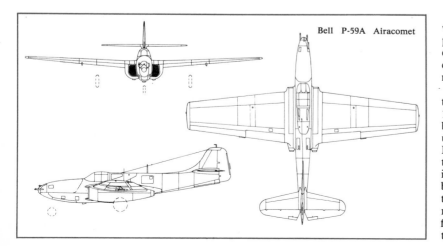

Bell P-59A Airacomet

went into service in May 1942. It was powerfully armed and was at first equipped with AI Mk IV radar with its characteristic arrow antenae in the nose.

The Mosquito shot down its first victim during the night of 28th–29th May 1942, thus starting a long list of combat successes which would proceed uninterruptedly for the rest of the war. Procurement of the Mosquito Mk II totalled 466, and these were followed in March 1943 by the Mk XII (97 built) which differed mainly in its electronics which included centimetric radar of the AI Mk VIII type for the first time, installation of which led to the elimination of the four machine

guns in the nose. In February 1944 a new version appeared, the Mk XIII, which had longer range, and 270 of these were constructed. The final variants were the Mk XVII, the Mk XIX and the Mk XXX, which were all different in their electronics, and the Mk XXX differed in giving improved performance at high altitudes.

The Germans, too, did not spare any effort. In the summer of 1943 the best night fighter of the *Luftwaffe* made its debut in combat: the Heinkel 219, which was to become one of the Mosquito's direct antagonists. It was fast, manoeuvrable and powerfully armed, and this aircraft too could perhaps have changed the course of the war if it had been available in larger numbers: less than 300 of them in fact reached units before the end of the war.

The He.219 project (nicknamed Uhu – Owl) had been commenced in the summer of 1940. The aircraft had been conceived as a multirole machine and it combined many very advanced features: pressurised cabin, tricycle landing gear, and defensive armament in a remote-control turret. Only towards the end of 1941, however, did the Reich's air ministry show some interest in the design, although it asked for it to be modified as a night fighter. The prototype flew a year later on 15th November 1942, and in the following March an initial order for 300 models was placed.

Before the construction of a few pre-series aircraft, numerous prototypes were built in which experiments were carried out with various types and combinations of armament and night radar installations. The A-1 reconnaissance variant was shelved and the first production model fighter was the A-2/R1, which was followed by A-5/R1, R2, R3 and R4 in which more powerful engines were introduced together with different types of armament.

The largest number of aircraft in any production series was the He.219 A-7, in which the armament was increased to 8 cannon: six 30 mm and two 20 mm, which was formidable firepower. The He.219 A-7s were also among the fastest machines; its sub-type R6 had been experimentally equipped with two Junkers Jumo 222 A/B 2,500 hp engines and it reached maximum speeds of 700 km/h (435 mph). An order was given, however, for production to be stopped towards the middle of 1944, in order to avoid a diffusion of production, although Heinkel continued to manufacture a few more aircraft on their own initiative.

Among the numerous modified German night fighters, the Junkers Ju.88 G merits an important place. This powerful twin-engine plane appeared in the spring of 1944, derived from the multirole Ju.88 bomber. It was heavily armed and equipped with various types of radar, and was a very fortunate combination of an excellent aircraft with good controls and handling, and powerful armament; it achieved many notable successes, especially against British bomber formations.

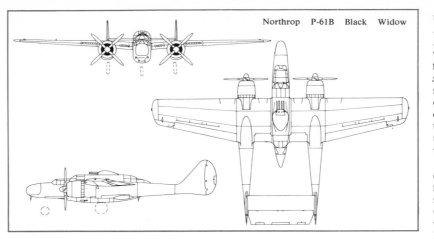

Northrop P-61B Black Widow

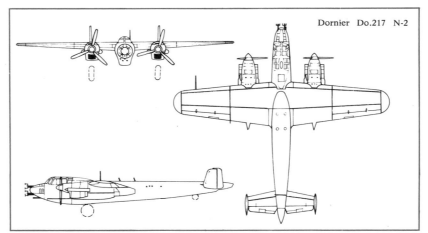

Dornier Do.217 N-2

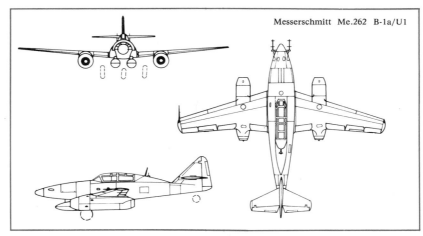

Messerschmitt Me.262 B-1a/U1

Plate 109
Second generation night fighters:
1943–45

The Germans converted another widely used twin-engine bomber into a night fighter, the Dornier Do.217. The first version to be modified for this particular role was the Do.217 J-1 which appeared towards the end of 1941. This aircraft was almost identical to the E-2 bomber, from which it differed only in the forward part of the fuselage, and in the radar antennae and the heavy armament installed in the nose.

The armament consisted of four 20 mm cannon and the same number of 7.9 mm machine guns. Produced almost simultaneously was another night fighter variant which was designated the Do.217 N and differed from its predecessor mainly in the adoption of Daimler Benz inline engines instead of the radial BMW engines. A total of 364 Dornier bombers, from various series, were converted into night fighters.

Unlike the corresponding versions of the Junkers Ju.88 and of the Messerschmitt Bf.110, these aircraft were never very popular with the crews. However, they remained in service up to the beginning of 1944 and were used very widely, especially when Allied bombing raids intensified. Among the various types of armament which were tried out on the night fighter Dorniers, one was the novel *schräge Musik* installation; this consisted of one or two pairs of 20 mm cannon mounted obliquely on the top of the fuselage. They were aimed through a special sight and fired upwards whilst flying underneath the waves of enemy bombers.

The last German attempt to produce an even more efficient night fighter was made with the Messerschmitt Me.262 jet aircraft in the October of 1944. The modification was carried out on an aircraft of the Me.262B trainer series and the result was the Me.262 B-1a/U1 variant, a twin-seater which was equipped with a whole battery of radar. The only drawback of the conversion was the noticeable reduction in speed brought about by the bulky antennae installed in the nose: no less than 60 km/h (37 mph).

Only one prototype of the definitive night fighter version, the Me.262 B-2a, was completed before the end of the war. The aircraft had undergone changes in the fuselage (which had been lengthened) and in the fuel tanks. Apart from this two 30 mm cannon had been installed on the top of the fuselage so that they could fire upwards and forwards.

The Germans and the British were not the only ones to pay particular attention to the development of night fighters. In the summer of 1944, first in the Pacific and then in Europe, an outstanding American aircraft made its debut. The first specifically designed night fighter of the US aircraft industry during the course of the Second World War, this was the Northrop P-61 Black Widow, given this sinister name not only because of the colour in which it was painted but also for its firepower and above-average overall performance, all of which made it a lethal weapon.

The interest of the American air force in this class of aircraft had been awakened in 1940 after the outbreak of war in Europe following British reports on the need for this specialised type of aircraft. In November of that year Northrop had submitted an interesting design to the technical branch of the USAAC: it concerned a heavy high-winged twin-engine aircraft with tricycle landing-gear, powered by two Pratt & Whitney Double Wasp 2,000 hp engines, which meant that this aircraft was large and powerful enough to carry a radar installation and a powerful armament.

The proposition was received with enthusiasm and the programme went ahead without delay: on 11th January 1941 two prototypes were ordered; on 10th March, 13 pre-series models; on 1st September, 150 production models; and on 12th February 1942, a further 450 aircraft. Time was short for the realisation of the project and

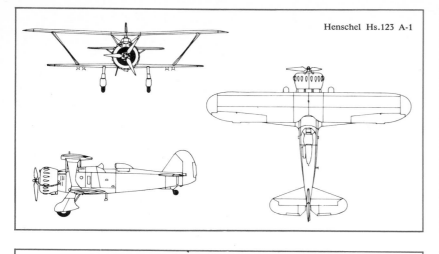

Henschel Hs.123 A-1

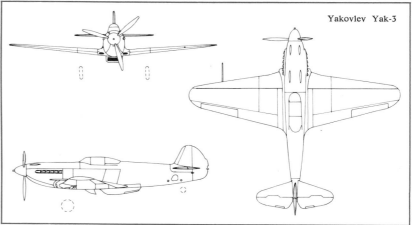

Henschel Hs.129 B-1

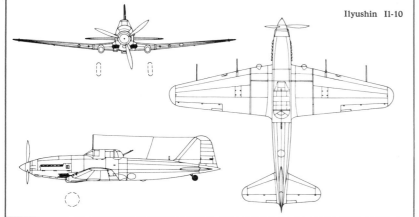

Ilyushin Il-10

Yakovlev Yak-3

the speed with which it was achieved reflected this.

The first prototype, XP-61, flew on 21st May 1942, followed a few months later by the pre-series models which were built for service trials. This last phase, however, was considerably delayed by the need to perfect the airborne radar which was based on the British designs and developed by the Massachusetts Institute of Technology. The first of the 200 P-61As to be constructed appeared towards the end of 1943 and went into operational service in the following year. They were followed by 450 of the second production, the P-61B, which had underwing pylons to carry bombs or additional fuel tanks. The next version, of which 41 were built, was the P-61 in which a 2,800 hp engine was installed.

In the period immediately after the war the fuselage was modified, the radar equipment dispensed with, and the reconnaissance version was developed, the F-15A Reporter, of which 36 were produced. It remained in service until 1952.

Plate 110
Close support and attack aircraft: the Germans lead the way but the Russian aircraft are more effective: 1936–44

The night fighter was not the only specialised aircraft to come to the fore during the course of the Second World War. Particular attention was also paid to ground attack aircraft by the various air forces, with an eye to the dependence on motor transport, and the ever-growing use of armoured vehicles, by land forces.

The Germans were among the first to produce fighter aircraft especially designed and constructed for this role. By the middle of the 1930s, the still clandestine *Luftwaffe* had expressed the need for an aeroplane which could also be used for ground attack. This was the Henschel Hs.123: the prototype flew on 8th May 1935, and the production model, the A-1, started to reach the fighter units of the German air force in the summer of 1936. The aircraft's military potential (it has its place in history as the last biplane fighter of the *Luftwaffe*) had been tried out in the Spanish Civil War, where five Hs.123s had been sent in 1937.

On the outbreak of the Second World War, despite its obsolescence, the Henschel fighter had a brief and intense operational career, taking part

in the Polish and French campaigns beside the more modern and powerful Junkers Ju.87 Stuka.

By that time Henschel had already prepared an improved successor to its ground attack fighter: the twin-engined Hs.129, which was in effect a sort of flying armoured car. Apart from the armament, which in the final version included a 30 mm or 40 mm cannon mounted under the fuselage, the aircraft was also exceptional for its armour plating. In fact the pilot was seated in what was nothing less than a steel capsule between 6 mm and 8 mm thick. The first prototype flew in the spring of 1939 and was followed by the machine of the first production series in 1940.

A radical change took place with the aircraft of series B, which appeared at the beginning of 1942, in which the engines were changed from the two Argus As 410 V-12 495 hp engines to two 700 hp Gnome-Rhône radials. Performance improved noticeably and in spite of some defects the Henschel served in the front line until 1944, especially in Russia.

It was the Russian front itself that saw a particularly intensive tactical use of air power against ground targets. The Red Army were very well aware of the great potential of specialised ground attack planes, and many were produced for this role. The best of all were those which were designed by Sergei Vladimorovich Ilyushin from

1938 onwards which have gone down in history under the name of Stormovik, accompanied by a phrase from Stalin: "They were as vital to the Russian army as oxygen and bread."

After the particular success of the Il-2 variant which went into service in the summer of 1941, a decision was taken to build a new version which would incorporate all the modifications and improvements which had been found necessary in operational use. Designated the Il-10 the aircraft appeared in prototype form in the summer of 1944. The new Stormovik kept the general lines of its direct predecessor which had proved so effective: the whole forward part of the fuselage from the engine mounting to the pilot's cockpit was armoured, which also gave the aircraft structural strength. Apart from protecting the engine and its ancillary parts, and of course the crew, this solution also permitted a compensatory saving of weight, the armour replacing parts of the structure as otherwise designed.

The principal modifications of the Il-10 compared with the Il-2 were in the engine, the landing-gear, the armament and streamlining. The motor was changed to a Mikulin 2,000 hp engine and the machine guns were replaced with three 20 mm cannon; the armour plating thickness was increased, and also its extent. The test flight results were so encouraging that the aircraft was chosen in preference to its direct competitor, the Sukhoi Su-6, and immediately put into production. After serving in the last phase of the war the Il-10 was a front-line fighter until the 1950s in the air forces of the allies of the Soviet Union. Over 35,000 Stormoviks were produced.

The Yakovlev Yak-3 was also converted for ground attack and, developed together with the Yak-9, was put into service in 1944. Originally it had been an interceptor but this aircraft benefited in its ground attack role from its excellent performance at low altitude, which made it a very handy, fast and formidable machine. At altitudes between 2,500 m (8,200 ft) and 3,500 m (11,480 ft) the Yak-3 was clearly superior to the British Supermarine Spitfire and to the German Messerschmitt Bf.109 G and Focke Wulf Fw.190 A.

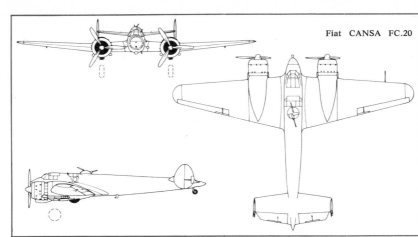

Fiat CANSA FC.20

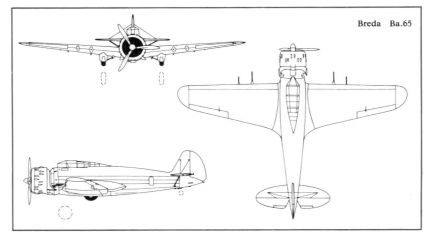

Breda Ba.65

Plate 111
Three unsuccessful Italian close support and attack aircraft: 1935–43

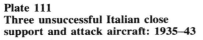

In Italy the *Regia Aeronautica* never succeeded in acquiring a particularly brilliant ground attack aircraft. The only one of the class which was specifically designed for this role and attained operational use was the Breda Ba.65 of 1935. Derived from the Ba.64 which had been produced in the first half of the thirties, the Breda made its debut in the Spanish Civil War, and then in June 1940 154 were in the front line. It was mainly used on the North African front, but confronted by the enemy's air supremacy it soon showed all its limitations. It was not very manoeuvrable, underpowered for the weight of its armament, and in the event the Ba.65 proved to be an easy prey for the British fighters. The aircraft was powered by two types of engine: the Fiat 1,000 hp A 80 RC 41 and the Gnome-Rhône of similar power. Two versions were produced, one a single-seater and the other a two-seater. In the latter a manually-aimed machine gun was installed in the rear of the cockpit.

In 1944 an attempt to produce a larger and more powerful machine for

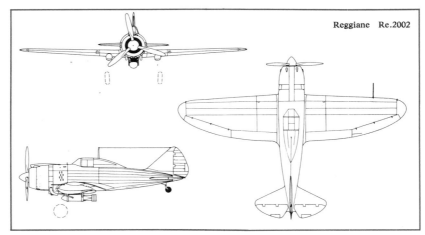

Reggiane Re.2002

use in an anti-tank role met with total failure. This aircraft was the twin-engine Fiat CANSA FC.20, which was originally conceived as a reconnaissance plane. Of the two prototypes, one was equipped with a 37 mm cannon installed in the nose. But the results of the tests proved disappointing, as did attempts to use the aircraft as an interceptor. Only 10 pre-series aircraft were built. Overall the Fiat CANSA FC.20 was always an inadequate aeroplane, with poor handling, flight instability and, since it was underpowered, generally unexciting performance.

In the last months of the war, however, a small and handy single-engine

aircraft met with considerable success. This was a direct descendant of an unfortunate fighter which had been too far ahead of its time, the Reggiane Re.2000. After the Reggiane 2001 had been manufactured with an inline engine, the designers Robert Lunghi and Antonia Alessio returned to the radial engine with the Re.2002. This was given the name of Ariete (the Ram) and was also ordered by the *Luftwaffe* which, in 1943, even planned the production of a version to be equipped with the BMW 1600 hp engine which powered the famous Focke Wulf Fw.190. This plan however came to nothing and the Germans confined themselves to using about 60 aircraft

of the Re.2002 series which were employed in the ground attack units of the *Luftwaffe* between the end of 1943 and 1944. Total procurement of the Ariete was 225, of which 149 went to the *Regia Aeronautica*. The project had been started off in the summer of 1940 and the prototype had flown in the month of October. After a long phase of development the Ariete became operational with the 5th *Stormo Tuffatori* in the July of 1943. After the Armistice about 40 surviving Re.2002s continued in operation with the Co-Belligerent Air Force until the summer of 1944.

Plate 112
Britain fields the best fighter-bombers: 1938–44

In Germany, throughout the entire duration of the war, every effort was made to produce a first-class tactical aircraft for close support. However, in this field the Messerschmitt Me.210–410 family proved, in the main, to be inadequate.

When, between the end of 1941 and the beginning of 1942, it became evident that the construction programme of the Me.210, which followed that of the Bf.110, would never achieve any satisfactory results because of serious defects of the aircraft, two alternative designs were proposed. Of these, the Me.410 was chosen, which was in essence a simplified and improved version of its predecessor. The prototype flew towards the end of 1942 and in January 1943 deliveries of the first production variants started: the Me.410 A-1 fighter-bomber and the Me.410 A-2 heavy fighter.

At the end of April 1943 48 models of these two variants went to the *Luftwaffe*, a figure which rose to 457 by the end of the year. The use of the Me.410s as fighter-bombers however was never widespread. The increasing frequency of Allied raids made the use of the aircraft in the role of heavy fighter a top priority. Various versions were developed to this end with the intention of further improving the offensive armament: the Me.410 A-1/U4 was armed with a 50 mm cannon; variants of the second B series were equipped with additional 30 mm cannon installed in pairs, or even with a multiple rocket launcher with 6 tubes (which, however, turned out to be a failure). The Me.410 fought right up to the end of the war. In all, 1,160 were constructed.

In Britain, too, the concept of a fighter bomber was given high priority. Indeed, the first monoplane which went into service with the Fleet Air Arm, the Blackburn Skua, was designed especially as a dive-bomber, a role which it was able to fulfil with some success at the same time as that of a fighter. The Skua project had been started off in 1935 and the first prototype flew on 9th February 1937.

Operational use on board HMS *Ark Royal* started in November 1938, and ended in 1941 when more modern and better-armed aircraft came on the scene. This monoplane had a metal skin and was powered by an 890 hp Bristol Perseus engine. Its defensive armament consisted of 5 machine guns, and it had 740 lb (335 kg) bomb capacity. Production totalled 190 aircraft. As a point of historical interest the first aircraft to be shot down by the Fleet Air Arm in the war (on 25th November 1939) was brought down off the coast of Norway by one of these planes.

A less fortunate project was that which in 1938 led to the creation of the Westland Whirlwind. The first twin-engine single-seat fighter to go into service with the RAF, this aircraft could have had a brilliant career had it not been for the inferior power of its Rolls-Royce Peregrine engines, which were never to be improved because of the priority given to the better Merlin engine. The prototype flew on 11 October 1938, and the first of the 112 aircraft to be constructed (Mk I) were delivered in the summer of 1940. Given its poor performance at high altitude, the Whirlwind was soon used as an escort fighter and in 1942 was adapted as a fighter-bomber.

But the best aircraft of this category were the Hawker Typhoon and Tempest. The Tempest also showed itself to be exceptional as an interceptor; a role in which it was widely used especially in the pursuit of the German flying bombs and the Me.262 jet aircraft.

The Typhoon was designed as an interceptor in 1937 but the programme was held back by the considerable and unexpected delay in the simultaneous production programme which had allowed for the manufacture of the two new 2,000 hp engines. When one of these engines, the Napier Sabre, was at last ready, it was discovered that these engine units were still very far from being perfected. In consequence, the first production Typhoons (the prototype had flown on 24th February 1940) were continuously plagued by technical problems. Added to this were structural weaknesses which were ultimately to put a stop to the use of the aeroplane.

In view of these limitations it was decided, in the second half of 1942, not to use the Typhoons as interceptors any longer but as fighter-bombers. In this capacity they went into action on 19th August 1942 and immediately showed themselves to be formidable at low altitude. They fought until the last day of the war and production of this aircraft ended in 1944 having totalled 3,330 models, mainly of the Mk I B series. This version had a 2,180 hp Napier Sabre engine which in spite of its high power did not improve the flight performance of the aircraft.

The problems of the Typhoon were completely overcome in the Tempest, the operational version of which, the Mk 5, flew in prototype form on 2nd September 1942 and went into service in April 1944. This was made possible thanks to a radical change in design and also to improvements in the Sabre engine. Powerful and fast, the Tempest had no effective enemies, either at low or high altitudes. Up to August 1945 procurement of the Mk 5 totalled just over 800: its best known use was in pursuit of the V-Is. From 13th June to 5 September 1944, the Tempests shot down 638 missiles out of 1,771 launched by the Germans.

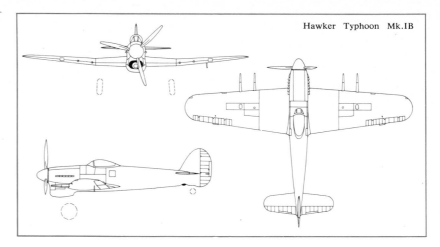

Hawker Typhoon Mk.IB

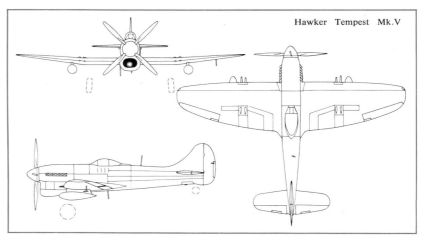

Hawker Tempest Mk.V

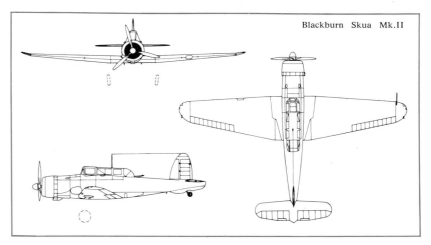

Blackburn Skua Mk.II

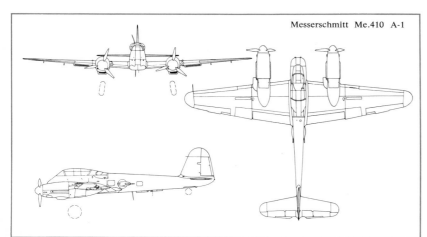

Messerschmitt Me.410 A-1

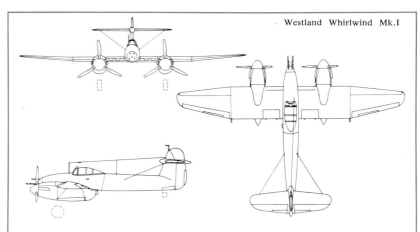

Westland Whirlwind Mk.I

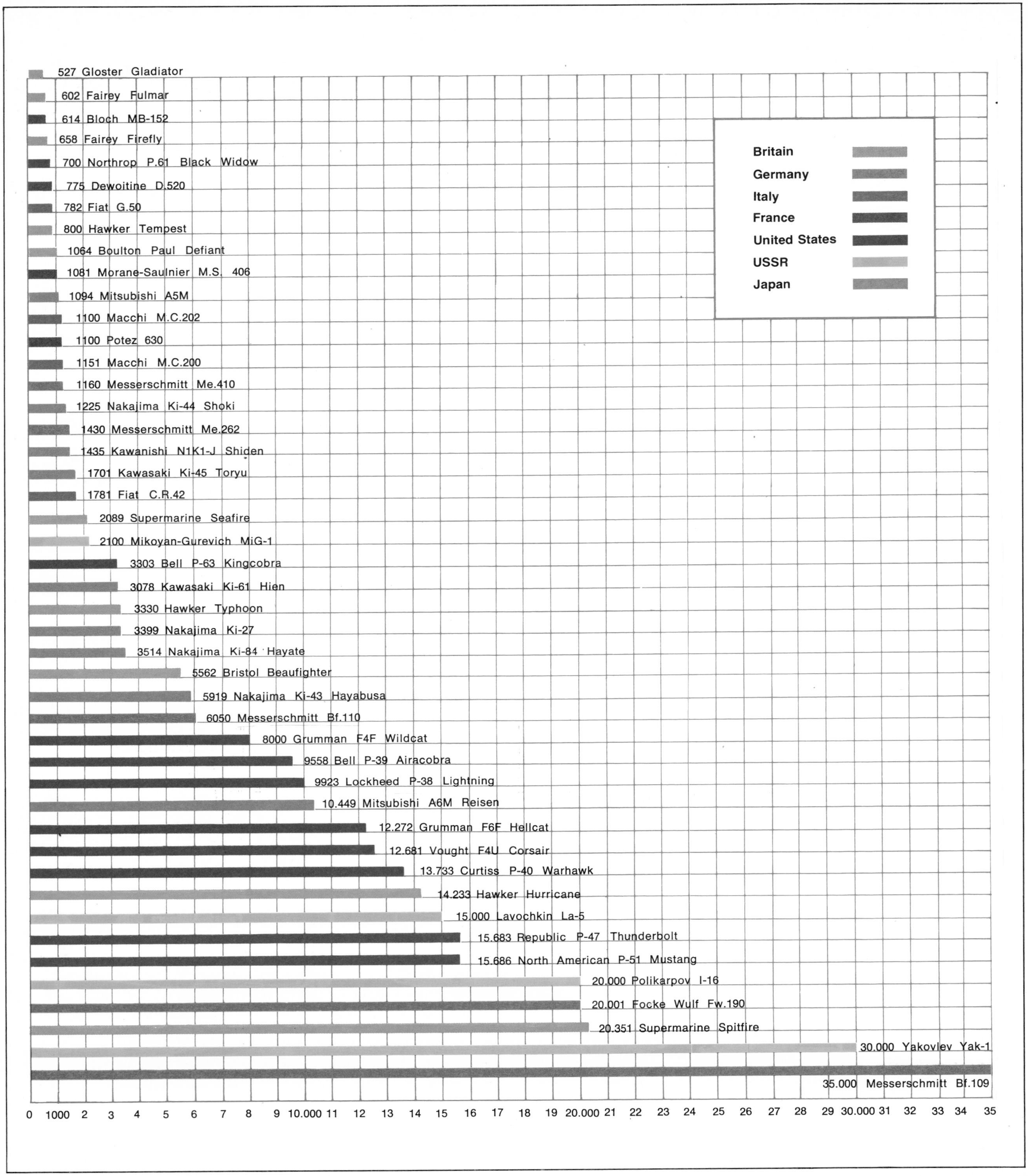

Plate 113

Fighter production in the Second World War

Legend:
- Britain
- Germany
- Italy
- France
- United States
- USSR
- Japan

- 527 Gloster Gladiator
- 602 Fairey Fulmar
- 614 Bloch MB-152
- 658 Fairey Firefly
- 700 Northrop P.61 Black Widow
- 775 Dewoitine D.520
- 782 Fiat G.50
- 800 Hawker Tempest
- 1064 Boulton Paul Defiant
- 1081 Morane-Saulnier M.S. 406
- 1094 Mitsubishi A5M
- 1100 Macchi M.C.202
- 1100 Potez 630
- 1151 Macchi M.C.200
- 1160 Messerschmitt Me.410
- 1225 Nakajima Ki-44 Shoki
- 1430 Messerschmitt Me.262
- 1435 Kawanishi N1K1-J Shiden
- 1701 Kawasaki Ki-45 Toryu
- 1781 Fiat C.R.42
- 2089 Supermarine Seafire
- 2100 Mikoyan-Gurevich MiG-1
- 3303 Bell P-63 Kingcobra
- 3078 Kawasaki Ki-61 Hien
- 3330 Hawker Typhoon
- 3399 Nakajima Ki-27
- 3514 Nakajima Ki-84 Hayate
- 5562 Bristol Beaufighter
- 5919 Nakajima Ki-43 Hayabusa
- 6050 Messerschmitt Bf.110
- 8000 Grumman F4F Wildcat
- 9558 Bell P-39 Airacobra
- 9923 Lockheed P-38 Lightning
- 10.449 Mitsubishi A6M Reisen
- 12.272 Grumman F6F Hellcat
- 12.681 Vought F4U Corsair
- 13.733 Curtiss P-40 Warhawk
- 14.233 Hawker Hurricane
- 15.000 Lavochkin La-5
- 15.683 Republic P-47 Thunderbolt
- 15.686 North American P-51 Mustang
- 20.000 Polikarpov I-16
- 20.001 Focke Wulf Fw.190
- 20.351 Supermarine Spitfire
- 30.000 Yakovlev Yak-1
- 35.000 Messerschmitt Bf.109

0 1000 2 3 4 5 6 7 8 9 10.000 11 12 13 14 15 16 17 18 19 20.000 21 22 23 24 25 26 27 28 29 30.000 31 32 33 34 35

Legend:
- Britain
- Germany
- Italy
- France
- United States
- USSR
- Japan

500 Dornier Do.17 Z
514 Fiat B.R.20
534 SIAI Marchetti S.M.81
560 Cant Z.1007 bis
602 Lioré et Olivier LeO 451
698 Mitsubishi Ki-67 Hiryu
800 Tupolev TB-3
819 Nakajima Ki-49 Donryu
852 Yokosuka MXY7 Ohka
854 Kawasaki Ki-32
870 Junkers Ju.86
1048 Mitsubishi G3M
1076 Junkers Ju.188
1098 Yokosuka P1Y Ginga
1169 Heinkel He.177
1217 SIAI Marchetti S.M.79
1430 Handley Page Hampden
1495 Aichi D3A
1528 Vultee A-35 Vengeance
1575 Martin Baltimore
1814 Armstrong Whitworth Whitley
1905 Dornier Do.217
1977 Kawasaki Ki-48
2038 Yokosuka D4Y Suisei
2064 Mitsubishi Ki-21
2185 Fairey Battle
2371 Short Stirling
2446 Mitsubishi G4M
2446 Douglas A-26 Invader
3970 Boeing B-29 Superfortress
5000 Ilyushin Il-4
5157 Martin B-26 Marauder
5213 Bristol Blenheim
5936 Douglas SBD Dauntless
6176 Handley Page Halifax
6439 de Havilland Mosquito
6600 Tupolev SB-2
7002 Curtiss SB2 Helldiver
7366 Avro Lancaster
7385 Douglas A-20 Havoc
7450 Heinkel He.111
8685 Boeing B-17 Flying Fortress
11.000 North American B-24 Mitchell
11.461 Vickers Wellington
14.980 Junkers Ju.88
18.188 Consolidated B-24 Liberator

x-axis: 0 1000 2 3 4 5 6 7 8 9 10.000 11 12 13 14 15 16 17 18 19 20.000 21

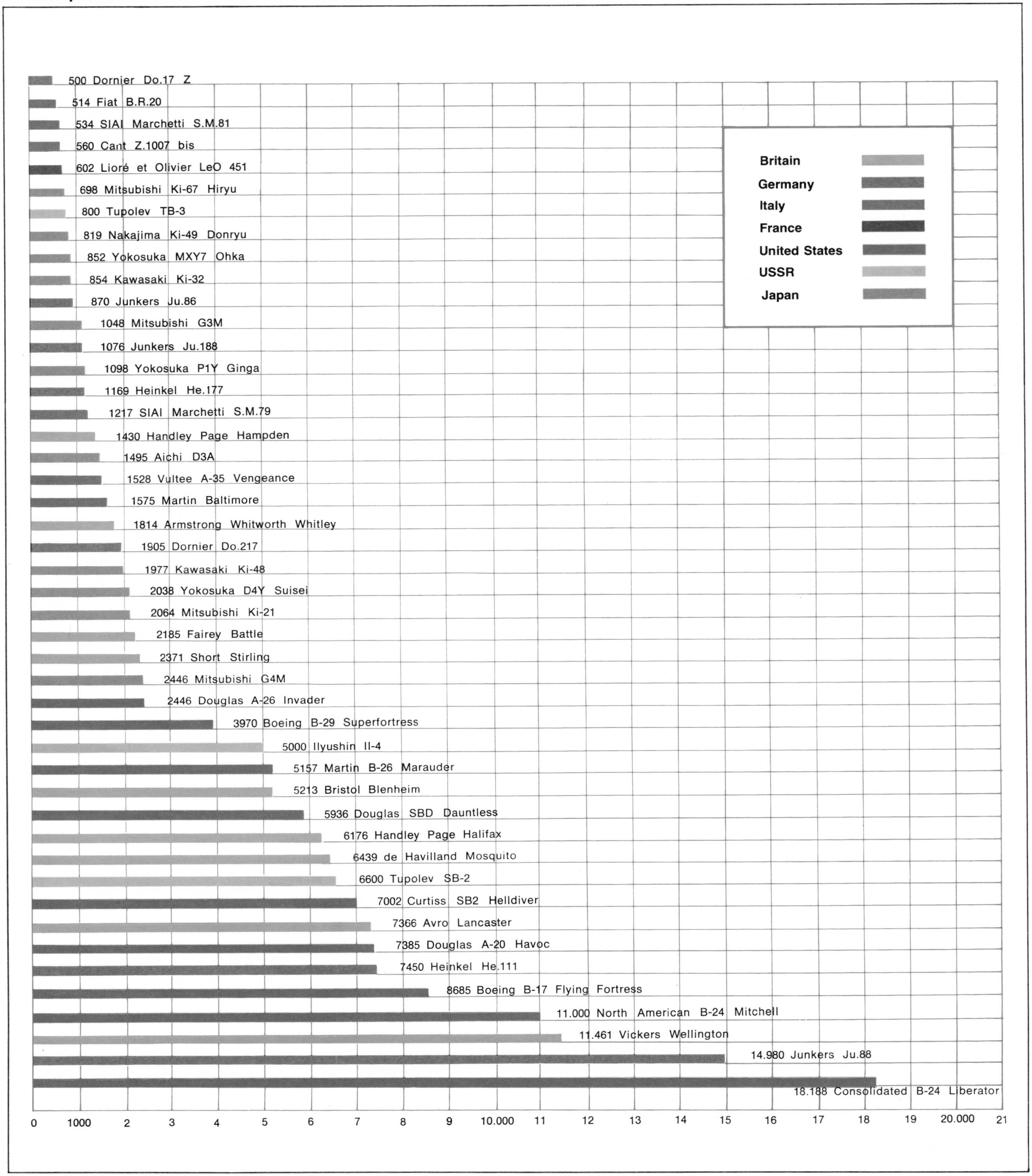

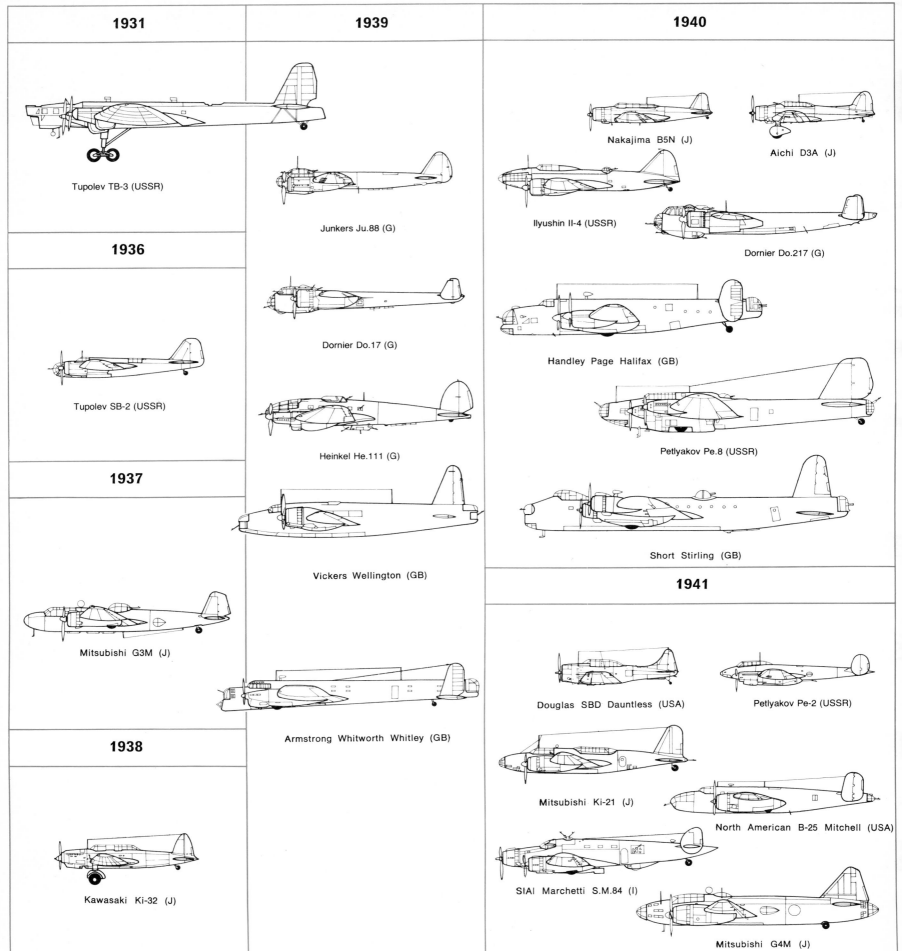

1931	1939	1940

1931

Tupolev TB-3 (USSR)

1936

Tupolev SB-2 (USSR)

1937

Mitsubishi G3M (J)

1938

Kawasaki Ki-32 (J)

1939

Junkers Ju.88 (G)

Dornier Do.17 (G)

Heinkel He.111 (G)

Vickers Wellington (GB)

Armstrong Whitworth Whitley (GB)

1940

Nakajima B5N (J)

Aichi D3A (J)

Ilyushin Il-4 (USSR)

Dornier Do.217 (G)

Handley Page Halifax (GB)

Petlyakov Pe.8 (USSR)

Short Stirling (GB)

1941

Douglas SBD Dauntless (USA)

Petlyakov Pe-2 (USSR)

Mitsubishi Ki-21 (J)

North American B-25 Mitchell (USA)

SIAI Marchetti S.M.84 (I)

Mitsubishi G4M (J)

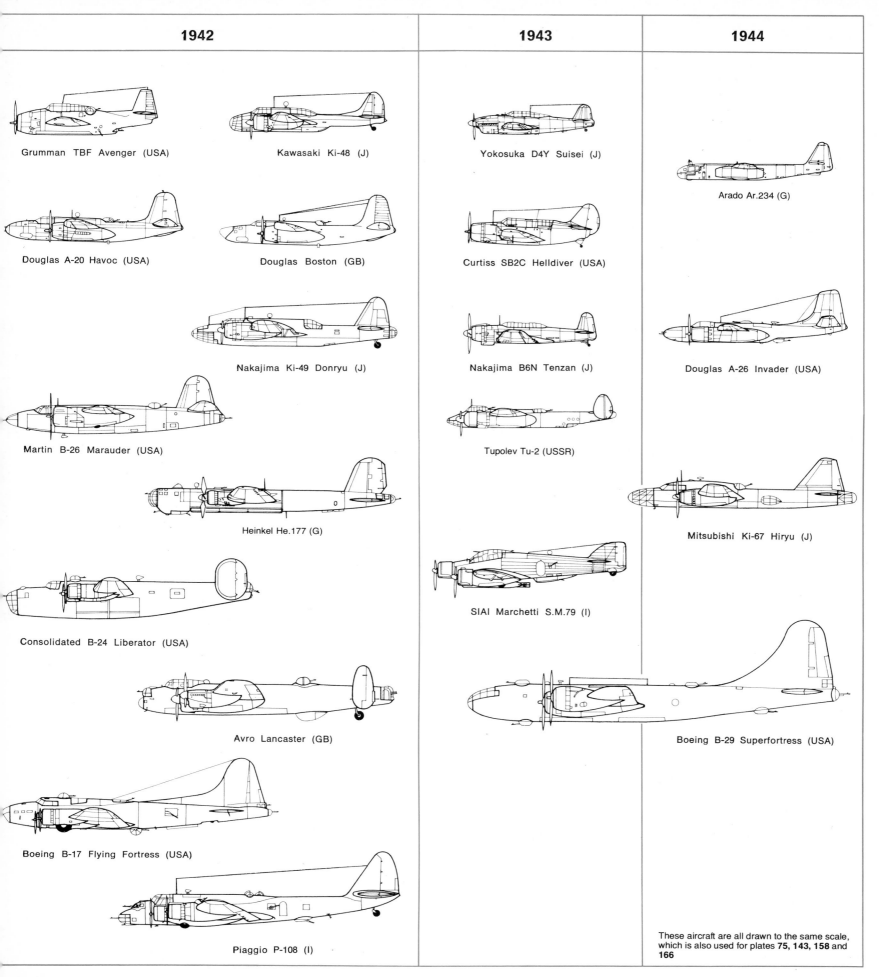

1942

Grumman TBF Avenger (USA)

Kawasaki Ki-48 (J)

Douglas A-20 Havoc (USA)

Douglas Boston (GB)

Nakajima Ki-49 Donryu (J)

Martin B-26 Marauder (USA)

Heinkel He.177 (G)

Consolidated B-24 Liberator (USA)

Avro Lancaster (GB)

Boeing B-17 Flying Fortress (USA)

Piaggio P-108 (I)

1943

Yokosuka D4Y Suisei (J)

Curtiss SB2C Helldiver (USA)

Nakajima B6N Tenzan (J)

Tupolev Tu-2 (USSR)

SIAI Marchetti S.M.79 (I)

1944

Arado Ar.234 (G)

Douglas A-26 Invader (USA)

Mitsubishi Ki-67 Hiryu (J)

Boeing B-29 Superfortress (USA)

These aircraft are all drawn to the same scale, which is also used for plates **75, 143, 158** and **166**

Plate 117   **Anatomy of a Second World War bomber: the Boeing B-17C**

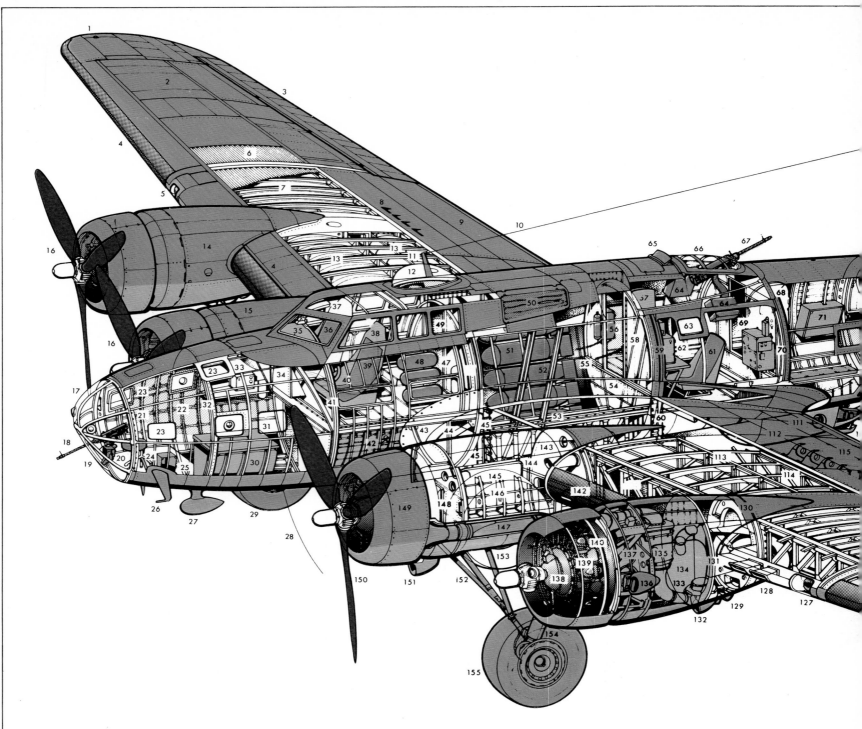

Boeing B-17C

1 Starboard navigation light
2 Wing skinning
3 Starboard aileron
4 Leading-edge de-icing boot
5 Starboard landing light
6 Wing corrugated inner skin
7 Starboard outer fuel tank
(9 inter-rib cells)
8 Cooling air slots
9 Starboard flaps
10 Aerial
11 Aerial mast
12 Astrodome
13 Starboard mid-wing tanks
(self-sealing)

14 No 4 engine nacelle
15 No 3 engine nacelle
16 Hamilton Standard
three-bladed constant-speed
propellers
17 Plexiglass nose-cone panels
18 0.30 in (7.62 mm)
machine gun
19 Optically flat bomb-aiming
panel
20 Bombsight
21 No 1 fuselage frame bulkhead
22 Forward fuselage structure
23 Nose windows
24 Bomb-aimer's seat

25 Bomb-aimer's panel
26 Pitot head
27 D/F bullet fairing
28 Whip aerial
29 Starboard mainwheel
30 Navigator's table
31 Window
32 No 2 fuselage frame bulkhead
33 Navigation equipment
34 Central control pedestal
35 Windscreen
36 Co-pilot's seat
37 Overhead control panel
38 Headrest/armour
39 Pilot's seat

40 Pilot's control column
41 No 3 fuselage frame bulkhead
43 Underfloor control runs
43 Wingroot/fuselage fairing
44 Battery access panels (in
wingroot)
45 Main spar/fuselage
attachment
46 No 4 fuselage frame bulkhead
47 Fire extinguisher
48 Oxygen cylinders
49 Flight-deck door
50 Dinghy stowage
51 Horizontal bomb-load
(starboard shown)

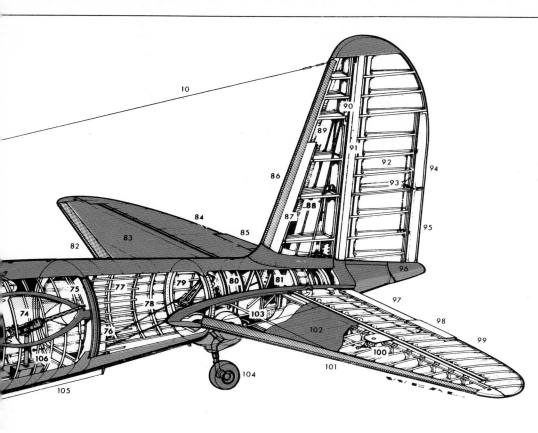

77 Fuselage structure
78 Control cables
79 Tailwheel retraction mechanism
80 Fuselage frame
81 Tailfin/fuselage attachment
82 Starboard tailplane de-icing boot
83 Starboard tailplane
84 Starboard elevator
85 Elevator tab
86 Tailfin de-icing boot
87 Tailfin front spar
88 Rudder control linkage
89 Tailfin construction
90 Rudder hinge (upper)
91 Rudder post
92 Rudder framework
93 Tab controls
94 Rudder tab (upper)
95 Rudder tab (lower)
96 Tail cone
97 Elevator tab (inner)
98 Elevator tab (outer)
99 Elevator construction
100 Elevator control linkage
101 Port tailplane de-icing boot
102 Tailplane skinning
103 Tailwheel (stowed/semi-retracted)
104 Tailwheel extended
105 Ventral aerial
106 Gun support mounting
107 Gunners catwalk
108 Ammunition box
109 Ventral gun position (twin 0.50 in/12.7 mm machine guns)
110 Hinged lower section
111 Circular vision port
112 Ventral bath
113 Auxiliary mid spar
114 Rear spar
115 Flap profile
116 Cooling air slots
117 Flap construction
118 Aileron tab (port only)
119 Port aileron construction

120 Port navigation light
121 Wingtip structure
122 Wing corrugated inner skin
123 Aileron control linkage
124 Wing ribs
125 Leading-edge de-icing boot
126 Port outer fuel tank (nine inter-rib cells)
127 Port landing light
128 Supercharger intake
129 Supercharger waste-gate
130 Spar bulkhead
131 Intercooler intake
132 Intake
133 Supercharger
134 Oil tank (outboard nacelle wall)
135 Intercooler
136 Intake
137 Engine bearers
138 Propeller reduction gear casing
139 Wright R 1820-73 radial engine
140 Firewall
141 Front spar web structure
142 Oil radiator intake
143 Spar bulkhead
144 Intercooler pressure ducting
145 Oil tank (inboard nacelle wall)
146 Nacelle structure
147 Exhaust
148 Firewall
149 No 2 engine cowling
150 Three-blade propeller
151 Intake
152 Retraction struts
153 Mainwheel (stowed/semi-retracted)
154 Mainwheel oleo
155 Port mainwheel

52 Vertical bomb stowage racks (port shown)
53 Central catwalk
54 Bulkhead step
55 Handrail ropes
56 Radio equipment
57 Communicating door
58 Bulkhead
59 No 5 fuselage frame bulkhead
60 Rear spar/fuselage attachment
61 Radio operator's seat
62 Radio rack
63 Window
64 Ammunition boxes (dorsal position)

65 Retractable wind deflector
66 Roof glazing
67 Dorsal gun position (0.50 in/12.7 mm machine gun)
68 Crew entry door (starboard)
69 Bulkhead door
70 No 6 fuselage frame bulkhead
71 Ammunition box
72 Starboard waist gun (0.50 in/12.7 mm machine gun)
73 Flush waist glazing
74 Port waist gun (0.50 in/12.7 mm machine gun)
75 Bulkhead
76 Toilet

Plate 118

The *Luftwaffe's* battle-seasoned bombers: 1937–39

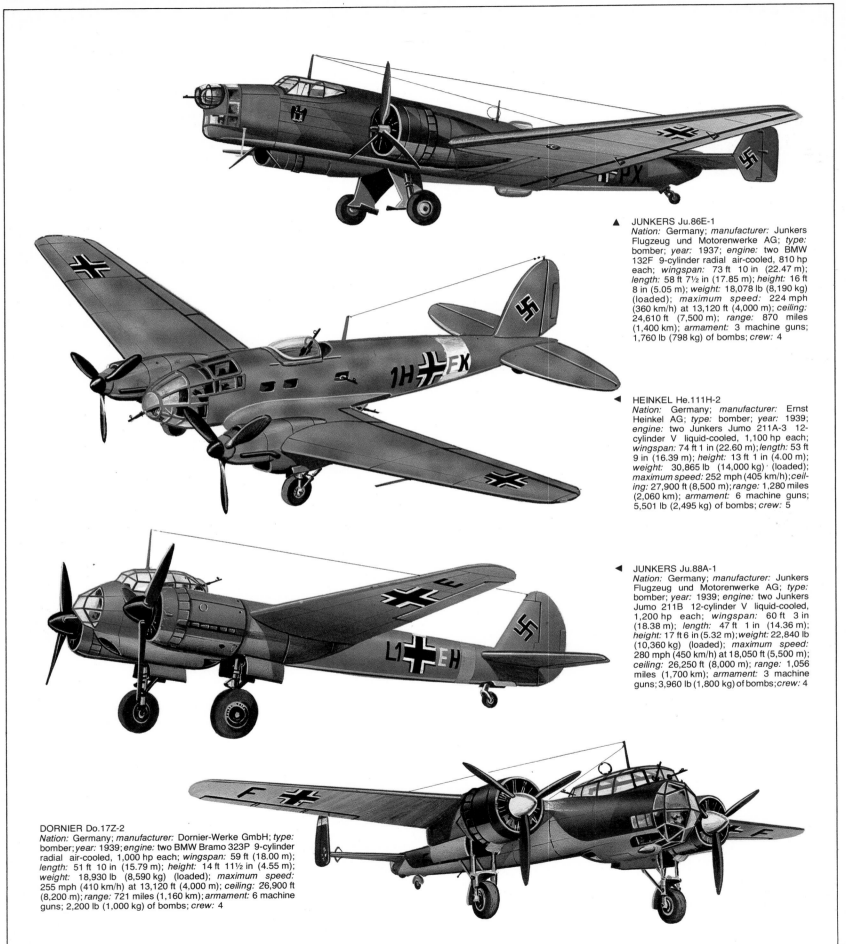

▲ JUNKERS Ju.86E-1
Nation: Germany; *manufacturer:* Junkers Flugzeug und Motorenwerke AG; *type:* bomber; *year:* 1937; *engine:* two BMW 132F 9-cylinder radial air-cooled, 810 hp each; *wingspan:* 73 ft 10 in (22.47 m); *length:* 58 ft 7½ in (17.85 m); *height:* 16 ft 8 in (5.05 m); *weight:* 18,078 lb (8,190 kg) (loaded); *maximum speed:* 224 mph (360 km/h) at 13,120 ft (4,000 m); *ceiling:* 24,610 ft (7,500 m); *range:* 870 miles (1,400 km); *armament:* 3 machine guns; 1,760 lb (798 kg) of bombs; *crew:* 4

◄ HEINKEL He.111H-2
Nation: Germany; *manufacturer:* Ernst Heinkel AG; *type:* bomber; *year:* 1939; *engine:* two Junkers Jumo 211A-3 12-cylinder V liquid-cooled, 1,100 hp each; *wingspan:* 74 ft 1 in (22.60 m); *length:* 53 ft 9 in (16.39 m); *height:* 13 ft 1 in (4.00 m); *weight:* 30,865 lb (14,000 kg) (loaded); *maximum speed:* 252 mph (405 km/h); *ceiling:* 27,900 ft (8,500 m); *range:* 1,280 miles (2,060 km); *armament:* 6 machine guns; 5,501 lb (2,495 kg) of bombs; *crew:* 5

◄ JUNKERS Ju.88A-1
Nation: Germany; *manufacturer:* Junkers Flugzeug und Motorenwerke AG; *type:* bomber; *year:* 1939; *engine:* two Junkers Jumo 211B 12-cylinder V liquid-cooled, 1,200 hp each; *wingspan:* 60 ft 3 in (18.38 m); *length:* 47 ft 1 in (14.36 m); *height:* 17 ft 6 in (5.32 m); *weight:* 22,840 lb (10,360 kg) (loaded); *maximum speed:* 280 mph (450 km/h) at 18,050 ft (5,500 m); *ceiling:* 26,250 ft (8,000 m); *range:* 1,056 miles (1,700 km); *armament:* 3 machine guns; 3,960 lb (1,800 kg) of bombs; *crew:* 4

DORNIER Do.17Z-2
Nation: Germany; *manufacturer:* Dornier-Werke GmbH; *type:* bomber; *year:* 1939; *engine:* two BMW Bramo 323P 9-cylinder radial air-cooled, 1,000 hp each; *wingspan:* 59 ft (18.00 m); *length:* 51 ft 10 in (15.79 m); *height:* 14 ft 11½ in (4.55 m); *weight:* 18,930 lb (8,590 kg) (loaded); *maximum speed:* 255 mph (410 km/h) at 13,120 ft (4,000 m); *ceiling:* 26,900 ft (8,200 m); *range:* 721 miles (1,160 km); *armament:* 6 machine guns; 2,200 lb (1,000 kg) of bombs; *crew:* 4

AMIOT 143
Nation: France; *manufacturer:* SECM; *type:* bomber; *year:* 1935; *engine:* two Gnome-Rhône 14 Kirs 14-cylinder radial air-cooled, 870 hp each; *wingspan:* 80 ft 6 in (24.51 m); *length:* 59 ft 11 in (18.26 m); *height:* 18 ft 8 in (5.68 m); *weight:* 21,385 lb (9,700 kg) (loaded); *maximum speed:* 193 mph (310 km/h) at 13,120 ft (4,000 m); *ceiling:* 25,920 ft (7,900 m); *range:* 746 miles (1,200 km); *armament:* 4 machine guns; 2,870 lb (1,300 kg) of bombs; *crew:* 5

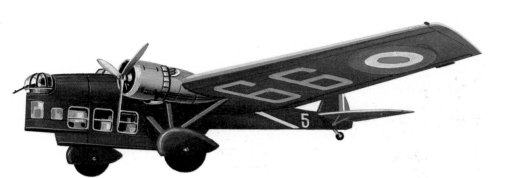

BLOCH 210
Nation: France; *manufacturer:* SNCASO; *type:* bomber; *year:* 1935; *engine:* two Gnome-Rhône 14N 14-cylinder radial air-cooled, 950 hp each; *wingspan:* 74 ft 10 in (22.80 m); *length:* 61 ft 9 in (18.82 m); *height:* 22 ft (6.70 m); *weight:* 22,487 lb (10,190 kg) (loaded); *maximum speed:* 200 mph (322 km/h) at 11,480 ft 3,500 m); *ceiling:* 32,480 ft (9,900 m); *range:* 808 miles (1,300 km); *armament:* 3 machine guns; 3,527 lb (1,600 kg) of bombs; *crew:* 5

FARMAN F.222
Nation: France; *manufacturer:* SNCAC; *type:* bomber; *year:* 1937; *engine:* four Gnome-Rhône 14N 14-cylinder radial air-cooled, 950 hp each; *wingspan:* 118 ft 1 in (36.00 m); *length:* 70 ft 4½ in (21.44 m); *height:* 17 ft (5.19 m); *weight:* 41,226 lb (18,675 kg) (loaded); *maximum speed:* 199 mph (320 km/h) at 13,120 ft (4,00 m); *ceiling:* 26,250 ft (8,000 m); *range:* 932 miles (1,500 km); *armament:* 3 machine guns; 9,260 lb (4,200 kg) of bombs; *crew:* 5

LATÉCOÈRE 298
Nation: France; *manufacturer:* Latécoère; *type:* bomber; *year:* 1938; *engine:* Hispano-Suiza 12 Ycrs 12-cylinder V liquid-cooled, 880 hp; *wingspan:* 50 ft 10 in (15.50 m); *length:* 41 ft 2½ in (12.59 m); *height:* 17 ft 1 in (5.20 m); *weight:* 9,960 lb (4,500 kg) (loaded); *maximum speed:* 180 mph (300 km/h) at 6,560 ft (2,000 m); *ceiling:* 19,685 ft (6,000 m); *range:* 932 miles (1,500 km); *armament:* 3 machine guns; 1,477 lb (670 kg) of bombs; *crew:* 2-3

Plate 120   **British bombers in service at the outbreak of war: 1937–39**

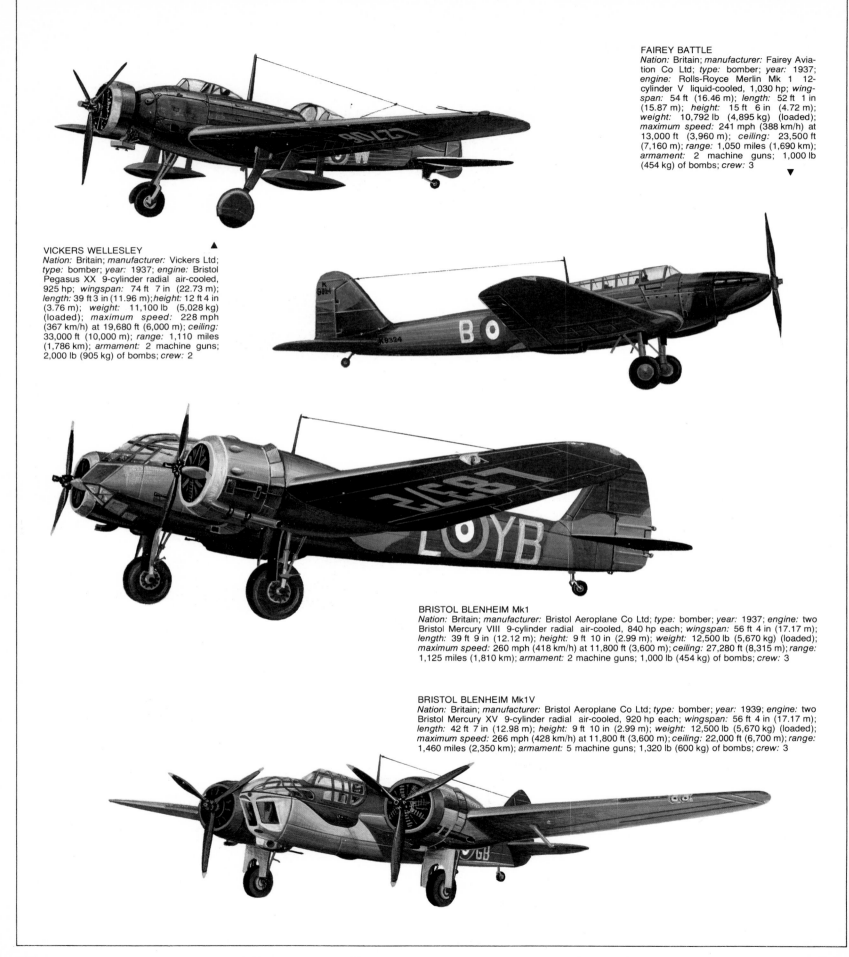

FAIREY BATTLE
Nation: Britain; *manufacturer:* Fairey Aviation Co Ltd; *type:* bomber; *year:* 1937; *engine:* Rolls-Royce Merlin Mk 1 12-cylinder V liquid-cooled, 1,030 hp; *wingspan:* 54 ft (16.46 m); *length:* 52 ft 1 in (15.87 m); *height:* 15 ft 6 in (4.72 m); *weight:* 10,792 lb (4,895 kg) (loaded); *maximum speed:* 241 mph (388 km/h) at 13,000 ft (3,960 m); *ceiling:* 23,500 ft (7,160 m); *range:* 1,050 miles (1,690 km); *armament:* 2 machine guns; 1,000 lb (454 kg) of bombs; *crew:* 3

VICKERS WELLESLEY
Nation: Britain; *manufacturer:* Vickers Ltd; *type:* bomber; *year:* 1937; *engine:* Bristol Pegasus XX 9-cylinder radial air-cooled, 925 hp; *wingspan:* 74 ft 7 in (22.73 m); *length:* 39 ft 3 in (11.96 m); *height:* 12 ft 4 in (3.76 m); *weight:* 11,100 lb (5,028 kg) (loaded); *maximum speed:* 228 mph (367 km/h) at 19,680 ft (6,000 m); *ceiling:* 33,000 ft (10,000 m); *range:* 1,110 miles (1,786 km); *armament:* 2 machine guns; 2,000 lb (905 kg) of bombs; *crew:* 2

BRISTOL BLENHEIM Mk1
Nation: Britain; *manufacturer:* Bristol Aeroplane Co Ltd; *type:* bomber; *year:* 1937; *engine:* two Bristol Mercury VIII 9-cylinder radial air-cooled, 840 hp each; *wingspan:* 56 ft 4 in (17.17 m); *length:* 39 ft 9 in (12.12 m); *height:* 9 ft 10 in (2.99 m); *weight:* 12,500 lb (5,670 kg) (loaded); *maximum speed:* 260 mph (418 km/h) at 11,800 ft (3,600 m); *ceiling:* 27,280 ft (8,315 m); *range:* 1,125 miles (1,810 km); *armament:* 2 machine guns; 1,000 lb (454 kg) of bombs; *crew:* 3

BRISTOL BLENHEIM Mk1V
Nation: Britain; *manufacturer:* Bristol Aeroplane Co Ltd; *type:* bomber; *year:* 1939; *engine:* two Bristol Mercury XV 9-cylinder radial air-cooled, 920 hp each; *wingspan:* 56 ft 4 in (17.17 m); *length:* 42 ft 7 in (12.98 m); *height:* 9 ft 10 in (2.99 m); *weight:* 12,500 lb (5,670 kg) (loaded); *maximum speed:* 266 mph (428 km/h) at 11,800 ft (3,600 m); *ceiling:* 22,000 ft (6,700 m); *range:* 1,460 miles (2,350 km); *armament:* 5 machine guns; 1,320 lb (600 kg) of bombs; *crew:* 3

BLOCH 131
Nation: France; *manufacturer:* SNCASO; *type:* bomber; *year:* 1938; *engine:* two Gnome-Rhône 14N 14-cylinder radial air-cooled, 950 hp each; *wingspan:* 66 ft 6 in (20.27 m); *length:* 58 ft 7 in (17.88 m); 13 ft 5 in (4.10 m); *height:* 18,960 lb (8,590 kg) (loaded); *weight:* 217 mph (349 km/h) at 12,300 ft (3,750 m); *maximum speed:* 23,785 ft (7,250 m); *range:* 808 miles (1,300 km); *armament:* 3 machine guns; 1,760 lb (800 kg) of bombs; *crew:* 4

LIORÉ ET OLIVIER 451
Nation: France; *manufacturer:* SNCASE; *type:* bomber; *year:* 1939; *engine:* two Gnome-Rhône 14N 14-cylinder radial air-cooled, 1,140 hp each; *wingspan:* 73 ft 10½ in (22.50 m); *length:* 56 ft 4 in (17.17 m); *height:* 17 ft 2 in (5.23 m); *weight:* 25,133 lb (11,385 kg) (loaded); *maximum speed:* 307 mph (494 km/h) at 15,748 ft (4,800 m); *ceiling:* 29,530 ft (9,000 m); *range:* 1,430 miles (2,300 km); *armament:* 1 × 20 mm cannon; 2 machine guns; 4,400 lb (2,000 kg) of bombs; *crew:* 4

AMIOT 354
Nation: France; *manufacturer:* SECM; *type:* bomber; *year:* 1940; *engine:* two Gnome-Rhône 14N 14-cylinder radial air-cooled, 1,060 hp each; *wingspan:* 74 ft 11 in (22.83 m); *length:* 47 ft 7 in (14.50 m); *height:* 13 ft 4½ in (4.06 m); *weight:* 24,912 lb (11,285 kg) (loaded); *maximum speed:* 298 mph (479 km/h) at 13,120 ft (4,000 m); *ceiling:* 32,810 ft (10,000 m); *range:* 1,553 miles (2,500 km); *armament:* 1 × 20 mm cannon; 2 machine guns; 2,200 lb (1,000 kg) of bombs; *crew:* 4

PZL P.37B
Nation: Poland; *manufacturer:* Panstwowe Zaklady Lotnicze; *type:* bomber; *year:* 1938; *engine:* two PZL-Bristol Pegasus XIIB 9-cylinder radial air-cooled, 873 hp each; *wingspan:* 58 ft 10 in (17.93 m); *length:* 42 ft 5 in (12.92 m); *height:* 16 ft 8 in (5.08 m); *weight:* 18,872 lb (8,560 kg) (loaded); *maximum speed:* 276 mph (445 km/h) at 11,154 ft (3,400 m); *ceiling:* 19,680 ft (6,000 m); *range:* 932 miles (1,500 km); *armament:* 19,680 ft (6,000 m); *range:* 932 miles (1,500 km); *armament:* 3 machine guns; 5,688 lb (2,580 kg) of bombs; *crew:* 4

FOKKER T.VIII
Nation: Netherlands; *manufacturer:* Fokker; *type:* bomber; *year:* 1940; *engine:* two Wright Whirlwind 9-cylinder radial air-cooled, 450 hp each; *wingspan:* 59 ft (17.98 m); *length:* 42 ft 8 in (13.00 m); *height:* 16 ft 5 in (5.00 m); *weight:* 11,030 lb (5,000 kg) (loaded); *maximum speed:* 177 mph (285 km/h); *ceiling:* 22,300 ft (6,800 m); *range:* 1,710 miles (2,750 km); *armament:* 2-3 machine guns; 1,330 lb (603 kg) of bombs; *crew:* 3

SIAI-MARCHETTI SM.81
Nation: Italy; *manufacturer:* SIAI-Marchetti; *type:*
bomber; *year:* 1935; *engine:* three Alfa Romeo 125
RC35 9-cylinder radial air-cooled, 680 hp each;
wingspan: 78 ft 9 in (24.00 m); *length:* 60 ft 1 in
(18.31 m); *height:* 14 ft 4 in (4.47 m); *weight:*
23,190 lb (10,505 kg) (loaded); *maximum speed:*
211 mph (340 km/h) at 13,120 ft (4,000 m); *ceiling:*
23,000 ft (7,000 m); *range:* 1,200 miles (1,931 km);
armament: 6 machine guns; 4,415 lb (2,000 kg) of
bombs; *crew:* 6

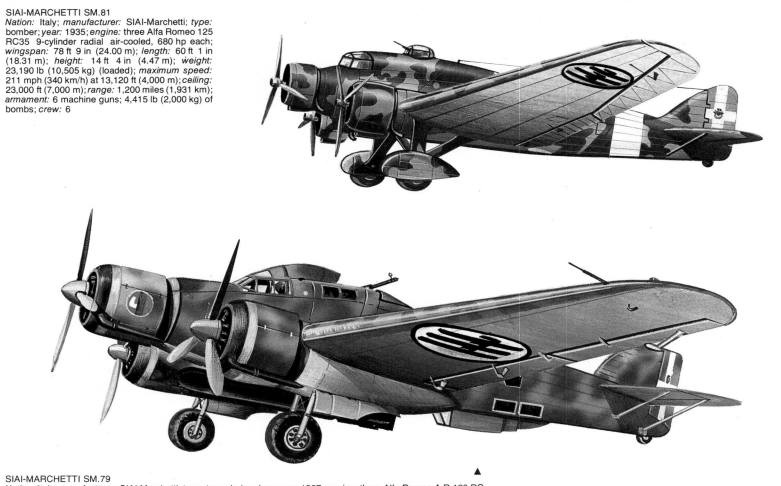

SIAI-MARCHETTI SM.79
Nation: Italy; *manufacturer:* SIAI Marchetti; *type:* torpedo-bomber; *year:* 1937; *engine:* three Alfa Romeo A.R.126 RC
34 9-cylinder radial air-cooled, 750 hp each; *wingspan:* 69 ft 7 in (21.20 m); *length:* 53 ft 2 in (16.20 m); *height:* 13 ft
5½ in (4.10 m); *weight:* 23,180 lb (10,500 kg) (loaded); *maximum speed:* 267 mph (430 km/h) at 13,120 ft (4,000 m);
ceiling: 23,000 ft (7,000 m); *range:* 1,180 miles (1,900 km); *armament:* 4-5 machine guns; 2,756 lb (1,250 kg) of bombs;
crew: 6

◄ **SIAI-MARCHETTI SM.79 III**
Nation: Italy; *manufacturer:* SIAI Marchetti; *type:*
torpedo-bomber; *year:* 1943; *engine:* three Piaggio
P.XI RC 40 14-cylinder radial air-cooled, 1,000 hp
each; *wingspan:* 69 ft 7 in (21.20 m); *length:* 51 ft
2 in (15.60 m); *height:* 15 ft 10 in (4.60 m); *weight:*
23,180 lb (10,500 kg) (loaded); *maximum speed:*
295 mph (475 km/h); *ceiling:* 23,000 ft (7,000 m);
range: 1,180 miles (1,900 km); *armament:* 4
machine guns; 1 × 20 mm cannon; 1 torpedo;
crew: 6

SIAI-MARCHETTI SM.84
Nation: Italy; *manufacturer:* SIAI Marchetti; *type:*
bomber; *year:* 1941; *engine:* three Piaggio P.XI RC
40 14-cylinder radial air-cooled, 1,000 hp each;
wingspan: 69 ft 7 in (21.20 m); *length:* 58 ft 10 in
(17.93 m); *height:* 15 ft 1 in (4.59 m); *weight:*
29,330 lb (13,288 kg) (loaded); *maximum speed:*
268 mph (432 km/h) at 15,000 ft (4,600 m); *ceiling:*
25,900 ft (7,900 m); *range:* 1,137 miles (1,830 km);
armament: 4 machine guns; 4,400 lb (2,000 kg) of
bombs; *crew:* 5

CANT Z.506B
Nation: Italy; *manufacturer:* Cantieri Riuniti dell'Adriatico; *type:* bomber; *year:* 1937; *engine:* three Alfa Romeo A.R.126 RC 34 9-cylinder radial air-cooled, 750 hp each; *wingspan:* 86 ft 11 in (26.50 m); *length:* 63 ft 1½ in (19.24 m); *height:* 24 ft 3 in (7.39 m); *weight:* 27,115 lb (12,299 kg) (loaded); *maximum speed:* 226 mph (364 km/h) at 13,120 ft (4,000 m); *ceiling:* 26,240 ft (7,997 m); *range:* 1,700 miles (2,745 km); *armament:* 4 machine guns; 2,650 lb (1,200 kg) of bombs; *crew:* 5

CANT Z.1007bis
Nation: Italy; *manufacturer:* Cantieri Riuniti dell'Adriatico; *type:* bomber; *year:* 1938; *engine:* three Piaggio P.XI RC 40 14-cylinder radial air-cooled, 1,000 hp each; *wingspan:* 81 ft 4 in (24.80 m); *length:* 61 ft (18.59 m); *height:* 17 ft 1 in (5.22 m); *weight:* 38,200 lb (17,327 kg) (loaded); *maximum speed:* 283 mph (456 km/h) at 15,100 ft (4,600 m); *ceiling:* 26,500 ft (8,100 m); *range:* 1,243 miles (2,000 km); *armament:* 4 machine guns; 2,430 lb (1,100 kg) of bombs; *crew:* 5

PIAGGIO P.108B
Nation: Italy; *manufacturer:* SA Piaggio & Co; *type:* bomber; *year:* 1942; *engine:* 4 Piaggio P.XII RC 35 18-cylinder radial air-cooled, 1,350 hp each; *wingspan:* 105 ft (32.00 m); *length:* 75 ft 2 in (22.92 m); *height:* 17 ft (5.18 m); *weight:* 65,970 lb (29,885 kg) (loaded); *maximum speed:* 261 mph (420 km/h) at 12,800 ft (3,900 m); *ceiling:* 26,400 ft (8,050 m); *range:* 2,190 miles (3,520 km); *armament:* 8 machine guns; 7,700 lb (3,500 kg) of bombs; *crew:* 6

CANT Z.1018
Nation: Italy; *manufacturer:* Cantieri Riuniti dell'Adriatico; *type:* bomber; *year:* 1943; *engine:* two Piaggio P.XII RC 35 18-cylinder radial air-cooled, 1,350 hp each; *wingspan:* 73 ft 10 in (22.50 m); *length:* 57 ft 9 in (17.60 m); *height:* 20 ft (6.10 m); *weight:* 25,400 lb (11,500 kg) (loaded); *maximum speed:* 325 mph (524 km/h) at 14,700 ft (4,500 m); *ceiling:* 23,800 ft (7,250 m); *range:* 830 miles (1,335 km); *armament:* 5 machine guns; 4,400 lb (2,000 kg) of bombs; *crew:* 4

FIAT BR.20
Nation: Italy; *manufacturer:* Fiat SA; *type:* bomber; *year:* 1937; *engine:* two Fiat A.80 R6 41 18-cylinder radial air-cooled, 1,000 hp each; *wingspan:* 70 ft 8 in (21.53 m); *length:* 52 ft 10 in (16.10 m); *height:* 14 ft 1 in (4.30 m); *weight:* 21,850 lb (9,900 kg) (loaded); *maximum speed:* 286 mph (460 km/h) at 16,400 ft (5,000 m); *ceiling:* 29,500 ft (9,000 m); *range:* 1,860 miles (3,000 km); *armament:* 3 machine guns; 3,527 lb (1,600 kg) of bombs; *crew:* 5

Plate 124

British bombers: 1938–40

HANDLEY PAGE HAMPDEN
Nation: Britain; *manufacturer:* Handley Page Ltd; *type:* bomber; *year:* 1938; *engine:* two Bristol Pegasus XVIII 9-cylinder radial air-cooled, 1,000 hp each; *wingspan:* 69 ft 2 in (21.08 m); *length:* 53 ft 7 in (16.33 m); *height:* 14 ft 11 in (4.55 m); *weight:* 18,756 lb (8,508 kg) (loaded); *maximum speed:* 254 mph (409 km/h) at 13,800 ft (4,200 m); *ceiling:* 22,700 ft (6,920 m); *range:* 1,885 miles (3,034 km); *armament:* 6 machine guns; 4,000 lb (1,815 kg) of bombs; *crew:* 4 ▶

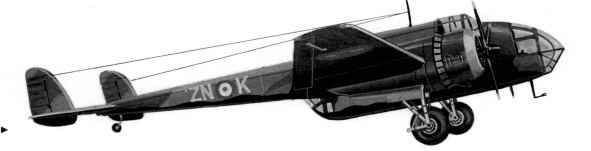

◀ **VICKERS WELLINGTON Mk 1**
Nation: Britain; *manufacturer:* Vickers-Armstrongs Ltd; *type:* bomber; *year:* 1938; *engine:* two Bristol Pegasus XVIII 9-cylinder radial air-cooled, 1,000 hp each; *wingspan:* 86 ft 2 in (26.26 m); *length:* 64 ft 7 in (19.68 m); *height:* 17 ft 5 in (5.31 m); *weight:* 28,500 lb (12,910 kg) (loaded); *maximum speed:* 235 mph (378 km/h) at 15,500 ft (4,700 m); *ceiling:* 18,000 ft (5,500 m); *range:* 2,200 miles (3,540 km); *armament:* 6 machine guns; 4,500 lb (2,000 kg) of bombs; *crew:* 6

ARMSTRONG WHITWORTH WHITLEY Mk V
Nation: Britain; *manufacturer:* Armstrong Whitworth Aircraft Ltd; *type:* bomber; *year:* 1939; *engine:* two Rolls-Royce Merlin X 12-cylinder V liquid-cooled, 1,145 hp each; *wingspan:* 84 ft (25.60 m); *length:* 70 ft 6 in (21.49 m); *height:* 15 ft (4.57 m); *weight:* 28,200 lb (12,792 kg) (loaded); *maximum speed:* 222 mph (357 km/h) at 17,000 ft (5,200 m); *ceiling:* 17,600 ft (5,365 m); *range:* 1,650 miles (2,655 km); *armament:* 5 machine guns; 7,000 lb (3,175 kg) of bombs; *crew:* 5 ▶

SHORT STIRLING Mk 1
Nation: Britain; *manufacturer:* Short Brothers Ltd; *type:* bomber; *year:* 1940; *engine:* four Bristol Hercules XI 14-cylinder radial air-cooled, 1,590 hp each; *wingspan:* 99 ft 1 in (30.21 m); *length:* 87 ft 3 in (26.60 m); *height:* 22 ft 9 in (6.93 m); *weight:* 59,400 lb (26,943 kg) (loaded); *maximum speed:* 260 mph (418 km/h) at 10,500 ft (3,200 m); *ceiling:* 17,000 ft (5,180 m); *range:* 2,330 miles (3,750 km); *armament:* 8 machine guns; 14,000 lb (6,350 kg) of bombs; *crew:* 7-8

TUPOLEV TB-3
Nation: USSR; *manufacturer:* State Industries; *type:* bomber; *year:* 1931; *engine:* four M-17F (BMW) 12-cylinder V liquid-cooled, 715 hp each; *wingspan:* 132 ft 10½ in (40.88 m); *length:* 83 ft (25.54 m); *height:* 27 ft 9 in (8.47 m); *weight:* 38,360 lb (17,400 kg) (loaded); *maximum speed:* 179 mph (288 km/h); *ceiling:* 12,470 ft (3,800 m); *range:* 1,939 miles (3,225 km); *armament:* 6 machine guns; 4,800 lb (2,200 kg) of bombs; *crew:* 8

TUPOLEV SB-2
Nation: USSR; *manufacturer:* State Industries; *type:* bomber; *year:* 1936; *engine:* two Klimov M-100A 12-cylinder V liquid-cooled, 830 hp each; *wingspan:* 66 ft 8½ in (20.33 m); *length:* 40 ft 3 in (12.27 m); *height:* 10 ft 8 in (3.25 m); *weight:* 12,637 lb (5,725 kg) (loaded); *maximum speed:* 255 mph (411 km/h) at 13,120 ft (4,000 m); *ceiling:* 31,200 ft (9,500 m); *range:* 745 miles (1,200 km); *armament:* 4 machine guns; 1,320 lb (600 kg) of bombs; *crew:* 3

◄ SUKHOI Su-2
Nation: USSR; *manufacturer:* State Industries; *type:* bomber; *year:* 1940; *engine:* Shvetsov M-82 14-cylinder radial air-cooled, 1,400 hp; *wingspan:* 46 ft 11 in (14.30 m); *length:* 33 ft 7½ in (10.25 m); *height:* 12 ft 3 in (3.75 m); *weight:* 8,965 lb (4,075 kg) (loaded); *maximum speed:* 302 mph (485 km/h) at 19,190 ft (5,850 m); *ceiling:* 28,900 ft (8,800 m); *range:* 746 miles (1,200 km); *armament:* 5 machine guns; 1,323 lb (600 kg) of bombs; *crew:* 2

ILYUSHIN Il-4
Nation: USSR; *manufacturer:* State Industries; *type:* bomber; *year:* 1940; *engine:* two M-88B 14-cylinder radial air-cooled, 1,000 hp each; *wingspan:* 70 ft 4 in (21.44 m); *length:* 48 ft 7 in (14.82 m); *height:* 13 ft 9 in (4.20 m); *weight:* 22,046 lb (10,000 kg) (loaded); *maximum speed:* 255 mph (410 km/h) at 21,000 ft (6,400 m); *ceiling:* 32,800 ft (10,000 m); *range:* 2,647 miles (4,260 km); *armament:* 3 machine guns; 5,512 lb (2,500 kg) of bombs; *crew:* 3-4

▶

Plate 126

Japanese bombers in service at the outbreak of war: 1937–41

MITSUBISHI G3M2
Nation: Japan; *manufacturer:* Mitsubishi Jukogyo KK; *type:* bomber; *year:* 1937; *engine:* 2 Mitsubishi Kinsei 41 14-cylinder radial air-cooled, 1,075 hp each; *wingspan:* 82 ft (25 m); *length:* 53 ft 11 in (16.45 m); *height:* 12 ft 1 in (3.68 m); *weight:* 17,637 lb (8,000 kg) (loaded); *maximum speed:* 232 mph (373 km/h) at 13,715 ft (4,180 m); *ceiling:* 29,950 ft (9,130 m); *range:* 2,722 miles (4,380 km); *armament:* 1 × 20 mm cannon; 4 machine guns; 1,764 lb (800 kg) of bombs; *crew:* 7

KAWASAKI Ki-32
Nation: Japan; *manufacturer:* Kawasaki Kokuki Kogyo KK; *type:* bomber; *year:* 1938; *engine:* Ha-9-11b 12-cylinder V liquid-cooled, 950 hp; *wingspan:* 49 ft 2½ in (15 m); *length:* 38 ft 2 in (11.64 m); *height:* 9 ft 6 in (2.90 m); *weight:* 8,294 lb (3,770 kg) (loaded); *maximum speed:* 263 mph (423 km/h) at 12,925 ft (3,840 m); *ceiling:* 29,265 ft (8,920 m); *range:* 1,218 miles (1,965 km); *armament:* 2 machine guns; 992 lb (450 kg) of bombs; *crew:* 2

MITSUBISHI Ki-21-IIb
Nation: Japan; *manufacturer:* Mitsubishi Jukogyo KK; *type:* bomber; *year:* 1941; *engine:* two Mitsubishi Ha-101 14-cylinder radial, 1,530 hp each; *wingspan:* 73 ft 10 in (22.50 m); *length:* 52 ft 6 in (16 m); *height:* 15 ft 11 in (4.85 m); *weight:* 23,392 lb (10,632 kg) (loaded); *maximum speed:* 302 mph (486 km/h) at 15,485 ft (4,720 m); *ceiling:* 32,810 ft (10,000 m); *range:* 1,680 miles (2,700 km); *armament:* 6 machine guns; 2,205 lb (1,000 kg) of bombs; *crew:* 5-7

AICHI D3A1
Nation: Japan; *manufacturer:* Aichi Kokuki KK; *type:* bomber; *year:* 1940; *engine:* Mitsubishi Kinsei 43 14-cylinder radial air-cooled, 1,000 hp; *wingspan:* 47 ft 2 in (14.38 m); *length:* 33 ft 5½ in (10.19 m); *height:* 12 ft 7½ in (3.84 m); *weight:* 8,047 lb (3,650 kg) (loaded); *maximum speed:* 240 mph (386 km/h) at 9,840 ft (3,000 m); *ceiling:* 30,050 ft (9,300 m); *range:* 915 miles (1,472 km); *armament;* 3 machine guns; 813 lb (370 kg) of bombs; *crew:* 2

MITSUBISHI G4M1
Nation: Japan; *manufacturer:* Mitsubishi Jukogyo KK; *type:* bomber; *year:* 1941; *engine:* two Mitsubishi MK4A Kasei 11 14-cylinder radial, 1,530 hp each; *wingspan:* 82 ft (25 m); *length:* 65 ft 7½ in (20 m); *height:* 19 ft 8 in (6 m); *weight:* 20,944 lb (9,500 kg) (loaded); *maximum speed:* 266 mph (428 km/h) at 13,780 ft (4,200 m); *ceiling:* 29,000 ft (8,840 m); *range:* 3,748 miles (6,030 km); *armament:* 1 × 20 mm cannon; 4 machine guns; 1,764 lb (800 kg) of bombs; *crew:* 7

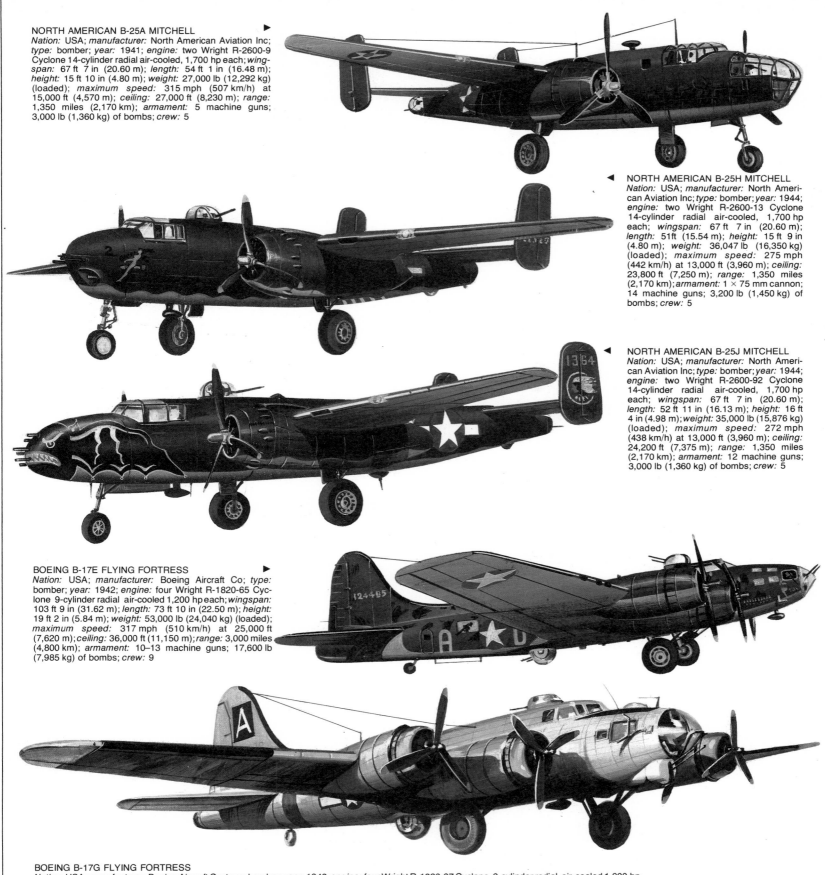

NORTH AMERICAN B-25A MITCHELL ▶
Nation: USA; *manufacturer:* North American Aviation Inc; *type:* bomber; *year:* 1941; *engine:* two Wright R-2600-9 Cyclone 14-cylinder radial air-cooled, 1,700 hp each; *wingspan:* 67 ft 7 in (20.60 m); *length:* 54 ft 1 in (16.48 m); *height:* 15 ft 10 in (4.80 m); *weight:* 27,000 lb (12,292 kg) (loaded); *maximum speed:* 315 mph (507 km/h) at 15,000 ft (4,570 m); *ceiling:* 27,000 ft (8,230 m); *range:* 1,350 miles (2,170 km); *armament:* 5 machine guns; 3,000 lb (1,360 kg) of bombs; *crew:* 5

◀ **NORTH AMERICAN B-25H MITCHELL**
Nation: USA; *manufacturer:* North American Aviation Inc; *type:* bomber; *year:* 1944; *engine:* two Wright R-2600-13 Cyclone 14-cylinder radial air-cooled, 1,700 hp each; *wingspan:* 67 ft 7 in (20.60 m); *length:* 51 ft (15.54 m); *height:* 15 ft 9 in (4.80 m); *weight:* 36,047 lb (16,350 kg) (loaded); *maximum speed:* 275 mph (442 km/h) at 13,000 ft (3,960 m); *ceiling:* 23,800 ft (7,250 m); *range:* 1,350 miles (2,170 km); *armament:* 1 × 75 mm cannon; 14 machine guns; 3,200 lb (1,450 kg) of bombs; *crew:* 5

◀ **NORTH AMERICAN B-25J MITCHELL**
Nation: USA; *manufacturer:* North American Aviation Inc; *type:* bomber; *year:* 1944; *engine:* two Wright R-2600-92 Cyclone 14-cylinder radial air-cooled, 1,700 hp each; *wingspan:* 67 ft 7 in (20.60 m); *length:* 52 ft 11 in (16.13 m); *height:* 16 ft 4 in (4.98 m); *weight:* 35,000 lb (15,876 kg) (loaded); *maximum speed:* 272 mph (438 km/h) at 13,000 ft (3,960 m); *ceiling:* 24,200 ft (7,375 m); *range:* 1,350 miles (2,170 km); *armament:* 12 machine guns; 3,000 lb (1,360 kg) of bombs; *crew:* 5

BOEING B-17E FLYING FORTRESS ▶
Nation: USA; *manufacturer:* Boeing Aircraft Co; *type:* bomber; *year:* 1942; *engine:* four Wright R-1820-65 Cyclone 9-cylinder radial air-cooled 1,200 hp each; *wingspan:* 103 ft 9 in (31.62 m); *length:* 73 ft 10 in (22.50 m); *height:* 19 ft 2 in (5.84 m); *weight:* 53,000 lb (24,040 kg) (loaded); *maximum speed:* 317 mph (510 km/h) at 25,000 ft (7,620 m); *ceiling:* 36,000 ft (11,150 m); *range:* 3,000 miles (4,800 km); *armament:* 10–13 machine guns; 17,600 lb (7,985 kg) of bombs; *crew:* 9

BOEING B-17G FLYING FORTRESS
Nation: USA; *manufacturer:* Boeing Aircraft Co; *type:* bomber; *year:* 1943; *engine:* four Wright R-1820-97 Cyclone 9-cylinder radial air-cooled 1,200 hp each; *wingspan:* 103 ft 9 in (31.62 m); *length:* 74 ft 9 in (22.70 m); *height:* 19 ft 1 in (5.82 m); *weight:* 65,500 lb (29,710 kg) (loaded); *maximum speed:* 287 mph (462 km/h) at 25,000 ft (7,620 m); *ceiling:* 35,600 ft (10,850 m); *range:* 3,400 miles (5,200 km); *armament:* 13 machine guns; 17,600 lb (7,985 kg) of bombs; *crew:* 10

Plate 128

Three famous American twin-engine aircraft: 1942–44

◀ MARTIN B-26B MARAUDER
Nation: USA; *manufacturer:* Glenn L. Martin
Co; *type:* bomber; *year:* 1942; *engine:* two
Pratt & Whitney R-2800-41 Double Wasp
18-cylinder radial air-cooled 2,000 hp
each; *wingspan:* 65 ft (19.81 m); *length:*
58 ft 3 in (17.75 m); *height:* 19 ft 10 in
(6.05 m); *weight:* 34,000 lb (15,422 kg)
(loaded); *maximum speed:* 317 mph
(510 km/h) at 14,500 ft (4,420 m); *ceiling:*
23,500 ft (7,200 m); *range:* 1,150 miles
(1,850 km); *armament:* 6 machine guns;
3,000 lb (1,360 kg) of bombs; *crew:* 7

MARTIN B-26G MARAUDER
Nation: USA; *manufacturer:* Glenn L. Martin
Co; *type:* bomber; *year:* 1944; *engine:* two
Pratt & Whitney R-2800-43 Double Wasp
18-cylinder radial air-cooled, 2,000 hp
each; *wingspan:* 71 ft (26.64 m); *length:*
56 ft 1 in (17.09 m); *height:* 20 ft 4 in
(6.19 m); *weight:* 38,200 lb (17,328 kg)
(loaded); *maximum speed:* 283 mph
(455 km/h) at 5,000 ft (1,500 m); *ceiling:*
19,800 ft (6,350 m); *range:* 1,100 miles
(1,780 km); *armament:* 11 machine guns;
4,000 lb (1,815 kg) of bombs; *crew:* 7

DOUGLAS A-20G HAVOC
Nation: USA; *manufacturer:* Douglas Aircraft Co; *type:* bomber;
year: 1942; *engine:* two Wright R-2600-23 Cyclone 14-cylinder
radial air-cooled, 1,600 hp each; *wingspan:* 61 ft 4 in (18.69 m);
length: 48 ft (14.63 m); *height:* 17 ft 7 in (5.63 m); *weight:* 27,200 lb
(12,338 kg) (loaded); *maximum speed:* 339 mph (545 km/h) at
12,400 ft (3,780 m); *ceiling:* 25,800 ft (7,800 m); *range:* 1,090 miles
(1,750 km); *armament:* 8 machine guns; 4,000 lb (1,815 kg) of
bombs; *crew:* 3

DOUGLAS A-26B INVADER
Nation: USA; *manufacturer:* Douglas Aircraft Co; *type:* bomber; *year:* 1944; *engine:*
two Pratt & Whitney R-2800-27 Double
Wasp 18-cylinder radial air-cooled,
2,000 hp each; *wingspan:* 70 ft (21.33 m);
length: 50 ft 9 in (15.45 m); *height:* 18 ft 6 in
(5.64 m); *weight:* 35,000 lb (15,876 kg)
(loaded); *maximum speed:* 355 mph
(571 km/h); *ceiling:* 31,300 ft (9,600 m);
range: 1,800 miles (2,900 km); *armament:*
10 machine guns; 4,000 lb (1,815 kg) of
bombs; *crew:* 3

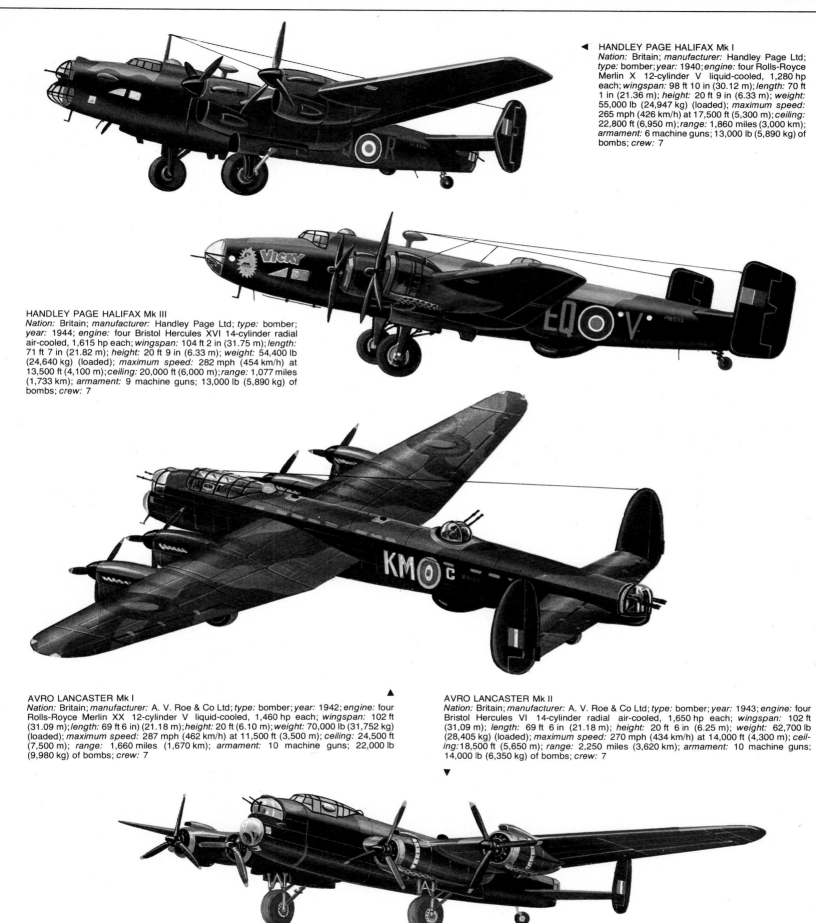

◄ HANDLEY PAGE HALIFAX Mk I
Nation: Britain; *manufacturer:* Handley Page Ltd;
type: bomber; *year:* 1940; *engine:* four Rolls-Royce
Merlin X 12-cylinder V liquid-cooled, 1,280 hp
each; *wingspan:* 98 ft 10 in (30.12 m); *length:* 70 ft
1 in (21.36 m); *height:* 20 ft 9 in (6.33 m); *weight:*
55,000 lb (24,947 kg) (loaded); *maximum speed:*
265 mph (426 km/h) at 17,500 ft (5,300 m); *ceiling:*
22,800 ft (6,950 m); *range:* 1,860 miles (3,000 km);
armament: 6 machine guns; 13,000 lb (5,890 kg) of
bombs; *crew:* 7

HANDLEY PAGE HALIFAX Mk III
Nation: Britain; *manufacturer:* Handley Page Ltd; *type:* bomber;
year: 1944; *engine:* four Bristol Hercules XVI 14-cylinder radial
air-cooled, 1,615 hp each; *wingspan:* 104 ft 2 in (31.75 m); *length:*
71 ft 7 in (21.82 m); *height:* 20 ft 9 in (6.33 m); *weight:* 54,400 lb
(24,640 kg) (loaded); *maximum speed:* 282 mph (454 km/h) at
13,500 ft (4,100 m); *ceiling:* 20,000 ft (6,000 m); *range:* 1,077 miles
(1,733 km); *armament:* 9 machine guns; 13,000 lb (5,890 kg) of
bombs; *crew:* 7

AVRO LANCASTER Mk I
Nation: Britain; *manufacturer:* A. V. Roe & Co Ltd; *type:* bomber; *year:* 1942; *engine:* four
Rolls-Royce Merlin XX 12-cylinder V liquid-cooled, 1,460 hp each; *wingspan:* 102 ft
(31.09 m); *length:* 69 ft 6 in) (21.18 m); *height:* 20 ft (6.10 m); *weight:* 70,000 lb (31,752 kg)
(loaded); *maximum speed:* 287 mph (462 km/h) at 11,500 ft (3,500 m); *ceiling:* 24,500 ft
(7,500 m); *range:* 1,660 miles (1,670 km); *armament:* 10 machine guns; 22,000 lb
(9,980 kg) of bombs; *crew:* 7

AVRO LANCASTER Mk II
Nation: Britain; *manufacturer:* A. V. Roe & Co Ltd; *type:* bomber; *year:* 1943; *engine:* four
Bristol Hercules VI 14-cylinder radial air-cooled, 1,650 hp each; *wingspan:* 102 ft
(31,09 m); *length:* 69 ft 6 in (21.18 m); *height:* 20 ft 6 in (6.25 m); *weight:* 62,700 lb
(28,405 kg) (loaded); *maximum speed:* 270 mph (434 km/h) at 14,000 ft (4,300 m); *ceiling:* 18,500 ft (5,650 m); *range:* 2,250 miles (3,620 km); *armament:* 10 machine guns;
14,000 lb (6,350 kg) of bombs; *crew:* 7

Plate 130

American bombers for the Allies: 1942–44

MARTIN BALTIMORE Mk I
Nation: USA; *manufacturer:* Glenn L. Martin Co; *type:* bomber;
year: 1942; *engine:* two Wright R-2600-A5B Cyclone 14-cylinder
radial air-cooled, 1,660 hp each; *wingspan:* 61 ft 4 in (18.69 m);
length: 48 ft 6 in (14.78 m); *height:* 17 ft 9 in (5.41 m); *weight:*
23,000 lb (10,432 kg) (loaded); *maximum speed:* 302 mph
(486 km/h) at 1,000 ft (3,350 m); *ceiling:* 24,000 ft (7,315 m);
range: 950 miles (1,530 km); *armament:* 8 machine guns; 2,000 lb
(907 kg) of bombs; *crew:* 4

MARTIN BALTIMORE Mk IV
Nation: USA; *manufacturer:* Glenn L. Martin Co; *type:* bomber;
year: 1944; *engine:* two Wright R-2600-29 Cyclone 14-cylinder
radial air-cooled, 1,700 hp each; *wingspan:* 61 ft 4 in (18.60 m);
length: 48 ft 6 in (14.78 m); *height:* 17 ft 9 in (5.41 m); *weight:*
22,600 lb (10,250 kg) (loaded); *maximum speed:* 320 mph
(515 km/h) at 14,760 ft (4,500 m); *ceiling:* 24,600 ft (7,500 m);
range: 950 miles (1,530 km); *armament:* 8 machine guns; 2,000 lb
(907 kg) of bombs; *crew:* 3

DOUGLAS BOSTON Mk III
Nation: USA; *manufacturer:* Douglas Aircraft Co;
type: bomber; *year:* 1942; *engine:* two Wright
Cyclone GR-2600-A5B 14-cylinder radial air-cooled,
1,600 hp each; *wingspan:* 61 ft 4 in (18.69 m);
length: 47 ft (14.31 m); *height:* 15 ft 10 in (4.83 m);
weight: 25,000 lb (11,325 kg) (loaded); *maximum
speed:* 304 mph (490 km/h) at 13,000 ft (4,000 m);
ceiling: 24,250 ft (7,400 m); *range:* 1,020 miles
(1,650 km); *armament:* 8 machine guns; 2,000 lb
(907 kg) of bombs; *crew:* 4

VULTEE A-35A VENGEANCE
Nation: USA; *manufacturer:* Vultee Aircraft Inc;
type: bomber; *year:* 1942; *engine:* Wright
R-2600-13 Cyclone 14-cylinder radial air-cooled,
1,700 hp; *wingspan:* 48 ft (14.63 m); *length:* 39 ft
9 in (12.12 m); *height:* 15 ft 4 in (4.67 m); *weight:*
16,400 lb (7,439 kg) (loaded); *maximum speed:*
279 mph (449 km/h) at 13,500 ft (4,100 m); *ceiling:*
22,300 ft (6,800 m); *range:* 2,300 miles (3,700 km);
armament: 5 machine guns; 2,000 lb (907 kg) of
bombs; *crew:* 2

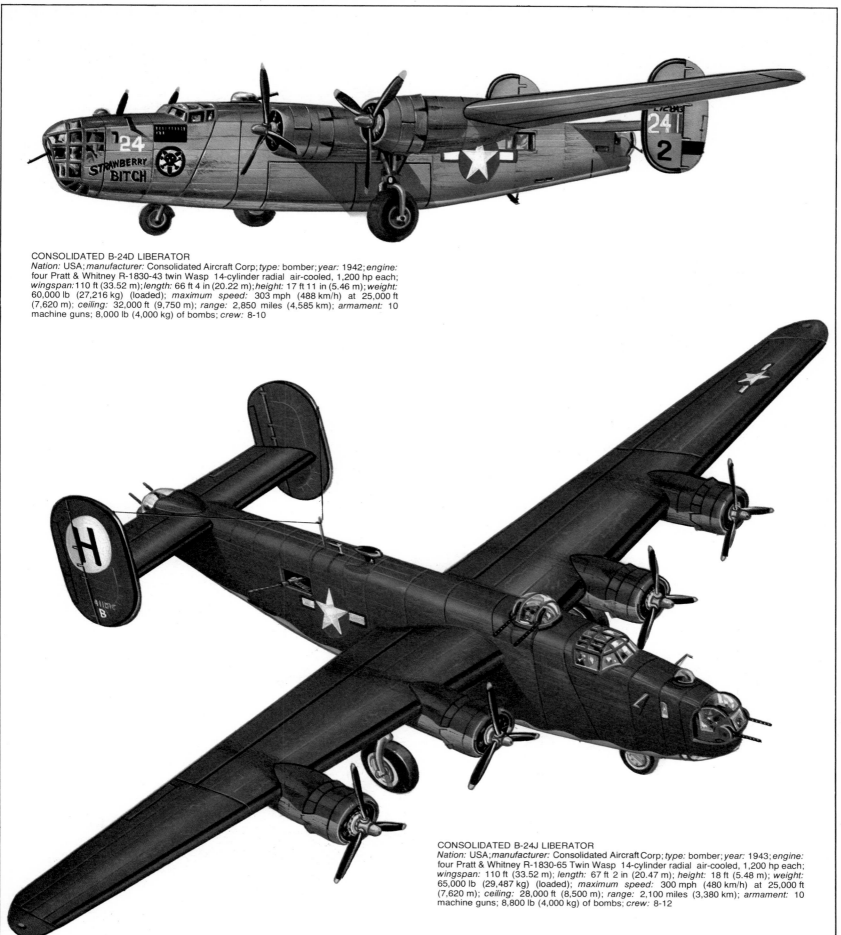

CONSOLIDATED B-24D LIBERATOR
Nation: USA; *manufacturer:* Consolidated Aircraft Corp; *type:* bomber; *year:* 1942; *engine:* four Pratt & Whitney R-1830-43 twin Wasp 14-cylinder radial air-cooled, 1,200 hp each; *wingspan:* 110 ft (33.52 m); *length:* 66 ft 4 in (20.22 m); *height:* 17 ft 11 in (5.46 m); *weight:* 60,000 lb (27,216 kg) (loaded); *maximum speed:* 303 mph (488 km/h) at 25,000 ft (7,620 m); *ceiling:* 32,000 ft (9,750 m); *range:* 2,850 miles (4,585 km); *armament:* 10 machine guns; 8,000 lb (4,000 kg) of bombs; *crew:* 8-10

CONSOLIDATED B-24J LIBERATOR
Nation: USA; *manufacturer:* Consolidated Aircraft Corp; *type:* bomber; *year:* 1943; *engine:* four Pratt & Whitney R-1830-65 Twin Wasp 14-cylinder radial air-cooled, 1,200 hp each; *wingspan:* 110 ft (33.52 m); *length:* 67 ft 2 in (20.47 m); *height:* 18 ft (5.48 m); *weight:* 65,000 lb (29,487 kg) (loaded); *maximum speed:* 300 mph (480 km/h) at 25,000 ft (7,620 m); *ceiling:* 28,000 ft (8,500 m); *range:* 2,100 miles (3,380 km); *armament:* 10 machine guns; 8,800 lb (4,000 kg) of bombs; *crew:* 8-12

Plate 132   **The last German bombers – one is a jet: 1940–44**

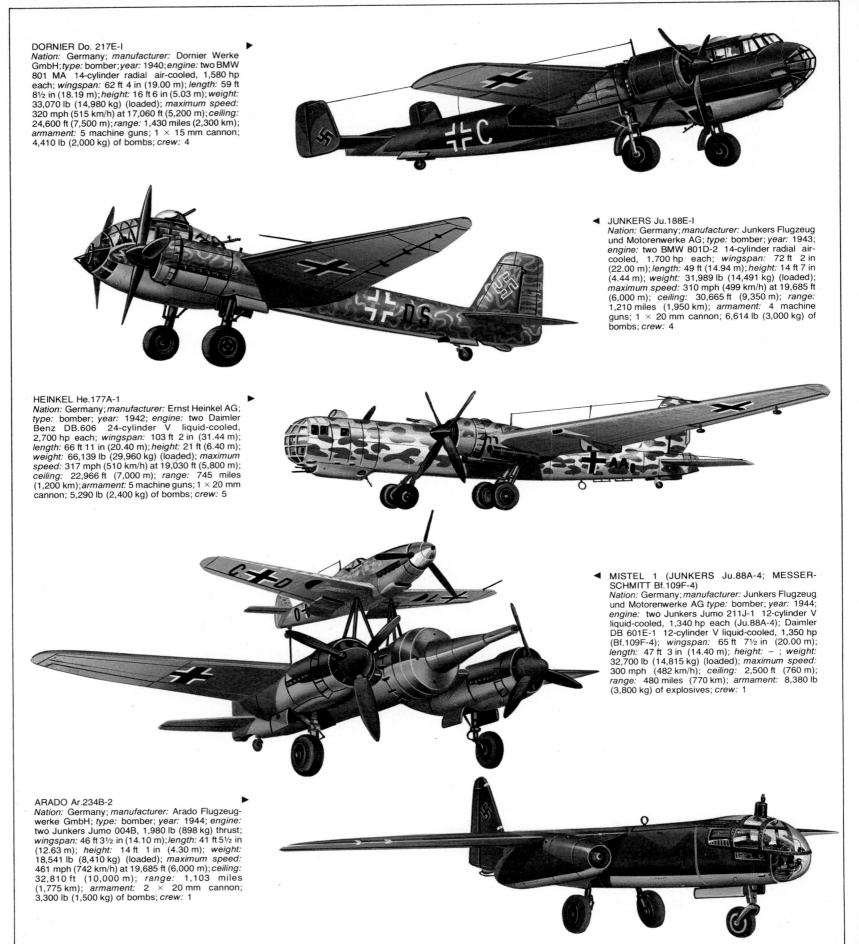

DORNIER Do. 217E-I
Nation: Germany; *manufacturer:* Dornier Werke GmbH; *type:* bomber; *year:* 1940; *engine:* two BMW 801 MA 14-cylinder radial air-cooled, 1,580 hp each; *wingspan:* 62 ft 4 in (19.00 m); *length:* 59 ft 8½ in (18.19 m); *height:* 16 ft 6 in (5.03 m); *weight:* 33,070 lb (14,980 kg) (loaded); *maximum speed:* 320 mph (515 km/h) at 17,060 ft (5,200 m); *ceiling:* 24,600 ft (7,500 m); *range:* 1,430 miles (2,300 km); *armament:* 5 machine guns; 1 × 15 mm cannon; 4,410 lb (2,000 kg) of bombs; *crew:* 4

JUNKERS Ju.188E-I
Nation: Germany; *manufacturer:* Junkers Flugzeug und Motorenwerke AG; *type:* bomber; *year:* 1943; *engine:* two BMW 801D-2 14-cylinder radial air-cooled, 1,700 hp each; *wingspan:* 72 ft 2 in (22.00 m); *length:* 49 ft (14.94 m); *height:* 14 ft 7 in (4.44 m); *weight:* 31,989 lb (14,491 kg) (loaded); *maximum speed:* 310 mph (499 km/h) at 19,685 ft (6,000 m); *ceiling:* 30,665 ft (9,350 m); *range:* 1,210 miles (1,950 km); *armament:* 4 machine guns; 1 × 20 mm cannon; 6,614 lb (3,000 kg) of bombs; *crew:* 4

HEINKEL He.177A-1
Nation: Germany; *manufacturer:* Ernst Heinkel AG; *type:* bomber; *year:* 1942; *engine:* two Daimler Benz DB.606 24-cylinder V liquid-cooled, 2,700 hp each; *wingspan:* 103 ft 2 in (31.44 m); *length:* 66 ft 11 in (20.40 m); *height:* 21 ft (6.40 m); *weight:* 66,139 lb (29,960 kg) (loaded); *maximum speed:* 317 mph (510 km/h) at 19,030 ft (5,800 m); *ceiling:* 22,966 ft (7,000 m); *range:* 745 miles (1,200 km); *armament:* 5 machine guns; 1 × 20 mm cannon; 5,290 lb (2,400 kg) of bombs; *crew:* 5

MISTEL 1 (JUNKERS Ju.88A-4; MESSER-SCHMITT Bf.109F-4)
Nation: Germany; *manufacturer:* Junkers Flugzeug und Motorenwerke AG *type:* bomber; *year:* 1944; *engine:* two Junkers Jumo 211J-1 12-cylinder V liquid-cooled, 1,340 hp each (Ju.88A-4); Daimler DB 601E-1 12-cylinder V liquid-cooled, 1,350 hp (Bf.109F-4); *wingspan:* 65 ft 7½ in (20.00 m); *length:* 47 ft 3 in (14.40 m); *height:* – ; *weight:* 32,700 lb (14,815 kg) (loaded); *maximum speed:* 300 mph (482 km/h); *ceiling:* 2,500 ft (760 m); *range:* 480 miles (770 km); *armament:* 8,380 lb (3,800 kg) of explosives; *crew:* 1

ARADO Ar.234B-2
Nation: Germany; *manufacturer:* Arado Flugzeug-werke GmbH; *type:* bomber; *year:* 1944; *engine:* two Junkers Jumo 004B, 1,980 lb (898 kg) thrust; *wingspan:* 46 ft 3½ in (14.10 m); *length:* 41 ft 5½ in (12.63 m); *height:* 14 ft 1 in (4.30 m); *weight:* 18,541 lb (8,410 kg) (loaded); *maximum speed:* 461 mph (742 km/h) at 19,685 ft (6,000 m); *ceiling:* 32,810 ft (10,000 m); *range:* 1,103 miles (1,775 km); *armament:* 2 × 20 mm cannon; 3,300 lb (1,500 kg) of bombs; *crew:* 1

PETLYAKOV Pe-2
Nation: USSR; *manufacturer:* State Industries;
type: bomber; *year:* 1941; *engine:* two Klimov
M-105R 12-cylinder V liquid-cooled, 1,100 hp
each; *wingspan:* 56 ft 3½ in (17.16 m); *length:* 41 ft
6½ in (12.66 m); *height:* 13 ft 1½ in (4 m); *weight:*
18,734 lb (8,515 kg) (loaded); *maximum speed:*
336 mph (540 km/h) at 16,400 ft (5,045 m); *ceiling:*
28,900 ft (8,800 m); *range:* 932 miles (1,500 km);
armament: 4 machine guns; 2,645 lb (1,000 kg) of
bombs; *crew:* 3

PETLYAKOV Pe-8
Nation: USSR; *manufacturer:* State Industries;
type: bomber; *year;* 1940; *engine:* four Mikulin
AM-35A 12-cylinder V liquid-cooled, 1,350 hp
each; *wingspan:* 131 ft (39,94 m); *length:* 73 ft 9 in
(22.49 m); *height:* 20 ft (6.10 m); *weight:* 73,469
lb (33,325 kg) (loaded); *maximum speed:* 272 mph
(438 km/h) at 24,930 ft (7,600 m); *ceiling:* 22,965 ft
(7,065 m); *range:* 3,383 miles (5,445 km); *armament:* 2 × 20 mm cannon; 4 machine guns; 8,818 lb
(4,000 kg) of bombs; *crew:* 10

◄ **TUPOLEV Tu-2**
Nation: USSR; *manufacturer:* State Industries;
type: bomber; *year:* 1943; *engine:* two Shvetsov
M-82 14-cylinder radial air-cooled, 1,850 hp each;
wingspan: 61 ft 10½ in (18.85 m); *length:* 45 ft 3 in
(13.80 m); *height:* 13 ft 11 in (4.25 m); *weight:*
28,219 lb (12,800 kg) (loaded); *maximum speed:*
342 mph (550 km/h) at 17,720 ft (5,400 m); *ceiling:*
31,200 ft (9,500 m); *range:* 1,243 miles (2,000 km);
armament: 2 × 20 mm cannon; 3 machine guns;
6,614 lb (3,000 kg) of bombs; *crew:* 4

COMMONWEALTH CA-11 WOOMERA (A23)
Nation: Australia; *manufacturer:* Commonwealth Aircraft; *type:*
bomber; *year:* 1944; *engine:* two Pratt & Whitney R-1830 S3C3- G
Twin Wasp 14-cylinder radial air-cooled, 1,200 hp each; *wingspan:* 59 ft 2½ in (18.03 m); *length:* 39 ft 7 in (12.06 m); *height:*
18 ft 2 in (5.53 m); *weight:* 22,287 lb (10,109 kg) (loaded); *maximum speed:* 282 mph (454 km/h); *ceiling:* 23,500 ft (7,230 m);
range: 2,220 miles (3,570 km); *armament:* 2 × 20 mm cannon; 7
machine guns; 3,200 lb (1,450 kg) of bombs; *crew:* 3

SAAB 18A
Nation: Sweden; *manufacturer:* Saab; *type:* bomber; *year:* 1944;
engine: two Pratt & Whitney Twin Wasp 14-cylinder radial air-
cooled, 1,065 hp each; *wingspan:* 55 ft 9 in (17.00 m); *length:* 43 ft
5 in (12.23 m); *height:* 14 ft 3 in (4.35 m); *weight:* 17,946 lb
(8,140 kg) (loaded); *maximum speed:* 289 mph (465 km/h) at
19,685 ft (6,000 m); *ceiling:* 26,250 ft (8,000 m); *range:* 1,367
miles (2,200 km); *armament:* 3 machine guns; 3,307 lb (1,500 kg)
of bombs; *crew:* 3

Plate 134

Japanese bombers: 1942–44

KAWASAKI Ki-48-II
Nation: Japan; *manufacturer:* Kawasaki Kokuki Kogyo KK; *type:* bomber; *year:* 1942; *engine:* two Nakajima Ha-115 14-cylinder radial air-cooled, 1,150 hp each; *wingspan:* 57 ft 3 in (17.45 m); *length:* 41 ft 10 in (12.75 m); *height:* 12 ft 6 in (3.80 m); *weight:* 14,880 lb (6,763 kg) (loaded); *maximum speed:* 314 mph (505 km/h) at 18,375 ft (5,600 m); *ceiling:* 33,135 ft (10,100 m); *range:* 1,491 miles (2,400 km); *armament:* 3 machine guns; 1,764 lb (800 kg) of bombs; *crew:* 4

◄ NAKAJIMA Ki-49-IIb DONRYU
Nation: Japan; *manufacturer:* Nakajima Hikoki KK; *type:* bomber; *year:* 1942; *engine:* two Nakajima Ha-109 14-cylinder radial air-cooled, 1,450 hp each; *wingspan:* 67 ft (20.42 m); *length:* 54 ft 1½ in (16.50 m); *height:* 13 ft 11 in (4.25 m); *weight:* 25,133 lb (11,424 kg) (loaded); *maximum speed:* 306 mph (492 km/h) at 16,400 ft (5.000 m); *ceiling:* 30,510 ft (9,300 m); *range:* 1,833 miles (2,950 km); *armament:* 1 × 20 mm cannon; 5 machine guns; 2,205 lb (1,000 kg) of bombs; *crew:* 8

YOKOSUKA D4Y1 SUISEI
Nation: Japan; *manufacturer:* Aichi Kokuki KK; *type:* bomber; *year:* 1943; *engine:* Aichi AE1A Atsuta 12-cylinder V liquid-cooled, 1,200 hp; *wingspan:* 37 ft 9 in (11.50 m); *length:* 33 ft 6½ in (10.22 m); *height:* 12 ft 1 in (3.67 m); *weight:* 9,370 lb (4,260 kg) (loaded); *maximum speed:* 343 mph (552 km/h) at 15,585 ft (4,750 m); *ceiling:* 32,480 ft (9,900 m); *range:* 978 miles (1,575 km); *armament:* 3 machine guns; 683 lb (310 kg) of bombs; *crew:* 2

MITSUBISHI Ki-67-I HIRYU
Nation: Japan; *manufacturer:* Mitsubishi Jukogyo KK; *type:* bomber; *year:* 1944; *engine:* two Mitsubishi Ha-104 14-cylinder radial air-cooled, 1,900 hp each; *wingspan:* 73 ft 10 in (22.50 m); *length:* 61ft 4 in (18.70 m); *height:* 25 ft 3 in (7.70 m); *weight:* 30,347 lb (13,765 kg) (loaded); *maximum speed:* 334 mph (537 km/h) at 19,685 ft (6,055 m); *ceiling:* 31,070 ft (9,470 m); *range:* 2,360 miles (3,800 km); *armament:* 1 × 20 mm cannon; 4 machine guns; 1,764 lb (800 kg) of bombs; *crew:* 6-8

NAKAJIMA C8N1 RENZAN
Nation: Japan; *manufacturer:* Nakajima Hikoku KK; *type:* bomber; *year:* 1944; *engine:* four Nakajima NK9K-L Homare 24 18-cylinder radial air-cooled, 2,000 hp each; *wingspan:* 106 ft 9 in (32.54 m); *length:* 75 ft 3 in (22.93 m); *height:* 23 ft 7 in (7.20 m); *weight:* 70,897 lb (32,150 kg) (loaded); *maximum speed:* 368 mph (592 km/h) at 26,245 ft (8,000 m); *ceiling:* 33,465 ft (10,200 m); *range:* 4,639 miles (7,500 km); *armament:* 6 × 20 mm cannon; 4 machine guns; 8,818 lb (4,000 kg) of bombs; *crew:* 10

DOUGLAS SBD-3 DAUNTLESS
Nation: USA; *manufacturer:* Douglas Aircraft Co; *type:* bomber; *year:* 1941; *engine:* Wright R-1820-52 Cyclone 9-cylinder radial air-cooled, 1,000 hp; *wingspan:* 41 ft 6 in (12.65 m); *length:* 32 ft 8 in (9.96 m); *height:* 13 ft 7 in (4.14 m); *weight:* 10,400 lb (4,717 kg) (loaded); *maximum speed:* 250 mph (402 km/h); *ceiling:* 27,100 ft (8,260 m); *range:* 1,345 miles (2,164 km); *armament:* 4 machine guns; 1,200 lb (544 kg) of bombs; *crew:* 2

CURTISS SB2C-1 HELLDIVER
Nation: USA; *manufacturer:* Curtiss-Wright Corp; *type:* bomber; *year:* 1943; *engine:* Wright R-2600-8 14-cylinder radial air-cooled, 1,700 hp each; *wingspan:* 49 ft 9 in (15.16 m); *length:* 36 ft 8 in (11.18 m); *height:* 13 ft 2 in (4.01 m); *weight:* 16,616 lb (7,537 kg) (loaded); *maximum speed:* 281 mph (452 km/h) at 16,700 ft (5,090 m); *ceiling:* 25,100 ft (7,650 m); *range:* 1,110 miles (1,785 km); *armament:* 2 × 20 mm cannon; 2 machine guns; 2,000 lb (907 kg) of bombs; *crew:* 2

BOEING B-29A SUPERFORTRESS
Nation: USA; *manufacturer:* Boeing Aircraft Co; *type:* bomber; *year:* 1944; *engine:* four Wright R-3350-57 Cyclone 18-cylinder radial air-cooled, 2,200 hp each; *wingspan:* 141 ft 3 in (43.05 m); *length:* 99 ft (30.18 m); *height:* 29 ft 7 in (9.02 m); *weight:* 141,000 lb (63,958 kg) (loaded); *maximum speed:* 358 mph (576 km/h) at 25,000 ft (7,620 m); *ceiling:* 31,850 ft (9,700 m); *range:* 4,100 miles (6,600 km); *armament:* 1 × 20 mm cannon; 10 machine guns; 20,000 lb (9,090 kg) of bombs; *crew:* 10

BOEING B-29-45-MO "ENOLA GAY"
Nation: USA; *manufacturer:* Boeing Aircraft Co; *type:* bomber; *year:* 1945; *engine:* four Wright R-3350-57 Cyclone 18-cylinder radial air-cooled, 2,200 hp each; *wingspan:* 141 ft 3 in (43.05 m); *length:* 99 ft (30.18 m); *height:* 29 ft 7 in (9.02 m); *weight:* 141,000 lb (63,958 kg) (loaded); *maximum speed:* 358 mph (576 km/h) at 25,000 ft (7,620 m); *ceiling:* 31,850 ft (9,700 m); *range:* 4,100 miles (6,600 km); *armament:* 1 × 20 mm cannon; 10 machine guns; 20,000 lb (9,090 kg) of bombs; *crew:* 10

Plate 136

The last Japanese bombers: 1945

YOKOSUKA P1Y1 GINGA
Nation: Japan; *manufacturer:* Nakajima Hikoki KK; *type:* bomber; *year:* 1945; *engine:* two Nakajima NK9C Homare 11 18-cylinder radial air-cooled, 1,825 hp each; *wingspan:* 65 ft 7 in (20 m); *length:* 49 ft 2 in (15 m); *height:* 14 ft 1 in (4.30 m); *weight:* 29,760 lb (13,530 kg) (loaded); *maximum speed:* 340 mph (547 km/h); *ceiling:* 30,840 ft (9,400 m); *range:* 3,338 miles (5,300 km); *armament:* 2 × 20 mm cannon; 2,205 lb (1,000 kg) of bombs; *crew:* 3

YOKOSUKA MXY7 OHKA 11
Nation: Japan; *manufacturer:* Dai-Ichi Kaigun Kokusho; *type:* suicide bomber; *year:* 1945; *engine:* three Type 4 Mk 1 Model 20 rockets, 1,764 lb (800 kg) thrust each; *wingspan:* 16 ft 9½ in (5.12 m); *length:* 19 ft 11 in (6.06 m); *height:* 3 ft 10 in (1.16 m); *weight:* 4,718 lb (2,140 kg) (loaded); *maximum speed:* 403 mph (648 km/h) at 11,485 ft (3,500 m); *terminal dive velocity:* 576 mph (926 km/h); *range:* 23 miles (37 km); *armament:* 2,646 lb (1,200 kg) of high explosive; *crew:* 1

AICHI B7A2 RYUSEI
Nation: Japan; *manufacturer:* Aichi Kokuki KK; *type:* bomber; *year:* 1945; *engine:* Nakajima NK9C Homare 12 18-cylinder radial air-cooled, 1,825 hp; *wingspan:* 47 ft 3 in (14.40 m); *length:* 37 ft 8 in (11.49 m); *height:* 13 ft 4½ in (4.07 m); *weight:* 14,330 lb (6,500 kg) (loaded); *maximum speed:* 352 mph (566 km/h); *ceiling:* 36,910 ft (11,250 m); *range:* 1,888 miles (3,000 km); *armament:* 2 × 20 mm cannon; 1 machine gun; 1,896 lb (860 kg) of bombs or 1 × 1,764 lb (800 kg) torpedo; *crew:* 2

NAKAJIMA KIKKA
Nation: Japan; *manufacturer:* Nakajima Hikoki KK; *type:* bomber; *year:* 1945; *engine:* two Ne-20, 1,047 lb (475 kg) thrust each; *wingspan:* 32 ft 9 in (10 m); *length:* 26 ft 8 in (8.12 m); *height:* 9 ft 8 in (2.95 m); *weight:* 7,716 lb (3,500 kg) (loaded); *maximum speed:* 443 mph (712 km/h) at 32,810 ft (10,000 m); *ceiling:* 39,370 ft (12,000 m); *range:* 586 miles (950 km); *armament:* 1,764 lb (800 kg) of bombs; *crew:* 1

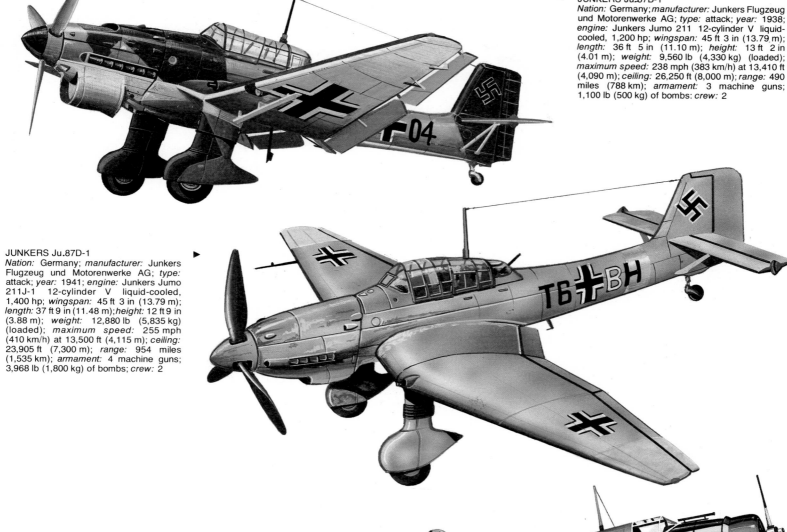

JUNKERS Ju.87B-1
Nation: Germany; *manufacturer:* Junkers Flugzeug und Motorenwerke AG; *type:* attack; *year:* 1938; *engine:* Junkers Jumo 211 12-cylinder V liquid-cooled, 1,200 hp; *wingspan:* 45 ft 3 in (13.79 m); *length:* 36 ft 5 in (11.10 m); *height:* 13 ft 2 in (4.01 m); *weight:* 9,560 lb (4,330 kg) (loaded); *maximum speed:* 238 mph (383 km/h) at 13,410 ft (4,090 m); *ceiling:* 26,250 ft (8,000 m); *range:* 490 miles (788 km); *armament:* 3 machine guns; 1,100 lb (500 kg) of bombs: *crew:* 2

JUNKERS Ju.87D-1
Nation: Germany; *manufacturer:* Junkers Flugzeug und Motorenwerke AG; *type:* attack; *year:* 1941; *engine:* Junkers Jumo 211J-1 12-cylinder V liquid-cooled, 1,400 hp; *wingspan:* 45 ft 3 in (13.79 m); *length:* 37 ft 9 in (11.48 m); *height:* 12 ft 9 in (3.88 m); *weight:* 12,880 lb (5,835 kg) (loaded); *maximum speed:* 255 mph (410 km/h) at 13,500 ft (4,115 m); *ceiling:* 23,905 ft (7,300 m); *range:* 954 miles (1,535 km); *armament:* 4 machine guns; 3,968 lb (1,800 kg) of bombs; *crew:* 2

PZL P.23B
Nation: Poland; *manufacturer:* Pantswowe Zaklady Lotnicze; *type:* attack; *year:* 1937; *engine:* PZL-Bristol Pegasus VIII 9-cylinder radial air-cooled, 680 hp; *wingspan:* 45 ft 9½ in (13.95 m); *length:* 31 ft 9½ in (9.68 m); *height:* 10 ft 10 in (3.30 m); *weight:* 7,773 lb (3,526 kg) (loaded); *maximum speed:* 198 mph (319 km/h) at 11,975 ft (3,650 m); *ceiling:* 23,950 ft (7,300 m); *range:* 782 miles (1,260 km); *armament:* 2 machine guns; 1,543 lb (700 kg) of bombs; *crew:* 3

NORTHROP A-17A
Nation: USA; *manufacturer:* Northrop Co; *type:* attack; *year:* 1936; *engine:* Pratt & Whitney R-1535-13 Wasp 9-cylinder radial air-cooled, 825 hp; *wingspan:* 47 ft 9 in (14.55 m); *length:* 31 ft 8 in (9.65 m); *height:* 12 ft (3.65 m); *weight:* 7,543 lb (3,421 kg) (loaded); *maximum speed:* 220 mph (354 km/h) at 2,500 ft (762 m); *ceiling:* 19,400 ft (5,900 m); *range:* 732 miles (1,180 km); *armament:* 5 machine guns; 400 lb (180 kg) of bombs; *crew:* 2

BREDA 88
Nation: Italy; *manufacturer:* Società Italiana Ernesto Breda; *type:* attack; *year:* 1938; *engine:* two Piaggio P.XI RC 40 14-cylinder radial air-cooled, 1,000 hp each; *wingspan:* 51 ft 2 in (15.60 m); *length:* 35 ft 5 in (10.79 m); *height:* 10 ft 3 in (3.10 m); *weight:* 14,900 lb (6,750 kg) (loaded); *maximum speed:* 304 mph (409 km/h); *ceiling:* 26,200 ft (8,000 m); *range:* 1,019 miles (1,640 km); *armament:* 4 machine guns; 2,200 lb (1,000 kg) of bombs; *crew:* 2

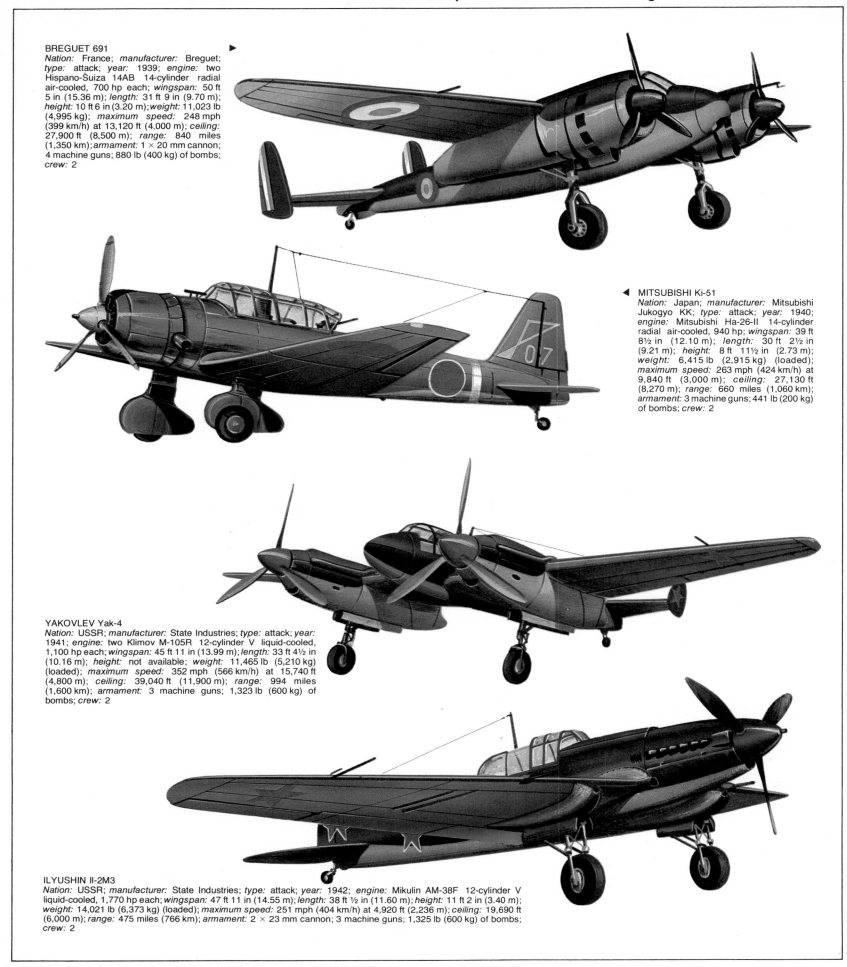

BREGUET 691
Nation: France; *manufacturer:* Breguet; *type:* attack; *year:* 1939; *engine:* two Hispano-Šuiza 14AB 14-cylinder radial air-cooled, 700 hp each; *wingspan:* 50 ft 5 in (15.36 m); *length:* 31 ft 9 in (9.70 m); *height:* 10 ft 6 in (3.20 m); *weight:* 11,023 lb (4,995 kg); *maximum speed:* 248 mph (399 km/h) at 13,120 ft (4,000 m); *ceiling:* 27,900 ft (8,500 m); *range:* 840 miles (1,350 km); *armament:* 1 × 20 mm cannon; 4 machine guns; 880 lb (400 kg) of bombs; *crew:* 2

MITSUBISHI Ki-51
Nation: Japan; *manufacturer:* Mitsubishi Jukogyo KK; *type:* attack; *year:* 1940; *engine:* Mitsubishi Ha-26-II 14-cylinder radial air-cooled, 940 hp; *wingspan:* 39 ft 8½ in (12.10 m); *length:* 30 ft 2½ in (9.21 m); *height:* 8 ft 11½ in (2.73 m); *weight:* 6,415 lb (2,915 kg) (loaded); *maximum speed:* 263 mph (424 km/h) at 9,840 ft (3,000 m); *ceiling:* 27,130 ft (8,270 m); *range:* 660 miles (1,060 km); *armament:* 3 machine guns; 441 lb (200 kg) of bombs; *crew:* 2

YAKOVLEV Yak-4
Nation: USSR; *manufacturer:* State Industries; *type:* attack; *year:* 1941; *engine:* two Klimov M-105R 12-cylinder V liquid-cooled, 1,100 hp each; *wingspan:* 45 ft 11 in (13.99 m); *length:* 33 ft 4½ in (10.16 m); *height:* not available; *weight:* 11,465 lb (5,210 kg) (loaded); *maximum speed:* 352 mph (566 km/h) at 15,740 ft (4,800 m); *ceiling:* 39,040 ft (11,900 m); *range:* 994 miles (1,600 km); *armament:* 3 machine guns; 1,323 lb (600 kg) of bombs; *crew:* 2

ILYUSHIN Il-2M3
Nation: USSR; *manufacturer:* State Industries; *type:* attack; *year:* 1942; *engine:* Mikulin AM-38F 12-cylinder V liquid-cooled, 1,770 hp each; *wingspan:* 47 ft 11 in (14.55 m); *length:* 38 ft ½ in (11.60 m); *height:* 11 ft 2 in (3.40 m); *weight:* 14,021 lb (6,373 kg) (loaded); *maximum speed:* 251 mph (404 km/h) at 4,920 ft (2,236 m); *ceiling:* 19,690 ft (6,000 m); *range:* 475 miles (766 km); *armament:* 2 × 23 mm cannon; 3 machine guns; 1,325 lb (600 kg) of bombs; *crew:* 2

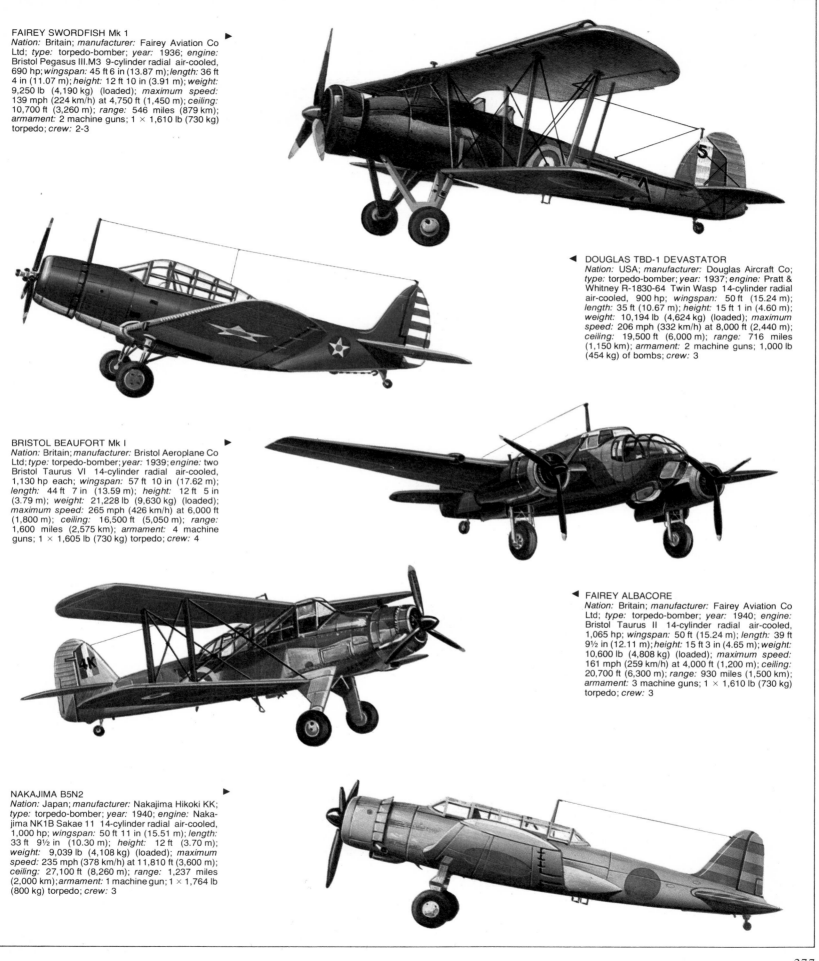

FAIREY SWORDFISH Mk 1
Nation: Britain; *manufacturer:* Fairey Aviation Co Ltd; *type:* torpedo-bomber; *year:* 1936; *engine:* Bristol Pegasus III.M3 9-cylinder radial air-cooled, 690 hp; *wingspan:* 45 ft 6 in (13.87 m); *length:* 36 ft 4 in (11.07 m); *height:* 12 ft 10 in (3.91 m); *weight:* 9,250 lb (4,190 kg) (loaded); *maximum speed:* 139 mph (224 km/h) at 4,750 ft (1,450 m); *ceiling:* 10,700 ft (3,260 m); *range:* 546 miles (879 km); *armament:* 2 machine guns; 1 × 1,610 lb (730 kg) torpedo; *crew:* 2-3

DOUGLAS TBD-1 DEVASTATOR
Nation: USA; *manufacturer:* Douglas Aircraft Co; *type:* torpedo-bomber; *year:* 1937; *engine:* Pratt & Whitney R-1830-64 Twin Wasp 14-cylinder radial air-cooled, 900 hp; *wingspan:* 50 ft (15.24 m); *length:* 35 ft (10.67 m); *height:* 15 ft 1 in (4.60 m); *weight:* 10,194 lb (4,624 kg) (loaded); *maximum speed:* 206 mph (332 km/h) at 8,000 ft (2,440 m); *ceiling:* 19,500 ft (6,000 m); *range:* 716 miles (1,150 km); *armament:* 2 machine guns; 1,000 lb (454 kg) of bombs; *crew:* 3

BRISTOL BEAUFORT Mk I
Nation: Britain; *manufacturer:* Bristol Aeroplane Co Ltd; *type:* torpedo-bomber; *year:* 1939; *engine:* two Bristol Taurus VI 14-cylinder radial air-cooled, 1,130 hp each; *wingspan:* 57 ft 10 in (17.62 m); *length:* 44 ft 7 in (13.59 m); *height:* 12 ft 5 in (3.79 m); *weight:* 21,228 lb (9,630 kg) (loaded); *maximum speed:* 265 mph (426 km/h) at 6,000 ft (1,800 m); *ceiling:* 16,500 ft (5,050 m); *range:* 1,600 miles (2,575 km); *armament:* 4 machine guns; 1 × 1,605 lb (730 kg) torpedo; *crew:* 4

FAIREY ALBACORE
Nation: Britain; *manufacturer:* Fairey Aviation Co Ltd; *type:* torpedo-bomber; *year:* 1940; *engine:* Bristol Taurus II 14-cylinder radial air-cooled, 1,065 hp; *wingspan:* 50 ft (15.24 m); *length:* 39 ft 9½ in (12.11 m); *height:* 15 ft 3 in (4.65 m); *weight:* 10,600 lb (4,808 kg) (loaded); *maximum speed:* 161 mph (259 km/h) at 4,000 ft (1,200 m); *ceiling:* 20,700 ft (6,300 m); *range:* 930 miles (1,500 km); *armament:* 3 machine guns; 1 × 1,610 lb (730 kg) torpedo; *crew:* 3

NAKAJIMA B5N2
Nation: Japan; *manufacturer:* Nakajima Hikoki KK; *type:* torpedo-bomber; *year:* 1940; *engine:* Nakajima NK1B Sakae 11 14-cylinder radial air-cooled, 1,000 hp; *wingspan:* 50 ft 11 in (15.51 m); *length:* 33 ft 9½ in (10.30 m); *height:* 12 ft (3.70 m); *weight:* 9,039 lb (4,108 kg) (loaded); *maximum speed:* 235 mph (378 km/h) at 11,810 ft (3,600 m); *ceiling:* 27,100 ft (8,260 m); *range:* 1,237 miles (2,000 km); *armament:* 1 machine gun; 1 × 1,764 lb (800 kg) torpedo; *crew:* 3

HEINKEL He.115B-1
Nation: Germany; *manufacturer:* Ernst Heinkel AG; *type:* torpedo-bomber; *year:* 1939; *engine:* two BMW 132K, 9-cylinder radial, air-cooled, 960 hp each; *wingspan:* 72 ft 2 in (22.00 m); *length:* 56 ft 9 in (17.30 m); *height:* 21 ft 8 in (6.60 m); *weight:* 20,065 lb (9,100 kg) (loaded); *maximum speed:* 220 mph (365 km/h) at 11,150 ft (3,400 m); *ceiling:* 18,040 ft (5,500 m); *range:* 2,080 miles (3,350 km); *armament:* 2 machine guns; 3,300 lb (1,500 kg) of bombs; *crew:* 3

GRUMMAN TBF-1 AVENGER
Nation: USA; *manufacturer:* Grumman Aircraft Engineering Corp; *type:* torpedo-bomber; *year:* 1942; *engine:* Wright R-2600-8 Cyclone 14-cylinder radial air-cooled, 1,700 hp; *wingspan:* 54 ft 2 in (16.51 m); *length:* 40 ft (12.19 m); *height:* 16 ft 5 in (5 m); *weight:* 15,905 lb (7,215 kg) (loaded); *maximum speed:* 271 mph (436 km/h) at 12,000 ft (3,660 m); *ceiling:* 22,400 ft (6,800 m); *range:* 1,215 miles (1,950 km); *armament:* 3 machine guns; 1,600 lb (725 kg) of bombs or torpedo; *crew:* 3

◄ **FAIREY BARRACUDA Mk II**
Nation: Britain; *manufacturer:* Fairey Aviation Co Ltd; *type:* torpedo-bomber; *year:* 1943; *engine:* Rolls-Royce Merlin 32 12-cylinder V liquid-cooled, 1,640 hp; *wingspan:* 49 ft 2 in (14.99 m); *length:* 39 ft 9 in (12.12 m); *height:* 15 ft 1 in (4.59 m); *weight:* 14,100 lb (6,394 kg) (loaded); *maximum speed:* 288 mph (463 km/h) at 1,750 ft (500 m); *ceiling:* 16,600 ft (5,000 m); *range:* 686 miles (1,100 km); *armament:* 2 machine guns; 1 × 1,620 lb (734 kg) torpedo; *crew:* 3

NAKAJIMA B6N2 TENZAN
Nation: Japan; *manufacturer:* Nakajima Hikoki KK; *type:* torpedo-bomber; *year:* 1943; *engine:* Mitsubishi MK4T Kasei 25 14-cylinder radial air-cooled, 1,850 hp; *wingspan:* 48 ft 10½ in (14.89 m); *length:* 35 ft 8 in (10.88 m); *height:* 12 ft 5½ in (3.80 m); *weight:* 12,456 lb (5,660 kg) (loaded); *maximum speed:* 299 mph (481 km/h) at 16,075 ft (4,900 m); *ceiling:* 29,660 ft (9,040 m); *range:* 1,892 miles (3,050 km); *armament:* 2 machine guns; 1,764 lb (800 kg) of bombs; *crew:* 3

Plate 118
The Luftwaffe's battle-seasoned bombers: 1937—39

For some time before its existence was officially admitted, the *Luftwaffe* had set up a massive expansion programme in preparation for the war which was to break out a few years after this began. In this expansion development of the bomber assumed great importance and it was in these years immediately preceding the war that the bombers with which the Third Reich was to fight up to the last day of the war came into being.

The first effective aircraft of this type dated from 1934 based on a request from the technical department of the air ministry which was designed to mask Germany's real military intentions quite convincingly. The Junkers Ju.86 started its career as a twin-engine civil airliner, but it could very easily be converted into a bomber. In fact the Ju.86 was in service simultaneously with the *Luftwaffe* and in commercial use by Deutsche Lufthansa.

The first aircraft of the A-1 version were delivered in the late spring of 1936 but they immediately revealed the inadequacies of the Junkers diesel engines with which the aircraft was equipped. In the E-1 variant of 1937 the engines were replaced with two BMW 810 hp radial engines which noticeably improved performance.

The Ju.86 was then replaced in service by the Heinkel He.111. This twin-engine aircraft had also started off in 1934 as a fast commercial transport but very soon its real role was revealed: together with the Dornier Do.17 and with the Junkers Ju.88, this aircraft formed the backbone of the bomber units of the *Luftwaffe* at the outbreak of war. Production continued for the duration of hostilities, a total of just under 7,000 being constructed in ten versions.

The first variants of the He.111 series appeared in 1939, when the aircraft assumed its definitive configuration, due mainly to the adoption of the Junkers Jumo engine which, in increasingly powerful versions, was to equip all the following sub-types of the H series. When war broke out no less than 400 aircraft were operational with front-line bomber units of the *Luftwaffe*. They were first used in the *Blitzkrieg* in Poland and in France and, when flown in large numbers and unopposed by any worthwhile enemy aircraft, the Heinkel did a great deal of damage. Their decline as strategic weapons began in the Battle of Britain when, confronted by the formidable British fighters, the He.111s proved to be very vulnerable, needing large numbers of escorting fighters. The H series variants were numerous: after the H-2 and the H-3, one of the most

widely used versions was the H-6 which appeared in 1941, which could also be used as a torpedo-bomber. In the H-10 and the H-12 variant of 1943, the defensive armament was increased whilst the final version, the H-23 of 1944, was used as a paratroop transport.

The Dornier Do.17 was another that had originated as a fast transport plane, and in 1937 it even won a speed competition, the Circuit of the Alps. The most important variant in the progression towards the Do.217 was the Z series in which the basic aircraft had its airframe and the shape of the forward part of the fuselage substantially modified, just as had been done with the Heinkel He.111H. The preceding variants, Do.17E and Do.17P had been tried out in the Spanish Civil War and had proved relatively vulnerable in their ventral and rear sections. This was remedied by introducing a gunner's position in the underside of the nose.

By the summer of 1940 500 Dornier 17Zs were produced; among the most interesting variants, two were designed as night fighters, the Z-6 and the Z-10, which served mainly to develop the *Luftwaffe*'s proficiency in this kind of operational use. Two-thirds of the 370 Dornier Do.17s which were in service at the outbreak of war were of the Z series. They took part in all operations of the first two years of the war and it was only towards the end of 1942 that they began to be withdrawn from service.

The last of the trio was the Junkers Ju.88, an aircraft which was eventually seen to be the most versatile of the entire arsenal of the *Luftwaffe*. Bomber, night fighter, reconnaissance plane, dive-bomber, close support plane, torpedo-bomber: in all these roles the Ju.88 acquitted itself brilliantly and from 1939 to 1945 the assembly lines continued uninterruptedly, completing over 16,000 in 10 variants.

The project started on 15th January 1936, and at that time was expressly designed as a bomber; the first prototype flew on 21st December 1936. The first production series (A-1) reached the *Luftwaffe* units in the summer of 1939 and was constructed in 17 variants. The C and G night fighter series were also developed. The last bomber version was the Ju.88S of 1943, when streamlining was improved and more powerful 1,700 hp BMW engines were adopted.

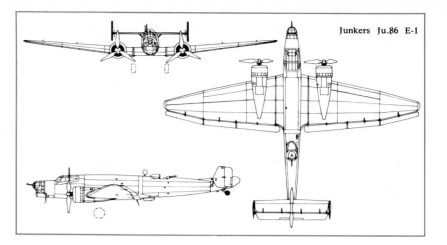
Junkers Ju.86 E-1

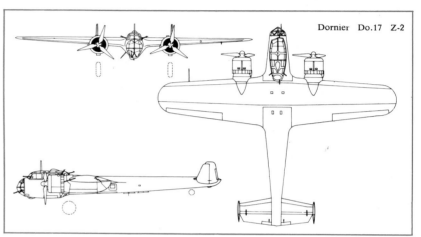
Dornier Do.17 Z-2

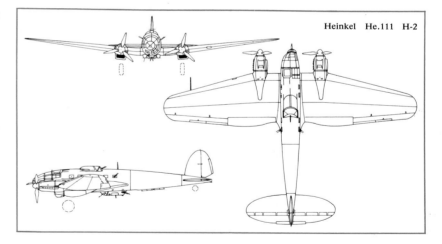
Heinkel He.111 H-2

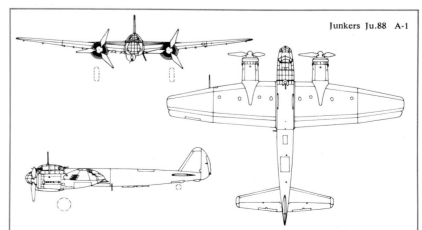
Junkers Ju.88 A-1

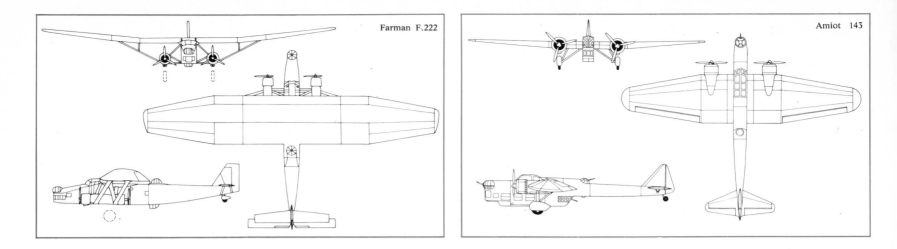

Farman F.222

Amiot 143

Plate 119
Obsolescent French bombers in service in 1938

Rarely, in a confrontation between two major industrial powers, has such disparity between opposing forces been so apparent as at the time of the German invasion of France. This was particularly true in the air, where the powerful and battle-seasoned *Luftwaffe* (at the time the most modern air force in the world) found itself facing the *Armée de l'Air* which was completely unprepared and insufficiently equipped. This was particularly obvious as regards bombers.

Among the few machines of this type to go into action before the Armistice was the Amiot 143. Outclassed by the more modern German aircraft, it was slow and unmanoeuvrable and this ugly twin-engine aircraft was involved in some of the most desperate actions during the defence of France. Among these was the day-time assault on the Sédan bridges on 14th May 1940: out of the 12 Amiots which took part in this action only one was to return to base.

The origins of this aircraft went right back to 1928, the year in which the air ministry had asked for a day and a night bomber to be built as part of a major production programme. Among the designs of four manufacturers (Blériot, Breguet, SPCA and Amiot) the Amiot 140 M was chosen and the prototype flew in 1931; two years afterwards 40 aircraft were ordered. Almost at the same time as the order was given, however, the original specification was changed: instead of a bomber a multirole aircraft was required which was also to be adapted for use as a heavy fighter and reconnaissance plane.

As a consequence the design was modified and two new prototypes which were designated Type 143 appeared in August 1934. At the end of the proving flights the aircraft was accepted and put into production. A number of orders were given and 178 aircraft were built: the day and night bomber variants were designated 143 BN4 and 143 B5. The first bombers of the final series flew in April 1935 and deliveries started in July 1935. Among the many units of the *Armée de l'Air* which were equipped with the Amiot 143, five bomber units were operational (with a total of 60 aircraft) at the outbreak of hostilities and the bombers' first flights started on the very same day that war was declared. By the time of the Armistice the Amiot 143 had dropped a total of 528 tonnes of bombs.

The 150 Bloch 210 aircraft which were in service with the *Armée de l'Air* on 3rd September 1939, however, were used on only a few operational missions. In fact this aircraft, even though superior in some ways to other contemporary machines, had come to be considered obsolete. Its design dated back to 1933 and the first prototype had flown on 23rd November of the following year. Series production was divided up amongst several manufacturers and a total of 253 aircraft were built, out of which 45 were for export. The Bloch 210 when it first appeared was the first low wing medium bomber with retractable undercarriage to be put into service by the *Armée de l'Air*.

The Farman F.222 which derived from the first 4-engine bomber of the *Armée de l'Air*, the F.221 of 1936, was also clearly obsolete. While keeping the general lines of its predecessor, the F.222 had a different landing gear, which was retractable unlike the fixed undercarriage of its forerunner. The 50 aircraft produced were delivered from the spring of 1937 onwards. During the first months of the war the Farman F.222s still in service were used on a series of reconnaissance missions and for leaflet raids over Germany, and in 1940 they were transferred to North Africa where they mainly operated as transports, and in some cases as naval reconnaissance planes. In their transport role these aircraft were used up to 1944.

The Latécoère 298 took an active part in the fighting in May 1940: this was a single-engine seaplane bomber which equipped units of the *Aéronavale*. The project had originated in 1935, based on a specification which called for a multirole aircraft which could be used as a reconnaissance plane, bomber and torpedo-bomber. The prototype had flown in May 1936 and about 200 were subsequently built in various versions, starting in the following year. It was powered by a Hispano-Suiza 880 hp engine and was capable of carrying a 670 kg (1,478 lb) bomb-load.

At the outbreak of hostilities the Latécoère 298 was in service with 8 units of the *Aéronavale*; one of these units subsequently joined Coastal Command of the RAF and was used in an anti-submarine role. Some models survived the Second World War and remained in service up till 1951, being used as trainers.

Plate 120
British bombers in service at the outbreak of war: 1937–39

The *Luftwaffe*'s complete superiority as regards bombers at the outbreak of war was obvious, even when compared with its principal adversary of that time, Britain. Among the aircraft in service with the RAF which clearly revealed their general obsolescence and their operational inadequacies, the Vickers Wellesley and the Fairey Battle were conspicuous; these two machines were fairly similar in their general concept.

The Wellesley flew in prototype form on 19th June 1935: it was a single-engine monoplane and had a very large wingspan which clearly showed the evolution of the light biplane bombers which were in service at the beginning of the thirties. A total of 106 of them were constructed and they went into operational service at the beginning of 1937. At the outbreak of the war, although obviously outdated, the Vickers Wellesley took part in a number of bombing missions in East Africa before being replaced in service by new and more effective twin-engine bombers.

More widespread – and eventful – was the use to which the Fairey Battle

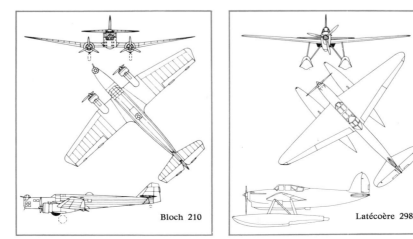

Bloch 210

Latécoère 298

was put, an aircraft which was only a little more modern than the Wellesley: in spite of its inferiority it was thrown into the fray in the first months of the war, especially in the Battle of France, suffering very heavy losses. The design had originated from an Air Ministry specification which had been issued in April 1933. At that time a light mono-plane bomber was required which was to be equipped with a retractable undercarriage, to replace the old Hawker Hart biplanes of 1930.

The prototype flew on 10th March 1936 and some months later, at the end of the tests and proving trials, was accepted by the RAF. The initial order was for 655 for the first Mk I production series, and very soon this was followed by other very large orders. To fulfill these requirements other manufacturers were called in and achieved a total production of 2,185 aircraft out of the 2,419 originally requested. The assembly lines were finally shut down in September 1940 in order to make way for more up-to-date machines.

The service use of the Battle started in March 1937 with the delivery of these aircraft to two squadrons, and a year later fifteen squadrons of Bomber Command had put the new aeroplane into service. Sent to France in 1939, these bombers carried out the first operational flights of the conflict and it was a Battle which achieved the RAF's first 'kill' of the war, a German aircraft on 20th September 1939. Combat experience, however, soon showed up the Battle's general inferiority. With-drawn from daytime operations but then put back into the line in response to the desperate pressures of this stage of the war, the Battles had their moment of glory in May 1940 in on-slaughts against the Germans. In the summer they were gradually with-drawn from the front line and used as trainers and as target tugs.

The Bristol Blenheim was far more outstanding, although it belonged to the same generation of combat air-craft; this was a twin-engine light bomber which originated in 1934 as a result of the initiative of the news-paper magnate Lord Rothermere, who wanted a commercial aircraft for his own use that would be faster than any other in the world. Indeed the pro-totype, which appeared on 12th April 1935, the Bristol Type 142, showed that it could exceed the speed of even the most advanced fighters in service at the time but when the Air Ministry, to whom Lord Rothermere then offered the aircraft, decided to develop it as a bomber, its originally brilliant performance was seriously reduced in the process of adaptation, and this resulted in the Blenheim turn-ing into a mediocre bomber.

Production (which reached a total of just under 5,500) started with the Mk I series which went into service in January 1937. A year later, the new bombers were sent overseas and at the outbreak of hostilities remained in the operational theatres of the Mediterra-

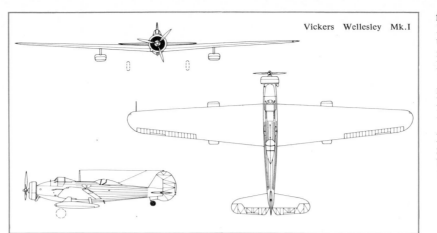

Vickers Wellesley Mk.I

nean, North Africa and the British colonies. It was the first admission of the inferiority of the Blenheim when confronted with the harsh reality of the war in Europe.

An attempt was also made to improve the aircraft by increasing the power of its armament and transform-ing it into a heavy fighter (Mk I F) but this version did not turn out satisfac-torily. At the beginning of 1939 the second production series, designated the Mk IV, appeared. The nose design was revised in these aircraft and the engines were changed to improved

Bristol Mercury XV engines of increased power (920 hp); the range was increased – it could comfortably stay in the air for a good 2,350 km (1,460 miles) – and defensive and offensive armament were stepped up to 5 machine guns and 600 kg (1,325 lb) of bombs.

The outbreak of war found 180 Blenheim Mk IV in service, spread over a night fighter squadron, two army co-operation squadrons and 7 bomber squadrons. Their use con-tinued for three years and, although some aircraft were modified to a

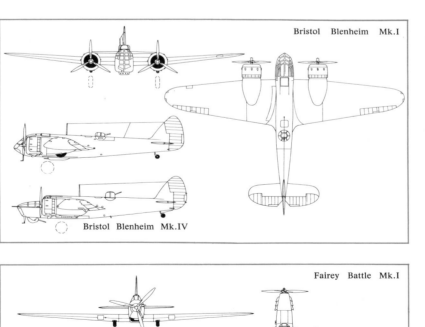

Bristol Blenheim Mk.I

Bristol Blenheim Mk.IV

Fairey Battle Mk.I

fighter version in the same way as the MK I Fs had been converted and were used with Coastal Command, the vast majority of Blenheims served with Bomber Command up till August 1942 when the twin-engine plane was replaced with the American Douglas Boston and with the de Havilland Mosquito.

As a point of historical interest the Blenheim Mk IVs of 107 and 110 Squadrons carried out the RAF's first bombing mission in the Second World War, on 3rd September 1939.

Plate 121
Only a few modern bombers are in service with the French, Polish and Dutch air forces: 1938–40

Turning to France: side by side with the clearly obsolete aircraft with which the bomber squadrons were equipped, the *Armée de l'Air* managed to put some modern aircraft into service as well, which had been developed dur-ing the second half of the thirties. Unfortunately enough, either they had their own inadequacies or they were delivered too late, so that the contribu-tion of even these bombers to the French war effort was virtually non-existent.

For example, the Bloch 131 was unsatisfactory; this was a twin-engine Marie which had been designed in 1935 and had appeared in prototype form on 16th August of the following year. The aircraft was derived from the preceding type 130 in an attempt to improve the performance of that aeroplane but the experiment showed itself to be a failure. At the time of its entry into service, the Bloch 131 was in fact almost immediately taken away from the bomber units and relegated to reconnaissance use. In all, 121 were constructed which remained in the front line up to the Armistice. Their usefulness was so doubtful that even the Germans preferred to destroy the aircraft they captured rather than use them. Some of them, however, remained in the use with the Vichy air force and were employed as target tugs.

The Lioré et Olivier LeO 451 turned out to be an excellent aircraft, but it arrived far too late; this was an elegant twin-engine plane which had been designed in 1934. The specification which had led to the design called for a day and night bomber capable of carrying up to 1,500 kg (3,300 lb) of bombs at a maxi-mum speed of 400 km/h (248 mph) and a range with bomb-load of 900 km (560 miles). The prototype of the LeO 45-01 flew for the first time on 16th

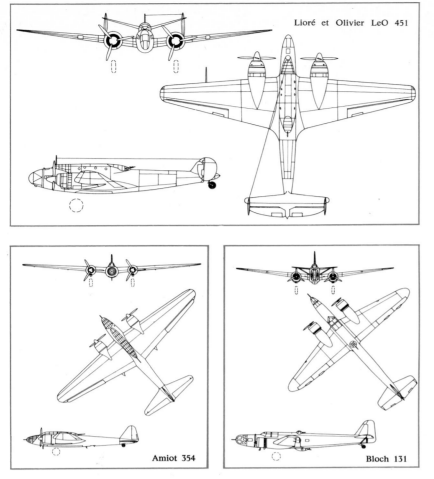

Lioré et Olivier LeO 451

Amiot 354

Bloch 131

Fokker T.VIII

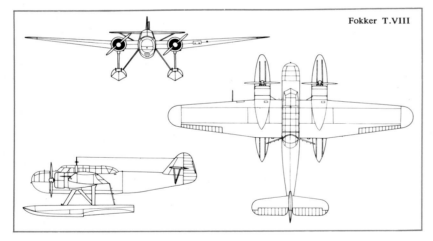

PZL P.37B

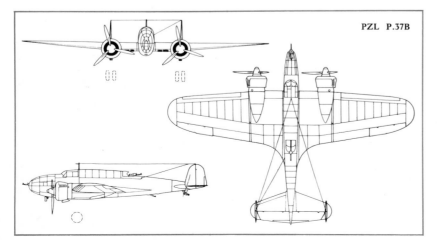

January 1937 and, apart from some problems of flight stability, it showed itself capable of excellent performance. In the course of testing, however, it became necessary to change the engines, replacing the two Hispano-Suiza 1,200 hp engines with two Gnome-Rhône 1,140 hp engines. It was therefore with these engines that the first series, designated LeO 451, was put into production. These aircraft appeared far later than had been foreseen by the production schedules because of serious supply problems and in September 1939 (the first LeO 451 of series production had flown on 24th March) a mere five aircraft were operational. On 10th May 1940, the *Armée de l'Air* had 222 of them at their disposal, but only half of these were ready for use. In total 452 aircraft were completed by the date of the French Armistice and another 150 were constructed during the Occupation. These were used by the Vichy Air Force and Navy.

The Germans did not take much interest in this bomber, converting some of them into transports and giving others to their allies. The *Regia Aeronautica* used 12 LeO 451s in its 51st Independent Bomber Wing. In spite of all this, after the war the surviving aircraft were put back into service in France, where they remained for another 12 years.

Another useful twin-engine bomber, the Amiot 354, had very limited operational use, being one of the numerous variants of the Series 350 which in turn had its origin in a design for an airmail carrier of 1934. The principal variants to be produced in quantity were the 351 (with Gnome-Rhône engines and twin fins), the 353 (two Rolls-Royce Merlin II engines and twin fins), the 354 (with new Gnome-Rhône radial engines but with a single fin). In 1939 total orders for these bombers amounted to 285 but the first Amiot 354 only flew in January 1940 and only 86 reached units before the Armistice.

An equally limited contribution was made to the course of the war by two other interesting aircraft, which were produced respectively in the Netherlands and in Poland. The Fokker T.VIII, which appeared in prototype form in 1938, was a twin-engined seaplane with large twin floats, giving good overall performance. About 40 of these were constructed, none of which was combat ready before the invasion. The majority were commandeered by the Germans and used in operations in the Mediterranean and in the North Sea. By an irony of fate, about 10 aircraft which had managed to flee to Britain joined RAF Coastal Command and filled the same role as the models which had been taken over by the Germans, and even did so in the same operational theatre – the North Sea.

Only 36 out of the 100 PZL P.37Bs which were constructed in Poland were in time to go into service at the outbreak of war. The aircraft had been designed in 1934 and the prototype had flown two years later. The first P.37A series had been delivered in 1938 and differed from its successor in its engines, which were less powerful. The PZL P.37s were among the best warplanes turned out by Polish industry.

Plate 122
SIAI Marchetti — the spearhead of the Italian bomber force: 1935–41

In Italy the bomber force of the *Regia Aeronautica* never equalled, either in the quality of their aircraft or in numbers, that of the other major powers, Axis or Allied. Typical examples of a series of aircraft which were eventually to be used very widely for the entire duration of the conflict were the three-engine bombers of SIAI Savoia-Marchetti, the designs of which were the result of the company's considerable experience in the field of commercial aviation, dating back to the early 1930s.

In 1935 the SIAI Savoia-Marchetti SM81 appeared, representing a considerable advance in the evolution of the warplanes which the *Regia Aeronautica* had at its disposal. Fast, well armed and with a good range, this three-engine aircraft was tested in action in the invasion of Abyssinia and in the Spanish Civil War, and its success (a very relative success, however, in view of the conditions in which the SM.81s were operating, which could not be compared with those of the fast approaching world war) led to orders for mass production and a total of 534 left the assembly lines. In the world war the SM.81 soon showed its limitations and it was clear that it was becoming obsolescent. In spite of this, it remained in service for the duration of the war and operated on all fronts where Italy was involved, although it was used as a transport after the appearance in large numbers of its successor, the SM.79 Sparviero.

Whereas the SM.81 was a military version of an airliner (the SM.73, of 1934) the Sparviero was a completely new design which shared only the general three-engine, low wing monoplane configuration with its predecessor. The prototype which had been designed as an 8-seat airliner to take part in the international London–Melbourne race, flew for the first time in October 1934. It was overall an excellent aircraft and in particular it had a high top speed, and in September 1935 managed to win as many as six world speed records over 1,000 and 2,000 km (620 and 1,240 miles), with respective payloads of 500, 1,000 and 2,000 kg (1,100, 2,200 and 4,400 lb).

As a result of these achievements the air force took an interest in it and they asked for a second prototype to be built in a bomber version. Once completed, this did not differ structurally from the civil version, the only variations being the addition of a ventral gondola and of a characteristic raised cockpit (which earned the SM.79s their nickname of "Hunchback" by which they were known to both their friends and enemies), these modifications being necessitated by the installation of defensive armament. Production, which was started in October 1936, proceeded uninterruptedly until June 1943, a total of 1,217 aircraft being constructed in all.

After its operational debut in the Spanish Civil War from February 1937 onwards, which was followed by a period when a number of appropriately modified versions took part in competitive events, the outbreak of the world war found 594 SM.79s in the front line. Soon the role of torpedo-bomber was added to their primary bomber role, and in this capacity the Sparviero was unequalled. After serving on all fronts, the aircraft continued in service after September 1943 as a torpedo-bomber. The Co-Belligerent Air Force, however, used this aircraft as a transport. The final variant, the SM.79 III, appeared in 1943 and had more powerful engines and better aerodynamic performance.

The SM.79 B was built for export and differed in that it had only two engines, and in consequence the fuselage was once more modified. Constructed in 1938 for commercial use, 113 of them were built, out of which 16 were constructed under licence in Romania; it was also sold to Iraq, Yugoslavia and Brazil.

From 1941 onwards the Sparviero was joined in operational service by a new, more up-to-date aircraft, the SM.84. This aircraft had been designed especially by Marchetti to replace the SM.79 but in the event this intention was never achieved. Whilst it was an adequate aircraft in its own right, it could not compare with the Sparviero. For example, its lack of manoeuvrability imposed serious limitations on its use as a torpedo-bomber.

The prototype flew on 5th June 1940 and production was immediately started with an order for 246 aircraft, which was increased to 309 later. The first of these became operational in February 1941. The SM.84 never shone in combat but gave good service in the Mediterranean up to the Armistice, mainly with bomber units. In spite of this a hybrid version, the SM.84 bis, was produced in 1942, in which an effort had been made to uprate the aircraft for use as a torpedo-bomber. Modifications included changes in the wing, the cockpit, the engine air inlets and the torpedo release controls.

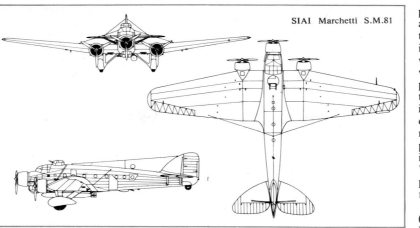

SIAI Marchetti S.M.81

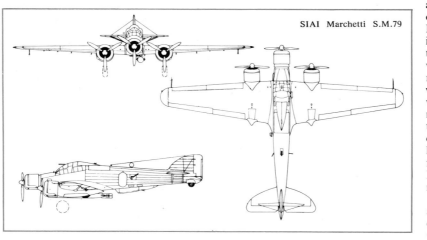

SIAI Marchetti S.M.79

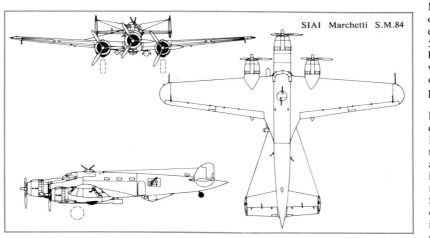

SIAI Marchetti S.M.84

Plate 123
The Italians produce only one four-engine bomber: 1937–43

The three-engine formula, besides being adopted by various Savoia-Marchettis, was also well-represented in the bombers produced by the Cantieri Riuniti dell'Adriatico (CANT). The patrol and bomber seaplane Z.506 B of 1937 derived from a civil aircraft, the CANT Z.506. Its particular good performance encouraged

production which, up to January 1943, also involved Piaggio and reached a total of 320 aircraft. Side by side with its use as a bomber the Z.506 B, which was called Erone (Heron), was worked hard as a reconnaissance plane, especially in the later phases of the war when the enemy's air superiority had become overwhelming. In the end these aircraft were used for air-sea rescue, an air ambulance version being produced, the Z.506S, and remained in service even after the end of the War. The last air ambulances were phased out in 1960 by the air-sea rescue service of the Italian air force.

The CANT Z.1007 Alcione (Kingfisher) was a better warplane, however, and together with the SM.79 and Fiat BR.20, typified the bombers of the *Regia Aeronautica*. Designed by Filippo Zappata, the first Z.1007 flew in the spring of 1937, but because of the inadequate power of the engines which were installed in it, it was soon replaced in production by a version with increased power, the Z.1007bis which was to become the standard model, and flew in both single-fin and twin-fin versions. The operational debut of the Kingfisher was not brilliant since it coincided with the ill-fated participation of the Corpo Aereo Italiano in operations over the Channel in September 1940.

A month later the first use of the aircraft in large numbers came about during the military operations against Greece and from then onwards the Mediterranean was the principal operational theatre for the three-engine CANT. Total procurement was 560 aircraft, the last 50 of which belonged to the the Z.1007 ter version which had appeared at the beginning of 1943 and had considerably more powerful engines.

The third Italian bomber was the Fiat BR.20 Cicogna (Stork) which was designed in 1936 by Celestino Rosatelli. Although it was modern and technically advanced at the time of its appearance (it first saw action in Spain in 1937), this twin-engine low-wing monoplane betrayed its obsolescence from the beginning of its operational career in the Second World War. But in spite of this, over 500 of them were constructed and served on all fronts up to the end of the war. Another, more powerful and more aerodynamically refined version was also built, the B.R.20 bis of 1942; overall performance was considerably improved but there was only time to produce 15 aircraft, which never saw operational service.

A similar fate was also suffered by an excellent prototype which never went into production: the CANT Z.1018, a machine in which Zappata abandoned the three-engine formula in order to produce a powerful and modern twin-engine bomber. The project was held up by a very lengthy period of development and by a succession of delays in the issuing of the ministerial specifications.

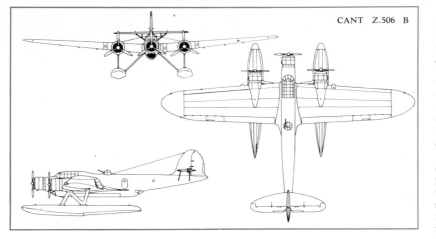

CANT Z.506 B

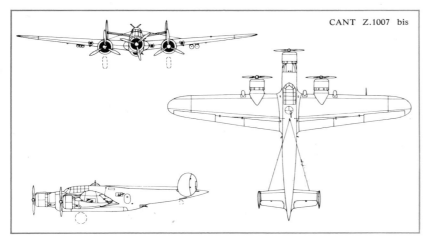

CANT Z.1007 bis

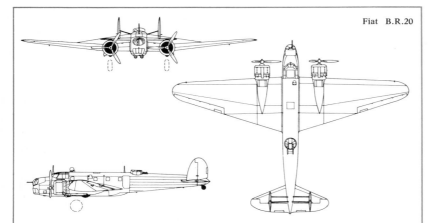

CANT Z.1018

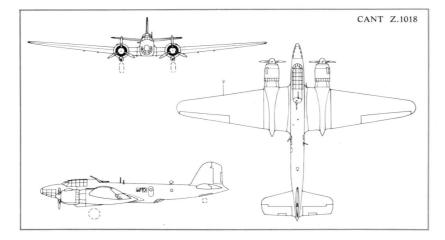

Fiat B.R.20

The Piaggio P.108 was totally competitive with other bombers in use anywhere in the world, and was the only four-engine bomber of the *Regia Aeronautica*. Designed by Giovanni Casiraghi, the P.108 flew for the first time on 24th November 1939 and went into service in May 1941. Crew training for conversion to this four-engine bomber proved more lengthy than foreseen and delayed entry into operational service until 9th June 1942, and service was intermittent during the last year of the war. The first production models of the P.108 were delivered in May 1941 to a specially-formed unit, the 274 Long-range Bomber Squadron. The main targets against which it flew were Gibraltar and Algeria, the latter at the time of the Allied landings in North Africa. In September 1943 the surviving P.108s were nearly all seized by the Germans, who never used them operationally.

Up to August 1943 production of this aircraft was: twenty-four P.108 Bs; a prototype (P.108A) armed with 102 mm cannon; another prototype (P.108C) for civil transport; and eight P.108 T military transports, which the Germans accepted.

Plate 124
British bombers: 1938–40

Among their medium bombers, the majority of the RAF's aircraft at the outbreak of war were of three types of twin-engine planes, all belonging to a generation of aircraft dating back to the middle of the 1930s: the Armstrong Whitworth Whitley, the Vickers Wellington and the Handley Page Hampden. These aircraft made up the British front-line bomber force until the arrival of the four-engine aircraft of the new generation which took over their strategic role.

The eldest of this trio was the Whitley. Based on a specification which had been issued in July 1934, this aeroplane flew in prototype form on 17th March 1936. Production was started immediately afterwards, and continued with the first series Mk I, Mk II and Mk III (34, 46 and 80 models respectively) differing from each other in their engines and armament. The largest series production was that of the Mk V (1,466 planes) which went into service in 1939, and in which the substantial modifications introduced in the preceding series, the Mk IV (40 built), were improved to the furthest possible extent, the most obvious being the replacement of the radial engines with two Rolls-Royce Merlin engines. The Merlin engines of the Whitley Mk V were in turn uprated later on, and as well as this change the fuselage, tailplane and fuel tanks were modified. The following version was the Mk VII, intended exclusively for Coastal Command and as such was equipped for an anti-submarine role. The Whitley Mk VIIs went into service at the end of 1941 and were the first bombers of Coastal Command to be fitted with radar for hunting submarines. They remained in service until the early months of 1943 while the Whitleys of Bomber Command were withdrawn from the front line in the spring of 1942.

The Vickers Wellington remained in service for the whole of the war,

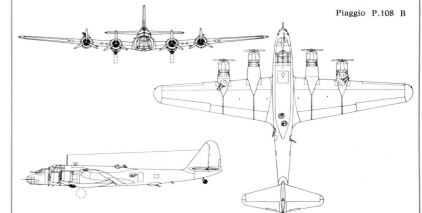

Piaggio P.108 B

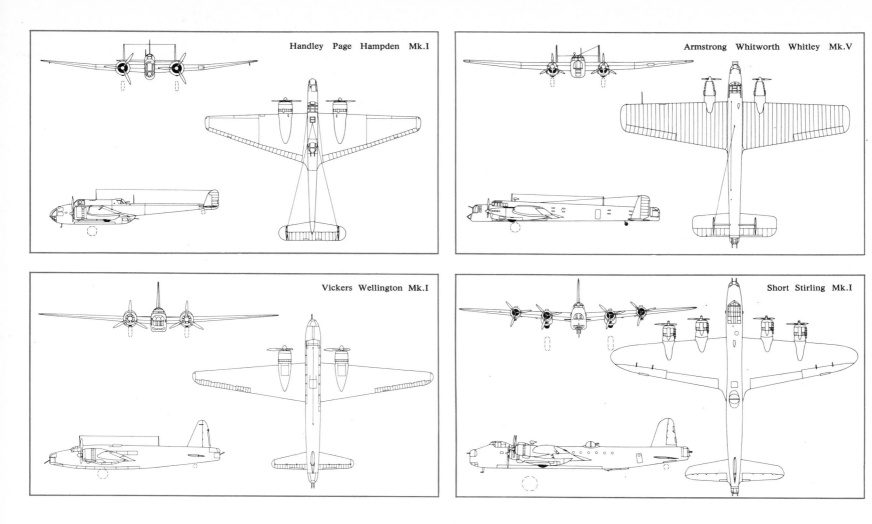

Handley Page Hampden Mk.I

Armstrong Whitworth Whitley Mk.V

Vickers Wellington Mk.I

Short Stirling Mk.I

being constructed from 1937 to 1945, reaching a total of 11,461 aircraft. The project had started off towards the end of 1932 and the prototype had flown on 15th June 1936. Undoubtedly one of the construction characteristics which made such an apparently elderly aeroplane so long-lived, compared with those with which it flew in the later stages of the war, was its geodetic design which gave it exceptional structural strength and enabled it to absorb considerable damage without having its operational capacities very much reduced.

The first series Mk I, Mk II and Mk III (which appeared as prototypes at the end of 1937 and in March and May 1939 respectively, and differed mainly in their engines) bore all the initial strain of the daytime bombing missions and were then used as night bombers, a role which they carried out up to October 1943. Their operational use however, continued uninterruptedly with the units of Coastal Command, for whom the subsequent mass production variants were manufactured from 1942 onwards.

The Mk VIII series was designed for reconnaissance, while the Mk XI, Mk XII, Mk XIII and Mk XIV (180, 58, 843 and 841 constructed) were used in a wide range of roles which varied from patrol and anti-

submarine, reconnaissance-bomber and mine-laying. The late series were used as transports: the Wellington Mk XV and Mk XVI, which were unarmed and had their bomb-bay sealed in order to accommodate a fuel tank. When the war was over the remaining Wellingtons were converted for use as trainers and remained in service with the RAF up to 1953.

The last of the three, the Handley Page Hampden, had a more limited career. It appeared in prototype form on 21st June 1936, and 1,430 aircraft were constructed in various production series, the first of which, Mk I, went into service in 1938. Even though it was fast and capable of carrying a considerable bomb-load, the Hampden proved inadequate as a day bomber, mainly due to its lack of defensive armament. After various modifications it was relegated to night bombing.

From August 1940 onwards a new, more powerful bomber joined the existing types in the RAF: the Short Stirling, the first four-engine British bomber. It was the first of another famous trio with the Handley Page Halifax and the Avro Lancaster; but the Stirling was never outstandingly successful, mainly because of its limited performance at high altitude.

The project commenced at the end

of 1936 and the prototype flew in May 1939. 712 of the first production series, the Mk I, were constructed and in 1942 it was joined by the Stirling Mk III, which had more powerful engines and armament. In its role of night bomber, this aeroplane remained in the front line up to half way through 1943 when it was relegated to a transport and target tug function; in 1944 and 1945 the two last series, Mk IV and Mk V, went into service specially equipped for these two roles. The Stirling Mk IVs which had absolutely no defensive armament were equipped with special towing gear: they were used for the first time on a massive scale on 6th June 1944, in the Allied invasion of Normandy. The aircraft of the MkV series (160 in all) were also completely unarmed and had a more streamlined nose: they went into service in January 1945 and were exclusively used as transports. They were replaced in the following year by the Avro York. In total 2,371 Stirlings were constructed.

Plate 125
At last in 1940, the arrival of Russia's first modern bombers: 1931–40

In the Soviet Union the commencement of war found the Russian army's air force short of modern bombers which could compete with the equivalent machines put into the field by the Germans. As in the case of the fighter, it was necessary to wait until the Soviet aircraft industry had recovered from the German attack and was capable of resuming production again before the front line was fully re-equipped with aeroplanes capable of resisting the *Luftwaffe*.

One of the oldest bombers in service at the moment of the German invasion was the Tupolev TB-3 (ANT-6), a gigantic four-engine aircraft designed by Andrei Nikolaivich Tupolev towards the end of the twenties which had gone into service in 1931. The development of this aircraft had been slow and beset by difficulties and only in 1935 had it been modified to assume its final form. At the outbreak of the Second World War when the obvious inadequacies of the TB-3 became apparent, it was decided to relegate the aircraft to a freight and

285

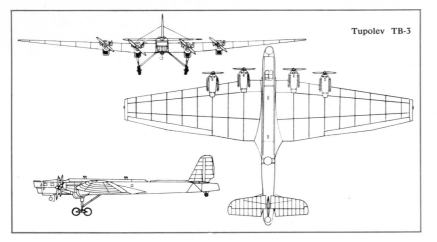

Tupolev TB-3

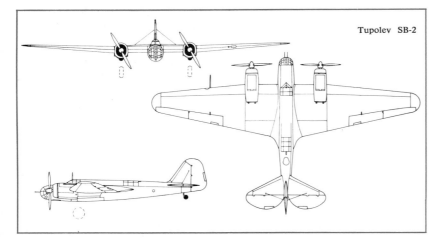

Tupolev SB-2

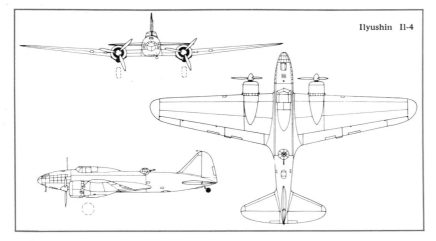

Ilyushin Il-4

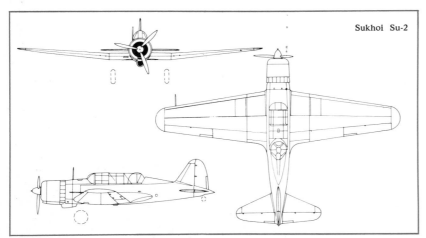

Sukhoi Su-2

paratroop transport role. Production ended on completion of the eight hundredth example and it was in front line service until 1944.

More modern (the design only went back to 1933) but still not really competitive when faced with more advanced enemy aircraft, was another Tupolev bomber, the SB-2 twin-engine which, on its operational debut in the Spanish Civil War in 1936 on the Republican side, had been impressive because of its excellent performance, especially its speed. Two prototypes, differing in their engines, had been prepared at the end of 1934, and mass production was ordered even before the commencement of the test flights. A total of over 6,600 aircraft of the SB-2 were constructed in various versions up to 1941. Among the principal variants were the SB-2 *bis* of 1938 and the SB-RK of 1940, a dive-bomber. After serving in actions against the Japanese in Mongolia in 1938 and 1939, the twin-engine Tupolevs took part in the attack on Finland, but subsequently, being hard-pressed by the German offensive, they began to show the limitations of their design and were transferred to night bombing. Gradually they were used in ever more secondary tasks, becoming trainers, target tugs and transports. A considerable number of SB-2s and SB-2 *bis* were converted for use as transports. Apart from serving in the Soviet air forces the Tupolev SB-2 was used by Nationalist China, Finland, Czechoslovakia and Bulgaria.

In 1940 a two-seat monoplane appeared, the Sukhoi Su-2, designed by Pavel Sukhoi in 1936 as a tactical attack bomber, and although it was hampered by a number of shortcomings it became operational whilst awaiting its replacement by the superior Ilyushin Il-2. At the time of the German invasion the first experiences of combat showed up these aircraft's shortcomings: poor manoeuvrability, mediocre general performance, and lack of adequate defensive armament which made it an easy prey for the powerful fighters of the *Luftwaffe*. An attempt was made to improve the aircraft by installing a more powerful engine, but even though performance did improve, the increased weight of the engine produced a negative effect on the aircraft's handling characteristics. In spite of all this, the Sukhois were kept in the front line up to 1942.

A major step forward was made among strategic bombers with the construction of the Ilyushin Il-4, a modern twin-engine plane which ended up by becoming the most widely used Soviet bomber of the war. Over 5,000 were built from 1939 to 1944. The Il-4 was designed in 1936 by Sergei Vladimirovich Ilyushin and went into service in 1940, but at the very moment when its presence in large numbers at the front would have been of the most use, production suffered a drastic cut (almost a suspension) because of two

problems: the necessity of evacuating the factories which manufactured the engines, and the serious lack of aluminium and other strategic materials.

As a consequence the designers tried to carry out a drastic structural revision, endeavouring to replace as many components of the aircraft as possible with wood, and changing the engine. This decision made it possible to recommence mass production after about a year, and thus modified the bomber was turned out in massive quantities up to 1944.

Besides the attack bomber version, a torpedo carrier variant was evolved for naval operations and destined for the *VVS-WMF* Soviet Navy. In this form the Ilyushin Il-4 was able to carry under its fuselage a torpedo of 940 kg (2,070 lb). In its bomber and anti-shipping roles, this twin-engine plane flew throughout the war, remaining in service for several years after the end of hostilities.

Plate 126
Japanese bombers in service at the outbreak of war: 1937–41

Hardened by combat against China, the Japanese air forces were prepared for a war of aggression, and were particularly advanced as regards their bomber force. The navy and the army both had at their disposal modern aircraft which were in general better than those of their adversaries and which contributed in no small way to the success of operations in the first stages of the Pacific war.

War with China was a good proving ground. In that conflict, in August 1937, the Mitsubish G3M (NELL in Allied code) made its debut and for the whole of the first year of the war constituted the backbone of the navy's units. Admiral Isoroku Yamamoto had been the one to push for the development of this twin-engine in 1933 and he had managed to convince the naval high command of the necessity of producing a long-range land-based bomber intended for use in the support of naval forces. The prototype (in a civil version) appeared in April 1934 and in the June of the following year the first of the 21 pre-series aircraft was developed to bring the bomber to its operational form, and

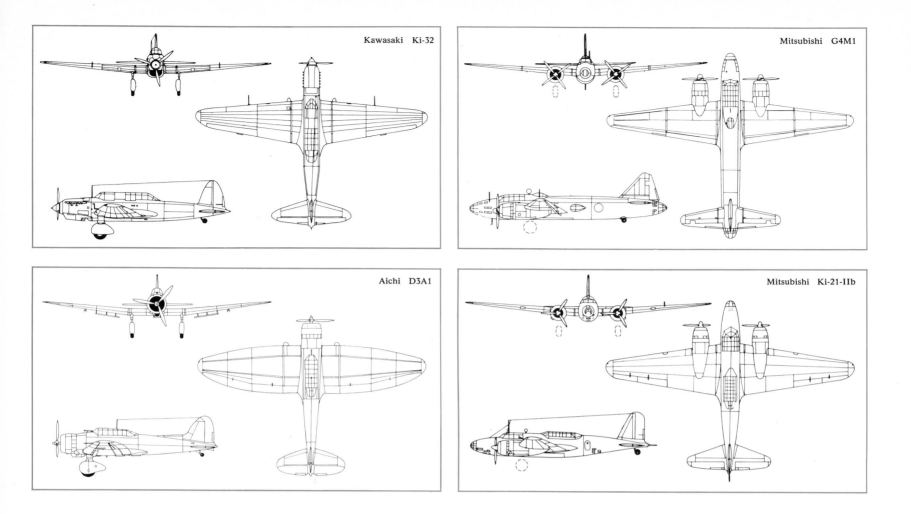

Kawasaki Ki-32

Mitsubishi G4M1

Aichi D3A1

Mitsubishi Ki-21-IIb

test flown. The initial version G3M1 was put into production in June 1936.

After 34 aircraft had been constructed the assembly line went on to the principal version, the G3M2, which had a more powerful engine and was developed in two sub-series, the 21 and the 22, of which 343 and about 400 were constructed respectively. A last version, made by Nakajima from 1941 onwards, was the G3M3-23, which was subsequently given more powerful engines and increased fuel capacity. Overall, up to 1943, 1,048 G3Ms were constructed.

In the course of its long operational life this bomber was used also as a transport, both civil and military; indeed in 1938 about 20 converted examples of the G3M2 were used by the two Japanese commercial airlines. As transports the G3Ms were identified in Allied code with the name of TINA.

On Japan's entry into the war the G3Ms were joined by a more modern aircraft which had been constructed especially to improve upon the G3Ms' excellent operational performance. The Mitsubishi G4M (BETTY in Allied code) was developed in the second half of 1937. This large twin-engine outclassed its immediate predecessor, especially in relation to speed and range, and in spite of some

limitations in the design, among them the lack of self-sealing fuel tanks which made the aircraft liable to catch fire under enemy attack, it ended up by becoming the most widely used Japanese bomber and was constructed in the greatest numbers: 2,446 were produced up to August 1945.

The first prototype flew on 23rd October 1939 and the aircraft of the intial production series, G4M1, left the assembly lines from April 1941 onwards. In the following year, the G4M2 version appeared which was more powerful, better armed and protected (1,154 aircraft), and at the end

of 1944 came the last variant, the G4M3, of which only 60 were built.

If the G3M and the G4M were typical of the bombers of the Imperial Navy, the Mitsubishi Ki-21 represented their equivalent in the Army's air force. Known in Allied code by the name of SALLY, the Ki-21 remained in the front line from the first to the last day of the war, in spite of its increasing inferiority in relation to its enemies. Production was sub-divided into five principal series and reached a high level: 2,064 were manufactured from March 1938 to September 1944.

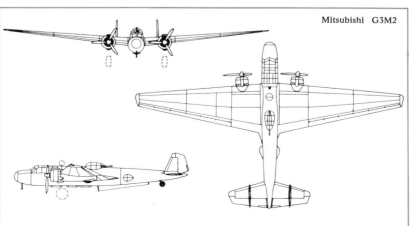

Mitsubishi G3M2

The first prototype flew on 18th December 1936 and the series of test flights to which it was subjected, together with two other aircraft, lasted for over a year. Production of the initial series Ki-21-Ia started in November 1937. This was followed by 120 Ki-21-Ibs and 160 Ki-21-Ics, which had more powerful defensive armament and increased fuel capacity. In December 1940 the first Ki-21-IIa appeared (590 constructed) in which the main modifications were to their engines and landing gear, and which were followed by 688 of the Ki-21-IIb sub-type which were later adapted and made more up to date.

The Japanese army and navy air forces also put excellent light bombers into the field. Up to 1942, for instance, the Kawasaki Ki-32 remained in the front line, one of the very few Japanese fighter aircraft to be powered by a liquid-cooled engine. Conceived in May 1936 following the same criteria which had led to the development in Britain of the Fairey Battle, the Ki-32 showed itself to be distinctly superior to the British aircraft. The prototype flew in March 1937 and the first production aircraft appeared in the second half of 1938. In all, 854 Ki-33s left the assembly lines. MARY was their name in Allied code.

Very much more distinguished was

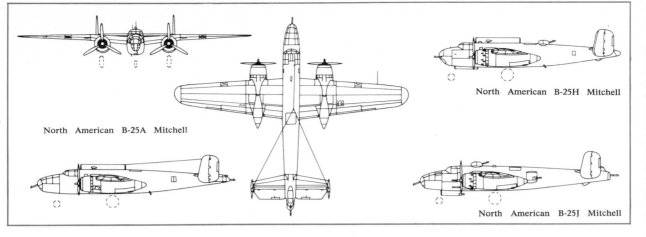

North American B-25A Mitchell

North American B-25H Mitchell

North American B-25J Mitchell

the navy's Aichi D3A (VAL) which was a contemporary of the Ki-32 and which proved to be one of the best dive-bombers of its time. The prototype flew in January 1938, and from December 1939 to August 1945 1,495 were built in three principal variants. The first, D3A1, went into service in 1940, and the second, D3A2, appeared two years later and had the highest production total, about 1,000. These aircraft had more powerful engines, the Kinsei 1,300 hp and also increased fuel capacity.

Plate 127
American bombers: the first serious threat to the enemy: 1941–43

In medium and heavy bombers the overwhelming strength of American industry soon made its weight felt during the progress of the war. On 19th August 1940 the aircraft which has been hailed as one of the best medium bombers of the war and the most widely used of its type among the Allies, appeared in prototype form: the North American B-25 Mitchell. Up to 1945 the production of this excellent and versatile twin-engine aircraft totalled over 11,000, of which slightly more than 9,800 carried United States insignia while the balance equipped air forces of the Allies, mainly Britain and the Soviet Union.

The design of the Mitchell (the name had been chosen in memory of General William "Billy" Mitchell, the man who in the early 1920s had exhorted the United States to increase its air power) was begun in 1938 and the definitive prototype had flown on 19th August 1940, and was ordered in large numbers straight off the drawing-board by the Army Air Corps. Production went forward at a rapid rate: after 24 initial aircraft it went on to the B-25A variant which

entered service in 1934 (40 produced); then on to the B-25B (120), the B-25C (1,619) and the B-25D (2,290). In all these production series which were gradually improved in equipment and general features, the armament was made considerably more powerful, especially its defensive armament, which in the D variant was notable for twin gun dorsal and ventral turrets.

During the course of 1942, as a result of the conversion of three B-25Cs into experimental prototypes, a new aircraft was produced which was to show itself to be an exceptional weapon, the B-25G (405 constructed) which was equipped with a 75 mm

cannon installed in the nose. The B-25H was then derived from these aircraft and went into service in the Pacific in February 1944: in this plane firepower was increased by the installation of 8 machine guns in the nose, which were added to the six which were in three defensive positions. These Mitchells, of which 1,000 were constructed, showed themselves to be deadly weapons in attack, whether over land or sea.

Still in 1944, the B-25J became operational; this was the final version, constructed in the greatest numbers, in which a return was first made to the traditional bomber with a glazed nose, then to that of ground attack aircraft

with the more powerful armament of the H variant.

If the Mitchell was impressive as a medium bomber, the Boeing B-17 Flying Fortress will always be remembered as one of the most celebrated four-engine American strategic aircraft of the war, only to be outdone, perhaps, by the Boeing B-29 which dropped the atomic bombs of Hiroshima and Nagasaki. The 299 project, as the B-17 was first coded by Boeing, began on 16th August 1934, on the basis of a specific request from the technical branch of the army which sought a new four-engine bomber to be ready before August of the following year.

The first prototype of the B-17 met the deadline, since it flew on 28th July 1935. It was followed by 13 pre-series aircraft which were delivered between 2nd December 1936 and 5th August 1937. Series production was started off in the following year with an order for 39 examples of the B-17B. The second order for 38 aircraft of the C series (which had more powerful armament, thicker armour plating and self-sealing fuel tanks) followed in 1939, and to this was added an order for 42 B-17 Ds in 1940. These aircraft were substantially the same as their predecessors and were the first to see action, together with the B-17Cs, in May 1941 in British hands, and afterwards under US colours at Pearl Harbor.

An important turning point in the course of production took place in 1941 with the appearance of the E variant, in which the rear section of the fuselage was completely redesigned in order to ensure greater flying stability at high altitude. In all 512 B-17Es left the assembly lines and the first ones saw operational service in the Pacific at the beginning of 1942. In the same year the F series (3,400 constructed) appeared with even more powerful armament, then in 1943 came the G series, which was produced in the greatest numbers. Intended almost entirely (8,685 aeroplanes) for the European front, this variant was characterised by the installation of a remote control chin turret.

Apart from these production variants there were many experimental types and other variants intended for various uses other than as bombers, such as photo-reconnaissance and air-sea rescue. Up to the last day of the war the name of the B-17s was linked to the daytime bombing raids on Germany.

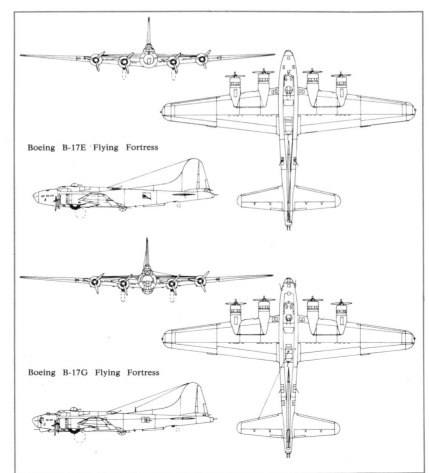

Boeing B-17E Flying Fortress

Boeing B-17G Flying Fortress

Plate 128
Three famous American twin-engine aircraft: 1942–44

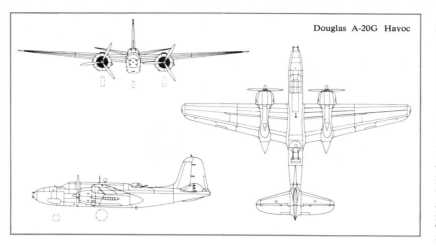

Douglas A-20G Havoc

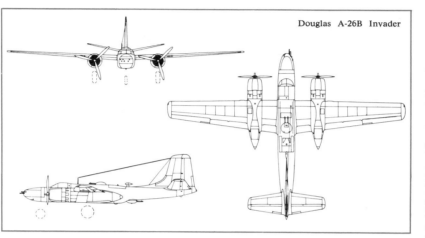

Douglas A-26B Invader

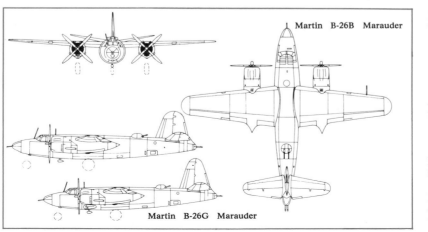

Martin B-26B Marauder

Martin B-26G Marauder

The twin-engine formula was applied with success in other medium bombers produced by the American aircraft industry. An equivalent of the B-25 Mitchell was the Martin B-26 Marauder, an aircraft which, although definitely more difficult to fly, gave outstanding service on all fronts from 1942 to 1945.

The specification which had brought the Marauder to life was issued by the USAAC on 25th January 1939. In this great stress was laid on the speed, range and operational altitude which the aircraft should achieve. The design which Martin presented a little under six months later fulfilled these requirements perfectly on paper and was accepted lock, stock and barrel – with an unprecedented order for 1,000 planes. The first prototype flew on 25th November 1940, and the first aircraft of the A version (139 built) were delivered in 1941. When it came to operational use, however, the B-26 immediately revealed the drawback that was to dog it throughout its career: the difficulty in training the crews and of maintaining their confidence, disconcerted as they were by certain features of the plane, notably an unprecedentedly high wing loading which necessitated high and dangerous landing speeds. After a number of accidents the point was even reached where production was shut down and a commission of inquiry appointed. In the end it was decided to continue with the production schedule but the aircraft was modified in order to make it easier to fly.

In May 1942 production began of the B variant (1,183 built) in which, apart from a number of improvements in the armament, in equipment, and in armour-plating for the crew, a substantial modification was adopted: an increase of 183 cm (60 in) in the wingspan in order to lessen the wing loading, accompanied by an enlargement of the tail surfaces.

This solution, however, was dropped in the following version, the B-26C, whilst the loaded weight of the aircraft was considerably increased with the addition of more defensive armament. 1,235 C variants were constructed, nevertheless, after which production went on to the final F and G versions, differing from each other only in details of equipment, and these went into service in 1944. In all 5,157 Marauders left the assembly lines between February 1941 and March 1945. Out of these, 522 saw service with the RAF and South African Air Force.

The Douglas family of twin-engines, built between 1938 and 1944, was far more prolific and versatile. These aircraft (7,385 constructed in many versions) were known under many names, according to the use to which they were put: in Britain the bomber and night fighter variants were known as the Boston and the Havoc while in the USA they were known as A-20, P-70 and F-3 and in France the DB-7 series. It was France which in 1938 placed the first order for the new twin-engine, which had only just appeared in prototype form and had been privately developed by Douglas two years previously. To begin with, the order was for 105 aircraft and then other orders were placed which brought the total up to 260 DB-7s and almost 700 DB-7As, a more powerful version. The majority of these machines finished up by going to the Royal Air Force after the fall of France.

In the USA it was thought better to fulfil these orders before starting production of the more powerfully engined variants (among them the F-3 photo-reconnaissance plane, the P-70 night fighter, and the A-20C which was the first to see combat service in American hands in May 1942). The variant which was produced in the largest number was the A-20G which was intended exclusively for the USAAF and for the Soviet air forces, to whom it was given in great numbers. The principal characteristics (common to the H variant which did, however, have more powerful engines) was the adoption of an unglazed nose in which the armament was concentrated. These aircraft were used mainly in the Pacific where they were indispensable in intruder and close-support missions. In the final variants, J and K, a return was made to the glazed nose of the previous models which was vital for its use as a traditional bomber.

The climax of the development of the A-20 line was embodied in the A-26 Invader which was designed in 1940 and which went into service half way through 1944. Powerful, very fast, heavily armed, the A-26s showed themselves to be the best ground attack and tactical bomber to be put into the field by the United States. They were the last of this category, too, since they were still in service to play an active part in the Korean and Vietnamese wars.

The first of the three prototypes flew on 10th July 1942 and production of the initial version, the A-26B (1,355 constructed), got under way immediately after the completion of proving flights. The principal characteristic of these machines lay in the heavy machine guns mounted in the nose section. Another four heavy machine guns were installed in remote control turrets and on certain missions it was also possible to add a further 10 externally mounted machine guns. This lethal firepower was added to an equally formidable bomb-load. In the last variant, the A-26C of 1945, however, the Invaders were constructed as conventional bombers with a glazed nose, and were less heavily armed. In all, 2,446 examples of the B and C versions came off the assembly lines. In the period after the war about 100 A-26 aircraft remained in service and were used in operations in the Korean War.

Plate 129
The Halifax and the Lancaster arrive: 1940–43

After the Short Stirling, the RAF's first four engine strategic bomber, the Handley Page Halifax and the Avro Lancaster were the aircraft which consolidated the use of four engines. Both were aircraft of outstanding quality and were the spearhead of Bomber Command for the duration of the war, linking their names with the continual, devastating raids over the territory of the Third Reich and to the tense

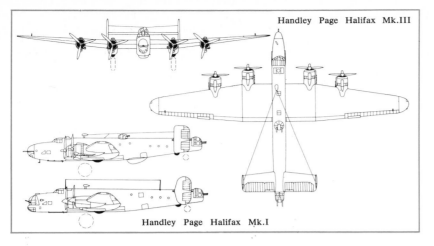

Handley Page Halifax Mk.III

Handley Page Halifax Mk.I

night-time battles against the German fighters who brought out new weapons all the time, including radar, to use on the bomber formations.

Taking these in chronological order, the Handley Page Halifax went into service barely three months after the Short Stirling, in November 1940, and it was a distinctly superior machine to its predecessor. The origins of the Halifax went back to a specification issued in September 1936 in which a twin-engine bomber was called for, to be powered by two Rolls-Royce Vulture engines which were, at the time, still being developed. A year later, because of the difficulties encountered by the Vulture programme, consider-able design modifications were required, including the adoption of four Rolls-Royce Merlin engines with a consequent increase in the wing-span and more than doubling of the all-up weight.

The first of two prototypes, there-fore, flew after a considerable delay, on the 25th October 1939 and the first production series Halifax flew on 11th October of the following year. The Mark I went into service at the end of 1940 and, from 1941 onwards, they were joined by the aircraft of the sec-ond series, Mk II, which had more powerful engines and more powerful armament. In all, 2,050 of these two versions were constructed.

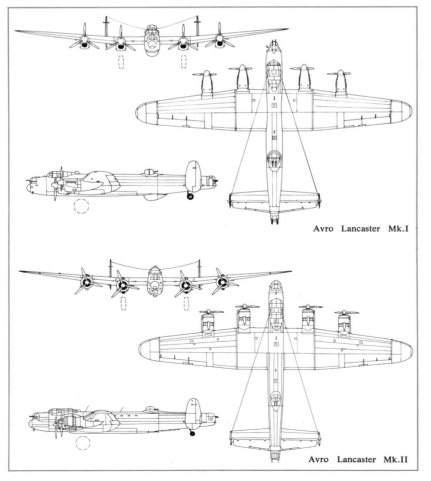

Avro Lancaster Mk.I

Avro Lancaster Mk.II

The series to be produced in the greatest number was the Mk III which was manufactured from 1943 onwards, and in which the Halifax underwent radical changes: the four Merlin engines were replaced with the same number of Bristol Hercules 1,615 hp radial engines. Other modi-fications were also carried out, which included a further increase of the wingspan. The Halifax Mk III, which had considerably improved perfor-mance and flight characteristics, went into service in February 1944 and remained in the front line up to the last day of the war, procurement totalling 2,060 aircraft.

Side by side with the bomber ver-sions (the last being the Mk VI and the Mk VII which had more powerful engines and longer range) another var-iant, the Mk V, was produced for Coastal Command. In operational use, however, the Halifax was also used as a paratroop carrier and as a glider tug, and for this purpose many aircraft of the Mk III, Mk V and Mk VII series were converted. In the period immediately following the war, two versions, the Mk VIII and the Mk IX, were specially built as military trans-port aircraft (500 approximately were produced). They remained in service up to 1952. In all 6,176 Halifaxes left the assembly lines from 1940 onwards.

The total number of Lancasters produced was even higher: 7,336 were constructed. This was the last, and without doubt the most famous war-time strategic bomber of the RAF. The origins of this four-engine aircraft had been similar to those of the Halifax, based on a request which asked for a twin-engine plane to be powered by two Rolls-Royce Vulture engines. However, unlike the Handley Page design, Avro's design was at first completed according to the ministerial specification and resulted in the rather inadequate Manchester, of which 200 were constructed.

It was only in the summer of 1940, following this aircraft's lack of success, which was mainly due to underpower, that the designers went back to work and had the idea of installing four Rolls-Royce Merlin engines. The first prototype (designated the Manchester III) flew on 9th January 1941, the sec-ond on 13th May (with the name changed to Lancaster) and the first of the production series flew on 31st October of that year. The aircraft sur-passed all expectations and mass pro-duction was immediately started, with many aircraft factories participating. 3,544 Lancaster Mk Is were com-pleted in total. Their operational use started in the first months of 1942.

In the summer of the following year two further versions were added: the Mk II (300 built) and the Mk III (2,990). The Lancaster Mk II differ-ent principally because of a substantial change in the engines (four Bristol Hercules radial engines), a modi-fication which was dictated by the need to avoid a possible scarcity of the Mer-lin engines. This danger receded with the arrival from the United States of the first Merlin engines to be manu-factured under licence by Packard, and the Lancaster Mk III was re-equipped with these units. Another two production series constructed in limited numbers were the Mk VI of 1944 for use as a counter-measure and radar spoof carrier, and the Mark VII (180 built) which had the dorsal turret modified. In addition, another 400 models were constructed under licence in Canada and these were given the designation of Lancaster Mk X.

The Lancaster also pursued its career after the end of the Second World War; and not only with Bomber Command, where various models were converted for photo reconnais-sance, remaining in service up to the 1950s, but also with Coastal Com-mand, the four-engine Avro serving as their principal maritime reconnais-sance aircraft in the years following the war.

Plate 130
American bombers for the Allies: 1942–44

A great part of the American bomber production was intended for her Allies in a similar fashion as with other com-bat aircraft. Among the Allies, the British were undoubtedly the ones to ask for the greatest numbers, and they put into service with the RAF not only nearly all the principal types of aircraft employed by the American air forces but also other models which were con-sidered of less importance by the

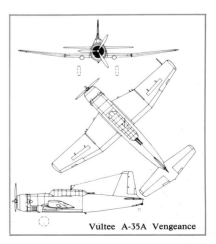

Vultee A-35A Vengeance

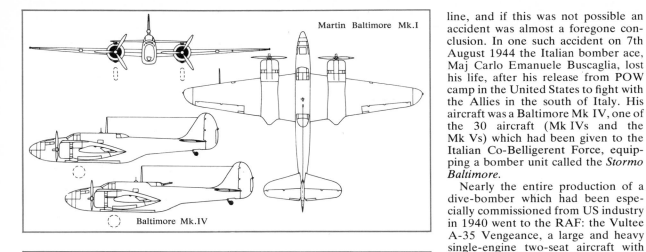

Martin Baltimore Mk.I

Baltimore Mk.IV

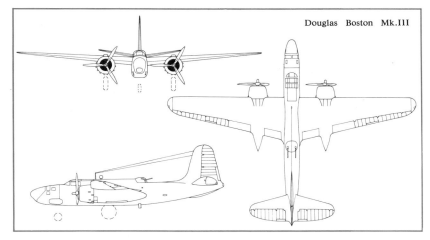

Douglas Boston Mk.III

line, and if this was not possible an accident was almost a foregone conclusion. In one such accident on 7th August 1944 the Italian bomber ace, Maj Carlo Emanuele Buscaglia, lost his life, after his release from POW camp in the United States to fight with the Allies in the south of Italy. His aircraft was a Baltimore Mk IV, one of the 30 aircraft (Mk IVs and the Mk Vs) which had been given to the Italian Co-Belligerent Force, equipping a bomber unit called the *Stormo Baltimore*.

Nearly the entire production of a dive-bomber which had been especially commissioned from US industry in 1940 went to the RAF: the Vultee A-35 Vengeance, a large and heavy single-engine two-seat aircraft with unimpressive overall performance. Out of the 1,528 Vengeances which were constructed, 1,205 were taken by the RAF, who used them in Burma up to the end of the war. The A-35A variant went into service in 1942. In the United States the remaining 323 planes were used for target tug and other secondary roles.

Plate 131
The most widely used American strategic bomber of the war: 1942–43

Up to the appearance, in the last year of the war, of the Boeing B-29 Superfortress, the strategic bombing component of the American air force was based on two types of aircraft: the Boeing B-17 Flying Fortress and the Consolidated B-24 Liberator.

The total production of the Liberator was the highest of any bomber aircraft produced by the United States industry: as many as 18,188 models left the assembly lines

under a massive production programme which was carried out by a series of factories belonging not only to the parent company, Consolidated, but also to other industrial giants such as Ford, Douglas and North American. This immense production was delivered to all operational theatres from 1942 onwards for duties which went far beyond those of the conventional bomber: the B-24s were also used for naval reconnaissance, anti-submarine warfare and as transports and subsequently revealed that they were excellent and versatile aircraft, even if they were not always popular with the crews. In contrast to the B-17, the Liberator was not able to take much punishment. This was due to its very complex construction: in particular, the wing was relatively weak and in many cases, if hit in the crucial places, it gave way completely. Photographic records of the Second World War show B-24s plummeting from the sky with their two wings folded upwards like those of a butterfly: in contrast, the sturdiness of the B-17 was almost unbelievable, sometimes returning to base with major components (tailplanes, engines, even wings) very badly damaged, and even on occasion partly missing.

The design of the B-24 went back to the beginning of 1939 and was based on a specification from the technical branch of the USAAC who wanted a more modern heavy bomber, with a better performance than the Boeing B-17 which was in production at the time. In particular the requirements placed special emphasis on speed, range and operational altitude. From feasibility studies assigned to Consolidated Aircraft Corporation's chief designer, Isaac M. Laddon, a high-wing monoplane emerged with twin fin, tricycle landing gear and deep fuselage with roomy bomb-bays fitted with bomb-door actuation track and rollers. The wing design itself was in advance of its time, with the introduction of laminated leading edges and high aerodynamic efficiency, the wings being very elongated; in such a way that carrying capacity and performance at high altitude were improved.

On 30th March 1939 a contract for

USAAF. For example, over 1,000 of the aircraft constructed to fulfil the large orders from France which were voided, the twin-engined Douglas, were diverted to Britain. In the RAF the bomber versions of these aircraft were designated Boston.

The first Bostons to arrive were the Mk Is and the Mk IIs, which were used as trainers and night interceptors respectively. The Boston Mk III followed which was to fill the role of light daytime bomber to take the place of the ageing Bristol Blenheim: these Bostons were in service from February 1942 and were widely used up to the end of the war.

Side by side with the Boston, the British also employed another aircraft of the same class, being the only nation who combined the two. This was the light twin-engined Martin Baltimore, of which 1,575 were constructed. Before the Baltimore the RAF had put 225 Maryland aircraft into service, the basic model of which had been developed in the USA in 1937, and although it had received an official designation from the USAAC (A-22) it had never been adopted for service use. It was in 1940 that the British authorities had asked their transatlantic colleagues to develop an improved and more powerful version of the Maryland. In particular they asked for more powerful engines and improved overall performance, and substantial modifications to the fuselage which

had to be widened and deepened, in order to allow more space both for the crew and the bomb-load. The prototype of the Baltimore flew on 14th June 1941 and in the following October it was sent to England.

150 of the intial Mk I and Mk II series followed, differing from each other only in the dorsal turret armament, one machine gun in the Baltimore Mk I and two in those of the second production series. This was produced up to 1944 going through three more series, the Mk III, the Mk IV and the Mk V, reaching a total of 1,575 aircraft. In these variants a dorsal fixed gun installation was adopted in place of the manually aimed guns of earlier models.

This aircraft went into operational use in the spring of 1942 and the Baltimore joined the other light bombers of the RAF in the Mediterranean. These aircraft distinguished themselves with the desert air force during the North African campaign and in the later Allied invasion of Sicily and at Anzio. The training of pilots to convert to this new machine had created some difficulties due to the power characteristics of the twin Wright Cyclone engines which were installed in it, and which were undoubtedly made worse by the aircraft's power-weight ratio. Take-off was particularly difficult for the pilot: on occasions it could be extremely difficult to apply and keep the aircraft on the straight

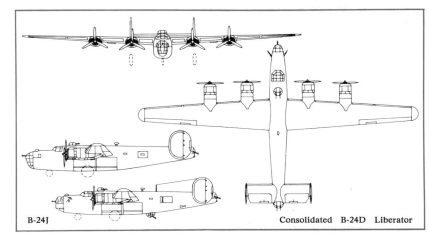

B-24J   Consolidated B-24D Liberator

the construction of a prototype was signed. This flew for the first time on 29th December, and to this were soon added seven pre-series models. In 1940 the first order for thirty-six series production aircraft was placed and twenty-seven of these were constructed as B-24Cs, which were powered by Pratt & Whitney R-1830 engines with turbo-superchargers and they were also more heavily armed.

The first major variant was the subsequent B-24D which between 1940 and 1941 had amassed orders for a total of 2,738 aircraft. In order to deal with these huge orders it was also decided to widen the production base, including Ford, Douglas and also North American in the production programme. This version of Liberator was the first to see combat service in April 1942, and the greater part of their early activity was concentrated in the Middle East and the Pacific theatre.

The B-24E and G followed the B-24D and these were powered by different engines and propellers and (from the twenty-sixth B-24G produced) also had a nose turret installed. After the B-24H (3,100 built) production passed on to the B-24J of 1943 which was the one to be produced in the greatest numbers, with improved equipment, engine controls and fuel tanks. The final versions, the B-24L and B-24M (1,667 and 2,593 built up to 31st May 1945) carried improved armament.

Among the numerous experimental variants the F-7 photo-reconnaissance plane is one of the more notable, as well as the C-87 transport, the AT-22 trainer, and the C-109 transport and re-fuelling plane. 1,694 Liberators in different versions, out of the total production, were to go to the RAF. A measure of the widespread combat use of the B-24 is to be seen in records of its use in the Pacific theatre in three years: it dropped 635,000 tonnes of bombs and shot down 4,189 enemy aircraft.

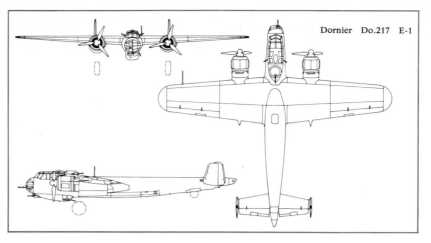

Dornier Do.217 E-1

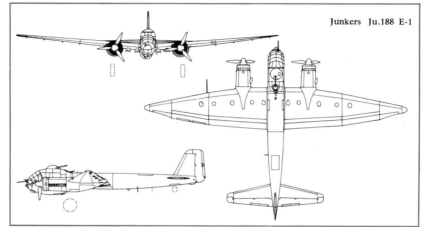

Junkers Ju.188 E-1

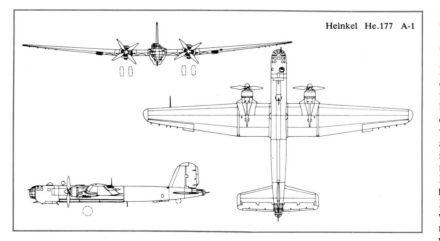

Heinkel He.177 A-1

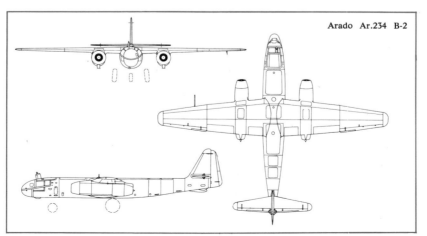

Arado Ar.234 B-2

Plate 132
The last German bombers — one is a jet: 1940–44

As the war proceeded, Germany found that she was increasingly in need of more modern and efficient bombers. The *Luftwaffe* succeeded in putting a few completely new designs into the field: the most useful aircraft continued to bear the brunt of front-line service and were mainly modifications of Junkers and Dornier basic models. The Dornier Do.217, for instance, was built to repeat, in a still further improved version, the outstanding qualities which had led to its direct predecessor's success, the Do.17, and although the Do.217 was a redesign, it only represented a larger and more powerful version of the Do.17. The prototype first flew in August 1938 but it was not until August 1940 that it reached its final configuration with the V-9 prototype.

The first production series (E) was constructed in several variants. The Do.217 E-1, which appeared towards the end of 1940, was the first; it was followed by the E-2 and by the E-3 which differed in their defensive armament and were intended for dive-bombing. Among other versions should be mentioned the E-2/R4 torpedo-bomber, the E-2/R10 for maritime patrol and the E-5 which was capable of carrying two Hs.293 air to ground missiles guided by radio control.

From 1941 onwards the production lines were also occupied with the production of the night fighter variants, the Do.217J and N (a total of 364 were built) but this did not impede the development of subsequent bomber versions: the Do.217 K which appeared half way through 1942 had its nose redesigned and was given more powerful armament; the Do.217 M which, like the N version night fighters, was equipped with inline Daimler Benz engines. Production, which went on up to June 1944, reached a total of 1,541 in all bomber variants.

Similar to the evolution of the twin-engine Dornier was that of the Junkers Ju.88 bomber. The best example of the basic model was provided by the Junkers Ju.188 developed in the autumn of 1941, derived from an E series Ju.88. The principal modifications consisted in the lengthening of the wing (which was now more pointed) and a larger and squarer tail, and by the option of installing either Junkers Jumo or BMW engines. The first production series (E) started to leave the assembly lines in February 1943 and went into operational service in the month of October. These aircraft – together with the subsequent F reconnaissance variants, the G bombers and the H

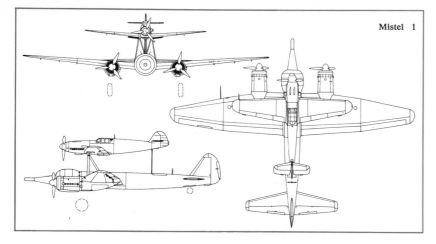

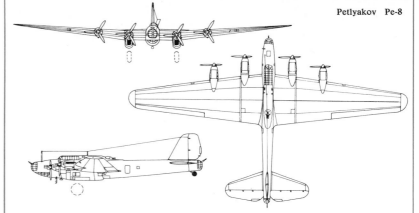

models (also for reconnaissance) – were all equipped with BMW 1,700 hp engines. At the same time, the production series of variants equipped with the Jumo 1,600 hp engine was developed. The first was the Ju.188 A which was delivered from the middle of 1943 onwards.

In January 1944 the A-2 variant appeared with more powerful engines and subsequently the A-3, which was constructed for use as a torpedo-bomber. The D series was to be for reconnaissance. The final series, which were completely experimental and therefore only constructed in very small numbers, were the R, the S and the T, for night-fighter, intruder and high altitude reconnaissance roles respectively. Production, which continued up to the end of the war, reached a total of 1,076 aircraft.

The project for the first and only strategic bomber to be fielded by the *Luftwaffe* was a complete failure: the Heinkel He.177. This appeared in prototype form on 19th November 1939, and was a large twin-engine plane. It was continually plagued by development problems which sprang from the very complicated nature of the design. Even when it went into service in 1944, the He.177 showed itself to be far from efficient. Approximately 1,000 aircraft in three variants were built (A-1, A-3 and A-5) and were, in the main, left unused on the ground and only 200 had an intermittent operational use.

A revolutionary aircraft which could certainly have had some impact on the course of the war had it arrived on the battlefield at an earlier stage was also relatively little used. The Arado Ar.234 Blitz was the second jet engined aircraft in the world to go into service and the first jet bomber. Planned from 1941 onwards, the prototype only flew on 15th June 1943, because of delays in the delivery of the new Junkers Jumo 004 turbojet engine. A year later the first aircraft of the first production series (B) were delivered and this was to become the principal production series. This production model was built in two variants, the B-1 photo-reconnaissance

aircraft, and the B-2 bomber.

The Ar.234 B-1 was the first to go into operational use in July of 1944. The bombers were only sent to an experimental unit at the end of the year and did not take an active part in the war until the first months of 1945, by then too late. In all, production reached a couple of hundred aircraft.

Among the desperate weapons thrown into the fray by Germany, the Mistel is worth mentioning, consisting of a composite aircraft combination armed with a powerful explosive charge. The pilotless missile was steered by the fighter originally mounted on top until it was near its target, against which it was then launched. The first Mistel (Mistel I) was built in 1943 and was made up of a Ju.88 A-4 and a Bf.109F-4, this latter fulfilling the role of parent aircraft. Experiments were, in general, successful, and were followed by the construction of numerous aircraft in various types. Among them were the Mistel II (which was composed of a parasite aircraft of the Junkers Ju.88 G-1 type and of its guiding aircraft, a Focke Wulf Fw.190 A-6) and the Mistel III: in this latter version the most important sub-types were the 3B and the 3C, in which the parent craft was still a Focke Wulf Fw.190 A-B but the parasite aircraft were in turn a Ju.88G-10 and a Ju 88 H-4 in which the wings and fuselage were considerably altered. In both cases the Fw.190 was equipped with supplementary fuel tanks since its engine could not use the lower octane fuel which fed the engines of the missile aircraft. These were ambitious plans, but the Mistel was only used during 1945.

Plate 133
Russian, Swedish and Australian attempts to produce modern bombers: 1941–44

The Russians were also unable to put an effective strategic bomber into the field which was up to the standard of the American and British aircraft.

The only aircraft of this type which went into service in the course of the Second World War was the large four-engined Petlyakov Pe-8, an aircraft which was always plagued by development problems, especially with the engines. The project was set in train in 1934 by the design bureau of Tupolev with the team head by Vladimir Petlyakov, and was based on a specification in which, among other things, optimum performance was required at an altitude of 8,000 m (17,640 ft). This requirement loomed large in the study and development of the new bomber from the very beginning. At that time engines capable of giving sufficient power above 5,000 m (11,025 ft) did not exist.

The solution was found by having recourse to the following expedient: four 1,100 hp M-105 engines, supercharged by a large blower driven by an M-100 engine in the rear fuselage. This was undoubtedly a complicated solution but in spite of this it worked: the prototype flew on 27th December

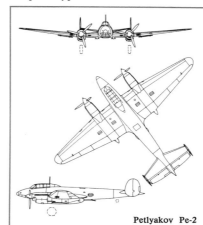

1936 and performed brilliantly. This major design achievement however proved completely unnecessary when it was decided, just as production started in 1939, that the engines should be replaced with others of the Am 35A type which did not need the complicated super-charging system.

The Pe-8 went into service in 1940 but the first operational mission worth noting was carried out in the summer of 1941 with a raid on Berlin. In the meantime, in an attempt to improve the performance of the plane it had been decided to replace the engines with M 30B diesels, although this experiment did not succeed. Production ended in 1944 after a relatively small number had been built.

The work of Vladimir Petlyakov as a designer was undoubtedly much more successful in the field of light bombers. The twin-engined Pe-2 which appeared in front-line service in 1941 proved to be one of the most versatile and outstanding combat planes to be put into the field by the Soviet Union in the course of the war and it remained in the front rank of the tactical bombers of the *VVS*, together with the Ilyushin Il-2, for the whole of the war. The origins of the Pe-2 went back to 1938 when the team headed by Petlyakov had started work on the design of a heavy twin-engine, high altitude fighter.

Then the specifications were changed, and a bomber rather than a fighter was required; the design was amended, although not to any great extent. The prototype, which appeared in 1939, showed itself to be very effective, above all in its flight characteristics, which were unusual for a bomber, and it was immediately put into production with but a few modifications which were mainly aimed at making the aircraft fit for its role as a dive-bomber.

The first model was followed by a heavy fighter variant which could also be used for reconnaissance and ground attack. From 1942 onwards, in view of the German fighters' increasing superiority, it was necessary to improve the aircraft's performance, which the following year culminated in

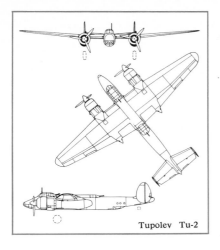

Tupolev Tu-2

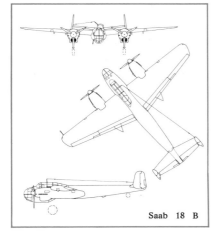

Saab 18 B

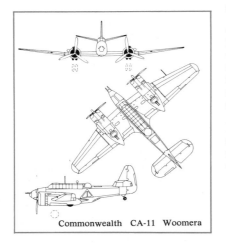

Commonwealth CA-11 Woomera

Ki-109 is worthy of note; intended to be a heavy fighter, it was armed with a 75 mm cannon in the nose. The twenty-two examples which were constructed, however, never saw operational use.

This all-metal plane was powered by 1,850 hp Shvetsov M.82 radial engines and apart from being used in the Soviet air force it served with those of Poland and China.

Up to well into the 1950s, another twin-engined bomber produced during the middle of the war remained in service: the Swedish Saab 18. The prototype of this aircraft, which was very similar to the German Dornier Do.217, flew for the first time on 19th June 1942, and at the end of its proving flights and tests it was put into production with an order for sixty aircraft of the A series. These went into service with the Swedish air force in the summer of 1944.

The aircraft's subsequent B series ran to 120 examples, production continuing long after the war was over. They differed from the first series mainly in their engines, which had been changed to two Daimler Benz DB 605 Bs built under licence, instead of the two Pratt & Whitney Twin Wasp radial engines which were also constructed under licence. In 1945 the last variant, the T 18 B, appeared which at first was intended for use as a torpedo-bomber but was then used for ground attack. The *Flygvapnet* (Swedish air force) took the Saab 18 out of service in 1956.

In Australia as well, the demands of war led to an attempt to produce a bomber which could also serve as a torpedo-bomber: the Commonwealth Ca-II Woomera. Design work began in 1939, but suffered from a very long development period. The aircraft only appeared in its final form on 7th July 1944. By that time the needs of the RAAF had already been amply satisfied by other Allied planes. As a result the Woomera programme was cancelled.

a new version, with better engines, armament, armouring and overall performance. The last variants to be constructed towards the end of the war, which took the overall production total to several thousands, were long-range reconnaissance planes, trainers and, finally, high-altitude fighters.

In operational use, from 1943 onwards, the twin-engine Petlyakov was joined by another useful aeroplane which had been created by another great designer, Andrei Nikolaevich Tupolev. The Tu-2 was the second most important medium bomber, both in its effectiveness and its numbers, produced in the Soviet Union. It was modern in its concept,

Plate 134
Japanese bombers: 1942–44

In the second half of the war the Japanese made a concerted effort to improve the composition of their bomber force. Besides the well-known types in the front line, numerous other aircraft appeared, but practically none of them proved able to compete effectively with the enemy aircraft. Indeed some of these bombers turned out to be inferior to those which they were meant to replace.

This was the case with the Nakajima Ki-49 Donryu (HELEN in Allied code) designed to be the successor to the Mitsubishi Ki-21 of the army air force. Although an improvement from many points of view and in particular as regards the armour plating for the crew and the fuel tanks, this twin-engine plane was always limited by its lack of power and by the consequent poor performance and the general inadequacy of its defensive armament.

The specification which brought the Ki-49 to life was issued at the beginning of 1938 and the prototype appeared a year later. But the proving flights and operational tests became protracted because of continued indecision on the part of the Army General Staff as to the eventual role of the aircraft. Only in the spring of 1941 was production started and the first Ki-49-Is reached units in the month of August. A year later the second variant, the Ki-49-II, went into service; this had increased power, was better armed and accounted for the greater part of production: 617 planes out of a total of 819. In an attempt to improve the performance of the aeroplane a third version was under consideration, equipped with Nakajima Ha-117 2,420 hp engines, but this remained at prototype stage because of difficulty in perfecting the engines.

Just as ineffective, in spite of continual attempts to eliminate its weak points, was the Kawasaki Ki-48 light bomber (Allied code-name LILY) an aircraft which was designed at the end

of 1937 and which went into action in the initial Ki-48-Ia version in 1940 in China. This aircraft was quite fast and handled well but these characteristics, which had earned it a better reputation than the average aircraft at the time of its entry into service, did not suffice as the war went on; in particular the Ki-48 had little defensive weaponry and therefore was very vulnerable when confronted by the modern Allied fighters.

After the construction of 557 aircraft of the first series, the designers tried to improve the plane, increasing the power of the engines, and installing better armament. From April 1942 the assembly lines started to build the second production variant, the Ki-48-II. There was little real change, not even when in 1943 the Ki-48-IIc series was developed which had still more powerful defence armament. Production continued up to October 1944 and 1,408 examples were completed out of a planned total of 1,997.

Quite different was the career of the last heavy bomber to be used in quantity by the Imperial Army: the Mitsubishi Ki-67 Hiryu, designed to replace the Ki-49. This was a very agile plane indeed, fast and well-armed, and this twin-engined bomber proved the best Japanese heavy bomber of the entire war.

However, this improvement had a very limited effect, for the time had arrived when nothing could be done to change the course of the war. The Ki-67 design (PEGGY in Allied Code) was started in February 1941, and the three prototypes were completed in December 1942 and in February and March 1943.

The aircraft made such a brilliant showing that it was decided to use it in the role of torpedo-bomber for the navy as well, and the operational debut of the Ki-67-I took place in this anti-shipping role in October 1944; from that moment onwards, the Ki-67-1 was used by both the army and the navy on both fronts. Production was assigned maximum priority and reached a total of 698 aircraft. Among the numerous experimental versions, the one which was designated

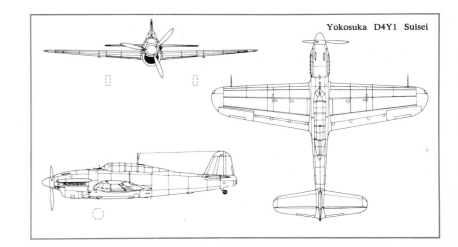

Yokosuka D4Y1 Suisei

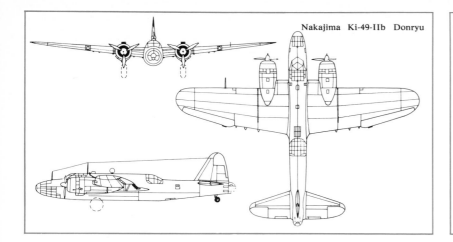

Nakajima Ki-49-IIb Donryu

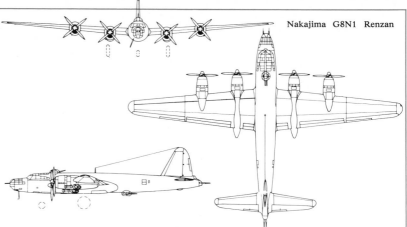

Nakajima G8N1 Renzan

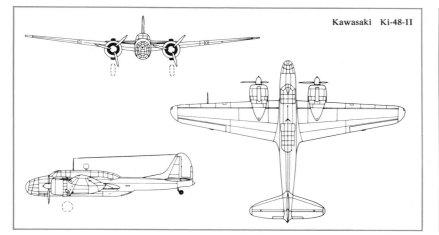

Kawasaki Ki-48-II

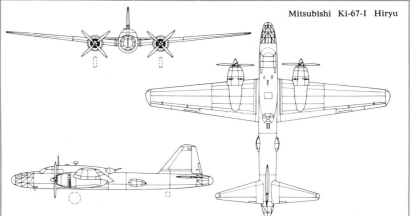

Mitsubishi Ki-67-I Hiryu

Ki-109 is worthy of note; intended to be a heavy fighter, it was armed with a 75 mm cannon in the nose. The twenty-two examples which were constructed, however, never saw operational use.

The Imperial Navy also used a small, carrier-based bomber very widely, the Yokosuka D4Y Suisei, designed in 1938; it appeared in prototype form in December 1940. The serious limitation of this aircraft (JUDY in Allied code), however, lay in the persistent unreliability of the engines, one of the very few V-12 liquid-cooled engines to be constructed by Japanese industry, and this continuously restricted its operational activity. The first D4Y1s (660 built) went into service as dive-bombers in March 1943 and were followed in October 1944 by the aircraft of the second production version D4Y2, of which 326 were constructed. In the D4Y3 a radical change was attempted, substituting the inline engine with a radial; but by now the aircraft was completely out-dated. In all 2,038 were built up to August 1945.

In a last-ditch effort, Japanese aircraft industry also undertook the construction of a four-engine strategic bomber: the Nakajima G8N Renzan. But this aircraft remained at the prototype stage: the first prototype

appeared at the end of 1944 and, out of a vast production plan, only four G8N1s were built. Although they never saw operational service, these planes were given the code-name RITA by the Allies.

Plate 135
The largest and the smallest American bombers used against Japan: 1941–44

The United States Navy attached great importance to the dive-bomber and kept efficient aircraft of this type in service for the duration of the war. The first and undoubtedly the most famous, stemming from its success in coping with the air battles of the first years of the war in the Pacific, was the Douglas SBD Dauntless. To this little single-engine plane must be ascribed the merit of the exploit which marked

the turning point in the progress of the struggle against the Japanese: the sinking of the aircraft carriers *Akagi*, *Kaga* and *Hiryu* on 4th June 1942 during the Battle of Midway.

The design of the Dauntless was directly derived from that of the Northrop BT-1 which was constructed in 1938 and it took on the designation of Douglas after that company had taken over the Northrop Corporation. The first orders for 57 SBD-1s and 87 SBD-2s for the US Marine Corps and the US Navy respectively were placed on 8th April 1938, and these aircraft went into service between the end

of 1940 and the first days of 1941.

In the following March a new version appeared, the SBD-3, which had a more powerful engine and armament and had improved armour-plating to protect the crew and the fuel tanks. In all 584 aircraft of this variant were constructed and, at the time when the United States came into the war against Japan, it equipped bomber units based on the aircraft carriers USS *Lexington*, *Enterprise*, *Yorktown* and *Saratoga*. In 1942 additional orders were placed and production went ahead on 780 SBD-4s and 2,409 SBD-5s; the latter had a more power-

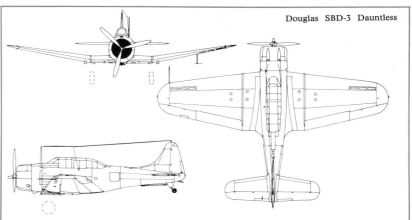

Douglas SBD-3 Dauntless

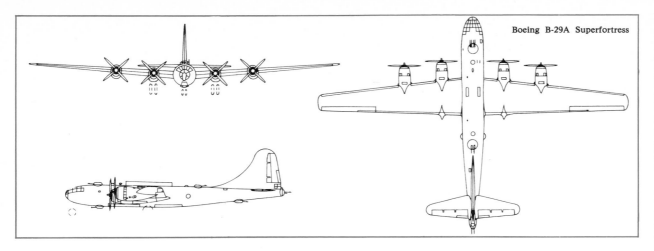
Boeing B-29A Superfortress

ful engine. The assembly lines only came to a half in July 1944, after completed a total of 5,936 aircraft. The final version was the SBD-6 with an even more powerful engine: 1,350 hp as compared with the 1,000 hp of the SBD-3.

From the second half of 1943 onwards the Dauntless were joined in operational use by a new dive-bomber, more modern and powerful: the Curtiss SB2C Helldiver, an aircraft of which 7,200 were constructed and which remained in service long after the Second World War and up to the 1950s. The order for the construction of the prototype had been given in May 1939 and the first aircraft had flown on 18th December of the following year. The proving flights and development, however, had lasted for much longer than had been foreseen and the first series aircraft was flown in 1942. There were also difficulties in getting mass production under way.

After entry into service of the first variants, the SB2C-1 Helldivers, on 11th November 1942, production concentrated on a more powerful version, the SB2C-3, of which 2,054 were built by Curtiss alone. The SB2C-4 variant, which was distinguished by its external bomb-racks under the wings, was for use in night operations; than a final version, the SB2C-5 which had increased range, appeared in the first half of 1945. Production was also entrusted to two Canadian companies,

Fairchild Aircraft Limited and the Canadian Car and Foundry Company Limited, who constructed a total of 300 and 894 aircraft respectively in several variants: by spreading production in this way it was possible to satisfy the ever-increasing demands from the US Navy and the US Marine Corps.

The best strategic bomber of all during the war was the Boeing B-29 Superfortress. The aircraft ended the war with the bombing of Hiroshima and Nagasaki and confronted humanity for the first time with the spectre of nuclear destruction. The studies which were to lead to the development of the B-29 started in 1937 but the definitive design was prepared in 1940. Three prototypes were ordered in that year and on 21st September 1942, the date of the first flight, orders were already being placed for a total of 1,500 aircraft. While the 14 pre-series models (YB-29) were constructed, Boeing set up a vast production programme which also involved the Bell Aircraft Company and the Glenn L. Martin Company, and this began in 1943.

The necessity of getting the new aircraft into the front line as soon as possible was all important, especially against Japan, and the decision to use the Superfortress exclusively in the Pacific theatre was taken at the end of the year. The first units to be equipped with the B-29s arrived in bases in Indian and in China in the spring of

1944. Missions were commenced on 5th June and ten days later the first raid on Japanese territory was carried out. These became increasingly frequent in the summer of 1945, operating from the new bases which were established on the Mariana Islands, and these bombing raids contributed in a decisive manner to the destruction of the Japanese industrial machine and the sapping of the civilian population's morale. The culmination was reached on the 6th and 9th August, with the missions on Hiroshima and on Nagasaki. For the record the two B-29s (out of the 3,970 built) were the first to carry nuclear weapons and were called *Enola Gay* and *Bockscar*.

which had been designed to replace the Nakajima B6N and the Yokosuka D4Y in carrier-based use. The first prototype flew in May 1942 and the principal production variant, the B7A-2, was produced a good two years later. When the first aircraft of the series appeared, the Imperial Navy no longer had any aircraft carriers and the 114 planes which had been built saw limited operational service with land-based units in the last months of the war.

The duration of the Yokosuka P1Y Ginga's useful life was also limited. This was a modern twin-engined land-based plane developed by the Navy almost at the same time as the Mitsubishi Ki-67 Hiryu of the Imperial Army. This aircraft (FRANCES in Allied code) appeared in prototype form in the summer of 1943 and went into production even before it had been officially accepted by the high command. In October 1944 it went into service, 453 aircraft of the initial P1Y1 version having been constructed. Its operational use was held up until the first months of 1945 because of difficulties in developing the engines. Production reached a total of 1,098 aircraft and in the brief period in which it saw combat the P1Y1 proved to be a very competitive and useful aircraft when faced with its adversaries.

The Imperial Navy initiated some very advanced projects by the Japanese

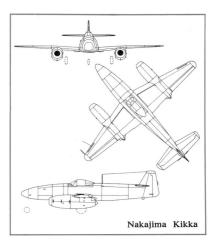
Nakajima Kikka

Plate 136
The last Japanese bombers: 1945

Even under the hail of American bombs in the last year of the war, the Japanese aircraft industry continued in its desperate efforts. In 1945 various types of bombers went into service; others reached the production stage when there were no longer any units left to use them or aircraft carriers to accommodate them.

This last was the case with the Aichi B7A Ryusei (GRACE in Allied code)

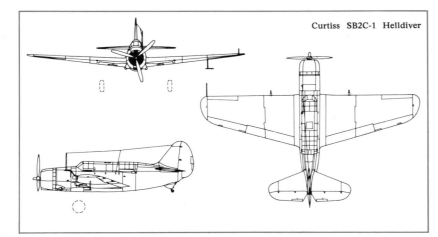
Curtiss SB2C-1 Helldiver

Yokosuka MXY7 Ohka 11

aviation industry in the last year of the war: the most modern of all, through it only reached the prototype stage, was a jet combat aircraft, developed from German technology. While the Mitsubishi J8M Shusui, an interceptor, was no more than a copy of the Messerschmitt Me.163B, the Nakajima Kikka originated as an entirely Japanese design, even though its external resemblance to the Messerschmitt Me.262A of the *Luftwaffe* was indisputable. Unlike its well-known relation, however, the Kikka was not a lucky aircraft; it was certainly the only jet aircraft which flew in Japan during the course of the Second World War but it only ever flew two test flights and the second one ended with the crash of the first prototype.

Patently fired with enthusiasm by the exceptional performance of the Me.262 as soon as it was in service with the *Luftwaffe*, the high command of the Imperial Navy decided in September 1944 that they would construct a fast jet bomber. Nakajima had been entrusted with developing the project and with the limited time at their disposal it was not at all surprising that the two designers concerned, Kazuo Ohno and Kenichi Matsumura, came up with an aircraft which echoed the configuration and general lines (if scaled down) of the German twin-engined aircraft.

The engine also, although of Japanese design, was derived from the

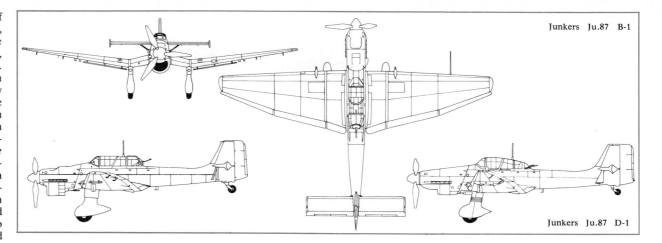

Junkers Ju.87 B-1

Junkers Ju.87 D-1

BMW 003 developed in Germany. The engines installed in the prototype, two Ne-12 340 kg (750 lb) thrust were subsequently replaced by two Ne-20 475 kg (1,050 lb) thrust. The first flight, made on 7th August 1945, met with success; the second and last took place four days later: a mistake in the installation of two auxiliary rockets which should have assisted the aircraft's take-off caused the crash, and so the project halted, to await the second prototype's completion. On 15th August, however, all activity was finally stopped.

By that date, not only the second Kikka was ready but also many of the 18 pre-series aircraft, at various stages

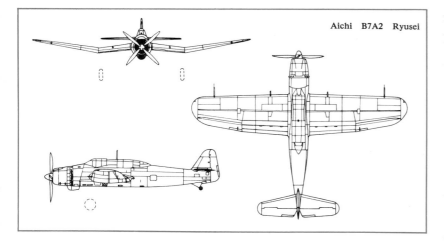

Aichi B7A2 Ryusei

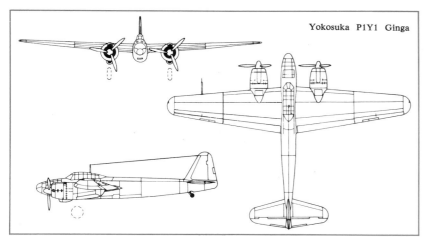

Yokosuka P1Y1 Ginga

of manufacture, were nearing completion. Subsequently the Allies discovered that the programme was far more ambitious than had at first appeared. Not only was Japanese industry planning jet engines of almost double the power of those which it had already had at its disposal, but also other variants of the Kikka: one two-seat trainer; a similar plane for reconnaissance, and a single-seat, very heavily-armed interceptor.

The armament planned for this last version included two 30 mm cannon whilst the power was to be furnished the engines of the Ne-130 or Ne-330 type, which could give 900 kg (1,985 lb) and 885 kg (1,950 lb) thrust respectively.

The final weapon was the Ohka flying bomb, powered by a rocket or jet-engine and used in desperate suicide missions. A total of 852 Yokosuka MXY7s were constructed in four versions in the last months of the war and the first success against an enemy vessel was scored on 12th April 1945. The MXY7, of which the eleventh model was produced in the largest numbers (755), was launched from near the target by a parent aircraft, generally a twin-engine Mitsubishi G4M2e. In Allied code it became all too well-known by the name of BAKA (Fool). These piloted bombs could only be controlled to a certain extent: once aimed at the target their great acceleration made only minor corrections of course possible and, above all, no evasive action could be taken.

Plate 137
The first dive-bombers — the most notorious in the Stuka: 1936–41

In the tactical bombing field the most effective propaganda machine of the whole conflict, the Junkers Ju.87 Stuka, was put into the field by the Germans. It was immediately identifiable by its fixed undercarriage and by its inverted gull wings with double wing ailerons following the typical pre-war Junkers configuration. Although it had been designed as far back as 1933, the Stuka remained in production for over nine years, being substantially unchanged in its structure and basic configuration for the entire war. This was the best proof of the general usefulness of the plane, and in spite of the enormous technical progress made over the years, German aircraft industry never managed to produce an effective replacement. Up to 1944 over 5,700 aircraft in about ten versions left the assembly lines and they fought on all fronts.

The request for a dive-bomber was bade by the German general staff in 1933 and four manufacturers submitted tenders: Arado, Blohm und Voss, Heinkel and Junkers. In March 1936 when competition had been narrowed down to the last prototypes, it was Junkers which triumphed. The first Ju.87 prototype had already flown at the beginning of 1935 and had been submitted to a long series of test flights resulting in substantial modifications. The most important was the replacement of the original Rolls-Royce Kestrel engine (which drove a wooden single-blade propeller) by a Junkers Jumo engine driving a three-blade metal variable pitch propeller; then the tailplanes were redesigned, having progressed from the twin fins of the original design to the single fin of the production models. These modifications had been incorporated in a second prototype and repeated, together with other improvements, in a third, final prototype.

The first production version, the

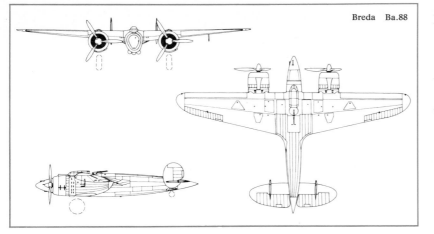

Breda Ba.88

Ju.87 A-1, appeared at the beginning of 1937 and, apart from training, it was intended for operational use in the Spanish Civil War. A year later the first variant of the following B series, Ju.87 B-1, was produced, which had a more powerful engine and was structurally and aerodynamically improved. This series became the first to go into mass production. Of equal importance were the following D and G series. The Ju.87 D-1 (1,940 of which reached the units in the spring of the following year), besides having an even more powerful engine installed, had improved armour-plating and armament. Aerodynamic refinements were also introduced, necessitating changes to the fuselage and cockpit.

The aeroplanes of the G series were developed along the general lines of the previous series and in these, for the first time, a Stuka was especially adapted to an anti-tank role. In the G-1 variant of 1942 the main offensive armament consisted of a pair of 37 mm cannon installed in under-wing fairings. In operational use, which was concentrated in Russia and on the Eastern Front, the Stuka proved deadly.

The fame of the Ju.87 remained linked to the first year of the war, when the overwhelming superiority of the German army and the general absence of any effective resistance in the air made the Stuka appear invincible. With the progress of the war and the changing balance of forces in the air, the Ju.87 remained in the German air arsenal as a good general machine which the *Luftwaffe* could not do without; and in fact they had no other type of aircraft of its kind.

The concept of a tactical bomber was taken up by practically all the principal nations involved in the war but the results did not always come up to expectations. This was the case with the Italian Breda Ba.88, a twin engine plane which, although giving excellent general performance, proved to be completely inadequate once it was loaded and armed. It appeared in prototype form in the spring of 1937 and 100 of them were built: these, after a brief and disappointing operational career in Libya in the summer of 1940, were taken back to Italy and parked on airfields to serve as decoys for enemy reconnaissance planes.

The Northrop A-17, which was designed in 1933 in the United States, was very limited in production and use, although it did serve with other air forces. This aircraft went into service as a tactical bomber two years later and the army air force took 110 examples. At the end of 1935 it was decided to produce an improved model, equipped with retractable undercarriage and with a more powerful engine. This was the A-17A of which 93 out of the 129 ordered remained in service for 18 months. Subsequently they were sold to France and Britain

and by the latter to South Africa in turn.

The Polish PZL P.23B was a single-engined tactical bomber which, although showing signs of its age in its general lines, proved to be an effective weapon. The design had been started off in 1932 and the prototype had flown in August 1934. Immediately afterwards it was put into production which, through successive orders, amounted to 250 aircraft. In service, the PZL P.23 B formed the spearhead of the Polish air force and at the time of the German invasion, twelve front-line units being equipped with this aircraft. About 30 examples were also exported to Bulgaria.

Plate 138
The Russians produce the last and the best ground attack aircraft: 1939–42

The French aviation industry was also successful in developing a light attack bomber and only the outcome of the war stopped some excellent machines from proving their worth. Among these the Breguet 691 was without doubt the most promising. The aircraft belonged to a family of twin-engined planes developed in the second half of the 1930s, intended to fulfil a wide range of functions, from reconnaissance to heavy fighter, to tactical bomber and ground attack. Its forerunner, the Breguet 690, had flown on 23rd March 1938, and the ground-attack variant, the Breguet 691 AB-2 was immediately ordered into production. The order for 205 aircraft was delayed by late delivery of engines. The first aircraft of the series only reached the forces at the end of 1939 and their operational use once war had broken out was very limited.

On the Pacific front Japan always accorded great importance to this role and in the course of its impressive and very varied aircraft production it managed to turn out some distinguished aircraft. One of these was the Mitsubishi Ki-51 (SONIA in Allied code) which, in spite of the apparent

obsolescence of its general lines (it had a fixed undercarriage, not particularly exciting performance and limited offensive armament) stayed in production from the first to the last day of the war, and in the event proved invaluable for ground attack and army co-operation. Further confirmation of this success lies in the fact that the Ki-51, unlike almost every other Japanese aircraft produced during the course of the war, remained substantially unaltered for its entire production span; as many as 2,385 aircraft left the assembly lines.

The design was embarked upon by Mitsubishi at the end of 1937 at the request of the army. The first and second prototypes were finished by the summer of 1939 and these were followed within the year by eleven pre-series models. The proving trials and test flights did not reveal any particular problems and the Ki-51 started its combat service in China. On the entry of Japan into the world war the aircraft was distributed to all front-line units and was not withdrawn even after more modern aircraft had made their appearance. Indeed, demands from the army for this plane reached such high levels that it was necessary in 1944 to open up a new assembly line at the army's Tachikawa arsenal.

Without doubt, however, the best close support aircraft of the entire war was put into the field by the Soviet Union. This was the Ilyushin Il-2 Stormovik, an aircraft which proved terribly effective in anti-tank use and which made a considerable impact on the course of the fighting, helping to contain the German invasion. The design of this "armoured attacker" as it was described was commenced by Sergei Vladimirovich Ilyushin and by his design bureau in 1938. At the same time the specification from the technical branch of the *VVS* brought a response from the team headed by Pavel Sukhoi, who designed the inferior Su-2.

The first prototype of the Il-2 appeared in the spring of 1939 but the proving trials and service test flights immediately revealed serious problems of stability and of inadequate engine power. This therefore necessitated a long development phase and partial redesign which ended in October of the following year with the appearance of the third and final prototype. Production was started immediately and the first Il-2s went into service in the summer of 1941. As a result of the operational experience acquired during the fierce fighting of that summer, it was decided to carry out further modifications to the aircraft, mainly aimed at improving its defensive and offensive armament: these led to the second production variant, the Il-2M3, which was to be the one produced in the greatest numbers.

Its principal characteristic, apart from the adoption of a more powerful engine, was provision for a second crew member who sat in the rear part

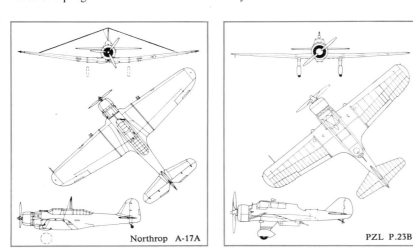

Northrop A-17A

PZL P.23B

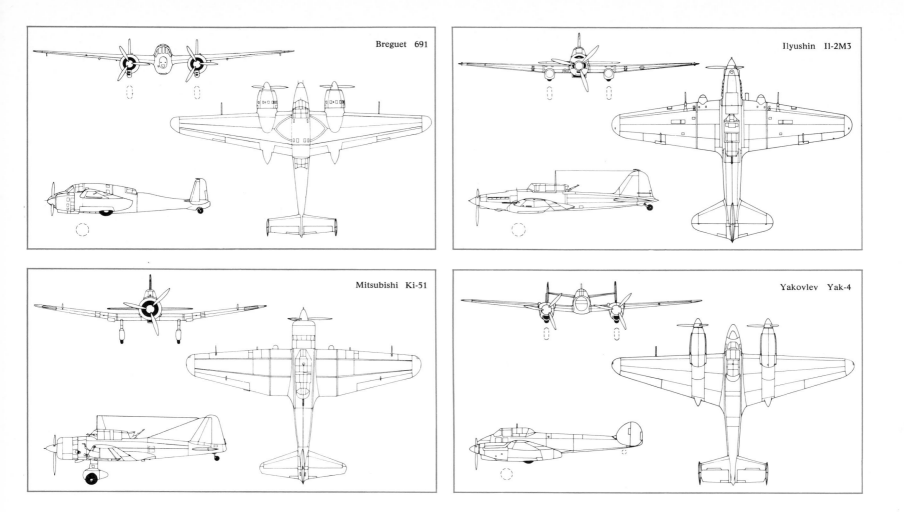

Breguet 691

Ilyushin Il-2M3

Mitsubishi Ki-51

Yakovlev Yak-4

of the cockpit and was armed with a machine gun. The structural design which was so original and had made the aircraft so practicable remained unchanged; the entire forward part of the aircraft was constructed in one single armour-plated shell, which besides giving an exceptional structural strength gave maximum protection to the crew and to the aircraft's vital components. The armour-plating in steel and duralumin had a maximum thickness of 13 mm in the rear part of the fuselage; the cockpit glass was reinforced and the windscreen was 65 mm thick.

The success of the Il-2 was to the detriment of another contemporary machine, the Yakovlev Yak-4. This twin-engine machine was derived from the Yak-2 of 1940 and had been designed by Alexander Sergeivich Yakovlev expressly as a ground attack and light bomber. Under operational conditions, however, the Yak-4 proved very vulnerable. Powered by two Klimov M 105R 1,100 hp engines it reached a maximum speed of 566 km/h (351 mph). It was taken out of production in 1942 and relegated to a high altitude reconnaissance role in which it remained until the end of the war.

Plate 139
The Swordfish and the B5N: the most effective torpedo-bombers: 1936–40

In an anti-shipping role an aircraft specifically designed as a torpedo-bomber proved to be a notable innovation of the Second World War. Nearly all the major powers developed effective aircraft of this type, some of which made a considerable contribution to the progress of the war.

In Britain one of the most well-known torpedo-bombers was the Fairey Swordfish, a carrier-borne biplane which was to stay in the front line of the Fleet Air Arm for nearly nine years, from July 1936 to May 1945, even after the appearance of more modern and sophisticated aircraft.

The Swordfish prototype flew on 17th April 1934 and was more or less directly derived from a model which had been privately developed by Fairey during the preceding year, the TSR 1. It was accepted for carrier-based use and the Swordfish was put into production immediately, the first

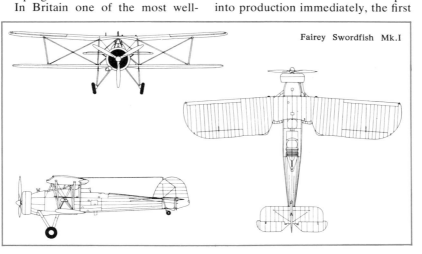

Fairey Swordfish Mk.I

Mk 1s going into service at the beginning of 1936. They were followed by aircraft of three other series: the Mk II of 1943, which had more power and was more robust; the Mk III, also in 1943, which was equipped with radar; and the Mk IV with closed cockpit which was built for Canada: in total 2,391 aircraft were built.

Operational used started in July 1936 and in the role of torpedo-bomber, continued until the beginning of 1942. The Swordfish were then switched to anti-submarine warfare, in which role they remained up to the end of the war. Among the great episodes of the war in which the Swordfish took a leading role were the attack on the Italian fleet at Taranto, the Battle of Cape Matapan, and the pursuit of the German battle-cruiser *Bismarck*.

From 1940 to 1943 another aircraft fought beside the Swordfish as a carrier-based torpedo-bomber, the Fairey Albacore, which was constructed for the express purpose of replacing the older biplanes. The Albacore was also a biplane but it was distinctly more modern; in spite of this it was never completely successful in fulfilling the purpose for which it had been designed. The prototype flew on 12th December 1938 and production continued until 1943, reaching a total of 800 aircraft. Its first use was from

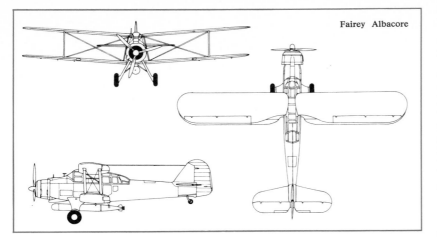

Fairey Albacore

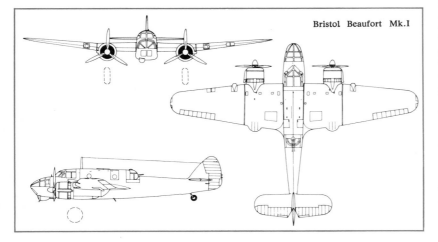

Bristol Beaufort Mk.I

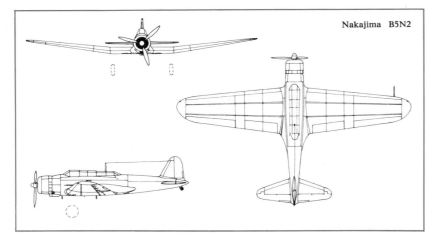

Nakajima B5N2

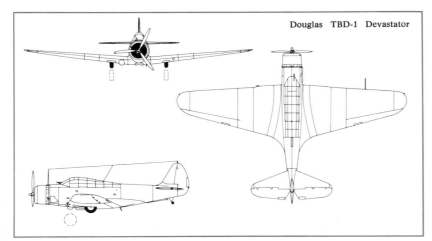

Douglas TBD-1 Devastator

land bases and only towards the end of 1940 did the Albacore become carrier-based. They operated mainly in the Mediterranean and Atlantic.

A contemporary in operational use which also served as a land-based torpedo-bomber was the Bristol Beaufort, a fast twin-engine machine which from 1940 to 1943 formed the standard equipment of Coastal Command in this function. Production reached 1,121 aircraft in two basic versions which had different engines. The project had been begun in 1935 and the first prototype had flown on 15th October 1938. The Beaufort Mk I (955 built) went into service in 1939 and its operational debut came in the April of the following year with a mine-laying mission. The second production series, the Mk II, reached a total of 166, in which the two Bristol Taurus 1,130 hp engines were replaced with two Pratt & Whitney Twin Wasp 1,200 hp engines, and with this aircraft the assembly lines closed in 1943.

The Beaufort operated mainly in the North Sea and in the Atlantic. Gradually they were moved to the Mediterranean. They were replaced by the more modern and powerful Bristol Beaufighter.

In the Pacific theatre the main type of warfare in which the principal adversaries – the Americans and the Japanese – were involved gave a primary importance to anti-shipping aircraft. As a result torpedo-bombers always played a dominant part in all operations. Japan in particular was very conscious of the offensive potential of these aircraft, both tactical and strategic, and used them very widely from the first day of the war onwards.

The most effective Japanese torpedo-bomber, one of the most outstanding of the entire war, began its career at Pearl Harbor: in that tragic day as many as 144 Nakajima B5Ns (Allied code name KATE) made a major contribution towards the devastation of the American fleet. The model in service at that time was the B5N2, the second production version, which had gone into service in 1940 and which was also the principal variant; a total of 1,149 were constructed between 1937 and 1943. The KATEs (the prototype had flown in January 1937) remained in the front line until 1944.

The operational career of the first carrier-borne American torpedo bomber, the Douglas TBD Devastator, came to a dramatic end in 1942 at the Battle of Midway. This aircraft had been designed as far back as 1934 (129 YBD-1s built) and in spite of its limitations had sustained the stresses of the first six months of the war in the Pacific whilst awaiting a more effective successor.

The prototype had flown for the first time on 15th April 1935, and on its appearance it had become the pride of the high command of the US Navy. It had fallen to the XTBD-1 to inaugu-

rate a new phase in the history of American naval aviation: not only was it the first carrier-based torpedo-bomber of the fleet, it was also the first low-wing all-metal monoplane to go into service. Its operational debut took place two and a half year later in November 1937 with the 3rd Torpedo Squadron, VT-3, based on the aircraft carrier USS *Saratoga*.

At the time of the Japanese attack on Pearl Harbor the US Navy had a total of one hundred Devastators at its disposal, but only 69 of these were combat-ready. This tiny attack force was distributed amongst the aircraft carriers in service at the time and they took part in all the air-sea operations of the first half of 1942. Their sad end came at Midway: between 4th and 7th June nearly all the Devastators of the USS *Hornet* and the USS *Enterprise* (36 aircraft out of 41) were destroyed in desperate, futile attacks on the Japanese fleet.

Plate 140
The Avenger: the best of the last wartime torpedo-bombers: 1939–43

The aircraft which replaced the Douglas TBD Devastator was the Grumman TBF Avenger; this gave the US Navy a weapon which was really effective in an anti-shipping role. It first saw battle at Midway on 4th June 1942, although it did not get off to an encouraging start: five out of 6 were shot down without hitting their targets. The Avenger was one of the mainstays of the fleet until the end of the war, 9,836 examples in a number of variants being built. After surviving the Second World war many of the TBF Avengers remained in active service until 1954 with the air forces and navies of many countries amongst

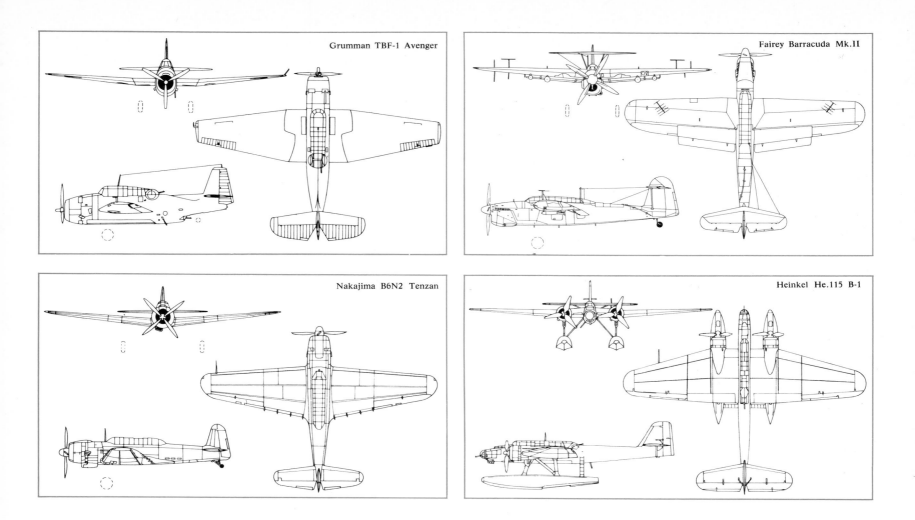

Grumman TBF-1 Avenger

Fairey Barracuda Mk.II

Nakajima B6N2 Tenzan

Heinkel He.115 B-1

which, paradoxically, was that of Japan.

The project was started in April 1940, and the prototype flew on 1st August of the following year, completing its proving trials and service test flights before the end of December. On 3rd January 1942 the first TBF1s left the assembly line and soon the production quotas were increased in order to satisfy growing orders from the US Navy.

Some quantities were built by Eastern Aircraft, a division of General Motors, and aircraft produced by this company took the specific designation of TBM. It was Eastern which built the 4,664 aircraft of the second main variant of the Avenger, the TBF-3 (this was its original designation) built from the spring of 1942 onwards. Besides this basic version many sub-series made their appearance, intended for various roles: photo-reconnaissance, night reconnaissance with early-warning equipment, and as transports. Many aircraft were also equipped with anti-submarine radar (TBM-3H and TBM-3W). The Avenger did not fight under American colours only: the British Fleet Air Arm used 958 of them from 1943 onwards whilst approximately another 60 went to the Royal New Zealand Air Force.

In Japan the substitute for the B5N aircraft-carrier-borne torpedo-

bomber was the B6N Tenzan which was also built by Nakajima. This large single-engine plane (Allied code-name JILL) kept up its predecessor's high standards: the only problem in its long operational career was the very long time it took to develop which was due to a succession of problems (which included unsatisfactory flight stability, problems with the engine and weaknesses in the landing gear) which took over two years to put right. The prototype in fact had appeared in the spring of 1941, before Japan's entry into the war, but production models of the first version, the B6N-1, were only delivered in 1943. After the construction of 133 of them the assembly lines went on to the second variant, the B6N-2, which reached units at the end of the year. In total 1,268 Tenzan were built, which stayed in the front line up to the end of the war.

As the war went on Britain also made every effort to produce new and more modern aircraft for use on board aircraft carriers to add to those which she already had. The successor to the old Swordfish and Albacore biplanes was a monoplane which was the first torpedo-bomber of this type to be put into service with the Fleet Air Arm. This was the Fairey Barracuda which commenced operational service in January 1943.

The project was undertaken in 1937 in response to a specific request from the Air Ministry which asked for a carrier-based torpedo-bomber to replace the Albacore. The prototype had flown on 7th December 1940, but development difficulties had made it necessary to build another (tested on 29th June the following year) from which the first production series was derived. Only 25 Barracuda Mk Is were built and were delivered from 18th May 1942 onwards: immediately afterwards they were replaced on the assembly lines by the aircraft of the second generation, Mk II, differing mainly in their engine, which was more powerful, and in their propeller, which changed from three-bladed to four-bladed. The first Mk II Barracuda flew on 17th August 1942, and production soon reached very high levels. The Mark III followed the Mk II and was specially designed for anti-submarine warfare and as such they were equipped with radar. In all 2,572 were built: they were used not only as torpedo-bombers but also as bombers until the last day of the war, some of them staying in service until 1953.

Among the wartime feats worthy of note in which the Barracuda of the Royal Navy played a leading role was the attack (one of many) carried out on 3rd April 1944, against the Ger-

man battle-cruiser *Tirpitz*, which had taken refuge in a fiord on the northern coast of Norway. As many as 42 aircraft were launched from the aircraft carriers HMS *Victorious* and HMS *Furious*, and, escorted by a strong fighter force, they took the defenders of the powerful German ship by surprise. The Barracuda struck the *Tirpitz* in the two waves with 15 bombs which, although they did not wreak a great deal of damage on the battleship, diminished the ship's operational capacities. According to historians this attack marked the beginning of the long death-agony of the *Tirpitz*, which was finally to be sunk on 12th November 1944 by the Lancasters of the RAF.

The Germans, unlike their adversaries, never attributed great importance to torpedo-bombers, perhaps for the very reason that their Navy did not have its own air force. Several aircraft were adapted to this role but few were conceived as such. Among these was the Heinkel He.115 of 1936. With the entry into service of the first production series, however (the B-1 became operational in 1939), the limitations of this large seaplane became all too apparent and it was used for mine-laying, and was taken out of front-line service in the summer of 1944.

Plate 141

Scale view of selected Second World War reconnaissance aircraft

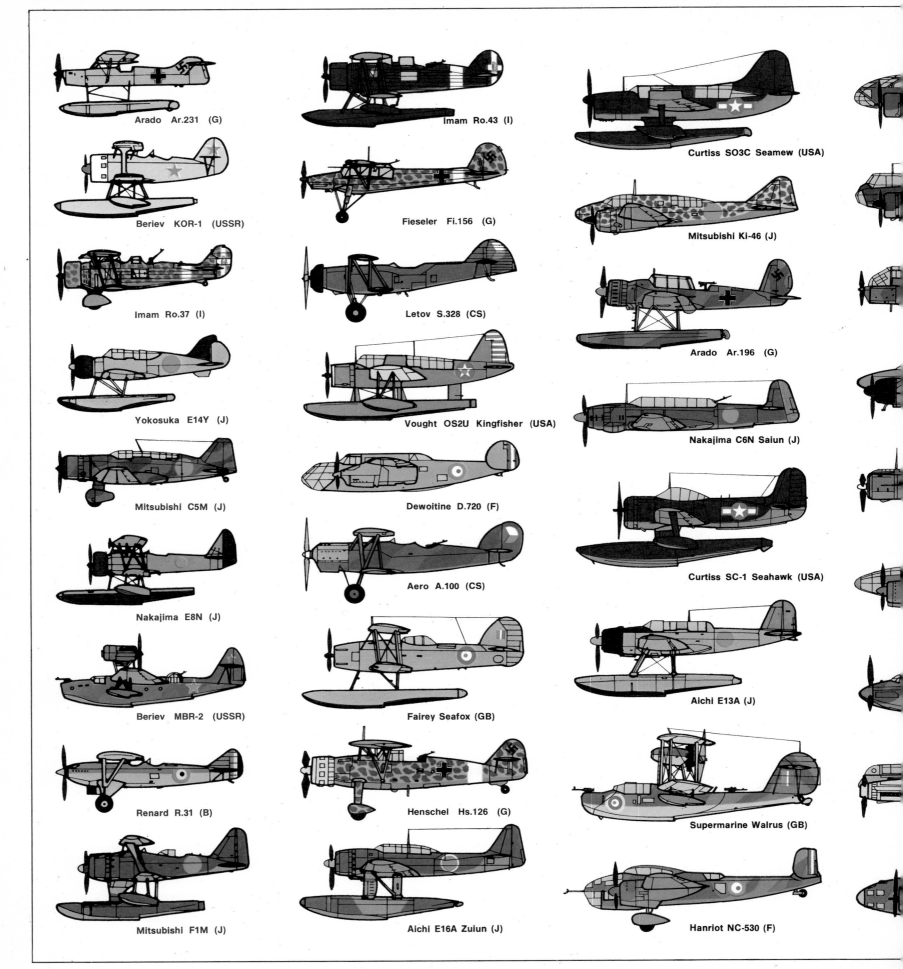

Arado Ar.231 (G)

Beriev KOR-1 (USSR)

Imam Ro.37 (I)

Yokosuka E14Y (J)

Mitsubishi C5M (J)

Nakajima E8N (J)

Beriev MBR-2 (USSR)

Renard R.31 (B)

Mitsubishi F1M (J)

Imam Ro.43 (I)

Fieseler Fi.156 (G)

Letov S.328 (CS)

Vought OS2U Kingfisher (USA)

Dewoitine D.720 (F)

Aero A.100 (CS)

Fairey Seafox (GB)

Henschel Hs.126 (G)

Aichi E16A Zuiun (J)

Curtiss SO3C Seamew (USA)

Mitsubishi Ki-46 (J)

Arado Ar.196 (G)

Nakajima C6N Saiun (J)

Curtiss SC-1 Seahawk (USA)

Aichi E13A (J)

Supermarine Walrus (GB)

Hanriot NC-530 (F)

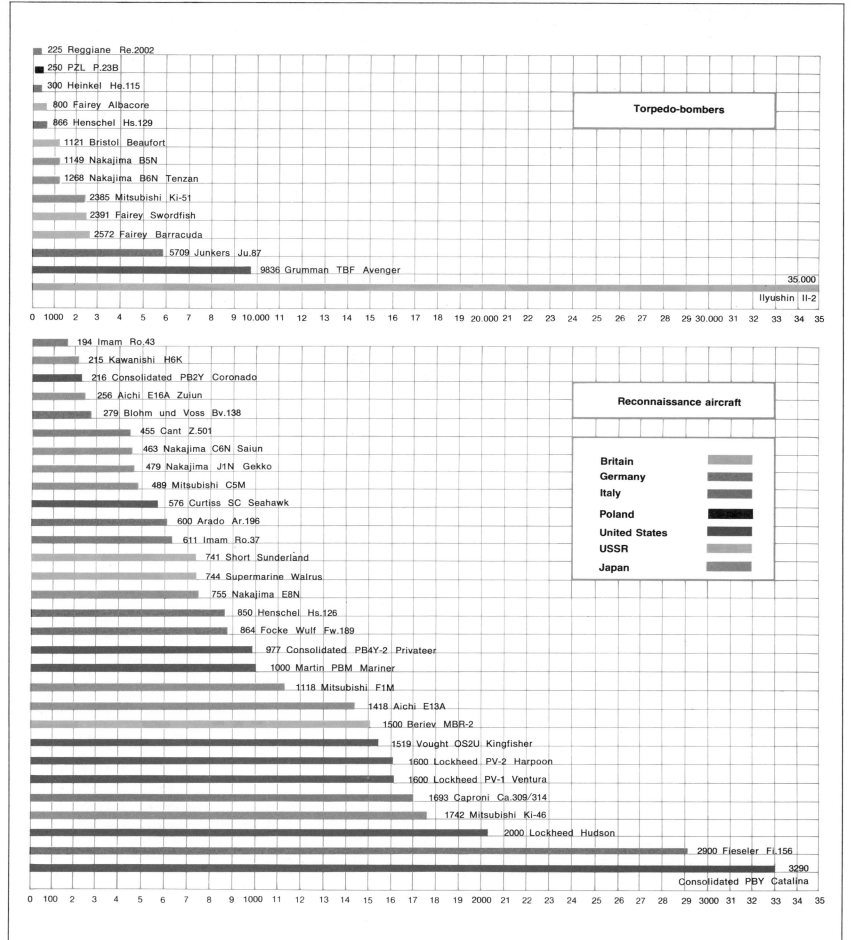

Torpedo-bombers

- 225 Reggiane Re.2002
- 250 PZL P.23B
- 300 Heinkel He.115
- 800 Fairey Albacore
- 866 Henschel Hs.129
- 1121 Bristol Beaufort
- 1149 Nakajima B5N
- 1268 Nakajima B6N Tenzan
- 2385 Mitsubishi Ki-51
- 2391 Fairey Swordfish
- 2572 Fairey Barracuda
- 5709 Junkers Ju.87
- 9836 Grumman TBF Avenger
- 35.000 Ilyushin Il-2

Reconnaissance aircraft

- 194 Imam Ro.43
- 215 Kawanishi H6K
- 216 Consolidated PB2Y Coronado
- 256 Aichi E16A Zuiun
- 279 Blohm und Voss Bv.138
- 455 Cant Z.501
- 463 Nakajima C6N Saiun
- 479 Nakajima J1N Gekko
- 489 Mitsubishi C5M
- 576 Curtiss SC Seahawk
- 600 Arado Ar.196
- 611 Imam Ro.37
- 741 Short Sunderland
- 744 Supermarine Walrus
- 755 Nakajima E8N
- 850 Henschel Hs.126
- 864 Focke Wulf Fw.189
- 977 Consolidated PB4Y-2 Privateer
- 1000 Martin PBM Mariner
- 1118 Mitsubishi F1M
- 1418 Aichi E13A
- 1500 Beriev MBR-2
- 1519 Vought OS2U Kingfisher
- 1600 Lockheed PV-2 Harpoon
- 1600 Lockheed PV-1 Ventura
- 1693 Caproni Ca.309/314
- 1742 Mitsubishi Ki-46
- 2000 Lockheed Hudson
- 2900 Fieseler Fi.156
- 3290 Consolidated PBY Catalina

Legend:
- Britain
- Germany
- Italy
- Poland
- United States
- USSR
- Japan

Plate 143

Entry into service of the most important reconnaissance aircraft of the Second World War

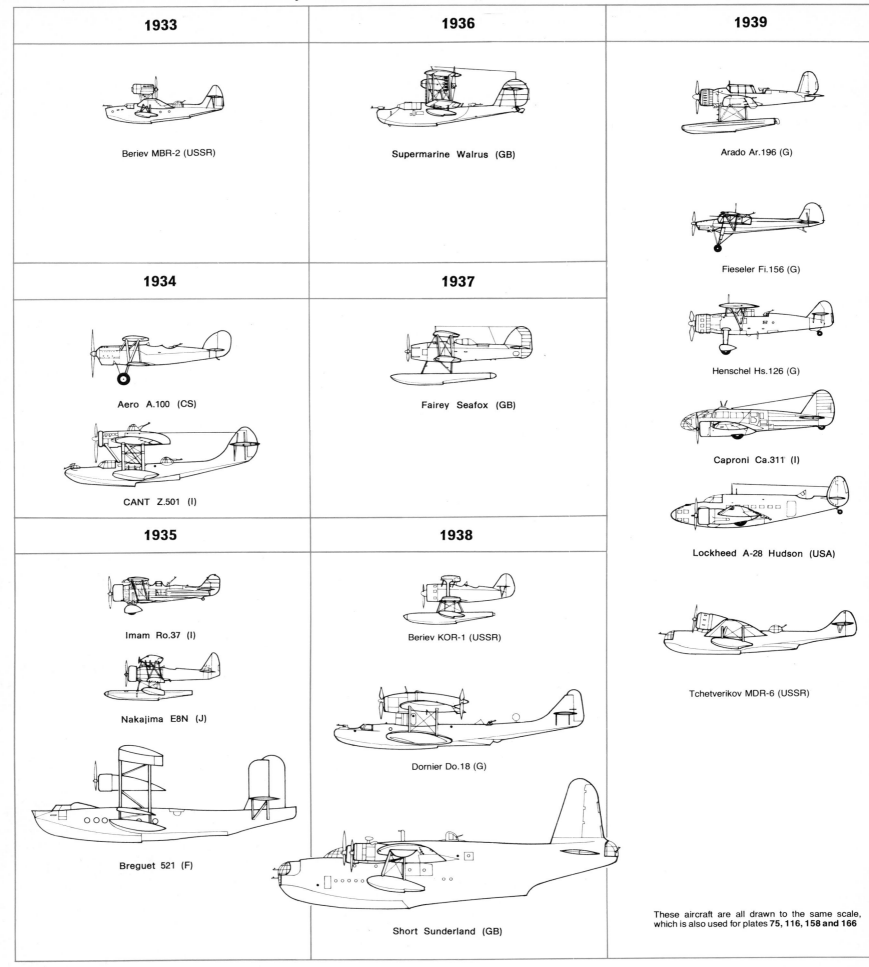

1933

Beriev MBR-2 (USSR)

1934

Aero A.100 (CS)

CANT Z.501 (I)

1935

Imam Ro.37 (I)

Nakajima E8N (J)

Breguet 521 (F)

1936

Supermarine Walrus (GB)

1937

Fairey Seafox (GB)

1938

Beriev KOR-1 (USSR)

Dornier Do.18 (G)

Short Sunderland (GB)

1939

Arado Ar.196 (G)

Fieseler Fi.156 (G)

Henschel Hs.126 (G)

Caproni Ca.311 (I)

Lockheed A-28 Hudson (USA)

Tchetverikov MDR-6 (USSR)

These aircraft are all drawn to the same scale, which is also used for plates **75, 116, 158 and 166**

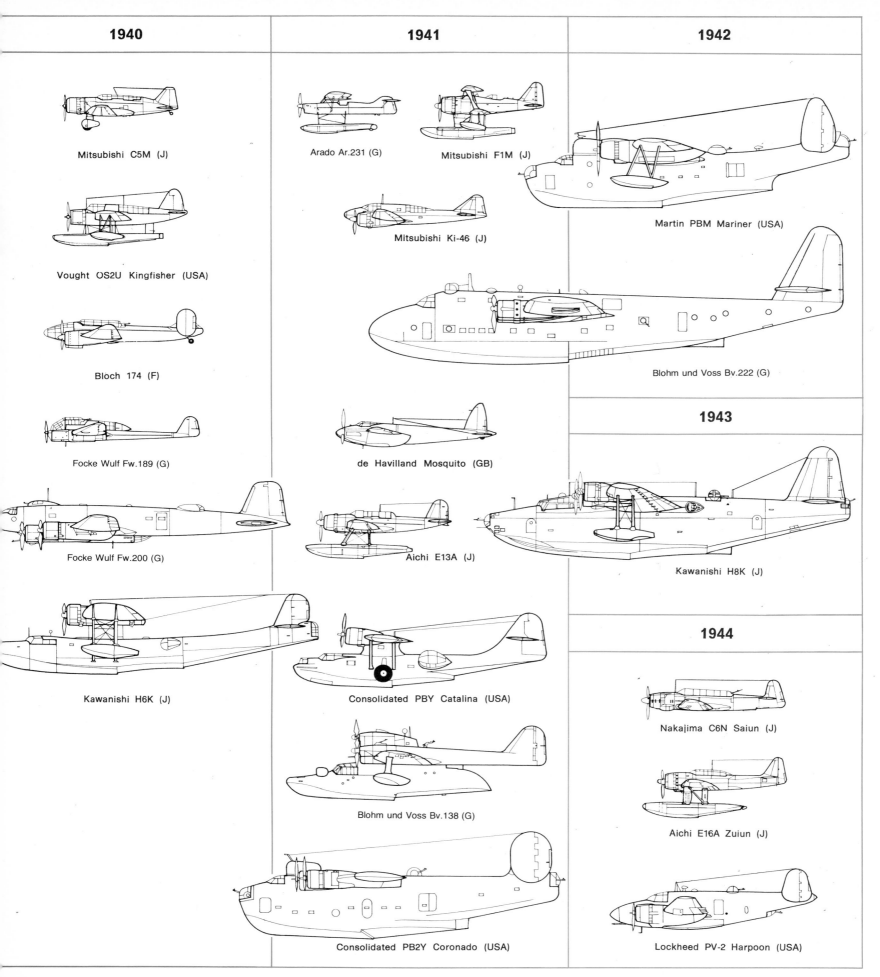

1940

Mitsubishi C5M (J)

Vought OS2U Kingfisher (USA)

Bloch 174 (F)

Focke Wulf Fw.189 (G)

Focke Wulf Fw.200 (G)

Kawanishi H6K (J)

1941

Arado Ar.231 (G)

Mitsubishi F1M (J)

Mitsubishi Ki-46 (J)

de Havilland Mosquito (GB)

Aichi E13A (J)

Consolidated PBY Catalina (USA)

Blohm und Voss Bv.138 (G)

Consolidated PB2Y Coronado (USA)

1942

Martin PBM Mariner (USA)

Blohm und Voss Bv.222 (G)

1943

Kawanishi H8K (J)

1944

Nakajima C6N Saiun (J)

Aichi E16A Zuiun (J)

Lockheed PV-2 Harpoon (USA)

Plate 144

Anatomy of a Second World War reconnaissance aircraft

Foche-Wulf Fw.189 A-2

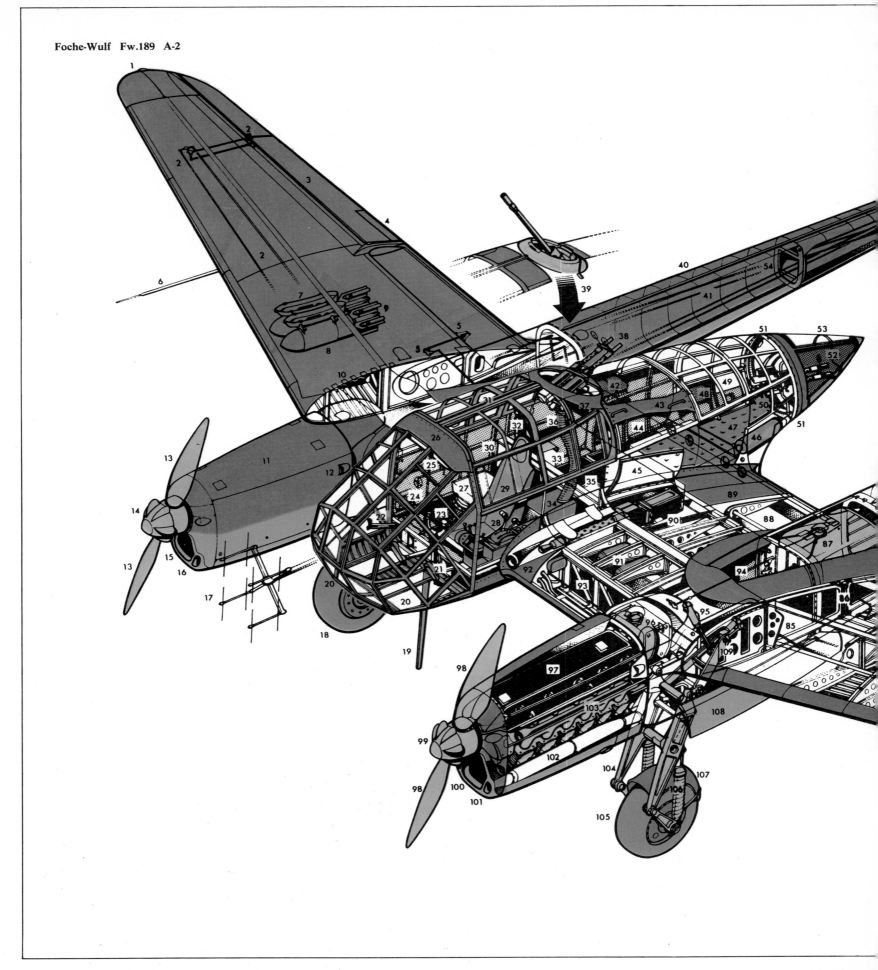

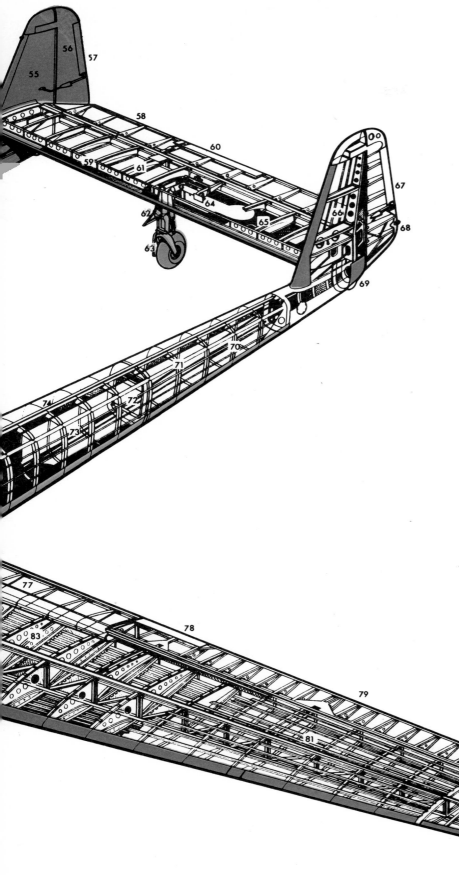

1 Starboard navigation light
2 Aileron control linkage (outer and inner)
3 Starboard aileron
4 Aileron tab
5 Starboard outer flap control linkage
6 Pitot tube
7 ETC 50/VIIId underwing rack fairings
8 Two 110 lb (50 kg) SC50 bombs
9 Papier-mache "screamers" attached to bomb fins
10 Wing centre/outer section join
11 Starboard engine nacelle
12 Air intake
13 Argus two-bladed controllable-pitch propeller
14 Pitch control vanes
15 Oil cooler intake
16 Engine air intake
17 FuG 212 Lichtenstein C-1 radar array (fitted to night fighter adaptation)
18 Starboard mainwheel
19 Ventral radio mast
20 Optically flat nose panels
21 Rudder pedals
22 GV 219d bomb sight
23 Control column
24 Bomb switch panel
25 Pilot's ring-and-bead sight (for fixed wing-root machine guns)
26 Padded overhead instrument panel
27 Navigator's swivel seat
28 Throttle levers
29 Pilot's seat
30 Mainspar carry-through
31 Centre hinged two-piece canopy hatch
32 Turnover bar with attached plasticised anti-glare curtain
33 Radio equipment
34 Shell collector box
35 Centre section camera well (one RB 20/30 RB 50/30 RB 21/18 or RB 15/18 camera)
36 Canvas shell collection chute
37 Dorsal turret
38 MG81Z twin 7.9 mm machine gun
39 MG 151 (15 mm) fixed cannon in "schräge Musik" installation (fitted to night fighter adaptation)
40 Starboard tailboom
41 Rudder and elevator control cables
42 Ammunition stowage (dorsal position)
43 Entry handholds
44 Centre-section flap below crew nacelle
45 Wing-root gun access panel (raised)
46 Rear turret-cone drive motor
47 Rear gunner's two-piece quilted pad
48 Ammunition stowage (rear position)

49 Rear canopy opening
50 MG 81Z twin 7.9 mm machine guns (trunnion mounted)
51 Revolving Ikaria powered cone turret
52 Field-of-fire cut-out
53 Aft glazing
54 Tailboom mid-section strengthening frame
55 Starboard tailfin
56 Starboard rudder
57 Rudder tab
58 Elevator construction
59 Tailplane forward spar
60 Elevator tab
61 Tailplane construction
62 Tailwheel hinged (two-piece) door
63 Tailwheel (swivelling)
64 Tailwheel retraction mechanism
65 Tailwheel well (offset to port)
66 Tailfin construction
67 Rudder tab
68 Rear navigation light
69 Tail bumper
70 Tailboom frames
71 Tailboom upper longeron
72 Mid-section strengthening frame
73 Tail surface control cables
74 External stiffening strake (upper and lower)
75 Master compass
76 Wing-root fairing
77 Port outer flap construction
78 Aileron tab
79 Aileron construction
80 Port navigation light
81 Wing stringers (upper shell)
82 Lower shell wing inner skin stringers
83 Two-piece shaped wing ribs
84 Mainspar structure
85 Mainspar/boom attachment point
86 Rear spar/boom attachment point
87 Port fuel tank (24.2 Imp gal/110 litre of 87° A-2)
88 Centre section one piece flap
89 Wing walkway
90 Fixed 7.9 mm MG 17 machine gun
91 Pilot's oxygen (3.5 pint/2 litre) bottles in port wing with navigator's and gunner's supply (four 2 litre bottles) in starboard wing
92 Gun port
93 Forward spar structure (with warm-air and oil-pressure lines)
94 Wheel well
95 Mainwheel retraction jack
96 Oil tank (99 Imp gal/45 litre capacity)
97 Argus As 410A-1 12-cylinder inverted-V air-cooled engine
98 Two-blade controllable-pitch Argus propeller
99 Pitch control vanes
100 Oil cooler air intake
101 Engine air intake
102 Oil cooler trunking
103 Exhaust collector
104 H-section hydraulically-operated main undercarriage members
105 Port mainwheel
106 Shock absorbers
107 Mudguard
108 Mainwheel door
109 Mainwheel retraction mechanism

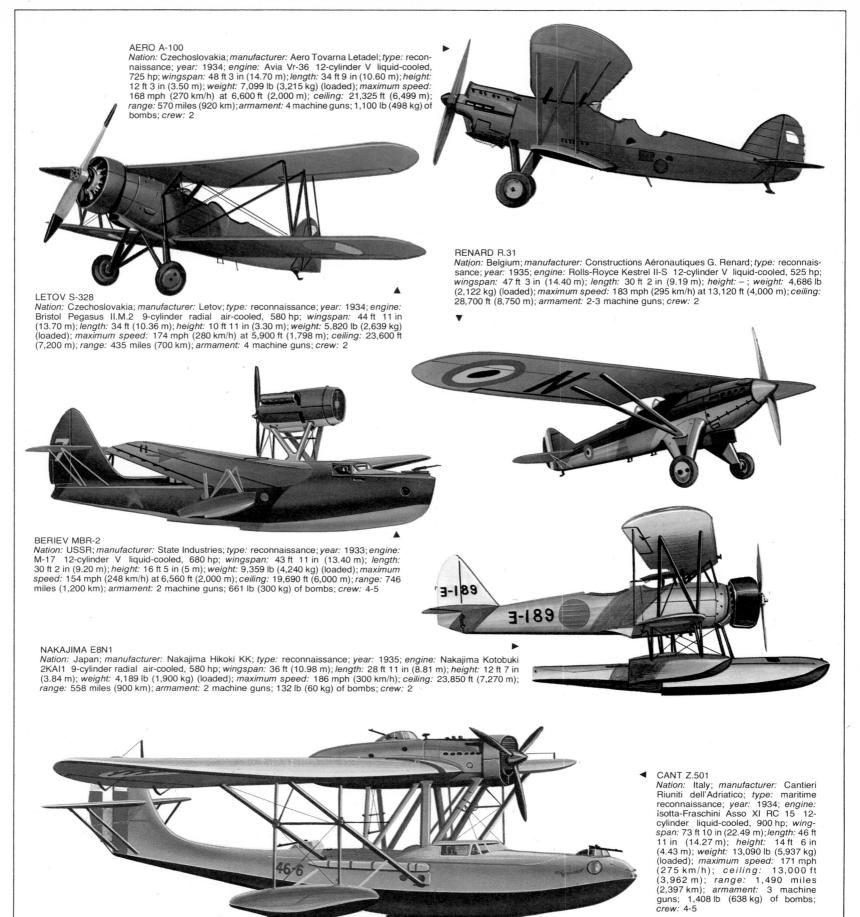

AERO A-100
Nation: Czechoslovakia; *manufacturer:* Aero Tovarna Letadel; *type:* reconnaissance; *year:* 1934; *engine:* Avia Vr-36 12-cylinder V liquid-cooled, 725 hp; *wingspan:* 48 ft 3 in (14.70 m); *length:* 34 ft 9 in (10.60 m); *height:* 12 ft 3 in (3.50 m); *weight:* 7,099 lb (3,215 kg) (loaded); *maximum speed:* 168 mph (270 km/h) at 6,600 ft (2,000 m); *ceiling:* 21,325 ft (6,499 m); *range:* 570 miles (920 km); *armament:* 4 machine guns; 1,100 lb (498 kg) of bombs; *crew:* 2

LETOV S-328
Nation: Czechoslovakia; *manufacturer:* Letov; *type:* reconnaissance; *year:* 1934; *engine:* Bristol Pegasus II.M.2 9-cylinder radial air-cooled, 580 hp; *wingspan:* 44 ft 11 in (13.70 m); *length:* 34 ft (10.36 m); *height:* 10 ft 11 in (3.30 m); *weight:* 5,820 lb (2,639 kg) (loaded); *maximum speed:* 174 mph (280 km/h) at 5,900 ft (1,798 m); *ceiling:* 23,600 ft (7,200 m); *range:* 435 miles (700 km); *armament:* 4 machine guns; *crew:* 2

BERIEV MBR-2
Nation: USSR; *manufacturer:* State Industries; *type:* reconnaissance; *year:* 1933; *engine:* M-17 12-cylinder V liquid-cooled, 680 hp; *wingspan:* 43 ft 11 in (13.40 m); *length:* 30 ft 2 in (9.20 m); *height:* 16 ft 5 in (5 m); *weight:* 9,359 lb (4,240 kg) (loaded); *maximum speed:* 154 mph (248 km/h) at 6,560 ft (2,000 m); *ceiling:* 19,690 ft (6,000 m); *range:* 746 miles (1,200 km); *armament:* 2 machine guns; 661 lb (300 kg) of bombs; *crew:* 4-5

NAKAJIMA E8N1
Nation: Japan; *manufacturer:* Nakajima Hikoki KK; *type:* reconnaissance; *year:* 1935; *engine:* Nakajima Kotobuki 2KAI1 9-cylinder radial air-cooled, 580 hp; *wingspan:* 36 ft (10.98 m); *length:* 28 ft 11 in (8.81 m); *height:* 12 ft 7 in (3.84 m); *weight:* 4,189 lb (1,900 kg) (loaded); *maximum speed:* 186 mph (300 km/h); *ceiling:* 23,850 ft (7,270 m); *range:* 558 miles (900 km); *armament:* 2 machine guns; 132 lb (60 kg) of bombs; *crew:* 2

RENARD R.31
Nation: Belgium; *manufacturer:* Constructions Aéronautiques G. Renard; *type:* reconnaissance; *year:* 1935; *engine:* Rolls-Royce Kestrel II-S 12-cylinder V liquid-cooled, 525 hp; *wingspan:* 47 ft 3 in (14.40 m); *length:* 30 ft 2 in (9.19 m); *height:* – ; *weight:* 4,686 lb (2,122 kg) (loaded); *maximum speed:* 183 mph (295 km/h) at 13,120 ft (4,000 m); *ceiling:* 28,700 ft (8,750 m); *armament:* 2-3 machine guns; *crew:* 2

CANT Z.501
Nation: Italy; *manufacturer:* Cantieri Riuniti dell'Adriatico; *type:* maritime reconnaissance; *year:* 1934; *engine:* isotta-Fraschini Asso XI RC 15 12-cylinder liquid-cooled, 900 hp; *wingspan:* 73 ft 10 in (22.49 m); *length:* 46 ft 11 in (14.27 m); *height:* 14 ft 6 in (4.43 m); *weight:* 13,090 lb (5,937 kg) (loaded); *maximum speed:* 171 mph (275 km/h); *ceiling:* 13,000 ft (3,962 m); *range:* 1,490 miles (2,397 km); *armament:* 3 machine guns; 1,408 lb (638 kg) of bombs; *crew:* 4-5

IMAM Ro. 37
Nation: Italy; *manufacturer:* SA Industrie Meccaniche e
Aeronautiche Meridionali (IMAM); *type:* reconnaissance;
year: 1935; *engine:* Fiat A.30 RA. 12-cylinder V liquid-
cooled, 550 hp; *wingspan:* 36 ft 4 in (11.08 m); *length:* 28 ft
3 in (8.62 m); *height:* 9 ft 9 in (2.95 m); *weight:* 5,269 lb
(2,390 kg) (loaded); *maximum speed:* 202 mph (325 km/h);
ceiling: 22,000 ft (6,700 m); *range:* 726 miles (1,168 km);
armament: 2-3 machine guns; *crew:* 2

IMAM Ro. 43
Nation: Italy; *manufacturer:* SA Industrie Meccaniche e
Aeronautiche Meridionali (IMAM); *type:* reconnaissance; *year:*
1936; *engine:* Piaggio P.XR 9-cylinder radial air-cooled, 700 hp;
wingspan: 37 ft 11½ in (11.57 m); *length:* 31 ft 10 in (9.71 m);
height: 11 ft 6 in (3.51 m); *weight:* 5,300 lb (2,400 kg) (loaded);
maximum speed: 186 mph (299 km/h) at 8,200 ft (2,499 m); *ceiling:* 21,600 ft (6,583 m); *range:* 678 miles (1,092 km); *armament:* 2
machine guns; *crew:* 2

SUPERMARINE WALRUS Mk 1
Nation: Britain; *manufacturer:* Saunders-Roe Ltd; *type:* reconnaissance; *year:* 1936; *engine:* Bristol Pegasus 11.M.2 9-cylinder
radial air-cooled, 775 hp; *wingspan:* 45 ft 10 in (13.97 m); *length:*
37 ft 7 in (11.45 m); *height:* 15 ft 3 in (4.65 m); *weight:* 7,200 lb
(3,261 kg) (loaded); *maximum speed:* 135 mph (217 km/h) at
4,750 ft (1,450 m); *ceiling:* 18,500 ft (5,650 m); *range:* 600 miles
(965 km); *armament:* 2-3 machine guns; *crew:* 4

TCHETVERIKOV ARK-3
Nation: USSR; *manufacturer:* State Industries; *type:* reconnaissance; *year:*
1936; *engine:* two M-25V 9-cylinder radial air-cooled, 730 hp each; *wingspan:* 65 ft 3½ in (19.90 m); *length:* 47 ft 7 in (14.50 m); *height:* not available; *weight:* 11,574 lb (5,243 kg) (loaded); *maximum speed:* 199 mph
(320 km/h) at 4,920 ft (1,500 m); *ceiling:* 27,890 ft (8,500 m); *range:* 932
miles (1,500 km); *armament:* 2 machine guns; 2,200 lb (1,000 kg) of
bombs; *crew:* 5

BREGUET 521
Nation: France; *manufacturer:* Breguet; *type:* maritime
reconnaissance; *year:* 1935; *engine:* three Gnome-
Rhône 14 Kirs 14-cylinder radial air-cooled, 900 hp
each; *wingspan:* 115 ft 4 in (35.18 m); *length:* 67 ft 2 in
(20.48 m); *height:* 24 ft 6½ in (7.50 m); *weight:*
35,320 lb (16,000 kg) (loaded); *maximum speed:*
151 mph (243 km/h) at 3,200 ft (980 m); *ceiling:*
19,700 ft (6,000 m); *range:* 1,305 miles (2,100 km);
armament: 5 machine guns; 660 lb (300 kg) of bombs;
crew: 8

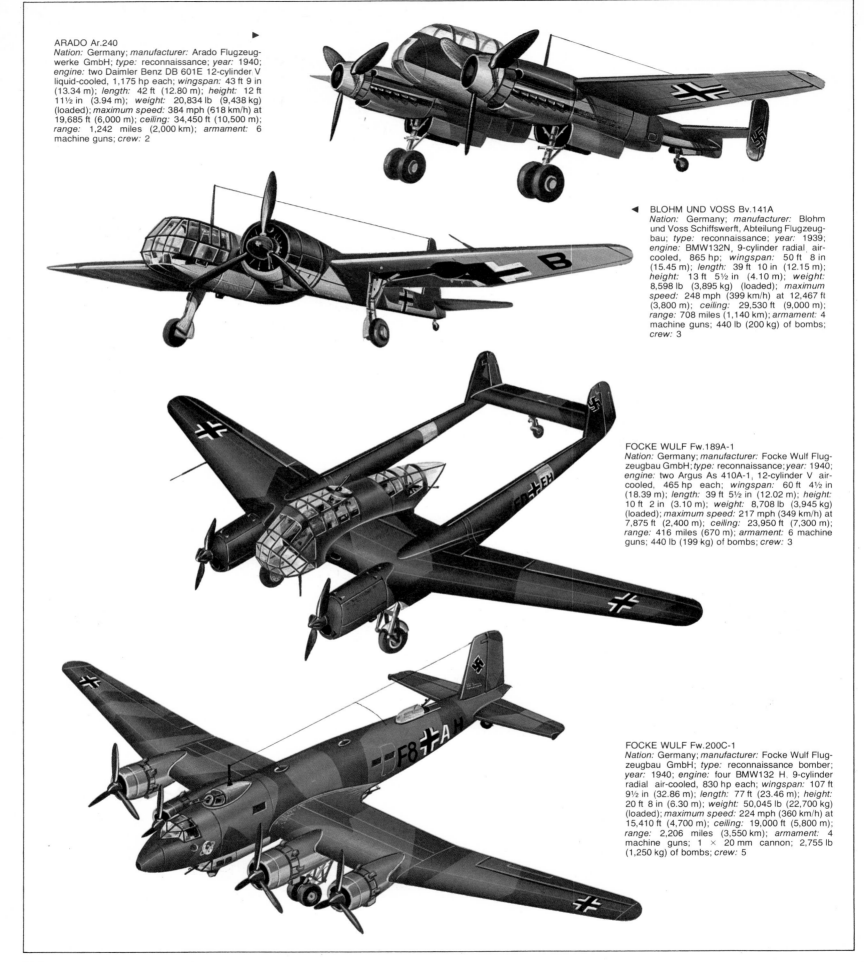

ARADO Ar.240
Nation: Germany; *manufacturer:* Arado Flugzeug-werke GmbH; *type:* reconnaissance; *year:* 1940; *engine:* two Daimler Benz DB 601E 12-cylinder V liquid-cooled, 1,175 hp each; *wingspan:* 43 ft 9 in (13.34 m); *length:* 42 ft (12.80 m); *height:* 12 ft 11½ in (3.94 m); *weight:* 20,834 lb (9,438 kg) (loaded); *maximum speed:* 384 mph (618 km/h) at 19,685 ft (6,000 m); *ceiling:* 34,450 ft (10,500 m); *range:* 1,242 miles (2,000 km); *armament:* 6 machine guns; *crew:* 2

BLOHM UND VOSS Bv.141A
Nation: Germany; *manufacturer:* Blohm und Voss Schiffswerft, Abteilung Flugzeug-bau; *type:* reconnaissance; *year:* 1939; *engine:* BMW132N, 9-cylinder radial air-cooled, 865 hp; *wingspan:* 50 ft 8 in (15.45 m); *length:* 39 ft 10 in (12.15 m); *height:* 13 ft 5½ in (4.10 m); *weight:* 8,598 lb (3,895 kg) (loaded); *maximum speed:* 248 mph (399 km/h) at 12,467 ft (3,800 m); *ceiling:* 29,530 ft (9,000 m); *range:* 708 miles (1,140 km); *armament:* 4 machine guns; 440 lb (200 kg) of bombs; *crew:* 3

FOCKE WULF Fw.189A-1
Nation: Germany; *manufacturer:* Focke Wulf Flug-zeugbau GmbH; *type:* reconnaissance; *year:* 1940; *engine:* two Argus As 410A-1, 12-cylinder V air-cooled, 465 hp each; *wingspan:* 60 ft 4½ in (18.39 m); *length:* 39 ft 5½ in (12.02 m); *height:* 10 ft 2 in (3.10 m); *weight:* 8,708 lb (3,945 kg) (loaded); *maximum speed:* 217 mph (349 km/h) at 7,875 ft (2,400 m); *ceiling:* 23,950 ft (7,300 m); *range:* 416 miles (670 m); *armament:* 6 machine guns; 440 lb (199 kg) of bombs; *crew:* 3

FOCKE WULF Fw.200C-1
Nation: Germany; *manufacturer:* Focke Wulf Flug-zeugbau GmbH; *type:* reconnaissance bomber; *year:* 1940; *engine:* four BMW132 H, 9-cylinder radial air-cooled, 830 hp each; *wingspan:* 107 ft 9½ in (32.86 m); *length:* 77 ft (23.46 m); *height:* 20 ft 8 in (6.30 m); *weight:* 50,045 lb (22,700 kg) (loaded); *maximum speed:* 224 mph (360 km/h) at 15,410 ft (4,700 m); *ceiling:* 19,000 ft (5,800 m); *range:* 2,206 miles (3,550 km); *armament:* 4 machine guns; 1 × 20 mm cannon; 2,755 lb (1,250 kg) of bombs; *crew:* 5

HANRIOT NC 530
Nation: France; *manufacturer:* SNCAC; *type:* reconnaissance; *year:* 1940; *engine:* two Gnome-Rhône 14M 14-cylinder radial air-cooled, 700 hp each; *wingspan:* 42 ft 11 in (13.08 m); *length:* 37 ft 3 in (11.35 m); *height:* – ; *weight:* 11,244 lb (5,095 kg) (loaded); *maximum speed:* 255 mph (410 km/h) at 16,900 ft (5,150 m); *ceiling:* 27,890 ft (8,500 m); *range:* 1,118 miles (1,800 km); *armament:* 3 machine guns; 1,100 lb (500 kg) of bombs; *crew:* 3

BLOCH 174
Nation: France; *manufacturer:* SNCASO; *type:* reconnaissance; *year:* 1940; *engine:* two Gnome-Rhône 14 14-cylinder radial air-cooled, 1,140 hp each; *wingspan:* 58 ft 9½ in (17.90 m); *length:* 40 ft 1½ in (12.22 m); *height:* 11 ft 8 in (3.58 m); *weight:* 15,784 lb (7,150 kg) (loaded); *maximum speed:* 329 mph (530 km/h) at 17,060 ft (5,200 m); *ceiling:* 36,090 ft (11,000 m); *range:* 1,025 miles (1,650 km); *armament:* 7 machine guns; 880 lb (400 kg) of bombs; *crew:* 3

VOUGHT OS2U-1 KINGFISHER
Nation: USA; *manufacturer:* United Aircraft Corp; *type:* reconnaissance; *year:* 1940; *engine:* Pratt & Whitney R-985-48 Wasp Junior, 9-cylinder radial air-cooled, 450 hp; *wingspan:* 35 ft 11 in (10.94 m); *length:* 33 ft 7 in (10.31 m); *height:* 15 ft 1 in (4.59 m); *weight:* 4,000 lb (1,815 kg) (loaded); *maximum speed:* 164 mph (264 km/h) at 5,500 ft (1,680 m); *ceiling:* 19,500 ft (5,950 m); *range:* 805 miles (1,300 km); *armament:* 2 machine guns; *crew:* 2

MITSUBISHI C5M2
Nation: Japan; *manufacturer:* Mitsubishi Jukogyo KK; *type:* reconnaissance; *year:* 1940; *engine:* Nakajima Sakae 12 14-cylinder radial air-cooled, 950 hp; *wingspan:* 39 ft 4½ in (12 m); *length:* 28 ft 6½ in (8.70 m); *height:* 11 ft 4 in (3.46 m); *weight:* 5,170 lb (2,345 kg) (loaded); *maximum speed:* 303 mph (487 km/h) at 14,930 ft (4,550 m); *ceiling:* 31,430 ft (9,580 m); *range:* 691 miles (1,100 km); *armament:* 1 machine gun; *crew:* 2

KAWANISHI H6K4
Nation: Japan; *manufacturer:* Kawanishi Kokuki KK; *type:* reconnaissance; *year:* 1940; *engine:* four Mitsubishi Kinsei 43 14-cylinder radial, air-cooled, 1,000 hp each; *wingspan:* 131 ft 3 in (40 m); *length:* 84 ft 1 in (25.64 m); *height:* 20 ft 7 in (6.27 m); *weight:* 47,399 lb (21,545 kg) (loaded); *maximum speed:* 211 mph (340 km/h) at 13,120 ft (4,000 m); *ceiling:* 31,530 ft (9,610 m); *range:* 3,779 miles (6,080 km); *armament:* 1 × 20 mm cannon; 4 machine guns; 2,205 lb (1,000 kg) of bombs; *crew:* 9

Plate 151   **German and American reconnaissance flying boats: 1941**

ARADO Ar.231
Nation: Germany; *manufacturer:* Arado Flugzeugw. GmbH; *type:* reconnaissance; *year:* 1941; *engine:* Hirth HM 501 6-cylinder inline air-cooled, 160 hp; *wingspan:* 33 ft 4½ in (10.16 m); *length:* 25 ft 7½ in (7.80 m); *height:* 10 ft 3 in (3.12 m); *weight:* 2,315 lb (1,050 kg) (loaded); *maximum speed:* 106 mph (170 km/h); *ceiling:* 9,840 ft (3,000 m); *range:* 310 miles (500 km); *armament:* – ; *crew:* 1

BLOHM UND VOSS Bv.138C-1
Nation: Germany; *manufacturer:* Blohm und Voss Schiffswerft, Abteilung Flugzeugbau; *type:* reconnaissance; *year:* 1941; *engine:* three Junkers Jumo 205 6-cylinder inline liquid-cooled, 880 hp each; *wingspan:* 88 ft 4 in (26.92 m); *length:* 65 ft 1½ in (19.65 m); *height:* 19 ft 4 in (5.90 m); *weight:* 31,967 lb (14,500 kg) (loaded); *maximum speed:* 177 mph (285 km/h); *ceiling:* 16,400 ft (5,000 m); *range:* 2,669 miles (4,295 km); *armament:* 2 machine guns; 2 × 20 mm cannon; 661 lb (300 kg) of bombs; *crew:* 5

CONSOLIDATED PB2Y-3 CORONADO
Nation: USA; *manufacturer:* Consolidated Aircraft Corp; *type:* reconnaissance; *year:* 1941; *engine:* four Pratt & Whitney R-1830-88 Twin Wasp 14-cylinder radial air-cooled, 1,200 hp each; *wingspan:* 115 ft (35.05 m); *length:* 79 ft 3 in (24.16 m); *height:* 27 ft 6 in (8.30 m); *weight:* 68,000 lb (30,845 kg) (loaded); *maximum speed:* 213 mph (343 km/h) at 20,000 ft (6,100 m); *ceiling:* 20,900 ft (6,400 m); *range:* 1,370 miles (2,200 km); *armament:* 8 machine guns; 12,000 lb (5,443 kg) of bombs; *crew:* 10

CONSOLIDATED PBY-5A CATALINA
Nation: USA; *manufacturer:* Consolidated Aircraft Corp; *type:* reconnaissance; *year:* 1941; *engine:* two Pratt & Whitney R-1830-82 Twin Wasp 14-cylinder radial air-cooled, 1,200 hp each; *wingspan:* 104 ft 2 in (31.70 m); *length:* 63 ft 10 in (19.45 m); *height:* 20 ft 2 in (6.14 m); *weight:* 35,420 lb (16,066 kg) (loaded); *maximum speed:* 175 mph (281 km/h) at 7,000 ft (2,135 m); *ceiling:* 18,100 ft (5,520 m); *range:* 2,350 miles (3,780 km); *armament:* 5 machine guns; 4,000 lb (1,814 kg) of bombs; *crew:* 7-9

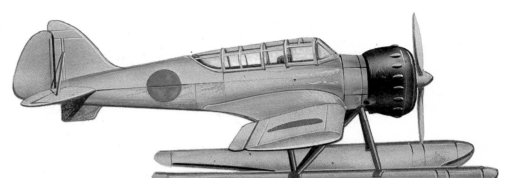

YOKOSUKA E14Y1
Nation: Japan; *manufacturer:* Watanabe Tekkosho KK; *type:* reconnaissance; *year:* 1941; *engine:* Hitachi Tempu 12 9-cylinder radial air-cooled, 340 hp; *wingspan:* 36 ft 1 in (11 m); *length:* 28 ft (8.54 m); *height:* 12 ft 6 in (3.82 m); *weight:* 3,527 lb (1,603 kg) (loaded); *maximum speed:* 153 mph (246 km/h); *ceiling:* 17,780 ft (5,420 m); *range:* 548 miles (880 km); *armament:* 1 machine gun; 132 lb (60 kg) of bombs; *crew:* 2

MITSUBISHI F1 M2
Nation: Japan; *manufacturer:* Mitsubishi Jukogyo KK; *type:* reconnaissance; *year:* 1941; *engine:* Mitsubishi Zuisei 13 14-cylinder radial air-cooled, 875 hp; *wingspan:* 36 ft 1 in (11 m); *length:* 31 ft 2 in (9.50 m); *height:* 13 ft 1½ in (4 m); *weight:* 6,926 lb (2,860 kg) (loaded); *maximum speed:* 230 mph (370 km/h) at 11,285 ft (3,440 m); *ceiling:* 30,970 ft (9,440 m); *range:* 460 miles (740 km); *armament:* 3 machine guns; 264 lb (120 kg) of bombs; *crew:* 2

AICHI E13A1
Nation: Japan; *manufacturer:* Aichi Kokuki KK; *type:* reconnaissance; *year:* 1941; *engine:* Mitsubishi Kinsei 43 14-cylinder radial air-cooled, 1,080 hp; *wingspan:* 47 ft 7 in (14.50 m); *length:* 37 ft 1 in (11.30 m); *height:* 15 ft 5 in (4.74 m); *weight:* 12,192 lb (5,542 kg) (loaded); *maximum speed:* 234 mph (376 km/h) at 7,155 ft (2,180 m); *ceiling:* 28,640 ft (8,730 m); *range:* 1,298 miles (2,090 km); *armament:* 1 machine gun; 550 lb (250 kg) of bombs; *crew:* 3

MITSUBISHI Ki-46-11
Nation: Japan; *manufacturer:* Mitsubishi Jukogyo KK; *type:* reconnaissance; *year:* 1941; *engine:* two Mitsubishi Ha-102 14-cylinder radial air-cooled, 1,080 hp each; *wingspan:* 48 ft 3 in (14.70 m); *length:* 36 ft 1 in (11 m); *height:* 12 ft 9 in (3.88 m); *weight:* 12,787 lb (5,812 kg) (loaded); *maximum speed:* 375 mph (604 km/h) at 19,030 ft (5,800 m); *ceiling:* 35,170 ft (10,720 m); *range:* 1,537 miles (2,474 km); *armament:* 1 machine gun; *crew:* 2

Plate 153

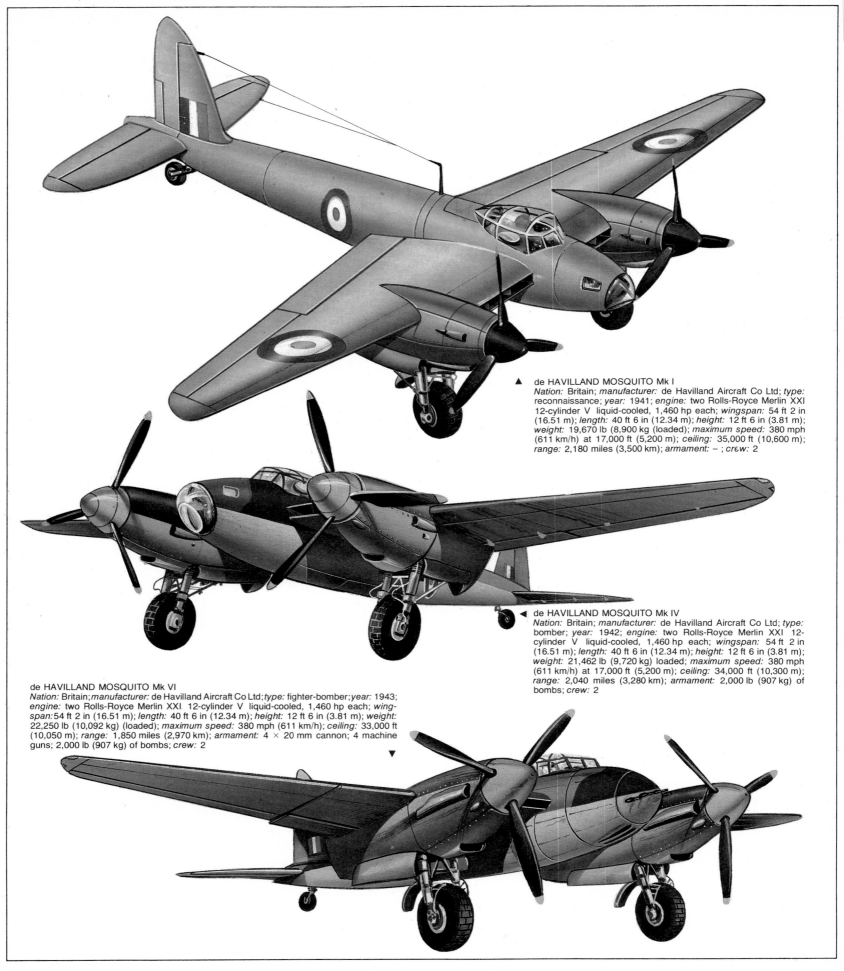

de HAVILLAND MOSQUITO Mk I
Nation: Britain; *manufacturer:* de Havilland Aircraft Co Ltd; *type:* reconnaissance; *year:* 1941; *engine:* two Rolls-Royce Merlin XXI 12-cylinder V liquid-cooled, 1,460 hp each; *wingspan:* 54 ft 2 in (16.51 m); *length:* 40 ft 6 in (12.34 m); *height:* 12 ft 6 in (3.81 m); *weight:* 19,670 lb (8,900 kg) (loaded); *maximum speed:* 380 mph (611 km/h) at 17,000 ft (5,200 m); *ceiling:* 35,000 ft (10,600 m); *range:* 2,180 miles (3,500 km); *armament:* – ; *crew:* 2

de HAVILLAND MOSQUITO Mk IV
Nation: Britain; *manufacturer:* de Havilland Aircraft Co Ltd; *type:* bomber; *year:* 1942; *engine:* two Rolls-Royce Merlin XXI 12-cylinder V liquid-cooled, 1,460 hp each; *wingspan:* 54 ft 2 in (16.51 m); *length:* 40 ft 6 in (12.34 m); *height:* 12 ft 6 in (3.81 m); *weight:* 21,462 lb (9,720 kg) loaded; *maximum speed:* 380 mph (611 km/h) at 17,000 ft (5,200 m); *ceiling:* 34,000 ft (10,300 m); *range:* 2,040 miles (3,280 km); *armament:* 2,000 lb (907 kg) of bombs; *crew:* 2

de HAVILLAND MOSQUITO Mk VI
Nation: Britain; *manufacturer:* de Havilland Aircraft Co Ltd; *type:* fighter-bomber; *year:* 1943; *engine:* two Rolls-Royce Merlin XXI 12-cylinder V liquid-cooled, 1,460 hp each; *wingspan:* 54 ft 2 in (16.51 m); *length:* 40 ft 6 in (12.34 m); *height:* 12 ft 6 in (3.81 m); *weight:* 22,250 lb (10,092 kg) (loaded); *maximum speed:* 380 mph (611 km/h); *ceiling:* 33,000 ft (10,050 m); *range:* 1,850 miles (2,970 km); *armament:* 4 × 20 mm cannon; 4 machine guns; 2,000 lb (907 kg) of bombs; *crew:* 2

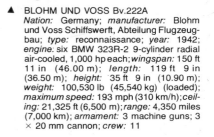

▲ BLOHM UND VOSS Bv.222A
Nation: Germany; *manufacturer:* Blohm und Voss Schiffswerft, Abteilung Flugzeugbau; *type:* reconnaissance; *year:* 1942; *engine:* six BMW 323R-2 9-cylinder radial air-cooled, 1,000 hp each; *wingspan:* 150 ft 11 in (46.00 m); *length:* 119 ft 9 in (36.50 m); *height:* 35 ft 9 in (10.90 m); *weight:* 100,530 lb (45,540 kg) (loaded); *maximum speed:* 193 mph (310 km/h); *ceiling:* 21,325 ft (6,500 m); *range:* 4,350 miles (7,000 km); *armament:* 3 machine guns; 3 × 20 mm cannon; *crew:* 11

FIAT RS.14
Nation: Italy; *manufacturer:* Costruzioni Meccaniche Aeronautiche SA; *type:* reconnaissance; *year:* 1942; *engine:* two Fiat A.74 RC 38 14-cylinder radial air-cooled, 840 hp each; *wingspan:* 64 ft 1 in (19.54 m); *length:* 46 ft 3 in (14.10 m); *height:* 18 ft 6 in (5.63 m); *weight:* 18,700 lb (8,470 kg) (loaded); *maximum speed:* 242 mph (390 km/h) at 15,400 ft (4,693 m); *ceiling:* 16,400 ft (5,000 m); *range:* 1,550 miles (2,500 km); *armament:* 3 machine guns; 880 lb (400 kg) of bombs; *crew:* 4-5

NAKAJIMA J1N1-C GEKKO
Nation: Japan; *manufacturer:* Nakajima Hikoki KK; *type:* reconnaissance; *year:* 1942; *engine:* two Nakajima NK1F Sakae 21 14-cylinder radial air-cooled, 1,130 hp each; *wingspan:* 55 ft 8½ in (16.98 m); *length:* 39 ft 11½ in (12.18 m); *height:* 15 ft (4.56 m); *weight:* 16,594 lb (7,542 kg) (loaded); *maximum speed:* 329 mph (530 km/h) at 19,685 ft (6,000 m); *ceiling:* 33,795 ft (10,300 m); *range:* 1,678 miles (2,700 km); *armament:* 1 machine gun; *crew:* 3

▲ CURTISS SO3C-1 Seamew
Nation: USA; *manufacturer:* Curtiss-Wright Corp; *type:* reconnaissance; *year:* 1942; *engine:* Ranger V-770-6 12-cylinder at V air-cooled, 600 hp; *wingspan:* 38 ft (11.58 m); *length:* 34 ft 9 in (10.50 m); *height:* 14 ft 2 in (4.31 m); *weight:* 7,105 lb (3223 kg); *maximum speed:* 168 mph (269 km/h) at 11,800 ft (3,600 m); *ceiling:* 16,500 ft (5,030 m); *range:* 640 miles (1,030 km); *armament:* 2 machine guns; 650 lb (295 kg) of bombs; *crew:* 2

MARTIN PBM-3 MARINER
Nation: USA; *manufacturer:* Glenn L. Martin Co; *type:* reconnaissance; *year:* 1942; *engine:* two Wright R-2600-12 Cyclone 14-cylinder radial air-cooled, 1,700 hp each; *wingspan:* 118 ft (35.97 m); *length:* 80 ft (24.38 m); *height:* 27 ft 6 in (8.38 m); *weight:* 58,000 lb (26,310 kg) (loaded); *maximum speed:* 198 mph (319 km/h) at 13,000 ft (3,960 m); *ceiling:* 16,900 ft (5,150 m); *range:* 2,137 miles (3,440 km); *armament:* 7 machine guns; 2,000 lb (907 kg) of bombs; *crew:* 7-8

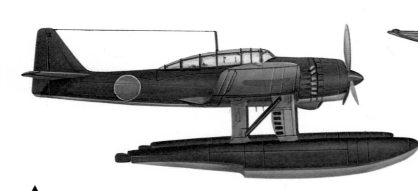

KAWANISHI H8K2
Nation: Japan; *manufacturer:* Kawanishi Kokuki KK; *type:* reconnaissance; *year:* 1943; *engine:* four Mitsubishi MK4Q Kasei 22 14-cylinder radial air-cooled, 1,850 hp each; *wingspan:* 124 ft 8 in (38 m); *length:* 92 ft 4 in (28.13 m); *height:* 30 ft (9.15 m); *weight:* 71,650 lb (32,570 kg) (loaded); *maximum speed:* 290 mph (466 km/h) at 16,400 ft (5,000 m); *ceiling:* 28,740 ft (8,850 m); *range:* 4,460 miles (7,190 km); *armament:* 5 × 20 mm cannon; 4 machine guns; 4,408 lb (2,000 kg) of bombs; *crew:* 10

KYUSHU Q1W1 TOKAI
Nation: Japan; *manufacturer:* Kyushu Hikoki KK; *type:* reconnaissance; *year:* 1944; *engine:* two Hitachi GK2C Amakaze 31 9-cylinder radial air-cooled, 610 hp; *wingspan:* 52 ft 6 in (16 m); *length:* 39 ft 8 in (12.08 m); *height:* 13 ft 6 in (4.11 m); *weight:* 11,724 lb (5,330 kg) (loaded); *maximum speed:* 200 mph (322 km/h) at 4,395 ft (1,340 m); *ceiling:* 14,730 ft (4,490 m); *range:* 834 miles (1,342 km); *armament:* 1 × 20 mm cannon; 1 machine gun; 1,102 lb (500 kg) of bombs; *crew:* 3

JUNKERS Ju.388L-1
Nation: Germany; *manufacturer:* Junkers Flugzeug und Motorenwerke AG; *type:* reconnaissance; *year:* 1944; *engine:* two BMW 801TJ 14-cylinder radial air-cooled, 1,800 hp each; *wingspan:* 72 ft 2 in (22.00 m); *length:* 49 ft 10½ in (15.19 m); *height:* 14 ft 3 in (4.34 m); *weight:* 30,450 lb (13,793 kg) (loaded); *maximum speed:* 383 mph (616 km/h) at 40,300 ft (12,290 m); *ceiling:* 44,100 ft (13,450 m); *range:* 1,414 miles (2,275 km); *armament:* 2 machine guns; *crew:* 3

AICHI E16A1 ZUIUN
Nation: Japan; *manufacturer:* Aichi Kokuki KK; *type:* reconnaissance; *year:* 1944; *engine:* Mitsubishi MK8D Kinsei 54 14-cylinder radial air-cooled, 1,300 hp; *wingspan:* 42 ft (12.81 m); *length:* 35 ft 6½ in (10.83 m); *height:* 15 ft 8½ in (4.79 m); *weight:* 10,038 lb (4,560 kg) (loaded); *maximum speed:* 273 mph (439 km/h) at 18,040 ft (5,500 m); *ceiling:* 32,810 ft (10,000 m); *range:* 1,504 miles (2,400 km); *armament:* 2 × 20 mm cannon; 1 machine gun; 551 lb (250 kg) of bombs; *crew:* 2

NAKAJIMA C6N1 SAIUN
Nation: Japan; *manufacturer:* Nakajima Hikoki KK; *type:* reconnaissance; *engine:* Nakajima HK9H Homare 21 18-cylinder radial air-cooled, 1,990 hp; *wingspan:* 41ft (12.50 m); *year:* 1944; *length:* 36 ft 1 in (11 m); *height:* 12 ft 11 in (3.96 m); *weight:* 11,596 lb (5,270 kg) (loaded); *maximum speed:* 379 mph (610 km/h) at 20,015 ft (6,100 m); *ceiling:* 35,326 ft (10,470 m); *range:* 3,300 miles (5,300 km); *armament:* 1 machine gun; *crew:* 3

LOCKHEED PV-1 VENTURA
Nation: USA; *manufacturer:* Lockheed Aircraft Corp; *type:* reconnaissance; *year:* 1942; *engine:* two Pratt & Whitney R-2800-31 Double Wasp 18-cylinder radial air-cooled, 2,000 hp each; *wingspan:* 65 ft 6 in (19.96 m); *length:* 51 ft 9 in (15.77 m); *height:* 11 ft 11 in (3.63 m); *weight:* 31,077 lb (14,100 kg) (loaded); *maximum speed:* 312 mph (502 km/h) at 13,800 ft (4,200 m); *ceiling:* 26,300 ft (8,000 m); *range:* 1,600 miles (2,670 km); *armament:* 6 machine guns; 5,000 lb (2,270 kg) of bombs; *crew:* 4-5

LOCKHEED PV-2 HARPOON
Nation: USA; *manufacturer:* Lockheed Aircraft Corp; *type:* reconnaissance; *year:* 1944; *engine:* two Pratt & Whitney R-2800-31 Double Wasp 18-cylinder radial air-cooled, 2,000 hp each; *wingspan:* 74 ft 11 in (22.83 m); *length:* 51 ft 1 in (15.55 m); *height:* 11 ft 11 in (3.63 m); *weight:* 36,000 lb (16,330 kg) (loaded); *maximum speed:* 282 mph (453 km/h); *ceiling:* 23,900 ft (7,285 m); *range:* 2,930 miles (4,700 km); *armament:* 9 machine guns; 4,000 lb (1,814 kg) of bombs; *crew:* 4-5

CURTISS SC-1 SEAHAWK
Nation: USA; *manufacturer:* Curtiss-Wright Corp; *type:* reconnaissance; *year:* 1944; *engine:* Wright R-1820-62 Cyclone 9-cylinder radial air-cooled, 1,350 hp; *wingspan:* 41 ft (12.50 m); *length:* 36 ft 4½ in (11.07 m); *height:* 18 ft (5.48 m); *weight:* 9,000 lb (4,082 kg) (loaded); *maximum speed:* 313 mph (504 km/h) at 28,600 ft (8,720 m); *ceiling:* 37,300 ft (11,400 m); *range:* 1,090 miles (1,750 km); *armament:* 2 machine guns; 750 lb (340 kg) of bombs; *crew:* 1

CONSOLIDATED PB4Y-2 PRIVATEER
Nation: USA; *manufacturer:* Consolidated Aircraft Corp; *type:* reconnaissance; *year:* 1944; *engine:* four Pratt & Whitney R-1830-94 Twin Wasp 14-cylinder radial air-cooled, 1,350 hp each; *wingspan:* 110 ft (33.53 m); *length:* 74 ft 7 in (22.73 m); *height:* 30 ft 1 in (9.17 m); *weight:* 35,000 lb (29,485 kg) (loaded); *maximum speed:* 237 mph (381 km/h); *ceiling:* 20,700 ft (6,300 m); *range:* 2,800 miles (4,500 km); *armament:* 12 machine guns; 12,800 lb (5,800 kg) of bombs; *crew:* 11

Plate 145
Obsolescent reconnaissance planes in service at the outbreak of war: 1933–45

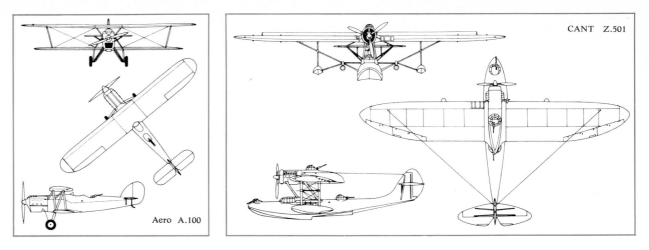

Aero A.100

CANT Z.501

Many of the front-line reconnaissance planes in service with the air forces at the outbreak of war date back well into the 1930s. Some of these, in spite of their obvious obsolescence, remained in service for a large part of the war, even after the appearance of more modern, highly specialised and efficient types: others were so inferior to the enemy aircraft that they disappeared from combat service, being relegated in many cases to much less demanding tasks, such as training and liaison.

This happened to the Czechoslovak Aero A-100, the last of a series of light bomber and reconnaissance biplanes constructed at the beginning of the thirties. Designed in 1933, this classic biplane with liquid-cooled engine was put into production the following year and up to 1935 44 had been constructed which equipped the Czechoslovak air force. The Aero A.100 was joined by a version with increased power, exclusively designed for bombing and designated A.101: the 29 planes which were constructed were amongst the last biplanes of this type to go into service with the Czech air force.

A contemporary of the Aero was the Letov S.328, a similar aircraft, which had been designed in 1933 in response to a request from Finland. The Finnish contract, however, never materialised and the Czechoslovak authorities decided to switch the production for the use of their own air force, placing an order for 445. Between 1934 and 1939 the Letov S.328 remained in service. Then, after the German invasion, all the aircraft of this type were commandeered by the *Luftwaffe*: they were used partially for training and a certain number were given to Bulgaria. The operational life of this aircraft lasted until 1944.

On the other hand, all 34 examples of the Renard R.31 with which the Belgian air force were equipped were

destroyed in the inferno of the first days of the war. This reconnaissance monoplane went down in history as the only aircraft of all-Belgian design to take part in the conflict. It was designed at the beginning of the 1930s (the prototype had flown on 16th October 1932) and was put into production in 1934 with an order for 28 aircraft; another six were ordered in August of the following year. Even though it was not considered an 'easy' aircraft to fly by the pilots and crews, the Renard R.31 fought hard in the brief period of resistance to the German invasion.

In the maritime reconnaissance field the typical construction formula of the 1930s lingered on for a very long time; particularly in the case of the aircraft which were based on large warships. The biplane proved invaluable for catapult launching. Many reconnaissance planes of this type remained operational for the whole of the war carrying out tasks which other aircraft could not perform so effectively.

In Japan, a typical example of this was given by the Nakajima E8N seaplane, a small biplane designed in 1933 which stayed in service on the largest ships of the Imperial Navy until well into the war. Production of the E8N (Allied code-name DAVE) came to an end in 1940 after the 775th

aircraft had been completed. Many of these aircraft were subsequently employed for training and liaison.

In the Soviet Union one of the most widely used marine reconnaissance (not carrier-based) planes was the Beriev MBR-2, a flying boat which had appeared in prototype form way back in 1931, and was put into service in 1933. In spite of its old-fashioned appearance, the Beriev flying boat proved to be a very versatile aircraft and outstandingly aerodynamic. Besides the 1,500 constructed for military use a large number of civil variants were also built, which were used on domestic routes. One of these flying boats set several altitude records for its class in May 1937, among other achievements reaching 8,864 m (29,080 ft) without any payload.

The life of a similar Italian machine, the CANT Z.501, was very much longer. It received much attention on 19th May 1934 when its prototype achieved a world distance record 4,130 km (2,566 miles) from Monfalcone to Massawa in Eritrea, in 26 hours 35 minutes flying time. This aircraft survived the war and stayed in service up to 1949. On Italy's entry into the war the CANT Z.501s were the standard equipment of the marine reconnaissance squadrons. A total of 202 were in service on 10th June 1940.

These aircraft were in continual use for the duration of the war for reconnaissance, escort of convoys, anti-submarine warfare and air-sea rescue.

Plate 146
Reconnaissance planes: 1933–36

Still in Italy, a typical family of light reconnaissance planes was built by Imam. The Ro.37, in spite of having first appeared in 1934, remained the standard aircraft for observation units for many years, and during the course of the war it was widely used, particularly in Africa and the Mediterranean; in emergencies this obsolete biplane was also assigned to a tactical support role and even used as a fighter.

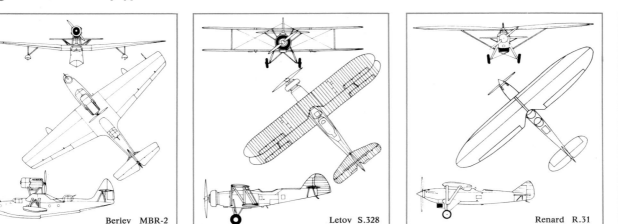

Beriev MBR-2

Letov S.328

Renard R.31

Nakajima E8N1

The Ro.37 appeared in two principal production series which were characterised by the adoption of very different engines: the V-12 Fiat A 30 RA *bis* 550 hp engine and the Piaggio P IX 560 hp radial engine, the latter being installed in the *bis* version of this aircraft.

The naval counterpart of the Ro.37 was the Imam Ro.43, a seaplane version of the land-reconnaissance plane. The Ro.43 was expressly designed for use on the capital ships of the *Regia Marina*, and in this, its major role, it was a participant in all the encounters of the sea war in the Mediterranean, staying in service up to September 1943. A notable feature of the Ro.43 was that its wings could be folded back in such a way that it was easily stowed on board ship: cruisers could carry two on board, and battleships up to four. Launching was by catapult and when a mission was completed the aircraft was picked up from the sea by its mother ship. A single-seater fighter version of the Ro.43, numbered Ro.44, was also built but the use of this aircraft was very limited because of its inferior performance, especially when compared with enemy fighters.

Like the Ro.43, particularly in its use, was the British Supermarine Walrus, a biplane flying boat designed towards the middle of the 1930s as a capapult-launched reconnaissance plane. In production from 1936 until 1944, this aircraft achieved a performance that was well ahead of its time and became one of the most useful all-purpose aircraft of the British carrier-based forces. During the course of its long career, taking part in the most important operations of the fleet, it was used for liaison, air-sea rescue and also bombing. The Walrus prototype, designed by Reginald J. Mitchell, flew under the name of Seagull V for the first time on 21st June 1933. The aircraft of the first production series (Mk I) went into service in 1936 and the assembly line built a total of 744.

A new Soviet flying boat appeared in prototype form in 1935 which was to join its comrade, the Beriev MBR-2, as a maritime reconnaissance plane. This was the Tchetverikov

ARK-3, a small twin-engine flying boat intended for use in Arctic waters. The Tchetverikov ARK-3 proved to be perfectly suited for the tasks which were assigned to it, and served during the war as an escort for the naval convoys in the far north. At the same time as the military version, a commercial variant was also made which could carry twelve passengers. This aircraft, like the Beriev MBR-2, set an international record for its class, reaching 9,160 metres altitude (30,000 ft) with 1,000 kg (2,200 lb) payload. This exploit took place in the April of 1937.

During the 1930s, interest in maritime reconnaissance aircraft was awakened in France. One of the most significant aircraft was the Breguet 521, a military version of the commercial transport plane, the Breguet 530 Saigon airliner which was, in its turn, derived from the British Short Calcutta flying boat. The prototype flew in September 1933, and two years later the first production models went into service. A total of 30 Breguet 521s were built, many of which were still operational in 1940 at the outbreak of war. This flying boat was powered by three Gnome-Rhône 900 hp radial engines and was armed with five machine guns and a 300 kg (660 lb) bomb-load. After the German invasion some Breguet 521s were taken over and used by the *Luftwaffe* for air-sea rescue.

Imam Ro.37 bis

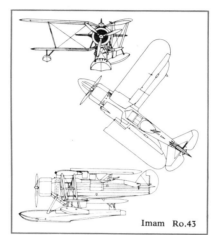
Imam Ro.43

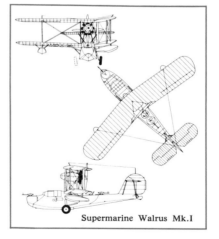
Supermarine Walrus Mk.I

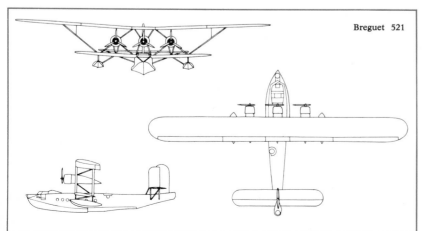
Breguet 521

Tchetverikov ARK-3

Plate 147
The age of the Flying Porcupine: 1937–39

In the Soviet Union Igor V. Tchetverikov repeated the success of the ARK-3 with a new flying boat, which was larger and more powerful and went into service in 1939: the MDR-6. This twin-engine plane was widely used by the navy for the whole of the war and remained operational right up to the 1950s. Such a long life (the aircraft was designed in 1936) was made possible by continual updating which was carried out on the production models and which mainly affected the engines. The MDR-6A of 1941 used two Klimov M 105A inline 1,100 hp engines instead of the M 63 radials of the basic model and although they had the same horsepower, aerodynamic refinements led to a noticeable improvement in performance: the final MDR-6B version of 1944 had M 105 1,260 hp power units and this further improved speed and payload capacity.

Just as well-known were the KOR-1 and KOR-2 biplanes designed by Georgi Mikailovich Beriev in the second half of the 1930s for marine reconnaissance. Both these aircraft, which were substantially similar, except for their engines, were to become the standard equipment of the Soviet fleet's cruisers in the postwar period. The Beriev KOR-1 flew for the first time in 1934 in prototype form, powered by an M 25 750 hp engine derived from the American Wright Cyclone. The KOR-2, however, appeared in 1939 powered by an M 62 900 hp radial engine and joined the KOR-1 in service, although in limited numbers.

Another carrier-based reconnaissance plane, one of the most widely used British aircraft of the first years of the war, was the Fairey Seafox seaplane, which from many points of view was comparable with the Soviet KOR-1. It was meant for catapult-launching on board the capital ships of the Royal Navy and the Seafox served in this capacity until the appearance of the first escort carriers. The prototype of this little biplane flew for the first time on 27th May 1936 and production continued until 1938. Among the most important naval actions in which the 31 Seafoxes took part, proving themselves to be indispensable for gunnery spotting, was the Battle of the River Plate in 1939.

Another of the most useful maritime patrol planes of the war was also British, the Short Sunderland: a gigantic four-engine plane derived from a line of commercial flying boats which had been prominent in British civil aviation in the 1930s. Called "the flying porcupine" by the Germans, because of its exceptional defensive

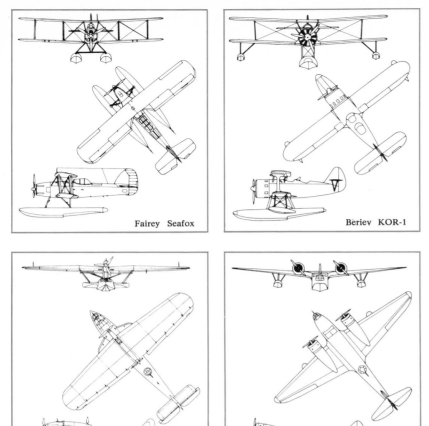

Fairey Seafox

Beriev KOR-1

Dornier Do.18 D-1

Tchetverikov MDR-6

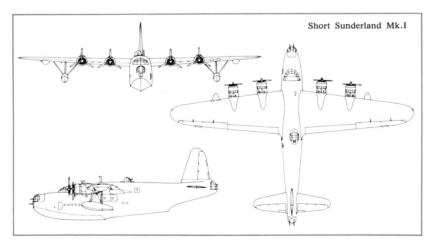

Short Sunderland Mk.I

can Pratt & Whitney Twin Wasp radial engines instead of the British Bristol Pegasus engines. Production continued until 1945, reaching a total of 741.

In the North Sea (which besides the Atlantic and the Mediterranean was one of the operational theatres in which the Sunderlands were most used) the large British flying boats often clashed with an enemy aircraft which was about the same business, the German Dornier Do.18 D, which was smaller, less powerful and less well-armed but nonetheless useful. The origins of this twin-engine flying boat went back to 1934: Deutsche Lufthansa had asked Dornier to develop a more modern successor to the Wal, to be used for transatlantic mail services. Six Dornier 18s were entrusted to the German airline between 1935 and 1937 and because of its exceptional range the aircraft aroused the interest of the *Luftwaffe* as well, who ordered a military version. This was designated the Do.18 D-1 and went into service in 1938, staying in the front line until 1942.

Plate 148
Reconnaissance planes of 1939

Another useful German maritime reconnaissance plane was the little Arado Ar.196 which, having been designed as an aircraft to be flown off capital ships of the *Kriegsmarine*, turned out to be just as useful in a coastal-based role. The project had been commenced in 1936 and the first pre-series Ar.196 was completed in November 1938. The first production series, Ar.196 A-1, reached the main naval units before the end of the following year.

The variant produced in the largest numbers was the A-3 of 1941, in which the armament was made more powerful mainly through the addition of a machine gun and two 20 mm cannon. A further machine gun was installed in the final A-5 series, which remained in production until August 1944, bringing the total of aircraft completed to over 600. Apart from its warship-based use, through which the Ar.196 took part in all the naval operations of the war, it was kept particularly busy in anti-submarine warfare.

The *Luftwaffe* also put excellent land-based reconnaissance planes into the field. The Henschel Hs.126, for

instance, made its mark as the best aircraft of its category, which was medium-range observation, during the first two years of the war. This big, high-wing monoplane went into service in 1938, as the A-1 version and after having seen operations in Spain, large numbers were built to replace the obsolete Heinkel He.45 and He.46. The B-1, which had a more powerful engine and better performance, appeared in 1939 and at the outbreak of war it was in widespread use. Production ended in 1941.

The Fieseler Fi.156 Storch was much more versatile, so much so that it was invaluable and was the real forerunner of all present STOL aircraft. The "Stork" was present on all fronts for the duration of the war and almost 2,900 of this aircraft left the assembly lines; besides reconnaissance and observation, it also carried out its tasks of liaison, transport and air-sea rescue outstandingly well.

The project was initiated in 1935 and immediately brought to light the exceptional aerodynamic qualities and performance of the aircraft. The minimum and maximum operating speeds were 50 km/h (32 mph) and 170 km/h (105 mph): it could take-off in under 50 m (165 ft) and land in less than 15 m (50 ft) and into the wind in 13 m (42 ft). Five prototypes were completed in 1936 and 1937 followed by ten pre-series models.

Production started with the A-1 variant which was soon replaced by the C series of which the greatest numbers of all were built: the Fi.156 C-O was the first to be armed, the Fi.156 C-1 of 1939 was used for liaison and its contemporary the Fi.156 C-2 was for photo-reconnaissance. In 1941 the D and E series appeared which were modified for air ambulance use and emergency landing strip operations respectively. The Storch was also constructed under licence in France and in Czechoslovakia. The French version was built by Morane-Saulnier in three variants: M.S.500, M.S.501 and the M.S.502; the Czechoslovak version was built by Mraz and was designated K-65 Cap.

In Italy the family of twin-engined reconnaissance planes built by Caproni from 1936 onwards was comparable with the Storch both as regards versatility and widespread use (although certainly not in performance) and in five principal models it was to equip the *Regia Aeronautica* as a trustworthy multirole aircraft. The forerunner was the Ca.309 Ghibli, designed in the second half of the thirties. In 1937 the Ca.310 Libeccio followed, which was a more streamlined and powerful version of its predecessor.

In 1939 the Ca.311 came on the scene in which the main modifications were to the forward part of the fuselage in order to give maximum visibility to the observer. A year later the Ca.313 was constructed which was equipped with two inline Isotta-

weaponry, the Sunderland had an intense and uninterrupted operational career from the first to the last day of the war and stayed in service with the RAF up to 1959.

The missions in which this aircraft specialised were those of convoy escort and anti-submarine warfare, assisted in this by their long range and powerful armament. The design (S.25 according to Short's own designation) had been embarked upon towards the end of 1934 and the prototype had flown on 16th October 1937. Five months later the first production series appeared, the Mk I. The aircraft of

this version were in use with three squadrons of Coastal Command at the outbreak of war.

Towards the end of 1941 the second series, the Mk II, was put into production, and in June 1942 the third, the Mk III: in these variants the engines and the armament were more powerful whilst the Sunderland Mk III also had structural modifications to its hull. The final version was the Mk V, the prototype of which flew in August 1943: in this series the operational capacities of the aircraft were noticeably improved. It was given more power with the adoption of the Ameri-

Fraschini Delta engines instead of the Piaggio radials: increased power and better aerodynamics led to a notice-able improvement in performance. The 215 Caproni Ca.313s built were followed by 425 Ca.314s which were subsequently improved and given increased power. The total of 1,693 twin-engine Capronis were used unin-terruptedly for the whole of the war and also met with considerable export success.

Another twin-engine plane, much more of a warplane than the Italian aircraft, which had a big operational success was the American Lockheed Hudson, effectively a military version of the Lockheed 14 Electra which had

been developed in 1938 in response to a British specification. The Royal Air Force were at that time searching for a naval reconnaissance plane to be used by Coastal Command and after much hesitation they had turned to the American aircraft industry.

The greater part of the production of this aircraft went to Britain which took no less than 2,000 planes of the five production series. Many Hudson Mk IIIs and Mk IVs were also used by the USAAF under the designations of A-28 and A-29. In front-line service from 1939 to 1943, the Hudsons were subsequently used for liaison and as transports and trainers.

A similar aircraft which was pro-

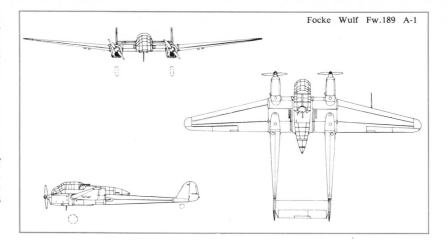
Focke Wulf Fw.189 A-1

duced in France between 1937 and 1939, however, remained at the pro-totype stage: the Dewoitine D.720 which was designed as a reconnais-sance plane, bomber and trainer. The original order for 1,000 planes never materialised because of the very long development phase of the prototype, which flew on 10th July 1939.

Plate 149
Four German reconnaissance planes of 1940

Recognising the need to put a very highly-specialised aircraft into service for tactical ground reconnaissance, the Germans produced an original light twin-engine plane between 1937 and 1938: the Focke Wulf Fw.189, in which the whole arrangement of the aircraft had been planned in order to give maximum possible visibility to the observer. The cockpit was completely glazed and formed a single transparent shell; the twin boom made for a very wide field of visibility towards the rear; flight stability, especially at lower speeds, was, moreover, almost ideal for observation.

The Fw.189 prototype flew in July 1938, and production went on through several series up to 1944, achieving a total of 864 aircraft. The first opera-tional version was the A-1, which went into service in 1940 and was widely used, particularly on the Russian front. The nickname, *das Fliegende Auge* (the flying eye) by which this reconnaissance plane was known, gives perhaps the best indication of its usefulness.

Comparison with the Focke-Wulf reconnaissance plane meant that a

similar aircraft remained at the pro-totype stage; this was the Blohm und Voss Bv.141 which had been pro-duced on the basis of the same specification and was undoubtedly the most unorthodox aircraft to be con-structed during the Second World War. In this aircraft, too, the cockpit was a glasshouse and very similar to that of the Fw.189, but it was asym-metrically positioned in relation to the fuselage and engine.

The first prototype flew on 25th February 1938, constructed at the company's expense, and it was fol-lowed by two further prototypes and by ten pre-series aircraft. The long proving trials did not suceed in freeing the technical staff of the German air ministry from their preconceptions induced by the unusual configuration of the aircraft, and although it showed that it had good general qualities, the Bv.141 was turned down.

Another very advanced twin engine also remained at the experimental stage, the Arado Ar.240, which was tested for a long time, not only as a reconnaissance plane but also as a heavy fighter, night fighter, dive-bomber and close support aircraft. Numerous prototypes were built of this machine (the first of which flew on 10th May 1940), which were evalu-ated in operational conditions for two years. This exhaustive experimental phase never managed to iron out its considerable problems, above all of

Fieseler Fi.156 C-2

Henschel Hs.126 B-1

Arado Ar.196 A-1

Lockheed A-28 Hudson

Caproni Ca.311

Dewoitine D.720

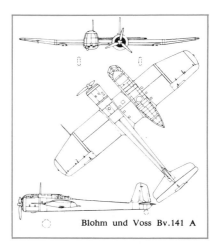
Blohm und Voss Bv.141 A

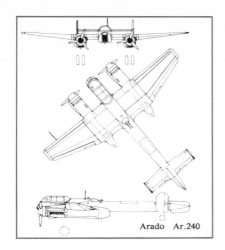

Arado Ar.240

who had been impressed by the aircraft during a propaganda flight to Tokyo. The first models of the pre-series C-O (ten built) appeared in 1939 and were followed by aircraft of the first production series C-1, which was the first to go into service. The other principal production variants were the C-3 of 1941 (more powerful and strengthened) and the C-4 of 1942 which was equipped with search radar. A total of 263 were built.

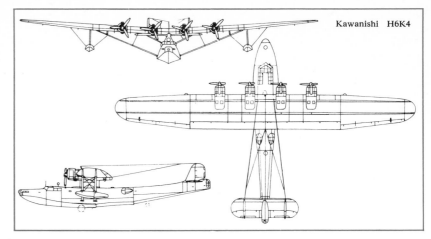

Kawanishi H6K4

flight stability, which had bedevilled the Ar.240 from the very start. It is interesting to note that the aircraft was equipped with a pressurised cabin and had its defensive armament installed in remote-controlled turrets.

In the category of long range marine reconnaissance planes, one of the few successful four-engine aircraft produced for the *Luftwaffe* during the war was the Focke Wulf Fw.200 Condor. Although it was derived from a commercial aircraft designed in 1936 for Deutsche Lufthansa, and had inherited certain limitations, for instance serious structural weakness, especially in the rear part of the fuselage, the Condor made its mark during its very full operational career among the best aircraft of its type.

Up till 1944 this large four-engine plane remained the nightmare of the Allied convoys and came to be known as "the scourge of the Atlantic", shadowing the convoys for hour after hour at a very high altitude waiting for the right moment to attack: in its first six months' service, from 1st August 1940 to 9th February 1941, the Condors sank 363,000 tonnes of shipping and these successes mounted until 1943 when, with improved convoy protection, the German reconnaissance planes were at last effectively challenged.

The idea of adapting the original Fw.200 to a military role came to the Germans in 1938 from the Japanese,

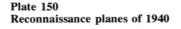

Plate 150
Reconnaissance planes of 1940

The Japanese also made wide use of long-range marine reconnaissance planes. An aircraft which belonged to the same category as the German Condor was the Kawanishi H6K, a large four-engine flying boat which in spite of having been designed in 1933 stayed in the front line until 1942, in which year it was replaced by a more modern aircraft and relegated to transport duties. The prototype had flown on 14th July 1936, and in the two following years three pre-series models were constructed; satisfactory proving trials had led to the first production variant and the aircraft were put into service under the designation H6K1.

In 1940 the H6K4 variant appeared, which was the most important and constructed in the greatest numbers, a total of 127. At the outbreak of war, 66 Kawanishi flying boats were in the front line and in the first months of the war, under the momentum of Japanese air supremacy, these aircraft were also used for bombing missions. As the war went on and as Japan's enemies gradually grew stronger, however, the limitations of the H6K appeared all too obvious.

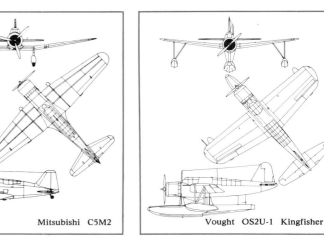

Mitsubishi C5M2

Vought OS2U-1 Kingfisher

In particular these aircraft were very vulnerable, both because of their lack of armouring for the protection of the crew and also because they did not have self-sealing fuel tanks. As a result, the Kawanishi flying boats were used exclusively for reconnaissance, a role which they carried out superbly well, thanks to their remarkably long range. In 1941 production was switched to a new variant, updated and more powerful: the H6K5, of which 36 were constructed and which brought the overall total to 215. In Allied code the H6K was called MAVIS.

Both the Japanese navy and army air forces made simultaneous use up till 1942 of a small single-engined light bomber derived from an aircraft which in 1937 had achieved a sensational long-distance flight: the Mitsubishi Ki-15 (the designation of the Japanese navy for this plane was C5M and its Allied code-name for both types was BABS).

The exploit which had led to such international fame for the aircraft was accomplished between 6th and 9th April 1937, by the second prototype which had been given the civil designation of J-BAA1 for the occasion and had been named Kamikaze (divine wind): with Masaaki Iinuma and Kenji Tsugakoshi at the controls, the aircraft had flown from Tachikawa to London in 94 hours 17 minutes and 57 seconds, covering 15,353 km (9,450 miles) in a net flying time of 51 hours 17

minutes and 23 seconds, at an average speed of 160.8 km/h (100 mph). The long-distance flight which had made a tremendous impression in the West was sponsored by the daily paper *Asahi Shimbun*.

It was only a very short step, however, from sporting feats to military use. The army immediately put the Ki-15 into service, putting it through its proving trials during the Sino-Japanese War and developing a second production variant, which was generally improved and made more powerful; this was the Ki-15-II. It was this version which started the Mitsubishi reconnaissance plane on its naval career: under the designation of C5M1 twenty aircraft were ordered by the navy and immediately put into service. In 1940 these were joined by the thirty C5M2s.

The greater part of production, however, went to the army: out of 489 aircraft built only 50 were of the navalised series, the C5M.

On the enemy's side the best and most widely used carrier-based reconnaissance plane of the war was the American Vought OS2U Kingfisher, a small seaplane which became standard on US Navy capital ships and which were operated in this role up to the last day of the war. Designed in 1937, the Kingfisher flew in prototype form in July of the following year and went into service in the first version, OS2U-1, in August 1940. The variant

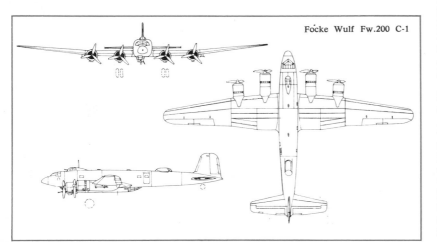

Focke Wulf Fw.200 C-1

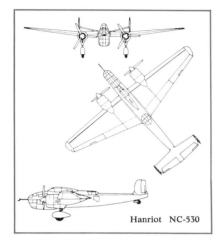

Bloch 174

Hanriot NC-530

Plate 151
German and American reconnaissance flying boats: 1941

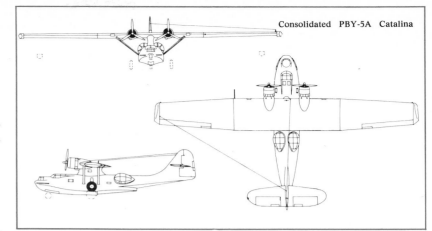

Consolidated PBY-5A Catalina

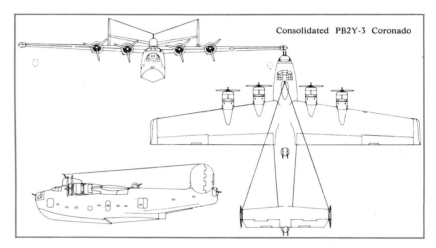

Consolidated PB2Y-3 Coronado

An American flying boat which came into existence because of particular wartime needs is still considered to this day as the most famous flying boat in the history of aviation. This is the Consolidated PBY Catalina which was not only worked extremely hard for the entire duration of the war, but went on being put to just as intense and versatile operational use for twenty years after the war, flying in the colours of half the countries in the world.

The origins of the "Cat" – this was to become the universal nickname by which the PBY was known – went back to a specification issued by the navy on 28th October 1933, which called for a new flying boat to replace the obsolete Martin P3M and Consolidated P2Y. The prototype flew on 28th March 1935, and three months later the first contract was signed for 60 aircraft of the first production variant, the PBY-1.

Before the end of 1937 three other models made their appearance: the PBY-2, the PBY-3 and the PBY-4 which had better engines and more powerful armament.

The outbreak of war meant that production was suddenly speeded up, partly in order to fill the substantial requirements of many Allied countries, amongst which were Britain, Canada, Australia and the Netherlands. The Soviet Union had been the first to make sure of having the PBY by buying the construction licence for the PBY-3 version in 1938 under which it built about two hundred of them.

In 1940 the PBY-5 variant came upon the scene which had more powerful engines and greater structural strength, and in 1941 the first amphibious version, the PBY-5A, appeared.

Production was extended by involving Canadian Vickers and the Canadian Boeing factories as well as the Naval Aircraft Factory of Philadelphia in the manufacture. In the latter factory, the basic design was considerably modified, as regards the structure of the hull, the tailplanes, armament and fuel capacity, and the new version was renamed the PBN-1 Nomad. From this aircraft was derived the final variant of the Catalina, the PBY-6A, of which 235 were built and which brought the total of aircraft built (excluding those built in the USSR) to 3,290. Production ended in April 1945.

The Consolidated PB2Y Coronado was developed in 1935 and was the successor to the Catalina. In the event this large four-engine flying boat never managed to equal the Cat's exceptional operational qualities. The prototype, XPB2Y-1, flew on 17th

produced in the largest numbers (over 1,000) was the OS2U-3 and the assembly lines were kept going up to 1942, when they had completed 1,519 aircraft. About 100 Kingfishers were also used by the British Royal Navy.

Returning once more to Europe, in 1940 a French reconnaissance plane appeared which, although it inevitably saw very limited use, had time to show its great qualities: the Bloch 174. In March and June only 50 of this fast and powerful twin-engine aircraft took part in operations, managing to compete with even the most advanced German fighters of the time. After the war, two bomber variants of this aircraft were developed, which were also derived from Bloch prototypes (Bloch 175 and 176) and had been developed in 1940.

Another twin-engine reconnaissance plane and tactical bomber, however, remained at the experimental stage, having reached the service test flight phase at the outbreak of war: the Hanriot NC-530. The more effective Potez 63.11 was chosen in preference to this aircraft.

September 1937 and the first aircraft of the production series, PB2Y-2, went into service in 1940. The principal variant was the PB2Y-3, of which 210 were ordered in November 1940, and which went into service in the following year. This aircraft did not have a particularly outstanding career and many of them were converted into transports following the example of the British Royal Navy, which had modified the Coronados received from the United States in this way. In all, 216 PB2Y Coronados were built.

In this category of aircraft mainly intended for anti-submarine warfare, there was one which became the principal helpmate of the submarines: the German Blohm und Voss Bv.138, a

maritime reconnaissance plane mainly used in close co-operation with the submarine force of the *Kriegsmarine*. Designed in 1935, the Bv.138 had a long development period and assumed its definitive form in 1937. Towards the end of 1940, the first series production models reached the maritime reconnaissance units of the *Luftwaffe*, and in the following year, when the principal version, the Bv.138 C, went into service, the new aircraft reached the peak of its performance. Production continued until 1943 and reached a total of 279.

The Germans developed a little reconnaissance seaplane in 1941, for the express purpose of increasing the operational capacities of submarines

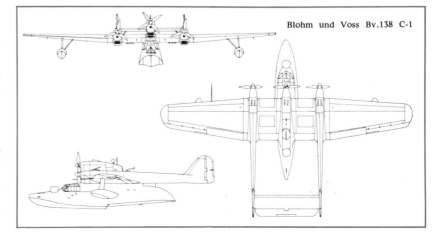

Blohm und Voss Bv.138 C-1

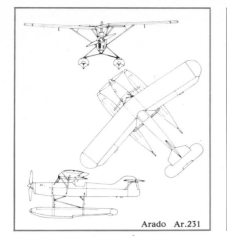

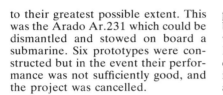

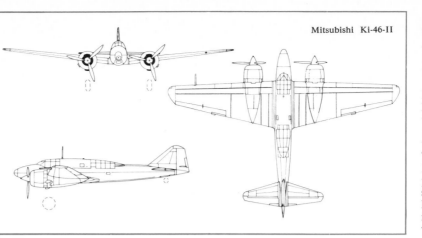

Mitsubishi Ki-46-II

Arado Ar.231

by detailed aerodynamic studies between 1938 and 1939, to which a great contribution had been made by the Institute of Aeronautical Research of the University of Tokyo.

In Ki-46 prototype appeared in November 1939 and at the end of a long development phase production of the first variant, the Ki-46-II, began. 1,093 of these were constructed and the aircraft went into service in 1941. Two years later the second version, Ki-46-III, was built which had more powerful engines and was still further streamlined. In total the assembly lines completed 1,742 of these, including the four prototypes of the final variant, Ki-46-IV.

to their greatest possible extent. This was the Arado Ar.231 which could be dismantled and stowed on board a submarine. Six prototypes were constructed but in the event their performance was not sufficiently good, and the project was cancelled.

Plate 152
Japanese reconnaissance planes of 1941

Similar to the German Arado Ar.231, but much more effective, was the small Japanese seaplane, the Yokosuka E14Y (GLEN in Allied code) designed to be carried on submarines. The aircraft could be easily dismantled and stowed inside a watertight stowage compartment on the deck of the larger submarines. The GLEN was mainly used for reconnaissance flights but in one sensational instance it was

pushed to its limits and was used as a bomber: in 1942 a Yokosuka E14Y-1 was launched from the submarine I-25, which was sailing off the American coast, with four 76 kg (168 lb) incendiary bombs instead of carrying an observer, and with United States territory as its target. The aircraft managed to reach the coast of Oregon and dropped its bombs in a vast forest with the object of starting off devastating fires. The practical results of this operation were very modest but its propaganda value was fully exploited by the Japanese: it was in fact the first time (and was also to remain the last) that a Japanese aircraft was to bomb American territory.

Less sensational but undoubtedly more far-reaching from a military point of view was the activity of another little naval reconnaissance plane, the Mitsubishi F1M. This biplane was designed in the middle of the 1930s as a catapult-launched seaplane carried on board capital ships of the Imperial fleet, and was also used in a great many roles which had been totally unforeseen by its designers and which went far beyond reconnaissance, such as use as a dive-bomber, close support aircraft and fighter. 1,118 were built (these were nearly all F1M-2 versions which went into service in 1941); they mainly saw service with units scattered among the small Pacific islands. Under these operational conditions the Mitsubishi F1M

showed its excellent qualities of sturdiness, versatility and ease of maintenance. In Allied code these aircraft went under the name of PETE.

An aircraft in the same class as the F1M but considerably more modern was the Aichi E13A which remained in the front line from the first to the last day of the war and of which 1,418 were constructed. The aircraft was designed at the beginning of 1938 and first saw combat towards the end of that year. Production went ahead, concentrating on the one basic version, the E13A-1 which, unusually for the Japanese aviation industry, did not undergo any significant changes. In 1944 two subseries appeared, the E13A-1a and E13A-1b, the former differing in its radio equipment and in the latter by the installation of magnetic detection gear. In Allied code the Aichi reconnaissance plane was called JAKE.

Among land-based planes, one of the best reconnaissance aircraft to be put into the field by the Imperial Army during the course of the war was the Mitsubishi Ki-46 (Allied code-name DINAH). The main characteristic of this elegant twin-engine plane was its speed which easily exceeded that of the best contemporary Japanese fighters; in February 1945 two Ki-45-IVs (prototypes of the final variant not put into production) covered 2,301 km at an average speed of 700 km/h (435 mph). This exceptional performance was made possible

Plate 153
A legendary all-rounder — the Mosquito: 1941

The de Havilland Mosquito deserves separate treatment since it was, perhaps, the most versatile combat aircraft of all to be produced during the whole of the war. Side by side with the night fighter versions, several reconnaissance and bomber variants were developed and in each of these roles this exceptional twin-engine aircraft constructed in wood by de Havilland proved equally indispensable and tremendously effective. From 1941 to 1950, 6,439 Mosquitoes were built by British industry and to these were added a further 1,342 constructed in Canada and Australia. This was a considerable number and gives further confirmation of the important part which this aircraft played in Allied air power: the last bomber Mosquitoes survived with RAF Bomber Command up to 1951, only giving way to the twin-jet Canberras.

The aircraft was planned in 1938 as a reconnaissance bomber which would be so fast that it could be considered safe from interception. Between 1940 and 1941 three prototypes appeared: a bomber on 25th November 1940; a

Yokosuka E14Y1

Mitsubishi F1M2

Aichi E13A1

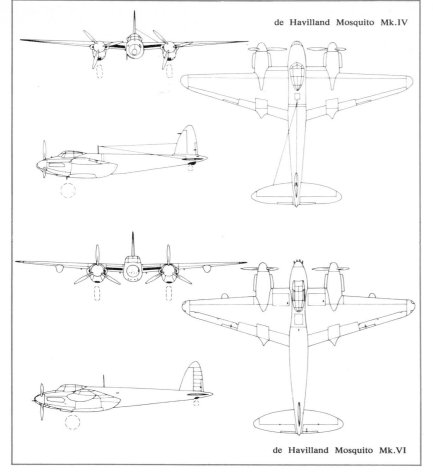

de Havilland Mosquito Mk.IV

de Havilland Mosquito Mk.VI

Plate 154
Reconnaissance planes of 1942

In Germany, the *Luftwaffe* attempted to strengthen their long-range maritime reconnaisance force in 1943, by putting several of the gigantic 6-engine Blohm und Voss Bv.222 flying boats, called Vikings, into service, the biggest aircraft of this kind to be produced during the course of the war. It was, however, an unsuccessful experiment, since the Viking which went into service in May 1942 as a strategic transport showed itself to be completely inadequate for the tasks demanded of it, mainly because of its vulnerability. After a few months in service operating from bases on the French Atlantic coast, the Bv.222 was withdrawn and relegated to its original role.

It was designed in 1938 at the request of Deutsche Lufthansa which wanted a commercial transport flying boat to put on their transatlantic routes. The prototype flew on 7th September 1940 but by that time commercial use across the Atlantic was no longer an issue and the aircraft was modified for military use. The manufacture of the first series, Bv.222 A totalled 7 aircraft which went into service during 1942. All development of

the Viking was abandoned in 1944, in spite of the fact that a prototype of a new version, the Bv.222 C, had already appeared, which was more powerful and better armed.

In Italy as well, a new seaplane went into service in 1942, also intended to strengthen the maritime reconnaissance force: the Fiat RS.14, a large twin-engine seaplane, which joined the various CANT planes which were already operational, taking part in all the air-sea operations of the last year of the war. A total of 152 Fiat RS.14s were built, nearly all of which were destroyed in the war. The project had been started in 1938 and the development of the aircraft had been very laborious, so much so that its entry into service was delayed for three years.

The troubled development of the Fiat RS.14 was mirrored by that of a Japanese twin-engine aircraft: the Nakajima J1N Gekko which, having been designed as a heavy, long-range fighter, ended up by being used mainly as a high-altitude reconnaissance plane. This aircraft was also designed in 1938 and went into service in the second half of 1942. Production continued until December 1944, turning out 479 aircraft in several variants. In the last versions the Nakajima J1N was finally used in its original combat role of night fighter, in which it met with a measure of success. In Allied coding, its designation was IRVING.

fighter on 15th May 1941; and a reconnaissance plane on 10th June 1941. The test flights immediately revealed the two main characteristics of the aircraft: great manoeuvrability and high maximum speed. Production began immediately and the first Mosquitoes that entered into service in September 1941 were the reconnaissance version, Mk I. In May of the following year it was the turn of the bomber version, Mk IV and then of a night fighter, Mk II.

From these basic types production series were in turn developed which were increasingly effective and powerful. The bomber and reconnaissance variants developed side by side. After the Mosquito IV, the two other principal bomber series made their appearance: the Mk IX and the Mk XVI, both in 1943, with more powerful engines and a larger bomb-load. The Mosquito Mk XVI, of which 1,200 were built, had a pressurised cockpit which enabled it to operate at 12,000 m (39,400 ft) and they could carry 1,800 kg (4,000 lb) of bombs.

The largest production series of the war period was the Mk VI of which over 2,500 were constructed. In this model the Mosquito's great versatility was enhanced and the potential of the aircraft was exploited to the full. The prototype was directly derived from a night fighter of the Mk II series, increasing the already impressive offensive armament and also adding to

the considerable bomb-carrying capacity of the bomber version. The first Mosquito Mk VIs, which went into service in 1943, could carry four 115 kg (250 lb) bombs on wing racks, but as production went on this bomb-load was doubled.

Thus armed the Mosquito fighter-bombers turned out to be deadly weapons, above all in an anti-shipping role (these aircraft were also used by Coastal Command to replace the Bristol Beaufighter) when the place of the bombs was taken by eight rockets. In the anti-submarine warfare version the Mosquito went so far as to carry a 57 mm cannon. This transformation did not affect many aircraft, perhaps because of serious structural problems which resulted from the installation of such a heavy weapon.

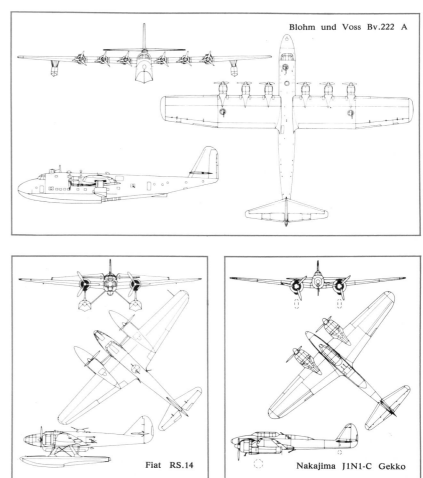

Blohm und Voss Bv.222 A

Fiat RS.14

Nakajima J1N1-C Gekko

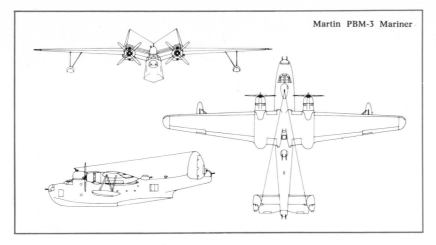
Martin PBM-3 Mariner

Still on the subject of sea patrol planes, the American attempt to replace the Catalina flying boats with more modern and challenging boats (which had failed with the PB2Y Coronado) was at least partially successful in the case of the Martin PBM Mariner, a large and powerful twin-engine plane which stayed in service up to the 1950s. The Mariner did not supplant the ubiquitous Cats, it simply joined them in operational use, proving only slightly superior in some respects.

The prototype had flown on 18th February 1939 and the first PBM-1 went into service in the course of 1941. Mass production settled down in 1942 with what was to become the principal variant of the war years, the PBM-3. At the beginning of 1944 the final version, the PBM-5 (589 built) appeared, which had more powerful armament and engines and improved radar equipment, and immediately after the war was also produced in an amphibious version (PBM-5A). Total production during the war years amounted to 1,289.

A small single-engined plane of the same class as the very widely used Vought OS2U Kingfisher appeared in 1942 as a light carrier-borne reconnaissance plane. This was the Curtiss SO3C Seamew, an aircraft which did not, however, manage to compete with the Kingfisher. 800 were constructed in three variants (SO3-1, SO3-2 and SO3-3) which remained in service until 1944. The principal limitation of the Seamew was always its poor performance, mainly due to the insufficient power of its engine, a Ranger V-7708 of only 600 hp. Many of these were transformed into remote control targets.

Plate 155
The last Japanese and German reconnaissance planes of the Second World War: 1943–44

In the last years of the war the Japanese navy increased its reconnaissance strength to the maximum. In the strategic class, in 1943, the optimum version of the best and largest Japanese flying boats, the Kawanishi H8K, appeared, which was an excellent aircraft, having very good overall performance and powerful defensive and offensive armament. It was designed at the beginning of the summer of 1938 at the request of the technical authorities of the Imperial Navy, who wanted a new aircraft which would replace the H6Ks which at that time were in their first stages of production.

Particular prominence was given to the necessity for speed and range as well as armour-plating. The first prototype was tested in January 1941, and its development was delayed for a few months because of serious problems of stability which had to be examined and solved by the redesign of the whole of the lower part of the hull. Production of the first variant, the H8K1, started before the end of the year and the aircraft went into service in early 1942. Only 14 production series aircraft were constructed, after which

manufacture was switched to the second principal variant, the H8K2, of which 148 were built. From 1943 onwards, up to the end of the war, these Kawanishi flying boats were worked hard and held in healthy respect by the Allies whose nickname for them aptly described their heavy armament, and was identical to that which the Germans had given to the British Short Sunderland: the "flying porcupine". In Allied code their official designation was EMILY.

Two new aircraft went into service in 1944 in the role of light carrier-based reconnaissance planes: the Nakajima C6N Saiun and the Aichi E16A Zuiun, two aeroplanes which, although satisfactory, arrived on the scene too late, being products of the Japanese aviation industry's desperate efforts in the last years of the war.

The Nakajima C6N appeared in prototype form on 15th May 1943, but only went into service more than a year later because of difficulty in developing the engine. 463 were built of one variant (C6N1) although in 1945 a few aircraft of a new night-fighter version were constructed and designated C6N1-X. In Allied code these aircraft were called MYRT.

A considerable delay in the development of the prototype was also experienced with the Aichi E16A, a floatplane which was ordered as a successor to the E13A model of 1941. The prototype in fact flew in August

1943, but it was only accepted a year later. Production of the PAUL, as it was referred to in Allied code, totalled 256 of one version, the E16A1, up to 1945.

In 1944 the Kyushu Q1W Tokai also went into service. This was a land-based twin-engine aircraft, expressly designed for reconnaissance and anti-submarine warfare. The design of this combat aircraft (the only one of its type to be produced by Japan) was started in 1942 and the first prototype had been flown in September of the following year. Production started in 1944 with the first and only variant to be produced, the Q1W1. Up to 1945, 153 had been built. These aircraft were mainly used for convoy escort duties. In operational use they were hampered by their inadequate overall performance and by their poor armament. In Allied code they were called LORNA. The Kyushu Q1W resembled the first version of the German twin-engine Junkers Ju.88 fairly closely.

In 1944 the final variants of this versatile aircraft were appearing in Germany: the Ju.388 J, K and L (being fighter, bomber and reconnaissance planes respectively) which brought the basic airframe to the peak of its development. In the event only the reconnaissance version was built. Thirty-seven Ju.388 L-1s left the assembly lines at the end of 1944. In use, which was very limited, they

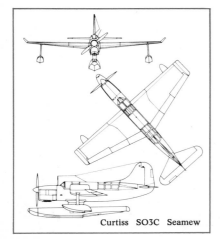
Curtiss SO3C Seamew

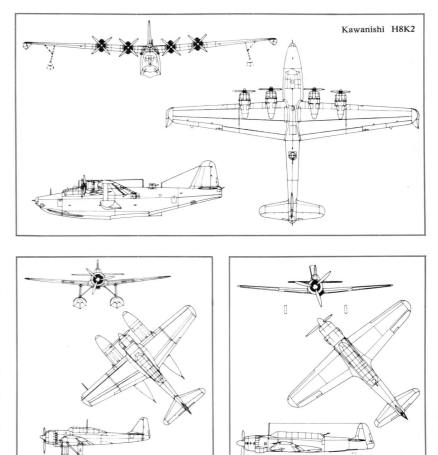
Kawanishi H8K2
Aichi E16A1 Zuiun
Nakajima C6N1 Saiun

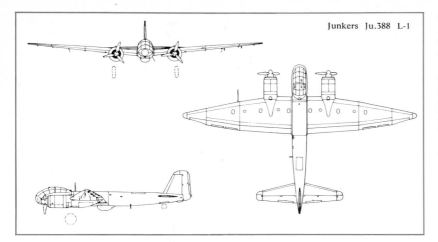

Junkers Ju.388 L-1

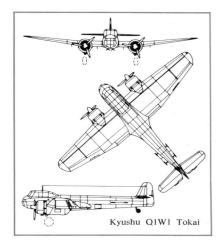

Kyushu Q1W1 Tokai

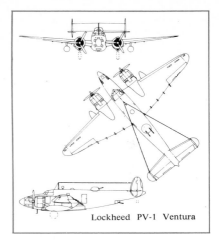

Lockheed PV-1 Ventura

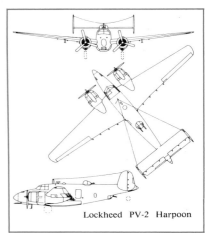

Lockheed PV-2 Harpoon

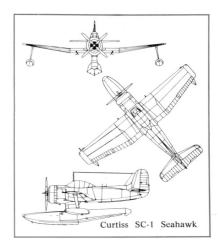

Curtiss SC-1 Seahawk

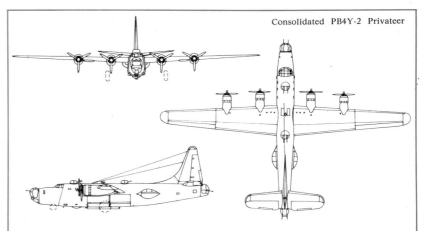

Consolidated PB4Y-2 Privateer

proved excellent aircraft at high altitudes. In the first months of 1945 the production of this handy twin-engine high-wing monoplane was abandoned.

Plate 156
The last American reconnaissance planes of the Second World War: 1942–44

The series of military aircraft derived from the commercial Lockheed models was considerably extended during the course of the war, starting off back in 1938 with the first Hudson which had been developed from the Lockheed 14 Electra. Once again it was the RAF which asked American industry to come up with a more effective successor to the Hudson. This was directly developed from the larger commercial twin-engine Lockheed Model 18s and was given the military designation of PV-1 Ventura.

The prototype of this new aircraft flew on 31st July 1941, and production began immediately on the massive order from the British, which was to total 400.

The aircraft also interested the American armed forces: the USAAF was first to put a couple of hundred of them into service, taken from the British procurement and designated B-34; immediately afterwards it was the turn of the US Navy, which from 1942 onwards absorbed the entire production for the use of land-based units. The PV-1 served as a reconnaissance bomber up to the end of the war. The American navy used 100 of them.

The PV-2 Harpoon was derived from the Ventura and was in effect a variant with more powerful armament, better performance and longer range. The aircraft was ordered in June 1943, with the first of a series of contracts which took the total production to 533. The Harpoon went into service in the following year and operated in the Pacific theatre up to the end of the war. In a subsequent attempt to increase the aircraft's combat potential came the PV-2D sub-series, of which 33 were built, equipped with 8 machine guns installed in the nose instead of the five of the other models.

The last reconnaissance plane produced by the American aviation industry during the course of the war to be based on capital ships also went into service in 1944. This was the Curtiss SC Seahawk, a modern and powerful single-engine aeroplane which bore more resemblance to a fighter than to a reconnaissance craft and was remarkable for the many uses to which it could be put, since it could be fitted with either floats or normal landing gear.

The project was commenced in March 1943, with an order for two prototypes and the first of these flew on 16th February of the following year. The development of these aircraft did not present any particular difficulties, and mass production was started immediately on the basis of an initial contract for 500. In the event, 566 SC-1s and 10 SC-2s were produced. The latter had more powerful engines and was better equipped.

In the strategic reconnaissance category, the US Navy needed not only the excellent seaplanes which it already had, it was necessary also to have a large number of effective land-based aircraft and this led the technical authorities of the US Navy to seek an aircraft which could be used in this role. The search resulted in an order issued in 1942 for a quantity of B-24 Liberator bombers. Subsequently, it was decided to use a larger number of these four-engine planes, which were already in use with the USAAF and were found particularly suited to anti-submarine warfare: in total 997 B-24s of this type were used by the navy. But this was not enough and an even more highly-specialised aircraft was needed. The final solution was provided by a special version of the B-24, produced on the bases of a US Navy requirement and designated the PB4Y-2 Privateer.

The production order for three prototypes was issued in May 1943, and the first of these flew on 20th September. Mass production began immediately afterwards to complete an order for 660 which was followed by a second order for 710. As it turned out, only 736 Privateers were delivered before the end of the war brought production to a halt. Although in service from 1944, these aircraft were not widely used. The principal difference compared with the normal B-24s lay in the redesign of the fuselage, the single fin and of the engine nacelles which housed four Pratt & Whitney engines.

Plate 157

Scale view of selected trainers and army co-operation aircraft of the Second World War

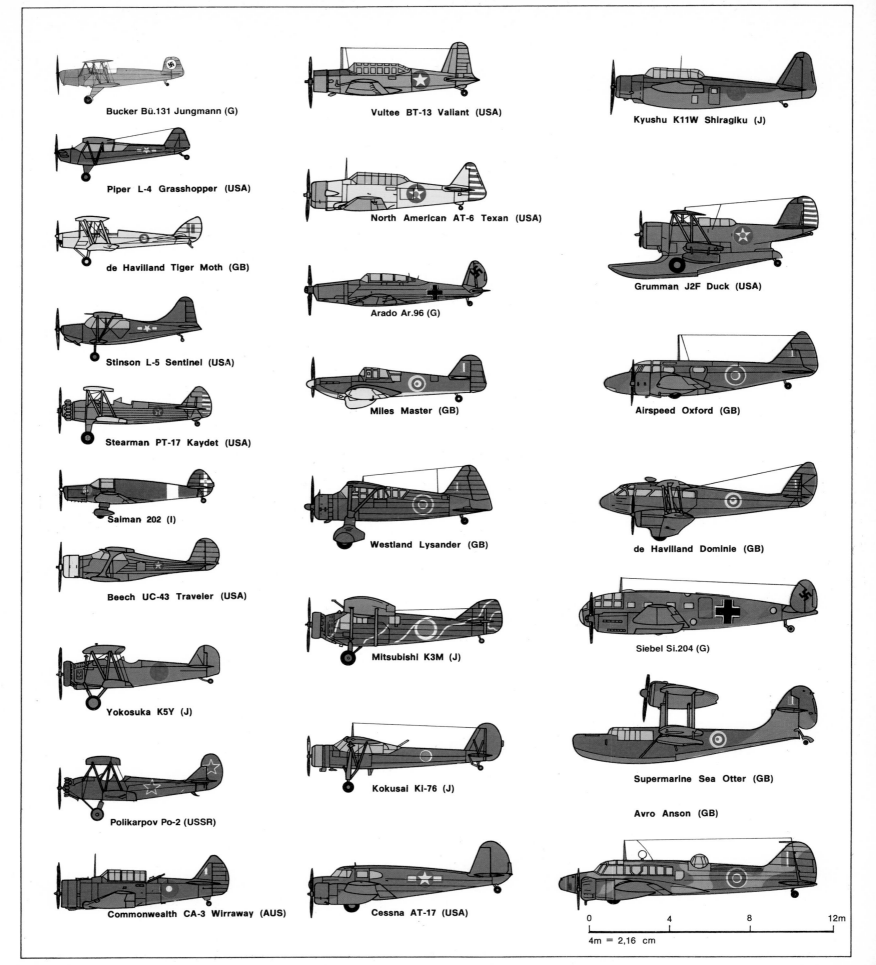

Bucker Bü.131 Jungmann (G)

Piper L-4 Grasshopper (USA)

de Havilland Tiger Moth (GB)

Stinson L-5 Sentinel (USA)

Stearman PT-17 Kaydet (USA)

Saiman 202 (I)

Beech UC-43 Traveler (USA)

Yokosuka K5Y (J)

Polikarpov Po-2 (USSR)

Commonwealth CA-3 Wirraway (AUS)

Vultee BT-13 Valiant (USA)

North American AT-6 Texan (USA)

Arado Ar.96 (G)

Miles Master (GB)

Westland Lysander (GB)

Mitsubishi K3M (J)

Kokusai Ki-76 (J)

Cessna AT-17 (USA)

Kyushu K11W Shiragiku (J)

Grumman J2F Duck (USA)

Airspeed Oxford (GB)

de Havilland Dominie (GB)

Siebel Si.204 (G)

Supermarine Sea Otter (GB)

Avro Anson (GB)

0   4   8   12m

4m = 2,16 cm

1928

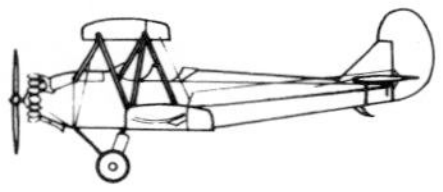

Polikarpov Po-2 (USSR)

1932

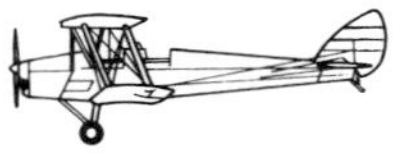

de Havilland Tiger Moth (GB)

1934

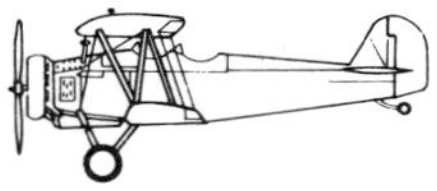

Yokosuka K5Y (J)

1935

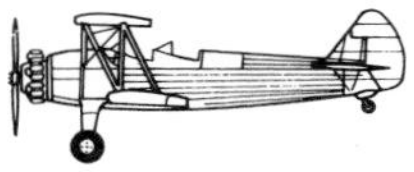

Stearman PT-17 Kaydet (USA)

1936

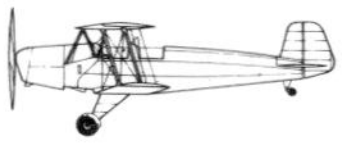

Bucher Bü.131 Jungmann (G)

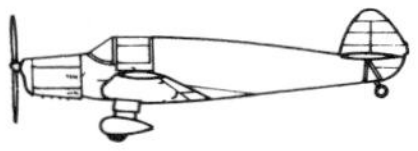

Saiman 202 (I)

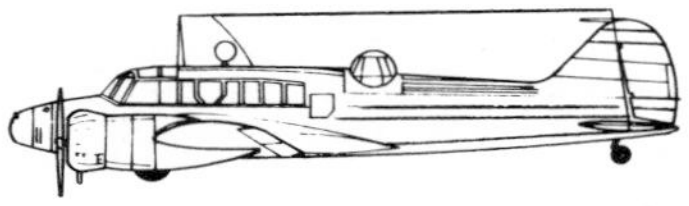

Avro Anson (GB)

1937

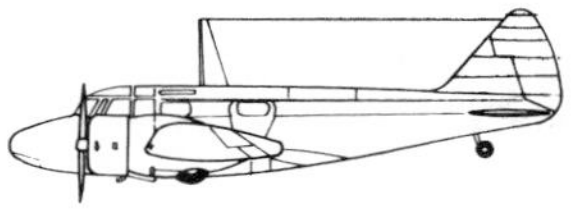

Airspeed Oxford (GB)

1938

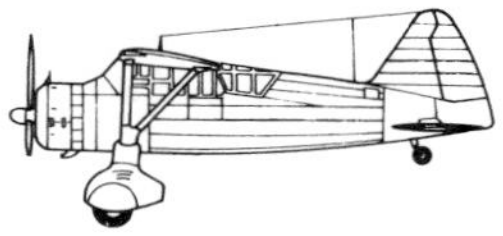

Westland Lysander (GB)

1939

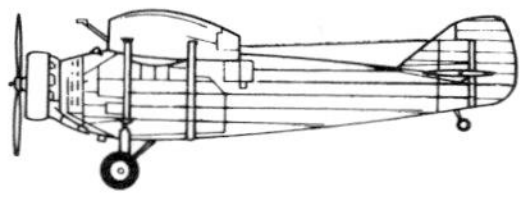

Mitsubishi K3M (J)

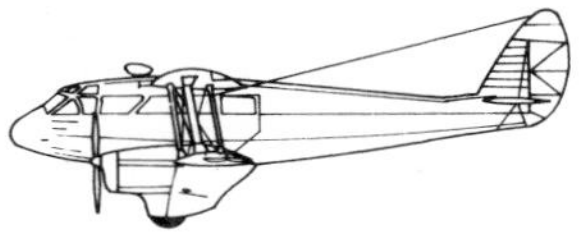

de Havilland Dominie (GB)

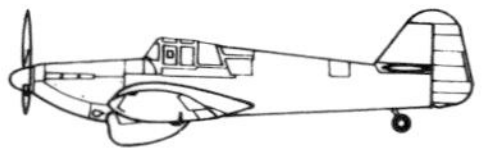

Miles Master (GB)

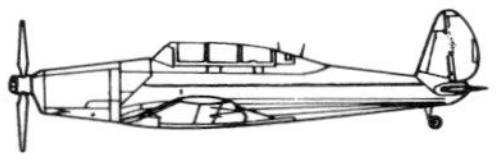

Arado Ar.96 (G)

1940

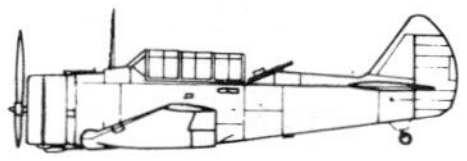

Commonwealth CA-3 Wirraway (AUS)

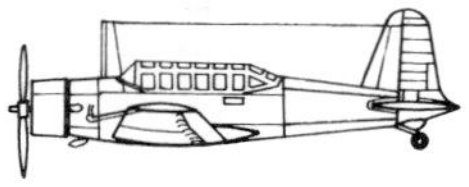

Vultee BT-13 Valiant (USA)

1941

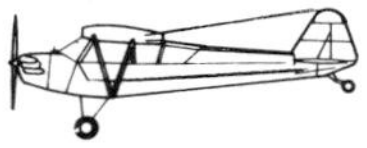

Piper L-4 Grasshopper (USA)

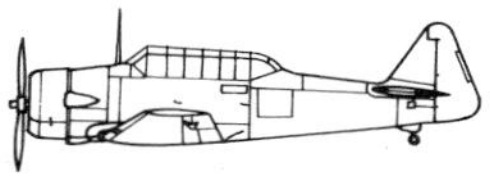

North American AT-6 Texan (USA)

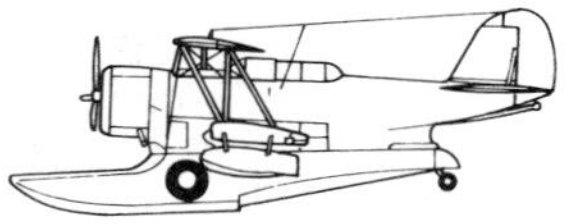

Grumman J2F Duck (USA)

1942

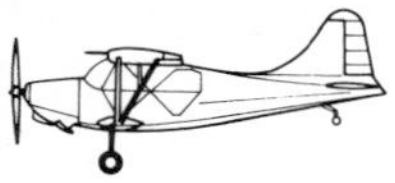

Stinson L-5 Sentinel (USA)

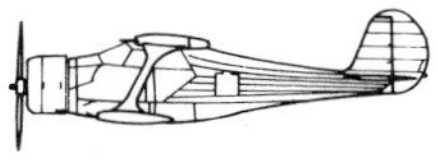

Beech UC-43 Traveler (USA)

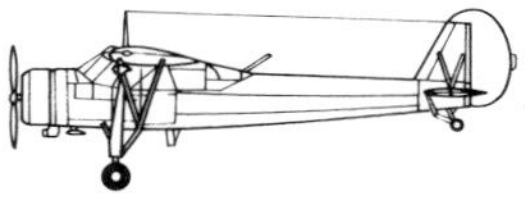

Kokusai Ki-76 (J)

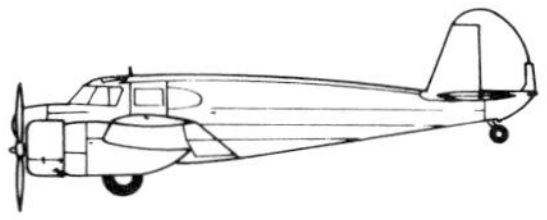

Cessna AT-17 (USA)

1943

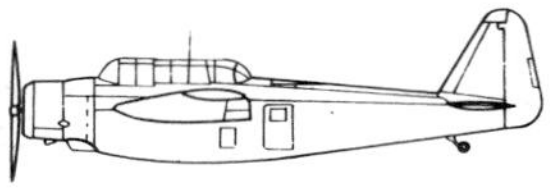

Kyushu K11W Shiragiku (J)

1944

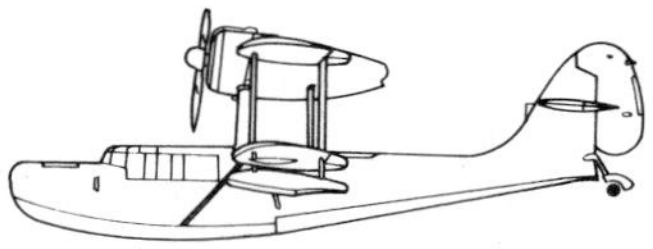

Supermarine Sea Otter (GB)

These aircraft are all drawn to the same scale, which is also used for plates **75**, **116**, **143** and **166**

Plate 159

Old but safe – Second World War trainers: 1928–40

◄ **BOEING-STEARMAN PT-17 KAYDET**
Nation: USA; *manufacturer:* Boeing Aircraft Co; *type:* trainer; *year:* 1940; *engine:* Continental R-670-5 7-cylinder radial air-cooled, 220 hp; *wingspan:* 32 ft 2 in (9.80 m); *length:* 25 ft (7.63 m); *height:* 9 ft 2 in (2.79 m); *weight:* 2,717 lb (1,232 kg); *maximum speed:* 124 mph (199 km/h); *ceiling:* 11,200 ft (3,415 m); *range:* 505 miles (812 km); *armament:* – ; *crew:* 2

POLIKARPOV Po-2 ►
Nation: USSR; *manufacturer:* State Industries; *type:* trainer; *year:* 1928; *engine:* M-11 5-cylinder radial air-cooled, 100 hp; *wingspan:* 37 ft 5 in (11.40 m); *length:* 26 ft 9 in (8.15 m); *height:* 9 ft 6 in (2.92 m); *weight:* 2,167 lb (981 kg) (loaded); *maximum speed:* 93 mph (149 km/h); *ceiling:* 13,120 ft (4,000 m); *range:* 329 miles (530 km); *armament:* 1 machine gun; 550 lb (250 kg) of bombs; *crew:* 2

de HAVILLAND TIGER MOTH Mk II ►
Nation: Britain; *manufacturer:* de Havilland Aircraft Co; *type:* trainer; *year:* 1932; *engine:* de Havilland Gipsy Major 4-cylinder inline air-cooled, 130 hp; *wingspan:* 29 ft 4 in (8.94 m); *length:* 23 ft 11 in (7.29 m); *height:* 8 ft 9½ in (2.66 m); *weight:* 1,770 lb (802 kg) (loaded); *maximum speed:* 109 mph (176 km/h); *ceiling:* 14,000 ft (4,267 m); *range:* 300 miles (482 km); *armament:* none; *crew:* 2

◄ **YOKOSUKA K5Y1**
Nation: Japan; *manufacturer:* Dai-Ichi Kaigun Koku Gijitsusho; *type:* trainer; *year:* 1934; *engine:* Hitachi Amakaze 11 9-cylinder radial air-cooled, 340 hp; *wingspan:* 36 ft 1 in (11 m); *length:* 26 ft 5 in (8.05 m); *height:* 10 ft 6 in (3.20 m); *weight:* 3,307 lb (1,500 kg) (loaded); *maximum speed:* 132 mph (212 km/h); *ceiling:* 18,700 ft (5,700 m); *range:* 633 miles (1,020 km); *armament:* 2 machine guns; *crew:* 2

◄ **BÜCKER Bü.131B JUNGMANN**
Nation: Germany; *manufacturer:* Bücker Flugzeugbau GmbH; *type:* trainer; *year:* 1936; *engine:* Hirth HW504 4-cylinder inline air-cooled, 100 hp; *wingspan:* 24 ft 3 in (7.40 m); *length:* 21 ft 9 in (6.62 m); *height:* 7 ft 5 in (2.25 m); *weight:* 1,474 lb (670 kg); *maximum speed:* 114 mph (183 km/h); *ceiling:* 14,000 ft (4,300 m); *range:* 400 miles (650 km); *armament:* – ; *crew:* 2

de HAVILLAND DOMINIE Mk I
Nation: Britain; *manufacturer:* de Havilland Aircraft Co Ltd; *type:* trainer; *year:* 1939; *engine:* two de Havilland Gipsy Six 6-cylinder inline, liquid-cooled, 200 hp each; *wingspan:* 48 ft (14.63 m); *length:* 34 ft 6 in (10.52 m); *height:* 10 ft 3 in (3.12 m); *weight:* 5,500 lb (2,491 kg) (loaded); *maximum speed:* 157 mph (253 km/h); *ceiling:* 16,700 ft (5,090 m); *range:* 580 miles (930 km); *armament:* – ; *crew:* 5/6-10

MILES MASTER Mk I
Nation: Britain; *manufacturer:* Miles Aircraft Ltd; *type:* trainer; *year:* 1939; *engine:* Rolls-Royce Kestrel XXX 12-cylinder V liquid-cooled, 715 hp; *wingspan:* 39 ft (11.88 m); *length:* 30 ft 5 in (9.27 m); *height:* 10 ft (3.05 m); *weight:* 5,573 lb (2,527 kg) (loaded); *maximum speed:* 226 mph (364 km/h) at 15,000 ft (4,500 m); *ceiling:* 27,000 ft (8,200 m); *range:* 500 miles (800 km); *armament:* 1 machine gun; *crew:* 2

ARADO Ar.96 B-1
Nation: Germany; *manufacturer:* Arado Flugzeugwerke GmbH; *type:* trainer; *year:* 1940; *engine:* Argus As.410 12-cylinder at V air-cooled, 450 hp; *wingspan:* 36 ft 1 in (11.00 m); *length:* 29 ft 11 in (9.13 m); *height:* 8 ft 6 in (2.60 m); *weight:* 3,747 lb (1,695 kg); *maximum speed:* 211 mph (340 km/h) at 9,840 ft (3,000 m); *ceiling:* 23,295 ft (7,100 m); *range:* 615 miles (990 km); *armament:* – ; *crew:* 2

MITSUBISHI K3M3
Nation: Japan; *manufacturer:* Mitsubishi Jukogyo KK; *type:* trainer; *year:* 1939; *engine:* Nakajima Kotobuki 2KAI2 9-cylinder radial air-cooled, 580 hp; *wingspan:* 51 ft 9 in (15.78 m); *length:* 31 ft 4 in (9.56 m); *height:* 12 ft 6 in (3.82 m); *weight:* 4,850 lb (2,200 kg) (loaded); *maximum speed:* 146 mph (240 km/h) at 3,280 ft (1,000 m); *ceiling:* 20,965 ft (6,390 m); *range:* 497 miles (800 km); *armament:* 1 machine gun; *crew:* 1-5

COMMONWEALTH CA-3 WIRRAWAY (A20)
Nation: Australia; *manufacturer:* Commonwealth Aircraft Corp; *type:* trainer; *year:* 1940; *engine:* Pratt & Whitney R-1340 S1H1-G Wasp 9-cylinder radial air-cooled, 600 hp; *wingspan:* 43 ft (13.10 m); *length:* 27 ft 10 in (8.48 m); *height:* 12 ft (3.70 m); *weight:* 6,595 lb (2,990 kg) (loaded); *maximum speed:* 220 mph (354 km/h) at 5,000 ft (1,525 m); *ceiling:* 23,000 ft (7,000 m); *range:* 720 miles (1,150 km); *armament:* 3 machine guns; 500 lb (227 kg) of bombs; *crew:* 2

Plate 161

Trainers: 1940–43

VULTEE BT-13A VALIANT
Nation: USA; *manufacturer:* Vultee Aircraft Inc; *type:* trainer; *year:* 1940; *engine:* Pratt & Whitney R-985-AN-1 9-cylinder radial air-cooled, 450 hp; *wingspan:* 42 ft 2 in (12.86 m); *length:* 28 ft 9 in (8.76 m); *height:* 12 ft 5 in (3.75 m); *weight:* 4,360 lb (1,980 kg); *maximum speed:* 166 mph (295 km/h); *ceiling:* 16,500 ft (5,030 m); *range:* 516 miles (826 km); *armament:* – ; *crew:* 2

NORTH AMERICAN AT-6A TEXAN
Nation: USA; *manufacturer:* North American Aviation Inc; *type:* trainer; *year:* 1941; *engine:* Pratt & Whitney R-1340-49 Wasp, 9-cylinder radial, air-cooled, 600 hp; *wingspan:* 42 ft (12.80 m); *length:* 29 ft (8.84 m); *height:* 11 ft 9 in (3.55 m); *weight:* 5,300 lb (2,404 kg) (loaded); *maximum speed:* 208 mph (335 km/h); *ceiling:* 24,200 ft (7,325 m); *range:* 750 miles (1,205 km); *armament:* 2 machine guns; *crew:* 2

CESSNA AT-17
Nation: USA; *manufacturer:* Cessna Aircraft Co; *type:* trainer; *year:* 1942; *engine:* two Jacob R-775-9 7-cylinder radial air-cooled, 245 hp each; *wingspan:* 41 ft 11 in (12.78 m); *length:* 32 ft 9 in (9.98 m); *height:* 9 ft 11 in (3.02 m); *weight:* 5,700 lb (2,600 kg) (loaded); *maximum speed:* 195 mph (314 km/h); *ceiling:* 22,000 ft (6,700 m); *range:* 750 miles (1,200 km); *armament:* – ; *crew:* 1-2; *passengers:* 4

KYUSHU K11W1 SHIRAGIKU
Nation: Japan; *manufacturer:* Kyushu Hikoki KK; *type:* trainer; *year:* 1943; *engine:* Hitachi GK2B Amakaze 21 9-cylinder radial, air-cooled, 515 hp; *wingspan:* 49 ft 2 in (14.98 m); *length:* 33 ft 7 in (10.24 m); *height:* 12 ft 10 in (3.93 m); *weight:* 6,173 lb (2,805 kg) (loaded); *maximum speed:* 143 mph (230 km/h) at 5,580 ft (1,700 m); *ceiling:* 18,440 ft (5,620 m); *range:* 1,093 miles (1,760 km); *armament:* 1 machine gun; 132 lb (60 kg) of bombs; *crew:* 5

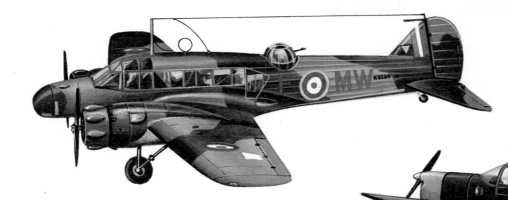

AVRO ANSON Mk I
Nation: Britain; *manufacturer:* A. V. Roe & Co Ltd; *type:* liaison; *year:* 1936; *engine:* two Armstrong Siddeley Cheetah IX 7-cylinder radial air-cooled, 350 hp each; *wingspan:* 56 ft 6 in (17.22 m); *length:* 42 ft 3 in (12.88 m); *height:* 13 ft 1 in (3.99 m); *weight:* 8,000 lb (3,630 kg) (loaded); *maximum speed:* 188 mph (303 km/h); *ceiling:* 19,000 ft (5,800 m); *range:* 790 miles (1,270 km); *armament:* 2 machine guns; 360 lb (165 kg) of bombs; *crew:* 3

SAIMAN 202
Nation: Italy; *manufacturer:* Società Anonima Industrie Meccaniche Aeronautiche Navali; *type:* liaison; *year:* 1936; *engine:* Alfa Romeo 110 4 cylinder inline air-cooled, 120 hp; *wingspan:* 35 ft 7 in (10.85 m); *length:* 25 ft 3 in (7.70 m); *height:* 6 ft 7 in (2.05 m); *weight:* 2,046 lb (928 kg) (loaded); *maximum speed:* 143 mph (230 km/h); *ceiling:* 16,400 ft (5,000 m); *range:* 435 miles (700 km); *armament:* none; *crew:* 2

WESTLAND LYSANDER Mk I
Nation: Britain; *manufacturer:* Westland Aircraft Ltd; *type:* liaison; *year:* 1938; *engine:* Bristol Mercury XII 9-cylinder radial air-cooled, 890 hp; *wingspan:* 50 ft (15.24 m); *length:* 30 ft 6 in (9.29 m); *height:* 11 ft 6 in (3.50 m); *weight:* 5,920 lb (2,685 kg) (loaded); *maximum speed:* 219 mph (352 km/h) at 10,000 ft (3,000 m); *ceiling:* 26,000 ft (7,900 m); *range:* 600 miles (965 km); *armament:* 3 machine guns; *crew:* 2

AIRSPEED OXFORD Mk I
Nation: Britain; *manufacturer:* Airspeed Ltd; *type:* trainer; *year:* 1937; *engine:* two Armstrong Siddeley Cheetah IX 7-cylinder radial air-cooled, 350 hp each; *wingspan:* 53 ft 4 in (16.25 m); *length:* 34 ft 6 in (10.51 m); *height:* 11 ft 1 in (3.38 m); *weight:* 7,600 lb (3,447 kg) (loaded); *maximum speed:* 182 mph (298 km/h); *ceiling:* 19,200 ft (5,852 m); *range:* 910 miles (1,464 km); *armament:* none; *crew:* 3

GRUMMAN J2F-5 DUCK
Nation: USA; *manufacturer:* Grumman Aircraft Engineering Corp; *type:* liaison; *year:* 1941; *engine:* Wright R-1820-50 Cyclone 9-cylinder radial air-cooled, 850 hp; *wingspan:* 39 ft (11.89 m); *length:* 34 ft (10.3€ m); *height:* 15 ft 1 in (4.60 m); *weight:* 6,711 lb (3,044 kg) (loaded); *maximum speed:* 188 mph (302 km/h); *ceiling:* 27,000 ft (8,230 m); *range:* 780 miles (1,255 km); *armament:* none; *crew:* 2

Plate 163

Army co-operation aircraft: 1941–44

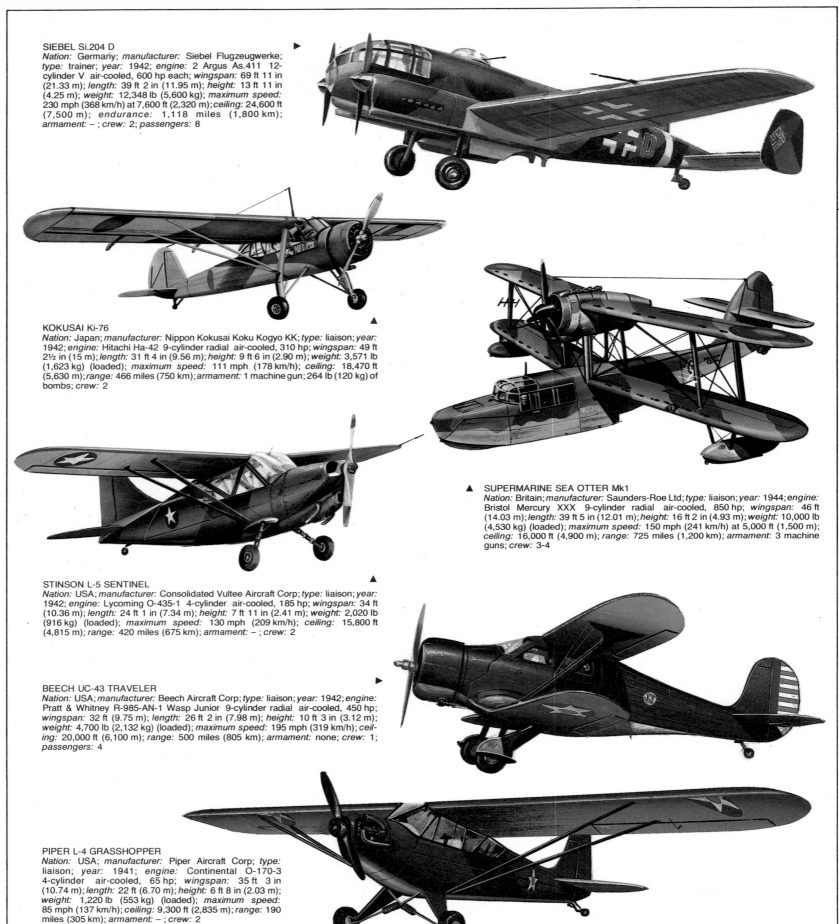

SIEBEL Si.204 D
Nation: Germany; *manufacturer:* Siebel Flugzeugwerke; *type:* trainer; *year:* 1942; *engine:* 2 Argus As.411 12-cylinder V air-cooled, 600 hp each; *wingspan:* 69 ft 11 in (21.33 m); *length:* 39 ft 2 in (11.95 m); *height:* 13 ft 11 in (4.25 m); *weight:* 12,348 lb (5,600 kg); *maximum speed:* 230 mph (368 km/h) at 7,600 ft (2,320 m); *ceiling:* 24,600 ft (7,500 m); *endurance:* 1,118 miles (1,800 km); *armament:* – ; *crew:* 2; *passengers:* 8

KOKUSAI Ki-76
Nation: Japan; *manufacturer:* Nippon Kokusai Koku Kogyo KK; *type:* liaison; *year:* 1942; *engine:* Hitachi Ha-42 9-cylinder radial air-cooled, 310 hp; *wingspan:* 49 ft 2½ in (15 m); *length:* 31 ft 4 in (9.56 m); *height:* 9 ft 6 in (2.90 m); *weight:* 3,571 lb (1,623 kg) (loaded); *maximum speed:* 111 mph (178 km/h); *ceiling:* 18,470 ft (5,630 m); *range:* 466 miles (750 km); *armament:* 1 machine gun; 264 lb (120 kg) of bombs; *crew:* 2

SUPERMARINE SEA OTTER Mk1
Nation: Britain; *manufacturer:* Saunders-Roe Ltd; *type:* liaison; *year:* 1944; *engine:* Bristol Mercury XXX 9-cylinder radial air-cooled, 850 hp; *wingspan:* 46 ft (14.03 m); *length:* 39 ft 5 in (12.01 m); *height:* 16 ft 2 in (4.93 m); *weight:* 10,000 lb (4,530 kg) (loaded); *maximum speed:* 150 mph (241 km/h) at 5,000 ft (1,500 m); *ceiling:* 16,000 ft (4,900 m); *range:* 725 miles (1,200 km); *armament:* 3 machine guns; *crew:* 3-4

STINSON L-5 SENTINEL
Nation: USA; *manufacturer:* Consolidated Vultee Aircraft Corp; *type:* liaison; *year:* 1942; *engine:* Lycoming O-435-1 4-cylinder air-cooled, 185 hp; *wingspan:* 34 ft (10.36 m); *length:* 24 ft 1 in (7.34 m); *height:* 7 ft 11 in (2.41 m); *weight:* 2,020 lb (916 kg) (loaded); *maximum speed:* 130 mph (209 km/h); *ceiling:* 15,800 ft (4,815 m); *range:* 420 miles (675 km); *armament:* – ; *crew:* 2

BEECH UC-43 TRAVELER
Nation: USA; *manufacturer:* Beech Aircraft Corp; *type:* liaison; *year:* 1942; *engine:* Pratt & Whitney R-985-AN-1 Wasp Junior 9-cylinder radial air-cooled, 450 hp; *wingspan:* 32 ft (9.75 m); *length:* 26 ft 2 in (7.98 m); *height:* 10 ft 3 in (3.12 m); *weight:* 4,700 lb (2,132 kg) (loaded); *maximum speed:* 195 mph (319 km/h); *ceiling:* 20,000 ft (6,100 m); *range:* 500 miles (805 km); *armament:* none; *crew:* 1; *passengers:* 4

PIPER L-4 GRASSHOPPER
Nation: USA; *manufacturer:* Piper Aircraft Corp; *type:* liaison; *year:* 1941; *engine:* Continental O-170-3 4-cylinder air-cooled, 65 hp; *wingspan:* 35 ft 3 in (10.74 m); *length:* 22 ft (6.70 m); *height:* 6 ft 8 in (2.03 m); *weight:* 1,220 lb (553 kg) (loaded); *maximum speed:* 85 mph (137 km/h); *ceiling:* 9,300 ft (2,835 m); *range:* 190 miles (305 km); *armament:* – ; *crew:* 2

Plate 159
Old but safe — Second World War trainers: 1928–40

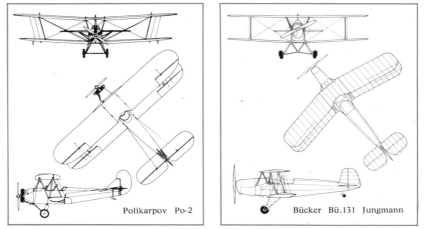

Polikarpov Po-2

Bücker Bü.131 Jungmann

Few aircraft in the entire history of aviation have been as long-lived as the Soviet Polikarpov Po-2. From 1928 to 1952 more than 20,000 of these fragile biplanes left the assembly lines in a production span which has remained a record for the Soviet state aviation industry. Although it was designed for training and as a general utility aircraft, during the world war the Po-2 was used in ways which could not have been remotely envisaged by its designer Nikolai Polikarpov, way back in 1927: these included reconnaissance, close support and bombing.

The aircraft reverted to its original role immediately after the end of the war, retaining a reputation for its excellent flight stability and safety which had made it familiar to thousands of pilots.

A very similar aircraft met with a similar success in the West: the British de Havilland Tiger Moth which for 15 years was the basic trainer of the RAF. The prototype of this elegant biplane first flew on 29th October 1931, and series production started soon afterwards: the first models went into service in February of the following year. Over 5,000 Tiger Moths went to British flying schools, of which no less than 4,000 were delivered during the course of the war. Its use was further extended to Canada, Australia and New Zealand, where they were manufactured under licence, in the context of a common training scheme for the Commonwealth countries. The Tiger Moth had a wooden airframe except for the forward part of the fuselage which was in metal, and it had a fabric skin. It was powered by a de Havilland Gypsy 130 hp engine and could reach an altitude of 5,180 m (16,995 ft).

Immediately after the war the de Havilland biplanes which had been taken out of service by the RAF literally invaded the flying clubs and the civil flying schools, achieving further success and popularity under a new

lease of life. Many of them are still flying today, scattered throughout the world.

During the war years the Tiger Moth was joined by a modern advanced trainer, the twin-engine Airspeed Oxford, derived from the commercial AS.6 Envoy of 1934. These aircraft were put into service in 1937 as the Mk I version with the Central Flying School and remained in service for as many as 17 years up to 1954. In all production totalled 8,751 aircraft in several series which were also used in Australia, Canada and New Zealand. The main attribute of the Oxford was its ability to respond to every type of training requirement, and it could be used to train both pilots and crews in a wide range of skills.

For basic training the biplanes remained unequalled for many years. Wherever there was an air force in existence throughout the world, aircraft of this type met with great success and popularity. In Japan, for instance, the most widely used trainer of the war years was the Yokosuka K5Y, a tough, sturdy and safe biplane which stayed in production uninterruptedly from 1933 to 1945, and a total of 5,770 were built in two principal variants; the K5Y1, a land-based model, and the K5Y2 which was built as a seaplane.

The project had started in 1932 when the Imperial Navy gave an order to Kawanishi for the joint development with the first naval air force

arsenal, Tachikawa Dai-Ichi Rikugun, of a basic trainer which could replace all those types which were in service at the time and remain in service for as long as possible. During production prototypes of another three variants were constructed, K5Y3, K5Y4 and K5Y5, which had more powerful engines, but these models were not followed up. In Allied code the Yokosuka trainers were designated WILLOW.

In the United States one of the most widely used basic trainers of the war period was a biplane: the Boeing-Stearman Kaydet which, based on the original Stearman design, was produced by Boeing until February 1945 in a total of 10,346 aircraft to meet the needs of the USAAF and the US Navy. Several versions were completed, differing in their engines and equipment: the PT-13 of 1935 had a Lycoming engine; the PT-17 of 1940 a Continental engine; the PT-18 had a Jacobs engine; and the PT-27, with different instrumentation and a closed cockpit, was made for Canada. In the US Navy these aircraft were given the basic designation of N2S.

Plate 160
Trainers: 1939–40

In Britain another de Havilland aircraft, the Dominie, had a similar career to the Tiger Moth. In essence this was a military version of the famous D.H.89 Dragon Rapide civil transport of 1934. The RAF's interest in this small twin-engine biplane was aroused on the very eve of the Second World War; the aircraft's excellent handling and its wide use by private owners and small companies led the military authorities to look favourably on the idea of using the D.H.89 as a trainer and liaison plane. Two production series were ordered (521 total built), the Mk I which appeared in 1939 for training, the Mk II as a general utility. At the end of the war many Dominies were sold to civil operators and when reconverted they joined the surviving Dragon Rapides. Their career went through a sort of third youth and continued for many years; BEA used a large fleet of them for feeder routes in Scotland and the Channel Islands.

Another advanced trainer, a contemporary of the Dominie, was the Miles Master, a modern monoplane of which 3,301 were built in three production series. The prototype first flew in 1938 and the assembly lines started work the next year, on the first of the 900 Master Mk Is which had been ordered. The British Air Ministry's order amazed aeronautical circles at the time, being the most massive ever given for an aircraft of this type. The Miles Master ended up by becoming one of the most widely used advanced trainers of the RAF. A horde of 1,799 Mk IIs joined the 900 Mk Is and were equipped with Bristol Mercury 820 hp radial engines instead of the Rolls-Royce Kestrel XXX 715 hp engines which powered the first series, and these were followed by a further 602 Master Mk IIIs in which the engine was changed yet again, to a Pratt & Whitney Wasp Junior 825 hp radial. Production ended in 1941.

In Germany the use of the Arado Ar.96 was even more widespread. This modern monoplane was chosen in 1940 to be the standard trainer of the *Luftwaffe*. The largest production version was the Ar.96 B of 1940 of which various sub-series were built, intended for various types of training and differing mainly in their equipment. Hardly any of these aircraft (11,546 in total) were constructed by the Arado company itself but by manufacturers associated with the production programme, such as the German AGO company up to half way through 1941, and the Czechoslovak factories of Avia and Letov.

In Japan an old high-wing monoplane was widely used for crew training:

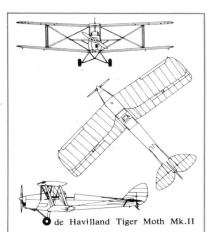

de Havilland Tiger Moth Mk.II

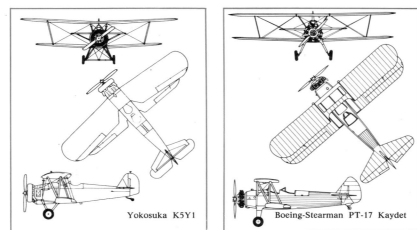

Yokosuka K5Y1

Boeing-Stearman PT-17 Kaydet

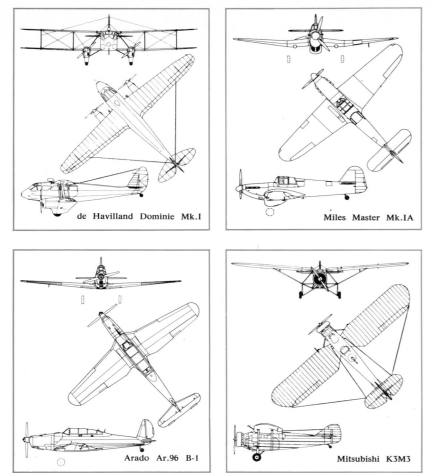

de Havilland Dominie Mk.I

Miles Master Mk.IA

Arado Ar.96 B-1

Mitsubishi K3M3

Plate 161
Trainers: 1940–43

The best and the most well-known trainer of the war was the "twin" aircraft of the Australian Wirraway: the North American AT-6, known by the name of Texan in the USA and Harvard in Britain. Over 15,000 of them were constructed and this sturdy and safe monoplane stayed in service with many military air forces for over twenty years after the end of the Second World War, and its career even today shows no sign of coming to an end.

The AT-6 project was derived directly from that of the BT-9, another successful trainer developed by North American in 1935 (an improved version of the BT-9 had been the NA-33 from which the Commonwealth Wirraway had come). Although it kept the general lines and structure of its predecessor and of its numerous variants, the new aircraft was definitely more up-to-date, in particular as regards its landing-gear which was retractable.

The first production models appeared in 1940, but because of the urgency of the rearmament programme the assembly lines were soon expanded and were working at top speed. The AT-6A followed, with different engine and fuel tanks, and went into service in 1941; 1,549 were built. Then came the AT-6B, unchanged but intended for air-gunner training; then the AT-6C with structural modifications in order to save aluminium (2,970); in the AT-6D the original structure was readopted (4,388); and the AT-6F, the final uprated variant, was more powerful (965 built).

In addition to these aircraft others were produced under licence in Australia, Sweden, Canada and in other countries; no less than 5,000 went to the RAF and to Commonwealth air forces. In Britain the last pilot to qualify in a Harvard did so on 22nd March 1955.

The success of the North American AT-6 was followed in turn by that of a very similar aircraft, the Vultee Valiant, which from September 1939 to the summer of 1944 was constructed in a total of 11,537 to meet the needs of the USAAF and the US Navy. There were numerous versions of the Valiant: the original, which was number BT-13, was followed in 1940 by the BT-13A and later by the BT-13B. The first two were designated SNV-1, the third SNV-2 by the navy. In all the USN used about 2,000 of these variants, which differed from each other only in equipment details. The final variant, which was only used by the USAAF, was the BT-15 in which a Wright R-975 radial was installed instead of the Pratt & Whitney R-985 Wasp Junior of the previous model.

For multi-engine training, a small and handy twin-engine aircraft was widely used which was directly adapted from civilian use: this was the Cessna AT-17. The original specification of the USAAF took shape in 1939 with an order for various militarised versions of the commercial T-50 model, which were designated AT-8. Two years later, when war was imminent, the army asked for a new version with different engines: this was the AT-17 (450 built) which went into service in 1942. This was followed by 223 AT-17As with metal propellers, 466 AT-17Bs, and 60 AT-17Cs, both of these two later variants being improved and carrying different equipment. Later on a transport, the UC-78 Bobcat, was also derived from those aircraft and remained in service up to 1949; its success was even greater, since over 3,000 were built, both for the USAAF and for the USN. In the navy, it was numbered JRC-1.

From 1943 to 1945 the Japanese Imperial Navy trained its air crews on the Kyushu K11W Shiragiku monoplane, designed towards the end of 1940 and of which 798 were built. The aircraft had a capacious fuselage and could be equally well used for the instruction of pilots, air-gunners, navigators, bomb-aimers and radio operators. There were two production series: K11W1 and K11W2, the latter used as a transport and for anti-submarine warfare.

the Mitsubishi K3M which dated back to 1929. Commissioned by the Imperial Navy, this aircraft aroused the interest of the army four years later but their enthusiasm for it subsequently waned. After the destruction of the prototype the whole production was switched to the Navy which employed a total of 624 of them in several variants. The final version, the K3M3, appeared in 1939 and was an improvement on the others both in its airframe and streamlining, as well as having a more powerful engine. Apart from being used as a trainer, various K3Ms were modified as light transports and designated K3M3-L. In

Allied code this aircraft was PINE.

A trainer was the first type of aircraft to be built in Australia with the advent of war and the menace of a Japanese invasion: this was the Commonwealth Wirraway, a construction licence version of the North American Na-33 (in its turn one of the forerunners of the prolific series of very well-known AT-6s). This aeroplane was certainly not a combat plane and yet it was put to uses which far exceeded its original role; bomber, ground attack plane, reconnaissance, fighter, all of which the Wirraway carried out effectively thanks to its enterprising crews. Production started in 1939 (the prototype had flown on 27th March) and continued, to reach a total of 755 in several series, which were given the factory designations of CA-1 to CA-16. As far as the RAAF was concerned, the Wirraway was designated A-20.

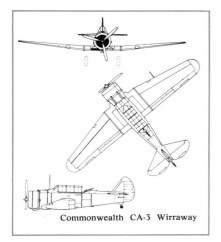

Commonwealth CA-3 Wirraway

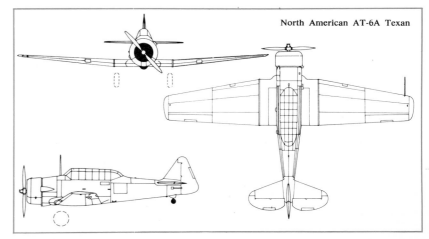

North American AT-6A Texan

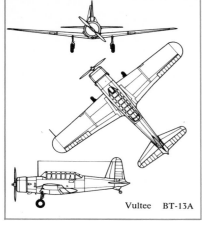

Vultee BT-13A

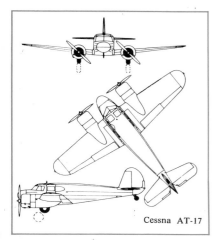

Cessna AT-17

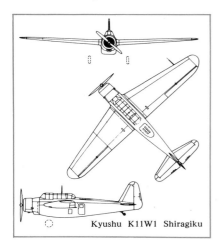

Kyushu K11W1 Shiragiku

Plate 162
Army co-operation aircraft: 1936–41

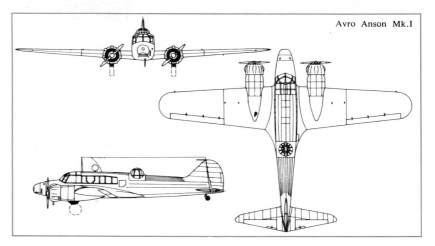

Avro Anson Mk.I

Many aircraft which had been demoted from roles of greater prestige were used for liaison or general utility during the course of the war; often too they were specially designed for their secondary tasks. The British Avro Anson belonged to the first category, a twin-engine aircraft derived from the civil Avro 652 of 1934 which the air force originally wanted to have at its disposal as a reconnaissance plane. As the war went on these aircraft were replaced by much more modern and powerful planes, and relegated to the role of trainer and general utility. Among its many merits, however, the Anson possessed that of longevity: 11,020 in all were built in Britain and Canada and 8,138 of these went to the RAF which used them for over 20 years; production, moreover, went on uninterruptedly for seventeen years, from 1935 onwards. From the time of entry into service of the first version, the Mk I which was operational from March 1936 with units of Coastal Command, the Avro Ansons were known by a very affectionate name which well reflected their safety and dependability, "Faithful Annie".

The Westland Lysander was one of those that were expressly designed for liaison and army co-operation, and was a real all-purpose plane which could be compared from many points of view with the German Fieseler Fi.156 Storch. The Lysander, a high-wing monoplane, acquired its own prestige during the course of the war for its clandestine missions, delivering and picking up secret agents in the most unlikely part of occupied territory, and it carried out these tasks, to which it was particularly well suited, with efficiency. The Lysander prototype flew in June 1936 and the aircraft went into service in its first production version, Mk I, two years later. At the outbreak of war Lysanders were widely used especially for tactical

reconnaissance, artillery spotting and supply drops.

The principal production variants beside the Mk I were the Mk II and the Mk III which differed mainly in the power of their engines and their armament. The Lysander Mk III led to the special variant for the transport of secret agents. It had a supplementary fuel tank which gave it eight hours' endurance and a small metal ladder in the fuselage to give easy access to the cockpit. Between the end of 1936 and January 1942 1,368 Lysanders came off the assembly lines.

In Italy one of the most well-known light aircraft to be used in the course of the war was the Saiman 202. Designed in the middle of the 1930s, this small low-wing monoplane had a long and busy operational career, and above and beyond its wartime use on all fronts, stayed in service with the air force up to the beginning of the 1950s. At that time the surviving models were taken out of service and sold to flying clubs which used them for a long time. The Saiman 202 was joined by an updated version, the 204, which was equipped with more powerful engines and was slightly larger, capable of carrying four people including the pilot: double the load of the 202.

In Germany the career of the Bücker Bü.131 Jungmann started in the period immediately preceding the war; it was a small, classic biplane

developed for flying schools as far back as 1934. In the course of the war the 4,000 aircraft which were constructed in three principal variants up to 1940 were widely used by the *Luftwaffe* for training and general utility. The production models were the A, then the B of 1936 with a more powerful engine, and the C of 1938 which was improved in detail. The Jungmann was constructed under licence in Switzerland, in Spain, in Czechoslovakia and in Japan and also exported to Yugoslavia, Romania and Bulgaria. Several dozen of them were still flying in the 1970s, prized for their aerobatic qualities.

The career of its contemporary, the Grumman J2F Duck, however, was strictly military; this was a small amphibian with a centre float, retractable undercarriage and wing floats which, although designed in 1933, served with the US Navy for the whole of the war. The prototype, designated JF-1, appeared in May 1933 and was followed by 27 series models. In 1937 the J2F-1 variant was built (20) which was followed by the J2F-2 (21), by the J2F-3 (20), and by the J2F-4 (32 built). At the outbreak of war the final versions, the J2F-5 and the J2F-6 appeared, of which 144 and 330 were built respectively. These differed from their predecessors in having more powerful engine and in general styling refinements.

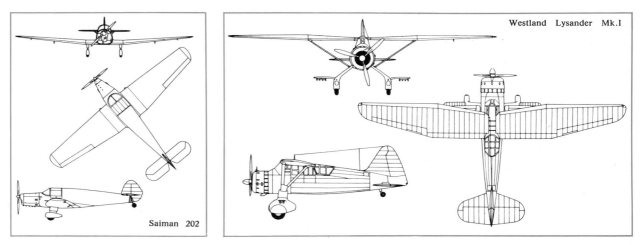

Saiman 202

Westland Lysander Mk.I

Airspeed Oxford Mk.I

Grumman J2F-5 Duck

several versions, which differed in equipment and construction details, the Piper L-4 (over 5,500 were built), having a busy and far-flung career up to the last days of the war.

The Stinson L-5 Sentinel was to continue in active service up to the Korean War. It was derived in 1942 from the commercial 105 Voyager. In a militarised form this aircraft had its fuselage slightly modified and was adapted to cope with greater loads than the civilian models. Over 3,000 were built for the needs of the USAAF. During the war the Sentinel was most widely used as an air ambulance/casevac.

Another very well-known aircraft among American aviation enthusiasts of the 1930s, the Beech 17, led to one of the most distinctive light aircraft of the USAAF: the Beech UC-43 Traveler. The first of this prolific family of "stagger-wings" as the Beech 17 was known had flown way back in 1932. The interest of the military authorities was aroused seven years later, when they placed an order for three of them, but towards the end of 1941 a larger contract for another 27 aircraft followed this nominal order. These were the first of a total of 270 which were to go to the USAAF and the US Navy. The AAF used 207, designating them UC-43, the Navy

taking remaining 63 which assumed the designation of GB-1. During the course of the war many civil aircraft requisitioned from airlines were added to these aircraft.

Similar to the Piper L-4 and the Stinson L-5 (but basically derived from the German Fieseler Fi.156 Storch) was the Japanese Kokusai Ki-76, a small high-wing monoplane which was put into production towards the end of 1942, and widely used by the Imperial Army for liaison and artillery spotting. The project had been inspired by the Storch but in the event this aircraft turned out to be better than its German counterpart from many points of view. In particular, following the adoption of a much more powerful engine (radial) compared with that which powered the famous Storch, and a different wing-flap system, the Ki-76 had better overall performance, including reduced landing distance requirement. The Allies code-named it STELLA. Production continued until 1944.

A general utility aircraft, which was larger than the Fieseler Fi.156, was used by the Germans from 1942 onwards. This was the Siebel Si.204, a light twin-engine plane which was soon issued to units and was popular thanks to its sturdiness and dependability. The largest production version

was the D. This, like the others, was constructed under licence in France during the German occupation by SNGAC and in Czechoslovakia by BMM and by Aero. French industry built 168, the two Czechoslovak manufacturers 492 and 515 respectively: production ceased at the end of 1944. In service the Siebel Si.204 was also used for multi-engine training.

In Britain the last liaison biplane of the Fleet Air Arm was the Supermarine Sea Otter, an amphibian derived from the Walrus which went into service at the end of 1944. Production continued until 1946, with 290 built in various series, and the aircraft remained operational up to the 1950s.

Plate 163
Army co-operation aircraft: 1941–44

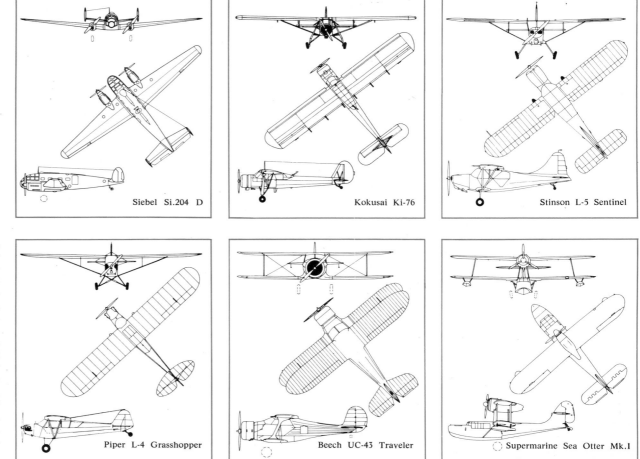
Siebel Si.204 D

Kokusai Ki-76

Stinson L-5 Sentinel

Piper L-4 Grasshopper

Beech UC-43 Traveler

Supermarine Sea Otter Mk.I

In the US Army Air Force the two most widely used light aircraft for observation and liaison were the Piper L-4 Grasshopper and the Stinson L-5 Sentinel which were very similar aircraft and were directly derived from models in production for the commercial market.

The Grasshopper (this name was apt in view of its ability to take off and land on any sort of terrain and in very limited spaces) was chosen by the USAAF in 1941: it was already in civil production under the name of Piper Cub and its military career only added more popularity to that which it had already achieved among flying clubs and private owners. It was produced in

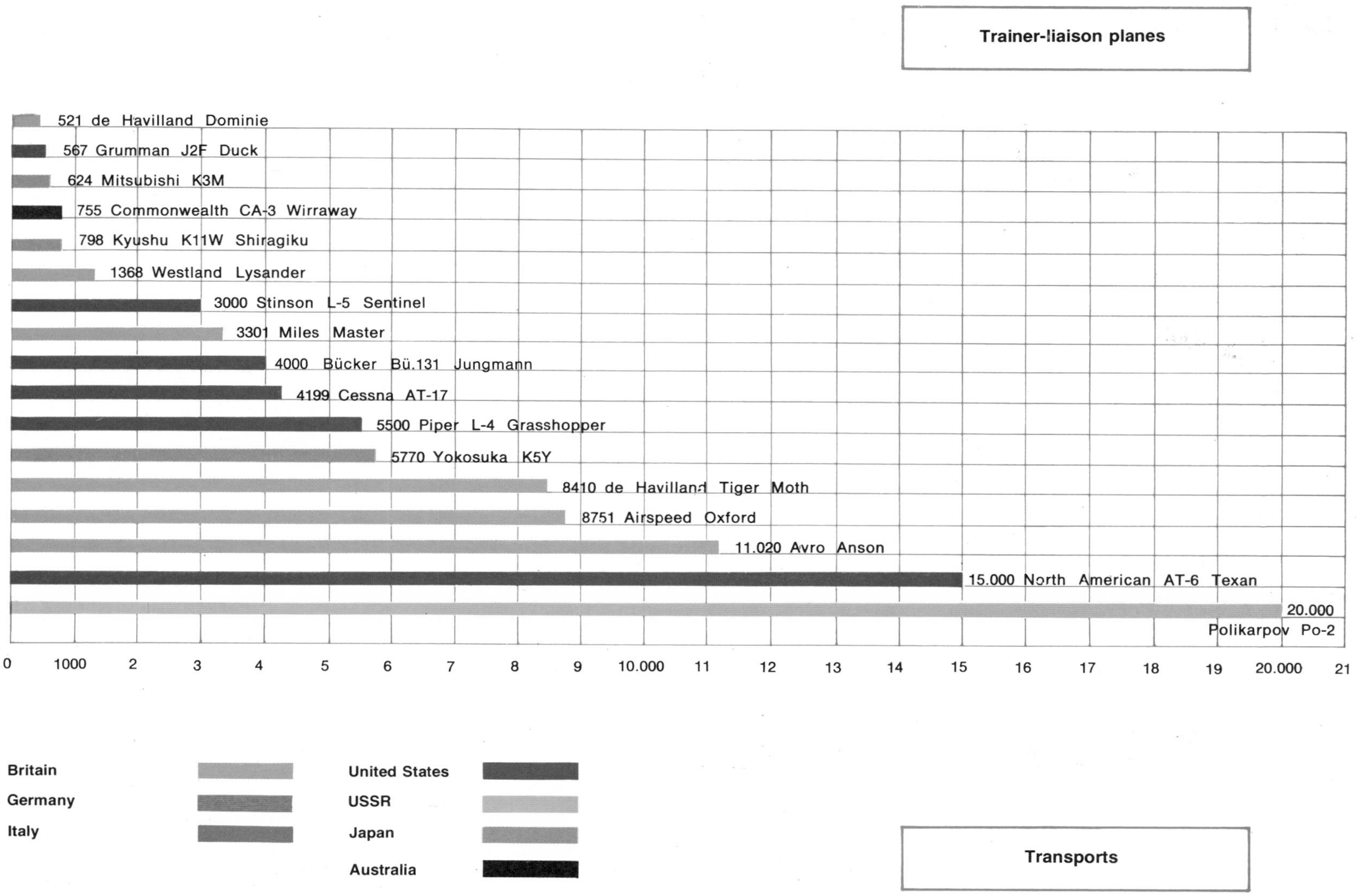

Trainer-liaison planes

521 de Havilland Dominie
567 Grumman J2F Duck
624 Mitsubishi K3M
755 Commonwealth CA-3 Wirraway
798 Kyushu K11W Shiragiku
1368 Westland Lysander
3000 Stinson L-5 Sentinel
3301 Miles Master
4000 Bücker Bü.131 Jungmann
4199 Cessna AT-17
5500 Piper L-4 Grasshopper
5770 Yokosuka K5Y
8410 de Havilland Tiger Moth
8751 Airspeed Oxford
11.020 Avro Anson
15.000 North American AT-6 Texan
20.000 Polikarpov Po-2

| 0 | 1000 | 2 | 3 | 4 | 5 | 6 | 7 | 8 | 9 | 10.000 | 11 | 12 | 13 | 14 | 15 | 16 | 17 | 18 | 19 | 20.000 | 21 |

Britain		United States	
Germany		USSR	
Italy		Japan	
		Australia	

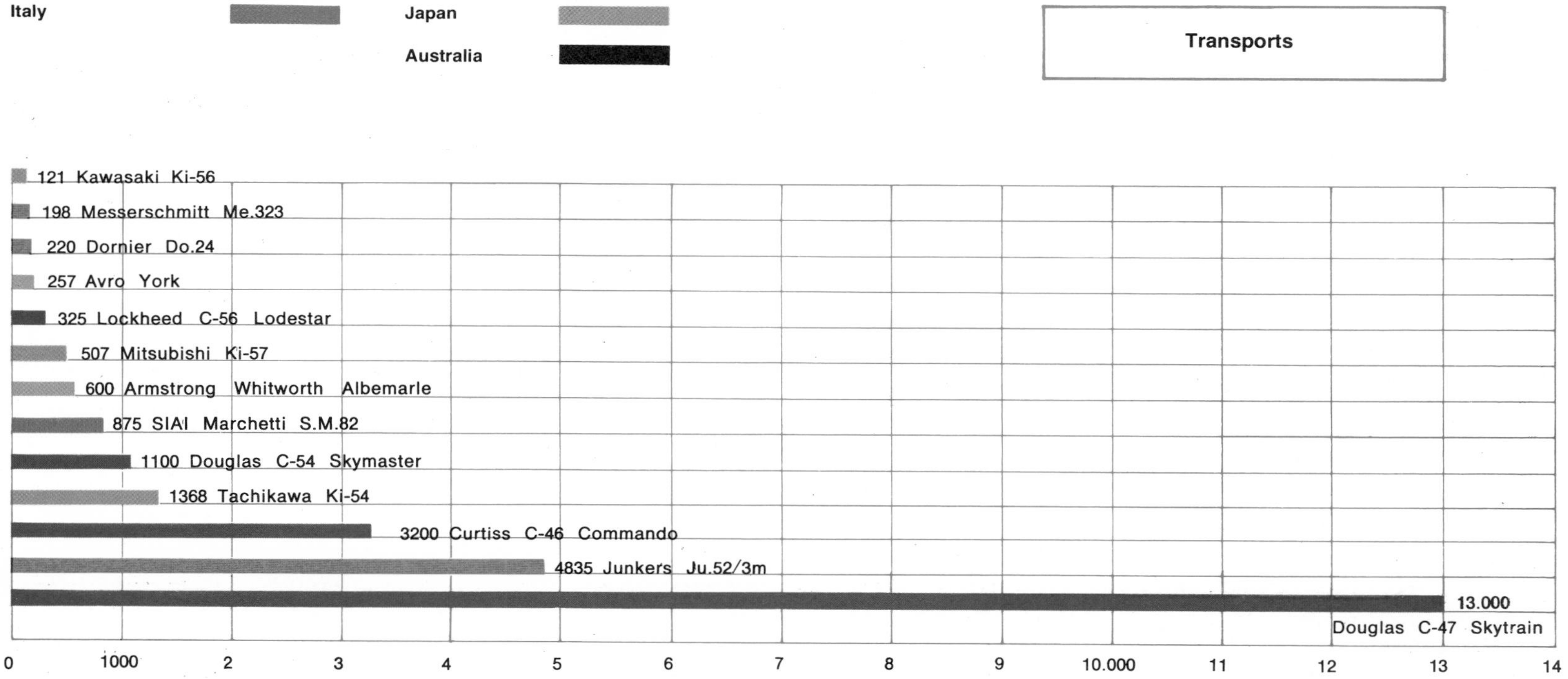

Transports

121 Kawasaki Ki-56
198 Messerschmitt Me.323
220 Dornier Do.24
257 Avro York
325 Lockheed C-56 Lodestar
507 Mitsubishi Ki-57
600 Armstrong Whitworth Albemarle
875 SIAI Marchetti S.M.82
1100 Douglas C-54 Skymaster
1368 Tachikawa Ki-54
3200 Curtiss C-46 Commando
4835 Junkers Ju.52/3m
13.000 Douglas C-47 Skytrain

| 0 | 1000 | 2 | 3 | 4 | 5 | 6 | 7 | 8 | 9 | 10.000 | 11 | 12 | 13 | 14 |

Plate 165

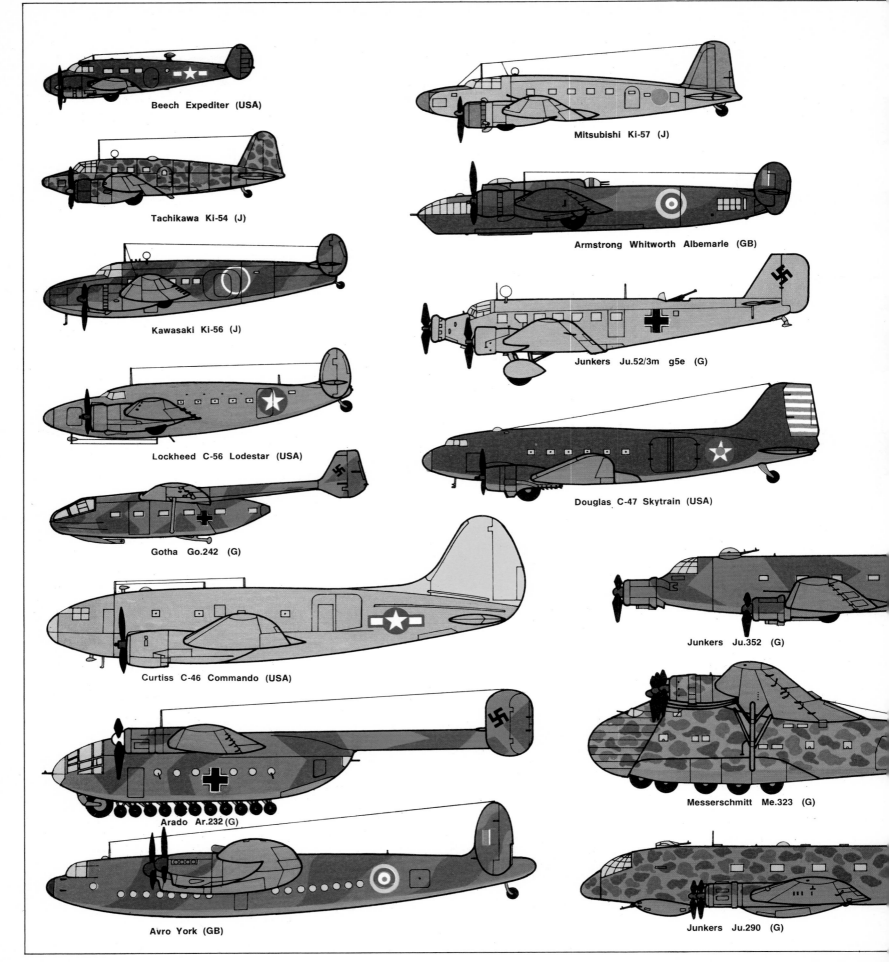

Beech Expediter (USA)

Tachikawa Ki-54 (J)

Kawasaki Ki-56 (J)

Lockheed C-56 Lodestar (USA)

Gotha Go.242 (G)

Curtiss C-46 Commando (USA)

Arado Ar.232 (G)

Avro York (GB)

Mitsubishi Ki-57 (J)

Armstrong Whitworth Albemarle (GB)

Junkers Ju.52/3m g5e (G)

Douglas C-47 Skytrain (USA)

Junkers Ju.352 (G)

Messerschmitt Me.323 (G)

Junkers Ju.290 (G)

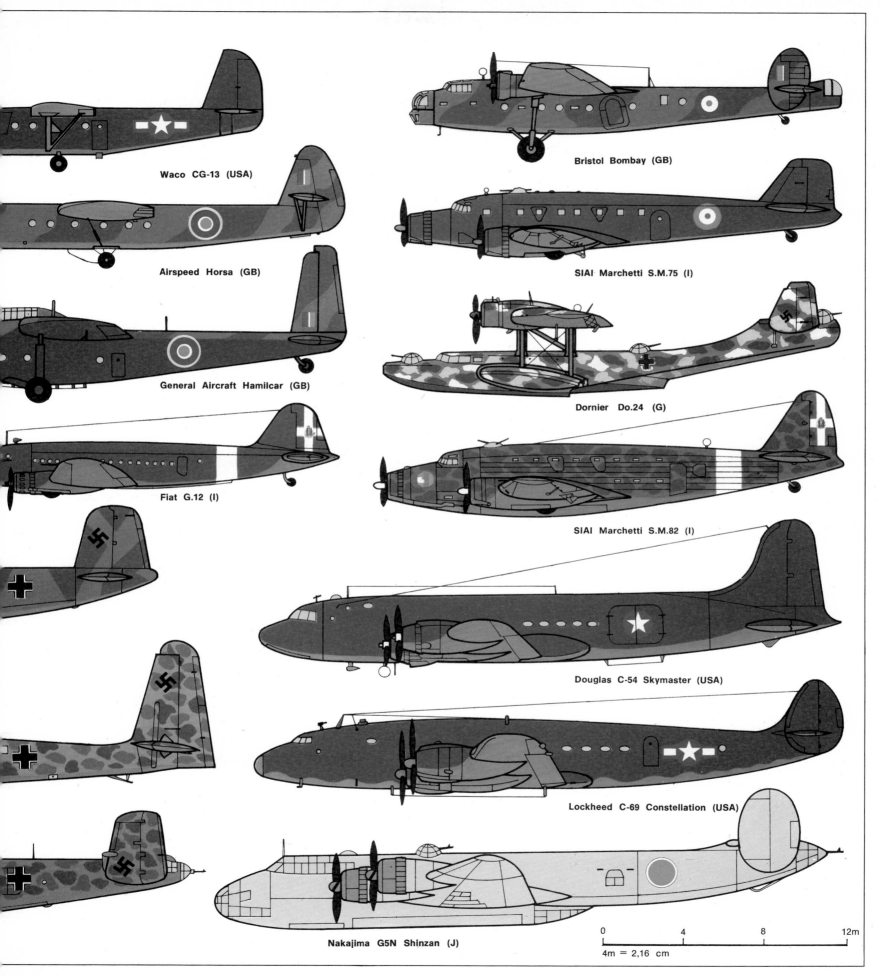

Waco CG-13 (USA)

Airspeed Horsa (GB)

General Aircraft Hamilcar (GB)

Fiat G.12 (I)

Bristol Bombay (GB)

SIAI Marchetti S.M.75 (I)

Dornier Do.24 (G)

SIAI Marchetti S.M.82 (I)

Douglas C-54 Skymaster (USA)

Lockheed C-69 Constellation (USA)

Nakajima G5N Shinzan (J)

0   4   8   12m

4m = 2,16 cm

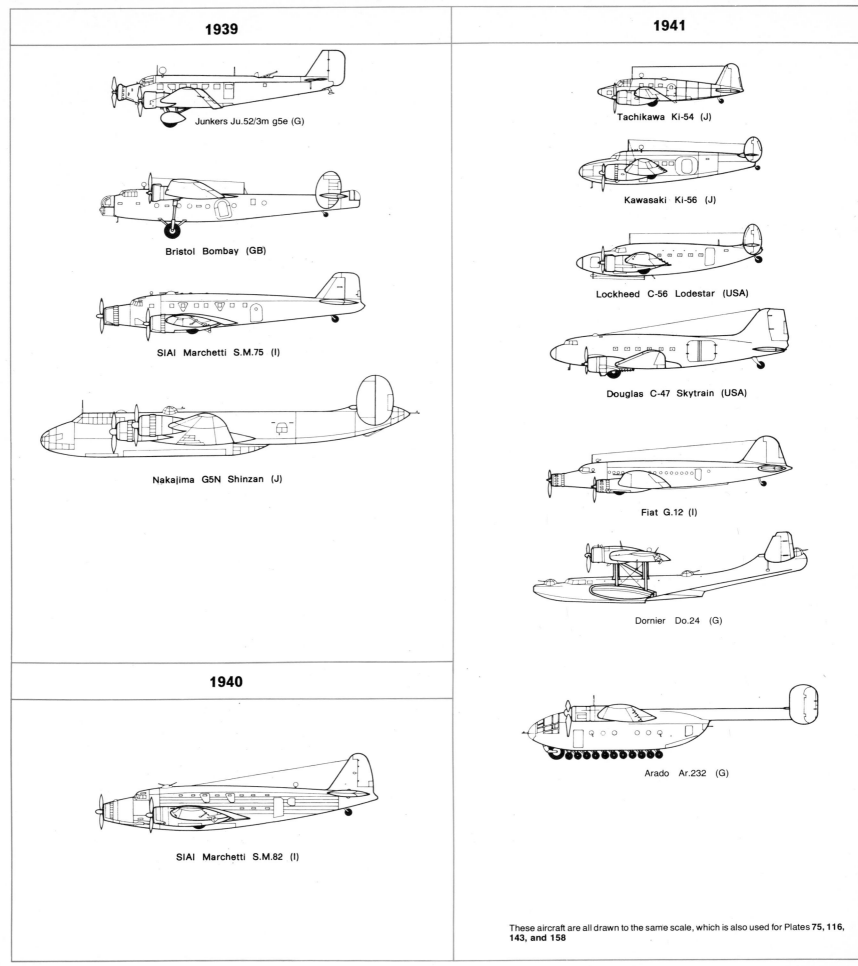

1939

Junkers Ju.52/3m g5e (G)

Bristol Bombay (GB)

SIAI Marchetti S.M.75 (I)

Nakajima G5N Shinzan (J)

1940

SIAI Marchetti S.M.82 (I)

1941

Tachikawa Ki-54 (J)

Kawasaki Ki-56 (J)

Lockheed C-56 Lodestar (USA)

Douglas C-47 Skytrain (USA)

Fiat G.12 (I)

Dornier Do.24 (G)

Arado Ar.232 (G)

These aircraft are all drawn to the same scale, which is also used for Plates **75, 116, 143,** and **158**

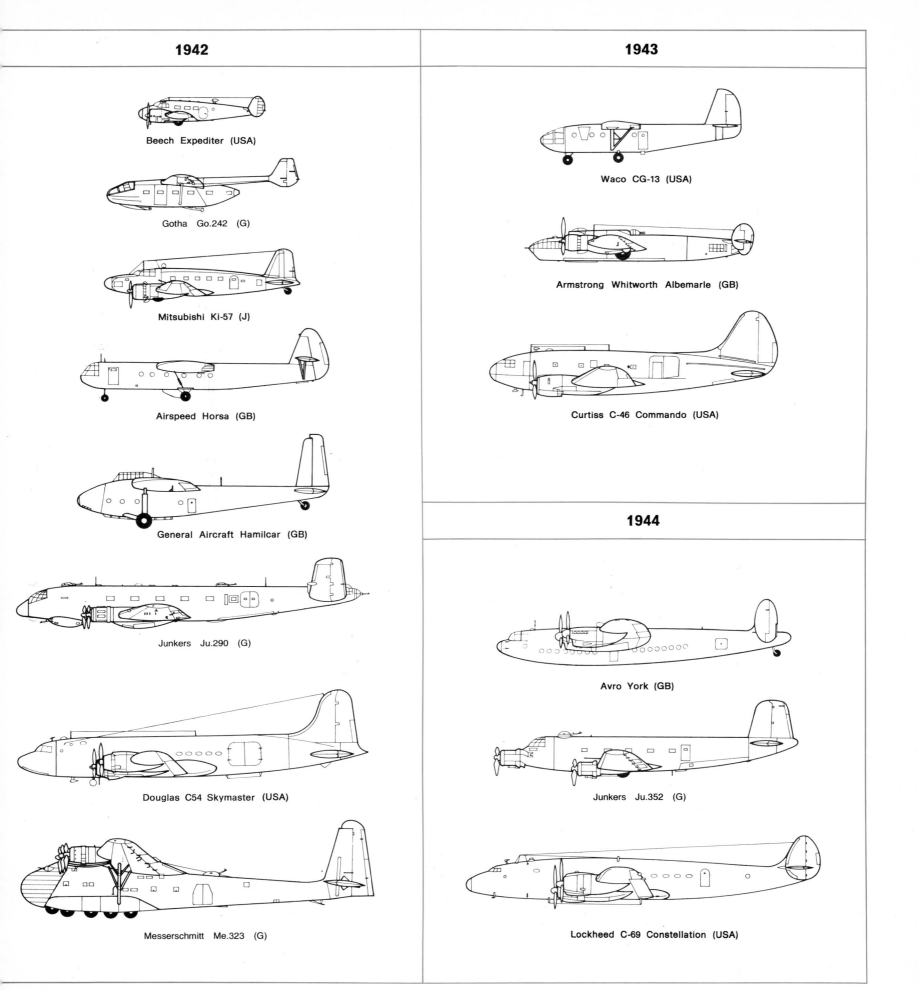

1942

Beech Expediter (USA)

Gotha Go.242 (G)

Mitsubishi Ki-57 (J)

Airspeed Horsa (GB)

General Aircraft Hamilcar (GB)

Junkers Ju.290 (G)

Douglas C54 Skymaster (USA)

Messerschmitt Me.323 (G)

1943

Waco CG-13 (USA)

Armstrong Whitworth Albemarle (GB)

Curtiss C-46 Commando (USA)

1944

Avro York (GB)

Junkers Ju.352 (G)

Lockheed C-69 Constellation (USA)

Plate 167

The Ju.52 was best among the prewar transports: 1934–39

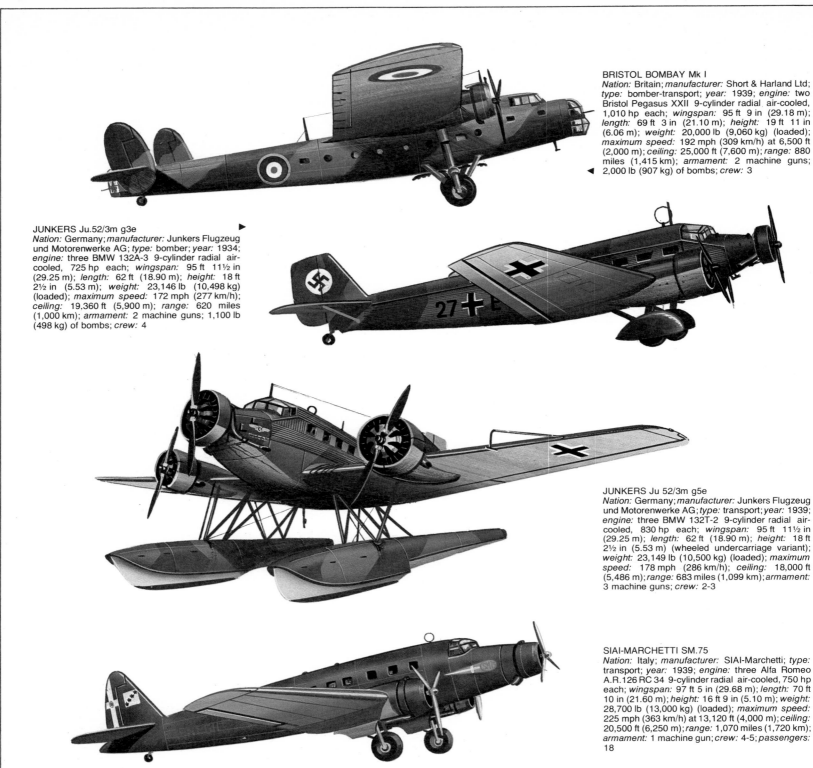

BRISTOL BOMBAY Mk I
Nation: Britain; *manufacturer:* Short & Harland Ltd;
type: bomber-transport; *year:* 1939; *engine:* two
Bristol Pegasus XXII 9-cylinder radial air-cooled,
1,010 hp each; *wingspan:* 95 ft 9 in (29.18 m);
length: 69 ft 3 in (21.10 m); *height:* 19 ft 11 in
(6.06 m); *weight:* 20,000 lb (9,060 kg) (loaded);
maximum speed: 192 mph (309 km/h) at 6,500 ft
(2,000 m); *ceiling:* 25,000 ft (7,600 m); *range:* 880
miles (1,415 km); *armament:* 2 machine guns;
2,000 lb (907 kg) of bombs; *crew:* 3

JUNKERS Ju.52/3m g3e
Nation: Germany; *manufacturer:* Junkers Flugzeug
und Motorenwerke AG; *type:* bomber; *year:* 1934;
engine: three BMW 132A-3 9-cylinder radial air-
cooled, 725 hp each; *wingspan:* 95 ft 11½ in
(29.25 m); *length:* 62 ft (18.90 m); *height:* 18 ft
2½ in (5.53 m); *weight:* 23,146 lb (10,498 kg)
(loaded); *maximum speed:* 172 mph (277 km/h);
ceiling: 19,360 ft (5,900 m); *range:* 620 miles
(1,000 km); *armament:* 2 machine guns; 1,100 lb
(498 kg) of bombs; *crew:* 4

JUNKERS Ju 52/3m g5e
Nation: Germany; *manufacturer:* Junkers Flugzeug
und Motorenwerke AG; *type:* transport; *year:* 1939;
engine: three BMW 132T-2 9-cylinder radial air-
cooled, 830 hp each; *wingspan:* 95 ft 11½ in
(29.25 m); *length:* 62 ft (18.90 m); *height:* 18 ft
2½ in (5.53 m) (wheeled undercarriage variant);
weight: 23,149 lb (10,500 kg) (loaded); *maximum
speed:* 178 mph (286 km/h); *ceiling:* 18,000 ft
(5,486 m); *range:* 683 miles (1,099 km); *armament:*
3 machine guns; *crew:* 2-3

SIAI-MARCHETTI SM.75
Nation: Italy; *manufacturer:* SIAI-Marchetti; *type:*
transport; *year:* 1939; *engine:* three Alfa Romeo
A.R.126 RC 34 9-cylinder radial air-cooled, 750 hp
each; *wingspan:* 97 ft 5 in (29.68 m); *length:* 70 ft
10 in (21.60 m); *height:* 16 ft 9 in (5.10 m); *weight:*
28,700 lb (13,000 kg) (loaded); *maximum speed:*
225 mph (363 km/h) at 13,120 ft (4,000 m); *ceiling:*
20,500 ft (6,250 m); *range:* 1,070 miles (1,720 km);
armament: 1 machine gun; *crew:* 4-5; *passengers:*
18

NAKAJIMA G5N1 SHINZAN
Nation: Japan; *manufacturer:* Nakajima Hikoki KK;
type: bomber; *year:* 1939; *engine:* four Nakajima
NK7A Mamoru 11 14,cylinder radial air-cooled,
1,870 hp each (bomber prototype); *wingspan:*
138 ft 3 in (42.14 m); *length:* 101 ft 9 in (31.02 m);
height: – ; *weight:* 70,768 lb (32,167 kg) (loaded);
maximum speed: 261 mph (420 km/h) at 13,450 ft
(4,100 m); *ceiling:* 24,440 ft (7,450 m); *range:*
2,647 miles (4,260 km); *armament:* 2 × 20 mm
cannon; 4 machine guns; 8,818 lb (4,000 kg) of
bombs; *crew:* 7-10

SIAI-MARCHETTI SM.82 ▶

Nation: Italy; *manufacturer:* SIAI-Marchetti; *type:* transport bomber; *year:* 1940; *engine:* three Alfa Romeo A.R.128 RC 18 14-cylinder radial air-cooled, 860 hp each; *wingspan:* 97 ft 5 in (29.68 m); *length:* 75 ft 4 in (22.95 m); *height:* 19 ft 8 in (6 m); *weight:* 39,340 lb (17,820 kg) (loaded); *maximum speed:* 230 mph (370 km/h); *ceiling:* 19,690 ft (6,000 m); *range:* 1,865 miles (3,000 km); *armament:* 4 machine guns; 8,800 lb (4,000 kg) of bombs; *crew:* 4-5

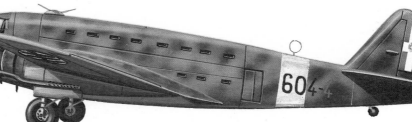

◀ FIAT G.12

Nation: Italy; *manufacturer:* Fiat SA; *type:* transport; *year:* 1941; *engine:* three Fiat A.74 RC 42 14-cylinder radial air-cooled, 800 hp each; *wingspan:* 93 ft 10 in (28.60 m); *length:* 65 ft 11 in (20.10 m); *height:* 16 ft 1 in (4.90 m); *weight:* 33,100 lb (15,000 kg) (loaded); *maximum speed:* 242 mph (390 km/h) at 16,400 ft (4,998 m); *ceiling:* 27,900 ft (8,500 m); *range:* 1,430 miles (2,300 km); *armament:* 2 machine guns; *crew:* 4

DORNIER Do.24

Nation: Germany; *manufacturer:* Dornier Werke GmbH; *type:* transport; *year:* 1941; *engine:* three BMW 323R-2 9-cylinder radial air-cooled, 1,000 hp each; *wingspan:* 88 ft 7 in (27 m); *length:* 72 ft 4 in (22.04 m); *height:* 18 ft 10 in (5.74 m); *weight:* 35,715 lb (16,180 kg) (loaded); *maximum speed:* 206 mph (331 km/h) at 8,530 ft (2,600 m); *ceiling:* 24,605 ft (7,500 m); *range:* 2,920 miles (4,700 km); *armament:* 2 machine guns; 1 × 20 mm cannon; *crew:* 4-5

ARADO Ar. 232

Nation: Germany; *manufacturer:* Arado Flugzeugwerke GmbH; *type:* transport; *year:* 1942; *engine:* two BMW 801MA 14-cylinder radial air-cooled, 1,600 hp each; *wingspan:* 109 ft 11 in (33.50 m); *length:* 77 ft 2 in (23.52 m); *height:* 18 ft 8 in (5.69 m); *weight:* 44,090 lb (20,000 kg) (loaded); *maximum speed:* 191 mph (307 km/h) at 13,120 ft (4,000 m); *ceiling:* 22,640 ft (6,900 m); *range:* 830 miles (1,335 km); *armament:* 3 machine guns; 1 × 20 mm cannon; *crew:* 2-5

KAWASAKI Ki-56

Nation: Japan; *manufacturer:* Kawasaki Kokuki Kogyo KK; *type:* transport; *year:* 1941; *engine:* two Nakajima Ha-25 14-cylinder radial air-cooled, 990 hp each; *wingspan:* 65 ft 6 in (19.96 m); *length:* 48 ft 10½ in (14.90 m); *height:* 11 ft 10 in (3.60 m); *weight:* 17,692 lb (8,025 kg) (loaded); *maximum speed:* 249 mph (400 km/h) at 11,480 ft (3,500 m); *ceiling:* 26,250 ft (8,000 m); *range:* not available; *crew:* 4; *payload:* 5,290 lb (2,400 kg)

▼

TACHIKAWA Ki-54c ▲

Nation: Japan; *manufacturer:* Tachikawa Hikoki KK; *type:* transport; *year:* 1941; *engine:* 2 Hitachi Ha-13a 9-cylinder radial air-cooled, 510 hp each; *wingspan:* 58 ft 9 in (17.90 m); *length:* 39 ft 2 in (11.94 m); *height:* 11 ft 9 in (3.58 m); *weight:* 8,591 lb (3,905 kg) (loaded); *maximum speed:* 234 mph (376 km/h) at 6,560 ft (2,000 m); *ceiling:* 23,555 ft (7,480 m); *range:* 597 miles (960 km); *crew:* 2; *passengers:* 8

Plate 169

American transport planes which helped win the war: 1941–42

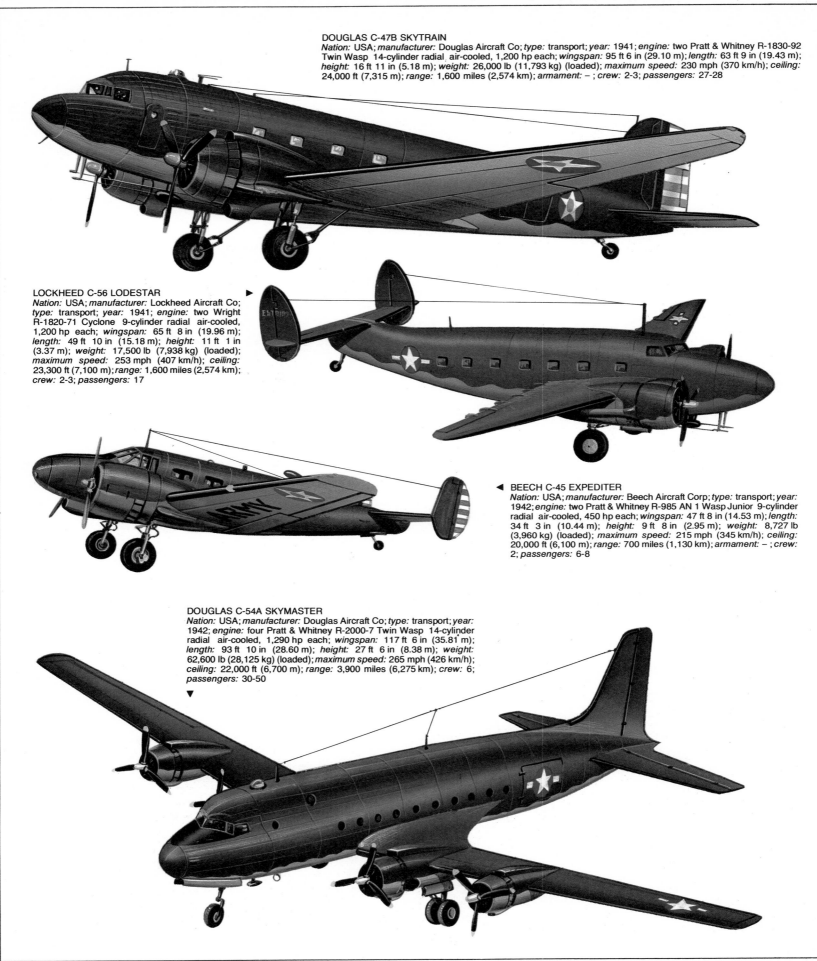

DOUGLAS C-47B SKYTRAIN
Nation: USA; *manufacturer:* Douglas Aircraft Co; *type:* transport; *year:* 1941; *engine:* two Pratt & Whitney R-1830-92 Twin Wasp 14-cylinder radial air-cooled, 1,200 hp each; *wingspan:* 95 ft 6 in (29.10 m); *length:* 63 ft 9 in (19.43 m); *height:* 16 ft 11 in (5.18 m); *weight:* 26,000 lb (11,793 kg) (loaded); *maximum speed:* 230 mph (370 km/h); *ceiling:* 24,000 ft (7,315 m); *range:* 1,600 miles (2,574 km); *armament:* – ; *crew:* 2-3; *passengers:* 27-28

LOCKHEED C-56 LODESTAR
Nation: USA; *manufacturer:* Lockheed Aircraft Co; *type:* transport; *year:* 1941; *engine:* two Wright R-1820-71 Cyclone 9-cylinder radial air-cooled, 1,200 hp each; *wingspan:* 65 ft 8 in (19.96 m); *length:* 49 ft 10 in (15.18 m); *height:* 11 ft 1 in (3.37 m); *weight:* 17,500 lb (7,938 kg) (loaded); *maximum speed:* 253 mph (407 km/h); *ceiling:* 23,300 ft (7,100 m); *range:* 1,600 miles (2,574 km); *crew:* 2-3; *passengers:* 17

BEECH C-45 EXPEDITER
Nation: USA; *manufacturer:* Beech Aircraft Corp; *type:* transport; *year:* 1942; *engine:* two Pratt & Whitney R-985 AN 1 Wasp Junior 9-cylinder radial air-cooled, 450 hp each; *wingspan:* 47 ft 8 in (14.53 m); *length:* 34 ft 3 in (10.44 m); *height:* 9 ft 8 in (2.95 m); *weight:* 8,727 lb (3,960 kg) (loaded); *maximum speed:* 215 mph (345 km/h); *ceiling:* 20,000 ft (6,100 m); *range:* 700 miles (1,130 km); *armament:* – ; *crew:* 2; *passengers:* 6-8

DOUGLAS C-54A SKYMASTER
Nation: USA; *manufacturer:* Douglas Aircraft Co; *type:* transport; *year:* 1942; *engine:* four Pratt & Whitney R-2000-7 Twin Wasp 14-cylinder radial air-cooled, 1,290 hp each; *wingspan:* 117 ft 6 in (35.81 m); *length:* 93 ft 10 in (28.60 m); *height:* 27 ft 6 in (8.38 m); *weight:* 62,600 lb (28,125 kg) (loaded); *maximum speed:* 265 mph (426 km/h); *ceiling:* 22,000 ft (6,700 m); *range:* 3,900 miles (6,275 km); *crew:* 6; *passengers:* 30-50

JUNKERS Ju.290A-1
Nation: Germany; *manufacturer:* Junkers Flugzeug und Motorenwerke AG; *type:* reconnaissance transport; *year:* 1942; *engine:* four BMW 801L 14-cylinder radial air-cooled, 1,600 hp each; *wingspan:* 137 ft 9½ in (42.00 m); *length:* 93 ft 11½ in (28.63 m); *height:* 22 ft 5 in (6.83 m); *weight:* 90,323 lb (40,970 kg) (loaded); *maximum speed:* 273 mph (439 km/h) at 19,030 ft (5,800 m); *ceiling:* 19,685 ft (6,000 m); *range:* 3,820 miles (6,150 km); *armament:* 1 machine gun; 6 × 20 mm cannon; *crew:* 7-9

JUNKERS Ju.352A-1
Nation: Germany; *manufacturer:* Junkers Flugzeug und Motorenwerke AG; *type:* transport; *year:* 1944; *engine:* three BMW 323R-2 9-cylinder radial air-cooled, 1,000 hp each; *wingspan:* 112 ft 3 in (34.21 m); *length:* 80 ft 8½ in (24.60 m); *height:* 18 ft 10 in (5.75 m); *weight:* 43,000 lb (19,510 kg) (loaded); *maximum speed:* 230 mph (370 km/h) at 16,565 ft (5,000 m); *ceiling:* 19,685 ft (6,000 m); *range:* 1,860 miles (2,993 km); *armament:* 1 × 20 mm cannon; *crew:* 3-4 ▶

MITSUBISHI Ki-57-II
Nation: Japan; *manufacturer:* Mitsubishi Jukogyo KK; *type:* transport; *year:* 1942; *engine:* two Mitsubishi Ha-102 14-cylinder radial air-cooled, 1,050 hp each; *wingspan:* 74 ft 2 in (22.60 m); *length:* 52 ft 10 in (16.10 m); *height:* 15 ft 8 in (4.80 m); *weight:* 18,600 lb (8,455 kg) (loaded); *maximum speed:* 292 mph (470 km/h) at 19,090 ft (5,800 m); *ceiling:* 26,250 ft (8,000 m); *range:* 1,865 miles (3,000 km); *crew:* 4; *passengers:* 11 ▶

MESSERSCHMITT Me.323D-1
Nation: Germany; *manufacturer:* Messerschmitt AG; *type:* transport; *year:* 1942; *engine:* six Gnome-Rhône 14N 14-cylinder radial air-cooled, 1,140 hp each; *wingspan:* 180 ft 5 in (55 m); *length:* 93 ft 6 in (28.50 m); *height:* 31 ft 6 in (9.60 m); *weight:* 96,050 lb (43,550 kg) (loaded); *maximum speed:* 144 mph (232 km/h); *ceiling:* 13,120 ft (4,000 m); *range:* 810 miles (1,300 km); *armament:* 7 machine guns; 2 × 20 mm cannon; *crew:* 5-7

Plate 171

The last Allied transports of the war: 1943–44

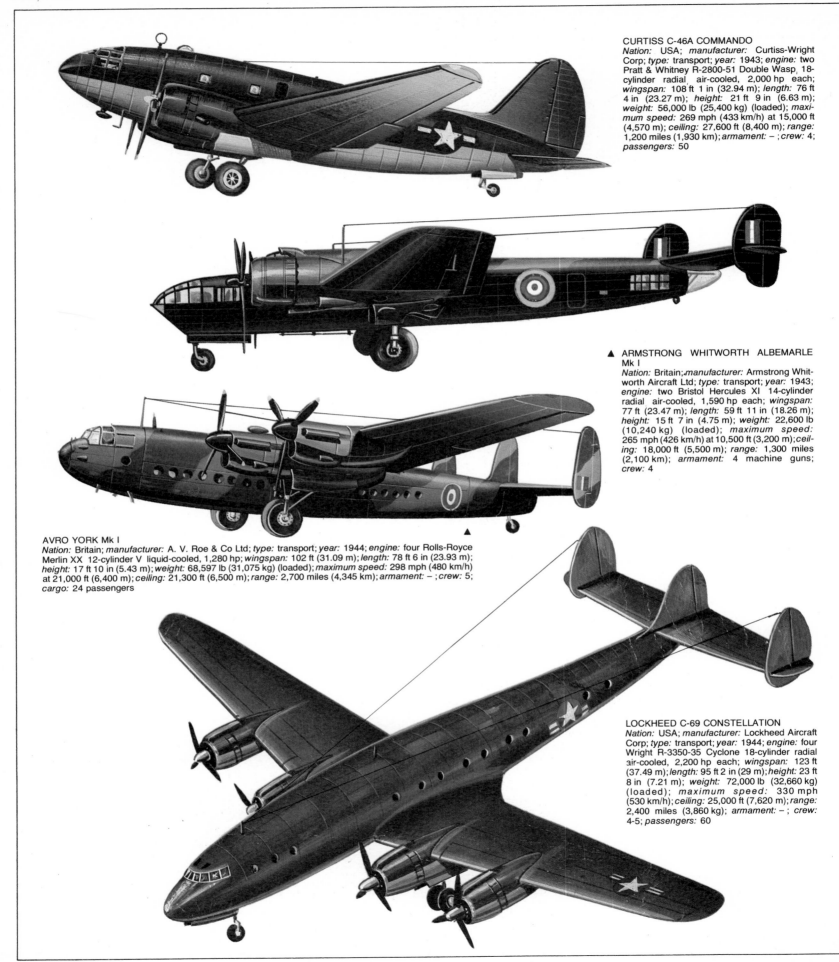

CURTISS C-46A COMMANDO
Nation: USA; *manufacturer:* Curtiss-Wright Corp; *type:* transport; *year:* 1943; *engine:* two Pratt & Whitney R-2800-51 Double Wasp, 18-cylinder radial air-cooled, 2,000 hp each; *wingspan:* 108 ft 1 in (32.94 m); *length:* 76 ft 4 in (23.27 m); *height:* 21 ft 9 in (6.63 m); *weight:* 56,000 lb (25,400 kg) (loaded); *maximum speed:* 269 mph (433 km/h) at 15,000 ft (4,570 m); *ceiling:* 27,600 ft (8,400 m); *range:* 1,200 miles (1,930 km); *armament:* – ; *crew:* 4; *passengers:* 50

▲ **ARMSTRONG WHITWORTH ALBEMARLE Mk I**
Nation: Britain; *manufacturer:* Armstrong Whitworth Aircraft Ltd; *type:* transport; *year:* 1943; *engine:* two Bristol Hercules XI 14-cylinder radial air-cooled, 1,590 hp each; *wingspan:* 77 ft (23.47 m); *length:* 59 ft 11 in (18.26 m); *height:* 15 ft 7 in (4.75 m); *weight:* 22,600 lb (10,240 kg) (loaded); *maximum speed:* 265 mph (426 km/h) at 10,500 ft (3,200 m); *ceiling:* 18,000 ft (5,500 m); *range:* 1,300 miles (2,100 km); *armament:* 4 machine guns; *crew:* 4

AVRO YORK Mk I
Nation: Britain; *manufacturer:* A. V. Roe & Co Ltd; *type:* transport; *year:* 1944; *engine:* four Rolls-Royce Merlin XX 12-cylinder V liquid-cooled, 1,280 hp; *wingspan:* 102 ft (31.09 m); *length:* 78 ft 6 in (23.93 m); *height:* 17 ft 10 in (5.43 m); *weight:* 68,597 lb (31,075 kg) (loaded); *maximum speed:* 298 mph (480 km/h) at 21,000 ft (6,400 m); *ceiling:* 21,300 ft (6,500 m); *range:* 2,700 miles (4,345 km); *armament:* – ; *crew:* 5; *cargo:* 24 passengers

LOCKHEED C-69 CONSTELLATION
Nation: USA; *manufacturer:* Lockheed Aircraft Corp; *type:* transport; *year:* 1944; *engine:* four Wright R-3350-35 Cyclone 18-cylinder radial air-cooled, 2,200 hp each; *wingspan:* 123 ft (37.49 m); *length:* 95 ft 2 in (29 m); *height:* 23 ft 8 in (7.21 m); *weight:* 72,000 lb (32,660 kg) (loaded); *maximum speed:* 330 mph (530 km/h); *ceiling:* 25,000 ft (7,620 m); *range:* 2,400 miles (3,860 km); *armament:* – ; *crew:* 4-5; *passengers:* 60

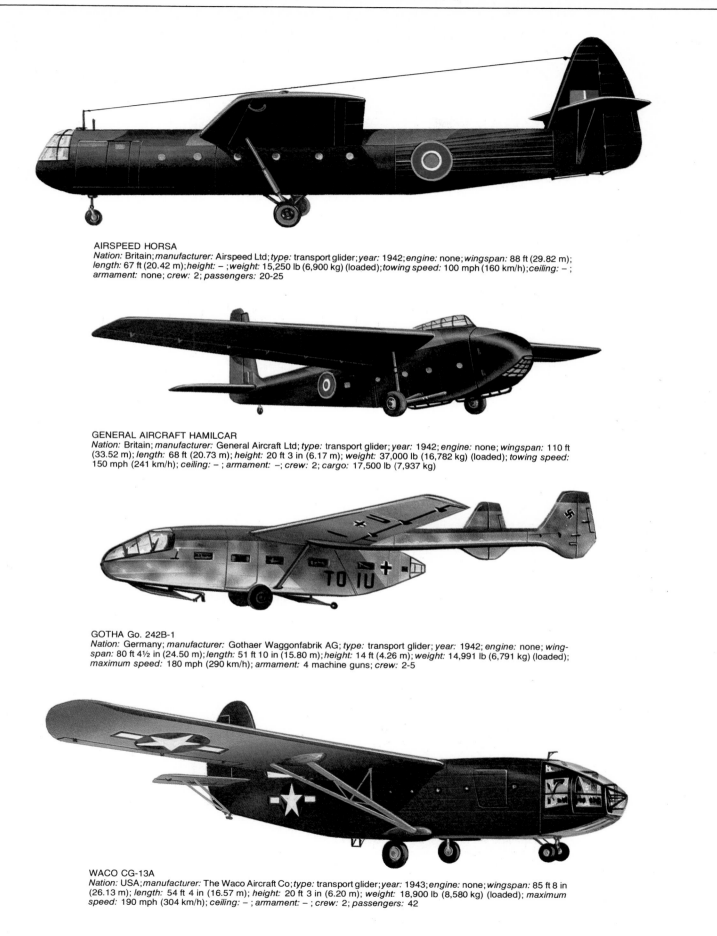

AIRSPEED HORSA
Nation: Britain; *manufacturer:* Airspeed Ltd; *type:* transport glider; *year:* 1942; *engine:* none; *wingspan:* 88 ft (29.82 m); *length:* 67 ft (20.42 m); *height:* – ; *weight:* 15,250 lb (6,900 kg) (loaded); *towing speed:* 100 mph (160 km/h); *ceiling:* – ; *armament:* none; *crew:* 2; *passengers:* 20-25

GENERAL AIRCRAFT HAMILCAR
Nation: Britain; *manufacturer:* General Aircraft Ltd; *type:* transport glider; *year:* 1942; *engine:* none; *wingspan:* 110 ft (33.52 m); *length:* 68 ft (20.73 m); *height:* 20 ft 3 in (6.17 m); *weight:* 37,000 lb (16,782 kg) (loaded); *towing speed:* 150 mph (241 km/h); *ceiling:* – ; *armament:* –; *crew:* 2; *cargo:* 17,500 lb (7,937 kg)

GOTHA Go. 242B-1
Nation: Germany; *manufacturer:* Gothaer Waggonfabrik AG; *type:* transport glider; *year:* 1942; *engine:* none; *wingspan:* 80 ft 4½ in (24.50 m); *length:* 51 ft 10 in (15.80 m); *height:* 14 ft (4.26 m); *weight:* 14,991 lb (6,791 kg) (loaded); *maximum speed:* 180 mph (290 km/h); *armament:* 4 machine guns; *crew:* 2-5

WACO CG-13A
Nation: USA; *manufacturer:* The Waco Aircraft Co; *type:* transport glider; *year:* 1943; *engine:* none; *wingspan:* 85 ft 8 in (26.13 m); *length:* 54 ft 4 in (16.57 m); *height:* 20 ft 3 in (6.20 m); *weight:* 18,900 lb (8,580 kg) (loaded); *maximum speed:* 190 mph (304 km/h); *ceiling:* – ; *armament:* – ; *crew:* 2; *passengers:* 42

Plate 167
The Ju.52 was best among prewar transports: 1934–39

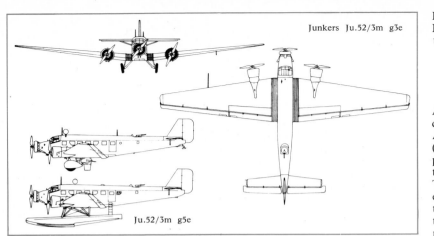

Junkers Ju.52/3m g3e

Ju.52/3m g5e

Plate 168
Italian, German and Japanese transports: 1940–41

Among the major powers the origin of many military transport planes went back to the 1930s, derived more or less directly from the great number of commercial aircraft which were in production at that time during the civil aviation boom. In Britain one of the oldest aircraft of this type was the Bristol Bombay, a twin-engine plane with fixed undercarriage, designed in 1931, but which went into service in 1939. The prototype had flown on 23rd June 1935, and its development had been fairly slow as had been the start of production. About 50 were constructed which were operationally used in secondary roles.

The destiny and the success of a contemporary German aircraft was very different: this was the Junkers Ju.52/3m, designed at the very beginning of 1930 for commercial use with Deutsche Lufthansa. Besides the 200 civil models built between 1932 and 1939, from 1934 onwards the assembly lines produced the first of the many military variants which were to reach a total of 4,835. "Tante Ju" (Auntie Ju), as the aircraft was soon nicknamed affectionately by the *Luftwaffe*, had no substantial alterations made to its

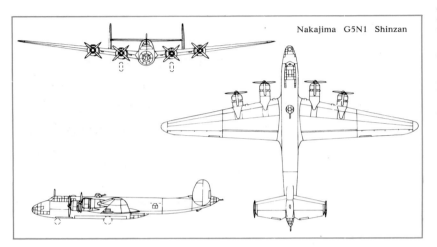

Nakajima G5N1 Shinzan

Another light Japanese transport directly derived from an American Aircraft was the Kawasaki Ki-56 (THALIA in Allied code) which in practice was a licence-built version of the well-known Lockheed 14 Electra. The first two prototypes of this twin-engine appeared in 1940, and showed that they were in general better than the original, mainly due to structural modifications carried out by the Japanese engineers. Series production continued until 1943 and reached a total of 121.

Another versatile Japanese twin-engine plane, constructed between 1940 and 1945, in a total of 1,368 aircraft, was the Tachikawa Ki-54 which in its first two versions (Ki-54a and Ki-54b) was mainly intended for training. The third variant (Ki-54c of 1941) was built for light transport and communications. In Allied code the aircraft was called HICKORY.

In Germany a flying boat transport built in 1935 was used for air-sea rescue, the Dornier Do.24. It appeared as a prototype on 3rd July 1937 and this large and sturdy three-engine flying boat was mainly constructed under licence in the

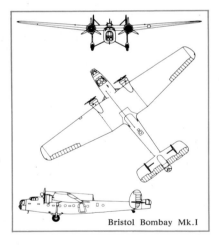

Bristol Bombay Mk.I

original configuration in the course of its long and busy operational career. It was everywhere, on all fronts, and this slow three-engine transport was a real all-purpose aircraft, used not only as a transport but also as an air ambulance, glider tug and for para-dropping, and even as a bomber.

It was as a bomber that the first military version, the Ju.52/3m g3e, went into service with the *Luftwaffe* towards the end of 1934. At the outbreak of war, however, the aircraft was adopted in its original transport role. The most significant production variants were the g5e of 1939, which had more powerful engines and interchangeable wheel/ski/float landing gear; the g7e of 1941, with better instrumentation and increased load capacity; and the g9e of 1942 with even more powerful engines, strengthened landing gear and a glider-towing hook as a standard installation. The g14e of 1943 was the final version which remained in production up to the middle of the following year, with improved armour plating and armament. Immediately after the war the Ju.52/3m was constructed under licence in France by the Ateliers Aéronautiques de Colombes and in Spain by CASA.

In Italy the SIAI Savoia-Marchetti S.M.75 had a similar use, although very much more limited: this was a

three-engine airliner designed in 1937 for the *Ala Littoria*. At the outbreak of war 34 of these aeroplanes were in use with the airlines and were requisitioned and assigned to the units of the *Servizi Aerei Speciali* and to communications centres of the *Regia Aeronautica*. Together with the rest of the production (a total of 90 were built) the S.M. 75 stayed in service until the end of the war, and some remained in service up to 1949.

In Japan the career of a large four-engine aircraft (one of the few which were produced by the Japanese aircraft industry) was completely the other way around: the Nakajima G5N Shinzan was built first as a bomber and subsequently relegated to transport. Designed in 1939, and almost entirely a copy of the American Douglas DC-4E, the Shinzan proved completely unsatisfactory for its intended use. Six were constructed (G5N1) which were called LIZ in the identification code used by the Allies.

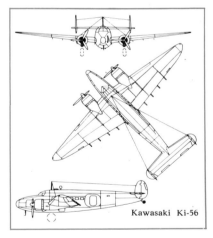

Kawasaki Ki-56

SIAI Marchetti S.M.75

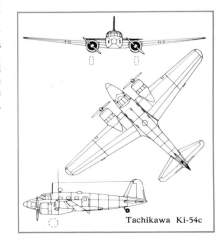

Tachikawa Ki-54c

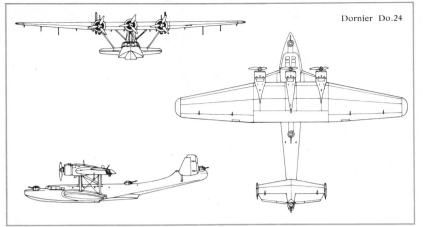
Dornier Do.24

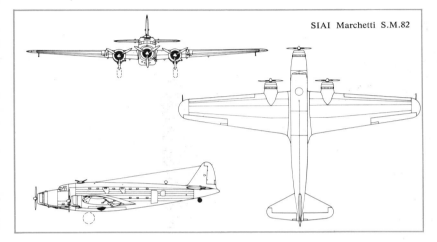
SIAI Marchetti S.M.82

Plate 169
American transport planes which helped to win the war: 1941–42

In the United States the best military transport planes were all derived from civil aircraft. The Lockheed C-56 Lodestar, for instance, was none other than the well-known Model 18, an aircraft which had shown itself, on its appearance in 1940, to be one of the most useful light twin-engine planes of the time. At the outbreak of war with Japan, the aircraft serving with the USAAF were former airline property that had been requisitioned and militarised, and in 1942 these aircraft (which had been designated according to the engines which powered them: the C-56, C-57 and C-59) were joined by a variant which was especially built for military use, designated C-60, of which 325 were built.

Out of a total of over 4,000 B-78s, as many as 1,400 aeroplanes were produced as Beech C-45 Expeditor transports, another light twin-engine plane. The army's interest in this versatile machine crystallised in 1941 with an order for 11 of them. The order was increased in the following year. The transport version was joined by training (AT-7 and AT-11) and photo-reconnaissance (F2) variants.

But the real workhorse of the

USAAF and the Allies was the Douglas C-47 Skytrain, the immortal DC-3, which had revolutionised civil transport in the second half of the 1930s. Over 13,000 of this aircraft were built in all and this immense production included 10,123 aircraft intended for military use. A large batch of 2,000 was built under licence in the USSR and 487 in Japan, as well as the 800 produced before the war for the commercial airlines of the world.

The first orders for a military version of the DC-3 were given in 1940 and the C-47 reached units in the course of the following year. The production variants were numerous, differing from each other in type of engine, cabin arrangement and their load capacity; the principal ones were the C-47B and the C-53 (Skytrooper) designed for the dropping of paratroops and as glider tugs. The twin-engine Douglas served everywhere under the colours of all the Allied air forces. The RAF, in particular, used 2,000 of them, giving them the name of Dakota. After the war the career of the C-47 was just as widespread and busy; the British did not take them out of service until 1970.

Another of Douglas's big successes was the C-54 Skymaster, derived from the four-engine commercial DC-4. This aircraft had been designed in 1935 and perfected in February 1942 with the appearance of the final prototype. The interest of the military was

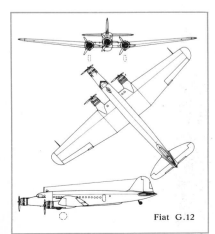
Arado Ar.232

Netherlands (about 170 of them) and in France (about 50). After the German invasion production continued and the aircraft were given to the *Luftwaffe*.

A land-based transport plane intended as a replacement for the Junkers Ju.52/3m, the Arado Ar.232, failed to achieve this. The main feature of the aircraft was its complex landing gear designed in such a way that the plane could be lowered in order to facilitate loading and unloading. The prototype flew in the summer of 1941 powered by two engines, but in production a four-engine variant was preferred (Ar.232B). About 20 of these were built.

In Italy a useful derivant of the S.M.75 was the SIAI Savoia-Marchetti S.M. 82 Marsupiale, which went into service in 1940. This was a robust plane capable of carrying a large load, and 875 of these three-engine machines were built, about half of which were used by the *Luftwaffe*. Fifty of these aircraft survived the war, staying in service with the *Aeronautica Militare* up to 1960.

Another three-engine plane designed in 1939 for commercial use had a similar career, the Fiat G.12. Militarised in 1941, this transport was manufactured in many variants.

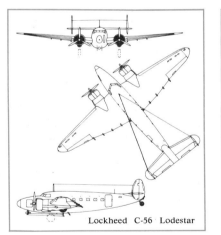
Lockheed C-56 Lodestar

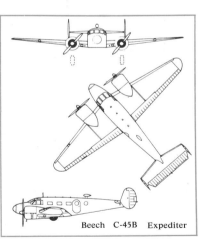
Beech C-45B Expediter

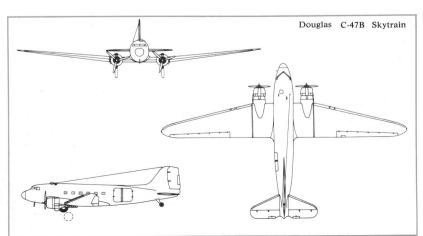
Douglas C-47B Skytrain

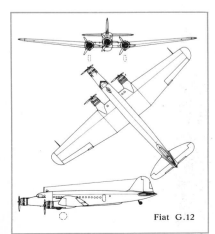
Fiat G.12

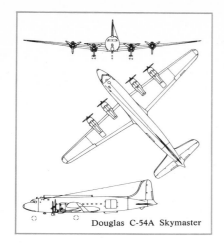
Douglas C-54A Skymaster

military transport) and after a brief trial with transport units of the *Luftwaffe* the 290 was developed for maritime reconnaissance and bombing. In these more demanding roles the aircraft showed that it was completely unsatisfactory and in 1944 those surviving out of the 50 built were once more adapted to their original use.

The prototype Ju.290 flew in August 1942. The principal variants were: the A-1, transport; the A-2, the A-3 and the A-4 for maritime reconnaissance; the A-7 and the A-9 were bombers, while the B-1 was a high-altitude bomber.

Another Junkers design was a failure: the three-engine Ju.352. Apart

from the prototype (which flew on 1st October 1943) and 10 pre-series models, 32 series A-1s were built during 1944. Because of the grave shortage of strategic materials the aircraft was constructed in steel, wood and fabric.

The enormous size which was typical of many German designs in the last years of the war was shared by another German aircraft which was original in other ways: the Messerschmitt Me.323, a monstrous six-engine transport plane which was originally a glider that could perform level flight at altitude after a rocket-assisted take-off. The project derived from the Me.321 glider of 1941 and the first

production series, the Me.323 D-1, appeared in September 1942. Up to April 1944, 198 had been built in several variants. The Me.323 was in service from the end of 1942 onwards and was widely used in the Mediterranean and on the Russian Front; their very large payload was invaluable in supplying troops trapped by the Russian counter-offensive.

immediately awakened with the result that the first airline orders were redirected. Over 1,100 served with the Air Transport Command from 1942 onwards; one of these, nicknamed "Sacred Cow", was President Roosevelt's personal aircraft.

Plate 170
The last German and Japanese transports of the war: 1942–44

A contemporary Japanese twin-engine transport plane also had commercial origins, the Mitsubishi Ki-57, developed in 1939 at the explicit request of the national airline, Dai Nippon Koku KK. The design, however, was immediately taken up by the army which changed the specifications in such a way that the aircraft could carry out military and civil tasks with equal efficiency.

The prototype Ki-57 appeared in July 1940 and the first production series (101 built) went into service with the army, the navy and the civil airline. In 1942 the principal variant was built, the Ki-57-II, which had more powerful engines and replaced its predecessors on the assembly lines up till January 1945, bring the production total to 507. These aircraft served with the Japanese army and with commercial companies. In Allied code they were called TOPSY.

The path followed by the Germans in developing the Junkers Ju.290 was more tortuous. This big, four-engine plane was derived from the Ju.90 of 1936 (which was designed as a bomber but in practice relegated to civil and

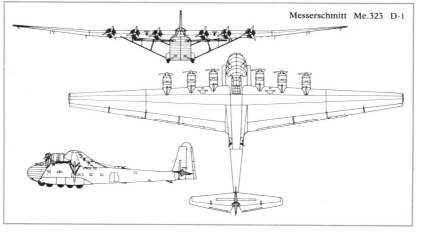
Messerschmitt Me.323 D-1

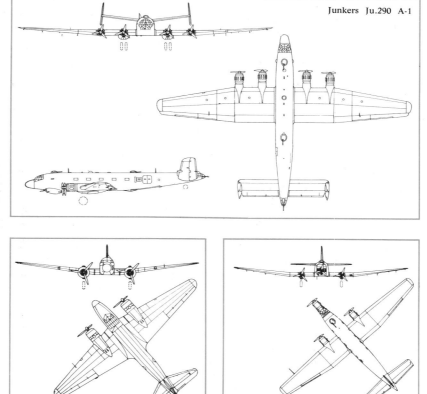
Junkers Ju.290 A-1

Mitsubishi Ki-57-II

Junkers Ju.352 A-1

Plate 171
The last Allied transports of the war: 1933–44

In the second half of the war, transport command of the USAAF was strengthened by two other important aircraft: the Curtiss C-46 Commando and the Lockheed C-69 Constellation. These aircraft had also been designed for commercial use and were now to make their debut in camouflage and military markings. Of the two, only the Constellation managed to make its mark as a major participant in civil aviation after the war; the Commando, however, was used by smaller companies.

The Curtiss C-46 had come into existence in 1937 and was meant to replace the Douglas DC-3 in American airlines. The prototype which flew on 26th March 1940 awakened the immediate interest of the army air force, mainly because of its excellent high altitude performance and its high load capacity. An initial order for 25 (the first of a series of orders which were to bring the total to almost 3,200) was issued immediately and deliveries started in July 1942. 1,491 C-46As and from 1944 onwards 1,410 C-46Ds (modified fuselage) were built. These principal variants were joined by 234 C-46Fs (more powerful engines), 17 C-46Es (one door only in the fuselage), and one C-46G built as a test bed for even more powerful engines. In service the C-46s were mainly used in the Pacific.

Only 22 of the Lockheed C-69 Constellation, however, reached the USAAF before the end of the war. This was destined to make its fortune in the commercial field since the other 51 aircraft ordered served as a basis for production for civil use in the immediate postwar period. The Constellation had been designed in 1939 at the request of Trans World Airlines and the prototype (L-049 in its Lockheed designation) flew on 9th January 1943. The first military version went into service in 1944. These were joined in 1948 and 1951 by militarised versions of the largest and most powerful civil variants built after the end of the war, the L-749 and the L-1049 which took the basic designation of C-121 and stayed in active service well into the 1960s.

In Britain the American aircraft which supplied most of the RAF Transport Command's requirements were joined in 1943 and 1944 by two new British aircraft: the Armstrong Whitworth Albemarle and the Avro York. The first was designed as a reconnaissance bomber and was adapted as a glider tug and for special transport duties (600 built in four production series); the second derived in

1942 from the Lancaster bomber and at first only a few were built; then it was put into mass production in 1944. 257 were built, about 50 of which had a very busy civil career up to the 1950s. In the postwar period the Avro Yorks were used in great numbers for the Berlin airlift.

Plate 172
The best glider transports of the Second World War: 1942–43

Side by side with the traditional transports, much use was made of the glider during the Second World War. These silent aircraft which managed to disgorge men and machines in surprise landings behind enemy lines proved indispensable in operations which needed airborne troops. The British and the Americans especially, in the last years of the war, used great numbers of gliders. The Germans were not far behind.

In the RAF the first of these to be used as an assault glider was the Airspeed Horsa which appeared in 1942 and of which 3,655 were built. It could carry 25 troops with full equipment or an equivalent load of supplies. The Horsa took part in all the principal Allied operations: the landings in Sicily, those in Normandy and in the final offensive on the territory of the Third Reich.

The General Aircraft Hamilcar was much larger and more capacious, and could carry a 7-tonne armoured car. The process of loading and unloading material and men was made easier by the installation of a very large door in the nose forming the entire front part of the fuselage. The Hamilcar prototype appeared on 27th March 1942 and procurement totalled 412. These gliders also took part in all the most important operations of the last two years of the war; they were usually pulled by four-engine aircraft.

The most widely used transport and assault glider of the USAAF was the Waco CG-4A of 1942: as many as 13,909 of these gliders were constructed by a consortium of sixteen manufacturers for the whole duration of the war. The CG-4A became the standard glider of the American air force and many of them were also supplied to the RAF, who called them Hadrian. Waco also built enlarged versions of this aeroplane (none of which met with similar success) such as the CG-13A of 1943, of which only 133 were constructed in spite of its excellent general qualities of high load capacity. The CG-4A was pulled by C-47s or by C-46s whereas the CG-13As needed a four-engine C-54.

Among the best and most extensively used German gliders was the Gotha Go.242 of 1941. It could carry 21 fully armed troops or an equivalent load, and 1,528 of this aircraft were constructed in numerous variants; it was usually pulled by a Ju.52/3m.

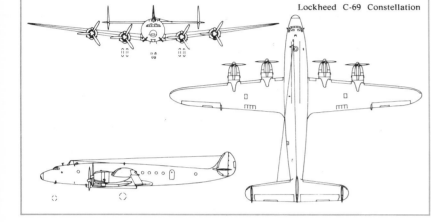
Lockheed C-69 Constellation

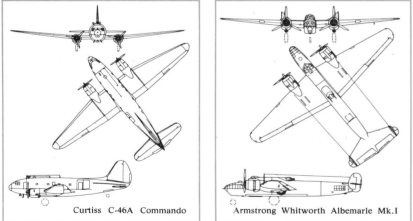
Curtiss C-46A Commando

Armstrong Whitworth Albemarle Mk.I

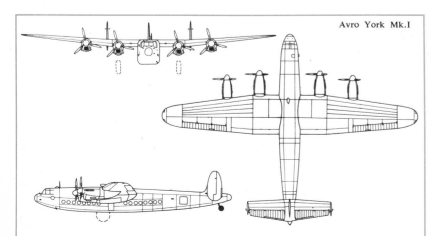
Avro York Mk.I

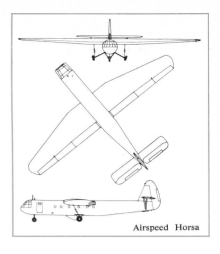
Airspeed Horsa

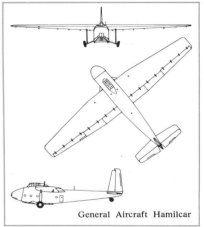
General Aircraft Hamilcar

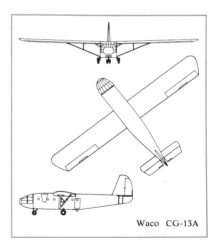
Waco CG-13A

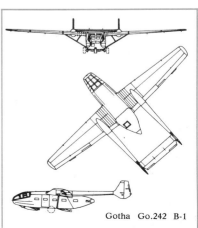
Gotha Go.242 B-1

Plate 173

Engines of the Second World War

BRISTOL MERCURY - 1927 (GB)
A derivant of the Jupiter engine of 1920, the Mercury was a 9-cylinder radial engine with reduction gear. The maximum power which could be sustained for 5 minutes of level flight ranged according to the different variants between 840 hp and 995 hp at 2,750 rpm. Power at take-off however was between 725 hp and 905 hp at 2,650 rpm. The capacity of the engine was 24.9 litres, its diameter 130 cm and the dry weight was 1,066 lb (483.5 kg). Between 1939 and 1945 20,700 Mercury engines were constructed in a number ◄ of variants

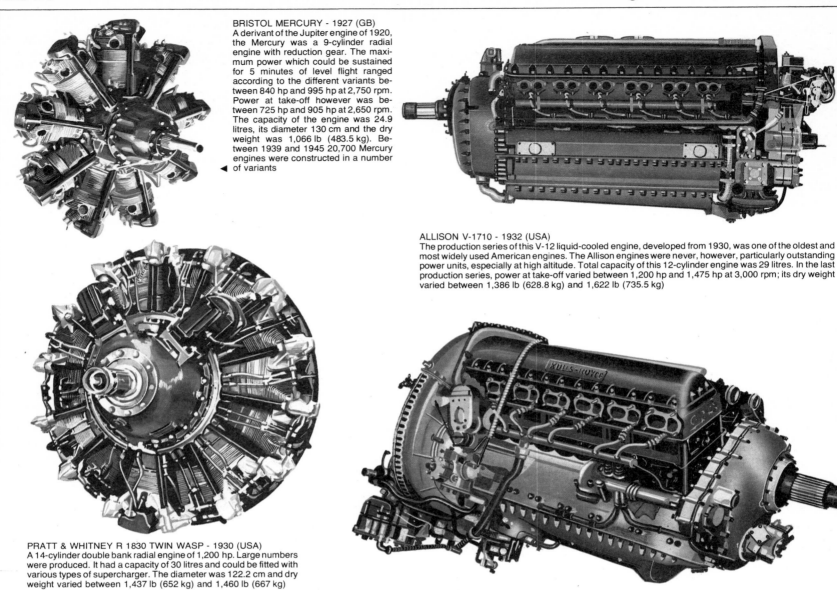

ALLISON V-1710 - 1932 (USA)
The production series of this V-12 liquid-cooled engine, developed from 1930, was one of the oldest and most widely used American engines. The Allison engines were never, however, particularly outstanding power units, especially at high altitude. Total capacity of this 12-cylinder engine was 29 litres. In the last production series, power at take-off varied between 1,200 hp and 1,475 hp at 3,000 rpm; its dry weight varied between 1,386 lb (628.8 kg) and 1,622 lb (735.5 kg)

PRATT & WHITNEY R 1830 TWIN WASP - 1930 (USA)
A 14-cylinder double bank radial engine of 1,200 hp. Large numbers were produced. It had a capacity of 30 litres and could be fitted with various types of supercharger. The diameter was 122.2 cm and dry weight varied between 1,437 lb (652 kg) and 1,460 lb (667 kg)

ROLLS-ROYCE MERLIN - 1936 (GB)
Probably the most famous engine of the war was the Merlin, of which 150,000 were constructed and were used in all the most important British aircraft of the war. It was a 12-cylinder, V-type liquid-cooled engine of 27 litres capacity with a supercharger and weighed between 1,375 lb (624 kg) and 1,650 lb (749 kg). The 1,030 hp of the Merlin was increased to 2,000 hp in the later versions.

BRISTOL HERCULES - 1936 (GB)
During the war 57,500 of these engines were produced in various types. It was a 14-cylinder double-bank radial engine in which power progressed from the initial 1,375 hp to 1,800 hp. Its capacity was 38.7 litres and it was supercharged. Diameter was 132 cm, weight between 1,872 lb (849 kg) and 1,991 lb (903 kg)

NAKAJIMA SAKAE - 1939 (J)
One of the most famous and widely used Japanese engines, which powered the Mitsubishi A6M Reisen, the well-known Zero fighter. The Sakae was a 14-cylinder double-bank radial engine with supercharger and its top performance varied between 1,100 and 1,200 hp. Total capacity was 27.8 litres, diameter 114.4 cm and its weight only just over 1,175 lb (533 kg)

JUNKERS JUMO 211 - 1938 (G)
An inverted V-12 liquid-cooled engine with supercharger and fuel injection. Total capacity was 35 litres, dry weight 640 kg. Many variants were manufactured, and power rose from 950 hp at 2,200 rpm in the type A to 1,500 hp at 2,700 rpm in the Q series.

PRATT & WHITNEY R-2800 DOUBLE WASP - 1939 (USA)
The series R-2800 developed from the earlier Wasp radial engines was one of the most outstanding power units in the 2,000 hp range. The Double Wasp was an 18-cylinder double bank radial engine. Total capacity was 45.9 litres, with supercharger and reduction gear.

BMW 801 - 1940 (G)
The BMW was one of the best radial engines produced by German industry and became famous for its high performance. It was a 14-cylinder double bank radial engine with supercharger and fuel injection. Power increased from 1,600 hp at 2,700 rpm in the earlier series to about 2,300 hp at 2,700 rpm in the latest series. Total capacity was 41.8 litres, diameter varied between 129 cm and 144 cm and dry weight rose from 1,055 kg in the 801 C model to 1,800 kg in the type R.

WRIGHT R-3350 CYCLONE - 1940 (USA)
The R-3350 became one of the best-known engines in the 2,200 hp range. It was an 18-cylinder double bank radial with supercharger and reduction gear. Total capacity was 54.56 litres; diameter 142 cm; dry weight approximately 1,200 kg. Maximum power of 2,200 hp was produced at 2,800 rpm

ROLLS-ROYCE GRIFFON - 1942 (GB)
This was a V-12 liquid-cooled engine, supercharged by a single- or two-stage, two-speed compressor. Total capacity was 36.7 litres, dry weight rose from 816 kg in the early single-stage compressor models to 898 kg in the last models with a two-stage compressor. Power rose from 1,730 hp to 2,300 hp in the last models.
▼

DAIMLER BENZ DB 605 - 1941 (G)
During the war Daimler Benz produced in the greatest numbers German's most widely used aircraft engines; the DB 605 was an inverted V-12 liquid-cooled engine with fuel injection and supercharger. Power was 1,475 hp at 2,800 rpm on take-off. Dry weight was approximately 756 kg. In the last types, power rose to 2,000 hp

Plate 174

Germany	
Poland	
France	
Britain	
Denmark	
Norway	
Belgium	
Netherlands	
Italy	
Yugoslavia	
USSR	
Romania	
Japan	
United States	

These totals are given in approximate form only, as
full documentation is not available for all countries

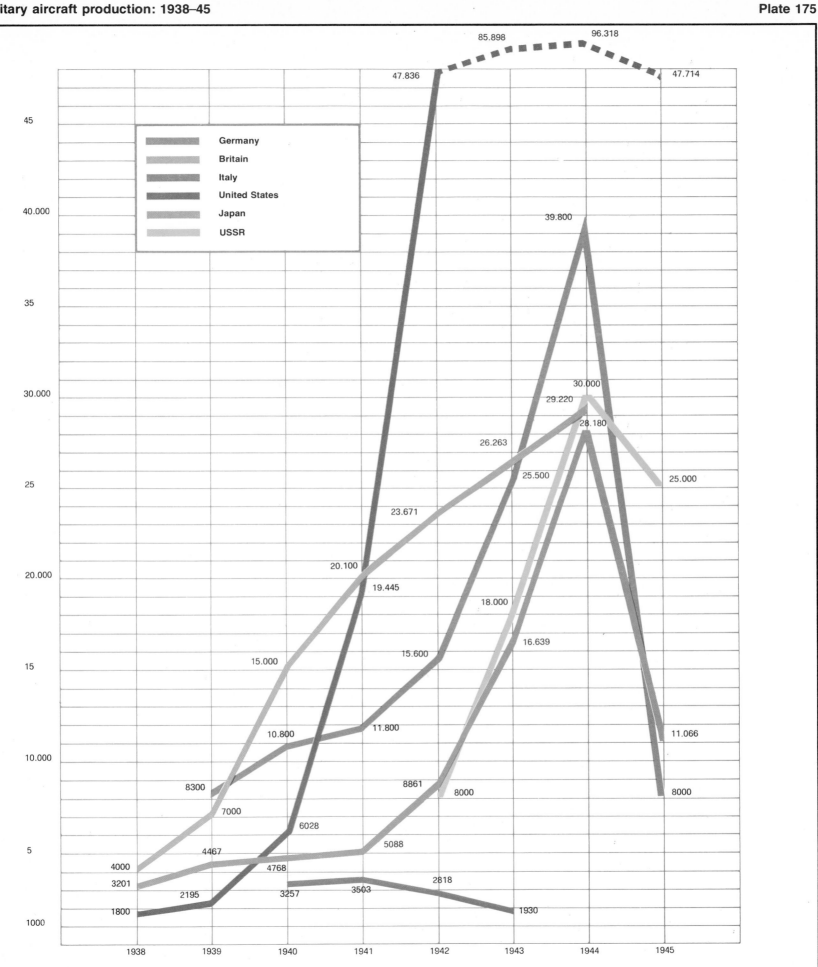

Legend:
- Germany
- Britain
- Italy
- United States
- Japan
- USSR

85.898 96.318

47.836 47.714

39.800

30.000
29.220
28.180
26.263
25.500 25.000

23.671

20.100
19.445
18.000
16.639
15.600
15.000

11.800 11.066
10.800
8300 8861 8000 8000
7000
6028
5088
4467
4000 4768 2818
3201 3503 1930
2195 3257
1800

1938 1939 1940 1941 1942 1943 1944 1945

45
40.000
35
30.000
25
20.000
15
10.000
5
1000

Plate 176

Comparative analysis of speeds of Second World War fighters

Avia B.534 (CS)

Gloster Gladiator Mk.I (GB)

PZL P.24 (PL)

Mitsubishi A5M4 (J)

Fiat C.R.42 (I)

Seversky P-35 (USA)

Fokker D.XXI (NL)

Polikarpov I-16/10 (USSR)

Nakajima Ki-27 (J)

Fiat G.50 (I)

Fokker G-1A (NL)

Morane-Saulnier M.S.406 (F)

Commonwealth CA-12 Boomerang (AUS)

Caudron C.714 (F)

Polikarpov I-17 (USSR)

Kawanishi N1K1 Kyofu (J)

Nakajima Ki-43-Ia (J)

Curtiss P-36C (USA)

Fairey Firefly Mk.I (GB)

I.A.R. 80 (R)

Macchi M.C.200 (I)

Bloch MB-152 (F)

Bristol Beaufighter Mk.IF (GB)

Brewster F2A-3 Buffalo (USA)

Hawker Hurricane Mk.I (GB)

Rogozarski IK-3 (YU)

Dewoitine D.520 (F)

Reggiane Re.2000 (I)

Reggiane Re.2002 (I)

Nakajima Ki-43-IIb (J)

Grumman F4F-3 Wildcat (USA)

Mitsubishi A6M2 Reisen (J)

Messerschmitt Bf.110 C-1 (G)

Kawasaki Ki-45 KAIa Toryu (J)

Messerschmitt Bf.109 E-1 (G)

Lavochkin LaGG-3 (USSR)

Republic P-43A Lancer (USA)

Reggiane Re.2001 (I)

Curtiss P-40B Warhawk (USA)

Kawasaki Ki-100--II (J)

| 1935 |
| 1937 |
| 1938 |
| 1939 |
| 1940 |
| 1941 |
| 1942 |
| 1943 |
| 1944 |
| 1945 |

km/h 300   400   500   600   700   800   900   100

Maximum speed comparison chart (km/h), axis from 300 to 1000:

- Supermarine Spitfire Mk.I (GB)
- Kawasaki Ki-102a (J)
- Kawanishi N1K1-J Shiden (J)
- Yakovlev Yak-1 (USSR)
- Mitsubishi J2M3 Raiden (J)
- Northrop P-61B Black Widow (USA)
- Kawasaki Ki-61-I Hien (J)
- Bell P-39D Airacobra (USA)
- Mikoyan-Gurevich MiG-5 (USSR)
- Yakovlev Yak-9D (USSR)
- Macchi M.C.202 (I)
- Grumman F6F-3 Hellcat (USA)
- Nakajima Ki-44-IIb Shoki (J)
- Curtiss P-40N (USA)
- Focke Wulf Fw.190 A-3 (G)
- Fiat G.55 (I)
- Focke Wulf Fw.190 A-1 (G)
- Mikoyan-Gurevich MiG-1 (USSR)
- North American P-51A Mustang (USA)
- Nakajima Ki-84-Ia Hayate (J)
- Lockheed P-38F Lightning (USA)
- Lavochkin La-5FN (USSR)
- Macchi M.C.205 (I)
- Mikoyan-Gurevich MiG-3 (USSR)
- Bell P-63A Kingcobra (USA)
- Heinkel He.219 A-2/R1 (G)
- Vought F4U-1 Corsair (USA)
- Reggiane Re.2005 (I)
- Lavochkin La-7 (USSR)
- Mikoyan-Gurevich MiG-7 (USSR)
- Republic P-47 Thunderbolt (USA)
- North American P-51D (USA)
- Supermarine Spitfire Mk.XIV (GB)
- Messerschmitt Bf.109 K-4 (G)
- Gloster Meteor Mk.III (GB)
- Heinkel He.162 A-2 (G)
- Messerschmitt Me.262 A-1a (G)
- Messerschmitt Me.163 B-1a (G)

Axis: 300 400 500 600 700 800 900 1000

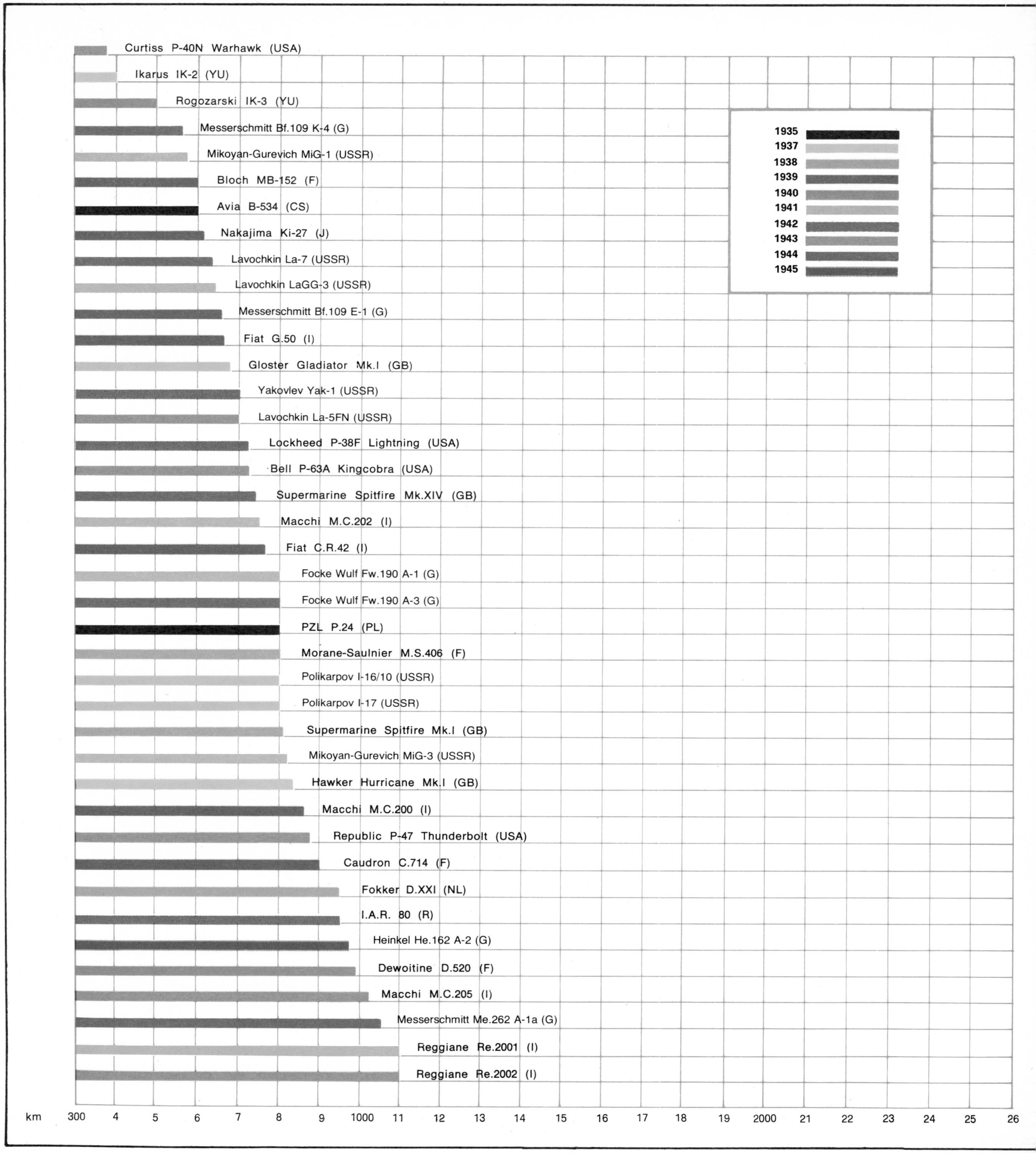

Plate 177

Comparative analysis of ranges of Second World War fighters

Curtiss P-40N Warhawk (USA)

Ikarus IK-2 (YU)

Rogozarski IK-3 (YU)

Messerschmitt Bf.109 K-4 (G)

Mikoyan-Gurevich MiG-1 (USSR)

Bloch MB-152 (F)

Avia B-534 (CS)

Nakajima Ki-27 (J)

Lavochkin La-7 (USSR)

Lavochkin LaGG-3 (USSR)

Messerschmitt Bf.109 E-1 (G)

Fiat G.50 (I)

Gloster Gladiator Mk.I (GB)

Yakovlev Yak-1 (USSR)

Lavochkin La-5FN (USSR)

Lockheed P-38F Lightning (USA)

Bell P-63A Kingcobra (USA)

Supermarine Spitfire Mk.XIV (GB)

Macchi M.C.202 (I)

Fiat C.R.42 (I)

Focke Wulf Fw.190 A-1 (G)

Focke Wulf Fw.190 A-3 (G)

PZL P.24 (PL)

Morane-Saulnier M.S.406 (F)

Polikarpov I-16/10 (USSR)

Polikarpov I-17 (USSR)

Supermarine Spitfire Mk.I (GB)

Mikoyan-Gurevich MiG-3 (USSR)

Hawker Hurricane Mk.I (GB)

Macchi M.C.200 (I)

Republic P-47 Thunderbolt (USA)

Caudron C.714 (F)

Fokker D.XXI (NL)

I.A.R. 80 (R)

Heinkel He.162 A-2 (G)

Dewoitine D.520 (F)

Macchi M.C.205 (I)

Messerschmitt Me.262 A-1a (G)

Reggiane Re.2001 (I)

Reggiane Re.2002 (I)

1935	
1937	
1938	
1939	
1940	
1941	
1942	
1943	
1944	
1945	

km 300 4 5 6 7 8 9 1000 11 12 13 14 15 16 17 18 19 2000 21 22 23 24 25 26

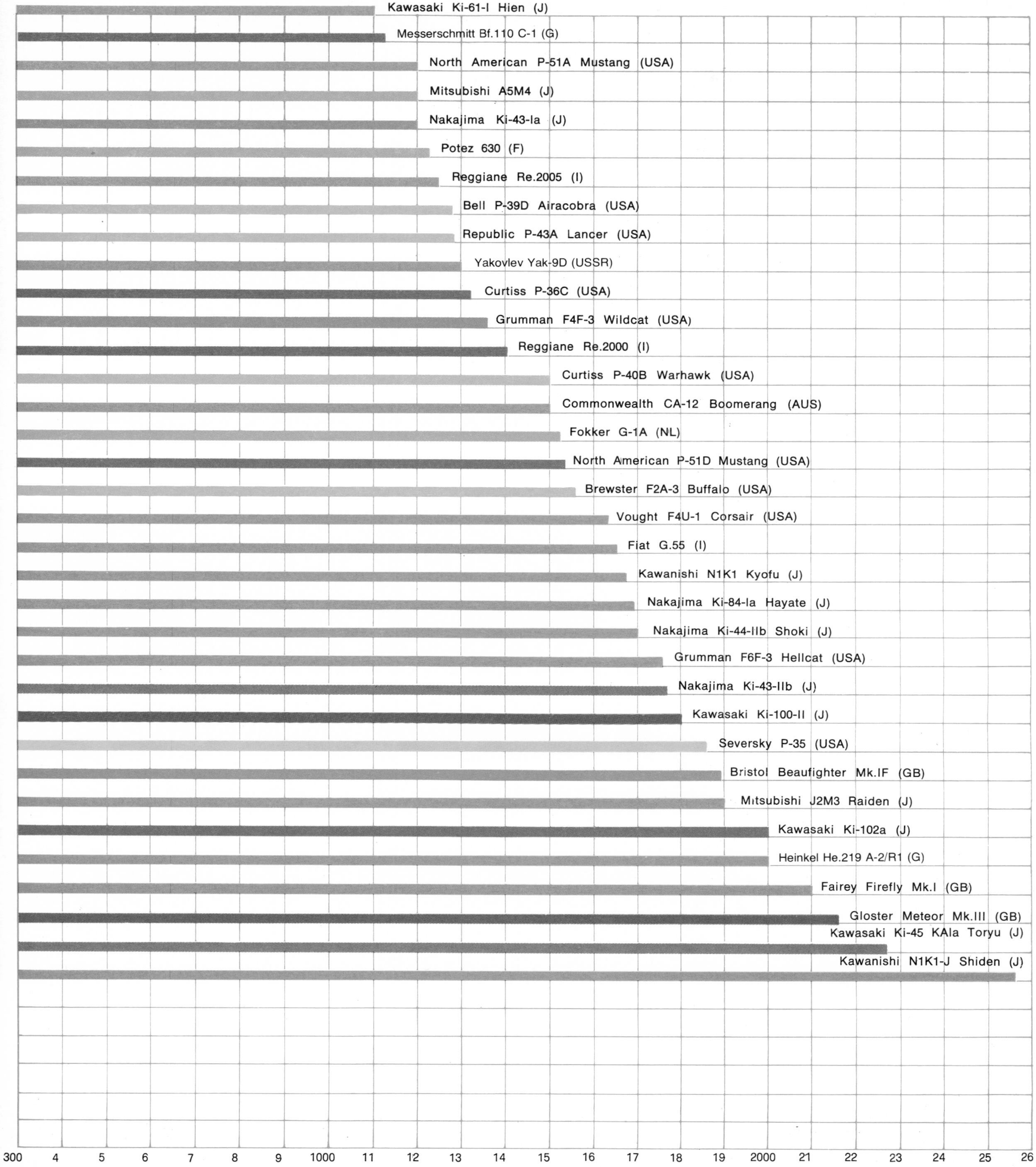

Kawasaki Ki-61-I Hien (J)

Messerschmitt Bf.110 C-1 (G)

North American P-51A Mustang (USA)

Mitsubishi A5M4 (J)

Nakajima Ki-43-Ia (J)

Potez 630 (F)

Reggiane Re.2005 (I)

Bell P-39D Airacobra (USA)

Republic P-43A Lancer (USA)

Yakovlev Yak-9D (USSR)

Curtiss P-36C (USA)

Grumman F4F-3 Wildcat (USA)

Reggiane Re.2000 (I)

Curtiss P-40B Warhawk (USA)

Commonwealth CA-12 Boomerang (AUS)

Fokker G-1A (NL)

North American P-51D Mustang (USA)

Brewster F2A-3 Buffalo (USA)

Vought F4U-1 Corsair (USA)

Fiat G.55 (I)

Kawanishi N1K1 Kyofu (J)

Nakajima Ki-84-Ia Hayate (J)

Nakajima Ki-44-IIb Shoki (J)

Grumman F6F-3 Hellcat (USA)

Nakajima Ki-43-IIb (J)

Kawasaki Ki-100-II (J)

Seversky P-35 (USA)

Bristol Beaufighter Mk.IF (GB)

Mitsubishi J2M3 Raiden (J)

Kawasaki Ki-102a (J)

Heinkel He.219 A-2/R1 (G)

Fairey Firefly Mk.I (GB)

Gloster Meteor Mk.III (GB)

Kawasaki Ki-45 KAIa Toryu (J)

Kawanishi N1K1-J Shiden (J)

300 4 5 6 7 8 9 1000 11 12 13 14 15 16 17 18 19 2000 21 22 23 24 25 26

Plate 178   **Analysis of the armament of Second World War fighters**

2 machine guns	Seversky P-35 - 1937 (USA) Mitsubishi A5M4 - 1938 (J) Nakajima Ki-27 - 1939 (J) Nakajima Ki-43-la Hayabusa - 1940 (J) Fiat C.R.42 - 1939 (I) Fiat G.50 - 1939 (I) Macchi M.C.200 - 1939 (I) Reggiane Re.2000 - 1939 (I) Macchi M.C.202 - 1941 (I)
3 machine guns	Mikoyan-Gurevich MiG-1 - 1940 (USSR) Mikoyan-Gurevich MiG-3 - 1941 (USSR)
4 machine guns	Bloch MB-152 - 1939 (F) Caudron C.714 -1939 (F) Avia B.534 - 1935 (CS) Fokker D.XXI - 1938 (NL) Curtiss P-36C - 1939 (USA) Blackburn Roc - 1940 (GB) Grumman F4F-3 Wildcat - 1940 (USA) Curtiss P-40B Warhawk - 1941 (USA) Brewster F2A-3 Buffalo - 1941 (USA) Republic P-43A Lancer (USA) North American P-51A Mustang - 1943 (USA) Kawasaki Ki-61-I Hien - 1943 (J) Nakajima Ki-44-IIb Shoki - 1943 (J) Polikarpov I-16/10 - 1937 (USSR) Gloster Gladiator Mk.I - 1937 (GB) Reggiane Re.2001 - 1941 (I) Reggiane Re.2002 - 1943 (I) Mikoyan-Gurevich MiG-5 - 1943 (USSR) Kawasaki Ki-61-I Hien - 1943 (J)
6 machine guns	Curtiss P-40N - 1943 (USA) North American P-51D Mustang - 1944 (USA) Vought F4U-1 Corsair - 1943 (USA) Grumman F6F-3 Hellcat - 1943 (USA)
8 machine guns	Hawker Hurricane Mk.I - 1937 (GB) Supermarine Spitfire Mk.I - 1938 (GB) Fairey Fulmar Mk.I - 1940 (GB) Republic P-47 Thunderbolt - 1943 (USA)
9 machine guns	Fokker G.1A - 1938 (NL)
1 × 20 mm cannon + 1 machine gun	Yakovlev Yak-9D - 1943 (USSR)
1 × 20 mm cannon + 2 machine guns	Morane-Saulnier M.S.406 - 1938 (F) Ikarus IK-2 - 1937 (YU) Rogozarski IK-3 - 1940 (YU) Polikarpov I-17 - 1937 (USSR) Yakovlev Yak-1 - 1942 (USSR) Mikoyan-Gurevich MiG-7 - 1944 (USSR)
1 × 20 mm cannon + 3 machine guns	Lavochkin LaGG-3 - 1941 (USSR) Kawasaki Ki-45 KAIa Toryu - 1942 (J)
1 × 20 mm cannon + 4 machine guns	Dewoitine D.520 - 1940 (F) Lockheed P-38 Lightning - 1942 (USA)

1 × 37 mm cannon + 4 machine guns	Bell P-39Q Airacobra - 1943 (USA) Bell P-63A Kingcobra - 1943 (USA)
1 × 37 mm cannon + 6 machine guns	Bell P-39D Airacobra - 1941 (USA)
2 × 20 mm cannon	Lavochkin La-5FN - 1943 (USSR) Messerschmitt Me.163 B-1a - 1944 (G) Heinkel He.162 A-2 - 1945 (G)
2 × 20 mm cannon + 1 machine gun	Potez 630 -1938(F)
2 × 20 mm cannon + 2 machine guns	PZL P.24 - 1935 (PL) Mitsubishi A6M2 Reisen - 1940 (J) Nakajima Ki-84-Ia Hayate - 1943 (J) Kawanishi N1K1 Kyofu - 1943 (J) Kawasaki Ki-100-II - 1945 (J) Messerschmitt Bf.109 E-1 - 1939 (G) Macchi M.C.205 - 1943 (I)
2 × 20 mm cannon + 4 machine guns	I.A.R. 80 - 1942 (R) Supermarine Spitfire Mk.XIV - 1944 (GB) Focke Wulf Fw.190 A-1 - 1941 (G)
2 × 20 mm cannon + 5 machine guns	Messerschmitt Bf.110 C-1 - 1939 (G)
1 × 30 mm cannon + 2 × 15 mm cannon	Messerschmitt Bf.109 K-4 - 1939 (G)
1 × 37 mm cannon + 2 × 20 mm cannon	Kawasaki Ki-102a - 1944 (J)
3 × 20 mm cannon	Lavochkin La-7 - 1944 (USSR)
3 × 20 mm cannon + 2 machine guns	Fiat G.55 - 1943 (I) Reggiane Re.2005 - 1943 (I)
4 × 20 mm cannon	Mitsubishi J2M3 Raiden - 1943 (J) Fairey Firefly Mk.I - 1943 (GB) Gloster Meteor Mk.III - 1945 (GB)
4 × 20 mm cannon + 2 machine guns	Focke Wulf Fw.190 A-3 - 1942 (G) Kawanishi N1K1-J Shiden - 1943 (J)
4 × 20 mm cannon + 4 machine guns	Northrop P-61B Black Widow - 1944 (USA)
4 × 20 mm cannon + 6 machine guns	Bristol Beaufighter Mk.IF - 1940 (GB)
4 × 30 mm cannon	Messerschmitt Me.262 A-1a - 1944 (G)
6 × 20 mm cannon	Heinkel He.219 A-2/R1 - 1943 (G)

Plate 179

Comparative analysis of ranges and bomb-loads of Second World War bombers

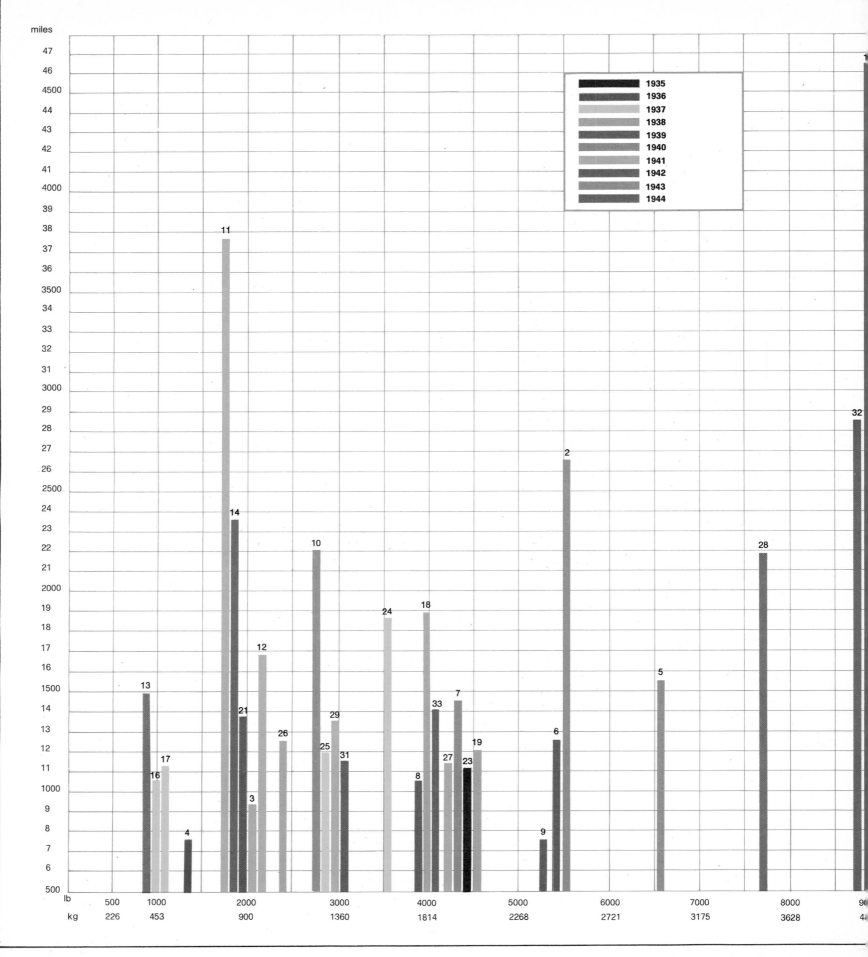

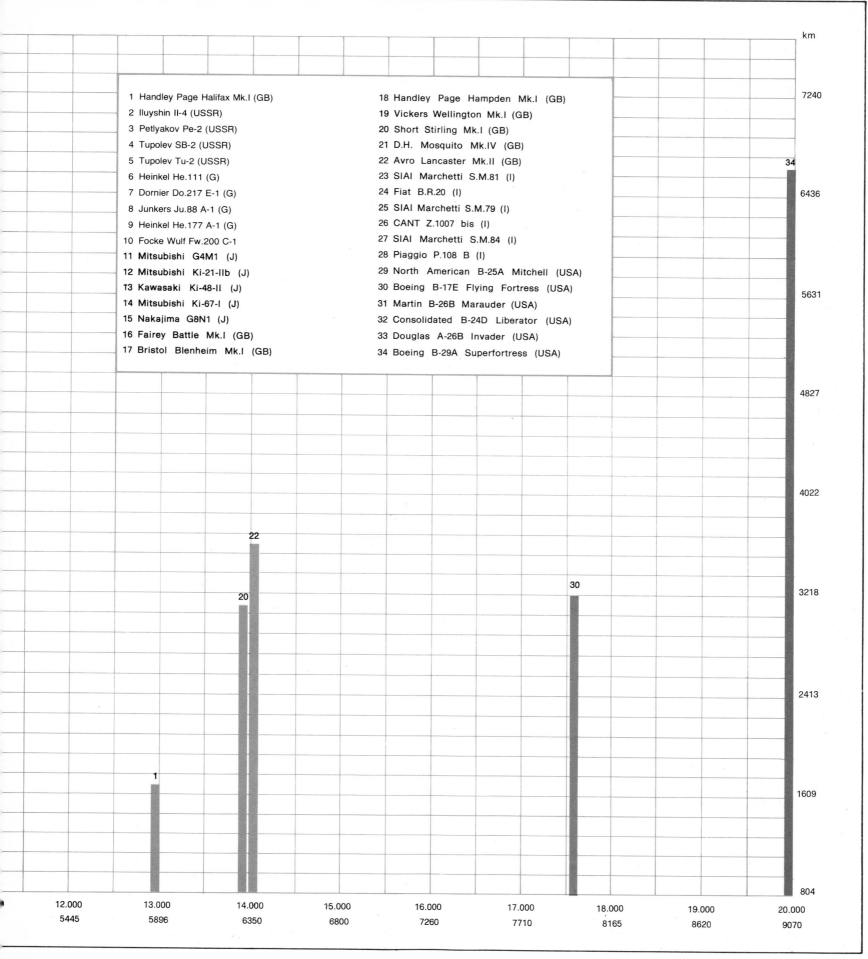

km

7240

6436

5631

4827

4022

3218

2413

1609

804

1 Handley Page Halifax Mk.I (GB)
2 Iluyshin Il-4 (USSR)
3 Petlyakov Pe-2 (USSR)
4 Tupolev SB-2 (USSR)
5 Tupolev Tu-2 (USSR)
6 Heinkel He.111 (G)
7 Dornier Do.217 E-1 (G)
8 Junkers Ju.88 A-1 (G)
9 Heinkel He.177 A-1 (G)
10 Focke Wulf Fw.200 C-1
11 Mitsubishi G4M1 (J)
12 Mitsubishi Ki-21-IIb (J)
13 Kawasaki Ki-48-II (J)
14 Mitsubishi Ki-67-I (J)
15 Nakajima G8N1 (J)
16 Fairey Battle Mk.I (GB)
17 Bristol Blenheim Mk.I (GB)

18 Handley Page Hampden Mk.I (GB)
19 Vickers Wellington Mk.I (GB)
20 Short Stirling Mk.I (GB)
21 D.H. Mosquito Mk.IV (GB)
22 Avro Lancaster Mk.II (GB)
23 SIAI Marchetti S.M.81 (I)
24 Fiat B.R.20 (I)
25 SIAI Marchetti S.M.79 (I)
26 CANT Z.1007 bis (I)
27 SIAI Marchetti S.M.84 (I)
28 Piaggio P.108 B (I)
29 North American B-25A Mitchell (USA)
30 Boeing B-17E Flying Fortress (USA)
31 Martin B-26B Marauder (USA)
32 Consolidated B-24D Liberator (USA)
33 Douglas A-26B Invader (USA)
34 Boeing B-29A Superfortress (USA)

12.000
5445

13.000
5896

14.000
6350

15.000
6800

16.000
7260

17.000
7710

18.000
8165

19.000
8620

20.000
9070

Plate 180

Allied bombing of Germany from 1939 to 1945

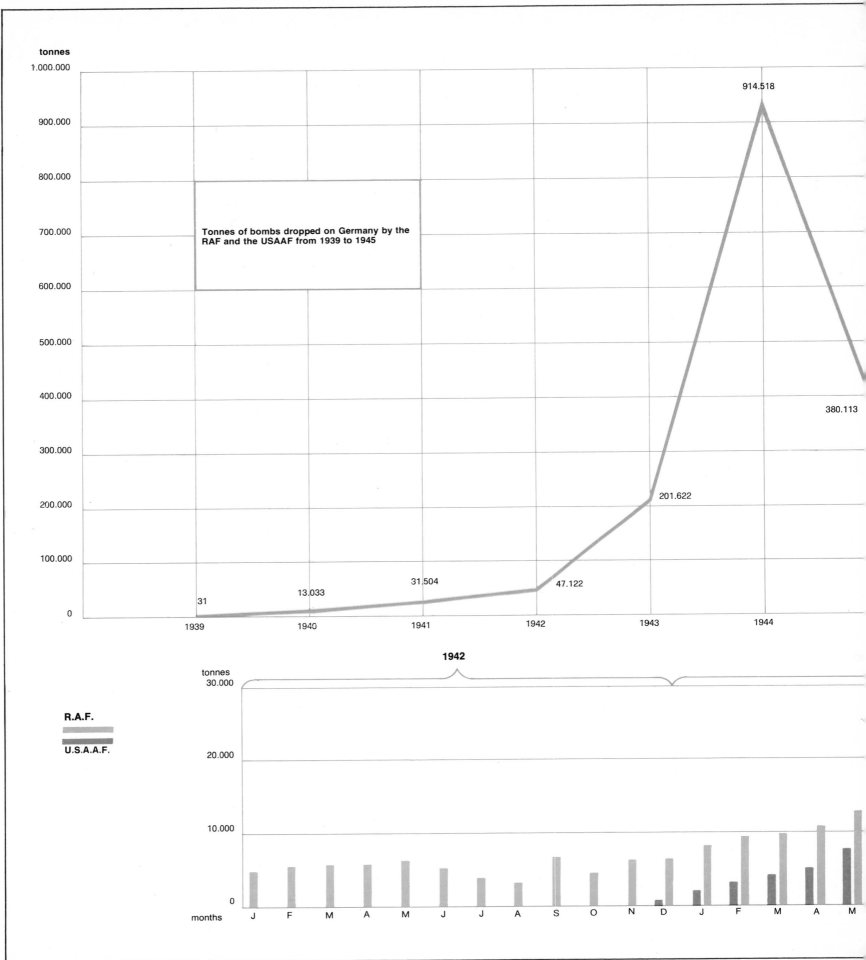

tonnes

1.000.000

Tonnes of bombs dropped on Germany by the
RAF and the USAAF from 1939 to 1945

914.518

900.000

800.000

700.000

600.000

500.000

400.000

380.113

300.000

201.622

200.000

100.000

31.504

47.122

13.033

31

0

1939   1940   1941   1942   1943   1944

1942

tonnes
30.000

R.A.F.

U.S.A.A.F.

20.000

10.000

0

months   J   F   M   A   M   J   J   A   S   O   N   D   J   F   M   A   M

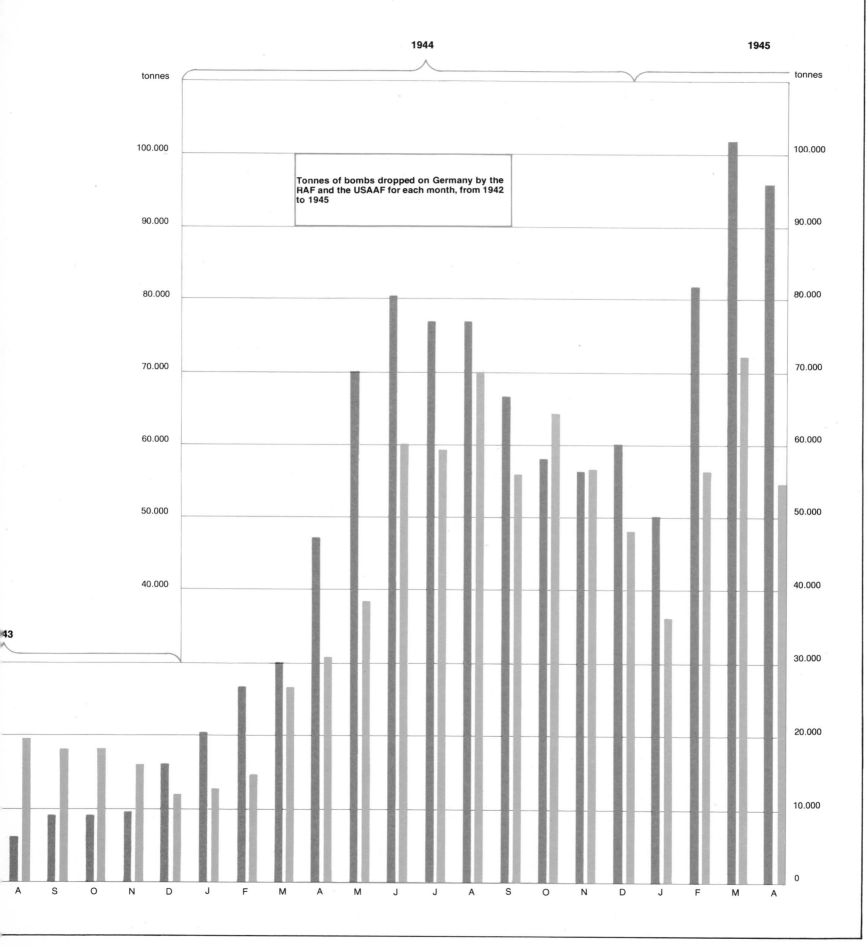

1944

1945

tonnes

tonnes

Tonnes of bombs dropped on Germany by the
RAF and the USAAF for each month, from 1942
to 1945

43

A S O N D J F M A M J J A S O N D J F M A

371

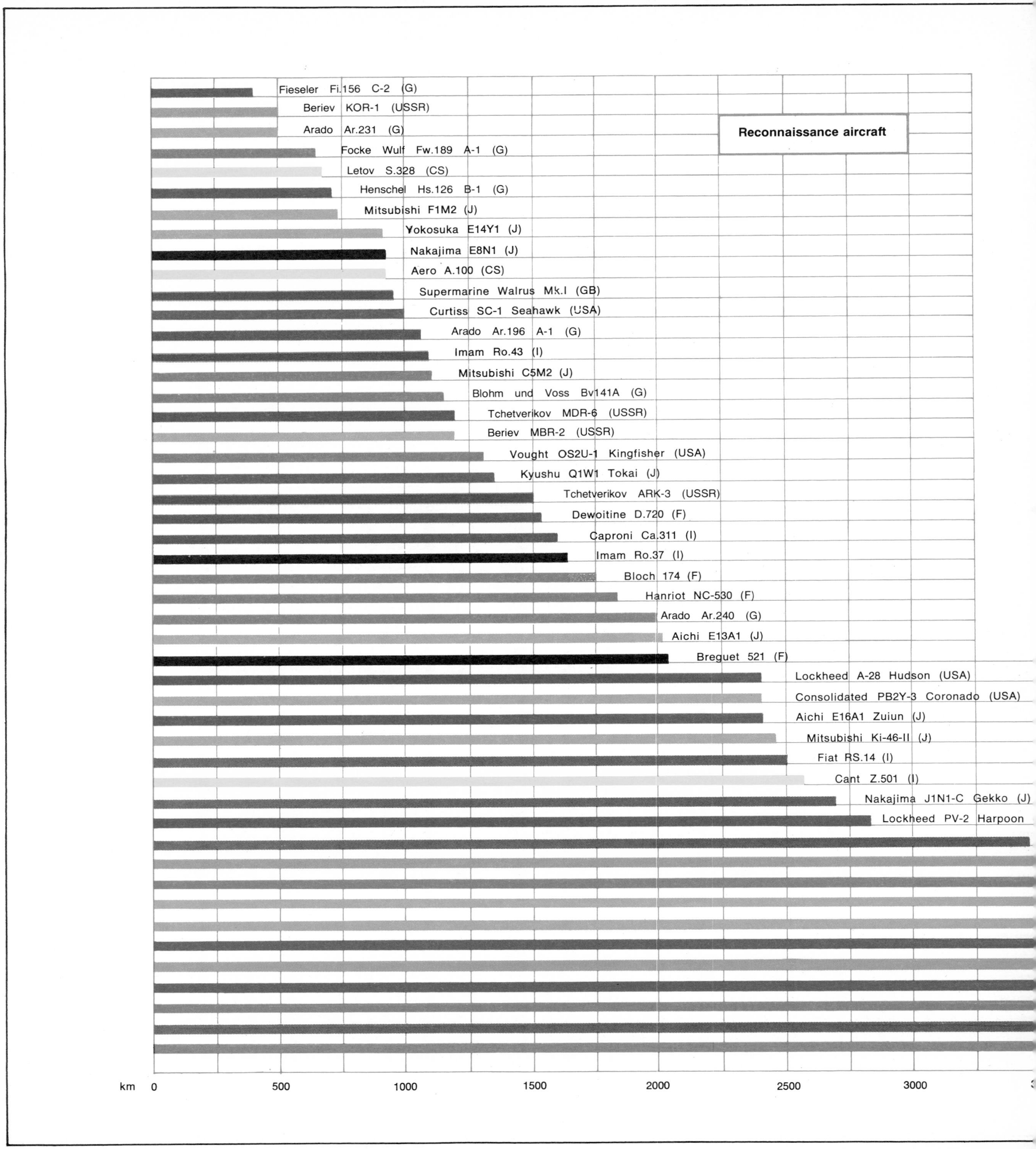

Fieseler Fi.156 C-2 (G)

Beriev KOR-1 (USSR)

Arado Ar.231 (G)

Focke Wulf Fw.189 A-1 (G)

Letov S.328 (CS)

Henschel Hs.126 B-1 (G)

Mitsubishi F1M2 (J)

Yokosuka E14Y1 (J)

Nakajima E8N1 (J)

Aero A.100 (CS)

Supermarine Walrus Mk.I (GB)

Curtiss SC-1 Seahawk (USA)

Arado Ar.196 A-1 (G)

Imam Ro.43 (I)

Mitsubishi C5M2 (J)

Blohm und Voss Bv141A (G)

Tchetverikov MDR-6 (USSR)

Beriev MBR-2 (USSR)

Vought OS2U-1 Kingfisher (USA)

Kyushu Q1W1 Tokai (J)

Tchetverikov ARK-3 (USSR)

Dewoitine D.720 (F)

Caproni Ca.311 (I)

Imam Ro.37 (I)

Bloch 174 (F)

Hanriot NC-530 (F)

Arado Ar.240 (G)

Aichi E13A1 (J)

Breguet 521 (F)

Lockheed A-28 Hudson (USA)

Consolidated PB2Y-3 Coronado (USA)

Aichi E16A1 Zuiun (J)

Mitsubishi Ki-46-II (J)

Fiat RS.14 (I)

Cant Z.501 (I)

Nakajima J1N1-C Gekko (J)

Lockheed PV-2 Harpoon

Reconnaissance aircraft

km   0   500   1000   1500   2000   2500   3000

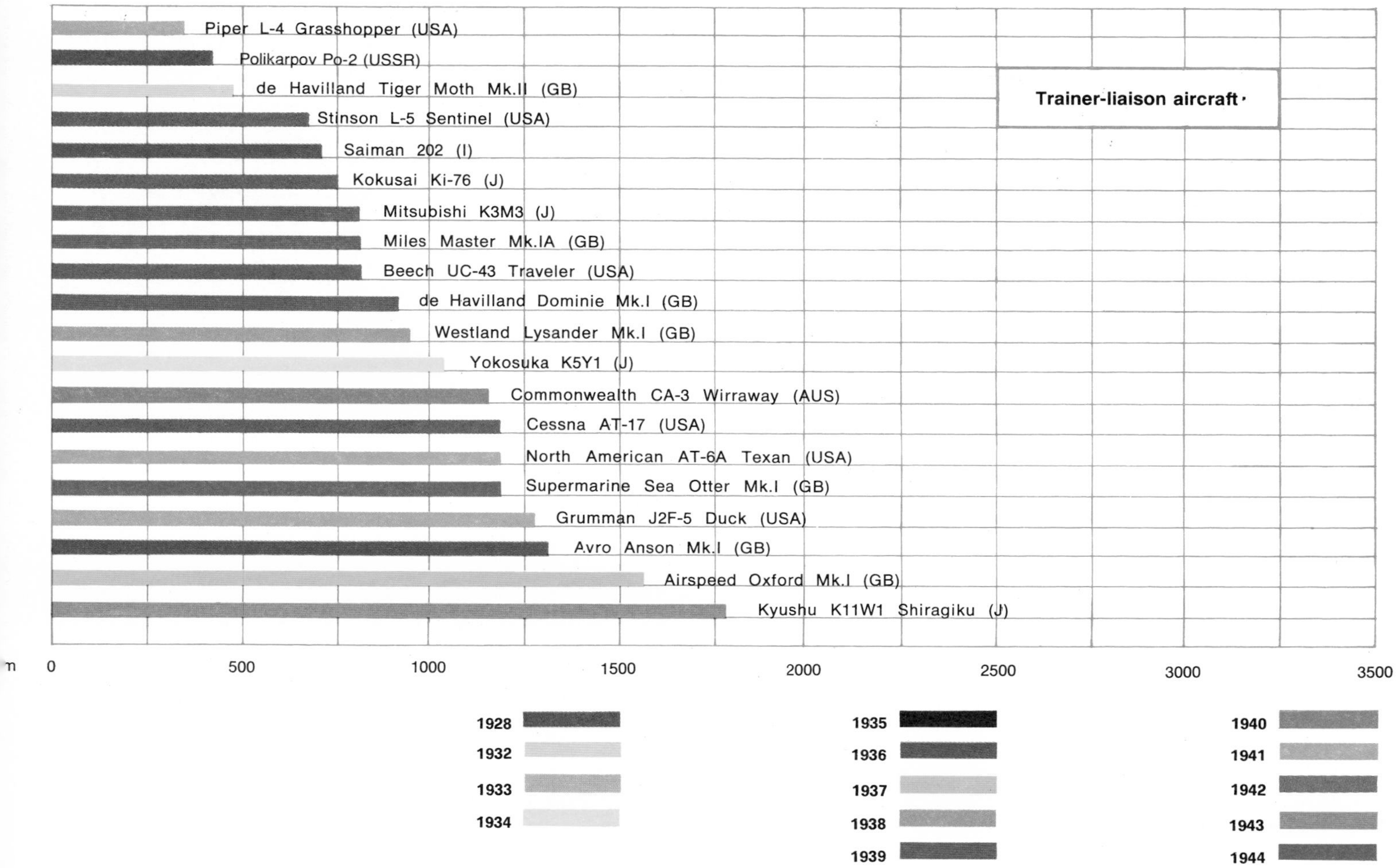

Trainer-liaison aircraft

Piper L-4 Grasshopper (USA)
Polikarpov Po-2 (USSR)
de Havilland Tiger Moth Mk.II (GB)
Stinson L-5 Sentinel (USA)
Saiman 202 (I)
Kokusai Ki-76 (J)
Mitsubishi K3M3 (J)
Miles Master Mk.IA (GB)
Beech UC-43 Traveler (USA)
de Havilland Dominie Mk.I (GB)
Westland Lysander Mk.I (GB)
Yokosuka K5Y1 (J)
Commonwealth CA-3 Wirraway (AUS)
Cessna AT-17 (USA)
North American AT-6A Texan (USA)
Supermarine Sea Otter Mk.I (GB)
Grumman J2F-5 Duck (USA)
Avro Anson Mk.I (GB)
Airspeed Oxford Mk.I (GB)
Kyushu K11W1 Shiragiku (J)

m   0   500   1000   1500   2000   2500   3000   3500

1928	1935	1940
1932	1936	1941
1933	1937	1942
1934	1938	1943
	1939	1944

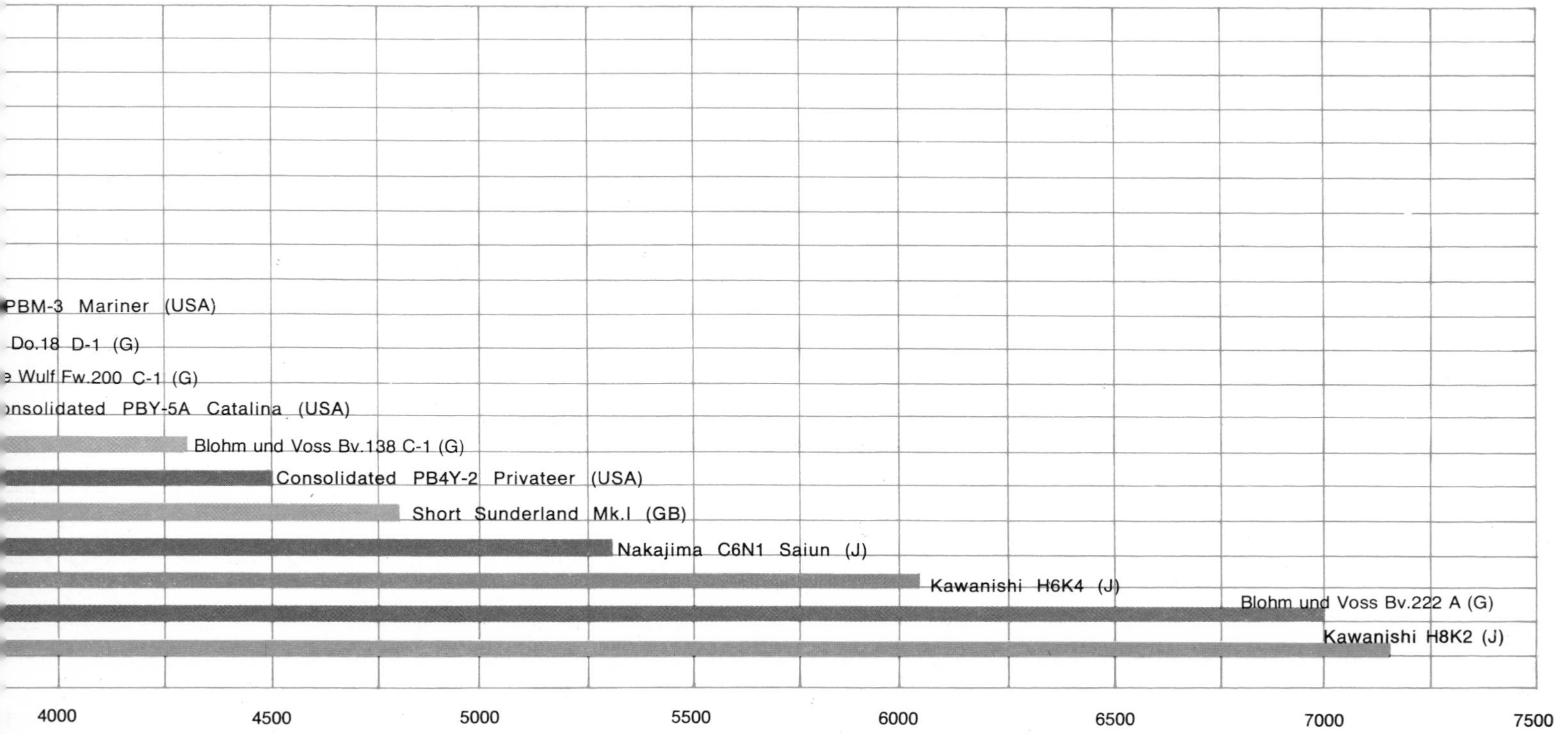

PBM-3 Mariner (USA)
Do.18 D-1 (G)
Focke Wulf Fw.200 C-1 (G)
Consolidated PBY-5A Catalina (USA)
Blohm und Voss Bv.138 C-1 (G)
Consolidated PB4Y-2 Privateer (USA)
Short Sunderland Mk.I (GB)
Nakajima C6N1 Saiun (J)
Kawanishi H6K4 (J)
Blohm und Voss Bv.222 A (G)
Kawanishi H8K2 (J)

4000   4500   5000   5500   6000   6500   7000   7500

Plate 182

Ranges and payloads of Second World War transports

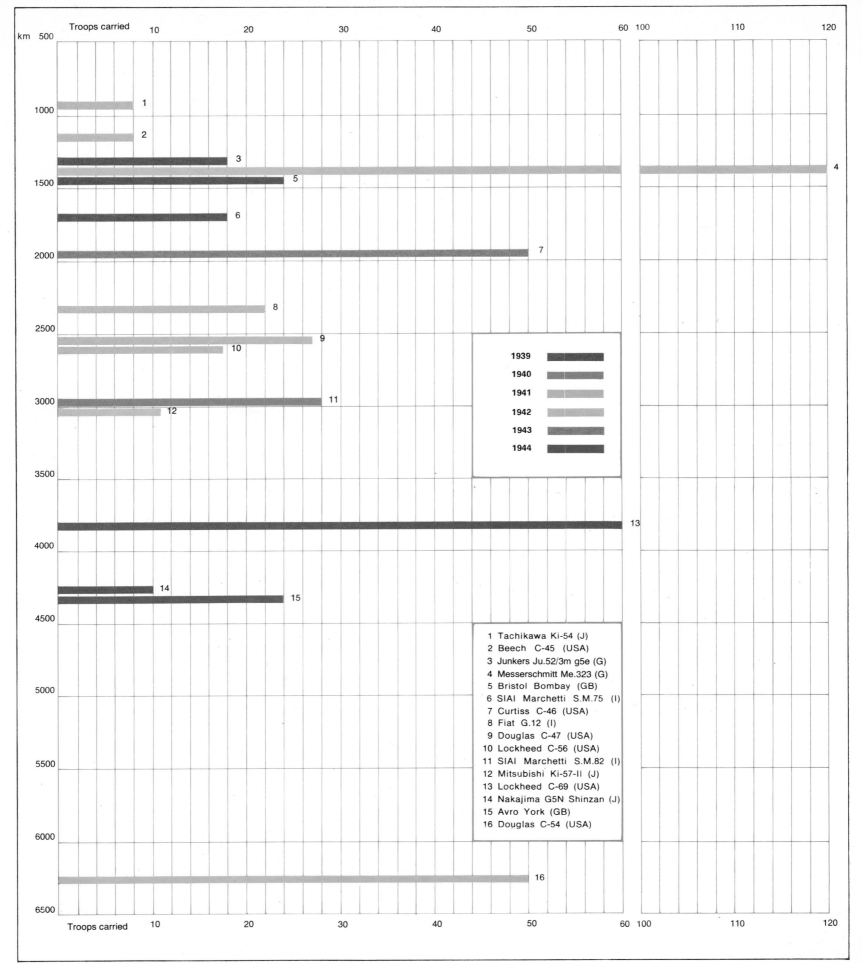

Troops carried

1 Tachikawa Ki-54 (J)
2 Beech C-45 (USA)
3 Junkers Ju.52/3m g5e (G)
4 Messerschmitt Me.323 (G)
5 Bristol Bombay (GB)
6 SIAI Marchetti S.M.75 (I)
7 Curtiss C-46 (USA)
8 Fiat G.12 (I)
9 Douglas C-47 (USA)
10 Lockheed C-56 (USA)
11 SIAI Marchetti S.M.82 (I)
12 Mitsubishi Ki-57-II (J)
13 Lockheed C-69 (USA)
14 Nakajima G5N Shinzan (J)
15 Avro York (GB)
16 Douglas C-54 (USA)

1939
1940
1941
1942
1943
1944

Fairey Swordfish-1936, GB (plate 139)

Gloster Gladiator-1937, GB (plate 81)

Vickers Wellesley-1937, GB (plate 120)

Westland Lysander-1938, GB (plate 162)

Vickers Wellington-1938, GB (plate 124)

de Havilland Tiger Moth-1938, GB (plate 159)

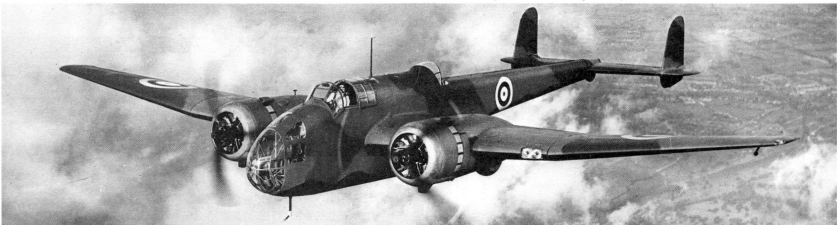
Handley Page Hampden-1938, GB (plate 124)

Short Sunderland-1938, GB (plate 147) & Short Stirling-1940, GB (plate 124)

Supermarine Spitfire-1940, GB (plate 84)

Bristol Beaufighter-1940, GB (plate 89)

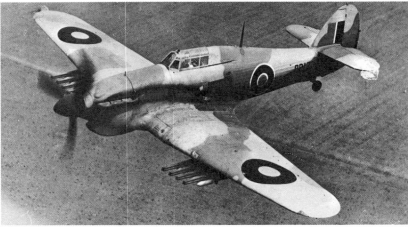

Hawker Hurricane-1941, GB (plate 83)

de Havilland Mosquito-1941, GB (plate 153)

Hawker Typhoon-1941, GB (plate 112)

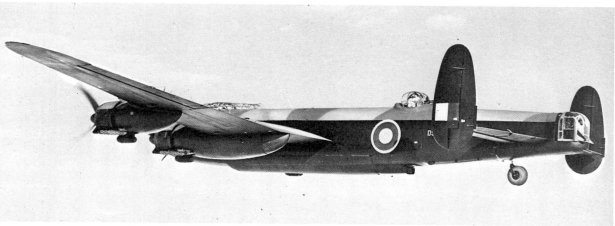

Avro Lancaster-1942, GB (plate 129)

Armstrong Whitworth Albemarle-1943, GB (plate 171)

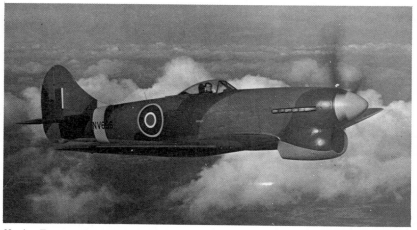

Hawker Tempest-1944, GB (plate 112)

Bloch 210-1935, F (plate 119)

Dewoitine D.520-1943, F (plate 88)

Photographic appendix

Morane-Saulnier M.S.406-1938, F (plate 79)

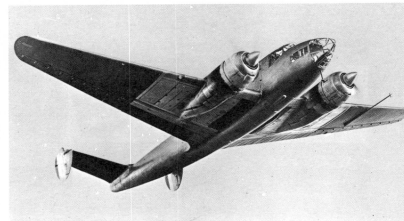

Lioré et Olivier LeO.45-1939, F (plate 121)

Potez 63-1940, F (plate 79)

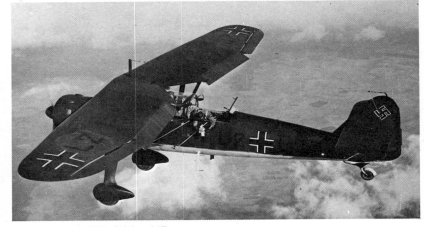

Junkers Ju.52-1934, G (plate 167)

Junkers Ju.87 B-1-1938, G (plate 137)

Henschel Hs.126-1939, G (plate 148)

Heinkel He.111-1939, G (plate 118)

Messerschmitt Bf.110-1939, G (plate 86)

Fieseler Fi.156-1939, G (plate 148)

Focke Wulf Fw.189-1940, G (plate 149)

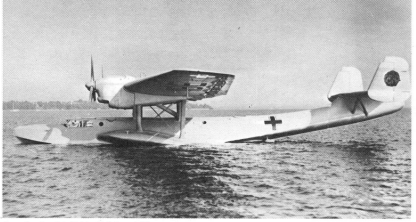

Dornier Do.217-1940, G (plate 132)

Blohm und Voss Bv.141-1940, G (plate 149)

Dornier Do.24-1940, G (plate 168)

Blohm und Voss Bv.138-1941, G (plate 151)

Blohm und Voss Bv.222-1942, G (plate 154)

Blohm und Voss Bv.222-1942, G (plate 154)

Messerschmitt Me.323-1942, G (plate 170)

Messerschmitt Bf.109-1942, G (plate 85)

Junkers Ju.290-1942, G (plate 170)

Focke Wulf Fw.190-1942, G (plate 86)

Heinkel He.219-1943, G (plate 108)

Messerschmitt Me.410-1943, G (plate 112)

Dornier Do.335-1944, G (plate 98)

Messerschmitt Me.262-1944, G (plate 105)

Messerschmitt Me.163B-1-1944, G (plate 105)

Heinkel He.162-1945, G (plate 105)

CANT Z.501-1934, I (plate 145)

Breda Ba.65-1935, I (plate 111)

SIAI Marchetti S.M.81-1935, I (plate 122)

Photographic appendix

SIAI Marchetti S.M.79-1936, I (plate 122)

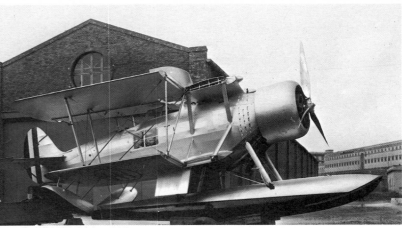

Imam Ro.43-1936, I (plate 146)

CANT Z.506-1937, I (plate 123)

CANT Z.1007 bis-1938, I (plate 123)

Fiat B.R.20-1938, I (plate 123)

Fiat C.R.42-1939, I (plate 81)

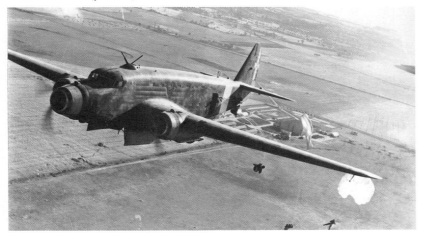

SIAI Marchetti S.M.82-1940, I (plate 168)

Fiat G.50-1939, I (plate 87)

Piaggio P.108-1942, I (plate 123)

Macchi M.C.202-1941, I (plate 87)

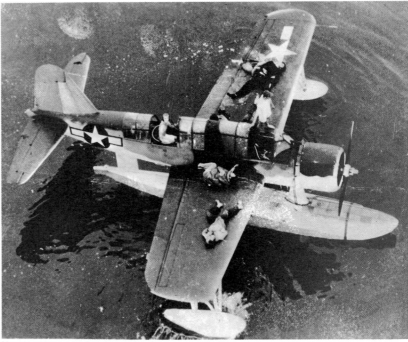

Vought OS2U-1-1940, USA (plate 150)

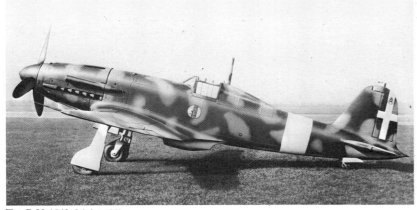

Fiat G.55-1942, I (plate 99)

Reggiane Re.2005-1943, I (plate 99)

Grumman 12F-4-1940, USA (plate 162)

Cessna AT-8-1940, USA (page 340)

Grumman F4F-3-1940, USA (plate 96)

Bell P-39-1941, USA (plate 92)

Republic P-43-1941, USA (plate 92)

Consolidated PBY-5-Catalina-1941, USA (plate 151)

Consolidated PB2Y-3-Coronado-1941, USA (plate 151)

Vultee A-35-1942, USA (plate 130)

Douglas A-20-1942, USA (plate 128)

Martin PBM-3 1942, USA (plate 154)

Lockheed PV-I-1942, USA (plate 156)

Boeing B-17G-1942, USA (plate 127)

Curtiss P-40D-1942, USA (plate 93)

Curtiss P-40F Warhawk-1942, USA (plate 93)

Vought F4U-1943, USA (plate 103)

Martin B-26-1943, USA (plate 128)

North American P-51-1943, USA (plate 100)

Republic P-47-1943, USA (plate 104)

North American A-36-1943, USA (page 234)

Bell P-59-1944, USA (plate 107)

Bell P-63-1944, USA (plate 104)

Northrop P-61-1944, USA (plate 109)

Curtiss C-46-1944, USA (plate 171)

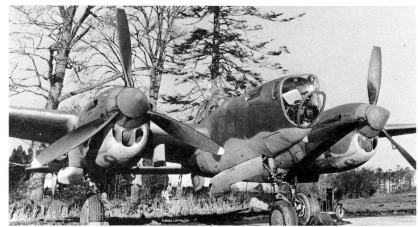

Lockheed P-38-1944, USA (plate 96)

North American B-25J-1944, USA (plate 127)

SAAB 18A-1944, S (plate 133)

Saab T18-B-1944, S (page 294)

Tupolev SB-2-1936, USSR (plate 125)

Yakovlev Yak-3-1944, USSR (plate 110)

Polikarpov I-16-1937, USSR (plate 82)

Mitsubishi Ki-21-II-1941, J (plate 126)

Yokosuka D4Y2-1943, J (plate 134)

Kawanishi N1K1 Shiden-1943, J (plate 102)

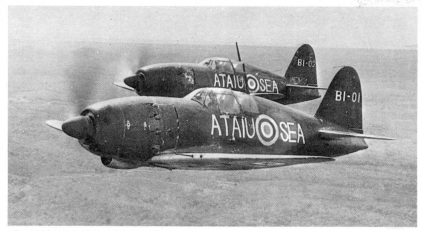

Mitsubishi J2M2-1943, J (plate 102)

Kawanishi N1K Kyofu-1943, J (plate 102)

Nakajima Ki-44-II Shoki-1943, J (plate 101)

Kawanishi H8K2-1943, J (plate 155)

4.

MILITARY AIRCRAFT FROM 1945 TO THE PRESENT DAY

A third of a century has now passed since the Second World War. The aeroplane is even more important in modern society than it has been before: always evolving and improving, it provides an unparalleled service to the consumer public on the one hand, and on the other it has a crucial role in the task of maintaining the military balance.

This frightening concept was first seen on the grand international scale in the policies adopted by the various powers after the end of the First World War; its logical conclusion was illustrated when the balance was lost, and the Second World War came; and it is still the basis of all foreign policy today. The balance being at least approximately maintained, no general hostilities have occurred since 1945 and, it is to be hoped, never will again.

The preservation of world peace, avowedly the main objective of the superpowers on either side, and of all other powers associated with them, in this way hinges on the balance between opposing forces whose ability to react and counter-attack with even more deadly weapons today carries the assured threat of total destruction.

The result of all this is a constant process of updating all military equipment on either side; and this in turn has been reflected in the development of the aeroplane, which has continued even faster since the Second World War, its strongest stimulus always coming from the needs of military aviation. Innovations arising in the military side of the industry have then shown the way for commercial aviation to follow.

The Second World War awakened world-wide recognition of the great strategic and military importance of the aeroplane; and it provided a new element which was to transform aviation once more: the jet engine. Invented by both the British and the Germans, this radically new form of propulsion has since then advanced to a fantastic degree. The achievements of the new era that it introduced are shown by the change in world records in 40 years, from 1938 to 1978.

In October 1938 the following world records had been ratified by the *Fédération Aéronautique Internationale*: distance, closed circuit: 7,240 miles (11,651 km) (Japan, Koken monoplane, 15th May 1938); distance in a straight line: 6,300 miles (10,148 km) USSR, Tupolev ANT 25, 15th July 1937); maximum speed: 441 mph (709.902 km/h) (Italy, Macchi-Castoldi MC72 seaplane, 23 October 1934). The world record for altitude was still held by a balloon, the American Explorer II which reached 72,400 feet (22,066 metres) on 11th November 1935, but on 22nd October 1938 the Italian Mario Pezzi reached 56,050 feet (17,083 metres) in a Caproni Ca161 *bis*.

By September 1978 these records had become: distance, closed circuit: 11,337 miles (18,245.05 km) (United States, Boeing B-52H Stratofortress, on 7th June 1962); distance in a straight line: 12,530 miles (20,168.78 km) (United States, in the same aircraft, 11th January 1962); maximum speed: 2,193 mph (3,529.56 km/h) (United States, Lockheed SR-71A, on 29th July 1976); altitude: 123,530 feet (37,650 metres) (USSR, MiG-25, 31 August 1977).

At the same time as this spectacular unfolding of the aeroplane's potential, its military application developed in new directions. Defensive and offensive weaponry became increasingly deadly and sophisticated and included nuclear warheads and successive generations of ever-improved and more "intelligent" missiles, operated in conjunction with complex electronic equipment which left only the decision to fire in the hands of the airman. This altered traditional concepts of the use of combat aircraft once again beyond all recognition from previous generations. The conventional bomber is now being superseded by strategic intercontinental missiles; more and more effective tactical fighters have emerged; the multirole combat aircraft (MRCA) has arrived, one of its advantages being economy, in view of today's enormous costs per single aircraft; instead of several aeroplanes, one MRCA can perform a wide range of operational tasks, from ground-attack to reconnaissance and interception. Meanwhile interceptors themselves have become even more sophisticated machines in their specialised role.

In the United States, the outcome of the war had reinforced the belief that America had become the custodian and guarantor of the liberty and peace of the world. To fulfil this role it was necessary to have a powerful strike force, which of course amounts to the same argument as the balance of power to which we have already referred.

This was the military posture that decided the course of development of American military aviation from the end of the Second World War. Only a short interval followed the victories of 1945 before the aircraft industry began to tighten up schedules under the new sense of urgency of the fast developing cold war. All efforts were directed to the modernisation of the industry, which included the introduction of jet-engine technology, where America had lagged behind in the war years. The air forces also saw some reorganisation.

On 18th September 1947 the USAAF dropped a letter A and became the USAF, United States Air Force, with its own chief of staff and general command at last. The US Naval squadrons remained a part of the Navy, still under the same structure since 1921 with senior officers holding direct responsibility to the Navy Chief of Staff. But it began to be re-equipped and developed.

Among America's first jet fighters were the F-80, F-84 and F-86 for the USAF and the F9F Panther and F2H Banshee for the US Navy. Giant strategic bombers came into service, the B-36 and the B-47.

The new aircraft did not wait long to see active service, for war broke out in Korea on 25th June 1950. It provided a testing ground, of aircraft, men and theories of strategy and tactics. It enabled the rival superpowers to compare each other's new equipment, too. The MiG-15 proved to be a very fast aircraft indeed, and showed that Russia could produce a few surprises.

The Korean War lasted for three years and America learnt to revise some of its theories of warfare, which for the aircraft industry meant new tasks, new designs, new development. Aircraft began to take shape in the 1950s which would last right through to the end of the next decade, leading the way for all the western aviation industries to follow.

The accent was on speed and this was the generation that achieved supersonic flight, reaching twice the speed of sound. For this to happen new materials had to be researched and new concepts in the application of electronics came into aviation: the word avionics was coined. The new fighters were the F-100 Super Sabre, the F-102 Delta Dagger, the F-104 Starfighter, the F-105 Thunderchief, the F-8 Crusader and the F-4 Phantom II. An even bigger bomber came, the strategic "flying battle-cruiser" or B-52 Stratofortress.

These aircraft all took part in the Vietnamese war, which began in South Viet-Nam in 1965 and continued for ten years, with all US forces being withdrawn in 1973. As in Korea, it was found that military theory, particularly in the field of counter-insurgency and combat against guerrilla forces, had to be revised, although in other areas such as the tactics of aerial combat there had not been so many changes. During the 1970s the use of the strategic bomber fell from favour, a new design of which, the B-1, being abandoned at the development stage in 1977. Instead, priority was given to the cruise missile which is purely a strategic weapon.

A third generation of American tactical aircraft was begun in the post-Viet-Nam period, even faster, even better equipped with computer fire control systems and many electronic aids to the pilot, who at speeds above Mach 2 can afford no error.

The development of military aviation in the Soviet Union was just as intensive and followed that of the Americans in a series of leaps forward as the superpowers vied with each other. Few western observers had realised, in the confusion of the immediate postwar period, what was going on in the USSR.

In 1945 the *VVS (Voenno Vozdushniye Sily)* or Soviet air force was far from possessing combat aircraft which could match the American and British warplanes of the time. However, they managed to recover lost ground in a very short time; they began a vast research programme in which they made use of designs and information they had captured from the Germans. There were also a number of German scientists who went to work in the Soviet Union. The Soviets were further able to learn from western technology through acquiring construction rights for some of the most advanced British jet engines. The result of this period of activity was the MiG-15. Progress did not cease there, and after so many years as a second rank air power, the USSR has come to the fore, as it is widely agreed in the West.

After the MiG-15 there was the more sophisticated MiG-17 which in turn was followed by the more powerful MiG-19 and MiG-21 of 1953 and 1956; in the sixties the MiG-23, 25 and 27 appeared which were even more advanced and whose military potential was enhanced not only by the quantities which were manufactured exceeding total western aircraft production, let alone American production, but also as a result of the large numbers which were distributed throughout the Warsaw Pact and other Moscow-oriented countries, either directly or through construction under licence.

Similarly large quantities of medium and heavy bombers were made, in an outstanding period for Yakovlev and Tupolev. The arms race slowed down for a short period in the 1960s and then the USSR developed more modern and efficient strategic bombers, amongst them the Tu-26 Backfire, capable of flying at two-and-a-half times the speed of sound and reaching any part of US territory. The *VVS* was reorganised during the 1960s, being divided in three: the *IAPVO (Aviatsiya protivovozdushnoi oborony strany*, for home defence); the *FA (Frontovaya aviatsiya*, tactical air force); and the *ADD (Aviatsiya dalnyevo deistviya*, strategic air force). To these was added the *AVMF (Aviatsiya voenno morskovo flota)*, the naval air force, whose tasks mainly consisted of marine reconnaissance, coastal patrol and anti-submarine warfare.

In Western Europe, the two countries which have retained the largest measure of independence as air powers are Britain and France: the former due to her aircraft industry's reputation and the continuation of a long tradition; the latter, apart from similar reasons, because of a determination to rebuild all that was lost in the war, and also an endemic mistrust of America's pre-eminence after the war, which formed a strand running through French politics for many years to come.

In Britain the postwar period saw the aircraft industry almost at a standstill. A radical new Labour government instituted drastic cuts in military spending, involving ruthless cancellation of orders. The whole industry marked time until 1948 when the tensions of the cold war began to justify a revived interest in defence. Those few years were in the meanwhile sufficient to relegate British air power to the second rank. Up to 1945 it had led the whole world, especially in its very high level of technological expertise; now it was ousted by the growth of American and Soviet air power.

In January 1945 the RAF had reached a peak in strength of 8,935 front line aircraft out of a total of 55,000 of all types, and over a million men. Three years later it had only just over 1,000 combat aircraft and 38,000 men. It was 1950 before the daytime fighter squadrons were fully converted to jet power and 1952 before the turn came of the night and all-weather fighter squadrons. A sad irony indeed for the first Allied air force to fly a jet aircraft against the Germans during the war. The bomber squadrons did hardly any better: only in 1951 did Bomber Command start to phase out their four-engine piston aircraft and replace them with the twin-jet Canberra; and the Fleet Air Arm suffered in much the same way.

The first rearmament programme was set in motion by the outbreak of the Korean War. In March 1951 it was announced that the RAF's strength would be increased, both in men and machines, by 50 per cent compared with 1948. New aircraft were ordered which became Britain's second generation of jet fighters in the late fifties: the

Hunter, Javelin and Lightning fighters and the Class V bombers such as the Valiant, the Vulcan and the Victor for the RAF, and the Scimitar, Sea Vixen and Buccaneer for the Fleet Air Arm.

During the 1960s expansion was once again curtailed by the government, anxious to keep spending under control. The two forces had to have recourse to American aircraft, for example the F-4 Phantom II, in order to maintain front line strength. The Fleet Air Arm suffered a reduction in both equipment and functions.

Ever since this period, for the British to modernise it has been necessary to form joint enterprises with the European industries: in 1965 British and French manufacturers together set up the Sepecat Consortium to build the Jaguar; in 1969 British, Federal German and Italian firms created the Panavia consortium to produce the Tornado. The only British-built prestige combat aircraft since then has been the vertical take-off Harrier, which went into service in 1969.

The renaissance of French military aviation after the war was mainly due to the efforts of Marcel Dassault, who managed to set up a concern which could produce exceptional aircraft, and also to the encouragement of General de Gaulle, who made a policy of being independent of the great powers, and emphasised the greatness of France itself. At the end of the Second World War the *Armée de l'Air* hardly existed at all, and the aircraft industry was in much the same position. However, a revival did get under way, with the help of some important measures of nationalisation.

State industry and private enterprise worked side by side, but in many ways it was the latter which took the lead. Dassault was the company which the aircraft manufacturer Marcel Bloch had started postwar, and which took the name assumed by Bloch on his return to France from German internment. The first French jet fighters came from Dassault: the Ouragan, the Mystère and the Etendard; so also did that even more distinguished family of jet aircraft, the Mirage jets, still being produced and developed in the 1980s. State industry complemented this successful revival particularly in manufacturing engines. The French *Aéronavale* force and the *Armée de l'Air* were to some extent to regain their place in the vanguard of military aviation, where they had always been until the mid 1930s, a position which after all is suited to France's traditional excellence in sophisticated engineering.

These four countries, the USA, USSR, Britain and France, are the world's major producers of aircraft, particularly military aircraft. Ever since the Second World War the majority of other nations, great and small, have become able to afford air forces; indeed only the true mini-state can afford to be without one. For most countries, and all third world countries, this means expensive imports, perhaps of second-hand aircraft, from the "big four" countries where investment is on hand for the huge costs of research and development, as well as production. By and large, the military aircraft market has thus remained the monopoly of the great powers.

Smaller industries in other countries, such as Japan and Czechoslovakia, are capable of producing simpler aircraft such as trainers, some forms of reconnaissance and transport planes, and even simple tactical aircraft. There is also Sweden, an interesting example of a small neutral state whch has a good technical base of her own and has chosen to develop her own defence system in complete independence. From the postwar period onwards Sweden has provided herself with a succession of very advanced combat aircraft which have been able to compete with the products of the most sophisticated industries.

Italy, as it has been noted, is a participant in the Tornado project. In Italian aviation this very advanced multirole aircraft is intended to replace the F-104 Starfighter in the 1980s. With the exception of the Fiat G.91 close support plane, the Tornado is the first really significant aircraft to serve with the *Aeronautica Militare Italiana* since the war which has not been of American or exclusively British manufacture.

The Federal Republic of Germany, while playing an important part in the Tornado project, is not otherwise a large producer of military aircraft. After the war the *Luftwaffe* was completely dismantled and the military aircraft manufacturing concerns were all dismantled too. They were reconstituted within set limits under Nato safeguards and supervision.

Finally the third world countries have bought increasing quantities of aircraft and now constitute a secondary market in the worldwide trade. The priority afforded to acquiring aircraft in the world's poorest countries is yet another sign of the dominant role which the aeroplane plays in the modern world.

Plate 183

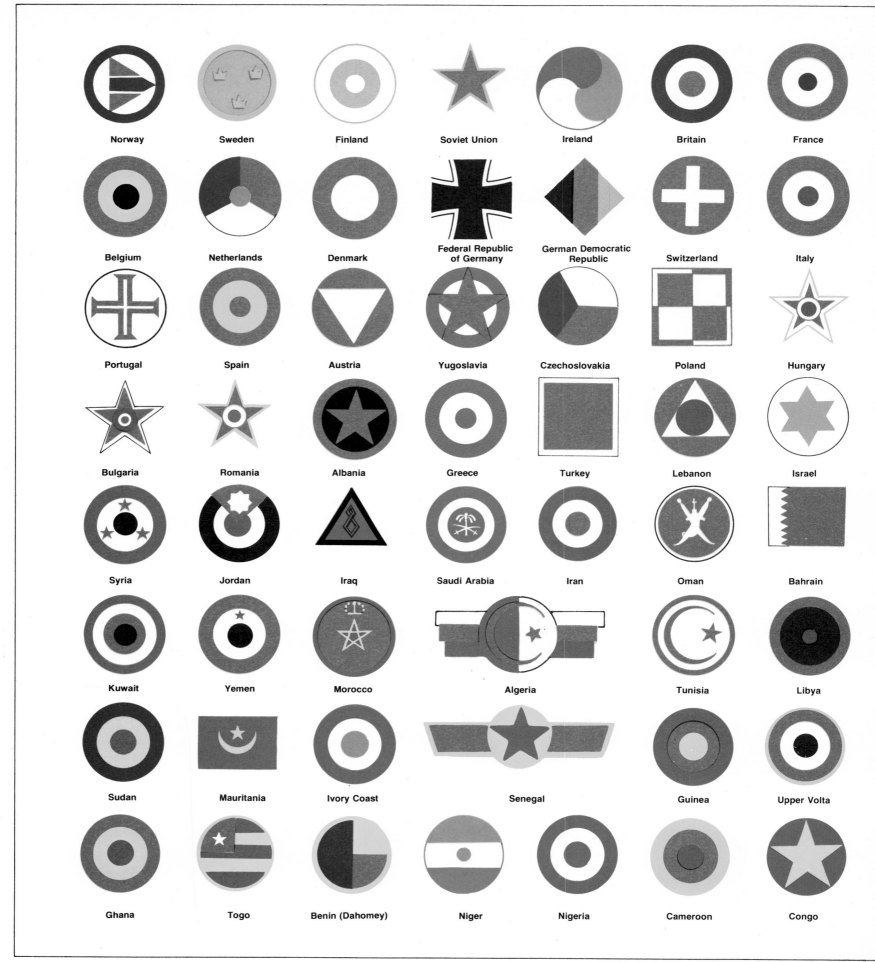

Norway

Sweden

Finland

Soviet Union

Ireland

Britain

France

Belgium

Netherlands

Denmark

Federal Republic of Germany

German Democratic Republic

Switzerland

Italy

Portugal

Spain

Austria

Yugoslavia

Czechoslovakia

Poland

Hungary

Bulgaria

Romania

Albania

Greece

Turkey

Lebanon

Israel

Syria

Jordan

Iraq

Saudi Arabia

Iran

Oman

Bahrain

Kuwait

Yemen

Morocco

Algeria

Tunisia

Libya

Sudan

Mauritania

Ivory Coast

Senegal

Guinea

Upper Volta

Ghana

Togo

Benin (Dahomey)

Niger

Nigeria

Cameroon

Congo

Ethiopia	Somalia	Kenya	Uganda	Zimbabwe	South Africa	Canada
United States of America		Mexico	Guatemala	Cuba		Dominican Republic
Honduras	El Salvador	Haiti		Panama	Nicaragua	Colombia
Ecuador	Venezuela		Peru	Bolivia	Brazil	Paraguay
Uruguay	Chile	Argentina	Australia	New Zealand	India	Japan
People's Republic of China		Taiwan	Mongolia	Afghanistan	Pakistan	DPR Korea (North)
Republic of Korea		Sri Lanka		Nepal	Burma	Thailand
Laos	Kampuchea	Vietnam	Philippines		Indonesia	Malaysia

Plate 184

Scale view of selected fighters from 1945 to the present day

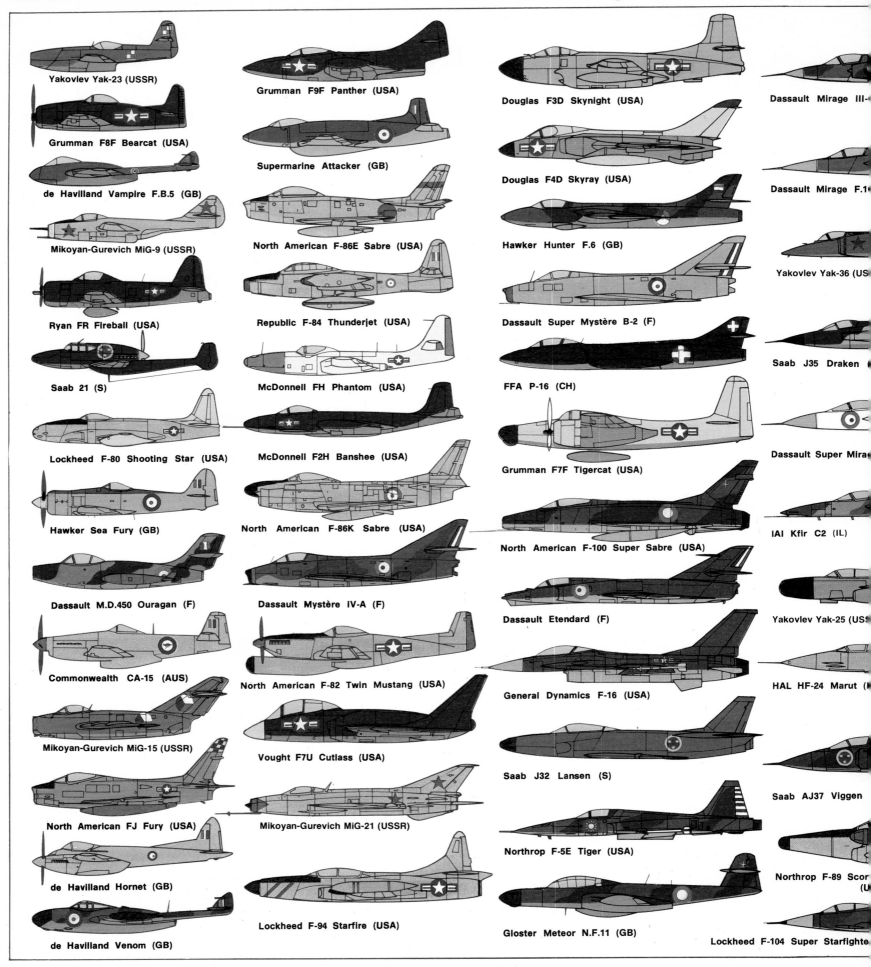

Yakovlev Yak-23 (USSR)

Grumman F8F Bearcat (USA)

de Havilland Vampire F.B.5 (GB)

Mikoyan-Gurevich MiG-9 (USSR)

Ryan FR Fireball (USA)

Saab 21 (S)

Lockheed F-80 Shooting Star (USA)

Hawker Sea Fury (GB)

Dassault M.D.450 Ouragan (F)

Commonwealth CA-15 (AUS)

Mikoyan-Gurevich MiG-15 (USSR)

North American FJ Fury (USA)

de Havilland Hornet (GB)

de Havilland Venom (GB)

Grumman F9F Panther (USA)

Supermarine Attacker (GB)

North American F-86E Sabre (USA)

Republic F-84 Thunderjet (USA)

McDonnell FH Phantom (USA)

McDonnell F2H Banshee (USA)

North American F-86K Sabre (USA)

Dassault Mystère IV-A (F)

North American F-82 Twin Mustang (USA)

Vought F7U Cutlass (USA)

Mikoyan-Gurevich MiG-21 (USSR)

Lockheed F-94 Starfire (USA)

Douglas F3D Skynight (USA)

Douglas F4D Skyray (USA)

Hawker Hunter F.6 (GB)

Dassault Super Mystère B-2 (F)

FFA P-16 (CH)

Grumman F7F Tigercat (USA)

North American F-100 Super Sabre (USA)

Dassault Etendard (F)

General Dynamics F-16 (USA)

Saab J32 Lansen (S)

Northrop F-5E Tiger (USA)

Gloster Meteor N.F.11 (GB)

Dassault Mirage III-

Dassault Mirage F.1

Yakovlev Yak-36 (US

Saab J35 Draken

Dassault Super Mira

IAI Kfir C2 (IL)

Yakovlev Yak-25 (USS

HAL HF-24 Marut (

Saab AJ37 Viggen

Northrop F-89 Scor
(U

Lockheed F-104 Super Starfighte

LTV F-8 Crusader (USA)

Grumman F-14 Tomcat (USA)

MRCA Tornado (G-GB-I)

Hawker Siddeley Harrier (GB)

Sepecat Jaguar (GB-F)

McDonnell F-4 Phantom II (USA)

English Electric Lightning (GB)

McDonnell - Douglas F-15 Eagle (USA)

Supermarine Scimitar (GB)

Republic F-105 Thunderchief (USA)

Hawker Siddeley Sea Vixen (GB)

McDonnell - Douglas F-18 Hornet (USA)

Sukhoi Su-15 (USSR)

Gloster Javelin (GB)

Convair F-102 Delta Dagger (USA)

McDonnell F3H Demon (USA)

Mikoyan-Gurevich MiG-23 (USSR)

Sukhoi Su-7 (USSR)

0   4   8   12m

4m = 2,16 cm

397

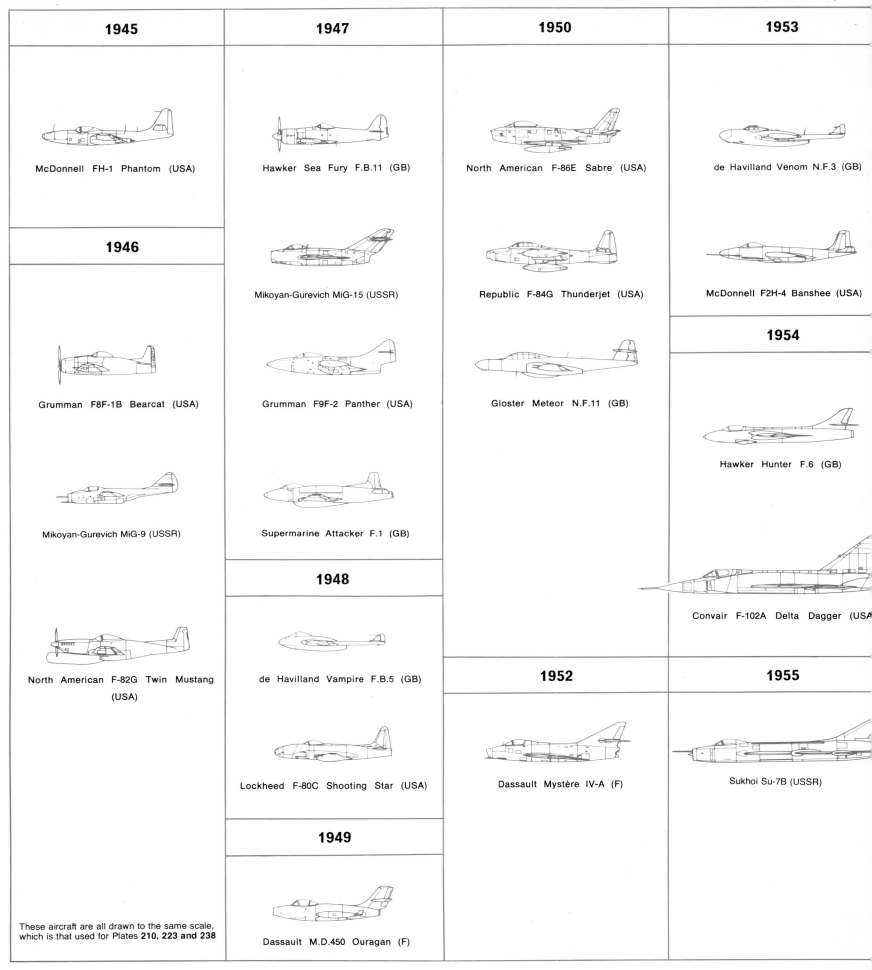

1945	1947	1950	1953
McDonnell FH-1 Phantom (USA)	Hawker Sea Fury F.B.11 (GB)	North American F-86E Sabre (USA)	de Havilland Venom N.F.3 (GB)

1945 — McDonnell FH-1 Phantom (USA)

1946 — Grumman F8F-1B Bearcat (USA); Mikoyan-Gurevich MiG-9 (USSR); North American F-82G Twin Mustang (USA)

These aircraft are all drawn to the same scale, which is that used for Plates **210**, **223 and 238**

1947 — Hawker Sea Fury F.B.11 (GB); Mikoyan-Gurevich MiG-15 (USSR); Grumman F9F-2 Panther (USA); Supermarine Attacker F.1 (GB)

1948 — de Havilland Vampire F.B.5 (GB); Lockheed F-80C Shooting Star (USA)

1949 — Dassault M.D.450 Ouragan (F)

1950 — North American F-86E Sabre (USA); Republic F-84G Thunderjet (USA); Gloster Meteor N.F.11 (GB)

1952 — Dassault Mystère IV-A (F)

1953 — de Havilland Venom N.F.3 (GB); McDonnell F2H-4 Banshee (USA)

1954 — Hawker Hunter F.6 (GB); Convair F-102A Delta Dagger (USA)

1955 — Sukhoi Su-7B (USSR)

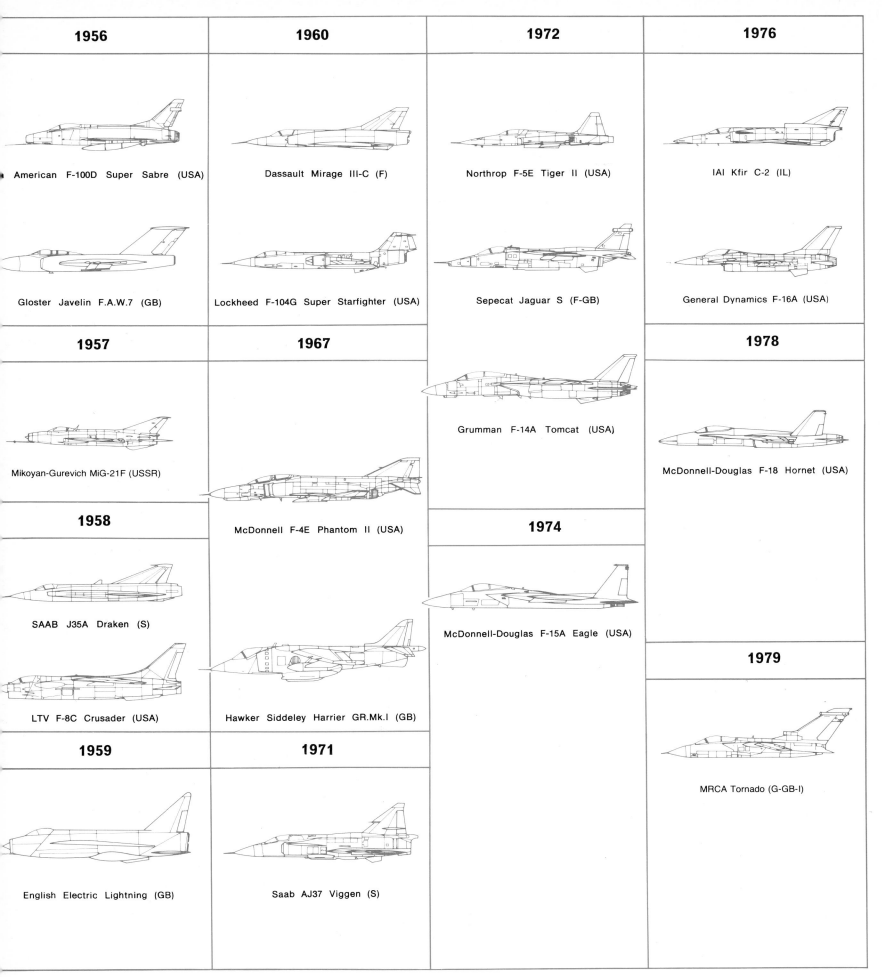

1956

American F-100D Super Sabre (USA)

Gloster Javelin F.A.W.7 (GB)

1957

Mikoyan-Gurevich MiG-21F (USSR)

1958

SAAB J35A Draken (S)

LTV F-8C Crusader (USA)

1959

English Electric Lightning (GB)

1960

Dassault Mirage III-C (F)

Lockheed F-104G Super Starfighter (USA)

1967

McDonnell F-4E Phantom II (USA)

Hawker Siddeley Harrier GR.Mk.I (GB)

1971

Saab AJ37 Viggen (S)

1972

Northrop F-5E Tiger II (USA)

Sepecat Jaguar S (F-GB)

Grumman F-14A Tomcat (USA)

1974

McDonnell-Douglas F-15A Eagle (USA)

1976

IAI Kfir C-2 (IL)

General Dynamics F-16A (USA)

1978

McDonnell-Douglas F-18 Hornet (USA)

1979

MRCA Tornado (G-GB-I)

MiG—21MF Cutaway Drawing Key

1 Pitot-static boom
2 Pitch vanes
3 Yaw vanes
4 Conical three-position intake centrebody
5 "Spin Scan" search-and-track radar antenna
6 Boundary layer slot
7 Engine air intake
8 Radar ("Spin Scan")
9 Lower boundary layer exit
10 Antennae
11 Nosewheel doors
12 Nosewheel leg and shock absorbers
13 Castoring nosewheel
14 Anti-shimmy damper
15 Avionics bay access
16 Attitude sensor
17 Nosewheel well
18 Spill door
19 Nosewheel retraction pivot
20 Bifurcated intake trunking
21 Avionics bay
22 Electronics equipment
23 Intake trunking
24 Upper boundary layer exit
25 Dynamic pressure probe for g-feel
26 Semi-elliptical armour-glass windscreen
27 Gunsight mounting
28 Fixed quarterlight
29 Radar scope
30 Control column (with tailplane trim switch and two firing buttons)
31 Rudder pedals
32 Underfloor control runs
33 KM-1 two-position zero-level ejection seat
34 Port instrument console
35 Undercarriage handle
36 Seat harness
37 Canopy release/lock
38 Starboard wall switch panel
39 Rear-view mirror fairing
40 Starboard-hinged canopy
41 Ejection seat headrest
42 Avionics bay
43 Control rods
44 Air conditioning plant
45 Suction relief door
46 Intake trunking
47 Wingroot attachment fairing
48 Wing/fuselage spar-lug attachment points (four)
49 Fuselage ring frames

50 Intermediary frames
51 Main fuselage fuel tank
52 RSIU radio bay
53 Auxiliary intake
54 Leading-edge integral fuel tank
55 Starboard outer weapons pylon
56 Outboard wing construction
57 Starboard navigation light
58 Leading-edge suppressed aerial
59 Wing fence
60 Aileron control jack
61 Starboard aileron
62 Flap actuator fairing
63 Starboard blown flap – SPS (sduva pogranichnovo sloya)
64 Multi-spar wing structure
65 Main integral wing fuel tank
66 Undercarriage mounting/pivot point
67 Starboard mainwheel leg
68 Auxiliaries compartment
69 Fuselage fuel tanks Nos 2 and 3
70 Mainwheel well external fairing
71 Mainwheel (retracted)
72 Trunking contours
73 Control rods in dorsal spine
74 Compressor face
75 Oil tank
76 Avionics pack
77 Engine accessories
78 Tumansky R-13 turbojet (rated at 14,550 lb/6,600 kg with full reheat)
79 Fuselage break/transport joint
80 Intake
81 Tail surface control linkage
82 Artificial feel unit
83 Tailplane jack
84 Hydraulic accumulator
85 Tailplane trim motor
86 Tailfin spar attachment plate
87 Rudder jack
88 Rudder control linkage
89 Tailfin structure
90 Leading-edge panel
91 Radio cable access
92 Magnetic detector
93 Tailfin mainspar
94 RSIU (radio-stantsiya istrebitelnaya ultrakorot-kykh vol'n – very short-wave fighter radio) antenna plate
95 VHF/UHF aerials
96 IFF antennae
97 Formation light

98 Tail warning radar
99 Rear navigation light
100 Fuel vent
101 Rudder construction
102 Rudder hinge
103 Braking parachute hinged bullet fairing
104 Braking parachute stowage
105 Tailpipe (variable convergent nozzle)
106 Afterburner installation
107 Afterburner bay cooling intake
108 Tailplane linkage fairing
109 Nozzle actuating cylinders
110 Tailplane torque tube
111 All-moving tailplane
112 Anti-flutter weight
113 Intake
114 Afterburner mounting
115 Fixed tailplane root fairing
116 Longitudinal lap joint
117 External duct (nozzle hydraulics)

118 Ventral fin
119 Engine guide rail
120 JATO assembly canted nozzle
121 JATO assembly thrust plate forks (rear mounting)
122 JATO assembly pack
123 Ventral airbrake (retracted)
124 Trestle point
125 JATO assembly release solenoid (front mounting)
126 Underwing landing light
127 Ventral stores pylon
128 Mainwheel inboard door
129 Splayed link chute
130 Twin 23 mm GSh-23 cannon installation
131 Cannon muzzle fairing
132 Debris deflector plate
133 Auxiliary ventral drop tank
134 Port forward air brake (extended)
135 Leading-edge integral fuel tank

136 Undercarriage retraction strut
137 Aileron control rods in
leading-edge
138 Port inboard weapons pylon
139 UV-16-57 rocket pod
140 Port mainwheel
141 Mainwheel outboard door
section
142 Mainwheel leg
143 Aileron control linkage
144 Mainwheel leg pivot point
145 Main integral wing fuel tank
146 Flap actuator fairing
147 Port aileron
148 Aileron control jack
149 Outboard wing construction
150 Port navigation light
151 Port outboard weapons pylon
152 "Advanced Atoll"
infrared-guided AAM
153 Wing fence
154 Radio altimeter antenna

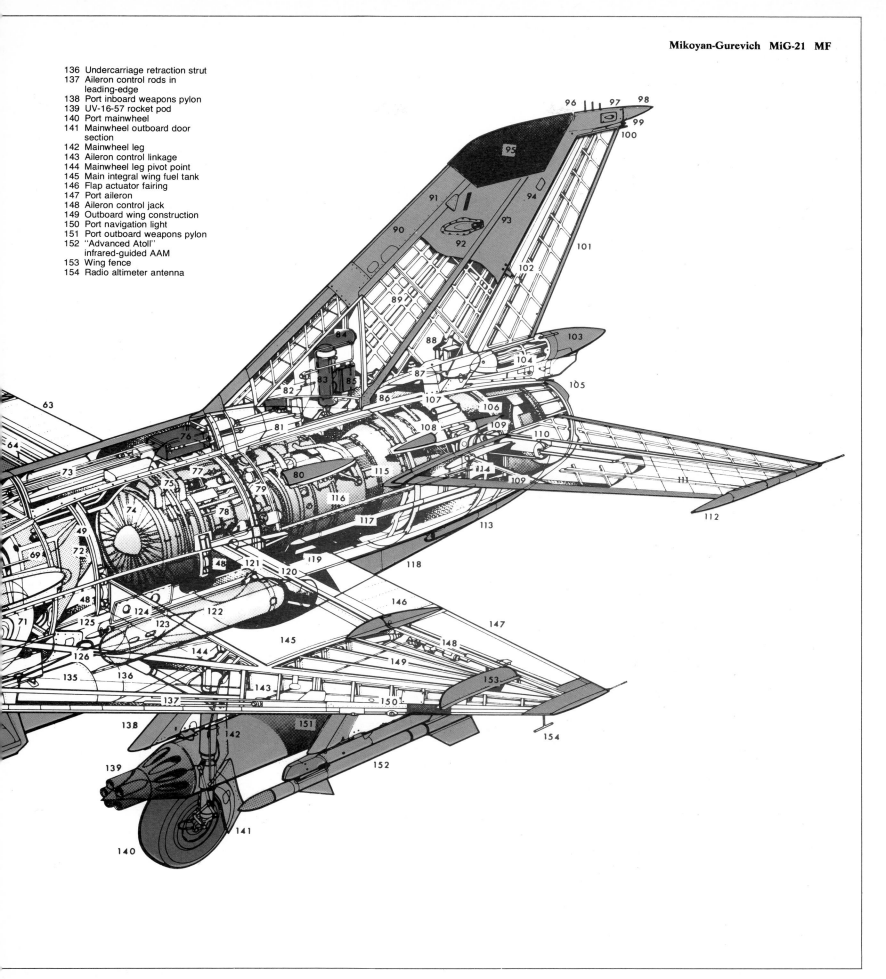

Plate 187

The last American piston-engine fighters: 1946

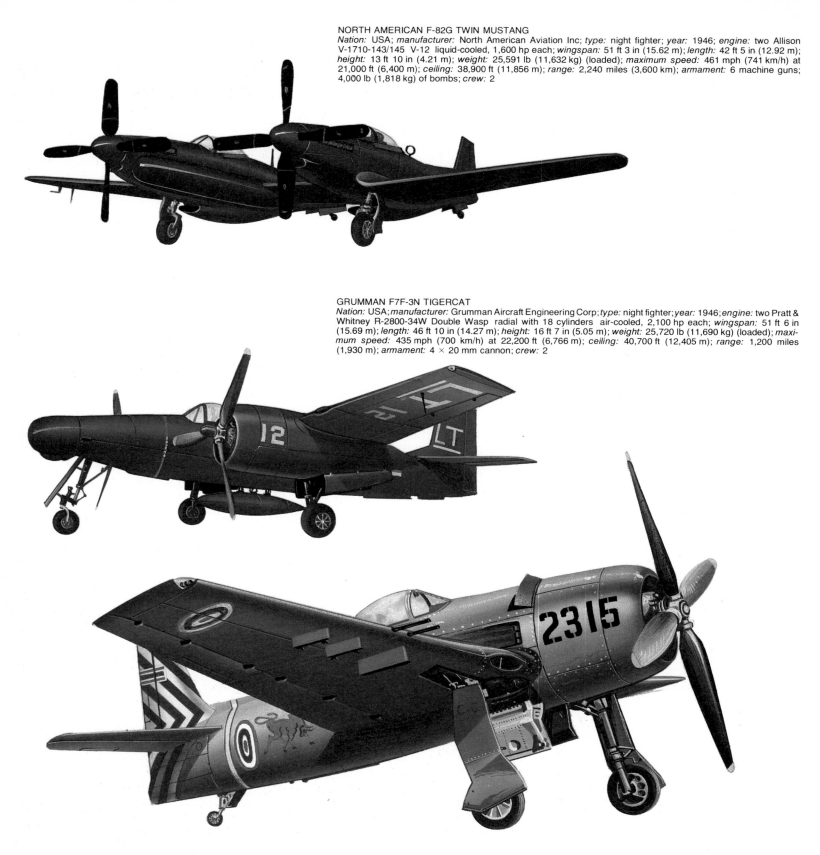

NORTH AMERICAN F-82G TWIN MUSTANG
Nation: USA; *manufacturer:* North American Aviation Inc; *type:* night fighter; *year:* 1946; *engine:* two Allison V-1710-143/145 V-12 liquid-cooled, 1,600 hp each; *wingspan:* 51 ft 3 in (15.62 m); *length:* 42 ft 5 in (12.92 m); *height:* 13 ft 10 in (4.21 m); *weight:* 25,591 lb (11,632 kg) (loaded); *maximum speed:* 461 mph (741 km/h) at 21,000 ft (6,400 m); *ceiling:* 38,900 ft (11,856 m); *range:* 2,240 miles (3,600 km); *armament:* 6 machine guns; 4,000 lb (1,818 kg) of bombs; *crew:* 2

GRUMMAN F7F-3N TIGERCAT
Nation: USA; *manufacturer:* Grumman Aircraft Engineering Corp; *type:* night fighter; *year:* 1946; *engine:* two Pratt & Whitney R-2800-34W Double Wasp radial with 18 cylinders air-cooled, 2,100 hp each; *wingspan:* 51 ft 6 in (15.69 m); *length:* 46 ft 10 in (14.27 m); *height:* 16 ft 7 in (5.05 m); *weight:* 25,720 lb (11,690 kg) (loaded); *maximum speed:* 435 mph (700 km/h) at 22,200 ft (6,766 m); *ceiling:* 40,700 ft (12,405 m); *range:* 1,200 miles (1,930 m); *armament:* 4 × 20 mm cannon; *crew:* 2

GRUMMAN F8F-1B BEARCAT
Nation: USA; *manufacturer:* Grumman Aircraft Engineering Corp; *type:* fighter; *year:* 1946; *engine:* Pratt & Whitney R-2800-34W Double Wasp 18-cylinder air-cooled radial, 2,100 hp; *wingspan:* 35 ft 10 in (10.92 m); *length:* 28 ft 3 in (8.61 m); *height:* 13 ft 10 in (4.21 m); *weight:* 12,947 lb (5,872 kg) (loaded); *maximum speed:* 421 mph (677 km/h) at 19,700 ft (6,000 m); *ceiling:* 38,700 ft (11,800 m); *range:* 1,105 miles (1,780 km); *armament:* 4 × 20 mm cannon; *crew:* 1

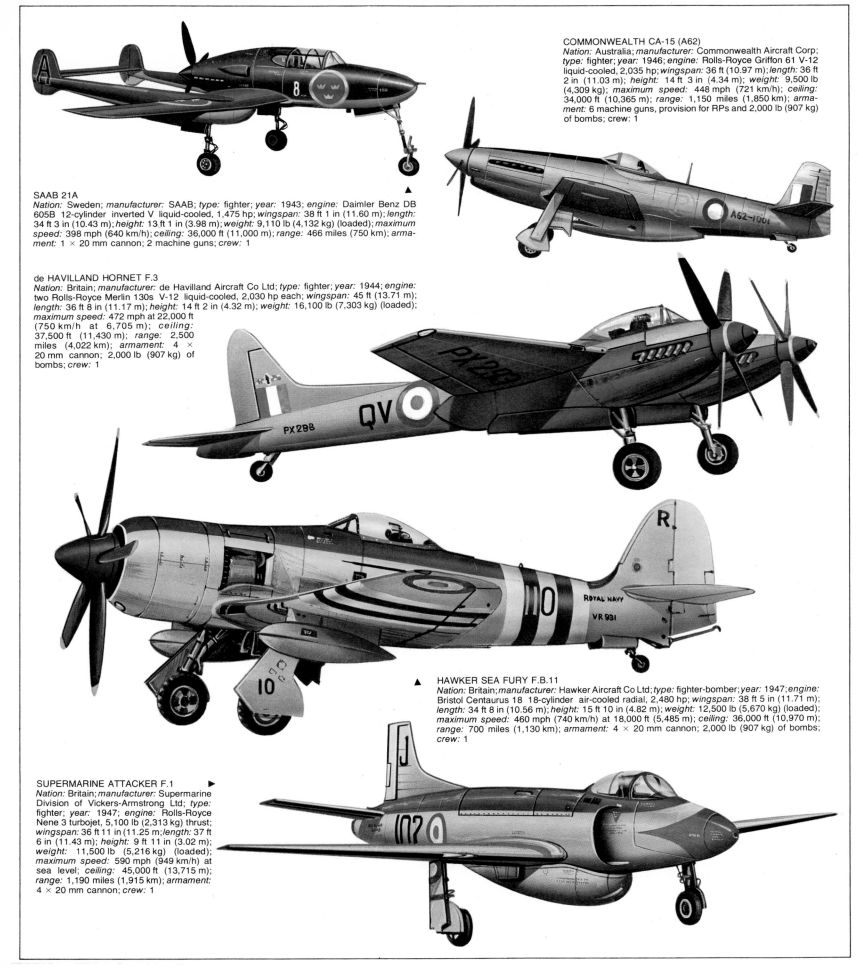

COMMONWEALTH CA-15 (A62)
Nation: Australia; *manufacturer:* Commonwealth Aircraft Corp; *type:* fighter; *year:* 1946; *engine:* Rolls-Royce Griffon 61 V-12 liquid-cooled, 2,035 hp; *wingspan:* 36 ft (10.97 m); *length:* 36 ft 2 in (11.03 m); *height:* 14 ft 3 in (4.34 m); *weight:* 9,500 lb (4,309 kg); *maximum speed:* 448 mph (721 km/h); *ceiling:* 34,000 ft (10,365 m); *range:* 1,150 miles (1,850 km); *armament:* 6 machine guns, provision for RPs and 2,000 lb (907 kg) of bombs; *crew:* 1

SAAB 21A
Nation: Sweden; *manufacturer:* SAAB; *type:* fighter; *year:* 1943; *engine:* Daimler Benz DB 605B 12-cylinder inverted V liquid-cooled, 1,475 hp; *wingspan:* 38 ft 1 in (11.60 m); *length:* 34 ft 3 in (10.43 m); *height:* 13 ft 1 in (3.98 m); *weight:* 9,110 lb (4,132 kg) (loaded); *maximum speed:* 398 mph (640 km/h); *ceiling:* 36,000 ft (11,000 m); *range:* 466 miles (750 km); *armament:* 1 × 20 mm cannon; 2 machine guns; *crew:* 1

de HAVILLAND HORNET F.3
Nation: Britain; *manufacturer:* de Havilland Aircraft Co Ltd; *type:* fighter; *year:* 1944; *engine:* two Rolls-Royce Merlin 130s V-12 liquid-cooled, 2,030 hp each; *wingspan:* 45 ft (13.71 m); *length:* 36 ft 8 in (11.17 m); *height:* 14 ft 2 in (4.32 m); *weight:* 16,100 lb (7,303 kg) (loaded); *maximum speed:* 472 mph at 22,000 ft (750 km/h at 6,705 m); *ceiling:* 37,500 ft (11,430 m); *range:* 2,500 miles (4,022 km); *armament:* 4 × 20 mm cannon; 2,000 lb (907 kg) of bombs; *crew:* 1

HAWKER SEA FURY F.B.11
Nation: Britain; *manufacturer:* Hawker Aircraft Co Ltd; *type:* fighter-bomber; *year:* 1947; *engine:* Bristol Centaurus 18 18-cylinder air-cooled radial, 2,480 hp; *wingspan:* 38 ft 5 in (11.71 m); *length:* 34 ft 8 in (10.56 m); *height:* 15 ft 10 in (4.82 m); *weight:* 12,500 lb (5,670 kg) (loaded); *maximum speed:* 460 mph (740 km/h) at 18,000 ft (5,485 m); *ceiling:* 36,000 ft (10,970 m); *range:* 700 miles (1,130 km); *armament:* 4 × 20 mm cannon; 2,000 lb (907 kg) of bombs; *crew:* 1

SUPERMARINE ATTACKER F.1 ▶
Nation: Britain; *manufacturer:* Supermarine Division of Vickers-Armstrong Ltd; *type:* fighter; *year:* 1947; *engine:* Rolls-Royce Nene 3 turbojet, 5,100 lb (2,313 kg) thrust; *wingspan:* 36 ft 11 in (11.25 m); *length:* 37 ft 6 in (11.43 m); *height:* 9 ft 11 in (3.02 m); *weight:* 11,500 lb (5,216 kg) (loaded); *maximum speed:* 590 mph (949 km/h) at sea level; *ceiling:* 45,000 ft (13,715 m); *range:* 1,190 miles (1,915 km); *armament:* 4 × 20 mm cannon; *crew:* 1

Plate 191

British and American jet fighters: 1948–50

► LOCKHEED F-80C SHOOTING STAR
Nation: USA; *manufacturer:* Lockheed Aircraft Corp; *type:* fighter-bomber; *year:* 1948; *engine:* General Electric J33-A-23 turbojet, 4,600 lb (2,086 kg) thrust; *wingspan:* 39 ft 11 in (11.85 m); *length:* 34 ft 6 in (10.51 m); *height:* 11 ft 4 in (3.45 m); *weight:* 16,856 lb (7,646 kg) (loaded); *maximum speed:* 580 mph (933 km/h) at 7,000 ft (2,133 m); *ceiling:* 42,750 ft (13,030 m); *range:* 1,380 miles (2,220 km); *armament:* 6 machine guns; 2,000 lb (907 kg) of bombs; *crew:* 1

GLOSTER METEOR F.8
Nation: Britain; *manufacturer:* Gloster Aircraft Co Ltd; *type:* fighter; *year:* 1949; *engine:* two Rolls-Royce Derwent 8 turbojets, 3,500 lb (1,587 kg) thrust each; *wingspan:* 37 ft 2 in (11.32 m); *length:* 44 ft 7 in (13.58; *height:* 13 ft (3.96 m); *weight:* 15,700 lb (7,121 kg) (loaded); *maximum speed:* 598 mph (962 km/h) at 33,000 ft (10,000 m); *ceiling:* 43,000 ft (13,106 m); *range:* 980 miles (1,580 km); *armament:* 4 × 20 mm cannon; *crew:* 1
▼

ARMSTRONG WHITWORTH METEOR N.F. 11
Nation: Britain; *manufacturer:* Armstrong Whitworth Aircraft Co Ltd; *type:* night fighter; *year:* 1950; *engine:* two Rolls-Royce Derwent 8 turbojets, 3,500 lb (1,587 kg) thrust each; *wingspan:* 43 ft (13.10 m); *length:* 48 ft 6 in (14.78 m); *height:* 13 ft 11 in (4.24 m); *weight:* 20,035 lbs (9.088 kg) (loaded); *maximum speed:* 579 mph (960 km/h); *ceiling:* 40,000 ft (12,192 m); *range:* 920 miles (1,480 km); *armament:* 4 × 20 mm cannon; *crew:* 2
▼

de HAVILLAND VAMPIRE F.B.5
Nation: Britain; *manufacturer:* de Havilland Aircraft Co Ltd; *type:* fighter-bomber; *year:* 1948; *engine:* de Havilland Goblin 2 turbojet, 3,100 lb (1,420 kg) thrust; *wingspan:* 38 ft (11.58 m); *length:* 30 ft 9 in (9.37 m); *height:* 8 ft 10 in (2.69 m); *weight:* 12,390 lb (5,620 kg) (loaded); *maximum speed:* 548 mph (882 km/h) at 30,000 ft (9,145 m); *ceiling:* 44,000 ft (13,410 m); *range:* 1,220 miles (1,960 km); *armament:* 4 × 20 mm cannon; 2,000 lb (907 kg) of bombs; *crew:* 1
▼

◄ de HAVILLAND VAMPIRE N.F.10
Nation: Britain; *manufacturer:* de Havilland Aircraft Co Ltd; *type:* night fighter; *year:* 1949; *engine:* de Havilland Goblin 3 turbojet, 3,350 lb (1,520 kg) thrust; *wingspan:* 38 ft (11.58 m); *length:* 34 ft 7 in (10.54 m); *height:* 6 ft 7 in (2 m); *weight:* 11,350 lb (5,148 kg) (loaded); *maximum speed:* 550 mph (885 km/h) at 20,000 ft (6,100 m); *ceiling:* 40,000 ft (12,190 m); *range:* 1,200 miles (1,960 km); *armament:* 4 × 20 mm cannon; *crew:* 2

YAKOVLEV YAK-30
Nation: USSR; *manufacturer:* State Industries; *type:* fighter; *year:* 1948; *engine:* RD-500 (Rolls-Royce Derwent V) turbojet, 3,505 lb (1,590 kg) thrust; *wingspan:* 28 ft 4 in (8.65 m); *length:* 29 ft 5 in (8.96 m); *height:* –; *weight:* 8,000 lb (3,630 kg) (loaded); *maximum speed:* 637 mph (1,025 km/h); *ceiling:* 50,000 ft (15,000 m); *range:* 932 miles (1,500 km); *armament:* 3 × 23 mm cannon; *crew:* 1

LAVOCHKIN La-15
Nation: USSR; *manufacturer:* State Industries; *type:* fighter; *year:* 1948; *engine:* RD-500 (Rolls-Royce Derwent V) turbojet, 3,500 lb (1,590 kg) thrust; *wingspan:* 29 ft (8.38 m); *length:* 29 ft 6 in (9 m); *height:* –; *weight:* 8,488 lb (3,850 kg) (loaded); *maximum speed:* 637 mph (1,026 km/h) at 16,400 ft (5,000 m); *ceiling:* 45,000 ft (13,700 m); *range:* 727 miles (1,170 km); *armament:* 2 × 23 mm cannon; *crew:* 1

MIKOYAN-GUREVICH MiG-17F
Nation: USSR; *manufacturer:* State Industries; *type:* fighter; *year:* 1950; *engine:* Klimov VK-1F turbojet, 7,495 lb (3,400 kg) thrust; *wingspan:* 31 ft 7 in (9.63 m); *length:* 36 ft 4 in (11.09 m); *height:* 11 ft (3.35 m); *weight:* 13,379 lb (6,069 kg) (loaded); *maximum speed:* 711 mph (1,145 km/h) at 9,840 ft (3,000 m); *ceiling:* 54,500 ft (16,600 m); *range:* 1,400 miles (2,250 km); *armament:* 3 × 23 mm cannon; 1,100 lb (500 kg) of bombs; *crew:* 1

YAKOVLEV Yak-25A
Nation: USSR; *manufacturer:* State Industries; *type:* fighter; *year:* 1952; *engine:* two Mikulin AM-9B turbojets, 5,730 lb (2,600 kg) thrust each; *wingspan:* 36 ft 1 in (11 m); *length:* 51 ft 5 in (15.67 m); *height:* 12 ft 6 in (3.80 m); *weight:* 21,826 lb (9,900 kg) (loaded); *maximum speed:* 630 mph (1,015 km/h); *ceiling:* 46,000 ft (14,000 m); *range:* 1,250 miles (2,000 km); *armanent:* 2 × 37 mm cannon; 50 × 50 mm air-to-air rockets; *crew:* 2

MIKOYAN-GUREVICH MiG-19
Nation: USSR; *manufacturer:* State Industries; *type:* fighter; *year:* 1953; *engine:* two Mikulin AM-5 turbojets, 6,700 lb (3,040 kg) thrust each; *wingspan:* 29 ft 6 in (9 m); *length:* 42 ft 11 in (13.08 m); *height:* 13 ft 2 in (4.02 m); *weight:* 19,180 lb (8,700 kg) (loaded); *maximum speed:* 920 mph (1,480 km/h) at 20,000 ft (6,100 m); *ceiling:* 58,725 ft (17,900 m); *range:* 1,367 miles (2,200 km); *armament:* 1 × 37 mm cannon; 2 × 23 mm cannon; 2,200 lb (1,000 kg) of bombs; *crew:* 1

DASSAULT M.D.450 OURAGAN
Nation: France; *manufacturer:* Avions Marcel Dassault; *type:* fighter; *year:* 1949; *engine:* Hispano-Suiza Nene 104B turbojet, 5,000 lb (2,270 kg) thrust; *wingspan:* 43 ft 2 in (13.16 m); *length:* 35 ft 3 in (10.74 m); *height:* 13 ft 7 in (4.14 m); *weight:* 17,416 lb (7,900 kg) (loaded); *maximum speed:* 584 mph (940 km/h) at sea level; *ceiling:* 43,000 ft (13,000 m); *range:* 570 miles (920 km); *armament:* 4 × 20 mm cannon; 2,000 lb (908 kg) of bombs; *crew:* 1

DASSAULT MYSTÈRE IV-A
Nation: France; *manufacturer:* Avions Marcel Dassault; *type:* fighter-bomber; *year:* 1952; *engine:* Hispano-Suiza Verdon 350 turbojet, 7,710 lb (3,497 kg) thrust; *wingspan:* 36 ft 6 in (11.12 m); *length:* 42 ft 2 in (12.85 m); *height:* 14 ft 5 in (4.40 m); *weight:* 16,535 lb (7,500 kg) (loaded); *maximum speed:* 695 mph (1,120 km/h) at sea level; *ceiling:* 45,000 ft (13,715 m); *range:* 570 miles (917 km); *armament:* 2,000 lb (908 kg) of bombs; *crew:* 1

DASSAULT SUPER MYSTÈRE B-2
Nation: France; *manufacturer:* Avions Marcel Dassault; *type:* fighter-bomber; *year:* 1956; *engine:* SNECMA Atar 101G turbojet, 9,920 lb (4,500 kg) thrust; *wingspan:* 33 ft (10.07 m); *length:* 46 ft 1 in (14.04 m); *height:* 15 ft 1 in (4.60 m); *weight:* 22,046 lb (10,000 kg) (loaded); *maximum speed:* 750 mph (1,200 km/h) at 36,000 ft (11,000 m); *ceiling:* 55,750 ft (17,000 m); *range:* 540 miles (870 km); *armament:* 2 × 30 mm cannon; 2,000 lb (908 kg) of bombs; *crew:* 1

FFA-P-16
Nation: Switzerland; *manufacturer:* Flug und Fahrzeugwerke AG; *type:* fighter-bomber; *year:* 1955; *engine:* Armstrong Siddeley Sapphire 200 turbojet, 11,000 lb (4,990 kg) thrust; *wingspan:* 36 ft 7 in (11.15 m); *length:* 46 ft 9 in (14.24 m); *height:* 13 ft 5 in (4.10 m); *weight:* 25,795 lb (11,700 kg) (loaded); *maximum speed:* 685 mph (1,100 km/h); *ceiling:* 46,000 ft (14,000 m); *range:* 620 miles (1,000 km); *armament:* 2 × 30 mm cannon; 4,400 lb (2,000 kg) of bombs; *crew:* 1

NORTH AMERICAN F-86E SABRE
Nation: USA; *manufacturer:* North American Aviation Inc; *type:* fighter; *year:* 1950; *engine:* General Electric J47-GE-13 turbojet, 5,200 lb (2,538 kg) thrust; *wingspan:* 37 ft 1 in (11.30 m); *length:* 37 ft 6 in (11.43 m); *height:* 14 ft 8 in (4.47 m); *weight:* 16,357 lb (7,419 kg) (loaded); *maximum speed:* 675 mph (1,086 km/h) at 2,500 ft (762 m); *ceiling:* 48,300 ft (14,720 m); *range:* 765 miles (1,260 km); *armament:* 6 machine guns; 2,000 lb (907 kg) of bombs; *crew:* 1

NORTH AMERICAN F-86D SABRE
Nation: USA; *manufacturer:* North American Aviation Inc; *type:* fighter; *year:* 1954; *engine:* General Electric J47-GE-17B turbojet, 7,500 lb (3,402 kg) thrust; *wingspan:* 39 ft 1 in (11.91 m); *length:* 40 ft 11 in (12.47 m); *height:* 14 ft 8 in (4.47 m); *weight:* 20,171 lb (9,150 kg) (loaded); *maximum speed:* 692 mph (1,113 km/h); *ceiling:* 50,000 ft (15,240 m); *range:* 850 miles (1,378 km); *armament:* 4 × 20 mm cannon; 2 air-to-air missiles; *crew:* 1

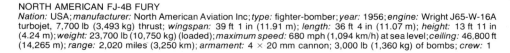

NORTH AMERICAN FJ-4B FURY
Nation: USA; *manufacturer:* North American Aviation Inc; *type:* fighter-bomber; *year:* 1956; *engine:* Wright J65-W-16A turbojet, 7,700 lb (3,493 kg) thrust; *wingspan:* 39 ft 1 in (11.91 m); *length:* 36 ft 4 in (11.07 m); *height:* 13 ft 11 in (4.24 m); *weight:* 23,700 lb (10,750 kg) (loaded); *maximum speed:* 680 mph (1,094 km/h) at sea level; *ceiling:* 46,800 ft (14,265 m); *range:* 2,020 miles (3,250 km); *armament:* 4 × 20 mm cannon; 3,000 lb (1,360 kg) of bombs; *crew:* 1

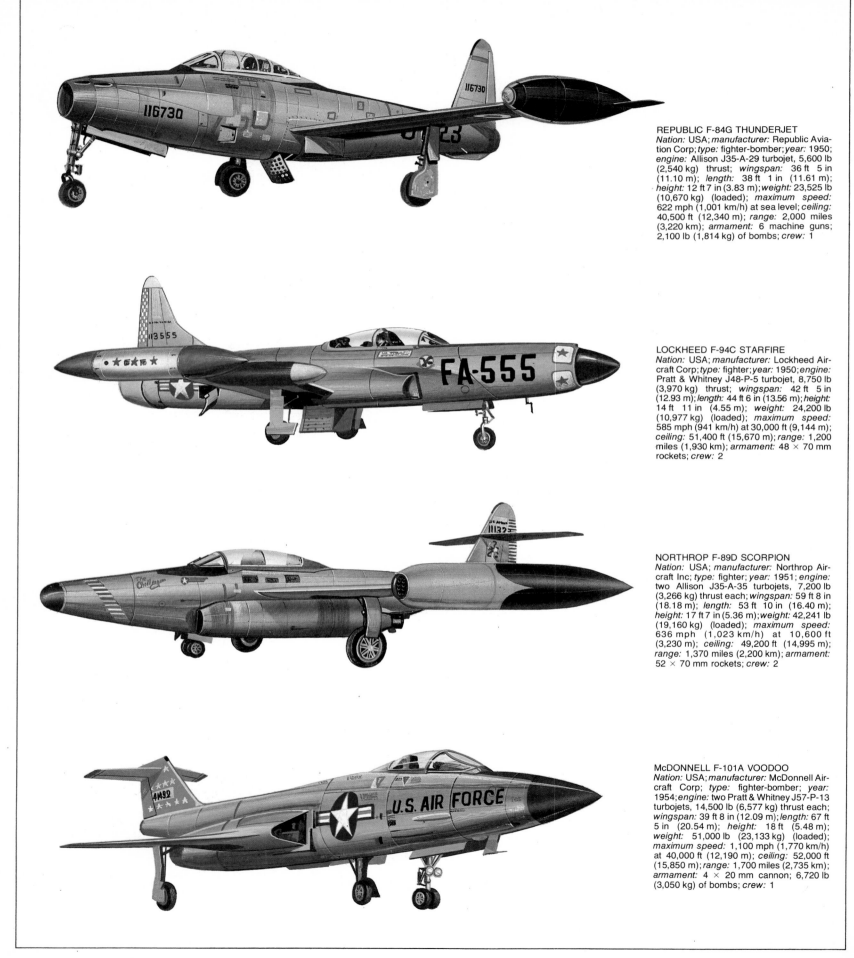

REPUBLIC F-84G THUNDERJET
Nation: USA; *manufacturer:* Republic Aviation Corp; *type:* fighter-bomber; *year:* 1950; *engine:* Allison J35-A-29 turbojet, 5,600 lb (2,540 kg) thrust; *wingspan:* 36 ft 5 in (11.10 m); *length:* 38 ft 1 in (11.61 m); *height:* 12 ft 7 in (3.83 m); *weight:* 23,525 lb (10,670 kg) (loaded); *maximum speed:* 622 mph (1,001 km/h) at sea level; *ceiling:* 40,500 ft (12,340 m); *range:* 2,000 miles (3,220 km); *armament:* 6 machine guns; 2,100 lb (1,814 kg) of bombs; *crew:* 1

LOCKHEED F-94C STARFIRE
Nation: USA; *manufacturer:* Lockheed Aircraft Corp; *type:* fighter; *year:* 1950; *engine:* Pratt & Whitney J48-P-5 turbojet, 8,750 lb (3,970 kg) thrust; *wingspan:* 42 ft 5 in (12.93 m); *length:* 44 ft 6 in (13.56 m); *height:* 14 ft 11 in (4.55 m); *weight:* 24,200 lb (10,977 kg) (loaded); *maximum speed:* 585 mph (941 km/h) at 30,000 ft (9,144 m); *ceiling:* 51,400 ft (15,670 m); *range:* 1,200 miles (1,930 km); *armament:* 48 × 70 mm rockets; *crew:* 2

NORTHROP F-89D SCORPION
Nation: USA; *manufacturer:* Northrop Aircraft Inc; *type:* fighter; *year:* 1951; *engine:* two Allison J35-A-35 turbojets, 7,200 lb (3,266 kg) thrust each; *wingspan:* 59 ft 8 in (18.18 m); *length:* 53 ft 10 in (16.40 m); *height:* 17 ft 7 in (5.36 m); *weight:* 42,241 lb (19,160 kg) (loaded); *maximum speed:* 636 mph (1,023 km/h) at 10,600 ft (3,230 m); *ceiling:* 49,200 ft (14,995 m); *range:* 1,370 miles (2,200 km); *armament:* 52 × 70 mm rockets; *crew:* 2

McDONNELL F-101A VOODOO
Nation: USA; *manufacturer:* McDonnell Aircraft Corp; *type:* fighter-bomber; *year:* 1954; *engine:* two Pratt & Whitney J57-P-13 turbojets, 14,500 lb (6,577 kg) thrust each; *wingspan:* 39 ft 8 in (12.09 m); *length:* 67 ft 5 in (20.54 m); *height:* 18 ft (5.48 m); *weight:* 51,000 lb (23,133 kg) (loaded); *maximum speed:* 1,100 mph (1,770 km/h) at 40,000 ft (12,190 m); *ceiling:* 52,000 ft (15,850 m); *range:* 1,700 miles (2,735 km); *armament:* 4 × 20 mm cannon; 6,720 lb (3,050 kg) of bombs; *crew:* 1

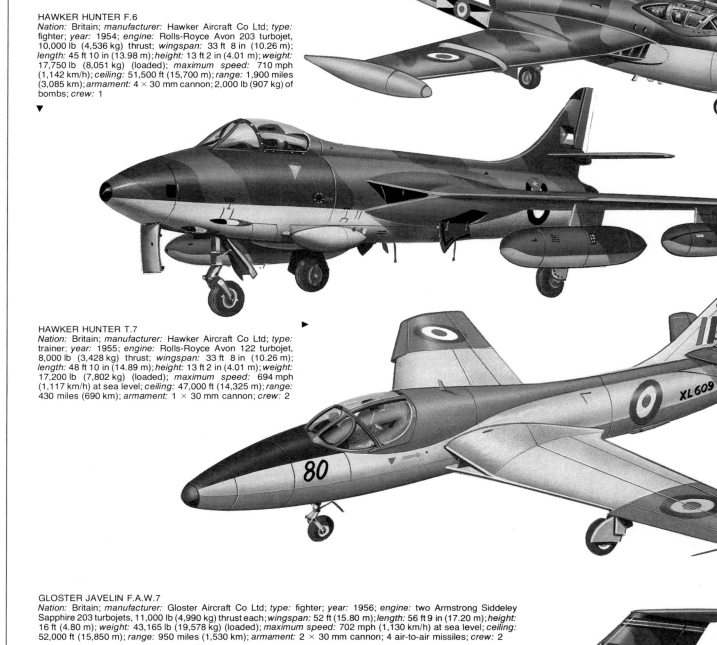

de HAVILLAND VENOM N.F.3
Nation: Britain; *manufacturer:* de Havilland Aircraft Co Ltd; *type:* night fighter; *year:* 1953; *engine:* de Havilland Ghost 104 turbojet, 4,950 lb (2,245 kg) thrust; *wingspan:* 41 ft 8 in (12.70 m); *length:* 36 ft 8 in (11.17 m); *height:* 6 ft 6 in (1.98 m); *weight:* 15,800 lb (7,166 kg) (loaded); *maximum speed:* 630 mph (1,013 km/h); *ceiling:* 49,200 ft (15,000 m); *range:* 1,000 miles (1,610 km); *armament:* 4 × 20 mm cannon; *crew:* 2

HAWKER HUNTER F.6
Nation: Britain; *manufacturer:* Hawker Aircraft Co Ltd; *type:* fighter; *year:* 1954; *engine:* Rolls-Royce Avon 203 turbojet, 10,000 lb (4,536 kg) thrust; *wingspan:* 33 ft 8 in (10.26 m); *length:* 45 ft 10 in (13.98 m); *height:* 13 ft 2 in (4.01 m); *weight:* 17,750 lb (8,051 kg) (loaded); *maximum speed:* 710 mph (1,142 km/h); *ceiling:* 51,500 ft (15,700 m); *range:* 1,900 miles (3,085 km); *armament:* 4 × 30 mm cannon; 2,000 lb (907 kg) of bombs; *crew:* 1

HAWKER HUNTER T.7
Nation: Britain; *manufacturer:* Hawker Aircraft Co Ltd; *type:* trainer; *year:* 1955; *engine:* Rolls-Royce Avon 122 turbojet, 8,000 lb (3,428 kg) thrust; *wingspan:* 33 ft 8 in (10.26 m); *length:* 48 ft 10 in (14.89 m); *height:* 13 ft 2 in (4.01 m); *weight:* 17,200 lb (7,802 kg) (loaded); *maximum speed:* 694 mph (1,117 km/h) at sea level; *ceiling:* 47,000 ft (14,325 m); *range:* 430 miles (690 km); *armament:* 1 × 30 mm cannon; *crew:* 2

GLOSTER JAVELIN F.A.W.7
Nation: Britain; *manufacturer:* Gloster Aircraft Co Ltd; *type:* fighter; *year:* 1956; *engine:* two Armstrong Siddeley Sapphire 203 turbojets, 11,000 lb (4,990 kg) thrust each; *wingspan:* 52 ft (15.80 m); *length:* 56 ft 9 in (17.20 m); *height:* 16 ft (4.80 m); *weight:* 43,165 lb (19,578 kg) (loaded); *maximum speed:* 702 mph (1,130 km/h) at sea level; *ceiling:* 52,000 ft (15,850 m); *range:* 950 miles (1,530 km); *armament:* 2 × 30 mm cannon; 4 air-to-air missiles; *crew:* 2

Plate 197

US Navy fighters: 1951–58

DOUGLAS F3D-2 SKYKNIGHT
Nation: USA; *manufacturer:* Douglas Air-craft Co; *type:* fighter; *year:* 1951; *engine:* two Westinghouse J34-WE-36 turbojets, 3,400 lb (1,542 kg) thrust each; *wingspan:* 50 ft (15.24 m); *length:* 45 ft 6 in (13.86 m); *height:* 16 ft (4.87 m); *weight:* 26,850 lb (12,179 kg) (loaded); *maximum speed:* 600 mph (965 km/h) at 20,000 ft (6,096 m); *ceiling:* 40,000 ft (12,190 m); *range:* 1,200 miles (1,930 km); *armament:* 4 × 20 mm cannon; *crew:* 2

McDONNELL F2H-4 BANSHEE
Nation: USA; *manufacturer:* McDonnell Aircraft Corp; *type:* fighter; *year:* 1953; *engine:* two Westinghouse J34-WE-38 tur-bojets, 3,600 lb (1,633 kg) thrust each; *wingspan:* 44 ft 10 in (13.66 m); *length:* 40 ft 2 in (12.24 m); *height:* 14 ft 6 in (4.42 m); *weight:* 22,312 lb (10,120 kg) (loaded); *maximum speed:* 532 mph (856 km/h) at 10,000 ft (3,048 m); *ceiling:* 44,800 ft (13,650 m); *range:* 1,475 miles (2,370 km); *arma-ment:* 4 × 20 mm cannon; 1,000 lb (454 kg) of bombs; *crew:* 1

DOUGLAS F4D-1 SKYRAY
Nation: USA; *manufacturer:* Douglas Air-craft Co; *type:* fighter; *year:* 1954; *engine:* Pratt & Whitney J57-P-2 turbojet, 9,700 lb (4,400 kg) thrust; *wingspan:* 33 ft 6 in (10.21 m); *length:* 45 ft 8 in (13.92 m); *height:* 13 ft (3.96 m); *weight:* 25,000 lb (11,340 kg) (loaded); *maximum speed:* 695 mph (1,118 km/h) at 36,000 ft (10,973 m); *ceiling:* 55,000 ft (16,760 m); *range:* 1,200 miles (1,930 km); *armament:* 4 × 20 mm cannon; 4,000 lb (1,814 kg) of bombs; *crew:* 1

McDONNELL F3H-2 DEMON
Nation: USA; *manufacturer:* McDonnell Air-craft Corp; *type:* fighter; *year:* 1955; *engine:* Allison J71-A-2E turbojet, 9,700 lb (4,400 kg) thrust; *wingspan:* 35 ft 4 in (10.77 m); *length:* 58 ft 11 in (17.95 m); *height:* 14 ft 7 in (4.44 m); *weight:* 33,000 lb (15,377 kg) (loaded); *maximum speed:* 647 mph (1,041 km/h) at 30,000 ft (9.145 m); *ceiling:* 42,650 ft (13,000 m); *range:* 1,370 miles (2,200 km); *armament:* 4 × 20 mm cannon; 6,600 lb (2,995 kg) of bombs; *crew:* 1

LTV F-8C CRUSADER
Nation: USA; *manufacturer:* LTV Aero-space Corp; *type:* fighter; *year:* 1958; *engine:* Pratt & Whitney J57-P-16A turbo-jet, 16,900 lb (7,665 kg) thrust; *wingspan:* 35 ft 2 in (10.72 m); *length:* 54 ft 3 in (16.54 m); *height:* 15 ft 9 in (4.80 m); *weight:* 27,550 lb (12,500 kg) (loaded); *maximum speed:* 1,120 mph (1,802 km/h) at 40,000 ft (12,190 m); *ceiling:* 58,000 ft (17,680 m); *range:* 1,100 miles (1,770 km); *armament:* 4 × 20 mm cannon plus 2 sidewinder air-to-air missiles, 32 rockets; *crew:* 1

◀ CONVAIR F-102A DELTA DAGGER
Nation: USA; *manufacturer:* Convair Division of General Dynamics; *type:* fighter; *year:* 1954; *engine:* Pratt & Whitney J57-P-23 turbojet, 17,002 lb (7,711 kg) thrust; *wingspan:* 38 ft 1½ in (11.61 m); *length:* 68 ft 4½ in (20.83 m); *height:* 21 ft 2½ in (6.45 m); *weight:* 31,505 lb (14,288 kg); *maximum speed:* 825 mph (1,327 km/h) at 36,000 ft (10,975 m); *ceiling:* 54,000 ft (16,460 m); *range:* 1,350 miles (2,170 km); *armament:* 6 air-to-air missiles; *crew:* 1

CONVAIR F-106B DELTA DART
Nation: USA; *manufacturer:* Convair Division of General Dynamics; *type:* fighter-trainer; *year:* 1958; *engine:* Pratt & Whitney J75-P-17 turbojet, 24,500 lb (11,113 kg) thrust; *wingspan:* 38 ft 3½ in (11.66 m); *length:* 70 ft 9 in (21.58 m); *height:* 20 ft 3 in (6.18 m); *weight:* 35,000 lb (15,876 kg) (loaded); *maximum speed:* 1,587 mph (2,454 km/h) at 40,000 ft (12,190 m); *ceiling:* 55,005 ft (16,765 m); *range:* 575 miles (925 km); *armament:* 4 air-to-air missiles; *crew:* 2 ▶

NORTH AMERICAN F-100D SUPER SABRE
Nation: USA; *manufacturer:* North American Aviation Inc; *type:* fighter-bomber; *year:* 1956; *engine:* Pratt & Whitney J57-P-21A turbojet, 17,000 lb (7,711 kg) thrust; *wingspan:* 38 ft 9 in (11.81 m); *length:* 47 ft (14.32 m); *height:* 15 ft (4.57 m); *weight:* 34,832 lb (15,800 kg); *maximum speed:* 864 mph (1,390 km/h) at 35,000 ft (10,670 m); *ceiling:* 45,015 ft (13,720 m); *range:* 1,500 miles (2,415 km); *armament:* 4 × 20 mm cannon; 7,500 lb (3,402 kg) external stores; *crew:* 1
▼

LOCKHEED F-104A STARFIGHTER
Nation: USA; *manufacturer:* Lockheed Aircraft Corp; *type:* fighter; *year:* 1956; *engine:* General Electric J79-GE-3B turbojet, 14,800 lb (6,713 kg) thrust; *wingspan:* 21 ft 11 in (6.68 m); *length:* 54 ft 9 in (16.68 m); *height:* 13 ft 6 in (4.11 m); *weight:* 22,422 lb (10,169 kg) (loaded); *maximum speed:* 1,532 mph (2,466 km/h) at 35,000 ft (10,668 m); *ceiling:* 60,000 ft (18,288 m); *range:* 580 miles (933 km); *armament:* 1 × 20 mm cannon; various external stores to total weight of 4,000 lb (1,814 kg); *crew:* 1

LOCKHEED F-104G SUPER STARFIGHTER ▶
Nation: USA; *manufacturer:* Lockheed Aircraft Corp; *type:* fighter-bomber; *year:* 1960; *engine:* General Electric J79-GE-11A turbojet, 15,800 lb (7,167 kg) thrust; *wingspan:* 21 ft 11 in (6.68 m); *length:* 54 ft 9 in (16.68 m); *height:* 13 ft 6 in (4.11 m); *weight:* 27,011 lb (12,250 kg) (loaded); *maximum speed:* 1,550 mph (2,494 km/h) at 40,000 ft (12,190 m); *ceiling:* 55,000 ft (16,765 m); *range:* 690 miles (1,100 km); *armament:* 1 × 20 mm cannon; various external stores to total weight of 4,000 lb (1,814 kg); *crew:* 1

Plate 199

Soviet fighters: 1955–60

SUKHOI Su-7B
Nation: USSR; *manufacturer:* State Industries; *type:* fighter-bomber; *year:* 1955; *engine:* Lyulka AL-7F TRD-31 turbojet, 22,045 lb (10,000 kg) thrust; *wingspan:* 30 ft 4 in (9.25 m); *length:* 60 ft 3 in (18.37 m); *height:* 16 ft 1 in (4.90 m); *weight:* 30,200 lb (13,700 kg) (loaded); *maximum speed:* 1,057 mph (1,700 km/h) at 39,370 ft (12,000 m); *ceiling:* 49,700 ft (15,150 m); *range:* 900 miles (1,450 km); *armament:* 2 × 30 mm cannon; 5,500 lb (2,500 kg) of bombs; *crew:* 1

SUKHOI Su-9
Nation: USSR; *manufacturer:* State Industries; *type:* fighter; *year:* 1956; *engine:* Lyulka AL-7F TRD-31 turbojet, 22,045 lb (10,000 kg) thrust; *wingspan:* 27 ft (8.23 m); *length:* 58 ft (17.68 m); *height:* 16 ft (4.88 m); *weight:* 30,000 lb (13,610 kg) (loaded); *maximum speed:* 1,190 mph (1,915 km/h) *ceiling:* 55,000 ft (16,765 m); *range:* 900 miles (1,450 km); *armament:* 4 air-to-air missiles; *crew:* 1

MIKOYAN-GUREVICH MiG-21F
Nation: USSR; *manufacturer:* State Industries; *type:* fighter; *year:* 1957; *engine:* Tumansky R-11 turbojet, 12,676 lb (5,750 kg) thrust; *wingspan:* 23 ft 6 in (7.15 m); *length:* 44 ft 2 in (13.46 m); *height:* 14 ft 9 in (4.50 m); *weight:* 16,700 lb (7,575 kg) (loaded); *maximum speed:* 1,243 mph (2,000 km/h); *ceiling:* 65,610 ft (20,000 m); *range:* 350 miles (560 km); *armament:* 1 × 30 mm cannon; 2 × K-13 air-to-air missiles; *crew:* 1

TUPOLEV Tu-28
Nation: USSR; *manufacturer:* State Industries; *type:* fighter; *year:* 1957; *engine:* two turbojets, 27,000 lb (12,250 kg) thrust each; *wingspan:* 65 ft (19.81 m); *length:* 85 ft (25.90 m); *height:* 23 ft (7.00 m); *weight:* 99,206 lb (45,000 kg) (loaded); *maximum speed:* 1,150 mph (1,850 km/h); *ceiling:* 60,000 ft (18,000 m); *range:* 1,800 miles (2,900 km); *armament:* air-to-air missiles; *crew:* 2

YAKOVLEV Yak-28P
Nation: USSR; *manufacturer:* State Industries; *type:* fighter; *year:* 1960; *engine:* two Tumansky RD-11 turbojets, 13,120 lb (5,950 kg) thrust each; *wingspan:* 42 ft 6 in (12.95 m); *length:* 71 ft (21.65 m); *height:* 12 ft 11 in (3.95 m); *weight:* 35,873 lb (16,000 kg) (loaded); *maximum speed:* 735 mph (1,180 km/h) at 35,000 ft (10,670 m); *ceiling:* 55,000 ft (16,750 m); *range:* 1,200 miles (1,930 km); *armament:* 2-4 air-to-air missiles; *crew:* 2

SUPERMARINE SCIMITAR F.1
Nation: Britain; *manufacturer:* Supermarine Division of Vickers-Armstrong Ltd; *type:* fighter/strike; *year:* 1957; *engines:* two Rolls-Royce Avon 202 turbojets, 11,250 lb (5,105 kg) thrust each; *wingspan:* 37 ft 2 in (11.33 m); *length:* 55 ft 4 in (16.87 m); *height:* 15 ft 3 in (4.65 m); *weight:* 40,000 lb (18,144 kg) (loaded); *maximum speed:* 710 mph (1,143 km/h) at 10,000 ft (3,050 m); *ceiling:* 50,000 ft (15,240 m); *range:* 600 miles (966 km); *armament:* 4 × 30 mm cannon or 4 missiles; 4,000 lb (1,814 kg) of bombs; *crew:* 1

HAWKER SIDDELEY SEA VIXEN F.A.W.1
Nation: Britain; *manufacturer:* Hawker Siddeley Aviation Ltd; *type:* fighter/strike; *year:* 1957; *engines:* two rolls-Royce Avon 208 turbojets, 11,250 lb (5,102 kg) thrust each; *wingspan:* 50 ft (15.24 m) *length:* 55 ft 7 in (17 m); *height:* 10 ft 9 in (3.30 m); *weight:* 31,000 lb (14,061 kg) (loaded); *maximum speed:* 650 mph (1,050 km/h) at 20,000 ft (6,100 m); *ceiling:* 48,000 ft (14,630 m); *range:* 600 miles (965 km); *armament:* 4 air-to-air missiles; 2,000 lb (907 kg) of bombs; *crew:* 2

HAWKER SIDDELEY (BAe) HARRIER GR.Mk 1
Nation: Britain; *manufacturer:* British Aerospace; *type:* fighter; *year:* 1967; *engine:* Rolls-Royce Bristol Pegasus Mk 101 turbofan, 19,000 lb (8,602 kg) thrust; *wingspan:* 25 ft 3 in (7.70 m); *length:* 45 ft 6 in (13.87 m); *height:* 11 ft 3 in (3.43 m); *weight:* 20,000 lb (9,979 kg) (loaded); *maximum speed:* 737 mph (1,186 km/h); *ceiling:* 50,000 ft (15,240 m); *range:* 2,300 miles (3,700 km); *armament:* 2 × 30 mm cannon; 5,000 lb (2,270 kg) of bombs; *crew:* 1

▲
McDONNELL F-4E PHANTOM II
Nation: USA; *manufacturer:* McDonnell Aircraft Co; *type:* fighter-bomber; *year:* 1967; *engines:* two General Electric J-79-GE-15 turbojets, 17,900 lb (8,120 kg) thrust each; *wingspan:* 38 ft 5 in (11.70 m) *length:* 62 ft 11 in (19.20 m); *height:* 16 ft 3 in (4.96 m); *weight:* 60,630 lb (27,500 kg) (loaded); *maximum speed:* 1,500 mph (2,413 km/h) at 40,000 ft (12,200 m); *ceiling:* 62,340 ft (19,000 m); *range:* 500 miles (800 km); *armament:* 1 × 20 mm cannon; 16,000 lb (7,257 kg) of bombs and missiles; *crew:* 2

McDONNELL F-4B PHANTOM II
Nation: USA; *manufacturer:* McDonnell Aircraft Co; *type:* fighter-bomber; *year:* 1958; *engines:* two General Electric J79-GE-8 turbojets, 16,000 lb (7,711 kg) thrust each; *wingspan:* 38 ft 5 in (11.70 m); *length:* 58 ft 3 in (17.76 m); *height:* 16 ft 3 in (4.96 m); *weight:* 54,600 lb (24,766 kg) (loaded); *maximum speed:* 1,583 mph (2,548 km/h) at 48,000 ft (14,630 m); *ceiling:* 62,000 ft (18,900 m); *range:* 500 miles (800 km); *armament:* 16,000 lb (7,257 kg) of bombs and up to 8 air-to-air missiles; *crew:* 2

▼

◄ One of the 5,000 Phantoms which had been manufactured as at 24th May 1978 is shown here in the special markings which were temporarily used during the Bicentenary Year of the USA.

McDONNELL F-4J PHANTOM II
Nation: USA; *manufacturer:* McDonnell Aircraft Co; *type:* fighter-bomber; *year:* 1966; *engines:* two General Electric J79-GE-10 turbojets, 17,900 lb (8,120 kg) thrust each; *wingspan:* 38 ft 5 in (11.70 m); *length:* 58 ft 3 in (17.76 m); *height:* 16 ft 3 in (4.96 m); *weight:* 54,600 lb (24,765 kg) (loaded); *maximum speed:* 1,485 mph (2,389 km/h) at 48,000 ft; *ceiling:* 62,000 ft (18,900 m); *range:* 900 miles (1,450 km); *armament:* 16,000 lb (7,257 kg) of bombs; *crew:* 2

▼

REPUBLIC F-105D THUNDERCHIEF
Nation: USA; *manufacturer:* Republic Aviation Corp; *type:* fighter-bomber; *year:* 1959; *engine:* Pratt & Whitney J75-P-19W turbojet, 26,500 lb (12,020 kg) thrust; *wingspan:* 34 ft 11 in (10.64 m); *length:* 64 ft 3 in (19.58 m); *height:* 19 ft 8 in (5.99 m); *weight:* 52,984 lb (24,033 kg) (loaded); *maximum speed:* 1,390 mph (2,237 km/h) at 36,000 ft (11,600 m); *ceiling:* 52,000 ft (15,850 m); *range:* 1,840 miles (2,960 km); *armament:* 1 × 20 mm cannon; 14,000 lb (6,350 kg) of bombs; *crew:* 1

ENGLISH ELECTRIC LIGHTNING T.4
Nation: Britain; *manufacturer:* English Electric Aviation Ltd; *type:* trainer; *year:* 1959; *engines:* two Rolls-Royce Avon 210 turbojets, 14,430 lb (6,545 kg) thrust each; *wingspan:* 34 ft 10 in (10.61 m); *length:* 55 ft 3 in (16.84 m); *height:* 19 ft 7 in (5.97 m); *weight:* 41,700 lb (18,915 kg); *maximum speed:* 1,500 mph (2,414 km/h) at 36,000 ft (10,970 m); *ceiling:* 60,000 ft (18,920 m); *range:* 895 miles (1,440 km); *armament:* 2 air-to-air missiles; *crew:* 2

ENGLISH ELECTRIC LIGHTNING F.1
Nation: Britain; *manufacturer:* English Electric Aviation Ltd; *type:* fighter; *year:* 1959; *engines:* two Rolls-Royce Avon 210 turbojets, 14,430 lb (6,545 kg) thrust each; *wingspan:* 34 ft 10 in (10.61 m); *length:* 55 ft 3 in (16,84 m); *height:* 19 ft 7 in (5.97 m); *weight:* 41,700 lb (18,915 kg) (loaded); *maximum speed:* 1,500 mph (2,414 km/h) at 36,000 ft (10,970 m); *ceiling:* 60,000 ft (18,920 m); *range:* 895 miles (1,440 km); *armament:* 2 × 30 mm cannon; 2 air-to-air missiles; *crew:* 1

Plate 203

The Swedish defence system relies on Saab: 1954–71

◄ SAAB 29F
Nation: Sweden; *manufacturer:* SAAB; *type:* fighter; *year:* 1954; *engine:* Svenska Flygmotor RM2 turbojet, 6,170 lb (2,800 kg) thrust; *wingspan:* 36 ft 1 in (11 m); *length:* 33 ft 2 in (10.10 m); *height:* 12 ft 3 in (3.73 m); *weight:* 17,637 lb (8,000 kg) (loaded); *maximum speed:* 659 mph (1,060 km/h); *ceiling:* 50,850 ft (15,500 m); *range:* 1,060 miles (1,700 km); *armament:* 4 × 20 mm cannon; 1,000 lb (500 kg) of bombs; *crew:* 1

▲
SAAB 35A DRAKEN
Nation: Sweden; *manufacturer:* SAAB; *type:* fighter; *year:* 1958; *engine:* Svenska Flygmotor RM6 turbojet, 15,000 lb (6,804 kg) thrust; *wingspan:* 30 ft 10 in (9.40 m); *length:* 50 ft 4 in (15.34 m); *height:* 12 ft 9 in (3.88 m); *weight:* 18,200 lb (8,255 kg) (loaded); *maximum speed:* 1,188 mph (1,910 km/h) at 36,000 ft (11,000 m); *ceiling:* 60,000 ft (18,000m); *range:* 800 miles (1,300 km); *armament:* 2 × 30 mm cannon; 4 air-to-air missiles; *crew:* 1

◄ SAAB 32B LANSEN
Nation: Sweden; *manufacturer:* SAAB; *type:* fighter; *year:* 1957; *engine:* Svenska Flygmotor RM6 turbojet, 15,190 lb (6,890 kg) thrust; *wingspan:* 42 ft 8 in (13 m); *length:* 47 ft 7 in (14.50 m); *height:* 15 ft 3 in (4.65 m); *weight:* 29,800 lb (13,517 kg) (loaded); *maximum speed:* 710 mph (1,142 km/h) at sea level; *ceiling:* 52,500 ft (16,000 m); *range:* 2,000 miles (3,200 km); *armament:* 4 × 30 mm cannon; 4 air-to-air missiles; *crew:* 2

SAAB AJ37 VIGGEN
Nation: Sweden; *manufacturer:* SAAB-Scania; *type:* fighter; *year:* 1971; *engine:* Volvo Flygmotor RM8A turbofan, 26,000 lb (11,800 kg) thrust; *wingspan:* 34 ft 9 in (10.60 m); *length:* 53 ft 6 in (16.30 m); *height:* 18 ft 4 in (5.60 m); *weight:* 35,275 lb (16,000 kg) (loaded); *maximum speed:* 1,320 mph (2,135 km/h); *ceiling:* 60,000 ft (18,300 m); *range:* 620 miles (1,000 km); *armament:* 13,200 lb (6,000 kg) of bombs; *crew:* 1
▶

DASSAULT ETENDARD IV-M
Nation: France; *manufacturer:* Avions Marcel Dassault; *type:* fighter; *year:* 1958; *engine:* SNECMA Atar 8 turbojet, 9,700 lb (4,400 kg) thrust; *wingspan:* 31 ft 6 in (9.60 m); *length:* 47 ft 3 in (14.40 m); *height:* 14 ft 1 in (4.30 m); *weight:* 22,486 lb (10,200 kg) (loaded); *maximum speed:* 683 mph (1,099 km/h) at sea level; *ceiling:* 49,200 ft (15,000 m); *range:* 1,056 miles (1,700 km); *armament:* 2 × 30 mm cannon; 3,000 lb (1,360 kg) of bombs; *crew:* 1

DASSAULT MIRAGE III-C
Nation: France; *manufacturer:* Avions Marcel Dassault; *type:* fighter; *year:* 1960; *engine:* SNECMA Atar 9B turbojet, 14,110 lb (6,400 kg) thrust; *wingspan:* 27 ft (8.22 m); *length:* 48 ft 6 in (14.77 m); *height:* 13 ft 11 in (4.25 m); *weight:* 26, 014 lb (11,800 kg) (loaded); *maximum speed:* 1,336 mph (2,230 km/h); *ceiling:* 54,135 ft (16,500 m); *range:* 745 miles (1,200 km); *armament:* 2 × 30 mm cannon; 3,000 lb (1,360 kg) of bombs; *crew:* 1

DASSAULT MIRAGE 5
Nation: France; *manufacturer:* Avions Marcel Dassault; *type:* fighter; *year:* 1967; *engine:* SNECMA Atar 9C turbojet, 13,670 lb (6,200 kg) thrust; *wingspan:* 27 ft (8.22 m); *length:* 51 ft (15.55 m); *height:* 14 ft 9 in (4.49 m); *weight:* 29,760 lb (13,500 kg) (loaded); *maximum speed:* 1,460 mph (2,350 km/h) at 40,000 ft (12,190 m); *ceiling:* 65,600 ft (20,000 m); *range:* 745 miles (1,200 km); *armament:* 2 × 30 mm cannon; 8,800 lb (4,000 kg) of bombs; *crew:* 1

DASSAULT MIRAGE F.1C
Nation: France; *manufacturer:* Avions Marcel Dassault; *type:* fighter; *year:* 1973; *engine:* SNECMA Atar 9K turbojet, 15,873 lb (7,200 kg) thrust; *wingspan:* 27 ft 7 in (8.40 m); *length:* 49 ft 2 in (15 m); *height:* 14 ft 9 in (4.50 m); *weight:* 24,030 lb (14,900 kg) (loaded); *maximum speed:* 1,450 mph (2,335 km/h) at 40,000 ft (12,190 m); *ceiling:* 65,600 ft (20,000 m); *range:* 560 miles (900 km); *armament:* 2 × 30 mm cannon; 8,800 lb (4,000 kg) of bombs; *crew:* 1

Plate 205

Minor fighters of the 1980s

IAI KFIR C2
Nation: Israel; *manufacturer:* IAI; *type:* multirole fighter; *year:* 1976; *engine:* General Electric J79-GE-17 turbojet, 17,900 lb (8,120 kg) thrust; *wingspan:* 26 ft 11 in (8.22 m); *length:* 51 ft (15.55 m); *height:* 13 ft 11 in (4.25 m); *weight:* 32,188 lb (14,600 kg) (loaded); *maximum speed:* 1,517 mph (2,442 km/h) at 36,000 ft (11,000 m); *ceiling:* 52,495 ft (16,000 m); *range:* 807 miles (13,000 km); *armament:* 8,820 lb (4,000 kg) of bombs; *crew:* 1

◄ **IAR-93 ORAO**
Nation: Yugoslavia, Romania; *manufacturer:* SOKO – CIAR; *type:* fighter; *year:* 1977; *engine:* two Rolls-Royce Viper Mk 632-40, turbojet, 5,950 lb (2,698 kg) thrust each; *wingspan:* 24 ft 10 in (7.56 m); *length:* 40 ft 10 in (12.45 m); *height:* 12 ft 5 in (3.78 m); *weight:* 22,700 lb (10,300 kg) (loaded); *maximum speed:* 1,089 mph (1,752 km/h); *ceiling:* 52,500 ft (16,000 m); *range:* 404 miles (650 km); *armament:* 2 × 30 mm cannon; 6,615 lb (3,000 kg) of bombs; *crew:* 1

HAL HF-24 Mk I MARUT
Nation: India; *manufacturer:* Hindustan Aeronautics Ltd; *type:* fighter; *year:* 1967; *engine:* two Rolls-Royce Orpheus 703 turbojets, 4,850 lb (2,200 kg) thrust each; *wingspan:* 29 ft 6 in (9 m); *length:* 52 ft 1 in (15.87 m); *height:* 11 ft 10 in (3.60 m); *weight:* 24,048 lb (10,908 kg) (loaded); *maximum speed:* 691 mph (1,112 km/h) at sea level; *ceiling:* 40,000 ft (12,200 m); *range:* 620 miles (1,000 km); *armament:* 4 × 30 mm cannon; 4,000 lb (1,815 kg) of bombs; *crew:* 1
▼

NORTHROP F-5E TIGER II
Nation: USA; *manufacturer:* Northrop Corp; *type:* fighter; *year:* 1972; *engine:* two General Electric J85-GE-21A turbojets, 5,000 lb (2,268 kg) thrust each; *wingspan:* 26 ft 8 in (8.13 m); *length:* 48 ft 2 in (14.68 m); *height:* 13 ft 4 in (4.06 m); *weight:* 24,664 lb (11,187 kg) (loaded); *maximum speed:* 1,060 mph (1,705 km/h); *ceiling:* 51,800 ft (15,790 m); *range:* 1,779 miles (2,863 km); *armament:* 2 × 20 mm cannon; 7,000 lb (3,175 kg) of bombs; *crew:* 1
▼

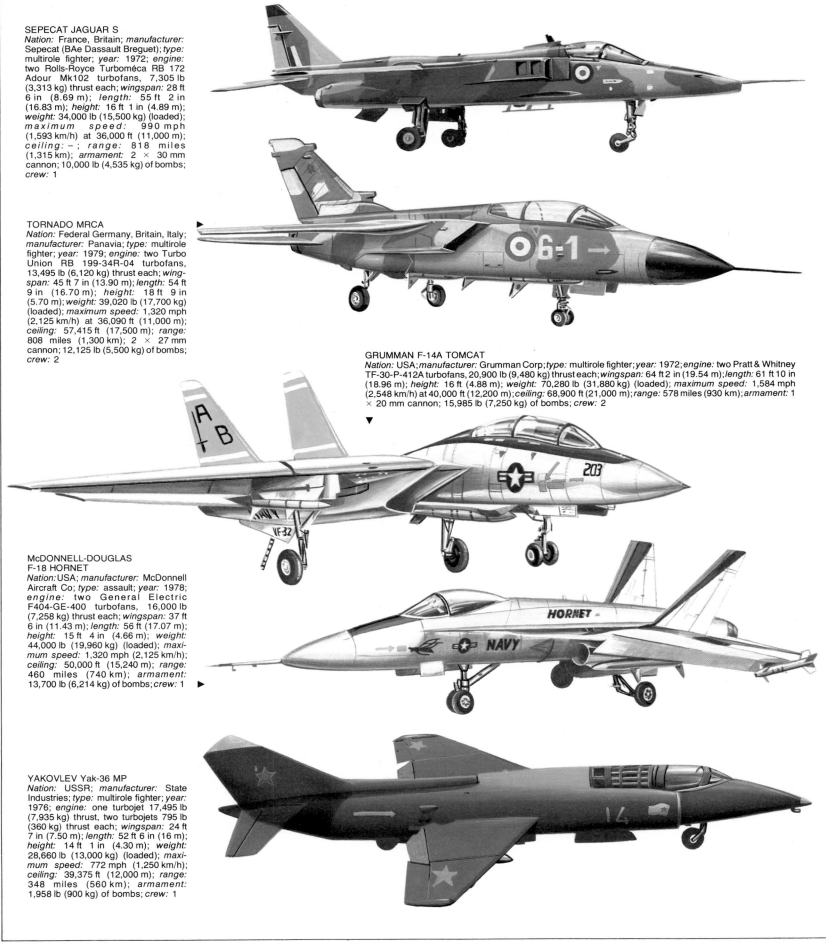

SEPECAT JAGUAR S
Nation: France, Britain; *manufacturer:* Sepecat (BAe Dassault Breguet); *type:* multirole fighter; *year:* 1972; *engine:* two Rolls-Royce Turboméca RB 172 Adour Mk102 turbofans, 7,305 lb (3,313 kg) thrust each; *wingspan:* 28 ft 6 in (8.69 m); *length:* 55 ft 2 in (16.83 m); *height:* 16 ft 1 in (4.89 m); *weight:* 34,000 lb (15,500 kg) (loaded); *maximum speed:* 990 mph (1,593 km/h) at 36,000 ft (11,000 m); *ceiling:* – ; *range:* 818 miles (1,315 km); *armament:* 2 × 30 mm cannon; 10,000 lb (4,535 kg) of bombs; *crew:* 1

TORNADO MRCA
Nation: Federal Germany, Britain, Italy; *manufacturer:* Panavia; *type:* multirole fighter; *year:* 1979; *engine:* two Turbo Union RB 199-34R-04 turbofans, 13,495 lb (6,120 kg) thrust each; *wingspan:* 45 ft 7 in (13.90 m); *length:* 54 ft 9 in (16.70 m); *height:* 18 ft 9 in (5.70 m); *weight:* 39,020 lb (17,700 kg) (loaded); *maximum speed:* 1,320 mph (2,125 km/h) at 36,090 ft (11,000 m); *ceiling:* 57,415 ft (17,500 m); *range:* 808 miles (1,300 km); 2 × 27 mm cannon; 12,125 lb (5,500 kg) of bombs; *crew:* 2

GRUMMAN F-14A TOMCAT
Nation: USA; *manufacturer:* Grumman Corp; *type:* multirole fighter; *year:* 1972; *engine:* two Pratt & Whitney TF-30-P-412A turbofans, 20,900 lb (9,480 kg) thrust each; *wingspan:* 64 ft 2 in (19.54 m); *length:* 61 ft 10 in (18.96 m); *height:* 16 ft (4.88 m); *weight:* 70,280 lb (31,880 kg) (loaded); *maximum speed:* 1,584 mph (2,548 km/h) at 40,000 ft (12,200 m); *ceiling:* 68,900 ft (21,000 m); *range:* 578 miles (930 km); *armament:* 1 × 20 mm cannon; 15,985 lb (7,250 kg) of bombs; *crew:* 2

McDONNELL-DOUGLAS F-18 HORNET
Nation: USA; *manufacturer:* McDonnell Aircraft Co; *type:* assault; *year:* 1978; *engine:* two General Electric F404-GE-400 turbofans, 16,000 lb (7,258 kg) thrust each; *wingspan:* 37 ft 6 in (11.43 m); *length:* 56 ft (17.07 m); *height:* 15 ft 4 in (4.66 m); *weight:* 44,000 lb (19,960 kg) (loaded); *maximum speed:* 1,320 mph (2,125 km/h); *ceiling:* 50,000 ft (15,240 m); *range:* 460 miles (740 km); *armament:* 13,700 lb (6,214 kg) of bombs; *crew:* 1

YAKOVLEV Yak-36 MP
Nation: USSR; *manufacturer:* State Industries; *type:* multirole fighter; *year:* 1976; *engine:* one turbojet 17,495 lb (7,935 kg) thrust, two turbojets 795 lb (360 kg) thrust each; *wingspan:* 24 ft 7 in (7.50 m); *length:* 52 ft 6 in (16 m); *height:* 14 ft 1 in (4.30 m); *weight:* 28,660 lb (13,000 kg) (loaded); *maximum speed:* 772 mph (1,250 km/h); *ceiling:* 39,375 ft (12,000 m); *range:* 348 miles (560 km); *armament:* 1,958 lb (900 kg) of bombs; *crew:* 1

Plate 207

Soviet fighters of the 1980s

MIKOYAN-GUREVICH MiG-23S
Nation: USSR; *manufacturer:* State Industry; *type:* multirole fighter;
year: 1970; *engine:* Tumansky turbofan, 22,050 lb (10,000 kg) thrust;
wingspan: 46 ft (14 m); *length:* 53 ft (16.15 m); *height:* 13 ft (3.95 m);
weight: 37,925 lb (17,200 kg) (loaded); *maximum speed:* 1,319 mph
(2,123 km/h) at 36,000 ft (11,000 m); *ceiling:* 50,035 ft (15,250 m);
range: 620 miles (1,000 km); *armament:* 2 × 23 mm cannon; 4 air-
to-air missiles; *crew:* 1
(Estimated)

◄ **SUKHOI Su-15**
Nation: USSR; *manufacturer:* State Industry; *type:* fighter; *year:* 1967; *engine:* two
Tumansky R-11F2-300 turbojets, 13,671 lb
(6,200 kg) thrust; *wingspan:* 30 ft (9.15 m);
length: 67 ft 2 in (20.50 m); *height:* 18 ft
11 in (5.79 m); *weight:* 35,280 lb
(16,000 kg); *maximum speed:* 1,519 mph
(2,445 km/h) at 36,000 ft (11,000 m); *ceiling:* 64,963 ft (19,800 m); *range:* 450 miles
(725 km); *armament:* 2 air-to-air missiles;
crew: 2
(Estimated)

◄ **SUKHOI Su-15**
Nation: USSR; *manufacturer:* State Industry; *type:* fighter; *year:* 1967; *engine:* two
Tumansky RD-13-300 turbo-
jets, 14,550 lb (6,600 kg)
thrust; *wingspan:* 35 ft
(10.65 m); *length:* 67 ft 3 in (20.50 m);
height: 19 ft (5.79 m); *weight:* 35,280 lb
(16,000 kg) (loaded); *maximum speed:*
1,519 mph (2,445 km/h) at 36,000 ft
(11,000 m); *ceiling:* 64,963 ft (19,800 m);
range: 450 miles (725 km); *armament:* 2
air-to-air missiles; *crew:* 1
(Estimated)

MIKOYAN-GUREVICH MiG-25S
Nation: USSR; *manufacturer:* State Industry; *type:* fighter; *year:* 1967; *engine:* two Tumansky R-266
turbojets, 27,300 lb (12,300 kg) thrust; *wingspan:* 45 ft 9 in (13.95 m); *length:* 73 ft 2 in (22.30 m);
height: 18 ft 6 in (5.60 m); *weight:* 79,820 lb (36,200 kg) (loaded); *maximum speed:* 2,100 mph
(3,380 km/h) at 62,995 ft (19,200 m); *ceiling:* 80,056 ft (24,400 m); *range:* 702 miles (1,130 km);
armament: 2 × 23 mm cannon; 4 air-to-air missiles; *crew:* 1
(Estimated)

SUKHOI Su-19
Nation: USSR; *manufacturer:* State Industry; *type:* multirole fighter; *year:* 1974;
engine: two Lyulka AL-21 F8 turbojets, 26,460 lb (12,000 kg) thrust; *wingspan:* 56 ft 3 in (17.15 m); *length:* 69 ft 10 in (21.29 m);
height: 20 ft 4 in (6.20 m); *weight:* 68,024 lb (30,850 kg) (loaded); *maximum speed:* 1,620 mph (3,380 km/h) at 36,000 ft
(11,000 m); *ceiling:* 62,339 ft (19,000 m); *range:* 1,211 miles (1,950 km); *armament:* 1 × 20 mm cannon; 16,537 lb (7,500 kg)
external stores; *crew:* 2
(Estimated)

McDONNELL-DOUGLAS F-15A EAGLE
Nation: USA; *manufacturer:* McDonnell Corp; *type:* multirole fighter; *year:* 1974; *engine:* two Pratt & Whitney
F100-PW-100 turbofans, 25,000 lb (10,800 kg) thrust
each; *wingspan:* 42 ft 10 in (13.05 m); *length:* 63 ft 9 in
(19.43 m); *height:* 18 ft 5 in (5.63 m); *weight:* 56,000 lb
(25,401 kg) (loaded); *maximum speed:* 1,678 mph
(2,701 km/h) at 47,210 ft (14,390 m); *ceiling:* 100,000 ft
(30,500 m); *range:* 995 miles (1,600 km); *armament:*
1 × 20 mm cannon; 16,800 lb (7,620 kg) of bombs;
crew: 1

GENERAL DYNAMICS F-16A
Nation: USA; *manufacturer:* General Dynamics Corp;
type: multirole fighter; *year:* 1976; *engine:* Pratt & Whitney F100-PW-100 turbofan, 25,000 lb (10,800 kg)
thrust; *wingspan:* 31 ft (9.45 m); *length:* 47 ft 8 in
(14.52 m); *height:* 16 ft 5 in (5.01 m); *weight:* 33,000
lb (14,968 kg) (loaded); *maximum speed:* 1,319 mph
(2,123 km/h) at 39,370 ft (12,000 m); *ceiling:* 50,000 ft
(15,420 m); *range:* 575 miles (925 km); *armament:* 1 ×
20 mm cannon; 10,500 lb (4,763 kg) of bombs; *crew:* 1

DASSAULT MIRAGE 2000
Nation: France; *manufacturer:* Dassault-
Breguet; *type:* multirole fighter; *year:* 1978;
engine: SNECMA M53-5 turbofan,
19,840 lb (9,000 kg) thrust; *wingspan:* 29 ft
6 in (9 m); *length:* 50 ft 3 in (15.33 m);
height: 15 ft 3 in (4.65 m); *weight:* 19,480 lb
(9,000 kg) (loaded); *maximum speed:*
1,265 mph (2,336 km/h) at 36,000 ft
(16,000 m); *ceiling:* 65,600 ft (20,000 m);
range: 932 miles (1,500 km); *armament:* 2
× 30 mm cannon; 11,025 lb (5,000 kg) of
bombs; *crew:* 1

DASSAULT SUPER MIRAGE 4000
Nation: France; *manufacturer:* Dassault-Breguet; *type:* multirole fighter; *year:* 1979; *engine:* two
SNECMA M53-5 turbofans, 19,840 lb (9,000 kg) thrust each; *wingspan:* 36 ft 1 in (11 m); *length:* 65 ft
8 in (20 m); *height:* 19 ft 8 in (6 m); *weight:* 44,100 lb (20,000 kg) (loaded); *maximum speed:* 1,650 mph
(2,650 km/h) at 36,100 ft (11,000 m); *ceiling:* 61,000 ft (20,000 m); *range:* 536 miles (861 km); *armament:* 2 × 30 mm cannon; 13,200 lb (6,000 kg) of bombs; *crew:* 1

Plate 187
The last American piston-engine
fighters: 1946

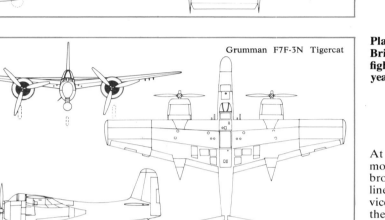

North American F-82G Twin Mustang

Grumman F7F-3N Tigercat

The American aircraft industry's tremendous surge forward in production and technology during the Second World War led to the best – and last – piston-engine fighters which represented the epitome of the formula which had originated in the First World War and which had evolved over thirty years. These aircraft were too late to make any noticeable contribution in the last stages of the war and in the postwar period they were soon pushed into the background by the introduction of the first modern jet fighters.

The North American F-81 Twin Mustang was one of the most original designs to emerge in response to the specific demands of the last years of the war. A specification issued in January 1944, which was the origin of this project, called for a long-range fighter as an escort for the latest American bomber, the Boeing B-29 Superfortress. Such a requirement assumed that the new fighter would have not only exceptional range, but also the ability to take on the newest agile and aggressive Japanese fighters at high altitude.

North American, when working out the design, chose a solution which from the outset was assured of success: using the fuselage, engine and wings of its outstanding P-51 Mustang as a starting point, since these were already proven, North American produced a twin-engine twin-boom plane which looked like two Mustangs joined together. A completely different aircraft emerged, however, with unique characteristics and a well-defined character of its own.

Three prototypes flew at the beginning of 1945 and immediately aroused the interest of the army: the Twin Mustangs were particularly prized for their speed, manoeuvrability, firepower and, naturally, for their long range.

The ending of the war, however, suddenly curtailed the production programme. There was no longer such a pressing need for an escort fighter, and after only 20 F-82Bs had been delivered to the USAAF the decision was taken to use the Twin Mustang as a night fighter. In 1946, after the manufacture of a few aircraft of the F-82C and D series, the first of 250 F-82Es, Fs and Gs appeared. The last two variants (in their final night fighter configuration) replaced the obsolescent Northrop P-61 Black Widows. The F-82's career ended with the Korean War. After short but intensive combat use, these aircraft gave way to jet fighters and were relegated to secondary roles, being taken out of service in 1953.

In the same class as the Twin Mustang – although of more conventional design – was the Grumman F7F Tigercat, a heavy multirole fighter which was developed for the US Navy during 1941 and which appeared in prototype in December 1943. The F7F broke completely away from the Grumman tradition and was a twin-engine aircraft with medium wing and a tricycle undercarriage, being the first of its kind to see carrier-borne service with the navy. It was exceptionally manoeuvrable, fast and powerful.

The first version, the F7F-1, was ordered at the beginning of 1944 and 34 were built, but the Tigercat was beset by operational problems which led to changes being made in the

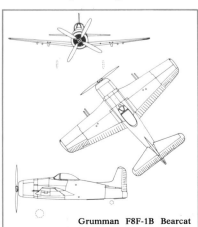

Grumman F8F-1B Bearcat

specifications. Production first centred on a two-seat night fighter variant, the F7F-2N, of which 65 were built, and then in 1945 reverted to a single-seat version, the F7F-3, of which 189 were built. This, however, was too late to go into service before the end of the war.

In 1946 the assembly lines built another 60 F7F-3Ns and 13 F7F-4Ns; both these models were in night fighter configuration for service with the US Marine Corps. The Tigercat's operational career also came to an end after the first stages of the Korean War.

Another of Grumman's "Cats" had a similar destiny, and to this day this aircraft is still considered the best single-seater carrier-borne piston-engine plane: this was the F8F Bearcat, designed in 1943 to replace the superb F6F Hellcat. The first prototype appeared on 21st August 1944 and two months later the US Navy ordered a large number.

With the coming of peace, the programme was revised: in 1945 the first of a total of 765 F8F-1s reached squadrons, followed in 1946 by 100 F8F-1Bs and 36 F8F-1Ns (night fighters). More than 24 squadrons of the US Navy were supplied with these fighters within the framework of a wide-ranging programme of modernisation whilst waiting for the first jet aircraft to come into service.

In 1948 the F8F-2 model was built which was more powerful and generally improved; 305 were built. Twelve

of these were night fighter variants (F8F-2N) and 30 were photo-reconnaissance planes (F8F-2P) which were taken out of service in 1952.

The Bearcats were used on operations in Indochina by the French *Armée de l'Air*, and were also flown by the Royal Thai Air Force.

At the beginning of the jet era the most aeronautically advanced nations brought the last examples of the long line of piston-engine aircraft into service alongside the new jets. In Britain the RAF and Fleet Air Arm, before replacing any of their front-line fighters with jet aircraft, for some time continued to use fighters which had been designed for the needs of the war which had just ended.

The de Havilland Hornet, for instance, which was derived from the famous Mosquito, was the last single-seat piston-engine plane of the Royal Air Force and as such it stayed in service until the middle of the 1950s. The design was undertaken in 1943 and the prototype flew on 28th July of the following year. The first Hornet F.1s were delivered in February 1945, too late to be made operational before the end of the war. After only five aircraft in a photo-reconnaissance variant (P.R.2) had been built, a second version, this time a fighter (F.3), appeared which had structural modifications and increased fuel capacity and immediately after this a new variant (F.R.4) which was further modified.

The aircraft's great qualities aroused the interest of the Royal Navy and in 1945 a navalised version of the Hornet was ordered. The principal variants which went to the Fleet Air Arm were the Sea Hornet F.20, the N.F.21 and the P.R.22, the first being a fighter, the second a night fighter and the third a photo-reconnaissance plane. In all, 391 Hornets were built excluding prototypes, of which 180 went to the Fleet Air Arm.

The last fighter with a piston engine to serve with the Royal Navy, however, was the single-seater Hawker Sea Fury, a powerful fighter of which 186 were built and which remained in front-line service for seven years, from 1947 until 1954. The Sea Fury's great

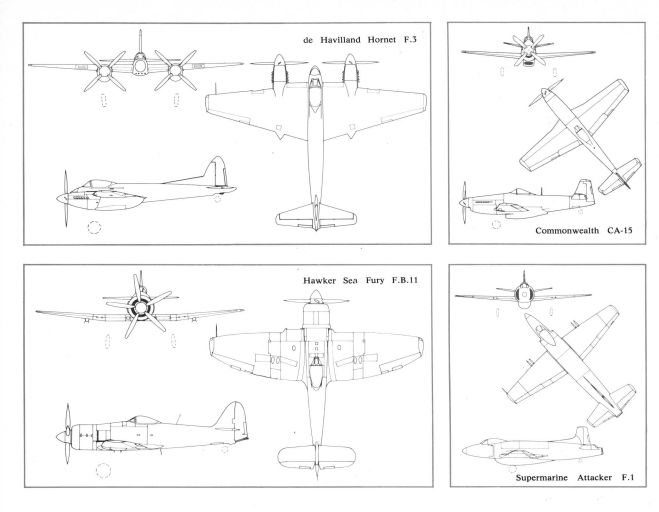

de Havilland Hornet F.3

Commonwealth CA-15

Hawker Sea Fury F.B.11

Supermarine Attacker F.1

Plate 189
The first jet fighters of the US Navy: 1944–53

With its traditionally cautious approach the US Navy gradually progressed to the use of jet combat planes in the immediate postwar period. Before the development and choice of a pure jet fighter, however, the naval staff wanted to try out a hybrid aircraft equipped with two different engines; a 1,350 hp radial engine and a turbojet of 725 kg (1,600 lb) thrust. The result of this prudent policy was the Ryan FR Fireball, a stubby single-seater which stood out from its contemporaries by having the jet engine exhaust located in the rear of the fuselage.

The prototype of the Fireball appeared on 25th June 1944, at which time a contract had already been drawn up for the supply of 100. At the end of proving trials this purchase order was increased to 600. In the event, only 66 aircraft of the Type FR-1 were built; these machines were used for a long series of experiments in order to test the effectiveness of a jet engine in carrier-borne use and they were also used for training until June 1947.

Immediately after the end of the war, the Fireball was joined by the US Navy's first carrier-borne pure jet, the McDonnell FH Phantom which had been designed in the late summer of 1943. This was also a transitional aircraft. The first of two prototypes flew on 26th January 1945 and two months later an order was placed for 100 aircraft (subsequently reduced to 60) of the first series, FH-1. The Phantom was the first pure jet aircraft to land on an American aircraft carrier on 21st July 1946.

The jet soon came of age. The first jets to see action with the US Navy, in Korea in the summer of 1950, were the first production aircraft of Grumman's F9F Panther-Cougar series, and these aeroplanes marked Grumman's first venture in the manufacture of jet aircraft. The design had been started in the closing stages of the Second World War in response to a specification from the Navy for a night fighter.

Progress was slow and delays were mainly linked to problems with the engine. By the time the first of the three prototypes took to the air on 24th November 1947, the specification had been changed, converting the aircraft to a day fighter. The F9F-2 variant was chosen for production, powered by a 2,270 kg (5,000 lb) thrust Pratt & Whitney J42-P6 turbojet constructed under licence from Rolls-Royce.

Following a purchase order for 567 aircraft, which went into service in May 1949, the two other versions were developed with more powerful

usefulness was confirmed during the Korean War, when it flew from British aircraft carriers and many "kills" of Soviet MiG-15 fighters were recorded.

The project had started in 1943 as a development of a design which had led to the Hawker Tempest: the aim was to built a lighter version of the aircraft, powered by a radial engine. After a long succession of experiments which led to the powerful Bristol Centaurus engine being chosen, the final prototype was prepared. By now, however, the war was over and the RAF (for whom the fighter had originally been intended) had lost all interest in it. Hawker, however, did not lose heart and built a navalised version of the aircraft, offering it to the Fleet Air Arm.

The aircraft was immediately accepted: 100 series aircraft were ordered and the first of these (F.10) went into service in August 1947. After the first 50, production was switched to a fighter-bomber variant (F.B.11) which was to become the principal variant: 615 were built up to November 1952: to these were added 60 Sea Fury T.20s for training which had a second cockpit. The remainder of the production was exported.

From 1951 onwards the Sea Fury was joined by the first jet to be used by the Fleet Air Arm, the Supermarine Attacker. The Attacker was a typical example of a first-generation jet air-

craft and 145 were built in three basic versions (plus another 36 in landplane configuration for the Pakistan Air Force): these were the F.1 fighter, the F.B.1 and the F.B.2 fighter-bomber variants (84 built). Work on the design had started at the end of 1944 with a view to offering the aircraft to the RAF. After the first prototype's proving flights, however (it made its maiden flight on 27th July 1946), the Royal Air Force's interest in the aircraft had waned and Supermarine modified the aircraft for carrier-borne use. The first navalised Attacker flew on 17th June 1947.

There were also two other interesting piston-engine fighters which, although developed in wartime, never saw combat service: the Swedish Saab 21 and the Australian Commonwealth CA-15. The Saab 21 flew on 30th July 1942, and went into production after the end of the war: 299 were built up till 1948. Saab's first jet fighter was a direct derivant of this aircraft, the model 21R which appeared in 1947.

The CA-15 was designed in 1943 but only completed three years later and was developed to equip the RAAF which a competent interceptor which could also be used as a long-range escort fighter. The prototype flew for the first time on 4th March 1946, and outclassed even the American P-51 Mustang, but this aircraft was not put into production.

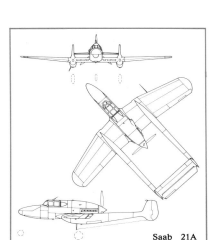

Saab 21A

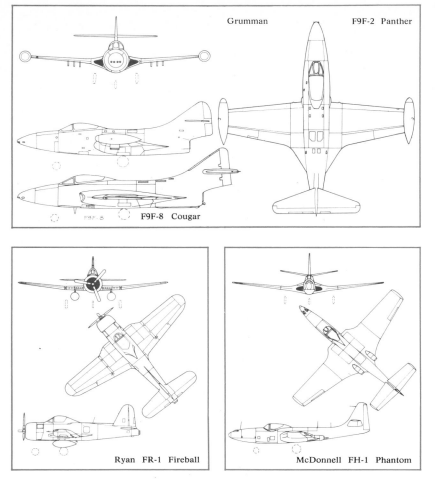

Grumman   F9F-2 Panther

F9F-8 Cougar

Ryan FR-1 Fireball

McDonnell FH-1 Phantom

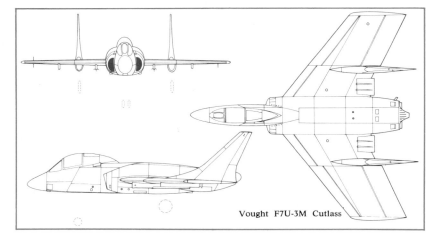

Vought F7U-3M Cutlass

Yakovlev Yak-15

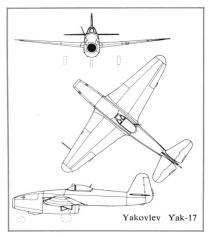

Yakovlev Yak-17

aircraft not to have the conventional tailplane and the first also to have an afterburner. It was developed immediately after the end of the war, using aerodynamic research carried out by the German Arado company, and the prototype Cutlass flew on 29th September 1948. Because of the difficulties encountered in perfecting the engines it was decided to cancel the order for the first two production series and to change the design. In its final configuration (F7U-3, 20th December 1951) 307 of these aircraft were built and production ceased in December 1955. Out of these, 180 were the F7U-3 variant, 12 were for photo-reconnaissance – the F7U-3P, and 98 were of the F7U-3M variant which was armed with air-to-air missiles. The Cutlass was replaced by the supersonic F8U Crusader from 1957 onwards.

Plate 190
The first Soviet jet fighters: 1946–47

The Soviet Union very quickly managed to bridge the technological gap which had separated her aircraft production from that of the other great powers during the war, succeeding within a short time and under great secrecy in equipping herself with machines comparable to, if not better than, those of the western world. The reasons underlying these exceptional results were in part to be found in the tremendous effort of organisation and production which had been made during the final phase of the war, and also to the availability of an enormous quantity of material and technical data, the booty of war captured from the more advanced German aeronautical industry.

In 1946, in a move which led to some resentment and fierce criticism, the British government supplied the USSR with several examples, together with the technical drawings, of the West's most advanced jet engine of the time, the Rolls-Royce Nene. With this unexpected technological assistance, Soviet designers made fast progress and in a short time they were competitive with western technology in this field as it advanced.

Yakovlev Yak-23

engines, designated F9F-4 and F9F-5. The assembly lines, however, only produced the F9F variant and, by the end of 1952, 761 of them had been completed, with the official name of Panther.

Meanwhile Grumman's engineers carried out a vast amount of work in order to bring the design up to date, give it more power and develop a new basic version of the fighter. This was designated F9F-6 Cougar and had a swept wing, with a sweep-back of 35°, and an engine which was 50 per cent more powerful.

The prototype flew on 20th September 1951 and shortly afterwards series production was started. The first

variants were the F9F-6 (706 built) and the F9F-7 (168 built, powered by a different type of engine). The first of these went into service in November 1952. The final version was the F9F-8 which appeared as a prototype on 18th December 1953: it had a longer fuselage in order to accommodate new fuel tanks and was equipped with radar which was installed in the nose. Cougars were also built for photo-reconnaissance, close support and training (F9F-8T – 399 built). The Cougar stayed in service until the late 1970s.

The life of another technically advanced fighter was short – this was the Vought F7U Cutlass, the first US

The first jet combat aircraft to fly in the USSR were the MiG-9 and the Yak-15, both of which were powered by engines of German origin. The Yak-15 was the first example by Alexander Sergeivitch Yakovlev, powered by this type of unit. The design was introduced in 1945, immediately after some turbojets which had been seized in Germany arrived in the Soviet Union. The engine chosen was the 900 kg (1,984 lb) thrust Junkers Jumo 004B, and in order to push forward with the development of the aircraft as quickly as possible the decision was taken to use as many components as possible from the Yak-3 piston-engine fighter. The prototype flew success-

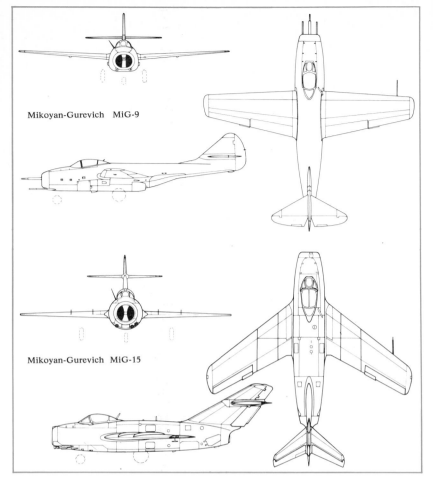

Mikoyan-Gurevich MiG-9

Mikoyan-Gurevich MiG-15

MiG-15, was Yakovlev's next design, the Yak-23, which echoed the configuration of his two preceding models. In appeared in prototype in 1947 and this fighter, which was called FLORA in NATO code, mainly equipped the air forces of the Soviet Union's eastern European allies for the whole of the 1950s. It was the first Soviet aircraft with an ejector seat for the pilot.

Plate 191
British and American jet fighters: 1948–50

After lengthy experiments with the Bell P-59 Airacomet, the American Air Force's first operational jet fighter was designed and built within the short space of six months. The Lockheed F-80 Shooting Star flew in prototype form on 8th January 1944 and only just missed the Second World War, but it proved its worth in a long and busy career which was still further widened by the success of the trainer variant the T-33. A total of 1,715

fighter aircraft in three principal versions were joined by as many as 5,691 trainers, built up till 1959 (plus 866 built under licence in Canada and Japan) which served with the air forces of about forty countries apart from the USA.

The P-80 design (the letter F was adopted in 1948) came to life in June 1943 when Lockheed received a request from the technical branch of the USAAF to design and build a single-seat jet fighter which could replace the P-59 Airacomet, which at that time was still encountering difficulties in its development. Lockheed's chief designer, Clarence "Kelly" Johnson, got a rough design ready in one week and asked for six months in which to complete a prototype. The time limit was met with time to spare when the XP-80 had its maiden flight and in the following June another two experimental aircraft appeared (YP-80A) with different engines. In October, 13 pre-series aircraft were delivered (YB-80A) and official proving trials were commenced with these. The end of the war meant an alteration in the size of the massive production programmes which were envisaged (5,000 aircraft of which some were to have been built by North American) and initial orders were for 917 P-80As. The first of these aircraft reached units in December 1945.

After the transitional 240 P-80Bs (which had a different engine and

fully on 24th April 1946, and production continued for two years completing about 400 aircraft which in the NATO code were given the name of FEATHER.

The MiG-9, too, was a first attempt in the field of jet propulsion, by Artem Mikoyan and Mikhail Gurevich. The prototype flew on the same day that the Yak-15 was tested and was powered by two BMW 003A 800 kg (1,760 lb) thrust engines. The development of the aircraft was troubled by a series of structural problems, and series production only started in 1946. For two years the assembly lines kept busy turning out about 550 aircraft in various versions. Amongst these were the MiG-9 UTI trainer, the MiG-9F which was more powerful, and the MiG-9FR with a pressurised cockpit. In NATO code, the MiG-9s were called FARGO.

Another fighter which belonged to the first generation of jet aircraft was the Yak-17, directly derived in 1947 from the Yak-15. It had a different undercarriage, structural improvements and was more powerful, and this aircraft was produced in a combat version and a trainer version (Yak-17 UTI) and as at August 1949, 700 had been built. The Yak-17s were also used by the Polish and Czechoslovak air forces: in NATO code they were also called FEATHER.

The first fighter of the second generation was the famous MiG-15 which

was almost completely developed in the few months which Soviet industry needed to get the production under licence of the Rolls-Royce Nene turbojet under way. Work on the project had started towards the end of 1945 and had remained practically at a standstill because of the lack of a suitable power plant. In the following year the aircraft achieved the final stage of its development with the signing of the trade agreement with Britain.

The first prototype flew on 30th December 1947 and at the end of the first test flights series production was started which in five years accounted for over 8,000 of these aircraft without taking into account those produced under licence in Poland, Czechoslovakia and the People's Republic of China. The MiG-15 was used from the end of 1948 and first saw combat service in November 1950, in Korea, where it clearly demonstrated its superiority over the contemporary American fighter planes, making the balance of air power shift decisively in favour of Russian-backed North Korea. The main versions of the MiG-15, which stayed in service until the second half of the 1970s, included the MiG-15 SD which had a more powerful engine; the MiG-15 UTI trainer, and the MiG-15 SB allweather fighter. In NATO code it was designated FAGOT.

Less well-known, and less outstanding, though a contemporary of the

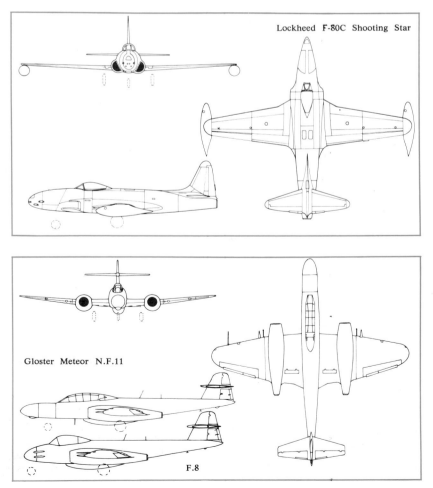

Lockheed F-80C Shooting Star

Gloster Meteor N.F.11

F.8

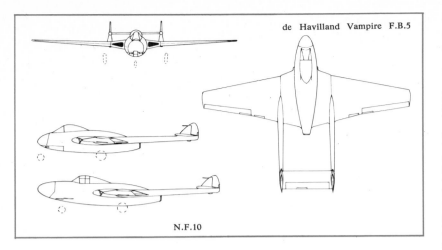

de Havilland Vampire F.B.5

N.F.10

improved armament) which went to make up the initial purchase order, in 1948 the second principal production variant appeared, the F-80C, which was more powerful and of which 798 were built. The Shooting Star first saw battle in Korea and stayed in first-line service until the arrival of the more modern F-84 and F-86. It was an F-80 on 8th November 1950 which took part in the first battle between jet fighters in the history of aviation.

British experience immediately after the war differed from that of the Americans. Whereas the US aircraft industry had to produce a new jet after the P-59 in order to have a fully operational jet fighter at its disposal, the British at first limited themselves to perfecting their first jet, the Gloster Meteor, in order that the RAF should have an effective and continually updated weapon.

The scope of the career of the first British jet aircraft is revealed by a few figures. Between 1942 and 1954 3,545 Meteors in eleven basic versions left the assembly lines to serve with the air forces of no less than twelve nations; these were joined by another 330 constructed under licence in the Netherlands by Fokker between 1951 and 1954. Amongst the front-line aircraft of the RAF these aeroplanes stayed in service as interceptors (F.8 until the spring of 1957) and night fighters (N.F.14 until August 1961).

After the wartime manufacture of

the first two production series, the development of this design quickly gathered momentum. The twenty Mk Is of 1944 and the 210 Mk IIIs of 1954 were joined by 685 Meteor F.4 models (almost twice as powerful: in service from 1948); 712 Meteor T.7 trainers (in service from 1949); 1,183 F.8 fighters (in service from June 1950 and which were much modified, with longer range). There were only two photo-reconnaissance variants: the F.R.9 (126 built) and the F.R.10 (58) whereas there were more numerous night fighter variants: the first, the N.F.11, appeared in prototype on 31st May 1950 and 335 were built; the second was the N.F.12, of which 100 were built; the third N.F.13 (40 built) and the last, the N.F.14 of which 100 were completed. The countries which used the Meteor were Argentina, the Netherlands, Belgium, France, Denmark, Egypt, Brazil, Syria, Israel and Sweden.

The second British jet fighter, the de Havilland Vampire, had as far-reaching a success and this too was developed during the war years but arrived too late to take part in hostilities. It was used by the air forces of about thirty countries and was constructed under licence in India, Australia, France and Italy (total production exceeded 4,000); it remained in service as a trainer until the second half of the 1970s, with the air forces of minor powers. The design originated

back in 1941 and had reached prototype stage on 26th September 1943; it was put into production in March 1944 as the F.1 version (120 built, in service from 1946).

Many other Vampire models followed: the F.3 which was another fighter; the F.B.5 for use as a fighter bomber (the prototype flew on 23rd June 1948) and the F.B.9 which was tropicalised; the N.F.10 (prototype appeared in 1949 and 95 were constructed) night fighter; the T.11 trainer (15th November 1950 – 800 built plus another 200 approximately under licence). The Vampire F.B.5 and N.F.10 were those exported in the largest numbers, in particular to the *Aeronautica Militare Italiana* in 1950 who took the F.B.5 and later also took several N.F.10s.

Plate 192
Soviet fighters begin to catch up: 1948–53

The MiG-15 marked a turning point in the evolution of postwar Soviet military aviation production. Mikoyan and Gurevitch's successful fighters became the forerunners of an entire generation of combat aircraft and in so doing eclipsed other worthwhile contemporary designs.

Among its unfortunate rivals were the Yakovlev Yak-30 and the Lavochkin La-15, both of which were designed in response to the same specification which had led to the MiG-15. The first, which was the logical step forward in a line of fighters which had started with the Yak-15 of 1946, remained at prototype stage, in spite of the fact that its general performance was completely satisfactory: the decision not to proceed with production was influenced by the long time it took to perfect the aircraft, the proving trials only starting in September 1948, when the MiG-15 was about to go into series production.

The Lavochkin La-15 (FANTAIL in NATO code) did achieve production status, but in limited numbers: this aircraft represented the culmination of a long period of research carried out by one of the leading Soviet

designers in the field of jet propulsion. Two prototypes were flown in 1948 and the aircraft went into service as a tactical fighter, continuing in use for a good part of the 1950s.

At the beginning of the 1950s a more powerful and modern successor to the MiG-15 made its appearance, the MiG-17, which was an interceptor developed to correct unsatisfactory aerodynamics in transonic flight which had come to light during the operational career of the MiG-15. Apart from its more powerful engine, the new Mikoyan and Gurevitch fighter had a completely redesigned wing and extensive modifications to the control surfaces. Tests started at the beginning of January in 1950 and proved completely satisfactory; the MiG-17 was immediately put into production and started to reach units of the *VVS* during 1952. Many variants were built in the Soviet Union, the basic type (FRESCO A in NATO code) was followed by the MiG-17P all-weather interceptor (FRESCO B) then the MiG-17F (FRESCO C) appeared which had an afterburner, as well as a range of streamlining and structural improvements; the next version was an all-weather fighter and finally, the last principal variant – the MiG17PFU (FRESCO E) which had guided air-to-air missiles. Procurement in the Soviet Union totalled over 9,000 aircraft, ending in 1958. To these must be added considerable numbers which were constructed under licence in Poland, Czechoslovakia and the People's Republic of China. The MiG-17 was in service with all the Warsaw Pact countries and many other third world and Asian countries.

The next logical step forward of the MiG-17 design appeared in prototype in September 1953, designated MiG-19. This aircraft was as aggressive and successful as those which had gone before, and it had just as busy a career. It was manufactured in the USSR from 1953 until the end of the 1960s (with an estimated total of over 5,000 built), it was constructed under licence in Czechoslovakia from 1957 and in China from 1961 to 1975, and the MiG-19 became the standard interceptor for all the Warsaw Pact air forces and many other countries.

The official debut of the MiG-19 came about when production had already started, in 1955, when it was first shown in the traditional air display at Tushino, but at that time its early operational use had already revealed problems of flight stability, and in order to solve these it was found necessary to built a second variant of the fighter (MiG-19S) which went into service in the second half of 1956, NATO observers giving it the same code-name as its predecessor, FARMER A. In 1958 an all-weather fighter variant appeared designated MiG-19P (FARMER B) and subsequently the MiG-19F (FARMER C) with a more powerful engine was developed, as well as the MiG-19PF

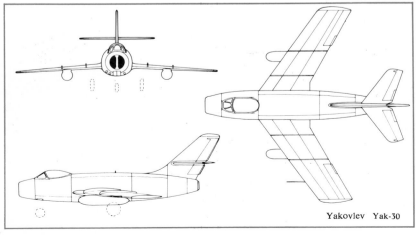

Yakovlev Yak-30

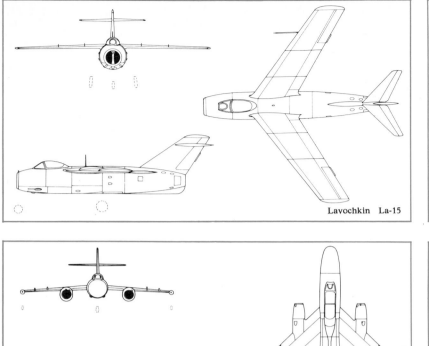

Lavochkin La-15

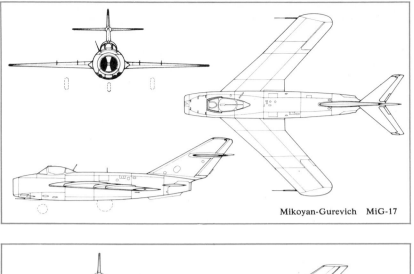

Mikoyan-Gurevich MiG-17

Yakovlev Yak-25A

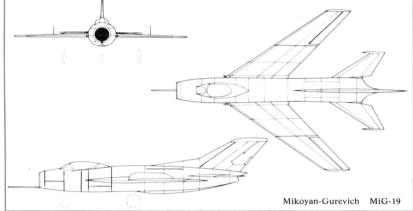

Mikoyan-Gurevich MiG-19

(FARMER D) which resembled the preceding model but was an all-weather fighter with all-missile armament, and the MiG-19 PM (FARMER E) night fighter, which stayed in service with the *VVS* until 1972.

Among all-weather interceptors the first two-seat twin-jet of the *VVS* was the Yakovlev Yak-25 (FLASH-LIGHT in NATO code) which remained in service for nearly twenty years, starting in 1955. The prototype appeared in 1952 and production was concentrated on another three basic versions apart from the first one (the Yak-25A). These were a reconnaissance and close support variant; an all-weather version and a tactical reconnaissance version, the Yak-25R. In 1959 a very high altitude strategic reconnaissance plane was derived from these aircraft (MANDRAKE in NATO code) which carried out similar surveillance duties to the American U2 planes.

Plate 193
First generation French jet fighter and Switzerland's sole venture: 1949–56

France soon caught up after the delays caused by the Second World War and became one of the limited number of air powers. Her first entirely nationally produced fighter, the Dassault M.D.450 Ouragan, was also the first of a long line of combat aircraft which were produced by a manufacturer which in the course of a few years was to reach the very forefront of aviation. The design was a private venture of Marcel Bloch and work began in 1946 immediately after his return to France from prison camp in Germany. This great technical achievement was rewarded on 29th June 1948, with an official order to build three prototypes. The first of these was successfully flown on 28th February the following year.

Series production was started in 1950 with an initial contract for 150 aircraft, followed within a short time by another two orders, each for 100 aircraft. These orders kept the assembly lines busy until 1954. In squadron service with the *Armée de l'Air*, the Ouragan started to replace the British Vampires in 1952, and stayed in first line service until May 1955. The Dassault fighter, apart from serving the

French air force, were also used by the Indian air force (104 ordered in June 1953) and by the Israeli air force (12 ordered in 1955).

In the spring of 1955 a new aircraft produced by Dassault started to replace the Ouragan in squadron service: this was the Mystère, an aircraft which was to go down in the history of aviation as the first fighter with slightly swept wings and was to become the first supersonic fighter to be built by the European aviation industry. The design had originated two years after that which had led to the Ouragan, and the Mystère was a further development of the Ouragan design.

The first prototype had its maiden flight on 23rd February 1951 and was

followed by another nine experimental aircraft and by eleven pre-series aircraft (Mystère II-C). It was this model which went into production in 1954 and 180 were built. The final variant was the Mystère IV of which the prototype appeared on 28th September 1952. Compared with its predecessor this version had a completely redesigned wing, a much stronger airframe and considerable changes made to its fuselage and tailplane. Eleven pre-series aircraft were constructed of the Mystère IV and then the final production series (IV-A) which brought the total to 483 by the time production ended in 1958. Nearly all went to the *Armée de l'Air*; 110 to the Indian air force and 50 to the Israeli air force.

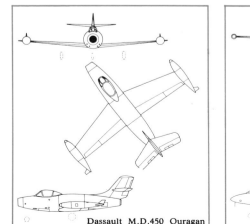

Dassault M.D.450 Ouragan

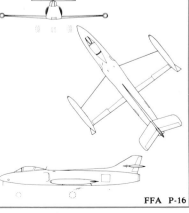

FFA P-16

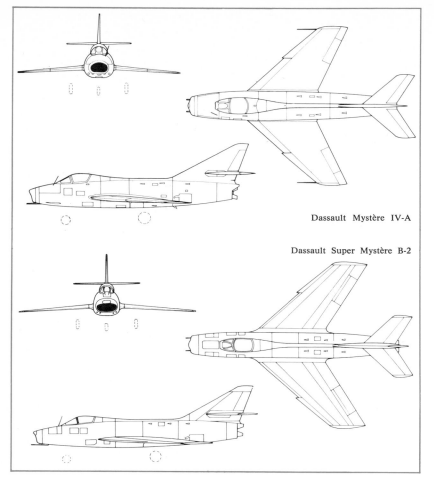

Dassault Mystère IV-A

Dassault Super Mystère B-2

Plate 194
The first great jet fighter of the USAF sees action in Korea: 1950–54

In the USAF the Lockheed F-80 Shooting Star was soon replaced in front-line service by a more modern, aggressive and powerful combat plane: the North American F-86 Sabre, the first swept-wing jet fighter to be adopted by the American air arm. In many respects this was also the last example of a long line of "classic" interceptors whose origins went back to the beginning of aerial warfare. It was fast and very manoeuvrable and gave a good account of itself in a dog-fight; the Sabre was to remain one of the best fighters of its time and was used in almost all Western countries, remaining in front-line service for almost twenty years. Various models of the F-86 were built in their thousands, including those built under licence in Canada, Australia, Japan and Italy. The *Aeronautica Militare* adopted the type E Sabre in 1956 (built under licence by Canadair), and the F-86K was produced by Fiat under licence in 1961.

Work began on the Sabre design in 1944. At that time North American was already working on a jet fighter for the US Navy (XFJ-1 Fury) and decided to develop a model for the USAAF. The project was accepted and after lengthy research into the swept wing (which was accepted only after the end of the war when an analysis of German research experiments indicated that a swept wing would significantly improve performance) a first prototype was completed which flew on 1st October 1947. It was an immediate success and was followed by an initial order for 221 aircraft of the first production variant, F-86A. In the event 554 Sabres were built which went into squadron service from February 1949. They first saw battle in Korea where they replaced the F-80 and won back air supremacy from the Soviet MiG-15.

The second principal production variant was the F-86E which appeared in prototype form on 23rd September 1950 and of which 336 were built. It was followed two years later (19th March 1952) by the prototype of the F variant which had a modified wing and a more powerful engine; as many as 2,450 of these Sabres were built; units of the USAF received them in the same month of March, and in autumn the F-86Fs arrived in Korea as replacements for the aircraft of the first production series. On 30th April 1953 the prototype of the subsequent day fighter variant appeared, the F-86H, which was more powerful, better armed and slightly larger: 473 were built and delivered to the USAF between January 1954 and August 1955.

The evolution of the Dassault family of fighter planes continued uninterruptedly. In the early versions the Mystère was barely supersonic; the next step led to an even more powerful and sophisticated fighter being built. The prototype which launched this new phase of research appeared in December 1953: this Mystère IV-B had an afterburner turbojet and considerable structural modifications. This prototype was followed by another two experimental aircraft and 16 pre-series aircraft which were subjected to lengthy trials in order to define the numerous structural modifications which were necessary to achieve optimum configuration and functioning of the more powerful engine which was to be installed. During these exhaustive proving trials, on 24th February 1954, a Mystère IBV was the first French aircraft to break the sound barrier in level flight.

These efforts were crowned by the creation of the Super Mystère, a fighter which fully justified the designers' hopes and repeated the success of the earlier plane. The first prototype flew on 2nd March 1955, and the first series model (B-2) appeared on 15th May the following year. The Super Mystère remained in production until October 1959 and 180 of them were built: it remained in first-line service with the *Armée de l'Air* until the middle of the 1960s. Twenty were sold to Israel and survived until 1975, being used in combat in the Middle East wars.

At this point it is worth mentioning, in the context of postwar European aeronautical activity, the first and only attempt by the Swiss to build a jet fighter. This aircraft was designated FFA P16 and had a British engine – the Armstrong Siddeley Sapphire turbojet of about 5,000 kg (11,025 lb) thrust. It appeared in prototype on 28th April 1955 but its development was disrupted by a number of serious accidents which in 1957 led the Swiss authorities to abandon the programme, although during its few test flights the P-16 had shown that it had good general flight characteristics and worthwhile development potential.

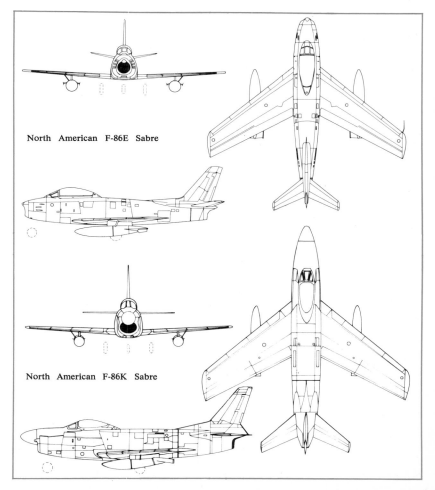

North American F-86E Sabre

North American F-86K Sabre

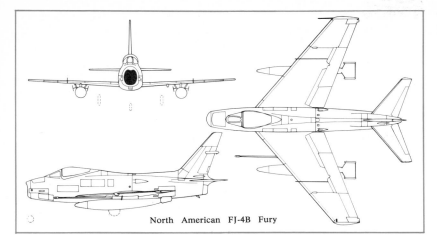

North American FJ-4B Fury

Apart from the day fighter variants other all-weather versions were produced which all had nose-installed radar. The first of these Sabres was the F-86D which appeared as a prototype on 22nd December 1949 and went into squadron service in March 1951. A total of 2,054 were built, 981 of which were subsequently modified by the USAF in an updated version (F-86L) based on the H day fighter model and equipped with more modern electronics.

For specific use by NATO countries, finally, in 1954, the F-86K variant was developed, the salient feature of which was the adoption of four 20 mm cannon instead of the air-to-air rockets of the Type D. The F-86K prototype was flown on 15th July 1954 and total production reached 341, 221 of which were built by Fiat (63 for the *Aeronautica Militare Italiana*, 60 for the *Armée de l'Air*, 88 for the *Luftwaffe*, 6 for the Royal Netherlands Air Force and 4 for the Royal Norwegian Air Force). The main manufacturer under licence in the F-86 programme was Canadair; from 1949 to October 1958 this Canadian manufacturer completed 1,815 aircraft in various versions.

The career of the plane which had led to all the Sabre aircraft was less outstanding: this was the FJ Fury. The US Navy, having at first encouraged the project and ordering 30 of the first straight-wing variant (the F-86 was derived from this particular model) stopped all production, preferring the aircraft chosen by the army. Only on 10th February 1951 was a contract signed for three new prototypes and the first of these (XFJ-2) flew on 27th December. Production was started in 1952 and involved several variants: these were the FJ-2, in service from 1954, 200 built; the FJ-3, in service from September 1954, 583 built (the prototype had flown on 11th December 1953); the FJ-4, in service from 1956, 152 built (first flight on 28th October 1954); the FJ-4B, in service from 1956, 222 built: this was

the final version which was for ground attack. The FJ-3 version was gradually modified during the course of production and the sub-series FJ-3M was the most important. Fury production ended in 1958.

Plate 195
The F-84 Thunderjet — the second outstanding USAF jet fighter: 1950–54

The F-86 Sabre was, together with the Republic F-84 Thunderjet, the best of the first generation jet fighters. It was designed by the creator of the outstanding P-47 Thunderbolt, Alexander Kartveli, and the F-84 echoed in a more modern and aggressive way the success of its illustrious predecessor. As many as 7,889 aircraft in numerous variants (amongst which the last one, the F-84F, was a major redesign of the original version, having a swept wing) left the assembly lines and of these almost half, 3,723 aircraft, equipped the air forces of NATO countries within the context of American postwar military aid programmes. In Italy for example the *Aeronautica Militare* put F-84s into service in 1952 and kept the RF-84F photo-reconnaissance variant in use until 1974. In the USAF the Thunderjet/Thunderstreak/Thunderflash (these were the names of the principal variants of the F-84) stayed in first-line service until the middle of the sixties.

The design of the F-84 had originated as far back as 1944 when Alexander Kartveli had started to think of developing a jet version of the P-47

Thunderbolt. The basic design of the F-84 was completed before the end of that year after a long series of experiments and plans using various power plants which were being developed at that time. The prototype was built round the General Electric TG-180 turbojet (subsequently called J35), and at the beginning of 1945 this design effort was rewarded by an order for three aircraft which were designated XP-84 and for 400 series aircraft.

The first prototype had its maiden flight on 28th February 1946 and the second followed in August. At the end of test flights production started off with 25 pre-series models designated YP-84 and subsequently went on to the manufacture of the definitive variant, the F-84B. The new fighter reached units from the summer of 1947 onwards and procurement was 226. The following version was the C model (which first flew in April 1948) which had structural details changed, and of which 191 were built. In November the following year the first F-84Ds appeared (154 built) which had stronger airframe and more powerful engines. These Thunderjets were the first to be used in the Korean War where they gave a good account of themselves.

On 18th May 1949 the prototype of the following production variant was flown, the F-84E (843 built) which was again modified and the fuselage

was about 30 cm longer. Finally, in November 1950, the fifth and last straight-wing version appeared, the F-84G (3,025 built) which was developed specifically at the request of Tactical Air Command who needed a light fighter-bomber able to deliver tactical nuclear weapons. The Thunderjets were the first single-seaters able to carry out such tasks.

In the following variant, the F-84F, the configuration of the aircraft was drastically changed when a 45° swept wing was adopted; the prototype flew on 5th June 1950 and the first series aircraft (named Thunderstreak) flew on 22nd November 1952. A total of 2,711 were built which went into service from 1954 onwards and represented the final stage of the design as a straight combat plane. The final version, the RF-84F, was for photo-reconnaissance.

A contemporary of the Thunderjet was the Lockheed F-94 Starfire, an all-weather interceptor which was derived from the trainer variant of the F-80 Shooting Star. This aircraft was clearly a transitional plane which was used almost exclusively within the United States. The prototype flew on 1st July 1949 and at the end of proving trials production of the first series, F-94A, was started (110 built). In 1951, 357 F-94Bs followed and subsequently 387 F-94Cs (the prototype of which had flown in 1950) and of which the wing had been substantially

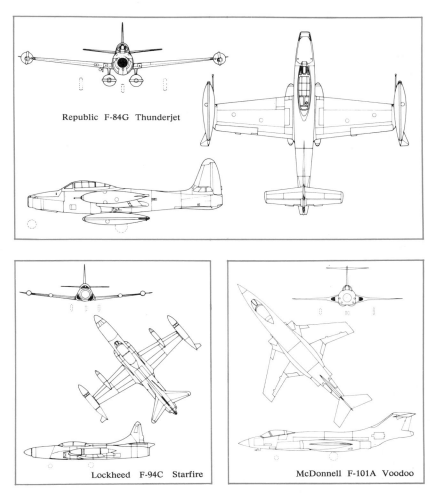

Republic F-84G Thunderjet

Lockheed F-94C Starfire

McDonnell F-101A Voodoo

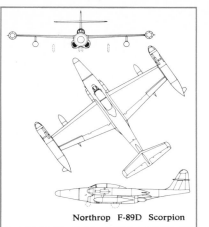

Northrop F-89D Scorpion

Plate 196
British fighters of the fifties: 1953–56

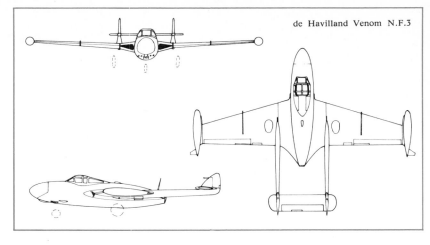

de Havilland Venom N.F.3

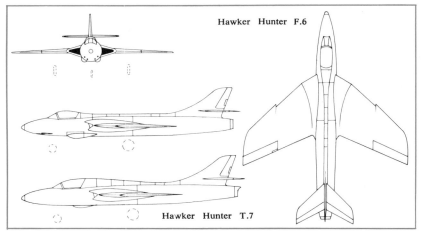

Hawker Hunter F.6

Hawker Hunter T.7

redesigned as had the fuselage and the tailplane; it had air-to-air missiles installed in the nose and in two wing-pods.

Another contemporary design led to the Northrop F-89 Scorpion: the first twin-seater all-weather interceptor of the USAF to be designed as such. The programme had got under way towards the end of 1945 with the aim of producing a successor to the P-61 Black Widow. The prototype flew on 16th August 1948 and 18 of the first production model (F-89A) were delivered two years later. 30 F-89Bs followed and 164 type Cs which were more powerful and generally improved. Subsequent versions had increasingly powerful armament.

The Scorpion F-89D (first flown in 1951 and of which 682 were built) was armed with rockets; 156 F-89Hs also had six missiles as well as 42 rockets: F-89Js could carry two nuclear warhead missiles, carried under the wings, and another four conventional warheads in under-wing racks. In all 1,050 Scorpions were built which stayed in service from 1951 till 1957.

The McDonnell F-101 Voodoo had a relatively limited success; this was a versatile single-seater which was hampered by a very long development process and by continual changes in the specifications. Although it was designed immediately after the end of the Second World War as a penetration fighter, the Voodoo only took on its final configuration in 1954, when it was adapted for close support.

The definitive prototype flew on 29th September of that year and production concentrated on six models, of which two (RF-101A and RF-101C) were photo-reconnaissance planes. 50 of the first version (F-101A) and 40 of the second (F-101C which went into service in, 1957) were built; 35 of the RF-101A and 166 of the RC-101C; a total of 478 of the final variant, the F-101B, were built. The Voodoo stayed in service with the USAF for a good part of the sixties; 133 of the 805 manufactured served with the Royal Canadian Air Force up till the middle of the following decade.

In Britain the development of the line of jet fighters went on uninterruptedly during the 1950s. A direct successor to the de Havilland Vampire was the Venom: an aircraft which repeated the twin-boom formula which had been so successful. The prototype was tested for the first time on 2nd September 1949 and series production soon got under way with the first fighter variant, the F.B.1, of which 373 were built. These Venoms were in service with the RAF from 1952 onwards but were not satisfactory. The optimum configuration was reached in the aircraft of the second series, F.B.4, the prototype of which had its maiden flight on 29th December 1953, with modified tailplanes and detail changes.

The Venoms were also successfully exported. 150 were constructed for the RAF and these were followed by numerous models for Iraq and Venezuela whilst 250 were built under licence in Switzerland between 1952 and 1955.

Production went on to two night fighter versions which had substantial fuselage modifications to accommodate a radar installation and a two-man crew. The first of these, N.F.2, appeared in prototype on 22nd August 1950, and was put into production two years later: about 80 aircraft left the assembly lines. The second, N.F.3, had detail structural changes and a total of 129 were built in 1953. Apart from the aircraft which were for export (notably to Australia and Sweden) and those constructed under licence abroad (France acquired the construction rights), 256 Sea Venoms were produced in total which were for the Fleet Air Arm and fell into three variants based on the RAF night fighter versions: the F.A.W.20, the F.A.W.21 and the F.A.W.22. The Sea Venoms remained in first line service until the end of 1960.

But the best British fighter of the first postwar generation was the Hawker Hunter, an aircraft of which just under 2,000 were constructed and which formed the backbone of Fighter Command from 1953 until 1964, staying in service until the beginning of the 1970s. This operational success with the RAF was echoed by the Hunter's success abroad: Belgium, the Netherlands, Sweden, Denmark and about 15 other countries adopted the versatile Hawker fighter. Production for export exceeded 400 (not counting 445 which were constructed under licence in the Netherlands) and apart from these no less than 700 Hunters in various versions had been taken out of service

with the RAF, updated and sold to foreign buyers, especially third world countries.

Work started on the design in 1946 under the supervision of Sydney Camm; two years later a specification was issued which called for the production of a replacement for the Gloster Meteor, which was followed by an order for three prototypes. The first prototype flew on 20th July 1951 and on 16th May 1953 the forerunner of the first series production model, the F.1, took to the air.

The development of the new fighter proceeded at great speed. The 139 Hunters of the first series were followed by 45 F.2s (first flown on 14th October 1953, with engine modi-

fications) and 365 F.4s (maiden flight 20th October 1954) with new wings, greater fuel capacity and pylons for external stores. The last two variants were the F.5 (105 built, first flight 19th October 1954) and the F.6 in which the basic airframe reached its full potential due to the adoption of a Rolls-Royce Avon turbojet which was more than 30 per cent more powerful. The first Hunter F.6 flew on 25th March 1955 and the RAF put 383 of them into service from January of the following year.

In 1959 a ground attack version was derived from the F.6 (designated F.G.A.9) which was achieved by modifying some aircraft which were already in service, arming them more

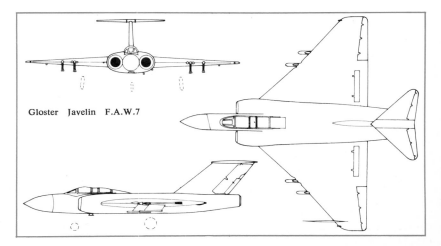

Gloster Javelin F.A.W.7

heavily and giving them greater fuel capacity. Apart from these basic fighter variants Hawker also developed a trainer version, the T.7, which appeared in July 1955. From this a sub-series was derived (T.8 – 41 built) for naval use.

For the role of all-weather fighter, the RAF kept a heavy twin-jet two-seater in service from 1956 until 1968, the Gloster Javelin. This was the first British aircraft to be made to this specific design. Six prototypes flew between 6th November 1951 and 31st October 1955 and series production was based on seven basic versions: the F.A.W.1 (40 built); the F.A.W.2 (30); the F.A.W.4 (50); the F.A.W.5 (64); the F.A.W.6 (33); the F.A.W.7 (96) and the F.A.W.8 (47).

These aircraft were progressively improved, had more advanced electronics and more powerful armament and updated engines, and they were joined by 35 trainer aircraft, designated T.3. The last variant was the F.A.W.9 which was structurally modified. Production ended in 1960.

Plate 197
US Navy fighters: 1951–58

After a period of indecision during the 1950s the US Navy set about strengthening its air arm.

Two aircraft which still belonged to the first generation but had a very busy and useful operational career were the Douglas F3D Skyknight and the McDonnell F2H Banshee. The first aircraft took shape on 3rd April 1946 in response to a navy specification which called for an all-weather jet

fighter which was to be the first of its type. The prototype was flown on 28th March 1948 and, at the end of proving trials and operational test flights, production was started on 28 of the first series, F3D-1.

These aircraft were delivered from February 1951 and in that same month the prototype of the second version appeared, the F3D-2 in which the most notable improvement was to the engine. These Skyknights accounted for nearly the whole of the procurement (237 out of a total of 268) and they only equipped units of the US Marine Corps. Their operational use was principally confined to the Korean War and the Skyknights remained in front line service until late in the 1950s.

The McDonnell F2H Banshee, however, lasted longer; this was a single-seater which had been designed as far back as 1945 as a replacement for the Phantom: the 892 aircraft constructed in four basic versions remained in service until the beginning of the 1960s. The first prototype flew on 11th January 1947 and the aircraft of the first series, F2H-1 – a total of 56 built – went into squadron service in March 1949.

In that year production of the second variant was started: the F2H-2, which had a more powerful engine and increased fuel capacity; as at September 1952, 364 of them had been built plus another fourteen night fighters (F2H-2N) and 58 for photo-reconnaissance (F2H-2P). The 250 Banshees of the third variant, F2H-3, had longer range, and the 150 aircraft of the final series, F2H-4, were more powerful and were built from 1953 onwards. The US Navy was not the only one to use the F2Hs (they were used a great deal in Korea); in 1955 39 F2H-3s which had been withdrawn from first-line service were sold to the Royal Canadian Navy.

In the second half of the 1950s two new fighters went into service with the US Navy: the Douglas F4D Skyray and the McDonnell F3H Demon. These were very modern and sophisticated aircraft which belonged to the second generation of jet fighters but, because of a whole series of circumstances which were basically linked to the failure of the development programme for the engine which was to power this aircraft, the Westinghouse J40, they had a short operational career as transitional aircraft.

The F4D Skyray – which was the first carrier-borne delta wing fighter – was developed from 1947 onwards but the definitive prototype only flew on 5th June 1954. Production of the first and only variant, F4D-1, started two years later as did deliveries to units. The assembly lines were closed in 1958 when 420 had been built. The Skyray stayed in service until 1962.

The FH3 Demon had a similar career; although it was ready in 1951 it had to await the outcome of the J40 programme for nearly four years and eventually it was adapted to be

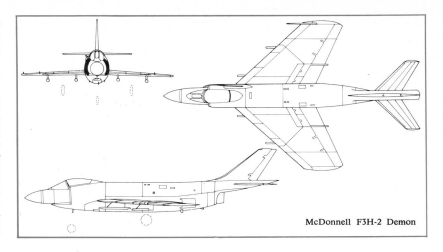

McDonnell F3H-2 Demon

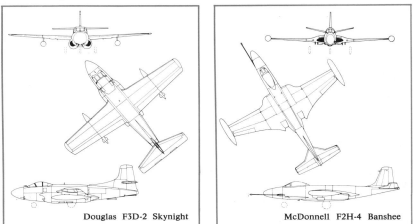

Douglas F3D-2 Skynight

McDonnell F2H-4 Banshee

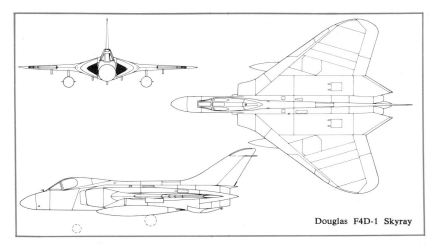

Douglas F4D-1 Skyray

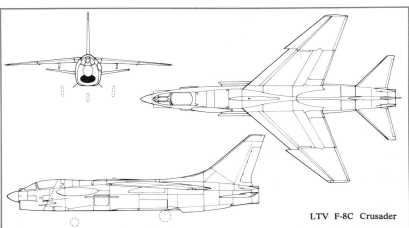

LTV F-8C Crusader

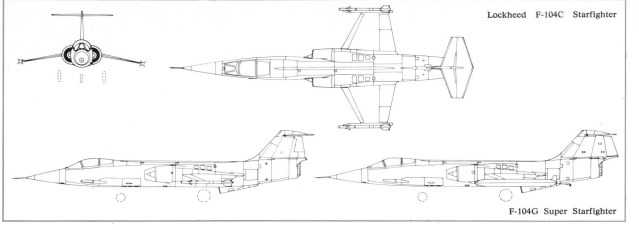

Lockheed F-104C Starfighter

F-104G Super Starfighter

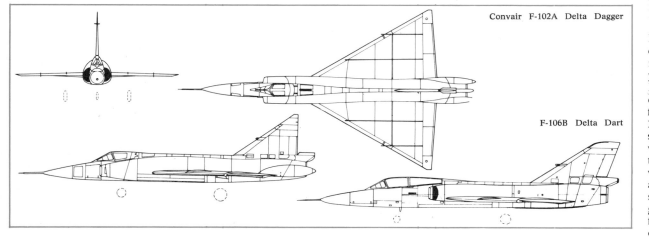

Convair F-102A Delta Dagger

F-106B Delta Dart

powered by a different engine. After the appearance of the original prototype, X3F-1 on 7th August 1951, the aircraft finally went into production under the designation of F3H-2 (231 built) in 1955 and was put into squadron service in the following year.

The main variants built up till 1959 were the F3H-2M (95) and the F3H-2N (125) which were armed respectively with Sparrow III and Sidewinder missiles. Total production, including 56 aircraft of the first F3H-1N series which was subsequently discontinued, totalled 507. The Demon stayed in first-line service until 1965.

The F-8 Crusader, on the other hand, was a resounding success and was one of the most widely used and effective carrier-borne supersonic fighters of its time. It was designed by Chance Vought in 1952 and remained in production from 1955 until 1965; the 1,259 aircraft built were in first-line service until late in the 1970s. After the prototype's maiden flight (25th May 1955) the development of the Crusader proceeded very rapidly. The first variant, F-8A (318 built which went into squadron service in 1957), was followed by 130 F-8Bs, 134 RF-8A photo-reconnaissance planes, 187 F-8Cs, 152 F-8Ds and 286 F-8Es.

The variants, the last of which appeared in June 1961, were all subjected to continual improvements in avionics and had more powerful engines, greater fuel capacity and better armament. In order to prolong the operational life of these aircraft between 1966 and 1968, 375 aircraft which were drawn from all production series were subjected to a very thorough updating programme and modifications were made to the landing gear, the wing and electronics. The French *Aéronavale* bought 42 aircraft of the type F-8E.

Plate 198
From the Delta Dagger to the Starfighter: 1954–60

A new generation of supersonic combat aircraft came to life in the 1950s in answer to the needs of the USAF. The first Delta wing interceptors to have all-missile armament were the Convair F-102 Delta Dagger and the F-106 Delta Dart, powerful and sophisticated aircraft which remained in first-line service until the second half of the 1970s.

The F-102 design was launched by Convair in 1950 on the basis of the experiments which had been carried out in the two preceding years into supersonic flight and the first prototype flew on 24th October 1953. After a laborious development phase which led to numerous modifications, on 20th December the following year the final prototype appeared, YF-102A, from which the first production series was directly derived. 975 F-102As were built which went into service half-way through 1956, staying in first-line service until 1974.

Side by side with this operational version a trainer variant was constructed (111 built) which was designated TF-102A and had a wider forward fuselage in order to enable the crew to sit side by side. The development of the basic design culminated in 1956 in the appearance on 26th December of the prototype F-106 Delta Dart, which was 50 per cent more powerful. Production went on until 1960 and 277 F-106s were built and 63 F-106Bs, this latter variant being a twin-seat operational trainer.

The real "thoroughbred" of the first generation of supersonic aeroplanes was the North American F-100 Super Sabre, an aircraft which was developed from the F-96 Sabre, and it equalled and outstripped its forerunner's success. 2,294 were built in four basic versions and the Super Sabre went into service with the USAF in 1954 and remained in service until 1972. Its career in some of the western countries' air forces was just as long; it was bought by Turkey, Denmark, France and Nationalist China.

The F-100 design was drawn up by North American in 1949 with the aim of perfecting the Sabre design and making it a supersonic aircraft. Two years later under the spur of the Korean War the USAF authorised construction of two prototypes and the first of these was successfully flown on 25th May 1953. The first production series was the F-100A, of which 203 were constructed from the autumn of that year onwards. Its operational use was held up, however, by a series of accidents which in 1954 led to the suspension of the Super Sabre programme and to a series of modifications to the structure and surfaces of the wing and tailplanes.

The second series was a fighter-bomber variant and the first of the 476 F-100Cs built flew on 17th January 1955. The third variant was the F-100D (first flight 24th January 1956 – production total 1,274) in which considerable changes were made to the aircraft's structure and avionics. Air-to-air missiles and air-to-ground missiles were added to its weaponry. The last version (3rd August 1956) was the F-100F which was for operational training and of which 339 were built up till October 1959. The long and active career of the Super Sabre reached its peak in the Viet-Nam War.

With the appearance of the Lockheed F-104 Starfighter in the middle of the 1950s a new phase had been

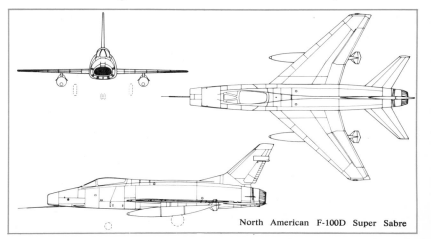

North American F-100D Super Sabre

attained in the long evolution of combat aircraft: the ability to operate at twice the speed of sound. As well as this great technological feat, the Starfighter was interesting as a joint industrial effort. Thousands of F-104s were constructed in Europe, Canada, Japan and the USA and were used by the air forces of almost all the allied nations. It is still in service at the beginning of the 1980s.

The first prototype flew on 7th January 1954, and production was at first concentrated on 155 F-104A and 26 F-104B trainers which went into squadron service in January 1958. In the same year the first of the 77 F-104Cs (which were more powerful and generally strengthened) were followed by 22 twin-seater trainer aircraft of the D series. In 1958 a new variant was developed especially for export (the G or Super Starfighter) which flew in prototype form on 7th June 1960 (this was strengthened, more powerful and had greater wing surface and more sophisticated avionics). Lockheed built 101 (96 for Germany, 3 to launch production under licence in Japan and 2 for the same purpose in Belgium and Italy); and also 200 in a two-seater trainer variant (TG-104G).

The remainder of the large production total was divided among a European consortium (1,300 built); Canada (378); Japan (239 built – these aircraft had more powerful armament and were designated F-104J). The air forces of Germany, Italy, the Netherlands, Belgium, Canada, Turkey, Norway, Denmark, Greece and Nationalist China were equipped with the Starfighter. The final version of the F-104 was the S variant, built in Italy by Aeritalia under licence. These aircraft had more powerful engines, better performance and armament and more up-to-date electronics; 205 of them were built for the *Aeronautica Militare* and 18 for the Turkish air force.

Plate 199
Soviet fighters: 1955–60

The evolution of Soviet combat planes proceeded along parallel lines. Towards the middle of the 1950s the old-established design bureau of Sukhoi came to the fore once more, having been overshadowed at the end of the Second World War, with two very remarkable aircraft, the Sukhoi Su-7 and the Sukhoi Su-9. These were constructed almost simultaneously and stayed in first-line service for many years providing the *VVS* with the useful tactical support (Su-7) and interceptor (Su-9) supersonic aircraft. Production numbers are known for only the first aircraft; over 3,000 were built which equipped all the Warsaw Pact air forces and those of Cuba, Syria, Egypt, India, North Korea, North Viet-Nam, Iraq and Afghanistan. The Su-9 was used in a defensive role until 1968 and it is thought that about 200 of them were built.

The Su-7 prototype appeared in the second half of 1955 and the first production variant, the Su-7B, reached units in 1961 (FITTER A in NATO code). Apart from a trainer version, Su-7U (MOUJIK), the other variants constructed in the USSR were the Su-7MF, which had a more powerful engine, and the more heavily-armed Su-7BMK of 1972. The Su-9 prototype (this aircraft differed from the Su-7 mainly in having a delta wing) flew in 1956 and deliveries to units started three years later. It was designated FISHPOT in NATO code and the Su-9 was constructed in a further three versions: two combat planes (FISHPOT C and D) which had better avionics and one trainer version, the Su-9U (MAIDEN).

The great success of the MiG family was continued in 1956 when the MiG-21 appeared. This fighter, which was still fully operational at the end of the 1970s, had a total procurement of over 4,000 and production, apart from the USSR, was also carried out in India, Czechoslovakia and in the People's Republic of China, and these planes were also used by the air forces of more than twenty countries.

The project was commenced around 1954 with the aim of turning out a light fighter which could fly at Mach 2. The development phase lasted for two years and in 1956 mass production was ordered. The first series aircraft (MiG-21F – FISHBED C) appeared a year later and at the beginning of 1958 deliveries to operational units were started.

Many variants were built: apart from a trainer version (MiG-21U – MONGOL A) the fighter versions which followed were the MiG-21P which was an all-weather interceptor; the MiG-21PFM which had improved

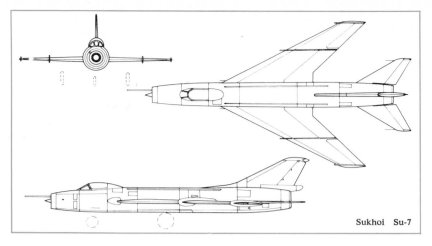
Sukhoi Su-7

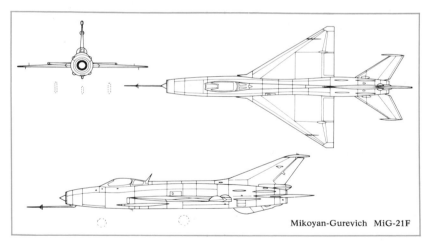
Sukhoi Su-9

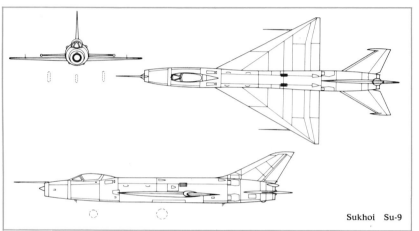
Mikoyan-Gurevich MiG-21F

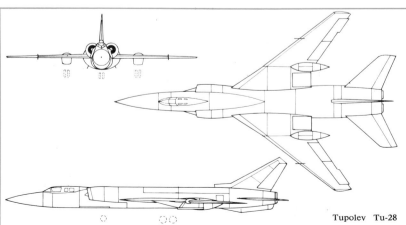
Tupolev Tu-28

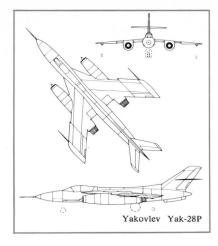

Yakovlev Yak-28P

Plate 200
British naval fighters: 1957–67

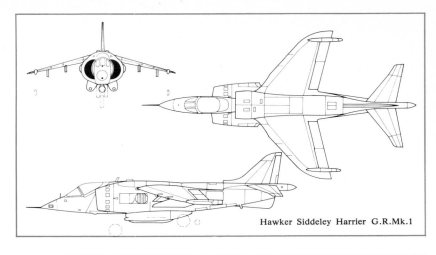

Hawker Siddeley Harrier G.R.Mk.1

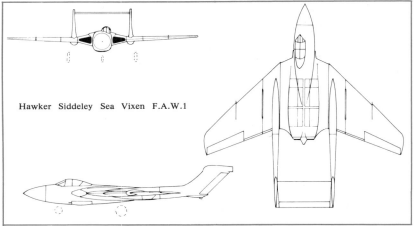

Hawker Siddeley Sea Vixen F.A.W.1

avionics and armament; the MiG-21 PFMA with considerably increased load capacity; the MiG-21R photo-reconnaissance electronic counter-measure; the MiG-21SMT which had a more powerful engine, strengthened wing, greater range and even more sophisticated avionics. In NATO code these variants had the suffixes of D to K added to their basic designations.

But the official appearance of an even more powerful and sophisticated fighter came about in 1961: the Tupolev Tu-28, a heavy missile-carrying fighter which was at first mistaken for a bomber by western observers. It is thought that the proto-type flew for the first time in 1957 and was derived from the Tu-98 bomber which had remained at pro-totype stage. It probably went into squadron service at the end of 1962 and two versions of the Tu-28 were observed; both were high altitude interceptors. Production is thought to have totalled about 130. In NATO code the Tu-28 was called FIDDLER.

Still in 1961, a new twin-jet of the family of the Yak-25 appeared in public; this was the Yak-28, a mar-kedly updated version and a more powerful aircraft. Several hundred of this aeroplane were built in two basic variants; one was an assault plane (BREWER in code) and the other was an all-weather interceptor variant (Yak-28P, FIREBAR) which had all missile armament. Derivants were the Yak-28U (MAESTRO) which was a trainer and the reconnaissance plane Yak-28R (BREWER D). These air-craft went into squadron service with the *VVS*, it is thought, in 1962.

Towards the end of the 1950s the Fleet Air Arm began to equip itself with particularly sophisticated combat air-craft. The Supermarine Scimitar went into service in 1958 and was the first carrier-borne fighter with swept wings and supersonic performance with nu-clear capability. The design was com-menced in the years immediately after the war and development proved to be much more difficult than was foreseen. As many as four prototypes were con-structed between 1951 and 1954 and only on 20th January 1956 was it poss-ible to test the fifth prototype (Type 544) which led to the production design.

The first series Scimitar F.1 appeared on 11th January 1957 and in total, up till September 1960, 76 air-craft of the original order for 100 were built: the remainder of the order had been cancelled because of lengthy delays. The Scimitars stayed in service until the late 1960s and proved par-ticularly useful and versatile, so much so that they were put to widely differ-ent uses, as tactical nuclear bombers, missile-armed high altitude intercep-tors and long-range reconnaissance aircraft.

A contemporary of the Scimitar was a powerful combat plane used as an all-weather fighter, the Hawker Sid-deley Sea Vixen, an aircraft which for over ten years, from 1960 onwards, was the most advanced weapon of the Fleet Air Arm. Work had begun on the original design in 1946 and as with the Scimitar its development was sub-ject to considerable delays. This was mainly due to an accident in 1951, in which the first prototype was des-troyed. Between 1952 and 1956 two other prototypes were built and tested, and finally on 25th March 1957 the first production Sea Vixen, designated F.A.W.1, had its maiden flight. The ensuing purchase purchase order total-led 114 examples.

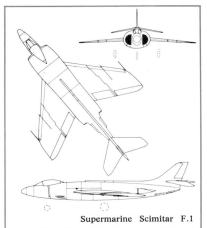

Supermarine Scimitar F.1

In 1961, justified by the aircraft's good operational record, the Royal Navy decided to develop another more powerful version of the aircraft, with longer range and also carrying more comprehensive armament. As a result two aircraft of the first series were modified and used as prototypes for the new variant: they flew on 1st June and 17th August 1962 and met the performance specification. In the event the production of the Sea Vixen F.A.W.2 totalled only 15 new aircraft: another 14 were modified directly on the assembly line from the first series; finally 67 F.A.W.1s were temporarily taken out of service and converted to F.A.W.2s between 1966 and 1968. Operational use continued until the beginning of the 1970s when all the Sea Vixens were withdrawn from active service and units were con-verted to the new and better Phantom fighter.

One of the most ambitious under-takings of the British aeronautical industry in the 1950s was the development of the Hawker Siddeley Harrier, the first V/STOL combat air-craft in the world, a revolutionary air-craft which, originally designed as a landplane; was also to prove extremely useful as a carrier-borne plane. The development programme was long and laborious. It started in 1957 in close collaboration with the designers of the Bristol Engine Company who had at that time started to develop a

version of the Orpheus turbofan engine in which the exhaust airflow could be vectored rearward, down-ward or at an intermediate angle to give jet lift to VTO.

The result of this phase of the design took shape on 21st October 1960, with the test flight of the first prototype, P.1127. This aircraft was followed by another five aircraft which until 1962 were subjected to a great many experi-ments. The next step led to the con-struction of nine further aircraft in an improved version called the Kestrel, which were tested by an experimental unit comprising American, German and British pilots.

The first of these aircraft flew on 7th March 1964, and operational tests started on 15th October. Eventually Germany withdrew from the pro-gramme and six Kestrels were sent to the USA where they continued joint proving flights. It was now no longer possible to continue the project as a joint international venture in the framework of NATO, so the British went on developing the plane alone. On 31st August 1966 the first pre-series aircraft of the final version, the Harrier, had its maiden flight; an air-craft which resembled the Kestrel in its external appearance, but otherwise the engine, avionics, equipment and armament were completely updated and redesigned. Production started with the GR.Mk I which was a close support and reconnaissance plane and of which 78 were built (first flight 28th December 1967) and went into service with the RAF on 1st April 1969. The second principal combat version was the GR.Mk 3 which had a more powerful engine: 36 were ordered in 1976, and by 1977 nearly all the GR.Mk 1s were equipped with a new engine and reclassified under the new series. In 1969 a two-seat trainer variant was also built, the T.Mk 2 of which 21 were ordered by the Royal Air Force.

These Harriers, which kept all their predecessors' best qualities, were subsequently equipped with the more powerful Pegasus 102 and 103 engines, as was the GR.Mk 1. In the 1970s the Harrier programme finally came into its own: the United States showed interest in the aircraft and in 1969 they ordered twelve Harrier Mk 50s (US designation AV-8A) for the US Marine Corps. Subsequent orders brought the production total to 110 (of which eight were trainers) delivered between 1971 and 1977; McDonnell Douglas later acquired the production rights for the USA. Through the United States, moreover, Spain bought eight Harriers in 1976 (including two trainers) which were designated T-AV-8S Matador. Finally, in 1975 the Royal Navy also decided to adopt the Harrier in a suitable navalised version, the F.R.S.1. The first of the 34 Sea Harriers ordered flew on 20th August 1978.

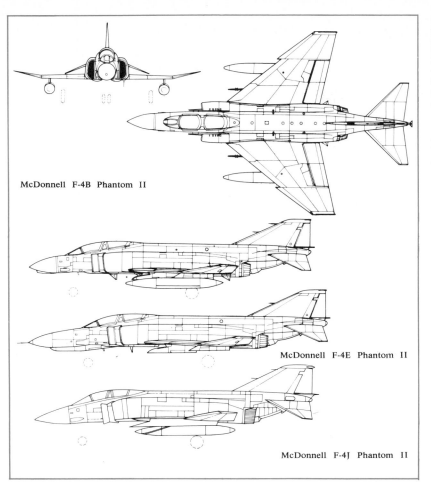

McDonnell F-4B Phantom II

McDonnell F-4E Phantom II

McDonnell F-4J Phantom II

craft: the first was the RF-4C of 1964 for the USAF of which 505 were built, followed by the RF-4B for the Marines (46 built) of 1965 and by the RF-4E of 1967 which was for export only and was bought by Federal Germany, Greece, Turkey, Iran, Israel and Japan.

In the photo-reconnaissance versions, night and day cameras were positioned in the forward part of the aircraft, replacing the fire controls and the guidance systems for the Sparrow missiles.

Among the updated combat versions which appeared during the 1970s, the F-4N and the F-4S were both for the US Navy and were converted from 228 F-4Bs and 260 F-4Js; these new versions were structurally strengthened, had their engines modified and their avionics updated. In the case of the F-4J conversion started in the spring of 1978.

Plate 201
The Phantom II — with 5,000 built it enters a class of its own: 1958

The McDonnell F-4 Phantom II is still to this day considered the best fighter-bomber ever built, and it has been one of the US aeronautical industry's greatest successes. It is still in service at the beginning of the 1980s with the main air forces of the non-communist world (after having seen action from Viet-Nam onwards) and this powerful and versatile Mach 2 aircraft reached a production total of 5,000 aircraft in dozens of versions.

An impressive position was reached on 24th May 1978, three days before the twentieth anniversary of the prototype's maiden flight, when the assembly lines of the St Louis factory completed the five-thousandth Phantom. At that date deliveries were as follows: 2,640 to the USAF; 1,264 to the US Navy and Marine Corps; 1,096 to foreign buyers. Amongst these were Britain, Federal Germany, Japan, Israel, Iran and Spain.

The project was started by McDonnell in 1953 in response to a request from the American Navy which called for a twin-jet all-weather assault fighter which had to be supersonic. The development phase was very long and laborious and was made longer by an unexpected change in the US Navy's specifications, announced after the contract for the production of two prototypes had been awarded on 18th October 1954.

The first of these prototypes was tested on 27th May 1958, with the designation of YF4H-1. Twenty-three pre-series aircraft followed and at the end of long proving trials the first of 649 aircraft of the first production variant F-4B were built which went into service in 1961. In the meantime the great potential of the aircraft had aroused the interest of the USAF, which asked McDonnell to develop an improved version. This substantially resembled the carrier-borne variant

and was designated F-4C; the prototype flew on 27th May 1963 and 583 were built. At the end of 1965 843 F-4Ds followed, which had more powerful engines and improved avionics; and from October 1967 580 F-4Fs were completed, which had better engines and armament, and increased fuel capacity.

Export began with the Phantom F-4E: several hundred were ordered by Israel and Iran, others went to Turkey and Greece and, apart from these, special variants were built for Allied countries. Amongst these was the F-4EJ of 1971 for Japan, for construction under licence (140 built); the F-4F of 1973 for Federal Germany (175 built between 1973 and 1976); the F-4K for the British Fleet Air Arm (powered by Rolls-Royce Spey engines) of which 52 were delivered from April 1968; and the F-4M which was substantially similar to the F-4K and 118 of which were supplied to the Royal Air Force from 1968.

Meanwhile the US Navy had decided to develop an improved version of its F-4B to be roughly the same as the USAF's F-4D. The prototype of this variant (F-4J) flew for the first time in May 1966 and had more powerful engines and more sophisticated fire control electronics. 518 were built up till December 1972. Photo-reconnaissance versions of the Phantom were also built in various versions parallel to the principal combat air-

Plate 202
Two great fighters — the American Thunderchief and the British Lightning: 1959

The end of the 1950s witnessed the debut of two other important combat aircraft produced in the West: the American Republic F-105 Thunderchief, one of the major combat aircraft used in the Viet-Nam War, and the English Electric Lightning, the spearhead of the RAF for over twenty years, due to be replaced only in the early 1980s by the Tornado MRCA.

The Thunderchief was a private venture for Republic and intended to be a replacement for the successful F-84. In 1954 the programme was officially approved by the USAF which had been impressed by the potential of the aircraft. Its main characteristics were certainly versatility and its formidable weaponry (almost 5.5 tonnes of stores in the prototype and just under 6.5 tonnes in the more advanced series models) apart from its very good performance at twice the speed of sound. The prototype flew for the first time on 22nd October 1955 and the first production model (F-105B) flew just over a year and a half later on 24th May 1957. Only 75 of this variant were built which reached units from May 1958.

About the same date the prototype

437

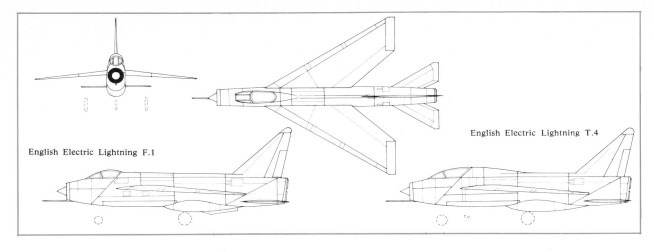

English Electric Lightning F.1

English Electric Lightning T.4

of the second more powerful version, the F-105D, was flown which was to become the principal production model. It had more advanced electronics and a Pratt & Whitney J75 engine which was almost 20 per cent more powerful; 600 of these Thunderchiefs were built and went into service in 1961.

A year later the following variant, F-105F, was ordered which was a two-seat development of the basic type equipped with complete dual control systems. From June 1963, 143 of these aircraft reached USAF units. The greater part of the operational career of the Thunderchiefs was spent in the Viet-Nam War; from 1963 to 1968 these aircraft carried out over 75 per cent of assault missions undertaken by the USAF.

The career of the British Lightning was much more peaceful. The design of this powerful Mach 2 interceptor was begun in 1949 on the basis of official specifications, but the development phase and the perfecting of the aircraft were made very much longer by a number of problems concerning aerodynamics and structure which confronted the designers.

Recourse even had to be made to an experimental scale prototype (flown in 1952) with which various wing configurations could be studied. Be-

tween 1954 and 1957 another three research prototypes (P.1A) and three operational prototypes (P.1B) were used to test manoeuvrability, armament, metal fatigue and various engines.

After the construction of 20 pre-series aircraft on 29th October 1959, the first production Lightning appeared, the F.1, which was followed on the assembly lines by another 19 aircraft of the same type. RAF squadrons received this aircraft from June 1960 onwards. 28 Lightning F.1As followed which had provision for flight refuelling and from July 1961 44 F.2s were built which had different engines, better electronics and detail alterations. The F.3, which was considered the definitive variant for use as an interceptor (first flight of the prototype on 16th June 1962, 62 aircraft put into service from April 1964 onwards) had further structural modifications, updated avionics and engines and had more powerful offensive weaponry. The last single-seat version was the F.6 (which appeared on 7th April 1964 and of which 62 were built); this had much greater fuel capacity and consequently greater operational range.

The first export version (F.53) was taken from this variant and went to Saudi Arabia and Kuwait (total 46).

These two countries also bought various aircraft and derivant versions (T.54, T.55 and T.56) of two twin-seat operational trainer variants developed for the RAF: the T.4 (first flight 6th May 1959, 20 built) and the T.5 (first flight 29th March 1962, 22 built). In all production totalled 338.

Plate 203
The Swedish defence system relies on Saab: 1954–71

Another European nation came well to the fore in the aeronautical field during the 1950s: Sweden, a country which, although traditionally neutral, decided to safeguard her position between the opposing blocs by equipping herself with a very advanced air force. The manufacturer which made this exceptional achievement possible was Saab; all the designs of this company after the Second World War led to

aircraft which were on a par with the most advanced contemporary production elsewhere.

The first successful aircraft was the Saab 29, a stubby but very aggressive fighter which appeared in prototype on 1st September 1948. Production was based on five versions, reaching a total of 661 and constructed up till 1956, going into service as from 1951. After the first A variant the evolution of the design led to the B series being built in 1953 (increased fuel capacity); the C (reconnaissance) and the E with a different wing and engine. The final version was the F (first flight 20th March 1954) which incorporated all the improvements of the preceding series.

On 3rd November 1952 the prototype of a new combat plane appeared: the Saab 32 Lansen. Production, which totalled 450 of this very worthwhile multirole plane, continued until May 1960. It went into service with the *Flygvapnet* in 1955. The first series was the 32A assault aircraft (operational designation A32A); the second was an all-weather fighter and was designated J32B (first flight 7th January 1957); the third, also of 1957, was a photo-reconnaissance plane and was designated F32C. These last Lansens were operational for the longest period of time; they were only finally taken out of first-line service in 1976, five years after the others.

In 1955 a great step forward towards the production of increasingly powerful and sophisticated aircraft was made when the prototype of the Saab 35 Draken had its maiden flight. This was designed to meet the very individual operational needs of the *Flygvapnet*, which apart from high performance and flexibility in armament also required extreme reliability and operational versatility.

The Draken was acknowledged to be one of the best interceptors of its time. Production was based on five basic variants and continued until 1969 totalling 606 aircraft which went into service from 1961 onwards. The first series was the J35A, the prototype of which had its maiden flight on 15th February 1958. On 29th November 1959 the first J35B followed which

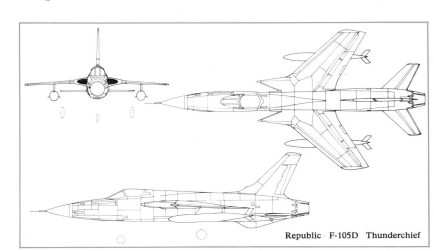

Republic F-105D Thunderchief

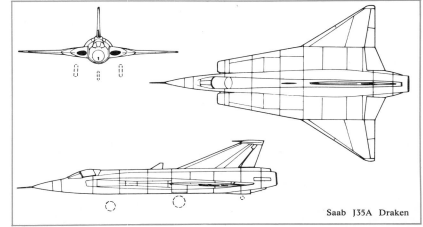

Saab J35A Draken

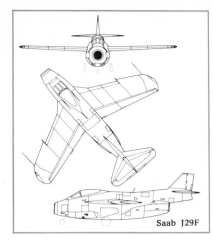

Saab J29F

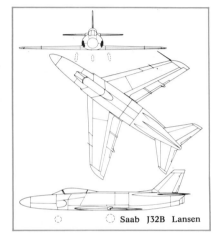

Saab J32B Lansen

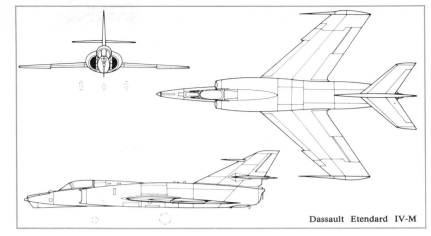

Dassault Etendard IV-M

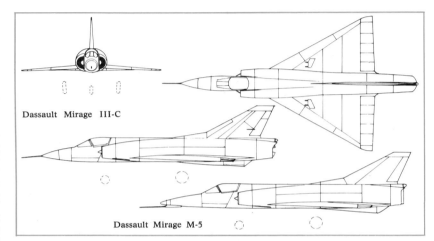

Dassault Mirage III-C

Dassault Mirage M-5

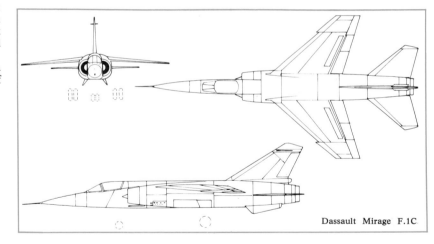

Dassault Mirage F.1C

was also the one that was constructed in the largest numbers – approximately 320. The *Flygvapnet* was not the only air force to use the Saab 35: forty were bought by Denmark and twelve were put into service by the Finnish air force.

The successor to the Draken brings one to the 1980s and this was a more formidable aircraft which was to replace the Draken completely; it appeared in prototype on 8th February 1967, and the first version became operational in June 1971, but production programmes are projected at least until 1985. This aircraft is the Saab 37 Viggen, a sophisticated multirole aircraft which is seen as a complete weapons system of its own within the framework of Swedish defence.

The evolution of this fighter progressed through seven prototypes before arriving at the first production variant, the AJ37, which was first designed as an attack plane. The second series led to the Saab JA37 in which its main roles were switched round compared with its predecessor, priority being given to interception.

The first JA37 production model flew on 4th November 1977 and deliveries started at the beginning of the following year; as at May 1978 orders totalled 149 in a production programme which allows for 180. Non-combat variants were the SF37 photo-reconnaissance plane (first flight 31st May 1973, deliveries from April 1977); the SH37 maritime reconnaissance plane (first flight 10th December 1973, operational from 19th June 1975); the SK37 two-seat trainer (prototype appeared on 2nd July 1970, deliveries from June 1972).

The *Flygvapnet* has plans to put a total of about 350 Saab 37 Viggens of different variants into service.

had a more powerful engine, a more up-to-date navigation system and improved fire control radar. On 30th December of the same year the prototype of the trainer version, the SK35C, appeared and a year later, on 29th December 1960, the J35D flew for the first time. This was a new variant of the fighter which had a more powerful engine, longer range and had more sophisticated avionics.

A photo-reconnaissance version (S35E) was derived from this Draken and 60 were built. The final series was the J35F in which the navigation electronics, the fire control radar and electronic counter measures underwent complete updating. The last Draken

JA37 Viggen

Plate 204
Dassault starts off with a carrier-based attack aircraft and progresses to the Mirage fighters: 1958–73

In France Dassault's leading position in world aviation, which was achieved during the course of the early 1950s, was further consolidated after the successful series of Mystère and Super Mystère (and before going on to the still more prolific family of Mirage jets), when this great French manufacturer designed a useful carrier-borne fighter. This aircraft, the Etendard, became the first supersonic plane

of its kind to be built in Europe.

The prototype, which flew in its final configuration on 24th July 1956, had been developed to answer the needs of NATO in general and in particular those of the *Armée de l'Air*. However, it was the *Aéronavale* which was to evince interest in the Etendard and a navalised prototype was ordered together with six pre-series aircraft. The first of these, which was designated IV-M, was tested on 21st May 1958 and at the end of proving trials was ordered into production. Two variants were completed, the IV-M fighter (69 built) and the IV-P photo-reconnaissance plane (21). The latter model of Etendard (first flight 19th

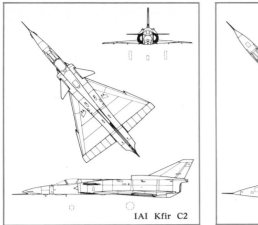

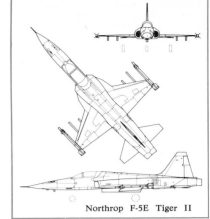

IAI Kfir C2

IAR-93 Orao

HAL HF-24 Mk.I Marut

Northrop F-5E Tiger II

November 1960) was delivered from 1962 to 1964.

The final development of the project came about with a new, more powerful and more sophisticated version, called the Super Etendard, which appeared in prototype on 28th October 1974. This was to replace the Etendard IV-M before the end of 1981 and 71 have been ordered, the first of which were delivered on 28th June 1978.

The most ambitious and prestigious of Dassault's programmes was that which in the middle of the 1950s led to the Mirage series. The production figures reflect this success very clearly. The Mirage had been in production since 1960 and a total of 2,000 had been ordered as at 1st January 1978 according to official figures, and orders for series III, 5 and 50 alone totalled 1,350 as at 1st January 1978 (official figures) and the Mirage was in service with some twenty air forces throughout the world.

The definitive prototype (Mirage III) was flown for the first time on 17th November 1956, and the programme for test flights continued for a long time before the best configuration for the aircraft was decided upon and a suitable engine was available which could enable the machine to fly at Mach 2. This spectacular result was attained for the first time on 24th October 1958 by Dassault's chief test pilot, Roland Glavarny, in the Mirage III-A. Series production was started immediately afterwards with an initial order for 100 aircraft of an interceptor version (Mirage III-C) and the first of these aircraft flew on 9th October 1960.

From that date the Dassault assembly lines were kept at work uninterruptedly. Very many variants and sub-variants of the Mirage III were constructed; the latter had a double designation which indicated the country for which it was bound. The III-C version, for example, was designated III-CJ for Israel and III-CZ for South Africa, while the III-B two-seat trainer (first flight 20th October 1959) became III-BL for the Lebanon and III-BS for Switzerland. The same process was adopted with the III-D series

of close support planes which were derived from the trainer variant and which were produced under licence in Australia.

A later version, which appeared on 20th April 1961, was the III-E which was a multirole aircraft and the first photo-reconnaissance version was the III-R which flew on 31st October of the same year. The *Armée de l'Air* put the Mirage III-Cs into service in 1960, the III-Bs and the III-Rs in 1962, and the III-Es in 1965.

The final developments of the series III were the Mirage 5 and the Mirage 50 which were for export. The Mirage 5 appeared in prototype form on 1st May 1967 and was in essence a simplified version of the III-E but had increased fuel capacity and armament. Three versions were constructed under licence in Belgium (assault, reconnaissance and trainer, a total of 106 built) and it was bought by many third world countries. On 1st January 1978, orders totalled 447 aircraft for eleven air forces. The Mirage 50, the prototype of which appeared in 1975, was effectively a more powerful Mirage 5 (16 per cent more thrust).

A new stage of development in the programme was marked on 20th March 1969 when the prototype Mirage F.1 took to the air. The delta wing which had been a feature of all the preceding versions was abandoned for the first time in this model and this led to far greater manoeuvrability and versatility. The first F.1 series plane flew on 15th February 1973 and at the end of the year the *Armée de l'Air* equipped an operational unit with the new interceptor. The basic versions were the F.1C multirole; the F.1B trainer, the F.1A assault plane and the F.1E which had more sophisticated avionics. In July 1978, 508 Mirage F.1s had been ordered: 185 by the *Armée de l'Air*, the rest by Ecuador, Greece, Iraq, Kuwait, Libya, Morocco, South Africa and Spain.

Plate 205
Minor fighters of the 1980s

In 1967, at the end of the Six Day War, Israel embarked upon a series of programmes which were aimed at updating the Mirage in service with its air force. One of these programmes led to a completely original variant of the French aircraft, the Kfir.

The project was initiated in 1970 when a Mirage III-CJ was equipped with an American General Electric J79 turbojet engine; a year later the same modification was carried out in a Mirage 5 which had already been altered to meet Israeli needs. The prototype, which flew in September, was immediately put into production. The first variant, Kfir 1, went into service in April 1975. A year later an improved version appeared, the Kfir C2 which had aerodynamic modifications, the most obvious of which was the addition of canard surfaces slightly ahead of and above the wings. By the beginning of the 1980s over 100 Kfirs had been produced and were also offered for export.

Another minor air power, India, built a combat aircraft within its own aviation industry during the 1960s; this was the HAL HF-24 Marut, a tactical fighter which was designed under the guidance of the German designer, Kurt Tank, the creator of so many Second World War Focke Wulf planes.

The first prototype of the Mk 1 series flew on 17th June 1961; the first production model on 15th November 1967. The assembly lines kept going for ten years and produced 100 HF-24 Mk 1s and 18 Mk 1T trainers. In 1978 plans were produced to develop a more powerful and improved version of the aircraft.

A joint programme between Yugoslavia and Romania gave rise, in 1974, to a single-seat fighter for tactical warfare, over 200 of which were to equip these two countries' air forces during the 1980s; the IAR-93 Orao. The first prototype was presented to the public

on 15th April 1975 and the first production model flew in 1977. A trainer variant is also envisaged.

In the USA the project which was to lead to one of the most widely used tactical fighters of the 1980s was started in 1955. This was the Northrop F-5 Tiger (or Freedom Fighter) an aircraft which was mainly manufactured for export to NATO countries.

The prototype F-5 flew on 30th July 1969 and production soon reached very high levels. The first basic variants were the A and the B (single-seater and twin-seater) which were delivered from 1974 and of which over 1,150 were built in various derivant series (construction licences were granted in Canada, the Netherlands and Spain).

In March 1969 the prototype of a new basic version was tested which was improved and more powerful, and was designated F-5E Tiger II. This aircraft was chosen the following year as the winner in a competition to find an international fighter aircraft (IFA), to be produced for export and to replace the Lockheed F-104 Starfighter and the first generation of F-105 jets. Its direct competitors were the Lockheed CL.1200 Lancer (an updated F-104), the F-4EF International Phantom and a simplified version of the Crusader carrier-borne fighter designated Vought V-1000.

The first series model flew on 11th August 1972 and deliveries started towards the end of the following year. In all (including the 1,138 examples of the T-38 Talon trainer which was produced exclusively for the USA) more than 3,000 F-5s had been delivered at the end of 1976. In the spring of 1978 orders for the F-5E and for the F-5F (two-seat variant) reached a total of over 1,000 of which 778 had already been delivered. At the beginning of the 1980s the Tigers were in service with the air forces of 25 countries, of which six were members of NATO.

Plate 206
Multirole and naval combat/strike fighters of the 1980s

Some of the most important combat aircraft of the 1980 generation have arisen out of collaborative multinational programmes. This is especially true in Europe. Two of the most prestigious examples are the Anglo-French Sepecat Jaguar and the Anglo-Italo-German Tornado MRCA.

The Jaguar design originated in 165 with an agreement between the British and French governments to produce a light tactical attack and training machine. A jointly owned company was formed, Sepecat, to develop the airframe and an international consortium of Rolls-Royce and Turboméca to produce the engine. In the event the new aircraft turned out to be much more powerful and effective than had been foreseen which meant that it could be classified as a multirole high-performance aircraft.

The first prototype was French (flown on 8th September 1968), as was the first series aircraft, a Jaguar E two-seater (2nd November 1971). Deliveries started in the following year and at the end of 1979 these totalled 426 in various versions: 165 Jaguar S single-seaters and 37 Jaguar B two-seaters for the RAF; 160 Jaguar A single-seaters and 40 Jaguar E two-seaters for the *Armée de l'Air* and in addition a total of 24 export variants had been ordered by Ecuador and Oman. The marketing campaign was carried out particularly aggressively by Britain, who had offered the Jaguar to many emergent nations, among which was India. The export version (International) had a more powerful engine.

The genesis of the Tornado MRCA project was more complex; this was a variable geometry wing multirole aircraft. A consortium of firms in Federal Germany, Britain and Italy was set up on 26th March 1969 and was called Panavia. Ownership of the company was shared out thus: 42.5 per cent BAC; 42.5 per cent German MBB; 15 per cent Aeritalia. Another consortium was formed to develop the engine: 40 per cent Rolls-Royce, 40 per cent MTU and 20 per cent Fiat; and this company was called Turbo-Union Limited. A NATO agency called NAMMO was formed to co-ordinate these activities. The actual definition of the programme itself took a long time to achieve because of the different needs of the three partners; and in the end they decided that two versions would be developed: the 100 single-seat air superiority aircraft and the 200 two-seat ground attack aircraft.

Only the latter was eventually chosen for joint production. The first prototype was German and flew on 14th August 1974, followed on 30th October by the second which was a British-built prototype. The first Italian aircraft (fifth prototype) appeared on the 5th December 1975. The forerunner of the 807 Tornados planned for production was flown in Britain for the first time on 10th July 1979. Production is planned as follows: 100 for Italy, 322 for Germany and the remainder for Britain.

For naval use, the USA was to develop a formidable interceptor at the beginning of the 1970s, the best of all in its category: the Grumman F-14 Tomcat. This also had variable geometry wings and this powerful and sophisticated combat aircraft flew in a final prototype form (F-14A) on 24th May 1971, at the end of a long and complicated development phase. Production got under way some time later and the first series models reached units of the US Navy in 1972. In 1979 total orders from the navy were 350.

In 1974 the US Navy mooted the idea of producing a new fighter to be put into service in 1982 which would replace all the F-4 Phantoms. The programme led to the McDonnell Douglas F-18 Hornet, a sophisticated combat aircraft which flew in prototype at the end of 1978. The first aircraft of the series F-18A started tests on 18th November 1979. Projected production will be about 800 aircraft.

In the opposing bloc the Soviets, after the introduction of the first aircraft carrier in their fleet, the *Kiev*, in 1976, developed a particular type of carrier-borne aircraft: the Yakovlev Yak-36 VTOL plane, similar to the British Harrier. These were seen for the first time by western observers on board the *Kiev* and there are two operational variants of the Yak-36: the MP single-seater multirole fighter (FORGER A in NATO code) and a second two-seat trainer version (FORGER B).

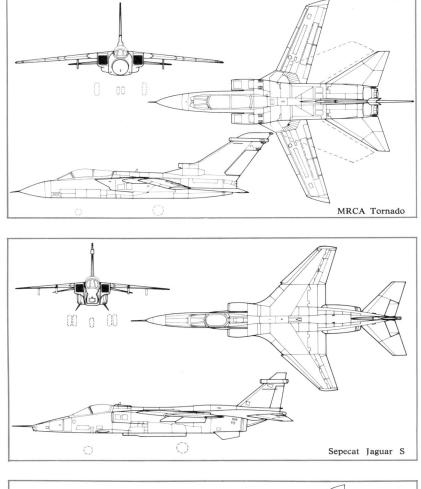

MRCA Tornado

Sepecat Jaguar S

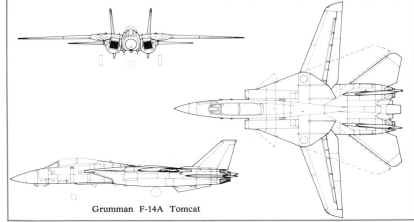

Grumman F-14A Tomcat

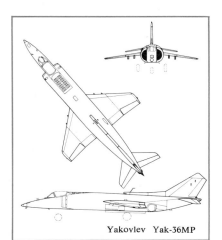

Yakovlev Yak-36MP

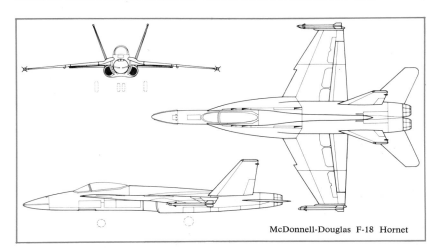

McDonnell-Douglas F-18 Hornet

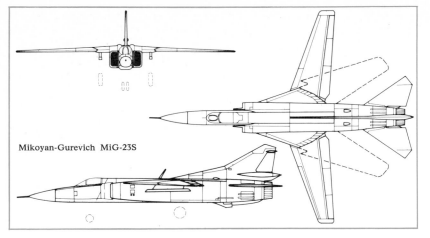

Mikoyan-Gurevich MiG-23S

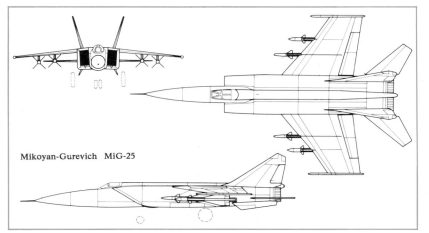

Mikoyan-Gurevich MiG-25

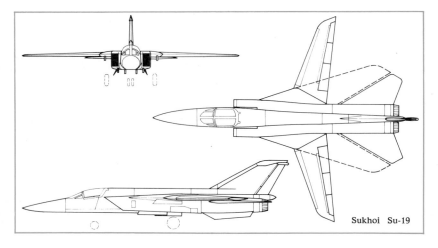

Sukhoi Su-19

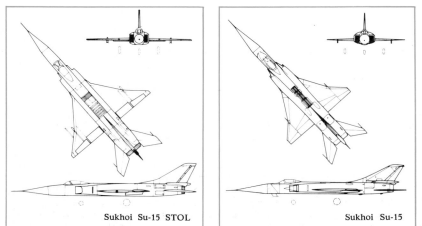

Sukhoi Su-15 STOL

Sukhoi Su-15

Plate 207
Soviet fighters of the 1980s

The Yakovlev Yak-36 is only one of the many Soviet combat aircraft which are to remain in first line use for a great part of the 1980s. Spurred on by increasingly serious confrontation with the western Allies, ever more powerful and sophisticated aircraft have been designed and built for the *VVS* in a real race with the American aeronautical industry. The long-lived MiG family was extended with two other outstanding aircraft at the end of 1960s, the MiG-23 (FLOGGER in NATO code) and the MiG-24 (FOX-BAT). The first appeared in prototype form, although not the definitive one, in 1967 and was put into service three years later with a total production of over 1,000 at the end of 1978, and many were exported (to Czecho-slovakia, Egypt, Iraq, Libya and Syria).

Six basic versions have been observed and classified by western experts; the MiG-23 prototype of 1967 (FLOGGER A); the MiG-23 S single-seat multirole fighter (FLOG-GER B); the MiG-23U two-seat trainer (FLOGGER C); the MiG 23S for export (FLOGGER E) which was a considerably simplified variant com-pared with that flown by the *VVS*; the MiG-23 ground attack plane (FLOGGER F) which in effect was an export version of the corresponding assault plane of the Soviet air arm, designated MiG-27 (FLOGGER D). The fundamental characteristic of the MiG-23 is the variable geometry wing which gives it great versatility.

The MiG-25 was developed almost simultaneously (FOXBAT in NATO code); this is an air superiority inter-ceptor which can fly at three times the speed of sound. The design of this formidable fighter was set in train at the same time as that of the American Mach 3 B-70 bomber at the end of the 1950s. The first prototype is thought to have flown in April 1965 and in its first proving trials set an impressive number of speed and altitude records. The exceptional performance of the aircraft was demonstrated twelve years later in August 1977 when a MiG-25 set the world altitude record at 37,650 m (123,530 ft). In 1967 the FOXBAT was seen for the first time in its definitive form and has been observed in five basic versions.

The versions are: MiG-25 FOX-BAT A interceptor; the MiG-25R FOXBAT B photo-reconnaissance plane; the MiG-25U FOXBAT C two-seat trainer which was revealed to western observers in 1975; the MiG-25R FOXBAT D, an improved reconnaissance version of the FOX-BAT B; and the E-266M experimen-tal aircraft which appeared in 1975 and holds the world record for altitude. At the end of 1979 produc-tion is estimated to have totalled about 500.

Another great designer of excep-tional combat aircraft is Pavel Ossipovich Sukhoi. The successful series of Su-9/11s was followed in the 1960s and 1970s by a new line of fighters which joined this already large family; these were the Su-15s, developed to equip the *VVS* with a good interceptor capable of Mach 2.5 which would replace the preceding types. The first public appearance of the Su-15s was in 1967 and the new aircraft was given the name FLAGON in NATO code.

Six basic variants were observed in the following years: the FLAGON A, which was clearly derived from the model 11 as could be seen from the simple delta wings which were identi-cal with those of the 11 and is thought to have been constructed in limited numbers; the FLAGON B, STOL version, which also appeared in 1967 and had a compound delta wing simi-lar to those of subsequent variants; the FLAGON C two-seat trainer; the FLAGON D (similar to the first series but with compound delta wing) which seems to have become the principal production version; the FLAGON E, operational from 1973 and equipped with more powerful engines and more sophisticated avionics, considered the second most important production variant; and the FLAGON F which was more powerful and improved and was the last to go into service. Accord-ing to Western estimates, at the end of 1979 the operational Su-15 first-line fighters based on Soviet territory total-led over 1,000.

The Sukhoi design bureau developed a parallel series of variable sweep wing aircraft. The first was the Su-17 derived from the Su-7 and was a low-level assault aircraft and desig-nated FITTER in NATO code. From this plane's experience a much more powerful and sophisticated aircraft was derived in 1974, The Sukhoi Su-19 (FENCER) a multirole fighter which was particularly effective in ground attack and considered to be the equal of the American F-111. It has only ever been flown over Soviet ter-ritory and never closely observed by western experts, but about 300 FENCERS are thought to have been constructed. First-line units of the *VVS* started to receive the Su-19 in December 1974, and in the spring of 1978 about 250 aircraft were in opera-tional service.

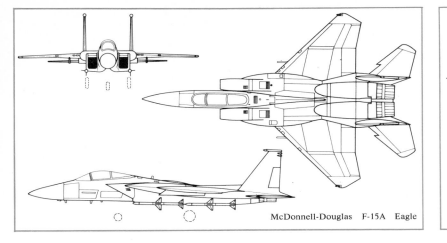

McDonnell-Douglas F-15A Eagle

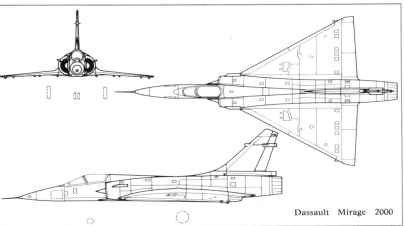

Dassault Mirage 2000

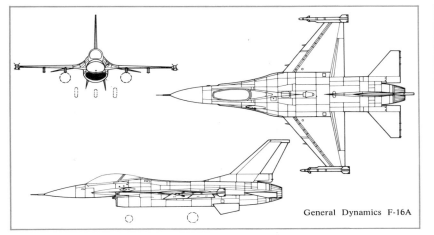

General Dynamics F-16A

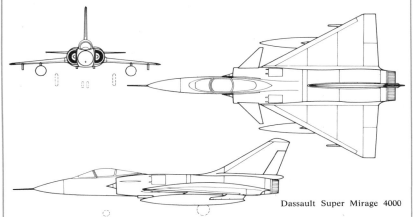

Dassault Super Mirage 4000

Plate 208
Western fighters of the 1980s

The race for air superiority also led to somewhat futuristic aircraft in the USA. The US Navy had to find a worthwhile substitute for the very well proven F-4 Phantom and this led first of all to the creation of the F-14 Tomcat and then to the development of the F-18 Hornet, and the USAF followed a similar route with the production of the McDonnell Douglas F-15 Eagle, and the General Dynamics F-16.

The F-15 programme originated in 1965 with an official specification issued to American aeronautical manufacturers. On 23 December 1969 the winning design was chosen and this was the McDonnell Douglas plane; less than three years later, on 27th July 1972 the first prototype F-15A was flown. The initial contract covered the construction of 18 series aircraft to be single-seaters and two two-seat trainers (T-15A) and the latter prototype (subsequently designated F-15B) appeared on 7th July of the following year. At that time an order had already been finalised for 30 fully operational aircraft. In the years which followed, orders for the combat variant topped 500, with a total production programme by 1983 of 749.

The first F-15As went into service in 1974 and the last versions, which are expected to be used in the middle of the 1980s, are the F-15C and the F-15D which have particularly sophisticated avionics and longer range. Apart from the USAF (the main user of the Eagle) the Israeli air force, the Saudi Arabians and the Japanese have chosen the McDonnell Douglas interceptor for re-equipment of their air forces. Japan in particular placed an order in 1978 for 109 F-15As and 14 F-15Bs. The Eagle is particularly sophisticated and versatile; it has been called the West's best interceptor.

More or less a contemporary of the F-15 but belonging to a different category, that of the light multirole fighter, is the General Dynamics F-16, an aircraft which won a competition in February 1972 in which it competed against the most advanced American aircraft. The first prototype started flight tests on 13th December 1973 and the second YF-16 appeared on 9th May 1974. The cycle of proving trials continued until January 1975 and, at that date, not only had the first order been placed for 11 F-16A single-seaters and 4 F-16B twin-seat pre-series aircraft for the USAF, but interest in the new aircraft had already been shown by four NATO nations: Belgium, Denmark, Norway and the Netherlands, which outside the context of the MRCA programme wanted a substitute for the F-104 Starfighter.

The F-16 was officially chosen on 7th June 1975.

The first definitive model of the F-16A version was flown on 8th December 1976, followed on 8th August 1977 by the first F-16B. Apart from the USAF's intention of producing at least 1,388 of these aircraft, another 348 F-16s have been ordered by four European countries as follows: 116 to Belgium, 102 to the Netherlands, 72 to Norway and 58 to Denmark. Of this total 58 were in two-seat trainer configuration. Belgium, the Netherlands, Norway and Denmark have formed a consortium for the construction of these machines. In the spring of 1980 orders were being discussed by Canada and Australia for 130 and 75 aircraft respectively.

The European industry's answer to this, however, was not long delayed. On 10th March 1978 the prototype of the new Dassault design flew for the first time, the Mirage 2000, which in effect was a more powerful and improved version of the series III-5 delta-wing Mirages. The aircraft, which was to be used mainly as an interceptor and air-superiority aircraft, had been chosen on 18th December 1975 as the standard type for the *Armée de l'Air*. Four other experimental aircraft followed, one of which was a two-seat trainer with which the development and perfecting phase was carried out. Programmes

for the 1980s allow for the initial production of 200 Mirage 2000s, to go into service in 1982 and to be fully operational in 1983. These machines will be joined by the same number for reconnaissance and assault.

Dassault's design was immediately followed by a further development which was a private venture of this French constructor, the Mirage 4000, a derivative of the model 2000 powered by two engines instead of one. This aircraft was at one time expected to go into service around 1984 and is thought of mainly as an interceptor and air superiority plane in the category of combat aircraft to which the American F-14 and F-15 belong. Furthermore, the French plane's performance in low-level assault and long-distance assault should be just as exceptional. The first prototype flew on 9th March 1979.

Plate 209

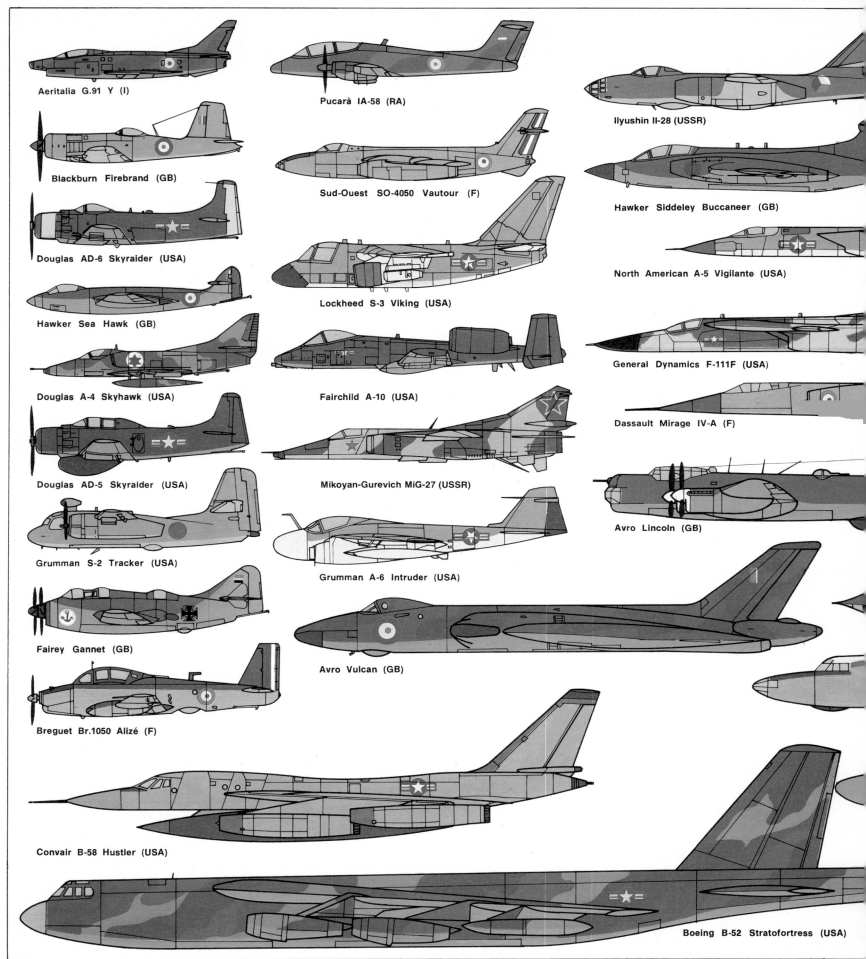

Aeritalia G.91 Y (I)

Pucarà IA-58 (RA)

Ilyushin Il-28 (USSR)

Blackburn Firebrand (GB)

Sud-Ouest SO-4050 Vautour (F)

Hawker Siddeley Buccaneer (GB)

Douglas AD-6 Skyraider (USA)

Lockheed S-3 Viking (USA)

North American A-5 Vigilante (USA)

Hawker Sea Hawk (GB)

Douglas A-4 Skyhawk (USA)

Fairchild A-10 (USA)

General Dynamics F-111F (USA)

Dassault Mirage IV-A (F)

Douglas AD-5 Skyraider (USA)

Mikoyan-Gurevich MiG-27 (USSR)

Avro Lincoln (GB)

Grumman S-2 Tracker (USA)

Grumman A-6 Intruder (USA)

Fairey Gannet (GB)

Avro Vulcan (GB)

Breguet Br.1050 Alizé (F)

Convair B-58 Hustler (USA)

Boeing B-52 Stratofortress (USA)

English Electric Canberra (GB)

Vickers Valiant (GB)

Boeing B-47 Stratojet (USA)

Tupolev Tu-16 (USSR)

Tupolev Tu-22 (USSR)

Handley Page Victor (GB)

Myasishchev Mya4 (USSR)

Tupolev Tu-20 (USSR)

Convair B-36 (USA)

4m = 2,16 cm

0   4   8   12m

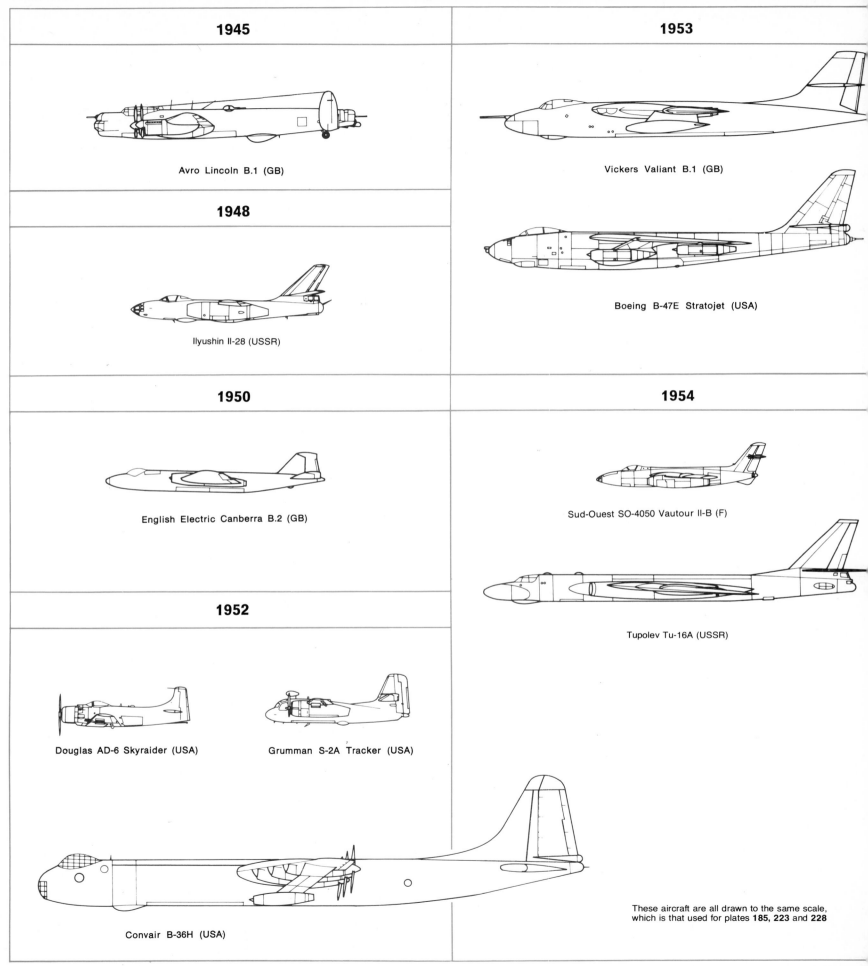

1945

Avro Lincoln B.1 (GB)

1948

Ilyushin Il-28 (USSR)

1950

English Electric Canberra B.2 (GB)

1952

Douglas AD-6 Skyraider (USA)

Grumman S-2A Tracker (USA)

Convair B-36H (USA)

1953

Vickers Valiant B.1 (GB)

Boeing B-47E Stratojet (USA)

1954

Sud-Ouest SO-4050 Vautour II-B (F)

Tupolev Tu-16A (USSR)

These aircraft are all drawn to the same scale,
which is that used for plates **185**, **223** and **228**

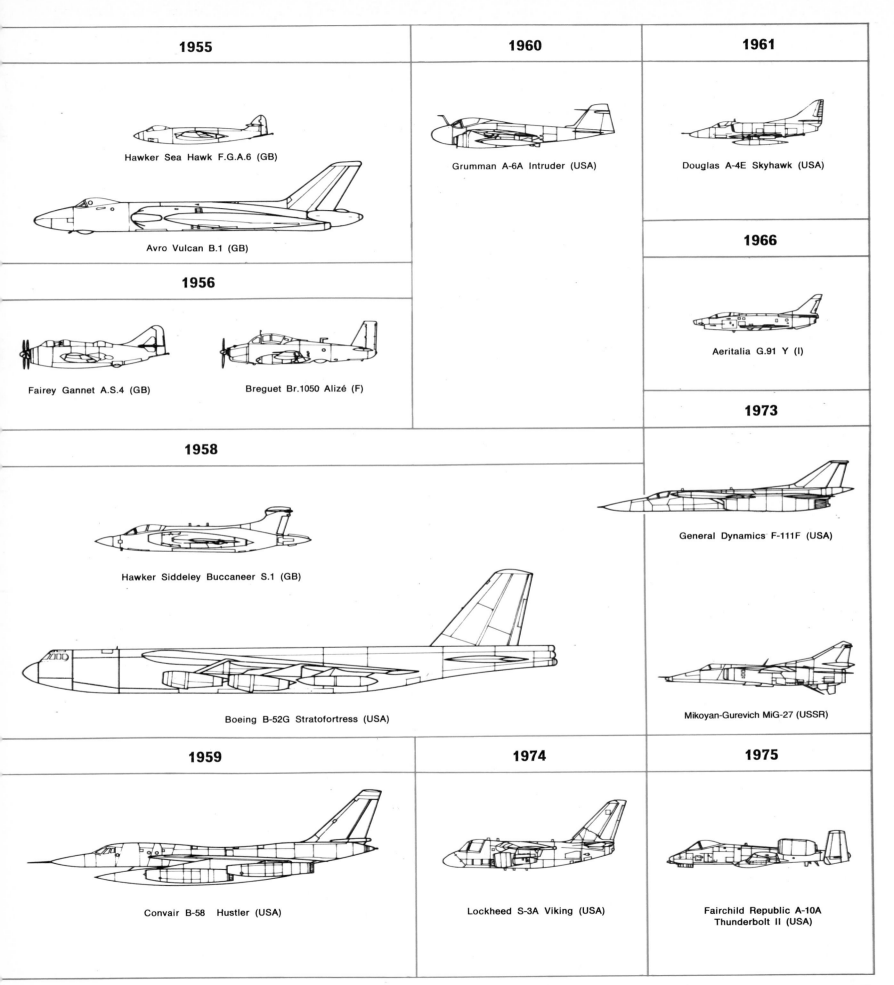

1955

Hawker Sea Hawk F.G.A.6 (GB)

Avro Vulcan B.1 (GB)

1956

Fairey Gannet A.S.4 (GB)

Breguet Br.1050 Alizé (F)

1958

Hawker Siddeley Buccaneer S.1 (GB)

Boeing B-52G Stratofortress (USA)

1959

Convair B-58 Hustler (USA)

1960

Grumman A-6A Intruder (USA)

1961

Douglas A-4E Skyhawk (USA)

1966

Aeritalia G.91 Y (I)

1973

General Dynamics F-111F (USA)

Mikoyan-Gurevich MiG-27 (USSR)

1974

Lockheed S-3A Viking (USA)

1975

Fairchild Republic A-10A
Thunderbolt II (USA)

447

Plate 211

Avro Vulcan B Mk.2

1 Wing tip antennae
2 Starboard navigation light
3 Starboard wing tip construction
4 Outboard aileron
5 Inboard aileron
6 Rear spar
7 Outboard wing panel ribs
8 Front spar
9 Leading edge ribs
10 Cranked leading edge
11 Corrugated leading-edge inner skin
12 Retractable landing and taxying lamp
13 Fuel tank fire extinguisher bottles
14 Outer wing panel joint rib
15 Honeycomb skin panel
16 Outboard elevator
17 Inboard elevator
18 Elevator hydraulic jacks
19 No 7 starboard fuel tank
20 No 5 starboard fuel tank
21 Diagonal rib
22 Leading edge de-icing air duct
23 Wing stringer construction
24 Parallel chord wing skin panels
25 No 6 starboard fuel tank
26 No 4 starboard fuel tank
27 No 3 starboard fuel tank
28 Main undercarriage leg
29 Eight-wheel bogie
30 Mainwheel well door
31 Fuel tank fire extinguishers
32 Inboard leading edge construction
33 De-icing air supply pipe
34 Fuel collectors and pumps
35 Main undercarriage wheel bay
36 Retracting mechanism
37 Airborne auxiliary power plant (AAPP)
38 Electrical equipment bay
39 Starboard engine bays
40 Rolls-Royce (Bristol) Olympus 301 engines
41 Air system piping
42 Engine bay dividing rib
43 Engine fire extinguishers
44 Jet pipes
45 Fixed trailing edge construction
46 Jet pipe nozzles
47 Rear equipment bay
48 Oxygen bottles
49 Batteries
50 Rudder power control unit
51 Rear electronics bay
52 Electronic countermeasures system equipment
53 Cooling air intake
54 Tail warning radar scanner

55 Tail radome
56 Twin brake parachute housing
57 Brake parachute door
58 Rudder construction
59 Rudder balance weights and seals
60 Fin de-icing air outlet
61 Di-electric fin tip fairing
62 Passive electronic countermeasures (ECM) antennae
63 Fin construction
64 Fin leading edge
65 Corrugated inner skin
66 Communications aerial
67 Fin de-icing air supply
68 Bomb-bay rear bulkhead
69 Bomb-bay roof arch construction
70 Flush air intake
71 Communications aerial
72 Port Olympus 301 engines
73 Engine bay top panel construction
74 Port jet pipe fairing
75 Electrical equipment bay
76 Chaff dispenser
77 "Green Satin" navigational radar bay
78 Elevator balance weights and seals
79 Elevator hydraulic jacks
80 Inboard elevator
81 Outboard elevator
82 Inboard aileron
83 Aileron balance weights
84 Control rods
85 Aileron power control jacks
86 Jack fairings
87 Outboard aileron
88 Port wing tip antennae
89 Retractable landing and taxying lamp

90 Cranked leading edge
91 Fuel tank fire extinguishers
92 Cambered leading edge profile
93 No 7 port fuel tank
94 No 5 port fuel tank
95 Leading edge de-icing air duct
96 No 6 port fuel tank
97 No 4 port fuel tank
98 No 3 port fuel tank
99 Port main undercarriage bay
100 Wing stringer construction
101 Port airbrakes

102 Airbrake drive mechanism
103 Intake ducts
104 Front wing spar attachment joints
105 Centre section front spar frame
106 Suppressed aerial
107 Anti-collision light
108 Bomb bay longerons
109 Forward limit of bomb bay
110 Starboard airbrake housings
111 Boundary layer bleed air duct
112 Starboard intake ducts

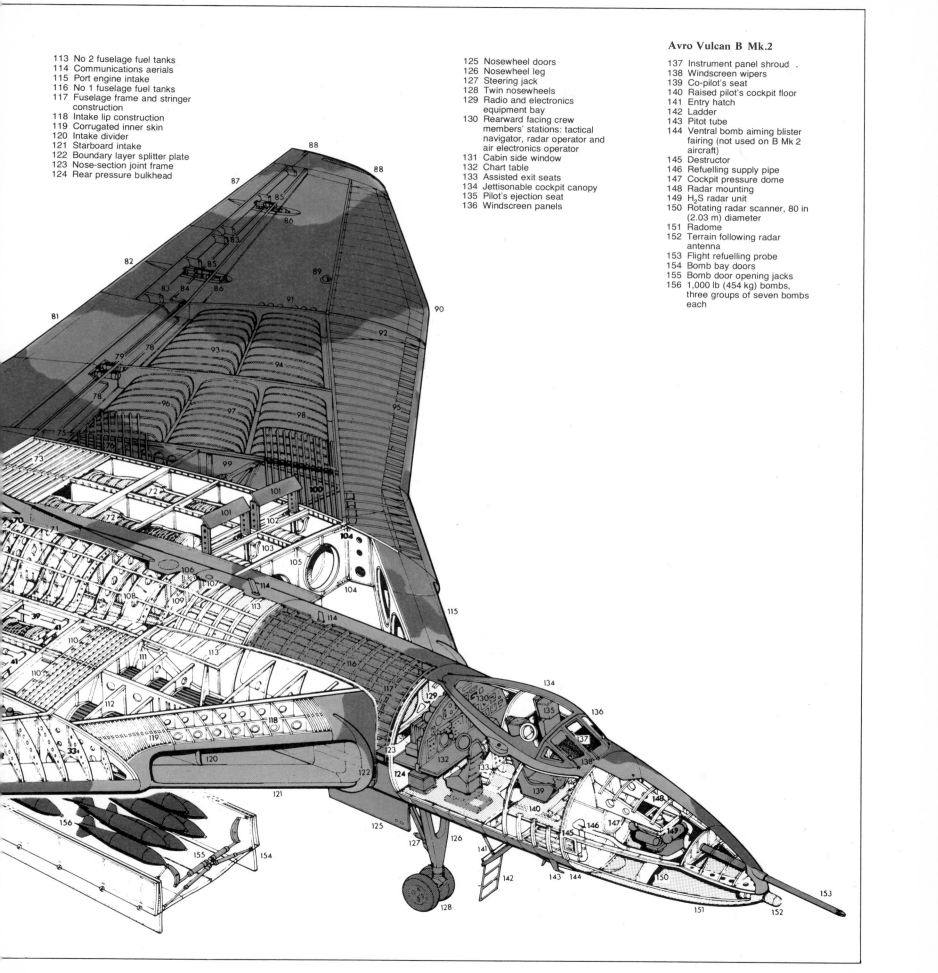

113 No 2 fuselage fuel tanks
114 Communications aerials
115 Port engine intake
116 No 1 fuselage fuel tanks
117 Fuselage frame and stringer construction
118 Intake lip construction
119 Corrugated inner skin
120 Intake divider
121 Starboard intake
122 Boundary layer splitter plate
123 Nose-section joint frame
124 Rear pressure bulkhead

125 Nosewheel doors
126 Nosewheel leg
127 Steering jack
128 Twin nosewheels
129 Radio and electronics equipment bay
130 Rearward facing crew members' stations: tactical navigator, radar operator and air electronics operator
131 Cabin side window
132 Chart table
133 Assisted exit seats
134 Jettisonable cockpit canopy
135 Pilot's ejection seat
136 Windscreen panels

Avro Vulcan B Mk.2

137 Instrument panel shroud
138 Windscreen wipers
139 Co-pilot's seat
140 Raised pilot's cockpit floor
141 Entry hatch
142 Ladder
143 Pitot tube
144 Ventral bomb aiming blister fairing (not used on B Mk 2 aircraft)
145 Destructor
146 Refuelling supply pipe
147 Cockpit pressure dome
148 Radar mounting
149 H₂S radar unit
150 Rotating radar scanner, 80 in (2.03 m) diameter
151 Radome
152 Terrain following radar antenna
153 Flight refuelling probe
154 Bomb bay doors
155 Bomb door opening jacks
156 1,000 lb (454 kg) bombs, three groups of seven bombs each

449

GRUMMAN AF-2A GUARDIAN
Nation: USA; *manufacturer:* Grumman Aircraft Engineering Corp; *type:* assault/anti-submarine; *year:* 1949; *engine:* Pratt & Whitney R-2800 48W Double Wasp 18-cylinder air-cooled radial, 2,400 hp; *wingspan:* 60 ft 8 in (18.49 m); *length:* 43 ft 4 in (13.20 m); *height:* 16 ft 2 in (4.92 m); *weight:* 25,500 lb (11,567 kg) (loaded); *maximum speed:* 317 mph (510 km/h); *ceiling:* 32,500 ft (9,900 m); *range:* 1,500 miles (2,410 km); *armament:* 2,000 lb (1,907 kg) torpedo; or 4,000 lb (1,814 kg) of bombs; *crew:* 2

DOUGLAS AD-5W SKYRAIDER
Nation: USA; *manufacturer:* Douglas Aircraft Co; *type:* reconnaissance; *year:* 1951; *engine:* Wright R-3350-26W Cyclone 18-cylinder air-cooled radial, 2,700 hp; *wingspan:* 50 ft (15.24 m); *length:* 40 ft 1 in (12.21 m); *height:* 15 ft 10 in (4.82 m); *weight:* 25,000 lb (11,340 kg) (loaded); *maximum speed:* 311 mph (501 km/h) at 18,000 ft (5,486 m); *ceiling:* 27,000 ft (8,230 m); *range:* 1,294 miles (2,080 km); *armament:* 2 × 20 mm cannon; *crew:* 3

DOUGLAS AD-6 SKYRAIDER
Nation: USA; *manufacturer:* Douglas Aircraft Co; *type:* assault; *year:* 1952; *engine:* Wright R-3350-26W Cyclone 18-cylinder air-cooled radial, 2,700 hp; *wingspan:* 50 ft (15.24 m); *length:* 39 ft 2 in (11.83 m); *height:* 15 ft 8 in (4.77 m); *weight:* 25,000 lb (11,340 kg) (loaded); *maximum speed:* 322 mph (518 km/h) at 18,000 ft 5,486 m); *ceiling:* 28,500 ft (8,690 m); *range:* 1,143 miles (1,840 km); *armament:* 4 × 20 mm cannon; 8,000 lb (3,628 kg) of bombs; *crew:* 1

GRUMMAN S-2A TRACKER
Nation: USA; *manufacturer:* Grumman Aircraft Engineering Corp; *type:* anti-submarine; *year:* 1952; *engine:* two Wright R-1820-82WA Cyclones 9-cylinder air-cooled radials, 1,525 hp each; *wingspan:* 69 ft 8 in (21.23 m); *length:* 42 ft 3 in (12.87 m); *height:* 16 ft 3 in (4.95 m); *weight:* 26,300 lb (11,930 kg) (loaded); *maximum speed:* 287 mph (461 km/h) at 5,000 ft 1,524 m); *ceiling:* 23,000 ft (7,010 m); *range:* 900 miles (1,450 km); *armament:* 4,810 lb (2,181 kg) of bombs; *crew:* 4

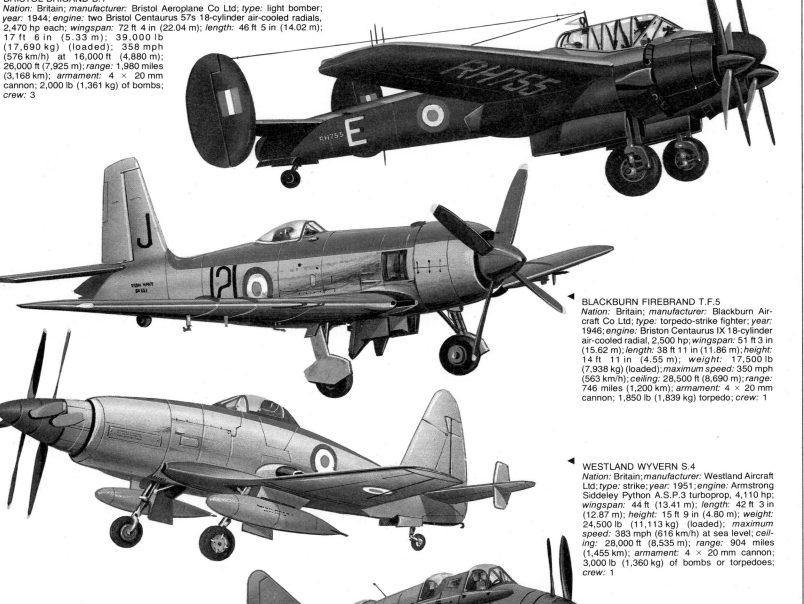

BRISTOL BRIGAND B.1
Nation: Britain; *manufacturer:* Bristol Aeroplane Co Ltd; *type:* light bomber; *year:* 1944; *engine:* two Bristol Centaurus 57s 18-cylinder air-cooled radials, 2,470 hp each; *wingspan:* 72 ft 4 in (22.04 m); *length:* 46 ft 5 in (14.02 m); 17 ft 6 in (5.33 m); 39,000 lb (17,690 kg) (loaded); 358 mph (576 km/h) at 16,000 ft (4,880 m); 26,000 ft (7,925 m); *range:* 1,980 miles (3,168 km); *armament:* 4 × 20 mm cannon; 2,000 lb (1,361 kg) of bombs; *crew:* 3

BLACKBURN FIREBRAND T.F.5
Nation: Britain; *manufacturer:* Blackburn Aircraft Co Ltd; *type:* torpedo-strike fighter; *year:* 1946; *engine:* Briston Centaurus IX 18-cylinder air-cooled radial, 2,500 hp; *wingspan:* 51 ft 3 in (15.62 m); *length:* 38 ft 11 in (11.86 m); *height:* 14 ft 11 in (4.55 m); *weight:* 17,500 lb (7,938 kg) (loaded); *maximum speed:* 350 mph (563 km/h); *ceiling:* 28,500 ft (8,690 m); *range:* 746 miles (1,200 km); *armament:* 4 × 20 mm cannon; 1,850 lb (1,839 kg) torpedo; *crew:* 1

WESTLAND WYVERN S.4
Nation: Britain; *manufacturer:* Westland Aircraft Ltd; *type:* strike; *year:* 1951; *engine:* Armstrong Siddeley Python A.S.P.3 turboprop, 4,110 hp; *wingspan:* 44 ft (13.41 m); *length:* 42 ft 3 in (12.87 m); *height:* 15 ft 9 in (4.80 m); *weight:* 24,500 lb (11,113 kg) (loaded); *maximum speed:* 383 mph (616 km/h) at sea level; *ceiling:* 28,000 ft (8,535 m); *range:* 904 miles (1,455 km); *armament:* 4 × 20 mm cannon; 3,000 lb (1,360 kg) of bombs or torpedoes; *crew:* 1

FAIREY GANNET A.S.4
Nation: Britain; *manufacturer:* Fairey Aviation Co Ltd; *type:* anti-submarine search and strike; *year:* 1956; *engine:* Armstrong Siddeley Double Mamba 101 turboprop, 3,035 hp; *wingspan:* 54 ft 4 in (16.56 m); *length:* 43 ft (13.10 m); *height:* 13 ft 8 in (4.16 m); *weight:* 22,506 lb (10,208 kg) (loaded); *maximum speed:* 299 mph (481 km/h) at sea level; *ceiling:* 25,000 ft (7,620 m); *range:* 943 miles (1,510 km); *armament:* 2,000 lb (907 kg) torpedoes, mines, depth charges etc; *crew:* 3

BREGUET Br.1050 ALIZÉ
Nation: France; *manufacturer:* Société des Ateliers d'Aviation Louis Breguet; *type:* anti-submarine; *year:* 1956; *engine:* Rolls-Royce Dart R.Da.21 turboprop, 2,100 shp; *wingspan:* 51 ft 2 in (15.60 m); *length:* 45 ft 6 in (13.86 m); *height:* 16 ft 5 in (5 m); *weight:* 18,078 lb (8,200 kg) (loaded); *maximum speed:* 292 mph (470 km/h); *ceiling:* 20,000 ft (6,100 m); *range:* 1,785 miles (2,850 km); *armament:* 3,000 lb (1,360 kg) of depth charges; *crew:* 3

Plate 214

Naval attack aircraft: 1954–61

DOUGLAS A-4A SKYHAWK
Nation: USA; *manufacturer:* Douglas Aircraft Co; *type:* assault; *year:* 1954; *engine:* Wright J65-W-4 turbojet, 7,700 lb (3,493 kg) thrust; *wingspan:* 27 ft 6 in (8.38 m); *length:* 39 ft 1 in (11.91 m); *height:* 15 ft (4.57 m); *weight:* 17,000 lb (7,711 kg) (loaded); *maximum speed:* 664 mph (1,069 km/h) at sea level; *ceiling:* 49,000 ft (14,935 m); *range:* 920 miles (1,480 km); *armament:* 2 × 20 mm cannon; 5,000 lb (2,268 kg) of bombs; *crew:* 1

DOUGLAS A-4E SKYHAWK
Nation: USA; *manufacturer:* Douglas Aircraft Co; *type:* assault; *year:* 1961; *engine:* Pratt & Whitney J52-P-6 turbojet, 8,500 lb (3,855 kg) thrust; *wingspan:* 27 ft 6 in (8.38 m); *length:* 40 ft 1 in (12.21 m); *height:* 15 ft 2 in (4.62 m); *weight:* 24,500 lb (11,113 kg) (loaded); *maximum speed:* 685 mph (1,102 km/h) at sea level; *ceiling:* 49,000 ft (14,935 m); *range:* 920 miles (1,480 km); *armament:* 2 × 20 mm cannon; 8,200 lb (3,719 kg) of bombs; *crew:* 1

GRUMMAN A-6A INTRUDER
Nation: USA; *manufacturer:* Grumman Aircraft Engineering Corp; *type:* assault; *year:* 1960; *engine:* two Pratt & Whitney J52-P-8A turbojets, 9,300 lb (4,218 kg) thrust each; *wingspan:* 53 ft (16.15 m); *length:* 54 ft 7 in (16.64 m); *height:* 15 ft 7 in (4.75 m); *weight:* 60,626 lb (27,500 kg); *maximum speed:* 685 mph (1,102 km/h) at sea level; *ceiling:* 41,660 ft (12,700 m); *range:* 1,920 miles (3,090 km); *armament:* 15,000 lb (6,804 kg) of bombs; *crew:* 2

HAWKER SEA HAWK F.G.A.6
Nation: Britain; *manufacturer:* Armstrong Whitworth Aircraft Ltd; *type:* attack fighter; *year:* 1955; *engine:* Rolls-Royce Nene 103 turbojet, 5,200 lb (2,359 kg) thrust; *wingspan:* 39 ft (11.89 m); *length:* 39 ft 8 in (12.08 m); *height:* 8 ft 8 in (2.79 m); *weight:* 13,785 lb (6,253 kg) (loaded); *maximum speed:* 560 mph (901 km/h) at 36,000 ft (10,970 m); *ceiling:* 44,500 ft (13,560 m); *range:* 740 miles (1,191 km); *armament:* 4 × 20 mm cannon; 1,000 lb (454 kg) of bombs; *crew:* 1

HAWKER SIDDELEY BUCCANEER S.1
Nation: Britain; *manufacturer:* Hawker Siddeley Aviation Ltd; *type:* strike; *year:* 1958; *engine:* two de Havilland Gyron 101 turbojets, 7,100 lb (3,220 kg) thrust each; *wingspan:* 44 ft (13.41 m); *length:* 63 ft 5 in (19.33 m); *height:* 16 ft 3 in (4.95 m); *weight:* 46,000 lb (20,865 kg) (loaded); *maximum speed:* 720 mph (1,158 km/h) at sea level; *ceiling:* 40,000 ft (12,190 m); *range:* 2,300 miles (3,700 km); *armament:* 8,000 lb (3,630 kg) of bombs; *crew:* 2

BAC 167 STRIKEMASTER
Nation: Britain; *manufacturer:* BAe; *type:* assault; *year:* 1967; *engine:* Rolls-Royce Viper Mk 535 turbojet, 3,410 lb (1,547 kg) thrust; *wingspan:* 36 ft 10 in (11.23 m); *length:* 33 ft 8 in (10.27 m); *height:* 10 ft 11 in (3.34 m); *weight:* 11,500 lb (5,215 kg) (loaded); *maximum speed:* 450 mph (774 km/h) at 18,000 ft (5,485 m); *ceiling:* 40,000 ft (12,200 m); *range:* 725 miles (1,166 km); *armament:* 2 machine guns; 3,000 lb (1,360 kg) of bombs; *crew:* 2

AERITALIA (FIAT) G.91 Y
Nation: Italy; *manufacturer:* Aeritalia SpA; *type:* assault; *year:* 1966; *engine:* two General Electric J85-GE-13A turbojets, 4,080 lb (1,850 kg) thrust each; *wingspan:* 29 ft 6 in (9.01 m); *length:* 38 ft 8 in (11.78 m); *height:* 14 ft 6 in (4.43 m); *weight:* 19,180 lb (8,700 kg) (loaded); *maximum speed:* 690 mph (1,110 km/h) at sea level; *ceiling:* 41,000 ft (12,500 m); *range:* 930 miles (1,500 km); *armament:* 2 × 30 mm cannon; 4,000 lb (1,814 kg) of bombs; *crew:* 1

FAIRCHILD REPUBLIC A-10A THUNDERBOLT II ▶
Nation: USA; *manufacturer:* Fairchild Republic Co; *type:* assault; *year:* 1975; *engine:* two General Electric TF34-GE-100 turbofans, 9,275 lb (4,207 kg) thrust each; *wingspan:* 57 ft 6 in (17.53 m); *length:* 53 ft 4 in (16.26 m); *height:* 14 ft 8 in (4.47 m); *weight:* 47,400 lb (21,500 kg) (loaded); *maximum speed:* 449 mph (722 km/h) at sea level; *ceiling:* –; *range:* 620 miles (1,000 km); *armament:* 1 × 30 mm cannon; 16,000 lb (7,257 kg) of bombs; *crew:* 1

CESSNA A-37B ▶
Nation: USA; *manufacturer:* Cessna Aircraft Co; *type:* assault; *year:* 1967; *engine:* two General Electric J85-GE-17A turbojets, 2,850 lb (1,293 kg) thrust; *wingspan:* 35 ft 10 in (10.93 m); *length:* 29 ft 3 in (8.93 m); *height:* 8 ft 10 in (2.70 m); *weight:* 14,000 lb (6,350 kg) (loaded); *maximum speed:* 507 mph (816 km/h) at 16,000 ft (4,875 m); *ceiling:* 41,765 ft (12,730 m); *range:* 460 miles (740 km); *armament:* 1 machine gun; 5,400 lb (2,450 kg) of bombs; *crew:* 2

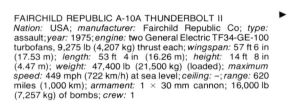

IA-58 PUCARA ▲
Nation: Argentine; *manufacturer:* FMA; *type:* assault; *year:* 1974; *engine:* two Turboméca Astazou XVIG turboprops, 1,022 hp each; *wingspan:* 47 ft 7 in (14.50 m); *length:* 46 ft 9 in (14.25 m); *height:* 17 ft 7 in (5.36 m); *weight:* 14,991 lb (3,600 kg) (loaded); *maximum speed:* 310 mph (500 km/h) at 9,845 ft (3,000 m); *ceiling:* 32,810 ft (10,000 m); *range:* 1,890 miles (3,042 km); *armament:* 2 × 20 mm cannon; 4 machine guns; 3,571 lb (1,620 kg) of bombs; *crew:* 2

LOCKHEED S-3A VIKING
Nation: USA; *manufacturer:* Lockheed Corp; *type:* assault; *year:* 1974; *engine:* two General Electric TF34-GE-2 turbofans, 9,275 lb (4,207 kg) thrust each; *wingspan:* 68 ft 8 in (20.93 m); *length:* 53 ft 4 in (16.26 m); *height:* 22 ft 9 in (6.93 m); *weight:* 42,500 lb (19,277 kg) (loaded); *maximum speed:* 518 mph (834 km/h); *ceiling:* 40,000 ft (12,200 m); *range:* 2,303 miles (3,705 km); *armament:* 7,715 lb (3,500 kg) of bombs; *crew:* 4

Plate 216

◀ BOEING B-50D SUPERFORTRESS
Nation: USA; *manufacturer:* Boeing Airplane Co; *type:* bomber;
year: 1949; *engine:* four Pratt & Whitney R-4360-35 Wasp
Majors 28-cylinder air-cooled radials, 3,500 hp each; *wingspan:* 143 ft 3 in (43.10 m); *length:* 100 ft (30.48 m); *height:*
34 ft 7 in (10.54 m); *weight:* 173,000 lb (78,472 kg) (loaded);
maximum speed: 380 mph (611 km/h) at 25,000 ft (7,620 m);
ceiling: 36,700 ft (11,190 m); *range:* 4,900 miles (7,880 km);
armament: 12 machine guns; 1 × 20 mm cannon; 20,000 lb
(9,072 kg) of bombs; *crew:* 10

NORTH AMERICAN RB-45C TORNADO
Nation: USA; *manufacturer:* North American Aviation Inc; *type:*
reconnaissance; *year:* 1950; *engine:* four General Electric
J47-GE-13 turbojets, 6,000 lb (2,721 kg) thrust each; *wingspan:* 96 ft (29.26 m); *length:* 75 ft 11 in (23.14 m); *height:* 25 ft
2 in (7.67 m); *weight:* 110,721 lb (50,223 kg) (loaded); *maximum speed:* 570 mph (917 km/h) at 4,000 ft (1,219 m); *ceiling:*
40,250 ft (12,270 m); *range:* 2,530 miles (4,070 km); *armament:* 2 machine guns; *crew:* 4
▼

CONVAIR B-36H
Nation: USA; *manufacturer:* Consolidated-Vultee Aircraft Corp;
type: bomber; *year:* 1952; *engine:* six Pratt & Whitney
R-4360-53 Wasp Majors 28-cylinder air-cooled radials,
3,800 hp each; and four General Electric J-47-GE-19 turbojets,
5,200 lb (2,358 kg) thrust each; *wingspan:*
230 ft (70.10 m); *length:* 162 ft 1 in (49.40 m);
height: 46 ft 8 in (14.22 m); *weight:* 410,000 lb
(185,976 kg) (loaded); *maximum speed:*
411 mph (661 km/h) at 36,400 ft (11,094 m);
ceiling: 39,900 ft (12,160 m); *range:*
6,800 miles (10,940 km); *armament:* 12 ×
20 mm cannon; 86,000 lb (36,000 kg) of
bombs; *crew:* 15
▼

BOEING B-47E STRATOJET
Nation: USA; *manufacturer:* Boeing Airplane Co; *type:* bomber;
year: 1953; *engine:* six General Electric J47-GE-25 turbojets,
6,000 lb (2,721 kg) thrust each; *wingspan:* 116 ft (35.35 m);
length: 109 ft 10 in (33.47 m); *height:* 27 ft 11 in
(8.50 m); *weight:* 206,700 lb (93,759 kg)
(loaded); *maximum speed:* 606 mph
(975 km/h) at 16,300 ft (4,968 m); *ceiling:*
40,500 ft (12,345 m); *range:* 4,000 miles
(6,435 km); *armament:* 2 × 20 mm cannon;
20,000 lb (9,072 kg) of bombs; *crew:* 3
▶

◀ DOUGLAS A3D-2 SKYWARRIOR
Nation: USA; *manufacturer:* Douglas Aircraft Co; *type:* bomber;
year: 1954; *engine:* two Pratt & Whitney J57-P-10 turbojets,
12,400 lb (5,625 kg) thrust each; *wingspan:* 72 ft 6 in
(22.10 m); *length:* 76 ft 4 in (23.36 m); *height:* 22 ft 9 in
(6.94 m); *weight:* 82,000 lb (37,195 kg) (loaded); *maximum
speed:* 610 mph (981 km/h) at 10,000 ft (3,048 m); *ceiling:*
41,000 ft (12,500 m); *range:* 2,100 miles (3,380 km);
armament: 2 × 20 mm cannon; 12,000 lb (5,443 kg) of bombs;
crew: 3

TUPOLEV Tu-14
Nation: USSR; *manufacturer:* State Industries
type: bomber; *year:* 1947; *engine:* two Klimov
VK-1 turbojets, 5,952 lb (2,700 kg) thrust each;
wingspan: 71 ft 1 in (21.68 m); *length:* 72 ft
(21.95 m); *height:* 21 ft 11 in (6.68 m); *weight:*
55,887 lb (23,350 kg) (loaded); *maximum
speed:* 525 mph (845 km/h); *ceiling:* 36,745 ft
(11,200 m); *range:* 1,870 miles (3,010 km);
armament: 2 × 23 mm cannon; 6,614 lb
(3,000 kg) of bombs; *crew:* 5 ▶

ILYUSHIN Il-28
Nation: USSR; *manufacturer:* State Industries;
type: bomber; *year:* 1948; *engine:* two Klimov
VK-1 turbojets, 6,040 lb (2,740 kg) thrust each;
wingspan: 70 ft 4 in (21.45 m); *length:* 57 ft
11 in (17.65 m); *height:* 22 ft (6.70 m); *weight:*
46,300 lb (21,000 kg) (loaded); *maximum
speed:* 559 mph (900 km/h) at 15,000 ft
(4,500 m); *ceiling:* 40,355 ft (12,300 m);
range: 715 miles (1,135 km); *armament:* 4 ×
23 mm cannon; 6,613 lb (3,000 kg) of bombs;
crew: 3 ▶

TUPOLEV Tu-16A
Nation: USSR; *manufacturer:* State Industries; *type:* bomber; *year:* 1954; *engine:* two Mikulin Am-3M turbojets,
20,940 lb (9,500 kg) thrust each; *wingspan:* 108 ft (32.93 m); *length:* 114 ft 2 in (34.80 m); *height:* 35 ft 6 in (10.80 m);
weight: 149,906 lb (68,000 kg) (loaded); *maximum speed:* 620 mph (1,000 km/h); *ceiling:* 42,650 ft (13,000 m); *range:*
3,580 miles (5,670 km); *armament:* 6 × 23 mm cannon; 19,800 lb (9,000 kg) of bombs; *crew:* 7

▲

MYASISHCHEV Mya-4A
Nation: USSR; *manufacturer:* State Industries; *type:* bomber; *year:* 1953; *engine:* four Mikulin AM-3D turbojets,
19,180 lb (8,700 kg) thrust each; *wingspan:* 167 ft 7 in (50.48 m); *length:* 154 ft 10 in (47.20 m); *height:* 46 ft (14.10 m);
weight: 352,740 lb (160,000 kg) (loaded); *maximum speed:* 560 mph (900 km/h); *ceiling:* 42,650 (13,000 m); *range:*
6,835 miles (1,000 km); *armament:* 10 × 23 mm cannon; 22,000 lb (10,000 kg) of bombs; *crew:* 6

Plate 218   The Canberra: Britain's first modern postwar bomber: 1950–55

AVRO LINCOLN B.1
Nation: Britain; *manufacturer:* A. V. Roe and Co Ltd; *type:* bomber; *year:* 1944; *engine:* four Rolls-Royce Merlin 85 V-12 liquid-cooled, 1,750 hp each; *wingspan:* 120 ft (36.57 m); *length:* 78 ft 3 in (23.85 m); *height:* 17 ft 3 in (5.25 m); *weight:* 75,000 lb (34,020 kg) (loaded); *maximum speed:* 319 mph (513 km/h) at 12,500 ft (5,640 m); *ceiling:* 30,500 ft (9,300 m); *range:* 1,470 miles (2,365 km); *armament:* 6 machine guns; 14,000 lb (6,350 kg) of bombs; *crew:* 7

ENGLISH ELECTRIC CANBERRA B.(I)8
Nation: Britain; *manufacturer:* English Electric Co Ltd; *type:* bomber intruder; *year:* 1954; *engine:* two Rolls-Royce Avon 109 turbojets, 7,500 lb (3,402 kg) thrust each; *wingspan:* 63 ft 11 in (19.49 m); *length:* 65 ft 6 in (19.96 m); *height:* 15 ft 7 in (4.75 m); *weight:* 51,000 lb (23,130 kg) (loaded); *maximum speed:* 580 mph (933 km/h) at 30,000 ft (9,144 m) *ceiling:* 48,000 ft (14,630 m); *range:* 800 miles (1,287 km); *armament:* 4 × 20 mm cannon; 5,000 lb (2,270 kg) of bombs; *crew:* 2

ENGLISH ELECTRIC CANBERRA B.2
Nation: Britain; *manufacturer:* English Electric Co Ltd; *type:* bomber; *year:* 1950; *engine:* two Rolls-Royce Avon 101 turbojets, 6,500 lb (2,948 kg) thrust each; *wingspan:* 63 ft 11 in (19.49 m); *length:* 65 ft 6 in (19.96 m); *height:* 15 ft 8 in (4.78 m); *weight:* 44,500 lb (20,185 kg) (loaded); *maximum speed:* 570 mph (917 km/h) at 40,000 ft (12,192 m); *ceiling:* 48,000 ft (14,630 m); *range:* 2,656 miles (4,274 km); *armament:* 6,000 lb (2,722 kg) of bombs; *crew:* 3

MARTIN RB-57D CANBERRA
Nation: USA; *manufacturer:* Glenn L. Martin Co; *type:* reconnaissance; *year:* 1955; *engine:* two Pratt & Whitney J57-P-37A turbojets, 11,000 lb (4,990 kg) thrust each; *wingspan:* 106 ft (32.30 m); *length:* 65 ft 6 in (19.96 m); *height:* 14 ft 10 in (4.52 m); *weight:* 55,000 lb (24,948 kg) (loaded); *maximum speed:* 582 mph (936 km/h) at 40,000 ft (12,190 m); *ceiling:* 65,000 ft (19,800 m); *range:* 3,000 miles (4,828 km); *armament:* –; *crew:* 2

SUD-OUEST SO-4050 VAUTOUR II-B
Nation: France; *manufacturer:* SNCASO; *type:* bomber; *year:* 1954; *engine:* two SNECMA Atar 101E-3, 7,716 lb (3,500 kg) thrust each; *wingspan:* 49 ft 7 in (15.11 m); *length:* 52 ft (15.84 m); *height:* 16 ft 2 in (4.95 m); *weight:* 45,635 lb (20,700 kg) (loaded); *maximum speed:* 685 mph (1,102 km/h) at sea level; *ceiling:* 49,200 ft (15,000 m); *range:* 1,600 miles (2,575 km); *armament:* 5,300 lb (2,400 kg) of bombs; *crew:* 2

VICKERS VALIANT B.1
Nation: Britain; *manufacturer:* Vickers-Armstrong Ltd; *type:* bomber; *year:* 1953; *engine:* four Rolls-Royce Avon 204 turbojets, 10,000 lb (4,536 kg) thrust each; *wingspan:* 114 ft 4 in (34.85 m); *length:* 108 ft 3 in (32.99 m); *height:* 32 ft 2 in (9.80 m); *weight:* 140,000 lb (63,504 kg) (loaded); *maximum speed:* 567 mph (912 km/h); *ceiling:* 54,000 ft (16,460 m); *range:* 3,450 miles (5,550 km); *armament:* 21,000 lb (9.525 kg) of bombs; *crew:* 5

AVRO VULCAN B.1
Nation: Britain; *manufacturer:* A. V. Roe and Co Ltd; *type:* bomber; *year:* 1955; *engine:* four Bristol Olympus 101 turbojets, 11,000 lb (4,990 kg) thrust each; *wingspan:* 99 ft (30.18 m); *length:* 97 ft 1 in (29.60 m); *height:* 26 ft 1 in (7.95 m); *weight:* 170,000 lb (77,112 kg) (loaded); *maximum speed:* 640 mph (1,030 km/h) at 40,000 ft (12,190 m); *ceiling:* 55,000 ft (16,765 m); *range:* 3,000 miles (4,830 km); *armament:* 21,000 lb (9,525 kg) of bombs; *crew:* 5

HANDLEY PAGE VICTOR B.1
Nation: Britain; *manufacturer:* Handley Page Ltd; *type:* bomber; *year:* 1956; *engine:* four Armstrong Siddeley Sapphire 200 turbojets, 11,000 lb (4,990 kg) thrust each; *wingspan:* 110 ft (33.53 m); *length:* 114 ft 11 in (35.05 m); *height:* 28 ft 1 in (8.59 m); *weight:* 180,000 lb (81,650 kg) (loaded); *maximum speed:* 640 mph (1,030 km/h) at 36,000 ft (10,973 m); *ceiling:* 55,000 ft (16,765 m); *range:* 2,700 miles (4,345 km); *armament:* 35,000 lb (15,876 kg) of bombs; *crew:* 5

DASSAULT MIRAGE IV-A
Nation: France; *manufacturer:* Avions Marcel Dassault; *type:* bomber; *year:* 1963; *engine:* two SNECMA Atar 9K turbojets, 15,432 lb (7,000 kg) thrust each; *wingspan:* 38 ft 10 in (11.84 m); *length:* 76 ft 10 in (23.41 m); *height:* 17 ft 8 in (5.46 m); *weight:* 69,665 lb (31,600 kg) (loaded); *maximum speed:* 1,454 mph (2,340 km/h) at 40,000 ft (12,190 m); *ceiling:* 65,600 ft (20,000 m); *range:* 770 miles (1,240 km); *armament:* 16,000 lb (7,257 kg) of bombs); *crew:* 2

Plate 220

Soviet bombers: 1954 to the present day

TUPOLEV Tu-20
Nation: USSR; *manufacturer:* State Industries; *type:* bomber; *year;* 1954; *engine:* four Kusnetsov NK-12MV turboprops, 15,000 hp each; *wingspan:* 159 ft (48.50 m); *length:* 155 ft 10 in (47.50 m); *height:* 38 ft 8 in (11.78 m); *weight:* 340,000 lb (154,000 kg) (loaded); *maximum speed:* 500 mph (805 km/h) at 41,000 ft (12,500 m); *ceiling:* 44,000 ft (13,400 m); *range:* 7,800 miles (12,550 km); *armament:* 6 × 23 mm cannon; 25,000 lb (11,340 kg) of bombs; *crew:* 10

TUPOLEV Tu-22
Nation: USSR; *manufacturer:* State Industries; *type:* bomber; *year:* 1960; *engine:* two turbojets, 27,000 lb (12,250 kg) thrust each; *wingspan:* 90 ft 10 in (27.70 m); *length:* 132 ft 11 in (40.53 m); *height:* 17 ft (5.18 m); *weight:* 184,970 lb (83,902 kg) (loaded); *maximum speed:* 920 mph (1,480 km/h); *ceiling:* 59,000 ft (18,000 m); *range:* 1,400 miles (2,250 km); *armament:* 1 × 23 mm cannon; 20,000 lb (9,070 kg) of bombs; *crew:* 3-5

TUPOLEV Tu-26
Nation: USSR; *manufacturer:* State Industries; *type:* bomber; *year:* 1970; *engine:* two Kuznetsov NK-144 turbofans, 48,500 lb (22,000 kg) thrust each; *wingspan:* 113 ft (34.45 m); *length:* 132 ft (40.23 m); *height:* 33 ft (10.06 m); *weight:* 270,000 lb (122,500 kg) (loaded); *maximum speed:* 1,520 mph (2,445 km/h); *ceiling:* 60,000 ft (18,920 m); *range:* 3,570 miles (5,475 km); *armament:* 1 × 30 mm cannon; air-to-ground missiles; *crew:* 4

SUKHOI Su-17
Nation: USSR; *manufacturer:* State Industries; *type:* assault; *year:* 1967; *engine:* Lyulka AL-21F-3 turbojet, 25,000 lb (11,340 kg) thrust; *wingspan:* 45 ft 11 in (14 m); *length:* 61 ft 6 in (18.75 m); *height:* 15 ft 7 in (4.75 m); *weight:* 41,887 lb (19,000 kg) (loaded); *maximum speed:* 1,432 mph (2,305 km/h); *ceiling:* 59,000 ft (18,000 m); *range:* 391 miles (630 km); *armament:* 2 × 30 mm cannon; 11,023 lb (5,000 kg) of bombs; *crew:* 1

MIKOYAN-GUREVICH MiG-27
Nation: USSR; *manufacturer:* State Industries; *type:* assault; *year:* 1973; *engine:* turbofan, 24,500 lb (10,000 kg) thrust; *wingspan:* 46 ft (14 m); *length:* 53 ft (16.15 m); *height:* 13 ft (3.95 m); *weight:* 39,130 lb (17,750 kg) (loaded); *maximum speed:* 1,320 mph (2,123 km/h) at 36,000 ft (11,000 m); *ceiling:* 50,000 ft (15,250 m); *range:* 620 miles (1,000 km); *armament:* 1 × 23 mm cannon; 4 air-to-ground missiles; *crew:* 1

BOEING B-52G STRATOFORTRESS
Nation: USA; *manufacturer:* Boeing Airplane Co; *type:* bomber; *year:* 1958; *engine:* 8 Pratt & Whitney J57-P-43W turbojets, 13,750 lb (6,248 kg) thrust each; *wingspan:* 185 ft (56.38 m); *length:* 157 ft 7 in (48.03 m); *height:* 40 ft 8 in (12.40 m); *weight:* 448,000 lb (221,500 kg) (loaded); *maximum speed:* 660 mph (1,062 km/h) at 20,000 ft (6,100 m); *ceiling:* 55,000 ft (16,765 m); *range:* 8,500 miles (13,680 km); *armament:* 4 machine guns; 66,000 lb (30,000 kg) max of bombs; *crew:* 6

CONVAIR B-58-A HUSTLER ▶
Nation: USA; *manufacturer:* Convair Division of General Dynamics Corp; *type:* bomber; *year:* 1959; *engine:* four General Electric J79-GE-5 turbojets, 15,600 lb (7,075 kg) thrust each; *wingspan:* 56 ft 10 in (17.32 m); *length:* 96 ft 9 in (29.49 m); *height:* 31 ft 5 in (9.58 m); *weight:* 160,000 lb (72,576 kg) (loaded); *maximum speed:* 1,385 mph (2,228 km/h) at 40,000 ft (12,190 m); *ceiling:* 64,000 ft (19,500 m); *range:* 5,125 miles (8,248 km); *armament:* 1 × 20 mm cannon; 19,450 lb (8,820 kg) of bombs; *crew:* 3

NORTH AMERICAN A-5A VIGILANTE
Nation: USA; *manufacturer:* North American Aviation Inc; *type:* bomber; *year:* 1958; *engine:* two General Electric J79-GE-4 turbojets, 16,150 lb (7,325 kg) thrust each; *wingspan:* 53 ft (16.15 m); *length:* 73 ft 3 in (22.33 m); *height:* 19 ft 5 in (5.92 m); *weight:* 62,000 lb (28,232 kg) (loaded); *maximum speed:* 1,385 mph (2,228 km/h) at 40,000 ft (12,190 m); *ceiling:* 64,000 ft (19,520 m); *range:* 3,200 miles (5,150 km); *armament:* 1 thermonuclear bomb; 5,000 lb (2,270 kg) of conventional bombs; *crew:* 2 ◀

GENERAL DYNAMICS F-111F
Nation: USA; *manufacturer:* General Dynamics; *type:* assault; *year:* 1973; *engine:* two Pratt & Whitney TF30-P-100 turbofans, 25,100 lb (11,385 kg) thrust each; *wingspan:* 63 ft (19.20 m); *length:* 23 ft 6 in (22.40 m); *height:* 17 ft 1 in (5.22 m); *weight:* 100,000 lb (45,359 kg) (loaded); *maximum speed:* 1,450 mph (2,335 km/h) at 35,000 ft (10,670 m); *ceiling:* 59,000 ft (18,000 m); *range:* 2,925 miles (4,707 km); *armament:* 1 cannon; 31,500 lb (14,290 kg) of bombs; *crew:* 2 ▶

ROCKWELL B.1
Nation: USA; *manufacturer:* Rockwell International; *type:* bomber; *year:* 1974; *engine:* four General Electric F101-GE-100 turbofans, 30,000 lb (13,600 kg) thrust each; *wingspan:* 136 ft 9 in (41.67 m); *length:* 150 ft 3 in (45.78 m); *height:* 33 ft 7 in (10.24 m); *weight:* 389,800 lb (176,810 kg) (loaded); *maximum speed:* 1,320 mph at 50,000 ft (2,125 km/h at 15,240 m); *ceiling:* 60,000 ft (18,300 m); *range:* 6,100 miles (9,815 km); *armament:* 115,000 lb (52,164 kg) of bombs; *crew:* 4 ▶

Plate 212
The last American piston-engine naval attack aircraft: 1949–52

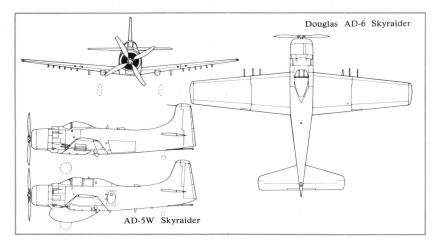

Douglas AD-6 Skyraider

AD-5W Skyraider

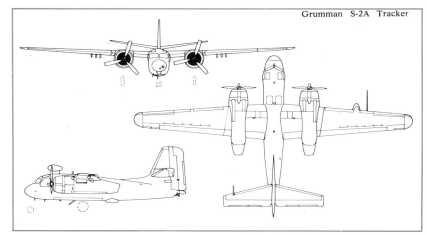

Grumman S-2A Tracker

Even well into the jet era, the old generation of piston-engine combat planes survived for a long time before being supplanted by their more modern rivals, the high-performance fighters, and among these aircraft was a long line of naval assault aircraft which had developed over the years.

In the USA one of the first attempts to develop a worthwhile naval assault plane was carried out at the end of the Second World War, when a scheme for using planes in pairs was put into practice: one being an AEW aircraft and the other a real assault aircraft. These aircraft were manufactured by Grumman and were called AF Guardians. The first definitive prototype appeared on 17th November 1949, and immediately afterwards production of the two basic variants started: the radar-equipped AF-2W and the armed AF-2S. They entered service in October 1950 and production ended three years afterwards. 156 AF-2Ws were built, 190 AF-2S, 16 AF-3Ws and 25 AF-3S. These last two series were more powerful and improved.

While the Guardian was designed to replace the Avenger torpedo-bomber, the Douglas AD Skyraider was developed to take the place of the Dauntless dive-bomber and was to become the last heavy single-seat piston-engine combat aircraft. For over twenty years the Skyraider stayed in first-line service with units of the US Navy and gave ample proof of its usefulness in two wars – the Korean War and the Viet-Nam War, proving unbeatable as a ground attack plane. From 1945 to 1957 the assembly lines built 3,180 aircraft in seven basic versions. The first of these (AD-1) reached units in December 1946 – a little over two years after the start of the project.

This had been begun in the summer of 1944 and the first prototype (XBT2D-1), had flown on 18th March of the following year and won a competition for a naval plane. After the first operational tests on the AD-1s, the airframe's great potential led to new variants being built. The 277 aircraft of the first series were therefore followed by 178 AD-2s (more powerful and structurally modified); 193 AD-3s (delivered from 1948 onwards, and which were further strengthened); 1,051 AD-4s (which appeared in 1949 and had a modified cockpit).

All these versions could be adapted for four main uses: day assault, all-weather assault, radar surveillance and electronic counter-measures. These functions were indicated by a special letter in the designation: N for all-weather version; W for radar sur-

veillance; Q for ECM. For the assault version, no extra letter was added to the designation.

The following variant of 1951, the AD-5, was even more sophisticated and had a wider cockpit, seating two side by side; 212 AD-5s were completed, 239 AD-5Ns; 218 AD-5Ws. In 1952 a return was made to the single-seat assault configuration with the AD-6 series: the Skyraider was improved and given simplified avionics; 716 were built. The last production variant was the AD-7 of 1955 which had a more powerful engine; 72 were constructed. In the Viet-Nam War the Skyraiders were used by the US Navy and the Marine Corps, the USAF, and by the air force of the Republic of Viet-Nam. France and

Grumman AF-2S Guardian

Britain were among the other countries which used this aircraft, apart from many lesser powers which kept the ADs in service until the second half of the 1970s.

The career of another family of piston-engine anti-submarine planes was just as long: the Grumman twin-engined S-2 Tracker, which was still in service with many countries at the beginning of the 1980s. Work began on the design in June 1950, in response to a request from the US Navy which wanted to provide itself with a new type of anti-submarine maritime reconnaissance plane which was also a search and attack aircraft.

The prototype (XS2F-1) flew on 2nd December 1952 and the first production aircraft, designated S2F-1 (a designation which was changed to S-2A in 1962), went into service in February 1954; 650 aircraft were built (Canada constructed 100 of them under licence), about 100 of which were sold to Allied countries, including Italy which put them into service in 1956.

In 1954 the first aircraft of the second production series S-2C also appeared (60 built) which had a modified fuselage. The second principal variant was the S-2D of May 1959, which was larger and had updated equipment; it was followed by the last series, the S-2E, which had improved avionics. A total of over 300 of this variant were constructed and they went into service in 1961.

Plate 213
The last of the piston-engine shipboard attack aircraft: 1956

In Britain the piston-engine planes also survived for a long time after the jet had come into its own. Immediately after the war, the British aeronautical industry set about developing combat aircraft which still belong to the wartime generation of planes and reached well into the 1960s with a new line of aircraft powered by turboprop engines.

The Bristol Brigand, for example, was designed to take part in the Second World War and this powerful and versatile twin-engine plane was derived from the Beaufighter which went down in history as the last light piston-engine bomber of the RAF.

The programme had started as early as 1942, and the first of four prototypes had flown on 4th December 1944. At the time, the original specification was changed: a torpedo-bomber was no longer called for and a bomber which could be a good ground attack and tactical support plane was wanted. Thus eleven aircraft were manufactured in the torpedo-bomber configuration (Brigand T.F.1), and then production switched to the bomber version. The Brigand B.1 went into service in 1949 and was used in the colonies, where they remained until the second half of the 1950s. These were used a great deal in Malaya and Kenya.

In total, including the various aircraft which were for meteorological reconnaissance (Met.3) and as trainers (T.4 and T.5), 147 Brigands were built up till 1950.

The Blackburn Firebrand carrier-borne torpedo-bomber was derived from an ill-fated project which had been started as far back as 1939; this was a powerful single-seater which was originally intended to be an interceptor. The development programme encountered many difficulties throughout the war years, being mainly held up by the scarcity of engines

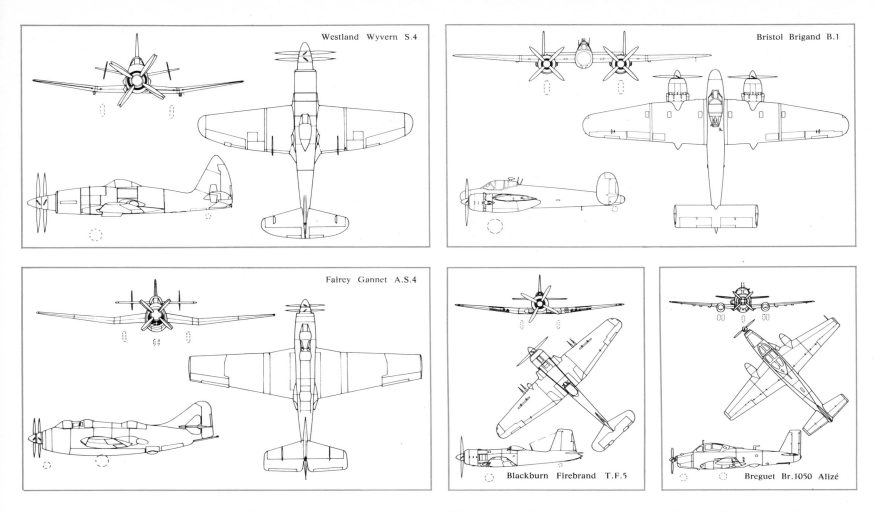

Westland Wyvern S.4

Bristol Brigand B.1

Fairey Gannet A.S.4

Blackburn Firebrand T.F.5

Breguet Br.1050 Alizé

which were to be used (the Napier Sabre). The first prototype Mk 1 flew on 27th February 1942 and was followed on 31st March of the following year by the Firebrand Mk II prototype in torpedo-bomber configuration. The definitive variants only appeared after the war and were powered by a Bristol Centaurus radial engine: these were the T.F.4 and the T.F.5 and a total of 220 were built. The Royal Navy kept these aircraft in service until 1953.

The career of the first turboprop combat aircraft of the Fleet Air Arm, the Westland Wyvern, had its share of problems, being hampered by the unsuccessful search for a reliable engine; this was a powerful single-seat assault plane which went into service in September 1954 and remained until March 1958.

The specification which led to the project had been issued in 1944 and called for the construction of a carrier-borne torpedo-bomber to be powered by one of the new turboprop engines which were being developed at the time. After a series of tests with a traditional piston engine, the Rolls-Royce Eagle, because of the enormous delays in the development of a suitable turbine engine, and after as many as 15 aircraft, consisting of prototypes and pre-production aircraft, had been built, at last on 18th January 1949 the first semi-definitive Wyvern was able to make its maiden flight.

Two months afterwards another prototype appeared on the basis of which it was decided to build twenty of the first torpedo-bomber version, the T.F.2. A whole series of technical and structural problems led to the cancellation of this programme and to the construction of an assault variant (S.4, first flight May 1951) with which production was finally started. In all, including the prototypes and experimental aeroplanes, 115 Wyverns were built, of which 90 were series S.4 planes.

The Fairey Gannet was a useful carrier-borne turboprop plane which stayed in first-line service with the Fleet Air Arm until 1960 in assault variants and until well into the seventies in AEW configuration. The programme was commenced in 1946 and the first of three prototypes flew on 19th September 1949. After a long cycle of operational proving flights, the first of 181 Gannets of the first series (A.S.1) appeared on 9th June 1953.

These aircraft entered service on 17th January 1955, and were followed by 38 trainers (T.2) and 75 A.S.4s (a more powerful assault version which appeared in April 1956); by another eight T.5 trainers (derived from the A.S.4) and by 44 AEW3 (operational from 1960). Production ceased in 1961.

The French Breguet Br.1050 Alizé resembled the Gannet very closely.

This was a turboprop carrier-borne attack aircraft, the definitive prototype of which appeared on 6th October 1956. The project had been started eight years previously, but its development had been slowed up by a change in specification which had made an almost complete redesign necessary. Series production started in 1959 with 75 aircraft for the *Aéronavale* and twelve for the Indian Navy. In its anti-submarine function, the Breguet Br.1050 Alizé was still in service at the beginning of 1980.

Plate 214
Naval attack aircraft: 1954–61

Except for the specific task of anti-submarine warfare, which has seen the replacement of the aircraft by the helicopter, carrier-borne roles have become the exclusive preserve of jet aircraft. One of the most versatile and worthwhile aircraft of this category is the American Douglas A-4 Skyhawk, a small but powerful single-seater which has been in service since 1955 and whose operational career with

units of the Marine Corps is projected into the 1980s. Nearly 3,000 of these planes have been built since 1954 and the Skyhawk has managed to retain its exceptional qualities undiminished by virtue of a policy of thorough updating and continuous improvement of the basic design.

The development programme got under way at the beginning the 1950s with a request from the US Navy for a close support fighter to replace the obsolescent Douglas Skyraider. A prototype and 19 pre-production aircraft were ordered on 21st June 1952 (designated A4D-1) and the first two of these were flown on 22nd June and 14th August 1954. At the end of proving trials series production started with 155 of the A4D-1 variant. These aircraft reached units from 26th October 1956. 526 A4D-2s followed (more powerful and with flight refuelling capability and more sophisticated avionics) and 638 A4D-Ns as an all-weather plane.

The prototype of the third production version, the A4D-5, which had a more powerful engine, improved avionics, increased range and could carry more stores, followed on 12th July 1961. These Skyhawks entered service at the end of 1962 and 480 were built. In the new designation system which came into effect in the US Navy in 1962, these four series were reclassified respectively as A-4A, A-4B, A-4C and A-4E.

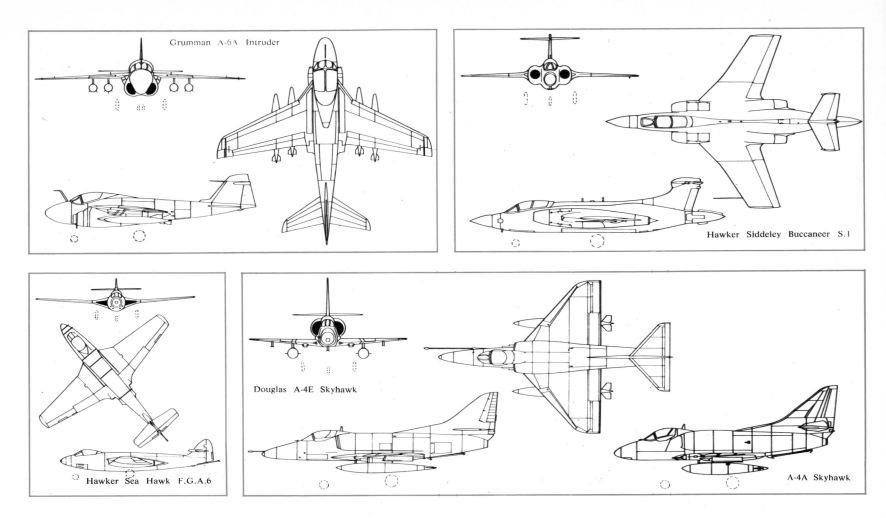

Grumman A-6A Intruder

Hawker Siddeley Buccaneer S.1

Hawker Sea Hawk F.G.A.6

Douglas A-4E Skyhawk

A-4A Skyhawk

On 31st August 1966 the prototype of a new variant had its maiden flight, the A-4F (146 built) which had a still more powerful engine and new avionics (installed in a distinctive humped fairing aft of the fuselage). Then 245 twin-seat trainers (TA-4F) followed and the first of many TA-4Js which were in simplified form for the needs of the US Naval Air Advanced Training Command.

Apart from the numerous sub-types for export, the basic variant of the 1970s was the A-4M (Skyhawk II) which had its first flight on 10th April 1970, and was built exclusively for the Marine Corps. These aircraft had more powerful engines and armament, had their instrumentation improved and were more versatile. Orders for 100 were gradually received; in particular a special variant (F-4N) was developed for Israel which had already received about 100 Skyhawks in 1969 and 1970. Among the other countries which received this aircraft were Australia, Argentina, New Zealand, Singapore and Kuwait.

From 1963 onwards the Skyhawk was joined by another versatile assault aircraft, the Grumman A-6 Intruder, which is still full operational at the beginning of the 1980s. The project took shape in 1957 and the first prototype had its maiden flight on 9th April 1960, followed after a short time by another seven pre-series aircraft. Production commenced in 1962 with the first variant, A-6A (488 built) which went into service the following year. From these aircraft were derived two versions for electronic countermeasures: the EA-6A (27 built) and the EA-6B Prowler, of which 77 were ordered. The last basic assault variant was the A-6E which flew in February 1970; a production programme of 318 was planned for this model. The Intruders have been continually updated.

Returning to the British Fleet Air Arm, one of the most useful assault jet aircraft of the 1950s was the Hawker Sea Hawk, a single-seater which stayed in first-line service from 1953 until the end of 1960, and of which 434 were built. The prototype flew on 3rd December 1948, and production comprised five basic variants: the F.1 and the F.2 fighters (95 and 40 constructed, built from 1951 and 1954); the F.B.3 fighter-bomber (1954, 116 built); the F.G.A.4 and the F.G.A.6 (fighter/ground attack – procurement 97 and 96, built from 1954 and 1955). The Sea Hawk also went for export: to India (74 which stayed in service until 1977), the Netherlands (22), and Federal Germany (64).

The Hawker Siddeley Buccaneer was more successful and had a longer career; this was a powerful and sophisticated twin-jet which was able to carry out high speed, low-level strike missions particularly effectively. The prototype appeared on 30th April 1958 and production consisted of two basic versions: the S.1 (40 built, in service from 1962) and the S.2 (which appeared in prototype on 19th August 1963 and was operational from 1965, 94 built). Apart from naval variants, 43 aircraft were ordered by the RAF and 16 by South Africa. At the end of the 1970s the Buccaneer was still in service with two air forces.

Plate 215
Attack aircraft — landplanes and carrier-based planes: 1966–75

During the 1960s and 1970s several assault aircraft were derived from aircraft which were originally conceived for training.. This is the case with the American Cessna A-37 and the British BAC 167 Strikemaster, two small twin-seaters which have achieved a definite success – specially in the export market – for counterinsurgency combat operations.

The Cessna A-37 was developed in 1963 by modifying two T-37 trainers (of which 1,268 were built between 1955 and 1977 in three basic versions) and equipping them with more powerful engines and thus with greater operational potential. The definitive production version was the A-37B which appeared in September 1967 and of which 577 were built over ten years. These aircraft, apart from their service with the USAF, were mainly used by Latin American countries.

The development of the BAC 167 Strikemaster was similar; this was derived from the BAC 145 Provost trainer by means of a general updating and increase in power. The prototype flew on 26th October 1967, and production was based on an initial order for 145. The Strikemaster has been constructed in various series for certain African countries, for Singapore, New Zealand and Ecuador.

Argentina has preferred to develop a light attack aircraft independently: the IA-58 Puccarà, a heavily armed twin-engine turboprop aircraft. The project started in 1966 and the first definitive prototype appeared in September 1970. Production began in 1974 with an initial order for 30 aircraft; another 15 followed three years later. The programme allows for the construction of 100 aircraft. The first two units to fly the Puccarà have been operational since 1978.

In Europe one of the most useful and successful light fighter tactical

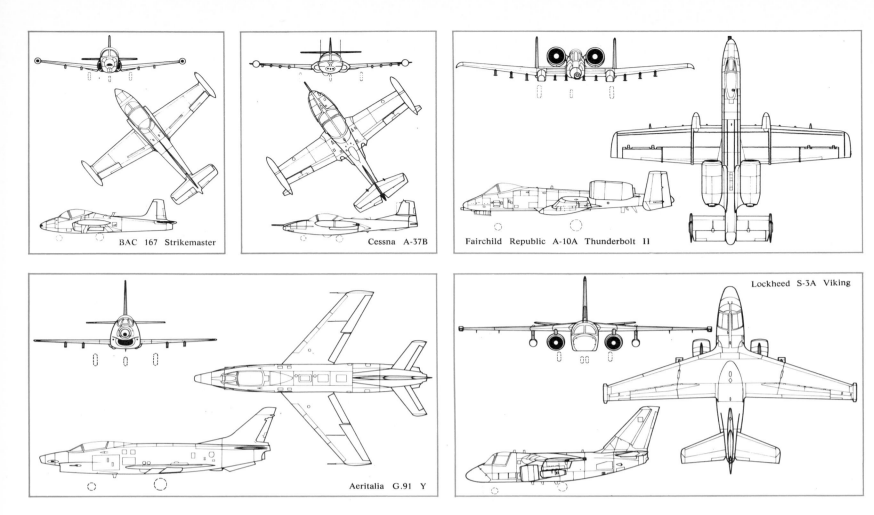

BAC 167 Strikemaster

Cessna A-37B

Fairchild Republic A-10A Thunderbolt II

Aeritalia G.91 Y

Lockheed S-3A Viking

support aircraft of the postwar years has been the Italian Fiat (Aeritalia) G.91 which won the NATO competition in 1953 and was constructed from 1956 until 1977 (total procurement 756). The first prototype was flown on 9th August 1956 and the initial version G.91 R was built in four subseries: R-1 for the *Aeronautica Militare Italiana* (40, in service from March 1971); R-3 for the *Luftwaffe* (50 built in Italy and 294 in Germany); R-4 for Turkey and Greece which was, however, subsequently delivered to the Germans (50); R-1B which in practice is a variant of the R-1 updated to the level of the R-3 for the AMI (50). These aircraft, although keeping their tactical support configuration, could also be used for photo-reconnaissance.

The second basic version was the G.91 T two-seat trainer (the prototype was flown on 31st May 1960) and two sub-series were produced: the T-1 for the *Aeronautica Militare Italiana* (99) and the T-3 for the *Luftwaffe* (66 built, 22 under licence). The last G-91 which was the most successful version of the design was the Y series: the prototype appeared on 13th December 1966 and 65 were built for the AMI. These aircraft were substantially redesigned and had two General Electric J85 turbojets instead of the single Bristol Siddeley Orpheus engine of earlier variants. The operational life of the G.91 will continue well into the 1980s.

The evolution of assault planes has gone ahead at a great rate. The most modern and powerful planes of the western world have been put into service by the USAF and by the US Navy into the second half of the 1970s: these are the Fairchild-Republic A-10 Thunderbolt II and the Lockheed S-3A Viking, two aircraft which although very different from each other and intended for tasks which only appear similar (ground attack/anti-tank capability), have their great manoeuvrability in common, and their almost incredible operational capacities.

The Fairchild-Republic A-10 was designed in 1967 and appeared in prototype on 10th May 1972. On 18th January 1973 the aircraft was chosen as the winner of a competition organised by the USAF and put into production. The first A-10A flew on 21st October 1975 (orders will soon have reached 339) and the first squadron became operational with the new aircraft in March 1977.

The Thunderbolt II is a twin-jet single-seat daytime close support plane which is at its most effective as an anti-tank platform and for this purpose it has been literally constructed around a special anti-tank gun with seven barrels which has exceptional firepower.

The Lockheed S-3A Viking on the other hand is a carrier-based hunter-killer aircraft and has been designed as

a flying electronic platform, carrying a truly impressive range of weapons. The first prototype was flown on 21st January 1972 and had been developed in response to a specification issued in 1968 which called for a replacement of the obsolescent Grumman S-2 Tracker. The first production model appeared at the beginning of 1974. At the end of the 1970s the US Navy had received 200 Lockheed Vikings.

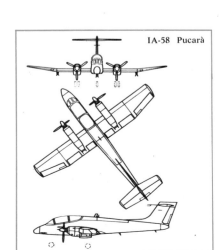

IA-58 Pucará

Plate 216
American bombers: 1949–54

As regards strategic bombers the progress from conventional piston-engine propulsion to jet propulsion was fairly gradual, at any rate in the western world. In the USA the first heavy bomber to be operational immediately after the war was a direct derivant of the Boeing B-29: this was the B-50 which was an enlarged Superfortress with engines which gave it over fifty per cent more power. Boeing and Pratt & Whitney started work together on the design in 1944. This first led to an experimental aircraft designated XB-44. From this (a B-29A powered by four radial Wasp Major 3,500 hp engines) was developed the B-50A production model which appeared on 25th June 1947. Strategic Air Command received 79 of this first model and then production went on to a second variant (B-50B, 45 constructed, first flown on 14th January 1949) which had structural modifications and an increase of total load capacity.

The last version had its maiden flight on 23rd May the same year: this was the B-50D which had increased fuel capacity and had in-flight refuelling capability. 222 of these Superfortresses

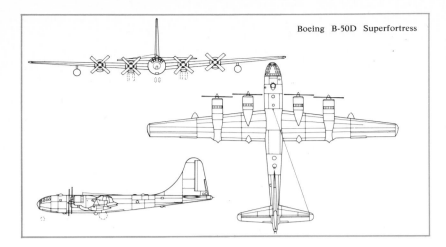

Boeing B-50D Superfortress

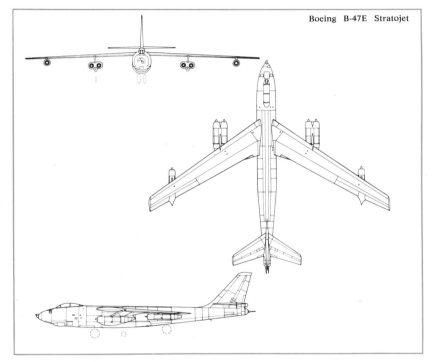

Boeing B-47E Stratojet

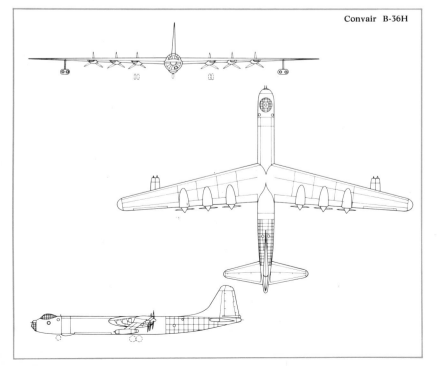

Convair B-36H

were built. At that time, however, the more powerful bomber types had already been developed and the career of the B-50 ended up by taking a different course as a photo-reconnaissance plane and tanker plane. After the conversion of many of these aircraft for strategic reconnaissance (and the production of 25 TB-50H trainers) the last B-50s were modified as flying tankers; they were designated KB-50 and entered service in 1957, remaining operational until the late 1960s.

In February 1959 Strategic Command took the last of 383 Convair B-36 planes out of service. This gigantic mixed propulsion bomber (6 piston engines and four turbojets) was the end product of a technical approach that had been formed during the years of World War II. The B-36 design went back to April 1941, when the USAAF had issued official requests for a bomber capable of carrying 4.5 tonnes of bombs for a distance of 8,000 km (4,970 miles). It was slowed down by development difficulties and above all by the course of the war, and the prototype B-36 only flew on 8th August 1946 when the war was already over.

In spite of this, production was started. In August 1947 the first of 22 B-36A trainers reached units. 73 fully operational B-36Bs followed (first flight 8th July 1948), and from 26th March 1949 aircraft of a new variant (B-36D), which had four J47 turbojets added to the six radial Wasp Major engines of the preceding series. With this change the B-36D showed a significant improvement in general performance and ended up by becoming the most important production version. A reconnaissance variant (RB-36D, 1949) was derived from the B-36D and built from 1950. The assembly lines built 28 B-36Fs (more powerful engines); 81 B-36Hs and 73 RH reconnaissance planes (first flight 5th April 1952) and 33 B-36Js with greater fuel capacity (prototype tested on 3rd September 1953). Production came to an end in August 1954.

Meanwhile the first jet bombers had gone into service. A transitional model was the North American B-45 Tornado: this was a four-engine plane with conventional structure and configuration which had been designed in 1945 and appeared in prototype in March 1947. Production started with 96 of the first variant B-45A, which went into service in November 1948, and with ten B-46Cs which were strengthened and made more powerful (1949). The final variant was a reconnaissance plane designated RB-45C: the prototype flew in April 1950 and deliveries of 33 aircraft of this series started two months later. These last Tornados were kept in service longer than the others: they were withdrawn in 1958.

At that time the final variants of the USAF's first worthwhile strategic jet bomber were fully operational, the

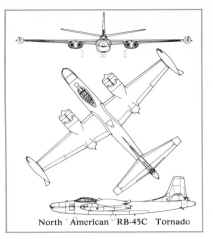

North American RB-45C Tornado

B-47 Stratojet. About 1,800 aircraft were completed between 1946 and 1957 and they stayed in service till half way through the 1960s. The aircraft had been designed in 1945 and production had gone through three principal versions: the B-47A of 1950 (10 built); the B-47B of 1951 (380); the B-47E of 1953 (1,359 built, followed by 255 photo-reconnaissance variants, RB-47E). The production lines closed on 15th February 1947 and in the same year the USAF started to relegate the B-47s to photo-reconnaissance and training. In these roles the last Stratojets were taken out of service in 1966.

The first strategic jet bomber of the US Navy was the Douglas A3D Skywarrior, an aircraft which went into service in 1956 and continued for the whole of the 1960s. the prototype flew on 28th October 1952 and series production was based on two principal versions: the A3D-1 of 1953 (50 operational from March 1956 and the A3D-3 of 1954 which had more powerful engines and a flight-refuelling probe.

164 of these bomber versions of the Skywarrior were built, and 30 A3D-2Ps, 24 A3D-2Q electronic surveillance planes and 4 A3D-2T trainers. These special variants, which were modified bombers, enabled the aircraft to continue its operational life into the next decade.

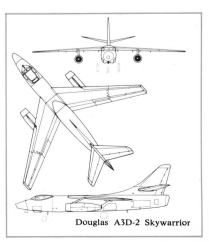

Douglas A3D-2 Skywarrior

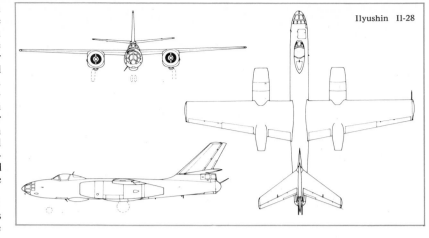
Ilyushin Il-28

postwar generation was the Ilyushin Il-28, an elegant twin-engine plane which appeared in prototype on 8th August 1948 and stayed in first-line service for about twenty years, over 10,000 of them being distributed among all the Eastern bloc countries. More or less an equivalent to the English 'Electric Canberra, the Ilyushin Il-28 was designed immediately after the end of the world war and, in much the same way as the MiG-15, reached its best configuration when the Rolls-Royce Nene engine was installed which was constructed under licence in the Soviet Union.

Mass production started in 1951 and was based on two basic variants besides the bomber variant: the Il-28U trainer, which appeared in 1951, and the Il-28R reconnaissance plane, which had the bomb-bay modified for installation of cameras and electronic equipment. The Soviet navy ordered the twin-engine Ilyushin in a torpedo-bomber variant, designated Il-28T. The use of the Il-28 (which was given the code-name of BEAGLE) by units of the *VVS* started in 1950; production for Russia's own use ended ten years later.

This, however, was not the end of the operational career of this bomber. Among the countries of the Warsaw Pact, great numbers of Il-28s were supplied to Czechoslovakia, East Germany, Hungary, Poland and Romania; and quantities were supplied to many other countries such as Algeria, Indonesia, Egypt, North Viet-Nam, North Korea and Finland. The People's Republic of China constructed several hundred of this aircraft during the 1960s.

The success of the Il-28 was repeated by a much more powerful aircraft, the Tupolev Tu-16, which was considered the classic Soviet bomber of the 1950s. Over 2,000 were built and the BADGER (NATO code-name) remained in service for over twenty years, its career being prolonged mainly through aircraft which were constructed under licence by the People's Republic of China.

The Tu-16 prototype appeared in public in 1954 and the first version to be seen by Western observers was called BADGER A: this was a basic bomber type from which were developed variants for photographic and electronic reconnaissance. The BADGER B followed which had missile armament and was used by the Naval Aviation. The following version as well (1961, BADGER C) was for use in an anti-shipping role whilst the BADGER D and the BADGER E were for maritime and electronic reconnaissance. The last two variants observed (BADGER F and BADGER G) differed from their predecessors in having better electronics and missile armament. The various derivants of the Tu-16 were not only used by the Soviet *VVS*; the A and B models were supplied in modest numbers to Indonesia between 1961 and

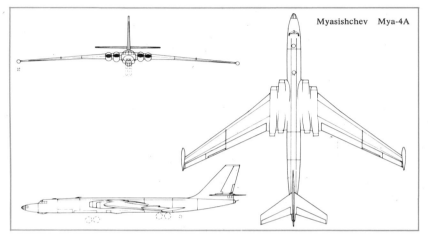
Myasishchev Mya-4A

Plate 217
The first postwar generation of Soviet bombers 1947–54

The Soviet Union was not content to stand aside watching while its ex-ally forged ahead building very large heavy bombers. Just as had been the case with the fighter, the Soviet designers were busy from the last phases of the Second World War onwards, working hard on a series of programmes which were aimed at achieving bomber air superiority as well.

One of the first designs was that which led the Tupolev Tu-14 (BOSUN in NATO code), a twin-engine plane of traditional structure and appearance which was immediately relegated to secondary tasks by much more effective contemporary aircraft. Although the development of this bomber had been particularly long and difficult, the military authorities decided to put it into production.

The BOSUN was built in three basic versions from 1947 onwards: the Tu-14, the Tu-14-R for reconnaissance and the Tu-14-T which had more powerful engines and some structural modifications. These aircraft were for units of naval aviation and stayed in service until the beginning of the 1960s.

The first successful bomber of the

1963, while Egypt and Syria used the bomber during the 1967 war with Israel.

The first giant bomber of the communist world was the Myasishchev Mya-4 which was developed in 1949 on the direct orders of Stalin who wanted a strategic bomber capable of reaching the USA and returning to base. In the event this aim was never fulfilled and the Mya-4 was eventually used as a reconnaissance plane. The prototype appeared in 1953 and the first bomber series aircraft (BISON A in NATO code) reached units two years later. Two other reconnaissance variants followed: the BISON B and

the BISON C, the latter appearing about the middle of the 1960s. According to Western estimates the total production of the Mya-4 was about 150. Some of these aircraft were subsequently modified for in-flight refuelling and used as tankers.

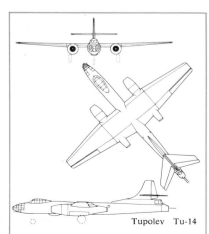
Tupolev Tu-14

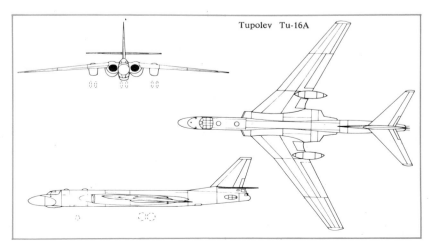
Tupolev Tu-16A

Plate 218
The Canberra — Britain's first modern postwar bomber: 1950–55

The last piston-engine strategic bomber of the RAF was the Avro Lincoln, the final stage in the development of a formula which had led to the famous Lancaster of the wartime period. The official specification had been issued in 1943 with the aim of constructing a successor to the "Lanc" which would have greater operational potential and which would be capable of flying at higher altitudes with a greater bomb-load. The first prototype flew on 9th June 1944 and had the appearance of a Lancaster but with longer fuselage and greater wingspan and was powered by the latest series of Merlin engines.

Otherwise, however, the design had been completely redrawn, especially as regards its defensive armament. The ending of the war meant that the massive production plans for the Lincoln were revised and two basic versions were constructed, the Mk I, powered by Merlin 85 engines and the Mk II, powered by Merlin 66 or 300 engines. The assembly lines completed a total of 528 for the RAF; another 54 were built in Australia, and were given the designation of Lincoln B.30. These four-engine planes stayed in first-line service with Bomber Command until 1955; and in Australian and Argentina until 1957. The Lincolns were subsequently assigned to secondary roles.

The new generation bomber which started to replace the Lincoln in the RAF in 1951 was the English Electric Canberra, a versatile twin-jet plane which was to show that it was one of the best combat aircraft of its category, and which was still operational at the beginning of the 1980s in roles other than its original one. The programme was commenced in 1945. English Electric was not at that time a well-known aircraft manufacturer but became famous with this design which was a great success. The first prototype flew on 13th May 1949 and greatly impressed those present with its structural simplicity, its excellent performance at low and high altitudes and its great flexibility and potential for development. Production was immediately started with the day bomber variant, the B.2, the first of which were completed in 1950 and entered service in 1951. Due to heavy demand for this aircraft, Handley Page, Avro and Short shared the production with English Electric.

The second version was the B.6 (in service from 1954 until 1961) which had more powerful engines and had greater operational range. On 23rd July 1954 the prototype of the B.8 variant appeared (in service with the RAF from May 1956) which had the

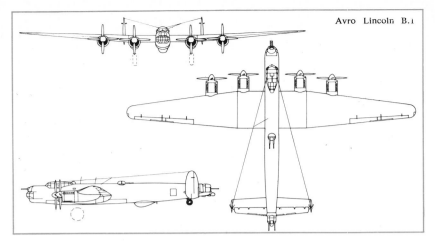

Avro Lincoln B.1

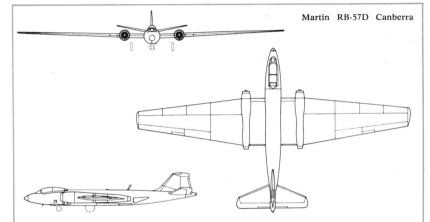

Martin RB-57D Canberra

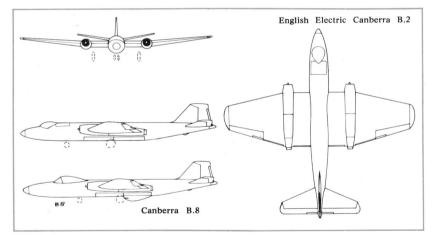

English Electric Canberra B.2

Canberra B.8

forward part of its fuselage considerably modified and could be used for a wide variety of tasks due to its considerable bomb-carrying capacity and its ventral installation for four cannon of either 20 mm or 30 mm calibre.

Numerous series and sub-types were developed from the B.8 which were for export; among the countries which ordered the Canberra were New Zealand, South Africa, Venezuela, Peru, Sweden and France. There were also several photo-reconnaissance variants: the P.R.3 (first flown on 19th March 1950) which was derived from the B.2 bomber: the P.R.7 (which appeared on 28th October 1953) derived from the B.6; the P.R.9 of

1955 which had a redesigned wing and more powerful engines. For training the T.4 and T.11 basic versions were constructed which resembled the first bomber variant fairly closely. Production totalled 925 including export aircraft; 49 Canberra B.20s (derived from the B.6) were built in Australia for the RAAF.

But the most convincing proof of this British bomber's excellence was to come from the United States. In 1951 it was decided to acquire construction rights and entrust production to Martin in order to meet the needs of the US Air Force for an effective assault aircraft. The American assembly lines constructed over 400 in various ver-

sions, and these aircraft were designated B-57 and repeated the great success of the British-built models.

The B-57A prototype flew on 20th July 1953 and was followed by 65 RB-57A reconnaissance planes by 202 B-57Bs to be used as night intruders by 38 B-57C trainers and 68 B-57E target tugs. For photo-reconnaissance and electronic counter measures the RB-57D was developed (1955) of which 20 were built and which had a very elongated wing and more powerful engines. The subsequent variant, constructed by General Dynamics, the RB-57F (21 built), was also for high altitude reconnaissance and had the structure of its wings, fuselage and tailplanes substantially modified. The last version was the B-57G which was in effect an updating of many aircraft of the first variant.

Plate 219
British and French bombers: 1953–63

The strategic bomber element of the RAF underwent a phase of thorough and ambitious development in the immediate postwar years. In 1946 the Air Ministry issued a specification which defined the basic requirements for a new generation of bombers (which were to be known as the V Class) and which were to be powered by four jet engines and capable of carrying nuclear weapons. This specification led to three heavy bombers: the Vickers Valiant, the Avro Vulcan and the Handley Page Victor; aircraft which marked an epoch in the history of British military aviation.

The Valiant was the first of the trio and the least successful. It was generally inferior in performance and general qualities and this bomber was relegated to secondary tasks after the appearance of the other two aircraft and for most of its operational career was used for in-flight refuelling as a tanker. About 100 Valiants went into service with Bomber Command between August 1954 and September 1957, staying operational until January 1965, after which they were all withdrawn and destroyed because of serious structural weaknesses.

The Valiant prototype flew on 18th May 1951. Production relied on four basic versions: the B.1 which appeared in December 1953 (30 built), the B(P.R)1 for strategic reconnaissance (11 built), the B(P.R)K.1 which was a multirole aircraft which could also be used for in-flight refuelling (14 built), and the B.K.1 bomber and tanker (48 built).

The second four-engine jet of the V Class was the Avro Vulcan, undoubtedly the best of the three: in service from 1957, it was still operational at the beginning of the 1980s, but due to be replaced by the Tornado MRCA. The main characteristic of the Vulcan was its large delta wing used for the first time in a strategic bomber which gave it very good flight characteristics. The first prototype appeared on 30th August 1952 and the first B.1 production aircraft on 5th February 1955. The following version which had more powerful engines, improved structure and better wing aerodynamics, was the B.2 which was flown for the first time on 31st August 1957. A total of about 100 Vulcans were built: their operational life was prolonged by means of continual updating and improvement. Modifications carried out on the B.2 variant mainly concerned the wing, which was made larger and completely restructured.

The Handley Page Victor had a very similar career to that of the Valiant and it had a very long development phase which delayed its entry into service: the first Victor B.1, in fact, only reached units in the spring of 1958, twelve years after the original specification had been issued. From 1965 the 80 aircraft constructed were relegated to the role of tankers which they continued to carry out for the whole of the 1970s. The Victor prototype was flown on the 24th December 1952 and had a structurally complex swept wing. The first production model appeared on 1st February 1956 (50 Victor B.1s were built) and three years later the prototype of the second series B.2 was tested which had more powerful engines and greater wingspan. About 30 of these aircraft were completed but their usefulness proved relatively limited. Once they

had been converted into tankers, the designations of the two Victor versions were changed to K.1A (the Victor B.1) and K.2 (the Victor B.2). Subsequently some B.2s were converted for strategic reconnaissance and called S.R.2.

France also, in its recovery from the war, paid particular attention to developing bombers for the *Armée de l'Air*. Side by side with the various Dassault designs, a versatile twin-engine plane from the state-owned sector of the industry, the Sud-Ouest SO-4050 Vautour, came to the fore because of its brilliant qualities. The 140 aircraft built between 1956 and 1959 were constructed in three basic versions: the II-N twin-seat all-weather fighter (70 built, first flight 16th October 1952); the II-A single-seat ground attack aircraft (30 built, first flight 4th December 1953) and the II-B twin-seat bomber (40 aircraft, first flight 4th December 1954).

The Vautours were operational with the *Armée de l'Air* from 1956, and the all-weather version stayed in service until 1973. Further production in 1960 were sold to Israel, who were still using them during the 1970s.

But France's first real strategic bomber was the Dassault Mirage IV-A, a heavy and powerful twin-jet aircraft which was developed towards the end of the 1950s as a platform for the nuclear warheads produced in France. The first prototype was flown on 17th June 1959 and the first of 62 production models ordered appeared on 7th December 1963. The Mirage IV-A entered service the following year.

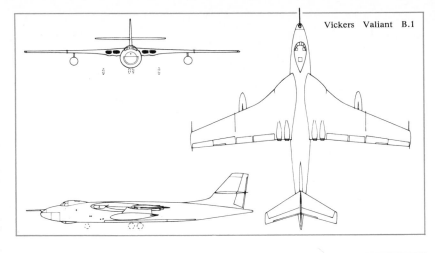

Vickers Valiant B.1

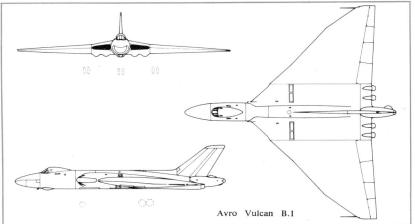

Avro Vulcan B.1

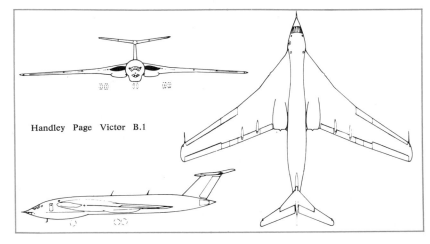

Handley Page Victor B.1

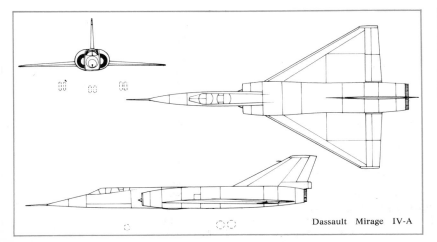

Dassault Mirage IV-A

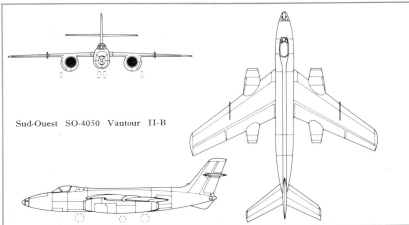

Sud-Ouest SO-4050 Vautour II-B

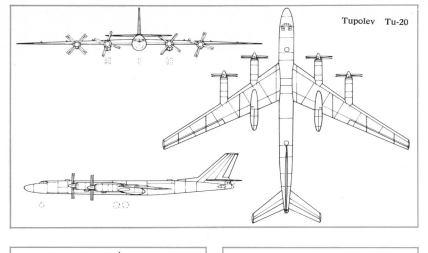
Tupolev Tu-20

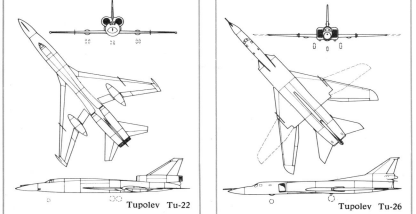
Tupolev Tu-22

Tupolev Tu-26

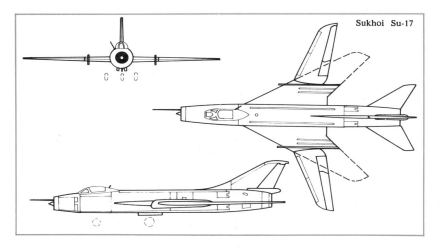
Sukhoi Su-17

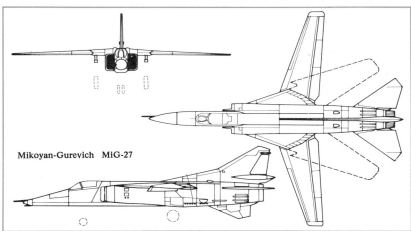
Mikoyan-Gurevich MiG-27

Plate 220
Soviet bombers: 1954 to the present day

In the Soviet Union another very large strategic bomber was the Tupolev Tu-20 basically developed from the same specifications which led to the Myasishchev Mya-4. The most interesting components of this enormous aeroplane were its power units. The designers abandoned the pure jet and chose four turboprop engines each driving two counter-rotating propellers. This solution, held to be the most suitable way to give the aircraft the exceptional range demanded of it, showed itself to be particularly inspired. Designed in the early 1950s, the Tu-20 (BEAR in NATO code) remained fully operational for nearly twenty-five years as a strategic reconnaissance plane.

The first prototype flew in 1954 and a year later five aircraft were shown in public at the traditional Tushino air display. The *VVS* put the Tu-20s into service in 1957 and four years later the Naval Aviation followed suit. Western observers have classified six basic versions of the BEAR: the initial A bomber; the Type B of 1961, a marine reconnaissance plane which has a very large fairing in the nose containing search radar and which can carry an anti-ship missile; the C of 1964 and the D which both specialised in maritime reconnaissance and electronic counter-measures; the last two BEAR E and F models were conversions of the first models up to a higher standard of equipment and avionics. The Tupolev Tu-20 had defensive armament consisting of six 23 mm cannon and a bomb-load of over 11 tonnes. Estimated production is about 300.

A more conventional plane, except that its engines were installed on the rear fuselage on either side of the rudder, was another design of Tupolev, the Tu-22 (BLINDER) which appeared for the first time in 1961.

This was considered the first supersonic Soviet bomber and has been classified in four versions: the BLINDER A bomber and reconnaissance plane with non-missile armament; the BLINDER B, similar to the former but equipped with air-to-ground missiles; the BLINDER C for maritime reconnaissance and ECM; the BLINDER D trainer which had a second cockpit above and behind the pupil's cockpit. Production is estimated to total 300, of which 200 were in the first versions and 60 in the maritime reconnaissance version. The Tu-22 has been exported, but the quantities are not well known to western experts: at the end of 1978 some were photographed in flight in Libyan national markings.

The serious inadequacy of the Tu-22 for long-range strategic missions led Tupolev to develop a new bomber design which was more suited to this role, the Tu-26 (BACKFIRE in NATO code). The most salient characteristic of this aircraft, apart from its being considerably larger than its predecessor, was its variable geometry wing. A prototype was observed for the first time in July 1970 and it is thought that the operational tests and proving flights were started three years later with a dozen pre-series aircraft.

Two basic versions have been classified by western observers: one designated BACKFIRE A, being the first version, which has large wing fairings containing stowage space for the main undercarriage, and the BACKFIRE B whose landing gear retracts into the fuselage. The first Tu-26s entered service in 1975 and some of them have been put into service with the Naval Aviation as maritime reconnaissance planes. At the end of 1979 total deliveries had reached nearly 200. The whole production programme is estimated by western sources to be approximately 400, being produced at the rate of 30 a year.

As regards tactical bombers, one of the most widely used Soviet planes is the Sukhoi Su-17 which is in fact a development of the Su-7 with a variable geometry wing. This was shown for the first time in 1967 and the Su-17 received the same NATO code-name as its predecessor, FITTER. It has been operational with units of the *VVS* from 1972 and this powerful and relatively unsophisticated single-seat assault plane has been classified in two basic versions: the FITTER C and the FITTER D of 1977 which is more powerful. An export variant (Su-20, simplified) has been seen in Egypt and in Poland.

Around 1973 the Russians derived a worthwhile assault aircraft from another well-known interceptor: the MiG-27 derived from the MiG-23. Designated FLOGGER D in NATO code, the MiG-27 has kept its predecessor's variable geometry wing but has a different engine and configuration of the nose, different avionics and armament. An export variant, FLOGGER F, has been used in Egypt.

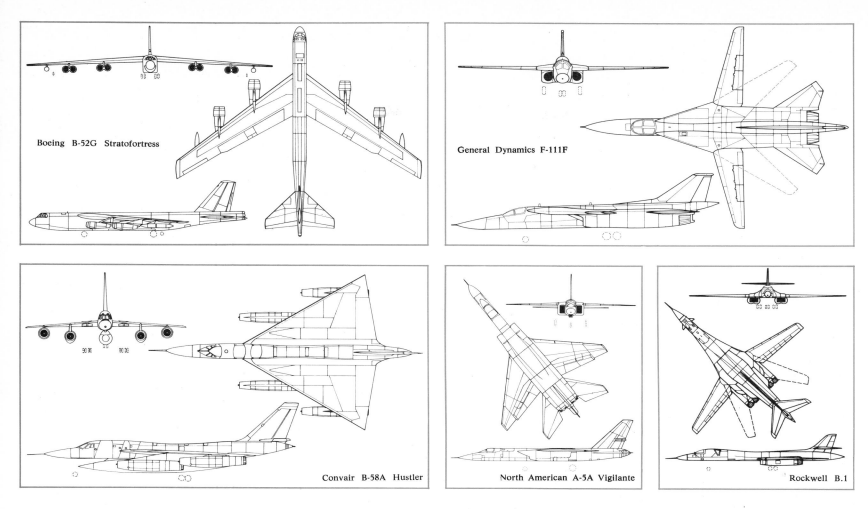

Boeing B-52G Stratofortress

General Dynamics F-111F

Convair B-58A Hustler

North American A-5A Vigilante

Rockwell B.1

Plate 221
American bombers: 1958 to the present day

America eagerly joined the race to build giant aircraft. For nearly 30 years the Boeing B-52 Stratofortress, a strategic bomber, has been seen as the symbol of US military power. This powerful and sophisticated warplane is powered by eight engines and is capable of reaching any forseeable or conceivable objective. Work on the design began as far back as 1945 and the first flight of the prototype was on 15th April 1952. A little over two years later the first of three initial production aircraft appeared, designated B-52A. Following versions were the RB-52B strategic reconnaissance plane (16 built); the B-52B reconnaissance bomber plane (38 built) the B-52C which was heavier, and had more fuel capacity (35 built, first flight 9th March 1956); the B-52D similar to the former plane but in bomber configuration only (170 built, first flight 4th June 1956); the B-52E with improved avionics (100 built, first flight 30th September 1957); the B-52F with more powerful engines (88 built, first flight 14th May 1958); the B-52G with redesigned wings and tailplanes (193 built, first flight 26th October 1958); the final version was

the B-52H which had more powerful engines and could carry all types of missile armament available at the time (102 built, first flight 6th March 1961).

The long operational life of the B-52 (which has lasted from 1957 and is still continuing at the beginning of the 1980s) included the most critical phase of the Indochina War, when the use of the Stratofortresses brought only temporary military gains, and lasting political criticism.

The career of the first supersonic bomber of the USAF, however, was relatively brief; this was the Convair B-58 Hustler. Although it had exceptional performance this powerful and sophisticated aircraft suffered from the change in strategic concepts which took place at the beginning of the 1970s, when the traditional bomber was superseded by smaller planes with greater operational flexibility. Only 116 B-58s were built which stayed in first-line service from 1960 to 1970. The design was commenced in 1948 and the first prototype flew on 11th November 1956. Three years later the first and only variant appeared: the B-58A. Eight of these aircraft were modified for training and were designated TB-58A.

In the naval sector the first nuclear bomber whose performance equalled that of its contemporary landplanes was the North American A-5 Vigilante. In spite of its qualities this heavy carrier-borne aircraft was, however,

developed and used almost exclusively in a completely different role, that of strategic reconnaissance.

Work started on the design in 1955 and the first prototype flew on 31st August 1958. Production was commenced immediately afterwards and 59 A-5A and 6 A-5B bombers were built before the decision was taken to develop the reconnaissance versions. On 30th June 1962, the RA-5C flew as a reconnaissance variant; 170 were built which went into service in January 1964. The Vigilantes showed themselves particularly useful and were subjected to continual updating, especially in their avionics, and they became the best reconnaissance platforms of the US Navy. They were still in service at the beginning of the 1980s.

The General Dynamics F-111 and the Rockwell B-1, which both have variable geometry wings, are examples of the latest generation of American strategic bombers. The first was developed in 1962 and had a long and troubled development phase and aroused a great deal of controversy because at the time it appeared the design was, in many respects, unsatisfactory. The prototype flew on 21st December 1964 and production continued through several variants: the F-111A strategic bomber (141 built) in service from 1967; the F-111C assault aircraft for the RAAF (24 built); the F-111D for close support

(96); the F-111E which was similar to the F-111D and had better engines (94); and the F-111F tactical fighter bomber which was more powerful (106 constructed as at November 1976, first flight of the prototype May 1973).

The Rockwell B-1 has been called the most expensive aircraft ever built; it was designed at the end of the 1960s to replace the B-52 in the role of low-altitude strategic bomber. The prototype flew on 23rd December 1974. The long and difficult development phase was brought to a halt on 30th June 1977 by President Carter, while priority was given to the development of late-generation intercontinental missiles. America's hopes of putting the B.1 into production as well as the missiles, however, had not been completely set aside at the end of the 1970s. The original proposal had been for a production run of 224 aircraft after the construction of three prototypes.

469

Plate 222

Scale view of selected reconnaissance planes and trainer/army co-operation aircraft from 1945 onwards

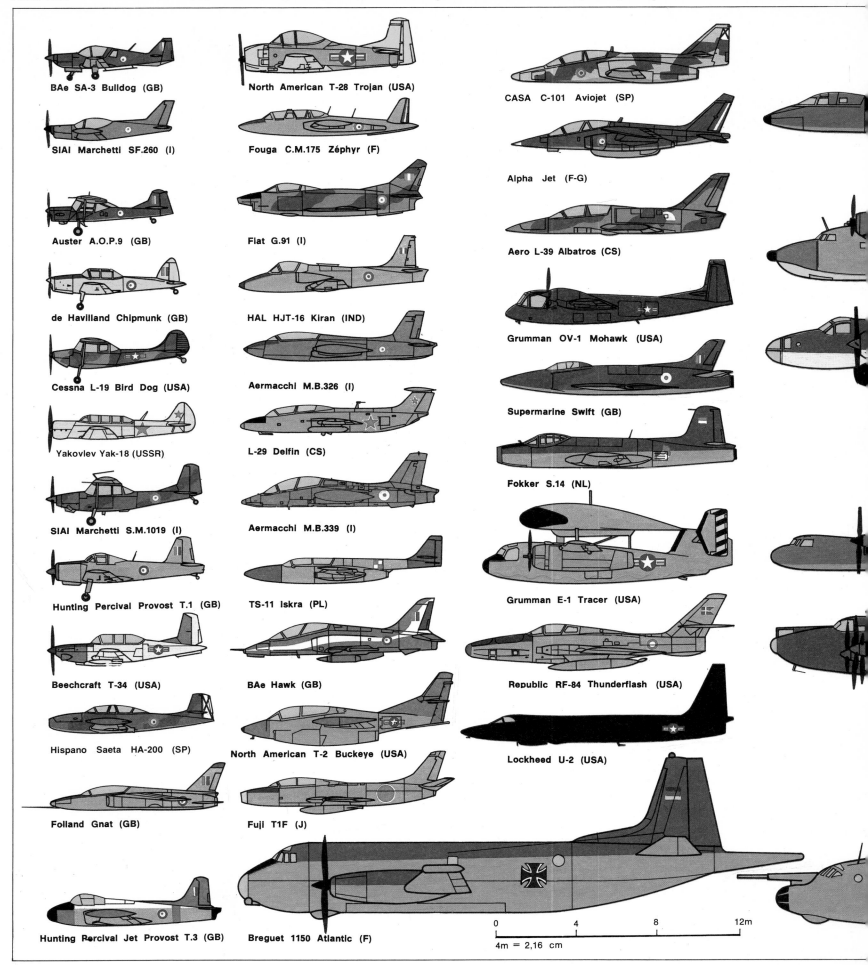

BAe SA-3 Bulldog (GB)

SIAI Marchetti SF.260 (I)

Auster A.O.P.9 (GB)

de Havilland Chipmunk (GB)

Cessna L-19 Bird Dog (USA)

Yakovlev Yak-18 (USSR)

SIAI Marchetti S.M.1019 (I)

Hunting Percival Provost T.1 (GB)

Beechcraft T-34 (USA)

Hispano Saeta HA-200 (SP)

Folland Gnat (GB)

Hunting Percival Jet Provost T.3 (GB)

North American T-28 Trojan (USA)

Fouga C.M.175 Zéphyr (F)

Fiat G.91 (I)

HAL HJT-16 Kiran (IND)

Aermacchi M.B.326 (I)

L-29 Delfin (CS)

Aermacchi M.B.339 (I)

TS-11 Iskra (PL)

BAe Hawk (GB)

North American T-2 Buckeye (USA)

Fuji T1F (J)

Breguet 1150 Atlantic (F)

CASA C-101 Aviojet (SP)

Alpha Jet (F-G)

Aero L-39 Albatros (CS)

Grumman OV-1 Mohawk (USA)

Supermarine Swift (GB)

Fokker S.14 (NL)

Grumman E-1 Tracer (USA)

Republic RF-84 Thunderflash (USA)

Lockheed U-2 (USA)

```
0        4        8        12m

4m = 2,16 cm
```

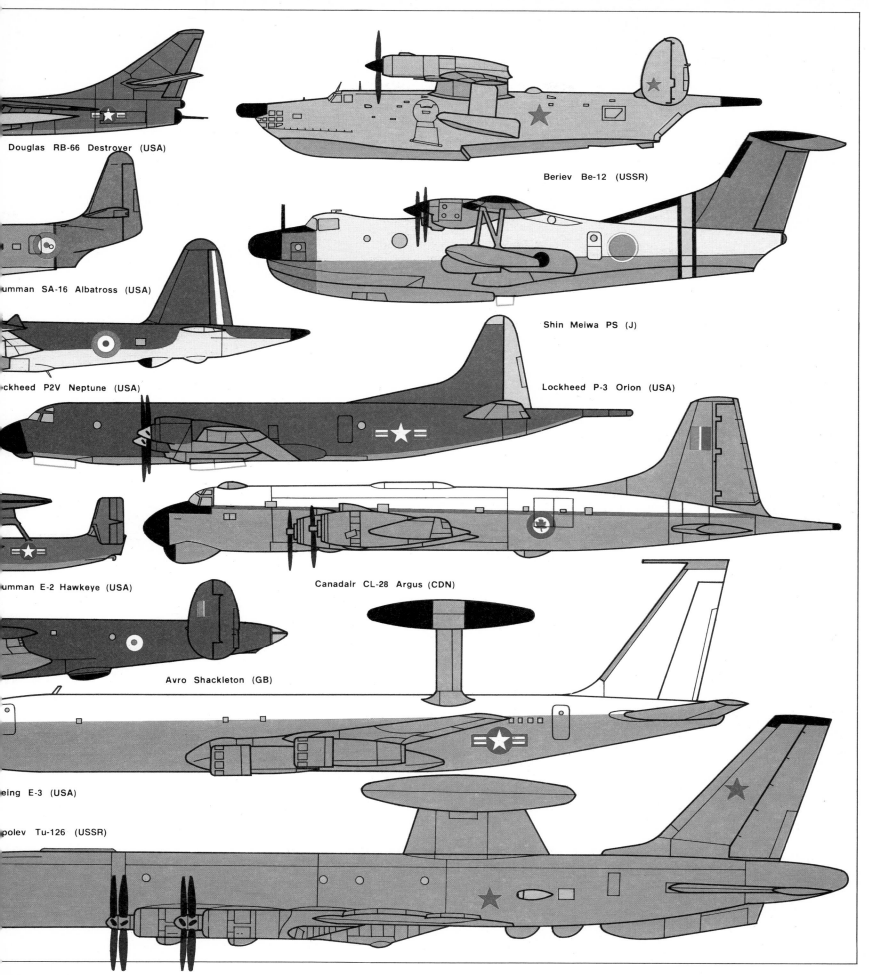

Douglas RB-66 Destroyer (USA)

Beriev Be-12 (USSR)

Grumman SA-16 Albatross (USA)

Shin Meiwa PS (J)

Lockheed P2V Neptune (USA)

Lockheed P-3 Orion (USA)

Grumman E-2 Hawkeye (USA)

Canadair CL-28 Argus (CDN)

Avro Shackleton (GB)

Boeing E-3 (USA)

Tupolev Tu-126 (USSR)

471

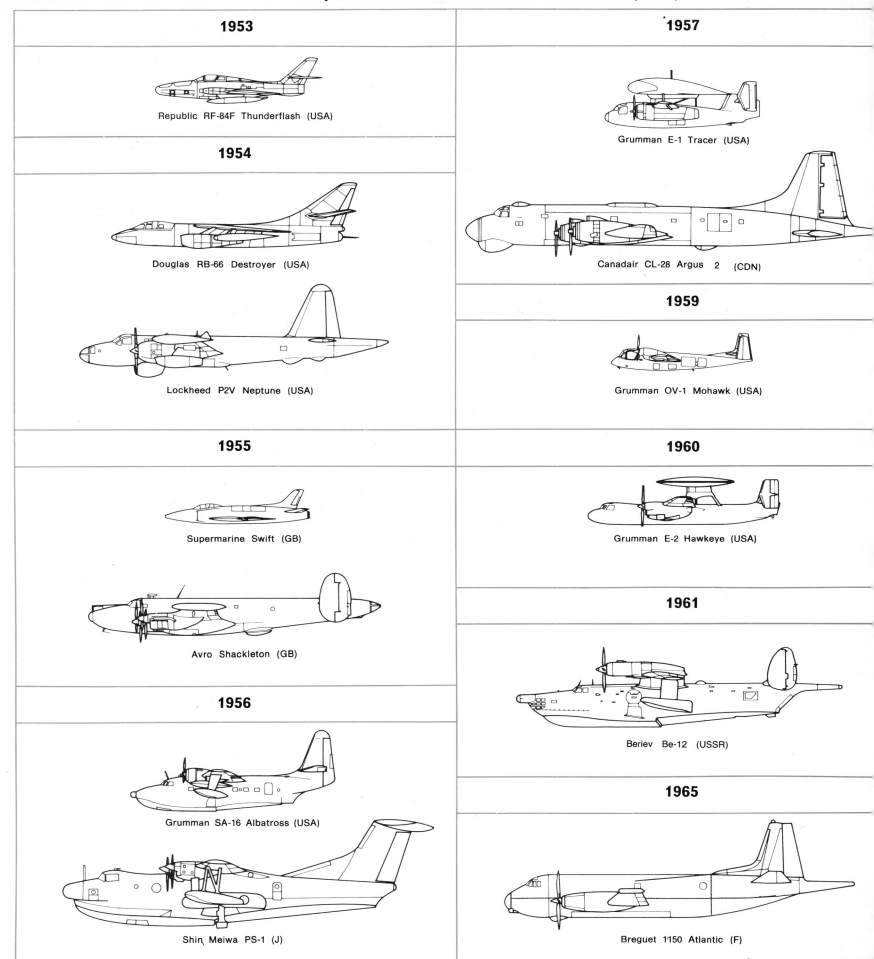

1953

Republic RF-84F Thunderflash (USA)

1954

Douglas RB-66 Destroyer (USA)

Lockheed P2V Neptune (USA)

1955

Supermarine Swift (GB)

Avro Shackleton (GB)

1956

Grumman SA-16 Albatross (USA)

Shin Meiwa PS-1 (J)

1957

Grumman E-1 Tracer (USA)

Canadair CL-28 Argus 2 (CDN)

1959

Grumman OV-1 Mohawk (USA)

1960

Grumman E-2 Hawkeye (USA)

1961

Beriev Be-12 (USSR)

1965

Breguet 1150 Atlantic (F)

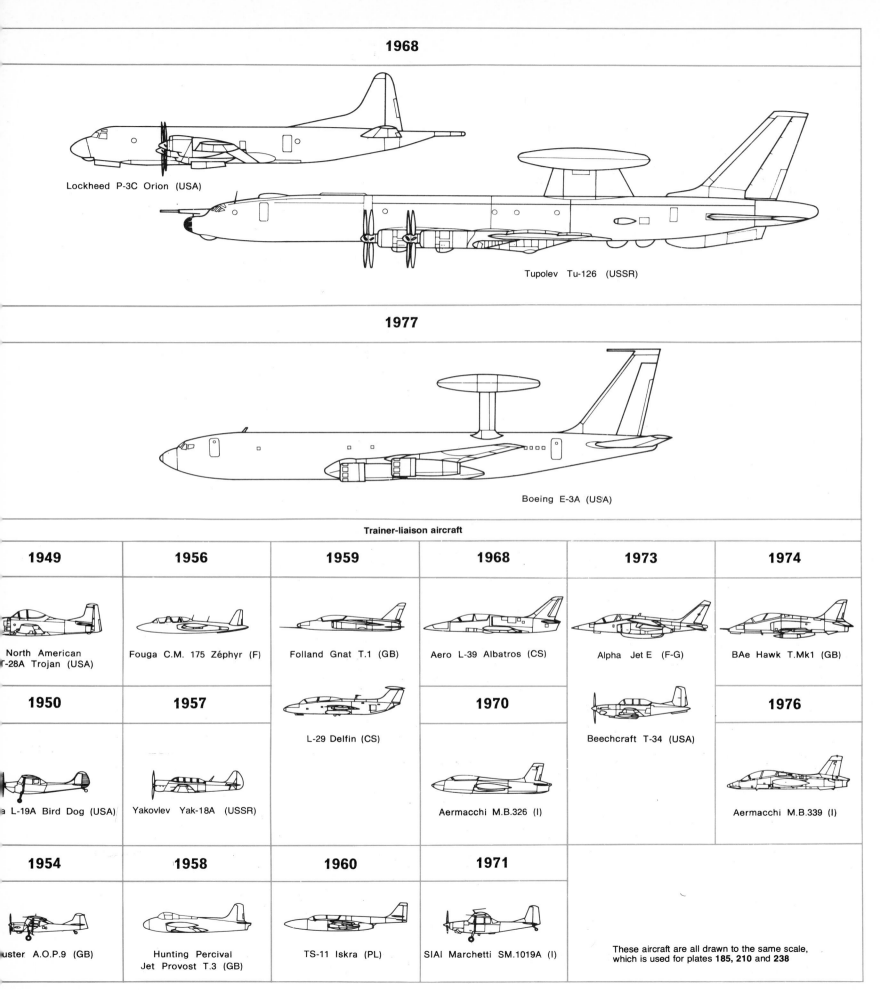

1968

Lockheed P-3C Orion (USA)

Tupolev Tu-126 (USSR)

1977

Boeing E-3A (USA)

Trainer-liaison aircraft

1949	**1956**	**1959**	**1968**	**1973**	**1974**
North American T-28A Trojan (USA)	Fouga C.M. 175 Zéphyr (F)	Folland Gnat T.1 (GB)	Aero L-39 Albatros (CS)	Alpha Jet E (F-G)	BAe Hawk T.Mk1 (GB)
1950	**1957**	L-29 Delfin (CS)	**1970**	Beechcraft T-34 (USA)	**1976**
L-19A Bird Dog (USA)	Yakovlev Yak-18A (USSR)		Aermacchi M.B.326 (I)		Aermacchi M.B.339 (I)
1954	**1958**	**1960**	**1971**		
uster A.O.P.9 (GB)	Hunting Percival Jet Provost T.3 (GB)	TS-11 Iskra (PL)	SIAI Marchetti SM.1019A (I)	These aircraft are all drawn to the same scale, which is used for plates **185**, **210** and **238**	

473

◄ MARTIN P5M-2 MARLIN
Nation: USA; manufacturer: Glenn L. Martin Co;
type: reconnaissance; year: 1953; engine: two
Wright R-3350-32WA Cyclones 18-cylinder
air-cooled radials, 3,450 hp each; wingspan:
118 ft 2 in (36.01 m); length: 100 ft 7 in
(30.65 m); height: 31 ft 8 in (9.96 m); weight:
85,000 lb (38,556 kg) (loaded); maximum
speed: 251 mph (404 km/h) at sea level; ceiling: 24,000 ft (7,315 m); range: 2,050 miles
(3,300 km); armament: 16,000 lb (7,257 kg) of
bombs; crew: 11

BERIEV Be-6
Nation: USSR; manufacturer: State Industries; type: reconnaissance; year:
1949; engine: two Shvetsov ASh-73TKs radial with 18 cylinders air-
cooled, 2,300 hp each; wingspan: 108 ft 4 in (33.00 m); length: 77 ft 3 in
(23.55 m); height: 24 ft 7 in (7.48 m); weight: 61,976 lb (28,112 kg)
(loaded); maximum speed: 258 mph (415 km/h) at 7,875 ft (2,400 m); ceiling: 20,000 ft (6,100 m); range: 3,045 miles (4,900 km); armament: 5 ×
23 mm cannon; 8,820 lb (4,000 kg) of bombs; crew: 7 ▼

▲ BERIEV Be-12
Nation: USSR; manufacturer: State Industries;
type: reconnaissance; year: 1961; engine: two
Ivchenko AI-20D turboprops, 4,000 hp each;
wingspan: 108 ft (32.91 m); length: 95 ft 9 in
(29.18 m); height: 21 ft 11 in (6.68 m); weight:
65,035 lb (29,500 kg) (loaded); maximum
speed: 379 mph (610 km/h); ceiling: 40,000 ft
(12,185 m); range: 2,485 miles (4,000 km);
armament: 22,250 lb (10,092 kg) of bombs;
crew: 5-6

SHIN MEIWA PS-1
Nation: Japan; manufacturer: Shin Meiwa
Industry Co; type: reconnaissance; year: 1968;
engine: four Ishikawajima (General Electric)
T64-IHI-10 turboprops, 2,850 hp each; wingspan: 107 ft 3 in (32.80 m); length: 109 ft 11 in
(33.50 m); height: 31 ft 10 in (9.70 m); weight:
86,862 lb (39,400 kg) (loaded); maximum
speed: 340 mph (547 km/h) at 5,000 ft
(1,500 m); ceiling: 29,500 ft (9,000 m); range:
1,347 miles (2,168 km); armament: torpedoes,
depth charges, missiles; crew: 10

▲
GRUMMAN SA-16B ALBATROSS
Nation: USA; manufacturer: Grumman Aircraft
Engineering Corp; type: rescue; year: 1956;
engine: two Wright R-1820-76A Cyclones
9-cylinder air-cooled radials, 1,475 hp each,
wingspan: 96 ft 8 in (29.58 m);
length: 61 ft 3 in (18.60 m); height:
25 ft 10 in (7.93 m); weight:
32,000 lb (14,400 kg) (loaded);
maximum speed: 236 mph
(379 km/h) at 18,800 ft (5,730 m);
ceiling: 25,000 ft (7,625 m); range:
3,200 miles (5,148 km); armament:
–; crew: 5-6

AVRO SHACKLETON M.R.3 ▶
Nation: Britain; *manufacturer:* A. V. Roe and Co Ltd; *type:* maritime reconnaissance and anti-submarine; *year:* 1955; *engine:* four Rolls-Royce Griffon 57A V-12 liquid-cooled, 2,450 hp each; *wingspan:* 119 ft 10 in (36.53 m); *length:* 92 ft 6 in (26.62 m); *height:* 23 ft 4 in (7.11 m); *weight:* 100,000 lb (45,360 kg) (loaded); *maximum speed:* 302 mph (486 km/h) at sea level; *ceiling:* 20,000 ft (6,100 m); *range:* 4,215 miles (6,780 km); *armament:* 2 × 20 mm cannon; 10,000 lb (4,536 kg) of bombs; *crew:* 10

CANADAIR CL-28 ARGUS 2 ▶
Nation: Canada; *manufacturer:* Canadair Ltd; *type:* reconnaissance; *year:* 1957; *engine:* four Wright R-3350-32W Turbo Compound radial with 18 cylinders air-cooled, 3,700 hp each; *wingspan:* 142 ft 3 in (43.77 m); *length:* 128 ft 3 in (39.09 m); *height:* 36 ft 9 in (11.20 m); *weight:* 148 000 lb (67,130 kg) (loaded); *maximum speed:* 315 mph (507 km/h) at 20,000 ft (6,100 m); *ceiling:* 29,000 ft (8,840 m); *range:* 5,900 miles (9,495 km); *armament:* 15,600 lb (7,076 kg) of bombs; *crew:* 15

SUPERMARINE SWIFT F.R.5 ▶
Nation: Britain; *manufacturer:* Supermarine Division of Vickers-Armstrong Ltd; *type:* fighter reconnaissance; *year:* 1955; *engine:* Rolls-Royce Avon 114 turbojet, 9,450 lb (4,285 kg) thrust; *wingspan:* 32 ft 4 in (9.86 m); *length:* 42 ft 3 in (12.88 m); *height:* 13 ft 6 in (4.11 m); *weight:* 21,400 lb (9,702 kg) (loaded); *maximum speed:* 685 mph (1,102 km/h) at sea level; *ceiling:* 25,000 ft (7,620 m); *range:* 480 miles (772 km); *armament:* 2 × 30 mm cannon (provision for light bomb-load); *crew:* 1

BREGUET 1150 ATLANTIC ▶
Nation: France; *manufacturer:* Breguet Aviation; *type:* reconnaissance; *year:* 1965; *engine:* two Rolls-Royce Tyne RTy.20 Mk 21 turboprops, 6,105 hp each; *wingspan:* 119 ft 1 in (36.30 m); *length:* 104 ft 2 in (31.75 m); *height:* 37 ft 2 in (11.33 m); *weight:* 95,900 lb (43,500 kg) (loaded); *maximum speed:* 409 mph (658 km/h); *ceiling:* 32,800 ft (10,000 m); *range:* 5,590 miles (9,000 km); *armament:* torpedoes, depth charges, missiles; *crew:* 12

HAWKER SIDDELEY NIMROD M.R. Mk 1
Nation: Britain; *manufacturer:* Hawker Siddeley Aviation Ltd; *type:* reconnaissance; *year:* 1968; *engine:* four Rolls-Royce RB.168 Spey turbojets, 11,500 lb (5,217 kg) thrust each; *wingspan:* 114 ft 10 in (35 m); *length:* 126 ft 9 in (38.63 m); *height:* 29 ft 8 in (9.01 m); *weight:* 177,500 lb (80,510 kg) (loaded); *maximum speed:* 575 mph (926 km/h); *ceiling:* 42,000 ft (12,800 m); *range:* 5,755 miles (9,265 km); *armament:* torpedoes, depth charges, missiles; *crew:* 12 ▼

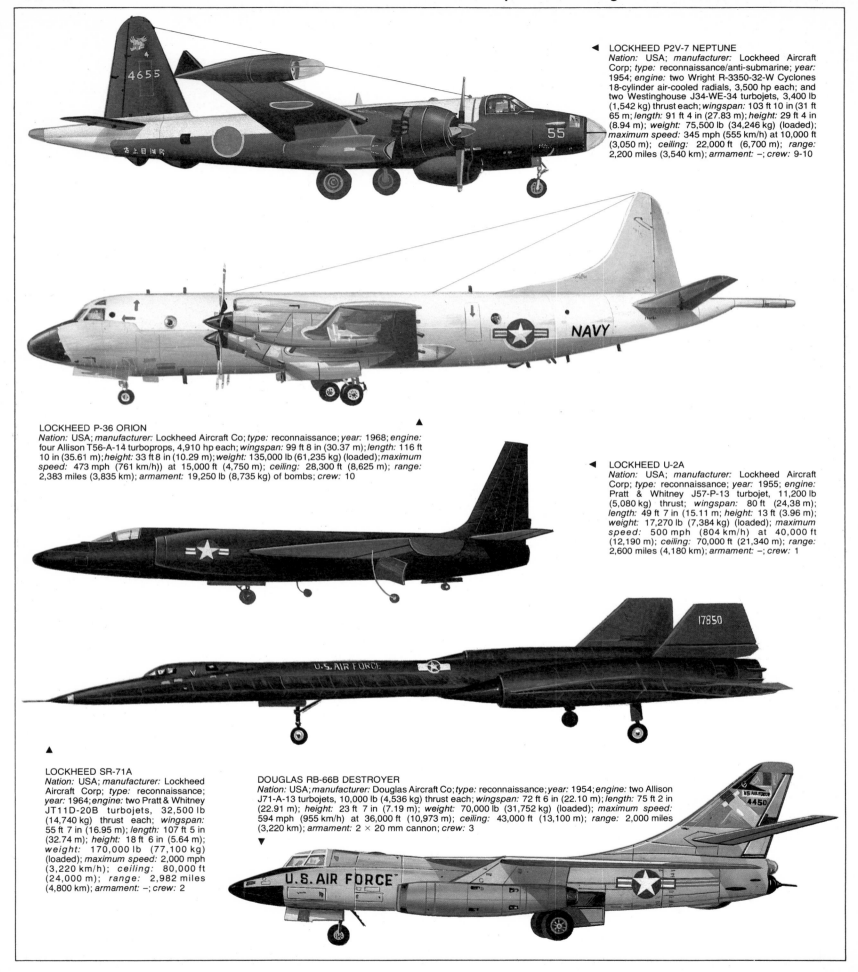

◄ LOCKHEED P2V-7 NEPTUNE
Nation: USA; *manufacturer:* Lockheed Aircraft Corp; *type:* reconnaissance/anti-submarine; *year:* 1954; *engine:* two Wright R-3350-32-W Cyclones 18-cylinder air-cooled radials, 3,500 hp each; and two Westinghouse J34-WE-34 turbojets, 3,400 lb (1,542 kg) thrust each; *wingspan:* 103 ft 10 in (31 ft 65 m); *length:* 91 ft 4 in (27.83 m); *height:* 29 ft 4 in (8.94 m); *weight:* 75,500 lb (34,246 kg) (loaded); *maximum speed:* 345 mph (555 km/h) at 10,000 ft (3,050 m); *ceiling:* 22,000 ft (6,700 m); *range:* 2,200 miles (3,540 km); *armament:* –; *crew:* 9-10

LOCKHEED P-36 ORION
Nation: USA; *manufacturer:* Lockheed Aircraft Co; *type:* reconnaissance; *year:* 1968; *engine:* four Allison T56-A-14 turboprops, 4,910 hp each; *wingspan:* 99 ft 8 in (30.37 m); *length:* 116 ft 10 in (35.61 m); *height:* 33 ft 8 in (10.29 m); *weight:* 135,000 lb (61,235 kg) (loaded); *maximum speed:* 473 mph (761 km/h) at 15,000 ft (4,750 m); *ceiling:* 28,300 ft (8,625 m); *range:* 2,383 miles (3,835 km); *armament:* 19,250 lb (8,735 kg) of bombs; *crew:* 10

◄ LOCKHEED U-2A
Nation: USA; *manufacturer:* Lockheed Aircraft Corp; *type:* reconnaissance; *year:* 1955; *engine:* Pratt & Whitney J57-P-13 turbojet, 11,200 lb (5,080 kg) thrust; *wingspan:* 80 ft (24,38 m); *length:* 49 ft 7 in (15.11 m; *height:* 13 ft (3.96 m); *weight:* 17,270 lb (7,384 kg) (loaded); *maximum speed:* 500 mph (804 km/h) at 40,000 ft (12,190 m); *ceiling:* 70,000 ft (21,340 m); *range:* 2,600 miles (4,180 km); *armament:* –; *crew:* 1

LOCKHEED SR-71A
Nation: USA; *manufacturer:* Lockheed Aircraft Corp; *type:* reconnaissance; *year:* 1964; *engine:* two Pratt & Whitney JT11D-20B turbojets, 32,500 lb (14,740 kg) thrust each; *wingspan:* 55 ft 7 in (16.95 m); *length:* 107 ft 5 in (32.74 m); *height:* 18 ft 6 in (5.64 m); *weight:* 170,000 lb (77,100 kg) (loaded); *maximum speed:* 2,000 mph (3,220 km/h); *ceiling:* 80,000 ft (24,000 m); *range:* 2,982 miles (4,800 km); *armament:* –; *crew:* 2

DOUGLAS RB-66B DESTROYER
Nation: USA; *manufacturer:* Douglas Aircraft Co; *type:* reconnaissance; *year:* 1954; *engine:* two Allison J71-A-13 turbojets, 10,000 lb (4,536 kg) thrust each; *wingspan:* 72 ft 6 in (22.10 m); *length:* 75 ft 2 in (22.91 m); *height:* 23 ft 7 in (7.19 m); *weight:* 70,000 lb (31,752 kg) (loaded); *maximum speed:* 594 mph (955 km/h) at 36,000 ft (10,973 m); *ceiling:* 43,000 ft (13,100 m); *range:* 2,000 miles (3,220 km); *armament:* 2 × 20 mm cannon; *crew:* 3

REPUBLIC RF-84F THUNDERFLASH
Nation: USA; *manufacturer:* Republic Aviation Corp; *type:* reconnaissance; *year:* 1953; *engine:* Wright J65-W-7 turbojet, 7,800 lb (3,540 kg) thrust; *wingspan:* 33 ft 7 in (10.24 m); *length:* 47 ft 7 in (14.52 m); *height:* 15 ft (4.57 m); *weight:* 28,000 lb (12,700 kg) (loaded); *maximum speed:* 679 mph (1,092 km/h) at sea level; *ceiling:* 46,000 ft (14,020 m); *range:* 2,200 miles (3,540 km); *armament:* 4 machine guns; *crew:* 1

FIAT G.91 R-3
Nation: Italy; *manufacturer:* Fiat SpA; *type:* reconnaissance/tactical support; *year:* 1959; *engine:* Bristol Siddeley Orpheus 801/02 turbojet, 5,000 lb (2,270 kg) thrust; *wingspan:* 28 ft 3 in (8.60 m); *length:* 33 ft 9 in (10.29 m); *height:* 13 ft 2 in (4 m); *weight:* 12,500 lb (5,670 kg) (loaded); *maximum speed:* 677 mph (1,090 km/h) at 6,560 ft (2,000 m); *ceiling:* 43,500 ft (13,260 m); *range:* 1,150 miles (1,850 km); *armament:* 2 × 30 mm cannon; 1,500 lb (680 kg) of bombs; *crew:* 1

GRUMMAN OV-1A MOHAWK
Nation: USA; *manufacturer:* Grumman Aircraft Engineering Corp; *type:* reconnaissance; *year:* 1959; *engine:* two Lycoming T53-L-3 turboprops, 1,005 hp each; *wingspan:* 42 ft (12.80 m); *length:* 41 ft (12.50 m); *height:* 12 ft 8 in (3.86 m); *weight:* 10,423 lb (4,728 kg) (loaded); *maximum speed:* 317 mph (510 km/h) at 5,000 ft (1,525 m); *ceiling:* 35,000 ft (10,670 m); *range:* 1,680 miles (2,700 km); *armament:* – ; *crew:* 2

ROCKWELL OV-10E BRONCO
Nation: USA; *manufacturer:* Rockwell International; *type:* reconnaissance; *year:* 1973; *engine:* two AiResearch T76-410/411 turboprops, 715 hp each; *wingspan:* 40 ft (12.19 m); *length:* 41 ft 7 in (12.67 m); *height:* 15 ft 2 in (4.62 m); *weight:* 14,466 lb (6,536 kg) (loaded); *maximum speed:* 281 mph (452 km/h) at sea level; *ceiling:* 30,000 ft (9,150 m); *range:* 600 miles (960 km); *armament:* 4 machine guns; 3,600 lb (1,632 kg) of bombs; *crew:* 2

Plate 228

Airborne radar systems for the 1980s

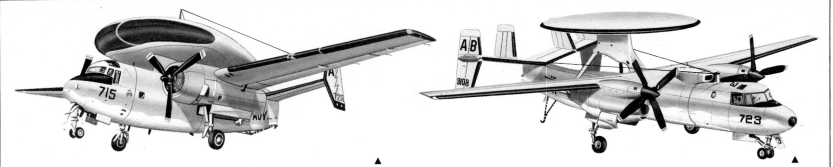

GRUMMAN E-1B TRACER
Nation: USA; *manufacturer:* Grumman Aircraft Engineering Corp; *type:* reconnaissance/early warning; *year:* 1957; *engine:* two Wright R-1820-82WA Cyclones 9-cylinder air-cooled radials, 1,525 hp each; *wingspan:* 72 ft 4 in (22.05 m); *length:* 45 ft 4 in (13.82 m); *height:* 16 ft 10 in (5.13 m); *weight:* 27,000 lb (12,247 kg) (loaded); *maximum speed:* 290 mph (466 km/h) at 5,000 ft (1,524 m); *ceiling:* 23,000 ft (7,010 m); *range:* 900 miles (1,450 km); *armament:* – ; *crew:* 4

GRUMMAN E-2A HAWKEYE
Nation: USA; *manufacturer:* Grumman Aircraft Engineering Corp; *type:* airborne early warning; *year:* 1960; *engine:* two Allison T56-A-8A turboprops, 4,050 hp each; *wingspan:* 80 ft 7 in (24.56 m); *length:* 56 ft 4 in (17.17 m); *height:* 18 ft 4 in (4.88 m); *weight:* 49,500 lb (22,453 kg) (loaded); *maximum speed:* 370 mph (595 km/h); *ceiling:* 31,700 ft (9,660 m); *range:* 1,900 miles (3,060 km); *armament:* – ; *crew:* 5

BAe NIMROD AEW Mk 3
Nation: Britain; *manufacturer:* British Aerospace; *type:* reconnaissance; *year:* 1977; *engine:* four Rolls-Royce RB-168 Spey turbojets, 11,500 lb (5,217 kg) thrust each; *wingspan:* 114 ft 10 in (35 m); *length:* 135 ft 9 in (41.37 m); *height:* 32 ft 10 in (10 m); *weight:* 192,000 lb (87,090 kg) (loaded); *maximum speed:* 575 mph (926 km/h); *ceiling:* 42,000 ft (12,800 m); *range:* 5,755 miles (9,625 km); *armament:* – ; *crew:* 12-18

BOEING E-3A SENTRY
Nation: USA; *manufacturer:* Boeing Aerospace Co; *type:* reconnaissance; *year:* 1977; *engine:* four Pratt & Whitney TF33-P-7 turbojets, 21,000 lb (9,525 kg) thrust each; *wingspan:* 145 ft 9 in (44.42 m); *length:* 152 ft 11 in (46.61 m); *height:* 42 ft 5 in (12.93 m); *weight:* 333,600 lb (151,315 kg) (loaded); *maximum speed:* 550 mph (886 km/h) at 25,000 ft (7,620 m); *ceiling:* 39,000 ft (11,885 m); *range:* 7,475 miles (12,000 km); *armament:* – ; *crew:* 17

TUPOLEV Tu-126
Nation: USSR; *manufacturer:* State Industries; *type:* reconnaissance; *year:* 1968; *engine:* four Kuznetsov NK-12MV turboprops, 14,795 hp each; *wingspan:* 168 ft (51.20 m); *length:* 181 ft 1 in (55.20 m); *height:* 50 ft 10 in (15.50 m); *weight:* 376,900 lb (170,000 kg) (loaded); *maximum speed:* 478 mph (770 km/h) at 29,500 ft (3,000 m); *ceiling:* 39,370 ft (12,000 m); *range:* 5,560 miles (8,950 km); *armament:* – ; *crew:* 10-15

Plate 224
Japan builds the latest reconnaissance flying boat: 1949–68

The flying boat with its links with the past and the Second World War years has experienced a new lease of life in the jet era, with new designs which fill very specific operational needs; the old formula of the flying boat has thus reappeared in a different, technologically more advanced guise. The most recent of these aircraft, the Japanese Shin Meiwa, can be compared in conception to the great Sunderlands of the late 1930s.

In the USA, however, this type of boat has gradually disappeared and the last great flying boat of the US Navy was the Martin P5M Marlin, developed in 1946 on the basis of the earlier PBM Mariner of which it was a more versatile derivant. The prototype flew on 30th May 1948 and the first series aircraft (P5M-1) flew on 22nd June of the following year. 114 of this first variant went into service in April 1952 before manufacture was switched to the production of the second variant, the P5M-2. This had more powerful engines, better equipment and a T-shaped tailplane; the prototype appeared in August 1953 and 145 were built. Ten of these were sold to France. In its role as an anti-submarine reconnaissance plane, the Marlin stayed in service until half way through the 1960s.

The Grumman SA-16 Albatross had just as long a career; this was a medium amphibious craft which appeared in prototype on 24th October 1947 and a large number of these craft were used, not only by the US Navy but also by the USAF and by numerous other allied air forces.

The basic production model was the SA-16A. This was followed in 1956 by the prototype of a second version which was structurally modified and more powerful (SA-16B), to whose standard many aircraft of the first series were subsequently converted.

Unlike the United States, the USSR continued to develop flying boats for reconnaissance use well after the end of the Second World War. The family of twin-engine Beriev boats, whose basic types were the Be-6 and Be-12, in fact enabled the Soviet naval aviation to keep useful flying boats in service for the whole of the 1970s. The Be-6 was designed in 1945 and was clearly inspired by the American Martin PMB Mariner; the definitive prototype appeared in 1949 and it stayed in first-line service even after the arrival of its more modern successor, the Be-12.

This was officially presented in 1961 and it had only its general configuration and its wing structure in common with the Be-6. Apart from this it was completely different; driven by twin

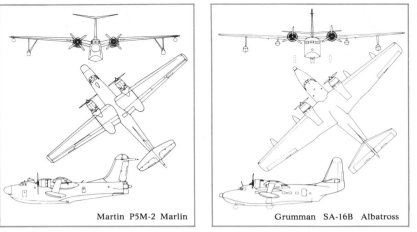

Martin P5M-2 Marlin

Grumman SA-16B Albatross

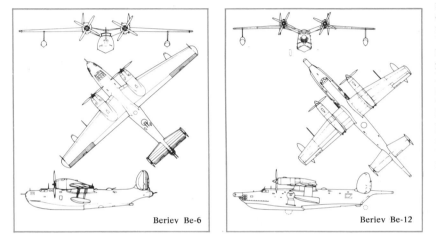

Beriev Be-6

Beriev Be-12

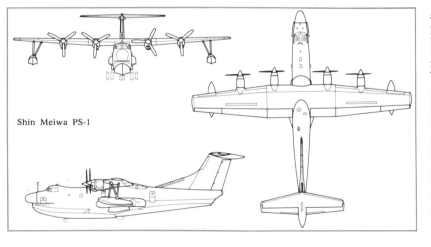

Shin Meiwa PS-1

turboprop 4,000 hp engines which gave it high performance, the Be-12 was designed to accommodate complex and sophisticated anti-submarine search radar. In the 1970s the Be-12s helped to weave a close mesh of surveillance along almost the whole of the Soviet coastline. In NATO code the Be-12 was designated MAIL while the Be-6 was MADGE.

Returning to the Japanese Shin Meiwa flying boat, this four-engine amphibian was designed in the first half of the 1960s, and two prototypes appeared, on 5th October 1967 and 14th June 1968. Twenty examples of

an anti-submarine version (PS-1) derived from these were built, and were in service from 1977. A second variant was for air-sea rescue (US-1) which flew as a prototype on 16th October 1974 and of which only a few were produced, built for the specific needs of the Japanese Maritime Self-Defence Force. The US-1s went into service in March 1975.

Plate 225
British, Canadian and French reconnaissance planes: 1955–68

After the war, Britain judged it particularly important to develop her maritime reconnaissance force. One of the most useful first generation aircraft of this type was the Avro Shackleton, a four-engine aircraft which was derived from the Avro bombers.

From 1951 until the end of the 1970s the Shackletons stayed in front-line service and were only replaced when the jet-engine Nimrods came into service. Work started on this design in 1946 and the first of three prototypes flew on 9th March 1949. Production centred on four basic variants: the M.R.1 (29 built, first flown on 24th October 1950); the M.R.1A which was powered by different engines (47 built); the M.R.2 which had its fuselage modified (70 built, first flight 17th June 1953, in production until September 1954); and the M.R.3 which was the final version which had structural modifications to the fuselage and the wing, and tricycle landing gear. 34 of the Shackleton M.R.3s were built for the RAF and eight for the South African Air Force. They went into service with Coastal Command towards the end of 1957.

From October 1969 a more modern and powerful naval reconnaissance plane started to join the Shackletons, the Hawker Siddeley Nimrod M.R.Mk 1 which was in fact derived from the four-jet Comet 4C airliner. The Nimrod design was started in June 1964 and the task of modifying two Comet 4C prototypes was completed in March and July 1967. Production was started immediately afterwards and the first Nimrod M.R.Mk 1 flew on 28th June of the following year. Deliveries of the total of 42 aircraft ordered by the RAF started on 2nd October 1969. Another three aircraft, which were originally ordered as M.R.Mk 1s, were used instead for the development of the later variants, Mk 2 and AEW Mk 3. The Nimrods are expected to continue their operational life until the 1990s.

A completely different aircraft should not be omitted, the Supermarine Swift, if only for its unusual operational career. It was designed in 1950 as an interceptor to join the Hawker Hunter, but this single-seat swept-wing aircraft did not manage to make its mark in this category and ended up by being used as a reconnaissance plane. The programme started in 1948 and the first prototype flew on 5th August 1951. After a total of 65 aircraft had been constructed in four fighter versions and after an unhappy operational career in 1954 and 1955, the aircraft were withdrawn from service and the decision was taken to

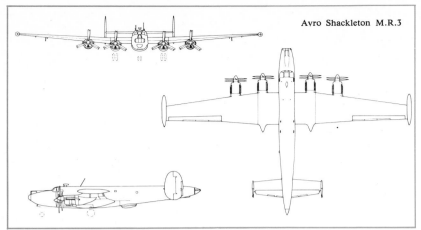

Avro Shackleton M.R.3

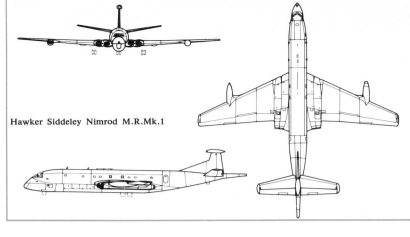

Hawker Siddeley Nimrod M.R.Mk.1

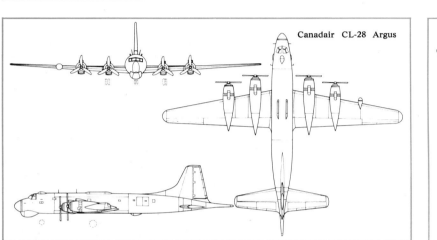

Canadair CL-28 Argus

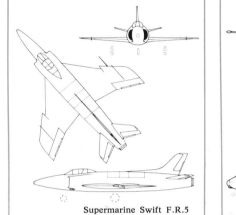

Supermarine Swift F.R.5

Breguet 1150 Atlantic

produce a reconnaissance variant (R.F.5). This appeared on 24th May 1955 and the 62 built equipped units of the RAF in Germany from 1956 to 1961.

Returning to maritime reconnaissance, another multi-engine plane which was derived from a civil aircraft was the Canadian Canadair CL-28 Argus developed in 1954 from the Britannia airliner. The prototype flew on 28th March 1957 and production got under way with twelve aircraft of the first series, followed by another 20 (Argus 2) which had their equipment modified. The Argus entered service in May 1958.

Within the framework of NATO a useful reconnaissance plane of the most recent generation whose service is expected to continue into the late 1980s is the French twin-engine turbo-prop Breguet 1150 Atlantic. This was developed in 1958 as part of a programme aimed at finding a successor to the Lockheed P2V Neptune; the Atlantic appeared in prototype on 21st October 1961 and the series aircraft on 19th July 1965. France ordered 40, Germany 20, the Netherlands 6 and Italy 18.

Plate 226
American maritime patrol and strategic reconnaissance aircraft: 1954–68

The standard maritime reconnaissance plane of the US Navy after the war until the beginning of the 1960s was the Lockheed P2V Neptune, a versatile twin piston-engine plane of which over 1,200 were built in seven basic versions and which was used by no less than eleven countries. The design was commenced in April 1944 and the prototype flew on 17th May 1945. Production aircraft were manufactured uninterruptedly for over 10

years: from the fifth variant P2V-5 onwards, the aircraft had twin turbojets in addition to its two piston-engines, and this arrangement was maintained even in the following variants. The last was the P2V-7 which appeared in prototype on 26th April 1954 and represented the final development of the design.

Another Lockheed aircraft, the P-3 Orion, replaced the Neptune and was derived from the piston-engine civil Electra. A second, definitive experimental aircraft was developed from the first prototype, which was in its turn a 1958 modification of the airframe of the third model of the civil version; the definitive prototype flew on 25th November 1959. Production,

which at the end of 1956 had reached a total of 446 aircraft, included several basic variants: the P-3A which was the first for the US Navy, began production in 1961 and was in service from August 1962; the P-3B which had modified engines, and was also for the US Navy; the P-3C which had particularly sophisticated electronics (first flight of the prototype on 18th September 1968) and was operational from 1969. The US Navy received 286 P-3As and P-3Bs and 132 P-3Cs. The rest of the production went to New Zealand, Australia, Norway, Canada and Iran.

Among the reconnaissance planes put into service by the USAF during the 1950s and 1960s, mention should

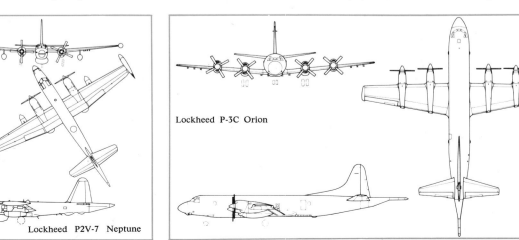

Lockheed P2V-7 Neptune

Lockheed P-3C Orion

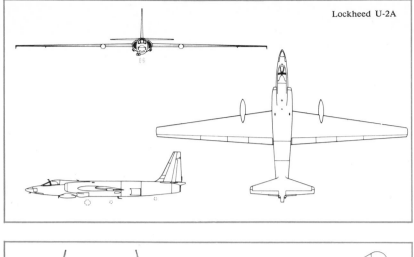

Lockheed U-2A

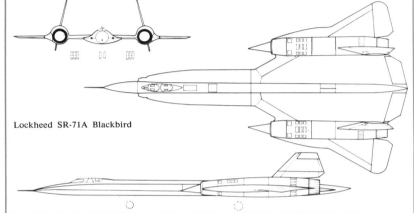

Lockheed SR-71A Blackbird

Plate 227
Observation and battlefield surveillance aircraft for the army: 1953–73

One of the most widely used and worthwhile tactical reconnaissance planes of the 1950s was the Republic RF-84F Thunderflash, a special version of the prolific family of Thunderjet/Thunderstreaks. The decision to develop this aircraft was taken in 1952 and the Thunderflash prototype flew in February 1953. Compared with the immediately preceding variant, the F-84F, the RF-84F had considerable modifications to the nose and wing which were made necessary by the installation of cameras in the forward fuselage and by the ensuing need to move the air-inlets of the turbojet to a new position in the wing. Deliveries to units started in March 1954. Production totalled 715, of which 386 were for NATO Allies. In Italy, the *Aeronautica Militare Italiana* received the RF-84F as well, and put it into service in 1956. Four years later the Thunderflash was joined by the first production series Fiat G.91R aircraft. They appeared in 1959 and were built in four variants: the R-1, the R-3, the R-4 and the R-1B.

The conception of an advanced tactical reconnaissance plane which was

to co-operate with ground forces was most successfully achieved by two American aircraft, the Grumman OV-1 Mohawk and the Rockwell OV-10 Bronco; two very specialised combat aircraft which had very similar characteristics to those of the helicopter. The Mohawk was designed in 1957 in response to a joint request from the US Army and the US Marine Corps. The first of nine pre-series aircraft which were ordered flew on 14th April 1959, and production was started immediately afterwards. Four basic versions were developed in a total of 375 aircraft which were all for the army: the OV-1A day and night photo-reconnaissance plane; the OV-1B which had side-looking airborne radar; the OV-1C with an infra-red surveillance system; and the OV-1D which incorporated the characteristics of the two preceding versions. The last Mohawk was completed in December 1970. The operational career of these aircraft was particularly active during the Viet-Nam War.

The Rockwell OV/10 Bronco was designed in 1962 in response to a joint request from the USAF, the US Navy and the US Marine Corps; the aim of the specification was to built an effective armed tactical reconnaissance plane which would take part in anti-insurgent operations. The definitive prototype of the Bronco flew on 15th August 1966 and the first example of

be made of the Douglas RB-66 Destroyer, a versatile twin-jet which although developed as a tactical bomber passed the main part of its career with reconnaissance units. Production was started in 1954 and the principal variant was the RB-66B (145 built) which went into service in February 1956. Another 77 aircraft of three further series completed the development of the reconnaissance versions. Only 72 aircraft of the other initial variant, the B-66B, which had appeared in 1955, were bombers.

One of the most well-known and controversial American strategic reconnaissance planes was the Lockheed U-2 which was secretly developed during the first half of the

1950s for the USAF and the prototype of which appeared in 1955. This spy plane (53 of which were built: 48 U-2As and 5 U-2D two-seaters) was at the centre of an international crisis in May 1960, when a U-2A was shot down by missile whilst carrying out a very high altitude mission over Soviet territory. The pilot, Francis Gary Powers, managed to save himself but when he landed he was captured and put on trial.

Another Lockheed aircraft was even more powerful and sophisticated and led to the SR-71 Blackbird, a titanium "monster" which could fly at 3,200 km/h (1,190 mph) at an altitude of 25,000 m (82,000 ft), outpace any known interceptor and also photograph continuously all the territory it flew over. The Blackbird was developed from the experimental aircraft YF-12A (whose existence was revealed by President Johnson in February 1964) which was in its turn derived from the A-11 interceptor which appeared as a prototype on 26th April 1962 and of which seven were built. The SR-71A had its first flight test on 22nd December 1964 and production totalled 30, of which some were trainers (SR-71B and SR-71C). Deliveries to an operational unit (9 Strategic Reconnaissance Wing) started in 1956.

Douglas RB-66B Destroyer

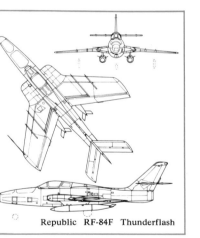

Republic RF-84F Thunderflash

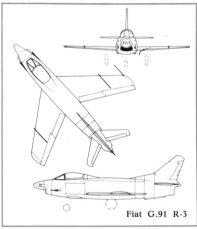

Fiat G.91 R-3

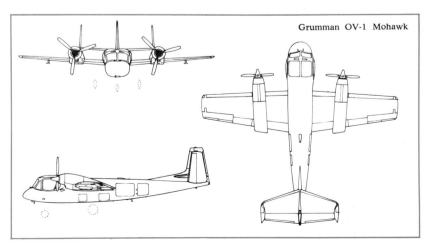

Grumman OV-1 Mohawk

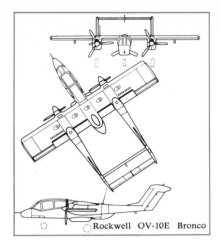
Rockwell OV-10E Bronco

Plate 228
Airborne radar systems for the 1980s

The traditional concept of photographic or electronic reconnaissance planes was extended from the end of the 1950s to cover that of an airborne platform which was really a complete strategic command post which would gather information for tactical forces and co-ordinate their action. This role has been given to particularly sophisticated aircraft which can carry out continual surface surveillance.

One of the first reconnaissance planes to be adapted for this very specialised use was the Grumman E-1B Tracer, a special version of the versatile twin-engine carrier-borne S-2 Tracker. The US Navy ordered this variant in 1956 and the prototype appeared on 1st March of the following year. The aircraft had a very large aerodynamic fairing above the fuselage which contained the large search radar antenna, and also had a different tailplane. Eighty were manufactured, which entered service in February 1958 and remained in use until 1965.

Whereas the Tracer was clearly the product of an adaptation, the Grumman E-2 Hawkeye, the aircraft which replaced it from January 1964, was specially designed as a flying command

post. The winner of a competition set up by the US Navy in 1956, this twin-engine turboprop aircraft appeared in prototype on 21st October 1960, and was put into production from February 1962 onwards; 59 of the first variant E-2A were built. Two other basic versions followed, beginning with E-2B of 1969 (which had a digital computer). All the E-2As were subsequently updated to the level of the E-2B; the E-2C, the final version and the most sophisticated, appeared in prototype on 20th January 1971, and twenty were built.

Soon, however, very much more powerful aircraft were developed with better operational capacities. Within the context of the AWACS programme (Airborne Warning and Control System) put in train by the USA at the beginning of the 1970s, the Boeing E-3A Sentry appeared which in practice was a derivant of the four-jet commercial Boeing 707-320. The first aircraft of the 22 production planes planned was delivered to the USAF on 24th March 1977 and entered service immediately with a specially created unit, 552 Airborne Warning and Control Wing based in Oklahoma. In operational use the Sentry has shown itself to be particularly efficient, mainly due to the complex and very advanced electronics and communications systems which it carries.

A similar aircraft has also been developed in Britain, the BAe Nimrod

AEW Mk 3 which is derived from the "conventional" Nimrod maritime reconnaissance plane. This aircraft differs from its American counterpart in having the radar antenna installed in the extreme nose in a very large bulbous fairing which has altered the lines of the fuselage considerably. The production of this aircraft started towards the middle of the 1970s by converting two Nimrods ordered by the RAF in M.R.Mk 1 configuration. The first of these made its first flight on 28th July 1977. Production is fixed at 11 planes whose operational life is to continue well into the 1990s, within the context of NATO's European defence system.

The Soviet Union has also produced an AWACS aircraft using a commercial plane; this is the Tupolev Tu-126 (MOSS in NATO code) which is derived from the civil transport Tu-114. It differs from its western equivalents in being a turboprop; the Tu-16 is, however, just as effective. According to western estimates at the end of the 1970s the *VVS* had in service about fifteen of these planes which were first observed in 1978.

the initial series OV-10A flew on 6th August of the following year. 271 of these aircraft were completed (114 for the USMC and 157 for the USAF) until April 1969. Production continued, however, for export: the OV-10B version was for Germany (24 built, first flight 21st September 1970); the OV-10C for the Royal Thai Air Force (36); the OV-10E which appeared in March 1973 was built for Venezuela (16); and 6 OV-10Fs (1976) went to Indonesia.

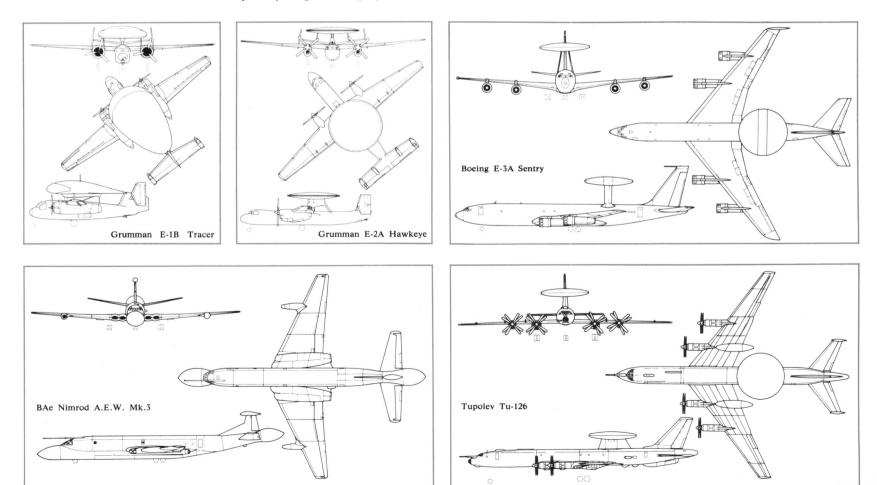

Grumman E-1B Tracer

Grumman E-2A Hawkeye

Boeing E-3A Sentry

BAe Nimrod A.E.W. Mk.3

Tupolev Tu-126

▲ AUSTER A.O.P.9 .
Nation: Britain; *manufacturer:* Auster Aircraft Ltd; *type:* observation; *year:* 1954; *engine:* Blackburn Cirrus Bombardier 203 4-cylinder inline air-cooled, 180 hp; *wingspan:* 36 ft 5 in (11.10 m); *length:* 23 ft 8 in (7.21 m); *height:* 8 ft 5 in (2.56 m); *weight:* 2,130 lb (966 kg) (loaded); *maximum speed:* 127 mph (204 km/h); *ceiling:* 18,500 ft (5,640 m); *range:* 246 miles (395 km); *armament:* – ; *crew:* 2-3

SIAI MARCHETTI SM. 1019A ▲
Nation: Italy; *manufacturer:* SIAI Marchetti; *type:* liaison; *year:* 1971; *engine:* Allison 250-B15G turboprop, 317 hp; *wingspan:* 36 ft (10.97 m); *length:* 27 ft 11 in (8.52 m); *height:* 7 ft 10 in (2.38 m); *weight:* 2,800 lb (1,270 kg) (loaded); *maximum speed:* 155 mph (250 km/h) at 9,845 ft (3,000 m); *ceiling:* 19,685 ft (6,000 m); *range:* 760 miles (1,225 km); *armament:* 500 lb (227 kg) of bombs; *crew:* 2

AERITALIA AM 3C ▶
Nation: Italy; *manufacturer:* Aeritalia; *type:* observation; *year:* 1969; *engine:* Lycoming GSO-480-B1B6 6-cylinder inline air-cooled, 340 hp; *wingspan:* 41 ft 6 in (12.64 m); *length:* 29 ft 5 in (8.98 m); *height:* 9 ft 11 in (2.72 m); *weight:* 3,858 lb (1,750 kg) (loaded); *maximum speed:* 173 mph (278 km/h) at 8,000 ft (2,440 m); *ceiling:* 27,550 ft (8,400 m); *range:* 880 miles (1,415 km); *armament:* 750 lb (340 kg) of bombs; *crew:* 2; *passengers:* 2

CESSNA L-19A BIRD DOG
Nation: USA; *manufacturer:* Cessna Aircraft Co; *type:* liaison; *year:* 1950; *engine:* Continental C-470-II, 4-cylinder horizontally opposed air-cooled, 213 hp; *wingspan:* 36 ft (10.97 m); *length:* 25 ft 9 in (7.85 m); *height:* 7 ft 3 in (2.21 m); *weight:* 2,400 lb (1,088 kg) (loaded); *maximum speed:* 151 mph (243 km/h) at sea level; *ceiling:* 18,500 ft (5,640 m); *range:* 530 miles
◀ (850 km); *crew:* 2

EMBRAER YC-95 BANDEIRANTE
Nation: Brazil; *manufacturer:* Embraer; *type:* liaison; *year:* 1968; *engine:* two Pratt & ▶ Whitney PT6A-20 turboprops, 550 hp each; *wingspan:* 50 ft 7 in (15.42 m); *length:* 41 ft 9 in (12.74 m); *height:* 16 ft 11 in (5.17 m); *weight:* 9,920 lb (4,500 kg) (loaded); *maximum speed:* 267 mph (430 km/h) at 8,200 ft (2,500 ft); *ceiling:* 29,500 ft (9,000 m); *range:* 1,150 miles (1,850 km); *armament:* – ; *crew:* 2; *passengers:* 7-9

Plate 230

Postwar trainers: 1946–50

PERCIVAL PRENTICE T.1
Nation: Britain; *manufacturer:* Percival Aircraft Ltd; *type:* trainer; *year:* 1946; *engine:* de Havilland Gipsy Queen 32 inline 6-cylinder air-cooled, 251 hp; *wingspan:* 46 ft (14.02 m); *length:* 31 ft 3 in (9.52 m); *height:* 12 ft 10 in (3.91 m); *weight:* 4,200 lb (1,905 kg) (loaded); *maximum speed:* 143 mph (230 km/h) at 5,000 ft (1,525 m); *ceiling:* 18,000 ft (5,490 m); *range:* 396 miles (637 km); *armament:* – ; *crew:* 2

FIAT G.46-4B
Nation: Italy; *manufacturer:* Fiat SpA; *type:* trainer; *year:* 1947; *engine:* Alfa Romeo 115 *ter* 6-cylinder inline air-cooled, 215 hp; *wingspan:* 34 ft 1 in (10.40 m); *length:* 27 ft 11 in (8.50 m); *height:* 7 ft 10 in (2.40 m); *weight:* 3,102 lb (1,410 kg) (loaded); *maximum speed:* 193 mph (312 km/h) at sea level; *ceiling:* 17,700 ft (5,400 m); *range:* 620 miles (1,000 km); *armament:* 1 machine gun; *crew:* 2

S.A.I. AMBROSINI S.7
Nation: Italy; *manufacturer:* Società Aeronautica Italiana Ambrosini; *type:* trainer; *year:* 1949; *engine:* Alfa Romeo 115 *ter* 6-cylinder inline air-cooled, 225 hp; *wingspan:* 28 ft 10 in (8.79 m); *length:* 26 ft 10 in (8.17 m); *height:* 9 ft (2.80 m); *weight:* 3,030 lb (1,376 kg) (loaded); *maximum speed:* 224 mph (358 km/h); *ceiling:* 17,220 ft (5,250 m); *range:* 620 miles (1,000 km); *armament:* 1 machine gun; *crew:* 2

NORTH AMERICAN T-28A TROJAN
Nation: USA; *manufacturer:* North American Aviation Inc; *type:* trainer; *year:* 1949; *engine:* Wright R-1300-1 Cyclone 7-cylinder air-cooled radial, 800 hp; *wingspan:* 40 ft 1 in (12.21 m); *length:* 32 ft (9.75 m); *height:* 12 ft 8 in (3.86 m); *weight:* 6,365 lb (2,887 kg) (loaded); *maximum speed:* 283 mph (455 km/h) at 5,900 ft (1,800 m); *ceiling:* 24,000 ft (7,300 m); *range:* 1,000 miles (1,600 km); *armament:* provision for 2 machine guns, 200 lb (90 kg) of bombs; *crew:* 2

de HAVILLAND CHIPMUNK T.10
Nation: Britain; *manufacturer:* de Havilland Aircraft Co Ltd; *type:* trainer; *year:* 1949; *engine:* de Havilland Gipsy Major 8 4-cylinder inline air-cooled, 145 hp; *wingspan:* 34 ft 4 in (10.46 m); *length:* 25 ft 8 in (7.82 m); *height:* 7 ft 1 in (2.16 m); *weight:* 2,000 lb (907 kg) (loaded); *maximum speed:* 138 mph (222 km/h) at sea level; *ceiling:* 16,000 ft (4,880 m); *range:* 300 miles (480 km); *armament:* – ; *crew:* 2

HUNTING PERCIVAL PROVOST T.1
Nation: Britain; *manufacturer:* Hunting Percival Aircraft Ltd; *type:* trainer; *year:* 1950; *engine:* Alvis Leonides 126 air-cooled 9-cylinder radial, 550 hp; *wingspan:* 35 ft (10.71 m); *length:* 28 ft 6 in (8.73 m); *height:* 12 ft (3.70 m); *weight:* 4,399 lb (1,995 kg); *maximum speed:* 200 mph (322 km/h) at sea level; *ceiling:* 25,000 ft (7,620 m); *range:* 650 miles (1,040 km); *crew:* 2

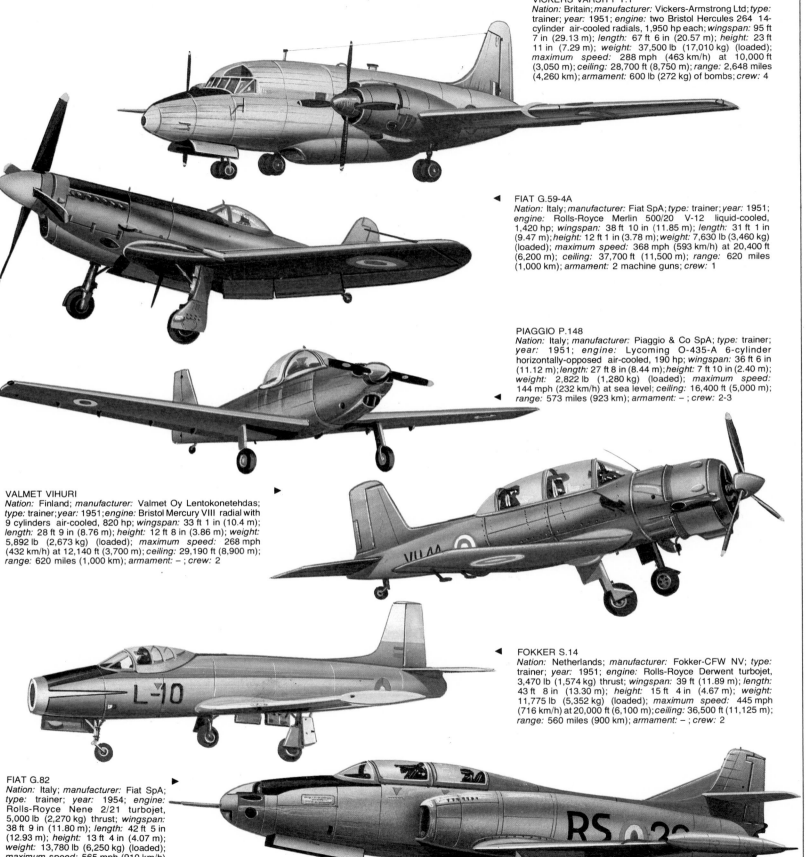

VICKERS VARSITY T.1
Nation: Britain; *manufacturer:* Vickers-Armstrong Ltd; *type:* trainer; *year:* 1951; *engine:* two Bristol Hercules 264 14-cylinder air-cooled radials, 1,950 hp each; *wingspan:* 95 ft 7 in (29.13 m); *length:* 67 ft 6 in (20.57 m); *height:* 23 ft 11 in (7.29 m); *weight:* 37,500 lb (17,010 kg) (loaded); *maximum speed:* 288 mph (463 km/h) at 10,000 ft (3,050 m); *ceiling:* 28,700 ft (8,750 m); *range:* 2,648 miles (4,260 km); *armament:* 600 lb (272 kg) of bombs; *crew:* 4

FIAT G.59-4A
Nation: Italy; *manufacturer:* Fiat SpA; *type:* trainer; *year:* 1951; *engine:* Rolls-Royce Merlin 500/20 V-12 liquid-cooled, 1,420 hp; *wingspan:* 38 ft 10 in (11.85 m); *length:* 31 ft 1 in (9.47 m); *height:* 12 ft 1 in (3.78 m); *weight:* 7,630 lb (3,460 kg) (loaded); *maximum speed:* 368 mph (593 km/h) at 20,400 ft (6,200 m); *ceiling:* 37,700 ft (11,500 m); *range:* 620 miles (1,000 km); *armament:* 2 machine guns; *crew:* 1

PIAGGIO P.148
Nation: Italy; *manufacturer:* Piaggio & Co SpA; *type:* trainer; *year:* 1951; *engine:* Lycoming O-435-A 6-cylinder horizontally-opposed air-cooled, 190 hp; *wingspan:* 36 ft 6 in (11.12 m); *length:* 27 ft 8 in (8.44 m); *height:* 7 ft 10 in (2.40 m); *weight:* 2,822 lb (1,280 kg) (loaded); *maximum speed:* 144 mph (232 km/h) at sea level; *ceiling:* 16,400 ft (5,000 m); *range:* 573 miles (923 km); *armament:* – ; *crew:* 2-3

VALMET VIHURI
Nation: Finland; *manufacturer:* Valmet Oy Lentokonetehdas; *type:* trainer; *year:* 1951; *engine:* Bristol Mercury VIII radial with 9 cylinders air-cooled, 820 hp; *wingspan:* 33 ft 1 in (10.4 m); *length:* 28 ft 9 in (8.76 m); *height:* 12 ft 8 in (3.86 m); *weight:* 5,892 lb (2,673 kg) (loaded); *maximum speed:* 268 mph (432 km/h) at 12,140 ft (3,700 m); *ceiling:* 29,190 ft (8,900 m); *range:* 620 miles (1,000 km); *armament:* – ; *crew:* 2

FOKKER S.14
Nation: Netherlands; *manufacturer:* Fokker-CFW NV; *type:* trainer; *year:* 1951; *engine:* Rolls-Royce Derwent turbojet, 3,470 lb (1,574 kg) thrust; *wingspan:* 39 ft (11.89 m); *length:* 43 ft 8 in (13.30 m); *height:* 15 ft 4 in (4.67 m); *weight:* 11,775 lb (5,352 kg) (loaded); *maximum speed:* 445 mph (716 km/h) at 20,000 ft (6,100 m); *ceiling:* 36,500 ft (11,125 m); *range:* 560 miles (900 km); *armament:* – ; *crew:* 2

FIAT G.82
Nation: Italy; *manufacturer:* Fiat SpA; *type:* trainer; *year:* 1954; *engine:* Rolls-Royce Nene 2/21 turbojet, 5,000 lb (2,270 kg) thrust; *wingspan:* 38 ft 9 in (11.80 m); *length:* 42 ft 5 in (12.93 m); *height:* 13 ft 4 in (4.07 m); *weight:* 13,780 lb (6,250 kg) (loaded); *maximum speed:* 565 mph (910 km/h) at 10,000 ft (3,000 m); *ceiling:* 41,000 ft (12,500 m); *range:* 1,000 miles (1,600 km); *armament:* 2 machine guns or cannon; *crew:* 2

Plate 232

Trainers: 1955–70

COMMONWEALTH CA-25 WINJEEL (A85)
Nation: Australia; *manufacturer:* Commonwealth Aircraft Corp; *type:* trainer; *year:* 1955; *engine:* Pratt & Whitney R-985-AN2 Wasp jr radial with 9 cylinders air-cooled, 450 hp; *wingspan:* 38 ft 7 in (11.76 m); *length:* 28 ft 1 in (8.56 m); *height:* 9 ft 1 in (2.77 m); *weight:* 4,265 lb (1,935 kg) (loaded); *maximum speed:* 186 mph (299 km/h); *ceiling:* 18,000 ft (5,490 m); *range:* 550 miles (825 km); *crew:* 3

HISPANO SAETA HA-200A
Nation: Spain; *manufacturer:* Hispano Aviación SA; *type:* trainer; *year:* 1955; *engine:* two Turboméca Marboré IIA turbojets, 880 lb (400 kg) thrust each; *wingspan:* 34 ft 2 in (10.42 m); *length:* 29 ft 2 in (8.88 m); *height:* 10 ft 8 in (3.26 m); *weight:* 6,995 lb (3,173 kg) (loaded); *maximum speed:* 435 mph (700 km/h) at 29,500 ft (9,000 m); *ceiling:* 40,000 ft (12,000 m); *range:* 1,056 miles (1,700 km); *armament:* 2 machine guns; *crew:* 2

FOUGA C.M.175 ZEPHYR
Nation: France; *manufacturer:* Potez Air-Fouga; *type:* trainer; *year:* 1956; *engine:* two Turboméca Marboré IIB turbojets, 880 lb (400 kg) thrust each; *wingspan:* 39 ft 10 in (12.15 m); *length:* 33 ft 6 in (10.21 m); *height:* 9 ft 6 in (2.95 m); *weight:* 7,496 lb (3,400 kg) (loaded); *maximum speed:* 403 mph (649 km/h) at 22,965 ft (7,000 m); *ceiling:* 36,088 ft (11,000 m); *range:* 478 miles (770 km); *armament:* two machine guns, 220 lb of bombs (100 kg); *crew:* 2

YAKOVLEV Yak-18A
Nation: USSR; *manufacturer:* State Industries; *type:* trainer; *year:* 1957; *engine:* Ivchenko AI-14R radial with 9 cylinders air-cooled, 260 hp; *wingspan:* 34 ft 9 in (10.60 m); *length:* 27 ft 5 in (8.35 m); *height:* 10 ft 8 in (3.25 m); *weight:* 2,901 lb (1,326 kg) (loaded); *maximum speed:* 163 mph (263 km/h) at sea level; *ceiling:* 16,600 ft (5,060 m); *range:* 441 miles (710 km); *crew:* 2

AERMACCHI M.B.326
Nation: Italy; *manufacturer:* Aeronautica Macchi SpA; *type:* trainer; *year:* 1957; *engine:* Bristol Siddeley Viper 11 turbojet, 2,500 lb (1,134 kg) thrust; *wingspan:* 34 ft 9 in (10.60 m); *length:* 35 ft (10.66 m); *height:* 12 ft 3 in (3.72 m); *weight:* 7,561 lb (3,430 kg) (loaded); *maximum speed:* 506 mph (815 mph) at 19,700 ft (6,000 m); *ceiling:* 41,000 ft (12,500 m); *range:* 680 miles (1,090 km); *armament:* – ; *crew:* 2

AERMACCHI M.B.326 K
Nation: Italy; *manufacturer:* Aeronautica Macchi SpA; *type:* trainer-tactical support; *year:* 1970; *engine:* Bristol Siddeley Viper 632 turbojet, 4,000 lb (1,814 kg) thrust; *wingspan:* 35 ft 3 in (10.74 m); *length:* 35 ft (10.66 m); *height:* 12 ft 3 in (3.72 m); *weight:* 12,000 lb (5,443 kg) (loaded); *maximum speed:* 576 mph (927 km/h); *ceiling:* 49,200 ft (15,000 m); *range:* 932 miles (1,500 km); *armament:* 2 × 30 mm cannon; 4,000 lb (1,814 kg) of bombs; *crew:* 1

FUJI T1F-2
Nation: Japan; *manufacturer:* Fuji Jukogyo Kabushiki Kaisha; *type:* trainer; *year:* 1958; *engine:* Bristol Siddeley Orpheus 805 turbojet, 4,000 lb (1,814 kg) thrust; *wingspan:* 34 ft (10.49 m); *length:* 39 ft 8 in (12.11 m); *height:* 13 ft 4 in (4.06 m); *weight:* 10,670 lb (4,840 kg) (loaded); *maximum speed:* 575 mph (926 km/h) at 20,000 ft (6,100 m); *ceiling:* 48,000 ft (14,630 m); *range:* 1,200 miles (1,950 km); *armament:* one machine gun, 1,500 lb of bombs (680 kg); *crew:* 2

NORTH AMERICAN T-2A BUCKEYE
Nation: USA; *manufacturer:* North American Aviation Inc.; *type:* trainer; *year:* 1958; *engine:* Westinghouse J-34-WE-36 turbojet, 3,400 lb (1,542 kg) thrust; *wingspan:* 35 ft 10 in (10.97 m); *length:* 38 ft 7 in (11.78 m); *height:* 14 ft 9 in (4.5 m); *weight:* 10,000 lb (4,536 kg) (loaded); *maximum speed:* 494 mph (795 km/h) at 25,000 ft (12,950 m); *ceiling:* 42,500 ft (12,950 m); *range:* 963 miles (1,550 km); *crew:* 2

BEECHCRAFT T-34C
Nation: USA; *manufacturer:* Beech Aircraft Corp.; *type:* trainer; *year:* 1973; *engine:* Pratt & Whitney PT6A-25 turboprop, 400 hp; *wingspan:* 33 ft 3 in (10.16 m); *length:* 28 ft 8 in (8.75 m); *height:* 9 ft 7 in (3.02 m); *weight:* 4,360 lb (1,978 kg) (loaded); *maximum speed:* 288 mph (464 km/h) at sea level; *ceiling:* 30,000 ft (9,145 m); *range:* 748 miles (1,205 km); *crew:* 2

BEECHCRAFT T-44A
Nation: USA; *manufacturer:* Beech Aircraft Corp.; *type:* trainer; *year:* 1976; *engine:* two Pratt & Whitney PT6A-34B turboprops, 550 hp each; *wingspan:* 50 ft 2 in (15.32 m); *length:* 35 ft 4 in (10.82 m); *height:* 14 ft 2 in (4.33 m); *weight:* 9,650 lb (4,377 kg) (loaded); *maximum speed:* 276 mph (445 km/h) at 15,000 ft (4,570 m); *ceiling:* 29,500 ft (8,990 m); *range:* 1,456 miles (2,344 km); *crew:* 2

CASA C-101 AVIOJET
Nation: Spain; *manufacturer:* CASA; *type:* trainer-tactical support; *year:* 1977; *engine:* Garret-AiResearch TFE 731-2-25 turbojet, 3,500 lb (1,588 kg) thrust; *wingspan:* 34 ft 8 in (10.60 m); *length:* 40 ft (12.25 m); *height:* 13 ft 10 in (4.25 m); *weight:* 12,345 lb (5,600 kg) (loaded); *maximum speed:* 420 mph (676 km/h) at sea level; *ceiling:* 40,500 ft (12,495 m); *range:* 730 miles (1,176 km); *armament:* 4,400 lb (2,000 kg) of bombs; *crew:* 2

Plate 234

British trainers and one from India: 1958–74

HUNTING PERCIVAL JET PROVOST T.3
Nation: Britain; *manufacturer:* Hunting Percival Aircraft Ltd; *type:* trainer; *year:* 1958; *engine:* Bristol Siddeley Viper ASV.8 turbojet, 1,750 lb (794 kg) thrust; *wingspan:* 35 ft 2 in (10.72 m); *length:* 31 ft 11 in (9.73 m); *height:* 12 ft 8 in (3.86 m); *weight:* 5,850 lb (2,654 kg) (loaded); *maximum speed:* 330 mph (530 km/h) at 20,000 ft (6,100 m); *ceiling:* 31,000 ft (9,450 m); *range:* 493 miles (793 km); *armament:* – ; *crew:* 2

BAe SA-3 BULLDOG T. Mk 1
Nation: Britain; *manufacturer:* British Aerospace; *type:* trainer; *year:* 1973; *engine:* Lycoming 10-360-A1B6 4-cylinder horizontal air-cooled, 200 hp; *wingspan:* 33 ft (10.06 m); *length:* 23 ft 3 in (7.09 m); *height:* 7 ft 6 in (2.28 m); *weight:* 2,350 lb (1,066 kg) (loaded); *maximum speed:* 150 mph (241 km/h) at sea level; *ceiling:* 16,000 ft (4,875 m); *range:* 621 miles (1,000 km); *armament:* 640 lb (290 kg) of bombs; *crew:* 2-3

FOLLAND GNAT T.1
Nation: Britain; *manufacturer:* Folland Aircraft Ltd; *type:* trainer; *year:* 1959; *engine:* Bristol Siddeley Orpheus 101 turbojet, 4,230 lb (1,920 kg) thrust; *wingspan:* 24 ft (7.32 m); *length:* 31 ft 9 in (9.65 m); *height:* 10 ft 6 in (3.20 m); *weight:* 8,560 lb (3,880 kg) (loaded); *maximum speed:* 636 mph (1,026 km/h) at 31,000 ft (9,450 m); *ceiling:* 48,000 ft (14,600 m); *range:* 1,180 miles (1,900 km); *armament:* 1,000 lb (454 kg) of bombs; *crew:* 2

BAe HAWK T. Mk 1
Nation: Britain; *manufacturer:* British Aerospace; *type:* trainer/tactical support; *year:* 1974; *engine:* Rolls-Royce/Turboméca RT.172-06-11 Adour 151 turbofan, 5,340 lb (2,422 kg) thrust; *wingspan:* 30 ft 10 in (9.39 m); *length:* 36 ft 8 in (11.17 m); *height:* 13 ft 1 in (3.99 m); *weight:* 17,097 lb (7,755 kg) (loaded); *maximum speed:* 621 mph (1,000 km/h) at sea level; *ceiling:* 50,000 ft (15,240 m); *range:* 645 miles (1,038 km); *armament:* 1 × 30 mm cannon; 2,000 lb (900 kg) of bombs; *crew:* 2

HAL HJT-16 Mk IA KIRAN
Nation: India; *manufacturer:* HAL; *type:* trainer/tactical support; *year:* 1964; *engine:* Rolls-Royce Viper 11 turbojet, 2,500 lb (1,134 kg) thrust; *wingspan:* 35 ft 1 in (10.70 m); *length:* 34 ft 9 in (10.60 m); *height:* 11 ft 11 in (3.64 m); *weight:* 9,039 lb (4,100 kg) (loaded); *maximum speed:* 432 mph (695 km/h) at sea level; *ceiling:* 30,000 ft (9,150 m); *range:* 463 miles (745 km); *armament:* 1,000 lb (453 kg) of bombs; *crew:* 2

L-29 DELFIN
Nation: Czechoslovakia; *manufacturer:* State Industries; *type:* trainer; *year:* 1959; *engine:* M-701 turbojet, 1,920 lb (870 kg) thrust; *wingspan:* 33 ft 1 in (10.08 m); *length:* 35 ft 6 in (10.82 m); *height:* 10 ft 2 in (3.10 m); *weight:* 7,736 lb (3,509 kg) (loaded); *maximum speed:* 422 mph (679 km/h) at 16,400 ft (5,000 m); *ceiling:* 39,700 ft (12,100 m); *range:* 800 miles (1,290 km); *armament:* 1,000 lb (454 kg) of bombs; *crew:* 2

AERO L-39 ALBATROS
Nation: Czechoslovakia; *manufacturer:* Aero; *type:* trainer; *year:* 1968; *engine:* Walter Titan turbojet, 3,792 lb (1,720 kg) thrust; *wingspan:* 31 ft 1 in (9.46 m); *length:* 40 ft 5 in (12.32 m); *height:* 15 ft 5 in (4.72 m); *weight:* 11,618 lb (5,270 kg) (loaded); *maximum speed:* 435 mph (700 km/h) at sea level; *ceiling:* 37,730 ft (11,500 m); *range:* 994 miles (1,600 km); *armament:* 2,425 lb (1,100 kg) of bombs; *crew:* 2

SIAI MARCHETTI SF.260W
Nation: Italy; *manufacturer:* SIAI Marchetti; *type:* trainer/tactical support; *year:* 1972; *engine:* Lycoming O-540-E4A5 6-cylinder inline air-cooled, 260 hp; *wingspan:* 27 ft 5 in (8.35 m); *length:* 23 ft 4 in (7.10 m); *height:* 7 ft 11 in (2.41 m); *weight:* 2,866 lb (1,300 kg) (loaded); *maximum speed:* 196 mph (315 km/h) at sea level; *ceiling:* 15,300 ft (4,665 m); *range:* 345 miles (556 km); *armament:* 661 lb (300 kg) of bombs; *crew:* 2

TS-11 ISKRA
Nation: Poland; *manufacturer:* State Industry; *type:* trainer; *year:* 1960; *engine:* SO-1 turbojet, 2,204 lb (1,000 kg) thrust; *wingspan:* 32 ft 8 in (9.98 m); *length:* 36 ft 11 in (11 m); *height:* 10 ft 9 in (3.30 m); *weight:* 8,712 lb (3,952 kg) (loaded); *maximum speed:* 497 mph (800 km/h); *ceiling:* 39,400 ft (12,000 m); *crew:* 2

AERMACCHI M.B.339
Nation: Italy; *manufacturer:* Aeronautica Macchi; *type:* trainer; *year:* 1976; *engine:* Rolls-Royce Viper Mk 632-43 turbojet, 4,000 lb (1,815 kg) thrust; *wingspan:* 35 ft 8 in (10.86 m); *length:* 36 ft (10.97 m); *height:* 13 ft 1 in (3.99 m); *weight:* 13,000 lb (5,895 kg) (loaded); *maximum speed:* 558 mph (898 km/h) at sea level; *ceiling:* 48,000 ft (14,630 m); *range:* 1,093 miles (1,760 km); *armament:* 4,000 lb (1,815 kg) of bombs; *crew:* 2

ALPHA JET E
Nation: France, Germany; *manufacturer:* Dassault-Breguet/Dornier; *type:* trainer; *year:* 1973; *engine:* two SNECMA/Turboméca Larzac 04-C5 turbofans, 2,976 lb (1,350 kg) thrust each; *wingspan:* 29 ft 11 in (9.11 m); *length:* 40 ft 4 in (12.29 m); *height:* 13 ft 9 in (4.19 m); *weight:* 13,448 lb (6,100 kg) (loaded); *maximum speed:* 621 mph (1,000 km/h) at sea level; *ceiling:* 49,200 ft (15,000 m); *range:* 273 miles (440 km); *armament:* 1 × 30 mm cannon; 4,960 lb (2,250 kg) of bombs; *crew:* 2

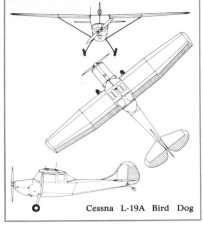

Cessna L-19A Bird Dog

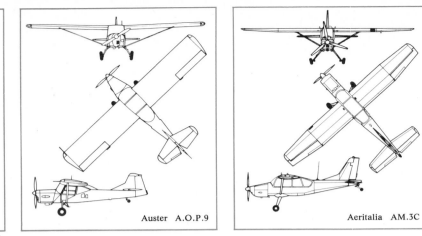

Auster A.O.P.9

Aeritalia AM.3C

Plate 230
Postwar trainers: 1946–50

Plate 229
Observation and liaison planes:
1954–71

With a very few exceptions the great majority of light observation and liaison planes were derived from models which were originally built for the civil market.

In the USA the Cessna L-19 Bird Dog, for instance, was none other than a militarised version of the Cessna 170, a commercial plane which was in production in 1950. This little high-wing monoplane, which became one of the most widely used light aircraft of the USAF, won a competition in 1950 and was put into production under a series of contracts which by October 1954 had already reached nearly 2,500 units ordered.

The first version, L-19A, was certainly the one produced in the largest numbers. Another important variant was the TL-19D trainer, ordered in 1956, of which 310 were built for operational use; the most up-to-date version was the L-19E of 1957, which had its equipment modified and had a more powerful engine; 376 L-19Es were ordered. Overall production exceeded 3,100 aircraft which stayed in service for nearly twenty years.

Britain's equivalent of the Cessna Bird Dog was the Auster A.O.P.9, a

tough and versatile monoplane with a fabric skin; it was a product of Auster's long experience in the field of light aircraft, both military and civil. The prototype appeared on 19th March 1954, and had been developed especially for advanced observation and liaison. At the end of proving trials the aircraft was accepted by the RAF and put into mass production. The first aircraft were delivered to units at the beginning of 1955 and the first order was followed by a second during 1959. The Auster was also sold to the Indian Air Force and Army, and to the South African Air Force.

In Italy the Savoia Marchetti SM.1019 was derived from the American Cessna L-19 Bird Dog. This project was started in January 1969 and the construction of the first prototypes started two months afterwards. The principal differences when comparing this aircraft with the Bird Dog lay mainly in the type of engine used, the fuselage and the tailplane. The first prototype, which flew on 24th May 1969, was followed by a second, improved prototype which was designated SM.1019A and appeared on 18th February 1971. At the end of proving trials a total of 80 aircraft was ordered by the Italian army. Production started in 1973 and deliveries to operational units began towards the end of 1975.

An unsuccessful competitor of the SM.1019 was the Aeritalia AM.3C,

which was developed jointly with Aeronautica Macchi. The first prototype flew on 12th May 1967 and was shown again in its definitive form two years later. An entirely Italian design, the AM.3C was put into production after an order had been received for 40 from South Africa and three from Rwanda. The Brazilian Embraer C-95 Bandeirante is a modern twin-engine turboprop transport which was developed in 1966 to replace the US Beechcraft C-45s in service with the air force. The first prototype YC-95 flew on 26th October 1968, and the first C-95 production model on 9th August 1972. Several military versions were built, including the R-95 photo-reconnaissance, C-95A freight transport and P-95 for maritime reconnaissance. The Bandeirante entered service with the Brazilian air force in 1973. It also met with considerable export success: over 200 aircraft which had been constructed by the end of 1979 were sold to about 35 operators.

The last American piston-engine trainer to be constructed as such was the North American T-28 Trojan, which was produced in 1948 to replace the old T-6 Texan. The first prototype flight was on 26th September 1949, and production started the following year, with a series of contracts totalling 1,194 examples of the initial T-28A variant for the USAF. The performance of this aircraft was very satisfactory and awakened the interest of the US Navy which in 1952 asked for a version to be built adapted for its specific needs. The T-28B appeared in prototype on 6th April 1953, the main change being the installation of a more powerful engine. After 489 had been built another 301 T-28Cs followed (the prototype flew on 19th September 1955) which could operate from aircraft carriers. The T-28 was taken out of service by the USAF in 1959 and by the US Navy during the 1960s. An unusual footnote to its career is the fact that a batch of 245 T-28As were taken out of service, transformed into ground attack aircraft and anti-insurgent aircraft and sold to France in 1960. They were used a great deal in Algeria, being given the name of Fennec.

In Britain one of the replacements of the famous Tiger Moth basic trainer was another de Havilland design, the Chipmunk, which was developed by the Canadian subsidiary of de Havilland in 1946; 158 were constructed in Canada. The RAF decided to use this plane in 1948; the production aircraft had some equipment changes carried out, and were then designated Chipmunk T.10. They reached units at the beginning of 1950 and soon were used by all flying schools. The 740 planes built were kept constantly busy for the greater part of the 1970s although relegated to secondary duties. A contemporary of the Chipmunk was the Percival Prentice, which stayed in service as a basic trainer from 1947 until 1953 and of which over 300 were built. The prototype flew on 31st March 1946. The instructor and the pupil sat side by side. The aircraft could also be used for night flying training.

In 1953 the Prentice started to be replaced by a more modern and powerful aircraft, the Hunting Percival Provost, with which the RAF standardised training methods, basing them on a piston-engine plane for basic training and on the Vampire for advanced training. The Provost prototype had flown in February 1950 and production had started a year later. The 461 Provosts that were built up till 1956 continued in service until the beginning of the 1960s.

In Italy, one of the first aircraft built

SIAI Marchetti SM.1019A

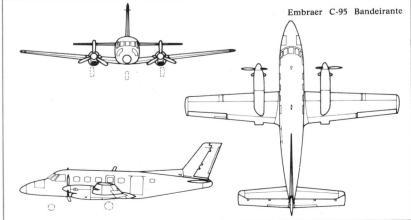

Embraer C-95 Bandeirante

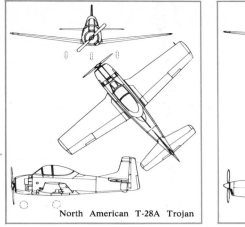

North American T-28A Trojan

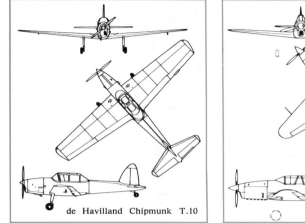

de Havilland Chipmunk T.10

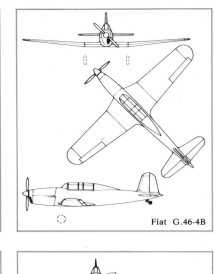

Fiat G.46-4B

S.A.I. Ambrosini S.7

Plate 231
Trainers: 1951–54

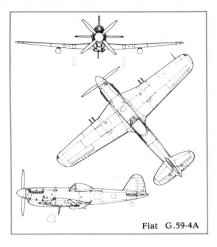

Fiat G.59-4A

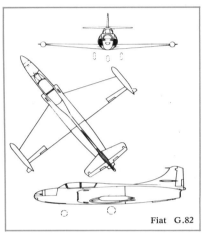

Fiat G.82

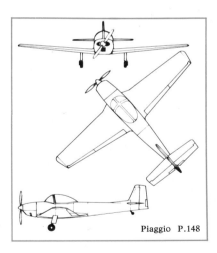

Piaggio P.148

Another excellent product of Italian manufacture in the immediate postwar years was the Fiat G.59. This trainer was tested in 1948 and went into production with an order for 30 aircraft designated G.59-1B. A year later the prototype of the single-seat version, the G.59-1A, appeared, which went into service together with the first version in 1950.

In the same year a second basic model appeared, and was built in two production series: the G.59-2B two-seater (19) and the G.59-2A single-seater. The latter had been developed in response to an order from Syria, for a combat version of the G.59. 36 G.59-2As were built, 26 of which went to Syria.

In 1951 the last basic model of the aircraft appeared which had a bubble hood, the G.59-4B, from which was derived the single-seat G.59-4A. 5 G.59-4Bs and 30 G.59-4As were built; the former all went to the *AMI* and some of the latter were exported to Syria.

The Fiat G.82 was less fortunate, failing to make its mark when entered in the NATO competition for a trainer to be used by all the countries of the Atlantic Alliance. The G.82 appeared in prototype on 23rd May 1954 and was derived from the first jet-engine aircraft to be constructed in Italy, the G.80, which flew on 10th December 1951 and of which three experimental aircraft had been built up till 1953. Only five G.82s were built and went into service in 1956: two years later they were transferred to an experimental unit, where they remained until 1959.

From 1952 the *Aeronautica Militare Italiana* put a trainer and liaison plane into service, the Piaggio P.148. This was designed in 1951 and was a small and versatile aircraft for which total procurement was about 100. In 1953 Piaggio made a more up to date and more powerful version of this plane, the P.149, which was selected by the *Luftwaffe*; 262 were built of which 190 were manufactured by Focke Wulf under licence.

Two other contemporary European trainers were the Finnish Valmet Vihuri piston-engine plane and the Dutch Fokker S.14 jet. The Valmet Vihuri appeared in prototype on 6th February 1951, and at the end of proving trials was put in series production for the Finnish air force. From 1956 a second version was built (Vihuri III) which had structural detail and instrumentation improvements.

The Fokker S.14 was designed with the specific aim of appealing to the export market. Exports however eluded this enterprising Dutch manu-

after the war was a trainer: the Fiat G.46, of which the prototype appeared in 1947 and was put into production the following year for the *AMI*. The 150 planes ordered were joined by 70 aircraft for export and were bought by Syria and Argentina. The G.46 was constructed in two basic versions, the A single-seater and the B two-seater and also in four sub-types which differed from each other in having different engines.

The SAI Ambrosini S.7 was not so fortunate: this was an elegant monoplane of wooden construction derived from a long succession of designs for light fighters which had been developed by Sergio Stefanuti during the war years. It appeared in prototype

form in 1949, and the S.7 was produced in small numbers for training units of the *AMI*, with whom it flew for only a few years. In 1952 a proposal for a more powerful version, the Super S.7, was turned down.

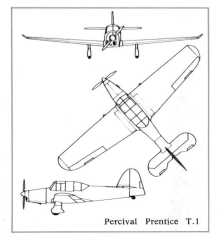

Percival Prentice T.1

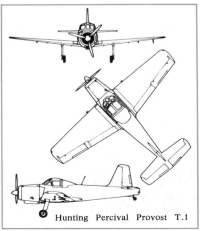

Hunting Percival Provost T.1

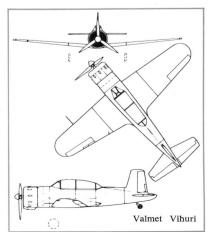

Valmet Vihuri

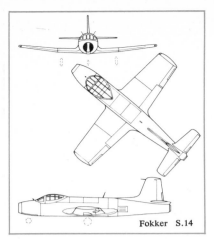

Fokker S.14

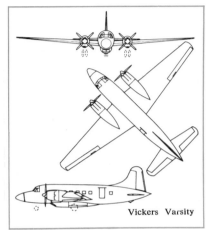

Vickers Varsity

Plate 232
Trainers: 1955–70

Among piston-engine trainers, mention must be made of the Australian Commonwealth CA-25 Winjeel and the Russian Yakovlev Yak-18

The Winjeel (which means "young eagle" in the Aboriginal language) was designed in 1948 at the request of the RAAF who wanted a replacement for the ageing Tiger Moths. The first prototype (CA-22) was flown on 3rd February 1951 and paradoxically it was the very fact that it had such outstanding flight stability – too much so for a trainer – which led to its being turned down. The design was therefore modified and it was only four years later (23rd February 1955) that the definitive CA-25 prototype could be tested. Only 62 were produced, which went into service in 1955.

The Yak-18 was designed even before the Second World War, and the design had been shelved and then taken up again in 1945. The first version went into service in 1947 and was followed in 1955 by the second principal production variant (Yak-18U) which had a tricycle undercarriage. In 1957 the third basic version (Yak-18A) appeared which was aerodynamically improved and was

more powerful. By 1969 6,760 Yak-18s had been built which were used not only in the USSR but also in most Eastern European countries, in China and in North Korea. In NATO code this aircraft was called MAX.

As training moved with the times, the gradual introduction of the concept of *ab initio* jet training led to the production of specialised jet aircraft for this purpose. In Europe one of the most widely used jet trainers of the 1950s was the French Fouga C.M.170 Magister of 1951. From this versatile aircraft (of which over 1,000 were built and used in Federal Germany, Belgium, the Netherlands, Austria, Finland and Israel) a carrier-borne version was derived in 1956 at the request of the *Aéronavale*. The prototype of this aircraft, which was designated C.M. 175 Zephyr, flew on 31st July 1956; 45 were built.

Spain also built a jet trainer: the Hispano Saeta HA-200, and this design marked the debut of the Spanish aeronautical industry in jet aircraft production. The prototype appeared on 12th August 1955, and the first HA.200A (35 built) went into service ten years later. These aircraft were first used for training and were then also used for tactical support. The D and E models of the aircraft of 1965 were used in this latter role and had more sophisticated engines, avionics and armament.

In Europe another successful

trainer was the Italian Aermacchi M.B.326, which was still in use at the end of the 1970s after over twenty years from the date of the prototype's first flight (10th December 1957) and had been highly successful: over 800 were sold to thirteen countries and were produced under licence in Australia, South Africa, and Brazil. The first air force to use the *Macchino* was the *Aeronautica Militare Italiana* (an initial order for 100 was signed in 1960) and these aircraft were delivered to flying training schools from 1962 onwards.

During its long production run, numerous variants were built, most of which were for export and had more powerful engines and armament and more or less sophisticated avionics according to the buyer's needs. Perhaps the most noteworthy version was the K single-seater of 1970 which, although built as an operational trainer, could also be used in a tactical support role. The principal users of the M.N. 326 (apart from Australia, South Africa and Brazil) were Tunisia, Ghana, Zaïre, Zambia, Dubai and Argentina.

facturer: only 20 S.14s were ordered by the military authorities and production came to an end towards the end of 1955, without any orders from foreign buyers.

In 1951 the RAF put a modern and versatile twin piston-engine plane into service for crew training, the Vickers Varsity, as a replacement for the obsolete Wellington T.10. The aircraft had been designed three years earlier in response to an Air Ministry specification and had been put into production once proving trials and operational tests had been completed. The most outstanding quality of the Varsity was that it could provide excellent training for pilots, flight engineers, radio officers, navigators and air gunners. These latter were seated in a very large ventral gondola which contained the fire controls and a small quantity of training bombs. As at February 1954 the assembly lines had completed 163 Varsity aircraft.

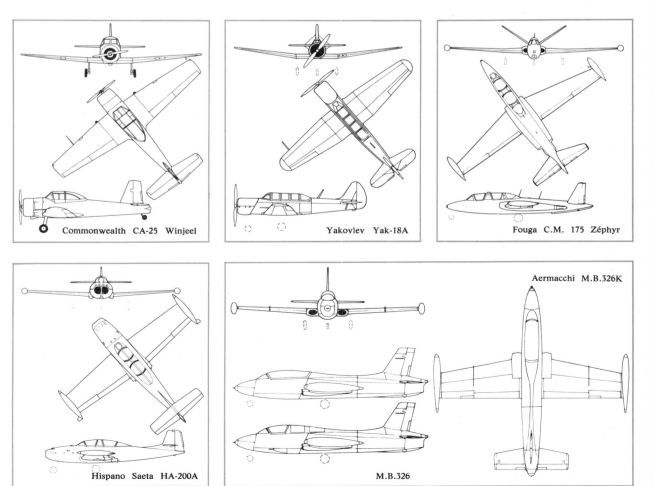

Commonwealth CA-25 Winjeel

Yakovlev Yak-18A

Fouga C.M. 175 Zéphyr

Hispano Saeta HA-200A

M.B.326

Aermacchi M.B.326K

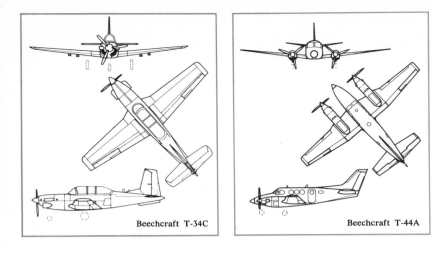

Beechcraft T-34C

Beechcraft T-44A

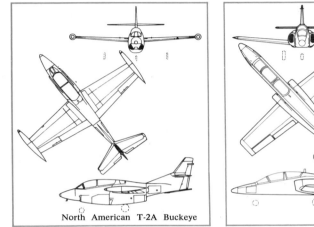

North American T-2A Buckeye

CASA C-101 Aviojet

basic versions: the T-2A which was the first model, of which 217 were built; the T-2B of 1962, which was powered by twin turbojets (97 went into service in 1966); the T-2C of 1968 which had different engines; and 207 which were produced and exported under the designation of T-2D.

Another trainer which was derived from a commercial Beechcraft was first used by the US Navy in 1977: the T-44A, which was in fact a militarised version of the twin-jet turboprop "executive" King Air 90. The first converted model flew in 1976. At the end of 1979 numbers ordered reached 61.

In Europe the Spanish air force's need to replace the Hispano HA-200 Saeta led, in 1975, to the design for a new aircraft, to be used both as a trainer and as an assault plane: the CASA C-101 Aviojet, which was developed in collaboration with the German Company MBB, and Northrop. The first of four prototypes flew on 17th June 1977, and production was started the following year with an initial order for 30 aircraft. The first Aviojet was completed in 1978, and deliveries began at the end of the following year.

Plate 234
British trainers — and one from India: 1958–74

Towards the middle of the 1950s Britain took steps towards adopting jet aircraft as trainers. Hunting Percival built the first aircraft of this type, the Jet Provost, which from 1959 was the RAF's basic trainer.

This aircraft was designed as a company venture in 1953, and this initiative was rewarded by an order for 9 experimental aircraft which were designated T.1. The first of these flew on 26th June 1954, followed by the first T.3 which flew on 22nd June 1958. Production continued until 1965 totalling over 450 aircraft. In 1967 a second basic version of the T.5 appeared, over 100 of which were ordered by the RAF. A sub-type which was armed (T.55) was derived from this variant and was exported to Sudan. In the same year the new assault variant, the Strikemaster, was built.

A contemporary of the Jet Provost — but used for advanced training — was the Folland Gnat, which was accepted by the RAF after it had been rejected as a fighter. Work started on the design in 1953 and a year later the first prototype appeared in single seat configuration. After a long series of

Plate 233
Trainers: 1958–77

The need to replace the old North American T-6 led Japan to design a worthwhile advanced jet trainer, the Fuji T1F, which was developed in the second half of the 1950s. Two versions of the aircraft were built: the T1F-1, which was powered by a Japanese engine; the second, T1F-2, was powered by a British Bristol Siddeley Orpheus engine. The second variant was the first one to fly (19th January 1958) and was followed over two years

later (19th May 1960) by the T1F-1. Production totalled 60: 40 T1F-2s and 20 T1F-1s. These aircraft went into service in 1962.

In the USA one of the most widely used groups of piston-engine trainers for over twenty-five years was the Beechcraft T-34. In 1953 450 were ordered by the USAF in T-34 configuration (this was the original design which had led in 1938 to the commercial Beechcraft prototype Model 45) and in 1954 the US Navy ordered 423 T-34Bs; these aircraft were, in 1973, subjected to a complete updating. The US Navy's requirement to modernise the T-34B prompted Beechcraft to change the original Continental piston engine for a turboprop engine which was nearly twice as powerful.

The new prototype T-34C had its first flight on 24th September 1973 and was put into production under a series of contracts which came to a total of 300 examples. The first T-34Cs entered service in 1977. The following year a derivant was produced which could also carry out assault missions (T-34C-1) and was exported to Morocco, Peru, Argentina, Indonesia and Ecuador.

The first jet-engine basic trainer of the US Navy was the North American T-2 Buckeye, which appeared in prototype on 7th February 1958 and entered service in the following year. Production was concentrated on three

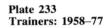

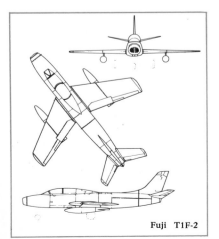

Fuji T1F-2

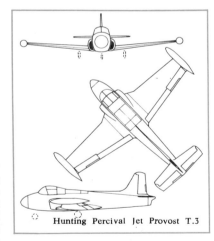

Hunting Percival Jet Provost T.3

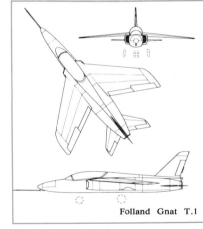

Folland Gnat T.1

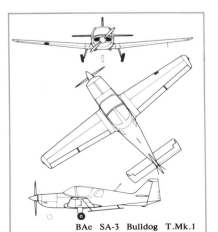

BAe SA-3 Bulldog T.Mk.1

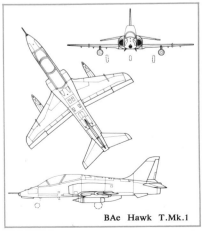

BAe Hawk T.Mk.1

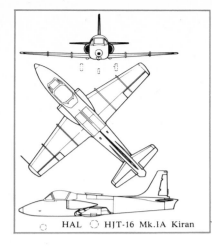

HAL ○ HJT-16 Mk.IA Kiran

proving trials the RAF turned down this lightweight fighter, but the aircraft was bought by India, together with the construction licence. In 1957, following this commercial success which affirmed the aircraft's good qualities, the RAF asked for a trainer version of the Gnat to be constructed; the first T.1 was flown on 31st August 1959 and these aircraft (105) entered service in February 1962.

Six years later the RAF decided to revert to a piston-engine trainer: the aircraft chosen was the small single-engined Beagle Pup in a militarised version. This was called the Bulldog, and it was an agile two-seater which appeared in definitive prototype form on 22nd June 1971 and was put into production for the RAF two years later in the T.Mk I version (130 built, first flight 30th January 1973). Up till the end of 1978, 76 Bulldogs had been built for export.

The last British jet trainer of the 1970s, the BAe Hawk, was designed in 1972 by Hawker Siddeley at the RAF's request, who wanted an aircraft to replace the Jet Provost and the Gnat. The first pre-production aircraft (there were no prototypes) was tested on 21st August 1974 and was followed by 135 production aircraft which were delivered from November 1976 onwards. Besides being used as a basic and advanced trainer (T.Mk I) the Hawk can also be used as a ground-attack aircraft.

A similar plane built in India by Hindustan Aeronautics followed much the same course of development; this was the HAL HJT-16 Kiran. This was designed in 1961 as a trainer (Mk I, first flight 4th September 1964) and put into production on the strength of an order for 190; in 1977 it was modified for light attack and weapons training, starting from the 119th series aircraft onwards and designated Mk IA. Subsequently a final variant, the Mk II, was derived from this.

Plate 235
European trainers: 1959–76

In Eastern Europe, Czechoslavakia was the only country which managed to make its mark in the manufacture of trainers. The first was the L-29 Delfin and this was followed by the Aero L-39 Albatros. The Delfin was designed towards the end of the 1950s and appeared in prototype on 5th April 1959. In 1963 the L-29 was submitted for a competition among the Warsaw Pact countries for the production of a standard trainer. It was the winner and was exported to Bulgaria, East Germany, Hungary, Romania and even to the Soviet Union. Production topped 3,000.

At the end of the 1960s the successor to the Delfin was designed, the Aero L-39 Albatros. The first of five prototypes had its maiden flight on 4th November 1968 and ten pre-series aircraft completed proving trials in 1971. These tests resulted two years later in the L-39 being accepted as a replacement for the Delfin with the Warsaw Pact air forces. The first production models went into service in the spring of 1974 in Czechoslovakia. At the end of 1979 over 1,000 of these aircraft had been ordered.

About ten years later the Polish TS-11 Iskra achieved a very modest success; this was the first Polish-designed jet aircraft and was the Delfin's unsuccessful rival. The prototype appeared on 5th February 1960, and this aircraft went into production towards the end of 1963, entering service at the beginning of the following year. Although various versions were available at the end of 1979, only 150 Iskras had been built.

In Italy, a light aircraft which was designed as a trainer, but met with great export success as a light attack aircraft, was the Savoia Marchetti SF.260. The first appearance of the civil prototype was on 15th July 1964, and this elegant single-engine plane was militarised six years later in the SF.260M variant (first flight 10th October 1970). Apart from 25 aircraft which were ordered by the *AMI*, production reached just under 400 and this aircraft was exported to as many as twelve countries including Belgium (36) and Libya (over 200). In May 1972 the SF.260SW version was developed. This variant was also exported, especially to countries such as the Philippines and Tunisia, and was mainly used in counter-insurgency and internal security roles. The last variant was the SF.260SW which was a maritime patrol and rescue variant. In all, production for military use had reached a total of 600 by the end of 1979.

The M.B.339 was the successor of the Aermacchi M.B.326 and inherited its excellent qualities; it was developed from 1972 onwards and was flown on 12th August 1976. It was more modern and versatile than the *Macchino* and the M.B.339 was ordered by the *Aeronautica Militare* in 1975 as a new basic and advanced trainer and the first two aircraft of the 100 planned for production were delivered on 8th August 1979. To make the aircraft more attractive to the export market, it has been designed to have good potential in a close support role as well as for training.

A similar type of plane is the Dassault-Breguet/Dornier Alpha Jet, developed jointly by France and Federal Germany from 1971 onwards with a production total of 400 aircraft in mind, made up of trainers (E) and light strike aircraft (A). The prototype appeared in June 1973 and the first production model for the *Armée de l'Air* appeared on 4th November 1977. The German strike version will replace the G.91R early in the 1980s. Orders have been placed by Belgium, Morocco, Togo, Nigeria and the Ivory Coast for a total of about fifty aircraft.

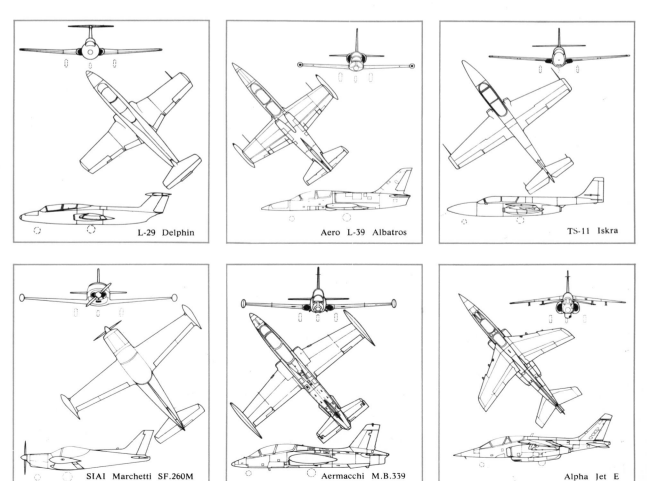

L-29 Delphin

Aero L-39 Albatros

TS-11 Iskra

SIAI Marchetti SF.260M

Aermacchi M.B.339

Alpha Jet E

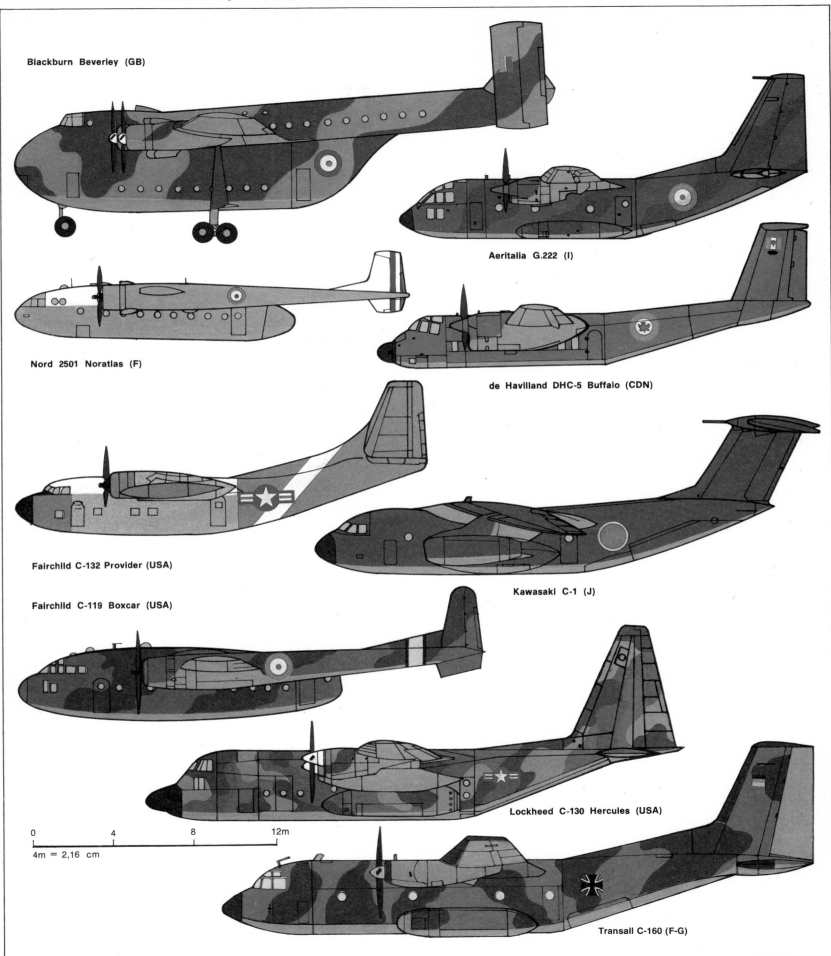

Blackburn Beverley (GB)

Aeritalia G.222 (I)

Nord 2501 Noratlas (F)

de Havilland DHC-5 Buffalo (CDN)

Fairchild C-132 Provider (USA)

Kawasaki C-1 (J)

Fairchild C-119 Boxcar (USA)

0   4   8   12m

4m = 2,16 cm

Lockheed C-130 Hercules (USA)

Transall C-160 (F-G)

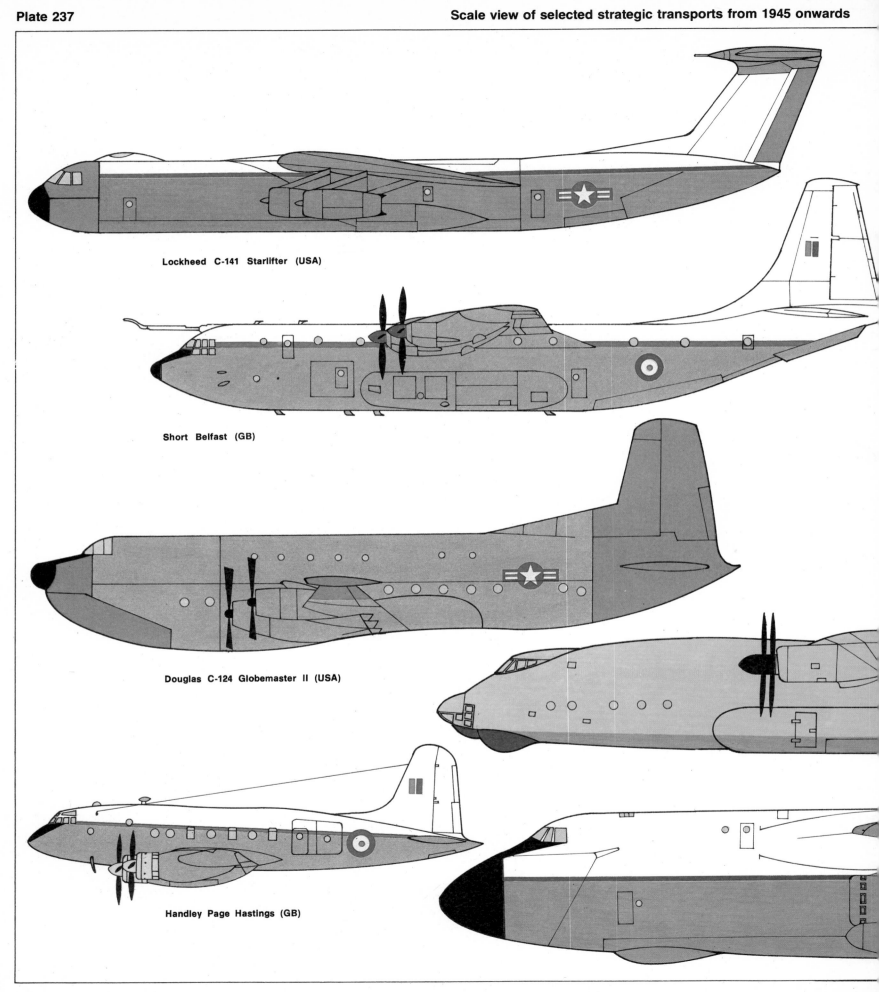

Lockheed C-141 Starlifter (USA)

Short Belfast (GB)

Douglas C-124 Globemaster II (USA)

Handley Page Hastings (GB)

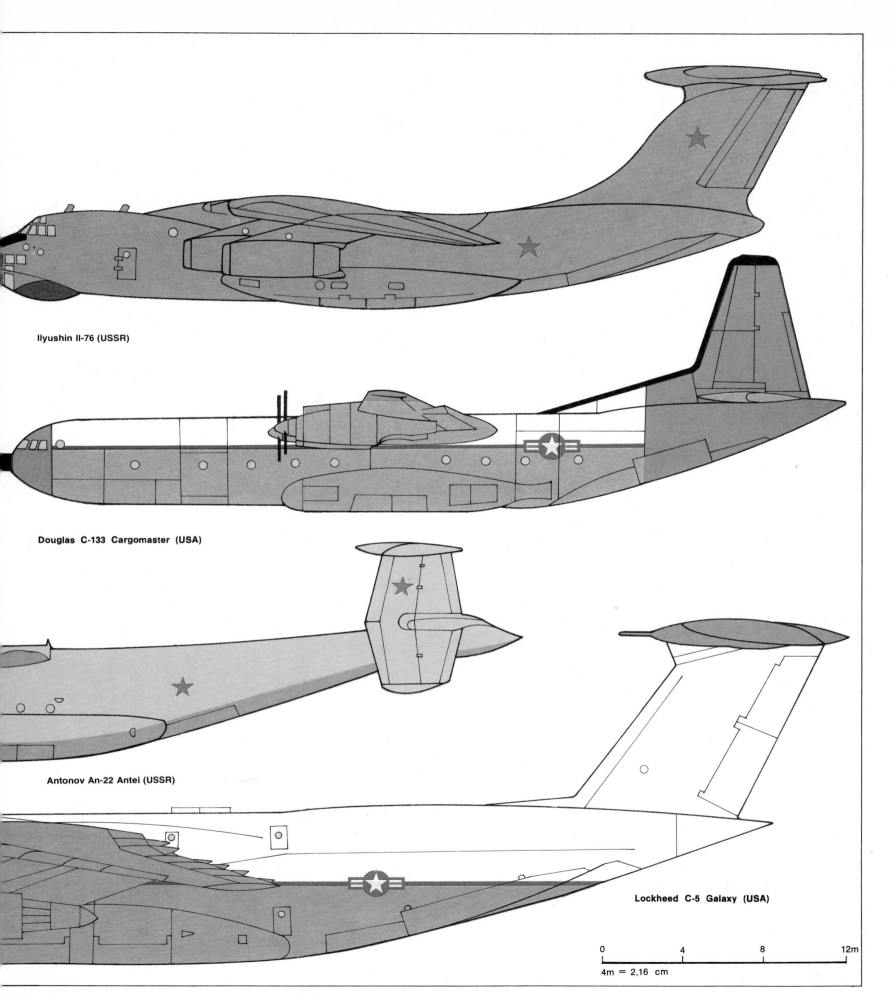

Ilyushin Il-76 (USSR)

Douglas C-133 Cargomaster (USA)

Antonov An-22 Antei (USSR)

Lockheed C-5 Galaxy (USA)

0   4   8   12m

4m = 2,16 cm

Plate 238

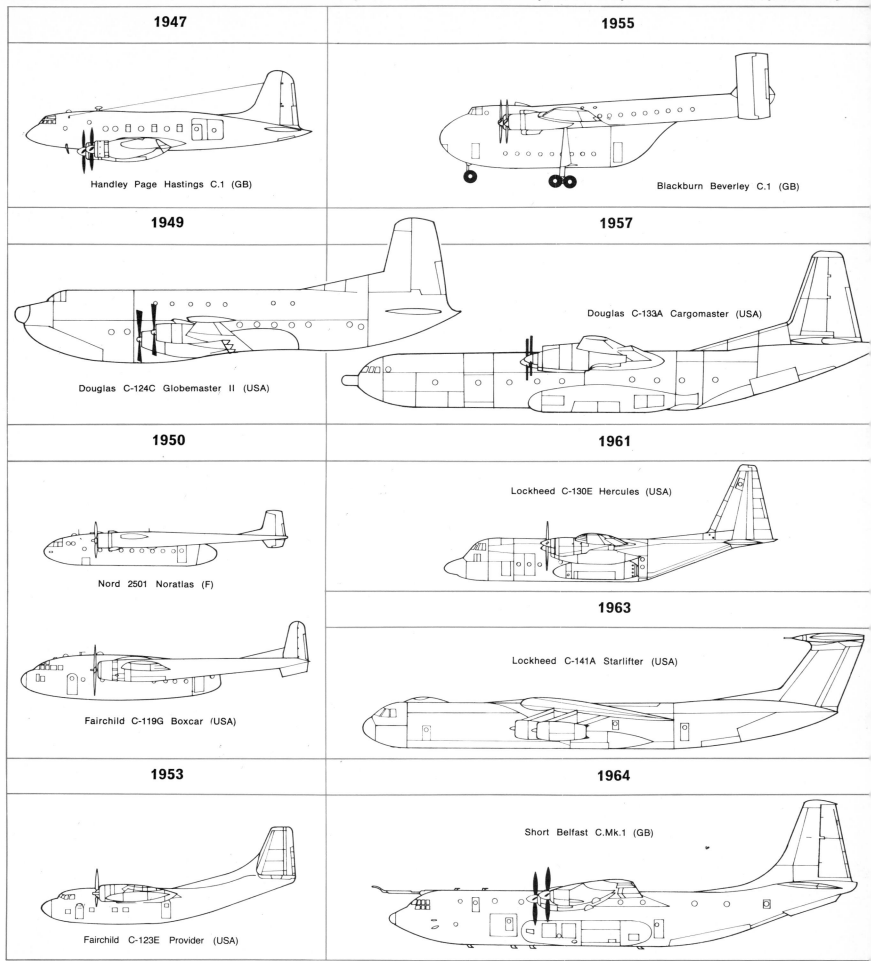

1947

Handley Page Hastings C.1 (GB)

1949

Douglas C-124C Globemaster II (USA)

1950

Nord 2501 Noratlas (F)

Fairchild C-119G Boxcar (USA)

1953

Fairchild C-123E Provider (USA)

1955

Blackburn Beverley C.1 (GB)

1957

Douglas C-133A Cargomaster (USA)

1961

Lockheed C-130E Hercules (USA)

1963

Lockheed C-141A Starlifter (USA)

1964

Short Belfast C.Mk.1 (GB)

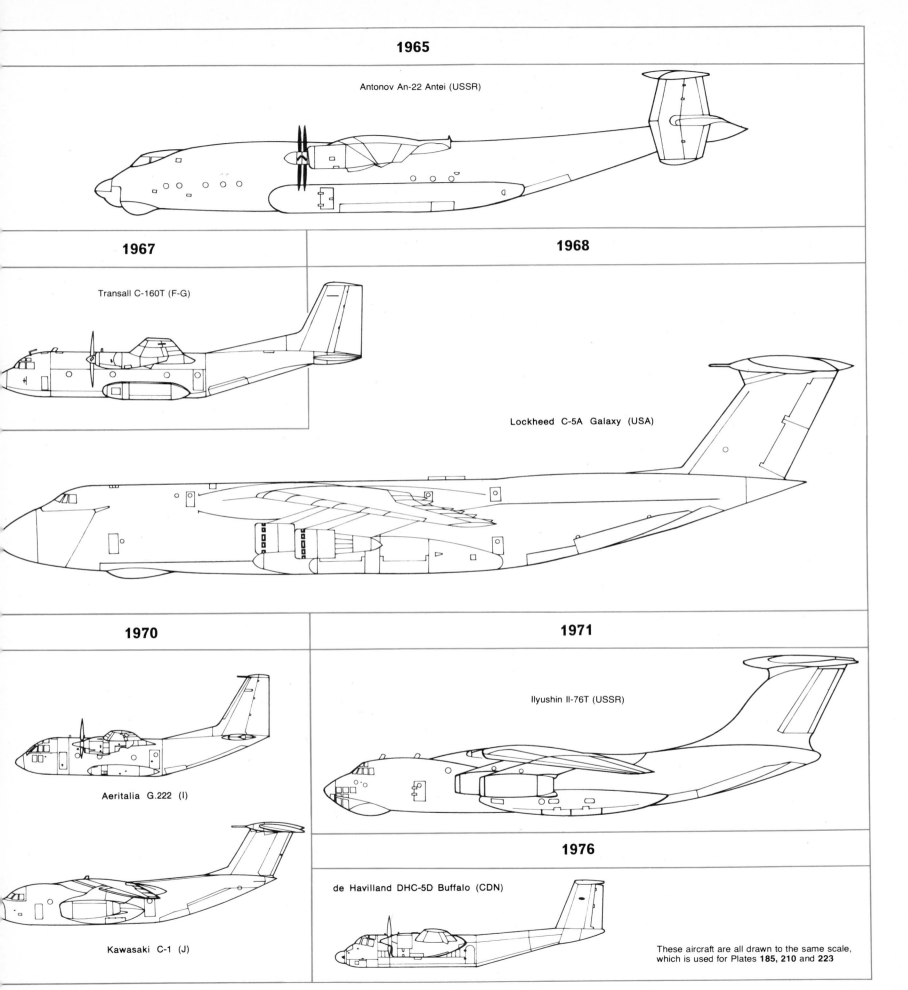

1965

Antonov An-22 Antei (USSR)

1967

Transall C-160T (F-G)

1968

Lockheed C-5A Galaxy (USA)

1970

Aeritalia G.222 (I)

Kawasaki C-1 (J)

1971

Ilyushin Il-76T (USSR)

1976

de Havilland DHC-5D Buffalo (CDN)

These aircraft are all drawn to the same scale, which is used for Plates **185**, **210** and **223**

Plate 239

European and American postwar transports: 1947–50

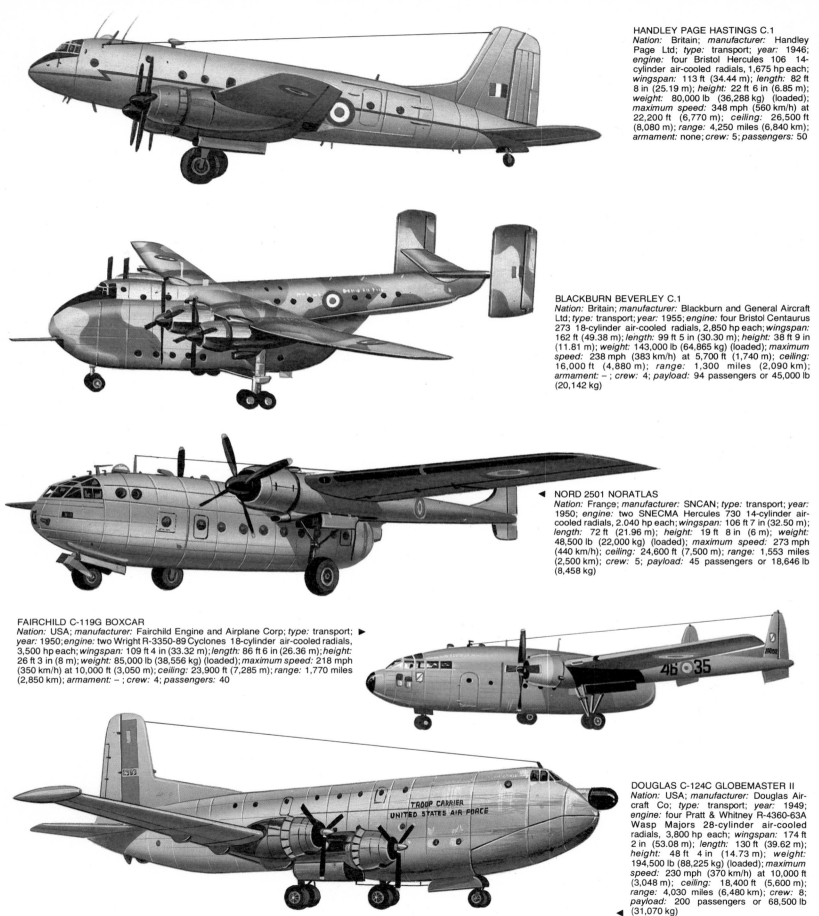

HANDLEY PAGE HASTINGS C.1
Nation: Britain; *manufacturer:* Handley Page Ltd; *type:* transport; *year:* 1946; *engine:* four Bristol Hercules 106 14-cylinder air-cooled radials, 1,675 hp each; *wingspan:* 113 ft (34.44 m); *length:* 82 ft 8 in (25.19 m); *height:* 22 ft 6 in (6.85 m); *weight:* 80,000 lb (36,288 kg) (loaded); *maximum speed:* 348 mph (560 km/h) at 22,200 ft (6,770 m); *ceiling:* 26,500 ft (8,080 m); *range:* 4,250 miles (6,840 km); *armament:* none; *crew:* 5; *passengers:* 50

BLACKBURN BEVERLEY C.1
Nation: Britain; *manufacturer:* Blackburn and General Aircraft Ltd; *type:* transport; *year:* 1955; *engine:* four Bristol Centaurus 273 18-cylinder air-cooled radials, 2,850 hp each; *wingspan:* 162 ft (49.38 m); *length:* 99 ft 5 in (30.30 m); *height:* 38 ft 9 in (11.81 m); *weight:* 143,000 lb (64,865 kg) (loaded); *maximum speed:* 238 mph (383 km/h) at 5,700 ft (1,740 m); *ceiling:* 16,000 ft (4,880 m); *range:* 1,300 miles (2,090 km); *armament:* – ; *crew:* 4; *payload:* 94 passengers or 45,000 lb (20,142 kg)

◀ **NORD 2501 NORATLAS**
Nation: France; *manufacturer:* SNCAN; *type:* transport; *year:* 1950; *engine:* two SNECMA Hercules 730 14-cylinder air-cooled radials, 2.040 hp each; *wingspan:* 106 ft 7 in (32.50 m); *length:* 72 ft (21.96 m); *height:* 19 ft 8 in (6 m); *weight:* 48,500 lb (22,000 kg) (loaded); *maximum speed:* 273 mph (440 km/h); *ceiling:* 24,600 ft (7,500 m); *range:* 1,553 miles (2,500 km); *crew:* 5; *payload:* 45 passengers or 18,646 lb (8,458 kg)

FAIRCHILD C-119G BOXCAR
Nation: USA; *manufacturer:* Fairchild Engine and Airplane Corp; *type:* transport; ▶ *year:* 1950; *engine:* two Wright R-3350-89 Cyclones 18-cylinder air-cooled radials, 3,500 hp each; *wingspan:* 109 ft 4 in (33.32 m); *length:* 86 ft 6 in (26.36 m); *height:* 26 ft 3 in (8 m); *weight:* 85,000 lb (38,556 kg) (loaded); *maximum speed:* 218 mph (350 km/h) at 10,000 ft (3,050 m); *ceiling:* 23,900 ft (7,285 m); *range:* 1,770 miles (2,850 km); *armament:* – ; *crew:* 4; *passengers:* 40

DOUGLAS C-124C GLOBEMASTER II
Nation: USA; *manufacturer:* Douglas Aircraft Co; *type:* transport; *year:* 1949; *engine:* four Pratt & Whitney R-4360-63A Wasp Majors 28-cylinder air-cooled radials, 3,800 hp each; *wingspan:* 174 ft 2 in (53.08 m); *length:* 130 ft (39.62 m); *height:* 48 ft 4 in (14.73 m); *weight:* 194,500 lb (88,225 kg) (loaded); *maximum speed:* 230 mph (370 km/h) at 10,000 ft (3,048 m); *ceiling:* 18,400 ft (5,600 m); *range:* 4,030 miles (6,480 km); *crew:* 8; *payload:* 200 passengers or 68,500 lb ◀ (31,070 kg)

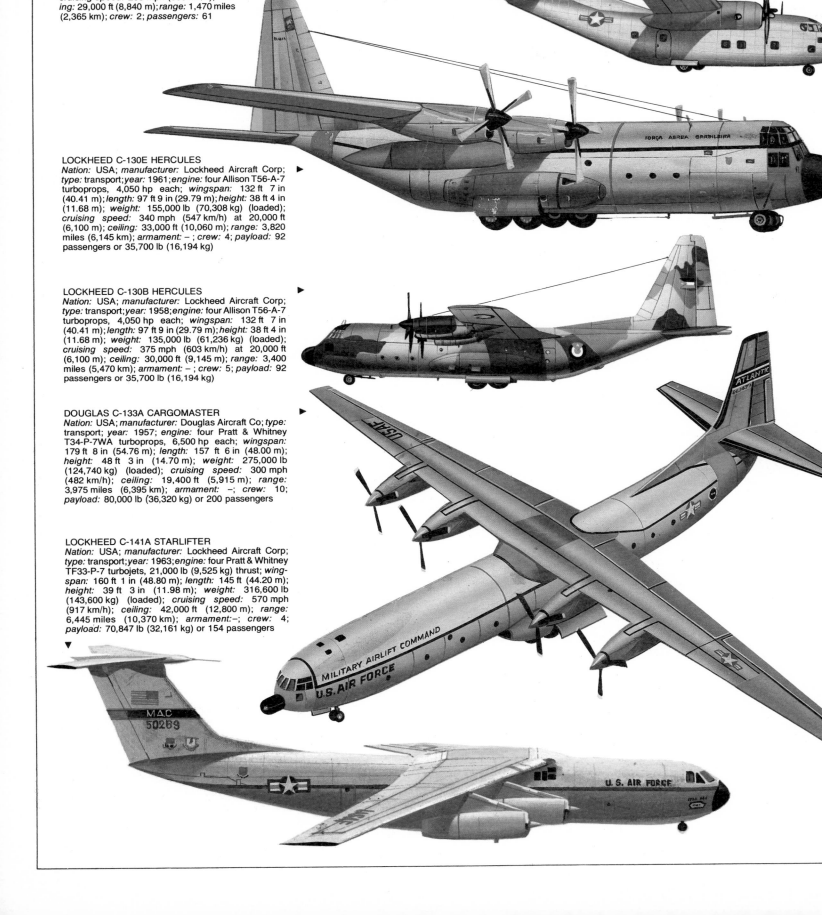

FAIRCHILD C-132B PROVIDER
Nation: USA; *manufacturer:* Fairchild Engine and Airplane Corp; *type:* transport; *year:* 1953; *engine:* two Pratt & Whitney R-2800-99W Double Wasp 18-cylinder air-cooled radials, 2,300 hp each; *wingspan:* 110 ft (33.53 m); *length:* 75 ft 9 in (23.08 m); *height:* 34 ft 1 in (10.38 m); *weight:* 60,000 lb (27,000 kg) (loaded); *cruising speed:* 205 mph (330 km/h); *ceiling:* 29,000 ft (8,840 m); *range:* 1,470 miles (2,365 km); *crew:* 2; *passengers:* 61

LOCKHEED C-130E HERCULES
Nation: USA; *manufacturer:* Lockheed Aircraft Corp; *type:* transport; *year:* 1961; *engine:* four Allison T56-A-7 turboprops, 4,050 hp each; *wingspan:* 132 ft 7 in (40.41 m); *length:* 97 ft 9 in (29.79 m); *height:* 38 ft 4 in (11.68 m); *weight:* 155,000 lb (70,308 kg) (loaded); *cruising speed:* 340 mph (547 km/h) at 20,000 ft (6,100 m); *ceiling:* 33,000 ft (10,060 m); *range:* 3,820 miles (6,145 km); *armament:* – ; *crew:* 4; *payload:* 92 passengers or 35,700 lb (16,194 kg)

LOCKHEED C-130B HERCULES
Nation: USA; *manufacturer:* Lockheed Aircraft Corp; *type:* transport; *year:* 1958; *engine:* four Allison T56-A-7 turboprops, 4,050 hp each; *wingspan:* 132 ft 7 in (40.41 m); *length:* 97 ft 9 in (29.79 m); *height:* 38 ft 4 in (11.68 m); *weight:* 135,000 lb (61,236 kg) (loaded); *cruising speed:* 375 mph (603 km/h) at 20,000 ft (6,100 m); *ceiling:* 30,000 ft (9,145 m); *range:* 3,400 miles (5,470 km); *armament:* – ; *crew:* 5; *payload:* 92 passengers or 35,700 lb (16,194 kg)

DOUGLAS C-133A CARGOMASTER
Nation: USA; *manufacturer:* Douglas Aircraft Co; *type:* transport; *year:* 1957; *engine:* four Pratt & Whitney T34-P-7WA turboprops, 6,500 hp each; *wingspan:* 179 ft 8 in (54.76 m); *length:* 157 ft 6 in (48.00 m); *height:* 48 ft 3 in (14.70 m); *weight:* 275,000 lb (124,740 kg) (loaded); *cruising speed:* 300 mph (482 km/h); *ceiling:* 19,400 ft (5,915 m); *range:* 3,975 miles (6,395 km); *armament:* –; *crew:* 10; *payload:* 80,000 lb (36,320 kg) or 200 passengers

LOCKHEED C-141A STARLIFTER
Nation: USA; *manufacturer:* Lockheed Aircraft Corp; *type:* transport; *year:* 1963; *engine:* four Pratt & Whitney TF33-P-7 turbojets, 21,000 lb (9,525 kg) thrust; *wingspan:* 160 ft 1 in (48.80 m); *length:* 145 ft (44.20 m); *height:* 39 ft 3 in (11.98 m); *weight:* 316,600 lb (143,600 kg) (loaded); *cruising speed:* 570 mph (917 km/h); *ceiling:* 42,000 ft (12,800 m); *range:* 6,445 miles (10,370 km); *armament:*–; *crew:* 4; *payload:* 70,847 lb (32,161 kg) or 154 passengers

Plate 241

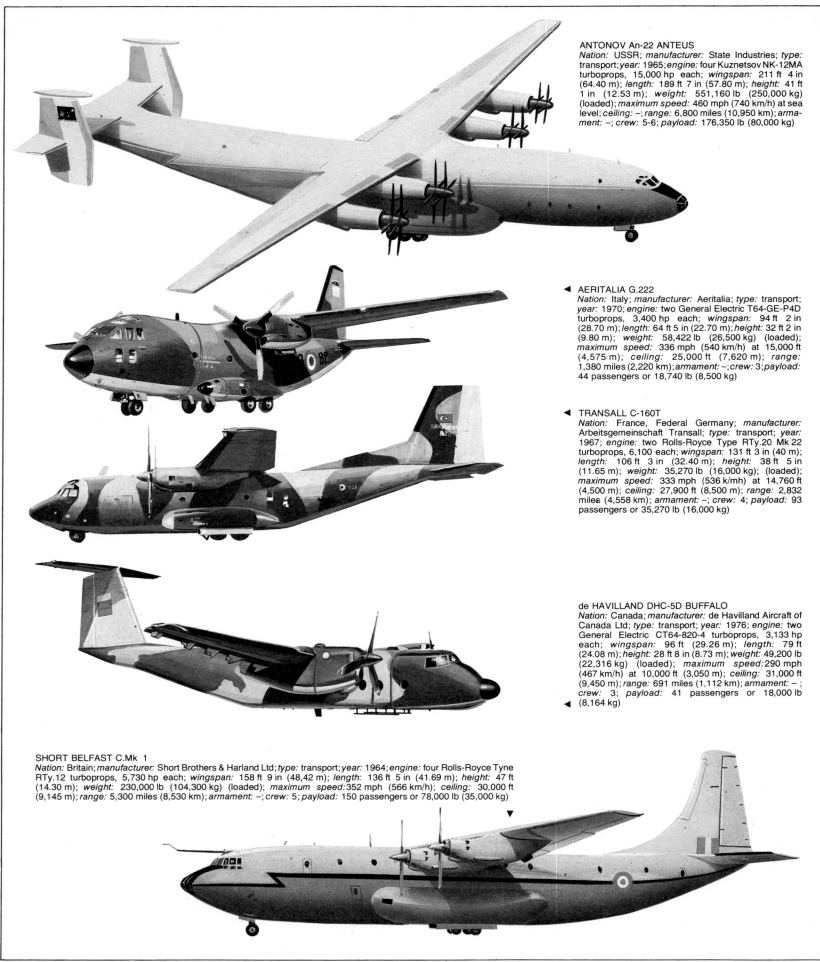

ANTONOV An-22 ANTEUS
Nation: USSR; *manufacturer:* State Industries; *type:* transport; *year:* 1965; *engine:* four Kuznetsov NK-12MA turboprops, 15,000 hp each; *wingspan:* 211 ft 4 in (64.40 m); *length:* 189 ft 7 in (57.80 m); *height:* 41 ft 1 in (12.53 m); *weight:* 551,160 lb (250,000 kg) (loaded); *maximum speed:* 460 mph (740 km/h) at sea level; *ceiling:* –; *range:* 6,800 miles (10,950 km); *armament:* –; *crew:* 5-6; *payload:* 176,350 lb (80,000 kg)

◄ **AERITALIA G.222**
Nation: Italy; *manufacturer:* Aeritalia; *type:* transport; *year:* 1970; *engine:* two General Electric T64-GE-P4D turboprops, 3,400 hp each; *wingspan:* 94 ft 2 in (28.70 m); *length:* 64 ft 5 in (22.70 m); *height:* 32 ft 2 in (9.80 m); *weight:* 58,422 lb (26,500 kg) (loaded); *maximum speed:* 336 mph (540 km/h) at 15,000 ft (4,575 m); *ceiling:* 25,000 ft (7,620 m); *range:* 1,380 miles (2,220 km); *armament:* –; *crew:* 3; *payload:* 44 passengers or 18,740 lb (8,500 kg)

◄ **TRANSALL C-160T**
Nation: France, Federal Germany; *manufacturer:* Arbeitsgemeinschaft Transall; *type:* transport; *year:* 1967; *engine:* two Rolls-Royce Type RTy.20 Mk 22 turboprops, 6,100 each; *wingspan:* 131 ft 3 in (40 m); *length:* 106 ft 3 in (32.40 m); *height:* 38 ft 5 in (11.65 m); *weight:* 35,270 lb (16,000 kg) (loaded); *maximum speed:* 333 mph (536 k/mh) at 14,760 ft (4,500 m); *ceiling:* 27,900 ft (8,500 m); *range:* 2,832 miles (4,558 km); *armament:* –; *crew:* 4; *payload:* 93 passengers or 35,270 lb (16,000 kg)

de HAVILLAND DHC-5D BUFFALO
Nation: Canada; *manufacturer:* de Havilland Aircraft of Canada Ltd; *type:* transport; *year:* 1976; *engine:* two General Electric CT64-820-4 turboprops, 3,133 hp each; *wingspan:* 96 ft (29.26 m); *length:* 79 ft (24.08 m); *height:* 28 ft 8 in (8.73 m); *weight:* 49,200 lb (22,316 kg) (loaded); *maximum speed:* 290 mph (467 km/h) at 10,000 ft (3,050 m); *ceiling:* 31,000 ft (9,450 m); *range:* 691 miles (1,112 km); *armament:* –; *crew:* 3; *payload:* 41 passengers or 18,000 lb (8,164 kg) ◄

SHORT BELFAST C.Mk 1
Nation: Britain; *manufacturer:* Short Brothers & Harland Ltd; *type:* transport; *year:* 1964; *engine:* four Rolls-Royce Tyne RTy.12 turboprops, 5,730 hp each; *wingspan:* 158 ft 9 in (48,42 m); *length:* 136 ft 5 in (41.69 m); *height:* 47 ft (14.30 m); *weight:* 230,000 lb (104,300 kg) (loaded); *maximum speed:* 352 mph (566 km/h); *ceiling:* 30,000 ft (9,145 m); *range:* 5,300 miles (8,530 km); *armament:* –; *crew:* 5; *payload:* 150 passengers or 78,000 lb (35,000 kg)

KAWASAKI C-1
Nation: Japan; *manufacturer:* Kawasaki Jukogyo Kabishiki Kaisha; *type:* transport; *year:* 1970; *engine:* two Mitsubishi JT8D-M-9 turbojets, 14,500 lb (6,577 kg) thrust each; *wingspan:* 100 ft 5 in (30.60 m); *length:* 95 ft 2 in (29 m); *height:* 32 ft 9 in (9.99 m); *weight:* 99,210 lb (45,000 kg) (loaded); *maximum speed:* 501 mph (806 km/h) at 25,000 ft (7,260 m); *ceiling:* 38,000 ft (11,580 m); *range:* 2,084 miles (3,353 km); *armament:* –; *crew:* 5; *payload:* 60 passengers or 17,415 lb (7,900 kg)

LOCKHEED C-5A GALAXY
Nation: USA; *manufacturer:* Lockheed Aircraft Corp; *type:* transport; *year:* 1968; *engine:* four General Electric TF39-GE-1 turbofans, 41,000 lb (18,600 kg) thrust each; *wingspan:* 222 ft 9 in (67.88 m); *length:* 247 ft 10 in) (75.54 m); *height:* 65 ft 2 in (19.85 m); *weight:* 769,000 lb (348,810 kg) (loaded); *maximum speed:* 571 mph (919 km/h) at 25,000 ft (7,620 m); *ceiling:* 34,000 ft (10,360 m); *range:* 3,749 miles (6,033 km); *armament:* –; *crew:* 5; *payload:* 345 passengers or 220,967 lb (100,228 kg)

ANTONOV An-26
Nation: USSR; *manufacturer:* State Industries; *type:* transport; *year:* 1969; *engine:* two Ivchenko AI-24T turboprops, 2,820 hp each; *wingspan:* 95 ft 9 in (29.20 m); *length:* 78 ft 1 in (23.80 m); *height:* 28 ft 2 in (8.58 m); *weight:* 52,911 lb (24,000 kg) (loaded); *maximum speed:* 270 mph (435 km/h) at 19,675 ft (6,000 m); *ceiling:* 26,575 ft (8,100 m); *range:* 1,398 miles (2,250 km); *armament:* –; *crew:* 5; *payload:* 121,250 lb (55,000 kg)

ILYUSHIN Il-76T
Nation: USSR; *manufacturer:* State Industries; *type:* transport; *year:* 1971; *engine:* four Soloviev D-30KP turbofans, 26,455 lb (12,000 kg) thrust each; *wingspan:* 165 ft 8 in (50.50 m); *length:* 152 ft 11 in (46.59 m); *height:* 48 ft 5 in (14.76 m); *weight:* 374,785 lb (170,000 kg) (loaded); *maximum speed:* 528 mph (850 km/h) at 39,350 ft (9,000 m); *ceiling:* 50,850 ft (15,500 m); *range:* 3,100 miles (5,000 km); *armament:* –; *crew:* 3; *payload:* 88,185 lb (40,000 kg)

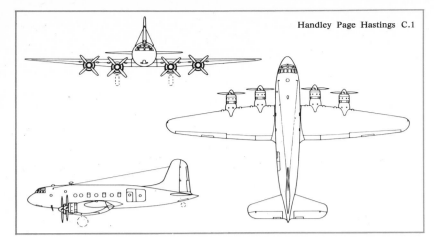
Handley Page Hastings C.1

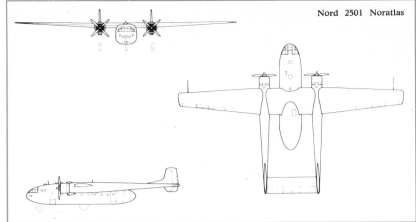
Nord 2501 Noratlas

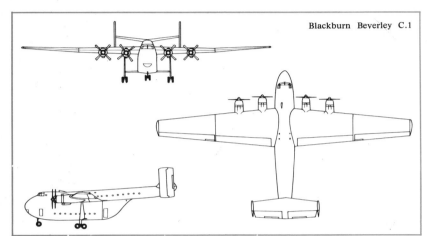
Blackburn Beverley C.1

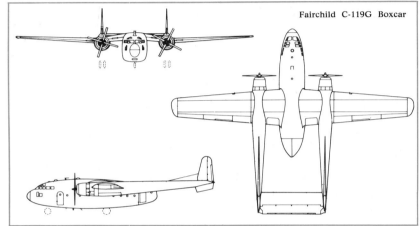
Fairchild C-119G Boxcar

Plate 239
European and American postwar transports: 1947–50

Immediately after the Second World War, the RAF paid close attention to the development of its Transport Command. Among the new designs was the Handley Page Hastings, a large four-engine piston-engine plane, built to replace the old Avro Yorks which were still in service. While the Hastings had already begun its career as an airliner, 25 being built for BOAC, while the Hastings had already begun its career as an airliner, 25 being built for BOAC, its military derivative was built in two basic versions: the C.1 of 1947 and the C.2 of 1950 of which 50 and 100 were built respectively. These aircraft stayed in first-line service as strategic transports until 1959 and for a large part of the sixties they were used in supporting roles.

This design had taken shape in 1945 and the prototype flew on 7th May 1946. Initial production started at the beginning of the following year and the first C.1 series aircraft flew on 25th April 1947. Its operational use started with the demanding and wearisome series of missions during the Berlin Airlift. Production was completed by several minor series aircraft: the Met.1 for meteorological reconnaissance;

the C.3 (four built for New Zealand) and the C.4 (four built as VIP transports).

From March 1956 a new and more specialised aircraft went into service with transport squadrons of the RAF: the Blackburn Beverley, the largest and most powerful military transport plane ever built in Britain. Until the beginning of the 1960s the forty-seven Beverley C.1s were the mainstay of Transport Command. The definitive prototype of this enormous four-engine high-wing plane with fixed undercarriage appeared on 14th June 1953 and the first C.1 series aircraft flew on 29th January 1955. Production continued until the beginning of 1958.

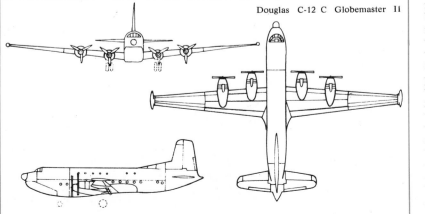
Douglas C-12 C Globemaster II

Another European transport plane which was usefully and widely employed was the French Nord 2501 Noratlas, a twin-engine twin-boom aircraft which, apart from flying with units of the *Armée de l'Air* and the *Aéronavale*, also equipped those of the *Luftwaffe*, for whom it was constructed under licence in Federal Germany.

The Noratlas prototype flew for the first time on 27th November 1950; production ran to 211 aircraft for the French air force and another 200 for the Federal German air force.

Subsequent derivants of the Nord 2501 were given more power by the addition of two small turbojets on the wingtips; this modification was made

to the model 2501 and the 2504 for the *Aéronavale* and to the 2508 in which the SNECMA .Hercules radials were replaced by American Pratt & Whitney engines. The Noratlas stayed in service for over twenty years.

The career of a transport plane which was very similar to the French aircraft was much longer: this was the American Fairchild C-119 Boxcar which was universally known as the "Flying Box-car". This was produced in 1947 and 1,112 were built up to October 1955. The C-119 was fully operational until the last years of the 1970s.

The basic design which led to the C-119 was commenced around the middle of the Second World War at the request of the USAAF which needed a tactical airlifter which would be particularly suited for troop carrying and heavy cargo. The aircraft which resulted from this specification was the C-82 Packet (first flight 10th September 1944) which was put into production, 220 being built. The C-82 was introduced too late to see service in the war but the needs which had led to this design still existed. Thus it was that in 1947 Fairchild developed an improved, more powerful, generally updated version of the C-82. This was designated C-119 and the prototype appeared in November. Four basic variants were built which were progressively updated and more powerful.

A contemporary of the C-119, but

used as a strategic transport plane, was the Douglas C-124 Globemaster, the last heavy piston-engine American military freighter. The prototype appeared on 27th November 1949, and production was based on two versions: the C-124A (204 built) and the C-124C, which was more powerful (243). The Globemaster II stayed in service until 1961.

Plate 240
American transports: 1953–63

The modernisation and strengthening of the USAF's Military Airlift Command continued uninterruptedly during the ensuing years. The twin-engine Fairchild C-132 Provider belonged to the same category as the C-119 and 300 were built, entering service in 1955. The origins of this aircraft went back to 1949 when the Chase Aircraft company designed a glider transport from which were derived two powered prototypes: the first had twin Pratt & Whitney R-2800 radial engines, the second had four General Electric J47 turbojets. The USAF chose the piston-engine variant for production and in 1952 five pre-series aircraft were ordered. The first of these aircraft, which was designated C-132B, flew in 1953. Development of the production programme was, however, held up by a financial crisis which hit the company and led to the temporary suspension of the project, but it was eventually started again by Fairchild, who completed production.

As regards strategic transports, the transition to turboprop aircraft was made with another heavy Douglas aircraft, the C-133 Cargomaster, which was the first of its category which could carry the giant strategic missiles of the 1950s in its fuselage. The programme was started in 1952 and the design followed the next year. There were no prototypes: the first C-133A production aircraft (35 of which were built) was flown on 29th August 1957. Two years later the USAF ordered a second variant to be developed, which was to be still more powerful and capable of carrying an increased payload. The first C-133B appeared on 31st October 1959 and deliveries of the fifteen built started the following year. The Cargomaster stayed in service until the late 1970s.

But the American aircraft which took over from the famous C-47 is the Lockheed C-130 Hercules, which is a versatile and reliable four-engine turboprop aircraft and is still, in the 1980s, considered to be the most widely used transport plane in the western world. It is used by no less than 32 nations and was still in production in 1979, with orders approaching a total of 1,700.

The Hercules has been built in a long series of variants and sub-types which have been employed in the most surprising roles: photo-reconnaissance, in-flight refuelling, air-sea rescue, and RPV launch and recover. But its role as a transport plane has been, and remains, its most important function.

On 2nd February 1951 a specification was issued which led to the Hercules. Fairchild, Douglas, Boeing and Lockheed entered aircraft for competitive evaluation and it was Lockheed's design which was chosen exactly five months later. The first of two prototypes was flown on 23rd August 1954.

The first variant was the A (7th April 1955) and the 219 initial series aircraft was followed by 242 C-130Bs which had more powerful engines and had longer range and could carry an increased payload. The third basic version was the E which was developed at the explicit request of the Military Airlift Command who wanted a transport which could supply bases outside the United States. The first C-130E flew on 25th August 1961 and deliveries of the 503 aircraft manufactured started in April of the following year. Production ended in February 1975.

The following basic variant was the H model which had more powerful 4,910 hp T56 engines. It appeared on 8th December 1964 and was the model which was exported in the greatest numbers. In January 1978, 518 aircraft had been delivered with orders still pending. The *Aeronautica Militare Italiana* bought 14 Hercules C-130Hs which were put into service on 26th March 1972. Sixty-six C-130Ks were built for the RAF which were actually C-130Hs which had been modified by the installation of different, British, equipment and electronics; the first of these aircraft flew on 19th October 1966. The one thousand five-hundredth Hercules, a

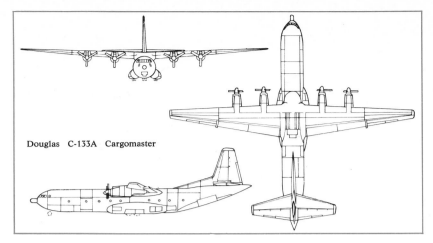

Douglas C-133A Cargomaster

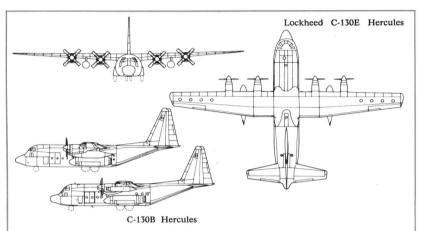

Lockheed C-130E Hercules

C-130B Hercules

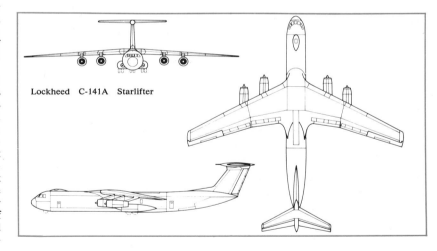

Lockheed C-141A Starlifter

C-130H, was delivered to Sudan on 13th March 1978. At that date 998 aircraft were in service in the USA and 433 in other countries.

Returning to the strategic transports, at the beginning of the 1950s the Lockheed C-141 Starlifter was built, a large four-jet-engine plane which was used by units of MATS (Military Air Transport Service). The first C-141A production aircraft flew on 17th December 1963, and deliveries of the 277 built started the following year. In 1976 a massive updating programme was started on these aircraft, elongating the fuselage and installing an in-flight refuelling system. The prototype YC-141B flew on 18th January 1977

and in June of the following year Lockheed implemented the conversion of all the C-141As to the new configuration: the production programme is scheduled to end in July 1982.

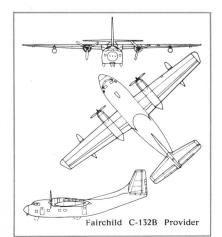

Fairchild C-132B Provider

Plate 241
European transports: 1964–76

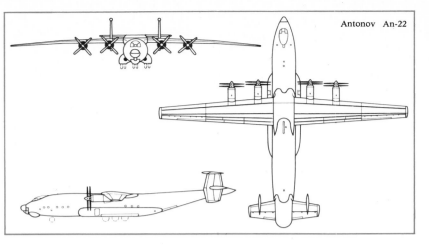
Antonov An-22

The USSR also put up good competition in the heavy transport sector. The designer who came to the fore during the 1960s was Oleg Antonov. Based on experience acquired building the An-10 and the An-12 (large four-engine turboprop aircraft which were used as airliners and also as military transports) he developed the mighty An-22 *Anteus*; this aircraft was shown at the Paris Air Show in 1965 and was the heaviest aircraft ever built at that date. The An-22 prototype was flown on 27th February of the same year. Production started in 1967 and by 1974 fifty aircraft had been completed. These served both with Aeroflot and with the *VVS*. They were designated COCK in NATO code.

The Short Belfast could be compared with the An-22, being also a military freighter designed to carry heavy loads, and ten were built for the Air Support Command of the RAF. The programme was started in February 1959 and the first prototype was produced in October. This aircraft flew on 5th January 1964 and was followed four months later by the second aircraft, which was the forerunner of the series C.Mk I. It entered service in January 1966.

At this time another useful European medium transport plane which had been designed and produced as a join venture by France and Federal Germany was the Transall 160, whose name was an abbreviated form of the name of the consortium Transporter Allianz. This programme had been started in January 1959 with an agreement between the two governments, and the companies of MBB, Aérospatiale and VFW-Fokker.

The prototype of this twin-engine turboprop flew for the first time on 25th February 1963, and series production started four years later. The basic variants were as follows: the C-160A (21st May 1965) pre-series aircraft of which 6 were built; the C-160D (first flight 2nd November 1967) for Federal Germany, of which 90 were built; the C-160F (13th April 1967) with 60 built for France; the C-160T which was similar to the preceding model but for export to Turkey (20); and the C-160Z for South Africa (9). In 1967 the Transall programme was extended for the development of a new, more powerful and improved variant.

Another European medium transport aircraft was developed in the first half of the 1970s: the Italian Aeritalia G.222, a versatile twin-engine turboprop aircraft which appeared in prototype on 18th July 1970; 44 were ordered two years later (August 1972) by the *Aeronautica Militare*. The first five series aircraft were delivered at the end of 1978, thus starting the replacement of the obsolescent C-119s. Meanwhile an intense promotional campaign had succeeded in gaining a consistent flow of orders from abroad: 1 aircraft for the United Arab Emirates (October 1976), 3 for Argentina (1974–76) four for Somalia, 20 for Libya. In 1976 a prototype of a fire-fighting variant was constructed which was designated G.222 SAMA. At the end of 1979 fifty G.222s had been delivered.

An equivalent of the G.222 is the de Havilland DHC-5 Buffalo, the prototype of which flew on 9th April 1964. Fifteen were ordered by Canada, 24 by Brazil and 16 by Peru in the initial DHC-5A version, and this twin-engine turboprop was updated in 1976 by a new variant, the DHC-5D which was more powerful and modern and was bought by Ecuador (2), Kenya (4), Togo (2), Zaïre (4) and Zambia (6).

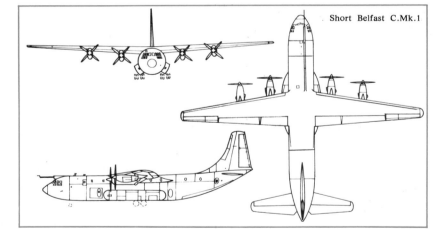
Short Belfast C.Mk.1

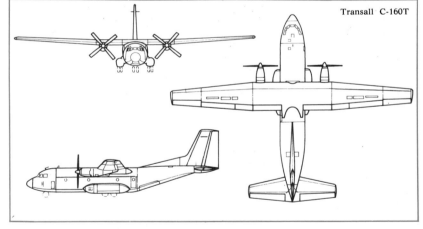
Transall C-160T

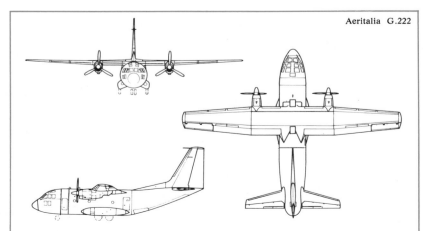
Aeritalia G.222

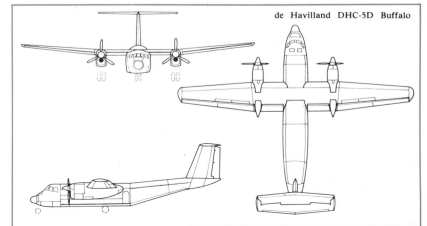
de Havilland DHC-5D Buffalo

Plate 242
American, Soviet and Japanese transports: 1968–71

Japan also took her place in the production of advanced transport aircraft to replace the obsolete piston-engine aircraft (including the Curtiss C-46) which were still in service at the end of the 1960s. Japan's new transport was the Kawasaki C-1, a twin-jet medium range aircraft which could carry nearly 8 tonnes of freight or 60 fully-equipped soldiers.

The programme was started in 1966 and two years later a contract was signed for the production of the prototype. This flew for the first time on 12th November 1970, and was followed two months later by the second experimental aircraft. At the end of proving trials and operational tests which lasted until March 1973, series production started with an initial order for 11 aircraft. The first Kawasaki C-1 was delivered in December 1974 and the last in March 1976. The second order brought the total to 36. At the end of the 1970s derivant versions of this aircraft were at the design stage. The C-1 programme has involved all the main Japanese aircraft manufacturers: Fuji for the outer wings, Mitsubishi for the fuselage, Shin Meiwa for the loading gear and Nikon Hikoki for the wing-control surfaces and the engine mountings.

The true giant of military transport aircraft of the 1980s is a product of the American aeronautical industry: the Lockheed C-5A Galaxy, a monstrous four-engine jet which can disgorge from its enormous forward ramp over 100 tonnes of cargo after having transported it for over 6,000 km (3,730 miles) at a speed of just under 1,000 km/h (620 mph). It is the largest aeroplane in the world.

The design took shape in 1963 and the three biggest American aircraft constructors competed for its development and production: Boeing, Douglas and Lockheed. In October 1965 Lockheed won the competition, and the construction of the first prototype started in August the following year.

The test flight was carried out on 30th June 1968. Production started some time later with the first of a series of orders from the USAF which was to bring the total to 81 aircraft. The last of these was delivered in May 1973. At the end of the 1970s, in response to requests for a new version of the Galaxy, Lockheed announced that within three years it would be able to deliver an even more powerful and capacious variant of the aircraft.

Contemporaries of the Galaxy, although they were generally inferior, were the Soviet Antonov An-26 and the Ilyushin Il-76 (designated respectively CURL and CANDID in NATO code). The former appeared in 1969 at the Paris Air Show and was classified by western observers as a variant of the well-known twin turboprop An-24 (which had been constructed ten years earlier). None the less, although the configuration and general structure were the same as in the earlier aircraft, the An-26 was an almost completely new design, developed to meet the most stringent requirements. It was particularly noteworthy for its versatility, and it could be easily adapted from the role of cargo carrier to paradropping, passenger transport or air-ambulance. Apart from being used with units of the *VVS* and Aeroflot, the An-26 went into service with the air forces of Yugoslavia, Poland and Bangladesh.

The Ilyushin Il-76T was even more specialised and up to date, powered by four jet engines, and made its first appearance at the Paris Air Show in May 1971, having had its first flight only six weeks previously on 25th March. According to western observers' estimates this aircraft can carry a 40-tonnes load for a distance of 5,000 km (3,100 miles) in less than six hours' flying time, and apart from this it can operate from semi-prepared landing strips. As well as being used by Aeroflot, the Il-76T has been observed with first-line units of Soviet military aviation as a replacement for the Antonov An-12.

In addition to the basic transport version, in-flight refuelling variants, strategic bombers and long range maritime reconnaissance variants of the Il-76 are planned for entry into service during the 1980s.

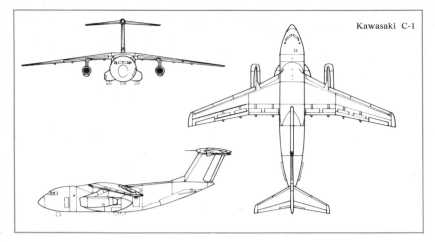
Kawasaki C-1

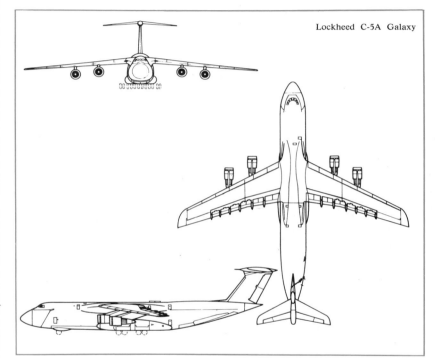
Lockheed C-5A Galaxy

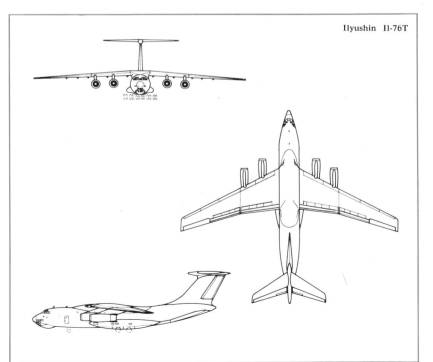
Ilyushin Il-76T

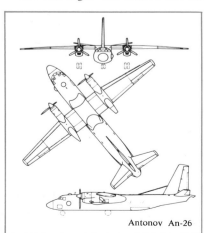
Antonov An-26

Plate 243

Engines of the 1960s

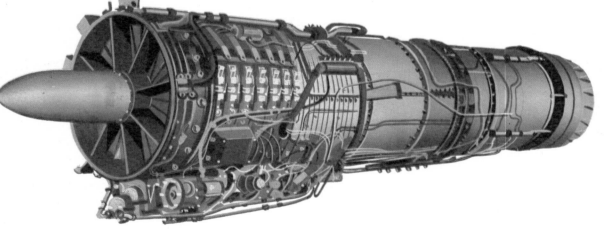

BRISTOL SIDDELEY OLYMPUS – 1953 (GB)
Series production of the Bristol Olympus began in 1953. This engine was developed to give the Avro Vulcan strategic bomber more power, and many versions were developed. Thrust rose from 4,990 kg in the Olympus Mk 101 to 7,710 kg in the series 201 of 1958. The Olympus 101 engine had an axial flow 15-stage compressor with a 2-stage turbine; maximum diameter 103.9 cm; length 261.1 cm; dry weight 1,632 kg; consumption at maximum power 0.8 kg of fuel per kg of thrust.

BRISTOL SIDDELEY ORPHEUS – 1954 (GB)
One of the most widely used medium power turbojets of the 1950s and 1960s, the Orpheus, had its first test flight in July 1955, when it powered the prototype of the Folland Gnat fighter, The 1,490 kg thrust of the original Orpheus engine was increased by over 100 per cent in later production models. Among the aircraft which were powered by the Orpheus was the Fiat G.91 (up to the G.91 Y variant). The Mk 803 engines had an axial flow 7-stage compressor and single-stage turbine; maximum diameter 82.3 cm; length 191.6 cm; dry weight 378 kg; consumption at maximum power 1.08 kg of fuel per kg of thrust.

GENERAL ELECTRIC J79 – 1958 (USA)
This turbojet engine was used in the most powerful American combat planes of the 1950s and 1960s (such as the Lockheed F-104, the McDonnell F-4 Phantom II and the Convair B-58 Hustler strategic bomber). The J79 was the first variable stator turbojet to be developed by the United States aircraft industry. J79 engines in the range 7,000 – 8,000 kg thrust with afterburner were constructed under licence in Federal Germany, Canada, Japan, Belgium and Italy. The J79-GE-17 engine had an axial flow 17-stage compressor and 3-stage turbine; maximum diameter 99.2 cm; length 530.1 cm; dry weight 1,740 kg; maximum power, with afterburner, 8,120 kg thrust.

SNECMA ATAR 9 – 1958 (F)
This was the turbojet which powered the most outstanding French combat planes of the 1950s and 1960s: the Mirage jets. The engine was designed by the "Atar group" (Atelier Aéronautique de Rickenbach) which was originally formed by a group of German scientists headed by the ex-director of BMW, Hermann Oestrich, and which subsequently became part of SNECMA. This engine produced thrust in the range of 7,000 kg and several increasingly powerful versions were developed. The SNECMA ATAR 9 had an axial flow 9-stage compressor and 2-stage turbine; maximum diameter 102 cm; length 627 cm; dry weight 1,250 kg; consumption at maximum power 2.075 kg of fuel per kg of thrust.

Grumman F8F Bearcat-1946, USA (plate 187)

Grumman F7F Tigercat-USA (plate 187)

North American F-82 Twin Mustang-1946, USA (plate 187)

Grumman F9F Panther-1947, USA (plate 189)

North American T-28-1949, USA (plate 230)

Douglas C-124 Globemaster-1949, USA (plate 239)

Gloster Meteor N.F.11-1950, GB (plate 191)

Ilyushin Il-28-1950, USSR (plate 217)

Nord 2501 Noratlas-1950, F (plate 239)

Vought F7U Cutlass-1951, USA (plate 189)

de Havilland Chipmunk-1951, GB (plate 230)

Grumman F9F Cougar-1953, USA (plate 189)

Dassault Mystère IV-A-1952, F (plate 193)

Douglas F4D Skyray-1954, USA (plate 197)

Douglas A-4F Skyhawk-1954, USA (plate 214)

Saab 29-1954, S (plate 203)

Saab 35 Draken-1955, S (plate 203)

Hawker Hunter-1955, GB (plate 196)

Avro Vulcan-1955, GB (plate 219)

Gloster Javelin-1956, GB (plate 196)

Hawker Hunter T.7-1956, GB (plate 196)

Dassault Super Mystère B-2-1956 F (plate 193)

Hispano Saeta HA-200-1956, E (plate 232)

511

Photographic appendix

Handley Page Victor-1956, GB (plate 219)

North American FJ-2-1956, USA (plate 194)

Supermarine Scimitar-1957, GB (plate 200)

Douglas C-133 Cargomaster-1957, USA (plate 240)

Vickers Valiant-1957, GB (plate 219)

Dassault Etendard IV/M-1958, F (plate 204)

Hawker Siddeley Buccaneer-1958, GB (plate 214)

Hawker Siddeley Buccaneer-1958, GB (plate 214)

Lockheed F-104 Starfighter-1958, USA (plate 198)

North American T2-1958, USA (plate 233)

North American A-5 Vigilante-1958, USA (plate 221)

Lockheed Hercules C-130-1958, USA (plate 240)

Fiat G.91 R-1958, I (plate 227)

Mikoyan-Gurevich MiG-21-1958, USSR (plate 199)

Grumman OV-1 Mohawk-1959, USA (plate 227)

Grumman S-2E Tracker-1954, USA (plate 212)

Grumman E2-A Hawkeye-1960, USA (plate 228)

Breguet 1150 Atlantic-1961, F (plate 225)

Dassault Mirage III-R-1961, F (plate 204)

Boeing B-52 Stratofortress-1958, USA (plate 221)

English Electric Lightning-1961, GB (plate 202)

Transall C.160-1963, F-G (plate 241)

Lockheed S.R.71-1964, USA (plate 226)

Short Belfast-1964, GB (plate 241)

Aermacchi M.B.326-1970, I (plate 232)

Antonov An-22 Antei-1965, USSR (plate 241)

General Dynamics F-111-1964, USA (plate 221)

Rockwell OV-10 Bronco-1973, USA (plate 227)

Dassault Mirage IV-A-1963, F (plate 219)

Hawker Siddeley Harrier-1967, GB (plate 200)

SIAI Marchetti SF.260-1966, I (plate 235)

McDonnell F-4 Phantom II-1967, USA (plate 201)

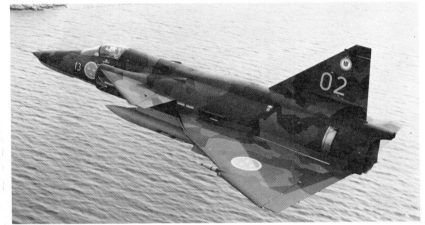

Saab A137 Viggen-1971, S (plate 203)

Sukhoi Su-15-1967, USSR (plate 207)

Shin Meiwa-1968, I (plate 224)

IA-58 Pucarà-1974, RA (plate 215)

Sepecat Jaguar-1968, F-GB (plate 206)

BAe Bulldog-1969, GB (plate 254)

Lockheed C-5 Galaxy-1968, USA (plate 242)

McDonnell Douglas F-15 Eagle-1974, USA (plate 208)

Alpha Jet-1973, F-G (plate 235)

General Dynamics F-16-1976, USA (plate 208)

Tornado MRCA-1974, G-GB-I (plate 206)

IAI Kfir C2-1975, IL (plate 205)

Embraer Bandeirante-1978, BR (plate 229)

5.

MILITARY AIRCRAFT FOR THE YEAR 2000

At the Farnborough Air Show in September 1988 the West had its first opportunity of seeing the MiG-29 Fulcrum, one of the most advanced fighter aircraft of the Soviet Union, of which only approximate information had been available until then on its characteristics and performance. The display of the Fulcrum was a particularly significant occasion in aviation, as it was the first sign of *glasnost*, or policy of openness, which was the new official line in Moscow and which, together with *perestroika* (restructuring), promised to put an end to 40 years of rivalry and antagonism between the two superpowers.

This historic change in the arms policy pursued by the two opposing blocs since the end of the Second World War, has already been dubbed the 'New East-West Revolution.' It is still far from clear what the final effects will be in political, economic and social terms. However, there is no doubt that the sweeping changes of the last decade have already altered the international balance of power, and the long dreamt-of process of disarmament does seem to have begun.

Positive signs of this thawing in relations are already visible in the world of aviation (the air force traditionally being regarded as the strategic weapon par excellence). This is particularly true in the United States, where changes in international policy on the one hand and financial constraints on the other have led to drastic cuts in military spending and hence uncertainty over the future of the most ambitious programmes.

The military potential of the world air forces in the scenario of the 1990s is nonetheless impressive. Major developments have taken place in the last decade, not just in response to strategic requirements, but also as a result of the staggering acceleration of technological research, particularly in the development of new materials and electronics. This progress is directly visible in the most advanced international projects of recent times: some are intended to optimise the performance of aircraft of 'traditional' design, which are most suitable for tactical use, and others have led to the creation of fighting machines which almost resemble something out of science fiction.

Of the latter, the American Northrop B-2 is undoubtedly the most sophisticated example, not just because of its concept, but mainly because of the considerable financial and research commitment which the programme required. Even if the future of the 'stealth bomber' now hangs in the balance, its development nevertheless represents a technological goal for the rest of the world to follow.

The United States are undoubtedly ahead of their former rivals, the Russians, as far as this particular project is concerned. The latter, however, have followed close behind, as can be seen from the latest additions to the prolific MiG, Sukhoi and Tupolev families. These are lethal weapons in their respective roles, fully capable of competing with their Western counterparts.

Whilst the United States and Soviet Union are still the undoubted leaders of the aeronautical world, other European countries are playing an increasingly important role, as can be seen from the military programmes of the French and Swedish aeronautical industries and international consortia of other countries. The powerful and sophisticated Rafale is a model of efficiency, even if success on the market has been delayed for purely economic reasons. Similarly, the Swedish Gripen was the first to exploit the clever formula of 'light multirole fighter,' and the EFA European fighter should prove a worthy successor to the Tornado at the end of the century.

This brief survey can of course only include the major programmes and most advanced machines, the ones with the highest 'added value' in technological and military terms. However, along with these undisputed leaders, the world market has witnessed unprecedented growth in the no less important sector of tactical aircraft, to which modern military theories attribute equally demanding roles. Here too, recent developments in electronics and progress in the materials and power plants have transformed the industry. One example speaks for all, the British Harrier (the first vertical takeoff fighter aircraft), whose complex technology has even been adopted by North American industry and which has been turned into a formidable weapon whose potential has yet to be fully explored.

Weaponry has kept pace with these other developments and electronics has played a vital role in this sector, too. The fighter aircraft of today, with its sophisticated missiles with active guidance and 'smart bombs', its fire control systems and ECM equipment, has virtually been transformed into a complex data processing unit, in which the pilot increasingly assumes the role of passive supervisor, carried on board purely to intervene in situations which the machine has not been programmed to handle.

If this represents the present, what will the future be like? At the end of the twentieth century, many are asking whether the development of aviation, formerly accelerated by military events, is destined to stop, or at least to slow down considerably. To give an answer to such a question would be premature at this stage. It is, however, reasonable to suppose that the growth of the aeroplane will, as in the past, be mainly fostered by the demands of civil development. This was the case in the golden age of aviation between the two world wars, and again to a certain extent in the 1960s, at the height of the first phase of the space race, in the bid to land the first man on the Moon. It could happen again, at the end of the second millennium, after barely a century of 'heavier-than-air' flight. The gateway to the year 2000 opens decidedly out on to space. The radical change in attitude between East and West, with all that has already been done to prepare the way for strategic disarmament, could cause all the accumulated resources and technology invested in the aeronautical field to be channelled into bridging the thin gap between the aeroplane and the spaceship, in order to abolish it altogether.

McDONNELL-DOUGLAS F-15E EAGLE
Nation: USA; *manufacturer:* McDonnell Aircraft Co; *type:* attack/air superiority; *year:* 1988; *engine:* two Pratt & Whitney F100-PW-100 turbofans, 23,829 lb (10,809 kg) thrust each; *wingspan:* 42 ft 10 in (13.05 m); *length:* 63 ft 9 in (19.43 m); *height:* 18 ft 5 in (5.63 m); *weight:* 81,000 lb (36,741 kg) (loaded); *maximum speed:* 1,650 mph (2,655 km/h) at over 35,990 ft (10,970 m); *ceiling:* 60,000 ft (18,300 m); *range:* 3,570 miles (5,745 km); *armament:* 1 × M61A1 Vulcan 20 mm cannon; 23,499 lb (10,659 kg) of stores; *crew:* 2

Harrier II GR. Mk. 7

McDONNELL-DOUGLAS/BAe AV-8B HARRIER II/HARRIER GR Mk. 7
Nation: USA, Britain; *manufacturer:* McDonnell-Douglas Corp./BAe; *type:* strike; *year:* 1984 (GR Mk. 7 1989); *engine:* Rolls-Royce F402-RR-406A Pegasus turbofan, 21,450 lb (9,729 kg) thrust (GR Mk. 7 Rolls-Royce Pegasus Mk. 105 turbofan), 21,750 lb (9,866 kg) thrust; *wingspan:* 30 ft 4 in (9.25 m); *length:* 46 ft 4 in (14.12 m); *height:* 11 ft 8 in (3.56 m); *weight:* 19,185 lb (8,702 kg) (vertical takeoff); 31,000 lb (14,061 kg) (short takeoff); *maximum speed:* 661 mph (1,075 km/h) at sea level; *ceiling:* 50,000 ft (over 15,240 m); *range:* 553 miles (889 km); *armament:* 7,000 lb (3,175 kg) of stores (vertical takeoff), 17,000 lb (7,710 kg) of stores (short takeoff); *crew:* 1

AV-8B Harrier II

LOCKHEED F-117A
Nation: USA; *manufacturer:* Lockheed Aircraft Corp; *type:* reconnaissance/attack; *year:* 1983; *engine:* two modified General Electric F404-GE-400 turbofans, 10,800 lb (4,899 kg) thrust each; *wingspan:* 45 ft (13.7 m); *length:* 25 ft (7.6 m); *height:* 16 ft (4.9 m); *weight:* 40,000 lb (approx. 18,000 kg) (loaded); *maximum speed:* 700 mph (1,127 km/h) at low altitude; *ceiling:*−; *range:*−; *armament:* 4,400 lb (2,000 kg) of internal stores instead of search sensors; air-to-surface missiles; *crew:* 1

*Estimated data

521

Plate 245

France and Russia in pursuit of air superiority

DASSAULT MIRAGE 2000N
Nation: France; *manufacturer:* Dassault-Breguet; *type:* attack; *year:* 1987; *engine:* Snecma M53-P2 turbofan, 21,385 lb (9,708 kg) thrust with afterburning; *wingspan:* 30 ft 5 in (9.26 m); *length:* 47 ft 9 in (14.55 m); *height:* 16 ft 11 in (5.15 m); *weight:* – ; *maximum speed:* 1,453 mph (2,338 km/h) at altitude; *ceiling:* – ; *range:* – ; *armament:* 1 × type ASMP air-to-surface nuclear missile; *crew:* 2

MIKOYAN-GUREVICH MiG-29
Nation: USSR; *manufacturer:* State Industries; *type:* interceptor; *year:* 1983; *engine:* two Tumansky R-33D turbofans, 18,300 lb (8,300 kg) thrust each with afterburning; *wingspan:* 37 ft 3 in (11.36 m); *length:* 56 ft 10 in (17.32 m); *height:* 15 ft 6 in (4.73 m); *weight:* 39,700 lb (18,000 kg) (loaded); *maximum speed:* 1,520 mph (2,440 km/h); *ceiling:* 56,000 ft (17,000 m); *range:* 1,300 miles (2,100 km); *armament:* 1 × 30 mm cannon, 6 wing pylons for AA-10 or AA-11 missiles, or other stores; *crew:* 1

MIKOYAN-GUREVICH MiG-31
Nation: USSR; *manufacturer:* State Industries; *type:* interceptor; *year:* 1981; *engine:* two Tumansky R-31F turbojets, 30,865 lb (14,000 kg) thrust each with afterburning; *wingspan:* 45 ft 11 in (14 m); *length:* 70 ft 6 in (21.50 m); *height:* 18 ft 6 in (5.63 m); *weight:* 90,725 lb (41,150 kg) (loaded); *maximum speed:* 1,568 mph (2,553 km/h) at altitude; *ceiling:* 75,500 ft (23,000 m); *range:* 1,305 miles (2,100 km); *armament:* 8 × AA-9 air-to-air missiles, or 4 × AA-9 missiles and 4 × R-23R or R-60 missiles; *crew:* 2

YAKOVLEV Yak-38
Nation: USSR; *manufacturer:* State Industries; *type:* attack; *year:* 1975; *engine:* one Lyulka AL-21 turbojet 17,985 lb (8,160 kg) thrust, two Koliesov ZM turbojets 7,875 lb (3,570 kg) thrust each; *wingspan:* 24 ft (7.32 m); *length:* 50 ft 10 in (15.50 m); *height:* 14 ft 4 in (4.37 m); *weight:* 25,795 lb (11,700 kg) (loaded); *maximum speed:* 608 mph (978 km/h) at sea level; *ceiling:* 39,375 ft (12,000 m); *range:* 230 miles (370 km); *armament:* 7,935 lb (3,600 kg) of stores; *crew:* 1

*Estimated data

SUKHOI Su-22
Nation: USSR; *manufacturer:* State Industries; *type:* attack; *year:* 1981; *engine:* Tumansky R-29B turbojet, 23,350 lb (11,500 kg) thrust with afterburning; *wingspan:* 45 ft 3 in (13.80 m); *length:* 61 ft 6 in (18.75 m); *height:* 16 ft 5 in (5 m); *weight:* 39,020 lb (17,700 kg) (loaded); *maximum speed:* 1,380 mph (2,220 km/h) at altitude; *ceiling:* 59,050 ft (18,000 m); *range:* – ; *armament:* 2 × NR-30 mm cannon; 7,000 lb (3,175 kg) of stores; *crew:* 1 ▶

*Estimated data

SUKHOI Su-24
Nation: USSR; *manufacturer:* State Industries; *type:* attack; *year:* 1974; *engine:* two Lyulka AL-21F turbofans, approx. 24,700 lb (11,340 kg) thrust with afterburning; *wingspan:* 57 ft 5 in (17.50 m) (maximum), 34 ft 5 in (10.50 m) (minimum); *length:* 69 ft 10 in (21.29 m); *height:* 19 ft 8 in (6 m); *weight:* 90,390 lb (41,000 kg) (loaded); *maximum speed:* 1,440 mph (2,315 km/h) at 36,000 ft (11,000 m); *ceiling:* 54,135 ft (16,500 m); *range:* 805 miles (1,300 km); *armament:* 1 × 30 mm cannon; 24,250 lb (11,000 kg) of stores; *crew:* 2

*Estimated data

SUKHOI Su-25
Nation: USSR; *manufacturer:* State Industries; *type:* attack/close support; ▶ *year:* 1981; *engine:* two Tumansky R-13-300 turbojets, 9,340 lb (4,237 kg) thrust each; *wingspan:* 46 ft 11 in (14.30 m); *length:* 50 ft 7 in (15.40 m); *height:* 15 ft 9 in (4.80 m); *weight:* 39,950 lb (18,120 kg) (loaded); *maximum speed:* 608 mph (980 km/h) at sea level; *ceiling:* – ; *range:* 345 miles (556 km); *armament:* 1 × 30 mm cannon; 9,920 lb (4,500 kg) of stores; *crew:* 1

*Estimated data

SUKHOI Su-27UB
Nation: USSR; *manufacturer:* State Industries; *type:* multirole/operational trainer; *year:* 1983; *engine:* two Tumansky R-32 turbofans, 29,955 lb (13,600 kg) thrust with afterburning; *wingspan:* 48 ft 3 in (14.70 m); *length:* 70 ft 10 in (21.60 m); *height:* 18 ft (5.50 m); *weight:* 60,000 lb (27,200 kg) (loaded); *maximum speed:* 1,555 mph (2,500 km/h) at altitude; *ceiling:* – ; *range:* 930 miles (1,500 km); *armament:* 1 × 30 mm cannon, 13,225 lb (6,000 kg) of stores; *crew:* 2

*Estimated data

Plate 247

Europe looks to its own defence

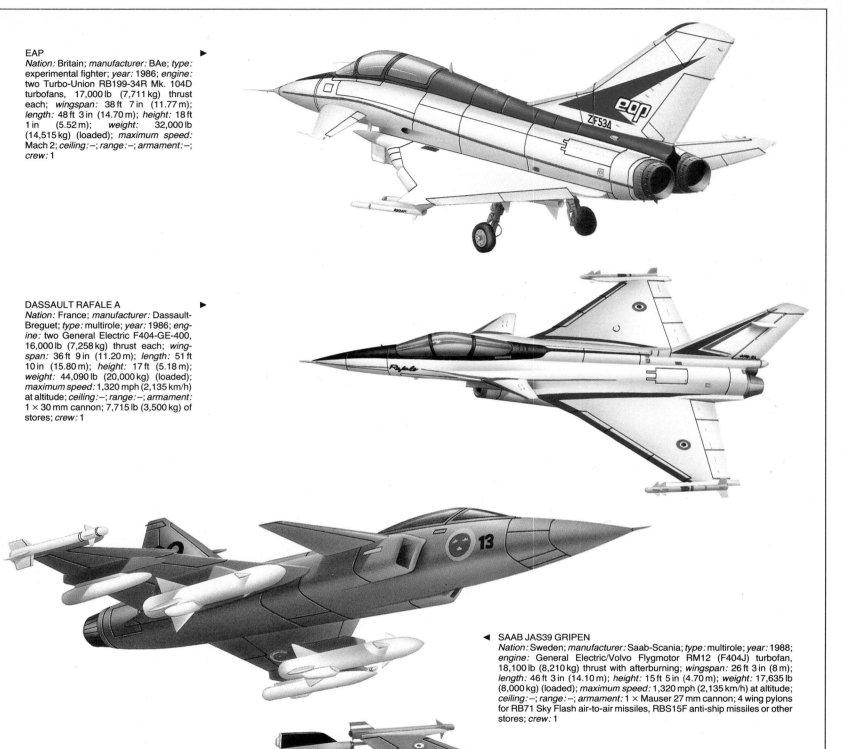

EAP
Nation: Britain; *manufacturer:* BAe; *type:* experimental fighter; *year:* 1986; *engine:* two Turbo-Union RB199-34R Mk. 104D turbofans, 17,000 lb (7,711 kg) thrust each; *wingspan:* 38 ft 7 in (11.77 m); *length:* 48 ft 3 in (14.70 m); *height:* 18 ft 1 in (5.52 m); *weight:* 32,000 lb (14,515 kg) (loaded); *maximum speed:* Mach 2; *ceiling:* –; *range:* –; *armament:* –; *crew:* 1

DASSAULT RAFALE A
Nation: France; *manufacturer:* Dassault-Breguet; *type:* multirole; *year:* 1986; *engine:* two General Electric F404-GE-400, 16,000 lb (7,258 kg) thrust each; *wingspan:* 36 ft 9 in (11.20 m); *length:* 51 ft 10 in (15.80 m); *height:* 17 ft (5.18 m); *weight:* 44,090 lb (20,000 kg) (loaded); *maximum speed:* 1,320 mph (2,135 km/h) at altitude; *ceiling:* –; *range:* –; *armament:* 1 × 30 mm cannon; 7,715 lb (3,500 kg) of stores; *crew:* 1

SAAB JAS39 GRIPEN
Nation: Sweden; *manufacturer:* Saab-Scania; *type:* multirole; *year:* 1988; *engine:* General Electric/Volvo Flygmotor RM12 (F404J) turbofan, 18,100 lb (8,210 kg) thrust with afterburning; *wingspan:* 26 ft 3 in (8 m); *length:* 46 ft 3 in (14.10 m); *height:* 15 ft 5 in (4.70 m); *weight:* 17,635 lb (8,000 kg) (loaded); *maximum speed:* 1,320 mph (2,135 km/h) at altitude; *ceiling:* –; *range:* –; *armament:* 1 × Mauser 27 mm cannon; 4 wing pylons for RB71 Sky Flash air-to-air missiles, RBS15F anti-ship missiles or other stores; *crew:* 1

AMX
Nation: Italy, Brazil; *manufacturer:* AMX (Aeritalia-Aermacchi SpA/Embraer); *type:* close support; *year:* 1988, *engine:* Rolls-Royce Spey MK807 turbofan, 11,030 lb (5,003 kg) thrust; *wingspan:* 29 ft 1 in (8.87 m); *length:* 44 ft 6 in (13.57 m); *height:* 14 ft 11 in (12.55 m); *weight:* 27,558 lb (12,500 kg) (loaded); *maximum speed:* 654 mph (1,052 km/h) at sea level; *ceiling:* 42,650 ft (13,000 m); *range:* 550 miles (890 km); *armament:* 1 or 2 cannon, 8,377 lb (3,800 kg) of stores; *crew:* 1

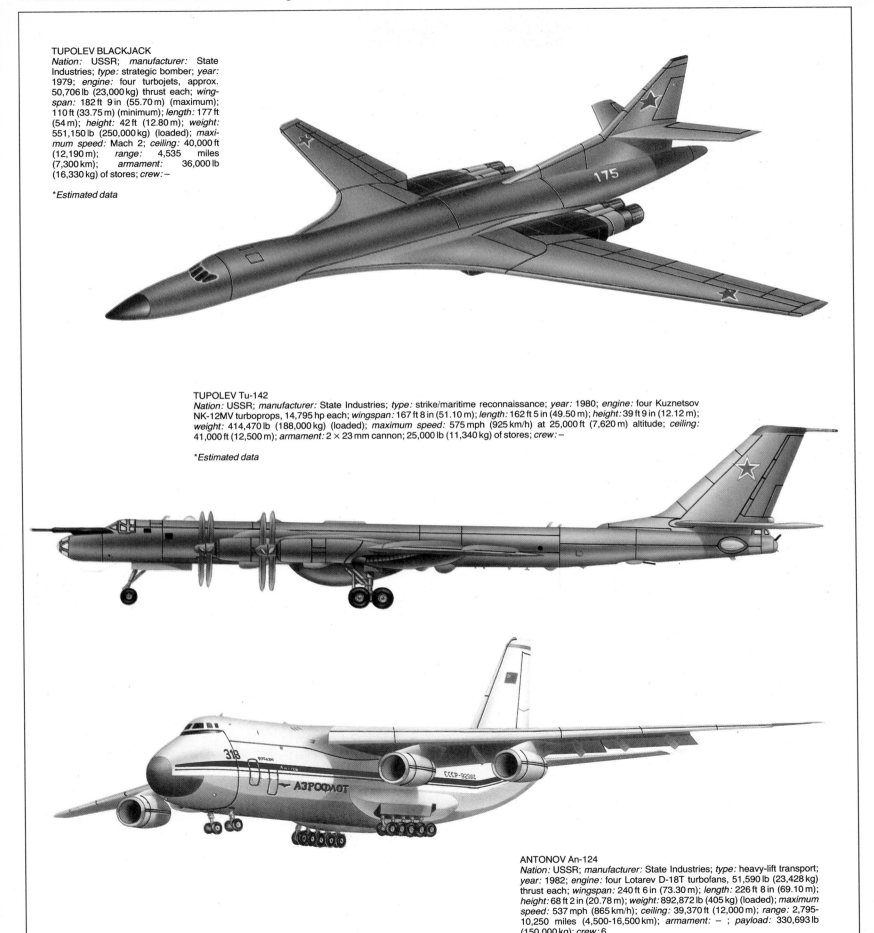

TUPOLEV BLACKJACK
Nation: USSR; *manufacturer:* State Industries; *type:* strategic bomber; *year:* 1979; *engine:* four turbojets, approx. 50,706 lb (23,000 kg) thrust each; *wingspan:* 182 ft 9 in (55.70 m) (maximum); 110 ft (33.75 m) (minimum); *length:* 177 ft (54 m); *height:* 42 ft (12.80 m); *weight:* 551,150 lb (250,000 kg) (loaded); *maximum speed:* Mach 2; *ceiling:* 40,000 ft (12,190 m); *range:* 4,535 miles (7,300 km); *armament:* 36,000 lb (16,330 kg) of stores; *crew:* –

*Estimated data

TUPOLEV Tu-142
Nation: USSR; *manufacturer:* State Industries; *type:* strike/maritime reconnaissance; *year:* 1980; *engine:* four Kuznetsov NK-12MV turboprops, 14,795 hp each; *wingspan:* 167 ft 8 in (51.10 m); *length:* 162 ft 5 in (49.50 m); *height:* 39 ft 9 in (12.12 m); *weight:* 414,470 lb (188,000 kg) (loaded); *maximum speed:* 575 mph (925 km/h) at 25,000 ft (7,620 m) altitude; *ceiling:* 41,000 ft (12,500 m); *armament:* 2 × 23 mm cannon; 25,000 lb (11,340 kg) of stores; *crew:* –

*Estimated data

ANTONOV An-124
Nation: USSR; *manufacturer:* State Industries; *type:* heavy-lift transport; *year:* 1982; *engine:* four Lotarev D-18T turbofans, 51,590 lb (23,428 kg) thrust each; *wingspan:* 240 ft 6 in (73.30 m); *length:* 226 ft 8 in (69.10 m); *height:* 68 ft 2 in (20.78 m); *weight:* 892,872 lb (405 kg) (loaded); *maximum speed:* 537 mph (865 km/h); *ceiling:* 39,370 ft (12,000 m); *range:* 2,795-10,250 miles (4,500-16,500 km); *armament:* – ; *payload:* 330,693 lb (150,000 kg); *crew:* 6

Plate 249

Research is paramount in the USA – not just for the B-2

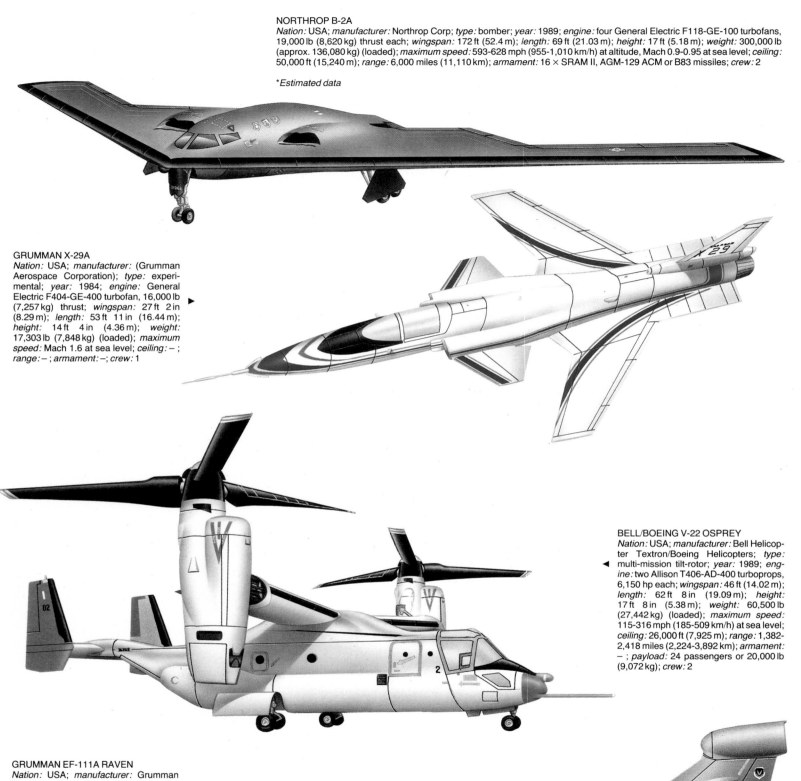

NORTHROP B-2A
Nation: USA; *manufacturer:* Northrop Corp; *type:* bomber; *year:* 1989; *engine:* four General Electric F118-GE-100 turbofans, 19,000 lb (8,620 kg) thrust each; *wingspan:* 172 ft (52.4 m); *length:* 69 ft (21.03 m); *height:* 17 ft (5.18 m); *weight:* 300,000 lb (approx. 136,080 kg) (loaded); *maximum speed:* 593-628 mph (955-1,010 km/h) at altitude, Mach 0.9-0.95 at sea level; *ceiling:* 50,000 ft (15,240 m); *range:* 6,000 miles (11,110 km); *armament:* 16 × SRAM II, AGM-129 ACM or B83 missiles; *crew:* 2

*Estimated data

GRUMMAN X-29A
Nation: USA; *manufacturer:* (Grumman Aerospace Corporation); *type:* experimental; *year:* 1984; *engine:* General Electric F404-GE-400 turbofan, 16,000 lb (7,257 kg) thrust; *wingspan:* 27 ft 2 in (8.29 m); *length:* 53 ft 11 in (16.44 m); *height:* 14 ft 4 in (4.36 m); *weight:* 17,303 lb (7,848 kg) (loaded); *maximum speed:* Mach 1.6 at sea level; *ceiling:* – ; *range:* – ; *armament:* – ; *crew:* 1

BELL/BOEING V-22 OSPREY
Nation: USA; *manufacturer:* Bell Helicopter Textron/Boeing Helicopters; *type:* multi-mission tilt-rotor; *year:* 1989; *engine:* two Allison T406-AD-400 turboprops, 6,150 hp each; *wingspan:* 46 ft (14.02 m); *length:* 62 ft 8 in (19.09 m); *height:* 17 ft 8 in (5.38 m); *weight:* 60,500 lb (27,442 kg) (loaded); *maximum speed:* 115-316 mph (185-509 km/h) at sea level; *ceiling:* 26,000 ft (7,925 m); *range:* 1,382-2,418 miles (2,224-3,892 km); *armament:* – ; *payload:* 24 passengers or 20,000 lb (9,072 kg); *crew:* 2

GRUMMAN EF-111A RAVEN
Nation: USA; *manufacturer:* Grumman Aerospace Corp; General Dynamics Co; *type:* electronic warfare; *year:* 1981, *engine:* two Pratt & Whitney TF30-P-3 turbofans, 18,500 lb (8,391 kg) thrust each; *wingspan:* 63 ft (19.20 m) (maximum), 31 ft 11 in (9.74 m) (minimum); *length:* 76 ft (23.16 m); *height:* 20 ft (6.10 m); *weight:* 89,947 lb (40,346 kg) (loaded); *maximum speed:* 1,412 mph (2,272 km/h); *ceiling:* 45,000 ft (13,715 m); *range:* 229-929 miles (370-1,495 km); *armament:* – ; *crew:* 2

SIAI MARCHETTI S.211
Nation: Italy; *manufacturer:* SIAI Marchetti; *type:* trainer/light attack; *year:* 1981; *engine:* Pratt & Whitney Canada JT15D-4D turbofan, 2,500 lb (1,135 kg) thrust; *wingspan:* 27 ft 8 in (8.43 m); *length:* 30 ft 6 in (9.31 m); *height:* 12 ft 6 in (3.80 m); *weight:* 6,063-6,944 lb (2,750-3,150 kg); *maximum speed:* 460 mph (740 km/h); *ceiling:* 40,000 ft (12,200 m); *range:* 1,036 miles (1,668 km); *armament:* 1,455 lb (660 kg) of stores; *crew:* 2

KAWASAKI T-4
Nation: Japan; *manufacturer:* Kawasaki Jukogyo Kabishiki Kaisha; *type:* trainer; *year:* 1988; *engine:* two Ishikawajima-Harima XF3-30 turbojets, 3,670 lb (1,664 kg) thrust each; *wingspan:* 32 ft 7 in (9.94 m); *length:* 42 ft 8 in (13 m); *height:* 15 ft 1 in (4.60 m); *weight:* 12,125 lb (5,500 kg) (loaded); *maximum speed:* 645 mph (1,038 km/h) at sea level; *ceiling:* 50,000 ft (15,240 m); *range:* 1,036 miles (1,668 km); *armament:* 2,502 lb (1,135 kg) of stores; *crew:* 2

1A–63 PAMPA
Nation: Argentina; *manufacturer:* FMA; *type:* trainer; *year:* 1984; *engine:* Garrett TFE731-2-2N turbofan, 3,500 lb (1,589 kg) thrust; *wingspan:* 31 ft 9 in (9.68 m); *length:* 35 ft 9 in (10.90 m); *height:* 14 ft 1 in (4.29 m); *weight:* 11,023 lb (5,000 kg) (loaded); *maximum speed:* 469 mph (755 km/h) at sea level; 509 mph (819 km/h) at 22,965 ft (7,000 m); *ceiling:* 42,325 ft (12,900 m); *range:* 932 miles (1,500 km); *armament:* 1 × DEFA 30 mm cannon, 2,557 lb (1,160 kg) of stores; *crew:* 2

RFB FANTRAINER 600
Nation: (West) Germany; *manufacturer:* RFB; *type:* trainer; *year:* 1984; *engine:* Allison 250-C30 turboprop, 650 hp; *wingspan:* 31 ft 11 in (9.74 m); *length:* 31 ft 1 in (9.48 m); *height:* 10 ft 4 1/2 in (3.16 m); *weight:* 5,070 lb (2,300 kg) (loaded); *maximum speed:* 259 mph (417 km/h) at 18,000 ft (5,490 m); *ceiling:* 25,000 ft (7,620 m); *range:* 646 miles (1,040 km); *armament:* –; *crew:* 2

Plate 251

From the basic trainer to the ultra-light fighter

◀ BAe HAWK 200
Nation: Britain; *manufacturer:* BAe; *type:* multirole; *year:* 1987; *engine:* Rolls-Royce/Turboméca Adour Mk871 turbofan, 5,845 lb (2,651 kg) thrust; *wingspan:* 30 ft 10 in (9.39 m); *length:* 37 ft 4 in (11.38 m); *height:* 13 ft 8 in (4.16 m); *weight:* 20,065 lb (9,101 kg) (loaded); *maximum speed:* 644 mph (1,037 km/h) at sea level; *ceiling:* 50,000 ft (15,250 m); *range:* 554 miles (892 km); *armament:* 1 or 2 × 25 mm cannon; 7,716 lb (3,600 kg) of stores; *crew:* 1

McDONNELL-DOUGLAS/BAe T-45A GOSHAWK
Nation: USA, Britain; *manufacturer:* McDonnell Aircraft Co/BAe; *type:* trainer; *year:* 1988, *engine:* Rolls-Royce/Turboméca Adour Mk 861-49 turbofan, 5,450 lb (2,472 kg) thrust; *wingspan:* 30 ft 10 in (9.40 m); *length:* 39 ft 3 in (11.97 m); *height:* 13 ft 6 in (4.12 m); *weight:* 12,758 lb (5,787 kg) (loaded); *maximum speed:* 620 mph (997 km/h) at 8,000 ft (2,440 m); *ceiling:* 42,250 ft (12,875 m); *range:* 1,150 miles (1,850 km); *armament:* –; *crew:* 2 ▶

◀ SHORT S312 TUCANO T Mk.1
Nation: Britain, Brazil; *manufacturer:* Short Brothers Ltd/EMBRAER; *type:* trainer; *year:* 1986; *engine:* Garrett TPE331-12B turboprop, 1,100 hp; *wingspan:* 37 ft (11.28 m); *length:* 32.34 ft (9.86 m); *height:* 11.15 ft (3.40 m); *weight:* 5,952 lb (2,700 kg) (loaded); *maximum speed:* 315 mph (507 km/h) at 10,000 ft (3,050 m); *ceiling:* 34,000 ft (10,365 m); *range:* 1,035 miles (1,665 km); *armament:* 992 lb (450 kg) of stores; *crew:* 2

PILATUS PC-7
Nation: Switzerland; *manufacturer:* Pilatus Flugzeugwerke AG; *type:* trainer; *year:* 1978; *engine:* Pratt & Whitney Canada PT6A-25A turboprop, 650 hp; *wingspan:* 34 ft 1 in (10.40 m); *length:* 32 ft 1 in (9.78 m); *height:* 10 ft 6 in (3.21 m); *weight:* 5,952 lb (2,700 kg) (loaded); *maximum speed:* 256 mph (412 km/h) at 20,000 ft (6,100 m); *ceiling:* 26,000 ft (7,925 m); *range:* 1,634 miles (2,630 km); *armament:* 2,292 lb (1,040 kg) of stores; *crew:* 2 ▶

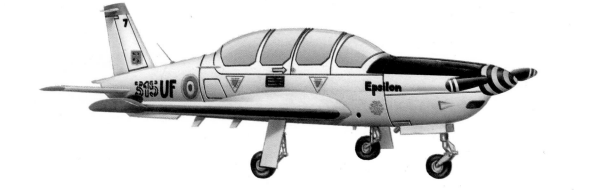

AÉROSPATIALE TB-30 EPSILON
Nation: France; *manufacturer:* Aérospatiale; *type:* trainer; *year:* 1983; *engine:* 300 hp, air-cooled, Textron Lycoming AE10-540-L1B5D flat-six (piston engine);
◀ *wingspan:* 26 ft (7.92 m); *length:* 24 ft 11 in (7.59 m); *height:* 8 ft 9 in (2.66 m); *weight:* 2,755 lb (1,250 kg) (loaded); *maximum speed:* 236 mph (378 km/h) at sea level; *ceiling:* 23,000 ft (7,010 m); *endurance:* 3 hours, 45 minutes; *armament:* 704 lb (320 kg) of stores; *crew:* 2

Plate 244
Western fighters from the Stealth Bomber to VTOLs

The power and versatility of the McDonnell-Douglas F-15 Eagle, which came into service in 1974, have earned it the reputation of the best interceptor in the West. This image can only be enhanced by the arrival of the latest and most sophisticated variant, the F-15E, the prototype of which appeared in December 1986. Originally designated Strike Eagle, it differs from the previous ones essentially in its role. If the F-15 started out as a single-seat air superiority fighter, the E version has been successfully turned into a two-seat dual-role aircraft. That is, a machine capable of carrying out long-range attack missions in all weathers, without compromising its proven air-to-air capabilities.

The most striking changes are to the avionics. The second crew-member has four multifunction displays for radar, weapon selection and monitoring of enemy activity; whereas the pilot, in addition to a latest-generation HUD (Head-Up Display), has three multifunction displays which control navigation, weapons delivery and on-board systems, including those regarding mission control and flight at very low altitude.

The F-15E was designed to exploit the potential of the aircraft's power plant and avionics. McDonnell-Douglas began developing the F-15E in 1982, production was authorised by the USAF on 24th February 1984, and it is planned to build 392.

While the strike capability of the F-15E is a highly successful addition to the original role for which the Eagle was designed, in the case of the AV8-B/Harrier II, development has been consistent with the initial intent. This powerful and original combat aircraft shows how it is possible to optimise the characteristics of an airframe, without changing its basic functions, namely attack, combined with the formidable potential of VTOL (vertical takeoff and landing).

The AV-8 programme started in the second half of the seventies, after McDonnell-Douglas acquired the licence to build the Hawker Siddeley (BAe) Harrier, the first vertical take-off combat aircraft in the world, which had been developed by the British company from 1957 and was in service with the US Marine Corps from the seventies. McDonnell-Douglas planned to develop an even more powerful machine from the Harrier, custom-built for the Marines. The programme started in collaboration with the British company and the first of the two YAV-8B prototypes flew on 9th November 1978. It was quite different from the original version in terms of structure, avionics and eng-

ines. The new wing in composite materials not only ensured greater manoeuvrability, but could hold more fuel and carry a heavier weapon load. The first AV-8B was rolled out on 16th October 1981 and the aircraft went into service on 12th January 1984. It is planned to build 300 single-seat AB-8Bs and 28 (TAV-8B) two-seat trainers. Towards the end of 1988, production focused on the AV-8D night-attack version with new avionics. The Spanish Navy has bought 12 specially-adapted aircraft (EAV-8B); the Italian Navy plans to use these machines on the Garibaldi aircraft carrier, and the RAF are to receive 94 special GR.Mk.5 and GR.Mk.7 Nightbird versions, with advanced avionics. These are in addition to the carrier-based versions already in service with the Royal Navy, designated Sea Harrier FRS.Mk.1. The main difference between these and the land-based versions is in the design of the nose, modified to take a Ferranti Blue Fox radar which can be folded back 180 degrees for stowage on board aircraft carriers, and in the cockpit, which has room for a more advanced navigation and attack system. The Royal Navy has received 57 FRS.Mk.1s, whose efficiency was proven in the Falklands War.

The Lockheed F-117A, the USAF's first 'stealth' fighter aircraft, is designed to penetrate strongly-defended enemy air space for re-

connaissance and precision-attack missions. The prototype of this highly-sophisticated aircraft appeared in June 1981 and was operational with the 4450th Tactical Group based at Nellis (Nevada) from October 1983, but little is known about it officially. It is a single-seat twin jet of an unusual, compact, angular design. It is built to reduce radar signature and infrared emissions to a minimum. The powerplant consists of two General Electric F404-GE-400s without afterburners and with specially shielded air intakes and exhausts. The programme was originally for 100 aircraft, but budget problems have reduced the number to 59.

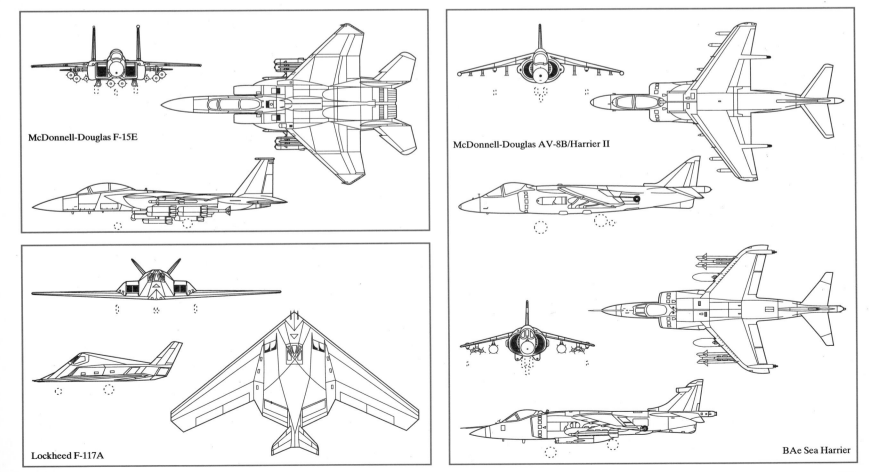

McDonnell-Douglas F-15E

McDonnell-Douglas AV-8B/Harrier II

Lockheed F-117A

BAe Sea Harrier

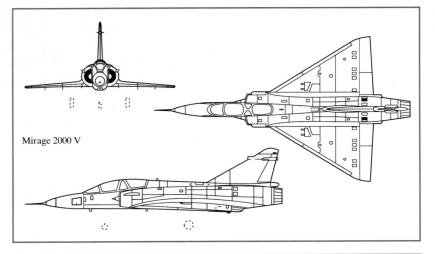

Mirage 2000 V

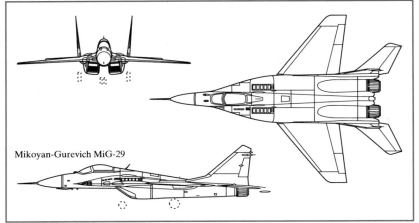

Mikoyan-Gurevich MiG-29

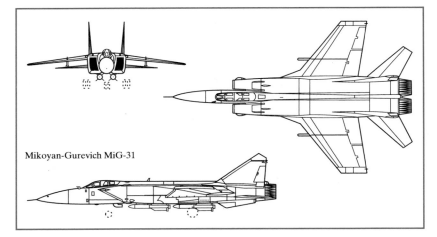

Mikoyan-Gurevich MiG-31

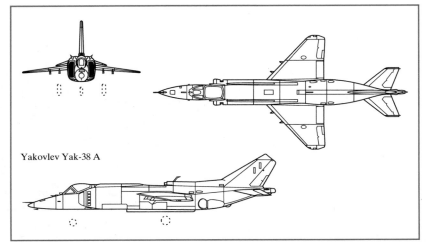

Yakovlev Yak-38 A

Plate 245
France and Russia in pursuit of air superiority

The French company Dassault has kept pace with North American industry in the intense competition for air superiority. The Mirage 2000 is a highly-sophisticated member of the prolific Mirage family, capable of competing with the Grumman F-14 and McDonnell-Douglas F-15. This new design by Dassault was chosen by the French government on 18th December 1975 to re-equip the front line of the *Armée de l'Air* in the mid eighties. The first of five prototypes took to the air on 10th March 1978 and the last on 11th October 1980. The latter machine (Mirage 2000B) was built as a two-seat trainer. First deliveries of the C variant began in December 1983 and the aircraft was operational by the following year. In the meantime, however, Dassault had developed a new, two-seat, low-altitude attack version, designated 2000N, the prototype of which first flew on 3rd February 1983. This aircraft, which was strengthened to withstand the stresses of a mission profile involving continuous flight at 690 mph (1,110 km/h) and an altitude of 200 ft (60 m), and equipped with highly sophisticated avionics, was designed to carry and use an ASMP air-to-surface nuclear missile. Delivery of the series aircraft began on 19th February 1987 and 36 were in service by the following year. At present it is planned to produce 112 Mirage 2000Ns (some of which will be designed for attack with conventional weapons) for a total of 300–400 in the different versions. Exports of the Mirage 2000 have been highly successful, with orders from Egypt, India, Peru, Greece, Abu Dhabi and Jordan.

The Russians have also been active in this sector and the prestigious Mikoyan and Gurevich bureau has designed two of the most lethal interceptors in the world in recent years. The MiG-29 (FULCRUM in NATO code) remained a mystery in the West until displayed at Farnborough and Le Bourget in 1988 and 1989 (thanks to Gorbachev's policy of *glasnost*), when it impressed observers with its efficiency as a fighting machine. This single-seat, twin-engined aircraft is regarded as being in the same class as the American McDonnell-Douglas F/A-18 Hornet. It has a distinctive shape with low-set wings and twin vertical tails; the engine nacelles are slung beneath the wings. The outstanding performance of these engines (18,300 lb–8,300 kg thrust each with afterburning) makes the MiG-29 an excellent fighter and a very good example of the effort the Soviet Union has made to bridge the gap between its technology and that of the West. The prototype was first seen in 1979 and about 500 MiG-29s are now in service, while others have been exported to India, Yugoslavia, Iraq and Syria. There are two versions: the FULCRUM A single-seat fighter and FULCRUM B two-seat trainer.

A worthy companion of the MiG-29 is the MiG-31 (FOXHOUND in NATO code). It is a completely-redesigned version of the MiG-25, with better manoeuvrability. The first news of this powerful fighter was received in 1978, when the Russians announced to the West that a 'modified MiG-25' had destroyed a small target cruise missile flying at very low altitude, from a distance of over 19,684 ft (6,000 m). Pictures of the MiG-31 were not available until August 1985 and only then was it possible to appreciate the novelty of the design. The main differences from its predecessor were the addition of a second crew member, changes to the structure of the wings and the fact that it could carry eight missiles. But above all, the MiG-31 was a real weapon system, for engaging multiple targets at all altitudes. By the end of 1986, about 150 FOXHOUNDS were operational in the Soviet Union, but production has continued at an intensive rate since then. There is also a reconnaissance version, and a special ECM variant is thought to have been developed.

The Soviet Union also felt the need for a maritime attack aircraft for anti-ship missions and missions against enemy reconnaissance. For this purpose, an aircraft very similar to the British Harrier and its United States derivative the AV-8B has been developed. Known as the Yak-38 (FORGER in NATO code), it is used on board Soviet aircraft carriers of the Kiev class and its VTOL capabilities make it particularly efficient. Unlike its Western counterparts, the Yak-38 has three engines instead of one: a Lyulka AL-21 turbojet of 18,000 lb (8,160 kg) thrust and two Koliesov ZM turbojets of 7,870 lb (3,570 kg) thrust each. The latter are needed for hovering during the transitional stage before horizontal flight. The Yak-38 has been produced in two versions, (FORGER A and FORGER B in NATO code). The first is a single-seat combat aircraft (in production since 1975), twelve of which are normally carried on each vessel; the second is a trainer with a second pilot seat in front of the main one (two of which are carried on each vessel).

Plate 246
The formidable bombers of the Sukhoi family

One of the most prolific families of Soviet combat aircraft is named after Pavel Osipovich Sukhoi, one of the world's top aircraft designers. After a period of obscurity following the Second World War, this engineer returned to the limelight in the fifties. One of his first models (the Su-7 close support aircraft) gave rise to a more modern and powerful attack aircraft in 1967 (NATO codename Su-17 FITTER) which, though directly derived from its predecessor, was in fact a much more efficient machine, with twice the weapon load, a 30 per cent increase in combat radius and greater flexibility thanks to the adoption of a partial swing-wing. The efficiency of the Su-17 is demonstrated not only by the sheer numbers built (these aircraft were one of the mainstays of the Soviet Air Force and Navy and Warsaw Pact forces in the eighties), but by the fact that the original design has been constantly updated, to cater for the most diverse requirements. The Sukhoi Su-20 and Su-22 are export versions with modified engines and avionics. The final sub-series (FITTER J in NATO code) has a Tumansky turbojet delivering 25,353 lb

(11,500 kg) thrust with afterburning. These aircraft also have a modified fuselage, which has increased fuel capacity and cockpit space and made room for additional avionics; they also have two extra hardpoints for external stores. The trainer variants have also been improved and the latest versions have an all-metal rear cockpit canopy with small, square windows at the sides.

The experience of the Sukhoi design bureau in the attack aircraft sector can also be seen from two subsequent models, the Su-24 (FENCER in NATO code) and Su-25 (FROGFOOT in NATO code). The first, which was operational from December 1974 as Su-19, has undergone continuous improvements and is now a powerful multirole aircraft, optimised for ground attack. It is a large, heavy, variable-geometry two-seater, capable of flying at speeds in excess of Mach 2, and is a lethal weapon at low altitude, thanks to its sophisticated avionics. About 1,000 Su-24s are in service in virtually all the border areas of the Soviet Union. The most outstanding variants are the FENCER C (of 1981) with improved avionics, the FENCER D (of 1983) with an in-flight refuelling probe and the E used by the Baltic Fleet. Another version designed for electronic warfare was tested in 1988.

The Sukhoi Su-25 is an altogether more specialised machine, designed

for close support of ground forces. It is a single-seat twin-engine aircraft very similar to the Northrop A-9A, an unsuccessful competitor of the Fairchild A-10A chosen by the USAF for the same purpose. Smaller, lighter and faster than the American design, the Su-25 (FROGFOOT in NATO code) is built for attack against ground targets, particularly heavily-armoured vehicles and protected targets, and has very good manoeuvrability and flexibility. Its armament consists of a 30 mm double-barrelled cannon and a maximum of 9,920 lb (4,500 kg) of external stores. The Sukhoi Su-25 first flew in 1976 and went into service four years later, after numerous adjustments had been made. In 1982, the aircraft received its baptism of fire in Afghanistan, where it was intensively used, often carrying out missions in cooperation with Mi-24 Hind attack helicopters. It has been in full-scale production since 1984 and about 600 are thought to have been delivered by the end of the eighties.

The Sukhoi design bureau has not confined itself to producing attack aircraft and the Su-27 is one of the largest and most powerful air superiority planes. This single-seat, twin-engine fighter (FLANKER in NATO code) has a speed of over Mach 2 and is based on the aerodynamics of the MiG-29 Fulcrum, despite being much larger, heavier and more powerful.

Furthermore, whilst the MiG-29 was designed to compete with American aircraft of the same class at close range, the Su-27 is optimised for engaging distant targets, particularly low-flying ones. This aircraft, powered by two Tumansky R-32 engines developing 29,983 lb (13,600 kg) thrust apiece and with a combat radius of 932 miles (1,500 km) with reduced armament, can carry 10 air-to-air missiles, including AA-10 Alamo laser and infrared guided types, which were the first Soviet missiles to have a homing system. The armament includes a 30 mm cannon in the root of the starboard wing. The Su-27 made its maiden flight in 1976 and went into production seven years later. According to Western estimates, over 200 had been delivered by the end of the eighties.

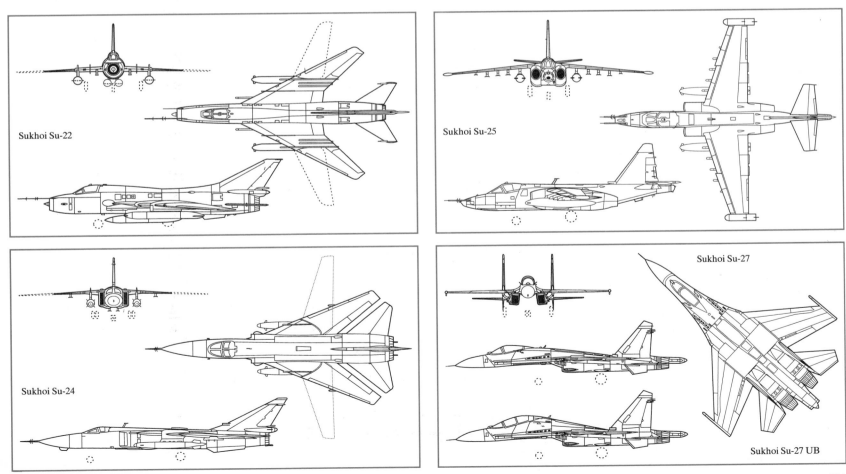

Sukhoi Su-22

Sukhoi Su-25

Sukhoi Su-24

Sukhoi Su-27

Sukhoi Su-27 UB

531

Plate 247
Europe looks to its own defence

Despite being dwarfed by the super-powers on either side of her, Europe developed high-technology aeronautical programmes of her own in the eighties. With the exception of France and Sweden (who have continued to develop completely independent designs), European countries have achieved results by international cooperation, to minimise expense and optimise resources. After the success of the first programme of this kind (for the Tornado multi-role combat aircraft [MRCA]) European governments began thinking in terms of a successor to form the new front line at the end of the century. The resulting project, designated EFA (European Fighter Aircraft), was started back in 1971 and was formally approved on 2nd August 1985 by the Ministries of Defence of Britain, Germany, Italy and Spain. These four countries formed the Eurofighter consortium for development of the airframe and the Eurojet consortium for that of the engine. British Aerospace is responsible for the right wing, front fuselage and canard foreplanes (33%); the German MBB and Dornier are responsible for the centre fuselage and tail unit (33%); Aeritalia the left wing and part of the fuselage (21%) and Casa in Spain part of the right wing and the rear fuselage (13%). Rolls-Royce, MTU, Fiat Aviazione and Sener are responsible for the engines. The programme made slow progress and only received the go-ahead for production in 1988. Prior to that (apart from appearing in the form of mock-ups) the future EFA was in a sense anticipated by an experimental prototype developed by British industry in conjunction with Aeritalia. This was the EAP (Experimental Aircraft Programme), construction of which was authorised in 1982 and which first flew on 8th August 1986. It is a highly sophisticated machine built to study the materials and aerodynamics for the European fighter. The EFA will however be a single-seat twin-jet with delta wing and canard foreplanes, optimised for air superiority. Eight prototypes will be built for the air forces of the four countries involved in the programme, for a planned initial requirement of 800.

A direct competitor of the above (given the repeated efforts of the French government to have it adopted as an alternative to the EFA) is the Dassault-Breguet Rafale. This is a powerful and sophisticated single-seat twin-jet Mach 2 combat aircraft, construction of which began in 1983. The first test model, Rafale A, appeared on 14th December 1985. Its first flight was on 4th July 1986 and it

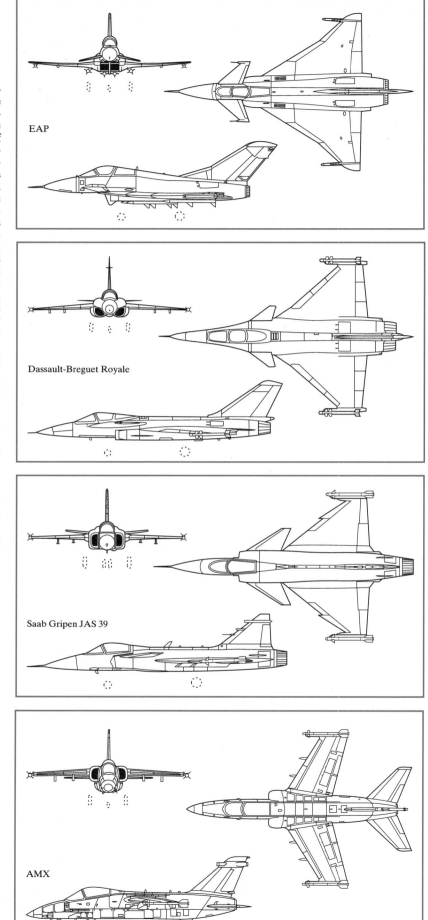

EAP

Dassault-Breguet Royale

Saab Gripen JAS 39

AMX

is planned to develop two variants for the French armed forces: the Rafale D for the *Armée de l'Air* and Rafale M for the *Aéronavale*. The Rafale is largely made of advanced materials and special alloys and is highly manoeuvrable, with voice-activated and 'fly-by-wire', computerised controls. The prototype has two General Electric F404-400 engines of 16,000 lb (7,258 kg) thrust each, but the production models should have two Snecma M-88s developing 16,860 lb (7,648 kg) thrust with afterburning.

The Saab Gripen JAS 39 is in a similar class. It is a small but powerful multirole aircraft and the latest of a series of prestigious fighters produced by Swedish industry since the war. The programme started towards the end of the seventies, the aim being to design an aircraft to replace all variants of the Saab-37 Viggen by the end of the century. The programme involved nearly all the country's major industries and was approved by the government on 6th May 1982. A total of 140 aircraft were ordered for the year 2000 (initially including 20 two-seat trainers). The first contract for 30 aircraft was signed on 30th June and building of the five prototypes began the following year. The first flight was in 1988, but the programme was badly delayed as the result of an accident in which the aircraft was practically destroyed. The Gripen has a delta wing and canards for greater manoeuvrability, and a speed of Mach 2. It is powered by a General Electric/Volvo Flygmotor RM12 developing 18,100 lb (8,210 kg). The sophisticated avionics include 'fly-by-wire' controls and fully-computerised on-board systems.

The AMX single-seat trainer developed by Italy and Brazil is in a very different class. It is a fairly orthodox design, optimised for close support, produced by Aeritalia and Embraer. The programme started towards the end of 1978 and three years later, Italy reached an agreement with her South-American partner to build 331 series aircraft, 187 of which were intended for the *Aeronautica Militare Italiana* (which introduced it in 1989 to replace the Fiat/Aeritalia G.91 tactical fighters) and 144 for the *Força Aerea Brasileira* (which later reduced the order to 79). The first of the seven prototypes flew in Italy in 1984, the one developed in Brazil a year later. The first production aircraft flew on 11th May 1988, and delivery to forces began the following year. A two-seater version is currently under development, and is intended for training, electronic warfare and anti-ship attack.

Plate 248
From the awesome bomber to the Russian giant

Research continued at a frenzied pace in the United States and Soviet Union in the eighties, in an effort to devise ever more lethal weapons to counter those being developed by the enemy. An example of this strategy is the latest project by the Tupolev design bureau, for the multirole strategic bomber known only by the NATO code-name BLACKJACK. This aircraft is very similar to the American Rockwell B-1, and like the latter, it can carry and launch cruise missiles and has great flexibility, due to the use of variable-geometry wings.

The BLACKJACK was first observed by satellite in 1979, but remained shrouded in mystery until one was photographed on 25th November 1981, next to a pair of Tupolev Tu-144 commercial jets. This gave some idea of the size of the aircraft, which appeared to be much larger than the B-1B. The Soviets only released the first official photograph of the BLACKJACK in August 1988, by which time eleven had been completed, ready for deployment with an operational unit which was still in the process of being formed. The Soviet bomber is in fact not just larger than its American competitor, but superior in terms of absolute speed. Compared with the Tupolev Tu-26 Backfire (of which it is a logical development), the BLACKJACK differs in the shape and struc-

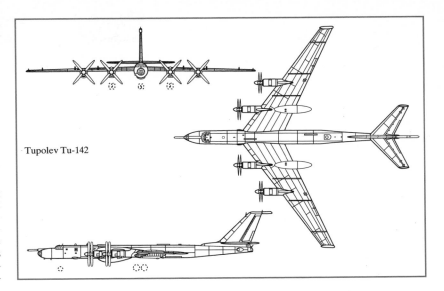

Tupolev Tu-142

ture of the wing and tailplane and in the engines, which appear to be fitted in a similar way to those of the Tu-144 supersonic jets. The BLACKJACK has sophisticated ECM systems and a terrain-following radar for flight at very low altitude, while the maximum weapon load is estimated at over 35,000 lb (16,000 kg). The main armament consists of AS-15 KENT and AS-X-19 cruise missiles, each of which has a range of 1,865 miles (3,000 km).

The highly sophisticated, futuristic BLACKJACK is in strong contrast to another plane in the Soviet arsenal which has earned a place in military history and is still fully operational 36 years after its maiden flight. This, the big Tupolev Tu-20 four-engine turboprop, the most recent versions of which, designated Tu-142, have proved invaluable, despite their age. As recently as 1988, the US Department of Defense warned of the potential of this aircraft, not to be underestimated in strategies regarding the Soviet bloc. Originally designed as a bomber, then gradually transformed into a strategic reconnaissance aircraft, an EW aircraft and an airborne warning and control system, the BEAR (as this entire family of aircraft is known to NATO), was turned into a lethal platform for launching cruise missiles. The version known as BEAR F is designated Tu-142. This was developed in 1970 for the needs of the Soviet Naval Air Force and had a much longer front fuselage section and modified wings. Production was resumed in 1980 and numerous variants were produced. Four years later, the BEAR H appeared. This had provision for launching six cruise missiles internally, including the AS-15 (KENT in NATO code) and improved avionics. Finally, in 1986, another version was identified, BEAR J, designed as a control platform for nuclear submarines. The Soviet Naval Air Force has at least 80 Tu-142s, in addition to the various earlier versions in service with the VVS (Soviet Air Force).

The Soviet predilection for huge aircraft, ever since the days of 'lighter than air' machines, is not confined to those directly intended for military use. The Antonov An-124 (CONDOR in NATO code) is one of the latest of numerous outsize airlift transports produced by Oleg Antonov. This colossal machine, with a maximum takeoff weight of 405 tonnes and payload of 150, is powered by four Lotarev D-18T turbofans of 51,649 lb (23,428 kg) thrust each; it has a range of 2,795 miles (4,500 km) fully loaded and 9,942 miles (16,000 km) empty and a wingspan of no less than 240 ft 6 in (73.30 m). Its complex main undercarriage with 24 wheels enables it to operate from rough airstrips, and even on snow and ice. The prototype first flew on 26th December 1982 and the second (named Ruslan, after a giant in Russian folklore) staggered Western observers when it appeared at the Paris Air Show in 1985. Two years later, ten had been built (including the two prototypes). The Antonov An-124, which is very similar in appearance to the American Lockheed C-5 Galaxy, bears the insignia of both Aeroflot and the Soviet Air Force. It began replacing the Antonov An-22 turboprop in 1987. Its capabilities were demonstrated in 1985 and 1987, when it set no fewer than 20 payload records, plus a record for covering 10,880.625 nautical miles (20,150.921 km) over a closed circuit in 25 hours, 30 minutes.

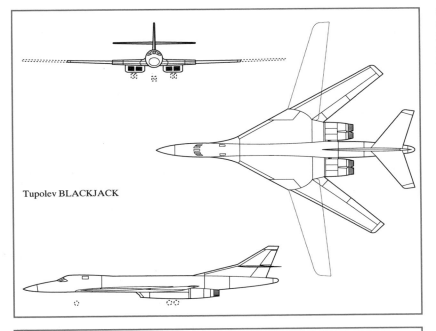

Tupolev BLACKJACK

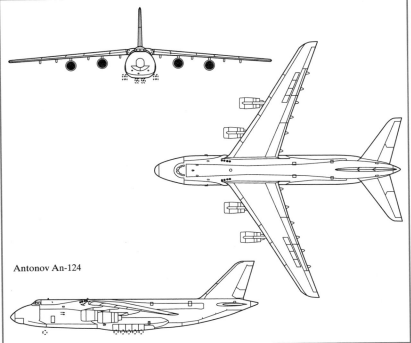

Antonov An-124

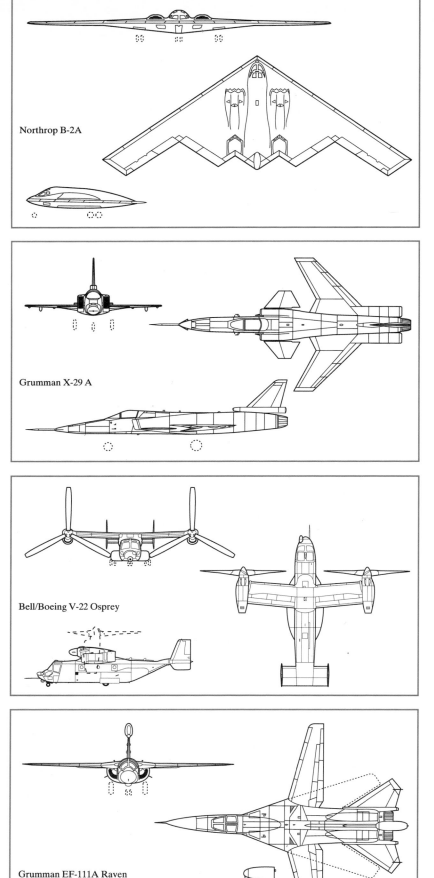

Northrop B-2A

Grumman X-29 A

Bell/Boeing V-22 Osprey

Grumman EF-111A Raven

Plate 249
Research is paramount in the USA – not just for the B-2

Technology and change have always been at the root of aeronautical development. But whereas the evolution of the aeroplane in the past was spurred on by world wars, in more recent times, the brutal demands of war have been replaced by a different type of incentive: the lure of space travel. The technological developments of the decade preceding the conquest of the Moon had a direct influence on the aeronautical field, mainly in the USA to begin with. This laid the foundations for a period of growth that is still in progress today. Of course the strategies of the two opposing blocs and intense competition of the arms race gave added impetus to the development of the aeroplane. It is nonetheless true that the boundary between aviation and space is now barely perceptible, and research covers both areas, above all in terms of materials, electronics and propulsive technology.

The Northrop B-2 'stealth' bomber is the fruit of this research and the latest product of the American aeronautical industry. Plans for this futuristic aircraft were first laid down at the end of the seventies, but it did not appear until the summer of 1989 (first flight 17th July). The USAF issued a specification for a new-generation strategic bomber to take over from the Rockwell B-1. The idea was to develop a combat aircraft which could reach deep into enemy air space, carry out its mission and return to base. To achieve all this, the aircraft would need to be of the 'low observable' type, that is, be hard to detect by either optical or electronic means. The design was entrusted to Northrop with the assistance of Boeing Aerospace and the LTV Vought Aero Production Division. It remained shrouded in the utmost secrecy until the USAF released an artist's impression of the new plane on 20th April 1988. Six months previously (on 19th November 1987) a contract had been signed for 135 such aircraft, 120 of which were to be capable of carrying nuclear weapons. The first B-2 was rolled out on 22nd November 1988. It was of a highly unorthodox design, strongly reminiscent of the B-35 and B-49 'flying wing' aircraft developed by Northrop in the postwar period. The first flight emphasised the basic features of the new bomber, which really was 'all wing', with an irregular-shaped trailing edge and fuselage carefully blended into the main profile. The General Electric F118-GE-100 turbofans of 19,000 lb (8,620 kg) thrust each are similarly 'buried' in the thickness of the wing and carefully shielded to reduce infrared signature to a mini-

mum. Extensive use has been made of advanced materials for the airframe (e.g. kevlar, carbon fibre and titanium), while the skin is made of special, radar-absorbent materials. Five more prototypes are to be built, which will later be adapted for operational use.

The Grumman X-29A project is also representative of current trends in aeronautical research, despite the fact that it remained at the experimental stage. The aim was to explore the potential of the forward-swept wing in combat aircraft. This type of aerodynamic solution had been studied by Junkers in 1942 in the project for the Ju.287 four-engine jet. It was now being re-examined, to try and exploit the considerable advantages of such a design, as established by German engineers in the Second World War. This project renewed the great American tradition of 'X-aircraft' (experimental aircraft to explore the confines of modern aviation, right to the frontier of space technology). The programme took off at the beginning of the eighties, when Grumman secured a contract for the development of two prototypes designated X-29A. The first of these flew on 14th December 1984 and on 2nd April of the following year the aircraft was delivered to NASA for assessment and trials. An enormous amount of information was obtained. The X-29A (a basically 'unstable' aircraft, constantly controlled by computer) showed excellent manoeuvrability and efficiency throughout the entire flight envelope, to the extent of being a very good starting point for development of a new generation of tactical aircraft, of much smaller size, weight and cost than that of a contemporary aircraft in the same class.

Another ambitious high-tech project was the one which led to the Bell/Boeing V-22 Osprey tilt-rotor aircraft, a cross between a helicopter and an aeroplane, developed at the request of the Department of Defense and chosen for production by the US Marine Corps, US Navy and USAF. The programme started in 1982 and trials began in 1989. Three production variants are planned: MV-22A for the Marines (552); HV-22A for the US Navy (50) and CV-22A for the USAF (55). Deliveries should commence at the end of 1991.

Finally, the Grumman/General Dynamics EF-111A Raven is an example of how an aircraft which is no longer new can be transformed by the addition of highly sophisticated avionics. It is a formidable electronic warfare aircraft produced by converting 42 models of the original F-111A attack variant. The programme started in 1975 and it took over four years to perfect the machine's complex electronics. The Raven was operational by November 1981 and the last one was delivered in 1985.

Plate 250
Advanced trainers

Training, the primary requirement by definition, has assumed particular importance in recent years, as a result of the rapid evolution of combat aircraft. Demand is very strong in this sector on the international market. One of the main reasons for this is because modern trainers, despite the fact that their military potential is limited by their size, weight and general performance, can be effectively used for aerial police work and light attack.

One of the most interesting products in this category is the Italian SIAI Marchetti S.211, an elegant two-seat trainer and close-support aircraft, with excellent capabilities and very low purchase and running costs. Yet despite these qualities, the S.211 has not been a great success. It was first exhibited in the form of a model at the Paris Air Show in 1977 and the prototype appeared on 10th April 1981. However, it failed to secure enough orders to justify mass production. It was beaten on to the Italian market by another aircraft in the same category: the Aermacchi M.B.339, which was chosen by the *Aeronautica Militare* as an advanced basic trainer. The prototype of the S.211 was followed by a second and

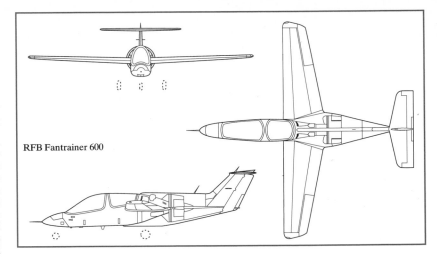

RFB Fantrainer 600

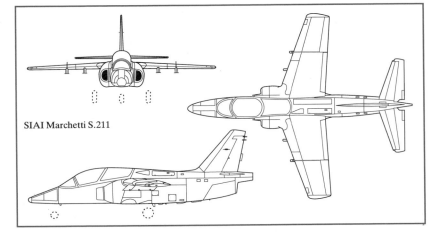

SIAI Marchetti S.211

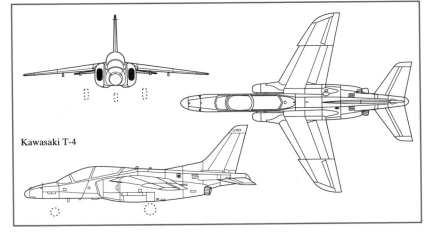

Kawasaki T-4

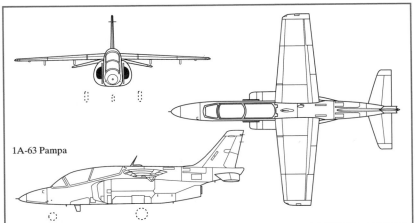

1A-63 Pampa

SIAI Marchetti undertook a long international demonstration programme with these two aircraft, in the hope of finding customers for its machine. An initial order was placed by the Singapore Government in 1985, for 30 SIAI S.211s for its Air Force (most of which were to be built under licence by Singapore Aircraft Industries). In September 1988, an order was signed for 18 (with an option on a similar number) for the Philippine Air Force. In 1989, after an agreement was reached with the Grumman Corporation, the S.211 was entered for the USAF's PATS (Primary Aircraft Training System) competition for a new-generation trainer.

The Kawasaki T-4 is a compact twin-jet trainer in the same class, developed from 1981 to replace the old Lockheed T-33A and Fuji T-1A/B in service with the JASDF. This project was a joint venture between Kawasaki (responsible for the forward fuselage, final assembly and tests), Fuji (wings, rear fuselage and tail unit) and Mitsubishi (centre fuselage and air intakes). The first of four prototypes flew on 29th July 1985 and the first production model, on 28th June 1988. About 200 should be produced for the JASDF.

The 1A-63 Pampa is a straightforward, robust, versatile trainer developed by the Argentine company FMA (Fabrica Militar de Aviones) in conjunction with the German Dornier as a replacement for the old Morane-Saulnier MS.760 of the *Fuerça Aerea*. The design was strongly influenced by the German manufacturer (the 1A-63 is very similar in appearance to the Alpha Jet by Dornier) apart from having a non-swept, supercritical wing and one Garrett TFE731-2-2N turbofan of 3,500 lb (1,588 kg) thrust instead of two. The wing is the result of a study carried out by Dornier using a specially-modified Alpha Jet. The prototype of the Pampa was first flown on 6th October 1984. The first order was for 64 planes. The aircraft is designed

to carry armament consisting of a container with a DEFA 30 mm cannon and a maximum of 2,557 lb (1,160 kg) of stores, distributed on four underwing pylons. This has led to the development of a second, armed trainer version, from which a close-support variant could be derived.

The Fantrainer of the 400/600 series is a wholly original design. It was developed by the German company RFB (Rehein Flugzeugbau GmbH) after an extended programme of research for a light aircraft powered by a ducted, pusher propeller. The shape of the aircraft was so unusual that it aroused the interest of the West German Ministry of Defence in 1975. A contract was signed in March of that year for the development of two prototypes, to be examined by the Luftwaffe as possible replacements for the Piaggio P.1490 basic trainers. The first of these aircraft flew on 27th October 1977, powered by two Wankel engines. An Allison turbine was subsequently fitted and the aircraft became known as the Model 400. The Luftwaffe did not in fact order the aircraft, despite its excellent capabilities. However, it went into production at the beginning of the eighties, thanks to an order from the Government of Thailand (in August 1982) for 47 aircraft for the Royal Thai Air Force (31 of which were to be from the 400 series and 16 from the 600 series, the latter having substantial changes to the powerplant). The first two models were built in Germany and delivered in 1984, while the others were assembled locally. In 1985, the Luftwaffe showed renewed interest in the Fantrainer and an example with a modified fan flew on 16th May 1986.

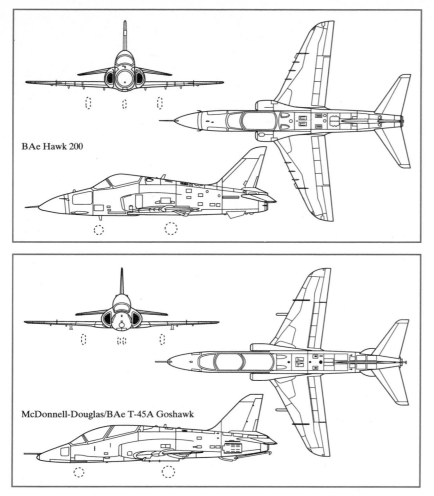

BAe Hawk 200

McDonnell-Douglas/BAe T-45A Goshawk

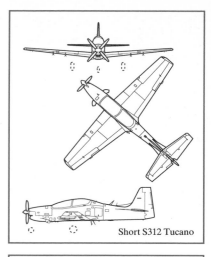

Short S312 Tucano

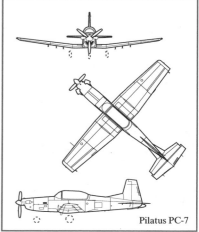

Pilatus PC-7

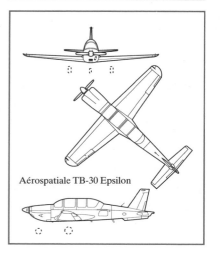

Aérospatiale TB-30 Epsilon

Plate 251
From the basic trainer to the ultra-light fighter

The thin dividing line between modern trainers and combat aircraft is demonstrated by the evolution of a very good British project: the one which led in the early seventies to the Hawk, a small, rugged, versatile trainer built for the Royal Air Force. Over the years, this aircraft has not only been a great success in terms of exports, but has also managed to cross the boundaries of its own specific market and enter the more ambitious multirole aircraft sector. The recent 200 version, which has been turned from a two-seater into a single-seater and given better avionics and armament, has in fact already achieved considerable market success (particularly in those countries which had already bought the trainer version and could thus exploit the logistic and operational advantages of having two such closely-related aircraft, with 80 per cent parts in common).

The programme for the Hawk 200 was launched by British Aerospace towards the end of 1983 and formally announced at the Farnborough Air Show the following year. The first (demonstration) model took to the air on 19th March 1986. It was destroyed in an accident but was replaced by the first pre-production aircraft ten months later, which flew on 24th April 1987. Although the main differences between the Hawk 200 and the trainer variant and two-seat attack variant (Hawk 100, first flight October 1987), are the fact that it is a single-seater and has a larger fin, it is a highly versatile machine from an operational standpoint. Many different tactical mission profiles are in fact possible, from battlefield interdiction (two air-to-air missiles), to close support; from long-range photoreconnaissance to anti-shipping strike. This is made possible by the provision of five hardpoints externally (the centreline one for a 592-litre [130 Imp. gallon/156 US gallon] auxiliary fuel tank, the ones under the wings for 2,000 lb [907 kg] of stores each) and the mounting of one or two 25 mm Aden guns internally, apart from the adoption of a highly diversified range of avionics: an FLIR (forward-looking infrared) and laser system and a multipurpose radar like the Westinghouse APG-66 can in fact be fitted into the nose. Initial orders include one from Saudi Arabia for 60 Hawk 200s. It is estimated that 600 of these aircraft will be built in a market in which one can foresee a demand for 2,000 planes in this category over the next 20 years.

The trainer version of the Hawk was a great success on the international market at the beginning of the eighties, when it was chosen by the US Navy as a new-generation trainer to replace the T-2C Buckeyes and TA-4J Skyhawks. An agreement was signed on 18th November 1981 for the production of 300 aircraft. Of these, BAe was to build the rear fuselage, windscreen, cockpit canopy and flight controls, while the rest, assembly included, was entrusted to McDonnell-Douglas. The first of two pre-production T-45A Goshawks (the name given to this aircraft by the US Navy) flew on 16th April 1988 and underwent a 19-month test cycle, together with the other model. The main differences between the T-45A and the original version are the fact that the airframe has been strengthened to enable it to operate from aircraft carriers, and the fact that it has been fitted with the avionics required by the US Navy.

There has also been a strong demand in recent years for propeller-driven trainers. Many successful designs have been developed. These include the Brazilian Embraer EMB-312 Tucano, which has even been chosen by the Royal Air Force with the designation Tucano TMk.1. 130 of these aircraft are to replace the Jet Provost. The project began in 1978, as part of a programme to develop a new basic trainer for the *Fuerça Aerea Brasileira* (Brazilian Air Force). The Tucano is a strong, highly manoeuvrable aircraft with excellent performance. Its first flight was on 16th August 1980 and delivery of an initial order for 118 (designated T-27) began on 29th September 1983, ending exactly three years later. The qualities of this aircraft and its low cost have stimulated considerable demand on the international market.

A direct competitor of the Tucano (notably in the competition for a trainer for the Royal Air Force) is the Swiss Pilatus PC-7, a highly aerobatic two-seat turboprop which has proved capable of satisfying all the demands of modern pilot training. The project for the PC-7 started in 1966, but was only completed ten years later, after a long period of research and development. The first production model flew on 18th August 1978 and the aircraft has attracted orders from many countries. From this basic aircraft, the Swiss industry developed a more advanced model in 1982, designated PC-9. Although similar in appearance to the PC-7, the PC-9 has only about 10 per cent parts in common with its predecessor. It has a more powerful engine, a different cockpit arrangement and modified fuselage and wings. The PC-9 was first flown on 7th May 1984 and was certified on 19th September of the following year. It has achieved considerable market success, the biggest orders coming from Saudi Arabia and Australia.

The French TB-30 Epsilon is a lighter and less powerful, two-seat trainer produced by Aérospatiale. It is unusual in being a piston-engined machine. It was developed in the late seventies at the request of the Armée de l'Air. The prototype was flown on 22nd December 1979 and the aircraft went into production with the designation TB-30B. The first series aircraft was flown on 23rd June 1983 and deliveries began the following year. A prototype of a turboprop variant (TB-30C) came out on 9th November 1985.

Lockheed F-117A-1988, USA (plate 244)

McDonnell-Douglas/BAe Harrier II Mk.7-1989, USA-GB (plate 244)

Mirage 2000S-1989, F (plate 245)

Mikoyan-Gurevich MiG 29-1983, USSR (plate 245)

Sukhoi Su-25-1981, USSR (plate 246)

Sukhoi Su-27-1983, USSR (plate 246)

EAP-1986, GB (plate 247)

AMX-1988, I-BR (plate 247)

Photographic appendix

Dassault Rafale A-1989, F (plate 247)

Saab JAS39 Gripen-1988, S (plate 247)

Northrop B-2A-1989, USA (plate 249)

Antonov An-124-1982, USSR (plate 248)

Bell/Boeing V-22 Osprey-1989, USA (plate 249)

SIAI Marchetti S.211-1981, I (plate 250)

Embraer EMB-312 Tucano-1983, BR (plate 251)

BIBLIOGRAPHY

INDEX BY COUNTRY

GENERAL INDEX

BIBLIOGRAPHY

Abate Rosario - Lazzati Giulio, *I velivoli Macchi dal 1912 al 1963*, Milano, Ali nel Tempo, 1963.

Ali Italiane, Milano, Rizzoli Editore, 1978

Achard André - Tribot-Laspierre, Jack, *Répertoire des Aéronefs de construction française pour la période 1890-1967,* Paris, Doc. Air Espace, Centre de Documentation de l'Armement, 1968.

Aircam «Specials» Series, vols. I-VII, Canterbury, Osprey Publications Ltd., 1969-71.

Aircam Aviation Series, vols. I-XVIII Canterbury, Osprey Publications Ltd., 1967-71.

Andrews C. F., *Vickers Aircraft since 1908,* London, Putnam & Co. Ltd, 1969.

Angelucci Enzo, *Gli Aeroplani,* Verona, Arnoldo Mondadori Editore, 1972

Angelucci Enzo - Matricardi Paolo, *Guida agli aeroplani di tutto il mondo « dalle origini alla prima guerra mondiale », « dal 1918 al 1935 », « la seconda guerra mondiale »* (parte prima e parte seconda), *« modelli civili dal 1935 al 1960 », « modelli militari dal 1945 al 1960 »,* Verona, Arnoldo Mondadori Editore, 1975-1979.

Arena N., *I caccia della serie 5 - Reggiane 2005 «Sagittario»,* Modena, Stem Mucchi, 1977.

Barbieri C., *Bombardieri del dopoguerra,* Parma, Delta Editrice, 1980.

Barnes C. H., *Shorts Aircraft since 1900,* London, Putnam & Co. Ltd., 1967.

Bekker T., *The Luftwaffe War Diaries,* London, Macdonald & Co. (Publishers) Ltd., 1966.

Bignozzi G. - Catalanotto B., *Storia degli aerei d'Italia,* Roma, Editrice Cielo, 1962.

Borgiotti Alberto, *I caccia della prima guerra mondiale,* Ermanno Albertelli Editore, Parma, 1970.

Bowers Peter M., *Boeing Aircraft since 1916,* London, Putnam & Co. Ltd., 1966.

Bowyer Michael J. F., *Fighting Colours: RAF Fighter Camouflage and Markings 1937-1969,* London, Patrick Stephens, 1969.

Boyd Alexander, *The Soviet Air Force since 1918,* London, Macdonald and Jane's Ltd., 1977.

Brown D., *Carrier Fighters,* London, Macdonald & Co. (Publishers Ltd., 1975.

Bruce J. M., *War Planes of the First World War: Fighters,* vols. I-III, London, Macdonald & Co. (Publishers) Ltd. 1965-69.

Caras Roger A., *Wings of Gold. The Story of the U.S. Naval Aviation,* Philadelphia, Lippincott Co., 1965.

Craven W. - Cate S., *U.S. Army Air Forces in World War II,* vols. I-VII, University of Chicago Press, 1954-1958

Cynk J., *History of the Polish Air Force, 1916-68,* Canterbury, Osprey Publications Ltd., 1972

Cornille Reni, *La guerre aérienne,* Paris, Les Editions de France, 1942.

Danel Raymond - Cuny Jean, *L'Aviation Française de Bombardement et de Renseignement (1918-1940),* Paris, Editions Larivière, 1978.

Desoutter D. M., *All about Aircraft,* London, Faber & Faber Ltd., 1955.

Dollfus C. - Bouché H., *Histoire de l'Aéronautique,* Paris, Edition Saint George, 1942.

Doll Thomas E., *U.S. Navy Markings W. W. II - Pacific Theater,* Sun Valley, Aeronautica Iohn W. Caler, 1967.

Dornier-Flugzeuge, München, Luftfahrt-Verlag, Walter Zuerl, s.d.

Duval G. R., *British Flying-Boats and Amphibians 1909-1952,* London, Putnam & Co. Ltd., 1966.

Ege L., *Balloons and Airships,* New York, MacMillan Publishing Co. Inc., 1974.

Emde Heimer - Demand Carlo, *Conquerors of the Air,* Lausanne, Edita S.A., 1968.

Fantonetti Rossi Carlo *Le grandi battaglie aeree della seconda guerra mondiale,* Milano, Arnoldo Mondadori Editore, 1970.

Feist Uve - Francillon René J., *Luftwaffe in World War II,* Fallbrook, California, Aero Publishers Inc., 1968.

Feutcher Georg W., *La guerra aerea,* Firenze, Sansoni Editore, 1968.

Fokker - The Man and the Aircraft, Letchworth, Herts, Harleyford Publications Ltd., 1961.

Francillon René J., *American Fighters of World War II.* Windsor, Hylton Lacy, 1968.

Francillon René J., *American Fighters of World War II,* Windsor, Hylton Lacy, 1968.

Freeman Roger A., *The Mighty Eighth - A History of the U.S. 8th Army Air Force,* London, Macdonald & Co. (Publishers) Ltd., 1970.

Galland Adolf, *Die Ersten und die Letzten,* Darmstadt, Schneekluth Verlag, 1953.

Gema José, *Historia de la aeronáutica española,* Madrid, Gráficas Huerfanos Ejército del Aire, 1950.

General View of Japanese Military Aircraft in the Pacific War, Tokyo, Aireview, Kantosha Co. Ltd., 1953.

Gentile Rodolfo, *Storia delle operazioni aeree nella Seconda Guerra Mondiale (1939-45),* Roma Editrice Ali, second edition, 1956.

Gentile Rodolfo, *Storia dell'Aeronautica,* Roma, Editrice Ali, 1958.

German Military, Aircraft in the Second World War, Tokyo, Aireview, Kantosha Co. Ltd., 1958.

Gibbs-Smith Charles H., *Aviation, an Historical Survey from its Origins to* the end of World War II, London, Science Museum. Her Majesty's Stationery Office, 1970.

Gibbs-Smith Charles H., The Wright Brothers, London, Science Museum, Her Majesty's Stationery Office, 1963.

Gibb-Smith Charles H., The Aeroplane: an Historical Survey of Its Origins and Development, London, Science Museum, Her Majesty's Stationery Office, 1960.

Gibbs-Smith Charles H., The World's First Aeroplane Flights, London, Science Museum, Her Majesty's Stationery Office, 1965.

Gibbs-Smith Charles H., The Invention of the Aeroplane 1799-1909, London, Faber & Faber Ltd., 1966.

Gray Peter - Thetford Owen, German Aircraft of the First World War, London, Putnam & Co. Ltd., 1962.

Green William - Gerald Pollinger, The Aircraft of the World, London, Macdonald & Co. (Publishers) Ltd., 3rd edition, 1965.

Green William, Warplanes of the Third Reich, London, Macdonald & Co. (Publishers) Ltd., 1970.

Green William, The World Guide to Combat Planes, vols. I, II, Garden City. N.Y., Doubleday & Co., 1967.

Green William, Famous Fighters of the Second World War, vols. I, II, London, Macdonald & Co. (Publishers) Ltd., 1957–62.

Green William, Famous Bombers of the Second World War, vols. I, II, London, Macdonald & Co. (Publishers) Ltd., 1959-60.

Green William, War Planes of the Second World War, voll. I-X, London, Macdonald & Co. (Publishers) Ltd., 1960-68.

Gurney Gene, The War in the Air, Los Angeles, Floyd Clymer, 1952.

Hébrard J., L'aviation des origines à nos jours, Paris, Robert Laffont, 1954.

Hébrard J., Vingt-cinq années d'aviation militaire (1920-1945), vols. I, II, Paris, Editions Albin Michel, 1946.

Historical Aviation Album, vols. I-VIII, Temple City California, Paul R. Matt, 1965-70.

Hooftman Hugo, Russian Aircraft, Fallbrook, California, Aero Publishers Inc., 1965

I primi voli di guerra nel mondo, a cura dell'Ufficio Storico dell'Aeronautica Militare, Roma, 1951.

Jackson A. J., Avro Aircraft since 1908, London, Putnam & Co. Ltd., 1965.

Jackson A. J. Blackburn Aircraft since 1909, London, Putnam & Co Ltd., 1968.

Jackson A. J., De Havilland Aircraft, London, Putnam & Co. Ltd., 1962.

James Derek N. Gloster Aircraft since 1917, London, Putnam & Co. Ltd., 1971.

Jane's 1909-1969: 100 Significant Aircraft, London, Jane's All the World's Aircraft Publishing Co. Ltd., 1969.

Jane's pocket book of Airship Development, London, Macdonald and Jane's, 1976.

Jane's World Aircraft Recognition Handbook, London, Macdonald and Jane's, 1979.

Jones Lloyd S., U.S. Bombers B-1, B-70, Fallbrook, California, Aero Publishers Inc., 1966.

Killen John, A History of Marine Aviation, London, Frederick Muller Ltd., 1969.

Killen John, The Luftwaffe, A History, London, Frederick Muller Ltd., 1967.

Kilmarx Robert A., A History of Soviet Air Power, London, Faber & Faber, 1962.

King H. F., The World's Fighters, London, The Bodley Head Ltd., 1971.

Lamberton W. M., Fighter Aircraft of the 1914-1918 War, Letchworth, Herts, Harleyford Publications Ltd., 1960.

Lamberton W. M., Reconnaissance & Bomber Aircraft of the 1914-1918 War, Letchworth, Herts, Harleyford Publications Ltd., 1962.

Larrazabal J. S., Air War over Spain, London, Ian Allan Ltd., 1974.

Lee Asher, The Soviet Air Force, New York, The John Day Co. Inc., 1962.

Lewis Peter, Squadron Histories: RFC, RNAS, & RAF since 1912, London, Putnam & Co. Ltd., 1959.

Lewis Peter, British Aircraft 1909-14, London, Putnam & Co. Ltd., 1962.

Mach 1, Enciclopedia dell'Aviazione, Novara, Edipem, 1978.

Mancini Luigi, Grande enciclopedia aeronautica, Milano, Edizioni Aeronautica, 1936.

Mason Francis K., Hawker Aircraft since 1920, London, Putnam & Co. Ltd., 1961.

Mason Francis K., British Fighters of World War II, Windsor, Hylton Lacy, 1969.

Mason Francis K. - Windrow Martin C., Air Facts and Feats, London, Guinness Superlatives Ltd., 1970.

Matt Paul R., U.S. Navy & Marine Corps Fighters 1918-62, Letchworth, Herts, Harleyford Publications Ltd., 1962.

Mermoz Jean, Mes vols, Paris, Flammarion, 1937.

Messerschmitt-Flugzeuge, München, Luftfahrt-Verlag, Walter Zuerl, s.d.

Miller Ronald - Sawers Davis, The Technical Development of Modern Aviation, London, Routledge & Kegan Paul, 1968.

Mizrahi J. V., Carrier Fighters vols. I, II, Northridge, California, Sentry Book, 1969.

Mizrahi J. V., Dive and Torpedo Bombers, Northridge, California, Sentry Book, 1967.

Moreau-Berillon E., L'aviation française 1914-1940, Ses escadrilles - Ses Insignes, vols. I-VIII, Paris, E. Moreau-Berillon, 1968.

Morris Lloyd - Smith Kendall - Ceiling Unlimited: The Story of American Aviation from Kitty Hawk to Supersonics, New York, Macmillan Co., 1953.

Leu Morgan, R. P. Shannon - The Planes the Ages Flew, New York, Arco Publishing Co. Inc., 1964.

Moyes Philip J. R. Royal Air Force Bombers of World War II, vols. I, II, Windsor, Hylton Lacy, 1964.

Moyes Philip J. R. Bomber Squadrons of the R.A.F., London, Macdonald & Co. (Publishers) Ltd., 1966.

Munson Kenneth, Fighters between the Wars 1919-39, London, Blandford Press Ltd., 1970.

Munson Kenneth, Pioneer Aircraft 1903-1914, London, Blandford Press Ltd., 1969.

Munson Kenneth, Aircraft the World Over, London, Ian Allan Ltd., 1963.

Munson Kenneth, Aircraft of World War I, London, Ian Allan Ltd., 1968.

Munson Kenneth, Bombers, Patrol and Transport Aircraft, London, Blandford Press Ltd., 1966.

Munson Kenneth, Fighters Attack and Training Aircraft, London, Blandford Press Ltd., 1966.

Nazawa Tadashi, Encyclopedia of Japanese Aircraft 1900-1945, 5 vols., Tokyo, Shuppan-Kyodo, 1958-66.

Nemecek Vaclav, Sowjet-Flugzeuge, Steinebach, 1969.

Nowarra Heinz J. Die Sowjetischen Flugzeuge 1941-1966, München, J. F. Lehmanus Verlag, 1967.

Nowarra Heinz J. - Duval G. R., Russian Civil and Military Aircraft 1884-1969, London, Fountain Press Ltd., 1971.

Nowarra Heinz J., The Messerschmitt 109 a Famous German Fighter, Letchworth, Herts, Harleyford Publications Ltd., 1963.

Penrose Harald, British Aviation: The Pioneer Years, London, Putnam & Co. Ltd., 1967.

Petit Edmond, Histoire mondiale de l'aviation, Paris, Libraire Hachette, 1967.

Piaggio & C., 75 anni di attività, Genova, Piaggio & C., 1960.

Postan M. - Hay D. - Scott J. D., Design and Development of Weapons, London, Her Majesty's Stationery Office, 1964.

Prato Piero, I caccia Caproni Reggiane 1938-1945, Roma, Intyrama 1971.

Price Alfred, German Air Force Bomber of World War II, vols I, II, Windsor, Hylton Lacy, 1968-69.

Rae B. John, Climb to Greatness. The American Aircraft Industry, 1920-1960, Cambridge, USA, Massachusetts Institute of Technology Press, 1968.

Rawlings John, Fighter Squadrons of the R.A.F., London, Macdonald & Co. (Publishers) Ltd., 1970.

Richard D. - Saunders H., The Royal Air Force 1939-45 (vols. I-III), London, Her Majesty's Stationery Office, 1964.

Ries Karl Jr., Markierungen und Tarnanstriche der Luftwaffe in 2. Weltkrieg, vols. I-III, Mainz, Verlag Dieter Hoffmann, 1967.

Robertson Bruce, Aircraft markings of the World 1912-1967, Letchworth, Herts, Harleyford Publications Ltd., 1967.

Robertson Bruce, Aircraft Camouflage and Markings 1907-1954, Letchworth, Herts, Harleyford Publications Ltd., 1956.

Robinson Douglas H. LZ 129 Hindenburg, Dallas, Morgan Aviation Books, 1964.

Rust Kenn C., The Ninth Air Force in World War II, Fallbrook Aero Publishers Inc., 1967.

Saladin Raymond, Les temps héroiques de l'aviation, Paris, Editions Arcadiennes, 1949.

Scharff Robert - Taylor Walter S., Over Land and Sea: Glenn A. Curtiss, New York, David McKay Co. Inc., 1968.

Schliepak H., The Birth of the Luftwaffe, London, Ian Allan Ltd., 1971.

Schmidt Heinz A. F., Historische Flugzeuge, vols. I, II, Stuttgart, Motorbuch-Verlag, 1968-1970.

Seventy Fighters of the II World War, Tokyo, Aireview, Kantosha Co. Ltd., 1963.

Simonson G.R., The History of the American Aircraft Industry (Anthology), Cambridge, USA, Massachusetts Institute of Technology Press, 1968.

Swanborough Gordon - Bowers Peter M., United States Military Aircraft since 1909, London, Putnam & Co. Ltd., 1963.

Swanborough Gordon - Bowers Peter M., United States Navy Aircraft since 1911, London, Putnam & Co., Ltd., 1963.

Taylor John W. R., Aircraft Annual, London, Ian Allan Ltd., 1962.

Taylor John W. R., Warplanes of the World, London, Ian Allan Ltd., 1960.

Taylor John W. R., - Philip J. R., Moyes, Pictorial History of the R.A.F., vols. I-II, London Ian Allan Ltd., 1969.

Taylor John W. R., Combat Aircraft of the World, London, George Rainbird Ltd., 1969.

The American Heritage History of Flight, New York, American Heritage Publ. Co. Inc., 1962.

The Lore of Flight, Gothenburg, Tre Tryckare Cagner & Co., 1970.

Thetford Owen, Aircraft of the Royal Air Force since 1918, Putnam & Co. Ltd., 3rd edition, 1962.

Thetford Owen, British Naval Aircraft since 1912, London, Putnam & Co. Ltd., 1962.

Thompson Jonathan, Italian Civil and

Military Aircraft 1930-45, Fallbrook, California, Aero Publishers Inc., 1963.

Thorpe Donald W., *Japanese Army Air Force Camouflage and Markings World War II,* Fallbrook, California, Aero Publishers Inc., 1968.

Tuck W. J., *Power to Fly,* London, Science Museum, Her Majesty's Stationery Office, 1966.

United States Army and Air Force Fighters 1916-1961, Letchworth, Herts, Harleyford Publications Ltd., 1961.

Villaves Henrique Dumont, *Foto história de Santos Dumont 1898-1910,* Sâo Paulo, Comp. Melhoramentos de Sâo Paulo, 1956.

Voyenno-Vozdushnye Sily SSSR, 1918-1948 (L'aeronautica militare della URSS, 1918-1948, in Russian), Mosca, Voenizdat, 1948.

Wagner Ray, *American Combat Planes,* Garden City, N.Y., Doubleday & Co., 1960-68.

Whitehouse Arch, *The Years of the War Birds,* Garden City, N.Y., Doubleday & Co., 1960.

Wilson Charles - Reader William, *Men and Machines - A History of D. Napier & Son, Engineers, Ltd., 1808-1958,* London, Weidenfeld and Nicolson, 1958.

Windrow Martin C., *German Air Force Fighters of World War Two,* vols. I, II, Windsor, Hylton Lacy, 1968–69.

Wood Derek - Dempster Derek, *The Narrow Margin, The Definitive Story of the Battle of Britain,* London, Arrow Books Ltd., 1961.

58 Bombers of the II World War, Tokyo, Aireview, Kantosha Co. Ltd., 1965.

60 Attack/Reconnaissance Aircraft of the II World War, Tokyo, Aireview, Kantosha Co. Ltd., 1966.

PERIODICALS

Aerospazio, Albenga.
« Air Classic » Canoga Park, Challange Publications, Inc.
« Aircraft Illustrated », Shefferton, Ian Allan Ltd.
« Air International », Leicester, Fine Scroll Ltd.
« Air Pictorial », London, Air League.
« Air Progress », New York, The Condé Nast Publication, Inc.
« Aviation Magazine International », Paris, Union de Presse Européenne.
«Aviation Week & Space Technology», New York, McGraw-Hill.
« Aviazione di Linea Aeronautica e Spazio », Roma.

«Flight International», London, IPC Business Press Ltd
« Flug Revue - Flugwelt », Stuttgart, Vereinigte Motor-Verlage GmbH.
« Flying Review International », London, Haymarket Press Ltd.
« Icare Revue de l'Aviation Française », Orly.
« Interconair Aviazione Marina », Genova, Interconair S.A.
« I primi cinquant'anni dell'aviazione Italiana », Roma, Rivista Aeronautica.
« l'Album du Fanatique de l'Aviation », Paris, Editions Larivière.
« Profile », Windsor, Profile Publications Ltd.
« The Aeroplane », London.

ANNUALS

«Jane's All the World's Aircraft», London, Jane's Publishing Company.

INDEX BY COUNTRY

GENERAL INDEX

552

563

565

T

Z